# The Law of Photography and Digital Images

**AUSTRALIA**
Law Book Co.—Sydney


**CANADA** and **USA**
Carswell–Toronto


**HONG KONG**
Sweet & Maxwell Asia


**NEW ZEALAND**
Brookers—Wellington


**SINGAPORE** and **MALAYSIA**
Sweet & Maxwell Asia
Singapore and Kuala Lumpur

# The Law of Photography and Digital Images

Christina Michalos MA, LLB

*Barrister*

LONDON
SWEET & MAXWELL
2004

Published in 2004 by
Sweet & Maxwell Limited of
100 Avenue Road, London, NW3 3PF
Typeset by YHT Ltd, London
Printed in Great Britain by TJ International

No natural forests were destroyed to make this product,
only farmed timber was used and replanted

A CIP catalogue record for this book is available from the British Library

ISBN 0421 764 708

*To my parents*

# Preface

It is a familiar phrase—a picture is worth a thousand words. Today a photograph is just as likely to be worth thousands of pounds in damages and an injunction—or in some circumstances, a criminal conviction and a prison sentence.

Changes in society have affected the frequency with which cases concerning photographs come before the courts. The modern rise of celebrity culture has resulted in the commercial value of image rights exceeding all expectation. The advent of the internet and digital images has enabled photographs to be copied and sent all round the world in a moment. The prevalence of CCTV cameras means that most of us will be captured on film hundreds of times a day as we go about our daily lives but the right to a private and family life is now part of UK domestic law. Practitioners are ever more frequently asked to advise in respect of these issues which encompass a number of areas of law.

The original idea for this book arose after I had been instructed in a series of unrelated cases, all of which involved photographic subject matter. Although the basic legal principles were dealt with by existing works, the particular problems in respect of which I had been asked to advise were not dealt with in any detail—and in some cases not dealt with at all. And these were problems likely to arise repeatedly in any comparable case concerning photographs. There was no text for the legal practitioner on this subject. The idea behind this work was to fill this gap for the litigation lawyer.

Each of the chapter topics in this work is the subject of a leading, frequently excellent, practitioner text in its own right. It is not the function of this book to seek to replace these works nor the arrogance of this author to even aspire to do so. The object is to address in detail particular legal problems posed by photographs and to place these issues in context with an overview of the relevant area of the law. The aim is to deal with specific questions relating to photographs and provide enough general information to allow the reader, for example, to identify likely defences and possible remedies. For more detailed information as to the general principles the reader is referred to other works.

It is important to emphasise that this is intended to be a book about the law in its application to *photographs*—that is to say still images and *not* moving images or stills from films. Thus copyright law in its application to films, which is an entirely separate subject, is not considered at all. The only real exception to this focus on still images is CCTV footage which is dealt with in the Data Protection chapter. The CCTV Code and the principles applicable are of direct relevance to still images of humans. I felt it would be unhelpful to exclude consideration of CCTV images in this area.

There is consideration of cases from other jurisdictions notably in the first part of the book—*Rights In The Image*. The United States of America in particular is the source of far more litigation concerning copyright in photographs than the United Kingdom. Much of the US case law can be regarded as persuasive precedent in this jurisdiction. Many legal conundrums which have yet to arise in UK reported case law have already been considered in other jurisdictions. Whilst the manner in which another common law jurisdiction has approached a particular issue is of course no guarantee that the courts here would adopt the same approach, I find that one can learn an enormous amount from arguments judiciary in other jurisdictions found persuasive, as well as being inspired by those arguments rejected. Where I have referred to cases from foreign jurisdictions, I have tried to include enough detail in the text, or in the footnote, for the reader to assess whether the case is on point or it is worthwhile obtaining a copy. I have no wish to send lawyers on wild goose chases for authorities that are of only tangential relevance to their case.

There is relatively little written that compares civil and common law approaches to photographic copyright. The analysis of the laws of the world that appears in the Tables and statute extracts began as an academic exercise to discover how many countries had a related right protecting non-creative photographs that were not otherwise protected by copyright. I was fascinated by both the variations and similarities in the laws of the world and the project expanded. I have also included analysis and comparison of case law from civil law jurisdictions in relation to copyright and moral rights. Whilst I do hope that this part of the work will be of use to those with a more academic interest in the subject, an understanding of the differing approaches is important for the practitioner. The United Kingdom is required to comply with European Directives and international treaties. The origins of the language and the ideas underpinning many of these instruments lie in civil law statutes, particularly those of France and Germany. As international copyright law becomes more harmonised, an understanding of the approach of other jurisdictions is of great assistance.

Although this work is primarily aimed at lawyers involved in litigation, I hope it is also accessible enough to be of assistance to photographers and non-lawyers working in this field. I anticipate that the practitioner is likely to dip into this work to seek answers to particular questions. However, I would hope that if a layman were interested, that reading a chapter from start to finish should result in a basic understanding of the relevant area of law and that the writing is clear enough to allow this. In certain places, I have also included some practical suggestions, ever aware that the lawyers' job is often to provide practical commercial advice in conjunction with legal analysis. These should be of interest to those working in the image business. There is detailed coverage of relevant decisions of the Press Complaints

Commission and the Advertising Standards Authority, which should also be of practical assistance to the non-lawyer.

There is an element of painting the Forth Bridge when it comes to writing law books. Virtually every day brings new case law and statutory instruments. After completion of the first draft of the text, the Copyright And Related Rights Regulations 2003 were published and came into force and the damages judgment was given in *Douglas v Hello!*. In December 2003, the Court of Appeal gave judgment in *Durant v Financial Services Authority* concerning the interpretation of important provisions of the Data Protection Act 1998. Even at the time of writing this preface, there are several relevant cases that are awaiting hearing or judgment that have the potential to change the law significantly. *Campbell v MGN* is due to be heard by the House of Lords in February 2004. The decision of the ECHR in *von Hannover v Germany* is also awaited in which an application was made by Princess Caroline von Hannover of Monaco complaining that the German Courts failed to accord her respect for Article 8 rights in not providing adequate protection from the publication of paparazzi photographs taken without her knowledge. Inevitably by the time this work finds its way onto a bookshelf the law will have moved on further, but this is a natural hazard of writing any law book. The law is intended to be stated as at November 1, 2003, but where possible later changes have been included.

For the most part, writing this book was a very enjoyable experience. Hopefully it will, for the first time, contain in one volume the relevant law and save others from a great deal of research work. I hope you find it useful.

Christina Michalos
Gray's Inn, London
January 2004

# Acknowledgments

I was assisted in my research by a number of people, all of whom were kind enough to give up their time to help me. In no particular order, I would like to thank: Sal Shuel, Collections Picture Library; Linda Royles, Chief Executive Officer, BAPLA; Mike Holderness; Tim Gopsill of the NUJ; Simon Quirk (Corporate Counsel, Getty Images); Joanne Hurley of Hurley Stanners; David Morgan (Head of Examination) and Anne Pritchard (Trade Marks Examination Team Leader) of The Patent Office; Inspector Brian Ward of the Obscene Publications Unit of the Metropolitan Police; Robin Cooper and Andrew McNamara of HM Customs and Excise; and Janet Tod, Membership and Development Officer, DACS.

I am also grateful to those organisations who kindly granted permission for reproduction of their respective materials including the Information Commissioner, the Press Complaints Commission, the Committee of Advertising Practice, the BBC, the National Union of Journalists and the Photo Marketing Association.

In addition I am grateful to Professor Adrian Sterling who kindly read and commented on the copyright chapters. I would particularly like to thank Sal Shuel for reading the Picture Libraries Chapter and for a very interesting afternoon at a picture library. Any errors or omissions are of course my responsibility.

I would like to thank those members of the Bar who spent time discussing difficult (and sometimes obscure and uninteresting!) points of law with me and sharing their opinions.

Thanks are also due to Sweet and Maxwell, particularly my publishing editors Jacqui Mowbrey and subsequently Anne Roper for their help and the Alexander Maxwell Trust for its assistance which was much appreciated.

I would like to thank my family for their support and encouragement throughout both my career and the writing of this book. When the book was nearly finished but the end never quite seemed in sight, my father inspired me by teaching me an amusing but apposite Greek adage. It became so associated with the completion of this book, it deserves to be included here as the last word: ἔφαγες τόν γάδαρο θά φάς και τήν οὐρά του.

# The Alexander Maxwell Law Scholarship Trust

Maurice W. Maxwell, whose family founded Sweet & Maxwell the law publishers, by his Will established a charitable trust to be known as the Alexander Maxwell Law Scholarship Trust in memory of both his great-great-grandfather and his great-grandfather.

The Trust is committed to promoting legal research and writing at various levels by providing financial assistance to authors whether they be experienced legal practitioners or those in the early years of practice. (The Trust does not assist towards the cost of any course or post-graduate work.)

The author of this book received an Award from the Trust.

The Trust calls for applications for awards from time to time (usually awards are made in the early part of each calendar year, with a deadline for applications on the preceding August 31). Anyone interested in the work of the Trust or wishing to discuss a possible application should contact:

The Clerk to the Trustees
Alexander Maxwell Law Scholarship Trust
c/o Sweet & Maxwell Limited
100 Avenue Road
London NW3 3PF

The Trust now has a website: http://www.amlst.org.uk and can be reached by email: clerk@amlst.org.uk.

# Contents

**Appendices**

# Table of Cases

# Table of PCC Reports

*All references are to paragraph numbers*

# Table of Statutes

*All references are to paragraph numbers*

# Table of Statutory Instruments

*All references are to paragraph numbers*

# Table of European Legislation

*All references are to paragraph numbers*

# Table of International Conventions

# Chapter 1

# A short history of the development of photography

1–001

The *camera obscura* technique has been known since the Renaissance. The pinhole camera, which uses the technique, is based on the principle that light entering a darkened room or box via a small hole produces a dim inverted image of the outside scene on the opposite wall (see Figure 1, below). It was referred to by Leonardo da Vinci[1] and in 1553 in his book *Natural Magic* Giovanni Battista della Porta published a description of the technique.[2]

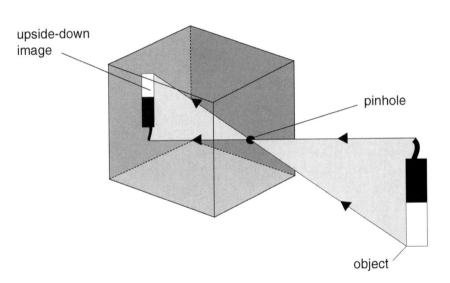

**Figure 1:** Camera obscura

The fact that certain materials either darkened or faded when left exposed to the sun had also been known for centuries. In 1727, Johann Schulze was experimenting with a mixture of phosphorous, chalk and nitric acid which contained an impurity—silver. He noticed that the compound turned a deep purple when exposed to the sun's light.[3] In about 1800, Thomas Wedgwood, son of the famous Staffordshire potter, aware of Schulze's experiments,

---

[1] M. Langford, *Story of Photography* (Focal Press, 1997), p.2.
[2] B. Newhall, *The History of Photography* (5th ed., Bulfinch Press, New York, 1982), p.9.
[3] *ibid.*, p.10.

created "sun pictures" by treating paper or leather with silver nitrate, placing objects in contact with it and then exposing to the sun. The exposed areas darkened while the area under the object remained white.

**1–002**   In 1826, Joseph Niépce succeeded in recording images using a *camera obscura* on to metal plates treated with white bitumen of Judea.[4] He named the process "heliograph"—literally "sun drawing". It was Niépce who created the world's oldest surviving picture produced with a camera in 1826 (see Figure 2, below).[5] A Frenchman, Louis Daguerre, had also experimented with recording images of a *camera obscura* using silver compounds. In 1829, he went into partnership with Niépce but little progress was made. After Niépce's death, his son took over the partnership but in reality Daguerre was working alone.[6]

**Figure 2:** Reproduction of Joseph Nicéphore Niépce's "View from the Window at Le Gras"—the world's oldest surviving "photograph".[6a]

**1–003**   By 1837, Daguerre had created an effective system using copper plates plated with silver and treated with iodine vapour creating a coating of silver iodide. Initially, a 30 minute exposure was necessary. After exposure the plate was held over warmed mercury which "developed" the image. The plate was then washed with a strong salt solution which rendered the unexposed silver iodide relatively insensitive to further light action. The

[4] Newhall, *op. cit.*, p.15.
[5] View from Niépce's window at Le Gras.
[6] Newhall, *op. cit.*, p.18.
[6a] Reproduced with permission of Gernsheim Collection, Harry Ransom Humanities Research Center, The University of Texas at Austin.

*daguerreotype* process, as this became known, was the first practical photographic process. In return for a state pension, Daguerre disclosed the technical details of his process at a meeting of the Academy of Science and the Academy of Art in August 1839. The meeting caused great excitement and an account in the London Morning Post of Friday August 23, 1839, revealed that "upward of two hundred persons who could not obtain admittance remained in the courtyard". Within five years of the announcement, portrait studios were established in principal cities in most European cities and America.[7] The subjects had their head kept still by a metal clamp, were instructed not to blink too much, and had to remain still for the one minute exposure.

In 1851, Frederick Scott Archer invented a new process by treating sheets **1–004** of glass with a mixture called collodion comprised of nitrated cotton dissolved in ether and alcohol, sensitising the plate and then exposing it in the camera while still damp. Thus, the collodion process became known as the "wet-plate" process. The negatives produced pictures with a high degree of clarity and could also be used to produce an unlimited number of prints, unlike the *daguerreotype*. The collodion process became the main photographic process in use in England almost immediately and then spread to Europe and America. The process was not easy to use and required some skill to flow the collodion mixture evenly over the glass, sensitise the plate, expose it and process it all within 10–20 minutes before it dried.[8]

The possibility of the mass production of prints lead to the "*carte-de-viste*" craze. These were calling cards with a photograph of the subject pasted on. They were taken by a four lens camera that took four poses at one time. The plate was then turned round and another four photographs taken—recording eight poses in all. Between 1861 and 1866, *carte-de-viste* were a popular obsession and newspapers named this "cardomania". The craze helped to promote professional photography. In 1855, London had 66 portrait studios, but six years later there were over 200—with 35 in Regent Street alone.[9]

The first major exhibition of photography was held in London in 1852. In **1–005** 1853 the Photographic Society of London was formed which is now the Royal Photographic Society. There persisted a general feeling that the most acceptable approach to "artistic" photography was to copy popular paintings of the period. Photographers would often choose a title (such as "Fading Away" by H. Peach Robinson, 1858, which depicts models posed as a dying girl and her family in a typical Victorian picture) and then construct a picture. Art critics did not accept photography and "often used the word in a negative way, to condemn painting and sculpture that to their eyes did not go beyond verisimilitude but merely recorded the outward appearance of the world".[10] In 1858, Charles Baudelaire reviewing an exhibition of the French Society of Photography wrote:

[7] Langford, *op. cit.*, p.12.
[8] Langford, *op. cit.*, p.23.
[9] Langford, *op. cit.*, p.35.
[10] Newhall, *op. cit.*, p.83.

"If photography is allowed to supplement art in some of its functions, it will soon have supplanted or corrupted it altogether … It is time, then, for it to return to its true duty which is to be the servant of the sciences and arts—but the very humble servant, like printing or shorthand, which have neither created nor supplemented literature."[11]

**1–006**   The attitude that photography was not art or creative prevailed for many years and was one of the main reasons why there was such a dispute as to the specific inclusion of photographs in the Berne Convention. Some countries, such as Germany, felt that photographs did not warrant protection as artistic works within copyright law.[12] As can be seen from the timeline below (see para. 1–012), copyright law lagged very far behind the developments in photography.

By 1878, dry plates made with a gelatin emulsion following the work of Richard Leach Maddox were available and for sale as ready-to-use manufactured plates in boxes. The invention of the first Kodak camera in 1888 gave the general public access to cameras and amateur photography in a way never seen before. Created by George Eastman, an American bank clerk and amateur photographer, the Kodak camera was small enough to carry. The price of $25 or 5 guineas (£25) was expensive but not prohibitive.

**1–007**   The first colour plates were sold in about 1907 by the Lumiere brothers in France and called autochromes.[13] Eastman Kodak in America and Agfa in Germany were experimenting in producing colour films. During World War II, Agfa and then Kodak began to produce multi-layer colour negative films. Kodakcolor and Agfacolor negative films did not become available in the UK until about 1950. By 1972, Dr Edwin Land's Polaroid Corporation invented the polaroid process which produces a photograph which ejects from the camera and develops in minutes.

Pyrotechnic flashpowder consisting of ground magnesium and other chemicals which were ignited was introduced as a light source for photographs in the 1880s. It was impractical to make the flashpowder ignite at the same time as the shutter. Use therefore required opening the shutter, igniting the powder, then closing the shutter. Flashbulbs were invented in 1925 and the first electronic flash tube was invented in 1931 by Harold Egerton.

**1–008**   In 1963, D. Gregg of Stanford University invented a videodisc type digital camera which was able to capture and store images for a few minutes. In 1969, Bell Laboratories invented the Charge-coupled device (known as a CCD) which accumulates charge according to the amount of light that falls on it. This charge is converted into binary code. The computer then uses the code to set the colour or brightness of the pixels that combine to reconstruct the image. It is the CCD which forms the basis of image production in

---

[11] Charles Baudelaire, *The Mirror of Art* (Phaidon Press Ltd, London, 1955), pp.228–231 quoted in Newhall, *op. cit.*, p.83.
[12] See below at paras 3–051 *et seq.*
[13] Langford, *op. cit.*, p.62.

digital cameras. The way in which the CCD produces an image is discussed further in Chapter 2.[14]

The invention of digital cameras and photographs signalled a move away from the traditional analogue process and the image quality produced by digital cameras was constantly improving as technology developed. In 1986, Kodak designed the megapixel CCD sensor that contained 1.4 million pixels and was capable of producing 5 × 7 inch digital prints that looked like photographs.[15] During the 1990s the first commercial digital cameras became available.

The modern development of cameras and films has lead to a wide variety of uses of photography including aerial photographs, underwater photography, "photofinish" sports photographs,[16] and speed cameras. In addition to the standard analogue and digital methods of producing a photograph, images can be created in a variety of different ways using different forms of radiation. This is particularly evident in the field of medicine where x-rays, magnetic resonance imaging, and ultrasound are all used to produce images.[17]   **1–009**

Today, the use of digital images means that photographs can be more easily transmitted, manipulated and, of course, copied. Image manipulation has moved on considerably since Leon Trotsky was removed from a photograph of Lenin leaving a noticeable gray gap. Adobe Photoshop 1.0, software allowing the user to edit and manipulate digital images, was launched in 1990;[18] by 2002, Adobe Photoshop version 7.0 was available. These types of image programmes are now so sophisticated that it is possible for a skilled user to alter photographs without leaving any trace of the fact the original has been edited.[19] The rapid development of the internet and the ease with which images can be accessed caused further problems for rights owners in facilitating copying. This in turn spawned its own industry with the development of watermarking software.   **1–010**

The extent of future turns in the development of photography and photographic methods cannot be foreseen. In 1826, when Joseph Niépce was creating heliographs, the concept of a digital camera was beyond the realms of fantasy. By what can be relatively certain is that copyright law will always be playing catch up. It was only in 2001 that the European Community passed a directive to harmonise certain aspects of Copyright and Related Rights in the Information Society.[20] The directive was aimed at addressing difficulties and lacuna caused by technological developments, in particular the internet. This was some 10 years after the internet had become well established. The directive was incorporated into the national law of the United Kingdom, on October 31, 2003 when the Copyright and Related Rights Regulations 2003 came into force.[21]   **1–011**

---

[14] See below at paras 2–014 *et seq.*

[15] *http://wwwca.kodak.com/US/en/corp/aboutKodak/kodakHistory/milestones80to94.shtml.*

[16] Now in fact, film stills rather than a traditional photograph.

[17] See below paras 2–028 and 2–033.

[18] *http://www.adobe.com/aboutadobe/pressroom/pdfs/adobe_timeline_7_9_02.pdf.*

[19] See below at paras 9–003 and 9–018 *et seq.*

[20] Directive 2001/29.

[21] SI 2003/2498.

## COPYRIGHT AND PHOTOGRAPHY TIME LINE

**1–012**

| Date | Development of Photography/Associated Technology | Developments in the Law of Copyright |
|---|---|---|
| 1709 | | First UK Copyright Statute passed. Copyright Act 1709 Statute of Anne. Came into force on April 10, 1710. |
| 1727 | Johann Schulze notices silver salts sensitive to light. | |
| 1800 | Thomas Wedgewood creates sun pictures on treated leather. | |
| 1826 | Joseph Niépce creates heliographs using camera obscura and the world's oldest surviving picture produced with a camera. | |
| 1839 | Daguerrotype process publicly announced in France. | |
| 1842 | | Copyright Act 1842. |
| 1851 | Archer invents collodion process. | |
| 1853 | Royal Photographic Society formed. | |
| 1855 | L.A. Poitevin invents photolithography. | |
| 1862 | | Photographs first granted statutory copyright in the UK by Fine Arts Copyright Act 1862. |
| 1865 | | Act of 1865: USA grant photographs copyright protection for the first time. |

| | | |
|---|---|---|
| 1869 | | *Graves' case*[22] (UK) held that a photograph of an engraving made from a painting was capable of being an original work. |
| 1876 | First manufactured dry plate appears in UK. | |
| 1884 | | *Burrow-Giles v Sarony* (USA) held that the Constitution permitted copyright protection of original photographs. |
| 1886 | | Berne Convention. Nine original member states. Photographs not specifically mentioned. |
| 5 Dec 1887 | | UK ratifies Berne Convention |
| 1888 | Kodak camera invented. | |
| 1895 | X-rays discovered by Roentgen. | |
| 1896 | | Berne Convention: Paris revision. Photographs still not specifically mentioned. |
| 1900 | Kodak Brownie goes on sale. | |
| 1903 | Perutz panchromatic plates invented in Germany. | |
| 1908 | | Berlin revision of Berne Convention. Photographs still not specifically mentioned. |
| 1 July 1912 | | UK Copyright Act 1911 came into force. |
| 1928 | | Rome revision of Berne Convention. |
| 1929 | Flashbulbs invented. | |

[22] (1868–1869) L.R. 4 Q.B. 715.

| | | |
|---|---|---|
| 1931 | Harold Egerton produces first electronic flash tube. | |
| 1934 | Chester F. Carlson invents "xerography"—the use of photoelectric phenomena to transfer an image from one sheet of paper to another. | |
| 1942 | Kodak and Agfa introduced colour film and printing. | |
| 1947 | Black and white Polaroid Camera invented. | |
| 1948 | | Brussels Revision of Berne Convention. |
| 1951 | | Berne Convention first specifically includes photographs following the Brussels Revision. |
| 1953 | | *Bauman v Fussell*[23] (UK) held that the positions of birds not under the photographers control in a photograph not a substantial part of the photograph. A painting copying those positions was not infringing. |
| 1 June 1957 | | UK Copyright Act 1956 came into force. |
| 1959 | The first office photocopier—the Xerox-914—goes on sale. | |
| 1963 | First digital camera. D. Gregg of Stanford University invented a videodisc type digital camera which was able to capture and store images for a few minutes. | |

---

[23] [1978] R.P.C. 485, CA.

| 1967 | | Berne Convention: Stockholm revision. |
|------|--|---------------------------------------|
| 1969 | Bell Laboratories invented the Charge-coupled device (CCD) used in digital cameras.<br><br>Advanced Research Projects Agency (ARPA) establishes first computer network system ARPANET with nodes at UCLA and Stanford—the origins of the internet.[24] | |
| 1971 | ARPANET had 15 nodes. First email sent. | Berne Convention: Second Paris revision |
| 1972 | ARPANET demonstrated publically. | |
| 1980 | Sony demonstrated first consumer camcorder. | |
| 1982 | Transmission Control Protocol (TCP) and Internet Protocol (IP), adopted by ARPANET. Birth of the internet as defined as a series of networks connected by TCP/IP. | |
| 1984 | Domain name server introduced developed giving .com names to websites instead of numbers. | |
| 1986 | Digital photography: Eastman Kodak designed the megapixel CCD sensor that contained 1.4 million pixels. | |

---

[24] For further information as to the structure of the internet see below at para.9–005.

| | | |
|---|---|---|
| 1987 | The world's first image editing software for personal computers—(Image Studio) released by Letraset for use on MacIntosh computers. | |
| 1988 | PhotoMac launched—the first image manipulation program for Macintosh computers.<br><br>Eastman Kodak announces a 4 megapixel CCD. | USA ratifies Berne Convention. |
| 1 August 1989 | | Copyright Designs and Patents Act 1988 came into force in the UK. |
| 1990s | Digital cameras first go on sale. | |
| 1990 | Adobe Photoshop 1.0 (TM) image manipulation program is launched. | |
| 1990/1 | World wide web developed by Tim Berners-Lee and scientists at CERN (Centre Européan pour la Recherche Nucléaire). | |
| 1992 | 50 web servers in the world.[25] | |
| 1993 | World wide web grows rapidly. 2 million internet hosts and 623 websites.[26] | |
| 1995 | 3 million internet hosts and over 10,000 websites.[27] | *Reject Shop v Manners*[28] (UK) Photocopy not an original work. |

---

[25] Robert Zakon, *http://www.zakon.org/robert/internet/timeline/*.
[26] Robert Zakon, *http://www.zakon.org/robert/internet/timeline/*;
Matthew Gray, *http://www.mit.edu/people/mkgray/net/web-growth-summary.html*.
[27] *ibid.*
[28] [1995] F.S.R. 870, QBD.

| | | |
|---|---|---|
| Jan 1, 1996 | | Duration of Copyright and Rights in Performances Regulations 1995 came into force extending the term of copyright from 50 yrs pma to 70 yrs pma. |
| 1996 | Advanced Photo System (APS) is introduced. | |
| 1997 | | *Creation Records v News Group Newspapers*[29] (UK) Independently created photograph of a scene was not a copy of an earlier photograph of the same scene. |
| 1999 | | *Bridgeman v Corel Corporation* (USA) Denying copyright protection to photographs of paintings. |
| 2000 | | *SHL Imaging Inc v Artisan House Inc* (USA) Photographs of mirror and picture frames held to be original and protected by copyright. |
| 2001 | | European Directive Copyright & Related Rights in the Information Society came into force (June 22, 2001) aimed at meeting the challenge of the internet and digital technology. *Antiquesportfolio.com v Rodney Fitch & Co Ltd* [2001] F.S.R. 23. Photographs of 3-D objects were protected by copyright. |

---

[29] [1997] E.M.L.R. 444.

| August 2003 | Over 42 million websites.[30] | UK has still not implemented the European Directive Copyright & Related Rights in the Information Society which should have occurred by December 22, 2002.[31] |
|---|---|---|
| October 31, 2003 | | Copyright and Related Rights in the Information Society Directive implemented in the UK by the Copyright and Related Rights Regulations 2003.[32] |

---

[30] Netcraft August 2003 survey *http://news.netcraft.com/archives/2003/08/01/august_2003_web_server_survey.html.*
[31] Directive 2001/29, Art.13.
[32] SI 2003/2498.

# Part A

# Rights in the Image

# Chapter 2

# Copyright

## INTRODUCTION

Photographic works present a challenge for the law of copyright. Although **2–001** there are variations within civil and common law jurisdictions, the concept of originality lies at the heart of copyright[1] law. Generally, a work is protected if it is original in the sense that it is creative. Yet every photograph is a copy of the image it represents and in that sense unoriginal. Given that copyright law is predominantly aimed at protecting original works, there is a real issue as to the extent to which photographs should be protected. Unsurprisingly, this has resulted in several different approaches to the protection of photography in national laws.

Problems arise not just because every photograph is a copy of something **2–002** else, but also because it is possible for a photograph to be non-creative and

---

[1] In Ch.3 and the section concerning International law, the term "copyright" is used generically, unless indicated otherwise, to include both "copyright" in its common law sense and the author's rights of the civil law system.

non-original to a degree not present in most other works. It is of course possible that any work of literature or art may be non-original but usually because it would be too simple, just reproduces an idea that can only be expressed in one way[2] or because it was a copy of something else. Photographs on the other hand have an inherent "non-original" potential due to the nature of the photographic process.

**2–003**    Some aspects of the process of taking a photograph are mechanical and a basic, ordinary photograph may just be a reflection of this process. Difficulties arise in the case of photographs due to the problem of ascertaining what degree of input by the author is necessary to attract copyright. At one end of the spectrum lies the truly original photograph with an original, and creatively arranged subject matter, artful lighting, unusual angle, and other artistic choices that reflect the personality of the photographer. At the other lies the simple photograph—"the point and press" work, for example a tourist taking a photograph of a landmark photographed by a thousand other tourists every day. Where a line should be drawn within this spectrum between works protected by copyright and those that are not is a difficult question which has troubled courts in many jurisdictions. Inevitably, the case law shows a lack of consistency across national jurisdictions. Originality in relation to photographs is considered in detail in Chapter 3.

**2–004**    The originality of a photograph is of crucial importance as it is the level of originality that will govern whether a photograph is protected by copyright. A photograph that is unoriginal and does not attract copyright may be copied with impunity. If only certain elements of a photograph are original, it is only the taking of those elements that will lead to infringement. In the United Kingdom it is rare for a photograph to be denied copyright because of a lack of originality. In practice, therefore, the question of what is original in a photograph tends to assume more importance in relation to infringement than subsistence of copyright.

**2–005**    As will be seen, there are a variety of different approaches to the protection of photographs in national laws, with some laws granting a "related" right to non-creative photographs.[3] This proves problematic in the international arena, as the principles of national treatment, which apply to copyright works only, leave some photographs protected in one jurisdiction but not in another. However, overall a picture emerges of photographic works as a "poor cousin" to other artistic works in the world of copyright law. Of the laws of 123 countries considered,[4] only 53 treat photographs in the same way as other copyright works and grant the same basic term of

---

[2] For example, a drawing of a hand making a cross on a voting slip *Kenrick v Lawrence* (1890) 25 Q.B.D. 99. But *cf.* the French case *PEP v Kerbouc'h Cass.* May 23, 1995, (1995) 166 R.I.D.A. 298 where an advertising image of a hand holding a visiting card was considered to be an original work even though it was an interpretation of a non-original idea.

[3] See Ch.3 below.

[4] Of those where information as to duration was obtained. See Ch.3 and Appendices 1 and 2, below. There are 125 countries referred to in Appendix 2, the author was unable to ascertain duration provisions in Liberia and Madagascar.

protection.[5] A further 15 countries[6] which have related rights for non-creative photographs, also provide the same term for creative photographs as for other copyright works. Fifty-four of the countries considered grant photographic works a shorter or different term than other works in their duration provisions. The continuing prevalence of affording photographic works a lesser term is in all probability due to the persistence of the idea that photography is not a "pure" art form being basically a mechanical process.[7] It appears that slowly, laws are changing to grant photographs the same term as other works.[8]

In 1971, the 11th edition of *Copinger* suggested copyright in a photograph would subsist as long as it was not a copy of an existing photograph and was original in the sense that it was a fresh photograph of some object. The authors continued: **2–006**

> "Some support for this view may also be found in the fact that the legislature has given to photographs only a relatively short term of protection, which would seem to suggest that copyright was not being conferred in respect of artistic qualities but only in respect of something in the nature of an industrial production."[9]

Obviously, at the time of writing, the 1956 Act with its shorter protection period of 50 years from first publication was in force in the United Kingdom. However the observation is of note for two reasons. First, because it indicates that as late as the 1970s, copyright lawyers were still regarding photography as an industrial process and not primarily artistic. Secondly, it reflects the fact that it is a logical inference that legislatures which award photographs a shorter period of protection than other artistic works are indicating that in some way photography is a "lesser" art. This attitude is still prevalent and albeit often at a minor level clearly influences decisions of judges in several jurisdictions when considering whether a photograph is original as a copyright work.

## SCOPE OF THIS CHAPTER

This chapter is concerned with copyright law in the United Kingdom, specifically in its application to photographic works. Specific issues con- **2–007**

---

[5] As noted below, this "basic term of protection" refers to the standard term of protection for any core copyright work produced by an identifiable natural author. Many countries have separate duration provisions for anonymous and pseudonymous works; works produced by legal entities; published and unpublished works, etc. These other provisions are not considered here.

[6] In 2000, 18 countries granted neighbouring rights including Jordan and Egypt. Both countries amended their laws in 2001 and 2002 and repealed the distinction between creative and non-creative photographs. See further below at para. 3–081 and Appendices 1 and 2.

[7] See above at para.1–006 and below at paras 3–051 *et seq.*

[8] In 2000, only 44 of the countries considered in Appendix 2 treated photographs the same way as other copyright works compared to 52 in 2003.

[9] *Copinger and Skone James on Copyright* (11th ed., Sweet & Maxwell, 1971) para.118.

cerning photographs are addressed and set in context by outlining the wider principles of copyright law. Originality which is particularly problematic is dealt with in Chapter 3. A detailed treatment of the wider principals of copyright is beyond the scope of this work and the reader is referred to Laddie, Prescott and Vitora, *The Modern Law of Copyright and Designs* (3rd ed., Butterworths) and *Copinger and Skone James on Copyright* (14th ed., Sweet & Maxwell).

**2–008**   In the United Kingdom, the present statute governing copyright law is the Copyright Designs and Patents Act 1988 (CDPA 1988). This Act will be referred to as the 1988 Act. Prior to the 1988 Act, the primary statutes were the Copyright Act 1956 and the Copyright Act 1911. These Acts remain of relevance, as in effect, they still govern copyright in older works.

## Definition of photograph

**2–009**   Copyright is a property right which is established by s.1 of the 1988 Act which provides:

> "1(1) Copyright is a property right which subsists in accordance with this Part in the following descriptions of work—
>
> (a) original literary, dramatic, musical or artistic works,
> (b) sound recordings, films or broadcasts,[10] and
> (c) the typographical arrangement of published editions."

**2–010**   In order to qualify for copyright protection, a work must be an *original* literary, dramatic, musical or artistic work. In addition, the qualification conditions as regards the status of the author or country of first publication must be met.[11] It is originality which frequently causes difficulty in the case of photographic works. Artistic works are further defined in s.4 which provides:

> "4(1) In this Part 'artistic work' means—
>
> (a) a graphic work, **photograph**, sculpture or collage irrespective of artistic quality,
> (b) a work of architecture being a building or a model for a building, or

---

[10] This section was amended by the Copyright And Related Rights Regulations 2003 (SI 2003/2598), reg. 5(2) which came into force on October 31, 2003. The Regulations implemented the EC Directive on the Harmonisation of Certain Aspects of Copyright and Related Rights in the Information Society (Directive 2001/29/EC). Prior to amendment s.1(1)(b) read "sound recordings, films, broadcasts or cable programmes". The distinction between broadcasts and cable programmes has now been removed. Note that the Regulations (and the amendments to the 1988 Act) apply to copyright works existing before October 31, 2003 but there are a few transitional provisions which provide, *inter alia*, that no pre-commencement act is to be regarded as an infringement of any new right. For further detail as to the transitional provisions see below at para. 2–149.

[11] See below, Qualifying Conditions at para. 2–038.

(c) a work of artistic craftsmanship

(2) In this Part—
'building' includes any fixed structure and a part of a building or fixed structure;
'graphic work' includes—

    (a) any painting, drawing, diagram, map, chart or plan, and
    (b) any engraving, etching, lithograph, woodcut or similar work.

**'photograph' means a recording of light or other radiation on any medium on which an image is produced or from which an image may be any means be produced, and which is not part of a film;**
'sculpture' includes a cast or model made for the purposes of sculpture."

Films are defined in s.5B as "a recording on any medium from which a moving image may by any means be produced." It should be noted however, that individual frames of films made before June 1957 are treated as photographs under the 1911 Act.[12]

## What types of image recordings are protected as photographs?

When considering whether a particular type of image recording is pro- **2–011** tected as a copyright work, there are two separate questions. First, is the medium capable of protection at all, *i.e.* is the record of the image produced by "a recording of light **or** other radiation on any medium on which an image is produced or from which an image may by any means be produced, ***and which is not part of a film***"? (emphasis added). If the image is produced by a recording of light or other radiation, the next question is whether the recorded image is original. This section is concerned with the first question—is the medium capable of protection? Originality is considered below at paras 3–001 *et seq.*

### *Analogue photographs and negatives*

The negative of a standard analogue photograph is protected by copy- **2–012** right if original.[13] The negative is a first generation record of the image, *i.e.* what is recorded by the camera on to the film from which positive prints are developed. The film in a camera is a medium upon which a recording of light is made. The film (the negative) has an image produced upon it and also enables the photograph to be produced from it. It is the negative which is the protected work within s.4 as it is the negative that records the light and from which the image is produced. Equally, a transparency is a protected

---

[12] CDPA 1988, Sch.1, para.7(3).
[13] *Pacific Film Laboratories Pty Ltd v Federal Commissioner of Taxation* (1970) 121 C.L.R. 154.

work.[14] Polaroid photographs or other "instant images", where the image is produced directly on to self developing film without a negative are also protected works.

**2–013**    In practical terms, when considering infringement, the fact that the negative is the protected work will usually make little difference as an infringing copy will usually be a copy of the image as recorded on the negative in any event. Developing photographic prints from a negative amounts to making copies of the artistic work embodied in the negative. Giving a film to a professional film developer for the purpose of making positive prints grants an implied licence to the developer to make prints of the negatives for the purpose of sale back to the negative owner.[15]

### Digital photographs

**2–014**    Digital photographs produced by a digital camera[16] are also protected if original. The definition of "a recording of light or other radiation on any medium on which an image is produced or from which an image may by any means be produced, and which is not part of a film" applies to a digital photograph created by a digital camera.

The image is produced from a light sensitive sensor in the digital camera.[17] Usually this is a charge-coupled device, known as a CCD which is designed to measure the amount of light hitting it. The CCD is a silicon chip bearing rows of silicon photo diodes (SPD), each of which accumulates a charge according to the quantity of light that falls on then.

**2–015**    Coloured filters are then placed over the top of the CCD, enabling each sensor to determine the colour of the light, in addition to the quantity. The filters are set in a pattern across the grid alternating between red (R) green (G) and blue (B)—known as the RGB model. From these additive primaries, it is possible for the camera to generate almost any colour. After the sensor has been exposed to the light and the image, the rows of electrical pulses are collected and converted to digital form and stored according to their position on the grid. The conversion uses a chip known as an analogue to digital converter (the ADC chip). This information is stored in the camera's memory as a file.

---

[14] For the difference between a transparency and a negative see below, paras 12–005 and 12–006.

[15] *Pacific Film Laboratories Pty Ltd v Federal Commissioner of Taxation* (1970) 121 C.L.R. 154. (High Court of Australia) Taxation case where the issue was whether the supply of prints by a developer amounted to sale of goods. It was argued that because the copyright in the negative belonged to the photographer, the developer had no property in the prints such as could be transferred by sale. This was rejected by the court observing "[Copyright] is not a right in an existing physical thing. It is a negative right, as it has been called, a power to prevent the making of a physical thing by copying."

[16] There are other ways of producing digital photographs: (1) scanning an analogue photograph into a computer and creating a digital version of the analogue picture; (2) generation of an image from pure data fed into a computer. See S. Corbett, *The Digital Photograph: Intellectual Property of . . . whom?* [2001] 6(2) Comm. Law 46.

[17] For further information as to the process by which a digital photograph is produced, see P. Andrews, *The Digital Photography Manual* (Carlton Books 2000); M. Freeman, *The Complete Guide to Digital Photography* (Thames & Hudson 2001).

In a digital camera sensor, the pixel receptors need to be laid out side by side. As a third of the receptors need to be allocated to each colour, this potentially reduces resolution by half. The CCD receptors individually filter the red, blue and green in groups. The missing information is "interpolated" by the nearby pixels. Accordingly, the more pixels the camera has, the better the potential quality of the image. **2–016**

There is also the newer complementary metal-oxide semi conductor (CMOS) which works on the same principles as the CCD, but is made using the same process used for making most computer memory chips. **2–017**

A digital photograph will fall within the definition of a photograph and, if original, be protected by copyright.

For the sake of completeness, although it is theoretically arguable, it is submitted that a digital photograph cannot be classified as a computer program and be protected as a literary work[18] under the 1988 Act. Computer program is not defined by the 1988 Act. Such definitions as have been suggested by legal commentators tend towards a series or a set of instructions to control a computer or to cause the machine to achieve a particular result.[19] It is submitted that the file storing a digital photograph would not qualify as a program within the meaning of the 1988 Act. It is however on one view a set of coded instructions that produces a particular result—the display of the photograph. There is as yet no definitive definition of what is protected as a computer program.[20] It is submitted that a digital photograph would not be protected as a computer program. By analogy, it has been held that a screen display is the product of a program and not the program itself.[21] **2–018**

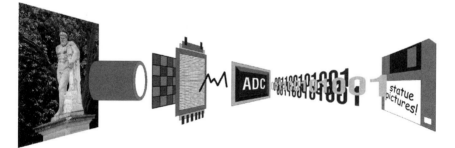

**Figure 3:** How a digital photograph is taken.[21a] Shooting skills are very similar with film and digital cameras. The difference is that the digital camera captures the image using a grid of electronic sensors rather than a piece of film.

---

[18] CDPA 1988, s.3(1)(b), "literary work" includes a computer progam.

[19] See for example Laddie, Prescott & Vitoria, *et al.*, *op. cit.*, at 34.19 "It is therefore submitted that the word 'program' in the Act should be taken to mean a series of instructions capable of being fed to a computer system by typing it in at a keyboard or in any other way, and, when so entered of controlling its operation in a desired manner."

[20] But see *Cantor Fitzgerald International v Tradition (UK) Ltd* [2000] R.P.C. 95 at 130 and the Appendix A to the judgment: *An introduction to computers and programming language* in which Pumfrey J. sets out some of the principal features of computer programs. A distinction is drawn between the program and the data manipulated by the program.

[21] *John Richardson Computers Ltd v Flanders (No. 1)* [1993] F.S.R. 497 at 527 *per* Ferris J.

[21a] Reproduced with permission of Philip Andrews, *The Digital Photography Manual* (Carlton Books Ltd London, 2000), p.23, Figure 9.

*Digitally manipulated photographs*

**2–019**   The initial digital photograph falls within the 1988 Act definition of a photograph. The digital image file is usually downloaded to a computer. Once the image is on the computer, editing packages such as Adobe Photoshop can be used to enhance the image.

The changes made using these types of programs are purely computerised alterations. There is no "recording of light or other radiation" at the point the computerised manipulation occurs.

Potentially, this may result in two copyrights in the final manipulated image—one in the initial digital photograph as a photographic work and a second copyright in the manipulated image recording, provided of course that the final image is itself original and not a mere copy of the photograph with minor amendments.

**2–020**   Section 4(2) defines graphic work but gives a non-exclusive list. Specifically the section defines graphic work as *including*:

a)   any painting, drawing, diagram, map, chart or plan, and

b)   any engraving, etching, lithograph, woodcut or similar work.

The classification of a digitally-manipulated photograph within one of the specific categories listed may prove problematic.

**2–021**   It is arguable that digital manipulation is a form of electronic painting. The only judicial guidance as to the definition of painting is in *Merchandising Corp of America v Harpbond Inc*[22] which concerned the 1956 Act. It was held that the distinctive makeup of Adam Ant, a pop singer, comprising three stripes on one cheek was not a painting. This decision has been criticised.[23] It was held that "painting" is a word is the ordinary usage of the English language and that it is a question of fact in each case whether a work is a painting.[24] This adds little to the 1988 Act.

**2–022**   Although one may think of painting as involving traditional "wet" paint, if a wider definition of paint as "to cover over with colouring matter; to represent in a coloured picture; to produce a coloured picture"[25] is considered—electronic painting may be included.

Is it a drawing? Again, it is clearly possible to draw, in the sense of creating a picture by application of lines, shading and colour, on a computer and digital manipulations may amount to drawing.

**2–023**   It is submitted that any original artistic work created on a computer would fall within the 1988 Act category "graphic work" as a form of elec-

---

[22] [1983] F.S.R. 32.

[23] The criticism arises from the fact that the court was influenced by the fact that the painting must be on a surface; the surface was the singer's face; therefore the painting must comprise the makeup plus the face and once the makeup was removed there could be no painting. It may very well be the case that the makeup design was too simple to be original but the fact that the design was capable of being removed should be immaterial to the subsistence of copyright. See Laddie, Prescott & Vitoria, *et al. (3rd ed.), op. cit.*, at 4.20 and n.4; *Copinger & Skone James on Copyright* (14th ed.), at 3–37 n.93.

[24] [1983] F.S.R. 32, 46.

[25] Chambers Dictionary, Chambers Harap.

tronic drawing or painting. A digital photograph is protected as a "photograph" as defined by the Act and not as a graphic work. Any original digital manipulation of that photograph may by analogy be regarded as a graphic work as electronic painting or drawing. A manipulated photograph will consist of two elements (1) the original photograph, and (2) the alterations to the photograph. It is submitted that a digital photograph that has been manipulated to create an original new image will be a copyright work and protected partly as a photograph (the original image) and partly as a graphic work (the original alterations). The precise categorisation is in fact unimportant as (a) the definition of graphic work is non-exclusive leaving it open for other works to be included, and (b) all graphic works are treated identically by the 1988 Act[26]—there is no distinction between painting or drawing or an etching. Potentially, copyright may subsist in a digitally-manipulated photograph where the alterations are original.

Whether the final manipulated image has a separate copyright will depend upon the nature and extent of the alteration—*i.e.* is the manipulated image itself an original work or is it a mere copy of the photograph? The manipulated image may very well be an infringement of the original image.   **2–024**

In an American case, *Mendler v Winterland Production Ltd*, a photograph of two yachts in the Americas Cup that had been digitally manipulated was held to be an infringement of the original image.[27]. The court held it was a reproduction of the original—"a filtered, posterised reproduction—but photographic none the less."[28]

## *Photocopiers*

A photocopier does record images by the use of light but is based on the principle that opposite charges attract.   **2–025**

Some substances, such as selenium, arsenic, and tellurium are photo conductors, *i.e.* they act as electrical insulators in the dark and are conductors in the light. A thin layer of photo conductor material is coated on a metal backing either in the form of a drum or a flat plate within the photocopier. The drum surface is given a uniform static electric charge. A beam of light moves across the paper placed on the copier's glass surface. The light is reflected from the white paper to the drum below. Where photons of light hit the drum, electrons are emitted from the positive charges above. Dark areas remain positively charged.

Negatively charged powder (the toner) is spread over the surface and adheres to the positively charged image area. A piece of paper is then given a positive charge and placed over the surface where it attracts the negatively charged powder. The paper is then heated to fuse the image to the paper's surface. Colour copying uses similar principles but works in stages. The   **2–026**

---

[26] "All graphic works" refers to graphic works created on or after August 1, 1989. The 1988 Act does have separate provisions for works existing at the date it came into force. See generally Term of Protection, below at para. 2–093.
[27] *Mendler v Winterland Production Ltd* (US Court of Appeals 9th Circ.) 207 F.3d 1119; 54 U.S.P.Q. 2d 1070. For facts of this case see below at para. 3–017.
[28] 207 F.3d 1119, 1124.

image is scanned through colour filters and then separate toners for magenta, cyan, yellow and black are applied.

The starting point is that due to the method of production, a photocopy is a photographic work within the meaning of s.4. The real issue will be whether the photocopy is original. It was held in *Reject Shop v Manners*[29] that an enlarged photocopy of an artistic work could not attract copyright as the photocopy lacked originality. It is submitted that a photocopy is capable of being an original artistic work if it involves copying of (for example) originally arranged objects. This is discussed further below at para. 3–018, in relation to originality.

### Scanners

**2–027**   Scanners work in much the same way as a digital camera[30] recording images by the use of a CCD. Potentially, a scanner image may be a photographic work but as with photocopies the problem is likely to be originality.

### X-rays

**2–028**   A radiographic machine works in a similar way to an analogue camera, but instead of light uses electromagnetic radiation to expose the film. The classes as "other radiation" within the meaning of s.4 and if original, an x-ray will be protected as a copyright work.

### Holograms

**2–029**   As with a photograph, a hologram is created by exposing a photosensitive surface to light. A hologram is essentially the interference pattern created when two beams of laser light interfere on the holographic plate. A laser beam is split into two beams by a device called a beamsplitter: see Figure 4 below. The first beam (the reference beam) strikes the plate directly or after bouncing off a mirror. The second beam (the object beam) strikes the plate after being reflected off the object which is the subject of the hologram. The two beams are initially in phase but when they hit the photographic emulsion plate are out of phase creating areas of light and dark.

Unlike a photograph which only records light intensity, a hologram records all the information about light reflecting off an object including phase and amplitude. This enables the hologram to display the object in three dimensions.

The image is produced by a recording of laser light and thus a hologram, if original, will be protected as a photographic work.[31]

---

[29] [1995] F.S.R. 870.
[30] See above at paras 2–014 *et seq.*
[31] *Hansard*, HL Vol.495, col.1065.

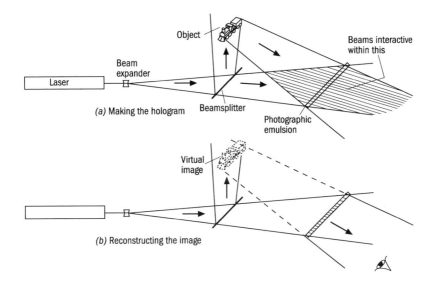

**Figure 4:** Diagram illustrating the mechanism of a hologram.[31a]

*Photo-booth pictures*

In principle, a photograph produced by a photo-booth is a protected work within s.4. The particular problem with such photographs is originality. Many photographs will be entirely non-creative. This is discussed below at para. 3–022.

*Automatic pictures: speed Cameras; photo-finish cameras and satellite images*

Automatic pictures present a particular problem again because of a potential lack of originality and also because in some cases they lack a human author. Common types of automatic photographs are photo-finish sports pictures which are in fact film frames; satellite images; security camera images (also film frames) and images from speed cameras. When considering whether copyright subsists in an "automatic" image, care should be taken to establish at the outset whether it is in fact a photograph within the meaning of the CDPA 1988 or whether it is a still from a video, film or other moving image and thus, if protected, will be protected as part of a film.

A photo-finish camera and automatic timing was used for the first time for track events at the 1932 Los Angeles Olympics. Originally, analogue cameras were used but obviously this meant athletes and spectators had to wait for the film to be developed before the results were known. Today photo-finish photographs at professional sporting events are taken from video film footage. The starter's pistol is linked to a transducer, which

**2–030**

**2–031**

**2–032**

---

[31a] Reproduced with permission of Graham Saxby, *The Science of Imaging* (Institute of Physics, 2001).

detects the sound made by the pistol. The transducer is connected to a timing computer which begins to run when it receives the signal. The timing system is connected to a video camera located at the finish line which produces the official time and a video image of the athletes as each one passes the finish line. The video camera scans a thin line which is aligned with the finish line up to 2000 times per second. The video image of each athlete as they actually cross the line is shown superimposed with a grid that records the time for each competitor. These images are stills from a moving image and would be protected as part of a film if considered original. They are not classed as photographs within the CDPA 1988.

A speed camera or Gatso unit takes a photograph of a speeding vehicle by the use of a radar beam. The speed of the passing vehicle is measured using a wide band Ka radar (also known as photoradar) emitted from the front of the camera across the road. The photoradar measures the speed and if the vehicle is travelling above a pre-determined limit, trips the camera which in turn takes two photographs of the vehicle. In principle, the image produced is a photograph as defined and capable of protection.

### Other types of imaging: ultrasonography; computed tomography and magnetic resonance imaging

**2–033**    Ultrasound images are produced using high frequency sound waves, some of which are reflected back to the probe when they encounter a barrier (bone, body tissue, etc.). The machine calculates the distance from the probe to the tissue or organ using the speed of sound in tissue and the time of each echo's return. The distances and intensities of the echoes on the screen form a two-dimensional image. Sound waves are not a form of radiation,[32] and it is therefore doubtful whether ultrasound images would fall within the statutory definition of a photograph.

**2–034**    Magnetic resonance imaging (MRI) works by altering the magnetic field in the tissue to be scanned. The image is produced by applying a radio frequency pulse to the tissue to be examined which causes hydrogen protons to absorb energy (see Figure 6, below). When the pulse is turned off, the protons slowly return to their natural alignment within the magnetic field of the MRI scanner. The signal given off by the protons is read by the magnetic coil and sent to the computer as data which is then converted into an image. Radio waves are a form of electro-magnetic radiation. It is submitted that an MRI image qualifies as a photograph within the meaning of the 1988 Act, subject to originality.

Computed tomography (from the Greek "tomos" meaning slice or section and "graphia" meaning writing) is based on the same principle as x-ray machines. Computed tomography is also known as CT scan or CAT Scan Computed Axial Tomography). The image is produced by x-rays passing

---

[32] The term "radiation" is generally applied to the emission of any rays, wave motion or particles from a source. It is usually applied to the emission of electromagnetic radiation. Sound is a mechanical wave requiring a medium through which to pass and is caused by a vibrating source. A wider non-scientific definition of "radiation" being something radiating from a source would encompass sound.

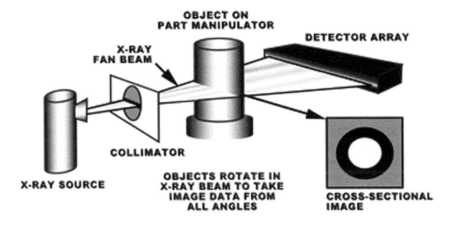

**Figure 5:** Computer Tomography[32a]

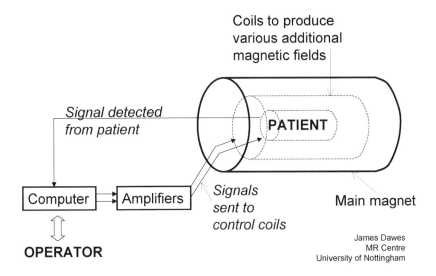

**Figure 6:** Magnetic Resonance Imaging[32b]

through the body of the subject. The x-rays are given precise definition by a collimator which defines the shape of the beam (see Figure 5, above). An x-ray machine performs a 360 degree rotation around the subject producing an image slice. The image is produced by use of radiation and potentially (if original) would class as a photographic work within the meaning of s.4 of the 1988 Act.

---

[32a] Reproduced with permission of *http://www.bio-imaging.com*.
[32b] Reproduced with permission of James Dawes, MR Centre, University of Nottingham.

*Photolithographs*

**2–035**    Photolithography is analogous to lithography where images were obtained from a flat surface by treating it so that ink would be repelled except where required when exposed to light. Historically, the 1911 Act defined a photograph as including a photolithograph.[33] A photolithograph is a recording of light on a medium upon which an image is produced and thus is potentially a protected work if original.

Today the technique of photolithography is used to imprint the patterns of an integrated circuit on a silicon wafer and the creation of semi-conductors. The process of photolithography involves the use of a material called "photo resist" to create a specific pattern on the surface of the wafer. Photo resist is a light-sensitive material which can be processed into a specific pattern after being exposed to light energy.

*Film frames*

**2–036**    Under the 1988 Act, a frame or a still from a film is not protected as a photograph. Section 4(2)(b) specifically defines a photograph as a recording of light or other radiation "which is not part of a film." Films are defined in s.5B as "a recording on any medium from which a moving image may by any means be produced."

**2–037**    Accordingly, still images or frames taken from films or videos may be protected as part of a film.[34] It has been held that a single frame of a film used on a poster was a copyright infringement of the film as a single frame amounted to a substantial part of the film.[35] This includes images from security cameras.[36] There is no requirement under the CDPA 1988 that a film be original to attract copyright.[37] It is questionable whether a photograph (rather than a film still) from a security type camera would be original within the meaning of the Act.[38]

## QUALIFYING CONDITIONS FOR COPYRIGHT PROTECTION UNDER THE 1988 ACT

**2–038**    An original photograph created on or after August 1, 1989, can qualify for copyright protection under the 1988 Act in one of two ways—either if the author is a qualifying person or by virtue of the place of first publication.

---

[33] s.35(1).

[34] *Spelling Goldberg Productions Inc v B.P.C Publishing* [1981] R.P.C. 280.

[35] *ibid.*

[36] *Hyde Park Residence Ltd v Yelland* [2001] Ch. 143,150C; [2000] 3 W.L.R. 215; [2000] E.C.D.R. 275; [2000] E.M.L.R. 363; [2000] R.P.C. 604. Subsistence of copyright in still photographs taken from a video of a security camera was not disputed. An allegation in the draft defence that the stills did not form a substantial part of the copyright work "appeared to have been abandoned".

[37] s.1(1)(b).

[38] See below at para. 3 023.

## Qualification by reference to author

When considering author qualification, the material time for an unpub- **2–039** lished photograph is when the work was made[39] and for a published photograph it is when the work was first published or if the author had died before publication, immediately before his death.[40]

A work qualifies for copyright protection if the author was, at the **2–040** material time, a qualifying person namely:

(a) a British citizen, a British Dependent Territories citizen, a British National (Overseas), a British Overseas Citizen, a British subject or a British protected person within the meaning of the British Nationality Act 1981,[41] or

(b) an individual domiciled or resident in the UK or another country to which the relevant provisions of the Act have been extended,[42] or

(c) a body incorporated under the law of a part of the UK or another country to which the relevant provisions of the Act have been extended.[43]

Broadly speaking for these purposes the countries to which the relevant **2–041** provisions have been extended are England, Wales, Scotland and Northern Island.[44] There is also power to extend the provisions to any of the Channel Islands, the Isle of Man or any Colony.[45] In addition, for unpublished works, protection has been extended to citizens or subjects of those foreign countries specified by order[46] under s.159 and those who are domiciled or resident there and to bodies incorporated under the laws of such a country. The countries are listed below, in Appendix 6.

For works of joint authorship, it is sufficient for any of the authors to be a **2–042** qualifying person for the work to attract protection.[47] However, only the qualifying persons are taken into account for the purposes of first owner-ship, duration and permitted acts in relation to anonymous and pseudon-ymous works.[48]

## Qualification by reference to country of first publication

Publication means the issue of copies of work to the public and includes **2–043** for the purposes of artistic works (including photographs) making it avail-

---

[39] CDPA 1988, s.154(4)(a).
[40] CDPA 1988, s.154(4)(b).
[41] CDPA 1988, s.154(1)(a).
[42] CDPA 1988, s.154(1)(b).
[43] CDPA 1988, s.154(1)(c).
[44] CDPA 1988, s.157(1).
[45] CDPA 1988, s.157(2).
[46] Copyright (Application to Other Countries) Order 1999 (SI 1999/1751).
[47] CDPA 1988, s.154(3).
[48] *ibid.*

able to the public by means of an electronic retrieval system.[49] Publication does not include any publication which is merely colourable and not intended to satisfy the reasonable requirements of the public.[50] Unauthorised acts of publication are also excluded.[51]

A photograph created on or after August 1, 1989, will qualify for copyright protection if it is first published in the United Kingdom or in another country to which the relevant provisions of the Act extend[52]—essentially England, Wales, Scotland and Northern Island.[53] There is also power to extend the provisions to any of the Channel Islands, the Isle of Man or any Colony.[54]

**2–044**   A work may also acquire copyright by first publication in foreign countries to which the provisions of the Act have been extended by Order in Council under s.159 of the CDPA 1988.[55] The foreign countries to which the provisions of the Act have been extended for the purposes of first publication of photographic works are listed in Appendix 6, below. Consideration of whether works of foreign origin are protected by copyright is outside the scope of this work and the reader is referred to other texts.[55a]

Where a work is simultaneously published in more than one country, the 1988 Act provides that publication in the UK or a qualifying country shall be treated as first publication.[56] Publication elsewhere within the previous 30 days is to be treated as simultaneous publication.[57]

### Qualifying conditions: Protection under the 1956 Act: Works created before August 1, 1989

**2–045**   The 1988 Act came into force on August 1, 1989.[58] The 1988 Act provided that the new provisions apply to works existing at commencement subject to any provisions to the contrary.[59] The 1988 Act also provides that every work in which copyright subsisted under the 1956 immediately before commencement is deemed to satisfy the qualification requirements of the 1988 Act.[59a]

When considering whether copyright subsists today in a photograph created before August 1, 1989, it is necessary to look at the provisions of the Copyright Act 1956 ('the 1956 Act"). This is because the transitional provisions of the 1988 Act provide that copyright does not subsist in a work that existed before the commencement of the 1988 Act unless copyright

---

[49] CDPA 1988, s.175(1).
[50] CDPA 1988, s.175(5).
[51] CDPA 1988, s.175(6).
[52] CDPA 1988, s.155(1).
[53] CDPA 1988, s.157(1).
[54] CDPA 1988, s.157(2).
[55] CDPA 1988, s.155(2).
[55a] See Laddie, Prescott & Vitoria, *et al.*, (3rd ed.), *op. cit.*, at 5.2 *et seq.* and 5.22 *et seq.*
[56] CDPA 1988, s.155(1).
[57] CDPA 1988, s.155(3).
[58] SI 1989/816.
[59] CDPA 1988, Sch.1, para.3.
[59a] CDPA 1988, Sch. 1, para. 35.

subsisted in it immediately before commencement.[60] Most of the provisions of the 1956 Act came into force on June 1, 1957.[61] For photographic works created before August 1, 1989, but after June 1, 1957, the question then is: did copyright subsist in the work under the 1956 Act? Photographs were protected under the 1956 Act if original, but there were differing provisions for published and unpublished works.

### Protection under the 1956 Act: General

The 1956 Act provided that copyright shall subsist in every original "artistic work which is unpublished".[62] The 1956 Act made a distinction between published and unpublished works which is discussed below. An artistic work was defined as:

**2–046**

"a work of any of the following descriptions that is to say—

(a) the following, irrespective of artistic quality, namely, paintings, sculptures, drawings, engravings and photographs" ...

"Photograph" is further defined under s.48 of the 1956 Act as:

"any product of photography or of any process akin to photography, other than a part of a cinematograph film."

As under the 1988 Act, a distinction is drawn between a photograph and a film frame which is protected as part of a cinematograph film.

### The 1956 Act: published works

Where a photograph had been published, then copyright subsists in the work under the 1956 Act if, but only if:

**2–047**

(a) the first publication of the photograph took place in the UK or in another country to which s.3 extended; or

(b) the author[63] was a qualified person at the time when the work was first published; or

(c) the author had died before that time but was a qualified person immediately before his death.[64]

It should be noted that the definition of the author of a photograph under the 1956 Act is different to that under the 1988 Act.[65] For published works, the relevant time for determining whether the author was qualified was at

---

[60] CDPA 1988, Sch.1, para.5(1).
[61] SI 1957/863.
[62] 1956 Act, s.3(2).
[63] For definition of author of a photograph under 1956 Act see below at para. 2–070.
[64] 1956 Act, s.3(3).
[65] See below at para. 2–070.

the time of publication. For unpublished works (see below) the relevant time is the date the work was made.

**2–048**    Under the 1956 Act "qualified person" is defined as:

(a) in the case of an individual a person who is a British subject or British protected person or a citizen of the Republic of Ireland or a person domiciled or resident in the UK or in another country to which that provision extended.[66]

(b) in the case of a company, a body incorporated under the laws of any part of the UK or another country to which that provision extended.[67]

However, for photographs taken before commencement of the 1956 Act where the qualified person is a company, the corporate body is a qualified person if it is a body corporate which has established a place of business in any part of the UK or another country to which those provisions extended.[68]

### 1956 Act: unpublished works

**2–049**    In the case of unpublished original photographs, copyright subsists under the 1956 Act if the author was a qualified person at the time the photograph was made.[69] The meaning of "Qualified person" under the 1956 Act is set out in the preceding paragraph. In order for copyright to subsist under the 1988 Act transitional provisions, it is necessary to establish that the 1956 Act "qualified person" criteria were satisfied to show that copyright subsisted immediately before commencement.

## Qualifying conditions: photographs created before June 1, 1957 and on or after July 1, 1912

**2–050**    The 1911 Act granted copyright protection to "every original literary dramatic musical and artistic work"[70] that met the qualifying conditions. Artistic works were defined as including photographs.[71] A photograph had a different definition from the later Acts and was defined as "including photolithograph and any work produced by any process analogous to photography."[72] This includes pre-1957 photographs which are stills from films.

**2–051**    The qualification provisions of the 1956 Act were not disapplied by the transitional provisions to works existing at commencement.[73] Thus for photographs created before June 1, 1957, the qualifying conditions of the 1956 Act apply—see above at paras 2–045 to 2–049. If the work was published before June 1, 1957, the 1956 Act limits conditions for qualification to

---

[66] 1956 Act, s.1(5)(a). "British Protected person" is stated to have the same meaning as in the British Nationality Act 1981 (previously British Nationality Act 1948): s.1(5).
[67] 1956 Act, s.1(5)(b).
[68] 1956 Act, Sch.7, para.39(4).
[69] 1956 Act, s.2(1).
[70] 1911 Act, s.1(1).
[71] 1911 Act, s.35(1).
[72] *ibid.*
[73] 1956 Act, Sch.7. NB: Sch. 7, para.1 in case of publication before June 1, 1957.

country of first publication and excludes national status of the author.[73a] It should be noted that where the qualifying person is a corporate body, the definition of corporate body in respect of photographs taken before commencement is different. For photographs taken before commencement of the 1956 Act, to be a qualifying person the body corporate needs to have established a place of business in any part of the UK or another country to which those provisions extended.[74]

## AUTHOR OF A PHOTOGRAPH

### Author of photograph taken on or after August 1, 1989

The author of a photograph taken on or after August 1, 1989, is the person **2–052** who creates it.[75] Usually this will be the photographer but difficulties may arise where one person arranges the subject matter of the photograph and a different person actually takes the photograph.[76] Interestingly, the Whitford Committee on Copyright and Designs Law which reported in March 1977[77] recommended that an author should be defined as the "person responsible for the composition of the photograph" but this was not implemented.

Older cases suggest that the author is the person who is the effective cause **2–053** of the photograph and that this may well be the person who arranges the composition[78] or the person who expended labour and skill in the production of the photograph.[79] However, where the person arranging the composition is merely acting as the assistant or agent of the principal photographer, the author is the principal photographer.[80] Many of these

---

[73a] 1956 Act, Sch.7, para.1.

[74] 1956 Act, Sch.7, para.39(4).

[75] CDPA 1988, s.9(1).

[76] See Y. Gendreau, *Copyright Ownership of Photographs in Anglo- American Law* [1993] 15(6) E.I.P.R. 207; K. Garnett, and A. Abbott, *Who is the "Author" of a Photograph?* [1998] E.I.P.R. 204.

[77] 1977 Cmnd. 6732.

[78] *Nottage v Jackson* (1883) 11 Q.B.D. 627 (see below at para.2–057) applied in *Wooderson v Raphael Tuck & Sons* (1887) 4 T.L.R. 57. (Photograph of two children in a photographer's shop. The assistant who "superintended the arrangements and actually formed the picture—he put people in position" was the author and not the shop proprietor who did nothing).

[79] *Ellis v Marshall (H.) & Son* (1895) 64 L.J.Q.B. 757 at 758 *per* Charles J. (Fine Arts Copyright Act 1862, photograph of an actress—mere permission of the sitter to allow photograph to be taken did not constitute a photograph "executed for on behalf of any other person for a good or valuable consideration" with s.1 of that Act.)

[80] *Melville v Mirror of Life Company* [1895] 2 Ch. 531; 13 R. 852; 65 L.J Ch. 531. The plaintiff photographer took a photograph of two well-known sporting personalities assisted by his son. The headnote in [1895] 2 Ch. 531 states that "The son posed [the subject] and performed all the manual acts, while the father stood by and looking on, and at the proper moment held up his hand so as to indicate to [the subject] the direction in which to look". It was contended by the plaintiff that the son acted as the father's agent and under his directions. Kekewich J. observed that: "The evidence is somewhat conflicting" but concluded that the author was the father who was the principal throughout. For discussion of this case see K. Garnett, and A. Abbott, *Who is the "Author" of a Photograph?* [1998] E.I.P.R. 204 at p.207 where the differing reports of the case are considered and the authors conclude "The decision is unsatisfactory because the factual basis for it is unclear."

cases were decided under the Fine Arts Copyright Act 1862 which did not define "author" and are of limited value when considering authorship under the 1988 Act. They do however shed some light on the court's approach to the general question of who is the author of a photograph and some of these cases are discussed below in more detail.

**2–054**    In *Creation Records v News Group Newspapers*[81] which concerned photographs taken for an album cover for the group Oasis it was said by Lloyd J. in the judgment:

> "It seems to me that ordinarily the creator of a photograph is the person who takes it. There may be cases where one person sets up the scene to be photographed (the position and angle of the camera and all the necessary settings) and directs a second person to press the shutter release button at a moment chosen by the first in which case it would be the first, not the second, who creates the photograph. There may also be cases of collaboration between the person behind the camera and one or more others in which the actual photographer has greater input, although no complete control of the creation of the photograph in which case it may be a work of joint creation and joint authorship."[82]

**2–055**    It is arguable that because the person who actually takes the photograph is the person who in fact creates it, the photographer will always be an author of the work. Even in circumstances where another person does everything other than press the shutter—arranges the composition of a photograph, chooses the film, sites the photographer, focuses the camera and tells the photographer when to take the photograph—it remains the case that the actual creation of the image occurs when the shutter is pressed.

**2–056**    It is submitted that where everything (other than pressing the shutter) is done by someone other than the actual shutter presser, that other person is the sole author of the photograph. All the creative work and the labour and skill to bring the image into being has been carried out by that other person. However, a very high degree of intervention by a third person would be necessary for the actual photographer to be denied joint authorship. Or to put it another way, where there is sufficient creative input from someone who arranges the composition of a photograph, if the photographer did anything other than just press the shutter (such as lighting or composing, the photograph) he should be regarded as a joint author. It is submitted that mere selection of angle for the photograph or choice of time to take the photograph would suffice. In most cases, joint authorship between the arranger and the photographer is more likely than sole authorship vested in an arranger.[83]

**2–057**    In *Nottage v Jackson*,[84] an 1883 case decided under the Fine Arts Copyright Act 1862, made some helpful observations on the authorship of a

---

[81] [1997] E.M.L.R. 444. Discussed in more detail below at para.2–060.
[82] [1997] E.M.L.R. 444 at 450–451.
[83] See Joint Authors below at para. 2–066.
[84] (1883) 11 Q.B.D. 627.

photograph. The plaintiffs were in partnership as a photographic business. They sent one of their photographer employees to photograph the Australian cricket team. The plaintiffs registered themselves as authors of the photograph under the Fine Arts Copyright Act 1862 which did not define "author". The defendant objected that the plaintiffs were not the authors of the photograph. It was held that they were not but the court did not need to decide who the author was and did not do so.

When considering who was the author of the photograph Brett M.R. said:

"The nearest I can come to is that it is the person who effectively is, as near as he can be, the cause of the picture which is produced—that is, the person who has superintended the arrangement, who has actually formed the picture by putting the people into position, and arranging the place in which the people are to be—the man who is the effective cause of that. Although he may only have done it by standing in the room and giving orders about it, still it is his mind and act as far as anybody's mind and act are concerned, which is the effective cause of the picture such as it is when it is produced. Therefore it will be question in every case who that man is. That will be a matter of evidence. That will be a question of fact."[85]

Cotton L.J. took the view that the word author should be given the same interpretation in respect of a photograph as for the author of a painting or drawing. He stated "In my opinion, "author" involves originating, making, producing, as the inventive or mastermind the thing which is to be protected whether it be a drawing or a painting or a photograph."[86] Bowen L.J. also considered that there was little difference between the author of a photograph and a painting. He agreed with Brett M.R.'s "effective cause" test and said that author was the man who "really represents or creates or gives effect to the idea or fancy or imagination."[87]    **2–058**

In *Stackemann v Paton*,[88] also decided under the Fine Arts Copyright Act 1862, concerned a photograph of a school cricket team. The proprietor of the school had arranged for a photographer to take photographs of the school. In relation to other photographs, the school proprietor had directed the photographer telling him which rooms he wished to be photographed and pointing out points of view from which it would be desirable to photograph the outside of the school house.[89] The school proprietor posed the cricket 11 himself as if they were playing a match and had them photographed. Farwell J. considered that the photographer was the author as he took the photographs. Although the school proprietor directed and guided the photographer, the court concluded that he could not be said to be the author of the photograph. It is submitted that if this case were to be decided today, that the photographer and the school proprietor would be held to be joint authors of the photograph.    **2–059**

---

[85] (1883) 11 Q.B.D. 627 at 632.
[86] *ibid.*, at 635.
[87] *ibid.*, at 637.
[88] [1906] 1 Ch. 774.
[89] *ibid.*, at 779.

**2–060**    In *Creation Records v News Group Newspapers*[90] a member of the pop group Oasis supervised the placing of various objects around a hotel swimming pool to be photographed as the basis for an album cover. A tabloid commissioned a freelance photographer to attempt to take pictures of the shoot. He managed to take photographs of the scene that were very similar to the one selected for the album cover but at a different angle— slightly to the left of the official photographer. It was argued for the plaintiffs that the subject matter had been created by the pop group member and therefore he created all photographs taken from it. This was rejected by the judge who concluded that on the facts, it was unarguable that anyone other than the photographer was the creator.[91] Merely bringing the subject matter of a photograph into existence did not make someone a creator of a photograph.[92]

### Authorship: automatic photographs

**2–061**    In the case of an artistic work which is computer-generated, the author is taken to be the person by whom the arrangements for the creation of the work are taken.[93] Computer-generated means that the work is generated by a computer in circumstances such that there is no human author of the work.[94] This would potentially include photographs taken automatically where there is truly no human author. Automatic photographs pose a particularly difficult problem as, in many cases, an image will be the product of both a computer and of human labour and skill. However, the 1988 Act does not permit joint authorship by a human with a computer.[95]

**2–062**    It remains an open question as to what extent and in what circumstances images taken automatically are computer-generated within the meaning of the 1988 Act. Consider a photo-finish image from an athletics race. As discussed above at para. 2–031, today this type of image will almost certainly be a still from video or film footage and protected under the 1988 Act as part of a film rather than a photograph.[96] It is not necessary for a film to satisfy any requirement for originality.[97] But say for the sake of argument, a photo-finish image is an automatically taken photograph. The person who selected the film, the type of camera, positioned the camera and focussed the camera has expended labour and skill in the creation of the image. In some ways this is analogous to the situation where one person sets up the photograph and carries out all the creative contribution to the photograph,

---

[90] [1997] E.M.L.R. 444.
[91] [1997] E.M.L.R. 444 at 451.
[92] *ibid*
[93] CDPA 1988, s.9(3).
[94] CDPA 1988, s.178.
[95] CDPA 1988, s.10(1) (joint authorship requires two or more authors); s.178 (computer-generated work arises where there is no human author).
[96] For the purposes of a film, the author is taken to be the producer and the principal director: CDPA, 1988, s.9(a)(b). This raises an interesting question when considering images that are stills from (say) a fixed focus security camera. There is in reality no human author and there is certainly no director.
[97] CDPA 1988, s.1(1)(b).

except for pressing the shutter. This may be the case with a time delayed photograph. In such circumstances, the image is not simply computer generated but has the contribution of human author.

Where photographs are taken with the aid of a computer whether a time 2–063 delay camera or a trip, but the machine is guided and directed by a person using it as a creative instrument, it is submitted that the work is not "computer-generated" within the meaning of the Act but rather the work is created by the person as author. It will be a question of fact in each case as to whether there is sufficient creative contribution from a human author for that person to be an author within the meaning of the Act.

In an Austrian case,[98] it was held that the test for authorship of a pho- 2–064 tograph produced mechanically was whether the claimant's contribution to the creation of the photograph is to be judged as merely subordinate, as being no more than an assistant function or a mere helper with no real contribution. The case concerned a camera set up to take automatic weather pictures at a mountain railway station. The claimant had installed and configured the cameras and carried out technical work necessary to transmit the photographs to the internet. The pictures were updated hourly. The defendant used various images in its own online services. The claimant's contribution was considered to be furnishing the necessary technical work (acquisition of the materials, installation and programming of the entire system, setting the camera, including the choice of its position and also the picture details). The only part of the process in which the claimant had made no contribution was during the actual shooting of the image. The court considered that the claimant provided more than a mere service of assistance and was a co-author of the photographs together with anyone who (using the system) chose the image content or the time at which an image was taken. This case is useful in a UK context for its consideration of what is required for authorship where images are produced automatically. Care should be taken when considering this case in a UK context as to originality and whether copyright subsists in a weather photograph, because it was decided under s.74 of the Austrian statute which grants a related right protection to non-original photographs[99] and the standard of creativity is judged under the author's rights system of Austria rather than a common law copyright standard.[1]

It is submitted that where a person has their photograph taken in an 2–065 automatic photo booth that they may be regarded as the author of the photograph under s.9(3) of the 1988 Act.[2] Although the photograph is taken automatically, the arrangements for the creation of a portrait are made by

---

[98] *Re Vorarlberg Online* [2001] E.C.D.R. 30, Oberster Gerichtshof (Austria).
[99] See below at para. 3–082 and Appendix 2 (Austria).
[1] See below at para. 3–102 and Appendix 2.
[2] See also Y. Gendreau, *Copyright Ownership of Photographs In Anglo-American Law* [1993] 15(6) E.I.P.R. 207 at p.210 citing *Fetherling v Boughner* (1978) 40 C.P.R. (2d) 253, a Canadian case where the author of a magazine article asked people to have their photographs taken in photo-booths. The court did not declare the article writer to be the author of the photographs but did not discuss who the author might be. "Had a provision similar to s.9(3) of the UK Act been in force, it is likely that the persons who put the coins into the machine would have been recognised as authors of their own photographs".

the person concerned. They put the coins into the machine and they arrange their own position before the camera.

### Joint authors

**2–066**    The 1988 Act defines a work of joint authorship as "a work produced by the collaboration of two or more authors in which the contribution of each other is not distinct from that of the other author or authors".[3] As discussed above, it is possible for two or more people to be authors of a photograph—in particular, a person who arranges the subject matter and directs the photographer together with the photographer.[4]

**2–067**    Each author must contribute a significant part of the labour and skill[5] but it is not necessary that each must contribute to the same extent as the others.[6] Collaboration requires furtherance of some common design.[7] Thus it would not be possible for an arranger of a scene to be a joint author of a photograph where he was unaware that the photograph was being taken as in *Creation Records v Newsgroup Newspapers*.[8] It is a question of fact not agreement whether a work is a work of joint authorship.[9]

It is a matter of fact and degree whether a person's contribution is sufficient to make him a joint author.[10] Trivial contributions do not qualify the contributor as a joint author and mere suggestions of ideas may not be enough.[11] It is submitted that in the case of photographs, the starting point is that the photographer is an author of the photograph and is likely to be, at a minimum, a joint author. Only where he merely presses the shutter at the direction of another and has done nothing else could he be denied author status.

**2–068**    The same matters that are taken into account in determining originality should be considered when assessing the photographer's labour and skill. Selection of angle, lighting, choice of film, moment to take the photograph and so forth are creative choices which confer originality on an image. If the photographer has input into some or all of these choices, he has contributed to creation of the image. In an American case where one person X had the idea and arranged the composition of the photograph, but Y, a professional photographer actually took the photograph, it was held X was a co-author with Y.[12] X had conceived the idea to photograph a particular subject; sourced the subject matter; arranged the composition of each photograph; directed the photographer to make changes to camera angles and gave final

---

[3] CDPA 1988, s.10(1).
[4] *Creation Records Ltd v News Group Newspapers Ltd* [1997] E.M.L.R. 444 at 450–451. See above at para. 2–060.
[5] *Ray v Classic FM plc* [1998] F.S.R. 622 at 636.
[6] *Levy v Rutley* (1871) L.R. 6 C.P. 523.
[7] *Ray v Classic FM plc* [1998] F.S.R. 622; *Levy v Rutley* (1871) L.R. 6 C.P. 523.
[8] [1997] E.M.L.R. 444. See above at para. 2–060.
[9] *Levy v Rutley* (1871) L.R. 6 C.P. 523; *Godfrey v Lees* [1995] E.M.L.R. 307.
[10] *Stuart v Barrett* [1994] E.M.L.R. 448.
[11] *Beckingham v Hodgens* [2002] EWHC 2143 at para.45; [2003] E.C.D.R. 6; [2003] F.S.R. 14 at 248.
[12] *Brod v General Publishing Group In* 2002 U.S. App. LEXIS 2544 (9th Cir., 2002).

approval of the positioning of the subject matter and the angle before the photographer triggered the shutter.

Whether another person's contribution is sufficient to confer on him joint authorship will depend upon the level of input. It is submitted that merely telling a photographer what to photograph or broadly deciding the place from which to take the photograph is insufficient.[13] **2–069**

### Author of photograph taken on or after June 1, 1957, but before August 1, 1989

The 1988 Act provides that for the purposes of copyright, the author of a work existing when that Act came into force on August 1, 1989, shall be determined in accordance with the law in force at the time.[14] This does not apply to moral rights[15] or determination of the identity of an author of an existing work for the purposes of determining the term of copyright under the Duration Regulations.[16] **2–070**

Under the 1956 Act, the author of a photograph was defined as the person who at the time when the photograph was taken is the owner of the material on which it is taken.[17] Under the 1956 Act (like the 1911 Act) it was possible for a corporation to be the author of photographic copyright. It is questionable whether this was compatible with Art.6 *bis* of the Berne Convention which granted moral rights to authors and contained the words "after his death" plainly indicating a person and not a corporation.[18]

For the purposes of transitional provisions the Term Directive (which calculates the term by reference to the author's death), the UK Regulations state that the author of existing photographs is to be determined in accordance with s.9 of the 1988 Act, *i.e.* the person who creates the photograph,[19] and not in accordance with the law in force at the time. This addresses potential problems where the author of a pre-1989 photograph was a corporation and hence did not have a date of death. **2–071**

The 1956 Act defined works of joint authorship as "a work produced by the collaboration of two or more authors in which the contribution of each author is not separate from the contribution of the other author or authors".[20] The wording is almost identical to the 1988 Act save that the word separate is replaced with "distinct" in the 1988 Act.

---

[13] See *e.g. Tate v Thomas* [1921] 1 Ch. 503 (idea for plot/comic routine to be included insufficient); *Evans v E. Hulton & Co Ltd* [1923–28] Mac.C.C. 51 (passing on reminiscences to ghost writer insufficient).

[14] CDPA 1988, Sch.1, para.10.

[15] *ibid.*

[16] Copyright and Related Rights Regulations 1996 (SI 1996/2967), reg.19.

[17] 1956 Act, s.48(1).

[18] As to Berne Convention see below at para. 3–051.

[19] Copyright and Related Rights Regulations 1996 (SI 1996/2967), reg.19.

[20] 1956 Act, s.11(3).

## Author of photograph taken on or after July 1, 1912, but before June 1, 1957

**2–072**    Under the 1911 Act, the author of a photograph is deemed to be the person who was the owner of the original negative from which the photograph was directly or indirectly derived at the time when the negative was made.[21] The 1911 Act expressly contemplated that the first owner of copyright in a photograph could be a company.[22] See previous paragraph for effect of Term Directive where author was a company.

The 1911 Act defined a work of joint authorship as "a work produced by the collaboration of two or more authors in which the contribution of one author is not distinct from the contribution of the other author or authors".[23]

### FIRST OWNERSHIP OF COPYRIGHT

## First owner of copyright in a photograph taken on or after August 1, 1989

**2–073**    Under the 1988 Act, generally the author of a work is the first owner of the copyright.[24] There are some exceptions to this rule, the main one being in the case of employees. Where a photograph is created by an employee in the course of his employment, his employer is the first owner of copyright in the work subject to any agreement to the contrary.[25] It is open to the employer and employee to make an agreement as to first ownership which will override the statutory provision.[26] In addition, under s.163 of the 1988 Act, copyright in any work made by an officer or servant of the Crown in the course of his duties belongs to the Crown.

**2–074**    Employment is defined as meaning employment under a contract of service or of apprenticeship.[27] A contract of service is distinguished from a contract for services where the contract is for the services of an independent contractor. The modern approach of the courts in determining whether a worker is engaged as a servant under a contract of service is to apply a multiple test.[28] Usually three questions will be considered[29]:

---

[21] 1911 Act, s.21.
[22] 1911 Act, s.21—"and where such owner is a body corporate".
[23] 1911 Act, s.16(3).
[24] CDPA 1988, s.11(1). As to who is the author of a photograph see above at paras 2–052 *et seq.*
[25] CDPA 1988, s.11(2).
[26] See for example *Christopher Bede Studios Ltd v United Portraits Ltd* [1958] N.Z.L.R. 250. A photographer's contract with customers which stated that in consideration for the supply of photographic proofs the customer agreed that the copyright in the photographs taken "shall be owned" by the photographer. It was held to be an agreement for consideration that the photographer was the first owner of the copyright and that it was not a transfer of an existing copyright.
[27] CDPA 1988, s.178.
[28] *Harvey on Industrial Relations and Employment Law* (Butterworths, Looseleaf) at A49.
[29] *Ready Mixed Concrete Ltd v Minister of Pensions & N.I* [1968] 2 Q.B. 497.

(1) Did the worker undertake to provide his own work and skill in return for remuneration?

(2) Was there a sufficient degree of control to enable the worker fairly to be called a servant?

(3) Were there any other factors inconsistent with the existence of a contract of service?

The degree of control exercised by the employer is an important con- **2–075** sideration. Factors the courts have considered as indicators of a contract of service and status are the presence of a regular salary for a full-time job; provision by employer of equipment; office and secretary provided by the employer; PAYE deductions and pension scheme deductions from salary made by employer; and the employee not using her own capital for the job.[30]

There is considerable case law both within the field of copyright law and outside it as to what constitutes a contract of service and what is meant by in the course of employment. These are more general issues concerning copyright rather than specifically pertaining to photographs. For detailed treatment of these questions the reader is referred to other texts.[31]

### First owner of copyright in photograph taken before August 1, 1989 and on or after June 1, 1957: commissioned photographs

The first ownership of copyright in works pre-dating the 1988 Act is **2–076** determined in accordance with the law in force at the time that the work was made.[32] For photographs taken between August 1, 1989, and after June 1, 1957, the 1956 Act applies.

Under the 1956 Act, generally the author[33] of a photograph was the first owner of the copyright in a photograph.[34] This was subject to three exceptions. First, where the photograph was created by the author in the course of his employment by the proprietor of a newspaper, magazine or similar periodical under a contract of service or apprenticeship *and* the photograph was made for the purpose of publication in that periodical the proprietor of the newspaper is entitled to copyright in the work. This is subject to any agreement to the contrary.[35]

Secondly, where a photograph is commissioned and the commissioner **2–077** pays or agrees to pay for the photograph in money or money's worth and the photograph is taken in pursuance of that commission, the commissioner

[30] *Beloff v Presdram* [1973] 1 All E.R. 241.
[31] *Copinger & Skone James on Copyright* (14th ed.) paras 5–08 *et seq.*; Laddie, Prescott & Vitoria, *et al.*, (3rd ed.), *op cit.*, Ch 21.
[32] CDPA 1988, Sch.1, para.11(1).
[33] Under the 1956 Act, the person who at the time when the photograph was taken is the owner of the material on which it is taken—see above at para. 2–070.
[34] 1956 Act, s.4(1).
[35] 1956 Act, s.4(5).

is the first owner of the copyright.[36] This is subject to any agreement to the contrary.[37] This provision applies to any photograph made pursuant to a commission agreement entered into before the 1988 Act commenced but taken after commencement.[38]

**2–078**   It is necessary for the commissioning agreement to pre-date the creation of the work.[39] An invitation by a photographer to have a photograph taken with no obligation to pay for the sitting does not amount to a commission.[40] A commission requires that one person shall give an order to another to do a particular piece of work, whether it be to take a photograph or to paint or draw a portrait.[41] It has been held that "commission" in the 1956 Act is just another word for order.[42]

**2–079**   An agreement to pay requires a consensus. A mere intention to pay from the commissioner and a mere expectation of payment from the commissioned without any promise to pay could not, even together, amount to an agreement to pay.[43]

**2–080**   Thirdly, in any other case (not falling within the first two situations) where a work is made in the course of the author's employment by another person under a contract of service or apprenticeship, the first owner is the employer.[44] Again, this is subject to any agreement to the contrary.[45]

### First ownership of copyright in a photograph taken before June 1, 1957, but after July 1, 1912

**2–081**   The first ownership of copyright in photographs taken before the commencement of the 1956 Act is governed by the 1911 Act.[46] The 1911 Act provided that the author of a work is the first owner of copyright but commissioned works had different provisions.

It was provided that in the case of a photograph where as "the original plate was ordered by some other person and was made for valuable consideration in pursuance of that order, then in the absence of any agreement to the contrary, the person by whom such plate or other original was

---

[36] 1956 Act, s.4(3).

[37] 1956 Act, s.4(5).

[38] CDPA 1988, Sch.1, para.11(2)(a).

[39] *Hartnett v Pinkett* (1953) 103 L.J. 204.

[40] *Sasha Ltd v G Stonesco* (1929) 45 T.L.R. 350 (decided under the 1911 Act).

[41] *Apple Corps Ltd v Cooper* [1993] F.S.R. 286 (photographs taken for the cover of the Beatles Sergeant Pepper's Lonely Hearts Club band were not commissioned as there was no agreement to pay). See also *Boucas v Cooke* [1903] 2 K.B. 227 (1911 Act); *Stackemann v Paton* [1906] 1 Ch. 774; *PS Johnson v Bucko Enterprises Ltd* [1975] 1 N.Z.L.R. 311; *James Arnold & Co Ltd v Miafern Ltd* [1980] R.P.C. 397; *Plix Products Ltd v Frank M Winstone (Merchants)* [1986] N.Z.L.R. 63; *Gabrin v Universal Music Operations Ltd* [2003] EWHC. 1335, Ch D (photograph taken at a photoshoot had not been commissioned).

[42] *Apple Corps Ltd v Cooper* [1993] F.S.R. 286 *per* HHJ Micklem sitting as a High Court Judge of the Chancery Division.

[43] *Loc. cit.*

[44] 1956 Act, s.4(4).

[45] 1956 Act, s.4(5).

[46] CDPA 1988, Sch.1, para.11(1).

ordered shall be the first owner of the copyright."[47] This provision still applies in determining the first ownership of a commissioned photograph made in pursuance of an agreement entered into before commencement of the 1956 Act.[48]

## First ownership of pre-1912 photographs

The provisions of the Fine Art Copyright Act 1862[49] apply to pre-1912    **2–082** photographs. The author of a photograph was the first owner copyright.[50] However, where a negative of any photograph was "sold or disposed of or shall be made or executed for or on behalf of any other person for a good or valuable consideration" the person selling or disposing or making the negative did not retain the copyright unless it was expressly reserved to the author in writing and signed by the person for whom it was made.[51] Equally, the assignee was not entitled to the copyright unless an agreement in writing was made signed by the person selling or disposing of the negative.

## Joint owners

One joint owner of copyright cannot grant an exclusive licence without    **2–083** the consent of the other owner or owners.[52] Such a licence could not possibly be an exclusive licence as one joint owner would not be able, without the consent of the others, to exclude the others or their licensees.[53]

## Extended copyright

The Duration of Copyright & Rights in Performances Regulations 1995[54]    **2–084** extended the copyright term from 50 years pma to 70 years pma. Many existing copyright works gained the benefit of an extended copyright term as a result.[55] The Regulations provide that the person who owned the copyright immediately before January 1, 1996, is the owner of any extended copyright.[56] If he was entitled to the copyright for a period less than the whole copyright term, then any extended copyright forms part of the reversionary interest and will belong to the owner of the reversion when the period expires.[57]

---

[47] 1911 Act, s.5(1)(a). For cases concerning the meaning of "commission" see above under 1956 Act at para. 2–078.
[48] CDPA 1988, Sch.1, para.11(1) and (2).
[49] (25 & 26 Vict. c.68).
[50] Fine Arts Copyright Act 1862, s.1.
[51] *ibid.*
[52] *Mail Newspapers plc v Express Newspapers plc* [1987] F.S.R. 90 at 93.
[53] *ibid.*
[54] SI 1995/3297. Came into force on January 1, 1996.
[55] As to the effect of the Regulations on duration see below at paras 2–093 *et seq.*
[56] regs 12, 17 and 18(1).
[57] reg.18(2).

## Revived copyright

**2–085**     Where copyright had expired before the Duration of Copyright & Rights in Performances Regulations 1995[58] but was revived by those Regulations, generally the person who owned the copyright immediately before it expired is the owner of any revived copyright.[59] However, if the former owner had died before January 1, 1996,[60] (or was a legal entity that ceased to exist before that date) then the revived copyright of a film will best in the principal director of the film or his personal representatives.[61] In the case of all other works, including photographs, the revived copyright vests in the author of the work or his personal representatives.[62]

Revived copyright that vests in personal representatives pursuant to the Regulations is to be held by them for the benefit of the person who would have been entitled to it had it been vested in the principal director or author immediately before his death and had devolved as part of his estate.[63]

Revived copyright is subject to a licence as of right for which a reasonable royalty is payable provided the requisite notice is served.[63a]

## Equitable ownership

**2–086**     Equitable ownership of the copyright may arise where the author of a work can, in the circumstances of the case, be regarded as holding the copyright on trust for another. In such circumstances the beneficial owner is entitled to have the copyright assigned to him. Insofar as photographs are concerned, equitable ownership may arise where the photograph has been commissioned.

**2–087**     The mere fact that a photograph is commissioned is not sufficient to give rise to equitable ownership.[64] Unlike its predecessor statutes,[65] the 1988 Act contains no provisions for the grant of copyright to a person commissioning a work. Whether it is possible to contend that a commissioned photograph beneficially belongs to the commissioner will depend on the circumstances of the case. A person who commissions a photograph and wishes to acquire the copyright is best advised to enter into a written agreement for the same prior to the photograph being created.

**2–088**     If there is equitable ownership of commissioned wedding photographs, in the absence of any direct evidence to the contrary, the court will infer that whomsoever of the husband and wife commissioned the photographs did so expressly or impliedly with the consent of the other and on behalf of them

---

[58] SI 1995/3297. Came into force on January 1, 1996.
[59] reg.19(1).
[60] The date of commencement of the Regulations.
[61] SI 1995/3297, reg.19(2).
[62] SI 1995/3297, reg.19(2)(b).
[63] SI 1995/3297, reg.19(3).
[63a] SI 1995/3297, reg. 24.
[64] *Ray v Classic FM plc* [1998] F.S.R. 622 at 641 *per* Lightman J.
[65] See above at para. 2–076.

both.[66] The natural understanding of prospective husband and wife would be that the wedding photographs were to belong to both of them and in the absence of evidence to the contrary the only reasonable inference is that the bride and groom intended to hold the copyright jointly.[67]

Where there has been no express agreement, in order for equitable ownership to arise, it is necessary to be able to imply a term that the intention of the parties was that the commissioner would be entitled to the copyright. The issue will be in every case what the client under the contract has agreed to pay for and whether that includes the copyright.[68] The possible alternatives are that the commissioner has bought the copyright, some form of copyright licence or nothing at all.

The law governing the conditions necessary for the implication of terms   **2–089**
into a contract is well settled and requires the following to be met[69]:

(1)  it must be reasonable and equitable;

(2)  it must be necessary to give business efficacy to the contract so that no term will be implied if the contract is effective without it;

(3)  it must be so obvious that "it goes without saying";

(4)  it must be capable of clear expression; and

(5)  it must not contract any express term of the contract.

The court will adopt a minimalist approach when implying terms. Thus, if   **2–090**
necessity requires only the grant of a licence, the ambit of the licence must be the minimum which is required to secure to the client the entitlement which the parties to the contract intended to confer.[70] The amount of the purchase price the commissioner is obliged to pay may be relevant[71]—a nominal fee may lead to the implication of a very limited licence[72] where as a higher fee may indicate a more extensive copyright licence.[73] The minimalist approach adopted by modern courts means that in most cases the grant of an exclusive licence will be sufficient and a full assignment of the copyright on the basis of equitable ownership is likely to be comparatively rare.[74] However, where the intention of the parties is that the only person entitled to exploit the

---

[66] *Mail Newspapers plc v Express Newspapers plc* [1987] F.S.R. 90 at 93 *per* Millett J. (application for interim injunction).
[67] *ibid.* at 94.
[68] *Ray v Classic FM plc* [1988] F.S.R. 622 at 640 *per* Lightman J.
[69] *BP Refinery (Westernport) Pty Ltd v The President, Councillors and Ratepayers of the Shire of Hastings* (1978) 52 A.L.J.R. 20 at 26 *per* Lord Simon of Glaisdale. Approved in *Philips Electronique v British Sky Broadcasting Ltd* [1995] E.M.L.R. 472 at 481. See also *Liverpool City Council v Irwin* [1977] A.C. 239.
[70] *Ray v Classic FM plc* [1998] F.S.R. 622 at 642 *per* Lightman J.
[71] *Ray v Classic FM plc* [1998] F.S.R. 622 at 643 *per* Lightman J.
[72] *Stovin-Bradford v Volpoint Properties Ltd* [1971] 1 Ch. 1007 (nominal fee to architect—licence limited to using plans for planning permission application only).
[73] *Blair v Tompkins & Osbourne* [1971] 2 Q.B. 78 (full RIBA scale fee licence extended to using architect plans for the building itself).
[74] *Ray v Classic FM plc* [1998] F.S.R. 622 at 644 *per* Lightman J.

work is the commissioner, the copyright is probably held on trust by the author for the commissioner.[75]

**2–091**    In *Durand v Molino*, a portrait was commissioned in a commercial context (by a restaurant owner for exhibition in the restaurant and reproduction on menus) and it was held that the commissioner was beneficially entitled to the copyright and entitled to have it transferred to him.[76] It was said that where the commissioner is the subject of the portrait, prima facie, he should have complete control of the work.[77] The two factors that seemed to have influenced the court most were (1) the fact that the painting was a portrait of the commissioner himself, and (2) the portrait had a clearly commercial purpose. The existence of a commercial purpose is important. This case is not authority for the proposition that a commission to take a photographic portrait of the commissioner is sufficient to establish equitable ownership. It is submitted that, by analogy, when a photographic portrait of an individual is commissioned for a commercial purpose or with some other intention that only the commissioner is entitled to exploit the photograph, in the absence of agreement, equitable ownership arises.[77a]

**2–092**    An equitable owner, whilst entitled to interim relief,[78] must join the legal owner before obtaining judgment[79] or otherwise obtain legal title by taking an assignment of the copyright and a right to sue for past infringements. If this is not done there is a risk that proceedings will be stayed.[80]

## THE TERM OF PROTECTION

**2–093**    The basic term of protection for copyright is 70 years from the end of the calendar year in which the author dies[81]—otherwise expressed as 70 years pma.[82] However, there are exceptions—particularly for older photographs, as discussed below. The extension of the term to 70 years pma was as a result of the amendment to the 1988 Act by the Duration of Copyright and Rights in Performances Regulations 1995[83] ("the Duration Regulations") which came into force on January 1, 1996. Previously, the term of protection had been 50 years after end of the year in which the author died. The Duration Regulations brought the European Term Directive[84] into force in the UK.

---

[75] *Massine v de Basil* (1936–45) M.C.C. 223 (composition of ballet); *Warner v Gestetner* [1988] E.I.P.R. 89 (advertising logo). See also *R. Griggs Group Ltd v Evans* [2003] EWHC 2914, Ch.
[76] *Durand v Molino* [2000] E.C.D.R. 320 at 329 *per* Pumfrey J.
[77] *Loc cit.*
[77a] See also *R. Griggs Group Ltd v Evans* [2003] EWHC 2914, Ch, December 2, 2003, Peter Prescott Q.C. (sitting as a deputy judge).
[78] *Mawman v Tegg* (1826) 2 Russ. 385; *Sweet v Shaw* (1838) 3 Jur. 217.
[79] *Performing Right Society Ltd v London Theatre of Varieties* [1924] A.C. 1; *Orwin v Attorney General* [1998] F.S.R. 415; [1998] 2 B.C.L.C. 693; (1998) 21(4) I.P.D. 21039; *Batjac Productions Inc v Simitar Entertainment (UK) Ltd* [1996] F.S.R. 139.
[80] *Weddell v J. A. Pearce & Major* [1988] Ch. 26.
[81] CDPA 1988, s.12(1)(2).
[82] *Post mortem auctoris.*
[83] SI 1995/3297.
[84] Council Directive of October 29, 1993, 93/98.

The Duration Regulations basically apply to all existing works and to    **2–094**
new works. In respect of existing works, the effect of the Regulations can be
summarised as follows:

a)  the term 70 years pma applies to all works in which copyright sub-
    sisted on December 31, 1995, (*i.e.* immediately before commence-
    ment).[85] However, if the 1988 Act prior to amendment by the
    Duration Regulations ("the old provisions") provided for a copyright
    expiry date later than that resulting from the new 70 years pma term,
    then copyright subsists for the duration of that longer term.[86]

b)  for works in respect of which copyright had expired by July 1, 1995,
    the new 70 years pma term will apply if the work was on July 1, 1995,
    protected in another state of the European Economic Area.[87] For
    works that were so protected in another EEA state, this results in the
    copyright that had expired being revived.

Any new copyright legislation needs to deal with existing works. When    **2–095**
the 1988 Act came into force, broadly speaking its transitional provisions
provided that copyright in existing works would continue to subsist until the
date it would have expired under the previous legislation—the Copyright
Act 1956. For existing works to acquire copyright under the 1988 Act,
copyright must have subsisted under the 1956 Act. It is therefore necessary
when considering whether the Duration Regulations apply to works made
before August 1, 1989, to trace back and see whether copyright did subsist
under the 1956 Act.

The following table and text applies to photographs which qualified for    **2–096**
UK copyright at the relevant time and where the identity of the author is
known. It assumes that the relevant qualification conditions have been met.
The term of protection can be established by reference to the flow chart (see
Figure 7, below). The explanation as to how the relevant term is arrived at is
explained in the relevant section.

## Photographs taken on or after January 1, 1996

**Duration.**    Copyright expires at the end of the period of 70 years from the    **2–097**
end of the calendar year in which the author dies.[88]

**Derivation.**    The Duration of Copyright and Rights in Performances Reg-    **2–098**
ulations 1995 ("the Duration Regulations 1995") came into force on January 1, 1996.[88a] The Regulations extended the period of copyright protection
from life of the author plus 50 years to life of the author plus 70 years.

---

[85] SI 1995/3297, regs 14(1) and 16.
[86] SI 1995/3297, reg.15.
[87] SI 1995/3297, reg.16(b).
[88] CDPA 1988, s.12(1)(2) as amended by Duration of Copyright and Rights in Performances
Regulations 1995, SI 1995/3297, reg.5.
[88a] SI 1995/3297, reg. 1(2).

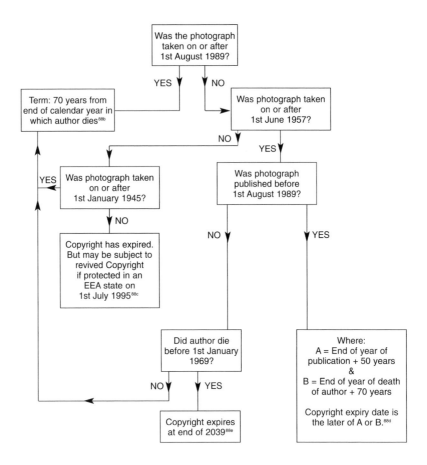

**Figure 7**: Flow Chart Showing Duration of Copyright In Photographs. NB: Flow chart assumes author is known and a qualified person at the relevant time. It does not apply to anonymous or pseudonymous photographs.

The Duration Regulations apply to works made after the Regulations came into force.[89]

---

[88b] For photographs taken after August 1, 1989 see above at para.2–097 and below at para.2–099.

For photographs taken on or after June 1, 1957 but before August 1, 1989 and unpublished before August 1, 1989 see below at para. 2–103.

For photographs taken on or after January 1, 1945 and before June 1, 1957 see below at para. 2–115.

[88c] See below at paras 2–120 and 2–126.

[88d] For photographs taken before January 1, 1945 see below at para. 2–120 and for photographs taken before July 1, 1912 see below at para. 2–126. The term under the 1956 Act for pre-commencement photographs was 50 years from the end of the calender year in which the photograph was taken.

[88e] See below at para. 2–103.

[89] SI 1995/3297, reg.16.

## Photographs taken on or after August 1, 1989, and before January 1, 1996

**Duration.** Copyright expires at the end of the period of 70 years from the 2–099 end of the calendar year in which the author dies.

**Derivation.** Duration Regulations 1995 extending term to 70 years came 2–100 into force on January 1, 1996.[90]

Regulations apply to existing copyright works (unless the date on which copyright would have expired under the old 1988 provisions is later than under the new provisions, in which case copyright subsists until the later date).[91]

"Existing" in relation to a work made before commencement (*i.e.* January 1, 1996). "Existing copyright work" means a work in which copyright subsisted immediately before commencement.[92]

Thus, for a photograph taken on or after August 1, 1989, but before 2–101 January 1, 1996, (an existing work) to claim the benefit of the extended period of 70 years, copyright must subsist in it immediately before commencement, *i.e.* under the 1988 Act pre-amendment by the Regulations.

The pre-amendment 1988 Act provided that copyright in an artistic work expired at the end of the period of 50 years from the end of the calendar year in which the author dies.[93]

All photographs in which copyright subsisted under the unamended 1988 2–102 Act taken after August 1, 1989, are subject to the 70-year period. The earliest possible date of death of the author in respect of a photograph taken on or after August 1, 1989, would be August 1, 1989, in respect of a photograph taken on the same day which under the old provisions would give a copyright period of life + 50 years until 2039. This means that (a) copyright subsisted in all photographs taken after August 1989 at the date the regulations came into force as it was not possible for it to have expired, and (b) the date on which copyright expired under the old provisions is not later than the date of expiry under the new provisions.

## Photographs taken on or after June 1, 1957, and before August 1, 1989, and unpublished before August 1, 1989

**Duration.** Copyright expires at the end of the period of 70 years from the 2–103 end of the calendar year in which the author dies. However, if the author died before January 1, 1969, the 70-year period does not apply as it gives a shorter period of protection and copyright will expire at the end of 2039 as provided for by the unamended 1988 Act. "Published" in this context has a specific legal definition—see below under photographs taken on or after

---

[90] SI 1995/3297, reg.1(2).
[91] SI 1995/3297, reg.15 and 16(c).
[92] SI 1995/3297, reg.14.
[93] CDPA 1988, s.12(1), pre-amendment by SI 1995/3297.

June 1, 1957, and before August 1, 1988, and published before August 1, 1989.

**2–104**   **Derivation.**   Duration Regulations 1995 extending the term to 70 years came into force on January 1, 1996.[94]

Regulations apply to existing copyright works (unless the date on which copyright would have expired under the old 1988 provisions is later than under the new provisions, in which case copyright subsists until the later date).[95]

"Existing" in relation to a work made before commencement (*i.e.* January 1, 1996). "Existing copyright work" means a work in which copyright subsisted immediately before commencement.[96]

Again, to claim the benefit of the extended period of 70 years, copyright must subsist in the photograph immediately before commencement of the Regulations, *i.e.* under the 1988 Act before amendment by the Regulations.

**2–105**   The 1988 Act provides that copyright does not subsist in works that existed before commencement of the 1988 Act (August 1, 1989[97]) unless copyright subsisted in it immediately before commencement.[98] This means that in order for copyright to subsist in a work already in existence by August 1, 1989, under the 1988 Act it is necessary to show that copyright subsisted under the 1956 Act.

**2–106**   As already discussed above, the 1956 Act granted copyright to photographs as artistic works.[99] The majority of the provisions came into force on June 1, 1957.[1]

The duration of copyright under the 1956 Act was 50 years from the end of the year of first publication,[2] but unpublished photographs were protected in perpetuity until such time as they were published when the 50-year term began to run.

The transitional provisions of the 1988 Act provided that copyright in unpublished photographs existing before August 1, 1989, that were taken on or after June 1, 1957, expired at the end of 2039 (*i.e.* 50 years from the end of the calendar year in which the 1988 Act came into force—1989).[3]

**2–107**   Thus, under the unamended 1988 Act, copyright subsisted in a photograph taken after June 1, 1957, (but before the commencement of the 1988 Act) and unpublished as at August 1, 1989, until the end of 2039. Hence, copyright subsisted at the date of commencement of the Duration Regulations and the duration regulation term of life + 70 years applies.

If however, the author died before January 1, 1969, then the unamended 1988 Act provisions give a later copyright expiry date than the Duration Regulations. Accordingly, the old 1988 Act provisions apply. For example,

---

[94] SI 1995/3297, reg.1(2).
[95] SI 1995/3297, reg.15 and 16(c).
[96] SI 1995/3297, reg.14.
[97] SI 1989/816.
[98] CDPA 1988, Sch.1, para.5(1).
[99] 1956 Act, s.3(1)
[1] SI 1957/863.
[2] 1956 Act, s.3(4).
[3] CDPA 1988, Sch.1, para.12(4)(c).

if the author died in 1968, the Duration Regulations term will mean copyright expires 70 years after the end of that year on December 31, 2038. This is shorter than the period provided for by the unamended 1988 Act which gives an expiry date of the end of 2039. The Duration Regulations provide that copyright in an existing work continues to subsist until the date on which it would have expired under the 1988 provisions if that date is later than the date on which copyright would expire under the new provisions.[4] Thus, if the author died before January 1, 1969, copyright would expire at the end of 2039 being a later date than 70 years pma as provided for by the Duration Regulations.

## Photographs taken on or after June 1, 1957, and before August 1, 1989, and published before August 1, 1989

**Duration.**  The starting point is that the Duration Regulations apply and   2–108
the period of protection is life of the author plus 70 years. However, in some instances, depending on the date of publication of the photograph and the date of death of the author, the old provisions will result in a longer term. If so, it is this longer term under the old provisions that gives the duration of copyright protection. To calculate the copyright term of such photographs where the author is deceased, it is essential to know the date of publication and the date of death of the author. If [end of year of publication + 50 years (old provisions)] is later than [end of year of death of the author + 70 years (duration regulations)], then the old provisions will apply.

**Derivation.**  Duration Regulations 1995 extending term to 70 years came   2–109
into force on January 1, 1996.[5]
Regulations apply to existing copyright works (unless the date on which copyright would have expired under the old 1988 provisions is later than under the new provisions, in which case copyright subsists until the later date).[6]
"Existing" in relation to a work made before commencement (*i.e.* January 1, 1996). "Existing copyright work" means a work in which copyright subsisted immediately before commencement.[7]
Again, to claim the benefit of the extended period of 70 years, copyright   2–110
must subsist in the photograph immediately before commencement of the Regulations, *i.e.* under the 1988 Act before amendment by the Regulations.
The 1988 Act provides that copyright does not subsist in works that existed before commencement of the 1988 Act (August 1, 1989[8]) unless copyright subsisted in it immediately before commencement.[9] This means that in order for copyright to subsist in a work already in existence by

---

[4] SI 1995/3297, reg.15(1).
[5] SI 1995/3297, reg.1(2).
[6] SI 1995/3297, regs 15 and 16(c).
[7] SI 1995/3297, reg.14.
[8] SI 1989/816.
[9] CDPA 1988, Sch.1, para.5(1).

August 1, 1989, under the 1988 Act it is necessary to show that copyright subsisted under the 1956 Act.

As already discussed above, the 1956 Act granted copyright to photographs as artistic works.[10]

The majority of the provisions came into force on June 1, 1957.[11]

The duration of copyright under the 1956 Act was 50 years from the end of the calendar year in which the photograph was first published.[12]

**2–111**    The transitional provisions of the 1988 Act provided that copyright in photographs published before August 1, 1989, continues to subsist until the date it would have expired under the 1956 Act[13], *i.e.* 50 years from the end of the year of first publication.

The earliest possible publication date for a photograph taken after June 1, 1957, is in 1957. Copyright would expire at the end of 2007. Obviously copyright in works published at later dates would expire later. It follows that copyright subsisted on January 1, 1996, in all photographs taken on or after June 1, 1957, but published before August 1, 1989. Hence the Duration Regulations apply.

**2–112**    However, the Duration Regulations provide that copyright in an existing work continues to subsist until the date on which it would have expired under the old 1988 Act provisions if that date is later than the date on which copyright would expire under the new provisions.[14] When considering the duration of copyright in works created after June 1, 1957, and published before August 1, 1989, it needs to be borne in mind that in some circumstances the unamended 1988 provisions will result in a longer term. For example:

Photograph taken in 1957. Author dies 1959. Photograph published 1988.

**2–113**    The old 1988 Act provisions protect the photograph for 50 years from the end of the year of publication, *i.e.* 1988 + 50 years = expires end of 2038.

The 1988 Act, as amended by the Duration Regulations protects the photograph for 70 years from the end of the year of the author's death, *i.e.* 1959 + 70 years = expires end of 2029.

The old provisions provide for a longer period of protection. By virtue of Reg.15(1) of the Duration Regulations, the copyright subsists until the date it would have expired under the old provisions if that date is later than the expiry date under the new provisions. Therefore, in this example copyright would expire at the end of 2038.

### *"Published"*

**2–114**    Published has a specific legal definition. The 1956 Act qualifying conditions for published works are as follows:

---

[10] 1956 Act, s.3(1).
[11] SI 1957/863.
[12] 1956 Act, s.3(4).
[13] CDPA 1988, Sch.1, para.12(2)(c).
[14] SI 1995/3297, reg.15(1).

(1) Copyright subsists only if the first publication of the work took place in the UK or in another country to which s.3 of the 1956 Act applies,[15] or

(2) the author of the work was a qualified person at the time when the work was first published[16], or

(3) the author had died before that time but was a qualified person before his death[17].

## Photographs taken on or after January 1, 1945, and before June 1, 1957

**Duration.**   The Duration Regulations apply and the period of protection is 70 years from the end of the calendar year in which the author died.   **2–115**

**Derivation.**   To claim the benefit of the Duration Regulations 1995 extending the term to life of the author plus 70 years, copyright must subsist in a work under the unamended 1988 Act immediately before the Duration Regulations came into force on January 1, 1996.[18]   **2–116**

The Regulations apply to existing copyright works (unless the date on which copyright would have expired under the old 1988 provisions is later than under the new provisions, in which case copyright subsists until the later date).[19]

The 1988 Act provides that copyright does not subsist in works that existed before commencement of the 1988 Act (August 1, 1989[20]) unless copyright subsisted in it immediately before commencement.[21] This means that in order for copyright to subsist in a work already in existence by August 1, 1989, under the 1988 Act it is necessary to show that copyright subsisted under the 1956 Act.   **2–117**

As already discussed above, the 1956 Act granted copyright to photographs as artistic works.[22]

The majority of the provisions came into force on June 1, 1957.[23]

The 1956 Act provided that photographs taken before commencement of the 1956 Act (*i.e.* before June 1, 1957) would be protected for 50 years from the end of the calendar year in which the photograph was taken.[24] There was no distinction between published and unpublished photographs.   **2–118**

The transitional provisions of the 1988 Act provided that copyright in photographs taken before 1957 continue to subsist until the date on which it

---

[15] 1956 Act, s.3(3)(a).
[16] 1956 Act, s.3(3)(b).
[17] 1956 Act, s.3(3)(c).
[18] SI 1995/3297, reg.14.
[19] SI 1995/3297, regs 15 and 16(c).
[20] SI 1989/816.
[21] CDPA 1988, Sch.1, para.5(1).
[22] 1956 Act, s.3(1)
[23] SI 1957/863.
[24] 1956 Act, Sch.7, para.2.

would have expired under the 1956 Act.[25] Thus, the unamended 1988 Act protects photographs taken before June 1, 1957 for 50 years from the end of the calendar year in which the photograph was taken.

2–119  Any copyright photograph taken on or after January 1, 1945, and before June 1, 1957, can claim the benefit of the Duration Regulation term of life of the author plus 70 years. This is because, for a photograph taken in 1945, copyright would expire under the unamended 1988 Act 50 years after the end of the year it was taken. Copyright would expire for a 1945 photograph under the unamended 1988 Act midnight on December 31, 1995. Copyright thus subsisted in a 1945 photograph immediately before the Duration Regulations came into force on January 1, 1996.[25a] The same is true for all photographs taken between 1945 and before June 1, 1957.

It is right that the Duration Regulations provide that copyright in an existing work continues to subsist until the date on which it would have expired under the old 1988 Act provisions if that date is later than the date on which copyright would expire under the new provisions.[26] However, for photographs in this category, it is not possible for the old 1988 Act to grant a longer term. This is because time runs under the old 1988 Act from the date the photograph was taken (*i.e.* 50 years from the end of the year the photograph was taken). The amended provision provides for life of the author plus 70 years. Even if the author died the same year the photograph was taken, the 70 year period from the date of the author's death is longer than the 50 year period from the date the photograph was taken.

## Photographs taken before January 1, 1945

2–120  **Duration.**  Prima facie, copyright has expired but photographs taken before January 1, 1945, may be subject to revived copyright under the 1988 Act as a result of the Duration Regulations. If such photographs are protected, the term is 70 pma. For photographs to be protected 70 pms, it is necessary to establish that as at July 1, 1995, the photograph was protected under legislation relating to copyright or related rights in another country that is a member of the European Economic Area.

2–121  **Derivation.**  The starting point is that copyright in photographs taken before January 1, 1945, had expired by the date the Duration Regulations came into force—January 1, 1996.

2–122  The transitional provisions of the 1988 Act provided that copyright in photographs taken before June 1, 1957, continue to subsist until the date on which it would have expired under the 1956 Act.[27] The 1956 Act provided

---

[25] 1988 Act, Sch.1, para.12(2)(c)

[25a] Time is a continuum and there is no break between the point immediately before commencement and commencement itself. Thus works in which copyright would have expired at midnight on December 31, 1995 were protected immediately before commencement of the Regulations on January 1, 1996. These copyrights are extended. See *Hansard* (6th Series) Vol. 268, col. 1265, December 18, 1995 *per* Ian Taylor, then Minister for Science and Technology.

[26] SI 1995/3297, reg.15(1).

[27] CDPA 1988, Sch.1, para.12(2)(c).

that photographs taken before the commencement of the 1956 Act (*i.e.* before June 1, 1957) would be protected for 50 years from the end of the calendar year in which the photograph was taken.[28] There was no distinction between published and unpublished photographs. Thus, the unamended 1988 Act protects photographs taken before June 1, 1957, for 50 years from the end of the calendar year in which the photograph was taken. Accordingly, under the unamended 1988 Act provisions, copyright would have expired for a photograph taken in 1944 on December 31, 1994. Thus, immediately before the Duration Regulations 1995 came into force, there was no subsisting copyright. Likewise copyright would have also expired in any photographs taken earlier than 1944. Copyright in a photograph taken on January 1, 1945 or at any time during 1945 would have expired at midnight on December 31, 1995, being 50 years from the end of the calendar year it was taken.[28a] Copyright subsisting at midnight on December 31, 1995 amounts to protection immediately before the Regulations came into force on January 1, 1996 and thus 1945 photographs can claim the benefit of extended copyright.[28b] Photographs taken before January 1, 1945 were not protected immediately before commencement and thus copyright had expired.

However, the Duration Regulations 1995 extending the term to 70 years pma, also applies to existing works in which copyright expired before December 31, 1995, but which were on July 1, 1995, protected in another EEA state under legislation related to copyright or related rights.[29]

To claim the benefit of revived copyright for photographs taken before June 1, 1957, it will be necessary to identify one state that is a member of the European Economic Area[30] in which it can be shown the photograph was protected on July 1, 1995.   **2–123**

The following are presently the EEA states: Austria, Belgium, Denmark, Finland, France, Germany, Greece, Iceland, Ireland, Italy, Liechtenstein, Luxembourg, The Netherlands, Norway, Portugal, Spain, Sweden and the UK.

To establish a photograph was protected by copyright in another EEA state on July 1, 1995, will require some investigation. It is possible that the photograph might have fallen into the public domain because the state did not have reciprocal copyright agreements with the country of which the author was a national or the country where the work was first published. Photographs are often subject to shorter periods of protection than other works. The Berne Convention still only requires protection of photographs for a period of 25 years from the making of the work.[31] The full title TRIPS   **2–124**

---

[28] 1956 Act, Sch.7, para.2.
[28a] 1956 Act, Sch.7 para.2.
[28b] Time being a continuum. See above at para.2–119, n.25a.
[29] SI 1995/3297, reg.16(b).
[30] Created by the Agreement on the European Economic Area (Cm. 2073; O.J. [1994] L1/3) signed on May 2, 1992, which came into force on January 1, 1994. The Agreement was brought into force in the UK by the European Economic Area Act 1993 which came into force on November 5, 1993.
[31] Art.7(4). See below at para.3–055.

Agreement permits members to exclude photographic works from the minimum term of protection of the life of the author plus 50 years.

When considering whether a photograph taken before January 1, 1946, can claim revived copyright, it will usually be prudent to take advice from lawyers specialising in copyright law of the relevant EEA state in respect of which it is sought to establish that it was protected, in order to ensure that copyright survives any transitional provisions or requirements for registration or otherwise.

**2–125**     Finally, obvious as it may be, before embarking on an exercise to establish whether a photograph was protected in an EEA state, the date of the author's death should be double checked with the date of infringement (or whatever is the cause of the attempt to establish copyright). For example:

Photograph taken in 1920. Author died 1930. Suspected infringement 2001.

Even if the photograph can be shown to be protected in an EEA state and thus be protected for 70 years following the death of the author, it would be a waste of time seeking to establish it in this instance. Copyright expired at the end of 2000. The suspected infringement occurred when copyright had expired.

## Photographs taken before July 1, 1912

**2–126**    **Duration.**    Prima facie, copyright has expired but as for photographs taken before January 1, 1945, photographs taken before July 1, 1912, may be subject to revived copyright under the 1988 Act as a result of the Duration Regulations. If such photographs are protected, the term is 70 pma. For photographs to be protected 70 pms, it is necessary to establish that as at July 1, 1995, the photograph was protected under legislation relating to copyright or related rights in another country that is a member of the European Economic Area.

**2–127**    **Derivation and Commentary.**    The Copyright Act 1911[32] ("the 1911 Act") came into force on July 1, 1912.[33] Photographs were protected under the 1911 Act. A photograph was defined as including "photo-lithograph and any work produced by any process analagous to photography".[34] The 1911 Act provided that photographs (including pre-1912 photographs) were protected for 50 years "for the making of the original negative from which the photograph was directly or indirectly derived".[35]

The 1956 Act effectively preserved the position and copyright subsisted in pre-July 1, 1912, photographs for 50 years from the date they were taken (provided copyright subsisted in the photograph immediately before com-

---

[32] (1&2 Geo. 5 c.46).
[33] 1911 Act, s.37.
[34] 1911 Act, s.35(1).
[35] 1911 Act, s.21, s.24 and First Sch.

mencement.)[36] Accordingly, copyrights in pre-July 1, 1912, photographs would all have expired by 1962 at the latest. Thus they would not have been copyright under the 1988 Act.

As the copyright had expired before January 1, 1995, to claim the benefit of the Duration Regulations extended term it is necessary to establish that the photograph was, on July 1, 1995, protected in another EEA state under legislation related to copyright or related rights.[37] See generally above under "Photographs Taken Before January 1, 1945."

**Works of unknown authorship**

A work is a work of "unknown authorship" if the identity of the author is unknown or, in the case of a work of joint authorship, if the identity of none of the authors is known.[38] The 1988 Act provides that the identity of an author shall be regarded as unknown if it is not possible for a person to ascertain his identity by reasonable inquiry.[39] If an author's identity was once known it shall not subsequently be regarded as unknown.[40]    **2–128**

If a work is of unknown authorship, copyright expires at the end of the period of 70 years from the end of the calendar year in which the work was made.[41] If, during that period, the work is made available to the public, copyright expires at the end of the period of 70 years from the end of the calendar year in which it was first made available to the public.[42] In the case of a photograph, being made available to the public includes exhibition in public but excludes unauthorised acts.[43] However, if the author becomes known before the end of either 70 years from the year in which it was made or 70 years from when it was made available to the public, then the normal rule applies—*i.e.* copyright expires 70 years pma.[44]

**Are the Duration Regulations 1995 *ultra vires* in part?**

This question is discussed in more detail in Chapter 3.[45] The short point is that the Directive (which the Duration Regulations implement in the UK) extends the term of protection of copyright to 70 years pma for all photographs as artistic works "irrespective of artistic quality". However, the Directive provides that an original photograph is only one which is "the author's own intellectual creation reflecting his personality".[46] The Directive extended the term of copyright protection only to photographs which are    **2–129**

---

[36] 1956 Act, Sch.7, paras 2, 35.
[37] SI 1995/3297, reg.16(b).
[38] CDPA 1988, s.9(4).
[39] CDPA 1988, s.9(5).
[40] *Loc. cit.*
[41] CDPA 1988, s.12(3)(a).
[42] CDPA 1988, s.12(3)(b).
[43] CDPA 1988, s.12(5)(b).
[44] CDPA 1988, s.12(4).
[45] See below at para. 3–064.
[46] Term Directive, Recital 17.

original in the sense that they are the author's own intellectual creation.[47] Insofar as the Duration Regulations purport to implement the directive, they exceed the ambit of the Directive.

**2–130**   This is because the UK statute has extended the protection to all "original" photographs. The test implemented by UK courts for originality does not require "intellectual creation". There is no requirement for "intellectual creation" in the 1988 Act either. In fact, the level of originality required for a photograph to be protected is very low. As can be seen from the case law of civil countries, "intellectual creation" denotes some genuine creativity. Indeed, the phrase "intellectual creation" is identical to the wording of the German author's right statute.[48] It is arguable that the Secretary of State has exceeded his power. Ultimately, it is capable of cure by the UK legislature as the directive permits the protection of "other" non-original photographs by Member States.

## Why does it matter?

**2–131**   If the reader is faced with a case where (1) the photographs in question are into the last 20 years of the 70 years of protection after the death of the author, and (2) the photographs are arguably not original in the sense of "an intellectual creation reflecting the author's personality" (*e.g.* satellite photographs, documentary photographs, photographs of two dimensional works of art), care should be taken when considering initiating copyright infringement proceedings if the infringement was in the last 20 years of the copyright term. It is possible that the copyright term could be challenged as deriving from a part of the Duration Regulations that is *ultra vires*.

Conversely, when defending an infringement claim, it may be worth considering whether to run an argument that the photographs are not copyright as the Regulations in that regard are *ultra vires*.

The obvious way round the problem for the UK court is to simply hold that "original" in the 1988 Act means the same as "original" in the Directive and that there is no difference. Whilst arguable, it is doubtful that "original" in the directive and "original" in the 1988 Act (as interpreted by the UK courts) have the same meaning. For further details the reader is referred to the comparison between the civil law and common law approach in Chapter 3, below.

## RIGHTS OF THE COPYRIGHT OWNER AND PRIMARY INFRINGEMENT

**2–132**   The owner of copyright in a photograph being an artistic work has the exclusive right to:

---

[47] Art.6.
[48] Law on Copyright and Neighbouring Rights (Copyright Law) of September 9, 1965, Art.2(2). Note Germany has author's right law not copyright in a common law sense. This wording is adopted from the WIPO translations. See Appendix 2 (Germany).

(a) copy the work (the reproduction right)[49];

(b) issue copies of work to the public (the distribution right)[50];

(c) rent or lend the work to the public (the rental and lending right)[51];

(d) communicate the work to the public (the right of communication to the public)[52];

Unless the use of the work is an act permitted by the statute or has been licenced, carrying out any of the above acts by someone other than the copyright owner amounts to an infringement.

Copyright is infringed not just by doing any of these acts in relation to the whole of the work, but also in relation to any substantial part of the work.[53] Copyright is also infringed by doing any of the acts indirectly as well as directly and it is immaterial whether any intervening acts themselves infringe copyright.[54]

**2–133**

Copyright is basically a "strict liability" tort in the sense that innocence is no defence to primary copyright infringement.[55] The fact that a defendant was unaware that his act infringed copyright is immaterial for the purposes of liability.[56]

## The reproduction right

Copyright is infringed by copying the work or a substantial part of the work in any material form.[57] This includes the making of copies which are transient or incidental to some other use of the work.[58] It also includes storing the work in any medium by electronic means[59] and would include

**2–134**

---

[49] CDPA 1988, ss.16 and 17.

[50] CDPA 1988, ss.16 and 18.

[51] CDPA 1988, ss.16 and 18A.

[52] CDPA 1988, ss.16 and 20 as amended. From October 31, 2003, the right contained in s.16(1)(d) became "to communicate the work to the public". This subsection was amended by the Copyright And Related Rights Regulations 2003 (SI 2003/2498), reg. 6(2) which came into force on October 31, 2003. The Regulations implemented the EC Directive on the Harmonisation of Certain Aspects of Copyright and Related Rights in the Information Society (Directive 2001/29/EC). Prior to amendment, the act restricted by s.16(1)(d) was "to broadcast the work or include it in a cable programme service". Note that the Regulations (and the amendments to the 1988 Act) apply to copyright works existing before October 31, 2003 but there are a few transitional provisions which provide, *inter alia*, that no pre-commencement act is to be regarded as an infringement of any new right. For further detail as to the transitional provisions see below at para. 2–149.

[53] CDPA 1988, s.16(3)(a).

[54] CDPA 1988, s.16(3)(b).

[55] *e.g. Francis Day & Hunter Ltd v Bron* [1963] Ch. 587; *Lady Anne Tennant v Associated Newspapers Group Ltd* [1979] F.S.R. 298; *Saphena Computing Ltd v Allied Collection Agencies* [1995] F.S.R. 616; *Linpac Mouldings Ltd v Eagleton Direct Export Ltd* [1994] F.S.R. 545.

[56] There is a very limited defence to a claim for damages where the defendant did not know and had no reason to believe copyright subsisted in the work: CDPA 1988, s.97(1).

[57] CDPA 1988, ss.16(2) and 17(1).

[58] CDPA 1988, s.17(1).

[59] CDPA 1988, s.17(6). "Electronic means" is defined in s.178 as meaning "actuated by electric, magnetic, electro-magnetic, electro-chemical or electro-mechanical energy". This is a very wide definition and in fact specifically includes photographs which are created by light which form electro-magnetic energy.

displaying an image on a television screen.[60] To establish infringement it is necessary to show that (1) there is sufficient objective similarity between the infringing work and the copyright work, and (2) the copyright work is the source from which the infringing work is derived.[61]

Copying in relation to a film or broadcast includes making a photograph of the whole or any substantial part of any image forming part of the film or broadcast.[62]

**2–135**   It is necessary to establish a causal connection between the claimant's work and the defendant's work. There is no infringement by an act of independent creation.[63] A photograph independently created of a particular monument or building would not infringe other photographs taken earlier. Direct or indirect copying is sufficient. Subconscious copying is also actionable but this tends to be of more relevance in cases concerning musical works.[64]

**2–136**   The question is whether the defendant has, in producing the alleged infringement made a substantial use of those features of the claimant's work in which copyright subsists.[65] For this reason photographic works cause particular difficulty as far as the reproduction right is concerned. As a photograph is itself a copy of the image it represents, some elements of a photograph may not be "original". If the only features copied from a photograph are not original, there can be no infringement.[66] Difficulties arise in distilling from an image precisely what elements of it are original and thus protected by copyright. The question of whether there is infringement of a photograph is therefore closely bound up with originality. As was said in the American case of *Rogers v Koons*:

> "Elements of originality in a photograph may include posing the subjects, lighting, angle, selection of film and camera, invoking the desired expression almost any other variant involved".[67]

The question of infringement therefore cannot be considered in isolation without consideration of what is original within a photograph. The aspects of a photograph which may be are original are discussed in more detail in Chapter 3, below, to which the reader is referred.

---

[60] *Bookmakers' Afternoon Greyhound Services Ltd v Wilf Gilbert (Staffordshire) Ltd* [1994] F.S.R. 723 at 737.
[61] *Francis Day & Hunter Ltd v Bron* [1963] Ch. 587 at 623.
[62] CDPA 1988, s.17(4) as amended by SI 2003/2498, reg. 5(5).
[63] *Francis Day & Hunter Ltd v Bron* [1963] Ch. 587 at 617.
[64] *EMI Music Publishing v Papathanasiou* [1993] E.M.L.R. 306; *Rees v Melville* [1911–1916] Mac. C.C. 168.
[65] *Kristarts S. A. v Briarfine Ltd* [1977] F.S.R. 557 at 562 *per* Whitford J.
[66] *Bauman v Fussell* [1978] R.P.C. 485; *Mattel Inc v Azrak Hamway Int'l Inc* 724 F.2d 357, 360 (2d Cir. 1983) (a superhuman muscle man doll crouched in a "traditional fighting pose" was an unprotectible idea); *Andersson v Sony Corp of Am* 1997 U.S. Dist. LEXIS No.96 Civ. 7975; 1997 WL 226310 (S.D.N.Y. 1997) ("idea of a woman in futuristic garb fascinated with an object held in her hand is simply not protectible").
[67] 960 F.2d 301, 306 (2nd Cir.).

## Substantial part

Copying an entire photograph is infringing even where the image is reduced in size so that the originality of the photograph is, to a degree lost.[68] The issue as to what forms a substantial part is a matter of fact and degree in each case.[69] The court will look at whether there has been a substantial appropriation of the skill and labour of the author.[70] As far as photographs are concerned, the question is whether there is copying of a substantial part of those elements of the photograph in which originality subsists. Thus, the quality of what has been appropriated is more significant than the quantity.[71] The court will concentrate on the similarities between the two works and not the differences at issue in what has been reproduced.[72]

**2–137**

## Recreation/re-shooting of original photograph

Where a second photographer recreates in a second photograph constituent elements of a first photograph that are original and form a substantial part of the first photograph, the second photograph will be an infringement of the first if the first is protected by copyright.[73] If the second photographer acts independently and merely photographs the same subject matter there will be no infringement.[74]

**2–138**

It is important to note that what is required for infringement to be established is recreation of the *original elements* of the first photograph. If all that is taken is the idea of the first photograph then there will be no infringement.[75] This is a difficult concept when considering photographs as often the idea and the expression are so closely connected as to be inseparable.[76] Broadly speaking, if the second photograph copies not just the idea but the exact expression of the first photograph (or a substantial part of the exact expression), there will be infringement unless the exact expression

**2–139**

---

[68] *Antiquesportfolio.com plc v Rodney Fitch* [2001] F.S.R. at 23 p.355. *Cf. Kelly v Arriba Soft Corporation* 336 F.3d 811 9th Cir., 2003, see below at paras 2–149 and 9–010 *et seq.*

[69] *Ladbroke (Football) Ltd v William Hill (Football) Ltd* [1964] 1 W.L.R. 273 at 283; *King Features Syndicate Inc v O.M.Kleeman* [1941] A.C. 417 at 424.

[70] *Ladbroke (Football) Ltd v William Hill (Football) Ltd* [1964] 1 W.L.R. 273.

[71] *ibid.*, at 276; *John Richardson Computers Ltd v Flanders (No. 1)* [1993] F.S.R. 497 (software); *Waterlow Directories Ltd v Reed Information Services Ltd* [1992] F.S.R. 409.

[72] *Baumann v Fussell* [1978] R.P.C. 485; *Entec (Pollution Control) Ltd v Abacus Mouldings* [1992] F.S.R. 332.

[73] *Gross v Seligman* 212 F. 930 (2d Cir. 1914) (photograph of model in a particular pose recreated using the same model in the identical pose was held to be an infringement even though there were slight differences—backgrounds not identical; model in one sedate and smiling in the other; model two years older and "some slight changes in her contour are discoverable"); *Turner v Robinson* (1860) 10 I. Ch. R. 121 and 510 (copyright in painting infringed by recreating scene with models and photographing them); *Ateliers Tango Argentin v Festival D'Espagne et D'Amerique* (1999) 84 C.P.R. (3d) 56 (recreation of photograph of tango dancers).

[74] *Creation Records Ltd v News Group Newspapers Ltd* [1997] E.M.L.R. 444.

[75] *Gentieu v John Muller & Co* 712 F. Supp. 740,742 (W.D.Mo. 1989) appeal dismissed 881 F. 2d 1082 (8th Cir., 1989) (idea of floating naked babies); *Great Importations Inc v Caffco Int'l Inc* 1997 U.S. Dist. LEXIS 10700 No.95 Civ. 0514; 1997 WL 414111 (S.D.N.Y., 1997) (no protection for baby angels as round-cheeked, smiling or bemused and wearing loose robes as these were stereotypical attributes of baby angels indispensible to the generalised idea of baby angels) *Cf. Ets-Hokin v. Skyy Spirits Inc* 323 F.3d 763 (9th Cir. 2003) (vodka bottle) discussed below at paras 3–036 *et seq.*

[76] See below at para: 3–005.

is either (a) unoriginal,[77] or (b) the only way of expressing that particular idea.[78] This approach has been adopted in the USA and it has been held where an idea for a photograph is capable of expression in "countless different layouts" but the exact layout of the claimant's photograph has been copied, a contention that the idea and the expression are indistinguishable will fail.[79] In reality, there are probably very few instances when it can genuinely be said a particular image is the only way of expressing the idea contained in the photograph. In many cases there will be options as to lighting, angle, choice of background, etc.

**2–140**     Copyright in a photograph cannot be used to monopolise poses used: only the particular photographic expression of the poses are protected and not the underlying ideas.[80] Thus, it has been held in an American case that the depiction of a businessman contemplating a leap from a tall building onto the street below is "a common concept unprotectible by copyright".[81]

**2–141**     Commonplace views or street scenes may be the subject of copyright if they are recorded in the work in an original way so that reproduction of the image may be an infringement.[81a] Copyright was held to subsist in a photograph of a street scene on Fifth Avenue in New York as originality was required to determine just when to take the photograph so as to capture people in "lifelike" and "artistic positions" and to bring out the features of light and shade.[82] It has also been said, in relation to paintings:

---

[77] *e.g.* photograph of the colour white or of a patch of cloudless sky. Equally, a photograph of the Eiffel Tower or Nelson's Column in itself would not give a copyright in the simple appearance of either monument or its setting.

[78] *e.g.* A photograph of a two-dimensional work of art intended to reproduce the full work can only really be taken in a limited number of ways—*i.e.* from the front. The idea and the expression to all intents and purposes merge. Thus, it is submitted that in any such photograph what is protected is only that specific recorded expression. All that is prohibited is reproducing that exact first photograph itself (*e.g.* by photocopying or reprinting the actual image) which would be an appropriation of the first author's labour and skill. Reproduction by taking another independent photograph of the same two-dimensional artwork would not infringe the earlier photograph. For full discussion of originality in relation to photographs of two-dimensional works of art see below at para. 3–038.

[79] *Wallace Computer Serv. v Adams Business Forms* 837 F. Supp. 1413 (N.D. Ill. 1993) (photograph of a hand writing on a phone message book for use on the cover of a phone message book. Court rejected the contention that there were a limited number of ways to express that idea.) *Cf. Ets-Hokin v. Skyy Spirits Inc* 323 F.3d 763 (9th Cir. 2003) discussed below at paras 3–036 *et seq.*

[80] *International Biotical Corp v Associated Mills Inc* 239 F. Supp. 511, 514 (N.D. Ill. 1964) (photographs of heat lamps in specific poses); *Kisch v Ammirati & Puris Inc* 657 F. Supp. 380, 382 (S.D.N.Y., 1987) (denying defendant's motion to dismiss copyright infringement claim. Photographs for lime juice advertisement taken in the same corner of a nightclub of a person seated holding a musical instrument in front of a striking mural. Subjects were different—plaintiff's was of a woman holding a concertina, defendant's was of a well-known musican holding a saxophone.).

[81] *Kaplan v The Stock Market Photoagency Inc* 133 F. Supp. 2d 317, 324 (S.D.N.Y., 2001).

[81a] Only the original elements are protected from infringement. Note that in the USA there is a doctrine of *scenes a faire* where the Court will not protect a copyright work from infringement if the expression necessarily flows from a common place idea: see *Ets-Hokin v Skyy Spirits Inc* 323 F.3d 763 (9th Cir. 2003) and 225 F.3d 1068, 1082 (9th Cir. 2000), discussed below at paras 3–036 *et seq.*

[82] *Pagano v Beseler* 234 F. 963, 964 (S.D.N.Y. 1916). The infringement constituted reproduction of the exact image by a lantern slide rather than re-creation.

"When one is considering a view of a very well-known subject like the Houses of Parliament with Westminster Bridge and part of the Embankment in the foreground, the features in which copyright is going to subsist are very often the choice of viewpoint, the exact balance of foreground features or features in the middle ground and features in the far ground, the figures which are introduced, possibly in the case of a river scene the craft may be on the river and so forth. It is in choices of this character that the person producing the artistic work makes his original contribution".[83]

It is the recreation of a substantial part of the original features of the photograph which will amount to infringement.

## Change of medium

Changing the medium of the photograph by drawing, painting, sculpting or filming[84] the image may amount to infringement but only where those elements of the photograph copied are (1) original and protected by copyright, and (2) form a substantial part of the photograph.  **2–142**

In *Bauman v Fussell*[85] it was held that where a painting based on a photo- graph of a cock fight only reproduced the relative positions of the birds to each other there was no infringement. It was held that the positions of the birds did not amount to a substantial part of the photograph. It should be noted that the decision did not specifically hold that positioning of elements of an incident beyond the photographer's control were not capable of forming part of the originality. It is submitted that the reasoning in this case is doubtful and to capture a fast-moving event like a cock fight requires a level of skill in respect of the composition and the decision as to when to take the photograph.[86] Although the relative positions are not the work of the photographer, capturing them in a particular way when skill is required may form part of the originality of the work. This will not always be the case—in some instances the relative positions of objects in a photograph will be commonplace.  **2–143**

Where photographs of antiques were copied by tracing the outline of the object and simplifying the object to an outline, there was no infringement as what was original in the original photographs (such as lighting, angle and focussing) were not reproduced.[87] If there is no appropriation of the original

---

[83] *Krisarts S.A. v Briarfine Ltd* [1977] F.S.R. 557 at 562 *per* Whitford J. (paintings of well-known views of London re-created by a second painter. Interlocutory relief refused as damages ade- quate remedy. Judge observed that it was arguable that the use of the original paintings was sufficiently substantial to amount to infringement).

[84] *Leigh v Warner Bros Inc* 212 F. 3d 1210, 1215 (11th Cir. 2000) (first instance decision at 10 F. Supp. 2d 1371) (where a contention that copyright in a photograph of a sculpture in a cemetery for the cover of the novel *Midnight in the Garden of Good and Evil* was infringed by sequences in a film of the novel was rejected. The court held that there was no substantial similiarity but impliedly accepted that in principle a photograph could be infringed by a film sequence).

[85] [1978] R.P.C. 485.

[86] *Bauman v Fussell* is discussed in more detail in relation to originality at para. 3–028 below.

[87] *Antiquesportfolio.com v Rodney Fitch* [2001] F.S.R. 23.

elements of the photograph or of the photographer's labour and skill in reproduction, there is no infringement.

**2–144**    In a Canadian case,[88] an artist entered a digital drawing in the Corel World Draw Design Contest depicting a native American Indian in profile with an American flag and a cowboy in the background which won the contest. The Indian in profile was based on a photograph by Nick Vedros entitled "the Potawatamie Indian". The photograph had been licenced to a photographic library who sued the artist and Corel for copyright infringement. Notwithstanding that in the digital drawing some details of the profile in the photograph had been altered and there had been a change of medium, the court granted summary judgment in favour of the plaintiff.

A sculpture or other three-dimensional representation of the original elements of a photographic image will amount to an infringement. This is specifically provided for in the 1988 Act which states copying includes the making of a copy in three dimensions of a two-dimensional work.[89]

A sculpture created by the artist Jeff Koons which was based on a photograph of a couple seated on a bench holding eight puppies was held to be an infringement of the original photograph.[90] Although there were differences between the sculpture and the photograph, there remained overwhelming similarity in composition, poses and expressions.

**2–145**    Converting analogue photographs to digital format by a person licenced by the original analogue photographer by scanning the original photograph for use in a CD-ROM may amount to copyright infringement where the original copyright permission was only for use of the analogue photograph in a magazine.[91]

### Digital manipulation

**2–146**    Taking an original photograph and making alterations to it through the use of digital manipulation which fails to destroy the elements of the photograph in which originality subsists will amount to an infringing copy.[92] Conversely, there is no infringement if all that is copied from the photograph is non-original material and there is no appropriation of the photographer's labour and skill.[93]

In *Tiffany Design Inc v Reno-Tahoe Specialty Inc*[94] six architectural images from a photograph of the Las Vegas strip were extracted from the plaintiff's

[88] *Tony Stone Images v Arscott and Corel Corporation* (unrep.) Court of Ontario (General Division), June 28, 1996, Day J.

[89] CDPA 1988, s.17(3).

[90] *Rogers v Koons* 960 F.2d 302 (2d Cir. 1992).

[91] *Greenberg v National Geographic Society* 244 F.3d 1267 (11th Cir. 2001) (at issue was the meaning of collective work under 17 U.S.C.S. 101); see also *New York Times v Tasini* 206 F.3d 161 (action by freelance authors in respect of digital use of their work produced for newspapers in an electronic database). Both cases are discussed below at paras 9–040 to 9–044.

[92] *Mendler v Winterland Production Ltd* (US Court of Appeals 9th Circ.) 207 F.3d 1119; 54 U.S.P.Q. 2d (BNA) 1070. Discussed below at para.3–017; see also *Antiquesportfolio.com plc v Rodney Fitch* [2001] F.S.R. 23.

[93] *Antiquesportfolio.com plc v Rodney Fitch* [2001] F.S.R. 23 at pp.355–356 *per* Neuberger J. (logos made by tracing outlines of objects in photographs and simplifying the image).

[94] 55 F. Supp. 2d 1113 (US District Court for District of Nevada, 1999). Motion for summary judgment by the plaintiff.

photograph and placed into the defendant's photograph. It was held that the scanned "precusor" image of the original photograph created by the defendant from which the architectural images were cropped amounted to copyright infringement notwithstanding only the briefest existence in the computer's RAM.[95] Summary judgment was granted for the plaintiff in respect of the scanned "precursor" image.

In respect of the use of the six cropped images, the defendant contended that it radically modified the appearance of the buildings to such an extent as they no longer resembled the elements from which they were scanned. It was argued that a copyright photograph could be reduced to its factual elements unprotected by copyright through the use of computer manipulation (*i.e.* the simple image of an architectural work in a public space). In declining to grant summary judgment on that point to the plaintiff, the court held the question of whether the defendant used a sufficient amount of recognisable elements to constitute substantial use was a question of fact that should be decided at trial. The issue was whether the defendant's modification of things such as lighting, perspective and shading were significant enough to render use of the original photographic image de minimis or unrecognisable in nature.[96]    **2–147**

### Reduction of image size

Infringement occurs where a whole photograph is reproduced even it is much reduced in size. *Antiquesportfolio.com v Rodney Fitch*[97] concerned photographs of various three-dimensional antiques. It was held that copyright subsisted in the photographs as there was originality in positioning, angle, lighting and the focus. Some of the photographs were reproduced in "very small scale" as icons on a website. It was argued by the defendant that this was not infringing use and the reproduction did not benefit from any of the photograph's originality such as the lighting or camera angle. This argument was rejected by Neuberger J. who, in finding infringing use said, "it would seem rather strange if, as I have concluded, copyright exists in the whole photograph, there is no infringement in a case involving reproduction of the whole photograph".[98]    **2–148**

This can be contrasted with the American case of *Kelly v Arriba Soft Corporation*[99] where an internet image search engine that created thumbnail images of photographs was held to be fair use under the USA statute.[1] The court observed that although exact replicas were created, they were much smaller, lower resolution and served an entirely different function to the original images, in particular improving access to information on the internet.    **2–149**

---

[95] *ibid.* at p.1121.
[96] *ibid.*
[97] [2001] F.S.R. 23, Neuberger J.
[98] [2001] F.S.R. 23 at p.355.
[99] 336 F.3d 811 (9th Cir., 2003). Remanded to the district court for further proceedings as to whether the full size images were infringing. See further below at paras 9–010 *et seq.*
[1] 17 U.S.C. 107, which provides four factors the court must take into account (1) the purpose and character of the use, including whether such use is of a commercial nature or is for nonprofit educational purposes; (2) the nature of the copyrighted work; (3) the amount and substantiality of the portion used in relation to the copyrighted work as a whole; and (4) the effect of the use upon the potential market for or value of the copyrighted work.

Prior to October 31, 2003, the use of thumbnail images by an internet search engine would have been be regarded as infringing on the authority of *Antiquesportfolio.com.* as the whole image is reproduced. It is very doubtful whether under the 1988 Act (prior to the 2003 amendment) there would have been a defence to this type of use. However, it is submitted that mere reproduction by an image search engine of thumbnails which link to the author's own site/ sites of lawful use will now be classified as the making of a temporary copy which is transient or incidental within the meaning of s.28A of the 1988 Act and would be non-infringing.[2]

Section 28A was inserted by the Copyright And Related Rights Regulations 2003[2a] which came into force on 31 October 31, 2003. The Regulations implemented the Copyright and Related Rights in the Information Society Directive 2001/29/EC which by Art. 5(1) required member states to provide a copyright exemption for transient or incidental temporary acts of reproduction which form an essential part of a technological process and have no independent economic significance. The Directive makes clear that this is intended to cover acts of internet browsing as well as caching insofar as they are transient and an integral part of a technological process.[2b]

Although the Copyright And Related Rights Regulations 2003[2c] came into force on October 31, 2003, they apply to copyright works made before or after commencement.[2d] They also apply to performances given, databases made and works first published either before or after October 31, 2003.[2e] However:

(1) no act done before October 31, 2003 is to be regarded as an infringement of any new or extended right.[2f]

(2) nothing in the regulations affects any agreement made before December 22, 2002.[2g]

---

[2] A new s.28A was inserted in the CDPA 1988 by the Copyright And Related Rights Regulations 2003 (SI 2003/2498), reg. 8 and reads as follows:

**Making of Temporary Copies**
28A. Copyright in a literary work, other than a computer program or database, or in a dramatic, musical or artistic work, the typographical arrangement of a published edition, a sound recording or a film, is not infringed by the making of a temporary copy which is transient or incidental, which is an integral and essential part of a technological process and the sole purpose of which is to enable—

(a) a transmission of the work in a network between third parties by an intermediary; or
(b) a lawful use of the work;

and which has no independent economic significance.

[2a] SI 2003/2598, reg. 8.
[2b] Recital 33.
[2c] SI 2003/2598.
[2d] *ibid.*, reg. 31.
[2e] *ibid.*, reg.31.
[2f] *ibid.*, reg. 31(2).
[2g] *ibid*, reg. 32(1).

(3) no act done after October 31, 2003 in pursuance of an agreement made before December 22, 2002 shall be regarded as an infringement of any new or extended right arising by virtue of these regulations.[2h]

## The distribution right

Copyright is infringed by issuing copies of the work to the public.[3] Issuing copies of work to the public means putting into circulation in the European Economic Area[4] copies not previously put into circulation in the EEA with the consent of the copyright owner.[5] It also includes the act of putting into circulation outside the EEA copies not previously put into circulation in the EEA or elsewhere.[6] "Copies" includes the issuing of the original which is prohibited without the consent of the copyright owner.[7]

**2–150**

"Issuing copies to the public" does not include any subsequent distribution, sale, hiring or loan of copies previously put into circulation nor subsequent importation of such copies into the UK or another EEA state.[8] The author's right of distribution is exhausted after first sale of a copy of the work in respect of that particular copy. Once a work is sold, the author has no further right to control circulation of that copy. Exhaustion of rights may be classified into three categories—national exhaustion, regional exhaustion, and international exhaustion. National exhaustion of rights is the exhaustion of the right to control further distribution after sale in a particular country and is recognised by many jurisdictions. Regional exhaustion arises where placing a copy on the market in a particular region exhausts the copyright owner's right to control further distribution throughout that region and applies (for example) in the European Union. There is also international exhaustion, where sale anywhere in the world results in exhaustion of rights and exhausts the distribution right in the country where the author claims to assert the right, but it is rare in national laws.

**2–151**

Infringement of the distribution right may occur by unauthorised issuing of copies which were lawfully made at the time they were created, for example by issuing copies to the public after the expiry of a licence agreement where this was not permitted.[9]

---

[2h] *ibid.*, reg. 32(2). The Directive states, in slightly different wording, that it shall apply "without prejudice to any acts concluded and rights acquired before December 22, 2002: 2001/29/EC, Art. 10(2).
[3] CDPA 1988, s.18.
[4] The following are presently (as at November 1, 2003) the EEA states: Austria, Belgium, Denmark, Finland, France, Germany, Greece, Iceland, Ireland, Italy, Liechtenstein, Luxembourg, The Netherlands, Norway, Portugal, Spain, Sweden and the UK.
[5] CDPA 1988, s.18(2).
[6] CDPA 1988, s.18(2)(b).
[7] CDPA 1988, s.18(4).
[8] CDPA 1988, s.18(3).
[9] *Nelson v Rye* [1996] F.S.R. 313 at 319.

## The rental and lending right

**2–152**     The rental or lending of copies to the public is an exclusive right of the owner of the copyright and applies to artistic works, including photographs.[10] This includes the rental or lending of the original work.[11]

Rental is defined as "making a copy of the work available for use on terms that it will or may be returned for direct or indirect economic or commercial advantage."[12] Lending is defined as "making a copy of the work available for use on terms that it will or may be returned otherwise than for direct or indirect economic or commercial advantage through an establishment which is accessible to the public."[13] Making available for "on the spot reference use" or for the purpose of exhibition in public or public performances are not included as lending or renting.[14]

## The Right of Communications to the Public (formerly Broadcasting and Cable Rights)

**2–153**     The right of communicating a copyright work (or a substantial part of it) to the public is a restricted act and will amount to infringement if done without the licence or consent of the copyright owner.[15] From October 31, 2003, the Copyright Designs and Patents Act 1988 was amended by the Copyright and Related Rights Regulations 2003[16] which replaced the right of broadcasting a work or including it in a cable programme with the right of communication to the public. The Regulations implemented the European Copyright and Related Rights in the Information Society Directive[17] which was designed to address the challenge of the internet and digital technology.

It is important to note that these changes to the 1988 Act apply to works already in existence before October 31, 2003 as well as to new works.[18] There are, however, some transitional provisions which provide that:

(1)   no act done before October 31, 2003 is to be regarded as an infringement of any new or extended right.[19]

(2)   nothing in the regulations affects any agreement made before December 22, 2002.[20]

(3)   no act done after October 31, 2003 in pursuance of an agreement made before December 22, 2002 shall be regarded as an infringement

---

[10] CDPA 1988, ss.16(1) and 18A.
[11] CDPA 1988, s.18A(6).
[12] S.18A(2)(a).
[13] S.18A(2)(b).
[14] CDPA 1988, s.18A(3).
[15] CDPA 1988, s.16 and s.20 as amended by The Copyright and Related Rights Regulations 2003 (SI 2003/2498), reg.6.
[16] SI 2003/2498.
[17] 2001/29/EC.
[18] The Copyright and Related Rights Regulations 2003 (SI 2003/2498), reg.31.
[19] *ibid.*, reg. 31(2).
[20] *ibid.*, reg. 32(1).

of any new or extended right arising by virtue of these regulations.[21]

Communication to the public is defined to mean communication to the public by electronic transmission and *includes*:[22]

(a) the broadcasting of the work;[23]
(b) the making available to the public of the work by electronic transmission in such a way that members of the public may access it from a place and at a time individually chosen by them.[23a]

The right to communicate the work to the public is an act restricted in respect of, inter alia, an artistic work and thus applies to photographs.[23b]

It is a very broadly worded right and the definition in the CDPA 1988 (as indicated by the word "includes") is plainly not exclusive. The intention of the Directive is clear from Recital 23 which reads: **2–154**

**Recital 23**

This Directive should harmonize further the author's right of communication to the public. *This right should be understood in a broad sense covering all communication to the public not present at the place where the communication originates.* This right should cover any such transmission or retransmission of a work to the public by wire or wireless means including broadcasting. This right should not cover any other acts.[23c] (emphasis added).

Transmission of images to the public by internet use, interactive television services, "pull" mobile phone services where images are downloaded on request to mobile phones will all fall within the definition of communication to the public.

A broadcast is a separate category of work in which copyright subsists[23d] and is given a new definition following the amendment of the 1988 Act.[23e] Broadly, broadcasting does not include any kind of interactive services. A

---

[21] *ibid.*, reg. 32(2). The Directive states, in slightly different wording, that it shall apply 'without prejudice to any acts concluded and rights acquired before December 22, 2002: 2001/29/EC, Art. 10(2).

[22] CDPA 1988, s.20(2).

[23] CDPA 1988, s.20(2)(a) as amended by SI 2003/2498, reg. 6.

[23a] CDPA 1988, s.20(2)(b) as amended by SI 2003/2498, reg. 6.

[23b] CDPA 1988, s.20(1) replacing the old s.20 which stated that the broadcasting of the work or its inclusion in a cable programme service was an act restricted by the copyright in a literary, dramatic, musical or artistic work, a sound recording or film, or a broadcast or cable programme.

[23c] See also Art. 3(1): Member States shall provide authors with the exclusive right to authorise or prohibit any communication to the public of their works, by wire or wireless means, including the making available to the public of their works in such a way that members of the public may access them from a place and at a time individually chosen by them.

[23d] CDPA 1988, s.1(1)(b) as amended by reg. 5(2).

[23e] Prior to October 31, 2003, "Broadcast" was defined by the CDPA 1988, s.6(1) as a transmission by wireless telegraphy of visual images, sounds or other information which is (a) capable of being lawfully received by members of the public or (b) is transmitted for presentation to members of the public. Wireless telegraphy was defined in turn as "the sending of electro-magnetic energy over paths not provided by a material substance constructed or arranged for the purpose, but does not include the transmission of microwave energy between terrestrial fixed points": s.178.

broadcast is defined as meaning "an electronic transmission of visual images, sounds or other information which—

    (a)  is transmitted for simultaneous reception by members of the public and is capable of being lawfully received by them,[23f] or

    (b)  is transmitted at a time determined solely by the person making the transmission for presentation to members of the public,[23g]

and which is not a specifically excluded transmission.[23h] Excluded from the definition of 'broadcast' is any internet transmission unless it is—

    (a)  a transmission taking place simultaneously on the internet and by other means,[23i]

    (b)  a concurrent transmission of a live event,[23j] or

    (c)  a transmission of recorded moving images or sounds forming part of a programme service offered by the person responsible for making the transmission, being a service in which programmes are transmitted at scheduled times determined by that person."[23k]

Only internet use that is simulcasting or otherwise falls within the previous categories (a) to (c) will be treated as a broadcast. Other internet use will class as "making available to the public by electronic transmission" within the meaning of s.20(2) of the CDPA 1988 and is thus a restricted act. Even prior to amendment on October 31, 2003, sending of copyright works via the internet was a restricted act as a cable service[23l] had been held to include the sending of web pages.[23m]

When considering alleged infringement of copyright in photographs used in broadcasts, the defence of incidental inclusion may apply and should be considered.[23n]

---

[23f] CDPA 1988, s.6(1)(a) as amended by SI 2003/2498, reg.4.
[23g] CDPA 1988, s.6(1)(b) as amended by SI 2003/2498, reg. 4.
[23h] CDPA 1988, s.6 as amended by SI 2003/2498, reg. 4.
[23i] CDPA 1988, s.6(1A)(a) as inserted by SI 2003/2498, reg. 4.
[23j] CDPA 1988, s.6(1A)(b) as inserted by SI 2003/2498, reg. 4.
[23k] CDPA 1988, s.6(1A)(c) as inserted by SI 2003/2498, reg. 4.
[23l] Prior to the October 31, 2003 amendment, the CDPA 1988 maintained a distinction between broadcasts and cable programme services which has now been abandoned. Cable programme was defined by s.7 (1) (now repealed) as any item included in a service which consists wholly or mainly in sending visual images, sounds or other information by means of a telecommunications system (other than by wireless telegraphy) for reception:

    (a)  at two or more places (whether for simultaneous reception or at different times in response to requests by different users) or

    (b)  for presentation to members of the public

and which was not a service excluded by the Act. Excluded services were set out in s.7(2) (also now repealed) and included any information sent via interactive services eg for internet shopping; internal business telecommunications systems used for the purposes of running the business or a service run for domestic purposes not connected to any other telecommunications system. For further detail see Laddie, Prescott & Vitoria, *et al.* (3rd ed.), *op cit.*, at 8.18 *et seq.* and *Copinger & Skone James on Copyright* (14th ed.), *op cit.*, at 3-68 *et seq.*
[23m] *Sony Music Entertainment (UK) Ltd v Easyinternetcafe Ltd* [2003] EWHC 62; [2003] F.S.R. 48; *Shetland Times v Wills* [1997] FSR 604 (Ct of Sess) (interlocutory decision).
[23n] See below at paras 2–168 and 5–054 *et seq.*

## SECONDARY INFRINGEMENT

The 1988 Act provides for secondary infringement where a person with-   **2–155**
out the licence of the copyright owner:

(a) imports into the UK otherwise than for his private and domestic use, an article which is and which he knows or has reason to believe is, an infringing copy of the work;[24]

(b) possesses or deals with an infringing copy—specifically in respect of an article which is and which he has reason to believe is an infringing copy:[25]

    (i) possesses in the course of business; or
    (ii) sells or lets for hire or offers or exposes for sale or hire; or
    (iii) in the course of business exhibits in public or distributes; or
    (iv) distributes otherwise than in the course of business to such an extent as to affect prejudicially the owner of the copyright.

(c) makes; imports into the UK; possesses in the course of business; or sells or lets for hire, or offers or exposes for sale or hire an article specifically designed or adapted for making copies of that work knowing or having reason to believe that it is to be used to make infringing copies.[26] Secondary infringement also arises where a person without the licence of the copyright owner transmits the work by means of a telecommunications system (other than by communication to the public) knowing or having reason to believe that infringing copies of the work will be made by means of the reception of the transmission in the UK or elsewhere.[27]

For the purposes of secondary infringement, an "infringing copy" means any article which when made constituted an infringement of the copyright in the work in question.[28]

In all cases of secondary infringement it is necessary to prove that the   **2–156**
defendant had knowledge or had reason to believe he was dealing with an infringing copy.

Secondary infringement does not pose any legal problems specifically pertaining to photographs and for that reason is not dealt with in detail here.[29]

---

[24] CDPA 1988, s.22.
[25] CDPA 1988, s.23.
[26] CDPA 1998, s.24(1).
[27] CDPA 1988, s.24(2), as amended by SI 2003/2498, reg.2(1), Sch. 1, Pt 1, paras 1 and 5(a).
[28] CDPA 1998, s.27(2).
[29] See *Copinger & Skone James on Copyright* (14th ed.), *op. cit.*, at 8–01 *et seq.* and Laddie, Prescott & Vitoria *et al.*, (3rd ed,) *op. cit.* at 19.1 *et seq.*

## Permitted acts and defences

**2–157**    The CDPA 1988 provides that certain "permitted acts" do not amount to copyright infringement. Not all the exceptions permitted acts in relation to every category of copyright work—some just concern literary, dramatic and musical works for example. The following section only deals with permitted acts that concern artistic works and thus include photographic works. In addition to the statutory exceptions, it is obviously a defence to show copyright does not subsist, the claimant does not have title or the defendant is licenced to use the work. It may also be a defence to show that the claimant's right to relief is barred by laches, acquiescence, delay,[30] or estoppel. A defence of public interest can apply to a copyright infringement claim.[30a]

### Fair dealing for purposes of research and private study

**2–158**    Fair dealing with an artistic work for the purpose of research for a non-commercial purpose does not infringe any copyright in the work provided that it is accompanied by a sufficient acknowledgment.[31] Sufficient acknowledgment means an acknowledgment identifying the work by its title or other description and identifying the author unless

(a) in the case of a published work it is published anonymously; or

(b) in the case of an unpublished work, it is not possible to ascertain the identity of the author by reasonable enquiry.[32]

However no acknowledgement is required in connection with fair dealing for research where this would be impossible for reasons of practicality or otherwise.[33]

In addition, fair dealing with a literary, dramatic, musical or artistic work for the purposes of private study does not infringe any copyright in the work.[34]

These permitted acts do not permit anyone other than a librarian to make multiple copies.[34a] Nor does it permit anyone other than the student or researcher himself to make copies if he has reason to believe that it will result in copies of substantially the same material being provided to more

---

[30] *e.g. Hoover plc v George Hulme Ltd* [1982] F.S.R. 565.

[30a] CDPA 1988, s.171(3). *Hyde Park v Yelland* [2001] Ch.143; *Ashdown v Telegraph Group* [2001] EWCA Civ 1142; [2002] Ch.149.

[31] CDPA 1988, s.29(1) as amended by the Copyright and Related Rights Regulations 2003 (SI 2003/2498), reg. 9. This section was amended on October 31, 2003. Prior to that date, commercial research was not excluded and there was no requirement for "sufficient acknowledgement". As to the transitional provisions of the amending regulations see above at para.2–153.

[32] CDPA 1988, s.178.

[33] CDPA 1988, s.29(1B) as inserted by SI 2003/2498, reg. 9.

[34] CDPA 1988, s.29(1C) as inserted by SI 2003/2498, reg. 9.

[34a] CDPA 1988, s.29(3)(a).

than one person at substantially the same time for substantially the same purpose.[34b]

### Fair dealing for the purpose of criticism, review but not news reporting

Fair dealing with a *published* work for the purpose of criticism or review **2–159** of that work or another work does not infringe any copyright in the work provided that it is accompanied by a sufficient acknowledgment.[34c] For alleged infringements prior to October 31, 2003 (when the CDPA 1988 was amended by the Copyright and Related Rights Regulations 2003[34d]), the defence of criticism and review could be claimed in respect of unpublished works.[34e] This was changed by the 2003 Regulations and s.30 now reads (with amendments shown in italics/strikeout):

#### Criticism, review and news reporting
**30.**–(1) Fair dealing with a work for the purpose of criticism or review, of that or another work or of a performance of a work, does not infringe any copyright in the work provided that it is accompanied by a sufficient acknowledgement *and provided that the work has been made available to the public.*

*(1A) For the purposes of subsection (1) a work has been made available to the public if it has been made available by any means, including—*

*(a) the issue of copies to the public;*
*(b) making the work available by means of an electronic retrieval system;*
*(c) the rental or lending of copies of the work to the public;*
*(d) the performance, exhibition, playing or showing of the work in public;*
*(e) the communication to the public of the work,*

*but in determining generally for the purposes of that subsection whether a work has been made available to the public no account shall be taken of any unauthorised act.*

(2) Fair dealing with a work (other than a photograph) for the purpose of reporting current events does not infringe any copyright in the work provided that (subject to subsection (3)) it is accompanied by a sufficient acknowledgement.

---

[34b] CDPA 1988, s.29(3)(b).
[34c] CDPA 1988, s.30(1) as amended by SI 2003/2498, reg. 10. This section was altered as a result of the implementation of the EC Directive on the Harmonisation of Certain Aspects of Copyright and Related Rights in the Information Society (Directive 2001/29/EC). Art. 5.3(d) provides that member states may provide for exceptions and limitations to rights in the case of: "quotations for criticism or review, provided they relate to a work or other subject matter which has already lawfully been made available to the public, that, unless this turns out to be impossible, the source, including the author's name, is indicated, and that their use is in accordance with fair practice, and to the extent required by the specific purpose". Note that the amendment to subsection (3) differs from the wording in the Directive, Art 5.3(c) which does not specify "for reasons of practicality or otherwise."
[34d] SI 2003/2498.
[34e] For the transitional provisions of Copyright and Related Rights Regulations 2003 (SI 2003/2498) see above at para 2–153.

(3) No acknowledgement is required in connection with the reporting of current events by means of a sound recording, film, ~~broadcast or cable programme~~ *or broadcast where this would be impossible for reasons of practicality or otherwise.*

Permitted criticism is not limited to the work itself but includes the underlying ideas, philosophy, doctrine or events.[35] It includes criticism of a decision to withdraw the work from circulation.[36] The use of the work must be for the purpose of criticism or review of the work itself; use for some other purpose is not fair dealing.[37] What is fair is a matter of degree and impression,[38] but use of the copies in commercial competition with the work itself is unlikely to be fair dealing.[39]

**2–160**    Sufficient acknowledgement means an acknowledgment identifying the work in question by its title or other description and identifying the author (unless for published works it was published anonymously or for unpublished works it is not possible to identify the author by reasonable enquiry).[40] Note that it is the author who is required to be identified by a sufficient acknowledgement.

The statute also provides no infringement for fair dealing with a work for the purpose of reporting current events provided there is sufficient acknowledgment. But this defence does not apply to photographs and use for reporting current events will amount to an infringement of a photograph.[41] It does extend to other works however and would include stills from a film or video including security cameras.[42]

**2–161**    It is submitted that the total failure of the 1988 Act to allow any use of photographs for the purpose of reporting current events is incompatible with Art.10 of the European Convention on Human Rights.[43] Article 10 reads as follows:

**"Article 10—Freedom of Expression**

1.    Everyone has the right to freedom of expression. This right shall include freedom to hold opinions and to receive and impart information and ideas without interference by public authority and

---

[35] *Hubbard v Vosper* [1972] 2 Q.B. 84; *Distillers Co (Biochemicals) Ltd v Times Newspapers Ltd* [1975] Q.B. 613; *Pro Sieben Media AG v Carlton UK Television* [1999] F.S.R. 610.
[36] *Time Warner Entertainments Co v Channel Four Television Corpn plc* [1994] E.M.L.R. 1 (Kubrick's film "A Clockwork Orange").
[37] *Ashdown v Telegraph Group Ltd* [2001] 4 All E.R. 666; [2002] Ch. 149 (confidential political memorandum used not to criticise the work but to criticise the actions of the claimant).
[38] *Hubbard v Vosper* [1972] 2 Q.B. 84 at 98.
[39] *ibid.; Johnstone v Bernard Jones Publications Ltd* [1938] Ch. 599 at 607; *Moorhouse v University of New South Wales* [1975] R.P.C. 454 (Aus).
[40] CDPA 1988, s.178.
[41] CDPA 1988, s.30(2).
[42] *Hyde Park v Yelland* [2001] Ch. 143, CA (on the facts rejecting argument that publication of stills from a security video of Diana Princess of Wales and Dodi Fayed the day before their deaths was fair dealing. Publication was for purpose of establishing timings of arrival and departure which could have been given by statements of people who had seen the photographs proving times.) As to distriction between photographs and film frames see above at para. 2–036.
[43] Given "further effect" in the UK by the Human Rights Act 1998 which came into force on October 2, 2000: *Human Rights Act 1998 (Commencement No.2) Order 2000* (SI 2000/1851).

regardless of frontiers. This Article shall not prevent States from requiring the licensing of broadcasting, television or cinema enterprises.

2. The exercise of these freedoms, since it carries with it duties and responsibilities, may be subject to such formalities, conditions, restrictions or penalties as are prescribed by law and are necessary in a democratic society, in the interests of national security, territorial integrity or public safety, for the prevention of disorder or crime, for the protection of health or morals, for the protection of the reputation or rights of others, for preventing the disclosure of information received in confidence, or for maintaining the authority and impartiality of the judiciary."

The right is not just that of expression in a literal sense but includes a right to receive and impart information and ideas.

It is well established that freedom of expression constitutes one of the essential foundations of a democratic society and that the safeguards to be afforded to the press are of particular importance.[44] The European Court of Human Rights has emphasised that "the freedom of the press affords the public one of the best means of discovering and forming an opinion of the ideas and attitudes of their political leaders".[45]   **2–162**

Where there is an interference with a Convention right, the court must determine whether the interference at issue is "proportionate to the legitimate aim pursued". and the reasons adduced to justify it are "relevant and sufficient".[46] A limitation is only lawful where it does not impair the very essence of the right.[47]   **2–163**

The principles of Art.10 have been applied to images and television broadcasts as well as to print media.[48] The European Court of Human Rights has said that in considering the "duties and responsibilities" of a journalist, the potential impact of the medium concerned is an important factor and it is commonly acknowledged that audio-visual media often has a much more immediate and powerful effect than print media. The audio visual media has means of conveying through images, meanings which the visual print media is not able to impart.[49]   **2–164**

An injunction granted in Austria under a copyright statute that prohibited publication of a politician's photograph has been held to be a vio-

---

[44] *Handyside v UK* (1979–80) 1 E.H.R.R. 737; *Jersild v Denmark* (1995) 19 E.H.R.R. 1.
[45] *Castells v Spain* (1992) 14 E.H.R.R. 445, para.43; *Özgür Gündem v Turkey* (2001) 31 E.H.R.R. 49.
[46] *Guardian Newspapers Ltd v United Kingdom* (1992) 14 E.H.R.R. 153, para.59; *Arslan v Turkey* App. No.23462/94 (2001) 31 E.H.R.R. 9.
[47] *Ashingdane v UK* (1985) 7 E.H.R.R. 528 at para.57.
[48] *Jersild v Denmark* (1995) 19 E.H.R.R. 1 prosecution of a journalist and a television broadcaster for broadcasting interviews with youths expressing racist views violated Art.10.
[49] *ibid.*, at 27. See also below at paras 7–006 and 7–007.

lation of Art.10. In *Krone Verlag Gmbh v Austria*,[50] the newspaper applicant published a photo-graph of a politician illustrating an article concerning his financial situation. It alleged he was unlawfully receiving a teacher's salary during his membership of the European Parliament, essentially alleging unjust enrichment. The politician obtained an injunction under a section of the Austrian author's right statute which prohibited publication of images of people where it would cause injury to the legitimate interests of the person concerned. It was common ground that the injunction was an interference, the issue was whether the interference was justified. The court accepted that the section of the statute pursued a legitimate aim, namely the protection of the rights and reputation of others.

**2–165**    The court observed that there was little scope for restrictions on political speech or questions of public interest.[51] It was said that the limits of acceptable criticism are wider with regard to a politician acting in his public capacity than in relation to a private individual, as the former inevitably lays himself open to close scrutiny of his every word and deed by both journalists and the public at large and must display a greater degree of tolerance. Accusing a politician that not all his income had been obtained lawfully was a matter of public concern.

The ECHR concluded that the reasons adduced by the Austrian courts for granting the injunction were relevant but not sufficient. The Austrian courts had failed to take into account the essential function the press fulfils in a democratic society and its duty to impart information and ideas on all matters of public interest. The politician had entered the public arena and had to bear the consequences. There was no valid reason why the newspaper should be prevented from publishing his picture and there had been a violation of Art.10.

**2–166**    Similarly, the Austrian Federal Supreme Court has held that the lack of a right to "quote" photographs was contrary to freedom of speech.[52] A weekly newspaper published an article about the plaintiff newspaper's attitude to a political group. The article featured five miniaturised pages of the front page of the plaintiff's newspaper (including the photographs). In one of these, the plaintiff paper had published a photograph of a youth suspected of arson in respect of which the plaintiff had not attempted to conceal the youth's identity. The plaintiff newspaper owned the copyright in the photograph and sought an injunction.

**2–167**    The Austrian Copyright statute recognised a right to quote text but made no mention of photographs. The court held that the lack of a defence permitting "quotation" of photographs was held to be a lacuna contrary to

---

[50] App. No: 34315/96, (2003) 36 E.H.R.R. 57, February 26, 2002. See also *News Verlags Gmbh & Co Kg v Austria* (App. No.31457/96) (2001) 31 E.H.R.R. 8, January 11, 2000, concerning the same provision of the Austrian Author's Right Act where a newspaper was subject to an injunction prohibiting publication of a photograph of a right-wing extremist later charged with various criminal offences in connection with a letter-bomb campaign against politicians. Later the suspect was convicted on some charges but acquitted on others and the proceedings were widely reported. Other newspapers were free to publish his picture but the applicant was subject to an injunction. This was held to be a violation of Art.10.

[51] Citing *Nilsen and Johnsen v Norway* App. No.23118/93.

[52] *Re Quotation of News Pictures* (4 Ob 224/00w) [2002] E.C.C. 20.

freedom of speech which the court would fill. Notwithstanding that this was a decision of an Austrian court, the following observations of the court could equally apply to the lack of a fair use defence for photograph in the UK and the right to freedom of speech. In giving judgment it was said:

"... the provisions governing the right of quotations do not do justice to the fact that in the interests of freedom of speech it may be just as necessary to quote a picture as to reproduce individual parts of a work of language and can promote intellectual discussion just as much as can the quotation of whole pictures in academic works. Contributions to newspapers and periodicals are increasingly illustrated with pictures, partly to draw attention to the contribution and partly to convey messages particularly effectively. Unlike in the case of quotations of words, there is normally no point in quoting in such a way that only parts of the picture are shown (small quotation). This applies not only to academic works in connection with which the legislature has taken account of the normal need to reproduce works of art, including pictures, complete, not merely details of them in the provision of free utilisation contained in s.54(1) no 3a Copyright Act which can also be applied to pictures.

The statute is therefore incomplete, if it permits the reproduction of individual parts of a work of language in the interests of freedom of speech and also large quotations in the interest of free academic argument in academic works, but at the same time does not permit pictures to be quoted in full in the interests of freedom of speech and of free intellectual discussion in the interest of the general public."[53]

It is doubtful whether the blanket exclusion of all photographs from a defence of fair use for the purpose of reporting current events in s.30(2) of the CDPA 1988 can be said to be legitimate or proportionate. There will inevitably be cases where, to prevent the media publishing a photograph for the purpose of reporting current events, would be an unjustifiable interference with freedom of expression. Each case will turn on its facts[54] but in principle, it is submitted that the total lack of a discretion in the statute to permit publication of photographs for the purpose of reporting current events is contrary to Art.10. In some cases, publication of an actual photograph will be essential to the exercise of free speech rather than a mere description of its contents. If publication of certain information is justifiable in the public interest then journalists must be given reasonable latitude as to

---

[53] *ibid.*, at 390.
[54] Compare the differing approaches of the Court of Appeal and the court of first instance in *Hyde Park Residence Ltd v Yelland.* See [1999] E.M.L.R. 654 at 662 where Jacob J. took the view that a picture says more than a thousand words and publication of image stills from a security camera showing the time at which people entered and departed from a property was necessary to refute allegations made that the time spent was much longer. The Court of Appeal took a different view concluding that publication was unnecessary, as the information therein could have been conveyed in a way that did not infringe copyright: [2001] Ch. 143; [2000] 3 W.L.R. 215; [2000] E.C.D.R. 275; [2000] E.M.L.R. 363.

the manner in which the information is conveyed to the public otherwise the Art.10 right to freedom of expression will be unnecessarily inhibited.[55]

### Incidental inclusion of copyright material

2–168    Copyright is not infringed by the incidental inclusion of the work in an artistic work, sound recording, film or broadcast.[56] Where there is no infringement by a second work because the use of the first work amounts to incidental inclusion of a first work, copyright in the first work is not infringed by issuing the second work to the public or playing, showing, communicating the second work to the public.[57]

Incidental is not defined, but commentators suggest that it has the ordinary meaning of "something casual or of secondary importance"[58] or "what is casual, not essential, subordinate, merely background etc".[59] Thus, a photographer taking a photographic portrait of a person in a room with a painting on the wall in the distant background would not infringe the copyright in the painting as it is of secondary importance to the portrait. Similarly, a film focussing on the director of a gallery walking through a room with photographs on the wall would not infringe the copyright in those photographs.

The relevant test for whether something is incidentally included is the question why has work "A" been included in work "B"?[60] The answer depends on an objective assessment of the circumstances in which the image was created and is not to be answered by considering what was in the mind of the photographer at the time when he took the photograph.[61]

### Making of Temporary Copies

2–168A    From October 31, 2003, the CDPA 1988 was amended by the Copyright and Related Rights Regulations 2003[61a] to provide a new permitted exception in respect of the making of temporary copies which are transient or

---

[55] *Campbell v Mirror Group Newspapers* [2002] EWCA Civ. 1373, at para.64; [2003] Q.B. 633; [2003] 2 W.L.R. 80; [2003] 1 All E.R. 224; [2003] E.M.L.R. 2. See also cases cited below at para. 7–007.

[56] CDPA 1988, s.31(1), as amended from October 31, 2003 by the Copyright and Related Rights Regulations 2003 (SI 2003/2498), reg. 2(1), Sch 1, Pt 1, paras 1 and 3(1)(d) replacing words "broadcast or cable programme" with "or broadcast". For transitional provisions and generally see above at para. 2–153.

[57] CDPA 1988, s.31(2), as amended from October 31, 2003 by the Copyright and Related Rights Regulations 2003 (SI 2003/2498), reg. 2(1), Sch 1, Pt 1, paras 1 and 6(2)(b) replacing words "broadcasting or inclusion in a cable programme service" with "communicating to the public". For transitional provisions see above at para. 2–153.

[58] *Copinger & Skone James on Copyright* (14th ed.), *op. cit.*, at 9–26.

[59] Laddie, Prescott & Vitoria *et al.* (3rd ed.) *op. cit.*, at 20.17.

[60] *The Football Association Premier League Ltd v Panini UK Ltd* [2002] EWCA Civ 995 *per* Chadwick L.J. at para.27; [2003] 4 All E.R. 1290; [2004] F.S.R. 1 (football club logos included in photographs of football players on collectible stickers held not to be incidental inclusion). This case is discussed more fully below at para. 5–054.

[61] *ibid.* at paras 25 and 27. See further, below at paras 5–054 *et seq.*

[61a] SI 2003/2498.

incidental and are an integral part of a technological process.[61b] In order to rely on this exception, the temporary copy must have no independent economic significance. In addition, its sole purpose must be either to enable a lawful use of the work or to enable a transmission of the work in a network between third parties by an intermediary. This exception is directed at copying that occurs during normal internet use by acts of caching and browsing and is discussed further below at paras 9–007 *et seq.*

## Copying for the Purpose of Instruction or Examination

Copyright in an artistic work is not infringed by being copied in the course of instruction or of preparation for instruction provided that the copying is:   **2–169**

(a)  done by a person giving or receiving instruction; and

(b)  is not done by the means of a reprographic process; and

(c)  is accompanied by a sufficient acknowledgement[62] (unless this would be impossible for reasons of practicality or otherwise)[63]

and provided that the instruction is for a non-commercial purpose.[64]

It is difficult to see how this can apply to photographs in any meaningful way. The exclusion of reprographic copying and the restriction to non-commercial purposes makes this permitted act very limited.

There is a slightly wider permission for the use of *published* artistic works which is not limited to non-commercial purposes. Copyright in a literary, dramatic, musical or artistic work which has been made available to the public[64a] is not infringed by its being copied in the course of instruction or of preparation for instruction, provided the copying:

(a)  is fair dealing with the work;

(b)  is done by a person giving or receiving instruction;

(c)  is not done by means of a reprographic process; and

(d)  is accompanied by a sufficient acknowledgement[64b] (unless this would be impossible for reasons of practicality or otherwise[64c]).

---

[61b] CDPA 1988, s.28A inserted by SI 2003/2498, regs 3 and 8(1).

[62] For meaning of "sufficient acknowledgment" see CDPA 1988, s.178 and above at para. 2–160.

[63] CDPA 1988, s.32(3A) inserted by SI 2003/2498, regs 3, 11(1)(c)

[64] CDPA 1988, s.32 (1) as amended from October 31, 2003 by the Copyright and Related Rights Regulations 2003 (SI 2003/2498), regs 3 and 11(1)(a). Prior to October 31, 2003, there was no requirement for a sufficient acknowledgment and the use was not restricted to non-commercial use. For transitional provisions and generally see above at para. 2–153.

[64a] By virtue of CDPA 1988, s.32(2B) (as inserted by SI 2003/2498) "made available to the public" has the same meaning as in s.30(1A) which is set out above at para. 2–159.

[64b] For meaning of "sufficient acknowledgment" see CDPA 1988, s.178 and above at para. 2–160.

[64c] CPDA 1988, s.32(3A) inserted by SI 2003/2498, regs 3 and 11(1)(c).

**2–170**    "Reprographic process" is defined as a process for making facsimile copies or involving the use of an appliance for making multiple copies.[64d] It includes in relation to a work held in electronic form any copying by electronic means not including making of a film or a sound recording.

In addition, copying is not infringed by anything done for the purposes of an examination by way of setting questions, communicating the questions to the candidates or answering the questions.[64e] From October 31, 2003, in order to rely on this permitted act, it is required that the questions be accompanied by a sufficient acknowledgement.[64f]

### Libraries and archives

**2–171**    There are various permitted acts that may be carried out by librarians and archivists specified in ss.37–43 of the CDPA 1988. These exceptions for the most part concern literary, dramatic, and musical works. Artistic works may only be copied when they accompany another work[65] such as an illustration accompanying a text. The exceptions do not permit copying the illustrations per se.

### Parliamentary and judicial proceedings and statutory inquiries

**2–172**    Copyright is not infringed by anything done for the purposes of parliamentary or judicial proceedings or for the purpose of reporting those proceedings.[66] That does not extend to authorising the copying of a work which is itself a published report of the proceedings.[67] Copyright in a work is also not infringed by anything done for the purposes of the proceedings of a Royal Commission or a statutory inquiry,[68] or by issuing to the public copies of a report containing the work or material from it.[69]

### Material open to public inspection or on an official register

**2–173**    Where material is open to public inspection pursuant to a statutory requirement or which is on a statutory register which contains information about matters of a general scientific, technical, commercial or economic interest, copyright is not infringed by the copying or issuing to the public of copies of the material, by or with the authority of the appropriate person for the purpose of disseminating that information.[70]

---

[64d] CDPA 1988, s.178.
[64e] CDPA 1988, s.32(3).
[64f] CDPA 1988, s.32(3) as amended by SI 2003/2498, regs 3 and 11(1)(b). For meaning of "sufficient acknowledgment" see CDPA 1988, s.178 and above at para. 2–160.
[65] CDPA 1988, ss.38(1) and 41(1).
[66] CDPA 1988, s.45(1).
[67] CDPA 1988, s.45(2).
[68] CDPA 1988, s.46(1).
[69] CDPA 1988, s.46(3).
[70] CDPA 1988, s.47(3).

## Material communicated to the Crown

The Crown has power to copy and issue previously unpublished works to **2–174** the public in certain cases without infringing copyright. The power applies where an artistic work (*inter alia*) has in the course of public business been communicated to the Crown for any purpose, by or with the licence of the copyright owner and a document or other material thing embodying the work is in the custody or control of the Crown.[71] In such cases, the Crown may issue copies of the work to the public provided it is for the purpose for which the work was communicated to the Crown or any related purpose which could reasonably have been anticipated by the copyright owner.[72]

## Public records

Public records within the meaning of the Public Records Act 1958 (and **2–175** other specific public record statutes) may be copied and a copy may be supplied to any person by or with the authority of any officer appointed under that Act without infringing copyright.[73]

## Acts done under statutory authority

Where the doing of a particular act is specifically authorised by an Act of **2–176** Parliament, whenever passed, then unless the Act provides otherwise, the doing of any such act does not infringe copyright.[74]

## Design documents and models

It is not infringement of copyright in a design document or model **2–177** recording or embodying a design (for anything other than artistic work or a typeface) to make an article to the design or copy an article made to the design.[75] Design means the design of any aspect of the shape or configuration (whether internal or external) of the whole part of an article, other than surface decoration.[76] A design document means any record of a design whether in the form of a photograph, a drawing, a written description, data stored in a computer or otherwise.[77] This is aimed at preventing the use of artistic copyright to protect utilitarian three-dimensional objects.

---

[71] CDPA 1988, s.48(1).
[72] CDPA 1988, s.48(2).
[73] CDPA 1988, s.49.
[74] CDPA 1988, s.50.
[75] CDPA 1988, s.51(1).
[76] CDPA 1988, s.51(3).
[77] CDPA 1988, s.51(3).

### Exploitation of designs derived from artistic works

**2–178**    This exception applies where an artistic work has been exploited, by or with the licence of the copyright owner by (a) making articles that are copies of the work by an industrial process, and (b) marketing such articles, in the United Kingdom or elsewhere.[78] At the end of 25 years from the end of the year in which such articles were first marketed, copyright will not be infringed by making articles of any description, or doing anything for the purpose of making articles of any description, and or by doing anything in relation to articles so made.[79]

### Reliance on registered designs

**2–179**    The copyright in an artistic work is not infringed by anything done (a) in pursuance of an assignment or licence made or granted by a person registered under the Registered Designs Act 1949 as the proprietor of a corresponding design, and (b) in good faith in reliance on the registration and without notice of any proceedings for the cancellation of the registration or for rectifying the relevant entry in the register of designs; and this is so notwithstanding that the person registered as the proprietor was not the proprietor of the design for the purposes of the 1949 Act.[80]

### Works in electronic form

**2–180**    There is an exception concerning electronic works which are purchased by one person and then transferred to another. There is no infringement by a transferee of a work where a work in electronic form has been purchased on terms which allow the purchaser to copy the work, or to adapt it or make copies of an adaptation, in connection with his use of it.[81] Provided there are no terms prohibiting transfer, anything which the purchaser was allowed to do may also be done without infringement of copyright by a transferee; but any copy, adaptation or copy of an adaptation made by the purchaser which is not also transferred shall be treated as an infringing copy for all purposes after the transfer.[82]

### Anonymous or pseudonymous works

**2–181**    Section 57 of the 1988 Act provides copyright in a literary, dramatic, musical or artistic work is not infringed by an act done at a time when or in pursuance of arrangements made at a time when:

---

[78] CDPA 1988, s.52(1).
[79] CDPA 1988, s.52(2).
[80] CDPA 1988, s.53.
[81] CDPA 1988, s.56(1).
[82] CDPA 1988, s.56(2).

(a) it is not possible by reasonable inquiry to ascertain the identity of the author, and

(b) it is reasonable to assume:

   (i) that copyright has expired, or

   (ii) that the author died 70 years or more before the beginning of the calendar year in which the act is done or the arrangements are made.[83]

This applies to photographs taken on or after August 1, 1989. In respect of photographs existing at the date of commencement, this section does not apply. In order for the section to apply it is necessary to establish the second limb—either copyright had expired or that the author died more than 50 years[84] ago. The transitional provisions provide that it is not a defence in respect of a photograph to establish that it was reasonable to assume copyright had expired and (b)(i) above is of no application.[85]

The result of the transitional provisions is also that (b)(ii) does not apply to existing photographs. This is because the Act specifies that it is only a defence to establish in respect of an existing anonymous work that the author died earlier than 50 years ago in two cases.[86] The first is where a particular paragraph (which expressly excludes photographs) applies; thus the first case is irrelevant to photographs.[87] The second is where the term of copyright is governed by s.12 of the 1988 Act and not by the transitional provisions.[88] Existing published and unpublished photographs are both governed by the transitional provisions and not by s.12.[89] Accordingly, s.57 does not apply to photographs which existed at the date of commencement.

## Representations of certain artistic works on public display

It is not copyright infringement to make a photograph, a film, or graphic work of buildings, or sculptures, models for buildings and works of artistic craftsmanship, which are permanently situated in a public place or in premises open to the public.[90] "Building" includes any fixed structure and a part of a building or fixture structure.[91] Copyright in a photograph of such a

**2–182**

---

[83] CDPA 1988, s.57(1). Note that (ii) "the author died" does not apply to a work in which Crown copyright subsists. Reference should be made to s.104 which sets out presumptions as to authorship.

[84] There was no change to the figure of 50 years in the transitional provisions: Sch.1, para.12.

[85] CDPA 1988, Sch.1, para.15(1) and (2).

[86] CDPA 1988, Sch.1, para.15(1) and (3).

[87] CDPA 1988, Sch.1, para.15(3)(a) which states it only applies if Sch.1, para.12(3)(b) applies. Para.12(3)(b) expressly excludes photographs ("other than photographs").

[88] CDPA 1988, Sch.1, para.15(3)(b) stating it only applies if para.12(6) (duration of copyright is the same under the new provisions as under the previous law) applies.

[89] Published photographs and photographs taken before June 1, 1957: Sch.1, para.12(2)(c). Unpublished photographs taken on or after June 1, 1957: Sch.1, para.12(4)(c).

[90] CDPA 1988, s.62(1) and (2).

[91] CDPA 1988, s.4(2).

work is also not infringed by issuing copies of the photograph to the public or communicating to the public.[92]

**2–183**     The Act provides copyright "in such a work" is not infringed by the taking of the photograph and logically is restricted to the building, structure, sculpture, or work of artistic craftsmanship itself. In theory, taking a photograph of a building would infringe the architect's drawings. The 1911 Act contained a similar provision which was not limited to copyright in the building itself and simply provided that taking a photograph of a building, etc. was not an infringement of copyright.[93] The 1956 Act provisions, like the 1988 Act, seem to be limited to the work itself and would not prevent such a photograph infringing plans or prepatory drawings.[94] This may be regarded as anomalous, particularly as the provision regarding reconstruction of buildings specifically states that reconstruction does not infringe any copyright in any drawings or plans in accordance with which the building was constructed with the licence of the copyright owner.[95]

### Advertisement for sale of artistic work

**2–184**     It is not an infringement of copyright in an artistic work to copy it or to issue copies to the public for the purpose of advertising the sale of the work.[96] This permits photographs or other copies of paintings to be published in sale catalogues without infringement. However, where a copy that is non-infringing under this provision is later dealt with for any purpose other than advertising the sale of the work, it shall be treated as an infringing copy and that dealing infringes copyright for all subsequent purposes.[97]

### Making of subsequent works by the same artist

**2–185**     Where the author of a work is not the copyright owner, he does not infringe the copyright by copying the work if he makes another artistic work, provided he does not repeat or imitate the main design of the earlier work. The exclusion of the main design tends to suggest that this is aimed at permitting copying minor features of the work. It has been said in Parliamentary debate that this would allow the painter of a group portrait to use his earlier work to produce individual portraits.[98] Like s.62 (works on public

---

[92] CDPA 1988, s.62(3) as amended by SI 2003/2498, Sch. 1, Pt 1, paras 1 and 14 with effect from October 31, 2003. For transitional provisions and meaning of communication to the public see above at para. 2–153.

[93] 1911 Act, s.2(1)(iii).

[94] 1956 Act, s.9(3) and (4).

[95] CDPA 1988, s.65(b).

[96] CDPA 1988, s.63(1).

[97] CDPA 1988, s.63(2). For this purpose "dealt with" means sold or let for hire, offered or exposed for sale or hire, exhibited in public, distributed or communicated to the public (following amendment by SI 2003/2498, regs 3 and 17).

[98] *Hansard* HL (5th series) Vol.491, cols 190–191, December 8, 1987; Vol.493, cols 1886–1887, February 23, 1988.

display) this provision also fails to deal with copyright in any preparatory photographs, studies or drawings, etc.

## Lending of works

The Secretary of State has power to order that the lending to the public of certain works including artistic works shall be treated as licensed by the copyright owner subject only to the payment of reasonable royalty.[99]    **2–186**

## Incidental recording for purposes of broadcast or cable programme

Where a person has been licenced to broadcast an artistic work, he is to be treated as licenced in the case of an artistic work to make a photograph of, or film the work.[1] The licence is subject to the condition that the photograph or copy in question shall not be used for any other purpose and shall be destroyed within 28 days of first broadcast.[2] A photograph or copy used for any other purpose or not so destroyed is to be treated as an infringing copy.[3]    **2–187**

## Photographs of television broadcasts or cable programmes

The making in domestic premises for private and domestic use of a photograph of the whole or any part of an image forming part of a broadcast, or a copy of such a photograph, does not infringe any copyright in the broadcast or in any film included in it.[3a]    **2–188**

From October 31, 2003, following the amendment of the CDPA 1988 by the Copyright and Related Rights Regulations 2003,[3b] any photograph (that if not for this exception would otherwise be an infringing copy) that is sold or let for hire, offered or exposed for sale or hire or communicated to the public, will be treated as an infringing copy for the purpose of that dealing.[3c] infringes copyright it shall be treated as an infringing copy for all subsequent purposes.

The amended s.71 of the Copyright Designs and Patents Act 1988, which provides this exception, together with the wording of the section prior to the October 31, 2003 amendment are set out in full and compared below at para. 9–046.

---

[99] CDPA 1988, s.66.
[1] CDPA 1988, s.68(1)(b) and (2)(b) as amended by SI 2003/2498, reg. 2(2), Sch.2.
[2] CDPA 1988, s.68(3).
[3] CDPA 1988, s.68(4).
[3a] CDPA 1988, s.71 as amended by SI 2003/2498, regs 3 and 20(1) Essentially (1) replacing words "broadcast or cable programme" with word "broadcast" and (2) adding a new s.71(2) making images acquired in this way infringing if dealt with commercially or communicated to the public—as to which see the following footnotes and accompanying text.
[3b] SI 2003/2498.
[3c] CDPA 1988, s.7(2) and (3) as inserted by SI 2003/2498, regs 3, 20(1). For transitional provisions see above at para. 2–153.

**Copying By and For Visually Impaired Persons**

2–188A    From October 31, 2003, the CDPA 1988 was amended to include new permitted acts that render certain copying by or on behalf of visually impaired persons non-infringing.[3d]

A visually impaired person is defined as meaning a person:

(a) who is blind

(b) who has an impairment of visual function which cannot be improved, by the use of corrective lenses, to a level that would normally be acceptable for reading without a special level or kind of light

(c) who is unable, through physical disability, to hold or manipulate a book; or

(d) who is unable, through physical disability, to focus or move his eyes to the extent that would normally be acceptable for reading.[3e]

If a visually impaired person has lawful possession or lawful use of a copy ("the master copy") of the whole or part of a literary, dramatic, musical or artistic work or a published edition which is not accessible to him because of the impairment, it is not an infringement of copyright in the work, or in the typographical arrangement of the published edition, for an accessible copy[3f] of the master copy to be made for his personal use.[3g] An accessible copy made pursuant to these provisions must carry a statement that it is made under the respective section of the 1988 Act and a sufficient acknowledgment.[3h]

If an accessible copy is available commercially by or with the authority of te copyright owner, this exception does not apply.[3i] In addition, it does not apply if the master copy is a database and the making of the copy would infringe copyright in the database.[3j] Nor does it apply if the master copy is a musical work and the accessible copy would involve recording a performance of the work or part of it.[3k]

There are similar provisions permitting the making of multiple copies by educational establishments or non-profit bodies for the personal use of visually impaired persons.[3l]

---

[3d] CDPA 1988, ss.31A to 31F as inserted by the Copyright (Visually Impaired Persons) Act 2002. Commencement October 31, 2003: Copyright (Visually Impaired Persons) Act 2002 (Commencement) Order 2003 (SI 2003/2499).
[3e] CDPA 1988, 31F(9) as inserted by the Copyright (Visually Impaired Persons) Act 2002, s. 6 (Commencement October 31, 2003: SI 2003/2499).
[3f] "Accessible copy" is defined as meaning a version which provides for a visually impaired person improved access to the work: CDPA 1988, s.31F(3).
[3g] CDPA 1988, s.31A(1)as inserted by the Copyright (Visually Impaired Persons) Act 2002, s. 1.
[3h] *ibid.*, s.31A(4).
[3i] *ibid.*, s.31A(3).
[3j] *ibid.*, s.31A(2)(b).
[3k] *ibid.*, s.31A(2)(a).
[3l] CDPA 1988, s.31B–31D as inserted by the Copyright (Visually Impaired Persons) Act 2002, ss. 2–4.

## Limited defence to claim for damages where no reason to believe copyright subsisted

Ignorance is no defence in an action for copyright infringement. Section **2–189** 97(1) provides an extremely limited defence to damages. Where the defendant did not know and had no reason to believe that copyright subsisted in the work to which the action relates, the claimant is not entitled to damages against him but without prejudice to any other remedy. It only concerns belief that copyright subsisted in the work and does not concern mistakes as to who the owner of the copyright is for example. The prevailing view of commentators is that this defence can only apply where (a) the work is so old that copyright is likely to have expired, (b) the work is not of a character in which copyright can subsist, or (c) possibly, the work is of obscure foreign origin.[4]

## REMEDIES

The remedies available for copyright infringement are[5]: **2–190**

(1) damages;

(2) statutory additional damages[6];

(3) account of profits;

(4) statutory delivery up[7];

(5) an interim injunction and a final injunction.

The claimant must elect between damages or an account of profits and is not entitled to both. If an account of profits is elected, the entitlement to statutory additional damages is lost.[8] The claimant is entitled to limited disclosure before making his election.[9] An account of profits is an equitable remedy and its award is a matter for the court's discretion.[10] Underlying an account of profits is the idea that the infringer is treated as carrying on his infringing business on behalf of the copyright owner and must therefore deliver up his profits to the owner. Taking an account is usually an expensive process and comparatively rare for copyright infringement cases.[11]

---

[4] *Copinger & Skone James on Copyright* (14th ed.), at 22–36; Laddie, Prescott & Vitoria (3rd ed.) *op. cit*; at 39.44.
[5] See CDPA, 1988, s.96(1). "In an action for infringement of copyright all such relief by way of damages injunctions accounts or otherwise is available to the plaintiff as is available in respect of the infringement of any other property right."
[6] CDPA 1988, s.97(2). See below at para. 2–195.
[7] CDPA 1988, s.99(1).
[8] *Redrow Homes Ltd v Betts Bros plc* [1999] 1 A.C. 197; [1998] 2 W.L.R. 198.
[9] *Island Records Ltd v Tring International plc* [1995] 3 All E.R. 444; *Brugger v Medicaid (No.1)* [1996] F.S.R. 362.
[10] *Hogg v Kirby* (1803) 8 Ves. 215; as to principles upon taking an account see C.L Kirby, *To account or not to account? An account* [1991] E.I.P.R. 13(10), 367 (Canada, patent infringement).
[11] But see *Potton Ltd v Yorkclose Ltd* [1990] F.S.R. 11.

In the vast majority of cases involving reproduction of single photographic works, it is unlikely to be a profitable exercise.[12]

## Damages

2–191      The purpose of damages in a copyright infringement action is to compensate for any harm to the claimant which flows directly and naturally from the tortious loss.[13] Damages have been defined as the amount by which the value of the copyright is diminished a chose in action.[14] Damages are recoverable in respect of all infringements whether proved to have resulted in lost sales or not.[15] The relevance of lost sales is to enable the court to assess the damage by reference to lost profits; it is not a limitation on the recoverable loss.

2–192      Where the claimant is in the habit of granting licences, the usual starting point for the assessment of damages is the royalty fee.[16] The court, in assessing a reasonable royalty or licence fee, will try to work out the fee which would have been arrived at as between a willing licensor and a willing licencee.[17] If the normal royalty rate is too low for the purposes of compensation, the court may increase the damages awarded.[18] The court will take into account any royalty fixed under licences actually granted, apply it so far as possible to the hypothetical bargain made between the rights owner and the infringer and to the extent which that does not provide a figure upon which the damage can be measured, will consider any other evidence according to its relevance and weight in order to assess the damages.[19] The ultimate process is one of judicial estimation of the available indications.[20]

2–193      In the case of photographs, a vast number of variables will affect the licence fee that would be payable for a particular photograph depending upon the nature of the use, size of the image, territories, etc.[21] The licence fee payable for the use of a stock image of a commonplace article or building will be able to be identified fairly accurately and relatively easily. A good starting point for a simple image of this type would be to contact the British Association of Picture Libraries and Agencies which collates information

---

[12] For further information as to account of profits see Laddie, Prescott & Vitoria, *et el.*, (3rd ed.), *op. cit.*, at 39.47 and Copinger & Skone James on Copyright (14th ed.), at 22–95.

[13] *General Tire and Rubber Co v Firestone Tyre and Rubber Co (No.2)* [1975] 2 All E.R. 173.

[14] *Sutherland Publishing Co v Caxton Publishing Co (No.1)* [1936] Ch. 323 at 336.

[15] *Blayney t/a Aardvark Jewelry v Clogau St. David's Gold Mines Ltd* [2002] E.W.C.A. Civ 1007; [2002] F.S.R. 14, CA.

[16] *ibid.*; *Stovin -Bradford v Volpoint* [1971] Ch. 1007; *Jones v Tower Hamlets LBC (No.2)* [2001] R.P.C. 23.

[17] *Irvine v Talksport Ltd (Damages)* [2003] 2 All E.R. 881, 900-902; *Nottinghamshire Healthcare NHS Trust v News Group Newspapers Ltd* [2002] EWHC 409 at para.[59] *per* Pumfrey J [2002] E.M.L.R. 33; [2002] R.P.C. 49.

[18] *Chabot v Davies* (1936) 155 L.T. 525; [1936] 3 All E.R. 221 (architect's plans standard scale fee of £52 increased to £100).

[19] *Meters Ltd v Metropolitan Gas Meters Ltd* (1911) 28 R.P.C. 157 at 165 (patent case) applied in a photographic copyright case in *Nottinghamshire Healthcare NHS Trust v News Group Newspapers Ltd* [2002] EWHC 409 at para. [29] *per* Pumfrey J. [2002] E.M.L.R. 33; [2002] R.P.C. 49.

[20] *General Tire and Rubber Co v Firestone Tyre and Rubber Co* (No.2) [1975] 2 All E.R. 173.

[21] For a list of factors for different types of image useage, see below at paras 12–040 to 12–048.

about the range of prices charged by its members for various types of usage.[22] Where the photograph is a particularly high value, newsworthy photograph, such as a one-off photograph of a politician or celebrity in a moment of indiscretion, the licence fee is not really open to any type of formulaic assessment and expert evidence as to the market value is advisable.

If the photograph in respect of which no licence would have been granted, **2–194** assessment is more difficult. Where the claimant refused to grant a licence he is entitled to damages, possibly additional damages, and an injunction against the infringer.[23] If there is no evidence of any practice of licensing a particular type of work or article, the compensation will still be assessed by reference to a notional fee for unauthorised use as to refuse compensation would be a denial of justice.[24] Where a photograph would not be licenced at all and is of no economic value to the claimant as it is not intended to be exploited commercially (*e.g.* a photograph forming part of confidential medical records), nonetheless the court will still approach the assessment of damages on the basis of a hypothetical bargain between the rights owner and the infringer.[25] However, additional damages may be justified.[26]

### Additional damages

Additional damages are provided for by s.97(2) of the 1988 Act which **2–195** provides as follows:

"The court may in an action for infringement of copyright having regard to all the circumstances, and in particular to—

(a) the flagrancy of the infringement, and
(b) any benefit accruing to the defendant by reason of the infringement, award such additional damages as the justice of the case may require."

Additional damages cannot be awarded where the claimant has elected an account of profits. They are only available to a claimant who has elected in favour of damages.[27]

"Flagrancy" it has been said, implies the existence of scandalous conduct, **2–196** deceit and such like, including deliberate and calculated copyright infringements.[28] It has also been described as "calculated disregard of the appli-

---

[22] For further information about BAPLA see below at paras 12–004 and 12–040.
[23] *Ludlow Music Inc v Williams (No.2)* [2002] EWHC 638; [2002] E.M.L.R. 29.
[24] *SPE International Ltd v Professional Preparation Contractors (UK) Ltd* [2002] EWHC 881 at para.[86] *per* Rimer J.
[25] *Nottinghamshire Healthcare NHS Trust v News Group Newspapers Ltd* [2002] EWHC 409 at paras [31]–[32]; [2002] E.M.L.R. 33; [2002] R.P.C. 49; *per* Pumfrey J.
[26] *ibid.*, at paras [59]–[60] and see below "Additional Damages" at para. 2–195.
[27] *Redrow Homes Ltd v Bett Brothers* [1999] 1 A.C. 197.
[28] *Ravenscroft v Herbert* [1980] R.P.C. 193, 208 *per* Brightman J. in relation to the predecessor section in the Copyright Act 1956.

cant's rights or cynical pursuit of benefit."[29] "Benefit" implies that the defendant has reaped a pecuniary advantage in excess of the damages he would otherwise have to pay.[30] Although flagrancy and benefit to the defendant are important factors, they are not mandatory pre-conditions for an award of additional damages.[31] However, it is unlikely in the absence of both, it would nevertheless be appropriate to award additional damages.[32] The authors of *Laddie* submit that additional damages may be awarded for such matters as injury to the author's reputation or feelings, such as the vulgarisation of his work.[33] It has been said that in the end it is a question of impression.[34]

There has been much debate[35] based on the legislative history of s.97(2) whether such additional damages are punitive (exemplary) or compensatory in nature or if the section is a codified discretion permitting the award of either. This question has been left open by the House of Lords.[36] In *Nottinghamshire Healthcare NHS Trust v News Group Newspapers Ltd*,[37] a decision of the High Court, it was held that the discretion is a wide one but an award of additional damages which was purely punitive is impermissible.[38] The question is free from higher authority and may still be regarded as arguable.[39]

**2–197**    A number of the cases in which the issue of additional damages has been raised concern photographs reproduced by newspapers.[40] This is perhaps unsurprising as photographs are a type of copyright work particularly open to flagrant infringement. In the absence of a defence or exemption where a whole photograph is reproduced by the media without a licence, there is usually no argument that (a) it is a copyright work, (b) a substantial part

---

[29] *Prior v Lansdowne Press Pty Ltd* (1975) 29 F.S.R. 59, 65; 12 A.L.R. 685. (SC. Vic).

[30] *Ravenscroft v Herbert* [1980] R.P.C. 193.

[31] *ZYX Music Gmbh v King* [1995] 3 All E.R. 1, 19 *per* Lightman J.

[32] *Cala Homes(South) Ltd v Alfred McAlpine Homes East Ltd* [1995] F.S.R. 818.

[33] Laddie, Prescott & Vitoria, *et al*; (3rd ed.), *op.cit*, 39.42 citing re: vulgarisation the South African case *Condé Nast Publications Ltd v Jaffe* 1951 (1) S.A. 81 at 87.

[34] *Pro Sieben Media AG v Carlton UK Television Ltd* [1998] F.S.R. 43. First instance decision reversed by CA [1999] 1 W.L.R. 605; [1999] F.S.R. 610 but no reference made by Court of Appeal to s.97(2) or additional damages.

[35] See *e.g. Redrow Homes Ltd v Bett Brothers* [1999] 1 A.C. 197; Laddie, Prescott Vitoria, *et al.* (3rd ed.) *op.cit.*, at 39.42 *Aggravated, Exemplary and Restitutionary Damages* Law Com. No. 247 (1997) paras 1.24, 4.21–4.22 and 5.284; C. Michalos, *Copyright and Punishment: The Nature of Additional Damages* [2000] E.I.P.R. 470.

[36] *Redrow Homes Ltd v Bett Brothers* [1999] 1 A.C. 197, 207E *per* Lord Jauncey. For discussion of availability of exemplary damages generally see *Kuddus v Chief Constable of Leicestershire* [2001] UKHL 29; [2002] 2 A.C. 122; [2001] 2 W.L.R. 1789, HL (concerning misfeasance in public office).

[37] [2002] EWHC 409; [2002] E.M.L.R. 33; [2002] R.P.C. 49.

[38] At paras [50]–[51] *per* Pumfrey J. *Cf.* Pumfrey J.'s comments at para.[60] to the effect that if after an award of £10,000 as additional damages future infringements occur, it would show that the advantage to the newspaper exceeds the damages suggesting that the court's intention was in fact deterrent, *i.e.* to punish and deter as in pure exemplary damages.

[39] For argument that the provision is a wide codified discretion that may permit exemplary damages see C. Michalos, *Copyright and Punishment: The Nature of Additional Damages* [2000] E.I.P.R. 470.

[40] *Williams v Settle* [1960] 2 All E.R. 806 (photograph of a murder victim taken at a wedding); *Lady Anne Tennant v Associated Newspapers Group Ltd* [1979] F.S.R. 298 (photographs of Princess Margaret taken at a private party); *Nottinghamshire Healthcare NHS Trust v News Group Newspapers Ltd* [2002] EWHC 409; [2002] E.M.L.R. 33; [2002] R.P.C. 49.

(commonly the entire photograph has been copied), and (c) there has been infringement. The publisher may often be aware that he does not have a licence to reproduce the photograph, therefore will do so knowing he is infringing copyright. Where there is copyright infringement by reproduction of a photograph completely, an application for additional damages should always be considered. Media organisations may have a defence of public interest to a claim for additional damages.[41]

Additional damages have been held to be appropriate under the 1988 Act against distributors of infringing copies of a musical work where there was evidence that the distributors knew that they were dealing with infringing copies.[42] Continuing to sell infringing copies following a warning by the copyright owner and without any attempt by the defendant to query the entitlement to copyright after the warning has also been held to be flagrant and justified an award of additional damages under the 1988 Act.[43] In an Australian case concerning a similar statutory section,[44] it was said that flagrancy was not established by proof of mere knowledge of copying alone.[45] It seems that in many of the cases where additional damages have been awarded, the defendant had both knowledge of infringement together with an element of bad faith or mala fides, whether express or implied from the circumstances.

**2–198**

Under the predecessor section in the Copyright Act 1956, additional damages have been awarded for flagrant unauthorised reproduction of photographs taken at private functions[46], for deliberate infringing of copy-

**2–199**

---

[41] See below at para. 2–199.

[42] *ZYX Music Gmbh v King* [1995] 3 All E.R. 1, 19. Lightman J. said "I can have no doubt as to the flagrancy of the infringement of [the distribution company] or that it determined without any pangs of conscience on exploiting for its own profit the infringing copies for all it was worth. If ever there was such a case, this is a proper case for the award of additional damages so far as the damages awarded on the inquiry before the Master do not adequately reflect either the profit obtained by [the distribution company] or the prejudice occasioned to the plaintiff by its deliberate and calculated infringement..." See also *Springsteen v Flute International* [1999] E.M.L.R. 180, 227.

[43] *Pachamama v Habibi Ltd* (unrep.) Chancery Division, February 26, 1998.

[44] Copyright Act 1968 of Australia, s.115(4) which reads:

"Where, in an action under this section (a) an infringement of copyright is established and (b) the court is satisfied that it is proper to do so having regard to (I) the flagrancy of the infringement (ii) any benefit shown to have to accrued to the defendant by reason of the infringement; (iii) or any other relevant matters, the court may in assessing damages for the infringement award such additional damages as it considers appropriate in the circumstances."

[45] *International Writing Institute Inc v Rimila Pty Ltd* (1994) 30 I.P.R. 255. See also *Cala Homes* [1995] F.S.R. 818, 838. For other Australian decisions where additional damages have been awarded under this section see *Bailey v Namol Pty Ltd* (1994) 125 A.L.R. 288 (award of $150,000—infringement following breach of fiduciary duties); *Milpurrurru v Indofurn Pty Ltd* (1995) I.P.R. 209; 130 A.L.R. 659 (unauthorised use of culturally sacred Aboriginal art; infringement "plainly deliberate and calculated") and *Led Builders Pty Ltd v Eagle Homes Pty Ltd* (1999) 44 I.P.R. 24 (clear attempt to gain commercial advantage by copying successful designs—additional damages of $20,000 where compensatory damages were $20,000). See also below at para.2–200, n.53.

[46] *Williams v Settle* [1960] 2 All E.R. 806—see above at para. 2–201; *Lady Anne Tennant v Associated Newspapers Group Ltd* [1979] F.S.R. 298 (photographs of Princess Margaret taken at a private party).

right in drawings of a racing car by a rival team, inflicting humiliation for which it was difficult to compensate,[47] and for "unethical and unlawful" behaviour in the use of the plaintiff's independent research work as the defendant's own.[48]

It has been held that where infringement is not deliberate but more the result of carelessness, additional damages are not appropriate.[49] Additional damages are a discretionary remedy and as such may be defeated by a defence of public interest.[50] An award of such damages has also been held inappropriate where the defendant held a sincere belief that the use of an infringing television clip was both permissible and for the public good in circumstances where the use did not compete with the original work[51].

2–200      The amounts awarded by courts under s.97(2) have typically been modest. There is as yet no readily discernable set of principles applied by the courts when assessing the amount of additional damages. In an Australian case,[52] an argument that additional damages are typically awarded in the same order of magnitude as compensatory damages was rejected.[53] It was held that as the circumstances giving rise to copyright infringement must always vary infinitely it is not desirable to adopt any principle which results in the broad general discretion carefully formulated in the statutory section being fettered in any arithmetic or mechanical way.

2–201      In *Williams v Settle* (1960),[54] which was decided in 1960, a professional photographer took some wedding photographs which incorporated the bride's father who was subsequently murdered. The murder attracted publicity and the photographer sold copies of the photographs which were then published in two daily newspapers. The groom, the owner of the copyright sued the photographer for copyright infringement. The plaintiff was awarded £1,000 "punitive" damages having regard to the flagrant infringement of his right, the intrusion into his life and disregard of his feelings.

2–202      In *Nottinghamshire Healthcare NHS Trust v News Group Newspapers*,[55] a newspaper published a photograph of a patient detained in hospital fol-

---

[47] *Nichols Advanced Vehicle Systems Inc v Rees (No.1)* [1979] R.P.C. 127; *Nichols Advanced Vehicle Systems v Rees (No.3)* [1988] R.P.C. 71.

[48] *Goswami v Hammons* 129 S.J. 653, CA, July 4, 1985 (award of £200).

[49] *Noah v Shuba* [1991] F.S.R. 14, 30 *per* Mummery J. Other reasons given in that case for the decision not to award additional damages under s.17(3) of the 1956 Act were (1) the scale and circumstances of the infringement were such that only a small amount of compensation was appropriate (publication with circulation of 4,500 copies), and (2) no benefit was shown to have accrued to the defendant by reason of the infringement. See also *Ravenscroft v Herbert* [1980] R.P.C. 193, 208—defendant did not intend to injure plaintiff and did not appreciate that he was so doing.

[50] *Hyde Park Residence Ltd v Yelland* [1999] R.P.C. 655, 671–672; [1999] E.M.L.R. 654.

[51] *Pro Sieben Media AG v Carlton UK Television Ltd* [1998] F.S.R. 43, 61–62. First instance decision reversed by CA on other grounds [1999] 1 W.L.R. 605; [1999] F.S.R. 610. No reference made by Court of Appeal to s.97(2) or additional damages.

[52] *Raben Footwear Pty Ltd v Polygram Records Inc* 145 A.L.R. 1; 37 I.P.R. 417.

[53] Examples cited were *Mafal Pty v Longuet* (1986) 8 I.P.R. 410 (compensatory damages $250; additional damages $250); *Autodesk Australia v Cheung* (1990) 17 I.P.R. 69 (compensatory damages $15,000; additional damages $35,000); *Bailey v Namol Pty Ltd*, (1994) 53 F.C.R. 102; 125 A.L.R. 228 (compensatory damages $350,000; additional damages $150,000); *Milpurrurru v Indofurn pty Ltd* 130 A.L.R. 659 (compensatory damages $12,000; additional damages $70,000).

[54] [1960] 2 All E.R. 806; [1960] 1 W.L.R. 1072, CA.

[55] [2002] EWHC 409 Pumfrey J.; [2002] E.M.L.R. 33; [2002] R.P.C. 49.

lowing his conviction in respect of the killing of two consultant surgeons. The photograph had been taken by the hospital, who owned the copyright in the photograph, and formed part of the patient's medical records. The judge considered that the photograph was obviously stolen. The court awarded £450 for infringement damages but awarded £9,550 additional damages which gave a total of £10,000.[56] Evidence was given of a settlement agreement in similar circumstances between the newspaper and a different hospital in respect of publication of "two illegitimate photographs of Peter Sutcliffe, the notorious murderer" where the newspaper paid £10,000.[57] The court observed that if the award of £10,000 exceeded the benefit to the defendant then no further infringements of that kind would take place. If further infringements consisting of the publishing of stolen photographs from medical records continues, the judge considered that it would show that the advantage to the newspaper still exceeds the damages.[58]

## Delivery up

The owner of the copyright in a work may apply for an order that **2–203** infringing copies of a work be delivered to him (or to such other person as the court may direct) against any person who has an infringing copy of the work in his possession, custody, or control in the course of a business.[59] Where a person has in his possession, custody, or control an article specifically designed or adapted for making copies of a particular copyright work knowing or having reason to believe that it has, or has been, or is to be used to make infringing copies, the copyright owner may apply for an order for delivery up of that article.[60]

An application for delivery up must be made before the expiry of six years from the date on which the infringing copy or article was made.[61] However, if the copyright owner is under a disability, he may apply at any time before the end of six years from when he ceased to be under a disability.[62] Where the copyright owner is prevented by fraud or concealment from discovering the facts entitling him to an order, he may apply before the end of six years the date on which he could, with reasonable diligence discover those facts.[63] No order for delivery up shall be made unless the court also makes or it

---

[56] [2002] EWHC 409 at paras [59]–[60].
[57] para.[60].
[58] *ibid.*
[59] CDPA 1988, s.99(1).
[60] *ibid.*
[61] CDPA 1998, ss.99(2) and 113(1). Save where the copyright owner is under a disability (as in the Limitation Act 1980) or is prevented by fraud or concealment from discovering the facts entitling him to apply for an order.
[62] CDPA 1988, s.113(2). Disability has the same meaning as in the Limitation Act 1980 (s.38), *i.e.* whilst an infant or of unsound mind, (being a person who, by reason of mental disorder within the meaning of the Mental Health Act 1983 is incapable of managing and administering his property and affairs).
[63] CDPA 1988, s.113(2).

appears to the court that there are grounds for making an order for disposal of the copies.[64]

## Interim injunctions

**2–204**    In order to obtain an interim injunction,[65] the court must be persuaded that (a) there is a serious question to be tried and that the claimant has a real prospect of success at trial in his claim for a permanent injunction, (b) that damages are not an adequate remedy, and (c) the balance of convenience favours the claimant.[66]

If the claimant would be adequately compensated by damages (including additional damages)[67] for any loss caused by the defendant and the defendant would be in a position to pay them, no interim injunction will be granted.[68] Where the court concludes damages would not be an adequate remedy, it proceeds to consider the balance of convenience—which is better described as the "balance of the risk of doing an injustice."[69] The court considers the injustice to both claimant and defendant if the injunction is refused or granted respectively. Whichever involves the least risk of ultimate injustice is the appropriate course.[70] Where all other factors are balanced, it is "a counsel of prudence" to preserve the status quo.[71] The relevant point of time for the purposes of the status quo may be difficult to determine and may vary.[72]

**2–205**    In cases involving press publication of photographs, the speed of the application for an interim injunction will often be everything. Once newspapers or magazines have gone to press and are into the distribution process, the cost and damage to the defendant of recalling the publications will militate against the granting of an interim injunction.[73]

The court may, in cases of extreme urgency, grant an injunction "without notice" on the application of the claimant where the defendant is not present and has not had notice of the application. Such an application may be granted if it appears to the court that there are good reasons for not giving notice[74] and the evidence in support must state the reasons why notice has

---

[64] CDPA 1988, ss.99(2) and 114.

[65] See generally Civil Procedure Rules 1998, Pt 25.

[66] *American Cyanamid Co v Ethicon Ltd* [1975] A.C. 396.

[67] *Monadress Ltd v Bourne & Hollingsworth Ltd* [1981] F.S.R. 118.

[68] *American Cyanamid Co v Ethicon Ltd* [1975] A.C. 396; *Fellowes & Son v Fisher* [1976] 1 Q.B. 122 at 137.

[69] *NWL Woods Ltd v Woods (No.2)* [1979] 3 All E.R. 614 at 625.

[70] *Mail Newspapers Plc v Express Newspapers plc* [1987] F.S.R. 90; *Shelley Films Ltd v Rex Features Ltd* [1994] E.M.L.R. 150.

[71] *American Cyanamid Co v Ethicon Ltd* [1975] A.C. 396; *Siskina v Distos Compania Naviera SA, The Siskina* [1979] A.C. 210.

[72] *Alfred Dunhill v Sunoptic SA* [1977] F.S.R. 337 at 376 *per* Megaw L.J.; *Mirage Studios v Counter-Feat Clothing Co Ltd* [1991] F.S.R. 145 at 153.

[73] See *e.g. Douglas v Hello! Ltd (No.1)* [2001] Q.B. 967; [2001] 2 W.L.R. 992; [2001] 2 All E.R. 289; [2001] E.M.L.R. 9 (breach of confidence, publication of un-authorised wedding photographs in magazine).

[74] Civil Procedure Rules 1998, r.25.3(1).

not been given.[75] Where an application is made without notice, the applicant has a "high" duty to make full and frank disclosure of all matters relevant to the application and to draw to the court's attention significant matters including those adverse to the applicant's case.[76]

If an interim injunction (where on notice or ex parte) is granted, the **2–206** claimant will invariably be required to give a cross-undertaking in damages in the event he is not entitled to an injunction and the defendant sustains loss.[77] A claimant should specifically give evidence in support of his application as to his ability to meet a cross-undertaking.[78]

A claimant whose position has been protected by an interlocutory injunction must proceed with the action with due diligence and without delay.[79]

## Permanent injunction

If the claimant succeeds at trial in his action for copyright infringement, **2–207** he will usually be entitled to a permanent injunction restraining future infringements.[80] An injunction is a discretionary remedy and may be refused on ground of public policy.[81] Generally, when considering the grant of a permanent injunction, the balance of convenience was irrelevant and the property rights of a copyright owner would be protected. However, an injunction would not be granted if the claimant's conduct had been such that there had been acquiescence and thus a waiver of the right to an injunction.[82]

Where only a part of the copyright work has been copied and that is separable from parts of the infringing work which have not been copied, an injunction will be granted only against the copied parts.[83]

---

[75] Civil Procedure Rules 1998, r.25.3(3).
[76] *Memory Corp Plc v Sidhu (No.1)* [2000] 1 W.L.R. 1443. There is a great deal of case law on this point, much of which arises out of applications for *Mareva*/freezing orders. See *e.g.* Gee, *Mareva Injunctions and Anton Piller Relief* (4th ed. Sweet & Maxwell).
[77] *Vapormatic Co Ltd v Sparex Ltd* [1976] R.P.C. 433.
[78] *Brigid Folley Ltd v Elliot* [1982] R.P.C. 433.
[79] *Newsgroup Newspapers Ltd v Mirror Group Newspapers Ltd* [1991] F.S.R. 487.
[80] *e.g. Weatherby & Sons v International Horse Agency and Exchange Ltd* [1910] 2 Ch. 297; *Samuelson v Producers Distributing Co Ltd* (1931) 48 R.P.C. 580 at 593; *Performing Right Society Ltd v Berman* [1975] F.S.R. 400 at 403 (High Court (Rhodesia)).
[81] *Lion Laboratories Ltd v Evans* [1985] Q.B. 526; *Beggars Banquet Records Ltd v Carlton Television* [1993] E.M.L.R. 349.
[82] *Ludlow Music Inc v Williams (No.1)* [2001] E.M.L.R. 7; [2001] F.S.R. 19.
[83] *Lamb v Evans* [1892] 3 Ch. 462.

## Assignment and licensing

### Assignment

**2–208**   Copyright is a property right[84] and the copyright title in a work can be transferred to another by assignment, testamentary disposition, or by operation of law, as personal or moveable property.[85] An assignment of copyright must be in writing, otherwise it is not effective.[86]

Transfer of the original copyright work itself is not enough alone to transfer the copyright.[87] The chattel itself (*e.g.* a photograph) is distinct from the copyright which subsists in the work. The exception to the general rule that transferring the work does not transfer copyright, is where a copyright owner bequeaths an unpublished work. Where an original document or material thing embodying an original literary, dramatic, musical, or artistic work which was not published before the death of the testator (if he owns the copyright), is bequeathed in a will to another, it shall be construed as including copyright in the work unless a contrary intention is indicated in the will or a codicil.[88]

### Licensing

**2–209**   Acts done with the licence of the copyright owner do not amount to infringement.[89] A licence is a permission that makes lawful that which would be unlawful.[90] Unlike an assignment, a licence transmits no interest in the copyright title.

There is no requirement in the statute that a licence be in writing. Copyright licences may be oral or implied. However, the 1988 Act provides that "an exclusive licensee" has specified rights, most importantly the right to bring proceedings for copyright infringement in his own name.[91] In addition, an exclusive licensee has the same rights against a successor in title who is bound by the licence as he has against the person granting the license.[92] An exclusive licence is defined by the Act and is required to be in writing to confer those rights.[93]

**2–210**   A license granted by a copyright owner is binding on every successor in title to his interest except a purchaser in good faith for valuable consideration and without notice (actual or constructive) or a person deriving

---

[84] CDPA 1988, s.1(1).
[85] CDPA 1988, s.90(1).
[86] CDPA 1988, s.90(3).
[87] *Nicol v Barranger* [1917–23] Mac C.C. 219.
[88] CDPA 1988, s.83.
[89] CDPA 1988, s.16(2).
[90] *Canon Kabushiki Kaisha v Green Cartridge Co (Hong Kong) Ltd* [1997] A.C. 728 at 735.
[91] CDPA 1988, s.101.
[92] CDPA 1988, s.92(2).
[93] CDPA 1988, s.92(1). "Exclusive licence" means "a license in writing signed by or on behalf of the copyright owner authorising the licensee to the exclusion of all other persons, including the person granting the licence, to exercise a right which would otherwise be exercisable exclusively by the copyright owner"

title from such a purchaser.[94] Where the copyright is owned by more than one person, the licence of all owners is required to be effective; a licence granted by one is not effective.[95]

It is doubtful whether a mere licensee (*i.e.* not an exclusive licensee[96] within the meaning of the Act) can bring proceedings in his own name.[97]

---

[94] CDPA 1988, s.91(3).
[95] CDPA 1988, s.173(2).
[96] s.92(1). See above at para. 2–209, n.93.
[97] See Laddie, Prescott & Vitoria, *et al.*, (3rd ed.), *op.cit.*, at 39.9 suggesting that notwithstanding older cases (pre-1911) to the contrary, the fact that there is special provision for exclusive licensees to sue but none for other licensees should be interpreted as showing a legislative intent not to give other licensees a right of action. *Cf* earlier cases where a licence might be entitled to sue if he joined the copyright owner: *Neilson v Horniman* (1909) 25 T.L.R. 684; *Power v Walker* (1814) 3 M. & S. 7; *Novello & Co Ltd v Ernst Eulenberg Ltd* [1950] 1 All E.R. 44.

# Chapter 3

# Copyright and originality

# INTRODUCTION

As discussed in the Introduction to Chapter 2, whether a photograph is **3–001** original within the meaning of the Copyright Designs And Patents Act 1988 can prove problematic. The problems arise because the Act protects only photographs which are "original". Every photograph is essentially non-original in the sense that it is itself a copy of the image it portrays. A photograph may be highly creative with original subject matter and obviously protected by copyright. On the other hand, it may not be original at all and a mere "tourist" copy of a landmark taken a million times before. In a photograph of the Tower of London, the Tower of London itself is not an original part of the image and is not protected by the photographic copyright. For images falling between the opposite ends of the scale, it is often difficult to distill from a photograph precisely what elements of it are original and hence infringed by reproduction

Difficulties also arise in international copyright law because the protection offered to photographic copyright works varies significantly from country to country. Some countries protect only creative photographs, whilst others provide, in addition, a neighbouring or related right for non-creative photographs. In this section the term "non-original photograph" is used to denote photographs which fall short of the originality requirement and are non-creative. Examples of such "non-original" photographs would be a straightforward passport photograph taken in a photo booth or a photograph of a car from a speed camera.

This section considers first, the position in the UK and other common law **3–002** jurisdictions. Then the provisions of the International Conventions, Treaties and European Directives are considered. The classification of photographic works by reference to originality under various national laws is reviewed. The approach of the civil law countries is considered and compared with the common law jurisdictions. Extracts from the national laws of 125 countries that are relevant to originality in photographic works are set out in Appendix 2 together with commentary in respect of selected jurisdictions. These national law provisions are summarised in the Table in Appendix 1.

Before considering the different approaches to originality in photographs in various national laws, in order to set modern law in context, it is helpful to consider briefly the history of photography as set out in Chapter 1 which post-dates the first copyright laws by some considerable period. For many years, photography was not considered an art form at all and this is reflected in the late incorporation of photographic works into international copyright laws.

## ORIGINALITY GENERALLY UNDER THE CDPA 1988

**3–003**     Section 1(1)(a) of the 1988 Act protects only "original" artistic works. For a photograph to acquire copyright protection under the 1988 Act it is a mandatory requirement that it be original. The 1956 Act and the 1911 Act also had the same requirement of originality.[1] The 1988 Act, like its predecessors, does not define originality. Reference must be made to case law to discover what is meant by original.

Generally, in the United Kingdom a low level of originality is required for copyright to subsist in a work. However, this in turn means that when considering whether there has been infringement, the originality of the part which has been copied will be paramount. There follows a summary[2] of the key principles of the general requirement for originality:

### Aesthetic merit immaterial

**3–004**     It is clear from the 1988 Act that the aesthetic merit of the photograph is immaterial. Section 4(1) provides that a photograph is protected "irrespective of artistic quality".

### Expression is protected not the idea

**3–005**     It is often said "copyright protects the form and not the idea".[3] When considering artistic works, this is an oversimplification and a maxim liable to lead to confusion. It is important to distinguish between (1) a mere idea—such as a technique or a vague concept—in which no copyright subsists, and (2) a specific collection of ideas, which together embody the artistic work.

The collection of ideas as manifested in the artistic work may be part of its originality and copying a substantial part of those ideas may lead to infringement. The distinction is as between (say) the idea of photographing a ballet dancer (mere idea) and (to take an extreme example) the idea of photographing a ballet dancer in a rainbow tutu, body painted in rainbow colours positioned in an arabesque holding an open umbrella on a plinth in Trafalgar Square (specific collection of ideas). Photographing a ballet dancer is an idea which copyright does not protect. Seeking to recreate a photograph replicating such specific idea elements of the second example is likely to be an infringement. In this way a specific collection of ideas

---

[1] ss.2(1), (2); 3(2), (3) and 1(1) respectively.

[2] This section primarily concerns originality specifically in its relation to photographs and the particular problems associated with photographic works. If further information as to originality generally and its application to other works is sought, see Laddie, Prescott & Vitoria *et al.*, (3rd ed.), *op.cit.*, and *Copinger and Skone James on Copyright* (14th ed.).

[3] "It is trite law that there is no copyright in ideas ... But ... it all depends on what you mean by ideas" *LB (Plastics) Ltd v Swish Products* [1979] R.P.C. 551, 629.

embodied in an artistic work may be protected by copyright. But simple, mere ideas will not be protected.

It was held in *Kenrick & Co v Lawrence*[4] that there was no copyright in the **3–006** idea of drawing a hand marking a cross on a ballot paper. The defendant produced a similar drawing but with slight differences thus not identical to the plaintiff's work. It was held that there was no infringement. The plaintiff's idea of a simple design did not entitle him to copyright in that idea.

There will be no copyright in the idea of a general technique. In *Norowzian v Arks Ltd (No.2)*[5] it was contended that the defendant's film which, like the plaintiff's film, used a cinematographic editing technique called jump cutting, was an infringement. It was held that no copyright subsists in mere style or technique.

## Independent labour, skill and judgment

The work must be the result of skill, labour and judgment on the part of **3–007** the author. The degree of skill, labour and judgment which is required will vary upon the facts of the case in issue.[6] Generally, the degree required is not high, but if it is negligible, no copyright will subsist.[7]

In *Cramp v Smythson*[8] the plaintiff and the defendant were both publishers of pocket diaries. A former employee of the plaintiff copied seven tables from the plaintiff's diary and inserted them into a diary published by the defendant. It was held that copyright did not subsist in the tables as they were nothing more than a commonplace selection or arrangement of scraps of information, neither of which involved any real exercise of labour, judgment or skill.[9] It was said[10]:

> "It is conceded that, if the work labour and skill required to make the selection and to compile the tables is negligible, then no copyright can subsist in it. Whether enough work labour and skill is involved, and what its value is, must always be a question of degree. Different minds will differ, as may be seen in the present case from the divergence of opinion in the courts below."

---

[4] (1890) 25 Q.B.D. 99; 38 W.R. 779. But *cf.* the French case *PEP v Kerbouc'h Cass* May 23, 1995; (1995) 166 R.I.D.A. 298 where an advertising image of a hand holding a visiting card was considered to be an original work even though it was an interpretation of a non-original idea.
[5] [2000] E.C.D.R. 205; [2000] E.M.L.R. 67; [2000] F.S.R. 363.
[6] *G.A. Cramp & Sons Ltd v Frank Smythson Ltd* [1944] A.C. 329, 335 and 340. *Ladbroke (Football) Ltd v William Hill (Football) Ltd* [1964] 1 W.L.R. 273.
[7] *G.A. Cramp & Sons Ltd v Frank Smythson Ltd* [1944] A.C. 329, 340 *per* Lord Porter. *Ladbroke (Football) Ltd v William Hill (Football) Ltd* [1964] 1 W.L.R. 273, 287 *per* Lord Hodson; 289 *per* Lord Devlin.
[8] *G.A. Cramp & Sons Ltd v Frank Smythson Ltd* [1944] A.C. 329.
[9] *per* Lord Porter quoting from the Court of Appeal judgment, [1944] A.C. 329, 340.
[10] [1944] A.C. 329, 340 *per* Lord Porter.

The last sentence encapsulates the problem—different judges will have different opinions on the facts of any one case. This is a particular problem in the area of photographic works.

**3–008**     There are, however, many cases where lists and compilations have been protected.[11] Mathematical tables have been said to be capable of protection where the author had independently calculated them, notwithstanding that previously identical tables had been published.[12]

Yet labour and investment on its own is not enough. Protection was refused to the word "Exxon" which had been created after extensive research into a suitable commercial name for an oil company on the basis that a word could not be an original literary work.[13]

## Mere copying not enough

**3–009**     The skill and labour necessary has to be more than that exerted in mere copying. In *Interlego AG v Tyco Industries*,[14] copyright was held not to subsist in redrawings of existing drawings of toy Lego bricks. It was observed:

> "There must in addition be some element of material alteration or embellishment which suffices to make the totality of the work an original work. But mere copying per se, however much skill or labour may be devoted to the process cannot make an original work."[15]

Copyright will not subsist in a mere photocopy of an existing work as copying involves "no such labour and skill as conferred an originality of an artistic character. The process was wholly mechanical".[16]

## Independent creation: no requirement that the work be unique

**3–010**     Originality does not require a work to be unique or novel. An independently created work which, by coincidence, is identical to an earlier work is not precluded from copyright protection. The comments of Peterson J. in *University of London Press v University Tutorial Press*[17] are often cited, namely:

---

[11] *e.g. Exchange Telegraph Co Ltd v Gregory & Co* [1896] 1 Q.B. 147; *Ladbroke (Football) Ltd v William Hill (Football) Ltd* [1964] 1 W.L.R. 273 (football pools coupons); *Football League Ltd v Littlewoods Pools Ltd* [1959] Ch. 637 (football fixture lists); *Express Newspapers v Liverpool Daily Post & Echo* [1985] 1 W.L.R. 1089; [1985] F.S.R. 306; [1985] 3 All E.R. 680 (newspaper competition grids).

[12] *Bailey v Taylor* (1830) 1 Russ. & My. 73; (1824) 3 L.J.O.S. 66.

[13] *Exxon Corp v Exxon Insurance Consultants International Ltd* [1981] 3 All E.R. 241; [1982] R.P.C. 69.

[14] [1989] A.C. 217.

[15] *per* Lord Oliver of Aylmerton at 371.

[16] *Reject Shop v Manners* [1995] F.S.R. 870, 876 *per* Leggatt L.J.

[17] [1916] 2 Ch. 601, 608–609.

"The originality which required relates to the expression of the thought. But the Act does not require that the expression must be in an original or novel form, but that the work must not be copied from another work— that it should originate from the author."

The classic example given in relation to photographs is that if two people independently take a photograph of the same building, both will have copyright in their respective photographs. The existence of one photograph does not prevent the second from having its own copyright, unless of course it was copied from the first. A photograph does not give rise to a copyright in the subject matter of the photograph.

## SPECIFIC DIFFICULTIES CONCERNING PHOTOGRAPHS AND ORIGINALITY

### Originality in photographic works: the UK

Under English law, for copyright to subsist in a photograph, the author must have exercised such labour, skill and judgment as confers originality.[18] A photocopy, being a mechanical process, lacks such originality.[19] The level required to establish originality is a low one and can be attained by the choices of the photographer as to the subject matter, film, the length of the exposure, lighting, filters, angle, camera and even the choice of the exact moment to take the photograph. It has been held that angle, lighting, focus, judgment as to the positioning albeit at "a very basic level", together with the aim of exhibiting specific details of the subject matter was sufficient to establish copyright.[20] Originality may be found in decisions taken at any of the three stages of creating a photograph namely, (1) pre-fixation in the arrangement of objects, choice of lighting, choice of camera, etc. (2) fixation when the photograph is taken such as the decision as to the exact moment to press the shutter and the angle of photography, (3) post-fixation in the development of the photograph and printing.

**3–011**

There are few English decisions which deal with this question in any depth.[21] Some assistance may derived from USA cases, discussed in more detail below, where sufficient skill or labour has been found to subsist in: posing and arrangement of subject and costume;[22] selection of the camera, the kind of film, the kind of lens, the area of photography, the time the photographs were to be taken and selection of the position from which to place the camera;[23] a decision when to take the photograph so as to bring

---

[18] *Reject Shop v Manners* [1995] F.S.R. 870 at 876; *Antiquesportfolio.com v Rodney Fitch* [2001] F.S.R 23 at p.352 *et seq.*
[19] *Reject Shop v Manners* [1995] F.S.R. 870. See below "Photocopies" at para.3–018.
[20] *Antiquesportfolio.com v Rodney Fitch* [2001] F.S.R 23 at pp.353–354 (paras 36–37) *per* Neuberger J; [2001] E.C.D.R. 5.
[21] *Antiquesportfolio.com v Rodney Fitch* [2001] F.S.R 23.
[22] *Burrow Giles Lithographic Company v Sarony* 111 US 53 (1884) (portrait of Oscar Wilde).
[23] *Time Inc v Bernard Geiss Assocs* 293 F.Supp 130, 143 (SDNY 1968).

out animate and inanimate objects and light and shade;[24] selection of background, lights, shading, positioning and timing;[25] selection of camera lenses, angles, exposures, height and direction from which to take the image;[26] and "almost any other variant involved".[27] Even where a third party has control over the subject matter and the composition of the images, the remaining choices of light sources, filters, lenses, camera, film, perspective, aperture setting, shutter speed and processing techniques amount to sufficient labour and skill for copyright to subsist.[28]

It has been said that analysing relatively amorphous characteristics of a photograph as a whole (such as "mood" or "combination of elements") creates a danger of unwittingly extending copyright protection to unoriginal aspects of the work.[29] It is safest to focus on the more concrete elements of the photographer's craft as mood is not so much an independent aspect of a photograph as the effect created by the lighting, shading, timing, angle and film.[30]

3–012   It is easy for a court to find elements in a photograph that constitute originality. It is always possible to say that any photograph, however simple and banal, involves some degree of originality or labour and skill. The mere decision as to which angle to take the photograph from or the decision as to the exact moment to take the picture, for example. For this reason perhaps, it is fairly rare for photographic works to be denied the status of a copyright work for lack of originality in the United Kingdom and common law jurisdictions because of the low level of originality required. The real problems arise in considering infringement where there has been a partial reproduction of elements of the original. This is highlighted by the English case of *Bauman v Fussell* considered below.[31]

## Originality in photographic works: other common law jurisdictions

3–013   In the USA (with the recent exception of photographs of art works) a similar low level of originality suffices. In *Burrow Giles Lithographic Company v Sarony*[32] it was held that a photographic portrait of Oscar Wilde

---

[24] *Pagano v Beseler* 234 F. 963, 964 (SDNY 1916).

[25] *Gentieu v John Muller & Co Inc* 712 F. Supp. 740, 742 (W.D. Mo 1989). Appeal dismissed 881 F.2d 1082 (8th Cir. 1989).

[26] *Los Angeles New Service v Tullo* 973 F.2d 791, 794 (9th Circ. 1992) (videotape footage).

[27] *Epic Metals Corp v Condec Inc* 867 F. Supp. 1009, 1013 (M.D. Fla. 1994).

[28] *Marco v Accent Publishing Co Inc* 969 F.2d 1547, 1551–1552 (3rd Cir. 1992) (photographs of jewellery for defendant trade journal. Journal supplied jewellery and props and sketched the shots. Held: copyright belonged to photographer).

[29] *Leigh v Warner Bros Inc* 212 F.3d 1210, 1215 (11th Cir. 2000) (first instance decision at 10 F.Supp 2d 1371) (copyright photograph of a sculpture in a cemetery for the cover of the novel *Midnight in the Garden of Good and Evil* allegedly infringed by sequences in a film of the novel and promotional photographs. Held (on D's motion for summary judgment) that the film sequences were not substantially similar but that the expressive elements in the promotional images had much in common with the elements protected by the plaintiff's copyright. In respect of those images, the defendant was not entitled to summary judgment).

[30] *ibid.*

[31] [1978] R.P.C. 485.

[32] 111 U.S. 53 (1884).

exhibited sufficient originality in the posing of the subject, selection and arrangement of costume, arranging the subject to present graceful outlines and arranging light and shade. The court, however, expressly declined to address the question of whether "the ordinary production of a photograph" received copyright protection.[33]

In *Bleistein v Donaldson Lithographic Co*[34] Judge Learned Hand held that a very modest expression of personality will constitute originality and concluded "no photograph, however simple, can be unaffected by the personal influence of the author". Nimmer (a leading USA copyright text) comments that this has become the prevailing view in the United States.[35] The majority of the case law does seem to support this view.

In *Los Angeles News Service v Tullo*[36] it was argued that raw, unedited news footage was not an original work deserving copyright protection as the camera simply captured whatever was before it without creativity or intellectual input. This argument was rejected as it was held that it was clear from the evidence that the preparation of the videotapes required intellectual and creative input. Elements referred to by the court as constituting such input included decisions about the newsworthiness of events; how best to tell the story succinctly; the selection of camera angles, lenses and exposures; the choice of the heights and directions from which to tape and what portions of the events to film and for how long.[37] A photograph of a public street has been held to have sufficient originality.[38] In *Rogers v Koons*[39] originality was found in posing a couple holding a litter of eight puppies, the selecting of angle, film and lighting.

The American copyright text Nimmer, suggests two situations in which a **3–014** photograph should be denied copyright for a lack of originality.[40] One situation is where a photographer, in choosing subject matter, camera angle and lighting, copies or attempts to duplicate all the elements of a previous photograph. This was the situation in *Gross v Seligman*[41] in which a photographer used the same model and posed her in a similar way as the first photograph with similarity in the lighting and shade was held to have infringed the first. Similarly, infringement was found in the Canadian case *Ateliers Tango Argentin v Festival D'Espagne et D'Amerique*.[42] The defendants employed a photographer to recreate a photograph of tango dancers as closely as possible. Sufficient originality was found in the original photograph in the choice, layout and posture of the subject, camera angles and lighting. The copying of these elements in the second photograph lead to a finding of infringement as it exhibited "a deliberate intention to imitate as slavishly as possible" the plaintiff's work. The other situation Nimmer

---

[33] *ibid.*, at 59.
[34] 188 U.S. 239 (1903).
[35] Nimmer on Copyright (Matthew Bender, Looseleaf) §2.08[E][1].
[36] 973 F.2d 791 (9th Cir. 1992).
[37] *ibid.*, at 794.
[38] *Pagano v Charles Beseler Co* 234 F. 963 (S.D.N.Y. 1916). See further below at para.3–033.
[39] 960 F. 2d 301.
[40] Nimmer on Copyright (Matthew Bender, Looseleaf) §2.08 [E][2].
[41] 212 F. 930 (2d Cir. 1914).
[42] (1999) 84 C.P.R. (3d) 56.

suggests is where the photograph amounts to "a slavish copy" of say, a photograph or printed material. He comments "A photograph of a painting or drawing, if a slavish copy, might be said to lack originality because of the predetermine subject matter and angle."[43]

**3–015**    Australian law is similar to English law and originality is fairly easy to establish. Lahore, considering the question of originality in photographs observes:

> "There is no reason why the most haphazard photograph of a scene in nature should not be regarded as 'original' for copyright purposes; anyone could take another photograph of that scene without infringing the photographer's copyright, provided that the photograph itself is not copied."[44]

By contrast, in Canada it has been held that a photograph still has to be original in the sense that some artistic quality must be given to it beyond a mere snapshot.[45] This is the exception rather than the rule in common law jurisdictions and indicative of the move towards a civil law "intellectual contribution" test that seems to be emerging in the US and Canadian case law.

Recently, the United States and Canada have moved away from a pure "work labour and skill" test. In *Feist*[46] the US Supreme Court held that "sweat of the brow" was not sufficient and that a "modicum of creativity" was required. Similarly, in Canada, mere "sweat of the brow" has been held as insufficient in and of itself to confer copyright.[47]

In general then, the level of originality required is low. However, a number of specific instances are illustrative of the problems in defining exactly what degree of originality is enough.

## Originality and specific types of photographs

### *Photographic print developed from negatives*

**3–016**    Unless the print is in some way itself original and more than a mere copy of the image in the negative by virtue of some labour and skill exercised during development, the photographic print will not be an original work.[48] Photographing a photograph similarly does not result in an original image.[49]

---

[43] *Loc.cit.*

[44] J. Lahore, Copyright and Designs (Butterworths Australia, Looseleaf) [10,140].

[45] *Ateliers Tango Argentin Inv v Festival d'Espagne et d'Amerique Latine Inc* (1997) 84 C.P.R. (3d) 56, 65–68 discussed below. And R.T. Hughes, *Hughes on Copyright and Industrial Design* (Butterworths Canada).

[46] See below at para. 3–074, n.51.

[47] *Tele-Direct (Publication) Inc v American Business Information Inc* (1997) 76 C.P.R. (3d) 296 at 307.

[48] *Pacific Film Laboratories Pty Ltd v Federal Commissioner of Taxation* (1970) 121 C.L.R. 154. (High Court of Australia) See above at para. 2–013, n.15.

[49] *Simon v Birraporetti's Restaurants Inc* 720 F. Supp. 85, 88 (S.D. Tex, 1989).

## Digitally manipulated photographs

Whether the final manipulated image has a separate copyright will depend    **3–017**
upon the nature and extent of the alteration—*i.e.* is the manipulated image
itself an original work or is it a mere copy of the photograph? Mere
retouching or minor alterations will not be enough to create a new copyright
in the manipulated photograph. An American case *Mendler v Winterland
Production Ltd* suggests that a high degree of substantive alteration will be
necessary before the manipulated photograph becomes an original image in
its own right. The manipulated image may very well be an infringement of
the original image if no licence has been obtained to manipulate or alter. In
*Mendler v Winterland Production Ltd*, a photograph of two yachts in the
Americas Cup that had been digitally manipulated was held to be an
infringement of the original image.[50] The plaintiff photographer had licenced
the use of the original to the defendant provided that the defendant only
used the image as a guide to achieve an illustration. The defendant digitally
manipulated the image and then reproduced the image on t-shirts. The
manipulated image had been reversed horizontally so that the foreground
vessel had moved from the right to the left; a missing tip of the sail cut off by
the frame had been reconstructed; the sky had been replaced with graduated
blue removing the original sky of white and grey clouds; shades of brown
were changed to shades of violet, whites to flourescent blues. The whole
image had been compressed through posterisation.[51]

The argument that these changes had transformed the image into an
illustration based on the photograph (which was permitted under the
licence) failed. The court held that the alterations made failed to destroy the
essentially photographic quality of the image. The precise shape of the two
boats, their positions relative to each other and the other elements of the
photograph all remained the same. Apart from the horizontal reverse, these
elements of the manipulated image remained identical. The court held it was
a reproduction of the original—"a filtered, posterised reproduction—but
photographic none the less."[52]

## Photocopies

It was held in *Reject Shop v Manners*[53] that an enlarged photocopy of an    **3–018**
artistic work could not attract copyright as the photocopy lacked originality
being a purely mechanical process. It was said that the copier had devoted to
their production "no such labour and skill as conferred an originality of an
artistic character. The process was wholly mechanical".[54] The court cited

---

[50] *Mendler v Winterland Production Ltd* (US Court of Appeals 9th Circ.) 207 F.3d 1119; 54
U.S.P.Q. 2d (BNA) 1070.
[51] A footnote in the judgment quotes from the Adobe Photoshop 5.0 User Guide (1998) as
follows: "The posterize command lets you specify the number of tonal levels (or brightness
values) for each channel in an image and then maps pixels to the closest matching level." 207
F.3d 1119, 1122. In layman's terms it reduces the number of levels of tones for each colour and
thus giving a flatter artificial "poster" appearance to the photograph.
[52] 207 F.3d 1119, 1124.
[53] [1995] F.S.R. 870.
[54] *Reject Shop v Manners* [1995] F.S.R. 870 at 876, CA, *per* Leggatt L.J.

*Interlego AG v Tyco Industries*[55] a Privy Council case concerning alterations to the original technical drawing of Lego bricks, where it was said in the judgment of Lord Oliver of Aylmerton at p.371 where he said "But copying, per se, however much skill or labour may be devoted to the process cannot make an original work."[56]

Generally, therefore, a straightforward photocopy (a mere copy of an existing work) will be devoid of originality. However, it is submitted that a photocopy is capable of being an original artistic work if it involves some elements of originality beyond mere copying of an existing work—copying of (for example) originally arranged objects.[57]

**3–019**    There is a school of artists who use photocopiers as art tools.[58] For example, the artist Doreen Lindsay created a triptych by photocopying a grouping of three apples placed directly on the glass surface of the machine. On each panel of Three Apples (1978) the tonal values were altered.[59] It is submitted that this type of photocopy involving arrangement of objects together with artistic choices as to the lightness or darkness of the image would properly be an original photographic work. At the Salt Mill Gallery in Yorkshire, works of art by David Hockney made using a photocopier are exhibited.

*Scanners*

**3–020**    A scanned image that is a mere copy of an existing photograph will not be original for the same reasons that a photocopy is not original as stated in *Reject Shop v Manners, i.e.* that it is a wholly mechanical process without the exercise of any relevant skill or labour. Thus there is no copyright in a digital photograph created by scanning an analogue photograph.[60]

It is arguable that the labour and skill required to obtain a good quality scanned image is enough to establish originality. Obtaining a good quality scan of an existing analogue image does require a certain level of skill. The level of resolution of the scan and the colouring may have to be adjusted to obtain a scan of the image of a high quality. The problem remains however, that the scan is not original, but a copy of an existing image. If adjustment of the lightness/darkness of the photocopier does not suffice as sufficient labour and skill, it is highly unlikely that a court would be persuaded that a scanner is any different.

The same observations made in relation to the originality of photocopies apply to scanners. It is submitted that if the scanner is used as an art tool to

---

[55] [1989] A.C. 217.
[56] *ibid.*, at 371 *per* Lord Oliver of Aylmerton.
[57] See also Laddie Prescott & Vitoria (3rd ed.) *et al.*, *op.cit.*, at 4.57 where it is submitted that an author may get copyright in a photocopy if he employed skill and labour in assembling the thing to be photocopied, such as a montage.
[58] See for example Firpo, P. *Copy Art*, (Richard Marekk Publishers, 1978); D. Liss, *Photocopy Art: Who Were the Pioneers?* ArtFocus/56 December 1995, reproduced at *http://www.artfocus.com/copyart.htm.*
[59] *ibid.*
[60] Obviously copyright would subsist in the analogue image if original.

record, for example an original arrangement created on the glass plate, copyright would subsist in the created image.

### X-rays

Radiography is a profession which requires a high degree of skill, labour **3–021** and judgment to produce a good quality x-ray, particularly to show contrast between bones and various soft tissues. The distance of the object from the plate and its position, the length of exposure, and the kilovolt setting (which governs the extent to which the x-rays penetrate the object) are all variables which may be altered depending on the size, weight and nature of the object to be x-rayed. In addition, any x-ray of a human or animal will be original in a "novel" sense because no two humans or animals will have the identical internal structure, in the same way that no two humans will have the same fingerprint.

There will of course be "simple" x-rays where little skill, labour and judgment is involved, such as the radiographic equivalent of the "point and press" photograph. It is submitted that as with analogue photographs, the denial of copyright on this basis for x-rays will be comparatively rare.

### Photo-booth pictures

"Photo-booth pictures" are photographs (commonly passport type pho- **3–022** tographs) taken in a booth where the person wishing to be photographed sits, and after having inserted the relevant payment is photographed automatically by a machine.

Difficulty arises as the photograph is taken automatically from a fixed point with an automatic flash. There is little scope for the standard indicia of skill and judgment that the court looks for, such as choice by the author as to the type of camera; the film; the precise moment to take the photograph; lighting, etc. The only real control of the person operating the machine lies in (a) the nature and arrangement of the subject matter being photographed which, in the majority of cases will be that person themself alone, and (b) the choice of angle to present to the fixed camera. Some machines also have a choice of colour of background curtain.

It is submitted that it is possible for a photograph taken by a photo-booth machine to be sufficiently original for copyright to subsist. However, such originality will need to be found in the choice and arrangement of subject matter and choice of angle to present to the fixed camera.

A straightforward, simple passport photograph where the subject simply sits in the standard position facing the camera directly, as dictated by the fixed positions of the camera and the booth seat, is unlikely to involve sufficient labour, skill and judgment. If there is any originality it will lie only in the image as a whole resulting in a "thin" copyright which would be infringed only by reproducing that specific image. "Thin" copyright is discussed further, below at para. 3–038.

*Automatic pictures: e.g. speed cameras; photo-finish cameras and satellite images*

3–023     Many modern automatic pictures are in fact film/video frames rather than photographs, such as photo-finish sports pictures, security camera images, and satellite camera images. The same questions of originality apply only if the images are photographs. If the images are stills from a film, they will be treated as films rather than photographs for the purposes of the 1988 Act. There is no requirement under the 1988 Act that a film be original for copyright to subsist in it.[60a] Unless security camera images are produced by photographic cameras controlled by a human (to zoom in, choose image, etc.), it is doubtful whether they are original within the meaning of the 1988 Act but there is presently no case law deciding this question.[61]

3–024     If a labour, skill and judgment test is being applied, it is submitted that many types of automatic photographs will qualify for copyright protection. This is because although the final image is automatically created, the camera has to be set up, calibrated, and positioned by a human in order to take the desired images. The automatic camera may be used as a creative tool. Time-delay photography is one example where this may occur. The author does not actually press the shutter, but provided he has made a sufficient creative contribution to the creation of the work, it will be original.[62] As discussed above, choice of subject matter and angle have been held sufficient to establish subsistence of copyright. Only where the human input is so low that there is no creativity will an image lack the requisite originality. Images taken by speed cameras for the most part remain photographic works but film image speed cameras are being introduced. It is submitted that a photograph of a car taken by a speed camera would lack originality. The subject matter does not exist at the time the camera is set up and the only human input is the calibration and angling of the camera.

*Aerial photographs and orthophotos*

3–025     The fact a photograph is taken from a helicopter or other aerial per-spective by a human author has no bearing on the issue of originality and the court will look for the same indicators of originality as in other pho-tographs. The photographer has to make choices as to the focus, time to

---

[60a] CDPA 1988, s.1(1)(b).

[61] *Hyde Park Residence Ltd v Yelland* [2001] Ch. 143, 150C; [2000] 3 W.L.R. 215; [2000] E.C.D.R. 275; [2000] E.M.L.R. 363; [2000] R.P.C. 604. Subsistence of copyright in still images taken from a video of a security camera was not disputed. An allegation in the draft defence that the stills did not form a substantial part of the copyright work "appeared to have been abandoned". Security camera images may arguably be regarded as computer generated works without a human author. Note that the CDPA 1988 states that in the case of a film, the author shall be taken to be the producer and the principal director, s.9(aab)—neither of which exist in relation to security camera images. See also computer generated works, above at para. 2–061.

[62] And see *Brod v General Publishing Group In* 2002 U.S. App. LEXIS 2544 (9th Cir. 2002) (person who conceived idea and arranged image but did not press the shutter was a co-author with the photographer). See also *Re Vorarlberg Online* [2001] E.C.D.R. 30, Oberster Gericht-shof (Austria) discussed above where more than mere assistance was required and setting up a camera to take automatic weather photographs and carrying out all the preparatory work sufficed to confer authorship.

take the photograph, angle, etc. Where, however, the images are taken automatically or are intended to be an accurate scale representation of land the position is more difficult.

A standard aerial photograph will have no uniform scale and will distort the image due to perspective and the topography of the land. An orthophoto corrects these distortions and produces an image with a uniform scale from which distances can be measured as they could be from a scale map. An orthophoto is intended to reproduce as accurately as possible various features of its subject topography. In some ways therefore orthophotos entirely lack originality as they are mere copies of geographical features. It is submitted that orthophotos are comparable to maps and should be treated for the purpose of assessing originality in a similar way to maps. Protection does not extend to the geographical features represented but only to the orthophotographer's selection of geographical data, presentation, use of symbols and annotation and any other artistic additions.[63]

In the Canadian case of *Weetman v Baldwin*[64] the claimant had produced **3–026** a recreational map combining aerial photography with topographical photography. He combined aerial photography digitally with trim data sets obtained from the British Columbia Government. Some roads and trails were missing on those maps and he set out to properly map them digitally from his orthophotos. After completing the map he deliberately mislabeled a lake in order to track any copyright infringement. About eight months after his map was released commercially, the defendant brought out a similar map which contained the same misspelling of the lake. The defendant's map contained a great number of similarities in the mapping of the roads and trails which the claimant contended could only have come from his map.

It was held that the differences in the claimant's orthophoto map which were the natural result of his selection of sources, interpretation of those sources and skill and judgment in depicting that information were capable of copyright protection.[65] The originality and creativity that was protected was the claimant's combination of the aerial photographs with the trim data sets using specially created software which achieved an accuracy of location and measurement on his map which had not previously been achieved by existing maps of the area. It was found on the evidence that the defendant had infringed the claimant's copyright by copying at least six features from the claimant's map, including the name of the mislabeled lake.

### Scientific photographs

Scientific photographs are open to the same criticism as orthophotos— **3–027** namely that they are intended to be an accurate copy of something else which lacks originality. Their purpose is usually to accurately reproduce images which exhibit the results of research. It is submitted that generally,

---

[63] *Cary v Longman* (1801) 1 East 357; *Geographia Ltd v Penguin Books Ltd* [1985] F.S.R. 208, 209.
[64] British Columbia Provincial Court, October 3, 2001; [2001] Carswell B.C. 2499; [2001] B.C.P.C. 292.
[65] Applying *Mason v Montgomery Data Inc* 967 F.2d 135 (5th Cir. 1992).

under UK law, such images will exhibit the requisite originality which can be found in the skill required to reproduce an image that is accurate and of the necessary quality. In addition, the labour and skill in the research arguably forms part of the originality of the final image.[66]

*Photograph of a random event over which the claimant has no control*

**3–028**    Where the photograph is of subject matter over which the photographer has no control—such as a news event—it is arguable that there is no originality, as all that is occurring is a reproduction of the scene. Conversely, it can be said that even in the simplest of photographs, there is a decision as to when to press the shutter which is sufficient. It is submitted that provided that some minimal element of skill is present in the decision as to when to take the photograph, this will suffice and copyright will subsist in such a photograph. Even where the photographer is present by luck, he still has to frame the subject with the camera and select the moment to take the photograph.

In *Bauman v Fussell*[67] the plaintiff took a photograph of a cock fight in Cuba. The defendant painted a picture based on the photograph. Although the photograph was of a scene over which the plaintiff had no control, it was not disputed that he had a copyright in the work. The report suggests that the painting was "entirely different" from the photograph, save for the position of the birds relative to one another.[68] It was held by a majority (Somervell and Birkett L.JJ. with Romer L.J. dissenting) that there had been no infringement of the photograph. The key issue was whether the defendant's painting reproduced a substantial part of the photograph.

**3–029**    Sommervell L.J. observed:

"It is an individual's work that the Act is intended to protect. I do not think that a painter who was minded to make a picture of [a procession from a photograph], in his own style, would be committing a breach of copyright if he used the photograph to enable him to get accurately the relatives positions of those taking part. What he would be taking would not be a substantial portion of the plaintiff's work. At the other end of the photographic scale one can imagine a case where the photographer has made an original arrangement of the objects animate and inanimate which he photographs in order to create a harmonious design representing for example, Spring. Here the design would be his work. The position of the birds here is betwixt and between. It is, I think nearer to the former than the latter category."[69]

**3–030**    Birkett L.J. observed that he found the question of whether the reproduction of the position of the birds:

---

[66] See comments of P. Soler Masota, *Photography and Copyright* (April 2000) 184 R.I.D.A. 60 at 94.
[67] [1978] R.P.C. 485.
[68] *ibid.*, at 488.
[69] *ibid.*, at 487.

One of the main contentions of the [plaintiff] was that the position of the birds was reproduced in the picture and that was the reproduction of a substantial part of the photograph. I am bound to say that it was this part of the case which occasioned me the most difficulty. The appellant did not arrange the position of the birds, but no doubt he waited for the moment to take the photograph when the birds were in the position he wanted them to be and his photograph produces the position.[70]

Birkett L.J. concluded that the county court judge had properly directed himself in asking whether a substantial part of the photograph had been reproduced and considered that his findings should not be disturbed.

Romer L.J. dissented as to whether, on the facts, a substantial part of the     **3–031**
picture had been reproduced and said:

Does then, the form of the birds, separately and relatively to one constitute a substantial part of the photograph? ... I have myself arrived at the conclusion it does ... The photograph is of two birds engaged in the one activity for which they were reared and trained. I cannot but think that the positions in which the camera caught them are the essence of the plaintiff's skilful presentation of that activity...

Is it to be said that any artist is entitled to trace from published photographs of this character the outline of forms of birds ... and use them as the basis for paintings of his own? I should have thought that by so doing, he would be infringing the copyright in the photographs—and none the less because he painted a background or feature of his own creation. Or assume the case of a man who preferred photographing big game to shooting them and was fortunate enough and sufficiently skilled to take a series of photographs of some incident which had rarely if ever been caught by a camera before, for example a battle between an elephant and a tiger; would the figures of the animals be at the disposal of any artist who wanted to paint a similar incident but was reluctant to visit the jungle for his material? Here again, the copying of the forms of the animals by the artist for his picture would, in my judgment constitute a reproduction of a substantial part of the photographer's work.[71]

The authors of *The Modern Law of Copyright & Designs* suggest that Birkett and Romer L.JJ. both thought that the capturing of the cocks' position was capable of being a substantial part of the photographer's work.[72] And further, that the Court of Appeal did not hold that an element of serendipity of choice or image capture is incapable of being part of the original work.

It is respectfully submitted that Birkett L.J. did not go so far as to suggest     **3–032**
the cocks' position was capable of being a substantial part. All he said was that it caused him some difficulty and declined to interfere with the judge's finding of fact. It is, however, correct that this case did not specifically hold

---

[70] *ibid.*, at 490.
[71] *ibid.*, at 492.
[72] Laddie, Prescott & Vitoria, *et al.* (3rd ed.) *op.cit.* at 4.60.

that positioning of elements of a captured incident beyond the photographer's control is not capable of forming part of the originality.

It is submitted that the dissent of Romer L.J. is to be preferred and if this specific question did fall to be determined under English law, it is likely that originality would be held to subsist in the relative positions. It is submitted that the decision in when to take the photograph and the angle to take it from, particularly in a fast moving event such as a cock fight, would require sufficient skill as to establish originality. This can be distinguished from a photograph where the relative positions of object do not form part of the protectable originality, such as buildings in relation to each other or the permanent setting of a monument.

**3–033** In the United States in the case of *Time Inc v Bernard Geis Associates*[73] copyright was held to subsist in the film frames of the Zapruder home movie of the assassination of President Kennedy. The argument that the images were devoid of creativity was rejected. It was observed that the film had "many elements of creativity"[74] including selection of the camera, the kind of film, the kind of lens, the area in which the pictures were to be taken, the time they were to be taken, and after testing several sites, the spot on which the camera would be operated.

Similarly in *Pagano v Charles Beseler Co*[75] copyright was held to subsist in a photograph of a scene on Fifth Avenue, New York. The court considered that to take such a photograph undoubtedly required originality stating:

"Anyone may take a photograph of a public building and the surrounding scene. It undoubtedly requires originality to determine just when to take the photograph, so as to bring out the proper setting for both animate and inanimate objects with the adjunctive features of light and shade etc."[76]

### Accidental photographs

**3–034** Where a photograph is created accidentally, for example, if a camera is dropped and a photograph taken or a camera is accidentally left with a timer on, it is unlikely that such images would attract copyright under UK law. This is because there has been no expenditure of work, labour or skill by the author. Such a photograph would plainly not satisfy the "author's own intellectual creation" test of the Term Directive.[77]

It is perhaps an academic debate as it is unlikely an accidentally created image would be of sufficient interest to warrant a third party infringing it by reproduction.

Accidental photographs are to be distinguished from photographs taken intentionally but where the content is of interest because the photographer

---

[73] 293 F. Supp. 130 (1968).
[74] *ibid.*, at 143.
[75] 234 F. 963 (S.D.N.Y. 1916).
[76] *ibid.*, at 964.
[77] See below at para. 3–063.

happens to be in the right place at the right time, such as being present when a newsworthy event taken place.[78] Copyright will generally subsist in such images as there will be scope for the court to find that work labour and skill was involved in choosing the angle and moment to take the photograph.

## Photographs of three-dimensional objects

The low level of originality required for copyright to subsist is illustrated by cases concerning photographs that document 3-dimensional (3-D) objects, such as sculptures. Copyright subsists in photographs of 3-D objects even where the photograph is merely intended to reproduce the object as accurately as possible.[79] It was held in respect of photographs of antiques designed to bring out particular features of the objects, that the positioning of the object, the angle, the lighting, focus were all matters of aesthetic or commercial judgment sufficient for copyright to subsist.[80]   **3–035**

In an American case, it was held that copyright subsisted in a series of photographs of a Vodka bottle.[81] Skyy Spirits hired Ets-Hokin, a professional photographer, to produce photographs of their Vodka bottle. The images were "straight on" images of the bottle, with the label centred, in front of a backlit backdrop with side lighting so that the left of the bottle was slightly shadowed. Skyy Spirits claimed they found the photographs unsatisfactory and then hired other photographers to photograph the bottle. The photographer issued proceedings against Skyy for copyright infringement.   **3–036**

Skyy applied for summary judgment contending that commercial images of a bottle were not worthy of copyright protection. The Court of Appeals for the 9th circuit disagreed. Reversing the district court's decision to grant summary judgment to Skyy Spirits and remanding the case back on the question of infringement, the Court of Appeals said:

"In view of the low threshold for the creativity element, and given that the types of decisions Ets-Hokin made about lighting, shading, angle, background and so forth have been recognized as sufficient to convey copyright protection, we have no difficulty in concluding that the defendants have not met their burden of showing that the invalidity of Ets-Hokin's copyright, and that Ets-Hokin's product shots are sufficiently creative and thus sufficiently original ... Finally, although Ets-Hokin took photos that undoubtedly resemble many other product shots of the bottle—straight-on, centered, with back lighting so that the word 'Skyy' on the bottle is clear—the potential for such similarity does not strip his work of the modicum of originality necessary for copyrightability. Indeed the fact that

---

[78] *Time Inc v Bernard Geis Associates* 293 F. Supp. 130 (1968) (film of assassination of President Kennedy) see above para.3–033.
[79] *Antiquesporfolio.com v Rodney Fitch* [2001] F.S.R. 23.
[80] *Antiquesporfolio.com v Rodney Fitch* [2001] F.S.R. 23 at pp.353–354.
[81] *Ets-Hokin v Skyy Spirits Inc* 225 F.3d 1068 (9th Cir. 2000).

two original photographs of the same object may appear similar does not eviscerate their originality or negate their copyrightability."[82]

The photographs were held to be original but the extent of that copyright and whether there had been infringement was left to the trial court.

The case was remanded to the District Court which then again granted summary judgment in favour of Skyy this time on the basis that there had been no copyright infringement. The photographer, Ets-Hokin, appealed again. The Court of Appeals of the 9th Circuit held, dismissing the appeal, that although the photographs were similar, that similarity was inevitable given the shared concept or idea of photographing a bottle.[82a] Although Ets-Hokin's initial photographs were protected by copyright, once the un-original elements were discounted, the photographer was left only with a "thin" copyright which protects against only virtually identical copying.[82b] Skyy's photographs were not identical—the lighting, shadows and high-lighting differed and the only constant was the bottle itself. The defence of the doctrine of merger applied, namely that the court will not protect a copyright work from infringement if the idea underlying the work can only be expressed in one way. The related defence of *scenes a faire*, where the court will not protect a copyright work from infringement if the expression embodied in the work necessarily flows from a common place idea was also applicable and the infringement claim failed.

3–037     It is submitted that, as for photographs of work of art discussed below, a non-original photograph of a mundane 3-D object taken "straight-on" which is intended to be an accurate copy of that object, any copyright that subsists is a "thin" copyright which is only infringed by actual reproduction of that image.[82c] It is the work labour and skill in creating *that* image which is protected. That work, labour and skill is only taken if the specific photograph or a substantial part of that photograph is reproduced by reprinting that photograph or photocopying it or otherwise reproducing *that exact* photograph. Re-creation of the image, in the sense of taking a new independent photograph of the same 3-D object, would not infringe. The "thin" copyright conferred on photographs intended to reproduce 3-D objects should protect only the work labour and skill and not the photograph's subject. Where the photograph is not just a simple copy of a single 3-D object but has other original elements in the image, re-creation may infringe.

### Photographs of works of art

3–038     Copyright subsists in photographs of 3-D works of art as the positioning of the object, the angle, the lighting, focus, etc. are matters of aesthetic or commercial judgment, particularly when the photographs are designed to

---

[82] *ibid.*, at 1077.
[82a] *Ets-Hokin v Skyy Spirits Inc* 323 F.3d 763 (9th Cir. 2003).
[82b] *ibid.* at 766.
[82c] *See SHL Imaging Inc v Artisan House* 117 F. Supp 2d 301 (SDNX 2000) and discussion below at paras 3–044 to 3–047, *Ets-Hokin v Skyy Spirits* 323 F.3d 763 (9th Cir. 2003).

exhibit specific details and features of the objects.[83] The position as far as photographs of 2-D works of art, such as paintings, is concerned is presently an open question in English law. The problem is that it can be contended that a photograph designed to record a painting as accurately as possible is not original—it amounts to effectively no more than a photocopy. It is said that the flat nature of 2-D artwork dictates that the camera can only be in one position—straight in front of the work and thus there is not sufficient skill and labour to create originality.[84] The American copyright text Nimmer suggests that a photograph of a work of art is one of two situations in which a photograph should be denied copyright for a lack of originality. It states: "A photograph of a painting or drawing, if a slavish copy, might be said to lack originality because of the predetermine subject matter and angle."[85]

It is submitted that the contention that photographs of 2-D works of art cannot be protected by copyright because they are bare copies is incorrect and an over-simplification. Photographing works of art to a professional standard is a matter in respect of which a high degree of skill and labour is often required.[86] Many of the choices of the photographer referred to as a basis for creativity apply to photographing works of art—choice of equipment including lighting, films, filters, and exposure control. It is submitted that in respect of a photograph of a 2-D work of art, copyright subsists but it is a "thin" copyright and only protects that exact image from verbatim copying.[87] Infringement would only arise where the reproduction was of that image itself, for example reprinting that photograph or photocopying it. The originality lies in the labour and skill expended by the photographer to create that specific image. As was said in *Marco v Accent Pub*: "Nonetheless something beyond owning a camera is necessary to make photographs suitable for a trade journal."[88] Equally, something beyond owning a camera is necessary to take a photograph of a 2-D work of art that accurately records that work of art. However, recreation by taking a second independent photograph of the 2-D artwork would not amount to infringement, as there is no originality in the subject matter.

The divergence of approach to issue of originality in photographs of **3–039** works of art is illustrated by comparing the US case *Bridgeman Art Library v Corel Corporation*,[89] a decision of the New York District Court, with

---

[83] *Antiquesporfolio.com v Rodney Fitch* [2001] F.S.R. 23 at pp.353–354. See also 3-D objects above at para. 3–035.

[84] For discussion of the problem of galleries and owners effectively obtaining monopoly rights in public domain art works through photography see R. Deazley, *Photographing Paintings in the Public Domain: A Response to Garnett* [2001] E.I.P.R. 179, 183. See also K. Connolly Butler, *Keeping the World Safe from Naked-Chicks-in-Art Refrigerator Magnets: The Plot to Control Art Images in the Public Domain through Copyrights in Photographic and Digital Reproductions* (Fall, 1998) 21 Hastings Comm. & Ent. L.J. 55. *Cf* below at para.3–052, n.18.

[85] *Loc.cit.*

[86] Indeed there are entire works devoted to the subject eg. William A. Titus, *Photographing Works of Art* (1982, Watson-Guptill).

[87] *SHL Imaging Inc v Artisan House* 117 F. Supp. 2d 301 (SDNY 2000) discussed below at para.3–044.

[88] 969 F.2d 1547, 1551.

[89] 25 F. Supp. 2d 421; 49 U.S.P.Q. 2d 1091 (S.D.N.Y. 1998) (first judgment); 36 F. Supp. 2d 191; 50 U.S.P.Q. 2d 1110 (S.D.N.Y 1999) (2nd judgment following motion for reconsideration and reargument.) See below.

another decision of the New York District Court, *SHL Imaging Inc v Artisan House*[90] and the English case *Antiquesportfolio.con v Rodney Fitch*.[91] Of these cases, *Bridgeman* conflicts with *SHL Imaging* and as discussed below, it is contended that the reasoning of *SHL Imaging* is to be preferred.

In *Bridgeman*, in rather unusual circumstances, two judgments were given. Following the first judgment, the plaintiff moved for reconsideration and re-argument. The motion was granted and following reconsideration, a second judgment was given confirming the first judgment. The facts were as follows:

The plaintiff Bridgeman was an art library which claimed to have exclusive rights in a number of well-known works of art which it had converted into digital images. It claimed that the defendant was marketing CDs containing a significant number of the images of the same works of art which Bridgeman claimed must have been copied from its transparencies in infringement of its copyrights. Bridgeman is an English company and contended that its rights were to be determined under English law on the basis that the initial copying and infringement occurred in England.

**3–040**    In the first judgment the court considered whether copyright subsisted in the transparencies under English law. The only text referred to was Nimmer & Geller on International Copyright and the only English case cited was *Interlego v Tyco*, the Privy Council Lego drawings case referred to above. The judge quoted the passage from *Interlego* to the effect that skill labour or judgment merely in the process of copying cannot confer originality and that "there must be some element of material alteration or embellishment which suffices to make the totality of the work an original work".[92] He concluded that the images were not copyright protected under English law as they did not satisfy the originality requirement as they were exact reproductions of public domain works, albeit in a different medium. There was no element of material alteration as referred to in *Interlego*. The judge stated:

"one need not deny the creativity inherent in the art of photography to recognize that a photograph which is no more than a copy of the work of another as exact as science and technology permits lacks originality. That is not to say such a feat is trivial, simply not original."[93]

The judge granted the defendant's motion for summary judgment. Following which the court was "bombarded with additional submissions"[94] and a motion for re-argument which was allowed and lead to the second judgment.[95]

**3–041**    The judge was extremely critical of the plaintiff and observed that it had "failed competently to address most of the issues raised" prior to entry of the first judgment. In particular it had failed to bring pertinent UK case law

---

[90] 117 F. Supp. 2d 301 (S.D.N.Y. 2000).
[91] [2001] F.S.R. 23.
[92] 25 F. Supp. 2d 421, 426.
[93] 25 F. Supp. 2d 421 at 427.
[94] 36 F. Supp. 2d 191, 192.
[95] *ibid.*

to the court's attention. The court had also received an unsolicited letter from Professor William Patry who argued that there was no "choice of law" issue because the copyright clause in the Constitution permitted Congress to enact legislation protecting only original works of authorship. Therefore only original works, with originality determined in accordance with the clause, are susceptible to protection in US courts. There was an issue as to whether the US courts were capable of giving effect to any provisions of international conventions which might require the determination of copyright under the laws of another nation. Following argument, the court now concluded that the law to be applied was the law of the United States.

The judge cited Nimmer's suggested exception mentioned above for a slavish copy. He observed that "there is little doubt that many photographs, probably the overwhelming majority, reflect at least the modest amount of originality required for copyright protection."[96] However, he considered that the photographs were slavish copies of the art works represented and copyright did not subsist under US law.

He then went on to conclude (albeit a moot point as he had concluded US    **3–042**
law applied) that the plaintiff's copyright claim would fail even if considered under UK law. This time Laddie, Prescott & Vitoria, *The Modern Law of Copyright & Designs* (2nd ed. 1995) was referred to, as was *Graves' Case*.[97] *Graves' Case* concerned photographs of engravings which had been made from paintings. Blackburn J. said (and this passage was cited in *Bridgeman*):

"The distinction between an original painting and a copy is well understood, but it is difficult to say what can be meant by an original photograph. All photographs are copies of some object such as a painting or a statue. And it seems to me that a photograph taken from a picture is an original photograph in so far that to copy it is an infringement of the statue."

The judge in *Bridgeman* then referred to a passage from the second edition of *The Modern Law of Copyright & Designs*[98] which questioned the authority of *Graves' Case* on two grounds. First, that there may have been special skill involved in setting up the equipment at that time (1869) due to the primitive nature of photography. Secondly, if that was incorrect, *Graves' Case* was, it was submitted, no longer good law, and should be explained as a decision made before the subject of originality had been fully developed by the courts.[99] On this basis and again citing *Interlego* the court concluded the images were not copyright under UK law. He concluded that the transparencies "stand in the same relationship to the original work of art as a photocopy stands to a page of typescript, a doodle, or a Michelangelo drawing".

[96] 36 F. Supp. 2d 191, 196.
[97] (1868–1869) L.R. 4 Q.B. 715, QB.
[98] Laddie, Prescott & Vitoria, (3rd ed.) *et al.*, *op.cit.*, 3.56.
[99] The second of these contentions (that the case is no longer good law) has been removed in the current edition of Laddie, Prescott & Vitoria, *et al.* (2nd ed.), *op. cit.*, although the first point concerning primitive materials remains: Laddie, Prescott & Vitoria, *et al.* 4.57 n.3.

**3–043**    This decision has been criticised by a number of English commentators[1] on the basis that *Interlego* is not authority for the proposition that a reproduction of an existing work of art cannot be original and the passage in *The Modern Law of Copyright & Designs* does not in fact question the authority of *Grave's Case* in so far as it relates to the type of photograph being considered. The current edition of *Copinger* states

> "In terms of what is original for the purpose of determining whether copyright subsists in a photograph, the requirement of originality is low and may be satisfied by little more than the opportunistic pointing of the camera and the pressing of the shutter button. There seems no reason of principle why there should be any distinction between the photograph which is the result of such a process and a photograph which is intended to reproduce a work of art, such as a painting or another photograph."[2]

The *Bridgeman* decisions, as reported, show a notable lack of discussion of possible elements of originality. Apparently (although this is not referred to in the report in the Federal Supplement), "evidence was led that in order to produce faithful and high quality photographs of such works of art (some of which were over 10 feet tall), photographers had to use considerable skill and labour in terms of lighting, choice of film, positioning of the camera".[3] Given the minimal requirements necessary in other cases in both the UK and the USA to constitute originality, it is surprising that this did not suffice. Reproducing a faithful photograph of an original work of art must require some degree of skill—for example arranging lighting so that there is no reflection.

**3–044**    In *SHL Imaging Inc v Artisan House*[4] the issue was whether copyright subsisted in photographs of mirrored picture frames for use in a catalogue. The photographs were described as accurate and precise copies of framed mirrors. In a full and interesting judgment, it was concluded that copyright did subsist in the photographs. It was considered that the photographer had made a number of creative decisions, including selecting the type of camera, film type, lenses, paper type, and lighting equipment. There was also creation of a "unique lighting design" so that the mirrors would not reflect any part of the factory or the photographer. The defendant's evidence was that none of this was unusual. The judge dealt with this by observing that "novelty" was not the test for copyrightability. He concluded:

> "While plaintiff's photographs meet the minimal originality requirements in *Feist*, they are not entitled to broad copyright protection. Plaintiff cannot prevent others from photographing the same frames or using the

---

[1] K. Garnett, *Copyright in Photographs* [2000] E.I.P.R. 229; R. Deazley, *Photographing Paintings in the Public Domain: A Response to Garnett* [2001] E.I.P.R. 179; S. Stokes, *Letter, Photographing Paintings in the Public Domain: A Response to Garnett* [2001] E.I.P.R. 354; S. Stokes, *Graves' Case Revisited in the USA* [2000] 11(5) Ent.L.R. 104.
[2] *Copinger and Skone James on Copyright* (14th ed.), at 3–104.
[3] K. Garnett, *Copyright in Photographs* [2000] E.I.P.R. 229, 230.
[4] 117 F. Supp. 2d 301 (S.D.N.Y. 2000).

same lighting techniques and blue sky reflection in the mirrors. What makes the plaintiff's photographs original is the totality of the precise lighting selection, angle of the camera, lens and filter selection. In sum, plaintiff is granted copyright protection only for its 'incremental contribution' ... Practically, the plaintiff's works are only protected from verbatim copying. However, that is precisely what defendants did."[5]

*SHL Imaging* is directly in conflict with *Bridgeman*. Although there is little discussion in the *Bridgeman* law report as to the "labour and skill" of the photographer, as referred to above it is apparent similar evidence was called. In circumstances where the defendant's evidence was that the method of photographing the mirrors was not unusual or original, it would be difficult to seriously contend *Bridgeman* is distinguishable on the basis that it involved paintings that required a less specific lighting design. It is submitted that to seek to do so would be artificial—in substance the differences between the two are extremely thin. It is submitted that in the light of other US case law, the decision in *SHL Imaging* is to be preferred. Sufficient labour and skill can be established by a "modicum" of creativity which can be found in such elements as choice of camera, film and lighting. **3–045**

The third case to be compared here is *Antiquesportfolio.com v Rodney Fitch*.[6] In that case the claimant had engaged the defendant to create a website. The defendant had used various photographs of individual antiques on the website that were in infringement of copyright images belonging to a third party. There was an issue as to whether copyright existed in photographs of single static items, such as a jug or candelabra or a sofa. The case did not involve issues of US law but nonetheless *Bridgeman* was cited and considered. The judge distinguished *Bridgeman* on the basis that it could be said in the case of 3-D objects that: **3–046**

"the positioning of the object (unless it is a sphere), the angle at which it is taken, the lighting and the focus and matters such as that, could all be matters of aesthetic or even commercial judgment, albeit in most cases at a very basic level.

Further, the instant photographs appear to have been taken with a view to exhibiting further qualities, including colour (in the case of some items), their features (eg. the glaze in pottery) and in the case of almost all the items the details. It may well be that, in those circumstances, some degree of skill was involved in the lighting, angling and judging the positioning"[7]

The judge concluded that copyright did exist in the photographs.

These three cases are illustrative of a lack of a uniform approach to the question of originality in photographs insofar as reproduction of works of art are concerned. Whilst there is a case to be made that there is more scope **3–047**

---

[5] *ibid.*, 311.
[6] [2001] F.S.R. 23.
[7] *ibid.*, at pp.353–354.

for selection of an angle from which to take the photograph in a 3-D object, the issues at the centre of these cases are the same—what is sufficient to establish originality? It cannot be the case that in photographing a 2-D work of art that the angle or exact positioning of the camera will always be in the same place, directly in front or that it is a simple matter not admitting any creative contribution of the photographer whatsoever. Some photographs of 2-D works will lack any skill and labour and be mere copies. But professional photographs of 2-D works are likely to require sufficient skill for originality to subsist. The copyright would only be in that exact image and it would only be protected from verbatim reproduction of the image itself and not re-creation. *Antiquesportfolio.com* and *SHL Imaging* both support the contention that there is no reason in principle why a photograph of a 2-D work of art would not attract copyright. Accordingly, it is submitted that *Bridgeman* in so far as it expresses an opinion as to the position in English law is incorrect.

### No infringement where only idea of photograph taken

**3–048**     There are many cases to the effect that where what is repeated in a second photograph is only the expression of an idea of the first, there will be no infringement.[8] In *Gentieu v Muller*[9] it was held that the idea of "floating naked babies" was not subject to copyright protection. The plaintiff was only protected from identical copying of her work. The defendants had photographed different naked babies in various poses by a photographer who had developed his own method and there was no infringement.

### Absence of originality

**3–049**     The CDPA 1988 only protects original photographs. It follows that not all photographs are eligible for protection. However, as discussed above, a low level of originality is required to satisfy this test. Non-original photographs are intended to be excluded, but under UK law very few photographs would be classed as non-original. A speed camera photograph of a car taken automatically or a simple passport photograph taken in a photobooth are two examples.

Some civil law countries[10] draw a distinction between original "creative" photographs protected by copyright and non-original non-copyright photographs which are protected by a related right. Thus, scientific or documentary photographs which are not creative are not afforded copyright but a lesser related right often with a shorter term. This causes difficulties under international treaties when foreign works are being considered. There

---

[8] *e.g. International Biotical Corp v Associated Mills Inc* 239 F. Supp. 511, 514 (N.D. Ill. 1964) (photographs of heat lamps in specific poses); *Kisch v Ammirati & Puris Inc* 657 F. Supp. 380, 382 (S.D.N.Y. 1987); *Wallace Computer Serv. v Adams Business Forms* 837 F. Supp. 1413, 1417 (N.D. Ill. 1993).
[9] 712 F. Supp. 740.
[10] See below at para. 3–081.

is no obligation under the Berne Convention for a country which protects non-original photographs (*i.e.* non-copyright photographs) to extend that protection to foreign works.[11]

## ORIGINALITY IN INTERNATIONAL LEGISLATION

The legislative provisions concerning photographic works, both at a national and an international level, should be considered against the historical background of the development of photography.[12] Right from the outset there was a strong body of opinion that considered that photography was not art. It is also particularly important to remember that photography (whilst the daguerreotype process as revealed in 1839 was the first modern workable system) did not really become accessible to the general public until the invention of the Kodak camera in 1888. The development of photography is of relevance in jurisdictions that apply a "labour and skill" test for originality. It has been suggested that there may have been a greater degree of labour and skill in the creation of early non-original photographs due to the primitive materials available.[13]

    In the light of the attitude held in many quarters that photography was not art, it is perhaps not entirely unexpected that the international treaties and conventions showed a hesitant reluctance to include photographs at all and then later a reluctance to accord them the same rights as other works.

3–050

### International Conventions and Treaties

*The Berne Convention 1886*

    The oldest of the international copyright Conventions only specifically named photographs as a protected work from 1951. Photographs were within the protection of the Convention from the outset, but only specifically named in 1951. "Photographs to which are assimilated works expressed by a process analogous to photography" were included in the list of protected works in Art.2(1) following the Brussels Revision.[14] It took six Conferences to get there—the initial Berne Conferences of 1884 and 1885, the Paris Conference (1896), the Berlin Conference (1908), the Rome Conference (1928) and the Brussels Conference (1948). This history is of interest as it illustrates the controversy surrounding photographs, originality and copyright protection.

3–051

    Photographic works divided countries during the 1884–1886 Berne Convention Conferences precisely because of the issues concerning the

3–052

---

[11] Further discussed below at para. 3–051.
[12] See above Ch.1.
[13] Laddie, Prescott & Vitoria, *et al.*, (2nd ed.), *op. cit*; at 3.56 in commenting on *Graves' Case* (1868–1869) L.R. 4 Q.B. 715 "there may have been special skill or labour in setting up the equipment to get a good photograph, especially with the rather primitive materials available in those days". Also Laddie, Prescott & Vitoria, *et al.*, (3rd ed.), *op. cit.*, 4.57 n.3.
[14] Brussels Act signed June 26, 1948, entered into force August 1, 1951.

capability of a photograph to be original. At the Conferences of 1884 and 1885, the French proposed the inclusion of photographic works in Art.4, but this was strongly opposed by Germany.[15] France, the United Kingdom and other countries protected photographs as artistic works. Germany did not grant photographs the status of artistic works. Ricketson states that the reasons for the dispute focussed on the "mechanical" nature of photography which were:

> "similar to those that exist in the case of cinematographic works. With photographic works, the skill required to produced the final picture may only be the simple manual operation of operating a shutter or pushing a button. On the other hand, there may be considerable elements of skill involved in relation to such matters as choice and arrangement of subject, lighting, perspective and so on. Whether these skills are those of authors is therefore something on which strong conflicting opinions can be held."[16]

It was agreed at the 1885 Conference that countries which protected photographs as artistic works could do so under the Convention but were not bound to protect photographs further than was permitted by their own national legislation or other international agreements. There was a rather bizarre provision in the Closing Protocol that:

> "It is understood that an authorized photograph of a protection work of art shall enjoy legal protection in all countries of the Union, as contemplated by the said Convention for the same period as the principal right of reproduction of the work itself subsists, and within the limits of private agreements between those who have legal rights."[17]

Strangely, the only photographic works which were to be protected were authorised photographs of "a protected work of art" such as a painting.[18]

**3–053**    At the Paris Conference in 1896, the French again proposed full protection for photographs, which again met German opposition. The protection given to photographic works varied enormously. Some countries expressly protected them as artistic works,[19] some did so impliedly, some, such as Germany, granted a limited special protection, and two countries Haiti and Tunis gave photographs no protection at all.[20] It is of no surprise that agreement to the French proposal could not be reached. Ultimately, an amendment proposed by Germany was adopted which provided that

---

[15] S. Ricketson, *The Berne Convention for the Protection of Literary and Artistic Works 1886– 1986* (Centre for Commercial Law Studies, Queen Mary College, Kluwer, 1987) at 6.33 (Hereafter "Ricketson (1987)"); and S. Ricketson, *International Conventions in Copyright and Photographs: An International Survey* (Y. Gendreau, A. Nordemann, and R. Oesch, eds) Kluwer Law International (1999) at p.18.

[16] Ricketson (1987) *op. cit.*, at 6.33.

[17] Quoted in Ricketson (1987) *op. cit.*, at 6.33.

[18] It is interesting that this was expressly provided for, *cf. Antiquesportfolio.com* [2001] F.S.R. 23 and *Bridgeman v Corel* 25 F. Supp. 2d 421 above at para. 3–039.

[19] *e.g.* the United Kingdom *Fine Arts Copyright Act 1862.*

[20] Ricketson (1987) *op cit.*, at 6.35.

photographic works were to be protected as under the respective State's legislation and "to the extent of the protection accorded by such laws to similar national works."[21] Previously, States had not been obliged to offer their national legislative protection for photographs to authors from other States. The effect of this amendment was to entitle foreign authors of photographs to claim whatever protection was granted to photographs by any given State.[22] The Convention did express the hope that all Union countries would eventually protect photographs.[23]

The Berlin Conference in 1908 adopted a German proposal that the Convention should protect photographic works irrespective of whether the law of a contracting country protected them as artistic works or otherwise.[24] This was significant progress given the previous history and each country was obliged to protect photographic works and works obtained by an analogous process under Art.3 of the Convention. There was no agreement as to duration. Photographs were still not included in the list of protected works in Art.2 and therefore could not claim the benefits of the Convention that applied to other artistic works. **3–054**

At the Rome Conference there were several proposals concerning photographs but no agreement was reached, again due to the fundamental differences between approaches in the different countries. Many of the civil law countries considered photographs should be protected only if they were original or creative as required for other works and protection should not be extended to a simple snapshot. The inherent problem of ascertaining the necessary level of creativity was (and continues today) to result in inconsistent court decisions. The United Kingdom protected all photographs as artistic works irrespective of artistic quality. During the 1930s there was a prevailing view in Germany that all photographs were "the result of purely mechanical operations involving technical skills and therefore could not fall within the scope of the expression 'literary or artistic works.' "[25]

In June 1935, an International Congress on Photographic Law held in Brussels advocated that the Berne Convention should protect photographic works as artistic works. The proposals of the Congress were used as a basis **3–055**

---

[21] Quoted in Ricketson (1987) *op. cit.*, at 6.34.
[22] This was not free from problems as Ricketson (1987) observes. It appeared that Art.2 resulted in an author from a country where there was no protection could not claim protection in a country that did protect photographs. The International Office expressed the view that the Conference had made it clear reciprocity was not required and therefore Art.2 did not apply to photographs. The anomalous consequence that such photographs would have the benefit of national treatment in all Union countries and thus receive greater protection than a work from a country with a shorter term than was granted in the country where protection was claimed. Ricketson noted that this interpretation was followed by the Civil Tribunal in Belgium and thus helped to highlight the need for a degree of uniformity in the Convention protection.
[23] *Actes de la Conférence de Paris de 1896*, Berne, International Office 1897, p.229 The resolution adopted was; "It is desirable ... that, in all countries of the Union, the law should protect photographic works and works obtained by an analogous process and that the length of such protection be at least fifteen years." See Ricketson (1987) at 6.34 and S. *Ricketson, International Conventions in Copyright and Photographs: An International Survey* (Y. Gendreau, A. Nordemann, and R. Oesch, eds, Kluwer Law International, 1999).
[24] Ricketson (1987) *op. cit.*, at 6.35.
[25] Ricketson (1987) *op. cit.*, 6.39.

for the French amendment that was proposed at the Brussels Conference in 1936.[26] A revised version of the French amendment was adopted but omitted the requirement that protection be extended to photographs which "constitute intellectual creations." Finally, photographic works were included in Art.2(1) and accorded the same status as other artistic works. The former Art.3 was now deleted from the Convention. It was not until 1971, following the Paris Act, that a minimum term of protection of 25 years was required for photographs. Article 7(4) of the Berne Convention states:

> "It shall be a matter for legislation in the countries of the Union to determine the term of protection of photographic works ... in so far as they are protected as artistic works; however this term shall last at least until the end of a period of twenty-five years from the making of such a work."

It remains the case that the Berne Convention potentially leaves gaps in the protection of photographic works. The Berne Convention operates on the principle of national treatment—namely that member countries of the Convention must grant to authors from other Convention countries the same rights which they grant their own nationals.[27] This can cause difficulties because the Convention protects "artistic" photographs but this is interpreted differently by different member countries. For example, the UK requires a very low level of originality for a photograph to be protected as an artistic work and applies a very loose interpretation to the term "artistic". Other countries, such as Italy and Germany, only protect creative photographs as copyright works and protect other photographs by a related right. The Convention does not allow foreign authors to force a foreign member country to apply the same interpretation of the law as the author's home country. The consequence is that an author may find his photograph is protected at home but not in a foreign Convention country. This is particularly so where the foreign country applies a related right to non-original photographs that are not copyright works.

**3–056**   Article 5(1), which sets out the principles of national treatment under the Berne Convention states: "authors shall enjoy, *in respect of works for which they are protected under this Convention*, the rights which their respective laws do now or may here grant to their nationals" (emphasis added). The Berne Convention is concerned with "intellectual creations" and it follows that a non-original photograph is not a work protected under the Convention. There is no obligation under Berne on countries that protect non-original photographs to extend that protection to foreign nationals.

This is illustrated by the *Beatles case*, a decision of the Higher Regional Court of Frankfurt where photographs of the pop group the *Beatles* were denied the status of copyright works under German law. It was held that the German related right for non-original photographs was also not available

---

[26] Ricketson (1987) *op. cit.*, 6.40.
[27] Berne Conventions For the Protection of Literary and Artistic Works, Art.5(1).

because of the lack of international provisions on the subject.[28] As Nimmer & Geller observe; "a production devoid of originality risks falling between the cracks of the framework of copyright treaties."[29] Non-original photographs under Berne are a paradigm example.

## Universal Copyright Convention (1952–1971)

Surprisingly, the Universal Copyright Convention (UCC) still does not   **3–057** require any kind of mandatory protection of photographs however minimal. Article I provides:

> "Each Contracting State undertakes to provide for the adequate and effective protection of the rights of authors and other copyright proprietors in literary, scientific and artistic works, including writings, musical, dramatic and cinematographic works, and paintings, engravings, and sculpture."

Photographs are obviously omitted from this list. In addition, Art.IV(3) provides:

> "The provisions of paragraph 2 [*term of protection not less than life of author plus 25 years*] shall not apply to photographic works or works of applied art; provided, however, that the term of protection in those Contracting States which protect photographic works, or works of applied art in so far as they are protected as artistic works, shall not be less than ten years for each of the said classes of works."

The UCC basically provided a bridging mechanism to bring the United   **3–058** States (which required various formalities and had a basic maximum term of 56 years) towards Berne and into the international copyright treaty arena. Its importance in the modern international copyright world is somewhat limited as it has been superseded by the TRIPS Agreement which requires members of the World Trade Organisation to comply with the Berne Convention. However, it is yet another example of the cautious way in which international treaties have approached the question of photographic works. This again has at its root the problems of originality and the varying approaches of different countries.

---

[28] A. Dietz, *Copyright Law Developments in Germany From 1993 to Mid-1997* (1998) 175 R.I.D.A. 96, 194. But cf. A. Nordemann, *Germany in Copyright and Photographs: An International Survey* (Y. Gendreau, A. Nordemann, and R. Oesch, eds, Kluwer Law International, 1999) at 142:

> "It is important to note that there is a court decision that grants protection pursuant to the Berne Convention and the German-US Copyright Treaty of 1896 not only for works of photography but also for simple photographs: OLG Hamburg (1983) AfP p.347 at pp.348–349".

[29] Nimmer & Geller, INT-106 para.4[2].

*TRIPS Agreement (1994)*

**3–059**   Following the Uruguay round of negotiations for revision of the General Agreement of Tarriffs and Trade, the World Trade Organisation Agreement was concluded in 1994. The Agreement on Trade related Aspects of Intellectual Property Rights ("the TRIPS Agreement") was adopted as part of the WTO Agreement. All members of the World Trade Organisation are bound by the TRIPS Agreement which provides that members shall comply with Arts 1–21 of the Berne Convention excluding the moral rights provisions in Art.6 *bis*.

Article 12 of the TRIPS Agreement allows members to exclude photographic works from the minimum requirement of a term of protection of the life of the author plus 50 years. Yet again, an international agreement treats photographs differently from other artistic works. The TRIPS Agreement does not contain any definition of originality.

*WIPO Copyright Treaty 1996*

**3–060**   Article 9 of the 1996 World Intellectual Property Organisation Copyright Treaty prevents signatories from applying Art.7(4) of the Berne Convention which provides that countries are free to determine the term of protection for photographs but that it shall last at least until the end of a period of 25 years from the making of such a work. The consequence of Art.9 of the WIPO Treaty is that photographs would fall under the standard duration provision of Berne under Art.7(1) whereby protection of works is now subject to the duration rule of life of the author plus 50 years after his death.

The WIPO Treaty has been a significant development in the international copyright protection of photographs. As at November 4, 2004, 43 countries were party to the WIPO Copyright Treaty including the USA.[30] The United Kingdom became a signatory on February 13, 1997. The Treaty does not define originality.

*Other international agreements*

**3–061**   There exist a number of bi-lateral agreements in the area of copyright law. As far as photographs are concerned, the only one of any real significance is the US-German Agreement of 1892[31] which specifically mentions "photographs" as well as "works".[32]

**European Directives**

**3–062**   It has been argued by at least one commentator that there is no common ground established in the European Directives which attempt to harmonise

---

[30] See *http://www.wipo.int/treaties/en/ip/wct/index.html*.
[31] The agreement was formally renewed by Germany by the law of May 18, 1922. Following World War II its continuing applicability was confirmed by diplomatic correspondence between the German Federal Government and the US High Commissioner for Germany in 1950. See Nimmer & Geller, GER-79 para.6[3].
[32] See Nimmer & Geller para.4[2] and below at Appendix 2 (Germany).

originality criteria.[33] There are three directives that explicitly refer to "originality", one of which—the Term Directive—specifically deals with photographs. The other two directives (the Database Directive and the Computer Program Directive) merit a brief mention as, although they do not deal with photographs, they do refer to originality and should be considered as a reflection of the European Union position as to originality generally. A fourth directive, the Copyright and Related Rights in the Information Society Directive,[34] which applies to photographs as authors' works, refers to intellectual creation and creativity but does not specifically refer to originality.

### The Term Directive

The Council Directive of October 29, 1993, harmonising the term of **3–063** protection of copyright and certain related rights[35] provides in Art.6:

"Photographs which are original in the sense that they are *the author's own intellectual creation* shall be protected in accordance with Article 1. No other criteria shall be applied to determine their eligibility for protection."

Recital 17 provides as follows:

"Whereas the protection of photographs in the Member States is the subject of varying regimes; whereas in order to achieve a sufficient harmonisation of the term of protection of photographic works, in particular those which, due to their artistic or professional character, are of importance within the internal market, it is necessary to define the level of originality required in this Directive; whereas a photographic work within the meaning of the Berne Convention is to be considered original if it is *the author's own intellectual creation reflecting his personality*, no other criteria such as merit or purpose being taken into account; whereas the protection of other photographs should be left to national law." (Emphasis added)

Primarily because of the difficulties arising in the differing treatment of photographs by Member States, the directive seeks to harmonise the definitions of originality as regards photographs. According to the Recital, a photographic work within the meaning of the Berne Convention in addition to "intellectual creation" is considered original if it reflects the personality of the author. "Intellectual creation" alone is thus not sufficient for a photograph to be considered original.

The law and courts of the United Kingdom for example are *prima facie* a **3–064** long way from considering "reflection of the personality of the author" as a

---

[33] G.W.G. Karnell, *European Originality: A Copyright Chimera.* in J.J.C. Kabel, and G. Mom, (eds) *Intellectual Property and Information Law* (Kluwer Law International, 1998) at 201.
[34] 2001/29.
[35] 93/98.

requirement for originality in photographic works. The authors of *The Modern Law of Copyright and Designs* suggest that in extending the term of protection to all photographs under the Copyright Designs and Patents Act 1988 the Secretary of State may have acted ultra vires as the Directive extension is limited to photographs which are original in the "intellectual creation" sense.[36] It is submitted that this is correct. It is apparent from the case law discussed above that the courts of the United Kingdom, when interpreting the UK Statute, do not apply the "intellectual creation" test to photographs when considering originality in any meaningful sense. The "intellectual creation" test is very much a civil law concept and embodies the same language as *inter alia* the German statute.[37]

The power of the Secretary of State to amend Acts of Parliament derives from s.2(2)(b) of the European Communities Act 1972.[38] The power is to make regulations either for the purpose of implementing any Community obligation,[39] or for the purpose of dealing with matters arising out of or related to any such obligation or rights.[40] The Duration Regulations were made in exercise of this power.

**3–065**   The Regulations purport to extend the term of protection to 70 yrs pma for all artistic works including all original photographs.[41] "Original" in the UK Statute has not so far been interpreted by the courts to mean the author's own intellectual creation reflecting his personality. The United Kingdom requires a very low level of originality and focuses on labour, skill and judgment. The application of the extension of the term to 70 yrs pma to photographs which are not the author's own intellectual creation exceeds the directive. This cannot be said to be permitted by the power allowing regulations to be made "for the purpose of implementing" the Community obligation as it exceeds the obligation. Unless it can be contended that this was "for the purpose of dealing with matters arising out of or related to any such obligation or rights" then in extending the term of 70 yrs pma to non-original photographs the Secretary of State has exceeded his power.

Member States continue to be permitted to protect other "non-original" photographs if they choose to do so under Art.6. It is therefore open to Parliament to protect non-original photographs in some way if it wishes to do so by amending the CPDA 1988.

---

[36] Laddie, Prescott and Vitoria, *et al.*, (3rd ed.), *op. cit.*, at 4.61A. and see also above at paras 2–129 to 2–131.

[37] See below at para. 3–076 and Appendices 1 and 2, Germany.

[38] Term Directive, Art.6.

[39] European Communities Act 1972, s.2(2)(a).

[40] European Communities Act 1972, s.2(2)(b).

[41] SI 1995/3297, reg.5(1), amending CDPA 1988, s.12(1); CDPA 1988, s.1(1) "copyright … subsists in … original … artistic works"; s.4 "artistic work" includes a photograph.

## Originality in other directives

*The Copyright and Related Rights in the Information Society Directive*[42]

This directive adopted on May 22, 2001, affects photographs as it applies to authors' works. The directive refers to intellectual creation and creativity but does not specifically refer to originality. Recitals 9 and 10 provide:

**3–066**

> "(9) Any harmonisation of copyright and related rights must take as a basis a high level of protection, since such rights are crucial to *intellectual creation*. Their protection helps to ensure *the maintenance and development of creativity* in the interests of authors, performers, producers, consumers, culture, industry and the public at large. Intellectual property has therefore been recognised as an integral part of property
>
> (10) If authors or performers are to continue *their creative and artistic work*, they have to receive an appropriate reward for the use of their work, as must producers in order to be able to finance this work. The investment required to produce products such as phonograms, films or multimedia products, and services such as 'on-demand' services, is considerable. Adequate legal protection of intellectual property rights is necessary in order to guarantee the availability of such a reward and provide the opportunity for satisfactory returns on this investment." (emphasis added).

*The Database Directive*

The European Council and European Parliament Directive on the Legal Protection of Databases[43] was adopted in March 1996. It too refers to "intellectual creation". Article 3 of the copyright provisions reads as follows:

**3–067**

> "In accordance with this Directive, databases which, by reason of the selection or arrangement of their contents, constitute *the author's own intellectual creation* shall be protected as such by copyright. No other criteria shall be applied to determine their eligibility for that protection." (emphasis added).

Recital 16 further provides:

> "Whereas no criterion other than originality in the sense of the author's intellectual creation should be applied to determine the eligibility of the database for copyright protection, and in particular no aesthetic or qualitative criteria should be applied."

---

[42] 2001/29.
[43] 96/9.

*Computer Program Directive*

**3–068**     The Council Directive on the Legal Protection of Computer Programs[44] was adopted in May 1991 and was required to be implemented by January 1, 1993. Article 3 provides:

> "A computer program shall be protected if it is original in the sense that it is *the author's own intellectual creation*. No other criteria shall be applied to determine its eligibility for protection." (emphasis added).

Recital 8 reads as follows:

> "Whereas, in respect of the criteria to be applied in determining whether or not a computer program is an original work, no tests as to the qualitative or aesthetic merits of the program should be applied."

The directives are superficially similar in their approach to originality as all three refer to "the author's own intellectual creation". This wording is indicative of the predominance of the civil law approach within the Member States—"personal intellectual creation" being the German statutory standard for copyright protection. The Recital in the Term Directive is slightly different in that it includes the reflection of the author's personality which the other directives do not. It is submitted that this is not of particular significance in so far as determining a common European approach as the other two directives deal with very different subject matter. Computer programs and databases are much more functional than creative. In reality, it would be meaningless to speak of a computer program that "reflects the author's personality." The sui generis protection for databases is indicative of this distinction. It was felt that there was a need to offer protection to databases which were not in the modern environment being adequately protected by copyright.

Karnell observes that the negative criteria in the directives are different namely; (1) no other criteria such as merit or purpose (photographs), (2) no test as to the qualitative or aesthetic merits (computer programs), and (3) no aesthetic or qualitative criteria (databases). He observes that EC law does not provide any explanation behind the varying drafting of the definitions of originality and concludes that there is no common ground of originality established by the directives.[45]

**3–069**     It is true that the standard set in "the author's own intellectual creation" test will vary from work to work in the sense that the indicia of intellectual creation will be different for say a painting as opposed to a book. The "reflection of the author's personality" test for truly creative works is an example of this. The establishment of originality will vary according to the facts of any given case. However, it follows that if copyright law as a whole (rather than on a work by work basis) has common justifications and aims,

---

[44] 91/250.
[45] G.W.G. Karnell, *European Originality: A Copyright Chimera, op. cit.*, at 203.

that the basic standard of originality for different works should in essence be the same. This is especially true when considering negative criteria—matters that cannot be taken into account for one work should also apply to another. To state that the originality of photographs on the one hand cannot be tested by merit or purpose whilst stating on the other that computer programs and databases cannot be tested by aesthetic or qualitative criteria is inconsistent. Logically, if there is a base standard of originality, photographs should also be subject to the same "no aesthetic or qualitative criteria" as well.

Although the European Union approach to originality as regards different works is not particularly unified, it is clear that the "intellectual creation" standard applies to all. Further, in so far as photographs as concerned, the Term Directive adds the gloss of "reflection of personality".

## Observations on photographs and originality in international and European legislation

All of the international and European treaties and directives (with the   **3–070** exception of the WIPO Copyright Treaty) treat, or at some point historically treated, photographs differently from other works. The shorter term of protection for photographs that is permitted under Berne, the UCC and TRIPS is a reflection of the very deep rooted conception that photographs are different from other works and do not warrant the same length of protection. This is relevant to originality as the starting point is that photographs are in effect a class below other artistic works. It is therefore likely that in considering questions of originality, this idea of the lesser status of photographs will influence national legislation and case law.

The test of "intellectual creation" is found in the Berne Convention and   **3–071** also the European Term Directive. In so far as any common approach to originality in international legislation can be found, it lies in this "intellectual creation" test. Thus we can conclude, before turning to consider individual national laws, that there is some unity in international and European law as to the standard of originality, namely that of "intellectual creation". The national legislation of many countries incorporates a similar standard, particularly in the civil law jurisdictions. However, the common law countries tend to apply a "labour and skill test" as the basis for originality.

ORIGINALITY AND PHOTOGRAPHIC WORKS UNDER NATIONAL LAWS

## Different schemes for protection of photographs in national laws

Gimeno identified four types of legal regime in relation to the protection   **3–072** of photographs:

(1) those that do not impose any special requirement to grant copyright protection and apply the general protection requirement: originality;

(2) those that impose special requirements (artistic or documentary character) to protect photographs by copyright;

(3) those that only protect photographs by a neighbouring or related right;

(4) finally, those that distinguish between different types of photographs: some protected by copyright others protected by a related right.[46]

**3–073**     Of the countries considered in Appendices 1 and 2, none fall into the third category.[47] Historically, some countries did, such as Germany and Switzerland which refused to accord photographs the status of artistic works protectable by copyright and did only offer a related rights protection.[48] Indeed, at one point Haiti and Tunis provided no protection for photographs at all.[49] Gimeno's third category does not to apply to any of the current copyright statutes considered in Appendix 2.

Accordingly, modern national legal regimes for the protection of photographs (with the emphasis on originality) can be re-classified as follows:

1.  Countries that protect photographs as an original artistic work under the basic national copyright/author's law divided into:

    (i)   countries that apply a "work, labour and skill test";
    (ii)  countries that apply a "creativity" or "work of the mind" test; and
    (iii) countries with a statutory test of "innovation" or "novel";[49a]

2.  countries that protect specified photographs only; and

3.  countries that protect some photographs by copyright/author's right but also have a related right for non-original photographs.

---

[46] L. Gimeno, *Photographs, Commercial Exploitation of the Image and Copyright in Spain* [1998] Ent. L.R. 131, 136.

[47] Gimeno cites the Nordic countries as an example. The Nordic Countries (Finland, Denmark, Norway & Sweden) granted a *sui generis* protection to photographs which was embodied in separate legislation to the main copyright legislation. Today, photographic works are also protected by copyright with a related for non-original photographs. See below in Appendix 2, for example Denmark Copyright Act, s.70(3) "where a photographic picture is subject to copyright ... such rights may also be enforced"; Sweden Art.49(a) "if such a picture is subject to copyright, copyright protection may also be claimed." See also R. Oesch, *Nordic Countries in Copyright and Photographs: An International Survey* in Y. Gendreau, Nordemann and R. Oesch, (eds) Kluwer Law Int. at p.231.

[48] German Law of January 10, 1897; Swiss law of April 23, 1883, Art.9—cited in S. Ricketson, *The Berne Convention for the Protection of Literary and Artistic Works 1886–1986* (Centre for Commercial Law Studies, Queen Mary College, Kluwer, 1987) at 6.33, n.139.

[49] See Ricketson (1987), *op. cit.*, at 6.35.

[49a] But this may be due to misleading translation from Arabic to English, see below at para. 3–078.

## Countries that protect photographs as an original artistic work under the basic national copyright law

These are countries which do not apply special regulations to photo-graphs and protect them as any other artistic work, provided they can establish originality. Within this category, there are a number of sub-categories.

### Countries that apply a "work, labour and skill test"

The most notable example of a country that applies a work, labour and skill test is the United Kingdom, but there are many others, usually common law countries, where the statutory origins of the copyright law can be traced to the United Kingdom, such as Australia. Mauritius actually defines "original" in its statute as "the product of a person's work, labour and skill."[50]

The United States would also fall within this category but with a caveat following the decision in 1991 in *Feist Publications v Rural Telephone Service Co Inc*[51] when the "sweat of the brow" test was rejected. It was held that rather than labour alone being able to constitute originality, a "modicum of creativity" was necessary. The United States, as a common law jurisdiction, is close in underlying philosophy to the law of the United Kingdom—indeed historically the USA copyright law originates from the UK. However, as far as originality is concerned following *Feist*, it is arguably moving towards being more appropriately classified with "countries that apply a creativity or work of the mind test". As far as the future prospect of world harmonisa-tion on standards of originality is concerned, this decision is of considerable significance as it represents a move by a common law country towards the civil law approach.[52]

### Countries that apply a "creativity" or "work of the mind" test

The specific statutory language varies from country to country in this category but references to creativity and intellectual creation predominate. These tend to be civil law jurisdictions where the emphasis is on the per-sonality of the author. Examples of the expressions used in the various statutes as translated into English[53] are "creation of any intellectual work"[54]; "any original intellectual work"[55]; "original intellectual productions"[56]; "the

---

[50] Copyright Act 1997 of Mauritius, s.2(1). See Appendix 2 below.
[51] 499 U.S. 340; 18 U.S.P.Q. 2d 1275.
[52] See below at para. 3–117.
[53] These examples are taken from Appendix 2 which is based on the statutes as translated into English. It should be noted that WIPO translates author's right as copyright although as has been discussed above, the two are different.
[54] For further information see Appendix 2 below. Algeria, Art.1.
[55] Guinea Art.1; Togo Art.2.
[56] For further information see Appendix 2 below. Costa Rica Art.1. Austria at para.1(1) also uses this term but is classified below with "Countries providing Related Rights".

production of creative effort"[57]; "creations of the mind"[58]; "works of the mind"[59]; "intellectual works"[60]; "works which involve creative activity"[61]; "the result of creative activity"[62]; "any expression of creative activity having individual character"[63]; "creative expression"[64]; "creative endeavour"[65]; "original creation"[66]; "original intellectual creation"[67]; "individual intellectual creations"[68]; "any original creation particularly as regards form which is a manifestation of the author's personality"[69]; "sufficient effort has been expended to give the work an original character"[70]; "all works manifesting human intelligence".[71] The rather florid description in the Indonesian Copyright Act of an author is a person "whose inspiration has called into being a creation based on intellectual capability, imagination, dexterity, proficiency or skillfulness, laid down in an exclusive and personal form".

**3-077**   Also within this category would fall two countries that have a statutory definition which refers to the identity of the author—Rwanda and Togo. As the emphasis is on the personality of the author, such countries are more properly included with the civil law "creativity" group. The Rwandan Copyright Law of 1983 provides in Art.1 " 'Original work' shall mean a work whose characteristic elements and whose form, or whose form alone, enable its author to be distinguished". Togo provides in Art.8 that " 'original work' means a work which, by its characteristic features and its form or by its form only, allows its author to be identified". Historically, Morocco also had a similar provision. The 1970 Moroccan Statute (now superseded by 2000 Statute referring to "original innovation") provided: "A work is original when its characteristic features and its form, or its form alone, make possible the identification of its author."[72]

*Countries with a statutory test of "innovation" or "novel"*

**3-078**   Within the countries considered in Appendix 2, those countries falling within the first category (protection of photographs as an artistic work) which have an "innovation" type of statutory test for copyright works tend

---

[57] For further information see Appendix 2 below. Bulgaria para.2; Kazakstan Art.2 and Art.6(1); Latvia Art.1; Russian Federation Art.4; Ukraine Art.4; Uzbekistan Art.5.

[58] Brazil Art.7; Switzerland Art.2.1. Also the statutes of Columbia (Art.2) and the Dominican Republic (Art.2) have this wording but both are classified below as countries protecting only specified works.

[59] El Salvador Art.12; France L111–1; Gabon Art.2; Moldova Art.4(1); Ecuador Law of 1998, Art.8. For further information see Appendix 2 below.

[60] Chile Art.1; Djibouti Art.1; Madagascar Art.3; Venezuela Art.1.

[61] Cuba Art.7.

[62] Czech Republic Art.2.(1); Estonia s.4(2).

[63] Poland Art.1–1.

[64] United Arab Emirates Law of 2002, Art.3.

[65] Bulgaria, Act of 1993, Art.3(1). For further information see Appendix 2 below.

[66] Greece Art.2(1); Mexico Art.4.

[67] Panama Art.2(14); Philippines Art.172.1; Romania Art.7; Paraguay Art.2.

[68] Slovenia Art.5(1).

[69] Mali Art.7.

[70] Kenya Art.3(2); Malaysia Art.7(3); Malta s.3(2); Nigeria Art.1(2); Uganda para.1(2); United Republic of Tanzania s.3(2)(a).

[71] Lebanon Art.138.

[72] Art.3. Appendix 2 below.

to be in the Middle East. This may however be as a result of difficulties in translation between Arabic and English rather than a true test of novelty.[72a]

The statutes of Bahrain and Saudi Arabia as translated into English respectively protect "innovative works"[73] and "any composition comprising novel elements or characterized by special features previously unknown".[74] Egypt protects "innovated works" and defines creativity as "the element of innovation that bestows authenticity upon the work".[75] Jordan similarly protects "innovated works". Morocco protects works which are "original innovations"[76] as does Oman.[77] Iraq also has similar statutory language— "innovated works"[78]—but is classed below as a country with related rights protection.

## Countries that protect specified types of photograph only

Historically, a number of countries drew a distinction between the type of    **3–079** photographs protected—commonly only artistic and documentary photographs were protected.[79] Today, of the countries considered in Appendix 2, only a few fall into this category. Benin only protects photographs of "an artistic or documentary nature"[80] as does the Democratic Republic of the Congo[81]; Columbia protects only "artistic photographs"[82] and the Dominican Republic protects only photographs that have "sufficient artistic

---

[72a] See for example in with regard to the Copyright Protection Act 1974 of Sudan, Professor Akolda M. Tier observes:

> " ... the Act ... shows signs of ill-considered translations from Arabic to English. The draftsman has obviously had difficulty with the word *mubtakar*, *i.e.* newly-created, novel, new or original according to the dictionary meaning. *Mubtakar* is translated as 'innovation' in s.4(1) on works of literature, arts or science; as 'novel' in s.4(3) on derivative works; and as 'novel style' and 'innovatory' in s.5 on collective works. Again, the definition section 2 contains *ibtikar* (the noun form of *mubtakar*) which is translated into 'creation although in no other section in the Arabic and English texts of the Act is that word used. In a future review of the Act, an opportunity should be taken to alter the wording of the English text. In this study, I prefer to use 'original' throughout".

M. Tier, Akolda, *Protection of Copyright Under Sudanese Law* 6 Arab Law Quarterly 161 at 169.

[73] For further information see Appendix 2 below. Bahrain Art.2(1).
[74] Saudi Arabia, Art.1; Appendix 2 below.
[75] Egypt Law No.82 of 2002, Art.138. Appendix 2 below.
[76] Law of 2000 of Morrocco, Art.3, Appendix 2 below.
[77] Decree No 37/2000, Arts 1 and 2. Appendix 2 below.
[78] Iraq Art.(1)1.
[79] For example the French law prior to 1985; Germany (historical documentary photographs)— the German Law of 1985 distinguished between photographic works, documentary photographs and other "simple photographs". See Ricketson (1987), *op. cit.*, 6.42 n.194. The duration of the protection accorded was respectively life of the author plus 70 years, 50 years post publication and 25 years post publication; Sweden Photography Act of 1960 (photographs of an artistic or scientific value). See Appendix 2 below, Sweden.
[80] Benin Law on the Protection of Copyright which came into force March 15, 1984, Art.8. See Appendix 2 below, Benin.
[81] Art.7, Law on Copyright and Neighbouring Rights Law No.24/82 of July 7, 1982. See Appendix 2 below, Democratic Republic of the Congo.
[82] See Appendix 2 below, Colombia Art.8.

merit".[83] Macau only protects works that are the "personal artistic creation of the author" and specifically excludes photographs that have "mere documentary value".[84]

**3–080**     Prior to amendment in 1998, the law of Paraguay in addition to protecting artistic creations had an unusual specific provision to the effect that "anyone who has produced an original photographic image of a panorama, a landscape or a view, shall likewise enjoy in his capacity as owner of such image all rights afforded by this Code to artistic production."[85] This may be regarded as a separate category from artistic works as being a reproduction of a scene but the use of the word "original" precluded it from being a related right. Paraguay historically would properly fall into this category but the 1998 law now provides for a true relate right.

## Countries that protect some photographs by copyright/author's right but also have a related right for non-original photographs

**3–081**     Of the 125 countries considered,[86] 15 have a variety of related right provisions for photographs. The criteria vary, but broadly speaking, copyright protects a creative original photograph and the related right protects an "ordinary", "simple", or "mere" photograph, *i.e.* a photograph devoid of creativity that does not attract copyright protection. This approach is taken in only a minority of countries which may prove problematic in the future in so far as harmonisation is concerned as discussed below.[87] Countries which have a type of related rights protection for photographs are set out below. In 2000, both Jordan and Egypt had a related right for non-copyright photographs, but this distinction was removed in both countries in 2001 and 2002 respectively when new laws were passed.[88] Hungary also had a related right for non-copyright photographs under the Act of 1969 but this has been repealed.[88a]

### Austria

**3–082**     The standard for protection of copyright works under para.1(1)[89] is "original intellectual productions". There is a distinction between "works of photography" (*i.e.* an original intellectual production) and photographs under para.73 being merely "images produced by a photographic process".[90] Under para.74 any photograph, not just "a work", is protected for 50 years

---

[83] Art.53, Copyright Statute (No.32–86) of July 4, 1986. See Appendix 2 below.
[84] Macau, SAR Copyright Decree of 1999 (2000) Art.149.
[85] Art.2175, the Copyright Law of Paraguay is contained in the Civil Code Law (No.1183): December 18, 1985, which came into force on January 1, 1987. See Appendix 2 below.
[86] See Appendices 1 and 2.
[87] See below at paras 3–100 and 3–114.
[88] For details as to the nature of the distinction of the related rights see Law of Jordan and Law of Egypt in Appendix 2 below.
[88a] Act No. LXXVI of 1999 as amended by Act No. XLVIII of 2001 on Designs and the Act No. LXXVII of 2001, see Hungary in Appendix 2, below.
[89] Copyright Act, Federal Law Gazette No.111/1936 as amended. See Appendix 2 below.
[90] And see J.A.L. Sterling, *World Copyright Law* (Sweet & Maxwell, 1998) 6.70 n.41.

after it has been taken, or, where the photograph is made public before the expiration of that term, 30 years from the date when it is first made public.

## Denmark

The basic standard is "creation" under s.1(1).[91] Under s.70 the producer of "a photographic picture" receives the exclusive right to make copies of it and make it available to the public. The right lasts for 50 years from the end of the year in which the picture was taken. It is clear that this is a separate right from the copyright in a photograph as the final sentence of s.70(3) provides; "Where a photographic picture is subject to copyright according to Section 1, such rights may also be enforced".

**3–083**

## Ecuador

The law of Ecuador distinguishes between a photograph that is "a work of the mind"[92] and "an ordinary photograph" that does not have the character of a photographic work.[93] Creative photographs are protected for 70 years pma. "Ordinary photographs" are protected for 25 years from January 1 following the date of making, disclosure or publication.[94]

**3–084**

## Finland

The basic standard for a copyright work is "creation" under Art.1.[95] Copyright subsists in photographs which are copyright works for 70 yrs pma. Article 49a provides that "a photographic picture" is protected for 50 years from the end of the year in which the photographic work was created. This is a different right from copyright as is made clear from the final sentence of Art.49a which provides. "If a photographic picture is subject to copyright, the corresponding rights may be claimed."

**3–085**

## Germany

The originality standard for copyright works is "personal intellectual creations" under Art.2(1).[96] Photographs are included as protected works in Art.2. Under German law from July 1, 1995, a non-creative photograph (*i.e.* one without sufficient creativity to attract copyright) is protected under s.72 for a term of 50 years from the year that the photograph is first made available to the public or if not published the year it is taken. Earlier law drew a related rights distinction between non-creative photographs and photographs of historical and documentary character, but this is no longer the case.[97] A minimum of creativity is required for simple photographs to be

**3–086**

---

[91] Act on Copyright 1995 which came into force on July 1, 1995. See Appendix 2 below.
[92] Intellectual Property Law 08/05/1998 No.83, Art.8. See Appendix 2 below.
[93] *ibid.*, Art.41 and 103.
[94] *ibid.*, Art.103.
[95] Copyright Act (Law No.404 of July 8, 1961, as last amended by Law No.365 of April 25, 1997). See Appendix 2 below.
[96] Law on Copyright and Neighbouring Rights (Copyright Law) of September 9, 1965, as amended. See Appendix 2 below.
[97] See Appendix 2 (Germany), below and Nimmer & Geller GER-36 para.[2][a][i].

protected by the related right in Germany.[98] Photographs reproducing other photographs[99] or photocopies are not protected by the related right.[1]

### Iceland

**3–087–88**    The Icelandic copyright statute[2-3] provides in Art.49 that the reproduction of photographs that are not protected as artistic works is prohibited without the consent of the photographer. There is no definition of the "non-copyright".photographs that are protected. The protection lasts for 25 years from the year in which the photograph was taken.

### Iraq

**3–089**    The basic copyright protection is afforded to "authors of innovated literary, artistic and scientific works"[4] and this includes photographic works. Under Art.20 there is a related right type of protection for non-copyright photographic works "which are limited to the mechanical transmission of scenery". Such photographs are protected for five years only from the date of first publication of the photograph.

### Italy

**3–090**    Copyright is afforded to "works of the mind having a creative character"[5] and upon "the creation of a work that constitutes the particular expression of an intellectual effort".[6] There is a related right protection for non-original photographs comprising "the images of persons or of aspects, elements or events of natural or social life". It has been suggested this would encompass, for example, banal snapshots or mechanically produced photographs.[7] However, the related right protection does not extend to photographs of writings, documents, business papers, material objects, technical drawings or other similar items.[8] This lead to one Italian court refusing to protect photographs of banknotes and documents illustrating a book on money.[9]

---

[98] A. Nordeman, *Germany in Copyright and Photographs: An International Survey* (Y. Gendreau, A. Nordemann, and R. Oesch, eds, Kluwer Law International, 1999) at p.140.

[99] *Bibelreproduktion BGH* (1990) G.R.U.R. 669 at 673 cited by A. Nordeman, *Germany in Copyright and Photographs: An International Survey* (Y. Gendreau, A. Nordemann, and R. Oesch, eds, Kluwer Law International 1999) at p.140.

[1] See W. Nordemann (1987) G.R.U.R. 15 at 17 cited by A. Nordeman, *Germany in Copyright and Photographs: An International Survey* (Y. Gendreau, A. Nordemann, and R. Oesch, eds, Kluwer Law International, 1999) at p.140.

[2-3] Copyright Act Law (No.73) of May 29, 1972, as amended. See Appendix 2 below.

[4] Art.1(1), Copyright Law No.(3) of 1971 for the Protection of Copyright. See Appendix 2 below.

[5] Art.1, Law for the Protection of Copyright and Neighbouring Rights (Law No.633 of April 22, 1941), as last amended by Decree Law No.154 of May 26, 1997. See Appendix 2 below.

[6] *ibid.*, Art.6.

[7] Dr Mario Fabian in Nimmer & Geller ITA-73 para. 9[1][a][v]. See also Luigi Carlo, Ubertazzi, *Italy in Copyright and Photographs: An International Survey* (Y. Gendreau, A. Nordemann, and R. Oesch, eds, Kluwer Law International, 1999) at pp.163 *et seq.*

[8] Art.87.

[9] Court of Cassation, January 13, 1988, Decision no.183, Giustizia civile, 1988, I, 955 cited in Nimmer & Geller ITA-73 para.9[1][a][v]. For further information as to the distinction between simple photographs in Italian law see Appendix 2 below, Italy.

The Supreme Court has distinguished between photographs which have "a mere documentary purpose", photographs which are not protected by the related right, and non-creative photographs which have a "figurative" purpose and are protected.[10] To claim the related right protection, copies of the photographs need to bear the name of the photographer, the year of production, and if a copy of a work of art, the name of the author of that work of art.[11] The right subsists for 20 years from the making of the photograph.[12]

## Libya

Copyright protection is granted to authors of "original literary, artistic and scientific works"[13] and photographic works are included. A related rights protection is granted to photographic works which "merely involve photographing or filming by technical means".[14] "Technical means" photographs are protected for five years from the date on which they are first made available to the public.

**3–091**

## Luxembourg

The protection of unoriginal photographs under the Luxembourg statute[15] seems to be implied by the wording of Art.4. It appears that Luxembourg affords some type of copyright protection to these "lesser" photographs, although this is not particularly clear from a translation of the statute. Article 4 provides as follows:

**3–092**

"The copyright in photographic works and works of applied art shall subsist for 50 years from the date on which such works were made. However, photographic works shall enjoy a term equal to that provided for in Article 2 if they are original in the sense that they are an intellectual creation specific to their author."

Article 2 sets out the basis term of life of the author plus 70 years. The qualification that photographs attract the 70 year term if they are "original in the sense that they are an intellectual creation specific to their author", implies that photographs that are not original in this sense are protected under the 50 year term. If only original photographs were protected under the 50 year term, the qualification for the 70 year term would be superfluous.

The wording of this section as translated[16] is anomalous as the first part refers to "copyright in photographic works". For copyright to subsist, then

---

[10] Supreme Court, April 16, 1975, No.1440 (1975) IDA 346 citied in Luigi Carlo, Ubertazzi, *Italy in Copyright and Photographs: An International Survey* (Y. Gendreau, A. Nordemann, and R. Oesch, eds, Kluwer Law International, 1999) at pp.163 *et seq.*

[11] Art.90.

[12] Art.92.

[13] Law on the protection of copyright law (No.9), Art.1: March 16, 1968. See Appendix 2 below.

[14] *ibid.*, Art.20.

[15] Law of March 29, 1972, on Copyright as last amended. See Appendix 2 below.

[16] This translation is from the UNESCO database of World Copyright Laws at *http://www.unesco.org/culture/copy/copyright/luxembourg/fr_page1.html.*

the photographic work must be original. If so, it makes little sense to go on to state that a longer term of protection is granted for photographs that are "original in the sense that they are an intellectual creation specific to their author". As the first part refers to "copyright in photographs" and the second to "original photographs" they both refer to the same thing—*i.e.* original copyright photographs. This is an unlikely construct as it would make the first part redundant. Prima facie, on a logical reading, the section appears to grant some sort of related right for 50 years for photographs that are not "original in the sense that they are an intellectual creation specific to their author" but terms it "copyright". This analysis is based on a translation of the statute and comes with a caution that it may not in fact be a true "related right".

### Norway

**3–093**   Photographic pictures are distinguished from photographs which are literary, scientific or artistic works.[17] Photographic pictures are granted a related right under s.43a which lasts for the life the photographer plus 15 years, but not less than 50 years from the production of the photograph. The section makes clear that this is a separate right from copyright as it states, "If a photograph is subject to copyright, such right may also be enforced."

### Peru

**3–094**   Copyright protection is granted to "works of the mind in the literary or artistic field"[18] and this includes photographic works. There is protection for a photograph or "another form of fixation by means of a comparable process" that does not qualify as a work.[19] The right granted is the exclusive right to authorise the reproduction, distribution and communication to the public on the same conditions as are accorded to the authors of photographs. The right lasts for 70 years from January 1 of the year following that of the taking of the photograph.

### Paraguay

**3–095**   Protected copyright works are "all intellectual works of creative character"[20] and such works are protected for the life of the author plus 70 years. However, the authors of photographs that do not qualify as "an intellectual work of creative character" still have the exclusive rights of reproduction, distribution and communication to the public on the same terms as are accorded to the authors of photographic works.[21] This related right endures for 50 years counted from January 1 of the year following that of the taking of the photograph.

---

[17] Act No.2 of May 12, 1961, Relating to Copyright in Literary, Scientific and Artistic Works, etc. as amended, s.1.
[18] Copyright Law (Legislative Decree No. 822 of April 24, 1996), Art.3.
[19] *ibid.*, Art.144.
[20] Law No.1328/98 on Copyright and Related Rights, Art.3.
[21] *ibid.*, Art.135.

*Spain*

The Spanish copyright statute[22] draws a distinction between photographic **3–096** works and "mere" pictures. Under Art.128, a photograph or other reproduction obtained by a process comparable to photography that does not have the character of a work (*i.e.* an original literary, artistic or scientific creation[23]) is protected by the author's exclusive right to authorise the reproduction, distribution and communication to the public under the same conditions as granted to authors of photographic works. The right lasts for 25 years from January 1 of the year following the making of the photograph.

*Sweden*

Copyright is granted to "anyone who has created a literary or artistic **3–097** work"[24] and this includes photographs. There is a type of related right granted to any photographic picture which is the exclusive right to reproduce the picture and to make it available to the public. This right lasts for 50 years from the year in which the picture was produced. If such a picture is subject to copyright, copyright protection may also be claimed. As with Denmark and Iceland, it is clear that this is a separate right from copyright as the section concludes, "If such a picture is subject to copyright, copyright protection may also be claimed."

The basic standard for copyright protections is "any intellectual production"[25] which applies to photographs. Copyright protection lasts for the life of the author plus 50 years. Article 20 provides that "photographic and cinematographic works having no original character, and limited to a simple mechanical reproduction of scenes" and are protected for 15 years from first publication of the work.

## Miscellaneous statutory provisions of national legislation that impact on originality

*No prohibition on taking a photograph of the same subject*

Several of the Arab countries have a specific statutory provision to the **3–098** effect that copyright in a photograph does not prohibit another person from taking a new photograph of the object depicted in the initial photograph even in the same place and circumstances as those in which the latter was made.[26] The law of Liechtenstein has a similar provision.[27] These types of

---

[22] Consolidated Text of the Law on Intellectual Property, April 12, 1996, as amended by Law 5/1998 of March 6, 1998.

[23] *ibid.*, Art.10(1).

[24] Art.1, Act on Copyright in Literary and Artistic Works (Law No.729, of December 30, 1960, as last amended).

[25] Art.1(1), Law (No.354): June 24, 1954, as amended by Law (No.34): June 17, 1975. See Appendix 2 below.

[26] See Appendix 2 below. Laws of Bahrain; Egypt; Iraq; Jordan; Libya; Saudi Arabia; Yemen.

[27] Art.16, Law concerning Copyright in Literary and Artistic Works of October 26, 1928, as amended by Law: August 8, 1959. See Appendix 2 (Liechtenstein), below.

provisions in fact add little to the law of copyright which automatically would not prohibit independent creation of a photograph of the same subject matter, unless the subject matter was itself a copyright work.[28] They have the aura of "for the avoidance of doubt" and are not strictly necessary.

### Exclusion of photographs of letters and documents

**3–099**    The law of Romania[29] specifies that photographs of letters, deeds, documents of any kind, technical drawings and other similar material, do not qualify for legal protection by copyright. Macau, SAR of China excludes photographs that have mere documentary value such as photographs of writings and documents, business papers and similar material from copyright protection.[30] Italian law also has a similar provision to the effect that photographs of writings, documents, business papers, material objects, technical drawings and similar products are excluded from even the related rights protection.[31] These provisions are consistent with the civil law approach requiring a degree of creativity. The common law approach is likely to lead to these sorts of photographs being protected.

### Observations on photographs and originality in national legislation

**3–100**    As can be seen, there are a number of different approaches. Although a small group of countries protect only specified photographs, the two main divides in copyright law concerning originality of photographs are between:

(1) broadly, the common law countries on the one hand and the civil law countries on the other applying respectively legislative standards for copyright works of (i) "original", and (ii) "intellectual creation" or "work of the mind"; and

(2) (a) those countries which assess the originality of photographs in the same way as other works and give no special treatment to non-original photographs, (b) those countries which, whilst protecting original photographs by copyright, afford some sort of related right for non-original photographs.

Although there are a relatively small number of countries that have a related right, this does not mean that the related rights protection for photographs is insignificant or that this is an issue that will die away. This is for a number of reasons. First, the fact that certain countries do protect

---

[28] *cf. Creation Records v News Group Newspapers Ltd* [1997] E.M.L.R. 444, 450 (photographer taking separate independent photograph of a non-copyright scene intended to form the cover of a music album). An injunction was granted but only on the basis of confidentiality not copyright.

[29] Art.85(1), Law on Copyright and Neighbouring Rights No.8 of March 14, 1996, which came into force on June 25, 1996.

[30] Copyright Decree of Macau 1999, Art.149(2). See Appendix 2, below.

[31] Art.87, Italian Law for the Protection of Copyright and Neighbouring Rights (Law No. 633 of April 22, 1941), as last amended by Decree Law No.154 of May 26, 1997.

non-creative photographs and others does not lead to difficulties and anomalies in international protection under principles of national treatment[32] and the risk Nimmer & Geller refer to such works "falling through the cracks"[33] of the international treaties.

Secondly, the 15 or so countries that protect such non-original photographs include Germany, which has a considerable influence internationally in matters of copyright law—as the language of the European legislation and the history of the inclusion of photographs in the Berne Convention shows.[34] Given that the number of countries that have a related rights protection for photographs is so small, it would obviously be quite a considerable feat to persuade over one hundred or so other nations that this type of protection should be included in international treaties. However, it is not as inconceivable as it may appear at first sight.

There is a modern trend towards protection of all aspects of intellectual **3–101** property that have a commercial value, even subject matter that previously has been outside the ambit of "traditional" copyright law. The classic example of this is the protection of non-original databases. What may be called the "directory cases" such as *Feist*[35] and others, showed that there were gaps in copyright protection for databases where they comprised non-original compilations. Strictly speaking, these types of bare factual compilations fall outside copyright law. In modern society, however, databases have great commercial value and for this reason the European Union introduced a *sui generis* protection for databases.[36] The Recitals to the European Database Directive places a great deal of emphasis on the financial investment in databases[37] and the importance of the commercial value is thus apparent. It is not too far into the realms of fantasy to predict that this "practical" attitude of protecting subject matter with a commercial value may spill over into the arena of photography, particularly as in the internet age copying and disseminating images is easier than ever. Decisions such as that in *Bridgeman Art Library v Corel Corporation*[38] (where photographs of works of art were held not to be protected as copyright works) may lead to organisations with a commercial interest in "non-original" photographs lobbying for national and international protection. Organisations with commercial interests in potentially non-original photographs do not just include "art" photographic libraries, but also, for example, producers of meteorological satellite photographs or other satellite photographs; aerial photographers; media organisations; sports organisations

---

[32] See discussion above concerning the Berne Convention at paras 3–055 and 3–056.

[33] See above at para.3–056.

[34] See history of Berne above at paras 3–051 *et seq.*

[35] See above at para. 3–074.

[36] Directive 96/9.

[37] See for example Recitals 7, 10, 11 and 12 "such investment in modern information storage and processing systems will not take place within the Community unless a stable and uniform legal protection regime is introduced for the protection of the rights of makers of databases"; Recitals 41 and 42 "thereby harm the investment".

[38] 25 F. Supp. 2d 421; 49 U.S.P.Q. 2d 1091 (S.D.N.Y. 1998) (first judgment); 36 F. Supp. 2d 191; 50 U.S.P.Q. 2d 1110 (S.D.N.Y 1999) (second judgment following motion for reconsideration and reargument.) The case is discussed fully above at paras 3–038 to 3–047.

producing "photo finish" pictures of athletics, horse racing and other sporting events to name a few.

Fourthly, of those countries that have related rights protection, seven of them—eight if Luxembourg is included[39]—are within the European Union. This is over half of the 15 Member States[40]—a large enough number of countries to conclude that a future directive on related rights in photography is a realistic possibility if and when questions of harmonisation fall to be addressed as eventually they no doubt will be.

These are matters affecting the possibility of future harmonisation. In so far as the existing national laws are concerned, problems arise when the courts are faced with deciding whether a particular photograph exhibits the necessary originality to qualify for copyright protection. The case law, even with the same jurisdictions, shows an inconsistency that is strongly suggestive of a need for further harmonisation.

## CASE LAW

### Originality in photographs: where courts draw the line

**3–102**    It should be noted at the outset that there is a marked difference in the legal philosophy underlying copyright law in the common law and civil countries. The author's rights systems of the civil law countries, which stem from the French Decrees of 1791 and 1793, place emphasis on the author's personality. It is considered that an original work should be protected as a human right—the work is an extension of the author's personality.

**3–103**    By contrast, the common law approach, which has its origins in the UK Act of Anne of 1709, is much more pragmatic and grounded in economic concepts. In common law theory, copyright is held necessary primarily to promote and protect labour and investment in the creative arts. The focus is said by some to be on commerce. The author's rights system places emphasis on the author whereas the common law theory places emphasis on the work. A full discussion of the differences between the author's right system and the common law system is outside the scope of this work.[41] However, for present purposes it suffices to note that it is easier to justify protection of a non-creative photograph if it has been obtained by labour and skill or has a commercial value due to its content under the common law system. For this reason, one would therefore expect the case law of the common law coun-

---

[39] See comments re: Luxembourg above at para. 3–091.

[40] The balance will change when the new Member States join on May 1, 2004. Of the 10 new Member States (Cyprus; Czech Republic; Estonia; Hungary; Latvia; Lithuania; Malta; Poland; Slovak Republic; Slovenia) none presently have a related right protecting non-original photographs. Hungary used to have such a related right but no longer does.

[41] There is considerable literature on this topic. See for example A., Franço, *Authors' Rights Beyond Frontiers: A Comparison of Civil Law and Common Law Conceptions* (1991) R.I.D.A. 2; A, Strowel, *Droit d'auteur et copyright: divergences et convergences* (Bruylant, 1993); S., Ricketson, *The Concept of Originality in Anglo-Australian Copyright Law* (1991) 9(2) Journal of Copyright Society of Australia 1; and Sterling (1998), *op. cit.*, at 1.15.

tries to have a lower standard of originality in photographs than the civil law countries and, with the exception of the United States, this is generally true.

## Where the courts draw the line: the common law approach

### *Originality generally*

As has been seen, the common law statutes tend to refer only to "original" or "originality" as the qualification for copyright protection.[42] The vast majority do not have any statutory definition of originality with the notable exception of Mauritius which defines original work as "the product of a person's work, labour and skill."[43] This absence of a statutory definition and the philosophical emphasis on the protection of the work has lead to the courts setting a fairly low standard of originality. The comments of Peterson J. in *University of London Press v University Tutorial Press*[44] to the effect that the originality required relates to the expression of thought but does not require novelty[45] are cited in treaties and cases from a number of common law jurisdictions.[46] In addition, the majority of common law countries require a degree of "work, labour and skill" before copyright protection will be accorded. In *Cramp v Smythson*[47] it was said:

> "It is conceded that, if the work labour and skill required to make the selection and to compile the tables is negligible, then no copyright can subsist in it. Whether enough work labour and skill is involved, and what its value is, must always be a question of degree. Different minds will differ, as may be seen in the present case from the divergence of opinion in the courts below."

The last sentence encapsulates the problem within the common law jurisdictions—different judges will have different opinions on the facts of any one case. This is a particular problem in the area of photographic works. For further discussion of the case law concerning originality in common law countries see above at paras 3–011 to 3–015.

## Where the courts draw the line: the civil law approach

### *Originality generally*

The Court de Cassation of France has expressed the opinion that a work is original when "it bears the mark of the personality of its author and

**3–104**

**3–105**

---

[42] See above at para.3–013.
[43] Copyright Act 1997 of Mauritius, s.2(1). See Appendix 2 below.
[44] [1916] 2 Ch. 601, 608–609.
[45] Quoted in full above at para.3–010.
[46] See for example UK (*e.g.* Laddie, Prescott & Vitoria, *et al.* (3rd ed.), 3.60); and Australia (*Copyright and Designs* (Butterworths Australia, Lahore [6085])).
[47] [1944] A.C. 329, 340 *per* Lord Porter.

confers on the created object a specific aspect". Other courts have referred to the "imprint of the personality of the author", "personal imprint", "reflection of the personality of the author" and "imprint of creative personal talent."[48]

In considering computer programs, in *Babolat v Pachot*[49] it was held that "intellectual contribution" rather than the mark of the author's personality was sufficient to establish originality. There is a modern trend in civil law jurisdictions, especially France, towards accepting the standard of "intellectual contribution" for certain works—particularly when considering technical subject matter such as computer programs.[50] Strictly speaking, this is a move away from the underlying philosophy of the "author's right" but is illustrative of the pragmatic approach of many courts when considering commercial issues.

### Originality in photographs

3–106    Similar matters (choices of the photographer as to angle, light, etc.) to those considered in the common law countries are considered when seeking to establish originality in the civil law jurisdictions. The following indicia have been used to determine originality: choosing and arrangement of the subject; camera angle; perspective; lighting; type of film, speed and lens aperture; and originality may also derive from the developing procedure and photomontage.[51] In an Austrian case, photographs of chimneys were held to be original due to their perspective, use of lenses and use of light.[52]

Although, in theory, only creative photographs reflecting the personality of the author should be protected by author's rights, there are a number of court decisions inconsistent with this approach where copyright has been granted for a bare record of a scene. In 1908, the French courts granted copyright protection to photographs taken by Amundsen at the South Pole which were unartistic but of commercial value due to the difficulty in obtaining them.[53] Conversely, protection has been denied in some cases where it would be expected under civil law principles.

3–107    In a Spanish case *Cristina B v José AM*[54] a professional model wanted to prepare a portfolio of her work and engaged a photographer to take photographs of her. The photographer then sold his reproduction rights in one of the photographs to a publisher to be used on a book cover. The model sued the photographer, book cover designer and the publisher The case was predominantly concerned with infringement of privacy and right to image. However, rather bizarrely, the court held that the photograph was not

---

[48] Sterling, *op cit.*, p.255.
[49] (1986) 129 R.I.D.A. 130.
[50] Sterling, *op cit.*, at 7.11.
[51] L., Gimeno, *Photographs, Commercial Exploitation of the Image and Copyright in Spain* [1998] Ent. L.R. 131, 136.
[52] [1999] Ent. L.R. N-1.
[53] *Amundsen v Juven* Civil Tribunal, Seine, November 28, 1908, affirmed by the Court of Appeal, Paris, November 5, 1908, cited in Ricketson (1987), *op. cit*, at 6.39 n.179.
[54] Decision of the Supreme Court of Spain, March 29, 1996 [1998] Ent. L.R. 131.

original as the photograph was not "the product of the photographers" mind and lacked:

"a personal character that transcends the mere reproduction of a beautiful person since the satisfaction here comes from there and not from the photograph itself nor from the merely reproductive labour of the photographer that fixes by chemical means the image".[55]

This decision has been criticised on the basis that it was based on the artistic quality of the photograph. Gimeno comments; "It is clear the court is trying to protect the image of the model but . . . it did not need to deny the existence of the copyright to protect the right to commercial exploitation of the image".[56]

This case is an illustration of both the inconsistency in civil law approaches to originality and the difference between the common law and civil law approaches. Given that choices by the photographer as listed above have been found sufficient in civil law jurisdictions to found originality, it seems inconceivable that a photographer taking portfolio pictures of a model, however beautiful, would not meet this criteria. It is clear from the common law cases, that it is relatively easy to establish originality in photographic portrait cases.[57] Again it is inconceivable that portfolio photographs of a model would be held to be unoriginal in common law countries. **3–108**

In a German case before the Higher Regional Court of Hamburg[58] a photograph was taken of a theatre production in Frankfurt am Main by a well-known theatre photographer. The photograph showed an actress wearing a crown with a tense expression on her face. The alleged infringer had recreated the scene using a model. The court classified the photograph as a photographic work (rather than a non-creative photograph protected only by related rights). The criteria for classification of a work were held to be the following, amongst others: the choice of theme; an unusual detail or an usual perspective; the distribution of light and shade; the contrasting, and the sharpness of the picture. **3–109**

The assessment of the individuality of the photograph was problematic in so far as the whole effect rested on the photograph's actress's performance. It was held that the subsequent photograph was a free use merely inspired by a model. The defendant had not used the theatre photographer's protected input—to do so he would have to have used the photograph itself as a model. Taken alone, the fact that the same scene had been used was irrelevant from a copyright viewpoint. The subject of a photographic work was not protected in principle. Only when the subject of the original work was

[55] Quoted in Gimeno [1998] Ent. L.R. at 136.
[56] *ibid.*, at 137.
[57] See for example *Burrow-Giles Lithographic Co v Sarony* 111 US 53 (portrait of Oscar Wilde); *Rogers v Koons* 751 F. Supp. 474 (couple with puppies); *Nottage v Jackson* (1883) 11 Q.B.D. 637 (copyright subsisted in photograph of the Australian cricket team); *Melville v Mirror of Life* [1895] 2 Ch. 531 (portrait of athlete).
[58] Cited in A., Dietz, *Copyright Law Developments in Germany From 1993 to Mid-1997* (1998) 175 R.I.D.A. 96, 190.

based on an artistic arrangement by the photographer and enjoyed copyright protection in its own right was it relevant for copyright purposes.

3–110    This case has elements in common with cases such as the "floating baby" case referred to above where an idea is not protectable. However, reconstruction of photographs by third parties has been held to be an infringement in many common law cases.[59] The arrangement of humans into various poses has in common law jurisdictions an element of a photograph sufficiently original to lead to an infringement claim if copied.[60] Arguably those cases can be distinguished, as here the pose was the work of the actress rather than the photographer. Posing the subject by a photographer has been held under civil law to be an element indicating originality in some cases[61] whereas copying of a typical posture of a model from a painting was held not lead to a finding of infringement.[62] However, it is submitted that in common law jurisdictions, theatre photography of actors performing would be infringed if recreation was attempted, even where the key element was the attitude of the actors where not controlled by the photographer. The originality and skill would, it is contended, lie in the angle of the photograph and the choice of when to take it at a minimum.

*Photographing of an event over which the photographer has no control*

3–111    In *R. Cauchetier v Les Cahiers du Cinéma*[63] it was held that a set photographer who was required to take photographs of scenes from a film was not a creator of an original work. The photographer's role was tied to the scene being shot which was determined by the director and the actors. The court considered that the task of the photographer did not reflect any creativity which bore the stamp of his personality, even if his name appeared in the credits of the film. The photographs could not be regarded as copyrightable intellectual works.

However, photographs of the film being shot where the photographer was not subject to any express instructions were capable of being original. The photographer was free to express his personality through the choice of situations and the determination of the characteristics of the lenses, angles, centring and lighting.

It is submitted that under the common law, even photographs by a set photographer are likely to attract copyright for the reasons discussed above as to the low level of creativity required. If, as a number of the common law texts suggest, merely pressing the shutter is enough, set photography requires considerably more skill.

3–112    In *Fédération française de Gymnastique v Cottret*[64] (1994) the Paris Court of Appeal held that copyright subsisted in photographs taken at athletic

---

[59] *e.g. Gross v Seligman* 212 F. 930 (2nd Cir. 1914) and *Ateliers Tango Argentin v Festival D'Espagne et D'Amerique* (1997) 84 C.P.R. (3d) 56.

[60] Compare *Gross v Seligman* 212 F. 930 (2nd Cir. 1914) and *Ateliers Tango Argentin v Festival D'Espagne et D'Amerique* (1997) 84 C.P.R. (3d) 56 discussed above at para.3–014.

[61] *Sté Arkadia v Jean Pierre Laloir* (France—photograph of Maria Callas) 180 R.I.D.A. 280.

[62] The German *Power of Blue* case OLG (Court of Appeal) Hamburg, October 12, 1995, cited in Sterling at 6.70, p.236.

[63] Paris *Tribunal de grande instance* June 18, 1997 (3rd chamber) 174 R.I.D.A. 180.

[64] 164 R.I.D.A. 244.

competitions. Although the photographed scenes were "without any true originality", the choice of angles of the shots, the lighting and the centring bore the mark of the author's personality and talent "conferring on the photographs an original character which makes them copyrightable works within the meaning of the law."

### Photographs of works of art

In Belgium it was held that a photograph of a work of art was not    **3–113**
protected by author's rights. It was held that to receive protection, a work should be an expression of its author's intellectual effort. The photograph was "simply the image of a work of art" and "had clearly been reproduced exclusively for information purposes".[65]

This decision accords broadly with the approach in *Bridgeman* but not that in either *SHL Imaging Inc v Artisan House*[66] or *Antiquesportfolio.com v Rodney Fitch*.[67] It is another example of the divergence and inconsistency between the common law and civil law jurisdictions in the assessment of the necessary originality.

By contrast, in the *Beuys-Fotografien* case in Germany, photographs of 3-D works and portraits of the artist Beuys were recognised as being protected photographic works under German law. The court considered that the degree of originality required for photographic works should not be set too low given the substantial 50 year protection which already exists for simple photographs.[68]

### OBSERVATIONS ON CASE LAW

It has been observed that although the approaches to originality under the    **3–114**
common law and civil law systems are different, the result will often be the same (other than in the "directory" cases).[69] This is generally true. However, the particular difficulty in ascertaining what constitutes originality in photographic works has led to a tangle of inconsistent case law—inconsistent both between the two systems and internal inconsistency within the two systems themselves.

It is right that a few common principles can be distilled. In both the common law and civil jurisdictions, matters of choice of the photographer are used to determine originality such as the angle of photography, choice of film and camera, lighting, etc. In both systems, there is internally conflicting

---

[65] Cass December 10, 1998, confirming Antwerp January 31, 1995; AM 1999/3 335 cited in J. Corbet, *Five Years Later: A First Assessment of the New Belgian Law on Author's Rights* (Jan. 200) 183 R.I.D.A. 200 at 212–214.

[66] 117 F. Supp. 2d 301 (S.D.N.Y. 2000).

[67] [2001] F.S.R. 23.

[68] Cited in A., Dietz, *Copyright Law Developments in Germany From 1993 to Mid-1997* 175 R.I.D.A. 96, 194.

[69] Sterling (1998), *op. cit.*, at 1.15, p.17.

case law as to whether a photograph of a work of art attracts copyright. This is obviously an area that causes particular difficultly.

However, there continue to be decisions that fail to fit properly into the originality mould of the system considered. The French protection of the *Amundsen* pole photographs which were properly "unoriginal" but were protected as a matter of practicality because they had a commercial value is a classic example. The *Cristina B* case where no copyright was held to subsist in portfolio photographs of a model is equally mystifying and totally contrary to civil law principles.

**3–115**    Almost every case that establishes originality in a particular type of photograph can be matched with one from the other legal system that holds the opposite. Just by way of illustration compare *Cristina B*[70] with *Burrow-Giles*[71] and *Melville v Mirror of Life*[72]; and the Belgian "works of art case"[73] with *SHL Imaging* and *Antiquesportfolio*.[73a] It is also possible to undertake the same exercise with some success within the respective systems. Again, by way of example, compare *Bridgeman* with *SHL Imaging* and *Antiquesportfolio*; the Belgian "works of art" case with the German *Beuys-Fotografien* case.[74]

We can conclude therefore that there remains a serious inconsistency in approach to originality in photographs. This goes beyond the odd "rogue" decision that is reasonably to be expected in most areas of case law. These cases show a much greater degree of inconsistency as to the level of originality necessary.

## THE FUTURE: THE PROSPECT OF FURTHER HARMONISATION

**3–116**    It is clear that there are varying standards of originality in photographs in both national legislation and in decisions of national courts. It seems inevitable that at some point in the future there will be attempts to harmonise these differences.

**3–117**    The first question is—is further harmonisation necessary or indeed desirable? It is submitted that it is, even if only to address the related rights problem. The inconsistency in approach between jurisdictions and the varying decisions of the courts would be assisted by some additional degree of harmonisation. It is inevitable that due to the nature of the subject matter, the issue of where the cut off point for originality should be in any given case will always be difficult. However, it is apparent that the existing international treaties with the "intellectual creation" standard have not resulted in any significant unanimity in the approach to the treatment of photographs by national jurisdictions. Although this may in part be due to

---

[70] See above at para. 3–107.
[71] See above at para. 3–013.
[72] See above at para. 2–053, n.80.
[73] See above at para. 3–113.
[73a] See above at paras 3–044 to 3–047.
[74] See above at para. 3–113.

the fact that some countries, for example the United Kingdom, do not truly apply this standard. Karnell points out, in a European context, that whilst national courts continue not to look at or even refer to case law as it develops in neighbouring countries this will perpetuate the lack of harmonisation of originality.[75]

It is apparent that the existence of related rights protection for non-original photographs in some jurisdictions but not others leaves gaps in the international protection of photographs. This results in some photographs without protection in some jurisdictions where national photographs would be protected—as in the *Beatles* case discussed above.[76] Irrespective of whether one contends non-original photographs should or should not be protected as a matter of principle, it remains true that the present system is unsatisfactory in its lack of uniformity and leads to uncertainty. Harmonisation in principle is desirable but whether it should be in support of non-original photographs receiving protection or contra is another matter entirely. It is the "related rights" aspect of photographic protection that remains one of the biggest differences of approach to photographs in the international arena.

The United States decision in *Feist*[77] is of considerable importance as far **3–118** as the question of future international harmonisation in originality is concerned. As discussed above, the United States previously had applied a "sweat of the brow" doctrine but has moved with the "modicum of creativity" closer to the civil law. This is a considerable step in closing the gaps between the common law and civil law approaches to originality. Already references in international and European legislation to "intellectual creation" reflect the civil law approach. The significance of the fact that the United States, a major producer of intellectual property, has in recent court decisions moved away from the traditional common law approach to originality, should not be underestimated.

The real difficulties in harmonisation will arise in addressing those countries that protect the "non-original" photograph by a related right. They are few in number which may prima facie suggest that ultimately weight of numbers will lead to the abandonment of a related right protection for non-original photographs. However, such countries include Germany which historically has been a powerful influence in international and particularly European law. Ultimately, this will require an international view as to whether such photographs are deserving of protection at all.

As with all copyright works, protection of photographic images involves a **3–119** number of competing and conflicting interests. On the one hand there is the right of the photographer to his work and its commercial value and the classic societal interests in all copyright law—the promotion of creativity and investment, etc.[78] On the other, there are a number of competing

---

[75] G.W.G., Karnell, *European Originality: A Copyright Chimera* in J.J.C. Kabel, and G. Mom, (eds) *Intellectual Property and Information Law* (Kluwer Law International, 1998) 201 at 209.
[76] Above at para. 3–056.
[77] Above at para. 3–075, n.51.
[78] For a discussion of traditional justifications for copyright law see Sterling (1998) *op. cit.*, at 2.27 *et seq.*

interests—the interest of the public in access to public domain works and photographic news images; rights of property owners in their property; privacy rights; and rights in image to name a few. Protection of photographs of works of public domain art works is particularly controversial. Some commentators argue that to protect such photographs results in galleries and other owners attaining a "de facto perpetual monopoly over the commercial reproduction of publicly owned works of art."[79] Nimmer suggests that the public interest in free speech and news photography could be addressed by a compulsory licencing approach to such photographs.[80] These are serious issues and it remains to be seen what views will be reached in the international arena as to the precise extent to which photographs should be protected.

It should be noted that the United States would face difficulties in protecting non-original photographs as the copyright clause[81] in the Constitution is considered to permit only protection of original works of authorship, as was held in *Feist*.[81a] This is not necessarily an insurmountable problem as the proposed Bill for the protection of databases shows. Due to the Constitutional issues of protecting works lacking originality, a misappropriation model based on the Commerce Clause[82] of the Constitution forms the basis of the proposed Bill.

In addition, several of the countries that apply a related right to photographs, require various formalities before such protection is granted. This too is likely to provide a problem in so far as harmonisation is concerned.

There are other concerns presently at the forefront of international and European intellectual property debate. Eventually, the problems presented by works of photography will fall to be further considered. The international path to be chosen, particularly with respect to related rights, remains to be seen.

## CONCLUSIONS

**3–120**   The two main areas of conflict in the protection of photographs by copyright internationally are first, the different approaches of the common and civil law systems generally and secondly, the division between countries that offer a related rights protection and those that do not.

There has been some attempt both in international and European legislation to address these divisions. Progress has been made but it has been

---

[79] R., Deazley, *Photographing Paintings in the Public Domain: A Response to Garnett* [2001] E.I.P.R. 179, 183. See also Connolly K., Butler, *Keeping the World Safe from Naked-Chicks-in-Art Refrigerator Magnets: The Plot to Control Art Images in the Public Domain through Copyrights in Photographic and Digital Reproductions* (Fall, 1998) 21 Hastings Comm. & Ent. L.J. 55.

[80] Nimmer para. 1.10[C][2].

[81] U.S. Const. Art.I, sec. 8, cl.8—"The Congress shall have the power to promote the progress of science and useful arts by securing for a limited time to authors and inventors the exclusive right to their respective writings and creations."

[81a] See above at para. 3–075, n.51.

[82] US Const. Art.I, sec.8, cl.3.

hampered by strong views of different countries as to the extent to which the "mechanical" nature of photographs deserves protection. This is illustrated by the history of the inclusion of photographic works in the Berne Convention.

There is a certain level of harmonisation at an international and European level in form—in the application of the "intellectual creation" standard. Practically, however, this has not resulted in harmonisation in the case law. As long as countries continue to be inward looking as to case law, this is likely to continue. It is difficult to see how further unity of approach can be achieved through international legislation as there is already an international standard test. It may be that the inconsistency in the case law will long continue due to the nature of the photographic work. The existence of digital photography is likely to further blur the boundaries of originality as creativity in digital manipulation is now possible. As was said in *Cramp v Smythson* when considering questions of originality, "Different minds will differ".[83]

The issue of related rights protection remains outstanding and needs to be resolved. It is highly unsatisfactory that a photograph may be protected in one country but not in another to the degree that presently exists. It is likely that with the passage of time this will be addressed, at the very least in the European Union,[84] if not internationally.

The opening remark of Chapter 2 was "Photographic works present a challenge for the law of copyright". The peculiar hybrid nature of a photograph as partly a mechanical and chemical reproduction, but partly the work of an author makes assessing the necessary element of originality extremely difficult. Valiant attempts in international and European law have been made in an effort to meet the challenge that photographic works pose. However, there remains gross inconsistency in the case law and a total failure to address properly the anomalies created by the lack of an international position on related rights. It is submitted therefore that despite making a valiant attempt, copyright law has not met the challenge—yet.

**3–121**

---

[83] [1944] A.C. 329 at 340 *per* Lord Porter.
[84] See above at paras 3–100 to 3–101.

# Chapter 4

# Moral rights

## Introduction

**4–001**     "Moral rights" is the name given to a bundle of rights, separate from copyright, that vest in the author of a work. Moral rights were really first introduced in to the United Kingdom in 1989 when the Copyright Designs and Patents Act 1988 came into force. Prior to that the Copyright Act 1956, s.43 had only provided for the prohibition of false attribution of authorship. The moral rights provided for in the 1988 Act are:

- the right to be identified as the author of a work (the right of paternity);

- the right to object to derogatory treatment of the work (the right of integrity);

- the right not to have a work falsely attributed to a person as author;

- the right to privacy of certain photographs and films.

Other jurisdictions (most notably civil law jurisdictions) grant other more extensive moral rights to authors which the UK does not, including the right of retraction or withdrawal of the work[1]; the right of divulging (publishing) the work.[2]

Moral rights originated in civil law jurisdictions and has traditionally been an area of conflict in international law between the common law and civil law jurisdictions. In civil law jurisdictions, the emphasis is more upon the need for copyright/moral rights as a human right—to protect the work as part of the extension of the author's personality. In the common law jurisdictions, justifications for copyright tend to focus on economic arguments and moral rights have been of little importance.   **4–002**

By Art.6 *bis* of the Berne Convention, member countries are required to provide that authors have the right to claim authorship of their works and the right to object to "any distortion, mutilation or other modification of, or other derogatory action" in relation to the work which would be prejudicial to the honour or reputation of the author.   **4–003**
Article 6 *bis*

> "1.   Independently of the author's economic rights, and even after the transfer of the said rights, the author shall have the right to claim authorship of the work and to object to any distortion, mutilation or other modification of, or other derogatory action in relation to, the said work, which would be prejudicial to his honour or reputation.
>
> 2.   The rights granted to the author in accordance with the preceding paragraph shall, after his death, be maintained, at least until the expiry of the economic rights, and shall be exercisable by the persons or institutions authorized by the legislation of the country where protection is claimed. However, those countries whose legislation, at the moment of their ratification of or accession to this Act, does not provide for the protection after the death of the author of all the rights set out in the preceding paragraph may provide that some of these rights may, after his death, cease to be maintained.
>
> 3.   The means of redress for safeguarding the rights granted by this Article shall be governed by the legislation of the country where protection is claimed."

Traditionally, moral rights have been objected to by common law countries because the overriding justification for copyright from a common law perspective is economic. Requiring commercial entities dealing with works to identify the author and so forth is a fetter on the economic use of copyright. The United States was particularly opposed to moral rights and Art.6 *bis* was one of the main reasons why it took such a long time to join the Berne Convention. Article 6 *bis* and moral rights are excluded from the TRIPS Agreement.[3]   **4–004**

---

[1] France—see French Intellectual Property Code of 1992, Art.L.121–4.
[2] *ibid.*, France, Art.L.121–2.
[3] World Trade Organisation *Agreement on Trade-Related Aspects of Intellectual Property Rights, including trade in counterfeit goods* ("TRIPS' Agreement"), Art.9(1).

Moral rights apply to all artistic works including photographs. In addition, photographs attract a particular right of privacy.

## Photographs taken before August 1, 1989

**4–005**   Authors of works that came into existence prior to August 1, 1989, do, in theory, have moral rights in respect of those works but the practical effect of these rights is very limited by the following statutory restrictions:

- No act done before commencement is actionable by virtue of any of the moral rights provisions.[4] It should be noted that 1956 Act prohibition against false attribution of authorship does continue to apply in relation to acts done before commencement.[5]

- The rights of paternity and integrity do not apply to photographs (nor indeed to any literary, dramatic, musical or artistic works) where the author died before commencement.[6]

- The rights of paternity and integrity do not apply in relation to literary, dramatic, musical or artistic works created before August 1, 1989, including photographs taken before August 1, 1989:

    (a) (where copyright first vested in the author) to anything which would not infringe copyright by virtue of an assignment of copyright made or licence granted before commencement[7];
    (b) (where copyright first vested in a person other than the author) to anything done by or with the licence of the copyright owner.[8]

- The right conferred by s.85 (right to privacy of certain photographs and films) does not apply to photographs taken before August 1, 1989.[9]

## The right of paternity

**4–006**   The right of paternity (the right to be identified as the author of a work) only exists in relation to a *copyright* work.[10] In the case of photographs where there may be argument as to whether a photograph is in fact sufficiently "original" to attract copyright,[11] it will be necessary to establish that the photograph is a copyright work before claiming any moral rights. The

---

[4] CDPA 1988, Sch.1, para.22(1).
[5] CDPA 1988, Sch.1, para.22(2).
[6] CDPA 1988, Sch.1, paras 23(1) and 23(2)(a).
[7] CDPA 1988, Sch.1, para.23(3)(a).
[8] CDPA 1988, Sch.1, para.23(3)(b).
[9] CDPA 1988, Sch.1, para.24.
[10] CDPA 1988, s.77(1).
[11] See generally Ch.3 above.

circumstances in which an author is entitled to the right varies according to the type of work in question.[12]

The author of a photograph has the right to be identified as the author of the work whenever the photograph is:

(a) published commercially or exhibited in public or a visual image of it is communicated to the public[13];

(b) a film including a visual image of the work is shown in public or copies of such a film are issued to the public.[14]

In addition, if a photograph of a work of architecture in the form of a building or a model for a building, a sculpture or a work of artistic craftsmanship is issued to the public, the author of the work depicted has the right to be identified as the author of that depicted work.[14a]

The right of paternity applies to the whole work and to any substantial part of the work.[15]

In relation to including a visual image of a photograph in a broadcast or   **4–007** film, it is important to appreciate that the right of paternity is not infringed by any act which would not infringe copyright by virtue of the incidental inclusion provisions in s.31 of the Copyright Designs and Patents Act 1988—see further below under exceptions.[16] The exception for incidental inclusion restricts the moral rights protection available for photographs included in the background of films or broadcasts.

## Extent of right to be identified as author

In the case of commercial publication of a work, the right of the author is   **4–008** to be identified in or on each copy or, if that is not appropriate, in some other manner likely to bring his identity to the notice of a person acquiring a copy.[17] The identification must be clear and reasonably prominent.[18] Commercial publication is defined in relation to an artistic works as "issuing copies to the public[19] at a time when copies made in advance of the receipt of orders are generally available to the public", or making the work available to the public by means of an electronic retrieval system.[20]

---

[12] CDPA 1988, s.77(2)—literary works other than lyrics; CDPA 1988, s.77(3)—musical works and literary works being lyrics; CDPA 1988, s.77(4)—artistic works.
[13] CDPA 1988, s.77(1) and (4)(a), as amended from October 31, 2003 by the Copyright and Related Rights Regulations 2003 (SI 2003/2498), reg. 2(1), Sch 1, Pt 1, paras 1 and 8(2)(a) replacing words "broadcast or include in a cable programme service" with "communicated to the public". As to the meaning of communication to the public see above at para. 2–153.
[14] CDPA 1988, s.77(1) and (4)(b).
[14a] CDPA 1988, s.77(1) and (4)(c).
[15] s.89(1).
[16] See below at para. 4–014.
[17] CDPA 1988 s.77(7)(a).
[18] Final words of CDPA 1988, s.77(7).
[19] For definition of issuing copies to the public see above at para. 2–150.
[20] CDPA 1988 s.175(2).

In any other case, the right of the author is to be identified in a manner likely to bring his identity to the attention of a person seeing or hearing the performance, exhibition, showing, broadcast, or cable programme in question.[21] Again, the identification must be clear and reasonably prominent.[22]

Unless the author, in asserting his right, specifies a pseudonym or other particular form of identification, any reasonable form of identification may be used.[23] If the author has asserted a particular form of identification then that form shall be used.[24]

### Right of paternity needs to be asserted

**4–009**    The right to be identified as an author of a work is not infringed unless the right has been asserted in accordance with s.78 of the CDPA 1988.[25]

The right can be asserted generally or in relation to any specified act or description of acts.[26] There are a number of ways specified in the statute by which the right to be identified as an author can be asserted:

1.  By expressly including in a written assignment of copyright in a work a statement that the author asserts his right to be identified in relation to that work.[27] On the face of the statute, all that is required is assertion in any assignment of copyright. The statute does not specify this is limited to the first assignment or even that the author has to be a party to the assignment.

2.  By an instrument in writing signed by the author.[28]

3.  In relation to public exhibition of an artistic work (which would include a photograph) the right may be asserted by:

    (a)  securing that when the author or other first owner of copyright parts with possession of the original, or of a copy made by him or under his direction or control, the author is identified on the original or copy, or on a frame, mount or other thing to which it is attached[29]; a signature or other form of identification would suffice, or

    (b)  including in a licence by which the author or other first owner of copyright authorises the making of copies of the work, a statement signed by or on behalf of the person granting the licence that the author asserts his right to be identified in the event of

---

[21] CDPA 1988, s.77(7)(c).
[22] Final words of CDPA 1988, s.77(7).
[23] CDPA 1988, s.77(8).
[24] *ibid.*
[25] CDPA 1988, s.77(1) and 78(1).
[26] CDPA 1988, s.78(2).
[27] CDPA 1988, s.78(2)(a).
[28] CDPA 1988, s.78(2)(b).
[29] CDPA 1988, s.78(3)(a).

the public exhibition of a copy made in pursuance of the licence.[30]

## Joint authors

Where there are joint authors of the work, a right of each joint author **4–010** must be asserted in one of the ways set out above by each joint author in relation to himself.[31]

## Right of paternity: illustrative cases

There is a paucity of case law in the UK concerning moral rights, prob- **4–011** ably illustrative of the traditional common law suspicion of moral rights and the view that they are an aberrant outshoot from the civil law systems. Some assistance may be derived from cases from other jurisdictions. The following have been held to be infringements of the right to be identified as the author of a work:

- Substituting "prepared by" instead of "written by" on a university case study paper downgraded the author by suggesting he was something less than the author.[32]

- Displaying a work that is a copyright infringement bearing the name of the infringer.[33] Copyright in a photograph was infringed by re-creating the poses of models and re-shooting the image. It was held that the display of the copyright infringing re-created photograph credited with the name of the second photographer and without the original author's name amounted to infringement of the author's right to be identified. It was said that "the photographer's right to recognition of his highly original work was held up to ridicule in a gross and flagrant manner."[34]

- Where an artist produced a graphic work for an advertisement on commission and his name was not included on the poster reproducing it.[35] The German Court of Appeals observed that the name of the artist did not need to appear in larger or more prominent type than was necessary in order to identify him. In a similar French case, it was

---

[30] CDPA 1988, s.78(3)(b).
[31] CDPA 1988, s.88(1).
[32] *Dolmage v Erskine* 23 C.P.R. (4th) 495 (Ont. Superior Court, Small Claims Court).
[33] *Ateliers Tango Argentin Inc v Festival d'Espagne & d'Amerique Latine Inc* (1997) 84 C.P.R. (3d) 56.
[34] *Ateliers Tango Argentin Inc v Festival d'Espagne & d'Amerique Latine Inc* (1997) 84 C.P.R. (3d) 56 at 81.
[35] *Oberlandesgericht Munich* (July 3, 1967) G.R.U.R. 1969; U.F.I.T.A. Bd. 57 S. 327 (1970) Court of Appeals. Cited in M.B. Nimmer and M.E. Price, *Moral Rights & Beyond: Considerations for the College Art Association.* Appendix B in *Occasional Papers In Intellectual Property* from Benjamin N. Cardozo School of Law, Yeshiva University, Number 3, *Resuscitating A Collaboration With Melville Nimmer: Moral Rights and Beyond.* Available on line at *http://www.cardozo.yu.edu/ip_program/papers/3.pdf* (hereafter "Nimmer & Price").

held that if the artist's signature was legible on the original, it must be legible on any reproduction of the work.[36]

- Where a collage intended for use on a full size poster was reproduced on a stamp without the artist's consent. The artist's signature was clearly visible on the original but on the stamp was "difficult if not impossible" to read.[37]

- Where photographs taken by photographers for the magazine *Paris Match* were used as the background for opening title sequences of a film and the photographers were not credited.[38] The court stated that the doctrine of moral rights required that it was necessary to indicate the name of each photographer in connection with his photograph or at the very least as part of the listing of other credits even if not juxtaposed with the photographs.

- Where a number of photographs of paintings were published in a book about the artist and there was only one mention of the photographers name.[39] It was held by the French court that the photographer's name must appear in juxtaposition with each of his photographs. Merely mentioning somewhere in the book that a number of photographs have been taken by the photographer was not sufficient. It should be noted that moral rights only apply to *copyright* works (*i.e.* original works). As discussed in Chapter 3, it is debatable whether photographs designed to accurately reproduce paintings are works in which copyright subsists.[40] In another French case, a photographer complained of moral rights infringement in respect of photographs of paintings and works of art reproduced without his consent and uncredited. The photographer failed on the basis that the photographs were documentary in nature and failed to evince either originality or creativity.[41]

**4-012** The following are cases where there was no violation of the right of paternity:

- No violation of the right of paternity was found where a number of photographs were reproduced where the photographer's name was not mentioned on or next to the photographs but the context made it

---

[36] *Tribunal de Grande Instance de la Seine* (December 19, 1961) (Court of First Instance) (1962) R.I.D.A. XXXV p.122. cited in Nimmer & Price, *op. cit.*
[37] *Echaurren Faranda v Italian Post Office* [2001] E.C.D.R. 14 Trib. (Rome). For facts see below at para.4–026.
[38] *Tribunal de Grande Instance de Paris* (December 13, 1966) (Court of First Instance) D.1969, 702 cited in Nimmer & Price, *op. cit.*
[39] *Tribunal de Grande Instance de Paris* (July 9, 1971) (Court of First Instance) D.1972 Somm. 84 cited in Nimmer & Price, *op. cit.*
[40] See above at paras 3–038 to 3–047 and 3–113.
[41] *Cours d'Amiens* (May 27, 1969) (Intermediate Appellate Court) R.T.D.C. 1969, 985 cited in Nimmer & Price, *op. cit.*

clear he was the photographer.[42] The photographs were accompanied by an article the text of which made clear that the photographer was the author of the photographs. The court inferred that readers could determine precisely that the photographer was the author.

- No violation of the right of paternity was found where extracts from works of the composer Rachmaninoff were used in the soundtrack of the film about a pianist who performed some of Rachmaninoff's works during his career.[43] His heirs contended that Rachmaninoff's name should have received the same treatment as that of the composer of the film music and given equal rank on the posters, cover of the video and in the film's opening credits. Rachmaninoff's name and the exact list of his works played in the film appeared in the closing credits. The court considered the references given to the name were adequate as only 11 minutes and 31 seconds of the total film comprising performances of Rachmaninoff's work out of a duration of 74 minutes and 24 seconds and this did not confer co-authorship. There was no possibility of confusion among members of the public between the works of Rachmaninoff and the music specially created for the film.

### Exceptions to the right of paternity relevant to photographs[44]

#### Employers

Where copyright originally vested in the author's employer[45] because the work was produced during the course of the author's employment, the right does not apply to anything done by the copyright owner or with the authority of the copyright owner.[46] This means that there is no right of paternity in respect of photographs taken by employed photo-journalists or other photographs taken by employees in the course of their employment.

Similarly, where the copyright vested in a film director's employer,[47] the right does not apply to anything done by the copyright owner or with the authority of the copyright owner.[48]

4–013

#### Acts which are non-infringing under the CDPA 1988

Certain acts that are permitted by the CDPA 1988 and do not infringe copyright are deemed not to infringe the right of paternity.[49] These are:

4–014

---

[42] *Arthus-Bétrand v Sté Panorama du Médecin* TGI Paris, July 6, 2001; (2002) 191 R.I.D.A. 196 at 198.
[43] CA Paris A. *Consus Rachmaninoff v Gaumount* June 12, 2002; (2003) 196 R.I.D.A. 284.
[44] There are other exceptions not referred to here, *e.g.* the right does not apply to computer program or typeface designs: see CDPA 1988, s.79 generally.
[45] By virtue of CDPA 1988, s.11(2).
[46] CDPA 1988, s.79(3)(a).
[47] CDPA 1988, s.9(2).
[48] CDPA 1988, s.79(3)(b).
[49] CDPA 1988, s.79(4).

(1) fair dealing so far as it relates to the reporting of current events by means of a sound recording, film, broadcast or cable programme[50];

(2) incidental inclusion of the work in an artistic work, sound recording, film, broadcast or cable programme[51];

(3) anything done for the purposes of setting examinations, communicating the questions to the candidates or by answering the question[52];

(4) anything done for the purpose of parliamentary or judicial proceedings or reporting such proceedings[53];

(5) anything done for the purposes of Royal Commission or statutory inquiry[54];

(6) making an article to the design of a design document or model[55];

(7) copying an artistic work by making articles by an industrial process or marketing them after the end of 25 years after the end of the calendar year in which such articles were first marketed[56];

(8) cases where acts are permitted in relation to anonymous or pseudonymous works.[57]

### Reporting current events

**4–015**    The right of paternity does not apply to any work made for the purposes of reporting current events.[58] This is a further restriction likely to affect photographers—in addition to the following restriction regarding newspaper and magazines.

### Newspapers, magazines and other collective works

**4–016**    The right to be identified as an author of a work does not apply in relation to the publication in a newspaper, magazine or similar periodical or an

---

[50] CDPA 1988, s.79(4)(a). Fair dealing within the meaning of CDPA 1988, s.30 as to which see above at paras 2–159 *et seq.*
[51] CDPA 1988, s.79(4)(b). Incidental inclusion within the meaning of CDPA 1988, s.31 as to which see above at para. 2–168 and below at para. 5–054.
[52] CDPA 1988, s.79(4)(c). Things done for the purpose of instruction with the meaning of CDPA 1988, s.32(3) as to which see above at para. 2–169.
[53] CDPA 1988, s.79(4)(d). Parliamentary and judicial proceedings: CDPA 1988, s.45, as to which see above at para. 2–171.
[54] CDPA 1988, s.79(4)(e). Within the meaning of CDPA 1988, s.46, as to which see above at para. 2–171.
[55] CDPA 1988, s.79(4)(f). Within the meaning of CDPA 1988, s.51 as to which see above at para. 2–177.
[56] CDPA 1988, s.79(4)(g). See CDPA 1988, s.52 and above at para. 2–178.
[57] CDPA 1988, s.79(4)(h). Within the meanings of CDPA 1988, ss.57 and 66A, as to which see above at para. 2–181.
[58] CDPA 1988, s.79(5). As to meaning of reporting current events, see discussion in cases about fair dealing under CDPA 1988, s.30, *e.g. Hyde Park Residence Ltd v Yelland* [2001] Ch. 143; [2000] 3 W.L.R. 215; *Newspaper Licensing Agency Ltd v Marks & Spencer Plc* [1999] E.C.C. 425; [1999] E.M.L.R. 369; [1999] R.P.C. 536; *Pro Sieben Media AG v Carlton UK Television Ltd* [1999] 1 W.L.R. 605; [2000] E.C.D.R. 110; [1999] E.M.L.R. 109.

encyclopaedia, dictionary, yearbook or other collective work of reference of literary, dramatic, musical or artistic work made for the purpose of such a publication or made available with the consent of the author for the purposes of such a publication.[59]

A collective work is a work of joint authorship or a work in which there are distinct contributions by different authors or in which works or parts of works by different authors are incorporated.[60]

### Crown copyright

The right of paternity does not apply in relation to a work in which Crown copyright or Parliamentary copyright subsists, or where copyright vested in an International organisation[61] unless the author has previously been identified as such in or on published copies of the work.

**4–017**

### Existing works: photographs taken before August 1, 1989

See above at para.4–005.

**4–018**

### Consent and waiver

There is no infringement of the right where the person entitled to the right has consented to the act.[62] The right of paternity can be waived.[63]

**4–019**

## THE RIGHT OF INTEGRITY

The author of a copyright artistic work (including a photograph) has the right not to have his work subjected to derogatory treatment.[64] In the case of an artistic work, the right is infringed by:

**4–020**

(a) commercial publication[65] or exhibition in public, a derogatory treatment of the work, or broadcasting or including in a cable programme service a visual image of a derogatory treatment of the work[66];

(b) showing in public a film including a visual image of a derogatory treatment of the work or issuing copies to the public of such a film[67]; or

(c) where the work is a model of a building of work of architecture, a sculpture or a work of artistic craftsman ship, issuing to the public

---

[59] CDPA 1988, s.79(6).
[60] CDPA 1988, s.178.
[61] By virtue of CDPA 1988, s.168.
[62] CDPA 1988, s.87(1). See below at para. 4–058.
[63] CDPA 1988, s.87(2). See below at para. 4–058.
[64] CDPA 1988, s.80(1).
[65] For meaning of commercial publication see above at para. 4–008.
[66] CDPA 1988, s.80(4).
[67] CDPA 1988, s.80(4)(b).

copies of a graphic work representing, or of a photograph of, a derogatory treatment of the work.

The right of integrity applies to the whole of the work and to any part of it.[68] Unlike the right to be identified as the author, the right to object to derogatory treatment in respect of part of a work is not restricted to "any *substantial* part".

It also extends to works that have been altered/treated by someone other than the author where the work is attributed to or is likely to be regarded as the work of an author.[69] This would cover, for example, a photograph that had been cropped or touched up by a newspaper and published as the work of a particular photographer. Any derogatory treatment of that cropped photograph by a third party would amount to infringement of the photographer's right of integrity, notwithstanding what had been derogatorily treated was not the original unaltered work.

**4–021**    The 1988 Act provides for secondary infringement of the right of integrity. The right of integrity is also infringed by a person who possesses or deals with an article which he knows or has reason to believe is an infringing article. Anyone who

(a)  possesses in the course of a business;

(b)  sells or lets for hire, or offers or exposes for sale or hire;

(c)  in the course of a business exhibits in public or distributes;

(d)  distributes otherwise than in the course of a business so as to affect prejudicially the honour or reputation of the author or director;

an article which is, and which he knows or has reason to believe is, an infringing article will be in infringement of the right to object to derogatory treatment of the work.[70] An "infringing article" for these purposes is a work or a copy of a work which has been subjected to derogatory treatment within the meaning of s.80 and has been or is likely to be the subject of any of the acts mentioned in that section in circumstances infringing the right.[71]

## Treatment

**4–022**    Treatment means any addition to, deletion from, or alteration to, or adaptation of the work.[72] Any kind of change to a photograph is likely to be classed as treatment. Scaling down or reduction of image size amounts to

---

[68] CDPA 1988, s.89(1).
[69] CDPA 1988, s.80(7).
[70] CDPA 1988, s.83(1).
[71] CDPA 1988, s.83(2).
[72] CDPA 1988, s.80(2)(a).

treatment.[73] Taking short sections of music (10–65 seconds) and very slight alterations to lyrics of a song (one or two words altered) was held to amount to treatment.[74] The issue is more likely to be whether the treatment is derogatory.

The narrow definition of "treatment" excludes display of a work in a manner damaging to the author's reputation. So for example, displaying a photograph in an unflattering context would not be classed as treatment within the definition of the statute. This is narrower than the obligation imposed by Art.6 *bis* of the Berne Convention which covers any derogatory action in relation to the work which would be prejudicial to his honour or reputation. Changes of context have been held to be moral rights infringement in other jurisdictions such as unauthorised use of music for advertising[75] and use of music in connection with an anti-Soviet film.[76]

## Derogatory

Treatment is derogatory if it amounts to distortion or mutilation of the work or is otherwise prejudicial to the honour or reputation of the author or director.[77] On a literal reading, it is unclear whether proof of distortion and mutilation alone is sufficient or whether they are qualified by the words "prejudicial to the honour or reputation of the author". It has been held that there is a qualification and only distortion or mutilation that is prejudicial to the honour or reputation of the author would amount to derogatory treatment.[78] The mere fact that a work has been distorted or mutilated gives rise to no claim, unless the distortion or mutilation prejudices the author's honour or reputation.[79] This is an accordance with Art.6 *bis* of the Berne Convention which qualifies all acts by the words "prejudicial to his honour or reputation".     **4–023**

Evidence will be necessary as to the reputation of the photographer/ author and the effect of the infringing work on his reputation in the minds of others.[80] Although it has been suggested that whether something is prejudicial to the author's honour or reputation involves "a certain subjective     **4–024**

---

[73] Conceded in *Tidy v Trustees of the Natural History Museum* (1995) 39 I.P.R. 501; [1996] E.I.P.R. D-81. Reduction of cartoons of dinosaurs to approximately one sixth of original size.

[74] *Morrison Leahy Music Ltd v Lightbond Ltd* [1993] E.M.L.R. 144 at 151 *per* Morritt J. Application for interlocutory injunction.

[75] *EMI Music v Brel* CA Paris, June 25, 1996; (1997) 171 R.I.D.A. 337. See also *Farinelli and BMG Ariola v Saatchi & Saatchi Advertising Srl* [2000] E.C.D.R. 309 where the Supreme Court of Italy said it was wrong to assume that infringement of the moral right of the author is a necessary consequence of the use of a musical work in a commercial. It could not be considered in the abstract and without reference the nature and the commercial purposes or the small scale of that kind of film. It has been acknowledged that commercials have a (sometimes even marked) artistic dignity.

[76] *Chant du Monde v Fox Europe* (1960) 28 R.I.D.A. 361 (Shostokovich).

[77] CDPA 1988, s.80(2)(b).

[78] *Confetti Records v Warner Music UK Ltd (t/a East West Records)* [2003] EWCH 1274, Ch. This was the approach adopted by HHJ Overend at Plymouth County Court in *Pasterfield v Denham* [1999] F.S.R. 168 at 182.

[79] *Confetti Records v Warner Music UK Ltd* [2003] EWCH 1274, Ch. *per* Lewison J. at para.150.

[80] *Tidy v Trustees of the Natural History Museum* (1995) 39 I.P.R. 501 *per* Rattee J.

element or judgment on the part of the author so long as it reasonably arrived at",[81] the author's view must be one which is reasonably held which involves the application of an objective test of reasonableness.[82] This requires an objective evaluation of the evidence based on public or expert opinion.[83] Even where an author is shocked and distressed by the treatment of his work, if he accepts that the publication did not do any harm and there is no evidence that objectively his reputation has been affected, there is no moral rights infringement.[84]

It has been said that it does not necessarily amount to a distortion or mutilation to take parts of a work and put them into a different context, but it is arguable.[85]

## Distortion or modification: illustrative cases

### Additions

**4–025**    *Snow v The Eaton Centre*[86]

Tying ribbons to the necks of a creation of a flight of 60 Canada Geese as part of a shopping centre Christmas display was held to be prejudicial to the author's honour and reputation. The artist contended that the naturalistic composition had been made to look ridiculous by the addition of the ribbons and it was not unlike dangling earrings from the Venus de Milo.[87]

### Reduction in size

**4–026**    *Tidy v Trustees of the Natural History Museum*[88]

It was arguable whether reduction of size of cartoons from original 420mm × 297mm to 67mm × 42mm was a distortion of a design if it was otherwise faithfully reproduced. Summary judgment was refused.

*Echaurren Faranda v Italian Post Office*[89]

The claimant was commissioned by the Italian Ministry for the Arts and the Environment to create a collage commemorating the fiftieth anniversary of the death of the painter Filippo Tommaso Marinetti for use on commemorative brochures and posters. Without the artist's permission the Italian Post Office issued a commemorative postage stamp which repro-

[81] *Snow v The Eaton Centre* (1982) 70 C.P.R. (2d) 105.
[82] *Tidy v Trustees of the Natural History Museum* (1995) 39 I.P.R. 501 *per* Rattee J.
[83] *Prise de Parole Inc v Guerin* 1995 A.C.W.S.J. Lexis 55821; 60 A.C.W.S. (3d) 390. Canadian Federal Court Trial Division (extracts of novel published as part of textbook for school children) at para.36.
[84] *Prise de Parole Inc v Guerin* 1995 A.C.W.S.J. Lexis 55821; 60 A.C.W.S. (3d) 390. Canadian Federal Court Trial Division (extracts of novel published as part of textbook for school children).
[85] *Morrison Leahy Music Ltd v Lightbond Ltd* [1993] E.M.L.R. 144 at 151 *per* Morritt J. Application for interlocutory injunction.
[86] 70 C.P.R. (2d) 105, Ontario High Court, O'Brien J.
[87] *ibid.*, at 106.
[88] 39 I.P.R. 501.
[89] [2001] E.C.D.R. 14 Trib. (Rome).

duced the collage in its entirety. The claimant contended that the reduced scale of the reproduction of the collage on the postage stamp was a reproduction in an imperfect and approximate manner which constituted a distortion of his work. The court considered that the claimant's complaint was justified with regard to the integrity and complete legibility of his work, which was originally intended to be reproduced on a full-sized poster.

### Cropping/re-touching/editing

*Pasterfield v Denham*[90]                                                                    **4–027**

Where differences are so trivial as to almost require inspection with a magnifying glass, there is no derogatory treatment. A copy of a cut-away drawing of the Plymouth Dome had two figures and a weather vane deleted; line rendering to the pavement altered; an absence of shadows from a number of figures and cars; and colour rendering was significantly altered.

*Lucie Saint-Clair v Malerbi*[91]

Photographs of hairstyles reproduced in a re-framed format, cutting off part of the photograph was held to be an infringement of moral rights.

*Le Nouvel Observateur du Monde v S Mirkine*[92]

Photograph published in a periodical which was created by inverting the original negative, reframing it and partly colouring it amounted to a "serious" violation of the author's right of integrity.

*Petit Jacqueline*[93]

A professional photographer took a photograph of a young woman which was exhibited in Cologne. As a result of the exhibition, the photographer achieved some fame and he consented to the inclusion of the photograph in a book entitled *Total Photography*. A part of the photograph—only the young woman's eyes—was reproduced on the cover of the book without his consent. It was held that the truncation of his work on the cover amounted to infringement of his moral rights.

*Opera Scenery*[94]

An artist designed 10 sets of scenery for 10 separate opera scenes. The producers cut one of the scenes from the production and accordingly did not use one of the sets. The artist claimed that deletion of one of the sets was an infringement of his moral rights. The court found that deletion of scenery from a particular scene could be a violation of moral rights if all the sets formed an integral unit and if in deleting one set, the public is not informed that they are not viewing the entire setting as created by the artist.

---

[90] [1999] F.S.R. 168, HHJ Overend, Plymouth County Court.
[91] CA Paris, June 11, 1990; (1990) 46 R.I.D.A. 293.
[92] CA Paris, January 23, 2001; (2001) 189 R.I.D.A. 288.
[93] Bundesgerichtshof (March 5, 1971) G.R.U.R. 1971, 525; Arch. Pr. 1971 541; D.B. 1971, 718; M.D.R. 1971, 459; N.J.W. 1971 885; U.F.I.T.A. B.D 60 P. 312 (1971) (Supreme Court of Germany) cited in Nimmer & Price, *op. cit.*, p.34.
[94] *Tribunal Civil de La Seine* October 15, 1954 (Court of First Instance) (1955) 6 R.I.D.A. 146.

*Isabelle Molinard v Les Fromagers Savoyards*[95]

An artist produced a drawing for the purposes of an advertisement of a large wheel of cheese in front of a village with a church, houses, trees and a single tree to the right in front of a fence. The cheese company reproduced the drawing in the advertisement but removed the single tree with the fence and replaced it with some bushes. The artist's action for moral rights infringement was dismissed by the court on the basis that (1) the changes were minor because they respected the drawings main them, and (2) when assessing moral rights violations it was necessary to take account of the work's advertising nature. It was said "the use of works of applied art in a commercial context does not imply the same inviolability as for works of pure art". The decision has been criticised because the advertiser did claim any commercial necessity to justify the alterations made to the work.[96] Only unavoidable technical constraints can justify departures from moral rights.[97] Note that in the UK, it is likely that artwork and photographs produced for advertisements would fall within the collective works exception[98] as a work made for the purpose of publication in a newspaper/magazine. This case is interesting however, as it indicates that the nature of the work and the purity of the artistic concept will be taken into account when considering moral rights violations.[99]

*Arthus-Bétrand v Sté Panorama du Médecin*[1]

Photographs which showed animals in competition with their owners were reproduced showing only the animals. This was held to amount to a distortion infringing the right of integrity because it had modified the photographer's artistic choice. The reproductions had also modified the background colour and affected the print quality of the reproduced photographs.

*Colourisation/changes in colour*

**4–028**    *Huston v Turner Entertainment*[2]

The film the "Asphalt Jungle" was made in black and white by John Huston, deceased. The rights to the film were acquired by Turner Entertainment who put the film into colour. The heirs to the estate of John Huston claimed that this was an infringement of his moral rights and contending that it was all the more flagrant because during his life he had been opposed to his work being colourised. The court held that colourisation was an infringement of the author's moral rights. It consisted of a

---

[95] *Tribunal de Grande Instance d'Annecy* September 10, 1998 (1999) 179 R.I.D.A. 318, 413.
[96] André Kerévér, September 10, 1998; (1999) 179 R.I.D.A. 318 at 319.
[97] *cf. AB Disques Vidéo* CA Paris, June 29, 2001; (2002) 191 RIDA 194 where a modified sound track of a film which affected its quality was held to infringe moral rights and there were "no technical reasons to justify" the change.
[98] See below at para. 4–034.
[99] For other cases concerning use of works in advertisements and commercials, see above at para. 4–022, n.75.
[1] TGI Paris, July 6, 2001; (2002) 191 R.I.D.A. 196 at 198.
[2] CA Versailles December 19, 1994; (1995) 164 R.I.D.A. 389; [1995] 6 Ent L.R. E-124; 23 IIC 702.

modification of the work by adding an element which was outside the author's artistic conception.

### Pasterfield v Denham[3]

Colour variations between the images in question were not such as to affect the honour or the reputation of the artist. The differences did not come anywhere near the gross differences between a black and white film and a colourised version of the same (considering *Huston v Turner Entertainment* above).

## Change of medium/digitisation

### Theberge v Galerie d'Art du Petit Champlain Inc[4]

A painter had licenced reproduction of certain works to a publisher of posters. The defendant purchased the posters and transferred the image to canvas. This "canvas backing" involved a chemical process which allowed the lifting of the ink layer from the poster paper leaving it blank. The ink layer was then applied to a canvas substrate. In an interlocutory decision refusing an injunction for seizure, it was impliedly doubted whether this was a moral rights infringement prejudicial to the painter's reputation because he had licenced the posters.[5] The court considered that it was an attempt to pursue a "droit de destination" (a right to control the manner of use of authorised copies of the work after sale) which did not exist under Canadian law. The primary claim was that the canvas transfers amounted to a reproduction which was rejected by the court as there was no multiplication of the image. The artist was seeking to assert a moral right in the guise of an economic right which should be rejected.

**4–029**

### Les Fleurs[6]

The painter George Braque entered into a contract with a publisher to reproduce engravings of his painting *Les Fleurs*. The engraver used a different type of paper for the copies than had been agreed. The court found there was no infringement of moral rights. Even though the paper used was less expensive than that agreed, it was still able to reproduce the colours more accurately that the agreed paper. The artist did have the right to supervise the process of colour reproduction in order to assure accuracy.

### Digitised Photographs[7]

Several hundred photographs were included on a CD-Rom without the authorisation of the photographer. He claimed that his right of paternity had been violated as his name was expressly mentioned on only a very small proportion of the photographs. He also asserted violation of the right of

---

[3] [1999] F.S.R. 168, HHJ Overend, Plymouth County Court.
[4] (2002) S.C.C. 34; [2002] S.C.C.D.J. 414, Supreme Court of Canada.
[5] Paras 23, 24, 68, 69 and 77. The question of whether there had in fact been a breach of economic or moral rights was left to the trial judge.
[6] *Tribunal Civil de La Seine* January 7, 1959; J.C.P. 1959, II 10965 cited in Nimmer & Price, *op. cit.*, p.36.
[7] TGI Paris April 29, 1998; (1999) 179 R.I.D.A. 320.

integrity as some of the photographs were "twisted" and included in a geometric framework. The court found that the photographer's moral rights had been violated. The argument of the CD-Rom producer that the moral rights provisions did not have to be applied strictly in the multimedia sector failed.

### R. Mihaileanu v Noé Productions[8]

A co-author of a film (screenplay and director) contended that a digital version of the film on DVD distorted the final version of the work. It had been recorded with an impaired digital recording with a "crushed" sound-track. The plaintiff contended that this could have easily been avoided as modern technology is capable of giving a faithful reproduction of the original version. The court found for the plaintiff and prohibited use of that version of the film.

### Destruction

**4–030**    It is unclear as to whether destruction of a work is something which would give rise to a claim for moral rights infringement. Can destruction be treatment within the meaning of s.80(2) of the CDPA 1988? Is destruction "any addition to, deletion from or alteration to or adaptation of the work"? The leading commentators are divided.[9]

Certainly, destruction of a work if prejudicial to the author's reputation *should* give rise to a moral right if Art.6 *bis* of the Berne Convention is to be complied with. Article 6 *bis* gives the right "to object to any distortion, mutilation or other modification of, or other derogatory action in relation to, the said work, which would be prejudicial to his honour or reputation." Destruction is mutilation or other derogatory action. It is submitted that on a strict reading of s.80(2) destruction cannot properly be classified as a "deletion from or alteration to" a work. Both imply that the work continues to exist. Even if destruction is prohibited, which is doubtful, it would be necessary for the act of destruction to be prejudicial to the honour or reputation of the creator of the work. Unless destruction is either carried out publically or accompanied by a public statement that the work has been destroyed or otherwise known to the public, it is hard to see how this would affect the author's honour or reputation. The following cases from other jurisdictions are illustrative of circumstances in which destruction has been held to be an infringement:

---

[8] TGI Paris November 3, 2000; (2001) 188 R.I.D.A. 298.
[9] Laddie, Prescott & Vitoria (3rd ed.), *op. cit.*, at 13.18 and p.598 *Example (4)* express the view that (1) it is doubtful whether an artist can prevent destruction under s.80(2), (2) this falls short of the requirements of the Berne Convention. The authors of *Copinger & Skone James on Copyright* (14th ed.) at 11–47 consider that destruction almost certainly amounts to a treatment of the work being a deletion or alteration from it but that unless a work is destroyed publically it is unlikely to be prejudicial to the honour or reputation of the author.

*Dubuffet v Regie Nationale Des Usines Renault (No.2)*[10]

Dubuffet was commissioned by Renault to make a model for a large 3-D monumental work to be erected outside their headquarters. Work began on the monument which was then stopped and it was decided to destroy the work. Dubuffet objected and the Cour de Cassation held that the work should be completed. The failure to complete the work would infringe the artist's moral rights in the integrity of his work. Further that the obligation to continue the construction of the uncompleted work implies an obligation not to demolish the work already carried out.

*Rousel v Grenoble*[11]

A sculpture in the Grenoble Municipal Park was disintegrating. The local authority destroyed it as it presented a safety risk to children who played on it. An administrative tribunal found for the authority on the basis that destruction was necessitated by public safety.

*Scrive v Rennes*[12]

A fountain in a commercial centre was dismantled by the owner who contended it posed a risk to customers. The court held that as no circumstances of force majeure warranted destruction, the artist's moral rights were infringed by destruction.

*RJE "La Ley"*[13]

In Spain, a building containing a mural painted on the walls was destroyed. The court held that as the "absolute need" to demolish the building because of its state of ruin, which was such as to prevent it from being preserved, that there had been no moral rights infringement.

*B. Aichouba v F Lecole*[14]

Squatters in a building had created a mosaic on the walls and floors of a building they had no right to occupy. The owner was threatening to destroy the building and in reliance on their right of integrity, the squatters requested that the owner compensate them for the cost of taking up the mosaic to offset the occupation indemnity they had to pay. The mosaic had been created in 1996 by the squatters. The owner had purchased the building in April 1998 and had notified the occupants they had to leave on November 18, 1998, following an eviction order. The premises were vacated in June 2000 during which time the creators of the mosaic had taken no steps to remove their work. The French court rejected the squatter's claim for compensation on the basis that the owner of a building "cannot be confronted with a right in a work made unlawfully on a medium which did not belong to the authors of the work". The squatters were granted a period of

---

[10] *Cour d'Appel* (Versailles) (1983) 117 R.I.D.A. 80; [1983] F.S.R. 31.
[11] T.adm Grenoble, February 18, 1976; (1977) 91 R.I.D.A. 116.
[12] CA Paris (1977) 91 R.I.D.A. 114.
[13] Court of Appeal of La Coruña (T.1999–4) Reference No.7691 cited in *News From Spain*, A., Delagado, (2002) 193 R.I.D.A. 148 at p.160.
[14] TGI Paris, October 13, 2000; (2003) 195 R.I.D.A. 280.

two months to remove the work at their own cost as it was not for the owner of the building to pay for it.

## Parody[15]

### *Fuensanta v Antena 3 TV SA*[16]

**4–031**    Where lyrics of a song had been re-written with humourous words referring to various members of the tabloid press, there was no moral rights infringement because the comedy was not directed at the original song or its authors but to third parties with no connection to them. The court took into account the fact that the claimants were not the authors of the song but their heirs.

## Exceptions to the right of integrity

### *Computer programs and computer generated works*

**4–032**    Both computer programs and computer generated works are excluded from the right of integrity.[17]

### *Reporting current events*

**4–033**    The right of integrity does not apply to any work made for the purpose of reporting current events.[18] For the exception to apply, the work must be *made* for the purpose of reporting current events as opposed to simply used for that purpose.

### *Newspapers, magazines and other collective works*

**4–034**    Like the right of paternity, the right to object to derogatory treatment of a work does not apply in relation to the publication in a newspaper, magazine or similar periodical or an encyclopaedia, dictionary, yearbook or other collective work of reference of a literary, dramatic, musical or artistic work made for the purpose of such a publication or made available with the consent of the author for the purposes of such a publication.[19]

A collective work is a work of joint authorship or a work in which there are distinct contributions by different authors or in which works or parts of works by different authors are incorporated.[20]

---

[15] TGI Paris gave a helpful definition of parody which fits in with the common law approach as a "travesty, which is at least humourous, if not burlesque or comical of *an identifiable* earlier work": *BMG Music v Lancelot Films* (2001) 189 R.I.D.A. 294 (emphasis added). *cf: Rogers v Koons* above at paras 2–136 and 2–144 where the fact that the original work was not referred to or identified was regarded as negating an argument of parody.

[16] [2001] E.C.D.R. 23, Audiencia Provincial (Spain).

[17] CDPA 1988, s.81(2). As to the meaning of "computer generated work" see above at para. 2–061

[18] CDPA 1998, s.81(3). For the meaning of "reporting current events" see cases cited above in para. 4–016.

[19] CDPA 1998, s.81(4).

[20] CDPA 1998, s.178.

The right does not apply in relation to any subsequent exploitation of such a work without any modification of the published version.[21]

### Anonymous and pseudonymous works

The right of integrity is not infringed by any act which would not be an infringement of copyright by reason of ss.57 or 66A which permit certain acts in respect of anonymous and pseudonymous works where it is reasonable to assume copyright has expired or the author died more than 70 years ago.[22]    **4–035**

### Particular purposes: avoiding the commission of an offence, etc.

The right to object to derogatory treatment is not infringed by anything done for the purpose of:    **4–036**

(a)  avoiding the commission of an offence,

(b)  complying with a duty imposed by or under an enactment, or

(c)  in the case of the British Broadcasting Corporation, avoiding the inclusion in a programme broadcast by them of anything which offends against good taste or decency or which is likely to encourage or incite to crime or to lead to disorder or to be offensive to public feeling,

provided, where the author or director is identified at the time of the relevant act or has previously been identified in or on published copies of the work, that there is a sufficient disclaimer.[23]

A "sufficient disclaimer" is defined as a clear and reasonably prominent indication given at the time of the act and if the author or director is then identified, appearing along with that identification, that the work has been subjected to treatment to which the author or director has not consented.[24]

### Existing works: photographs taken before August 1, 1989

See above at para. 4–005.    **4–037**

### Consent and waiver

There is no infringement of the right where the person entitled to the right has consented to the act.[25] The right of integrity can be waived.[26]    **4–038**

---

[21] CDPA 1988, s.81(4). As to anonymous and pseudonymous works see above at para. 2–181.
[22] CDPA 1988, s.81(5).
[23] CDPA 1988, s.81(6).
[24] CDPA 1988, s.178.
[25] CDPA 1988, s.87(1). See below at para. 4–058.
[26] CDPA 1988, s.87(2). See below at para. 4–058.

*Qualification of right in cases of employees, Crown and parliamentary copyright and international organisations*

**4–039**      Where copyright originally vests in the author's employer,[27] or an international organisation,[28] or the work is one in which Crown or Parliamentary copyright subsists, the right to object to derogatory treatment does not apply to anything done by or with the authority of the copyright owner, unless the author (a) is identified at the time of the relevant act, or (b) has previously been identified in or on published copies of the work.[29] Further, if the right does apply, it is not infringed if there is a sufficient disclaimer.[30]

FALSE ATTRIBUTION OF AUTHORSHIP

**The right not to have authorship of a work falsely attributed**

**4–040**      A person has the right not to have a literary, dramatic, musical or artistic work falsely attributed to him as author.[31] Attribution means a statement express or implied as to who is the author.[32] The right also applies to copies of artistic works falsely represented as being a copy made by the author of the work as well as to the false attribution of the original work.[33] The right is actionable *per se* without proof of damage.[34] Unlike the right to be identified as the author, the right to object to false attribution relates to the whole of the work or any part of a work and it is not restricted to "any *substantial part*".

The right is infringed by a person who issues to the public copies of works containing a false attribution or exhibits in public an artistic work or a copy of an artistic work in or on which there is a false attribution.[35] Issuing to the public or public display of any material containing a false attribution of authorship in connection with any of those acts is also an infringement.[36] Thus, publishing leaflets advertising an exhibition of photographs falsely attributed to a different photographer would amount to an infringement. Literary, dramatic and musical works are infringed by a person performing the work in public, broadcasting it or including it in a cable programme who knows or has reason to believe the attribution is false.[37] There is no equivalent infringement provided for artistic works.

---

[27] By virtue of CDPA 1988, s.11(2) works produced in the course of employment. As to which see above at para. 2–073.
[28] By virtue of CDPA 1988, s.168.
[29] CDPA 1988, s.82(1).
[30] CDPA 1988, s.82(2). For the meaning of sufficient disclaimer see above at para. 4–036.
[31] CDPA 1988, s.84(1).
[32] CDPA 1988, s.84(1).
[33] CDPA 1988, s.84(8)(b).
[34] *Clark v Associated Newspapers* [1998] 1 W.L.R. 1558 at 1564; [1998] 1 All E.R. 959.
[35] CDPA 1988, s.84(2).
[36] CDPA 1988, s.84(4).
[37] CDPA 1988, s.84(3).

A person also infringes the right if, in the course of business, he possesses or deals[38] with an artistic work when there is a false attribution in or on it knowing or having reason to believe that there is such an attribution and that it is false.[39]

Artistic works that have been altered by someone other than the author and are held out as being the original unaltered work also infringe the right. A person infringes the right if, in the course of business, he deals with a work which has been altered after the author parted with it as being the unaltered work of the author (or as a copy of the unaltered work) if he knows or has reason to believe that that is not the case.[40] The alteration must be a material alteration such as to affect the character and reputation of the artist.[41]

The proper approach of the court is to determine what is the single    **4–041** meaning the work conveys to the national reasonable reader, *i.e.* would a reasonable person understand the work as presented with any attributions to amount to a false attribution of authorship to the claimant.[42] A newspaper column parodying the diaries of an MP with a heading "Alan Clark's Secret Political Diaries" and the MP's photograph was held to amount to false attribution.[43] It was held that a statement below the heading that the column was the work of a journalist imagining what the MP's new diaries might contain did not cure the false attribution. In order for a counter statement to neutralise the effect of a prima facie false attribution it would have to be as bold, precise and compelling as the false statement.[44]

The right not to have a work falsely attributed was held to be infringed by publication of an interview with a singer written in the first person when, in fact, it was written by a journalist who had interviewed her.[45] Where a quotation from the claimant included two additional sentences not written by him that gave the impression that he had given medical advice that was uselessly vague and in part grossly incompetent and dangerous, the fact that whole passage was attributed to the claimant amounted to a false attribution of the extra words.[46]

---

[38] Dealing in this context is defined as "selling or letting for hire, offering or exposing for sale or hire, exhibiting in public or distributing": CDPA 1988, s.84(8).

[39] CDPA 1988, s.84(5).

[40] CDPA 1988, s.84(6). For the meaning of dealing see n.38 above.

[41] *Carlton Illustrators v Coleman* [1911] 1 K.B. 771 at 780 (drawings enlarged and coloured. Decided under s.7 of the Fine Arts Copyright Act 1862); see also *Preston v Raphael Tuck & Sons* [1926] Ch. 667.

[42] *Clark v Associated Newspapers* [1998] 1 W.L.R. 1558 at 1568; [1998] 1 All E.R. 959.

[43] *ibid.*

[44] *ibid.*, at 1571. *cf. Fabris v Barthelmy* Cour de Cassation July 18, 2000; 188 R.I.D.A. 308 where it was held that putting a false signature of a painter on a painting by another artist (which wasn't a copy or imitation of the famous painter's work) did not infringe the well-known painter's moral right because the seller drew to the attention of purchases the inauthentic nature of the signature and the identity of the real painter.

[45] *Moore v News of the World* [1972] 1 Q.B. 441; [1972] 1 All E.R. 915 (under s.43 of the 1956 Act).

[46] *Noah v Shuba* [1991] F.S.R. 14.

### Existing works: photographs taken before August 1, 1989

**4–042**    The right not to have a work falsely attributed to a person applies to photographs taken before August 1, 1989, in respect of acts taking place after August 1, 1989.[47]

A similar right was provided for in s.43 of the Copyright Act 1956 and this section governs and continues to apply to acts of infringement before August 1, 1989.[48]

### Joint authors

**4–043**    The right to object to false attribution is infringed by any false statement as to the authorship of a work of joint authorship and by the false attribution of joint authorship in relation to a work of sole authorship.[49] Any such false attribution infringes the right of every person to whom authorship of any description is, whether rightly or wrongly, attributed.[50]

RIGHT OF PRIVACY OF PHOTOGRAPHS AND FILMS TAKEN ON OR AFTER AUGUST 1, 1989 COMMISSIONED FOR PRIVATE AND DOMESTIC PURPOSES

### The right of privacy in certain photographs

**4–044**    A person who, for private and domestic purposes, commissions the taking of a photograph or the making of a film has the right not to have copies of the work issued to the public, the work exhibited or shown in public, or the work communicated to the public.[51] The right only attaches to photographs and films in which copyright subsists.[52] Thus, if a photograph is not "original" within the meaning of the Copyright Designs and Patents Act 1988, no copyright will subsist in the photograph and there will be no right to privacy under s.85.[53] Subject to the exceptions below, it is an infringement to issue (or to authorise) copies to the public, exhibit or show the work in public or to communicate the work to the public.[54] The right to privacy

---

[47] CDPA 1988, Sch.1, para.22(2).
[48] *ibid.*
[49] CDPA 1988, s.88(4).
[50] *ibid.*
[51] CDPA 1988, s.85(1) as amended from October 31, 2003 by the Copyright and Related Rights Regulations 2003 (SI 2003/2498), reg. 2(1), Sch 1, Pt 1, paras 1 and 8(2)(b) replacing words "broadcast or included in a cable programme service" with "communicated to the public". As to the meaning of communication to the public and transitional provisions see above at para. 2–153.
[52] CDPA 1988, s.85(1).
[53] Because a photograph is a copy of the image it records, what renders a photograph original is a difficult question and subject to debate. Some photographs, such as automatic camera images/ security camera images may not be "original" and not copyright works. See Ch.3 above.
[54] CDPA 1988, s.85(1). See also n.51, above.

relates to the whole or any *substantial* part of the commissioned photograph or film.[55]

The right does not apply to photographs taken before the 1988 Act came into force on August 1, 1989, or to films made before that date.[56]

## Meaning of commission

"Commission" is not defined in the part of the Act dealing with moral   **4-045** rights and copyright. There is a definition contained in Pt III relating to design right where commission is stated to mean "a commission for money or money's worth".[57]

The Copyright Act 1956 provided that the first owner of copyright of a photograph taken pursuant to a commission was the commissioner.[58] Cases decided under that section tend to support the view that commission requires an agreement pre-dating the taking of the photograph for money or money's worth.[59]

## Private and domestic purposes

"Private and domestic purposes" is not defined by the statute. It would   **4-046** presumably encompass commissioned wedding photographs[60] or commissioned photographs taken at a private party.[61]

In a different context it has been said that "private" means for domestic, pleasure or social purposes as opposed to the purposes of trade.[62] If there is commercial gain, this will not amount to private and domestic purposes.[63]

## Jointly commissioned photographs

In cases of jointly commissioned photographs[64] or films, the statutory   **4-047** right to privacy is that of each person who commissioned the photographs.[65] The right of each is satisfied if he consents to the act in question.[66] A waiver

---

[55] CDPA 1988, s.89(1).
[56] CDPA 1988, Sch.1, para.24.
[57] CDPA 1988, s.263(1).
[58] Copyright Act 1956, s.4(3). See above at para.2-077.
[59] See discussion of meaning of commission above at paras 2-077 to 2-080 and 2-086 to 2-092.
[60] *Williams v Settle* [1960] 1 W.L.R. 1072—copyright infringement under 1956 Act; *Mail Newspapers Plc v Express Newspapers Plc* [1987] F.S.R. 90.
[61] *Lady Anne Tennant v Associated Newspaper Group Ltd* [1979] F.S.R. 298 copyright infringement under 1956 Act. Photographs of HRH Princess Margaret at a private party.
[62] *Roberts (Inspector of Taxes) v Granada TV Rentals* [1970] 2 All E.R. 764 at 771, s.16(3) of the Finance Act 1964.
[63] *Sony Music Entertainment (UK) Ltd v Easyinternetcafé Ltd* [2003] EWHC 62, (Ch), para.41 considering meaning of "private and domestic use" under CDPA 1988, s.70.
[64] The classic example would be wedding photographs. See *Mail Newspapers Plc v Express Newspapers Plc* [1987] F.S.R. 90 above at para. 2-088.
[65] CDPA 1988, s.88(6).
[66] CDPA 1988, s.88(6)(a).

of the rights of one does not affect the rights of the other.[67] Accordingly, to avoid infringing the privacy right in respect of photographs jointly commissioned for private and domestic purposes, the consent of each and every joint commissioner is required.

## Exceptions to the right to privacy of photographs

### Incidental inclusion

4–048    The right is not infringed by an act which would not infringe copyright because it amounted to incidental inclusion in an artistic work, sound recording, film or broadcast.[68]

### Parliamentary and judicial proceedings

4–049    The right to privacy in respect of photographs/films commissioned for private and domestic purposes is not infringed by an act which would not infringe copyright because it was done for the purposes of Parliamentary or judicial proceedings or reporting such proceedings.[69]

### Royal Commissions and statutory inquiries

4–050    The right is not infringed by an act which by virtue of s.46 would not infringe copyright because is was done for the purpose of the proceedings of a Royal Commission or a statutory inquiry or for the purpose of reporting such proceedings held in public.[70]

### Acts authorised by statute

4–051    The right to privacy in respect of photographs/films commissioned for private and domestic purposes is not infringed by an act which would not infringe copyright because it is specifically authorised by an Act of Parliament and, unless that Act provides otherwise, the doing of the act does not infringe copyright.[71]

### Anonymous and pseudonymous works

4–052    The right is not infringed by any act which would not be an infringement of copyright by reason of ss.57 or 66A which permit certain acts in respect of anonymous and pseudonymous works where it is reasonable to assume copyright has expired or the author died more than 70 years ago.[72]

---

[67] CDPA 1988, s.88(6)(b).
[68] CDPA 1988, s.85(2)(a). As to the meaning of incidental inclusion see CDPA 1988, s.31, above at para. 2–168 and below at para. 5–054.
[69] CDPA 1988, s.85(2)(b). As to the Parliamentary & judicial proceedings exception see CDPA 1988, s.45 and above at para. 2–171.
[70] CDPA 1988, s.85(2)(c). See above at para. 2–171.
[71] CDPA 1988, s.85(2)(d). As to acts done under statutory authority see CDPA 1988, s.50 and above at para. 2–176.
[72] CDPA 1988, s.85(2)(e). See above at para. 2–181.

*Consent and waiver*

See below at paras 4–058 *et seq.*                                    **4–053**

## DURATION OF MORAL RIGHTS

The right to be identified as an author, the right to object to derogatory   **4–054**
treatment, and the right to privacy of certain photographs/films continues to
subsist as long as copyright subsists in the work.[73]
   The right to object to false attribution continues to subsist until 20 years
after a person's death.
   From January 1, 1996, the Duration of Copyright & Rights in Perfor-   **4–055**
mances Regulations 1995 extended the copyright term from 50 yrs pma to
70 yrs pma.[74] Moral rights apply under the 1988 Act to the extended term.[75]
If copyright had expired by January 1, 1996, provided on July 1, 1995 the
work was protected in another State of the European Economic Area,[76]
copyright was revived. For further information as to duration, extended
copyright, and revived copyright see above at paras 2–093 *et seq.*
   The 1995 Regulations provide that, in respect of works where copyright
was revived, moral rights are exercisable after commencement by the author
of a work in which revived copyright subsists as with any other copyright
work.[77] However, the Regulations provided that nothing in them shall be
construed as causing a moral right to be exercisable if it was excluded by
paras 23 or 24[78] of Sch.1 of the 1988 Act.[79] Paragraph 23 of Sch.1 of the 1988
Act provides that the right of paternity and the right of integrity do not
apply to works where the author died before commencement.[80] There is no
right of integrity or paternity prior to January 1, 1996, if the author died
before August 1, 1989, but after January 1, 1996, the rights are exercisable
by his personal representatives.[81]
   Paragraph 24 of Sch.1 provides that the right to privacy in certain photo-
graphs/films does not apply to photographs taken or films made before
August 1, 1989. This is also not affected by the Regulations,[82] so even if
there is a revived copyright, if the photograph was taken before August 1,
1989, there is no statutory right to privacy.

---

[73] CDPA 1988, s.86(1). For duration of copyright see above at paras 2–093 *et seq.*, esp. Figure 7.
[74] SI 1995/3297. Came into force on January 1, 1996. For meaning of pma, see above at para. 2–093.
[75] Note SI 1995/3297, reg.21(1) which provides that any waiver subsisting prior to January 1, 1996, continues to have effect for the period of any extended copyright subject to any agreement to the contrary.
[76] SI 1995/3297, reg.16(b).
[77] SI 1995/3297, reg.22(3).
[78] Right to privacy in certain photographs/films does not apply to ones taken/made before August 1, 1989. See above at para. 4–044.
[79] SI 1995/3297, reg.22(6).
[80] CDPA 1988, Sch.1, para.23.
[81] SI 1995/3297, regs 22(3) and 22(4).
[82] SI 1995/3297, reg.22(6).

Any waiver or assertion of moral rights which subsisted immediately before the expiry of copyright shall continue to have effect during the period of revived copyright.[83]

## TRANSMISSION OF MORAL RIGHTS

**4–056**    Moral rights are the rights of the author and as discussed above have their root in the civil law philosophy that a work is an extension of the author's personality. Moral rights are essentially a species of human rights and are in principle the rights of *that* author alone. Accordingly, moral rights are not assignable during the life of the author or moral rights owner.[84]

The right to be identified as the author of a work, the right to object to derogatory treatment of a work, and the right to privacy in certain photographs and films can be transmitted upon the death of the rights owner.[85] The rights pass to such a person as the person entitled to the right directs by testamentary disposition.[86] If there is no such direction, but the copyright in the work forms part of his estate, the rights pass to the person to whom the copyright passes.[87] In default of either specific testamentary disposition or passing of the copyright as part of the estate, the rights are exercisable by the personal representatives of the author.[88] Any consent or waiver given by the author binds any successor in title of the rights.[89]

**4–057**    If on death of the rights owner, the copyright becomes owned by two or more people, for example where the rights are divided by a bequest (either with respect to the rights owned or where ownership is for part but not all of the period of copyright), the moral rights transmitted with the copyright are also divided.[90]

Where, under a testamentary disposition or by passing of the copyright, the right becomes exercisable by more than one person, the right to identification of the author can be asserted by any of them and the rights of integrity and privacy of certain photographs/films are exercisable by each of them.[91]

The right of false attribution is not transmissible on death, but it is actionable after a person's death by his personal representatives.[92]

---

[83] SI 1995/3297, reg.22(2).
[84] CDPA 1988, s.94.
[85] CDPA 1988, s.95(1).
[86] CDPA 1988, s.95(1)(a).
[87] CDPA 1988, s.95(1)(b).
[88] CDPA 1988, s.95(1)(c).
[89] CDPA 1988, s.95(4).
[90] CDPA 1988, s.95(2).
[91] CDPA 1988, s.95(3).
[92] CDPA 1988, s.95(5).

## WAIVER AND CONSENT

It is not an infringement of any of the moral rights conferred by the 1988    **4–058**
Act to do anything to which the person entitled to the right has consented.[93]
There is no statutory requirement for consent to be in writing and it can be
made orally.

Any of the moral rights can be waived by an instrument in writing signed
by the person giving up the right.[94] This is in contrast to many of the civil
law countries where moral rights are inalienable and cannot be waived.[95]
Under the 1988 Act, a waiver may relate to a specific work, to works of a
specified description, or to works generally, and may relate to existing or
future works.[96] A waiver may also be may be conditional or unconditional
and may be expressed to be subject to revocation.[97] Where a waiver is made
in favour of the owner or prospective owner of the copyright in the work or
works to which it relates, it shall be presumed to extend to his licensees and
successors in title unless a contrary intention is expressed.[98] A waiver by one
joint author does not affect the rights of other joint authors.[99]

The statutory provisions concerning waiver are not to be construed as
excluding the operation of the general law of contract or estoppel in relation
to an informal waiver or other transaction in relation to any of the moral
rights.[1]

## LIMITATION

Moral rights infringement is actionable as a breach of a statutory duty.[2]    **4–059**
Breach of statutory duty is properly classified as an action founded on a
tort.[3] The limitation period for moral right infringement is six years from the
date on which the cause of action arose.[4]

It is an academic question as to whether an action for moral rights
infringement falls within s.2 (torts) or within s.9 of the Limitation Act 1980
which concerns actions for sums recoverable by statute, as both provide for
a period of limitation being six years from the date on which the cause of
action accrued. Section 9(1) reads:

---

[93] CDPA 1988, s.87(1).
[94] CDPA 1988, s.87(2).
[95] *e.g.* French Copyright Code L.121–1 where the author's right to respect for his name, his authorship and his work is expressed to be "perpetual, inalienable and imprescriptible." Interestingly, the amendment to the Australian Copyright Act 1968 introducing moral rights which came into force at the end of 2000 does not specifically provide for waiver.
[96] CDPA 1988, s.87(3).
[97] CDPA 1988, s.87(3)(b).
[98] *ibid.*
[99] CDPA 1988, s.88(3).
[1] CDPA 1988, s.87(4).
[2] CDPA 1988, s.103(1).
[3] *R. v Secretary of State for Transport Ex p. Factortame Ltd (No.6)* [2001] 1 W.L.R. 942 at 965.
[4] S.2, Limitation Act 1980.

"An action to recover any sum recoverable by virtue of any enactment shall not be brought after the expiration of six years from the date on which the cause of action accrued."

It has been said that s.9 refers to cases where the sums which are recoverable by the claimant are specified in or directly ascertainable from the enactment as contrasted with damages.[5] This would not encompass a claim for moral rights where damages are at large and not restricted by the statute. Conversely, it has been held that s.9(1) is not limited to liquidated damages and its intention is to distinguish between a claim for money (whether liquidated or unliquidated) and a claim for non-monetary relief under a speciality.[6]

It is submitted that where the claim is for breach of statutory duty because the action is founded on a tort, s.2 applies. Whichever is the case, the limitation period for moral rights infringement is six years from the date the cause of action accrued.

## REMEDIES

**4–060**   Any infringement of moral rights is actionable as a breach of a statutory duty owed to the person entitled to the right.[7] Moral rights are actionable *per se* without proof of damage.[8] The person entitled to the right has access to the normal remedies for breach of statutory duty, namely damages and an injunction. The Australian statute specifically provides for an order for a public apology[9] and it is submitted that there is no reason in principle why such an order would not be available in England and Wales under the power of the court to grant mandatory injunctions.

Where there is infringement of the paternity right, when considering remedies the court shall take into account any delay in asserting the right.[10]

In proceedings for infringement of the right to object to derogatory treatment of the work, the court may, if it thinks it is an adequate remedy in the circumstances, grant an injunction on terms prohibiting the doing of any act unless a disclaimer is made, in such terms and in such manner as may be approved by the court, dissociating the author or director from the treatment of the work.[11]

If the claimants are "second generation" claimants, being the heirs and successors in title to the original authors, it should be taken into account when determining whether an infringement of a moral right should be

---

[5] *R. v Secretary of State for Transport. Ex p. Factortame Ltd (No.6)* [2001] 1 W.L.R. 942 at 967 *per* Judge John Toulmin Q.C.
[6] *Rowan Companies Inc v Lambert Eggink Offshore Transport Consultants VOF (The Gilbert Rowe) (No.2)* [1999] 2 Lloyd's Rep. 443 *per* David Steel J.
[7] CDPA 1988, s.103(1).
[8] *Clark v Associated Newspapers* [1998] 1 W.L.R. 1558 at 1564; [1998] 1 All E.R. 959.
[9] Australian Copyright Act 1968, s.195AA(1).
[10] CDPA 1988, s.78(5).
[11] CDPA 1988, s.103(2). As to "sufficient disclaimer" see CDPA 1988, s.178 and above at para. 4–036.

remedied.[12] Where the rights are exercisable by the personal representatives, any damages recovered form part of the deceased's estate.[13]

## Damages

Writers, artists, and photographers who live by getting known to the public are entitled to recover damages for loss of publicity where they are not identified as the author of a work.[14] In a Canadian case of copyright infringement, where a designer's building plans were used without his permission, the court in awarding damages took into account the loss of publicity.[15] It was said:

**4–061**

"An important additional element of damage is the loss to him of the opportunity to enhance his reputation. His plans have been used and yet his has had no credit for that. To be given such credit in a timely and appropriate way is a matter of obvious importance, particularly to a young designer seeking to make his reputation. Had he given a licence, it would likely have been a term of that that he be allowed to have a sign on the project. Having in mind that the buildings are on a very prominent intersection, that would have been an advantage of considerable potential value."[16]

It has been observed that quantification for infringement of moral rights is problematic.[17] Awards in common law jurisdictions have tended to be fairly modest.[18] However, in one Canadian case where a unique and unreproducible artwork 12ft to 16ft high created by a renowned artist, described as culturally very significant, was totally destroyed intentionally, the equivalent of £50,400 was awarded.[19] The German Court of Appeals has

**4–062**

---

[12] *Fuensanta v Antena 3 TV SA* [2001] E.C.D.R. 23, Audiencia Provincial (Spain).

[13] CDPA 1988, s.95(6).

[14] *Tolnay v Criterion Film Production Ltd* [1936] 2 All E.R. 1625. Screen play authors not given screen credit in breach of contract. Not nominal damage. Awarded £100 each in respect of loss of publicity in 1936. *Cf.* Failure to credit fee in same photographic licence standard terms and conditions below at para. 12–008, n.8

[15] *Kafka v Mountain Side Developments Ltd* 62 C.P.R. (2d) 157, British Columbia Supreme Court.

[16] 62 C.P.R. (2d) 157 at 163 *per* Esson J.

[17] *Boundreau v Lin* (1997) 75 C.P.R. (3d) 1, Ontario Gen Div.

[18] e.g. *Moore v News of the World* [1972] 1 Q.B. 441; [1972] 1 All E.R. 915 (£100 awarded for false attribution of interview where £4,300 awarded for primary claim of libel); *Noah v Shuba* [1991] F.S.R. 14 (£250 for false attribution where £7,250 awarded for primary claim of libel); *Dolmage v Erskine* 23 C.P.R. (4th) 495, Ont. Superior Court, Small Claims Court (Canadian $3,000 awarded for paternity right infringement (equivalent to £1,200 at the date of judgment: For facts see above at para. 4–011, n.32 and associated text); *Ateliers Tango Argentin Inc v Festival d'Espagne & d'Amerique Latine Inc* (1997) 84 C.P.R. (3d) 56 Canadian $2,000 (equivalent to £880 at date of judgment) awarded for paternity right infringement for display of a copyright infringing photograph. For facts see above at para. 4–011.

[19] *Vaillancourt c Carbone 14* (June 8, 1999) no. C.Q. Montreal 500–22–003682–971 cited in *Dolmage v Erskine* 23 C.P.R. (4th) 495, Ont. Superior Court, Small Claims Court. Award was Canadian $120,000.

said that the amount of damages should depend upon how extensively the work was distributed.[20]

It is submitted that when assessing damages, the court should take into account the following factors:

(1) the nature and purpose of the work, for example, derogatory treatment of a work produced for an advertising poster should receive a lower award of damages than that of a purely artistic work;

(2) the actual effect on the author's honour and reputation;

(3) the defendant's state of mind. Deliberate, flagrant and malicious infringement should result in a higher award than inadvertent breach;

(4) the number and type of people who have seen the work and their relevance/proximity to the author's reputation;

(5) any acts of mitigation or other conduct by the defendant.

**4–063**    A particular problem with the award of damages in moral rights infringement is that in many cases there will be other overlapping causes of action such as breach of contract, passing off, defamation, and copyright infringement. These primary causes of action are likely to lead to more substantial damages than that attributable solely to the moral rights infringement. There is a risk of double recovery if an additional award for moral rights infringement is also made. Where damages for breach of contract include damages for loss of publicity/association, no further award for moral rights infringement will be awarded as this would amount to double damages.[21] Similarly, in cases of false attribution, if there is also a cause of action in libel or passing off in many cases the damages awarded for those causes of action will cover false attribution as well.[22] In a proper case it may be appropriate to award an additional sum for the false attribution of authorship if that does not amount to double damages.[23]

---

[20] *Oberlandesgericht Munich* (July 3, 1967) G.R.U.R. 1969; U.F.I.T.A. Bd. 57 S. 327 (1970) Court of Appeals. Cited in Nimmer & Price, *op. cit.*

[21] *Adams v Quasar Management Service* (2002) 56 I.P.R. 385 (Sup. Ct Queensland).

[22] *Moore v News of the World* [1972] 1 All E.R. 915 at 920.

[23] *ibid.*, at 922j.

# Chapter 5

# Photographs and trade marks

## SCOPE OF THE CHAPTER

This Chapter contains an outline of the law relating to trade marks and focusses on two particular issues relevant to photography. First, the registerability of a photograph as a trade mark, and secondly, problems that may
**5–001**

arise in taking photographs of trade marks. These are fairly narrow issues and the treatment of the general law is for this reason in outline only. This chapter does not deal at all with the procedure governing applications to register trademarks which is comprehensively covered in other works. For detailed treatment of the law relating to trade marks, the reader is referred to *Kerly's Law of Trade Marks and Trade Names* (Sweet & Maxwell) and Morcom, Roughton & Graham, *The Modern Law of Trade Marks* (Butterworths).

## TRADE MARKS

5–002    A trade mark is any sign which is capable of distinguishing goods or services as emanating from a particular business or source. A registered trade mark gives the proprietor a prima facie right to the exclusive use of the mark without the necessity of having to prove goodwill or that in fact distinguishes goods. The UK trade mark system is governed by the Trade Marks Act 1994 (TMA 1994) which implemented the European Directive[1] and the Council Regulation on the Community Trade Mark 40/94. The directive provided for harmonisation of trade mark laws of the Member States and the Regulation set up the Community Trade Mark System.[2]

The UK Register of Trade Marks is maintained by the Registrar who is the Comptroller-General of Patents, Designs and Trade Marks.[3]

The Register is divided into different classes of goods and services and a prescribed system of classification is a statutory requirement.[4] Any application for a trade mark must state the goods or services in respect of which it is sought to register the mark.[5]

Once registered, a trade mark remains registered for an initial period of 10 years and may be renewed for further periods of 10 years.[6]

## DEFINITION OF A TRADE MARK

5–003    Section 1 of the Trade Mark Act 1994 defines a trademark as follows:

> "1(1) In this Act a 'trade mark' means any sign capable of being represented graphically which is capable of distinguishing goods or services of one undertaking from those of other undertakings.
>
> A trade mark may, in particular, consist of words (including personal names), designs, letters, numerals or the shape of goods or their packaging."

---

[1] Directive 89/104 adopted on December 21, 1988.
[2] For further information about Community Trade Marks see the website of the Office for the Harmonisation of the Internal Market (OHIM) at *www.oami.eu.int.*
[3] TMA 1994, ss.62 and 63.
[4] TMA 1994, s.34.
[5] TMA 1994, s.32.
[6] TMA 1994, ss.42 and 43.

A photograph is capable of being represented graphically and in principle is registerable as a trade mark. As discussed below, a number of photographs have indeed been registered as trade marks in the United Kingdom. Moving images can also be represented graphically as a series of still images. Qualification in s.1 of the word "represented" by the word "graphically" does not restrict the means by which the representation is made, provided it is in graphical form, for example by way of writing, drawing, musical notation, or written description.[7] A trade mark can consist of a sign which is not in itself capable of being perceived visually (*e.g.* a sound) provided that it can be represented graphically.[8] The graphic representation must enable the sign to be represented visually by means of images, lines or characters so that it can be precisely identified.[9] The representation must be clear, precise, self-contained, easily accessible, intelligible, durable and objective.[9a]

A hologram has been rejected under s.3(1)(a). However, the applicant conceded that it was "very unlikely that a relatively low number of photographic views would suffice for a complete description of the mark" and therefore the mark was not graphically represented.[10] The list of types of marks is non-exhaustive[11] so other types of images which are capable of being represented graphically are not necessarily excluded if they can fulfill the other requirements. It is submitted that, in principle, provided that the other requirements of s.1 are met, there is no reason why a hologram should not be registerable if the graphical representation is sufficiently precise.[12]

**5–004**

It is the second requirement that the mark must be "capable of distinguishing goods or services" that tends to be more problematic when considering registering photographs as trademarks. This is especially the case when considering photographs of famous people as trade marks because a single photograph of a particular person is unlikely to be regarded as an indication of trade source. This is discussed further below.

**5–005**

A mark must be capable of distinguishing goods as its essential purpose and function. It has been said that this provision means that the sign must simply be "not incapable" of distinguishing goods or services of one undertaking from those of other undertakings.[13]

---

[7] *Swizzels Matlow Ltd's Three Dimensional Trade Mark Application* [2000] E.T.M.R. 58; [1999] R.P.C. 879 (Appointed Person, Simon Thorley Q.C.). See also *Shield Mark BV v Kist* (C283/01) ECJ Nov 27, 2003 holding that a sequence of notes without more did not meet the requirements and a stave, clef, notes and rests which constituted a faithful representation of the sound sequence was required.

[8] *Shield Mark BC v Kist* (C283/01) ECJ Nov 27, 2003 (see n.7 above); *Sieckmann v Deutsches Patent- und Markenamt* [2003] Ch.487; [2003] 3 W.L.R. 424; [2003] ETMR 37 (ECJ) at paras 45–46. It was held that a description of an odour although it is graphic, is not sufficiently clear, precise and objective to satisfy the requirements.

[9] *ibid.*

[9a] *ibid.*

[10] *Checkpoint Security Services Ltd's Application*, June 7, 1999, App. No. 2031496, 0/181/99. A copy of the decision is available online at *http://www.patent.gov.uk* under Trade Marks; Legal Decisions: Ex parte 1999.

[11] *Sieckmann v Deutsches Patent und Markenamt* (C273/00) [2003] E.T.M.R. 37 at 44 (considering the list in the directive at Art.2 and recital 7) see above at para.5–003, n.5.

[12] This was submitted in *Sieckmann v Deutsches Patent und Markenamt* (C273/00) at para.26.

[13] *AD2000* [1997] R.P.C. 168.

In order for a trade mark to be registerable, it needs to comply with the requirements of s.1 of the 1994 Act. The Act specifies circumstances in which a trade mark will be refused registration.

## ABSOLUTE GROUNDS FOR REFUSAL OF REGISTRATION

**5–006**   The absolute grounds for refusal of registration of a trade mark are set out in s.3 of the Trade Marks Act 1994 which provides as follows:

"**Absolute grounds for refusal of registration**
   **3.**—(1) The following shall not be registered—

   (a) signs which do not satisfy the requirements of section 1(1),
   (b) trade marks which are devoid of any distinctive character,
   (c) trade marks which consist exclusively of signs or indications which may serve, in trade, to designate the kind, quality, quantity, intended purpose, value, geographical origin, the time of production of goods or of rendering of services, or other characteristics of goods or services
   (d) trade marks which consist exclusively of signs or indications which have become customary in the current language or in the bona fide and established practices of the trade:

Provided that, a trade mark shall not be refused registration by virtue of paragraph (b), (c) or (d) above if, before the date of application for registration, it has in fact acquired a distinctive character as a result of the use made of it.

   (2) A sign shall not be registered as a trade mark if it consists exclusively of—

   (a) the shape which results from the nature of the goods themselves,
   (b) the shape of goods which is necessary to obtain a technical result, or
   (c) the shape which gives substantial value to the goods.

   (3) A trade mark shall not be registered if it is—

   (a) contrary to public policy or to accepted principles of morality, or
   (b) of such a nature as to deceive the public (for instance as to the nature, quality or geographical origin of the goods or service).

   (4) A trade mark shall not be registered if or to the extent that its use is prohibited in the United Kingdom by any enactment or rule of law or by any provision of Community law.

   (5) A trade mark shall not be registered in the cases specified, or referred to, in section 4 (specially protected emblems).

   (6) A trade mark shall not be registered if or to the extent that the application is made in bad faith."

The absolute grounds set out above are not mutually exclusive and there is much overlap.[14] Of the above absolute grounds, those most likely to be relevant to photographs are s.3(1)(b) (devoid of distinctive character), s.3(1)(c) (descriptive), and s.3(6) (bad faith).

## Signs which do not satisfy the requirements of s.1

The requirements of s.1 are as set out above namely, (a) a sign, (b) capable **5–007** of being represented graphically, and (c) which is capable of distinguishing the goods/services of one undertaking from those of other undertakings. The third requirement is essentially covered by s.3(1)(b) of the absolute grounds for refusal of registration (lack of distinctiveness) which is discussed below.

## Signs devoid of any distinctive character: s.3(1)(b)

The often quoted dictum of Jacob J. in *British Sugar*[15] describes what is **5–008** meant by "devoid of distinctive character":

"What does devoid of any distinctive character mean? I think the phrase requires consideration of the mark on its own, assuming no use. Is it the sort of word (or other sign) which cannot do the job of distinguishing without first educating the public that it is a trade mark? A meaningless word or a word inappropriate for the goods concerned ('North Pole' for bananas) can clearly do. But a common laudatory word such as 'Treat' is, absent use and recognition as a trade mark itself (I hesitate to borrow the word from the old Act but the idea is much the same) devoid of any inherently distinctive character".

He concluded that a word is incapable of distinguishing when a word is so descriptive that it is incapable of distinguishing properly, even if it does so partially. It was held "Treat" for dessert sauces and syrups was devoid of distinctive character. It has also been said that the mark must have a character which enables it to be distinctive of one trader's goods in the sense that it has a meaning denoting the origin of the goods.[16]

In *Canon v Mgm*,[17] the European Court of Justice confirmed that: **5–009**

"... according to the settled case-law of the Court, the essential function of a trade mark is to guarantee the identity of the origin of the marked products to the consumer or end user by enabling him, without any possibility of confusion, to distinguish the product or service from others which have another origin. For the trade mark to be able to fulfil its

---

[14] *BACH and BACH FLOWER REMEDIES Trade Marks* [2000] R.P.C. 513 at 525.
[15] *British Sugar v James Robertson & Sons* [1996] R.P.C. 281 at 306.
[16] *Philips v Remington (No.1)* [1999] R.P.C. 809.
[17] [1999] E.T.M.R. 1 at 8, para.28.

essential role in the system of undistorted competition which the Treaty seeks to establish, it must offer a guarantee that all the goods or services bearing it have originated under the control of a single undertaking which is responsible for their quality..."

Section 3(1)(b) is directed at any visible sign or combination of signs which can by itself readily distinguish one trader's product from another competing trader. If the differences become apparent only on close examination and comparison, neither can be said to be distinctive.[18]

Photographs of people in particular are susceptible to falling foul of the distinctiveness requirement as the photograph tends to signify the subject matter rather than the trade source. The particular difficulties of seeking register images of people and distinctiveness are discussed below at para.5–027.

**5–010**   Similarly, photographs or images simply showing the actual product are likely to be refused for a lack of distinctiveness. These types of images are likely to be used legitimately by other traders. This will overlap with s.3(1)(c) where images of the product may be refused as being descriptive. For examples of cases where pictures of the product have been refused see the following paragraph.

An objection under s.3(1)(b) can be overcome by establishing that before the date of application the mark has in fact acquired a distinctive character as a result of the use made of it.[19]

### Signs which designate the kind, quality, etc. or other characteristics of the goods or services: s.3(1)(c)

**5–011**   Essentially, this prohibits the registration of descriptive marks and it prevents the registration of words and marks which other traders may legitimately want to use in the course of trade. If a mark does not consist "exclusively" of one of the categories listed, it cannot fall foul of s.3(1)(c). The Works Manual states that the Registrar considers that the word "exclusively" relates to the content of the mark and not to whether the mark serves more than one purpose.[20] Thus the word *Jumper* together with a distinctive device would be registerable for clothing as the whole mark (device and word) does not consist *exclusively* of a word that is descriptive, but the word alone would not be registerable.

A photograph merely showing a product may be refused as descriptive. A mark showing toothpaste being squeezed from the tube on to a brush was held to be a purely descriptive pictorial device and accordingly not registerable.[21] A mere pictorial representation of a product is not a trade mark.

---

[18] *Procter & Gamble Ltd's Trade Mark Applications (Detergent Bottles)* (CA) [1999] R.P.C. 673 at 680.
[19] TMA 1994, Concluding words of s.3(1).
[20] Ch.6, para.4 at p.64 citing *FROOT LOOPS Trade Mark* [1998] R.P.C. 240. See also *West (t/a Eastenders) v Fuller Smith & Turner Plc* [2003] EWCA Civ 48.
[21] *Unilever plc's Trade Mark* [1984] R.P.C. 23.

Similarly, an application to register a picture of coffee beans and six leaves in respect of coffee was refused[22] as was a picture of a bunch of herbs for herbal capsules.[23] Other manufacturers will legitimately wish to use such images to illustrate their products.

Under this ground the following types of marks have been refused: lau-   **5–012** datory words[24]; descriptive words[25]; and words denoting geographical origin.[26] The Trade Mark Registry Works Manual gives the following examples for non-registerable marks within the other categories listed in s.3(1)(c):

| | |
|---|---|
| kind[27] | Jumbo, Mini, Personal (for computers), Vertical (for blinds) |
| quality[28] | Good, Best, High Tech (for computers or other highly technical goods) |
| quantity[29] | 12 (for wine as 12 bottles = a case) or 200 for cigarettes |
| intended purpose[30] | Kettle Clean (for kettle cleaners); Twist and Curl (hair curlers); Marine or Rustfree for paints |
| value[31] | Two For One; Worth Their Weight in Gold. |
| geographical origin[32] | Sahara for Dates; Kalahari for diamonds; Billingsgate for fish; Covent Garden for fruit and vegetables; Bond Street for clothing. |
| the time of production of goods or of rendering of services[33] | Vintage 1996 for wines; Eight Til Late for restaurant services; Overnight Delivery for transport services and "24 Hours Service" for emergency plumbing services. |
| other characteristics of goods/ services[34] | mere representations of the goods *e.g.* illustrations of cars for car cleaning preparations. |

---

[22] Trade Marks Registry, November 1, 1996, *CIPA Journal*, December 1996, p.1017.
[23] *Re General Nutrition Investment Co's Application*, Trade Marks Registry, January 23, 1998, New Law Digest 698058209.
[24] *e.g.* "Supreme" for photographic products [1999] E.T.M.R. 505; "Treat" for dessert sauces *British Sugar plc v James Robertson & Sons Ltd* [1996] R.P.C. 281.
[25] *e.g.* "Baby-Dry" for disposable nappies *BABY DRY Trade Mark* [2002] Ch. 82; [2002] 2 W.L.R. 485; "Froot Loops" for cereal [1998] R.P.C. 240.
[26] *e.g.* "Savile Row" [1998] R.P.C. 155; "Eurolamb" [1997] R.P.C. 279.
[27] Trade Marks Registry Works Manual, Ch.6, para.4.8.1 at p.72.
[28] *ibid.*, para.4.8.2 at p.73.
[29] *ibid.*, para.4.8.3 at p.74.
[30] *ibid.*, para.4.8.4 at p.75.
[31] *ibid.*, para.4.8.5 at p.76.
[32] *ibid.*, para.4.9 at pp.78 *et seq.*
[33] *ibid.*, para.4.8.6 at p.77.
[34] *ibid.*, para.4.10 at p.92.

An objection under s.3(1)(c) can be overcome by establishing that before the date of application the mark has in fact acquired a distinctive character as a result of the use made of it.[35]

## Signs which have become customary: s.3(1)(d)

**5–013**    This is directed at preventing registration of signs which have become generic. Some trade marks are incorrectly used by the consuming public instead of the generic word, for example Kleenex for tissues instead of the true generic word tissues, Hoover for vacuum cleaner, Xerox for photo-copier and RollerBlades for in-line skates. Owners of such marks often spend time and money policing their trade mark and seeking to stop the use of it in a generic way.

The Trade Mark Registry Works Manual gives examples of devices of grapes for wine or stars for hotel services.[36] The Works Manual states that representations of people connected with relevant goods or services would also be covered, such as devices of chefs which are not generally distinctive of foodstuffs or restaurant services.

An objection under s.3(1)(d) can be overcome by establishing that, before the date of application, the mark has in fact acquired a distinctive character as a result of the use made of it.[37]

## Shapes: s.3(2)

**5–014**    A sign shall not be registered as a trade mark if it consists *exclusively* of:

(a)  the shape which results from the nature of the goods themselves,

(b)  the shape of goods which is necessary to obtain a technical result, and

(c)  the shape which gives substantial value to the goods.

Marks that comprise a shape with something else such as a word or a 2-D device do not consist exclusively of a shape. This section equates to Art.3(1)(e) of the directive.[38] The purpose of preventing registration of the specified shapes is to prevent monopoly on technical solutions or functional characteristics of a product which a user is likely to seek in the products of competitors.[39]

---

[35] Concluding words of TMA 1994, s.3(1).
[36] Trade Marks Registry Works Manual, Ch.6 p.106.
[37] Concluding words of TMA 1994, s.3(1).
[38] See above at para.5–002, n.1.
[39] *Koninklijke Philips Electronics NV v Remington Consumer Products Ltd* [2003] Ch. 159; [2003] 2 W.L.R. 294; [2003] R.P.C. 2, at para.78.

It has been said that it is difficult to envisage shapes which result from the nature of the goods themselves under s.3(2)(a) "except for those that are produced in nature such as bananas".[40]

Where the essential functional characteristics of the shape of a product are attributable solely to the technical result, s.3(2)(b) precludes registration of a sign consisting of that shape, even if that technical result can be achieved by other shapes.[41] Accordingly, objection under s.3(1)(b) cannot be overcome by establishing that there are other shapes which allow the same technical result to be obtained.

The question of whether the only shapes to be excluded from registration are shapes "natural, functional or ornamental" as opposed to artificially created shapes has been referred to the ECJ.[42]

As to s.3(1)(c) and what is meant by substantial value, it has been said that this subsection:  **5–015**

> "... is intended to exclude functional shapes and the former aesthetic-type shapes. Thus the fact that the technical result of a shape is excellent and therefore the article can command a high price does not mean that it is excluded from registration by subsection (c). The subsection is only concerned with shapes having 'substantial value'. That requires a conclusion as to whether the value is substantial, which in my view requires that a comparison has to be made between the shape sought to be registered and shapes of equivalent articles. It is only if the shape sought to be registered has, in relative terms, substantial value that it will be excluded from registration."[43]

## Contrary to public policy or deceptive: s.3(3)

A trade mark shall not be registered if it is (a) contrary to public policy or to accepted principles of morality, or (b) of such a nature as to deceive the public (for instance as to the nature, quality or geographical origin of the goods or service).  **5–016**

The Trade Marks Registry Works Manual states that it is not possible to define what is contrary to public policy or principles of morality and that the Registrar must exercise his judgment in each case.[44] The Manual gives examples of marks which would be objected to under this ground and they include marks which encourage drug use; promote pornography and murder; and offensive bad language.

---

[40] *Philips Electronics NV v Remington Consumer Products Ltd (No.1)* [1999] E.T.M.R. 816; [1999] R.P.C. 809; *Societe De Produits Nestle Sa v Unilever Plc* [2002] EWHC 2709; [2003] E.T.M.R. 53.

[41] *Koninklijke Philips Electronics NV v Remington Consumer Products Ltd* [2003] Ch. 159; [2003] 2 W.L.R. 294; [2003] R.P.C. 2, para.83.

[42] *Societe De Produits Nestle Sa v Unilever Plc* [2002] EWHC 2709; [2003] E.T.M.R. 53 ("Viennetta" ice cream).

[43] *Philips Electronics NV v Remington Consumer Products Ltd (No.1)* [1999] R.P.C. 809 at 822; [1999] E.T.M.R. 816.

[44] Ch.6, para.9.1.

In respect of s.3(3)(b) (deceptive marks), if the mark indicates a particularly desirable quality of the goods, then it should be restricted to goods which have that quality. For example, Orlwoola for suits would be deceptive if the suits were not all wool.[45]

## Marks the use of which is prohibited by law: s.3(4)

**5–017**    A trade mark shall not be registered if or to the extent that its use is prohibited in the United Kingdom by any enactment or rule of law or by any provision of Community law.

## Specially protected emblems: ss.3(5) and 4

**5–018**    Section 4 of the Trade Marks Act 1994 lists various specially protected emblems, in particular royal arms, royal and national flags and the Olympic symbol. Section 3(5) prohibits registration of such marks outside the circumstances specified in s.4. Photographs of any member of the Royal family are prohibited from registration by virtue of s.4(1)(c). Section 4 would exclude from registration photographs of those emblems listed and it is set out below for the sake of completeness.

   **"Specially protected emblems**
       **4.**—(1) A trade mark which consists of or

  (a) the Royal arms, or any of the principal armorial bearings of the Royal arms, or any insignia or device so nearly resembling the Royal arms or any such armorial bearing as to be likely to be mistaken for them or it,

  (b) a representation of the Royal crown or any of the Royal flags,

  (c) a representation of Her Majesty or any member of the Royal family, or any colourable imitation thereof, or

  (d) words, letters or devices likely to lead persons to think that the applicant either has or recently has had Royal patronage or authorisation,

   shall not be registered unless it appears to the registrar that consent has been given by or on behalf of Her Majesty or, as the case may be, the relevant member of the Royal family.
       (2) A trade mark which consists of or contains a representation of

  (a) the national flag of the United Kingdom (commonly known as the Union Jack), or

  (b) the flag of England, Wales, Scotland, Northern Ireland or the Isle of Man,

   shall not be registered if it appears to the registrar that the use of the trade mark would be misleading or grossly offensive.

---

[45] Works Manual, Ch.6, para.9.3.

Provision may be made by rules identifying the flags to which paragraph (b) applies.

(3) A trade mark shall not be registered in the cases specified in section 57 (national emblems, &c of Convention countries), or section 58 (emblems, &c of certain international organisations).

(4) Provision may be made by rules prohibiting in such cases as may be prescribed the registration of a trade mark which consists of or contains

    (a) arms to which a person is entitled by virtue of a grant of arms by the Crown, or

    (b) insignia so nearly resembling such arms as to be likely to be mistaken for them,

unless it appears to the registrar that consent has been given by or on behalf of that person.

Where such a mark is registered, nothing in this Act shall be construed as authorising its use in any way contrary to the laws of arms.

(5) A trade mark which consists of or contains a controlled representation within the meaning of the Olympic Symbol etc (Protection) Act 1995 shall not be registered unless it appears to the registrar

    (a) that the application is made by the person for the time being appointed under section 1(2) of the Olympic Symbol etc (Protection) Act 1995 (power of Secretary of State to appoint a person as the proprietor of the Olympics association right), or

    (b) that consent has been given by or on behalf of the person mentioned in paragraph (a) above."

## Bad faith: s.6

There is no statutory definition of what constitutes bad faith. It includes   **5–019** dishonesty,[46] no intention to use the registered mark[47] or registration of a mark to which someone does not have title with the intention to interfere with the rights of others.[48] Bad faith thus may arise where the mark sought to be registered comprises a photograph where the image represented is something or someone to which the applicant has no connection (*e.g.* a celebrity) or title (*e.g.* a building or a copyright work).

In *Growmax Plasticulture v Don & Low Nonwovens Ltd*[49] Lindsay J. said:   **5–020**

"I shall not attempt to define bad faith in this context. Plainly it includes dishonesty and, as I would hold, includes also some dealings which fall short of the standards of acceptable commercial behaviour observed by reasonable and experienced men in the particular area being examined.

---

[46] *Gromax Plasticulture Ltd v Don & Low Nonwovens Ltd* [1999] R.P.C. 367; *Knoll AG's Trade Mark (No. 698501)* [2002] EWHC 899; [2003] R.P.C. 10.
[47] *DEMON ALE Trade Mark* [2000] R.P.C. 345 (Appointed Person: Geoffrey Hobbs Q.C.).
[48] *Byford v Oliver* [2003] EWHC 295, Ch.; [2003] E.M.L.R. 20 (former band member registering name of band after they had left the band).
[49] [1999] R.P.C. 367.

Parliament has wisely not attempted to explain in detail what is or is not bad faith in this context; how far a dealing must so fall- short in order to amount to bad faith is a matter best left to be adjudged not by some paraphrase by the courts (which leads to the danger of the courts then construing not the Act but the paraphrase) but by reference to the words of the Act and upon a regard to all material surrounding circumstances."

Reprehensible behaviour that is not actually dishonest is sufficient to trigger the application of s.3(6).[50] Thus an applicant (aware of a third party using a mark abroad with an intention to apply in the UK) applying to register a mark in the UK to pre-empt the third party and to improve its bargaining position vis á vis the third party, acts in bad faith.[51]

It has been said that an allegation that a trade mark application has been made in bad faith is a serious allegation equatable to an allegation of commercial fraud.[52] No such allegation should be made unless it could be fully and properly pleaded and it could certainly not be proved by inference alone.[53]

**5–021**   The Trade Mark Registry Works Manual states as follows in relation to images and bad faith:

> "9.11.3 **Portraits or pictures of individuals**
> Where a sign consists of or contains a portrait or picture of a famous living or recently deceased person the examiner should object under section 3(6) of the Act unless the permission of that person, or if recently deceased their legal representative, has been obtained. In the case of persons who are not well known, the examiner should *not* object and permission is *not* required. (see also paragraph 3.12.10)
> 9.11.4 **Representations of famous paintings**
> If a sign contains a representation of a famous painting it is *not* necessary to object under Section 3(6). Objections based on copyright should normally be left to the opposition.
> 9.11.5 **Pictorial representations or names of well known buildings**
> It will NOT be necessary to take an objection under Section 3(6) except in the case of applications to register the names or pictures of well known buildings for films and videos, printed matter and photographs falling within Classes 9 and 16 and tourist services within Classes 35, 39 and 42. In these circumstances the consent of the owner of the building will be required. There will also be questions of distinctiveness for goods in classes 9 & 16."

There is also a statement in relation to pictures of Royal Palaces which should not be registerable without the consent of the Queen or the relevant member of the Royal family.[54]

---

[50] *DAAWAT Trade Mark* [2003] R.P.C. 11 (Appointed Person: Geoffrey Hobbs Q.C.).
[51] *ibid.*
[52] *ROYAL ENFIELD Trade Marks* [2002] R.P.C. 24 (Appointed Person: Simon Thorley Q.C.)
[53] *ibid.*
[54] Trade Marks Registry Works Manual, Ch.6, para.9.11.4.

## RELATIVE GROUNDS FOR REFUSAL OF REGISTRATION

Section 5 sets out relative grounds for refusal of registration. Its provisions **5–022** broadly prevent registration of marks that conflict with pre-existing registered marks or common law unregistered marks. It should be noted that an "earlier trade mark" for these purposes is defined in s.11 of the Act.[55]

If a proposed trade mark that is identical with an earlier trade mark and the goods/services for which the trade mark is applied for are identical with the goods or services for which the earlier trade mark is protected, the proposed trade mark shall not be registerable.[56]

If the trade mark is either (a) identical to the earlier mark but the regis- **5–023** tration sought is for similar goods/services, or (b) similar to the earlier mark and the registration sought is for similar or identical services, the mark shall not be registered if there exists a likelihood of confusion on the part of the public, which includes the likelihood of association with the earlier trade mark.[57]

If the trade mark is either identical to or similar to an earlier trade mark, and it is to be registered for goods or services which are *not* similar to those for which the earlier trade mark is protected, the mark shall not be registered where the use of the later mark, without due cause, would take unfair advantage of, or be detrimental to the distinctive character or the reputation of the earlier trade mark.[58]

A trade mark shall not be registered if, or to the extent that, its use in the **5–024** United Kingdom is liable to be prevented:

(a) by virtue of any rule of law (in particular, the law of passing off) protecting an unregistered trade mark or other sign used in the course of trade, or

(b) by virtue of an earlier right (excluding those earlier trade mark rights listed in s.5(1) to (3)) in particular by virtue of the law of copyright, design right or registered designs.

None of the relative grounds for refusal of registration prevents the registration of a trade mark where the proprietor of the earlier trade mark or other earlier right consents to the registration.[59]

---

[55] Essentially earlier registered UK, Community and international trade marks, pending applications where the date of application pre-dates the mark in question, and unregistered trade marks.
[56] TMA 1994, s.5(1).
[57] TMA 1994, s.5(2).
[58] TMA 1994, s.5(3).
[59] TMA 1994, s.5(5).

## PHOTOGRAPHS GENERALLY

**5–025**   In principle, any photograph can be registered as a trade mark if it satisfies the requirements of the 1994 Act. The key thing is that the image must be distinctive. As noted above,[60] photographs merely of a product itself (such as a simple squeeze of toothpaste or coffee beans) would not be registerable as other traders would legitimately wish to use such pictures in respect of their products.

It has to be remembered that the function of a trade mark is to guarantee the trade mark as indication of origin.[61] Many failed attempts at registering photographs are essentially a collateral attempt to acquire trade mark rights in the subject of the photograph—whether that be the image of a person or a building or product.

**5–026**   As Lord Simonds L.C. said in *Yorkshire Copper Works Ltd's Application*[62]:

"Paradoxically perhaps, the more apt a word to describe the goods of a manufacturer, the less apt it is to distinguish them: for a word that is apt to describe the goods of A, is likely to be apt to describe the similar goods of B."

The same principle can be applied to photographs. So the more that a photograph comprises a mere non-distinctive image of goods or services (*e.g.* just coffee beans or a waiter serving at a table), the less apt it is to distinguish them.

Section 32(3) of the 1994 Act and the application form require an applicant for a trade mark to state that the mark is being used in relation to the classes of goods and services applied for or that he has a *bona fide* intention so to use it. Applications will be accepted if they cover many classes.[63] But blanket applications for vast numbers of classes may result in the Registrar raising an objection under s.3(6). The applicant would then need to demonstrate that he intended to use the mark in connection with all the goods and services claimed.

## PHOTOGRAPHS OF PEOPLE

**5–027**   Photographs and other portraits of people are registerable as trade marks if they satisfy the requirements of s.1 of the 1994 Act set out above. The main points to note are:

---

[60] See above at para.5–011.
[61] *Canon Kabushiki Kaisha v Metro-Goldwyn Mayer Inc* (Case C-39/97) [1999] R.P.C. 117. See also Recital 10 of the Directive.
[62] (1953) 71 R.P.C. 150 at 153.
[63] Trade Marks Works Registry Manual, Ch.6, para.9.11.1.

(1) only the image that is registered is protected; registration of one image of a person does not give a monopoly right on their appearance;

(2) the image must be distinctive in the sense that it would be taken by the public as an indication of trade source;

(3) if the applicant is not the person represented in the photograph or does not have the consent of the person in the photograph (where the person is still alive), registration may be refused on the basis of bad faith;

(4) applications to register a large number of different photographs of a person in respect of a large number of classes of goods are equally at risk of an objection under s.3(6) (bad faith).

It is worth observing at the outset however, that the Trade Marks Registry Works Manual in relation to registration of images of people states "Such cases raise complex issues. Unit Managers should be consulted in all cases."[64]

Registration of images of people as trade marks is not a new phenomenon. In 1897, a registered trade mark for "Army & Navy Paregoric tablets" consisting of a portrait of the manufacturer in an oval with the words "The New Conqueror. Never known to fail" was held to be distinctive.[65] The argument that a photograph of a human being was not capable of being a distinctive device was rejected. The Court of Appeal approved the findings of the judge below who said:

**5–028**

"In the case before me the photograph is distinctive. I can see no reason why the photograph of a person who invents a Trade Mark should not be in itself distinctive."[66]

In the same case, Lindley L.J. said:

**5–029**

"Why cannot a portrait of a human face be a distinctive device? . . . I can understand that [Counsel for the defendant] might be right if he had evidence to show that a portrait like this—a photograph more or less substantially like it—was common in the trade, so that it did not, in fact distinguish, and could not be registered as distinguishing the Plaintiff's goods . . . There might be already on the Register a face more or less like this so that the Registrar might say, "I cannot register another, because it is very likely to deceive.' I can understand that. But, in the absence of any circumstance of that kind, I cannot conceive upon what ground we could justify a decision to the effect that a face like this cannot be registered because it is not or cannot be a distinctive device. Distinctive of what? The object is to distinguish the Plaintiff's goods from other people's. Why

---

[64] Ch.6, para.3.12.10.
[65] *Rowland v Mitchell* (1897) 14 R.P.C. 37. See also *Re Anderson* (1884) LR 26 Ch. D. 409.
[66] *ibid.*, at 39 (*per* Romer J.) quoted and approved by Lord Russell C.J.

cannot the Plaintiff use this which has never been used before to distinguish this class of goods from other classes of goods, or goods of one maker from goods of another when it is registered and used for that purpose? I fail to appreciate the difficulty I confess; but I do protest against the notion that we are to lay down a general proposition that the photographs of human faces cannot be registered because it is not within the Act of Parliament."[67]

Photographs of the Queen or members of the Royal Family are prima facie not registerable unless they have consented. This is due to s.4(1) of the 1994 Act which is set out above.[68]

**5–030**    A number of photographs of famous people have been registered in the United Kingdom as trade marks. They include the pop group Abba[69]; footballers Allan Shearer,[70] Eric Cantona,[71] and Jakob Stam[72]; Formula 1 racing drivers Damon Hill,[73] Jacques Villeneuve,[74] and Alexander Wurz[75]; gardener Alan Titchmarsh[76]; and Claire Rayner, "agony aunt" and writer.[77] Images of deceased celebrities registered as trade marks include Marilyn Monroe[78]; S.F. Cody, inventor and Wild West show man[79]; and author Dale Carnegie.[80]

Applications to register images of people that have been refused include an application by the Executors of the will of Diana, Princess of Wales to register 26 photographs of Diana, Princess of Wales in 25 different classes.[81] The photographs were all head shots.[82] An application to register an image of the head of a Christ like figure was also refused.[83]

## Distinctiveness in human image as a trade mark

**5–031**    A major difficulty with registration of photographs of celebrities as trade marks is that the use of a person's image in connection with memorabilia

---

[67] *ibid.*, at 45.
[68] See above at para.5–018.
[69] Trade Mark No.1071440. See below at para.5–031, n.84.
[70] Trade Mark No.2117215.
[71] Trade Mark No.2120277.
[72] Trade Mark No.2176748.
[73] Trade Mark No.2036489.
[74] Trade Mark No.2050596.
[75] Trade Mark No.2165095.
[76] Trade Mark No.2277288.
[77] Trade Mark No.2224661A.
[78] Trade Mark No.1308839.
[79] Trade Mark No.2150320. S.F Cody (died 1913).
[80] Trade Mark No.785089. Dale Carnegie (1888–1955).
[81] Application No.2149520. Refused following an ex parte hearing in 1998 which was not appealed. Accordingly, the reasons for refusal were not published. For discussion of the applications concerning Diana, Princess of Wales and whether a registration of a certification mark should have been considered see B. Isaac, *Merchandising or Fundraising? Trade Marks and the Diana, Princess of Wales Memorial Fund* [1998] 20 E.I.P.R. 441.
[82] The images can be viewed by inputting the application number into the UK Trade Mark Database search for a Trade Mark Number available via the Patent Office website at *http://www.patent.gov.uk/*.
[83] Application No.2307467.

and merchandise has a prima facie tendency to identify the goods with a particular subject matter (*i.e.* the celebrity) rather than a particular trade source.[84] It is not an insurmountable difficulty and such photographs have been registered.[85] If it is proposed to contend that the mark is indicative of "genuine source", in practice this is more likely to be effective if the photograph is used in combination with words indicating that the products are "Official" merchandise.[86]

Cases dealing with registration of the names of celebrities are instructive as the approach of the Trade Mark Registry and the courts in considering distinctiveness in connection with images and celebrity reputation.

In *Elvis Presley Trade Marks*,[87] an American company (accepted to be the successor in title to the merchandising activities of Elvis Presley when he was alive) applied to register a manuscript signature of Elvis Presley together with the words "Elvis" and "Elvis Presley" in Class 3 (toilet preparations, soaps, etc). On appeal from the Trade Mark Registry, holding that the marks were not registerable, Laddie J. observed:  **5–032**

> "Just as Elvis Presley did not own his name so as to be able to prevent all and any uses of it by third parties, so Enterprises can have no greater rights. Similarly, Elvis Presley did not own his appearance. For example, during his life he could not prevent a fan from having a tattoo put on his chest or a drawing on his car which looked like the musician simply on the basis that it was his appearance which was depicted. For the same reason under our law. Enterprises does not own the likeness of Elvis Presley. No doubt it can prevent the reproduction of the drawings and photographs of him in which it owns copyright, but it has no right to prevent the reproduction or exploitation of any of the myriad of photographs, including press photographs, and drawings in which it does not own the copyright simply by reason of the fact that they contain or depict a likeness of Elvis Presley. Nor could it complain if a fan commissioned a sculptor to create a life-size statue of the musician in a characteristic pose and then erected it in his garden. It can only complain if the reproduction or use of the likeness results in the infringement of some recognised legal right which it does own."[88]

Laddie J. refused to accept an argument that use of the name "Elvis" would be taken by the public to distinguish "genuine" goods from a "genuine source". In considering this aspect, he said:  **5–033**

---

[84] See for example comments of Laddie J. in *Elvis Presley Trade Marks* [1997] R.P.C. 543 at 556. Upheld on appeal at [1999] R.P.C. 567; *Diana, Princess of Wales Trade Mark* [2001] E.T.M.R. 25.

[85] See the list above in para.5–030.

[86] Although cf. *Diana, Princess of Wales Trade Mark* [2001] E.T.M.R. 25 at para.62 *per* Allan James, Trade Marks Registry (use of other signs such as an "official" logo suggested that the name *per se* was not capable of guaranteeing connection in trade of the goods).

[87] [1999] R.P.C. 567; [1997] R.P.C. 543, CA (Laddie J.).

[88] [1997] R.P.C. 543 at 547.

"It may be that in some cases a plaintiff in a passing off action or an applicant for a registered trade mark will be able to show that to be the case. But I am not willing to assume that that is the public perception generally. On the contrary, my own experience suggests that such an assumption would be false. When people buy a toy of a well known character because it depicts that character, I have no reason to believe that they care one way or the other who made, sold or licensed it. When a fan buys a poster or a cup bearing an image of his star, he is buying a likeness, not a product from a particular source. Similarly the purchaser of any one of the myriad of cheap souvenirs of the royal wedding bearing pictures of Prince Charles and Diana, Princess of Wales, wants mementoes with likenesses. He is likely to be indifferent as to the source. Of course it is possible that, as a result of the peculiarities of the way goods are marketed or advertised, an inference of association with a particular trader may be possible to draw. This may be the case when the proprietor's products bear the word 'Official'. But that does not mean that absent that word members of the public would draw any such inference."[89]

Where there is a trade in the image of a person in its own right (*i.e.* because the public want a product with an image of the person on irrespective of the source), that person has no right to stop others legitimately trading in products bearing such images:

"there is no reason why Mr. Shaw or anyone else for that matter should not sell memorabilia and mementoes of Elvis Presley, including products embellished with pictures of him, and such traders are likely, in the ordinary course of their business and without any improper motive, to desire to use the name Elvis or Elvis Presley upon or in connection with their own such goods."[90]

**5–034**    The Court of Appeal upheld the judgment of Laddie J. Morritt L.J. observed:

"In the field of memorabilia, which I consider includes consumer items bearing the name or likeness of a famous figure, it must be for that person to ensure by whatever means may be open to him or her that the public associate his or her name with the source of the goods. In the absence of evidence of such association in my view the court should be very slow to infer it."[91]

Similarly, Simon Brown L.J. stated:

"In addressing the critical issue of distinctiveness there should be no *a priori* assumption that only a celebrity or his successors may ever market

---

[89] [1997] R.P.C. 543 at 554.
[90] *ibid.*, at 552.
[91] [1999] R.P.C. 567 at 594.

(or licence the marketing of) his own character. Monopolies should not be so readily created."[92]

Robert Walker L.J. said:

"In my judgment the judge was right to conclude that the Elvis mark has very little inherent distinctiveness. That conclusion was reached by a number of intermediate steps, one of which was the judge's finding that members of the public purchase Elvis Presley merchandise not because it comes from a particular source, but because it carries the name or image of Elvis Presley. Indeed the judge came close to finding (although he did not in terms find) that for goods of the sort advertised by Elvisly Yours (or by Enterprises in the United States) the commemoration of the late Elvis Presley is the product, and the article on which his name or image appears (whether a poster, a pennant, a mug or a piece of soap) is little more than a vehicle."[93]

It can be seen from the above dicta that (1) evidence of an existing merchandising practice and that the public associate a mark with a particular "genuine" or "official" source is vital in opposition proceedings, and (2) there is no inherent distinctiveness in a person's appearance or image.

In a decision of the Trade Marks Registry refusing (under s.3(1)(b)) an   **5–035**
application to register "Jane Austen" for toiletries, it was said that there were a number of factors which were likely to have a bearing on how the use of a well-known figure's name on goods was perceived and accordingly whether such use signified trade origin.[94] The factors might include[95]:

(i)   the nature and extent of the individual's reputation;

(ii)   whether there are any surrounding reasons why a trade in souvenirs, etc. may have developed, for instance, because of an individual's strong association with an area (Hardy's Wessex or Bronte country) or a particular style (William Morris say);

(iii)   whether, in the case of contemporary figures, the individual established any trade mark rights during his or her lifetime;

(iv)   whether any existing trade in souvenirs, memorabilia, etc. exists or (in the case of someone recently deceased) can be expected to arise;

(v)   whether descendants, the estate, trustees or other such body have, through use, established any rights in relation to the name of the individual (and, if so, whether to the exclusion of others);

---

[92] *ibid.*, at 598.
[93] [1999] R.P.C. 567 at 585.
[94] *Jane Austen Trade Mark* [2000] R.P.C. 879.
[95] *ibid.*, at 886 *per* Mr M. Reynolds, Trade Marks Registry.

(vi) the extent to which the life and works of the individual are kept alive either by general public interest or media coverage, etc. in such a way as to generate demand for commercial consumer items;

(vii) the nature of the goods in respect for which registration is sought.

There are indications that considerations differ if the image in question is that of a living person or recently deceased or whether it is that of an historical figure or someone who has been dead for a long time. The Trade Marks Registry Manual states that in the cases of pictures of people who are alive or recently deceased, objection should be taken unless the permission of the person or their estate has been obtained.[96] Where the image is of an historical figure, such as William Shakespeare, it is more likely that there will be a high level of existing trade in commercial consumer items bearing his image and that the name/image would not be taken as an indication of trade source.[97]

### Choice of photograph of a person to register as a trade mark

**5–036**    The reality is that a simple photograph of a famous person will, in most cases, have a comparatively low inherent distinctiveness. "Simple photograph" in this context is used to mean any photograph of an individual (whether full length or head shot) that is a mere portrait in the sense that it is simply a typical record of the person's image. In other words, a photograph of a person that is like any other photograph of that person bar minor changes such as clothes or angle. So, in the absence of an unusual pose or faux pas, a paparazzi shot of a celebrity on a red carpet arriving at one premiere will be very like a different photograph of the same person arriving at another premiere on a different day. These types of "simple photographs" are more likely to face objection as being non-distinctive as opposed to more visually distinctive photographs.

Simple photographs of a celebrity, including those of them "at work" whether performing in concert, scoring a goal or whatever, are images that will almost certainly appear on all kinds of memorabilia such as posters and t-shirts. Accordingly, they are images which other traders are likely in the ordinary course of the business and without any improper motive to want to use on goods.[98] The vast majority of celebrities in the modern world are regularly photographed by the media in circumstances where the copyright in the photograph vests in the photograph or the media organisation.[99] Where the copyright owner is not the celebrity, absent any breach of confidence or contractual provisions arising from a photoshoot, the celebrity has no rights or control over the image. It is therefore relatively easy to obtain a licence to reproduce a photograph of a particular celebrity, whether

---

[96] Ch.6, para.9.11.3 quoted in full above at a para.5–021.
[97] *Jane Austen Trade Mark* [2000] R.P.C. 879 at 887 *per* Mr M. Reynolds, Trade Marks Registry.
[98] *Elvis Presley* [1997] R.P.C. 543 at 552 *per* Laddie J.
[99] As to ownership of copyright in photographs see above at paras 2–073 *et seq.*

from a picture library or otherwise, because so many photographs outside the control of the person featured are in existence. "Simple photographs" for this reason have a low inherent distinctiveness and risk being refused trade mark status because such an image would not be taken by the public as an indication of trade source.

The Trade Marks Registry Works Manual states that where (prior to the date of application) other traders are already producing souvenirs and memorabilia in relation to a famous person, even if not of the same type as the applicant's goods, there is a particular risk that the public will be unlikely to regard a picture of that person as indicative of origin.[1] If so, there will be an objection under s.3(1)(b) and (d).   **5–037**

The ideal type of photograph of a person to select to use as a trademark is one that has a high degree of visual distinctiveness and is not just a "simple photograph" or mere portrait. A good example of such a mark is one of Damon Hill, the Formula 1 racing driver,[2] which shows just his eyes and part of his racing helmet. An image of Marilyn Monroe with her skirt blowing up in the scene from the film the Seven Year Itch is a registered UK trade mark owned by her estate.[3] This is another example of an image that is not a mere portrait.

Mere portraits are not automatically excluded from being registered trade marks. Examples of simple photographs of a person registered as trade marks include footballers Allan Shearer[4] and Jakob Stam[5] and racing driver Alexander Wurz.[6] Other ways of seeking to make a simple portrait photograph more visually distinctive for the purposes of trade mark registration include turning the photograph sideways[7]; combining one or more photographs into one mark such as a series of three portraits side by side[8]; or adding words or a logo.[9]

### PHOTOGRAPHS OF BUILDINGS

The trade marking of images of buildings and building facades is relatively uncommon in the United Kingdom. This contrasts with the USA[10] where a   **5–038**

---

[1] Ch.6, para.3.12.10.
[2] Trade Mark No.2036489. Can be viewed via the Trade Mark Registry online database, see above at para.5–030, n.82.
[3] Trade Mark No.1308839.
[4] Trade Mark No.2117215.
[5] Trade Mark No.2176748.
[6] Trade Mark No.2165095.
[7] Eric Cantona, Trade Mark No.2120277.
[8] Jacques Villeneuve, Trade Mark No.2050596.
[9] Alan Titchmarsh, Trade Mark No.2277288. Dale Carnegie, Trade Mark No.785089.
[10] For discussion of registration of building facades as trade marks in the USA see: K. Christ, *Eddifice Complex: Protecting Landmark Buildings As Intellectual Property—A Critique of Available Protections and A Proposal.* (2002) 92 Trademark Reporter 1041; A. Lesieutre Honan, *The Skyscraping Reach of the Lanham Act: How Far Should the Protection of Famous Building Design Trademarks Be Extended?* (2000) 94 Northwestern University Law Review 1509; and L.B. Burgunder, *Commercial Photographs of Famous Buildings: The Sixth Circuit Fails to Make the Hall of Fame* (1999) 89 Trademark Reporter 791.

large number of building facades are registered as trade marks, for example the Chrysler Building[11]; the Empire State Building[12]; the Wrigley Building in Chicago[13]; and Monticello,[14] to name but a few. The building marks registered in the USA tend to take the form of black and white line drawings in a logo style recording the architectural features of the building rather than actual photographs. Even limited registration of the facade as a logo type drawing can cause difficulties for photographers as discussed below at para.5–053.

In the United Kingdom, some buildings or land marks have been registered as trade marks. As with the USA, virtually all of these are "logo-ised" line drawings of the buildings rather than photographs. The following are examples of representations of buildings or structures registered as trade marks in the UK:

the Houses of Parliament for HP sauce[15]; the Dome in 15 classes ranging from soaps to clothing to confectionery[16]; the Royal Albert Hall[17]; Blenheim Palace[18]; Chatsworth House[19]; Glasgow School of Art[20]; Shakespeare's Globe Theatre[21]; Balmoral Castle[22]; Windsor Castle for pallets and packing cases[23]; Castle Howard York for furniture[24]; a representation of Durham Cathedral with the words "Durham City Golf Club"[25]; Ripon Cathedral[26]; the Eiffel Tower for various preservatives and food stuffs[27]; the Roman Colleseum for various clothing[28]; a triumphal arch for spectacles[29] a trilithon for newspapers and printed matter[30]; and a police public call box.[31]

---

[11] Registered November 20, 1979, USA Trademark Reg No.1,126,888. A copy of the registered image of this trade mark and all the following marks can be viewed on the United States Patent & Trade Mark Office website trade mark database at *http://www.uspto.gov/*.

[12] Registered February 27, 2001, USA Trademark Reg No.2,430,828.

[13] Registered February 11, 1997, USA Trademark Reg No.2,037,110.

[14] Registered April 18, 2000, USA Trademark Reg No.2,342,042.

[15] Trade Mark No.275688. See also a representation of a tower turret with the words "The House of Commons" for videotapes Trade Mark No.2291018. A copy of the registered image of this trade mark and all the following marks can be viewed on the UK Patent Office website trade mark database accessible via the home page at *http://www.patent.gov.uk/*.

[16] Trade Mark No.2211005.

[17] Trade Mark No.2003138.

[18] Trade Mark No.2197001.

[19] Trade Mark No.1427280.

[20] Trade Mark No.2111810.

[21] Trade Mark No.2258480.

[22] Trade Mark No.2184260.

[23] Trade Mark No.949529. Also registered to a different proprietor for fish and fish products: Trade Mark No.990874.

[24] Trade Mark No.1389105.

[25] Trade Mark No.2173440.

[26] Trade Mark No.2190938.

[27] Trade Mark No.244411.

[28] Trade Mark No.2163448.

[29] Trade Mark No.1315467.

[30] Trade Mark No.853402.

[31] In some quarters known as a Tardis. Trade Mark No.2104259. Proprietor, the BBC.

There is however, no reason in principle why a photograph of a building    **5–039**
could not be registered as a trade mark subject to compliance with the 1994
Act and in particular the requirement for distinctiveness. Again, as with
images of people, the most common problem is likely to be the risk that a
photograph of a famous building would not necessarily be taken as an
indication of trade source. The observations above concerning distinctiveness in relation to human image are equally applicable to images of public
buildings.[32] As with celebrity memorabilia, in respect of many famous
"landmark" buildings there will already be an existing trade in souvenir
items bearing photographs of the building which would militate against the
Registry taking a view that any one photograph would be taken by the
public as indicative of trade origin. For example, photographs of Buck-
ingham Palace and the Houses of Parliament can be found on a myriad of
souvenir items including postcards, mugs, t-shirts, etc. The more famous a
building, the more unlikely it is that a single photograph would be an
effective trade mark. It is probably for this reason that the majority of trade
marks of buildings are logo type drawings of a building rather than a
photograph. However, a visually distinctive photograph of a building
should, in principle, be registerable.

See also the Trade Marks Registry Work Manual statement as to pictorial
representations of buildings and bad faith quoted above at para.5–021 as to
policy and the circumstances where the consent of the building owner is
required.

## GROUNDLESS THREATS OF TRADE MARK INFRINGEMENT

Making groundless threats of proceedings for infringement of a registered    **5–040**
trade mark is actionable under the Trade Marks Act 1994 unless it is a
threat concerning (1) the application of the mark to goods or their packaging, (2) the importation of goods to which the mark has been applied or to
the packaging, (3) the supply of services under the mark.[33] Mere notification
that a mark is registered or that an application for registration has been
made does not constitute a threat of proceedings.[34]

Relief available for groundless threats is any of the following: (a) a
declaration that the threats are unjustifiable, (b) an injunction restraining
continuance of the threats, and (c) damages for any loss sustained by the
threats.[35] However, no relief is available if the acts in respect of which the
defendant threatened proceedings constitute (or if done would have constituted) infringement of the registered trade mark[36] concerned unless the
mark is invalid or liable to revocation.[37]

---

[32] See above at paras 5–031 to 5–037.
[33] TMA 1994, s.21.
[34] TMA 1994, s.21(5).
[35] TMA 1994, s.21(2).
[36] TMA 1994, s.21(2).
[37] TMA 1994, s.21(3).

CRIMINAL PROCEEDINGS

**5–041**   The Trade Marks Act 1994 creates various criminal offences. First, offences concerning unauthorised use of the trade mark (*i.e.* counterfeiting)[38] and secondly, offences concerning misrepresenting the status of a mark.[39]

In particular, it should be noted that it is a criminal offence to falsely represent that a mark is a registered trade mark knowing or having reason to believe that a mark is false.[40] The use of the word "registered" or of any other word or symbol importing a reference (express or implied) to registration shall be deemed to be a representation as to registration under the 1994 Act unless it is shown that the reference is to a registration elsewhere in the UK and the mark is in fact so registered for the relevant goods/services.[41] A person guilty of this offence is liable on summary conviction to a fine not exceeding level 3 on the standard scale.[42]

INFRINGEMENT

**5–042**   Section 10 of the Trade Marks Act 1994 provides as follows:

**"Infringement of registered trade mark**
**10.**—(1) A person infringes a registered trade mark if he uses in the course of trade a sign which is identical with the trade mark in relation to goods or services which are identical with those for which it is registered.

(2) A person infringes a registered trade mark if he uses in the course of trade a sign where because

(a) the sign is identical with the trade mark and is used in relation to goods or services similar to those for which the trade mark is registered, or

(b) the sign is similar to the trade mark and is used in relation to goods or services identical with or similar to those for which the trade mark is registered,

there exists a likelihood of confusion on the part of the public, which includes the likelihood of association with the trade mark.

(3) A person infringes a registered trade mark if he uses in the course of trade a sign which

(a) is identical with or similar to the trade mark, and

(b) is used in relation to goods or services which are not similar to those for which the trade mark is registered,

---

[38] TMA 1994, ss.92 and 93.
[39] TMA 1994, ss.94 (falsification of the register) and 95 (falsely representing a mark as registered).
[40] TMA 1994, s.94(1).
[41] TMA 1994, s.94(2).
[42] TMA 1994, s.94(3).

where the trade mark has a reputation in the United Kingdom and the use of the sign, being without due cause, takes unfair advantage of, or is detrimental to, the distinctive character or the repute of the trade mark.

(4) For the purposes of this section a person uses a sign if, in particular, he

(a) affixes it to goods or the packaging thereof;
(b) offers or exposes goods for sale, puts them on the market or stocks them for those purposes under the sign, or offers or supplies services under the sign;
(c) imports or exports goods under the sign; or
(d) uses the sign on business papers or in advertising.

(5) A person who applies a registered trade mark to material intended to be used for labelling or packaging goods, as a business paper, or for advertising goods or services, shall be treated as a party to any use of the material which infringes the registered trade mark if when he applied the mark he knew or had reason to believe that the application of the mark was not duly authorised by the proprietor or a licensee.

(6) Nothing in the preceding provisions of this section shall be construed as preventing the use of a registered trade mark by any person for the purpose of identifying goods or services as those of the proprietor or a licensee.

But any such use otherwise than in accordance with honest practices in industrial or commercial matters shall be treated as infringing the registered trade mark if the use without due cause takes unfair advantage of, or is detrimental to, the distinctive character or repute of the trade mark."

The proprietor of a registered trade mark has exclusive rights in the trade mark which are infringed by the use of the trade mark in the United Kingdom without his consent.[43] The acts amounting to infringement are set out in s.10[44] which is reproduced above.   **5–043**

A trade mark is infringed if it is used in the course of trade in respect of exactly the same goods or services for which the mark is registered.[45] "Use" in this context is defined in s.10(4) above. The ECJ has stated that Art.5(1)(a) of the directive (from which s.3(1) derives) must be interpreted as meaning that a sign is identical with the trade mark where it reproduces, without any modification or addition, all elements constituting the trade mark or where, viewed as a whole, it contains differences so insignificant that they may go unnoticed by an average consumer.[46]

If a non-identical but similar sign is used for the same or similar goods for which the mark is registered, there is no infringement unless there is a

---

[43] TMA 1994, s.9(1).
[44] *ibid.*
[45] TMA 1994, s.10(1).
[46] *LTJ Diffusion SA v Sadas Verbaudet AS* (Case 291/00) (Arthur et Felicie) [2003] F.S.R. 34. For AG Jacobs Opinion see [2003] F.S.R. 1.

likelihood of confusion on the part of the public.[47] The same is true where an identical sign is used for similar goods.[48]

If either an identical mark or a similar mark is used in respect of goods/ services which are *not* similar to those for which the trade mark is registered, there is no infringement unless the use of the sign in the course of trade takes unfair advantage of or is detrimental to the reputation of the registered trade mark in the UK.[49]

## Trade mark use and the nature of use amounting to infringement

**5–044**      There has been much debate and consideration by the courts[50] as to whether it is a requirement of infringement under the 1994 Act to establish that the infringing use of a trade mark was "trade mark use", *i.e.* use of the mark in a way which indicates trade origin.

This issue arose in the case of *Arsenal Football Club v Reed* which concerned the use by a street trader of a football club's trade marks on souvenirs. This case has had an initial hearing in the Chancery Division,[51] a reference to the ECJ,[52] a further hearing in the Chancery Division in the light of the ECJ ruling,[53] and then an appeal to the Court of Appeal[54] in respect of the latter Chancery Division hearing. Although some principles can be distilled from these decisions, at the time of writing the situation was somewhat complicated by a decision of the House of Lords in a criminal case *R v Johnstone*[55] which interpreted the decision of the ECJ in a different way to the Court of Appeal.

It is fair to say that at the time of writing, the question as to what extent infringement requires the use to be "trade mark use" or even what exactly is encompassed by the term "trade mark use" is not particularly clear. In the words of Lord Walker, "The law is therefore in something of a state of disarray."[56] The starting point should be the ECJ's observations which take precedence. However, in order to understand the conflicting dicta, it is necessary to consider the background to the Court of Appeal decision.

**5–045**      In *Arsenal Football Club v Reed*, Arsenal football club had registered various trade marks, in particular a club crest and a cannon logo, which were used by the defendant, a street trader, on football scarves and other memorabilia. Arsenal issued proceedings for passing off and trade mark

---

[47] TMA 1994, s.10(2).
[48] *ibid.*
[49] TMA 1994, s.10(3).
[50] *e.g. Holterhoff v Freiesleben* (C2/00) (ECJ) [2002] All E.R. (EC) 665; [2002] E.T.M.R. 79; [2002] F.S.R. 52; *Philips Electronics NV v Remington Consumer Products Ltd (No.1)* (CA prior to reference to ECJ) [1999] E.T.M.R. 816; [1999] R.P.C. 809; *Bravado Merchandising Services Ltd v Mainstream Publishing (Edinburgh) Ltd* (Scotland, Outer House) [1996] F.S.R. 205; *British Sugar Plc v James Robertson & Sons Ltd* [1996] R.P.C. 281; [1997] E.T.M.R. 118.
[51] [2001] E.T.M.R. 77; [2001] R.P.C. 46.
[52] [2003] All E.R. (EC) 1; [2003] E.T.M.R. 19; [2003] R.P.C. 9. Advocate General's opinion at [2002] E.T.M.R. 82.
[53] [2002] EWHC 2695; [2003] 1 All E.R. 137; [2003] E.T.M.R. 36.
[54] [2003] EWCA Civ 696; [2003] 3 All E.R. 865; [2003] E.T.M.R. 73; [2003] R.P.C. 39.
[55] [2003] UKHL 28; [2003] 1 W.L.R. 1736; [2003] 3 All E.R. 884.
[56] *R v Johnstone (Robert Alexander)* [2003] UKHL 28 at para.85.

infringement. At first instance,[57] Laddie J. dismissed the claim for passing off. In relation to trade mark infringement, he expressed the view that the use of the marks on the defendant's products was as a badge of support and not as an indication of origin. His lordship concluded that in order for the claimant to succeed, it would be necessary for s.10 to be widely construed to mean infringement occurred even where there was non-trade mark use of the sign. In other words, s.10 would include as infringement use of a trade mark by a third party even where that sign was not being used as an indication of trade source. Laddie J. stayed the action pending reference of the question to the ECJ of whether it was a defence to an action for infringement (identical mark/identical goods) that the use of the trade mark did not indicate trade origin or a connection in trade between the goods and the trade mark proprietor.

The ECJ did not answer the question as formulated. In its judgment, the ECJ stated that a trade mark, in addition to guaranteeing origin, also offered a guarantee that all the goods or services bearing a trade mark had been manufactured or supplied under the control of a single undertaking, which is responsible for their quality.[58] The ECJ said that:

> "It follows that the exclusive right under Art 5(1)(a) of the Directive was conferred in order to enable the trade mark proprietor to protect his specific interests as proprietor, that is, to ensure that the trade mark can fulfill its functions. The exercise of that right must therefore be reserved to cases in which a third party's use of the sign affects or is liable to affect the functions of the trade mark, in particular its essential function of guaranteeing to consumers the origin of the goods."[59]

and later

> "A proprietor may not prohibit the use of a sign identical to a trade mark for goods identical to those for which the mark is registered if that use cannot affect his own interests as proprietor of the mark, having regard to its function."[60]

The ECJ took the view that it did not matter for these purposes whether the goods were sold with a disclaimer stating they were not official Arsenal products as there was a possibility consumers would come across the goods after sale and interpret the trade mark as a designator of origin. It was immaterial whether, in the context of that use, the sign is perceived as a badge of support or loyalty to the trade mark owner.

Back in the Chancery Division, after the ECJ reference, Laddie J. took the view that the ECJ had exceeded its jurisdiction by seeking to overturn the High Court's finding of fact that the trade marks would not be perceived as

---

[57] [2001] R.P.C. 46; [2001] E.T.M.R. 77.
[58] [2003] R.P.C. 9; [2003] All E.R. (EC) 1; [2003] E.T.M.R. 19 at para.48.
[59] *ibid.*, at para.51.
[60] *ibid.*, at para.54.

indicators of trade origin but as badges of support. Laddie J. interpreted the ECJ's ruling to mean that where the defendant's use of a mark is not intended by the defendant or understood by the public to be a designation of origin, there could be no infringement because such use does not prejudice the essential function of the trade mark.[61] He found there was no infringement and dismissed the claimant's claim.

**5–046**    Arsenal appealed to the Court of Appeal which allowed the appeal. The Court of Appeal interpreted the ECJ's judgment as follows:

> "In summary the ECJ held that registration of a trade mark gave to the proprietor a property right ... The relevant consideration was whether the use complained about was likely to damage the property right or, as the ECJ put it, is likely to affect or jeopardise the guarantee of origin which constitutes the essential function of the mark. That did not depend on whether the use complained of was trade mark use."[62]

The Court of Appeal observed that the ECJ was not concerned with whether the use was "trade mark use" but merely whether the third party use affects or was likely to affect the functions of the trade mark.[63] This would include where a competitor wished to take unfair advantage of the reputation of the trade mark by selling products bearing the mark, whether that was trade mark use or not. Where goods not coming from the trade mark owner are in circulation, this affects the ability of the trade mark to guarantee the origin of the goods.[64]

**5–047**    However, the day after the Court of Appeal gave judgment in the *Arsenal* case, the House of Lords gave judgment in *R. v Johnstone*[65] (criminal prosecution under s.92 of the Trade Marks Act 1994). After considering the ECJ judgment in *Arsenal v Reed*, the House of Lords stated that s.10 did not include "non-trade mark use".[66] This was expanded upon by Lord Walker, who, unlike the Court of Appeal, considered that ECJ in the *Arsenal* case had concluded that Mr Reed's use was trade mark use where he said:

> "The [ECJ] stated that Mr Reed's use of the Arsenal sign took place in the context of sales to consumers and was obviously not intended for purely descriptive purposes. The use was such as to create the impression that there was a material link in the course of trade between Mr Reed's goods and AFC. AFC could therefore rely on what Mr Reed has done as trade mark use."[67]

**5–048**    It is submitted, that although it is not particularly clear, the following is the present state of the law:

---

[61] [2002] EWHC 2695 at para.20.
[62] [2003] EWCA Civ 696 at para.33; [2003] 3 All E.R. 865; [2003] R.P.C. 39.
[63] *ibid.*, para.37.
[64] *ibid.*, para.48.
[65] [2003] UKHL 28; [2003] 1 W.L.R. 1736; [2003] 3 All E.R. 884; [2003] F.S.R. 42.
[66] *ibid.*, para.17 *per* Lord Nicholls.
[67] *ibid.*, at para.83.

(1) in order for trade mark infringement to arise, it is necessary that the third party activity in using the mark *affects* the function of the trade mark as a guarantee of origin;

(2) this includes use, where even if at the point of sale the trade mark is not being used as a guarantee of origin, the nature of the trade mark's use by the third party is such that it would give the impression to the public coming across the goods after sale that there was a link between the trade mark owner and the goods;

(3) purely descriptive use of a mark is excluded from s.10 infringement.[68]

The term "trade mark use", meaning use of a trade mark to guarantee origin, is unhelpful given the differing interpretations of the Court of Appeal and House of Lords of the ECJ judgment. Only if the term "trade mark use" is to be taken to have a slightly wider definition than is traditional to mean not only use of the trade mark by the third party to guarantee origin but any use of the trade mark reasonably capable of being interpreted thereafter as a guarantee of origin, could it still be said that s.10 is restricted to trade mark use.

It is to be hoped that the position is clarified by the courts as soon as possible.

## PHOTOGRAPHS OF TRADE MARKS

*"To prevent filmmakers, novelists, painters, and political satirists from*    **5–049**
*including trademarks in their works is to cordon off an important part of*
*modern culture from public discourse."*[69]

A photograph of a trade mark may infringe the proprietor's legal rights in a number of ways:

(1) if the photograph represents the trade mark in a manner affecting the trade mark as a guarantee or origin and infringes under the Act;

(2) if the photograph, in using the trade mark, misrepresents the source of the photograph as being that of the proprietor in the sense of passing off the photograph as the goods of the trade mark proprietor[70];

---

[68] *Arsenal Football Club Plc v Reed* (C206/01) [2003] All E.R. (EC) 1; [2003] E.T.M.R. 19; [2003] R.P.C. 9 at para.54.
[69] Robert N. Kravitz, *Trademarks, Speech, and the Gay Olympics Case*, 69 B.U.L.Rev. 131 at 152 quoted by McKenna J. in *Girl Scouts of US v Bantam Doubleday Dell Publ'g Group, Inc*, 808 F. Supp. 1112 (S.D.N.Y.1992).
[70] This probably would also amount to trade mark infringement. As to passing off see below at Ch.10.

(3) if the trademark is itself a copyright work (for example a logo being an original artistic work in which copyright subsists), a photograph of the trade mark may amount to copyright infringement.

The law of passing off is discussed elsewhere in this work. This section considers photographs of trade marks that may amount to trade mark infringement and photographs of trade marks that may amount to copyright infringement.

### Photographs of trade marks amounting to trade mark infringement

**5–050**    It is clear that, notwithstanding the present confusion as to the law concerning "trade mark use" discussed above at paras 5–044 *et seq.* descriptive use is excluded from infringement. Accordingly, photographs of trade marks in which the trade mark appears in some sort of descriptive way or in any manner which does not affect the trade mark as a badge of origin would not amount to infringement. So, a photograph of a footballer wearing a shirt with a trade mark on it would not constitute trade mark infringement. It may amount to copyright infringement and this is discussed further below at paras 5–054 to 5–056.

It has been said that where companies sponsor sports stars and place trade marks on their shirts, the use of the trade mark is not as a trade mark for shirts but as a form of advertising for the company's artistic work or other emblem or device in which copyright subsists.[71]

**5–051**    In *Trebor Bassett Ltd v The Football Association*,[72] Trebor Bassett produced children's collectible cards bearing photographs and descriptions of famous footballers. Some of the photographs depicted footballers wearing the England football strip with the England team crest of three Lions. The Football Association ("FA") objected on the grounds that this infringed a registered trade mark of the FA. Trebor Bassett issued wrongful threats proceedings under s.21 against the FA who issued a cross-action alleging infringement. In granting summary judgment in favour of Trebor Bassett on the threats action and striking out the FA's infringement action, Rattee J. found that there was no infringement because the sign was not being *used* by Trebor in relation to any goods or services at all. In finding there was no "use" *per se*, Rattee J. stated (and impliedly distinguished) that it was unnecessary to consider whether, in order to infringe, there had to be "trade mark use". His Lordship said:

"In deciding the questions before me, I consider it unnecessary, and therefore inappropriate, for me to decide whether I should adopt the view adopted by Jacob J. in the *British Sugar Plc* case on the question whether use of a sign, to be within section 10(1), has to be used as a trade mark. I express no view on the point. I accept the argument put forward ... on

---

[71] *Arsenal Football Club Plc v Reed (No.1)* [2001] R.P.C. 46 at 939.
[72] [1997] F.S.R. 211.

behalf of Trebor Bassett, that it cannot seriously be argued that by publishing and marketing, on the cards concerned, photographs of players wearing the England team football strip (including the three lions logo) Trebor Bassett is in any sense using the logo in respect of the cards on which the photographs appear. In my judgment it plainly is not. The logo appears on the card only because it is worn by the player whose photograph appears on the card as part of that player's England team football strip, to show that the player himself is an England team player. The reproduction of the photograph on the card inevitably reproduces the England logo on the garments which the player was wearing when the photograph was taken. By such reproduction, in my judgment. Trebor Bassett is not even arguably using the logo, as such, in any real sense of the word 'uses', and is certainly not, in my judgment, using it as a sign in respect of its cards."[73]

It is submitted that this case remains good law and that where there is no "use" per se of a trade mark at all, there is no trade mark infringement. This type of apparently incidental inclusion of trade marks in photographs may amount to copyright infringement if the trade mark is an original logo or copyright work.[74]

The types of photographs of trade marks that, in the light of *Arsenal v*   **5–052**
*Reed*[75] would amount to trade mark infringement are most likely to be photographs where the mark would be taken as an indicator of source rather than simply viewed as the subject of the photograph. If the trade mark is merely part of the subject of the photograph, then the use is properly characterised as descriptive. If, for example, a photograph was taken of a Coca-Cola bottle and that image alone was placed on a poster with the words Coca Cola underneath, that, it is submitted would amount to trade mark infringement.[76] Purchasers of the poster may believe the poster was an official product of the Coca Cola company. There is a risk that where the trade mark is the only or dominant feature of a photograph sold commercially, that the use would be treated as infringing. Ultimately however, whether use of a trade mark amounts to "trade mark use" or other infringing use is a question of fact to be decided on a case by case basis.[77]

The prevalence in the USA for the trade marking of images of public   **5–053**
buildings has caused difficulties for photographers in that jurisdiction.[78] In

---

[73] [1997] F.S.R. 211 at 216.
[74] See below at paras 5–054 to 5–056.
[75] Discussed above at paras 5–044 *et seq.*
[76] An example used in *Rock and Roll Hall of Fame and Museum Inc v Gentile Productions* (6th Cir.) 134 F.3d 749. For facts of this case see below at para.5–053. See also *Coca-Cola Co v Gemini Rising Inc* 346 F. Supp. 1183 (poster showing Coca-Cola script trademark altered to read "Enjoy Cocaine". Injunction granted as use impaired the plaintiff's mark as a selling device).
[77] *R. v Johnstone (Robert Alexander)* [2003] UKHL 28 at paras 36–37 *per* Lord Nicholls and para.87 *per* Lord Walker.
[78] See also *New York Stock Exchange Inc v New York, New York Hotel* 293 F.3d 550 (Las Vegas hotel including a replica of the New York Stock Exchange facade) and the articles cited at above at para.5–038, n.10.

*Rock and Roll Hall of Fame and Museum Inc v Gentile Productions*[79], the Rock and Roll Hall of Fame designed by the architect I.M. Pei had trade marked its "unique and distinctive design". The defendant, Charles Gentile, a professional photographer, took a photograph of the museum against a colourful sunset and sold the image as posters. The Hall of Fame issued trade mark infringement proceedings against the photographer and sought an injunction on the basis that the photograph and the words on the poster identifying the museum were likely to lead consumers to believe the poster was sponsored by the museum. The Sixth Circuit Court of Appeals refused to grant injunction. Although obviously this case was decided under the law of the United States, the following observations by the court are equally applicable to the law of trade marks in the United Kingdom and may be of assistance to practitioners faced with a similar factual situation:

> "... when we view the photograph in Gentile's poster, we do not readily recognise the design of the Museum's building as an indicator of source or sponsorship. What we see rather, is a photograph of an accessible, well-known public landmark. Stated somewhat differently, in Gentile's poster, the Museum's building strikes us not as a separate distinct mark *on the good* but rather, as the good itself."[80]

The ever expanding rights of intellectual property owners should not be permitted to conflict with freedom of expression to the point where photographers cannot freely photograph public buildings. This would amount to an unjustifiable fetter on artistic freedom that cannot be in the public interest. The quotation above at para.5–049, sums this up very well. It is to be hoped that if similar issues fall to be considered by the courts in the United Kingdom, they will adopt a similar approach to that of the US Court of Appeals for the 6th Circuit in *Rock and Roll Hall of Fame and Museum Inc v Gentile Productions*.

### Copyright infringement and photographs of trade marks

5–054    Even where a photograph incorporating a trade mark does not itself amount to trade mark infringement, it may never the less amount to copyright infringement if the trade mark is in itself an artistic work or other original copyright work.[81] This is most likely to be a problem where the trade mark incorporates a logo, picture or other artistic device. However, even if the trade mark is simply words, if the words are represented in an artistic or stylised way, the mark may amount to an original copyright work.

In *Football Association Premier League v Panini UK Ltd*,[82] the Football Association obtained an injunction restraining the defendant from selling stickers featuring photographs of footballers on the basis of copyright

---

[79] (6th Cir) 134 F.3d 749.
[80] (6th Cir) 134 F.3d 749 at 752 *per* Circuit Judge Ryan.
[81] For definition of copyright works see above at paras 2–009 *et seq.*
[82] [2003] EWCA Civ 995; [2003] 4 All E.R. 1290; [2004] F.S.R. 1.

infringement. Many were registered trade marks but the claim was not for trade mark infringement. The FA and 14 of the clubs in the premier league claimed to own copyright in the FA emblem and their respective club badges. Topps (another producer of collectible sticker albums) entered into an exclusive deal with the FA to sell an "official" album. Panini described its album as "Unofficial" and it featured photographs of footballers in their kit which usually have the club badge on the left breast.

The FA, 14 clubs and Topps sought an injunction restraining Panini from infringing copyright in the logos. Panini argued that the inclusion of the logos within the photographs amounted to "incidental inclusion" within the meaning of s.31 of the Copyright Designs and Patents Act 1988. The Court of Appeal considered that it was impossible to say the inclusion of the individual badges was "incidental," as the inclusion of the badge was essential to the object for which the image of the player was created, *i.e.* something attractive to the collector. The relevant question for testing whether the inclusion was "incidental" was why has work "A" been included in work "B"? The answer depends on an objective assessment of the circumstances.

*Football Association Premier League v Panini UK Ltd*[83] can be contrasted with *Trebor Bassett Ltd v The Football Association*[84] where the claim for trade mark infringement was dismissed. The decision in *Football Association Premier League v Panini UK Ltd*[85] means effectively that any photograph of a footballer featuring a club copyright logo can be restrained on the basis of copyright infringement, absent any defence. It is submitted that this decision is regrettable and contrary to basic principles of freedom of expression. As was accepted by the Court of Appeal, "A photographic image of a player in action in a club strip will almost invariably include the club badge. It must do so unless the badge is obscured (say by the player's hand or arm) or the angle of the photograph is such that it does not show a clear front view of the player." Accordingly, this decision is tantamount to restricting any reproduction of a substantive image of a player in club kit. It is surprising when the object of the photograph was to record *the football player* rather than his dress and when the logo appears simply as a small but inevitable part of that dress, that the defence of incidental inclusion did not succeed.

**5–055**

This raises serious issues of freedom of speech and the conflict between intellectual property rights and the public's right to receive information. The vast majority of professional sports teams, venues, and sports leagues operate an accreditation system whereby only accredited photographers are permitted to enter the venue and take photographs. In addition, the terms of the licence are often very restricted and will include limitations as to what the resultant photographs can be used for, invariably excluding any kind of

**5–056**

---

[83] [2003] EWCA Civ 995; [2003] 4 All E.R. 1290; [2004] F.S.R. 1.
[84] [1997] F.S.R. 211.
[85] [2002] EWCA Civ 995.

commercial use. Breach of such conditions will often lead to the accreditation being withdrawn and disputes between photographers and the sports industry are not unknown.[86]

National sports are big business and plainly, intellectual property rights owners are entitled to police their rights and protect their trade interests. However, sports matches are not simply a private enterprises carried out behind closed doors. Premier League football in common with many other sports has a huge audience, both in terms of those in the stadium and those who watch the games on television. Restrictions in respect of photographs can be imposed because the sports events take place on private property and the organisers and owners are free to impose contractual conditions.[87] There is a tension between the reliance on private property rights to impose such restrictions when what is taking place on the private property is of public interest and has a massive public audience. In the context of judicial review, the question of whether sports governing bodies are public bodies has been the subject of much case law which has generally held that the relationship between the body and the members is a private contractual one.[88] However, sporting bodies may be regarded as public authorities subject to the Human Rights Act 1998 and thus required to act in accordance with the rights granted by the European Convention on Human Rights.[89]

The extent to which the imposition of restrictive licence conditions in respect of sports photographs and other public interest matters are contrary to freedom of expression (including the public's right to receive information) and/or laws of competition, has not been the subject of litigation as yet in the United Kingdom. There has been comparable litigation in the United States which has tended to support the rights of the property owners rather than the rights of the photojournalists.[90] The issues raised overlap to a degree with the same problems concerning broadcasting rights which,

---

[86] For example R. Greenslade, "Pitch Battle", *Guardian*, July 29, 2002, (reporting how no Scottish papers published photographs of a particular football match following a dispute as to licence terms with Celtic); *British Journal of Photography*, November 18, 1998, (reporting how a photographic agency had its Premier League licence suspended after supplying a photograph of a footballer to a newspaper used in a double page spread which the Premier League contended amounted to a poster (*i.e.* commercial use)).

[87] *Sports & General Press Agency Ltd v "Our Dogs" Publishing Company Ltd* [1916] 2 K.B. 880; affirmed CA [1917] 2 K.B. 125 and see below at paras 6–002 *et seq.*

[88] *R. v Disciplinary Committee of the Jockey Club Ex p. Aga Khan* [1993] 1 W.L.R. 909; *R. v Football Association Ltd Ex p.* and *Football League Ltd* [1993] 2 All E.R. 833. And see A. Lewis and J. Taylor, *Sport: Law and Practice* (Butterworths, 2003) at A3.62 and Ch.A3 generally.

[89] Home Secretary Jack Straw stated in Parliament that the Jockey Club would count as a public authority for the purposes of the Human Rights Act 1998 (*Hansard*, HC col.1018 (May 29, 1998)) but *cf.* cases cited above in n.88. As to meaning of public authority see below at paras 14–009 and 14–011 to 14–012.

[90] *e.g. D'Amario v Providence Civic Center Authority* 639 F. Supp. 1538 (D. Rhode Island 1986) (civic centre's refusal to permit commercial photojournalist to take photographs at a rock concert did not impinge impermissably on his First Amendment freedom of press rights); *WIPX v League of Women Voters* 595 F.Supp 1484 (S.D.N.Y. 1984) (right of equal access to televising presidential debate is not absolute); *Post-Newsweek Stations Connecticut v Travelers Insurance Co* 510 F. Supp. 81 (D. Conn. 1981) (upholding restriction on television coverage of figure-skating contest because state was acting in proprietary capacity in operating rink.)

unsurprisingly given the great financial value, have been the subject of litigation in Europe and the UK.[91] Detailed consideration of these complex issues concerning competition law are outside the scope of this work[92] but flagged for consideration in any case concerning copyright infringement arising out of a restrictive sports photography licence (or other licence affecting public interest subject matter) should be freedom of expression/ the public's right to receive information,[93] and European and UK laws concerning competition.

## DEFENCES TO TRADE MARK INFRINGEMENT

As indicated under "Scope of the Chapter", this chapter focuses on the narrow issues of registration of photographs and issues arising from photographing trademarks. This section merely lists the main defences available in respect of an action for trade mark infringement in order that the reader can ascertain whether any apply or are likely to apply. The majority of these defences are the subject of considerable case law consideration which is outside the scope of this chapter. Reference should be made to the works identified as the beginning of this chapter for further detail.   **5–057**

The following are the main defences to an action for trade mark infringement:   **5–058**

- The use was with the consent of the trade mark owner.[94]

- The registration of the trade mark is itself invalid[95] or should be revoked.[96]

- No infringement—in the sense that the requirements of s.10 are not met.

- Use complained of is in fact use of another registered trade mark in respect of the goods/services for which that mark is registered.[97]

- Honest use of own name or address.[98]

---

[91] As to broadcasting and competition see A. Lewis and J. Taylor, *Sport: Law and Practice* (Butterworths, 2003) at B2.236 *et seq* and Ch.D4; M.J. Beloff, *et al. Sport Law* (Hart Publishing, 1999) Ch.6.

[92] See works cited above in n.91 and on competition law: *e.g.* Bellamy and Child *European Community Law of Competition* (5th ed., Sweet & Maxwell 2001) and Coleman and Grenfell *The Competition Act 1998* (Oxford University Press).

[93] See above at paras 2–161 *et seq.* and below at paras 7–008 and 7–106.

[94] TMA 1994, s.9.

[95] Grounds for invalidity are set out in s.47 of the Act. (*e.g.* registered in breach of s.3 requirements (but will not be declared invalid if has acquired distinctive character through use), earlier trade mark.

[96] Grounds for revocation are set out in s.46 of the Act *e.g.* non-use, become common name in trade, used in a way liable to mislead public.

[97] TMA 1994, s.11(1).

[98] TMA 1994, s.11(2)(a). See *Asprey & Garrard Ltd v WRA (Guns) Ltd (t/a William R Asprey Esquire)* [2001] EWCA Civ 1499; [2002] E.T.M.R. 47; [2002] F.S.R. 31; *Premier Luggage and Bags Ltd v The Premier Company (UK) Ltd* [2002] EWCA Civ 387; [2002] E.T.M.R. 69; [2003] F.S.R. 5 (own name defence in relation to companies); *Euromarket Designs Inc v Peters* [2000] E.T.M.R. 1025; [2001] F.S.R. 20 (own name defence in relation to companies).

- Honest use of indications concerning the kind, quality, quantity, intended purpose, value, geographical origin, the time of production of goods or services or the use of a trademark where it is necessary to indicate the intended purpose of a product or service (*e.g.* accessories or spare parts).[99]

- The use complained of is in fact use in the course of trade in a particular locality of an unregistered earlier right which applies only in that locality.[1] Essentially, the defendant has to establish enough use to create passing off rights (*i.e.* goodwill)[2] prior to the earliest of either the first use of the trade mark by the proprietor or the registration of the mark.

- The use was is respect of aspects of the trade mark that had been disclaimed or limited.[3]

- Exhaustion of rights. A mark is not infringed by the use of the trade mark in relation to goods which have been put on the market in the European Economic Area under that trade mark by the proprietor or with his consent.[4]

- Laches and acquiescence.[5]

It should be noted that in respect of earlier rights that where the proprietor of an earlier mark/earlier right has acquiesced for a continuous period of five years in the use of a registered trade mark in the UK where he is aware of that use, he ceases to be entitled to apply to have the registered mark declared invalid or oppose the use of that mark (in relation to goods/services for which it had been used).[6]

## REMEDIES

**5–059**   A claimant in an action for trade mark infringement may seek:

(a) an interim and permanent injunction restraining further infringement by the defendant[7];

(b) a declaration that the defendant has infringed the mark[8];

---

[99] TMA 1994, s.11(2)(b) and (c).
[1] TMA 1994, s.11(3).
[2] *Hart v Relentless Records Ltd* [2002] EWHC 1984; [2003] F.S.R. 36.
[3] TMA 1994, s.13.
[4] TMA 1994, s.12(1).
[5] *Habib Bank v Habib Bank AG Zurich* [1981] 1 W.L.R. 1265; [1981] 2 All E.R. 650; [1982] R.P.C. 1; *Cluett Peabody & Co v McIntyre Hogg Marsh & Co* [1958] R.P.C. 335; *Wilmott v Barber* (1880) 15 Ch. D. 97.
[6] TMA 1994, s.48(1).
[7] TMA 1994, s.14(2).
[8] *Treasure Cot Co Ltd v Hamley Bros Ltd* (1950) 67 R.P.C. 89.

(c)  an order for erasure, removal or obliteration of the offending sign[9];

(d)  an order for delivery up of infringing material[10];

(e)  damages (damages are compensatory and assessed to put the claimant in the position he would have been in but for the infringement)[11];

(f)  in the alternative to damages, an account of profits.[12]

It should be noted that there are also schemes in place to enable a trade mark owner to have infringing goods seized by Customs and Excise on entry into the United Kingdom.[13]

---

[9] TMA 1994, ss.15 and 17.

[10] TMA 1994, ss.16–19.

[11] *General Tire & Rubber Co v Firestone Tyre & Rubber Co Ltd (No.2)* (HL, patent infringement) [1975] 1 W.L.R. 819; [1975] 2 All E.R. 173; [1975] F.S.R. 273; [1976] R.P.C. 197.

[12] The claimant's election can be postponed until after disclosure: *Island Records Ltd v Tring International plc* [1995] 3 All E.R. 444.

[13] TMA 1994, s.89 and Trade Marks (Customs) Regulations 1994. See also the European Council Regulation, Counterfeit and Pirated Goods Regulation 3295/94.

# Part B

# Place and Subject Matter of Photographs

# Chapter 6

# Restrictions on the right to take a photograph

## SCOPE OF THIS CHAPTER

This chapter deals with restrictions on the right to take a photograph and publish a photograph once taken. Broadly, but not exclusively, this chapter is focussed on the place of photography or conduct of the photographer (for example, trespass and nuisance). It does not deal with the law of confidence or privacy issues arising in connection with image of people which are considered in the next chapter. **6–001**

## THE RIGHT TO TAKE A PHOTOGRAPH

It has been said, citing *Sports & General Press Agency Ltd v "Our Dogs" Publishing Company Ltd*,[1] that there is a basic freedom or a right to take a photograph. First, this is an oversimplification of the ratio of *Sports & General Press*. Secondly, what is in fact established by the case is, in modern times, subject to so many exceptions and caveats that its effect is much watered down. **6–002**

*Sports & General Press* concerned a dog show run by the Ladies' Kennel Association. The plaintiff was a publishing company who entered into a contract with the Kennel Association for sole photographic rights of the dog show. The defendant, another publisher, took its own photographs of the dog show knowing they were infringing rights of at least someone, if not the plaintiff. The plaintiff issued proceedings seeking an injunction restraining the defendant's from publishing any photographs taken at the dog show other than those taken by the plaintiffs. It was held, and affirmed on appeal, that there was no exclusive right of property in the taking of photographs of the show and therefore the Kennel Association could not grant, as property, the exclusive photographic rights to the defendant. However, the court made clear that it was open to a property owner or the promoter of a show to prevent the taking of photographs by contract, such as a condition of entry that no photographs should be taken.[2] **6–003**

---

[1] [1916] 2 K.B. 880; affirmed CA [1917] 2 K.B. 125.
[2] [1916] 2 K.B. 880 at 883; [1917] 2 K.B. 125 at 128 *per* Swinfen Eady L.J. and Lush J.

The ratio therefore is that in the absence of a contractual term preventing others from photographing, there is no exclusive property right to take photographs vested in the possessor of land. It was said at first instance:

"no one possesses a right of preventing another person photographing him any more than he has a right of preventing another person giving a description of him, provided the description is not libellous or otherwise wrongful".[3]

It was an *obiter* comment in any event as the issue in question was the right of a possessor of land to photograph activities on the land, not prevention of a photograph of an individual. This case was decided in 1916. The spirit of the quote remains true in the sense that the starting point is that there is a freedom to take a photograph of any person or any place if contract, statute or the common law does not provide otherwise. Similarly, it was said in *Bernstein v Skyviews*, "there is ... no law against taking a photograph".[4]

**6–004**    However, today there are many instances in which, certainly publication of photographs of an individual, can be prevented, if not the taking of the photograph itself. In addition to statutory and common law restrictions, property owners or those organising private events are free to impose contractual terms or conditions of entry regulating the taking of photographs.[5] For this reason, the brandishing of *Sports & General Press v "Our Dogs"* as an authority for the bare unqualified proposition that there is an absolute right to take a photograph is misguided. In some circumstances, where photography is precluded by contractual terms on private property by public bodies if the subject matter concerns matters of public interest, it may be arguable that the contractual terms are contrary to the right of freedom of expression.[6]

The various exceptions to the freedom to take a photograph as provided for by statute and the common law are considered below. Statutory and tortious exceptions that relate primarily to the place of photography. Restrictions publishing pictures of those involved in court proceedings are included with the general prohibition on taking photographs in court. For exceptions concerning privacy and images of people, see Chapter 7 below.

---

[3] [1916] 2 K.B. 880 at 884.

[4] *Bernstein v Skyviews & General Ltd* [1978] 1 Q.B. 479 at 488C *per* Griffiths J.

[5] The vast majority of museums, sports stadia, theatres, etc. impose such conditions in one form or another. Private parties or celebrity weddings may also have such conditions, particularly if exclusive rights to photographs have been sold to magazines/tabloids. If there are conditions of entry, the "right to take a photograph" principle in *Sports & General Press Agency* is of no application: *Douglas v Hello! Ltd (No.6)* [2003] EWHC 786 at para.222 *per* Lindsay J.; [2003] 3 All E.R. 996; [2003] E.M.L.R. 31. See also *Victoria Park Racing and Recreation Grounds Co Ltd v Taylor* (1937) C.L.R. 479 and cases cited above at para.5–056.

[6] For example, restrictions concerning sporting events or political meetings: see above at para.5–056.

### COURT PROCEEDINGS

As is well known, photography in courts is prohibited by statute.[7] In **6–005** addition, various statutes prohibit the media from publishing photographs or other material identifying certain participants in litigation. The court has power in some circumstances to order that cases be heard in private and also to order that no identifying material be published, which again may include photographs of or containing participants in legal proceedings. Thus, the well established general principle that proceedings in courts and tribunals should be held in public[8] is subject to exceptions.

There are three categories of cases: those heard in open court, those heard **6–006** in private, and those heard in secret where information disclosure, identity of the parties and the proceedings are protected as confidential even after the end of the case.[9] Orders protecting the identity of parties (including publication of photographs of the individuals) are more likely to arise in the latter category of case. Simply because a case is heard in private does not necessarily mean that publication of the proceedings is barred. The starting point is that justice should be open and that publicity in the administration of justice is an important guarantee of civil liberties.[10] However, this does not prevent the enactment of statutes or rules to regulate court procedure.[11] Information about children cases will invariably remain confidential subject to, in cases of wider interest, anonymised judgements being given in public.[12]

### Prohibition on taking photographs in court

Section 41 of the Criminal Justice Act 1925 prohibits the taking of pho- **6–007** tographs in any court:

> **"Prohibition on taking photographs, etc, in court**
> **41.**—(1) No person shall
>
> (a) take or attempt to take in any court any photograph, or with a view to publication make or attempt to make in any court any portrait or sketch, of any person, being a judge of the court or a juror or a witness in or a party to any proceedings before the court, whether civil or criminal; or
> (b) publish any photograph, portrait or sketch taken or made in contravention of the foregoing provisions of this section or any reproduction thereof;

---

[7] Criminal Justice Act 1925, s.41, see below at para.6–007.
[8] *Clibbery v Allan* [2002] EWCA Civ 45; [2002] Fam. 261; [2002] 2 W.L.R. 1511; *R. v Denbigh Justices Ex p. Williams* [1974] 1 Q.B. 759.
[9] *Clibbery v Allan* [2002] EWCA Civ 45; [2002] 2 W.L.R. 1511; [2002] 1 All E.R. 865.
[10] *Scott v Scott* [1913] A.C. 417 at 476; *Clibbery v Allan* [2002] EWCA Civ 45 at paras 41–42; [2002] 2 W.L.R. 1511; [2002] 1 All E.R. 865.
[11] *Clibbery v Allan* [2002] EWCA Civ 45 at paras 41–42; [2002] 2 W.L.R. 1511; [2002] 1 All E.R. 865.
[12] *Clibbery v Allan* [2002] EWCA Civ 45 at para.48; [2002] 2 W.L.R. 1511; [2002] 1 All E.R. 865.

and if any person acts in contravention of this section he shall, on summary conviction, be liable in respect of each offence to a fine not exceeding level 3[13] on the standard scale.

(2) For the purposes of this section—

   (a)  the expression 'court' means any court of justice, including the court of a coroner:

   (b)  the expression 'judge' includes … registrar, magistrate, justice and coroner:

   (c)  a photograph, portrait or sketch shall be deemed to be a photograph, portrait or sketch taken or made in court if it is taken or made in the court-room or in the building or in the precincts of the building in which the court is held, or if it is a photograph, portrait or sketch taken or made of the person while he is entering or leaving the court-room or any such building or precincts as aforesaid."

**6–008**      Photography is prohibited in the court room itself, anywhere in the court building, or in the precincts of the court building, including custody areas to which the public do not have general access.[14] The prohibition attaches to photographs of a person entering or leaving the court room, the court building or its precincts.

Court includes a church used for a consistory court.[15] The Judicial Committee of the Privy Council, whilst its decision takes the form of a recommendation to Her Majesty, is in truth an appellate court.[15a] The Appellate Committee of the House of Lords also in practice operates as an appellate court. However, given that both the Privy Council and the House of Lords are not technically courts, there may be doubt as to whether s.41 of the Criminal Justice Act 1925 applies.[15b] Apart from the televising of summaries of the judgments in the Pinochet case[15c] which were given in the Chamber of the House of Lords, other recent applications to televise proceedings in either the House of Lords or Privy Council have not been successful.[15d]

---

[13] At the time of writing, £1,000: Criminal Justice Act 1982, s.37.
[14] *R. v Loveridge (William) (Appeal against Conviction)* [2001] EWCA Crim 973; [2001] 2 Cr. App. R. 29.
[15] *Re St Andrew's Heddington* [1977] 3 W.L.R. 286; 121 Sol. J. 286 (footage of a consistory court sitting in a village church to be included in a documentary on rural life was prevented by s.41).
[15a] *British Coal Corpn v R.* [1935] A.C. 500 at 510-511. See also Halsbury's Laws (4th ed.) Vol.10 at 404.
[15b] See further J. Rozenburg, *The Pinochet case and cameras in court* [1999] Public Law 178–184 observing by giving consent in 1989 to the filming of proceedings by the BBC to illustrate the work of the House of Lord, the House of Lords demonstrated that it did not consider itself to be a court for the purposes of the Criminal Justice Act 1925, s.41.
[15c] *R. v Bow Street Metropolitan Stipendiary Magistrate Ex p. Pinochet Ugarte (No.3)* [2000] 1 A.C. 147.
[15d] See J. Rozenburg, *The Pinochet case and cameras in court* [1999] Public Law 178–184. In November 2003, an application to the Privy Council to televise proceedings in *Belize Alliance of Conservation Non-Governmental Organizations v Department of the Environment and others* (Appeal No. 47 of 2003) (the Chalillo Dam case) was refused.

The prohibition against sketching in court with a view to publication only applies to portraits of judges, jurors, witnesses and parties and not to the parties, representatives. It is an arguable point of construction as to whether the qualification of judges, jurors, witnesses and parties applies to photographs, but the absurdity that would result militates against such a construction.[16] It is submitted that the only logical construction is a total prohibition against photographing anyone not just judges, jurors, witnesses or parties.

There is often uncertainty as to how far the precincts of the court extend   **6–009** which can pose difficulties for photographers. In *Re St Andrews Heddington*[17] it was considered that "precincts" covered the church and the small area of churchyard which physically adjoined the church. In a case where the meaning of the word "precincts" in a different statute[18] was considered, it was said

> "It was conceded that the words 'close' and 'precincts' import the notion of a boundary surrounding an inclosure but that the boundary might be a line or notional surround. The first meaning of 'precinct' given in the *Shorter Oxford English Dictionary* is: 'The space enclosed by the walls or other boundaries of a particular place or building, or an imaginary line drawn around it; esp. the ground immediately surrounding a religious house or place of worship.' The word can also be used to mean 'the environs'."[19]

A photograph of a judge, juror or witness which includes in the back-   **6–010** ground part of the court building would strictly be within the court precincts. Although this type of photograph is as a matter of practice frequently tolerated—for example the frequent filming and photographing of litigants approaching and leaving the Royal Courts of Justice—it is dangerous to assume that such photographs will not be the subject of a s.41 prosecution.[20] It is unclear whether it is in contravention of the section to photograph the judge and the court whilst on a site visit.[21]

The Phillimore Committee appointed in 1971 to consider whether any   **6–011** changes were required in the law relating to contempt of court reported in 1974[22] and stated in its report:

---

[16] C. J. Milller *Contempt of Court* (3rd ed., Oxford University Press, 2000) at 4.101.
[17] [1978] Fam. 121, 123.
[18] Factories Act 1937.
[19] *Walsh v Allweather Mechanical Grouting Co Ltd* [1959] 1 All E.R. 588 at 592; [1959] 2 Q.B. 300. Factories Act 1937, s.151(1) now repealed. See Factories Act 1961, s.175(1).
[20] According to the authors of *Borrie & Lowe The Law of Contempt* (3rd ed., Butterworths, 1996) "apparently serious consideration was given to prosecuting under s.41" a tabloid which published a photograph of a defendant in front of a court. The prosecution was in fact on the basis of strict liability contempt: *AG v News Group Newspapers Ltd* (1984) 6 Cr. App. Rep. (S) 418.
[21] Such photographs have been known to be taken. See *Borrie & Lowe The Law of Contempt, op. cit.*, at 26 n.4 observing Megarry J. was extensively photographed whilst visiting Ocean Island in the course of *Tito v Waddell* [1975] 3 All E.R.
[22] *Report of the Committee on Contempt of Court* (1974) Cmnd. 5794

"We have considered whether it would be possible to devise some definition of general application [as to how far precincts extend] which would remove such uncertainty as may exist. The difficulty is that court buildings vary greatly throughout the country ... We consider that it would be impracticable to attempt to define for all purposes what are the precincts of the court. However, no doubt in many cases it may be possible by means of a map or plan displayed in the court premises to define the extent of what will normally be treated as the court and its precincts. We recommend that this should be done whenever practicable for the guidance and assistance of all having business in the court. This should not however, in any way limit or prejudice the court's powers to determine and declare the limits of its own precincts or to extend them if, for example, an actual or threatened demonstration in the highway outside should interfere with proceedings in court."[23]

In some cases involving a high level of media interest, the court will issue guidelines as to how far the precincts of the court in question extend.[24] In the trial of the defendants charged with the murder of Oluwadamilola (Damilola) Taylor which took place at the Central London Criminal Court (the Old Bailey) during 2002, it was ordered that precincts "shall mean Old Bailey, the road at the front of the court building, Newgate street, the street beside the court building, and Warwick Square, the square behind the court building."[25]

**6–012** Although the 1925 Act does not specifically refer to video recordings or film, the section is applied in a way to include such modern developments in photography.[26] Covert filming by the police of suspects in custody at a magistrate's court for the purpose of comparison with CCTV evidence contravened s.41.[27]

Prosecutions under s.41 seem to be comparatively rare. The DPP instituted proceedings for publication in February 1973 of a picture from a photograph of the judge and jury in an obscenity trial.[28] In July 1986, the wife of a solicitor was fined £100 for photographing a judge in court.[29] In

---

[23] *ibid.*, para.41.

[24] See for example *Media Court Guides* in the trials of Rosemary West (October 1995); Szymon Serafinowicz (February 1996); Bruce Grobbelar (January 1997) referred to in *Arlidge Eady and Smith On Contempt* (2nd ed.) at 10–194 n.24.

[25] Order of Hooper J., November 12, 2001, quoted in Court Service *Media Court Guide* for trial of the defendants charged with the murder of Oluwadamilola (Damilola) Taylor, p.10, January 2002.

[26] *R. v Loveridge* [2001] EWCA Crim 973, para.25; [2001] 2 Cr. App. R. 592, 597; *J. Barber & Sons v Lloyd's Underwriters* [1987] 1 Q.B. 103, 105. Cf. "Photograph" in the Obscene Publication Act 1959 and Protection of Children Act 1978 interpreted to include developments in photography post-dating the statute—video cassettes and digital photography: *A-G's Reference (No.5 of 1980)* [1980] 3 All E.R. 816; *R. v Fellows* [1997] 2 All E.R. 548 at 557; [1997] 1 Cr. App. R. 244. See below at paras 8–007 to 8–008 and 8–044.

[27] *R. v Loveridge* [2001] EWCA Crim 973, para.25; [2001] 2 Cr. App. R. 592, 597. See also police Code of Practice for identification of persons by police officers (Code D) paras D4.1 *et seq.* (circumstances in which photographs of arrested persons can be taken without their consent).

[28] *The Times*, February 10, 1973, cited in C. J. Miller *Contempt of Court* (3rd ed., Oxford University Press, 2000) at 4.102.

[29] *The Times* July 15, 1986, cited in C. J. Miller, *op. cit.*, at 4.102.

April 2003, a man was fined £250 for taking a photograph of a defendant in court using a mobile phone capable of taking photographs.[30]

## Tribunals of inquiry

Inquiry tribunals do not fall within the definition of court in s.41(2)(a) of the Criminal Justice Act 1925. The Tribunals of Inquiry (Evidence) Act 1924 does not contain any prohibition of photography. Thus the tribunal has a discretion to permit photography or filming of its proceedings.   **6–013**

However, if a person does anything which would, if the tribunal had been a court of law had power to commit for contempt, have been contempt of court then the chairman of the tribunal may certify the offence to the High Court and the court may punish the person as if he had been guilty of contempt of the court.[31] In addition, the Contempt of Court Act 1981 (except for s.9(3)—forfeiture of tape recordings) applies to inquiry tribunals as they do in relation to courts and legal proceedings.[32] Accordingly, it will be essential to obtain the permission of the inquiry tribunal to film or photograph, otherwise the photographer will expose himself to being found guilty of contempt of court.   **6–014**

Recently, there has been a move towards televising inquiries. The Southall Rail Enquiry for example was televised, as were the opening submissions at the Victoria Climbie and Ladbrook Grove enquiries. The opening statement of the Bloody Sunday Inquiry was televised. CNN also televised the testimony of witnesses who did not object at the Harold Shipman inquiry after Dame Janet Smith reversed her original decision to exclude broadcasters.[33]

Permission was given by Lord Hutton, chairing the 2003 inquiry into the death of Dr David Kelly, the UK government weapons expert, to televise his Lordship's opening statement and the opening addresses of counsel. An application by a group of broadcasters to televise all or part of the inquiry into the death of Dr David Kelly, the UK government weapons expert, was refused by Lord Hutton who in giving his ruling said:   **6–015**

"The Inquiry relates to matters of very great public interest and will be attended with very widespread publicity and comment. Those who give evidence will be placed under strain even if their evidence is not filmed and broadcast on television. But the strain will be all the greater if they know that their evidence is being filmed and broadcast and that every answer, every qualification or correction of an answer, every hesitation, every facial expression and every alteration of their posture will be watched by hundreds of thousands of people on their television screens and will be liable to be replayed on television on a number of occasions ... I think

---

[30] April 17, 2003, Merthyr Tydfil Crown Court, order of Judge John Cowan: *Guardian*, April 24, 2003; *The Times*, April 24, 2003, p.2.
[31] Tribunals of Inquiry (Evidence) Act 1921, s.1(2)(c).
[32] Contempt of Court Act 1981, s.20(1).
[33] Application by CNN to televise proceedings of the Shipman Inquiry: Decision cited in G. Robertson, and A. Nicol, *Media Law* (4th ed., Sweet & Maxwell, 2000) in "Stop Press" at p.xxii.

that this knowledge might well inhibit some witnesses from speaking as frankly as they would otherwise do, and that filming them would not assist me in my task of trying to determine as precisely as is possible what happened during the period which preceded Dr Kelly's death. It is relevant to observe that this is one of the reasons which influenced the decision of Sir Richard Scott (as he then was) that witnesses in his inquiry on Arms to Iraq would not be filmed. In paragraph B 2.33 of Vol 1 of his Report, he stated:

'I had particularly in mind the possible effect on witnesses. It was foreseeable that there would be considerable media interest in the evidence to be given to the inquiry by Ministers, ex-Ministers and senior officials. There seemed to be a danger that the presence of television cameras might unfairly increase the inevitable pressure on witnesses resulting from the public character of the hearings.'[34]

**6–016**   Lord Hutton went on to observe that the practice of filming some witnesses' evidence but not others' was undesirable saying:

"Obvious problems could arise if there was a significant difference on a particular issue between the evidence of a witness who was filmed and a witness who was not. Indeed the procedure of filming some witnesses at a public inquiry, but not others, depending on their public prominence or their willingness to be filmed, appears to me to be an undesirable one. Moreover, in an Inquiry which requires to be conducted urgently, the need to ask some witnesses if they were willing to be filmed, and then to consider what should be done in the light of their replies, would add a time consuming burden to the work of the tribunal and its secretariat."

**6–017**   His Lordship also held that the applicants had no right under Art.10 (freedom of expression) to film proceedings.[35] He citied Dame Janet Smith's decision in an application by Cable News Network (CNN) to broadcast the public hearings of the Shipman inquiry to the effect that Art.10 does not guarantee the right to receive information which is in the possession or control of one who is not willing to impart it. In so far as the inquiry is in possession or control of the information under discussion, those who wish to televise it must seek permission to receive it rather than assert a right to receive it.

### Employment tribunals

**6–018**   The Employment Tribunals Act 1996 states that Employment Tribunal Regulations may include provision in cases involving allegations of the commission of sexual offences to prevent the identification of any person

---

[34] *In the Matter of Applications by ITN, BSkyB, Channel 4, Channel 5, ITV and Irn Radio*, ruling by Lord Hutton, August 5, 2003, at para.19: *http://www.the-hutton-inquiry.org.uk/*.
[35] *ibid.*, at para.10.

making, or affected by the allegation, and to allow the tribunal to make a restricted reporting order.[36] If any "identifying matter" is published in contravention of a restricted reporting order, that is an offence for which a person is liable on summary conviction to a fine not exceeding level 5 on the standard scale.[37] Identifying matter means "any matter likely to lead members of the public to identify him as a person affected by or as the person making the allegation". There is also power to make a restricting reporting order in disability cases.[38]

The procedural rules governing reporting restriction orders are set out in r.14 of the Rules of Procedure 1993. In cases involving allegations of misconduct, the tribunal may make a restricted reporting order any time before the promulgation of its decision in respect of an originating application, either of its own motion or on the application of a party.[39] In proceedings under s.8 of the Disability Discrimination Act 1995, in which evidence of a personal nature is likely to be heard, an order can be made on the application of a complainant (not a party) or by the tribunals' own motion.[40]

A restricted reporting order can be made in respect of a body corporate.[41]   **6–019**
If a restricted reporting order is made, it will invariably include a photograph for obvious reasons.[42] If orders are made, the terms should be clear and exactly what is meant by "identifying matter" spelt out in the order.[43]

## Defendants

Publication of photographs of defendants in criminal cases may give rise   **6–020**
to a strict liability contempt under s.2(2) of the Contempt of Court Act 1981.[44] Section 1 of the Act provides for strict liability contempt and s.2 sets out limitations as follows:

> **"The Strict Liability Rule**
>    (1) In this Act "the strict liability rule" means the rule of law whereby conduct may be treated as a contempt of court as tending to interfere with

---

[36] Employment Tribunals Act 1996, s.11.
[37] Employment Tribunals Act 1996, s.11(2). At the time of writing, a level 5 fine is £5,000. Criminal Justice Act 1982, s.37.
[38] Employment Tribunals Act 1996, s.12.
[39] Rules of Procedure, r.14(1).
[40] Rules of Procedure, r.14(2).
[41] *M v Vincent* [1999] I.C.R. 73 applying the Interpretation Act 1978, Sch.1, which provides that unless the contrary appears, the presumption is that the word "person" includes a body of persons corporate or unincorporate; *Leicester University v A* [1999] I.C.R. 701. But *cf. R. v London (North) Industrial Tribunal Ex p. Associated Newspapers Ltd* [1998] I.C.R. 1212 at 1225–1226 where Keene J. doubted whether a corporate body was intended by Parliament to be included.
[42] For example *Leicester University v A* [1999] I.C.R. 701.
[43] *R. v Southampton Industrial Tribunal Ex p. INS News Group Ltd* [1995] I.R.L.R. 247. Suggested wording by QBD in that case was "an order prohibiting the publication of any matter, whether by way of the written or spoken word, or by photographic representation, which was likely to lead members of the public to identify the respondent as a person affected by or the complainant as a person making an allegation of sexual misconduct."
[44] If publication "creates a substantial risk that the course of justice in the proceedings in question will be seriously impeded or prejudiced": s.2(2).

the course of justice in particular legal proceedings regardless of intent to do so.

2. Limitation of scope of strict liability

(1) The strict liability rule applies only in relation to publications, and for this purpose "publication" includes any speech, writing, [programme included in a programme service] or other communication in whatever form, which is addressed to the public at large or any section of the public.

(2) The strict liability rule applies only to a publication which creates a substantial risk that the course of justice in the proceedings in question will be seriously impeded or prejudiced.

(3) The strict liability rule applies to a publication only if the proceedings in question are active within the meaning of this section at the time of the publication.

(4) Schedule 1 applies for determining the times at which proceedings are to be treated as active within the meaning of this section.[45]

(5) In this section "programme service" has the same meaning as in the Broadcasting Act 1990"

**6–021**    The publication of a photograph of a defendant will fall foul of the strict liability rule if it "creates a substantial risk that the course of justice in the proceedings in question will be seriously impeded or prejudiced".[46] Substantial risk means a risk that is not remote[47] or "not insubstantial or not minimal".[48] The risk must be a practical risk and not a theoretical risk.[49]

**6–022**    In some circumstances, courts will stay proceedings or quash convictions as a result of prejudicial pre-trial publicity or court reporting which has resulted in an unfair trial.[50] A court will stay a trial on the grounds of adverse pre-trial publicity only if satisfied on a balance of probabilities that the effect of the pre-trial publicity is such as to render a future hypothetical guilty verdict unsafe and unsatisfactory.[51] Accordingly, care must be taken when using photographs of a defendant before and during a trial until a final verdict is reached.

---

[45] Broadly, any time between arrest or issue of a warrant and until acquittal, a verdict or order ending the proceedings or discontinuance. For full definitions see Sch.1.

[46] See Contempt of Court Act 1981, s.2(2) above at para.6–020.

[47] *AG v English* [1983] A.C. 116.

[48] *AG v News Group Newspapers Plc* [1987] Q.B. 1, 15.

[49] *AG v Guardian Newspapers plc (No.3)* [1992] 1 W.L.R. 874, 881.

[50] *Reade, Independent*, October 19, 1993, (stay of proceedings against policemen in Birmingham six case); *Attorney-General v MGN Ltd* [1997] 1 All E.R. 456; [1997] E.M.L.R. 284 (A-G's application to punish several newspapers for contempt following stay of murder trial due to pretrial publicity); *R. v Stone (Michael John)* [2001] EWCA Crim 297; [2001] Crim. L.R. 465 (appeal against conviction allowed; retrial ordered). See further *Arlidge Eady & Smith on Contempt* (2nd ed.) 2–65 *et seq.* and N. Lowe, and B. Sufrin, *Borrie & Lowe The Law of Contempt* (3rd ed.) (1996 Butterworths) pp.123 *et seq.*

[51] *Maxwell* (unrep) March 6, 1995, (Phillips J.) approved in *R. v Stone (Michael John)* [2001] EWCA Crim 297; [2001] Crim. L.R. 465. See also s.4(1) Contempt of Court Act 1981 ("a person is not guilty of contempt of court under the strict liability rule in respect of a fair and accurate report of legal proceedings held in public published contemporaneously and in good faith").

Publication of a defendant's photograph is in contempt of court where there is an issue as to identification.[52] A newspaper was held in contempt for publication of a defendant on the day of an identification parade where at the time "it was reasonably clear a question of identity might arise."[53]

The test is whether, at the time when the photograph was published, there   **6–023**
was a likelihood that the identity of the accused would come into question in some aspect of the case.[54] Until it is reasonably clear that a question of identity will *not* arise, publication of a photograph of a defendant is at risk of being in contempt of court.

Where a photograph of a defendant was published two days before an   **6–024**
identification parade, the newspaper and the editor were held in contempt of court. The editor was fined £20,000 and the newspaper £80,000. In giving judgment, Steyn L.J. said:

> "The photograph was published at a time when [the editor] knew (a) that a defendant had been arrested and charged with murder; (b) that he was probably pleading not guilty, and (c) that identity was likely to be an issue in the case. It was palpably a situation in which an identification parade was a real prospect and any editor should have known that. And it was manifest that the publication of the photograph might gravely undermine any identifications. It also raised a different risk, namely a risk of an erroneous identification and an unjustified conviction. For my part, I regard all the essentials of liability under s 2(2) of the 1981 Act as established. I would find both defendants guilty of contempt in respect of the publication of the photograph."[55]

In considering the level of penalty the judge said:

> "There was here a vetting system, and that the Newspaper and its Editor had shown some responsibility in setting up a system of night lawyers. . . . and I will take that into account. On the other hand, that in no way can derogate from the individual responsibility of the Editor and the Journalist. I also take into account the acceptance of guilt on the part of both respondents and the unqualified apologies that have been tendered to us. The scale of the penalties must, however, be sufficient to mark the seriousness of these particular contempts and to discourage others who might place at risk the integrity of the criminal justice system. And the penalty must underline the individual responsibility of the Editor."[56]

---

[52] *R. v Daily Mirror, Ex p. Smith* [1927] 1 K.B. 845; *R. v Evening Standard Ex p. AG, The Times,* November 3, 1976, (publication of photograph of defendant on the day he was to attend and identification parade. Serious risk of prejudicing the trial by increasing the likelihood that he would be picked out at the identification parade. It was immaterial that the caption was "He's No Bank Robber". Newspaper fined £1,000).

[53] *R. v Daily Mirror Ex p. Smith* [1927] 1 K.B. 845.

[54] *AG v Times Newspapers Ltd* [1992] 1 A.C. 191, 215; *Re Consolidated Press Ex p. Auld* (1936) 36 S.R. N.S.W. 596, 598.

[55] *Attorney-General v News International plc* (unrep) QBD, Crown Office List) CO 2643/93, 1855/94 July 5, 1994, Steyn L.J. and Kay J.

[56] *ibid.*

Photographs of "wanted" individuals issued by the police can be published by the media without risk of contempt.[57]

**6–025**   Publication of prejudicial photographs (as part of general "sensational, inaccurate and misleading" press coverage) which had no relevance to the trial and were not used at trial was criticised as not reporting at all but comment which assumed guilt.[58] In that case, the press coverage included a still photograph taken from a video of the victim's wedding which showed one of the defendant's kissing the groom who was her lover. The frame had been frozen in such a manner as to give a false impression that it was a mouth to mouth kiss when in fact it was a kiss on the cheek. The convictions were quashed on the basis that it was impossible to say that the jury were not influenced in their decision by what they read in the press.

**6–026**   Publication of a photograph of a person awaiting trial under the Race Relations Act 1965 with "a highly derogatory caption" describing him as a "brothel-keeper, procurer and property racketeer" was held to be a contempt of court.[59] It was described as undoubtedly something which is likely to prejudice the fair trial of the accused before the jury. The newspaper was fined £5,000. The editor was not punished personally on the basis that it was clear that he knew nothing about it and it could not be said that he acted recklessly or turned a blind eye. As in *Attorney-General v News International plc*,[60] regard was had to the fact that the newspaper had a system in place to avoid contempts. The defendant in question was convicted. His appeal against conviction was dismissed on the basis that, in evidence, he admitted using the words of the character he was charged with, it was inevitable that the jury would conclude as they did and there was no possible prejudice affecting the result of the trial.[61]

Publication of a photograph of a defendant charged with assaulting a baby under a misleading headline "Baby was blinded by Dad" was held to be contempt of court and a fine of £5,000 imposed.[62]

**6–027**   Whether publication will lead to a stay or if there is a conviction, a successful appeal, will turn on the particular facts of the case in question. It has been acknowledged by the Court of Appeal that a common way of dealing with such problems arising during the course of the trial is "for the judge to assess what is the likelihood of prejudice to the accused arising from a publication in the press which there ought not to have been and then either to discharge the jury or to say to them: 'This has arisen. It has got nothing to do with this case. Put it out of your minds, as I am sure you will and we will get on with the case.'"[63]

---

[57] Hansard, HC Debs [1981] Vol.1000, col.34.

[58] (1993) 98 Cr. App. R. 361, 369.

[59] *R. v Thompson Newspapers Ltd Ex p. AG* [1969] 1 All E.R. 268; [1968] 1 W.L.R. 1.

[60] See above at para.6–024, n.55 and accompanying text.

[61] *R. v Malik* [1968] 1 All E.R. 582; [1968] 1 W.L.R. 353; 52 Cr. App. Rep. 140. See also *R. v Hemming* [1985] Crim. L.R. 395 (publication of photograph of defendant in punk "gear" with raised clench fist and caption "Defiant". Judge asked the jury whether they had been prejudiced, an action which was described on appeal as "unfortunate". Appeal against conviction dismissed).

[62] *AG v News Group Newspapers* (1984) 6 Cr. App. R. (S) 418.

[63] *R. v Hemming* [1985] Crim. L.R. 395.

Innocent publication is a defence to strict liability contempt. A person is **6–028** not guilty of contempt "as the publisher of any matter to which [the strict liability rule] applies if at the time of publication (having taken all reasonable care) he does not know and has no reason to suspect that relevant proceedings are active."[64] Equally, a person is not guilty of contempt as a distributor of a publication if "at the time of distribution (having taken all reasonable care) he does not know that it contains such matter and has no reason to suspect that it is likely to do so."[65] In both cases, the burden of proof lies upon the person asserting the defence.[66] There is also a defence in respect of fair and accurate reporting of legal proceedings under s.4(1) of the 1981 Act which provides:

"Subject to this section a person is not guilty of contempt of court under the strict liability rule in respect of a fair and accurate report of legal proceedings held in public, published contemporaneously and in good faith."

It is doubtful whether this defence could apply to publication of a photo-  **6–029** graph that is in contempt of court as "report of legal proceedings" is almost certainly confined to the actual proceedings in court.[67] A photograph taken in court is prohibited by s.41 of the Criminal Justice Act 1925 in any event. So this defence could only apply to a photograph taken outside court either pre-existing photographs such as an earlier photograph of the defendant or of the offence taking place or photographs of witnesses and the defendant arriving at court provided not within the court precincts. Pre-existing photographs of that type would not be considered a report of legal proceedings.[68] It is arguable that photographs of people arriving at court or of activity outside the court such as (for example) the defendant and a defence witness engaging in a fight, could fall within this definition, but it is doubtful.[69] The section concerns "a fair and accurate report *of legal proceedings*" not "matters in connection with legal proceedings". As the case law suggests, it is probably confined to what occurs within the court as part of the legal proceedings.

---

[64] Contempt of Court Act 1981, s.3(1).
[65] Contempt of Court Act 1981, s.3(2).
[66] Contempt of Court Act 1981, s.3(3).
[67] *Delegal v Highley* (1837) 3 Bing. N.C. 950 at 960 in relation to defamation common law qualified privilege in respect of fair and accurate reports of judicial proceedings. See also *R. v Rhuddlan Justices Ex p. HTV Ltd* [1986] Crim. L.R. 329 regarding an order under s.4(2) (power of court to order postponement of reporting of legal proceedings) where it was held that " 'legal proceedings held in public' mean proceedings which are held in court at a hearing of a charge of a person for a criminal offence" and a film of an arrest did not fall within that definition.
[68] *R. v Rhuddlan Justices Ex p. HTV Ltd* [1986] Crim. L.R. 329.
[69] *cf: Re G (Celebrities: Publicity)* [1999] 1 F.L.R. 409, 413G, concerning the Administration of Justice Act 1985, s.12.

## Witnesses

6–030   In the absence of any statutory power affecting the proceedings concerned[70] or a specific court order imposing reporting restrictions, there is no general prohibition against photographing witnesses outside court or publishing their photograph. Of course, photographing witnesses in court or within its precincts is forbidden under the general prohibition of photography in s.41 of the Criminal Justice Act 1925 as to which see above at para.6–007.

It is plain that interference with a witness may be contempt of court. The general principle is that those who give evidence in court should be protected from abuse. It has been said that the administration of justice depends on witnesses coming forward and that they must be confident in doing so that the law will protect them.[71] Interviewing and filming interviews of witnesses after they have given evidence but before the trial has concluded has been restrained where several of the witnesses were impressionable and vulnerable and there was a risk that they would be recalled to give further evidence.[72]

6–031   An allegation of contempt was made against a press photographer who had been trying to photograph two defendants on their way to court.[73] One defendant ran off with his face covered pursued by the photographer and collided with scaffolding. On appeal it was held that although the photographer's behaviour was offensive, rude and uncivilised and wholly reprehensible, it was not capable of amounting to interference sufficient to constitute the necessary acts for contempt. However, Lord Lane C.J. stated:

> "It should be made clear at the outset that the law insists that a defendant and witnesses and indeed anyone else who has a duty to perform at Court, whether in a criminal trial or in a civil trial, is entitled to go to and from the Court, that is between his home and the Court, whether on foot or otherwise, without being molested or assaulted or threatened with molestation."

## Court's power to restrict publicity: Contempt of Court Act 1981, ss.11 and 4(2)

6–032   The court has a common law power to prohibit publicity which is recorded in s.11 of the Contempt of Court Act 1981.[74] The section reads as follows:

---

[70] See below at paras 6–032 *et seq.*
[71] *Smithers v Bowen* (1983) Cr. App. R. 243, 254.
[72] *Ex p. HTV Cymru (Wales)* [2002] E.M.L.R. 11.
[73] *R. v Runting* (1989) 89 Cr. App. R. 243, 245; [1989] Crim. L.R. 282.
[74] See *Arlidge Eady & Smith on Contempt* (2nd ed.) at 7–58 observing that "the section confers no powers but simply refers to a common law jurisdiction to restrict publication assumed to exist without defining it."

"In any case where a court (having power to do so) allows a name or other matter to be withheld from the public in proceedings before the court, the court may give such directions prohibiting the publication of that name or matter in connection with the proceedings as appear to the court to be necessary for the purpose for which it was so withheld."

Magistrates' courts, where they consider there is a reasonable risk to the administration of justice because a witness feared for his safety, have inherent power to take steps to protect the witness so that he is not deterred from giving evidence.[75]

The power has been exercised in cases involving grave distress and embarrassment arising out of a medical condition.[76] However, orders have been refused where an application was "no more than a plea for privacy"[77]; where a defendant was afraid of harassment by a former wife[78]; and where a solicitor's firm argued that public disclosure of the Legal Aid Board's reasons would be immensely damaging and result in its professional reputation being seriously compromised.[79]    **6–033**

Although s.11 does not specifically provide that breach of an order made under it is contempt, once an order has been made, anyone who knowingly acts contrary to the order is likely to be held in contempt of court.[80]

The court also has power under s.4(2) of the Contempt of Court Act 1981    **6–034**
to postpone media coverage of all or part of the proceedings[81] which contrasts with the s.11 power to "prohibit" publication. The power is restricted to "any report of the proceedings or any part of the proceedings". Pre-existing photographs (*i.e.* historical photographs taken before the proceedings begin) of a defendant or party to litigation do not amount to a report of the proceedings and cannot be restrained under this section.[82]

When considering whether to make such an order, there is nothing which precludes the court from hearing a representative of the press and it is likely that the court will wish to do so.[82a] Any order must state (a) its precise scope (b) the time at which it shall cease to have effect, if appropriate and (c) the

---

[75] *R. v Watford Magistrates Court Ex p. Lenman* [1993] Crim. L.R. 388.
[76] *H v Ministry of Defence* [1991] 2 Q.B. 103; *R. v Criminal Injuries Compensation Board Ex p. A* [1992] C.O.D. 379. For further discussion of the proper exercise of power under s.11 see *Arlidge Eady & Smith on Contempt* (2nd ed.) pp.7–69 *et seq.* and Borrie and Lowe, *The Law of Contempt* (3rd ed., Butterworths, 1996) at pp.299 *et seq.*
[77] *R. v Westminster City Council Ex p. Castelli and Tristan-Garcia (No.1)* [1996] 1 F.L.R. 534, 538 (anonymity sought as HIV positive).
[78] *R. v Evesham Justices ex part McDonagh* [1988] Q.B. 553.
[79] *R. v Legal Aid Board Ex p. Kaim Todner* [1999] Q.B. 966; [1998] 3 W.L.R. 925; [1998] 3 All E.R. 541.
[80] [1988] Ch. 333, 380D-F.
[81] The power is limited to restriction of reports of the legal proceedings, *i.e.* the actual court proceedings. An earlier film of the arrest of a person is not a report of the legal proceedings: *R. v Rhuddlan Justices Ex p. HTV Ltd* [1986] Crim. L.R. 329 see above at para.6–029. For further information see *Arlidge Eady & Smith on Contempt* (2nd ed.) pp.7–82 *et seq.* and Borrie and Lowe, *The Law of Contempt* (3rd ed.) at pp.284 *et seq.*
[82] See cases cited above at para. 6–029, nn.67–69 above and accompanying text.
[82a] *Practice Direction (Criminal Proceedings: Consolidation)* at 3.2 [2002] 1 W.L.R. 2870; [2002] 3 All E.R. 904; [2002] 2 Cr. App. R. 35.

specific purpose of making such an order.[82b] It remains the responsibility of those reporting cases and their editors to ensure that no breach of any order occurs and the onus rests on them to make inquiry in case of doubt.[82c]

## Inherent jurisdiction and the court's power to grant injunctions to restrain an anticipated contempt

6–035    The inherent jurisdiction of the court has been defined as:

> "the inherent jurisdiction of the court may be defined as being the reserve or fund of powers, a residual source of powers, which the court may draw upon as necessary whenever it is just or equitable to do so, and in particular to ensure the observance of the due process of law, to prevent improper vexation or oppression, to do justice between the parties and to secure a fair trial between them."[83]

The court enjoys such powers in order that it can enforce its rules of practice and suppress any abuse of its process and to defeat any attempt at thwarting its process.[84]

6–035A    *The House of Lords*
The House of Lords has power under its inherent jurisdiction to make any order which the Court of Appeal is by statute empowered to make.[85]

6–036    *The Court of Appeal*
The Court of Appeal (Civil and Criminal Division) has all such jurisdiction that was conferred upon it immediately before the Supreme Court Act 1981 came into force.[86] The civil division has all the authority and jurisdiction of the court or tribunal from which the appeal was brought.[87] The Court of Appeal criminal division has granted an injunction prohibiting the broadcast of a television programme based on reconstruction of excerpts from the appeal hearing.[88]

*The High Court*
6–037    The High Court has all such jurisdiction, whether civil or criminal, that was exercisable by it immediately before the Supreme Court Act 1981 came

---

[82b] ibid., at 3.3. See also *R. v Horsham Justices ex p Farquharson* [1982] 2 All E.R. 269.
[82c] Loc. cit.
[83] *Grobbelaar v News Group Newspapers Ltd* [2002] UKHL 40 at para.37 *per* Lord Bingham quoting I.H. Jacob *The Inherent Jurisdiction of the Court* (1970) 23 Current Legal Problems 27. For discussion of the inherent jurisdiction powers in relation to reporting restrictions see G. Busuttil, *Inherent Jurisdiction: Power for Use "When Necessary"* [2002] Nov/Dec Issue 42 Media Lawyer 40.
[84] *Connelly v DPP* [1964] A.C. 1254 at 1301 *per* Lord Morris.
[85] *Grobbelaar v News Group Newspapers Ltd* [2002] UKHL 40 at para.25; [2002] 1 W.L.R. 3024; [2002] 4 All E.R. 732 *per* Lord Bingham.
[86] Supreme Court Act 1981, s.15(1)(b).
[87] Supreme Court Act 1981, s.15(2).
[88] *Attorney-General v Channel 4 Television Co Ltd* [1988] Crim. L.R. 237.

into force.[89] This provision incorporates the inherent jurisdiction of the court. The High Court does have power to grant injunctions to restrain a contempt before it takes place.[90]

The Family Division of the High Court has an inherent jurisdiction to protect children from publicity and may make orders in connection with criminal proceedings.[91]

### The County Court

The county court has no inherent jurisdiction to grant injunctions as it is a creature of statute.[92] Any power the county court has to grant injunctions must derive from s.38 of the County Courts Act 1984 which provides that "in any proceedings in a county court the court may make any order which could be made in the High Court if the proceedings were in the High Court" excluding mandamas, certiorari and prohibition.    **6–038**

The county court has no power to deal with contempt of court other than contempt in the face of the court at common law[93] and by statue under ss.14 (assaults on officers of the court); 92 (rescuing seized goods) and 118–121 (wilful insults and interruptions) of the County Courts Act 1984. However, it is submitted that the general power to grant orders which the High Court could make would cover threatened contempt and hence the county court would have jurisdiction to grant such an injunction by virtue of s.38 of the County Courts Act 1984. See also power to order non-disclosure of identity of any party or witness under the Civil Procedure Rules 1998, below at para.6–081.

### The Crown Court

It has been held that the Crown Court has power to grant an injunction to restrain a threatened contempt of court under s.45(4) of the Supreme Court Act 1981 which grants the Crown Court the same power as the High Court to deal with any contempt of court.[94] Section 45(4) limits the power of the Crown Court to grant an injunction and if a proposed publication of a photograph would not amount to a contempt of court or otherwise fall within s.45(4), the Crown Court has no power to grant an injunction prohibiting publication of that photograph.[95] Accordingly, if the proposed publication anticipated is outside either s.4(2) or s.11 of the Contempt of Court Act 1981, the appropriated tribunal to grant an injunction would be the High Court.[96]    **6–039**

---

[89] Supreme Court Act 1981, s.19(2)(b).
[90] *Attorney-General v Times Newspapers Ltd* [1974] A.C. 273; [1973] 3 W.L.R. 298; [1973] 3 All E.R. 54.
[91] *Re S (A Child)* [2003] EWCA Civ 963 (order permitting report of criminal proceedings concerning mother charged with murder of her child which inevitably led to identification of sibling); *Venables v News Group Newspapers Ltd* [2001] 2 W.L.R. 1038; [2001] 1 All E.R. 908; [2001] E.M.L.R. 10. See also cases cited below at para.6–048, nn.6 and 7.
[92] *Ali v Westminster City Council* [1999] 1 W.L.R. 384; [1999] 1 All E.R. 450.
[93] *Brompton County Court Judge* [1893] 2 Q.B. 195.
[94] *Ex p. HTV Cymru (Wales) Ltd* [2002] E.M.L.R. 11.
[95] *ibid.*, at para.23.
[96] *R. v Rhuddlan Justices Ex p. HTV Ltd* [1986] Crim. L.R. 329. This is discussed more fully in *Arlidge, Eady & Smith on Contempt, op. cit.*, at pp.13–37, 7–84 and 7–58.

*Magistrates' court*

**6–040**    Magistrates' courts have no inherent jurisdiction to prohibit publication of photographs or reports of proceedings and can only act pursuant to specific statutory powers.[97] In addition to the various statutory restrictions concerning children set out below at paras 6–044 *et seq.* and the Contempt of Court Act 1981,[98] magistrates' courts are subject to s.8 of the Magistrates' Court Act 1980 which restricts the right to report committal proceedings but grants the power to the justices to direct that the restrictions do not apply. If the proposed publication is outside the specific statutory powers, a magistrates' court has no general power to grant injunctions prohibiting publication of photographs of defendants, parties or witnesses.

There is authority in a different context to the effect that the High Court can fill a gap where a magistrates' court has no power to grant an injunction.[99] By analogy with the Crown Court, it is submitted that the High Court should consider that it has power to grant an injunction in respect of a threatened contempt if the magistrates have no power to do so.

## Civil proceedings: power of court to order non-disclosure of identity of any party or witness

**6–041**    The Civil Procedure Rules 1998 ("CPR") governing civil litigation in county courts, the High Court and the Civil Division of the Court of Appeal[1] grants the court power to order non-disclosure of the identity of any party or witness. This is provided for by r.39.2(4). Part 39 in full reads as follows:

"**39.2 General rule—hearing to be in public**
(1) The general rule is that a hearing is to be in public.
(2) The requirement for a hearing to be in public does not require the court to make special arrangements for accommodating members of the public.
(3) A hearing, or any part of it, may be in private if—

   (a) publicity would defeat the object of the hearing;
   (b) it involves matters relating to national security;
   (c) it involves confidential information (including information relating to personal financial matters) and publicity would damage that confidentiality;
   (d) a private hearing is necessary to protect the interests of any child or patient;

---

[97] *R. v Newtownabbey Magistrates Court Ex p. Belfast Telegraph Newspapers Ltd* [1997] N.I. 309 (QBD Northern Ireland).
[98] *R. v Horsham Justices Ex p. Farquharson* [1982] 2 All E.R. 269. See also above at paras 6–032 and 6–020 *et seq.*
[99] *West Mercia Constabulary v Wagener* [1981] 3 All E.R. 378 (injunction freezing bank account suspected to be profits of crime).
[1] CPR 1998, r.2.1. Excludes: insolvency proceedings; non-contentious/common form probate proceedings; High Court acting as a prize court; proceedings before a judge within the meaning of Pt VII of the Mental Health Act 1983; Family Proceedings and Adoption Proceedings.

(e) it is a hearing of an application made without notice and it would be unjust to any respondent for there to be a public hearing;

(f) it involves uncontentious matters arising in the administration of trusts or in the administration of a deceased person's estate; or

(g) the court considers this to be necessary, in the interests of justice.

(4) The court may order that the identity of any party or witness must not be disclosed if it considers non-disclosure necessary in order to protect the interests of that party or witness."

The Part 39 Practice Direction lists a number of types of hearings that in the first instance should be held in private.[2]  **6–042**

(1) a claim by a mortgagee against one or more individuals for an order for possession of land;

(2) a claim by a landlord against one or more tenants or former tenants for the repossession of a dwelling house based on the non-payment of rent;

(3) an application to suspend a warrant of execution or a warrant of possession or to stay execution where the court is being invited to consider the ability of a party to make payments to another party;

(4) a redetermination under CPR r.14.13 or an application to vary or suspend the payment of a judgment debt by instalments;

(5) an application for a charging order (including an application to enforce a charging order), third party debt order, attachment of earnings order, administration order, or the appointment of a receiver;

(6) an oral examination;

(7) the determination of an assisted person's liability for costs under reg.127 of the Civil Legal Aid (General) Regulations 1989 or the liability of an LSC funded client under regs 9 and 10 of the Community Legal Service (Costs) Regulations 2000;

(8) an application for security for costs under s.726(1) of the Companies Act 1985;

(9) proceedings brought under the Consumer Credit Act 1974, the Inheritance (Provision for Family and Dependants) Act 1975 or the Protection from Harassment Act 1997; and

(10) an application by a trustee or personal representative for directions as to bringing or defending legal proceedings (see CPR PD 39A).

---

[2] Practice Direction 39A—Miscellaneous Provisions Relating to Hearings, at para.1.5.

**6–043**    Committal proceedings may also be heard in private: RSC Ord.52 r.6 and CCR.

The power of the court to sit in private does not breach Arts 6 or 10 of the ECHR as it does not comprise a blanket ban upon publicity but simply permits judges to sit in private in very limited circumstances.[3] The general rule is, however, that a hearing should be in public.[4]

If an order was made under CPR r.39.2(1) prohibiting identification of a witness or party, publication of a photograph of that person would be in breach of the order and in contempt of court.

## Children and young persons

**6–044**    There are a number of different statutory restrictions governing publicity and children. The majority prohibit identification of the child involved in legal proceedings and thus publication of a photograph is prohibited. The law is unnecessary complicated by the existence of these different provisions which have developed in an apparently random and patchwork style over many years. In some circumstances, the provisions overlap and are difficult to reconcile. To further complicate matters, further provisions and some amendments will be introduced as a result of the Youth Justice and Criminal Evidence Act 1999. At the time of writing, the sections of that Act concerning reporting restrictions are not yet in force.[5]

**6–045**    The main statutory provisions which concern children and family proceedings and broadly the areas they cover are:

- s.1(1), Judicial Proceedings (Regulation of Reports Act) 1926 (a criminal offence to publish in proceedings for dissolution or nullity of marriage or judicial separation anything other than name, address, occupations of witnesses or parties);

- s.39(1), Children and Young Persons Act 1933 (youth court proceedings plus discretion to direct no identification of a child involved in any adult proceedings as party or witness);

- s.12(1), Administration of Justice Act 1960 (proceedings in private);

- s.1, Domestic and Appellate Proceedings Act 1968 (appellate court power to sit in private);

- s.71(1), Magistrates' Court Act 1980 (proceedings in magistrates' courts);

---

[3] *R. (on the application of Pelling) v Bow County Court (No.2)* [2001] U.K.H.R.R. 165.
[4] CPR r.39.2(1); *R. (on the application of Pelling) v Bow County Court (No.2)* [2001] U.K.H.R.R. 165; *Scott v Scott* [1913] A.C. 417.
[5] Save for the purpose only of the exercise of any power to make rules of court—see below at para.6–065. The Government has indicated a date of implementation is likely to be Spring 2004. See *Hansard*, HL (5th series) Vol.657, Col. GC472, February 9, 2004, *per* Baroness Scotland of Asthal.

- s.97(2), Children Act 1989 (criminal offence to publish material identifying a child, (and his address or school) involved in any proceedings before a High Court, County court or magistrates' court).

Publication of photographs of children or young people will rarely be appropriate or permitted. This is particularly so in respect of family cases and Children Act proceedings where cases will usually be held in private.[6] **6–046**

In addition to the above, the court also has an inherent jurisdiction to grant injunctions to restrain publication of information about its wards or other children[7] and jurisdiction to restrain any act by a parent that, if unrestrained would or might adversely affect the welfare of the child, the subject of proceedings.[8] Where there is such an injunction in place prohibiting publication of a photograph of the ward or child concerned, publication will be in contempt of court. **6–047**

## Children and Young Persons Act 1933

*Children in youth courts, etc.*[9]

There are several sections of the Children and Young Persons Act 1933 that impose restrictions on court reporting about children involved in legal proceedings. The provisions provide that no picture of any child or young person involved in specified legal proceedings can be published or included in a programme service. A child is a person under the age of 14 years and a young person is a person who has attained the age of 14 but is under 18.[10] The prohibition is set out in s.49(1), Children and Young Persons Act 1933: **6–048**

"(1) The following prohibitions apply (subject to subsection (5) below) in relation to any proceedings to which this section applies,[11] that is to say—

(a) no report shall be published which reveals the name, address or school of any child or young person concerned in the proceedings

---

[6] *Clibbery v Allan* [2002] EWCA Civ 45 at para.48; [2002] 2 W.L.R. 1511; [2002] 1 All E.R. 865; *P-B (A Minor) (Child Cases: Hearing in Open Court)* [1997] 1 All E.R. 58.
[7] *Re X (A Minor) (Wardship: Injunction)* [1984] 1 W.L.R. 1422 (Mary Bell); *R. v Central Independent Television plc*; sub nom *Mrs R. v Central Independent Television plc* [1994] Fam. 192; [1994] 2 F.L.R. 151; *Re C (A Minor) (Wardship: Medical Treatment) (No.2)*; sub nom *Re C (A Minor) (No.2) (Wardship: Publication of Information)* [1990] Fam. 39; [1990] 1 F.L.R. 263; *Re Z (A Minor) (Identification: Restrictions on Publication)*; sub nom *Re Z (A Minor) (Freedom of Publication)* [1997] Fam. 1; [1996] 1 F.L.R. 191; *Kelly v BBC* [2001] 1 F.L.R. 197; *Re S (A Child)* [2003] EWCA Civ 963.
[8] *Re G (Celebrities: Publicity)* [1999] 1 F.L.R. 409, 414–415; *A v M (Family Proceedings: Publicity)* [2000] 1 F.L.R. 562; *Kelly v BBC* [2001] 1 F.L.R. 197, 216.
[9] See below at para.6–048, n.11.
[10] Children and Young Persons Act 1933, s.107(1).
[11] Children and Young Persons Act 1933, s.49(2) provides the proceedings to which s.49 applies are proceedings in a youth court; on appeal from a youth court (including by way of case stated); proceedings for varying or revoking supervision orders under the Children and Young Persons Act 1969, s.15 or 16 and proceedings on appeal from a magistrates' court arising out of proceedings under s.15 or 16 of that Act (including proceedings by way of case stated).

or includes any particulars likely to lead to the identification of any child or young person concerned in the proceedings; and

(b) no picture shall be published or included in a programme service as being or including a picture of any child or young person concerned in the proceedings."

Picture is defined as including "a likeness however produced" and thus will include analogue and digital photographs as well as sketches.[12]

**6–049**    Section 49(5) provides that, in certain circumstances, the restrictions can be lifted by the court—if it is satisfied either that it is appropriate to do so for the purpose of avoiding injustice to the child/young person or where it is necessary to apprehend a child or young person charged with or convicted of a violent or sexual offence or an offence punishable with 14 years or more imprisonment who is unlawfully at large. It has been said that this power should be exercised with great caution.[13] The restriction can also be lifted where the child or young person has been convicted of an offence and the court considers it is in the public interest to do so.[14]

### Children in adult proceedings

**6–050**    Protection is also provided at the court's discretion[15] for children appearing as defendants or witnesses in adult courts. This is set out is s.39 of the Children and Young Persons Act 1933 and the relevant part provides as follows:

"(1) In relation to any proceedings in any court ... the court may direct that—

(a) no newspaper report of the proceedings shall reveal the name, address or school or include any particulars calculated to lead to the identification, of any child or young person concerned in the proceedings, either, as being the person by or against, or in respect of whom the proceedings are taken or as being a witness therein;

(b) no picture shall be published in any newspaper as being or including a picture of any young child or young person so concerned in the proceedings as aforesaid;

except insofar (if at all) as may be permitted by the court."

---

[12] Children and Young Persons Act 1933, s.49(11).
[13] *McKerry v Teesdale and Wear Valley Justices* [2001] E.M.L.R. 5; [2000] Crim. L.R. 594; [2000] C.O.D. 199. (the tension between the need to protect juvenile offenders against unnecessary and adverse publicity (Art.8 European Convention on Human Rights) and freedom of expression (Art.10) could be resolved by dispensing with anonymity only where it was in the public interest to do so).
[14] Children and Young Persons Act 1933, s.49(4A) added by Crime (Sentences) Act 1997, s.45.
[15] *R. v Central Criminal Court Ex p. Godwin and Crook* [1995] 1 F.L.R. 132.

There is a maximum penalty of £5,000.[16] It is therefore open to the court to make a direction under this section and if so, publication of any photograph of the child/young person concerned would be prohibited unless specifically permitted by the court, which is unlikely.

The court has a complete discretion to hear anybody in support of or in opposition to an application under s.39.[17] There is a strong and proper public interest in knowing the identity of those who have committed crimes, particularly serious and detestable crimes.[18] Orders preventing the disclosure of the identity of defendants or other persons concerned in criminal proceedings should be restricted and only made when they are justified.[19] It is not the case that orders will only be made in "rare and exceptional cases" but there must be good reason to make such an order.[20] The offender's age and welfare have to be taken into account, but it might be appropriate, particularly after conviction, to place greater weight on the public interest in knowing as much as possible about the criminal proceedings.[21]   **6–051**

The Court of Appeal has suggested that the following procedure should be followed when making orders under s.39[22]:   **6–052**

(1) The terms of the order should be made clear. Normally, it will suffice to use the words of s.39(1) of the Act of 1933, or a suitable adaptation, and to relate the order to, for example, "the child/children named in the charge/indictment." But, if there is possible doubt as to which child or children the order relates, the judge (or magistrate) should identify the relevant child or children with clarity.

(2) A written copy of the order should be drawn as soon as possible after the judge or magistrate has made the order orally and made available in the court office for representatives of the press to inspect.

(3) The fact that an order has been made should be communicated to those who were not present when it was made, perhaps best be done by a short notice included in the daily list, alert the press to the fact that the order has been made.

This section will be amended by the Youth Justice and Criminal Evidence Act 1999[23] which (when it comes into force) will provide that it no longer applies to criminal proceedings by a new subs.(3):   **6–053**

"(3) In this section proceedings means proceedings other than criminal proceedings"

---

[16] A fine not exceeding level 5 on the standard scale: Children and Young Persons Act, s.39(2). See below at para.6–055, n.26.
[17] *R. v Central Criminal Court Ex p. Crook* [1995] 1 W.L.R. 139; [1995] 1 All E.R. 537; [1995] 2 Cr. App. R. 212.
[18] [1995] 1 W.L.R. 139 at 145.
[19] *ibid.*
[20] *R. v Lee (A Minor)* [1993] 1 W.L.R. 103.
[21] *R. v Central Criminal Court Ex p. P* [1999] 1 F.L.R. 480; [1999] Crim. L.R. 159.
[22] *R. v Central Criminal Court Ex p. Crook* [1995] 1 W.L.R. 139 at 146.
[23] Sch.2, para.2.

*Future amendment of Children and Young Person Act 1933, ss.39 and 49.*

**6–054**    The Youth Justice and Criminal Evidence Act 1999 provides for the future amendment of ss.39 and 49 of the Children and Young Person Act 1933.[24] At the time of writing, the amendments are not yet in force.

The main proposed amendments are to add to s.39 a new subs.(3) "In this section 'proceedings' means proceedings other than criminal proceedings."[25] This will not affect the operation of s.39 to proceedings instituted before the day on which the amendment comes into force. The main amendments to s.49 are as follows:

A new s.49(1) which reads:

"(1) No matter relating to any child or young person concerned in proceedings to which this section applies shall while he is under the age of 18 be included in any publication if it is likely to lead members of the public to identify him as someone concerned in the proceedings."

Section 49(3) is substituted as:

"(3) In this section 'publication' includes any speech, writing, relevant programme or other communication in whatever form, which is addressed to the public at large or any section of the public (and for this purpose every relevant programme shall be taken to be so addressed), but does not include an indictment or other document prepared for use in particular legal proceedings.

(3A) The matters relating to a person in relation to which the restrictions imposed by subsection (1) above apply (if their inclusion in any publication is likely to have the result mentioned in that subsection) include in particular—

(a)  his name,
(b)  his address,
(c)  the identity of any school or other educational establishment attended by him,
(d)  the identity of any place of work, and
(e)  any still or moving picture of him."

Section 49(4) for the words from "whether as being" onwards substitute "if he is—

(a)  a person against or in respect of whom the proceedings are taken, or

(b)  a person called, or proposed to be called, to give evidence in the proceedings."

---

[24] Youth Justice and Criminal Evidence Act 1999, s.48(a) and Sch.2.
[25] Youth Justice and Criminal Evidence Act, Sch.2, para.2.

In s.49(4A), for "requirements of this section" substitute "restrictions imposed by subsection (1) above".

By the substituted subsection (9), where publication is in contravention of s.49(1), the following people shall be guilty of an offence and liable on summary conviction to a fine not exceeding level 5[26] on the standard scale: **6–055**

(a) where the publication is a newspaper or periodical, any proprietor, any editor and any publisher of the newspaper or periodical;

(b) where the publication is a relevant programme—

    (i) any body corporate or Scottish partnership engaged in providing the programme service in which the programme is included; and

    (ii) any person having functions in relation to the programme corresponding to those of an editor of a newspaper;

(c) in the case of any other publication, any person publishing it.

A new subsection (9A) provides a defence to an offence under s.49(9)— that it shall be a defence to prove that at the time of the alleged offence that the accused was not aware, and neither suspected nor had reason to suspect, that the publication included the matter in question.[27] **6–056**

Where an offence under s.49(9) is committed by a body corporate and it is proved (a) to have been committed with the consent or connivance of, or (b) to be attributable to any neglect on the part of, an officer, the officer as well as the body corporate is guilty of the offence and liable to be proceeded against and punished accordingly.[28] "Officer" means a director, manager, secretary or other similar officer of the body, or a person purporting to act in any such capacity.[29] Section 49(11) substitutes for the definition of "programme" and "programme service" **6–057**

" 'picture' includes a likeness however produced;
    'relevant programme' means a programme included in a programme service, within the meaning of the Broadcasting Act 1990"

## Children Act 1989

Section 97(2) of the Children Act 1989 as amended[30] provides that: **6–058**

---

[26] At the time of writing, £5,000: Criminal Justice Act 1982, s.37.
[27] Youth Justice and Criminal Evidence Act 1999, Sch.2, para.7.
[28] New Children and Young Persons Act 1933, s.49(9B) as inserted by the Youth Justice and Criminal Evidence Act 1999, Sch.2, para.7.
[29] New Children and Young Persons Act 1933, s.49(9B) as inserted by the Youth Justice and Criminal Evidence Act 1999, Sch.2, para.7.
[30] Access to Justice Act 1999, s.72. From September 27, 1999, extended provision to High Court and county court in addition to the magistrates' court.

"No person shall publish any material which is intended, or likely, to identify—

(a) any child as being involved in any proceedings before the High Court, a county court or a magistrates' court in which any power under this Act may be exercised by the court with respect to that or any other child; or

(b) an address or school as being that of a child involved in any such proceedings."

The prohibition includes publication via inclusion in a programme service.[31] "Material" includes any picture or representation.[32] Not just photographs of the child are prohibited, but pictures of anything which is likely to identify the child or its address or school. Photographs of the school itself or identifiable relatives would fall within this section.

There is power, where the welfare of the child requires it, to make an order dispensing with the requirements of s.97(2) to such extent as specified.[33] This will be rarely exercised as the court or the Lord Chancellor have to be satisfied the welfare of the child requires it.[34] Reporting restrictions were lifted for example in one case so the father could seek to raise money to fund a child's treatment.[35]

**6–059**    It is a defence to a charge under s.97 to prove that the person accused did not know and had no reason to suspect that the published material was intended or likely to identify the child.[36] A person convicted under the section is liable on summary conviction not a fine not exceeding level 4 on the standard scale.[37]

### Proceedings in private: Administration of Justice Act 1960, s.12

**6–060**    Section 12(1) provides:

"The publication of information relating to proceedings before any court sitting in private shall not of itself be contempt of court, that is to say—

(a) where proceedings—
    (i) relate to the exercise of the inherent jurisdiction of the High Court with respect to minors;
    (ii) are brought under the Children Act 1989;
    (iii) otherwise relate wholly or mainly to the maintenance or upbringing of a minor."

---

[31] Children Act 1989, s.97(5).
[32] Children Act 1989, s.97(5).
[33] Children Act 1989, s.97(4).
[34] Children Act 1989, s.97(5).
[35] *R. v Cambridge District Health Authority Ex p. B (No.2)* [1996] 1 F.L.R. 375, CA (Children and Young Persons Act 1933, s.39, restrictions revoked).
[36] Children Act 1989, s.97(3).
[37] At the time of writing, £2,500: Criminal Justice Act 1982, s.37(2) as amended by Criminal Justice Act 1991, s.17(2).

This section prevents the publication of information in respect of child law cases which are heard in private. These restrictions are for the purpose of protecting the proper functioning of the court's own jurisdiction and the court will not use the provision more widely.[38] The prohibition is construed strictly and by direct reference to the mischief at which it is directed.[39]

It is the publication of information *relating to the proceedings* which is prohibited. If information published relates to the parties but not to the proceedings, there is no contempt under this section.[40] The section protects the privacy and confidentiality of (i) documents on the court file,[41] and (ii) what goes on in front of the judge in his court room.[42]

6–061

Information will include photographs relating to the proceedings[43] such as photographs from the court file. As regards photographs and documents on the court file, it should be noted that confidentiality of documents in family proceedings is also governed by r.4.23 of the Family Proceedings Rules 1991 which provides that no documents held by the court relating to proceedings can be disclosed to non-parties without the leave of the court.[44] Whether confidentiality continues between the parties after a case heard in private is over depends upon the type of proceedings and whether they (or part of the information) comes within the ambit of s.12 of the 1960 Act or whether the administration of justice will otherwise be impeded or prejudiced by publication.[45]

6–062

Section 12 of the Administration of Justice Act 1960 does not prohibit the media from reporting the comings and goings of the parties or witnesses as well as any incident that may occur under the pressure of litigation either outside the court or within the court precincts[46] but outside the room in which the judge conducts the case.[47] In the absence of prohibition under

---

[38] *Scott v Scott* [1913] A.C. 417; *Re F (OrseA) (A Minor) (Publication of Information)* [1977] Fam. 58; *M v BBC* [1997] 1 F.L.R. 51 (adult seeking to use section to prevent publication of his own infertility).

[39] *X v Dempster* [1999] 1 F.L.R. 894, 898H *per* Wilson J.

[40] *X v Dempster* [1999] 1 F.L.R. 894, 898F citing *Re F (Otherwise A) (A Minor) (Publication of Information)* [1977] Fam.58.

[41] Confidentiality of documents is protected in addition by r.4.33 of the Family Proceedings Rules 1991, see below at para.6–062.

[42] *Kelly v BBC* [2001] 1 F.L.R. 197, 214B.

[43] See *Handyside Films (Production) Ltd v Express Newspaper Ltd* [1986] F.S.R. 463 (a decision under s.10 of the Contempt of Court Act 1981—disclosure of sources). It was argued that photographs were not "information". Sir Nicholas Brown Wilkinson V.C. rejected the argument saying at 486:

> "photographs are the same as oral or written communications. They are merely a different form of communicating information. Photographs communicate visually: writing does it through words. But in either case what is contained in the publication is information".

[44] There is no objection for a litigant to provide non-identifiable information about a problem that affected himself and his family to those from whom he sought advice: *Re G (A Child (2003))* [2003] EWCA Civ 1055.

[45] *Clibbery v Allan* [2002] EWCA Civ 45 at para.75; [2002] Fam. 261; [2002] 2 W.L.R. 1511; [2002] 1 All E.R. 865. All cases of ancillary relief will be protected as will information about children cases: Re G (A Child (2003)) [2003] EWCA Civ 1055.

[46] Obviously this does not include photographs with the court precincts which remain prohibited under the Criminal Justice Act 1925, s.41, see above at para.6–007.

[47] *Re G (Celebrities: Publicity)* [1999] 1 F.L.R. 409, 413G.

some other statute or an injunction, this section does not prohibit publication of the photograph of a child[48] or a photograph of the parties.[49]

**6–063**     The prohibition is not limited in time. It remains a contempt of court to publish such information even after proceedings are discharged.[50]

### Family proceedings in magistrates' courts: Magistrates' Court Act 1980, s.71

**6–064**     In the case of family proceedings in magistrates' courts, it is unlawful to publish in any newspaper or periodical or include in a programme any particulars other than:

(a)  the names, addresses, and occupations of the parties and witnesses;

(b)  the grounds of the application and a concise statement of charges, defences and counter-charges in support of which evidence has been given;

(c)  submissions on any point of law arising in the course of proceedings and the decision of the court on the submissions;

(d)  the decision and any observations of the court in giving its decision.[51]

In the case of proceedings in a magistrate's court under the Adoption Act 1976, particulars of the proceedings include any picture of or including any child concerned in the proceedings.[52] Thus, in Adoption Act 1976 proceedings, it is unlawful to publish a picture of the child. Contravention is an offence punishable on summary conviction to a fine not exceeding level 4 on the standard scale.[53]

### Youth Justice And Criminal Evidence Act 1999: under 18 year olds and certain witnesses

**6–065**     At the time of writing, the sections of this Act which concern reporting restrictions, Ch.IV (ss.44–52) are not yet in force, save for the power to make rules of court[54] and s.47 which governs reporting of any directions or applications for directions for (1) special measures (*e.g.* screening) to apply

---

[48] *Re W (Wards) (Publication of Information)* [1989] 1 F.L.R. 246, 257H; *X v Dempster* [1999] 1 F.L.R. 894, 899A.

[49] *Re De Beaujeu's Application for Writ of Attachment Against Cudlipp* [1949] 1 Ch. 230; *X v Dempster* [1999] 1 F.L.R. 894, 898B.

[50] *Re E (A Minor) (Child Abuse: Injunctions)* [1991] 1 F.L.R. 420, 455B.

[51] Magistrates' Court Act 1980, s.71(1) and (1A).

[52] Magistrates' Court Act 1980, s.71(1B) and (2).

[53] Magistrates' Court Act 1980, s.71(1B) and (3). At the time of writing, a level 4 fine is £2,500: Criminal Justice Act 1982, s.37 as amended.

[54] For the purpose only of the exercise of any power to make rules of court s.44 came into force on July 27, 1999: s.68(4)(c). As to implementation, see above at para.6–044, n.5.

to witness, or (2) prevent the accused from cross-examining particular witnesses.[55]

Once these sections come into force, the main change that will be introduced is that reporting restrictions will apply once a criminal investigation has begun. Presently, as set out above, reporting restrictions only applied once proceedings had begun. This exposed children and young people to potential identification by the media if they had been suspected but not charged. Children who had witnessed criminal offences could not be protected from identification until they were called as witnesses in criminal proceedings.

The main relevant provisions are as follows:

### Reporting criminal investigations involving persons under 18

Where a criminal investigation has begun no matter can be published  **6–066** relating to any person under the age of 18 involved (suspect, victim or witness[56]) which is likely to lead members of the public to identify him.[57] Still and moving pictures are included in the restriction.[58] A picture includes a likeness however produced.[59] This restriction ceases to apply once court proceedings have commenced.[60] The court has power to dispense with the restrictions if it is satisfied "it is necessary in the interests of justice to do so" having regard to the welfare of the person concerned.[61]

### Reporting criminal proceedings involving person under 18 to which the Children and Young Persons Act 1933, s.49 does not apply

In relation to proceedings to which s.49 of the Children and Young  **6–067** Persons Act 1933 does *not* apply,[62] the court has power in criminal proceedings or any proceedings in a service court to direct to such extent specified that no matter relating to any person whilst under the age of 18 be included in any publication if it is likely to lead members of the public to identify him as a person concerned in the proceedings.[63] Any such direction may be revoked by that court or an appellate court.[64] Restricted matters include any still or moving picture of the person concerned.[65] A picture includes a likeness however produced.[66]

---

[55] Came into force July 24, 2002. Youth Justice and Criminal Evidence Act 1999 (Commencement No.7) Order 2002 (SI 2002/1739).
[56] Youth Justice and Criminal Evidence Act 1999, s.44(4). It does not include a victim covered by s.1 of the Sexual Offences (Amendment) Act 1992.
[57] Youth Justice and Criminal Evidence Act 1999, s.44. Criminal offence includes civil offences committed by a person subject to service law.
[58] Youth Justice and Criminal Evidence Act 1999, s.44(6)(e).
[59] Youth Justice and Criminal Evidence Act 1999, s.63(1).
[60] Youth Justice and Criminal Evidence Act 1999, s.44(3).
[61] Youth Justice and Criminal Evidence Act 1999, s.44(7), (8).
[62] For those proceedings presently covered by the Children and Young Persons Act 1933, s.49. Note that future amendment of the Children and Young Persons Act 1933, s.49, is provided for by the Youth Justice and Criminal Evidence Act 1999, s.48(a) and Sch.2.
[63] Youth Justice and Criminal Evidence Act 1999, s.45(1)–(3).
[64] Youth Justice and Criminal Evidence Act 1999, s.45(9).
[65] Youth Justice and Criminal Evidence Act 1999, s.45(8).
[66] Youth Justice and Criminal Evidence Act 1999, s.63(1).

*Power to restrict reporting concerning adult witnesses needing protection*

**6–068**   In criminal proceedings or any proceedings in a service court there is also a power to restrict reports about those adult witnesses who are eligible for protection.[67] A witness is eligible for protection if the court is satisfied the quality of their evidence or their level of co-operation given to any party is likely to be diminished by fear or distress on the part of the witness in connection with being identified by the public as a witness.[68] Still and moving pictures are included in any reporting direction given.[69] A picture includes a likeness however produced.[70] The factors that the court must take into account in determining whether a witness is eligible for protection are set out in the Act.[71]

---

YOUTH JUSTICE AND CRIMINAL EVIDENCE ACT 1999, ss.44–52

CHAPTER IV

REPORTING RESTRICTIONS

*Reports relating to persons under 18*

**6–068A**   **44.**—(1) This section applies (subject to subsection (3)) where a criminal investigation has begun in respect of—

(a)  an alleged offence against the law of—

(i)  England and Wales, or
(ii)  Northern Ireland; or

(b)  an alleged civil offence (other than an offence falling within paragraph (a)) committed (whether or not in the United Kingdom) by a person subject to service law.

(2) No matter relating to any person involved in the offence shall while he is under the age of 18 be included in any publication if it is likely to lead members of the public to identify him as a person involved in the offence.

---

[67] Youth Justice and Criminal Evidence Act 1999, s.46(1), (2).
[68] Youth Justice and Criminal Evidence Act 1999, s.46(3).
[69] Youth Justice and Criminal Evidence Act 1999, s.46(7)(e).
[70] Youth Justice and Criminal Evidence Act 1999, s.63(1).
[71] Youth Justice and Criminal Evidence Act 1999, s.46(4) nature and circumstances of offence; age of witness; in so far as appears relevant to the court—social and cultural background and ethnic origins of the witness, domestic and employment circumstances of the witness, religious beliefs or political opinions of the witness; any behaviour towards the witness by the accused, members of the accused's family or associates and any other person who is likely to be an accused or witness in any proceedings. The court must also consider any views expressed by the witness: s.44(5).

YOUTH JUSTICE AND CRIMINAL EVIDENCE ACT 1999, ss.44–52
CONT.

(3) The restrictions imposed by subsection (2) cease to apply once there are proceedings in a court (whether a court in England and Wales, a service court or a court in Northern Ireland) in respect of the offence.

(4) For the purposes of subsection (2) any reference to a person involved in the offence is to—

(a) a person by whom the offence is alleged to have been committed; or

(b) if this paragraph applies to the publication in question by virtue of subsection (5)—

   (i) a person against or in respect of whom the offence is alleged to have been committed, or

   (ii) a person who is alleged to have been a witness to the commission of the offence;

   except that paragraph (b)(i) does not include a person in relation to whom section 1 of the Sexual Offences (Amendment) Act 1992 (anonymity of victims of certain sexual offences) applies in connection with the offence.

(5) Subsection (4)(b) applies to a publication if—

(a) where it is a relevant programme, it is transmitted, or

(b) in the case of any other publication, it is published,

on or after such date as may be specified in an order made by the Secretary of State.

(6) The matters relating to a person in relation to which the restrictions imposed by subsection (2) apply (if their inclusion in any publication is likely to have the result mentioned in that subsection) include in particular—

(a) his name,

(b) his address,

(c) the identity of any school or other educational establishment attended by him,

(d) the identity of any place of work, and

(e) any still or moving picture of him.

(7) Any appropriate criminal court may by order dispense, to any extent specified in the order, with the restrictions imposed by subsection (2) in relation to a person if it is satisfied that it is necessary in the interests of justice to do so.

(8) However, when deciding whether to make such an order dispensing (to any extent) with the restrictions imposed by subsection (2) in relation to a person, the court shall have regard to the welfare of that person.

(9) In subsection (7) "appropriate criminal court" means—

(a) in a case where this section applies by virtue of subsection (1)(a)(i) or (ii), any court in England and Wales or (as the case may be) in Northern Ireland which has any jurisdiction in, or in relation to, any criminal

## Youth Justice and Criminal Evidence Act 1999, ss.44–52 CONT.

proceedings (but not a service court unless the offence is alleged to have been committed by a person subject to service law);

(b)  in a case where this section applies by virtue of subsection (1)(b), any court falling within paragraph (a) or a service court.

(10) The power under subsection (7) of a magistrates' court in England and Wales may be exercised by a single justice.

(11) In the case of a decision of a magistrates' court in England and Wales, or a court of summary jurisdiction in Northern Ireland, to make or refuse to make an order under subsection (7), the following persons, namely—

(a)  any person who was a party to the proceedings on the application for the order, and

(b)  with the leave of the Crown Court, any other person,

may, in accordance with rules of court, appeal to the Crown Court against that decision or appear or be represented at the hearing of such an appeal.

(12) On such an appeal the Crown Court—

(a)  may make such order as is necessary to give effect to its determination of the appeal; and

(b)  may also make such incidental or consequential orders as appear to it to be just.

(13) In this section—

(a)  "civil offence" means an act or omission which, if committed in England and Wales, would be an offence against the law of England and Wales;

(b)  any reference to a criminal investigation, in relation to an alleged offence, is to an investigation conducted by police officers, or other persons charged with the duty of investigating offences, with a view to it being ascertained whether a person should be charged with the offence;

(c)  any reference to a person subject to service law is to—

(i)  a person subject to military law, air-force law or the Naval Discipline Act 1957, or

(ii)  any other person to whom provisions of Part II of the Army Act 1955, Part II of the Air Force Act 1955 or Parts I and II of the Naval Discipline Act 1957 apply (whether with or without any modifications).

**6–068B**

**45.**—(1) This section applies (subject to subsection (2)) in relation to—

(a)  any criminal proceedings in any court (other than a service court) in England and Wales or Northern Ireland; and

(b)  any proceedings (whether in the United Kingdom or elsewhere) in any service court.

(2) This section does not apply in relation to any proceedings to which section 49 of the Children and Young Persons Act 1933 applies.

## YOUTH JUSTICE AND CRIMINAL EVIDENCE ACT 1999, SS.44–52
### CONT.

(3) The court may direct that no matter relating to any person concerned in the proceedings shall while he is under the age of 18 be included in any publication if it is likely to lead members of the public to identify him as a person concerned in the proceedings.

(4) The court or an appellate court may by direction ("an excepting direction") dispense, to any extent specified in the excepting direction, with the restrictions imposed by a direction under subsection (3) if it is satisfied that it is necessary in the interests of justice to do so.

(5) The court or an appellate court may also by direction ("an excepting direction") dispense, to any extent specified in the excepting direction, with the restrictions imposed by a direction under subsection (3) if it is satisfied—

(a) that their effect is to impose a substantial and unreasonable restriction on the reporting of the proceedings, and

(b) that it is in the public interest to remove or relax that restriction;

but no excepting direction shall be given under this subsection by reason only of the fact that the proceedings have been determined in any way or have been abandoned.

(6) When deciding whether to make—

(a) a direction under subsection (3) in relation to a person, or

(b) an excepting direction under subsection (4) or (5) by virtue of which the restrictions imposed by a direction under subsection (3) would be dispensed with (to any extent) in relation to a person,

the court or (as the case may be) the appellate court shall have regard to the welfare of that person.

(7) For the purposes of subsection (3) any reference to a person concerned in the proceedings is to a person—

(a) against or in respect of whom the proceedings are taken, or

(b) who is a witness in the proceedings.

(8) The matters relating to a person in relation to which the restrictions imposed by a direction under subsection (3) apply (if their inclusion in any publication is likely to have the result mentioned in that subsection) include in particular—

(a) his name,

(b) his address,

(c) the identity of any school or other educational establishment attended by him,

(d) the identity of any place of work, and

(e) any still or moving picture of him.

(9) A direction under subsection (3) may be revoked by the court or an appellate court.

(10) An excepting direction—

## YOUTH JUSTICE AND CRIMINAL EVIDENCE ACT 1999, ss.44–52 CONT.

(a)  may be given at the time the direction under subsection (3) is given or subsequently; and

(b)  may be varied or revoked by the court or an appellate court.

(11) In this section "appellate court", in relation to any proceedings in a court, means a court dealing with an appeal (including an appeal by way of case stated) arising out of the proceedings or with any further appeal.

### *Reports relating to adult witnesses*

**6–068C**

**46.**—(1) This section applies where—

(a)  in any criminal proceedings in any court (other than a service court) in England and Wales or Northern Ireland, or

(b)  in any proceedings (whether in the United Kingdom or elsewhere) in any service court,

a party to the proceedings makes an application for the court to give a reporting direction in relation to a witness in the proceedings (other than the accused) who has attained the age of 18.

In this section "reporting direction" has the meaning given by subsection (6).

(2) If the court determines—

(a)  that the witness is eligible for protection, and

(b)  that giving a reporting direction in relation to the witness is likely to improve—

   (i)  the quality of evidence given by the witness, or
   (ii)  the level of co-operation given by the witness to any party to the proceedings in connection with that party's preparation of its case,

the court may give a reporting direction in relation to the witness.

(3) For the purposes of this section a witness is eligible for protection if the court is satisfied—

(a)  that the quality of evidence given by the witness, or

(b)  the level of co-operation given by the witness to any party to the proceedings in connection with that party's preparation of its case,

is likely to be diminished by reason of fear or distress on the part of the witness in connection with being identified by members of the public as a witness in the proceedings.

(4) In determining whether a witness is eligible for protection the court must take into account, in particular—

(a)  the nature and alleged circumstances of the offence to which the proceedings relate;

YOUTH JUSTICE AND CRIMINAL EVIDENCE ACT 1999, SS.44–52
CONT.

(b) the age of the witness;

(c) such of the following matters as appear to the court to be relevant, namely—

    (i) the social and cultural background and ethnic origins of the witness,
    (ii) the domestic and employment circumstances of the witness, and
    (iii) any religious beliefs or political opinions of the witness;

(d) any behaviour towards the witness on the part of—

    (i) the accused,
    (ii) members of the family or associates of the accused, or
    (iii) any other person who is likely to be an accused or a witness in the proceedings.

(5) In determining that question the court must in addition consider any views expressed by the witness.

(6) For the purposes of this section a reporting direction in relation to a witness is a direction that no matter relating to the witness shall during the witness's lifetime be included in any publication if it is likely to lead members of the public to identify him as being a witness in the proceedings.

(7) The matters relating to a witness in relation to which the restrictions imposed by a reporting direction apply (if their inclusion in any publication is likely to have the result mentioned in subsection (6)) include in particular—

(a) the witness's name,

(b) the witness's address,

(c) the identity of any educational establishment attended by the witness,

(d) the identity of any place of work, and

(e) any still or moving picture of the witness.

(8) In determining whether to give a reporting direction the court shall consider—

(a) whether it would be in the interests of justice to do so, and

(b) the public interest in avoiding the imposition of a substantial and unreasonable restriction on the reporting of the proceedings.

(9) The court or an appellate court may by direction ("an excepting direction") dispense, to any extent specified in the excepting direction, with the restrictions imposed by a reporting direction if—

(a) it is satisfied that it is necessary in the interests of justice to do so, or

(b) it is satisfied—

    (i) that the effect of those restrictions is to impose a substantial and unreasonable restriction on the reporting of the proceedings, and
    (ii) that it is in the public interest to remove or relax that restriction;

YOUTH JUSTICE AND CRIMINAL EVIDENCE ACT 1999, ss.44–52
CONT.

but no excepting direction shall be given under paragraph (b) by reason only of the fact that the proceedings have been determined in any way or have been abandoned.

(10) A reporting direction may be revoked by the court or an appellate court.

(11) An excepting direction—

(a)  may be given at the time the reporting direction is given or subsequently; and

(b)  may be varied or revoked by the court or an appellate court.

(12) In this section—

(a)  "appellate court", in relation to any proceedings in a court, means a court dealing with an appeal (including an appeal by way of case stated) arising out of the proceedings or with any further appeal;

(b)  references to the quality of a witness's evidence are to its quality in terms of completeness, coherence and accuracy (and for this purpose "coherence" refers to a witness's ability in giving evidence to give answers which address the questions put to the witness and can be understood both individually and collectively);

(c)  references to the preparation of the case of a party to any proceedings include, where the party is the prosecution, the carrying out of investigations into any offence at any time charged in the proceedings.

*Reports relating to directions under Chapter I or II*

**6–068D**

**47.**—(1) Except as provided by this section, no publication shall include a report of a matter falling within subsection (2).

(2) The matters falling within this subsection are—

(a)  a direction under section 19 or 36 or an order discharging, or (in the case of a direction under section 19) varying, such a direction;

(b)  proceedings—

(i)  on an application for such a direction or order, or

(ii)  where the court acts of its own motion to determine whether to give or make any such direction or order.

(3) The court dealing with a matter falling within subsection (2) may order that subsection (1) is not to apply, or is not to apply to a specified extent, to a report of that matter.

(4) Where—

(a)  there is only one accused in the relevant proceedings, and

(b)  he objects to the making of an order under subsection (3),

the court shall make the order if (and only if) satisfied after hearing the representations of the accused that it is in the interests of justice to do so; and if

YOUTH JUSTICE AND CRIMINAL EVIDENCE ACT 1999, SS.44–52
CONT.

the order is made it shall not apply to the extent that a report deals with any such objections or representations.

(5) Where—

(a)  there are two or more accused in the relevant proceedings, and

(b)  one or more of them object to the making of an order under subsection (3),

the court shall make the order if (and only if) satisfied after hearing the representations of each of the accused that it is in the interests of justice to do so; and if the order is made it shall not apply to the extent that a report deals with any such objections or representations.

(6) Subsection (1) does not apply to the inclusion in a publication of a report of matters after the relevant proceedings are either—

(a)  determined (by acquittal, conviction or otherwise), or

(b)  abandoned,

in relation to the accused or (if there is more than one) in relation to each of the accused.

(7) In this section "the relevant proceedings" means the proceedings to which any such direction as is mentioned in subsection (2) relates or would relate.

(8) Nothing in this section affects any prohibition or restriction by virtue of any other enactment on the inclusion of matter in a publication.

## *Other restrictions*

**48.** Schedule 2, which contains amendments relating to reporting restrictions under—          **6–068E**

(a)  the Children and Young Persons Act 1933,

(b)  the Sexual Offences (Amendment) Act 1976,

(c)  the Sexual Offences (Northern Ireland) Order 1978,

(d)  the Sexual Offences (Amendment) Act 1992, and

(e)  the Criminal Justice (Northern Ireland) Order 1994,

shall have effect.

## *Offences*

**49.**—(1) This section applies if a publication—          **6–068F**

(a)  includes any matter in contravention of section 44(2) or of a direction under section 45(3) or 46(2); or

YOUTH JUSTICE AND CRIMINAL EVIDENCE ACT 1999, ss.44–52
CONT.

(b)  includes a report in contravention of section 47.

(2) Where the publication is a newspaper or periodical, any proprietor, any editor and any publisher of the newspaper or periodical is guilty of an offence.
(3) Where the publication is a relevant programme—

(a)  any body corporate or Scottish partnership engaged in providing the programme service in which the programme is included, and

(b)  any person having functions in relation to the programme corresponding to those of an editor of a newspaper,

is guilty of an offence.
(4) In the case of any other publication, any person publishing it is guilty of an offence.
(5) A person guilty of an offence under this section is liable on summary conviction to a fine not exceeding level 5 on the standard scale.
(6) Proceedings for an offence under this section in respect of a publication falling within subsection (1)(b) may not be instituted—

(a)  in England and Wales otherwise than by or with the consent of the Attorney General, or

(b)  in Northern Ireland otherwise than by or with the consent of the Attorney General for Northern Ireland.

**6–068G**    **50.**—(1) Where a person is charged with an offence under section 49 it shall be a defence to prove that at the time of the alleged offence he was not aware, and neither suspected nor had reason to suspect, that the publication included the matter or report in question.
(2) Where—

(a)  a person is charged with an offence under section 49, and

(b)  the offence relates to the inclusion of any matter in a publication in contravention of section 44(2),

it shall be a defence to prove that at the time of the alleged offence he was not aware, and neither suspected nor had reason to suspect, that the criminal investigation in question had begun.
(3) Where—

(a)  paragraphs (a) and (b) of subsection (2) apply, and

(b)  the contravention of section 44(2) does not relate to either—

(i)  the person by whom the offence mentioned in that provision is alleged to have been committed, or

(ii)  (where that offence is one in relation to which section 1 of the Sexual Offences (Amendment) Act 1992 applies) a person who is alleged to be a witness to the commission of the offence,

it shall be a defence to show to the satisfaction of the court that the inclusion in the publication of the matter in question was in the public interest on the ground that, to the extent that they operated to prevent that matter from being

## YOUTH JUSTICE AND CRIMINAL EVIDENCE ACT 1999, ss.44–52
### CONT.

so included, the effect of the restrictions imposed by section 44(2) was to impose a substantial and unreasonable restriction on the reporting of matters connected with that offence.

(4) Subsection (5) applies where—

(a)   paragraphs (a) and (b) of subsection (2) apply, and

(b)   the contravention of section 44(2) relates to a person ("the protected person") who is neither—

    (i)   the person mentioned in subsection (3)(b)(i), nor
    (ii)   a person within subsection (3)(b)(ii) who is under the age of 16.

(5) In such a case it shall be a defence, subject to subsection (6), to prove that written consent to the inclusion of the matter in question in the publication had been given—

(a)   by an appropriate person, if at the time when the consent was given the protected person was under the age of 16, or

(b)   by the protected person, if that person was aged 16 or 17 at that time,

and (where the consent was given by an appropriate person) that written notice had been previously given to that person drawing to his attention the need to consider the welfare of the protected person when deciding whether to give consent.

(6) The defence provided by subsection (5) is not available if—

(a)   (where the consent was given by an appropriate person) it is proved that written or other notice withdrawing the consent—

    (i)   was given to the appropriate recipient by any other appropriate person or by the protected person, and
    (ii)   was so given in sufficient time to enable the inclusion in the publication of the matter in question to be prevented; or

(b)   subsection (8) applies.

(7) Where—

(a)   a person is charged with an offence under section 49, and

(b)   the offence relates to the inclusion of any matter in a publication in contravention of a direction under section 46(2),

it shall be a defence, unless subsection (8) applies, to prove that the person in relation to whom the direction was given had given written consent to the inclusion of that matter in the publication.

(8) Written consent is not a defence if it is proved that any person interfered—

(a)   with the peace or comfort of the person giving the consent, or

(b)   (where the consent was given by an appropriate person) with the peace or comfort of either that person or the protected person,

YOUTH JUSTICE AND CRIMINAL EVIDENCE ACT 1999, ss.44–52
CONT.

with intent to obtain the consent.

(9) In this section—

"an appropriate person" means (subject to subsections (10) to (12))—

(a) in England and Wales or Northern Ireland, a person who is a parent or guardian of the protected person, or

(b) in Scotland, a person who has parental responsibilities (within the meaning of section 1(3) of the Children (Scotland) Act 1995) in relation to the protected person;

"guardian", in relation to the protected person, means any person who is not a parent of the protected person but who has parental responsibility for the protected person within the meaning of—

(a) (in England and Wales) the Children Act 1989, or

(b) (in Northern Ireland) the Children (Northern Ireland) Order 1995.

(10) Where the protected person is (within the meaning of the Children Act 1989) a child who is looked after by a local authority, "an appropriate person" means a person who is—

(a) a representative of that authority, or

(b) a parent or guardian of the protected person with whom the protected person is allowed to live.

(11) Where the protected person is (within the meaning of the Children (Northern Ireland) Order 1995) a child who is looked after by an authority, "an appropriate person" means a person who is—

(a) an officer of that authority, or

(b) a parent or guardian of the protected person with whom the protected person is allowed to live.

(12) Where the protected person is (within the meaning of section 17(6) of the Children (Scotland) Act 1995) a child who is looked after by a local authority, "an appropriate person" means a person who is—

(a) a representative of that authority, or

(b) a person who has parental responsibilities (within the meaning of section 1(3) of that Act) in relation to the protected person and with whom the protected person is allowed to live.

(13) However, no person by whom the offence mentioned in section 44(2) is alleged to have been committed is, by virtue of subsections (9) to (12), an appropriate person for the purposes of this section.

(14) In this section "the appropriate recipient", in relation to a notice under subsection (6)(a), means—

(a) the person to whom the notice giving consent was given,

(b) (if different) the person by whom the matter in question was published, or

YOUTH JUSTICE AND CRIMINAL EVIDENCE ACT 1999, ss.44–52
CONT.

(c) any other person exercising, on behalf of the person mentioned in paragraph (b), any responsibility in relation to the publication of that matter;

and for this purpose "person" includes a body of persons and a partnership.

**51.**—(1) If an offence under section 49 committed by a body corporate is proved—

**6–068H**

(a) to have been committed with the consent or connivance of, or

(b) to be attributable to any neglect on the part of,

an officer, the officer as well as the body corporate is guilty of the offence and liable to be proceeded against and punished accordingly.

(2) In subsection (1) "officer" means a director, manager, secretary or other similar officer of the body, or a person purporting to act in any such capacity.

(3) If the affairs of a body corporate are managed by its members, "director" in subsection (2) means a member of that body.

(4) Where an offence under section 49 is committed by a Scottish partnership and is proved to have been committed with the consent or connivance of a partner, he as well as the partnership shall be guilty of the offence and shall be liable to be proceeded against and punished accordingly.

## *Supplementary*

**52.**—(1) Where for the purposes of any provision of this Chapter it falls to a court to determine whether anything is (or, as the case may be, was) in the public interest, the court must have regard, in particular, to the matters referred to in subsection (2) (so far as relevant).

**6–068I**

(2) Those matters are—

(a) the interest in each of the following—

    (i) the open reporting of crime,

    (ii) the open reporting of matters relating to human health or safety, and

    (iii) the prevention and exposure of miscarriages of justice;

(b) the welfare of any person in relation to whom the relevant restrictions imposed by or under this Chapter apply or would apply (or, as the case may be, applied); and

(c) any views expressed—

    (i) by an appropriate person on behalf of a person within paragraph (b) who is under the age of 16 ("the protected person"), or

    (ii) by a person within that paragraph who has attained that age.

(3) In subsection (2) "an appropriate person", in relation to the protected person, has the same meaning as it has for the purposes of section 50.

## Complainants in certain sexual offences

**6–069**   Identification of complainants in rape cases is prohibited by the Sexual Offences (Amendment) Act 1976, s.4. Identification of victims of certain other offences is prohibited by the Sexual Offences (Amendment) Act 1992, ss.1–4. Section 4 of the Sexual Offences (Amendment) Act 1976 will be repealed when Sch.2 to the Youth Justice and Criminal Evidence Act 1999 comes into force.[71a] The substance of its provisions will be superceded by the amended provisions of the Sexual Offences (Amendment) Act 1992.[72] The sections below appears as they will be following the coming into force of the amendments. Words in square brackets are substituted for italicised words which show the current wording.

---

### SEXUAL OFFENCES (AMENDMENT) ACT 1992, ss.1–6

**Anonymity of victims of certain offences**[73]

**6–070**   **1.**—(1) Where an allegation has been made that an offence to which this Act applies has been committed against a person, *neither the name nor address, and no still or moving picture, of that person shall during that person's lifetime—*

> *(a)  be published in England and Wales in a written publication available to the public; or*

> *(b)  be included in a relevant programme for reception in England and Wales*

[no matter relating to that person shall during that person's lifetime be included in any publication], if it is likely to lead members of the public to identify that person as the person against whom the offence is alleged to have been committed.

(2) Where a person is accused of an offence to which this Act applies, no matter likely to lead members of the public to identify a person as the person against whom the offence is alleged to have been committed ('the complainant') shall during the complainant's lifetime [be included in any publication.]–

> *(a)  be published in England and Wales in a written publication available to the public; or*

> *(b)  be included in a relevant programme for reception in England and Wales*

*(3) Subsections (1) and (2) are subject to any direction given under section 3.*
[(3) This section—

> (a)  does not apply in relation to a person by virtue of subsection (1) at anytime after a person has been accused of the offence, and

---

[71a] As to likely implementation, see above at para.6–044, n.5.
[72] Youth Justice and Criminal Evidence Act 1999, s.48(b); s.68(4); Sch.2, para.4.
[73] Amended by Youth Justice and Criminal Evidence Act 1999, Sch.2, para.7.

## SEXUAL OFFENCES (AMENDMENT) ACT 1992, ss.1–6 CONT.

(b) in its application in relation to a person by virtue of subsection (2), has effect subject to any direction given under section 3.

(3A) The matters relating to a person in relation to which the restrictions imposed by subsection (1) or (2) apply (if their inclusion in any publication is likely to have the result mentioned in that subsection) include in particular—

(a) the person's name,

(b) the person's address,

(c) the identity of any school or other educational establishment attended by the person,

(d) the identity of any place of work, and

(e) any still or moving picture of the person.]

(4) Nothing in this section prohibits the *publication or inclusion in a relevant programme* [inclusion in a publication] of matter consisting only of a report of criminal proceedings other than proceedings at, or intended to lead to, or on an appeal arising out of, a trial at which the accused is charged with the offence.

**Offences to which this act applies**[74]

**2.**—(1) This Act applies to the following offences [against the law of England and Wales—

   (aa) rape;

   (ab) burglary with intent to rape;]

   (a) any offence under any of the provisions of the Sexual Offences Act 1956 mentioned in subsection (2);

   (b) any offence under section 128 of the Mental Health Act 1959 (intercourse with mentally handicapped person by hospital staff etc);

   (c) any offence under section 1 of the Indecency with Children Act 1960 (indecent conduct towards young child);

   (d) any offence under section 54 of the Criminal Law Act 1977 (incitement by man of his grand-daughter, daughter or sister under the age of 16 to commit incest with him);

   (e) any attempt to commit any of the offences mentioned in paragraphs (a)[(aa)] to (d);

   [(f) any conspiracy to commit any of those offences;

   (g) any incitement of another to commit any of those offences.]

   [(h) aiding, abetting, counselling or procuring the commission of any of the offences mentioned in paragraphs (aa) to (e) and (g);]

(2) The provisions of the Act of 1956 are—

   (a) section 2 (procurement of a woman by threats);

   (b) section 3 (procurement of a woman by false pretences);

   (c) section 4 (administering drugs to obtain intercourse with a woman);

   (d) section 5 (intercourse with a girl under the age of 13);

   (e) section 6 (intercourse with a girl between the ages of 13 and 16);

**6–071**

---

[74] Amended by Youth Justice and Criminal Evidence Act 1999, Sch.2, para.8.

SEXUAL OFFENCES (AMENDMENT) ACT 1992, ss.1–6 CONT.

(f) section 7 (intercourse with a mentally handicapped person);
(g) section 9 (procurement of a mentally handicapped person);
(h) section 10 (incest by a man);
(i) section 11 (incest by a woman);
(j) section 12 (buggery);
(k) section 14 (indecent assault on a woman);
(l) section 15 (indecent assault on a man);
(m) section 16 (assault with intent to commit buggery);
[(n) section 17 (abduction of woman by force)].

[(3) Northern Ireland ]

**Power to displace section 1**[75]

**6–072**   **3.**—(1) If, before the commencement of a trial at which a person is charged with an offence to which this Act applies, he or another person against whom the complainant may be expected to give evidence at the trial, applies to the judge for a direction under this subsection and satisfies the judge—

   (a) that the direction is required for the purpose of inducing persons who are likely to be needed as witnesses at the trial to come forward: and

   (b) that the conduct of the applicant's defence at the trial is likely to be substantially prejudiced if the direction is not given, the judge shall direct that section 1 shall not, by virtue of the accusation alleging the offence in question, apply in relation to the complainant.

   (2) If at a trial the judge is satisfied—

   (a) that the effect of section 1 is to impose a substantial and unreasonable restriction upon the reporting of proceedings at the trial, and

   (b) that it is in the public interest to remove or relax the restriction, he shall direct that that section shall not apply to such matter as is specified in the direction.

   (3) A direction shall not be given under subsection (2) by reason only of the outcome of the trial.

   (4) If a person who has been convicted of an offence and has given notice of appeal against the conviction, or notice of an application for leave so to appeal, applies to the appellate court for a direction under this subsection and satisfies the court—

   (a) that the direction is required for the purpose of obtaining evidence in support of the appeal; and

   (b) that the applicant is likely to suffer substantial injustice if the direction is not given, the court shall direct that section 1 shall not, by virtue of an accusation which alleges an offence to which this Act applies and is specified in the direction, apply in relation to a complainant so specified.

---

[75] Amended by Youth Justice and Criminal Evidence Act 1999, Sch.2, para.9.

## SEXUAL OFFENCES (AMENDMENT) ACT 1992, ss.1–6 CONT.

(5) A direction given under any provision of this section does not affect the operation of section 1 at any time before the direction is given.

(6) In subsections (1) and (2), "judge" means—

(a) in the case of an offence which is to be tried summarily or for which the mode of trial has not been determined, any justice of the peace acting for the petty sessions area concerned; and

(b) in any other case, any judge of the Crown Court [in England and Wales.]

[(6A) Northern Ireland]

(7) If, after the commencement of a trial at which a person is charged with an offence to which this Act applies, a new trial of the person for that offence is ordered, the commencement of any previous trial shall be disregarded for the purposes of subsection (1).

**Special rules for cases of incest or buggery**

**4.**—(1) In this section—

"section 10 offence" means an offence under section 10 of the Sexual Offences Act 1956 (incest by a man) or an attempt to commit that offence;

"section 11 offence" means an offence under section 11 of that Act (incest by a woman) or an attempt to commit that offence;

"section 12 offence" means an offence under section 12 of that Act (buggery) or an attempt to commit that offence.

(2) Section 1 does not apply to a woman against whom a section 10 offence is alleged to have been committed if she is accused of having committed a section 11 offence against the man who is alleged to have committed the section 10 offence against her.

(3) Section 1 does not apply to a man against whom a section 11 offence is alleged to have been committed if he is accused of having committed a section 10 offence against the woman who is alleged to have committed the section 11 offence against him.

(4) Section 1 does not apply to a person against whom a section 12 offence is alleged to have been committed if that person is accused of having committed a section 12 offence against the person who is alleged to have committed the section 12 offence against him.

(5) Subsection (2) does not affect the operation of this Act in relation to anything done at any time before the woman is accused.

(6) Subsection (3) does not affect the operation of this Act in relation to anything done at any time before the man is accused.

(7) Subsection (4) does not affect the operation of this Act in relation to anything done at any time before the person mentioned first in that subsection is accused.

[(8) Northern Ireland]

**Offences**[76]

**5.**—(1) *If any matter is published or included in a relevant programme in contravention of section 1, the following persons shall be guilty of an offence and*

**6–073**

**6–074**

---

[76] As amended by Youth Justice and Criminal Evidence Act 1999, Sch.2, para.11. Amendments not in force at November 1, 2003.

SEXUAL OFFENCES (AMENDMENT) ACT 1992, ss.1–6 CONT.

*liable on summary conviction to a fine not exceeding level 5 on the standard scale—*

> *(a)   in the case of publication in a newspaper or periodical, any proprietor, any editor and any publisher of the newspaper or periodical;*
>
> *(b)   in the case of publication in any other form, the person publishing the matter; and*
>
> *(c)   in the case of matter included in a relevant programme—*
>
>> *(i)   any body corporate engaged in providing the service in which the programme is included; and*
>> *(ii)   any person having functions in relation to the programme corresponding to those in relation to the of an editor of a newspaper.*

[(1) If any matter is included in a publication in contravention of section 1, the following persons shall be guilty of an offence and liable on summary conviction to a fine not exceeding level 5 on the standard scale—

> (a)   where the publication is a newspaper or periodical, any proprietor, any editor and any publisher of the newspaper or periodical;
>
> (b)   where the publication is a relevant programme—
>
>> (i)   any body corporate or Scottish partnership engaged in providing the programme service in which the programme is included; and
>> (ii)   any person having functions in relation to the programme corresponding to those of an editor of a newspaper;
>
> (c)   in the case of any other publication, any person publishing it.]

(2) Where a person is charged with an offence under this section in respect of *the publication of any matter or the inclusion of any matter in a relevant programme* [inclusion of any matter in a publication], it shall be a defence, subject to subsection (3), to prove that the publication or programme in which the matter appeared was one in respect of which the person against whom the offence mentioned in section 1 is alleged to have been committed had given written consent to the appearance of matter of that description.

(3) Written consent is not a defence if it is proved that any person interfered unreasonably with the peace or comfort of the person giving the consent, with intent to obtain it[, or that person was under the age of 16 at the time when it was given].

(4) Proceedings for an offence under this section shall not be instituted except by or with the consent of the Attorney General [if the offence is alleged to have been committed in England and Wales or of the Attorney General for Northern Ireland if the offence is alleged to have been committed in Northern Ireland.]

(5) Where a person is charged with an offence under this section it shall be a defence to prove that at the time of the alleged offence he was not aware, and neither suspected nor had reason to suspect, that the publication *or programme in question was of, or (as the case may be) included,* the matter in question [included the matter in question].

[(5A) Where—

> (a)   a person is charged with an offence under this section, and
>
> (b)   the offence relates to the inclusion of any matter in a publication in contravention of section 1(1),

## SEXUAL OFFENCES (AMENDMENT) ACT 1992, ss.1–6 CONT.

it shall be a defence to prove that at the time of the alleged offence he was not aware, and neither suspected nor had reason to suspect, that the allegation in question had been made.]

(6) Where an offence under this section committed by a body corporate is proved to have been committed with the consent or connivance of, or to be attributable to any neglect on the part of—

(a)  a director, manager, secretary or other similar officer of the body corporate, or

(b)  a person purporting to act in any such capacity, he as well as the body corporate shall be guilty of the offence and liable to be proceeded against and punished accordingly.

(7) In relation to a body corporate whose affairs are managed by its members "director", in subsection (6), means a member of the body corporate.

[(8) Where an offence under this section is committed by a Scottish partnership and is proved to have been committed with the consent or connivance of a partner, he as well as the partnership shall be guilty of the offence and shall be liable to be proceeded against and punished accordingly.]

**Interpretation**[77]

6.—(1) In this Act—                                                                                          **6–075**

"complainant" has the meaning given in section 1(2);

"picture" includes a likeness however produced;

["publication" includes any speech, writing, relevant programme or other communication in whatever form, which is addressed to the public at large or any section of the public (and for this purpose every relevant programme shall be taken to be so addressed), but does not include an indictment or other document prepared for use in particular legal proceedings;]

"relevant programme" means a programme included in a programme service, within the meaning of the Broadcasting Act 1990; and

*"written publication" includes a film, a sound track and any other record in permanent form but does not include an indictment or other document prepared for use in particular legal proceedings.*

(2) For the purposes of this Act—

(a)  where it is alleged that an offence to which this Act applies has been committed, the fact that any person has consented to an act which, on any prosecution for that offence, would fall to be proved by the prosecution, does not prevent that person from being regarded as a person against whom the alleged offence was committed; and

(b)  where a person is accused of an offence of incest or buggery, the other party to the act in question shall be taken to be a person against whom the offence was committed even though he consented to that act.

---

[77] As amended by Youth Justice and Criminal Evidence Act 1999, Sch.2, para.12. Amendments not in force as at November 1, 2003.

---

## Sexual Offences (Amendment) Act 1992, ss.1–6 cont.

(2A) For the purposes of this Act, where it is alleged or there is *an accusation that an offence of conspiracy or incitement of another to commit an offence mentioned in section 2(1)(a) to (d) has been committed, the* [accusation—

    (a) that an offence of conspiracy or incitement of another to commit an offence mentioned in section 2(1)(aa) to (d) or (3)(a) to (h) has been committed, or

    (b) that an offence of aiding, abetting, counselling or procuring the commission of an offence of incitement of another to commit an offence mentioned in section 2(1)(aa) to (d) or (3)(a) to (h) has been committed,

the] person against whom the substantive offence is alleged to have been intended to be committed shall be regarded as the person against whom the conspiracy or incitement is alleged to have been committed.

In this subsection, "the substantive offence" means the offence to which the alleged conspiracy or incitement related.]

(3) For the purposes of this Act, a person is accused of an offence if—

    (a) an information is laid[, or (in Northern Ireland) a complaint is made,] alleging that he has committed the offence,

    (b) he appears before a court charged with the offence,

    (c) a court before which he is appearing commits him for trial on a new charge alleging the offence, or

    (d) a bill of indictment charging him with the offence is preferred before a court in which he may lawfully be indicted for the offence,

and references in [subsection (2A) and in] section 3 to an accusation alleging an offence shall be construed accordingly.

(4) Nothing in this Act affects any prohibition or restriction imposed by virtue of any other enactment upon a publication or upon matter included in a relevant programme.

---

## Sexual Offences (Amendment) Act 1976, s.4

**6–076**    This entire section is to be repealed by the Youth Justice and Criminal Evidence Act 1999, ss.48, 67(3), Sch.2, para.4(1), (2), Sch.6 from a day to be appointed. At the time of writing it remains in force. Provision is made for the substance of this section in the *Sexual Offences (Amendment) Act 1992* as amened by the *Youth Justice and Criminal Evidence Act 1999* as set out above at paras 6–068A, *et seq.*

**Anonymity of complainants in rape cases**

**6–077**    **4.**—(1) Except as authorised by a direction given in pursuance of this section—

    (a) after an allegation that a woman or man has been the victim of a rape offence has been made by the woman or man or by any other person,

## SEXUAL OFFENCES (AMENDMENT) ACT 1976, s.4 CONT.

neither the name nor the address of the woman or man nor a still or moving picture of her or him shall during that person's lifetime–

   (i)  be published in England and Wales in a written publication available to the public; or

   (ii)  be included in a relevant programme for reception in England and Wales, if that is likely to lead members of the public to identify that person as an alleged victim of such an offence; and

 (b)  after a person is accused of a rape offence, no matter likely to lead members of the public to identify a woman or man as the complainant in relation to that accusation shall during that person's lifetime–

   (i)  be published in England and Wales in a written publication available to the public; or

   (ii)  be included in a relevant programme for reception in England and Wales;

but nothing in this subsection prohibits the publication or inclusion in a relevant programme of matter consisting only of a report of criminal proceedings other than proceedings at, or intended to lead to, or on an appeal arising out of, a trial at which the accused is charged with the offence.

(1A) In subsection (1) above "picture" includes a likeness however produced.

(2) If, before the commencement of a trial at which a person is charged with a rape offence, he or another person against whom the complainant may be expected to give evidence at the trial applies to a judge of the Crown Court for a direction in pursuance of this subsection and satisfies the judge—

 (a)  that the direction is required for the purpose of inducing persons to come forward who are likely to be needed as witnesses at the trial; and

 (b)  that the conduct of the applicant's defence at the trial is likely to be substantially prejudiced if the direction is not given, the judge shall direct that the preceding subsection shall not, by virtue of the accusation alleging the offence aforesaid, apply in relation to the complainant.

(3) If at a trial the judge is satisfied that the effect of subsection (1) of this section is to impose a substantial and unreasonable restriction upon the reporting of proceedings at the trial and that it is in the public interest to remove or relax the restriction, he shall direct that that subsection shall not apply to such matter as is specified in the direction; but a direction shall not be given in pursuance of this subsection by reason only of the outcome of the trial.

(4) If a person who has been convicted of an offence and given notice of appeal to the Court of Appeal against the conviction, or notice of an application for leave so to appeal, applies to the Court of Appeal for a direction in pursuance of this subsection and satisfies the Court—

 (a)  that the direction is required for the purpose of obtaining evidence in support of the appeal; and

 (b)  that the applicant is likely to suffer substantial injustice if the direction is not given,

## SEXUAL OFFENCES (AMENDMENT) ACT 1976, s.4 CONT.

the Court shall direct that subsection (1) of this section shall not, by virtue of an accusation which alleges a rape offence and is specified in the direction, apply in relation to a complainant so specified.

(5) If any matter is published or included in a relevant programme in contravention of subsection (1) of this section, the following persons, namely—

(a)   in the case of a publication in a newspaper or periodical, any proprietor, any editor and any publisher of the newspaper or periodical;

(b)   in the case of any other publication, the person who publishes it; and

(c)   in the case of matter included in a relevant programme, any body corporate which is engaged in providing the service in which the programme is included and any person having functions in relation to the programme corresponding to those of an editor of a newspaper, shall be guilty of an offence and liable on summary conviction to a fine not exceeding level 5 on the standard scale.

(5A) Where a person is charged with an offence under subsection (5) of this section in respect of the publication of any matter or the inclusion of any matter in a relevant programme, it shall be a defence, subject to subsection (5B) below, to prove that the publication or programme in which the matter appeared was one in respect of which the woman or man had given written consent to the appearance of matter of that description.

(5B) Written consent is not a defence if it is proved that any person interfered unreasonably with the peace or comfort of the woman or man with intent to obtain the consent.

(6) For the purposes of this section a person is accused of a rape offence if—

(a)   an information is laid alleging that he has committed a rape offence; or

(b)   he appears before a court charged with a rape offence; or

(c)   a court before which he is appearing commits him for trial on a new charge alleging a rape offence; or

(d)   a bill of indictment charging him with a rape offence is preferred before a court in which he may lawfully be indicted for the offence,

and references in this section and section 7(5) of this Act to an accusation alleging a rape offence shall be construed accordingly; and in this section—

"complainant" , in relation to a person accused of a rape offence or an accusation alleging a rape offence, means the woman or man against whom the offence is alleged to have been committed; and

"relevant programme" means a programme included in a programme service within the meaning of the Broadcasting Act 1990; and

"written publication" includes a film, a sound track and any other record in permanent form but does not include an indictment or other document prepared for use in particular legal proceedings.

(6A) For the purposes of this section, where it is alleged or there is an accusation that an offence of incitement to rape or conspiracy to rape has been committed, the person who is alleged to have been the intended victim of the rape shall be regarded as the alleged victim of the incitement or conspiracy or, in the case of an accusation, as the complainant.

(7) Nothing in this section—

---

SEXUAL OFFENCES (AMENDMENT) ACT 1976, S.4 CONT.

(a) [repealed by *Criminal Justice Act 1988,* Sch.16]

(b) affects any prohibition or restriction imposed by virtue of any other enactment upon a publication or upon matter included in a relevant programme;

and a direction in pursuance of this section does not affect the operation of subsection (1) of this section at any time before the direction is given.

---

### Attorney-General's appeal on a point of law: respondent not to be identified

In criminal cases where the Attorney-General appeals on a point of law, the appellate tribunal is required to take steps so as to prevent the respondent from being identified. The relevant rules provide that in any Attorney-General's reference no mention shall be made in the reference of the proper name of any person or place which is likely to lead to the identification of the respondent.[78] The obligation on the court is as follows:   **6–078**

> "The court shall ensure that the identity of the respondent is not disclosed during the proceedings on a reference except where the respondent has given his consent to the use of his name in the proceedings."[79]

The Court of Appeal or the House of Lords will make an order to ensure this, typically stating that no mention shall be made in any broadcast or publication of the proper name of any person or place which is likely to lead to the identification of the respondent.

The objective of the provisions is to protect the respondent's privacy and maintain the presumption of innocence by avoiding the undermining or qualifying of an acquittal by anything said by the appellate tribunal in clarifying the law.[80] It has been held that breach of a such a court order (by publication of an interview with a rape victim naming the acquitted respondent) does not give rise to a civil claim for damages.[81]   **6–079**

### Jigsaw identification

"Jigsaw identification" is the problem that arises, often in sexual offences cases and cases involving children, where various news sources and reports when read together can lead to the identification of the child or the victim. Various bodies have considered this issue.   **6–080**

---

[78] Criminal Appeal (Reference of Points of Law) Rules 1973 (SI 1973/1114), r.3.
[79] Criminal Appeal (Reference of Points of Law) Rules 1973 (SI 1973/1114), r.6.
[80] *B v H Bauer Publishing Ltd* [2002] E.M.L.R. 8 at para.12 *per* Eady J.
[81] *ibid.*

**6–081**     The Committee on Privacy and Related Matters considered the issue but did not recommend legislation due to the difficulties with drafting and implementation.[82] The Judicial Studies Board issued guidelines on reporting restrictions in the Crown Court which addressed the question of jigsaw identification[83]:

> "Particular problems may arise where an order restricts publication of the identity of a victim or witness, and different reports, each complying with the requirement not to identify the victim or witness provide information which when put together makes the restricted identification clear. For example, if one report refers to an unnamed defendant having been convicted of rape of his daughter, and another report names the defendant but does not identify the relationship between the defendant and the witness. However, newspapers, magazines, broadcasters and their regulators have aligned their respective codes so that the media adopt a common approach which avoids such problems when reporting sexual offences (see Code of Practice upheld by the Press Complaints Commission, BBC Producers Guidelines, Independent Television Commission Programme Code, Radio Authority Programme Code). Media organisations may also agree to follow the same approach in reporting other offences involving children. This enables identification of the defendant by name but requires that no details should be given of any relationship which would link the offence to the alleged victim or otherwise identify the victim or the witness. It is recognised that this restriction may handicap the reporting of proceedings but the uniform approach protects the victim or the witness in the way required by the court. Since reports may already have appeared before the case reaches the Crown Court, the court should be very slow to interfere with this agreed practice (even where interference is possible—see *R. v Southwark Crown Court Ex p. Godwin*[83a]) since it may result in the sort of identification that the agreement is designed to prevent.
>
>     Article 6 (right to a fair hearing), Art.8 (right to respect for private and family life) and Art.10 (right to freedom of expression) of the European Convention on Human Rights may need to be considered. Section 12 of the Human Rights Act 1998 making provision for protection of journalistic and literary material against prior restraint does not apply to criminal proceedings."

**6–082**     The BBC Producers Guidelines states as follows in relation to jigsaw identification[84]:

---

[82] (1990) Cmnd. 1102.
[83] *Reporting Restrictions in the Crown Court*, Judicial Studies Board (2000) para.6.1. Available at *http://www.jsboard.co.uk/represt.htm # 1.*
[83a] [1991] 3 All E.R. 818.
[84] BBC Producers Guidelines, Ch. 37, para.4.4. Available at *http://www.bbc.co.uk/info/editorial/prodgl/chapter37.shtml # iden.*

"It is not enough that we do not name the victims of sexual crime. We need to take special precautions to avoid what is known as the 'jigsaw effect'. This happens when different news organisations give different facts about the victim, which can then be pieced together. The risk is at its highest when reporting sexual crime within the family, where naming the accused and the alleged offence could in effect identify the victim. In 1993 most newspapers and broadcasters agreed in principle that in such cases we will report the name of the accused/convicted person but we will refer to the crime merely as 'a serious sexual offence'. Where the accused and the victim are related, if we identify the accused we should refer to the victim merely as 'a young woman', 'a child' and so on.

The objective, however, is to protect the victim. In some individual cases some sections of the media have published details of the offence. In these circumstances it may be necessary for the BBC to follow suit and avoid naming the offender. One way or another, we must not complete the jigsaw. In such situations Programme Legal Advice and Editorial Policy should be consulted.

In other cases where there is a danger of the jigsaw effect, we should avoid any detail that might, with corroborating facts, lead to identification. Take care not to give an address, any link with another person in the story, or any link between the victim and the scene of the assault.

These restrictions may make it difficult or impossible to convey in our reporting the incidence of certain sexual crimes by reference to individual cases. Programmes should still address these issues but without referring to identifiable instances."

The Press Complaints Commission have also upheld allegations for breach of their Code of Practice where there has been identification of a child through jigsaw identification.[85] In *R. v Bradshaw (Simon)* editors of local papers were fined £2,500 each for breaching s.39 of the Children and Young Persons Act 1933 act on the basis that persons reading the newspaper reports could identify the child involved in court proceedings due to background knowledge or associations with family.[86]

## OFFICIAL SECRETS ACT

The law relating to official secrets is set out in three statutes—the Official Secrets Acts 1911, 1920 and 1989. The provisions that affect the right to take a photograph lie in the 1911 Act. The 1920 Act is of little relevance here as it **6–083**

---

[85] *Hazzledine v The Times* PCC Report No.30 (May–July 1995) p.6 (Clause 13 (Children in Sex Cases) of the pre-1998 Code). See below at para.14–050.
[86] *Media Lawyer Newsletter* (2001) 33, 7–8, 24–25.

primarily deals with falsification of reports and other documents.[87] Similarly, the 1989 Act concerns unlawful disclosure of documents or other articles relating to security or intelligence.[88]

## Official Secrets Act 1911

**6–084**     Section 1 provides:

"(1) If any person for any purpose prejudicial to the safety or interests of the State—

   (a) approaches inspects, passes over or is in the neighbourhood of, or enters any prohibited place within the meaning of this Act; or
   (b) makes any sketch, plan, model, or note which is calculated to be or might be or is intended to be directly or indirectly useful to an enemy; or
   (c) obtains, collects, records, or publishes, or communicates to any other person any secret official code word or pass word, or any sketch, plan, model, article, or note, or other document or information which is calculated to be or might be or is intended to be directly or indirectly useful to an enemy;

he shall be guilty of felony...

(2) On a prosecution under this section, it shall not be necessary to show that the accused person was guilty of any particular act tending to show a purpose prejudicial to the safety or interests of the State, and, notwithstanding that no such act is proved against him, he may be convicted if, from the circumstances of the case, or his conduct, or his known character as proved, it appears that his purpose was a purpose prejudicial to the safety or interests of the State; and if any sketch, plan, model, article, note, document, or information relating to or used in any prohibited place within the meaning of this Act, or anything in such a place or any secret official code word or pass word, is made, obtained, collected, recorded, published, or communicated by any person other than a person acting under lawful authority, it shall be deemed to have been made, obtained, collected, recorded, published or communicated for a purpose prejudicial to the safety or interests of the State unless the contrary is proved."

---

[87] Official Secrets Act 1920, s.6(1), does provide a power to a chief officer of police to apply to the Secretary of State to require a person believed to be able to furnish information to give any information in his power relating to the offence or suspected offence. This obviously could involve production of photographs or disclosure of sources. Detailed consideration is outside the scope of this work. For further information see *Archbold* 2004 (Sweet & Maxwell) at 25–313 *et seq.*

[88] Official Secrets Act 1989, s.5(1), makes it an offence for any person into whose possession any information, document or article (which would include a photograph) protected against disclosure by the Act to disclose it himself without lawful authority knowing or having reasonable cause to believe that it is protected against disclosure. Detailed consideration of the Official Secrets Act 1989 is outside the scope of this work. For further information see *Archbold* 2004 (Sweet & Maxwell) at 25–325 *et seq.*

The section encompasses a wide variety of matters. In fact it has been said **6–085** that it managed by "tortuous drafting" to create over 2,000 different offences.[89] In case there was any doubt, "sketch" is defined to include "any photograph or other mode of representing any place or thing".[90]

The definition of "prohibited place" is equally as wide. Section 3 provides: **6–086**

"For the purposes of this Act, the expression 'prohibited place' means—

(a) any work of defence, arsenal, naval or air force establishment or station, factory, dockyard, mine, minefield, camp, ship, or aircraft belonging to or occupied by or on behalf of His Majesty, or any telegraph, telephone, wireless or signal station, or office so belonging or occupied, and any place belonging to or occupied by or on behalf of His Majesty and used for the purpose of building, repairing, making, or storing any munitions of war, or any sketches, plans, models, or documents relating thereto, or for the purpose of getting any metals, oil, or minerals of use in time of war;

(b) any place not belonging to His Majesty where any munitions of war, or any sketches, models, plans or documents relating thereto, are being made, repaired, gotten or stored under contract with, or with any person on behalf of, His Majesty, or otherwise on behalf of His Majesty; and

(c) any place belonging to or used for the purposes of His Majesty which is for the time being declared by order of a Secretary of State to be a prohibited place for the purposes of this section on the ground that information with respect thereto, or damage thereto, would be useful to an enemy; and

(d) any railway, road, way, or channel, or other means of communication by land or water (including any works or structures being part thereof or connected therewith), or any place used for gas, water, or electricity works or other works for purposes of a public character, or any place where any munitions of war, or any sketches, models, plans or documents relating thereto, are being made, repaired, or stored otherwise than on behalf of His Majesty, which is for the time being declared by order of a Secretary of State to be a prohibited place for the purposes of this section, on the ground that information with respect thereto, or the destruction or obstruction thereof, or interference therewith, would be useful to an enemy."

Any place belonging to the Civil Aviation Authority is deemed to be a **6–087** prohibited place,[91] as is any telecommunications station or office belonging

---

[89] G. Robertson and A. Nicol, *A Media Law* (4th ed., Sweet & Maxwell, 2000) p.555.
[90] Official Secrets Act 1911, s.12.
[91] Civil Aviation Authority Act 1982, s.18(2).

to or occupied by a public telecommunications operator.[92] The Official Secrets (Prohibited Places) Order 1994[93] declares places in its schedule to be prohibited places. Currently these are British Nuclear Fuels plc sites at Sellafield, Cumbria and Capenhurst, Cheshire and the Urenco site at Capenhurst; the UK Atomic Energy Authority site at Harwell, Oxfordshire and Windscale, Cumbria.

Prosecutions under the Act can only by instituted by or with the consent of the Attorney General.[94]

## ATOMIC ENERGY ACT 1946

**6–088**    Under the Atomic Energy Act 1946, it is an offence to communicate to any unauthorised person any photograph of existing or proposed atomic energy plant without the consent of the Secretary of State. A person committing such an offence is liable on summary conviction to a term of imprisonment not exceeding three months or a fine or both and on conviction on indictment to a term of imprisonment not exceeding five years or a fine or both.[95]

The offence is set out in s.11 which provides:—

"(1) Subject to the provisions of this section, any person who without the consent of the Minister communicates to any other person except an authorised person any document, drawing, photograph, plan, model or other information whatsoever which to his knowledge describes, represents or illustrates—

(a) any existing or proposed plant used or proposed to be used for the purpose of producing or using atomic energy;

(b) the purpose or method of operation of any such existing or proposed plant; or

(c) any process operated or proposed to be operated in any such existing or proposed plant;

shall be guilty of an offence under this Act:

Provided that it shall not be such an offence to communicate information with respect to any plant of a type in use for purposes other than the production or use of atomic energy, unless the information discloses that plant of that type is used or proposed to be used for the production or use of atomic energy.

In this subsection 'authorised person' means, in relation to information on any subject to which this subsection applies, a person to whom, by virtue of a general authority granted by the Minister, information on that subject may be communicated.

---

[92] Telecommunications Act 1984, s.109(1) and Sch.4, para.12(2).
[93] SI 1994/968. See Atomic Energy Authority Act 1954, s.6(3) enabling the Secretary of State to declare places belonging to or used by the authority prohibited places.
[94] Official Secrets Act 1911, s.8.
[95] Atomic Energy Act 1946, s.14(1).

(2) The Minister shall not withhold consent under the last foregoing subsection, if he is satisfied that the information proposed to be communicated is not of importance for purposes of defence.

(3) The Minister may by order grant exemption from this section in such classes of cases, and to such extent and subject to such conditions, as may be specified in the order.

(4) Where any information has been made available to the general public otherwise than in contravention of this section, any subsequent communication of that information shall not constitute an offence under this Act."

## TRESPASS TO LAND

Another restriction upon the right to take a photograph is the tort of trespass which means (1) photographers are not free to enter private property without permission for the purposes of taking photographs, and (2) even where permission to enter has been granted, acting in a way beyond the permission granted is a trespass. Thus, if a person is permitted to enter on the proviso that they shall take no photographs and then do so, they commit a trespass when they begin to photograph.  **6–089**

For further information as to trespass to land generally, beyond the specific application to photography see *Clerk & Lindsell on Torts* (18th ed.) pp.18–01 *et seq.*

### Definition of trespass

Every unlawful entry by one person on land in the possession of another is a trespass giving rise to a cause of action even though no actual damage is done.[96] A trespass occurs even where there is minor encroachment on to the land such as only part of the defendant's foot.[97] The lack of damage or the trivial nature of the trespass is no defence.[98] The subject matter of trespass is real property, namely land and its subsoil and buildings.[99] Crops and other herbage attached to the soil may be the subject of a different possession from the soil and the owner can maintain an action in trespass.[1] Trespass does not lie for disturbance of an incorporeal right such as a right of common, fishing rights or a right of way.[2]  **6–090**

---

[96] *Ashby v White* (1703) 2 Ld. Raym. 938, 955; *Bush v Smith* [1953] C.P.L. 670.
[97] *Ellis v Loftus Iron Co* (1874) L.R. 10 C.P. 10 at 12 *per* Coleridge J.
[98] *Stoke on Trent City Council v W & J Wass Ltd (No.1)* [1988] 3 All E.R. 394, 398; *Yelloly v Morley* (1910) 27 T.L.R. 20; *Bush v Smith* [1953] C.P.L. 670.
[99] *Burt v Moore* (1793) 5 Term. Rep. 329; *Wellaway v Courtier* [1918] 1 K.B. 200.
[1] *Richard v Davies* [1911] 1 Ch. 90; *Wellaway v Courtier* [1918] K.B. 200 (turnips); *Back v Daniels* [1925] K.B. 526 (potatoes).
[2] *Wilson v Mackreth* (1766) 3 Burr. 1824; *Stocks v Booth* (1786) 1 Term Rep. 428; *Bryan v Whistler* (1828) 8 B. & C. 288.

### Distinction between nuisance and trespass

**6–091**    Direct intrusion by an individual onto another's property is a trespass. If there is no such direct intrusion there is no trespass, however, there may be a cause of action in nuisance. So where a cricket ball lands in a garden[3] or where tree roots or branches encroach on to neighbour's land,[4] the cause of action lies in nuisance not trespass. It is also necessary to prove damage to succeed in nuisance,[5] but proof of damage is not required for trespass.

### Acts constituting trespass

**6–092**    A trespass occurs when a person wrongfully sets foot on land or rides or drives through the property.[6] Taking possession of land or wrongfully expelling the person in possession is a trespass.[7] Destroying anything permanently fixed to the land or removing such things from the land is a trespass,[8] as is placing or fixing anything on or in the land[9] such as propping a ladder against a wall.[10] A photographer leaning a ladder against a wall for the purposes of using it to take a photograph over the wall commits a trespass if he does so without consent.

**6–093**    Where a person has been granted a right of entry and whilst on the land acts in excess of his right or remains there after his right has expired, he becomes a trespasser *ab initio* and may be sued as if his original entry were unlawful.[11] The fact that business premises are open to the public where there is a licence to enter does not necessarily imply a licence to photograph or film. The implied invitation extends only to bona fide customers of the business and thus those who exceed the licence by filming or photographing or harassing customers with a film camera become trespassers.[12] Any implied licence to be on the land is revoked when the occupier asks the licencee to leave.[13]

---

[3] *Miller v Jackson* [1977] Q.B. 966.
[4] *e.g. Lemmon v Webb* [1894] 3 Ch. 1; *McCombe v Read* [1955] 2 Q.B. 429.
[5] *Sedleigh-Denfield v O'Callaghan* [1940] A.C. 880.
[6] *Blundell v Catterall* (1821) 5 B. & Ald. 268 (crossing seashore on foot or with bathing machine); *League Against Cruel Sports Ltd v Scott* [1986] Q.B. 240; [1985] 2 All E.R. 489 (foxhunt hounds entering land—master of hounds is liable in trespass if he knew there was a real risk of the hounds entering the prohibited land); *Chamberlain v Sandeman, The Times,* October 24, 1962, (hounds entering garden and causing damage. Damages awarded of £30).
[7] *Murray v Hall* (1894) 7 C.B. 441; *Watson v Murray & Co* [1955] 2 Q.B. 1.
[8] *Lavendar v Betts* [1942] 2 All E.R. 72 (removing doors and windows).
[9] *Lawrence v Obee* (1815) 1 Stark 22; *Simpson v Weber* (1925) 41 T.L.R. 302; *Mace v Philcox* (1864) 15 C.B.N.S. 600 (bathing machine); *Kynoch v Rowlands* [1912] 1 Ch. 527 (tipping rubbish); *Gregory v Piper* (1892) 9 B. & C. 591 (rubbish against wall).
[10] *Westripp v Baldock* [1938] 2 All E.R. 779, affirmed [1939] 1 All E.R. 279.
[11] *Six Carpenters Case* (1610) 8 Co. Rep. 146a; *Hillen v ICI (Alkali) Ltd* [1936] A.C. 65.
[12] *Lincoln Hunt Australia Pty Ltd v Willesee* (1986) 4 N.S.W.L.R. 457, 460F; *Le Mistral Inc v Columbia Broadcasting System* 402 N.Y.S. 2d 815 (1978) (film crew in restaurant); *Belluomo v Kake TV & Radio Inc* 596 P. 2d 832 (1979) (film crew in restaurant).
[13] *Emcorp Pty Ltd v Australian Broadcasting Corp* 2 Qd. 169, 174 (Supreme Court of Brisbane).

Invasion of airspace may amount to a trespass where the airspace is   **6–094**
necessary for the full use of the land below.[14] However, it is not a trespass to
fly over a private property at a reasonable height. In *Bernstein v Skyviews*
where an aircraft flew over a property "many hundreds of feet above the
ground" in order to photograph it without the owners permission, it was
held that the mere entry by an aircraft into the airspace above a person's
land is not trespass.[15] The court made it plain that the judgment was not
authority for the proposition that in no circumstances could the activities of
an aerial photographer be restrained.[16] It was suggested that harassment of
constant surveillance might very well amount to an actionable nuisance.[17]
Low altitude flying or hovering helicopters may constitute a trespass.[18]

However s.76(1) of the Civil Aviation Act 1982 provides that:

"No action shall lie in respect of trespass or nuisance by reason only of
the flight of an aircraft over any property at a height above the ground
which, having regard to wind, weather and all the circumstances of the
case is reasonable or the ordinary incidents of such flight so long as the
provisions of any Air Navigation Order and of any orders under s.62
above have been complied with and there has been no breach of section 81
below."

It is not clear what precisely is meant by the words "by reason only of the   **6–095**
flight" or "the ordinary incidents of the flight". The authors of *Shawcross
and Beaumont: Air Law* observe that one view is the section confers no more
than a right of innocent passage which would mean that it provides no
defence to aircraft flown over land for the purpose of obtaining unauthorised photographs.[19] However, this approach was not followed in *Bernstein v
Skyviews*[20] where the corresponding section in the Civil Aviation Act 1949
was considered. It was held that the provision extended to all flights at a
reasonable height and complying with statutory requirements.

Taking a photograph from adjoining land by a photographer who did not
cross the boundary for an innocent, as opposed to a criminal, purpose

---

[14] *Anchor Brewhouse Developments Ltd v Berkley House (Docklands Developments)* (over-
hanging crane boom) (1987) 2 E.G.L.R. 173, *The Times*, April 3, 1987; *Woollerton and Wilson v
Richard Costain* [1970] 1 All E.R. 483 (crane 50ft above property); *Kelsen v Imperial Tobacco Co
(of Great Britain and Ireland)* [1957] 2 All E.R. 343 (advertising sign).
[15] *Bernstein v Skyviews and General Ltd* [1978] Q.B. 479; [1977] 2 All E.R. 902, [1977] 3 W.L.R.
136.
[16] *ibid.*, at 489G.
[17] *ibid.*
[18] *Smith v New England Aircraft Co* 170 N.E. (Mass. 1930) (flight at 100 feet a trespass);
*Swetland v Curtiss Airports Corpn* 55 F.2d 201 (6th circ., 1932) (flight over 500 feet no trespass);
*Gardener v County of Allegheny* 114 A.2d 491 (P.A. 1955) (flight below minimum altitude of safe
flight set by Civil Aeronautics Board held to be a trespass. And see other cases cited in
*Shawcross and Beaumont: Air Law* (4th ed., Butterworths) at V(131) n.18.
[19] At V (137) citing *Cory v Physical Culture Hotel* 88 F.2d 411 (2nd Cir. 1937).
[20] [1978] Q.B. 479; [1977] 2 All E.R. 902.

cannot be prevented by the law of trespass.[21] It is not a trespass to look across a boundary or to sketch what one sees[22] or to photograph it.[23]

## Entitlement to sue

**6-096**     Only the person who is or was in actual possession of the land (or deemed to be) at the time of the trespass is entitled to sue in trespass.[24] The slightest amount of possession is sufficient.[25] Thus, a tenant in possession can sue, but not a landlord except, where there is injury to the reversion.[26]

## Defences

**6-097**     The following are defences to a claim of trespass:

(a) justification of the trespass either because the defendant had a right of possession or a right to be on the land or because he had the licence of the possessor;

(b) necessity to be on the land to preserve life or property[27];

(c) entry for the purposes of retaking own goods unlawfully placed on the land[28];

(d) expiry of limitation period.[29]

Neither lack of damage nor the trivial nature of the trespass,[30] nor mere delay by the claimant complaining of the defendant's action[31] are valid defences.

**6-098**     Necessity to be on the land concerns specifically attendance on the land where it was reasonably necessary in order to prevent harm to the defendant

---

[21] *Bernstein v Skyviews and General Ltd* [1978] Q.B. 479, 488F.

[22] *Hickman v Maisey* [1900] 1 Q.B. 752, 756.

[23] *Sports & General Press Agency Ltd v "Our Dogs" Publishing Company Ltd* [1916] 2 K.B. 880; affirmed CA [1917] 2 K.B. 125; *Bernstein v Skyviews and General Ltd* [1978] Q.B. 479; [1977] 2 All E.R. 902; [1977] 3 W.L.R. 136; *Lincoln Hunt Australia Pty Ltd v Willisee* (1986) 4 N.S.W.L.R. 457, 461.

[24] *Thompson v Ward* [1953] 2 Q.B. 153, 163 (non-occupying tenant not able to maintain action).

[25] *Bristow v Cormican* (1878) 3 App. Cas. 641 at 657.

[26] See *Clerk & Lindsell on Torts* (18th ed.) at pp.18–10 and 18–24.

[27] *Cope v Sharpe (No.1)* [1910] 1 K.B. 168 (entry to extinguish fire); *Cope v Sharpe (No.2)* [1912] 1 K.B. 496 (entry to extinguish fire); *Rigby v Chief Constable of Northamptonshire* [1985] 2 All E.R. 985; [1985] 1 W.L.R. 1242 (police firing CS gas canister into building in order to move out a dangerous psychopath. Building caught fire. Defence of necessity succeeded).

[28] *Anthony v Haney* (1832) 8 Bing. 186; *Rea v Sheward* (1837) 2 M. & W. 424; *Patrick v Colerick* (1838) 3 M. & W. 483.

[29] In actions founded on tort generally six years from accrual of the cause of action: Limitation Act 1980, s.2.

[30] *Stoke on Trent City Council v W & J Wass Ltd (No.1)* [1988] 3 All E.R. 394, 398; *Yelloly v Morley* (1910) 27 T.L.R. 20; *Bush v Smith* [1953] C.P.L. 670.

[31] *Jones v Stones* [1999] 1 W.L.R. 1739. To successfully rely on estoppel it is necessary to demonstrate assurance, reliance by the defendant and detriment to the defendant. As to proprietary estoppel see S. Wilken and T. Villiers *Waiver Variation & Estoppel* (John Wiley & Sons Ltd, 1998) at 11.001.

or a third party. There is no general "public interest" defence of trespassing in order to (say) take photographs to expose some newsworthy story. In any event, it is not a defence that finds much favour with modern courts.[32]

As far as photography is concerned, the most likely defence will be jus- **6–099** tification of trespass on the basis that there was a licence to be present on the land. A person present on the land with the licence of the person entitled to possession is not a trespasser.[33] However, a licensee who remains on the land after his licence has expired or has been terminated is a trespasser.[34] Once a licence has expired or been withdrawn, the licencee has a reasonable time to leave the premises in default of which they become a trespasser and what is a reasonable time will depend on the circumstances of the case.[35] A licence may be express or implied, a bare licence or a contractual licence.

An occupier of a dwelling grants an implied licence to anyone coming on **6–100** lawful business to come through the front gate and knock on the front door.[36] If the licence is withdrawn, he is not a trespasser during the reasonable time it takes to leave the premises.[37] Any bare licence to enter land which does not grant an interest in the land is revocable at will.[38]

Whether a licence to enter exists will depend upon an analysis of any invitation, express or implied, given by the occupier in each case, but most implied invitations will be held to be for limited purposes.[39] In most cases, there will be no implied licence permitting photography. Commercial business premises which extend an implied licence to customers to enter their premises is limited to members of the public bona fide seeking information or business with it or to clients of the firm.[40] Accordingly, such a licence would not extend to the taking of photographs or filming without permission.[41] Covert filming in a hotel open to the public is also likely to be a trespass.[42]

Conversely, there was no trespass where film rental inspectors bought two **6–101** tickets and entered a cinema for the purposes of collecting evidence to crosscheck with the returns of the cinema.[43] In that case the evidence the inspectors obtained amounted to the numbers printed on the tickets bought and a head

---

[32] See *Clerk & Lindsell on Torts* (18th ed.) at pp.3–100 *et seq.* and 18–64.
[33] *Thomas v Sorrell* (1674) Vaugh. 330, 351; *Kavanagh v Gudge* (1844) 7 Man. & G. 316; *Hyde v Graham* (1862) 1 H. & C. 593.
[34] *Wood v Leadbitter* (1845) 13 M. & W. 838 (but *cf. Hurst v Picture Theatres* [1915] 1 K.B. 1 holding *Wood v Leadbitter* no longer good law in the light of the Judicature Acts); *Thompson v Park* [1944] K.B. 408.
[35] *Winter Garden Theatre (London) v Millenium Products Ltd* [1948] A.C. 173 at 196 and 204.
[36] *Robson v Hallett* [1967] 2 All E.R. 407.
[37] *ibid.*
[38] *Wood v Leadbitter* (1845) 13 M. & W. 838; *Thompson v Park* [1944] K.B. 408; *Armstrong v Sheppard and Short Ltd* [1959] 2 Q.B. 384.
[39] *Lincoln Hunt Australia Pty Ltd v Willisee* (1986) 4 N.S.W.L.R. 457, 460D.
[40] *Lincoln Hunt Australia Pty Ltd v Willisee* (1986) 4 N.S.W.L.R. 457 at 460F. The licence did not extend "for instance, to people who wished to enter to hold up the premises and rob them or even to people whose motives were to go onto the premises with video cameras and associated equipment or a reporter to harass the inhabitants by asking questions which would be televised throughout the state."
[41] *ibid.*
[42] *Savoy Hotel Plc v BBC The Times*, December 18, 1982. For facts see below at paras 6–104 and 6–105, n.61 and 67
[43] *Byrne v Kinematographer Renters Society Ltd* [1958] 1 W.L.R. 762 at 777.

count of patrons neither of which were excessively outside the terms of the licence. It is submitted that this case can be distinguished on the basis that a licence to attend the cinema impliedly includes a right to do anything which a bona fide patron attending the cinema would be entitled to do. Thus, anyone is entitled to buy a ticket and retain it. A person attending a cinema would not be prohibited from looking around to see how many other people were there and in fact counting them if he chose to do so. A bona fide customer of a cinema, theatre, or any business would not be expected or permitted to enter with a camera and take photographs or to film.

**6–102**    A sale of a ticket to enter premises to witness a particular event such as a theatre production or sports event entitles a well behaved purchaser to remain on the premises until the end of the event which he has paid to witness.[44] He shall not be treated as a trespasser until the event is over and he has had reasonable time to depart.[45]

Where the licence is contractual, there is an implied obligation by the grantor not to revoke the licence otherwise than in accordance with the contract.[46] It is a matter of construction of the contract whether the licence is revocable and if so, an issue remains as to whether it has been validly determined in accordance with the contract.[47] Many contractual licences to enter premises such as tickets for sports events or the theatre will contain specific terms prohibiting photography. If photography is prohibited under the terms of the licence, a licensee who photographs acts outside his licence is a trespasser.

## Remedies

**6–103**    The remedies available for trespass are:

(a) "Self-help" expulsion using no more force than reasonably necessary where the trespasser refuses to leave upon request.[48] It is rarely justified—only in clear and simple cases or in an emergency[49] and is only available where the possessor acts promptly as soon as he is aware of the wrongful intrusion.[50]

(b) Damages. The claimant is entitled to recover nominal damages even if he has not suffered any actual loss.[51]

---

[44] *Hurst v Picture Theatres* [1915] 1 K.B. 1; *Winter Garden Theatre (London) Ltd v Millenium Productions Ltd* [1947] A.C. 173, 189.

[45] *Winter Garden Theatre (London) Ltd v Millenium Productions Ltd* [1947] A.C. 173, 189.

[46] *Hounslow LBC v Twickenham Garden Developments Ltd* [1970] 1 Ch. 233; [1970] 3 W.L.R. 538.

[47] *Hurst v Picture Theatres* [1915] 1 K.B. 1; *Winter Garden Theatre (London) Ltd v Millenium Productions Ltd* [1948] A.C. 178 173; *Hounslow LBC v Twickenham Garden Developments Ltd* [1970] 1 Ch. 233; [1970] 3 W.L.R. 538.

[48] *Hall v Davis* (1825) 2 C. & P. 33; *Thomas v Marsh and Nest* (1833) 5 C. & P. 596; *Hemmings v Stoke Poges Golf Club Ltd* [1920] 1 K.B. 720.

[49] *Burton v Winters* [1993] 1 W.L.R. 1077, 1082.

[50] *ibid.*

[51] *Hanina v Morland* (2000) 97(47) L.S. Gaz. 41; *Nelson v Nicholson, Independent*, January 22, 2001.

(c) Exemplary damages. Exemplary damages are available for trespass[52] which falls within the three categories where such damages may be awarded set out by Lord Devlin in *Rookes v Barnard (No.1)*[53] namely: (1) those cases where there has been oppressive arbitrary or unconstitutional action by servants of the government[54]; (2) cases where the defendant's conduct has been calculated by him to make a profit for himself which may exceed the compensation payable to the plaintiff[55]; and (3) cases where exemplary damages are expressly authorised by statute.[56] In circumstances where a photographer cynically trespasses on land in order to obtain a photograph of high commercial value, such conduct may very well fall within the second category. The power to award exemplary damages is no longer limited to cases where the cause of action had been recognised before 1964 as justifying such an award as long as one of the three limbs of *Rookes v Barnard (No.1)* are satisfied.[57]

(d) Aggravated damages.[58]

(e) Injunction and declaration. The court may grant an inunction to prevent continuance or repetition of the trespass[59] and to restrain a future or threatened trespass.[60] It is submitted that the court also has power to grant an injunction to restrain publication of photographs obtained while trespassing as discussed below.

## Restraining publication of photographs obtained whilst trespassing

The court has power to grant an injunction to prevent publication of **6–104** images obtained whilst trespassing[61] but will probably only do so if publication is unconscionable.[62] If publication of the images would be in breach

---

[52] *Drane v Evangelou* [1978] 2 All E.R. 437.
[53] [1964] A.C. 1129. And see *Broome v Cassell & Co.* [1972] A.C. 1027.
[54] [1964] A.C. 1129 at 1226.
[55] *Loc.cit.*
[56] *ibid.*, at 1227.
[57] *Kuddus v Chief Constable of Leicestershire* [2001] UKHL 29; [2001] 2 W.L.R. 1789; [2001] 3 All E.R. 193 overruling *AB v South West Water Services Ltd* [1993] Q.B. 507 (which restricted awards of exemplary damages to those causes of action where such awards had already been made before the decision in *Rookes, i.e.* before 1964).
[58] *Bisney v Swanston* (1972) 225 E.G. 2299; *Drane v Evangelou* [1978] 2 All E.R. 437; [1978] 1 W.L.R. 455.
[59] *Kelsen v Imperial Tobacco Co (of Great Britain and Ireland) Ltd* [1957] 2 Q.B. 334; [1957] 2 All E.R. 343.
[60] *Hooper v Rogers* [1975] Ch. 43 (mandatory *quia timet* injunction).
[61] *Savoy Hotel Plc v BBC The Times*, December 18, 1982 (see below); (1983) 133 New L.J. 1100. Transcripts of both decisions are available on Lexis: Comyn, J. (December 17, 1982); Court of Appeal (December 20, 1982). See also *Bradley v Wingnut* 24 I.P.R. 205 (High Court of New Zealand, 1992. Horror film including footage of actor trespassing by sitting on a low wall surrounding a family tomb. Injunction refused on balance of convenience. Would have been unable to show film at Cannes); *Rinsale Pty Ltd v Australian Broadcasting Corp* (1993) Aust. Torts Reports 81–230 at 62,830; *Emcorp Pty Ltd v Australian Broadcasting Corp* [1988] 2 Qd. 169 (Supreme Court of Brisbane).
[62] *Lincoln Hunt Australia Pty Ltd v Willesee* (1986) 4 N.S.W.L.R. 457.

of confidence, this may give rise to a right to a separate claim for an injunction,[63] but it is not axiomatic that images obtained whilst trespassing will be confidential. Where the cause of action is trespass, the claimant needs to establish a prima facie case of trespass and then the question of whether an injunction will be granted will depend on the normal principles upon which the court acts in granting such relief.[64] There is a public interest that unfair, tortious, and illegal methods should not be used in general, but this must be balanced with other considerations such as insurers preventing fraudulent claims[65] and freedom of speech.[66]

**6–105**    An injunction was granted at first instance in respect of covert filming by the BBC of a barman at the Savoy Hotel allegedly serving short measures on the basis that the BBC should not be allowed to take advantage of a wrongful act.[67] Comyn J. said "the BBC entry with concealed cameras and television equipment could well be said to amount to trespass". The injunction was reversed on appeal on the basis of new evidence, namely a new proposed version of the film. The Court of Appeal took the view that a shortened film would cause no damage and the injunction lifted on the undertaking of the BBC that it would show only the revised and restricted version. However, the Court of Appeal did not disapprove Comyn J.'s comments that the entry could amount to a trespass nor on the basis that an injunction was an available remedy.

In an Australian case, *Lincoln Hunt Australia Pty Ltd v Willesee*,[68] Young J. said:

> "... the Court has power to grant an injunction in the appropriate case to prevent publication of a videotape or a photograph taken by a trespasser even though no confidentiality is involved. However, the Court will only intervene if the circumstances are such to make publication unconscionable."[69]

**6–106**    *Lincoln Hunt* concerned entry into the lobby of an investment business by a film crew with cameras rolling. It was argued that there could be no trespass as the lobby was open to members of the public wishing to seek the business services of the plaintiff. This was rejected on the basis that the film crew had exceeded the implied licence which was limited to members of the public bonafide seeking information or business with it or to clients of the firm.[70] Young J. went on to say

---

[63] See *e.g. Douglas v Hello! Ltd (No.6)* [2003] EWHC 786; [2003] 3 All E.R. 996; [2003] E.M.L.R. 31 and below at Ch. 7.
[64] As to which see *American Cyanamid Co v Ethicon Ltd* [1975] A.C. 396.
[65] *Jones v University of Warwick* [2003] 3 All E.R. 760 at 764j approved 776c (video evidence in personal injury case obtained by trespasser).
[66] *e.g. Australian Broadcasting Corp v Lenah Game Meats Pty Ltd* [2001] H.C.A. 63 at para.221.
[67] *The Times*, December 18, 1982. CA: (1983) 133 New L.J. 1100. Transcripts of both decisions are available on Lexis: Comyn, J. (December 17, 1982); Court of Appeal (December 20, 1982). The Court of Appeal judgment is extremely short and adds little.
[68] (1986) 4 N.S.W.L.R. 457.
[69] *ibid.*, at 463G.
[70] *ibid.*, at 460F.

"I would have thought that there is a lot to be said in the Australian community where a film is taken by a trespasser, made in circumstances as the present, upon private premises in respect of which there is some evidence that publication of the film would affect goodwill, that the case is one where an injunction should seriously be considered. However there is a long way to go from that point to the point where the court actually grants an injunction. The court will only grant an injunction if it can be seen that irreparable damage will be suffered by the plaintiff is such an injunction is not given. Such may occur where the damages are virtually impossible of quantification. It is not only that the plaintiff merely shows that there is a strong prima facie case that the trespass is committed and that it is the sort of case where the court may grant an injunction, it must also show that irreparable damage is likely to be suffered if an injunction is not granted and that the balance of convenience favours the grant of an injunction."[71]

An injunction was declined in that case on the basis that it was a case for large exemplary damages and that damages were an adequate remedy.

Even where the media are investigating matters of great public importance, that will not justify entry as a trespasser.[72] In an Australian case where investigative journalists obtained film footage as trespassers, an injunction restraining publication was granted. Williams J. said:     **6–107**

"... because the audio-visual material was obtained in breach of the legal rights of the plaintiffs it is appropriate for the court to conclude that considerations of freedom of speech which might otherwise operate in favour of the defendants are overcome. By abusing its right of freedom of speech in the way in which the material was obtained, the defendants are deprived of the right to rely on that as a material consideration."[73]

In *Australian Broadcasting Corporation v Lenah Game Meats Pty Ltd*,[74]     **6–108**
the High Court of Australia overturned an injunction granted by the Supreme Court of Tasmania. Hidden video cameras had been installed in a licenced possum killing and processing abbattoir by unidentified trespassers. The operations filmed were not secret and the fact they were licenced suggested that the information was not confidential.[75] The film was supplied to an animal liberation organisation which then supplied it to the Australian Broadcasting Corporation. The operators of the abbattoir applied for an injunction restraining publication of the film. The full court of Tasmania on appeal granted an injunction. In very full judgments, four judges allowed the appeal on the basis that the court had no power to grant an injunction if

---

[71] *ibid.*, at 464C.
[72] *Emcorp Pty Ltd v Australian Broadcasting Corp* [1988] 2 Qd. 169 at 174 (Supreme Court of Brisbane, *per* Williams J.).
[73] *Emcorp Pty Ltd v Australian Broadcasting Corp* [1988] 2 Qd. 169 at 178 (Supreme Court of Brisbane, *per* Williams J.).
[74] [2001] H.C.A. 63.
[75] *ibid.*, para.25.

there was no equitable right or legal right being infringed.[76] *Lincoln Hunt* was not disapproved as such. But it was held that if (as in the *Lenah* case) the information was merely tortiously obtained in the first place but there was no breach of confidence[77] or claim to equitable copyright,[78] the court had no power to grant an injunction.[79]

**6–109**     It is respectively submitted that the powerful dissents of Callinan J. and Kirby J. on this point are to be preferred. Kirby J. agreed that the appeal should be allowed but on the basis of freedom of speech and a wrong exercise of discretion. Callinan J. considered that the appeal should be dismissed entirely.

In considering the court's power to grant such an injunction, Kirby J. expressed the view that, following *Lincoln Hunt*, the equitable jurisdiction which exists to restrain the publication of a videotape or a photograph made by a trespasser is equally applicable where such materials have passed into the hands of third parties.[80] He went on to say:

> "To hold that a superior court in Australia lacks the power to grant an interlocutory injunction to restrain a media defendant from broadcasting information acquired illegally, tortiously, surreptitiously or otherwise improperly simply because it was only a receptacle and not directly involved in the wrongful acquisition of the information would involve an unjustifiable abdication of the large powers afforded to such courts by their enabling statutes."[81]

**6–110**     It is submitted that this reasoning is to be preferred. It would be contrary to basic principles of justice and the deterrent of unlawful conduct, if the products of unlawful conduct in respect of which there would be a cause of action (*i.e.* the initial trespass) was something that a court had no power to sanction or regulate. It would also render the right to a private and family life under Art.8 of the ECHR meaningless. In the UK, it has been stated that there is a public interest that unfair, tortious and illegal methods should not be used in general to obtain images or evidence.[82]

**6–111**     Callinan J. agreed that there was power to grant an injunction but considered that the appeal should be dismissed contending:

> "Equity should, and in my opinion is right to, indeed it has no choice but to, regard the relationship created by the possession of the appellant of a tangible item of property obtained in violation of the respondent's right of possession, and the exploitation of which would be to its detriment, and to the financial advantage of the appellant, as a relationship of a fiduciary

---

[76] *ibid.*, Gleeson C.J. at 52–55; Gaudron J. at 61; Gummow & Hayne J.J. at 105.
[77] *ibid.*, paras 52–55 *per* Gleeson C.J.
[78] *ibid.*, paras 101–103 *per* Gummow & Hayne J.J.
[79] *ibid.*, paras 52–55 *per* Gleeson C.J.
[80] *ibid.*, para.178.
[81] *ibid.*, para.182.
[82] *Jones v University of Warwick* [2003] 3 All E.R. 760 at 764j approved 776c (video evidence in personal injury case obtained by trespasser).

kind and of confidence. It is a relationship that the appellant could immediately terminate by delivering up the film to the respondent. The circumstances are ones to which equity should attach a constructive trust."[83]

"... The film was brought into existence, and the appellant acquired it, in circumstances in which it cannot in good conscience use it without the permission of the respondent. If the facts remain at the trial as they appear to be now, the appellant should then be obliged to deliver up the film to the respondent. There is therefore an underlying remedy sufficient to support an interlocutory injunction."[84]

He went on to express the view that this could be framed as a claim for breach of confidence stating:  **6–112**

"There is no reason why the claim in an appropriate case should not be framed as a claim for breach of confidence, being the misuse of a relationship arising out of the acquisition or retention or use by the defendant of a film made in violation of the plaintiff's right of exclusive possession of which the defendant knew or ought to have known and to which a constructive trust should be attached. The ultimate remedy, to which the plaintiff would be entitled, is delivery up of the film, and an account of any profits made from it."[85]

In a UK case, *Service Corporation International plc v Four Television Corporation*[86] covert film footage was obtained of alleged disrespectful treatment of corpses at a funeral home. The funeral home applied for an injunction on various grounds including trespass. With respect to the allegation of trespass, Lightman J. said:

"The second claim is in trespass. It is to the effect that Mr Anderson having obtained access to the Salisbury Funeral Home to undertake covert filming by a trick, was a trespasser 'ab initio' from the moment of his entry and that he should not be permitted to profit from his trespass; but whether this is so or not, that cannot confer upon the Plaintiff's the right to prevent the Defendant's showing the film. As Glidewell LJ said in *Kaye v Robertson* [1991] F.S.R. 62 at 69 the argument has its attractions but is not maintainable."

It is respectfully submitted, on the basis of the authorities set out above, that this is incorrect and that a possessor of land can, in some circumstances prevent a trespasser from publishing photographs or film obtained while trespassing, particularly where publication would be unconscionable. The covert filming was carried out by an employee of the funeral home who was  **6–113**

[83] *Australian Broadcasting Corporation v Lenah Game Meats Pty Ltd* [2001] H.C.A. 63, para.297.
[84] *Loc cit.*
[85] *ibid.*, para.311.
[86] [1999] E.M.L.R. 83.

working undercover for the defendant. As an employee, he had a licence to be on the premises, but there was no discussion in judgment as to whether covert filming (an act outside his licence) did in fact render him a trespasser. All that was said in judgment was, as above, whether or not he was a trespasser, there was no right to prevent the defendant showing the film without any analysis as to the consequence of trespass such as the possiblity of a constructive trust arising. There was no reference in the judgment to *Savoy v BBC* or to any of the Australian authorities in support of the proposition that an injunction was an available remedy.

**6–114**    The citation of *Kaye v Robertson* does not take matters much further as the allegation was trespass to the person by flashbulbs where there was no evidence of any damage and thus an injunction would not be granted in any event on that basis. *Kaye v Robertson* is a decision subject to much criticism and doubts have been expressed as to whether it would be decided the same way today.[87] The comments of Glidewell L.J. referred to which the judge in *Service Corporation International* made reference were:

> "Moreover the injunction sought in relation to this head of action would not be intended to prevent another anticipated battery, since none was anticipated. The intention here is to prevent the defendants from profiting from the taking of photographs, ie. from their own trespass. Attractive thought this argument may appear to be, I cannot find as a matter of law that an injunction should be granted in these circumstances. Accordingly, I would not base an injunction on this cause of action."[88]

Glidewell L.J. concluded that he could not "find as a matter of law" that an injunction should be granted in such circumstances. But it is submitted that the authorities cited above, none of which were referred to in *Kaye v Robertson*, establish that where images have been obtained by trespassers to land, an injunction may be granted in some circumstances.

### Copyright in images obtained whilst trespassing

**6–115**    It is arguable that a copyright work made in circumstances involving the invasion of the legal or equitable rights of another may mean it is inequitable and against good conscience for the maker to assert copyright in that work. In addition, the maker may be regarded as a constructive trustee of the copyright on behalf of the person whose rights he has invaded.[89] The law is not clear and it appears to be the case that if a trust does arise it will do so

---

[87] See below at paras 7–038 and 7–134.
[88] *Kaye v Robertson* [1991] F.S.R. 62 at 69.
[89] *Missing Link Software v Magee* [1989] F.S.R. 361 (arguable that a software program written by an employee for a rival software company whilst still employed to write programs for his employers, then the copyright in the new would belong to his employer on a constructive trust); *A-G v Blake* [1996] F.S.R. 727 at 738 (breach of fiduciary duty) and see Laddie, Prescott & Vitoria, *et al.* (2000), *op. cit.*, at 21.74–21.75; *Australian Broadcasting Corp v Lenah Game Meats Pty Ltd* [2001] H.C.A. 63 at paras 101–103 *per* Gummow & Haynes J.J. (majority), and at para.297 *per* Callinan J.

where there is a breach of a fiduciary duty or a duty of good faith owed to ones employer.[90] Trespass may involve breaches of other duties, such as confidentiality, if it is clear that what is taking place on the premises is in some way secret or confidential, such as a closed film set or a celebrity wedding where only official photography was permitted.

An argument that copyright in a covert film belonged to the employer of a man who secretly took the covert film failed.[91] It is submitted that, unless the trespass involves a breach of fiduciary duty or duty of confidentiality, which in most trespass cases will be unlikely,[92] copyright in any images obtained will belong to the trespasser photographer and not the land owner. Whether the claimant is entitled to rely on the copyright of such images in an infringement action or otherwise is a separate question.

The contractual maxim *ex turpi causa non oritur actio* that no cause of action arises from illegal or immoral acts also applies to tort claims.[93] A court may refuse to entertain a claim that is founded on an illegal act of the claimant or where his conduct was grossly immoral or reprehensible.[94] It has been pointed out that there is some confusion as to the circumstances in which a defence of *ex turpi causa* will succeed in tort and there are three different competing tests.[95]     **6–116**

In summary, these three competing tests are that the defence should apply (1) where it is impossible for the court to determine a standard of care and thus concludes no duty of care is owed to the claimant[96]; (2) where it would be an affront to public conscience to grant the relief sought as it would encourage other similar acts[97]; (3) where the claimant had to rely on the illegality to succeed on his cause of action.[98] Any party seeking to contend that they have an *ex turpi causa* defence to a copyright infringement action on the basis that the image is obtained by trespassing should approach the matter with caution as the law is far from clear.[99]     **6–117**

In so far as the reliance test is concerned, it is submitted that it would rarely, if at all, be necessary to rely on the illegal act to establish copyright. The copyright arises by virtue of the fact it is an original artistic work created by a qualifying person. Other than the fact it was taken in England or Wales, the precise location where the photograph was taken is immaterial. It would be possible to frame a claim for copyright infringement without relying on or reference to the trespass.

---

[90] *Service Corporation International plc v Channel Four Television Corporation* [1999] E.M.L.R. 83.

[91] *ibid.*

[92] Although see the observations of Callinan J. in *Australian Broadcasting Corp v Lenah Game Meats Pty Ltd* [2001] H.C.A. 63 at para.297 quoted above at para. 6–111.

[93] *Pitts v Hunt* [1991] 1 Q.B. 24, 25; *Kirkham v Chief Constable of Greater Manchester Police* [1990] 2 Q.B. 283.

[94] *Kirkham v Chief Constable of Greater Manchester Police* [1990] 2 Q.B. 283.

[95] *Clerk & Lindsell on Torts* (18th ed.) pp.3–04 *et seq.*

[96] *Pitts v Hunt* [ 1991] 1 Q.B. 24. See *Clerk & Lindsell on Torts* (18th ed.) pp.3–05.

[97] *Kirkham v Chief Constable of Greater Manchester Police* [1990] 2 Q.B. 283, 291. See *Clerk & Lindsell on Torts* (18th ed.) pp.3–06.

[98] *Tinsley v Milligan* [1994] 1 A.C. 340.

[99] A detailed discussion of the competing theories, case law and the current uncertainty is to be found in *Clerk & Lindsell on Torts* (18th ed.) pp.3–04 *et seq.*

## Criminal liability for trespass: public order offences

### Summary of public order powers

**6–118**    The Criminal Justice and Public Order Act 1994 creates powers to remove trespassers on land (ss.61–62); powers to deal with disruptive trespassers (ss.68–9); and trespassory assemblies (ss.70–71). The Public Order Act 1986 gives police powers to impose conditions on processions and assemblies (ss.12 and 14), to prohibit processions and trespassory assemblies (ss.13 and 14A), and to stop people proceedings to trespassory assemblies (s.14C). Breaches of any conditions imposed is a criminal offence.

**6–119**    In addition to these statutory powers, there remains a common law power to restrain any person who is breaching the peace.[1] A breach of the peace occurs whenever harm is actually done or likely to be done to a person, or in his presence, his property or a person is in fear of being harmed through an assault, an affray, a riot, unlawful assembly or other disturbance.[2] The right to take reasonable steps to make a person refrain from breaching the peace is that of every citizen, whether policeman or not.[3]

### Photojournalists and public order

**6–120**    These provisions (together with statutory provisions concerning obstruction[4]) sometimes cause difficulties for photojournalists seeking to cover and photograph processions and assemblies. Those who get unwittingly caught up with the participants can end up being arrested by the police or held with participants in a cordon.

Many of the provisions set out below apply only to organisers or participants. The best advice to photojournalists seeking to cover marches or assemblies is to ensure that they have identification showing that they are a journalist and, if faced with arrest, immediately show their identification and clearly assert that they are a journalist (*i.e.* not a participant).[5] The National Union of Journalists (NUJ) Press Card has a Metropolitan Police telephone number on it which any police officer can call to confirm a journalist's identity using a PIN number. Even showing an NUJ Press Card will not necessarily avoid arrest.[6] Police officers may be sceptical of any identification shown where there is a history of protesters claiming to be journalists or having forged identification.

---

[1] Public Order Act 1986, s.40(4) which provides that noting in the Act affects the common law powers to prevent a breach of the peace.
[2] *R. v Howell* [1982] Q.B. 416.
[3] *Albert v Lavin* [1982] A.C. 546.
[4] As to which see below at paras 6–151 *et seq.*
[5] For further practical advice see Freelance (the newsletter of the London Freelance Branch of the NUJ) at *http://www.londonfreelance.org/fl/streets.html.*
[6] See *e.g.* Mike Holderness, *Nicked if you do, Nicked if You Don't* by Freelance, above (para.6–120, n.5) at *http://www.londonfreelance.org/9901nick.html.* Photographer arrested for leaving a demonstration after asserting he was a journalist and showing a press card.

## *Public processions*

A public procession within the meaning of the Public Order Act 1986 is a **6–121** procession in any public place, specifically any highway or place to which, at the material time, the public or any section of the public has access, on payment or otherwise, as of right or by virtue of express or implied permission.[7]

The senior police officer or Chief officer of police has power to impose conditions on the people organising or taking part in the procession as appear to him necessary to prevent public disorder, damage, disruption, or intimidation, including conditions as to the route of the procession or prohibiting it from entering any public place specified in the directions.[8] The senior police offer has power to impose such conditions where he reasonably believes that the public procession:

(1) may result in serious public disorder, serious damage to property or serious disruption to the life of the community, or

(2) the purpose of the persons organising it is the intimidation of others with a view to compelling them not to do an act they have a right to do, or to do an act they have a right not to do.[9]

Any organiser or participant who knowingly fails to comply with any **6–122** such condition imposed is guilty of an offence but it is a defence to show that the failure arose from circumstances beyond his control.[10] A constable in uniform may arrest, without warrant, anyone he reasonably suspects of committing such an offence.[11]

## *Public assemblies*

A public assembly is an assembly of 20 or more persons in a public place **6–123** which is wholly or partly open to the air.[12] Public place has the same definition as for public processions, namely, a highway or any place to which at the material time the public or any section of the public has access, on payment or otherwise, as of right or by virtue of express or implied permission.[13]

The senior police officer or chief officer of police has power to impose conditions on the persons organising or taking part in the assembly as to the place at which the assembly may be (or continue to be) held, its maximum duration, or the maximum number of persons who may constitute it, as

---

[7] Public Order Act 1986, s.16.

[8] Public Order Act 1986, s.12(1).

[9] Public Order Act 1986, s.12(1).

[10] Public Order Act 1986, s.12(4) (Organisers: Person convicted liable on summary conviction to three months imprisonment or fine not exceeding level 4 on the standard scale: s.12(8)); s.12(5) (Participants: Person convicted liable on summary conviction to a fine not exceeding level 3 on the standard scale: s.12(9)). As to which see above at para.6–059, n.37 (level 4) and below para.6–152, n.20 (level 3).

[11] Public Order Act 1986, s.12(7).

[12] Public Order Act 1986, s.16.

[13] *ibid.*

appear to him necessary to prevent public disorder, damage, disruption, or intimidation.[14] The power to impose conditions arises where the police officer reasonably believes that the public assembly:

(1) may result in serious public disorder, serious damage to property or serious disruption to the life of the community; or

(2) the purpose of the persons organising it is the intimidation of others with a view to compelling them not to do an act they have a right to do, or to do an act they have a right not to do.[15]

**6–124**   Any organiser or participant who knowingly fails to comply with any such condition imposed is guilty of an offence but it is a defence to show that the failure arose from circumstances beyond his control.[16] A constable in uniform may arrest, without warrant anyone he reasonably suspects of committing such an offence.[17]

*Trespassory assemblies*

**6–125**   The power to make or obtain an order banning assemblies arises in relation to trespassory assemblies. Trespassory assemblies are those where the chief officer of police/Commissioner of the Police for the Metropolis/ Commissioner of Police for the City of London has a reasonable belief that the assembly is (1) intended to be held in any district at a place on land to which the public has no right of access or only a limited right of access, and (2) that the assembly is likely to be held without the permission of the occupier of the land or to conduct itself in such a way as to exceed the limits of any permission of his or the limits of the public's right of access.[18]

The power to make a banning order only arises where there is reasonable belief that the trespassory assembly may result in either:

(1) serious disruption to the life of the community, or

(2) where the land, or a building or monument on it, is of historical, architectural, archaeological, or scientific importance, in significant damage to the land, building or monument,[19]

he may apply to the council of the district for an order prohibiting for a specified period the holding of all trespassory assemblies in the district or a part of it, as specified.

---

[14] Public Order Act 1986, s.14(1).
[15] Public Order Act 1986, s.14(1).
[16] Public Order Act 1986, s.14(4) (Organisers: Person convicted liable on summary conviction to three months imprisonment or fine not exceeding level 4 on the standard scale: s.14(8)); s.14(5) (Participants: Person convicted liable on summary conviction to a fine not exceeding level 3 on the standard scale: s.14(9)). See above at para.6–122, n.10.
[17] Public Order Act 1986, s.14(7).
[18] Public Order Act 1986, s.14A(1).
[19] Public Order Act 1986, s.14A(1) and (4).

Provided the above requirements are met, in London, the Commissioner **6–126** of the Police for the Metropolis or the Commissioner of Police for the City of London may, with consent of the Secretary of State make an order prohibiting for a specified period the holding of trespassory assemblies in an area or part of an area.[20] Outside of London, the Chief Officer of Police must apply to the relevant district council for an order.[21]

Any order made can only prohibit the holding of assemblies for a period **6–127** of four days or less and cannot exceed an area represented by a circle with a radius of five miles from a specified centre.[22] Any order made operates to prohibit any assembly which:

(1) is held on land to which the public has no right of access or only a limited right of access, *and*

(2) takes place in the prohibited circumstances, *i.e.* without the permission of the occupier of the land or so as to exceed the limits of any permission of his or the limits of the public's right of access.[23]

The extent of the public's right of access is an important part of assessing what can be prohibited. If the assembly is taking place on a public highway, any activity which is reasonable, does not involve a public or private nuisance, and does not obstruct the highway should not be regarded as a trespass.[24] A right of peaceful assembly on the public highway could therefore exist subject to those restrictions.[25]

Organising a trespassory assembly which is prohibited by such an order or **6–128** taking part in such an assembly is an offence.[26] A person convicted of organising such an assembly is liable on summary conviction to imprisonment of up to three months or a fine not exceeding level 4 on the standard scale, or both.[27] A person convicted of taking part in such an assembly is liable on summary conviction to a fine not exceeding level 3 on the standard scale.[28] A constable in uniform may arrest, without warrant, anyone he reasonably suspects of committing such an offence.[29]

## Criminal liability for trespass: miscellaneous

Many different specific types of property are the subject of statutes which **6–129** render trespass on to them criminal. The following are some examples, but not an exhaustive list:

---

[20] Public Order Act 1986, s.14A(3) and (4).
[21] Public Order Act 1986, s.14A(1) and (2).
[22] Public Order Act 1986, s.14A(6).
[23] Public Order Act 1986, s.14A(5).
[24] *DPP v Jones (Margaret)* [1999] 2 A.C. 240; [1999] 2 W.L.R. 625; [1999] 2 All E.R. 257.
[25] *ibid.*
[26] Public Order Act 1986, s.14B(1) (organising); s.14B(2) (participating).
[27] Public Order Act 1986, s.14A(5).
[28] Public Order Act 1986, s.14A(6).
[29] Public Order Act 1986, s.14B(4).

- aerodromes,[30]

- railways,[31]

- the Channel Tunnel,[32]

- certain gardens and ornamental grounds in public squares,[33]

- diplomatic residences and consular premises,[34]

- military establishments and army encampments,[35]

- certain designated areas of special protection,[36]

- explosives factories and stores.[37]

## NUISANCE

**6–130**  For further information as to nuisance generally, beyond the specific application to photography see *Clerk & Lindsell on Torts* (18th ed.) pp.19–01 *et seq.* and *Halsbury's Laws of England* Vol.34 (4th ed., 1997) at paras 1 *et seq.*

## General

**6–131**  An actionable private[38] nuisance is any act or omission which interferes with a person's use or enjoyment of his land or any right connected with the land.[39] Damage is an essential requirement of a cause of action in nuisance,[40] although presumed damage will suffice.[41] Private nuisance usually involves

---

[30] Civil Aviation Act 1982, s.39.

[31] Railway Regulation Act 1840, s.16; Regulation of Railways Act 1868, s.23.

[32] Railway Regulation Act 1840, s.16 and Channel Tunnel Act 1987, Sch.6.

[33] Town Gardens Protection Act 1863, s.5.

[34] Criminal Law Act 1977, s.9.

[35] Official Secrets Act 1911, s.1; Military Lands Act 1892, s.14 and byelaws made under it: *R. v Barnet London Borough Ex p. Johnson* (1989) 88 L.G.R. 73.

[36] Wildlife and Countryside Act 1981, s.3(1)(b).

[37] Explosives Act 1875, s.77.

[38] Nuisance may be private or public nuisance; for present purposes the consideration here is of private nuisance only. A public nuisance arises where a person does an act not warranted by law or omits to discharge a legal duty where the effect is to endanger the life, health, property, morals or comfort of the public or to obstruct the public in the exercise of its enjoyment of rights common to all: 1 Hawk. c.75. The likelihood of photography constituting a public nuisance (other than obstruction, as to which see below) is such that consideration here is not warranted. A public nuisance is a criminal offence at common law: *Archbold* 2004, 31–33 *et seq.*

[39] The term is not capable of exact definition *Bamford v Turnley* (1862) 3 B. & S. 66 at 79.

[40] *AG v Kingston-on-Thames Corpn* (1865) 34 L.J. Ch. 481; *Salvin v North Brancepeth Coal Co* (1874) 9 Ch. App. 705; *Sedleigh-Denfield v O'Callaghan* [1940] A.C. 880.

[41] Where an absolute legal right has been infringed, the law will presume damage: *Nicholls v Ely Beet Sugar Factory Ltd (No.2)* [1936] Ch. 343 at 350.

an encroachment on to land[42]; causing physical damage to land[43] or interfering with the comfortable enjoyment of land.[44] However, the forms nuisance may take are protean.[45] If photography or the acts of a photographer are to amount to a nuisance at all, it would probably be on the basis of interfering with the comfortable enjoyment of land. When considering damage to health and comfort, it is necessary to determine whether the acts complained of interfere with the complainant's comfortable and convenient enjoyment of his land with regard being had to the usage of civilised society and the character of the neighbourhood.[46] The question is whether it is an inconvenience materially interfering with the ordinary comfort physically of human existence, not merely according to elegant or dainty modes and habits of living, but according to plain, sober and simple notions.[47]

## Photographers and nuisance

The taking of a single photograph is not an actionable nuisance.[48] **6–132** However, noise and vibration such as materially interferes with the ordinary comfort of the inhabitants, will amount to a nuisance.[49] Mere noise of music lessons and practice has been held not to constitute a nuisance.[50] It has been suggested that harassment of constant surveillance by an aerial photographer might very well amount to an actionable nuisance.[51] Low flying aircraft or hovering helicopters where there is noise may also amount to a nuisance. It is not necessary for the nuisance to be continuing. A temporary but substantial interference with enjoyment is sufficient to create a cause of action.[52]

It is arguable that a group of photographers engaged in surveillance from **6–133** the highway outside private premises amounts to a nuisance. Whenever a person is using a highway other than purely as a means of passage, he is only entitled to use it for a purpose which is reasonably incidental to the right of passage.[53] A person's right to enjoy his property includes the right to have access to the property both for himself and his invitees, but a temporary or

---

[42] *e.g.* tree branches or tree roots: *Butler v Standard Telephones and Cables Ltd* [1940] 1 K.B. 399.
[43] *e.g.* allowing drains to become blocked and overflow onto neighbouring land: *Sedleigh-Denfield v O'Callaghan* [1940] A.C. 880.
[44] *e.g.* right to light: *Lazarus v Artistic Photographic Co* [1897] 2 Ch. 214 (access of light to his premises for a special or extraordinary purpose namely taking photographic portraits).
[45] *Sedleigh-Denfield v O'Callaghan* [1940] A.C. 880 at 903.
[46] *Thompson-Schwab v Costaki* [1956] 1 All E.R. 652 (use of house for prostitution).
[47] *Walter v Selfe* (1851) 4 De G. & Sm. 315 at 322, 64 E.R. 849 at 852.
[48] *Bernstein v Skyviews and General Ltd* [1978] Q.B. 479 at 489; [1977] 2 All E.R. 902; [1977] 3 W.L.R. 136.
[49] *e.g. Heath v Brighton Corp* (1908) 98 L.T. 718 (electrical generators); *Hardman v Holberton* [1866] W.N. 379 (church bells).
[50] *Christie v Davey* [1893] 1 Ch. 316.
[51] *Bernstein v Skyviews and General Ltd* [1978] Q.B. 479; [1977] 2 All E.R. 902; [1977] 3 W.L.R. 136. See also provisions of the Civil Aviation Act 1982.
[52] *Crown River Cruises Ltd v Kimbolton Fireworks Ltd* [1996] 2 Lloyd's Rep. 533 (firework debris falling onto barge. Firework display lasting 20 minutes held to be actionable in nuisance).
[53] *Hubbard v Pitt* [1976] Q.B. 142 at 149H–150A *per* Forbes J.

reasonable obstruction will not amount to a nuisance.[54] A gathering of persons may be held to be a nuisance.[55] There is no law permitting assembly or meetings on the highway.[56] For example, picketing business premises may amount to a nuisance if accompanied by obstruction or violence.[57] Picketing is in a slightly different category to a group of photographers however as picketing, like the right to demonstrate, is part of the right to free speech.[58] Where the stationing of people on the highway renders the highway less commodious as a means of passage, it amounts to a nuisance.[59] Watching or besetting a man's house with a view to compelling him to not do something which is lawful for him to do without reasonable justification is unlawful as it interferes with the ordinary enjoyment of the house.[60] However, it has also been said that watching a man's house is only wrongful if combined with other conduct such as obstruction as to render the whole conduct a nuisance.[61]

### Entitlement to sue

**6–134**    It is necessary to have an interest in the land affected in order to maintain an action for nuisance.[62] A person in possession or occupation of the land, including tenants,[63] can sue, as can a reversioner for damage to the reversion[64] but those with no proprietary interest cannot.[65]

---

[54] *Hubbard v Pitt* [1976] Q.B. 142 at 158C *per* Forbes J.; *Harper v GN Haden & Sons Ltd* [1933] Ch. 298, 304 (temporary obstruction does not give rise to a remedy where reasonable); *Dwyer v Mansfield* [1946] K.B. 437, 441 (no nuisance where shopkeeper distributing food when in short supply. Not responsible for queues).

[55] *Lippiatt v South Gloucestershire Council* [1994] 4 All E.R. 149. And see *Rex v Carlile* 6 C. & P. 636 (display in window of effigies attracting crowds); *Walker v Brewster* (1867) L.R. 5 Eq. 25; *Bellamy v Wells* (1891) 39 W.R. 158; *Barber v Penley* [1893] 2 Ch. 447 (theatre); *Lyons, Sons & Co v Gulliver* [1914] 1 Ch. 631 (theatre).

[56] *Ex parte Lewis* (1881) 21 QBD 191.

[57] *J. Lyons & Sons v Wilkins (No.2)* [1899] 1 Ch. 255; *Ward, Lock & Co Ltd v Operative Printers' Assistants' Society* (1906) 22 T.L.R. 327 at 329 (no nuisance where pickets "watching or besetting" premises without violence or obstruction); *Hubbard v Pitt* [1976] 1 Q.B. 142 at 175G *per* Lord Denning M.R. (dissenting).

[58] *Hubbard v Pitt* [1976] 1 Q.B. 142 at 177F *per* Lord Denning M.R. (dissenting).

[59] *Hubbard v Pitt* [1976] 1 Q.B. 142 at 157D. A colourable pretence at passage by having pickets move around does not prevent a nuisance: *Tynan v Balmer* [1967] 1 Q.B. 91.

[60] *J. Lyons & Sons v Wilkins* [1899] 1 Ch. 255 at 267. The discussion here relates to the law of nuisance only. Watching a house may also involve breach of confidence or infringement of the right to a private and family life as to which see below at paras 7–048 to 7–052 and 7–062.

[61] *Hubbard v Pitt* [1976] 1 Q.B. 142 at 175G *per* Lord Denning M.R. (dissenting).

[62] *Khorasandjian v Bush* [1993] Q.B. 727; [1993] 3 All E.R. 669; *Hunter v Canary Wharf Ltd* [1997] A.C. 655; [1997] 2 W.L.R. 684.

[63] *Inchbald v Robinson, Inchbald v Barrington* (1869) 4 Ch. App. 388; *Jones v Chappell* (1875) L.R. 20 Eq. 539.

[64] *Tucker v Newman* (1829) 11 A. & E. 40.

[65] *Hunter v Canary Wharf Ltd* [1997] A.C. 655; [1997] 2 W.L.R. 684.

## Liability for nuisance

The person who creates or causes a nuisance, or continues or adopts it,[66]   **6–135**
or who authorises[67] its creation or continuance is liable for nuisance whether
or not he is in actual occupation of the land.[68] An employer is liable for a
nuisance committed by his employee or agent acting in the course of their
employment.[69]

## Defences

In addition to standard defences to tort claims (act of God, causation,   **6–136**
etc.), the following are defences to an action for nuisance:

(a) statutory authority where an act or omission is specifically authorised
by statute[70];

(b) prescriptive right acquired in respect of the nuisance[71];

(c) nuisance caused by a trespasser[72];

(d) ignorance of the nuisance (only where ignorance is not due to failure
to use reasonable care to discover the nuisance)[73];

(e) contributory negligence where nuisance based on negligence[74];

(f) consent[75];

(g) limitation where nuisance is not continuing.

Where nuisance is alleged against a photographer or group of photo-   **6–137**
graphers, few of these defences will be relevant. A successful defence is more
likely to be found in contending the acts complained of do not amount to a
nuisance at all.

---

[66] *Ryppon v Bowles* (1616) Cro. Jac. 373; *Leakey v National Trust* [1980] Q.B. 485; *Page Motors Ltd v Epsom v Ewell BC* (1982) 80 L.G.R. 337.
[67] *King v Ford* (1816) 1 Stark. 421; *R. v Longton Gas Co* (1860) 2 E. & E. 651; *White v Jameson* (1874) L.R. 18 Eq. 303.
[68] *Hall v Beckenham Corp* [1949] 1 K.B. 716 (noise from model aeroplanes in a public park).
[69] *Laugher v Pointer* (1826) 5 B. & C. 547.
[70] *e.g.* local highway authority legalising obstructions to right of passage.
[71] See *Halsbury's Laws* Vol.34 at para.67.
[72] *Barker v Herbert* [1911] 2 K.B. 633. Occupier not liable where he did not know or ought to have known of the nuisance.
[73] *Ilford Urban DC v Beal and Judd* [1925] 1 K.B. 671; *Caswell v Powell Duffryn Associated Collieries Ltd* [1940] A.C. 152; *Hicks v British Transport Commission* [1958] 1 W.L.R. 493.
[74] *Trevett v Lee* [1955] 1 All E.R. 406 at 412.
[75] *Pwllbach Colliery Co Ltd v Woodman* [1915] A.C. 634.

**Remedies**

6–138   (a) "Self-help" abatement where it is possible to lawfully end the nuisance. It is not usually advisable and not encouraged by the courts.[76]

(b) Damages. Damages for private nuisance are usually assessed on the basis of the loss of the amenity value of the land affected.[77]

(c) Injunction to restrain the continuance of a nuisance. Where the injury caused by the nuisance is not serious and is capable of compensation in damages, an injunction will not normally be granted,[78] nor where the nuisance is occasional or temporary.[79]

It is submitted that there is no basis in the law of nuisance to seek to restrain publication of photographs obtained whilst causing a nuisance, unlike trespass.[80] A photographer is free to take photographs in a public place across a boundary[81] and thus the fact he has caused a nuisance has no bearing on his right to photograph or to the photographs themselves.

## HARASSMENT

6–139   The main provisions of the Protection From Harassment Act 1997 came into force on June 16, 1997.[82] The Act created a civil remedy for harassment and also created a criminal offence of harassment.

The Act prohibits a course of conduct which amounts to harassment of another and which the defendant knows or ought to have known amounts to harassment.[83] Conduct that ought to be known to amount to harassment arises where a reasonable person in possession of the same information

---

[76] *Earl of Lonsdale v Nelson* (1823) 2 B. & C. 302 at 311. See *Clerk & Lindsell on Torts* (18th ed.) at pp.31–23 *et seq.* where the authors suggest the right of abatement is subject to a number of modern limitations including (i) it must be possible to abate the nuisance peacefully, (ii) the court has not or would not refuse a mandatory injunction, (iii) it must be carried out so as to cause as little damage as possible, (iv) the right must be exercised promptly, (v) the wrongdoer should be given notice.

[77] *Hunter v Canary Wharf Ltd* [1997] A.C. 655; [1997] 2 W.L.R. 684; [1997] 2 All E.R. 426.

[78] *Haines v Taylor* (1846) 10 Beav. 75; *Sampson v Hodson-Pressinger* [1981] 3 All E.R. 710; *Jaggard v Sawyer* [1995] 1 W.L.R. 269; [1995] 2 All E.R. 189.

[79] *Swaine v Great Northern Rly Co* (1864) 4 De J. & Sm. 211; *Cooke v Forbes* (1867) L.R. 5 Eq. 166.

[80] See above at paras 6–104 to 6–114.

[81] *Sports & General Press Agency Ltd v "Our Dogs" Publishing Company Ltd* [1916] 2 K.B. 880; affirmed CA [1917] 2 K.B. 125; *Bernstein v Skyviews and General Ltd* [1978] Q.B. 479; [1977] 2 All E.R. 902; [1977] 3 W.L.R. 136; *Lincoln Hunt Australia Pty Ltd v Willisee* (1986) 4 N.S.W.L.R. 457, 461; *Hickman v Maisey* [1900] 1 Q.B. 752, 756.

[82] ss.13–16 came into force upon receipt of the Royal Assent on March 21, 1997. Excluding s.3(3)–(9), the remainder came into force on June 16, 1997: Protection From Harassment Act 1997 (Commencement) (No.1) Order 1997 (SI 1997/1418); Protection From Harassment Act 1997 (Commencement) (No.2) Order 1997 (SI 1997/1498). ss.3(3)–(9) came into force on September 1, 1998, Protection From Harassment Act 1997 (Commencement) (No.3) Order 1997 (SI 1998/1902).

[83] Protection from Harassment Act 1997, s.1(1).

would think the course of conduct amounted to harassment.[84] It is a defence to show that the conduct was (a) pursued to prevent or detect crime, (b) pursued under any statute or law, or (c) reasonable in the particular circumstances.[85]

The Act is not contrary to Arts 10 and 11 of the ECHR as the rights provided for are not absolute and could be restricted by the domestic law to prevent disorder or crime or to protect the reputation or rights of others.[86]

## Conduct amounting to harassment

There is no exhaustive definition of harassment in the statute. However, the statute provides that references to harassing a person include alarming the person or causing the person distress.[87] It has been held that this includes negative emotion caused by repeated molestation, such as annoyance and worry.[88] Harassment includes an element of intent to cause distress or harm.[89]   **6–140**

The test whether a course of conduct is one which a reasonable person would think amounted to harassment is an objective one and therefore the mental illness of the defendant is immaterial.[90] It has been said that because of the wide potential and far-reaching meaning of harassment, it is legitimate for the court to have recourse to the Hansard as an aid to construction.[91] Hansard makes clear that the behaviour that Parliament was aiming to control was stalking, anti-social behaviour by neighbours and racial harassment. The oppressive conduct of litigation was not behaviour the act was directed at.[92] Although no more than two incidents were needed to constitute harassment, the fewer the number of incidents and the wider the time lapse, the less likely such a finding would be justified.[93] Three telephone calls made within five minutes will suffice.[94]   **6–141**

It is plain that photographing and filming is capable of being conduct   **6–142**

---

[84] Protection from Harassment Act 1997, s.1(2).

[85] Protection from Harassment Act 1997, s.1(3).

[86] *Silverton v Gravett* (unrep.) October 19, 2001, QBD, HHJ Bentley Q.C.; Lawtel: AC0102102.

[87] Protection from Harassment Act 1997, s.7(2).

[88] *DPP v Ramsdale* February 12, 2001 [2001] EWHC Admin 106 at [16].

[89] *Johnson v Walton* [1990] 1 F.L.R. 350, 352H.

[90] *R. v Colohan*, *The Times* June 14, 2001.

[91] *Tuppen v Microsoft*, *The Times* November 15, 2000 (reference made by court to speeches of Michael Howard HC, Debates, December 17, 1996 cols 781–784 and of Lord Mackay of Clashfern HL Debates January 24, 1997).

[92] *Tuppen v Microsoft*, *The Times*, November 15, 2000.

[93] *Lau v DPP* [2000] 1 F.L.R. 799; [2000] Crim. L.R. 580; [2000] Fam. Law. 610 (two incidents separated by four months); *R. v Gavin Spencer Hills* [2001] 1 F.L.R. 580; (2001) Crim. L.R. 318 (assaults in April and October were not a course of conduct). Cf. *Bacon v CPS* (Lawtel 13/6/2000) (two letters to a civil servant sent 4½ months apart amounted to harassment. It was said that whilst a court would normally be slow to find 2 letters sent over 4½ months apart amounted to harassment, everything depended on the facts of the individual case).

[94] *Kelly v DPP* [2002] EWHC 1428; [2003] Crim. L.R. 45.

amounting to harassment.[95] Persistent stalking in an attempt to obtain a photograph also amounts to harassment and is sufficient basis to obtain an ex parte injunction.[96] Going through rubbish bags and covert filming has been held to be capable of amounting to harassment.[97]

**6–143**     Where threats of violence are made, the issue is whether the threats caused the victim to be in fear of violence and whether the defendant ought to have known that, and not whether particular threats are capable of falling within the section.[98] Obstructing access to an animal research laboratory by anti-vivisection campaigners involving standing in front of cars, shouting obscenities at drivers together with threats such as "we know where you live", photographing people using video cameras, taking down registration numbers of vehicles and following vehicles after they had left the premises has been held to amount to harassment.[99] Publication of a series of articles calculated to incite racial hatred were capable of being harassment.[1]

However, the Act was not intended to clamp down on the discussion of matters of public interest or upon the rights of political protest and public demonstration which are part of the democratic tradition and the courts will resist such a wide interpretation.[2]

**6–144**     A course of conduct could amount to the harassment of more than one victim as the use of the singular in s.1 of the Act was to be construed as including the plural. Where a person pursues a course of conduct against two or more people which amounts to harassment of them, a single offence is committed and it is immaterial that individual acts forming part of that course of conduct are directed at one only of the victims.[3]

---

[95] See *King v DPP* [2001] A.C.D. 7; *Independent*, July 31, 2000 (covert filming); *Huntingdon Life Sciences Ltd v Curtin* (October 15, 1997, Lexis) (1998) Env. L.R. D9, CA; and decision of Eady J. (November 28, 1997, Lexis) *The Times*, December 11, 1997 (photographing people entering a leaving animal research laboratory).

[96] In August 1996, Diana, Princess of Wales obtained an *ex parte* High Court injunction against Martin Stenning, a freelance photographer, whom she accused of persistent harassment. According to a newspaper report which reproduced her affidavit, the conduct complained of by the claimant took place over a period of 6–8 months and included frequent pursuit of the claimant's car on a motorcycle driven closely to the car on occasion causing damage and collision; obstruction of her path when leaving a restaurant and pointing a camera in her face; regularly following the claimant's movements and approaching the claimant and shouting abuse: *The Times*, August 16, 1996, p.1 and August 17, 1996, p.2.

[97] *King v DPP* [2001] A.C.D. 7; *Independent*, July 31, 2000.

[98] *Howard v DPP* [2001] EWCA Admin 17 at [13]; [2001] Crim. L.R. 396 (threats towards a dog in its owners presence which caused the owner to be in fear of violence).

[99] *Huntingdon Life Sciences Ltd v Curtin* (October 15, 1997, Lexis) (1998) Env. L.R. D9, CA; and decision of Eady J. (November 28, 1997, Lexis) *The Times*, December 11, 1997. *Cf.*: *DPP v Dziurzynski* [2002] EWHC 1380, QBD (Admin. Ct) Rose, L.J.; Gibbs, J.—holding a company was not a person for the purposes of the Act and not following *Huntingdon Life Sciences Ltd v Curtin*.

[1] *Thomas v News Group Newspapers Ltd* [2001] EWCA Civ 1233; [2002] E.M.L.R. 4.

[2] *Huntingdon Life Sciences Ltd v Curtin* Eady J. (November 28, 1997, Lexis) *The Times*, December 11, 1997.

[3] *DPP v Dunn* [2001] 1 Cr. App. R. 22; (2001) 165 J.P. 130; [2001] Crim. L.R. 130.

## Corporations and associations

Case law is divided as to whether a company is capable of being the **6–145** subject of harassment under the Protection From Harassment Act 1997.[4] However, the prevailing view appears to be that a company is capable of obtaining an injunction under the Act, even if only acting on behalf of its employees.[5] It has been said that the Interpretation Act 1978 presumption that "person" included bodies corporate should prevail.[6]

No cause of action for harassment will lie against a members association simply by virtue of the conduct of one of its members unless there is "a modicum of evidence" to show that the acts were performed with "the approval, authority or encouragement" of the association.[6a] The court has power to make an order that binds non-parties who are acting in concert with the defendant and who have notice of the injunction.[6b]

## Threatened harassment

By s.7(2), the Act requires conduct on at least two occasions before a right **6–146** to the civil remedy arises. However, an application for an injunction *quia timet* may be made for a threatened tort where evidence shows a commission of the tort is likely.[7]

## Defence that course of conduct was reasonable: s.1(3)(c)

As with the test as to whether a course of conduct was one which a **6–147** reasonable person would think amounted to harassment, the test under s.1(3)(c) is clearly an objective one.[8] There is no basis to attach to the word "reasonable" the standards or characteristics of the particular defendant.[9] Mental illness is thus no defence, but will go to the question of sentence.

It is not reasonable for the purposes of s.1(3)(c), to pursue a course of conduct in breach of an injunction without exceptional circumstances, such

---

[4] *cf. Huntingdon Life Sciences Ltd v Curtin* (October 15, 1997, CA) (1998) Env. L.R. D9 (holding a company fell within the Act) and: *DPP v Dziurzynski* [2002] EWHC 1380 (QBD (Admin Ct) Rose, L.J.; Gibbs, J.—holding a company was not a person for the purposes of the Act and not following *Huntingdon Life Sciences Ltd v Curtin.*

[5] *Huntingdon Life Sciences v Stop Huntingdon Animal Cruelty (SHAC)* [2003] EWHC 1967 (QBD) (Gibb J.); *Emerson Developments Ltd v Avery and Others* (Field J.) (January 26, 2004).

[6] *Huntingdon Life Sciences Ltd v Curtin* (October 15, 1997, CA) (1998) Env. L.R. D9. But see above at n.4.

[6a] *Huntingdon Life Sciences Ltd v Curtin* (November 28, 1997) (Eady J.) *The Times*, December 11, 1997.

[6b] *Silverton & Others v Paul Gravett & Others* (QBD, HH Judge Bentley Q.C., October 19, 2001) citing *Huntingdon Life Sciences Ltd v Curtin* (October 15, 1997, CA) (1998) Env. L.R. D9 and *DPP v Moseley (Joanna)* (June 9, 1999) *The Times*, June 23, 1999.

[7] As to *quia timet* injunctions in tort cases see *Clerk & Lindsell on Torts* (18th ed.) at pp. 30–14 *et seq.*; *South Carolina Insurance Co v Assurantie Maatschappij "De Zeven Provincien" NV* [1987] A.C. 24; [1986] 3 W.L.R. 398; *Morris v Redland Bricks Ltd* [1970] A.C. 652, 655; *Khorasandjian v Bush* [1993] 2 F.L.R. 66.

[8] *R. v Colohan, The Times* June 14, 2001.

[9] *ibid.*

as the need to rescue a person in imminent danger.[10] Conduct that constituted harassment for the purposes of the Act could not in general be reasonable and such action could not be justified merely because the defendant believed it to be reasonable.[11]

### Restraining orders: s.5

**6–148**    An order under s.5 must identify the person intended to be protected.[12]

### Criminal sentencing guidelines

**6–149**    It was held in *R. v Liddle*[13] that when passing sentence under the Act the court should consider:

(1)  whether the offence was under s.2 or s.4;

(2)  whether there was a history of disobeying court orders;

(3)  the seriousness and range of the conduct complained of;

(4)  whether there was a persistent course of conduct or a solitary instance of behaviour;

(5)  the effect of the offence on the victim;

(6)  the degree of future risk posed to either the victim or their family and whether protection was necessary;

(7)  the mental health of the offender and whether he was willing to undergo treatment, and

(8)  whether the offender had pleaded guilty, expressed remorse or recognised the need for help.

Although very much dependent upon the facts, a first offence would normally merit a short sharp sentence. For second offences, 15 months' imprisonment would be the appropriate starting point where the offender pleaded guilty and between three and five years for a not guilty plea.

### Civil Proceedings

**6–149A**    A breach of s.1 of the Protection From Harassment Act 1997 (whether actual or apprehended) may be the subject of civil proceedings.[13a] Only the

---

[10] *DPP v Moseley (Joanna)* (June 9, 1999) *The Times*, June 23, 1999 (protestors outside a mink farm in breach of an injunction).
[11] *DPP v Moseley (Joanna)* (June 9, 1999) *The Times*, June 23, 1999.
[12] *R. v Mann* (2000) 97(14) L.S.G. 41; (2000) 144 S.J.L.B. 150.
[13] [1999] 3 All E.R. 816; [2000] 1 Cr. App. R. (S) 131; [1999] Crim. L.R. 847.
[13a] Protection From Harassment Act 1997, s.3(1). Reproduced in full below at para. 6–150B.

person who is or may be the victim of the course of conduct may bring the claim.[13b] In addition to an injunction, damages may be awarded for inter alia any anxiety caused by the harassment and any financial loss resulting from the harassment.[13c]

---

## PROTECTION FROM HARASSMENT ACT 1997, ss.1–7, AND 12

**Prohibition of harassment**                                                 6–150
  **1.**—(1) A person must not pursue a course of conduct—

  (a)  which amounts to harassment of another, and

  (b)  which he knows or ought to know amounts to harassment of the other.

  (2) For the purposes of this section, the person whose course of conduct is in question ought to know that it amounts to harassment of another if a reasonable person in possession of the same information would think the course of conduct amounted to harassment of the other.
  (3) Subsection (1) does not apply to a course of conduct if the person who pursued it shows–

  (a)  that it was pursued for the purpose of preventing or detecting crime,

  (b)  that it was pursued under any enactment or rule of law or to comply with any condition or requirement imposed by any person under any enactment, or

  (c)  that in the particular circumstances the pursuit of the course of conduct was reasonable.

**Offence of harassment**                                                     6–150A
  **2.**—(1) A person who pursues a course of conduct in breach of section 1 is guilty of an offence.
  (2) A person guilty of an offence under this section is liable on summary conviction to imprisonment for a term not exceeding six months, or a fine not exceeding level 5 on the standard scale, or both.
  (3) In section 24(2) of the Police and Criminal Evidence Act 1984 (arrestable offences), after paragraph (m) there is inserted– '(n) an offence under section 2 of the Protection from Harassment Act 1997 (harassment).'.

**Civil remedy**                                                              6–150B
  **3.**—(1) An actual or apprehended breach of section 1 may be the subject of a claim in civil proceedings by the person who is or may be the victim of the course of conduct in question.
  (2) On such a claim, damages may be awarded for (among other things) any anxiety caused by the harassment and any financial loss resulting from the harassment.
  (3) Where—

---

[13b] *ibid.*, s.3(1).
[13c] *ibid.*, s.3(2).

## PROTECTION FROM HARASSMENT ACT 1997, SS.1–7, AND 12
### CONT.

(a) in such proceedings the High Court or a county court grants an injunction for the purpose of restraining the defendant from pursuing any conduct which amounts to harassment, and

(b) the plaintiff considers that the defendant has done anything which he is prohibited from doing by the injunction,

the plaintiff may apply for the issue of a warrant for the arrest of the defendant.

(4) An application under subsection (3) may be made—

(a) where the injunction was granted by the High Court, to a judge of that court, and

(b) where the injunction was granted by a county court, to a judge or district judge of that or any other county court.

(5) The judge or district judge to whom an application under subsection (3) is made may only issue a warrant if—

(a) the application is substantiated on oath, and

(b) the judge or district judge has reasonable grounds for believing that the defendant has done anything which he is prohibited from doing by the injunction.

(6) Where—

(a) the High Court or a county court grants an injunction for the purpose mentioned in subsection (3)(a), and

(b) without reasonable excuse the defendant does anything which he is prohibited from doing by the injunction,

he is guilty of an offence.

(7) Where a person is convicted of an offence under subsection (6) in respect of any conduct, that conduct is not punishable as a contempt of court.

(8) A person cannot be convicted of an offence under subsection (6) in respect of any conduct which has been punished as a contempt of court.

(9) A person guilty of an offence under subsection (6) is liable–

(a) on conviction on indictment, to imprisonment for a term not exceeding five years, or a fine, or both, or

(b) on summary conviction, to imprisonment for a term not exceeding six months, or a fine not exceeding the statutory maximum, or both.

**6–150C**

**Putting people in fear of violence**

**4.**—(1) A person whose course of conduct causes another to fear, on at least two occasions, that violence will be used against him is guilty of an offence if he knows or ought to know that his course of conduct will cause the other so to fear on each of those occasions.

(2) For the purposes of this section, the person whose course of conduct is in question ought to know that it will cause another to fear that violence will be used against him on any occasion if a reasonable person in possession of the

PROTECTION FROM HARASSMENT ACT 1997, SS.1–7, AND 12
CONT.

same information would think the course of conduct would cause the other so to fear on that occasion.

(3) It is a defence for a person charged with an offence under this section to show that—

(a) his course of conduct was pursued for the purpose of preventing or detecting crime,

(b) his course of conduct was pursued under any enactment or rule of law or to comply with any condition or requirement imposed by any person under any enactment, or

(c) the pursuit of his course of conduct was reasonable for the protection of himself or another or for the protection of his or another's property.

(4) A person guilty of an offence under this section is liable—

(a) on conviction on indictment, to imprisonment for a term not exceeding five years, or a fine, or both, or

(b) on summary conviction, to imprisonment for a term not exceeding six months, or a fine not exceeding the statutory maximum, or both.

(5) If on the trial on indictment of a person charged with an offence under this section the jury find him not guilty of the offence charged, they may find him guilty of an offence under section 2.

(6) The Crown Court has the same powers and duties in relation to a person who is by virtue of subsection (5) convicted before it of an offence under section 2 as a magistrates' court would have on convicting him of the offence.

**Restraining orders**                                                      **6–150D**

5.—(1) A court sentencing or otherwise dealing with a person ('the defendant') convicted of an offence under section 2 or 4 may (as well as sentencing him or dealing with him in any other way) make an order under this section.

(2) The order may, for the purpose of protecting the victim of the offence, or any other person mentioned in the order, from further conduct which—

(a) amounts to harassment, or

(b) will cause a fear of violence,

prohibit the defendant from doing anything described in the order.

(3) The order may have effect for a specified period or until further order.

(4) The prosecutor, the defendant or any other person mentioned in the order may apply to the court which made the order for it to be varied or discharged by a further order.

(5) If without reasonable excuse the defendant does anything which he is prohibited from doing by an order under this section, he is guilty of an offence.

(6) A person guilty of an offence under this section is liable—

(a) on conviction on indictment, to imprisonment for a term not exceeding five years, or a fine, or both, or

---

PROTECTION FROM HARASSMENT ACT 1997, ss.1–7, AND 12
CONT.

(b) on summary conviction, to imprisonment for a term not exceeding six months, or a fine not exceeding the statutory maximum, or both.

**6–150E**  **Limitation**
6.—In section 11 of the Limitation Act 1980 (special time limit for actions in respect of personal injuries), after subsection (1) there is inserted—

'(1A) This section does not apply to any action brought for damages under section 3 of the Protection from Harassment Act 1997.'

**6–150F**  **Interpretation of this group of sections**
7.—(1) This section applies for the interpretation of sections 1 to 5.
(2) References to harassing a person include alarming the person or causing the person distress.
(3) A 'course of conduct' must involve conduct on at least two occasions.
(4) 'Conduct' includes speech.

**Sections 8–11 [*Scotland*]**

**6–150G**  **National security, etc**
12.—(1) If the Secretary of State certifies that in his opinion anything done by a specified person on a specified occasion related to—

(a) national security,

(b) the economic well-being of the United Kingdom, or

(c) the prevention or detection of serious crime,

and was done on behalf of the Crown, the certificate is conclusive evidence that this Act does not apply to any conduct of that person on that occasion.
(2) In subsection (1), 'specified' means specified in the certificate in question.
(3) A document purporting to be a certificate under subsection (1) is to be received in evidence and, unless the contrary is proved, be treated as being such a certificate.''

---

## OBSTRUCTION

**6–151**  It is a public nuisance to obstruct or hinder the free passage of the public along the highway.[14] In theory, it is possible that a group of photographers on the highway waiting outside a property for a particular individual could be causing a public nuisance. It is more likely that they would be asked to move rather than face a prosecution for public nuisance. A private individual will only have a cause of action for public nuisance where he has sustained direct and substantial damage over and above the general public

---

[14] See generally *Clerk & Lindsell on Torts* (18th ed.) pp.19–106 *et seq.*

inconvenience.[15] Mere inconvenience without pecuniary damage such, as a delay due to an obstruction, is not sufficient.[16]

Obstruction is also a criminal offence under various statutes and it is not unknown for photographers to be arrested for causing an obstruction or obstructing a police constable in the course of his duty.[17]

## Obstruction: Highways Act 1980

Under s.137 of the Highways Act 1980[18] it is an offence for a person without lawful authority or excuse in any way to willfully obstruct the free passage along the highway.[19] The offence is punishable by a fine not exceeding level 3 on the standard scale.[20]

**6–152**

Lawful excuse includes activities otherwise lawful in themselves which may or may not be reasonable in the circumstances.[21] The test as to whether there is an obstruction is whether the use of the highway is unreasonable having regard to all the circumstances including its position, duration and purpose and whether it caused actual as opposed to potential obstruction.[22]

Obstruction of only part of the highway which makes the highway less convenient and commodious to the public is an offence even where there is space around the obstruction for people to pass.[23] If stopping on the highway is merely part and parcel of reasonably passing and repassing there is no obstruction.[24] The fact that police do not prosecute in respect of a particular obstruction for some years does not grant a licence to perform unlawful obstruction.[25]

**6–153**

There is no right to demonstrate in a way which obstructs the highway, and sitting down in the road in order to block traffic will amount to an obstruction,[26] as will causing a crowd to collect.[27] Where a tout approached groups of pedestrians in such a way that members of the public were forced to step into the roadway, it was held to be an unreasonable use of the

**6–154**

---

[15] *Benjamin v Storr* (1874) L.R. 9 C.P. 400; *Vanderpant v Mayfair Hotel Co* [1930] 1 Ch. 138.
[16] *Winterbottom v Lord Derby* (1867) L.R. Eq. 2 Ex 316.
[17] See for example *Reporters win £18,000 payout after wrongful arrest*, Guardian January 21, 2002 (compensation awarded for wrongful arrest in 1998 of photographers covering an animal rights dispute. Detained when trying to leave a police cordon); *Camera Crews In The Firing Line*, Daily Telegraph, October 22, 1990; *Photographers Target For Police Violence*, Independent, January 26, 1987; *Flash, Bang Wallop!—You're nicked*, Guardian, November 18, 1985.
[18] As amended by the Criminal Justice Act 1982, ss.38 and 46 and Police and Criminal Evidence Act 1984, Sch.7.
[19] "Highway" is defined in Highways Act 1981, s.328 as "the whole or part of a highway other than a ferry or waterway" and includes a bridge or tunnel over or through which a highway passes.
[20] At the time of writing, £1,000: Criminal Justice Act 1982, s.37(2) as amended.
[21] *Hirst and Agu v Chief Constable of West Yorkshire* [1987] Crim. L.R. 726.
[22] *Nagy v Weston* [1965] 1 All E.R. 78.
[23] *Homer v Cadman* (1886) 50 J.P. 454 (lecturer standing on chair addressing attracted crowd was rightly convicted even where there was room for a vehicle to pass round the crowd).
[24] *Waite v Taylor* (1985) 149 J.P. 551.
[25] *Redbridge London Borough v Jacques* [1971] 1 All E.R. 260.
[26] *Birch v DPP* [2000] Crim. L.R. 301.
[27] *Back v Holmes* (1887) 57 L.J.M.C. 37 (singing); *Fabbri v Morris* [1947] 1 All E.R. 315 (queue of customers).

roadway and amounted to an obstruction.[28] Accordingly, stopping or waiting on the highway to take a photograph or for the opportunity to take a photograph may very well amount to an obstruction.

### Obstruction: police constables

6–155    Section 89(2) of the Police Act 1996 provides:

> "Any person who resists or wilfully obstructs a constable in the execution of his duty or a person assisting a constable[29] in the execution of his duty shall be guilty of an offence and liable on summary conviction to imprisonment for a term not exceeding six months or to a fine not exceeding level 5[30] on the standard scale or to both."

A person wilfully obstructs a police constable in the execution of his duty where he does something which prevents or makes it more difficult for the police to carry out their duties and where the defendant intended his conduct to have that effect.[31] It is not necessary for the defendant's actions to be aimed at or hostile to the police constable.[32] It is immaterial that the defendant does not appreciate that his action amounted to an obstruction.[33] However, where the defendant reasonably believes a person is not a police officer he cannot be guilty of obstructing him in the course of his duty.[34] The police officer must be acting in the execution of his duty at the material time of the alleged obstruction in order to give rise to the offence.[35]

Refusal to move upon request by a police office may amount to an obstruction.[36] It is in this regard that photographers are most at risk of arrest for obstructing a police constable in the execution of his duty.

6–156    If none of the general arrest conditions under s.25 of the Police and Criminal Evidence Act 1984 apply, there is no specific statutory power of arrest for the offence of obstructing a police constable in the course of his duty. There is a common law power to arrest where the nature of the obstruction was such that it caused or was likely to cause a breach of the

---

[28] *Cooper v Metropolitan Police Comr* (1985) 82 Cr. App. Rep. 238.
[29] Includes a person who is a member of an international joint investigation team that is led by a member of a police force or by a member of the National Criminal Intelligence Service or of the National Crime Squad: s.89(4) and (5) inserted by the Police Reform Act 2002, s.104(1).
[30] At the time of writing, a level 5 fine is £5,000: Criminal Justice Act 1982, s.37 as amended.
[31] *Lewis v Cox* [1985] Q.B. 509 at 515–17.
[32] *ibid.*
[33] *Moore v Green* [1983] 1 All E.R. 663 at 666f.
[34] *Ostler v Elliot* [1980] Crim. L.R. 584.
[35] *Chapman v DPP* (1989) Cr. App. R. 190; *Riley v DPP* (1989) 91 Cr. App. R. 14; *Kerr v DPP* [1995] Crim. L.R. 394.
[36] *Despard v Wilcox* (1910) 74 J.P. 115 (group known as "Women's Freedom League waiting outside Prime Minister's residence in Downing Street for two days, arrested after refusing to leave); *Pankhurst v Jarvis* (1910) 74 J.P. 64 (referred to in *Despard v Wilcox*, but *quaere* citation); *Piddington v Bates* [1960] 3 All E.R. 660 (pickets refusing to move where police officer limiting number of pickets in order to prevent an anticipated breach of the peace).

peace or was calculated to prevent the lawful arrest or detention of another.[37]

## Obstruction: miscellaneous

### Town Police Clauses Act 1847

The Town Police Clauses Act 1847[38] grants local authorities power to make orders to prevent obstructions in the street during public processions or in any case where the streets are "thronged" or liable to be obstructed.[39] The power is confined to particular and extraordinary occassions and does not cover the circumstances of ordinary day to day traffic conditions, nor does it enable an order for a continuous period to be made.[40]    **6–157**

It applies throughout England and Wales, except in Greater London.[41] Every wilful breach of such an order is an offence and the offender liable to a penalty not exceeding level 3 on the standard scale.[42] In order to establish an offence, it is not necessary to allege or prove that any particular person was in fact obstructed.[43]    **6–158**

The Act also creates, under s.28, a vast array of offences to the "obstruction, annoyance or danger of the residents or passengers."[44] Many of these offences are of little relevance to either photography or modern society.[45] However, it does create an offence of, by any means, wilfully interrupting any public crossing, or wilfully causing any obstruction in any public footpath or public thoroughfare.[46] Stopping to talk unless done wilfully and pertinaciously in not an offence of obstruction.[47] The obstruction does need to be intentional[48] but a belief that the obstruction is lawful is not a defence.[49]

An person convicted is liable to a penalty not exceeding level 3[50] on the standard scale or 14 days' imprisonment.[51] It is not necessary to prove that    **6–159**

---

[37] *Wershof v Metropolitan Police Comr* [1978] 3 All E.R. 540; *R. v Redman* [1994] Crim. L.R. 914.
[38] 10 & 11 Vict. c.89.
[39] Town Police Clauses Act 1847, s.21.
[40] *Brownsea Haven Properties Ltd v Poole Corporation* [1958] 1 Ch. 574 at 597.
[41] Public Health Act 1875, s.171; Local Government Act 1972, Sch.14, paras 23 and 26.
[42] Town Police Clauses Act 1847, s.21. At the time of writing, a level 3 fine is £1,000: Criminal Justice Act 1982, s.37 as amended.
[43] *Wolverton UDC v Willis* [1962] 1 All E.R. 243 at 246F.
[44] Town Police Clauses Act 1847, s.28.
[45] *e.g.* keeping a pigstye to the front of a street; slaughtering or dressing cattle, causing any beast of burden to stand longer than is necessary for loading; making use of a slide upon ice or snow: s.28.
[46] Town Police Clauses Act 1847, s.28, unnumberd sub-para.6. See also sub-para.4.
[47] *Wemyss v Black* 1881, 8 R. (Ct. of Sess.) 25.
[48] *Eaton v Cobb* [1950] 1 All E.R. 1016.
[49] *Arrowsmith v Jenkins* [1963] 2 Q.B. 561 at 567 ("wilfully obstructs" under Highways Act 1959).
[50] At the time of writing, £1,000: Criminal Justice Act 1982, s.37(2) as amended.
[51] Town Police Clauses Act 1847, s.28.

specific individuals were actually annoyed or obstructed.[52] A police officer who goes to a public place to perform a specific duty is not a passenger.[53]

## Metropolitan Police Act 1839

**6–160**   The Metropolitan Police Act 1839, s.54 applies only to the Metropolitan Police District[54] and creates similar offences to those in the Town Police Clauses Act 1874. It creates an offence of wilfully causing any obstruction in any thoroughfare.[55] Unlike the Town Police Clauses Act 1874 there is no requirement that the offence be committed to "the obstruction, annoyance or danger of residents or passengers". The offence is triable summarily only and subject to a maximum fine not exceeding level 2 on the standard scale.[56] If there is obstruction, it is irrelevant that no one was inconvenienced.[57]

## MISCELLANEOUS RESTRICTIONS

### Wildlife photography

**6–161**   The Wildlife & Countryside Act 1981 makes it an offence to disturb certain species of wild animals and birds. "Disturbing" is not defined by the Act, but this would certainly cover disturbing such species whilst photographing or attempting to photograph them. Broadly speaking, photography of these species is permitted whilst they are away from their nest or place of shelter. In order to photograph protected wild animals and birds in or near their nests or places of shelter it is necessary to apply for a licence from the relevant authority.[58]

**6–162**   Photographers wishing to photograph wild animals or birds would be well advised to obtain copies of the following leaflets (1) *The Nature Photographers' Code of Practice* which is produced by the Nature Group of the Royal Photographic Society and is also available from English Nature, and (2) *Bird Photography and the Law* produced by the RSPB.

## Wild birds and their nests

**6–163**   It is an offence to intentionally—

(a) kill, injure or take any [specified] wild bird;

(b) take, damage or destroy the nest of any wild bird while that nest is in use or being built; or

---

[52] *Wooley v Corbishley* (1860) 24 J.P. 773; *Read v Perrett* (1876) 1 Ex. D. 349; *Hinde v Evans* (1906) 96 L.T. 20; *Lees v Stone* (1919) 88 L.J.K.B. 1159.
[53] *Cheeseman v DPP* [1991] Crim. L.R. 297, 93 Cr. App. R. 145.
[54] Greater London (excluding the City of London, the Inner Temple and the Middle Temple): London Government Act 1963, s.76.
[55] Metropolitan Police Act, 1839, s.54(6).
[56] At the time of writing, a level 2 fine is £500: Criminal Justice Act 1982, s.37 as amended.
[57] *Read v Perrett* (1876) 1 Ex. D. 249.
[58] See below at para.6–169.

(c) take or destroy an egg of any wild bird.[59]

A person is also guilty of an offence if he intentionally or recklessly—

(a) disturbs any [specified] wild bird while it is building a nest or is in, on or near a nest containing eggs or young; or

(b) disturbs dependent young of such a bird.[60]

A "wild bird" does not include any bird which is shown to have been bred in captivity.[61] Both offences require intention, or in the case of disturbing birds, recklessness.[62]

A person found guilty of any of these offences is liable on summary conviction to a term of imprisonment not exceeding six months or a fine not exceeding level 5[63] on the standard scale, or to both.[64] Where an offence was committed in respect of more than one bird, nest or egg the maximum fine shall be determined as if the person had been convicted of a separate offence in respect of each bird, nest or egg.[65]

## Areas of special protection

The Secretary of State has power to make an order defining an area of special protection.[66] He also has power to order that within any such area, any person who disturbs a wild bird whilst building a nest or is in, on or near a nest containing eggs or young or disturbs the dependent young of such bird is guilty of an offence.[67]

**6–164**

## Protected birds

The vast majority of wild birds are protected. Common species that are not protected from disturbance include poultry,[68] blackbirds, jackdaws, jays and woodpigeons.[69]

The following are birds that are protected under the Wildlife and Countryside Act 1981 and may not be disturbed (and hence photographed) at or near their nest without a licence.[70] The Act states that the common

**6–165**

---

[59] Wildlife and Countryside Act 1981, s.1(1).

[60] Wildlife and Countryside Act 1981, s.1(5).

[61] Wildlife and Countryside Act 1981, s.1(6).

[62] Unlike Wildlife and Countryside Act 1981, s.1(2) (possession of live or dead birds) which is a strict liability offence requiring no *mens rea*: *Kirkland v Robinson* 151 J.P. 377 (QBD, December 2, 1986).

[63] At the time of writing, £5,000: Criminal Justice Act 1982, s.37.

[64] Wildlife and Countryside Act 1981, s.21(1) as amended by Countryside and Rights of Way Act 2000, s.81, Sch.12, para.10 other than in relation to any offence committed before January 30, 2001.

[65] Wildlife and Countryside Act 1981, s.21(5) as amended by Countryside and Rights of Way Act 2000, s.81, Sch.12, para.10.

[66] Wildlife and Countryside Act 1981, s.3.

[67] Wildlife and Countryside Act 1981, s.3(1)(a)(iv) and (v).

[68] Wildlife and Countryside Act 1981, s.27(1) definition of "wild bird".

[69] Wildlife and Countryside Act 1981, Sch.3 Pt.2, may be sold dead.

[70] Wildlife and Countryside Act 1981, Sch.1. See above at para.6–161

names of birds given in Schedule 1 are included for guidance only and in the event of any dispute or proceedings, the common name or names shall not be taken into account.

| Common name | Scientific name |
| --- | --- |
| Avocet | Recurvirostra avosetta |
| Bee-eater | Merops Alister |
| Bittern | Botaurus stellaris |
| Bittern, Little | Ixobrychus minutus |
| Bluethroat | Luscinia svecica |
| Brambling | Fringilla montifringilla |
| Bunting, Girl | Emberiza circus |
| Bunting, Lapland | Calvaries lapponicus |
| Bunting, Snow | Plectrophenax nivalis |
| Buzzard, Honey | Pernis apivorus |
| Chough | Pyrrhocorax pyrrhocorax |
| Corncrake | crex |
| Crake, Spotted | porzana |
| Crossbills (all species) | Loxia |
| Curlew, Stone | Burhinus oedicnemus |
| Divers (all species) | Gavia |
| Dotterel | Charadrius morinellus |
| Duck, Long-tailed | Clangula hyemalis |
| Eagle, Golden | Aquila chrysaetos |
| Eagle, White-tailed | Haliaetus albicilla |
| Falcon, Gar | Falco rusticolus |
| Fieldfare | Turdus pilaris |
| Firecrest | Regulus ignicapillus |
| Garganey | Anas querquedula |
| Godwit, Black-tailed | Limosa |
| Goshawk | Accipiter gentilis |
| Grebe, Black-necked | Podiceps nigricollis |
| Grebe, Slovenian | Podiceps auratus |
| Greenshank | Tringa nebularia |
| Gull, Little | Larus minutus |
| Gull, Mediterranean | Larus melano cephalus |
| Harriers (all species) | Circus |
| Heron, Purple | Ardea purpurea |
| Hobby | Falco subbuteo |
| Hoopoe | Upupa epops |
| Kingfisher | Alcedo atthis |
| Kite, Red | Milvus |
| Merlin | Falco columbarius |
| Oriole, Golden | oriolus |
| Osprey | Pandion haliaetus |
| Owl, Barn | Tyto alba |
| Owl, Snowy | Necktie scandiaca |

| | |
|---|---|
| Peregrine | Falco peregrinus |
| Petrel, Leach's | Oceanodroma leucorhoa |
| Phalarope, Red-necked | Phalaropus lobatus |
| Plover, Kentish | Charadrius alexandrinus |
| Plover, Little Ringed | Charadrius dubius |
| Quail, Common | Coturnix coturnix |
| Redstart, Black | Phoenicurus ochruros |
| Redwing | Turdus iliacus |
| Rosefinch, Scarlet | Carpodacus erythrinus |
| Ruff | Philomachus pugnax |
| Sandpiper, Green | Tringa ochropus |
| Sandpiper, Purple | Calidris maritima |
| Sandpiper, Wood | Tringa Glareola |
| Scaup | Aythya marila |
| Scoter, Common | Melanitta nigra |
| Scoter, Velvet | Melanitta fusca |
| Seri | Serinus |
| Shoreward | Eremophila Aletris |
| Shrike, Red-backed | Lanius collaris |
| Spoonbill | Platalea leucorodia |
| Stilt, Black-winged | Himantopus Himantopus |
| Stint, Temmincki's | Calidris temminckii |
| Swan, Bewick's | Cygnus bewickii |
| Swan, Whooper | Cygnus cygnus |
| Tern, Black | Chlidonias niger |
| Tern, Little | Sterna albifrons |
| Tern, Roseate | Sterna dougallii |
| Tit, Bearded | Panurus biarmicus |
| Tit, Crested | Parus cristatus |
| Treecreeper, Short-toed | Certhia brachydactyla |
| Warbler, Cetti's | Cettia cetti |
| Warbler, Dartford | Sylvia undata |
| Warbler, Marsh | Acrocephalus palustris |
| Warbler, Savi's | Locustella luscinioides |
| Whimbrel | Numenius phaeopus |
| Woodlark | Lullula arborea |
| Wryneck | Jynx torquilla |

The following birds are protected during the close season[71] for the respective bird:

---

[71] The "close season" is different for some species and the Secretary of State has power to make orders varying close seasons for any wild bird: Wildlife and Countryside Act 1981, s.2. Where the close season is not specified, it is the period in the year commencing with February 1, and ending with August 31: s.2(4)(d).

| Common name | Scientific name |
|---|---|
| Goldeneye | Bucephala clangula |
| Goose, Greylag (in Outer, Hebrides, Caithness, Sutherland and Wester Ross only) | Anser anser |
| Pintail | Anas acuta |

*Wild animals*

**6–166**     Similar provisions exist in respect of specified wild animals. Thus, is it is an offence to intentionally kill, injure or take any wild animal.[72] It is also an offence to intentionally or recklessly:

(a) damage or destroy, or obstruct access to, any structure or place which any [specified] wild animal uses for shelter or protection; or

(b) disturb any such animal while it is occupying a structure or place which it uses for that purpose.[73]

**6–167**     In addition, it is an offence to intentionally or recklessly disturb at any time or place a dolphin or whale or a basking shark.[74] In any proceedings for disturbing a wild animal, there is a statutory presumption that the animal was a wild animal unless the contrary is shown.[75] Disturbing or trapping a protected animal for the purposes of photography is thus an offence under the Act as the purpose is immaterial.

A person found guilty of any of these offences is liable on summary conviction to a term of imprisonment not exceeding six months or a fine not exceeding level 5[76] on the standard scale, or to both.[77] Where an offence was committed in respect of more than one animal, the maximum fine shall be determined as if the person had been convicted of a separate offence in respect of each animal.[78]

*Protected animals*

**6–168**     Below is set out a list[79] of the animals that are protected under the Wildlife and Countryside Act 1981. The Act states that the common names of animals given in Schedule 1 are included for guidance only and in the event of

---

[72] Wildlife and Countryside Act 1981, s.9(1).
[73] Wildlife and Countryside Act 1981, s.9(4).
[74] Wildlife and Countryside Act 1981, s.9(4A) as inserted by Countryside and Rights of Way Act 2000, s.81(1) and Sch.12 para.5(b) other than in relation to any offence committed before January 30, 2001.
[75] Wildlife and Countryside Act 1981, s.9(5).
[76] At the time of writing, £5,000: Criminal Justice Act 1982, s.37.
[77] Wildlife and Countryside Act 1981, s.21(1) as amended by Countryside and Rights of Way Act 2000, s.81 and Sch.12, para.10 other than in relation to any offence committed before January 30, 2001.
[78] Wildlife and Countryside Act 1981, s.21(5) as amended by Countryside and Rights of Way Act 2000, s.81 and Sch.12, para.10.
[79] Wildlife and Countryside Act 1981, Sch.5.

any dispute or proceedings, the common name or names shall not be taken into account.[80]

Some animals are only protected for the purposes of killing or injuring (s.9(1)) or selling or offering for sale whether alive or dead (s.9(5)). It is s.9(4) which is of most relevance to photography as subsection (a) provides that it is an offence to intentionally or recklessly destroy or obstruct access to any structure or place that any specified wild animal uses for shelter and protection. Section 9(4)(b) provides that an animal may not be disturbed whilst occupying any structure or place it uses for shelter or protection. This prohibits all disturbance, including that caused by photographing the animal. For the sake of completeness, the entire Schedule 5 list of protected animals is set out below even where the protection only extends to killing or injuring rather than disturbing.

| Common name | Scientific name |
| --- | --- |
| Adder (in respect of s.9(1) (in part), 9(5) only) | Vipera berus |
| Allis shad (in respect of s.9(1) and (4)(a) only) | Alosa alosa |
| Atlantic Stream Crayfish (in respect of s.9(1) (so far as it relates to taking), 9(5), only) | Austropotomobius pallipes |
| Anemone, Ivell's Sea | Edwardsia ivelli |
| Anemone, Startlet Sea | Nematosella vectensis |
| Apus | Triops cancriformis |
| Bats, Horseshoe (all species) | Rhinolophidae |
| Bats, Typical (all species) | Vespertilionidae |
| Beetle | Graphoderus zonatus |
| Beetle | Hypebaeus flavipes |
| Beetle | Paracymus aeneus |
| Beetle, Lesser Silver Water | Hydrochara caraboides |
| Beetle, Mire Pill (in respect of s.9(4)(a) only) | Curimopsis nigrita |
| Beetle, Rainbow Leaf | Chrysolina cerealis |
| Beetle, Stag (in respect of s.9(5) only) | Lucanus cervus |
| Beetle, Violet Click | Limoniscus violaceus |
| Burbot | Lota Lota |
| Butterfly, Heath Fritillary | Mellicta athalia (otherwise known as Melitaea athalia) |
| Butterfly, Large Blue | Maculinea arion |
| Butterfly, Swallowtail | Papilio machaon |
| Butterfly, Northern Brown Argus (in respect of s.9(5) only) | Aricia artaxerxes |
| Butterfly, Adonis Blue (in respect of s.9(5) only) | Lysandra bellargus |

---

[80] Wildlife and Countryside Act 1981, Sch.5, Note.

| | |
|---|---|
| Butterfly, Chalkhill Blue (in respect of s.9(5) only) | Lysandra coridon |
| Butterfly, Silver-studded Blue (in respect of s.9(5) only) | Plebejus argus |
| Butterfly, Small Blue (in respect of s.9(5) only) | Cupido minimus |
| Butterfly, Large Copper | Lycaena dispar |
| Butterfly, Purple Emperor (in respect of s.9(5) only) | Apatura iris |
| Butterfly, Duke of Burgundy (in respect of s.9(5) only) | Hamearis lucina |
| Butterfly, Glanville Fritillary (in respect of s.9(5) only) | Melitaea cinxia |
| Butterfly, High Brown Fritillary (in respect of s.9(5)only) | Argynnis adippe |
| Butterfly, Marsh Fritillary | Eurodryas aurinia |
| Butterfly, Pearl-bordered Fritillary (in respect of s.9(5) only) | Boloria euphrosyne |
| Butterfly, Black Hairstreak (in respect of s.9(5) only) | Strymonidia pruni |
| Butterfly, Brown Hairstreak (in respect of s.9(5) only) | Thecla betulae |
| Butterfly, White Letter Hairstreak (in respect of s.9(5) only) | Stymonida w-album |
| Butterfly, Large Heath (in respect of s.9(5) only) | Coenonympha tullia |
| Butterfly, Mountain Ringlet (in respect of s.9(5) only) | Erebia epiphron |
| Butterfly, Chequered Skipper (in respect of s.9(5) only) | Carterocephalus palaemon |
| Butterfly, Lulworth Skipper (in respect of s.9(5) only) | Thymelicus acteon |
| Butterfly, Silver Spotted Skipper (in respect of s.9(5) only) | Hesperia comma |
| Butterfly, Large Tortoiseshell (in respect of s.9(5) only) | Nymphalis polychloros |
| Butterfly, Wood White (in respect of s.9(5) only) | Leptidea sinapis |
| Cat, Wild | Felis silvestris |
| Cicada, New Forest | Cicadetta montana |
| Cricket, Field | Gryllus campestris |
| Cricket, Mole | Gryllotalpa gryllotalpa |
| Damselfly, Southern | Coenagrion mercuriale |
| Dolphin, Bottle-nosed | Tursiops truncatus (otherwise known as Tursiops tursio) |
| Dolphin, Common | Delphinus delphis |
| Dolphins (all species) | Cetacea |

| | |
|---|---|
| Dormouse | Muscardinus avellanarius |
| Dragonfly, Norfolk Aeshna | Aeshna isosceles |
| Frog, Common (in respect of s.9(5) only) | Rana temporaria |
| Goby, Couch's | Gobius couchii |
| Goby, Giant | Gobius cobitis |
| Grasshopper, Wart-biter | Decticus verrucivorus |
| Hatchet Shell, Northern | Thyasira gouldi |
| Hydroid, Marine | Clavopsella navis |
| Lagoon Snail | Paludinella littorina |
| Lagoon Snail, De Folin's | Caecum armoricum |
| Lagoon Worm, Tentacled | Alkmaria romijni |
| Leech, Medicinal | Hirudo medicinalis |
| Lizard, Sand | Lacerta agilis |
| Lizard, Viviparous | Lacerta vivipara |
| (in respect of s.9(1) (so far as it relates to killing and injuring), 9(5) only) | |
| Marten, Pine | Martes martes |
| Mat, Trembling Sea | Victorella pavida |
| Moth, Barberry Carpet | Pareulype berberata |
| Moth, Black-veined | Siona lineata (otherwise known as Idaea lineata) |
| Moth, Essex Emerald | Thetidia smaragdaria |
| Moth, Fiery Clearwing | Bembecia chrysidiformis |
| Moth, Fisher's Estuarine | Gortyna borelii |
| Moth, New Forest Burnet | Zygaena viciae |
| Moth, Reddish Buff | Acosmetia caliginosa |
| Moth, Sussex Emerald | Thalera fimbrialis |
| Mussel, Fan (in respect of s.9(1), (2) and (5) only) | Atrina fragilis |
| Mussel, Freshwater Pearl | Margaritifera margaritifera |
| Newt, Great Crested (otherwise known as Warty newt) | Triturus cristatus |
| Newt, Palmate (in respect of s.9(5) only) | Triturus helveticus |
| Newt, Smooth (in respect of s.9(5) only) | Triturus vulgaris |
| Otter, Common | Lutra lutra |
| Porpoises (all species) | Phocaena phocaena |
| Sandworm, Lagoon | Armandia cirrhosa |
| Sea Fan, Pink (in respect of s.9(1), 9(2) and 9(5)only) | Eunicella verrucosa |
| Sea Slug, Lagoon | Tenellia adspersa |
| Shad, Twaite (in respect of s.9(4)(a) only) | Alosa fallax |
| Shark, Basking | Cetorhinus maximus |
| Shrimp, Fairy | Chiroephalus diaphanus |
| Shrimp, Lagoon Sand | Gammarus insensibilis |
| Slow-worm | Anguis fragilis |
| (in respect of s.9(1) (so far as it relates to killing and injuring), 9(5) only) | |
| Snail, Glutinous | Myxas glutinosa |

| | |
|---|---|
| Snail, Sandbowl | Catinella arenaria |
| Snake, Grass | Natrix helvetica |
| (in respect of s.9(1) (so far as it relates to killing and injuring), 9(5) only) | |
| Snake, Smooth | Coronella austriaca |
| Spider, Fen Raft | Dolomedes plantarius |
| Spider, Ladybird | Eresus niger |
| Squirrel, Red | Sciurus vulgaris |
| Sturgeon | Acipenser sturio |
| Toad, Common (in respect of s.9(5) only) | Bufo bufo |
| Toad, Natterjack | Bufo calamita |
| Turtles, Marine (all species) | Dermochelyidae and Cheloniidae |
| | |
| Vendace | Coregonus albula |
| Vole, Water (in respect of s.9(4) only) | Arvicola terrestris |
| Walrus | Odobenus rosmarus |
| Whale (all species) | Cetacea |
| Whitefish | Coregonus lavaretus |

*Licences*

**6–169**   In order to photograph protected wild animals and birds in or near their nests or places of shelter it is necessary to apply for a licence from the relevant authority.

The relevant authorities are:

English Nature,
Northminster House
Peterborough,
PE1 1UA
Telephone: 01733 455 000

Countryside Council for Wales,
Maes-y-ffynnon
Penrhosgarnedd
Bangor
Gwynedd
LL57 2DW
Telephone: 01248 385 500

Scottish Natural Heritage
Research and Advisory Service
Bonnington Bond
2/5 Anderson Place
Edinburgh
EH6 5NP
Telephone: 0131 554 9797

A licence may be granted for the purpose of photography of both pro-  **6–170**
tected birds and animals.[81] Pursuant to statute, the authority shall not grant
a licence with respect to protected birds unless it is satisfied that there is no
other satisfactory solution.[82] The authority will only grant a licence for bird
photography on a selective basis and in respect of a small number of birds.[83]
Any licence granted may be general or specific or subject to conditions and
can be modified or revoked at any time.[84] A licence in respect of wild bird
photography will specify the species of wild bird and the conditions subject
to which action may be taken and the methods, means or arrangements
which are authorised for the taking of photographs.[85]

## City of London: street trading

Under the City of London (Various Powers) Act 1987, the Corporation of  **6–171**
the City of London has the power to designate areas in or near Middlesex
Street in the City within which photographing by way of business without
the consent of the Corporation is an offence.[86]
Designation of an area does not prohibit the taking of photographs for
publication in newspapers or periodicals if the photographer is employed by
the publisher or is employed in a business which includes selling or supplying photographs for newspaper/periodical publication.[87] It also does not
prohibit taking of photographs on land by the owner or occupier of land or
with the consent of the owner or occupier.[88] Nor does it prohibit the doing
of anything on land forming part of the highway by the owner or occupier
of land fronting that part.[89]
The parts of the City which are capable of designation are places within  **6–172**
that part of Middlesex Street which lies within the City (or within 45 metres
of that part of Middlesex Street) and are:

(a) a public off-street car park, garden or other park or open space under
the management and control of the Corporation of London;

(b) a street, parade or way to which the public commonly have access,
whether or not as of right; and

(c) a road or any unenclosed land adjacent to, and within 15 metres of,
any road.[90]

[81] Wildlife and Countryside Act 1981, s.16(1)(h) (birds) and s.16(3)(e) (wild animals).
[82] Wildlife and Countryside Act 1981, s.16(1A), (a).
[83] Wildlife and Countryside Act 1981, s.16(1A), (b).
[84] Wildlife and Countryside Act 1981, s.16(5).
[85] Wildlife and Countryside Act 1981, s.16(6).
[86] City of London (Various Powers) Act 1987, s.26.
[87] City of London (Various Powers) Act 1987, s.26(9)(b).
[88] City of London (Various Powers) Act 1987, s.26(9)(a).
[89] City of London (Various Powers) Act 1987, s.29(9)(a).
[90] City of London (Various Powers) Act 1987, s.26(1).

Before designating a place, the Corporation must give notice of their proposal by advertisement in a newspaper circulating in the City, and by posting it in the place to which it relates stating that objections may be made to the proper officer of the Corporation within a period not less than 28 days after the notice was given.[91] After considering any objections and consulting with the Commissioner of Police, the Corporation may designate the place specified notice as a place to which s.26 of the City of London (Various Powers) Act 1987 applies.[92]

**6–173**     Any person who in a designated place without the written consent of the Corporation, or in breach of any condition subject to which the Corporation's consent is given, photographs, or purports to photograph, any person by way of trade or business is guilty of an offence and liable on summary conviction to a fine not exceeding level 3 on the standard scale.[93]

**6–174**     It is a defence for the person charged to prove that he took all reasonable precautions and exercised all due diligence to avoid the commission of the offence.[94] In order to rely on a defence that the commission of the offence was due to the act or default of another person, it is necessary to serve notice on the prosecution seven clear days before the hearing identifying or assisting in the identification of that other person.[95] In the absence of such a notice, the defendant is not entitled to rely on that defence without the leave of the court.[96]

Where the Corporation refuse consent to photograph or to renew consent or revoke consent, a person aggrieved may appeal to a magistrates' court.[97] It is also possible to appeal about the conditions subject to which the Corporation give such consent.[98]

### Trafalgar Square and Parliament Square

**6–175**     On October 1, 2000, the Greater London Authority (GLA) took over the care, control, management and regulation of Trafalgar Square and Parliament Square from the Secretary of State for the Department of Media, Culture and Sport.[99] The powers of the Secretary of State under s.2 of the Trafalgar Square Act 1844 were transferred to the GLA.[1]

From May 8, 2000, the GLA had power to make byelaws for preserving order in, prevention of abuses in, and securing the proper management of

[91] City of London (Various Powers) Act 1987, s.26(7)(a).
[92] City of London (Various Powers) Act 1987, s.26(7)(b).
[93] City of London (Various Powers) Act 1987, s.26(2). Level 3 on the standard scale is currently £1,000: Criminal Justice Act 1982, s.37.
[94] City of London (Various Powers) Act 1987, s.26(3)(a).
[95] City of London (Various Powers) Act 1987, s.26(3)(b).
[96] City of London (Various Powers) Act 1987, s.26(3)(b).
[97] City of London (Various Powers) Act 1987, s.26(6).
[98] City of London (Various Powers) Act 1987, s.26(6)(a)(iv).
[99] Greater London Authority Act 1999, ss.383 and 384, brought into force on October 1, 2000, by Greater London Authority Act 1999 (Commencement No.4 and Adaptation) Order 2000 (SI 2000/801). And see Royal Parks and Other Open Spaces Regulations 1997 (SI 1997/1639).
[1] Greater London Authority Act 1999, s.383(1).

the Squares.[2] The GLA also has power to make byelaws for the licensing of any trading and the seizure, retention or disposal or any property in connection with any contravention of or failure to comply with a trading byelaw.[3]

Trafalgar Square and Parliament Square Garden are currently regulated **6–176** by the Trafalgar Square and Parliament Square Byelaws 2000[4] which provide that unless acting in accordance with written permission of the Mayor or a person authorised by the Mayor under s.380 of the Greater London Authority Act, no person shall within either square (*inter alia*):

> "use any apparatus for the transmission, reception, reproduction or amplification of sound, speech or images, except apparatus designed and used as an aid to defective hearing, or apparatus used in a vehicle so as not to produce sound audible to a person outside that vehicle, or apparatus where the sound is received through headphones[5]
>
> take photographs or any other recordings of visual images for the purpose of or in connection with a business, trade, profession or employment or any activity carried on by a person or body of persons, whether corporate or unincorporate"[6]

People wishing to take photographs in either Square for the purpose of or **6–177** in connection with business, etc. need to apply for permission from the GLA by submitting a proposal form.[7] At the time of writing the fee for such use of Trafalgar Square was £420 per hour and anyone using Trafalgar Square must obtain public liability insurance with a minimum of £5 million cover for each act or occurrence or series of acts or occurrences.

Contravention of such byelaws is an offence and if the byelaw is a trading byelaw, punishable on summary conviction to a fine not exceeding level 3 on the standard scale.[8] In any other case, the offender is liable on summary conviction to a fine not exceeding level 1 on the standard scale.[9]

## Royal parks and other specified gardens

The Royal Parks Agency has responsibility for the eight Royal Parks **6–178** comprising Hyde Park, Kensington Gardens, Green Park, St. James's Park, Regent's Park, Bushy Park, Richmond Park and Greenwich Park. The

---

[2] Greater London Authority Act 1999, s.385(1) brought into force on May, 8 2000, by *Greater London Authority Act 1999 (Commencement No.4 and Adaptation) Order 2000* (SI 2000/801).
[3] Greater London Authority Act 1999, s.385(4).
[4] As amended by *Trafalgar Square and Parliament Square (Amendment No.1) Byelaws 2002*.
[5] *Trafalgar Square and Parliament Square Byelaws 2000, Byelaw 5(5)*.
[6] *ibid.* Byelaw 5(11).
[7] For further details as to the procedure: *http://www.london.gov.uk/mayor/trafalgar_square/guidelines_filming.jsp*.
[8] Greater London Authority Act 1999, s.385(3)(a). At the time of writing, level 3 on the standard scale is £1,000: Criminal Justice Act 1982, s.37.
[9] Greater London Authority Act 1999, s.385(3)(b). At the time of writing, level 1 on the standard scale is £500: Criminal Justice Act 1982, s.37.

Royal Parks Agency is a non-departmental public body for which the Department for Culture, Media and Sport is responsible. The Agency performs the Secretary of State's duty of care for the Royal Parks. In addition, the Agency has responsibility for other areas including Primrose Hill, Brompton Cemetery, Victoria Tower Gardens and Poet's Green.

By the Royal Parks and Other Open Spaces Regulations 1997[10] unless the Secretary of State's written permission has first been obtained, no person using one of the Royal Parks (or other areas specified in the Regulations[11]) shall:

"use any apparatus for the transmission, reception, reproduction or amplification of sound, speech or images, except apparatus designed and used as an aid to defective hearing, or apparatus used in a vehicle so as not to produce sound audible to a person outside that vehicle, or apparatus used where the sound is received through headphones[12]

take photographs of still or moving subjects for the purpose of or in connection with a business, trade, profession or employment or any activity carried on by a body of persons whether corporate or unincorporate".[13]

**6–179**    Those wishing to film or photograph commercially within the Royal Parks should contact the Royal Parks Agency in advance to obtain permission.[14] A fee is usually charged.

In addition to the above Regulations, many other public parks and gardens prohibit commercial photography or filming without payment being made.[15] It is prudent to check with the relevant park authorities in advance.

## Bank notes

**6–180**    In addition to the law of copyright, production of any photographs of British currency notes is specifically prohibited by statute unless permission has first been obtained from the Bank of England. This is by virtue of s.18(1) of the Forgery and Counterfeiting Act 1981 which makes it a criminal

---

[10] SI 1997/1639.

[11] Areas specified in Sch.1 to the Regulations which in addition to the Royal Parks include the following areas: Abingdon Street Garden including the lawn surrounding the King George V Memorial; Brompton Cemetery; the Longford River and those parts of its banks which are for the time being under the control or management of the Secretary of State; Grosvenor Square Garden; Hampton Court Gardens; Hampton Court Green; Hampton Court Park; the Natural History Museum Gardens; Parliament Square Gardens; Primrose Hill; Tower Gardens; Trafalgar Square, being that part of Trafalgar Square in the City of Westminster which is for the time being under the control or management of the Secretary of State; Victoria Tower Gardens.

[12] reg.4(10).

[13] reg.4(18).

[14] For contact details see Royal Parks Agency website at *http://www.royalparks.gov.uk/*.

[15] *e.g.* Parks and gardens (excluding Royal Parks) within the City of Westminster. Scale of fees negotiable. As at August 2003, the guideline fee stated for commercial photography was £155 per hour. See further: *http://www.westminster.gov.uk/environment/parksgardens/Holding-Events-in-Parks.cfm.*

offence for "any person, unless the relevant authority has previously consented in writing, to reproduce on any substance whatsoever, and whether or not on the correct scale, any British currency note or any part of a British currency note."

The Bank of England has an application form for those who wish to apply to reproduce images of Bank of England bank notes which is available on its website.[16] In Scotland, notes are issued by three banks, namely Bank of Scotland, the Royal Bank of Scotland, and Clydesdale Bank.[17] There are four note issuing banks in Northern Ireland: the Bank of Ireland, the Ulster Bank, Northern Bank, and First Trust Bank. Similar provisions apply to currency in the Republic of Ireland.[18]

---

[16] *http://www.bankofengland.co.uk/* under "Banknotes and Banking".
[17] *http://www.scotbanks.org.uk/*.
[18] For further information as to how to apply for permission see the website of the Central Bank of Ireland at *http://www.centralbank.ie/notesandcoins1.asp*.

# Chapter 7

# Images of people

## SCOPE OF THE CHAPTER

**7–001**   This chapter concerns rights and liabilities arising in connection with photographs of people. It is intended to provide an outline of relevant areas of law and to address in more detail specific problems raised by photographs. In addition, although not strictly falling within the title topic, this chapter is a convenient place for consideration of photographs of property which raises similar issues of confidentiality and privacy.

For detailed consideration of the law of privacy beyond the confines of photography, the reader is referred to *The Law of Privacy & the Media*.[1] For the law of defamation see *Gatley on Libel and Slander*.[2]

## PHOTOGRAPHS, PRIVACY AND CONFIDENTIALITY: GENERAL

**7–002**   Photographic images raise particularly difficult questions for the law of confidentiality and privacy. The popular language of photography suggests

---

[1] M. Tugendhat Q.C. and I. Christie (eds) (Oxford University Press, 2002).
[2] (10th ed., Sweet & Maxwell, 2003).

invasive activity in itself—a photograph is said to be "taken". The associated language is also aggressive—for example "snap", "shoot", and "capture on film". It is said that there are primitive tribes who fear the taking of a photograph from a belief that it captures a part of the soul. The law of copyright gives the photographer a property right in the image he creates. But there is a tension between the fact that a complete stranger can derive profit from an image of a person taken without their consent and the personal autonomy and rights of the subject.

The problem is perhaps encapsulated by the fact that a photograph creates a permanent record of something that might otherwise be forgotten. A person who falls over or otherwise embarrasses themselves in a public street is subjected to momentary embarrassment in front of a limited audience. The creation of a photograph of the incident that is then published on the front page of a newspaper may result in humiliation before an audience of millions. The nature of the accurate and detailed information recorded in a photograph also means that the information it contains is on a different plain to a mere description of the image. It has been said that "a photograph is more than the information you get from it".[3] A classic example would be a photograph of a person in the nude. For this to be described is one thing but even an unflattering description is unlikely to be regarded as much of an invasion of privacy as publication of such a photograph.

**7–003**

It is clear that in appropriate circumstances publication of a photograph that contains confidential information will be restrained by the court.[4] At the time of writing, the present state of UK domestic law, as held by the House of Lords in *Secretary of State for the Home Department v Wainwright*,[5] is that there is no free standing tort of invasion of privacy. The Human Rights Act 1998 does not create a cause of action for infringement of privacy.[6] Any cause of action can only be founded in the tort of breach of confidence as expanded by the courts to include cases where there is no confidential relationship.[6a]

**7–004**

There is however some dicta that suggests to the contrary.[6b] There remains the possibility that the law may yet develop to recognise a free standing right of privacy arising from the Human Rights Act 1988. If such development is to occur, it is most likely to arise if UK domestic law is held to be inadequate to protect the right to a private and family life under Article 8 of the ECHR whether by domestic courts or in Europe.

---

[3] *D v L* [2003] EWCA Civ 1169, at paras 23–24.
[4] e.g. *Douglas v Hello! Ltd (No.6)* [2003] EWHC 786 (wedding photographs); *Theakston v MGN Ltd* [2002] EWHC 137; [2002] EMLR 22 (photographs of a TV presenter in a brothel); *Creation Records Ltd v News Group Newspapers Ltd* [1997] EMLR 444 (album cover photoshoot).
[5] *Wainwright v Secretary of State for the Home Department* [2003] UKHL 53; [2003] 3 W.L.R. 1137; [2003] 4 All E.R. 969, HL.
[6] *Secretary of State for the Home Department v Wainwright* [2001] EWCA Civ 2081; [2002] Q.B. 1334, CA upheld by the HL.
[6a] *Wainwright v Secretary of State for the Home Department* [2003] UKHL 53; [2003] 3 W.L.R. 1137; [2003] 4 All E.R. 969, HL.
[6b] See below at para. 7–042.

On November 6, 2003 The European Court of Human Rights heard the case of *Von Hannover v Germany*.[6c] At the time of writing, the decision of the court had not yet been published, but this case is likely to be significant in the development of the law in this area. The application is Princess Caroline von Hannover of Monaco. She had on several occasions applied to German courts for an injunction preventing further publication of photographs about her private life in the sensationalist press. In 1999 the Federal Constitutional Court granted an injunction only in respect of photographs in which the applicant appeared with her children, on the basis that their need for protection of intimacy was great than that of adults. The German Court considered that the applicant as a public figure had to tolerate photographs of herself in a public place even if the photographs showed scenes from her daily life rather than showing her engaged in official duties. In the application to the ECHR it was asserted that the decision of the German Court infringed the applicant's right to respect for her private and family life. The applicant asserts that the courts have failed to protect her adequately from the publication of photographs taken without her knowledge by paparazzi. The decision of the ECHR is awaited with interest and it remains to be seen if a breach of Art. 8 will be found.

## PHOTOGRAPHS AND BREACH OF CONFIDENCE

**7–005**  The classic test for breach of confidence derives from *Coco v Clark*[7] and states that three elements are required:

(1) the information must have the "necessary quality of confidence about it";

(2) the information must be imparted in circumstances importing an obligation of confidence; and

(3) there must be unauthorised use of that information.

**7–006**  It is now well established that a photograph contains information and as such can be the subject of a duty of confidence.[8] Photographs convey

---

[6c] App. No. 59320/00

[7] *Coco v A.N. Clark (Engineers) Ltd* [1969] R.P.C. 41, 47.

[8] *Douglas v Hello! Ltd (No.6)* [2003] EWHC 786; [2003] 3 All E.R. 996; [2003] E.M.L.R. 31 (celebrity wedding photographs); *Theakston v MGN Ltd* [2002] EWHC 137 (photographs of a TV presenter in a brothel); [2002] E.M.L.R. 22; *Nicholls v BBC* [1999] E.M.L.R. 791 (film); *Creation Records Ltd v News Group Newspapers Ltd* [1997] E.M.L.R. 444 (album cover photoshoot); *Shelley Films Ltd v Rex Features Ltd* [1994] E.M.L.R. 314 (closed film set); *Hellewell v Chief Constable* [1995] 1 W.L.R. 804 at 807; *Pollard v Photographic Co* (1888) 40 Ch. D. 345. And cf. *Handyside Films (Production) Ltd v Express Newspaper Ltd* [1986] F.S.R. 463 (Contempt of Court Act 1981; disclosure of sources). An argument that photographs were not "information" was rejected by Sir Nicholas Browne Wilkinson V.C. saying at p.486: "photographs are the same as oral or written communications. They are merely a different form of communicating information. Photographs communicate visually: writing does it through words. But in either case what is contained in the publication is information".

information as to what the subject looks like and the photographic content may be confidential even if the subject could have been described in words and drawings.[9]

Indeed, the ECHR has acknowledged that audio-visual media often have a much more immediate and powerful effect that the print media.[10] The UK courts have also shown a willingness to treat photographs differently from bare reporting of facts[11] and as more deserving of protection, even where the media are free to describe the facts depicted.

A photograph can make a greater impact than a written account of the matter depicted by a photograph, just as the recorded details of the very words of a private conversation can make more impact and cause more embarrassment and distress than a mere account of the conversation.[12] It has been said that a picture says more than a thousand words and that a description of image content may not have anything like the same impact and force as actual publication of the images.[13]     **7–007**

The fact that a photograph makes more impact than a mere description of its content is something of a double-edged sword. It may be a reason to justify imposition of an injunction where the media is free to describe the facts or matters shown therein precisely because the actual image may be more embarrassing and intrusive.[14] Conversely, if publication of the photograph is necessary to lend credibility to support journalistic allegations, it may be a reason to permit publication. Journalists are to be permitted reasonable latitude in taking decisions as to the method of reporting and the information reproduced.[15] It is not for the court to substitute their own views for those of the press as to what technique of reporting should be adopted by journalists.[16]

In *Fressoz and Roire v France*[17] the publisher of a satirical magazine was prosecuted in France for reproducing sections of the head of Peugeot's tax returns in connection with an article about a self-awarded salary rise. The ECHR held that Art.10 had been infringed and observed:     **7–008**

"In essence that article leaves it for journalists to reproduce such documents to ensure credibility. It protects journalists' right to divulge information on issues of general public interest provided that they are

---

[9] *Douglas v Hello! Ltd (No.6)* [2003] EWHC 786 at para.186(xii); [2003] 3 All E.R. 996; [2003] E.M.L.R. 31; *Douglas v Hello! Ltd (No.1)*, [2001] Q.B. 967, 1005; [2001] 2 W.L.R. 992; [2001] 2 All E.R. 289; [2001] E.M.L.R. 9 at para.138; *D v L* [2003] EWCA Civ 1169 at para.23 *per* Walter L.J.

[10] *Jersild v Denmark* (1995) 19 E.H.R.R. 1 at para.31. See also case discussed above at paras 2–164 to 2–166.

[11] *Theakston v MGN Ltd* [2002] E.M.L.R. 22 discussed below.

[12] *D v L* [2003] EWCA 1169 at para.24 *per* Walter L.J.; [2004] E.M.L.R. 1.

[13] Observations of Jacob J. in *Hyde Park Residence Ltd v Yelland* [1999] E.M.L.R. 654 at 662; [1999] R.P.C. 655. Decision reversed by Court of Appeal [2001] Ch. 143; [2000] 3 W.L.R. 215; [2000] E.M.L.R. 363.

[14] *Theakston v MGN Ltd* [2002] E.M.L.R. 22.

[15] *Campbell v MGN Ltd* [2002] EWCA Civ 1373 at para.64; [2003] Q.B. 633, 662.

[16] *Jersild v Denmark* (1995) 19 E.H.R.R. 1 at para.31.

[17] (1999) 31 E.H.R.R. 28.

acting in good faith and on an accurate factual basis and provide 'reliable
and precise' information in accordance with the ethics of journalism".[18]

Thus, freedom of expression protects both the right to publish information and the right of the public to receive it.

**7–009**     If the use of the photograph containing confidential information is merely
to add colour and flavour to an article to appeal to the readership of a
newspaper, it is doubtful whether publication of the photograph (as
opposed to the fact of the information contained in it) would be permitted.[19]

## THE NECESSARY QUALITY OF CONFIDENCE

**7–010**     An action for breach of confidence is only sustainable where the information
has the necessary quality of confidence about it, namely that it must not be
something which is public property or public knowledge.[20] The quality of
confidence is not susceptible to exhaustive definition and as it has been said,
whether there is a private interest worthy of protection will usually be
obvious.[21]

There are four main categories of information that have been traditionally
protected by breach of confidence: (1) trade secrets; (2) personal confidences; (3) government information; and (4) artistic and literary confidences.[22]

**7–011**     Certain types of information about a person may be easy to identify as
private such as information relating to health, personal relationships, or
finances.[23] Personal information concerning health contained in medical
records and reports is confidential[24]; as is information about a person's
sexual life.[25] Mere "trivial tittle-tattle" will not be protected however confidential.[26] Disclosure of confidential information may be objectionable even
when it shows the claimant in a good light, such as those who wish dona-

---

[18] (1999) 31 E.H.R.R. 28 at 60, para.54.
[19] *Ashdown v Telegraph Group Ltd* [2001] EWCA Civ 1142, para.82; [2002] Ch. 149, 176
(copyright, no justification for extensive reproduction of author's own words).
[20] *Saltman Engineering Co Ltd v Campbell Engineering Co* (1948) R.P.C. 203 at 215.
[21] *A v B plc* [2002] EWCA Civ 337 at para.11(vii); [2003] Q.B. 195 at 206; [2002] E.M.L.R. 21 *per*
Lord Woolf at 382; approved in *Campbell v MGN Ltd* [2002] EWCA Civ 1373 at para.51; [2003]
Q.B. 633 at 660 *per* Lord Phillips M.R.
[22] *R. v Department of Health ex p. Source Informatics Ltd (No. 1)* at para.23 [2001] Q.B. 424,
436; [2000] 2 W.L.R. 940 citing F. Gurry, *Breach of Confidence* (1984).
[23] *Australian Broadcasting Corp v Lenah Game Meats Pty* 185 A.L.R. 1; [2001] H.C.A. 63 (High
Court of Australia) at para.42; approved in *A v B plc* [2002] EWCA Civ 337; [2003] Q.B. 195;
[2002] E.M.L.R. 21.
[24] *Venables v News Group Newspapers* [2001] 2 W.L.R. 1038; [2001] 1 All E.R. 908; [2001]
E.M.L.R. 1; [2001] Fam. 430 at para.48; *Cornelius v De Taranto* [2001] E.M.L.R. 12; *X v Y*
[1988] 2 All E.R. 648.
[25] *Stephens v Avery* [1988] 2 All E.R. 477; [1988] 2 W.L.R. 1280; *Barrymore v News Group
Newspapers Ltd* [1997] F.S.R. 600; *Argyll (Duchess) v Argyll (Duke)* [1965] 1 All E.R. 611.
[26] *Coco v AN Clark (Engineers) Ltd* [1969] R.P.C. 41 at 48: *AG v Guardian Newspapers (No.2)*
[1990] 1 A.C. 109.

tations to charity to remain anonymous.[27] There must be some interest of a private nature which is worthy of protection.[28]

## Physical appearance

The extent to which the physical appearance of a person at a particular **7–012** time is capable of having the necessary quality of confidence to found an action for breach of confidence is unclear. If the physical appearance in itself has a commercial value and is being revealed in circumstances where it is clear to all concerned that it is being done so in confidence, it is protected as a commercial confidence—as in the case of celebrity wedding photographs.[29] It is doubtful whether a photograph of the mere physical appearance of a person without more, whether in a public place or in a private place, is capable of amounting to confidential information. Note that this is a separate question from whether such appearance can be protected by a free standing right of privacy beyond the law of confidence.[30] The decision of the House of Lords in *Secretary of State for the Home Department v Wainwright*[30a] held that there was no free standing tort of invasion of privacy in the UK.

It has been suggested that the underlying rationale of the cases *Prince* **7–013** *Albert v Strange*[31] and *Pollard v Photographic Co*[32] is that a person's appearance or image in a private place is confidential and he should be able to control how it is used.[33] It is respectfully submitted that this is incorrect and neither case is authority for this proposition.

In *Prince Albert v Strange*[34] Queen Victoria and Prince Albert had made **7–014** drawings and etchings "principally of subjects of private and domestic interest to themselves" of which they had copperplate impressions made. For greater privacy, such impressions had been made by a private press kept for that purpose and the plates were ordinarily kept by the Queen under lock. The etchings included not just portraits of members of the Royal Family and friends but also portraits of their dogs and etchings from old and rare engravings owned by the Queen. The plates were entrusted to a printer at Windsor for the purpose of printing off impressions. The printer took impressions for himself and in violation of trust and sold the impressions to the defendant who published a catalogue of them. It was held that the plaintiff was entitled to an injunction restraining publication of the catalogue.

[27] *Campbell v MGN Ltd* [2002] EWCA Civ 1373 at para.52; [2003] Q.B. 633, 660.
[28] *A v B plc* [2002] EWCA Civ 337 at para.11(vii); [2003] Q.B. 195 at 206; [2002] E.M.L.R. 21 *per* Lord Woolf at 382.
[29] *Douglas v Hello! Ltd (No.6)* [2003] EWHC 786; [2003] 3 All E.R. 996; [2003] E.M.L.R. 31, discussed below at para. 7–017.
[30] Discussed below at para. 7–037.
[30a] [2003] UKHL 53; [2003] 3 W.L.R. 1137; [2003] 4 All E.R. 969, HL. See below at para. 7–037.
[31] (1849) 2 De Gex. & Sm. 652; 64 E.R. 293.
[32] (1888) 40 Ch. D. 345.
[33] *The Law of Privacy & the Media* (Michael Tugendhat Q.C. and Iain Christie ed., 2002, Oxford University Press) at 6.50.
[34] (1849) 2 De Gex. & Sm. 652; 64 ER 293.

**7–015**     The rationale of this decision is that confidentiality lay in the fact that these were unpublished works that the owner had retained in a state of privacy.[35] The content of the works (whether personal appearances or otherwise) was not a basis for this decision nor indeed something the court placed any emphasis on at all. And in fact, as indicated above, the etchings contained other subjects beyond portraits. The focus of the court was very much on the property rights in the etchings as unpublished works.[36]

**7–016**     In *Pollard v Photographic Co*[37] the plaintiff was a woman who had engaged a photographer to take photographs of her and other members of her family. The photographer exhibited one of the photographs of the plaintiff in his shop window for sale "got up as a Christmas card". It was held that the contract between a photographer and his customer includes an implied term that the prints taken from the negative are for the use of the customer only.[38] Underpinning the court's decision was the implied term arising from the contract. It was said that "where a person obtains information in the course of a confidential employment, the law does not permit him to make any improper use of the information so obtained" but the focus of the decision was on a right of property. As with *Prince Albert v Strange*, the content of the images was not material to the decision.

**7–017**     In *Douglas v Hello*[39] it was held that physical appearance can have the necessary quality of confidence about it. The facts of this case are now well-known and can be stated shortly. The film actors, Michael Douglas and Catherine Zeta Jones held their wedding ceremony in the New York Plaza. They had sold the exclusive photographic rights to the event to OK! magazine. There were extensive security arrangements[40] surrounding the event which in the words of the judge "were intended to serve the three-fold purposes of confining the event to family and friends, of ensuring that only authorised photographs were taken and of preserving the exclusivity of the photographic rights for which OK! had paid £1m."[41] An unauthorised photographer had managed to gain access to the event and surreptitiously took some relatively poor quality photographs which were then bought by and published in Hello! a rival publication.

---

[35] See 64 E.R. 293 at 309.
[36] 64 E.R. 292 at 312–13.
[37] (1888) 40 Ch. D. 345.
[38] (1888) 40 Ch. D. 345 at 350.
[39] [2003] EWHC 786; [2003] 3 All E.R. 996; [2003] E.M.L.R. 31.
[40] These included: entry cards for each guest marked with a code indicating only to the event planner the identity of the guest; an invisible ink design on the back of each card; late delivery of the entry cards to reduce the risk of them being copied; employment of 3 private security companies; sweeping of the rooms to be used for hidden sound or video devices; a sign at the entrance reminding guests no photography was to be permitted; checking of entry cards against the code; authorised guests being given a gold wedding pin of a secret design; arrangements to check in any cameras found at the cloakroom; a computer on hand to obliterate shots of the wedding from any digital cameras found but not any other shots stored; arrangements to ensure that no unauthorised copies could be made from the official photographers film which were taken off for processing and processed under the eyes of security staff; the "locking down" of every corridor on the relevant floor of the hotel; security staff being *in situ* for the entire weekend of the wedding beginning on the Friday night including in stair wells.
[41] [2003] EWHC 786 at para.1; [2003] 3 All E.R. 996; [2003] E.M.L.R. 31.

In *Douglas v Hello*[42] in considering what was required for "the necessary quality of confidence", Lindsay J. applied the test of whether the information has "the basic attribute of inaccessibility". Lindsay J also quoted Megarry J.'s observation that Lord Greene's sentence from *Saltman* "necessary quality of confidence" **7–018**

"is a citation that stops mid-sentence. Lord Greene M.R.'s sentence in full read (with emphasis added):—

'The information, to be confidential must, I apprehend, apart from contract, have the necessary quality of confidence about it, *namely, it must not be something which is public property and public knowledge*'."[43]

He found that the photographic representation of the wedding had the necessary quality of confidence about it. This basis of this conclusion was commercial confidence. The judge observed that the claimants had "a valuable trade asset, a commodity the value of which depended, in part at least, upon its content at first being kept secret and then its being made public in ways controlled by Miss Zeta-Jones and Mr Douglas for the benefit of them and [OK!]."[44] He went on to say: **7–019**

"I thus regard photographic representation of the wedding reception as having the quality of confidence about it. Of course the general appearance of both Mr Douglas and Miss Zeta-Jones was no secret; what they looked like was well known to the public. But that does not deny the quality of commercial confidentiality to what they looked like on the exceptional occasion of their wedding".[45]

He concluded that the event was of a private character and that the elaborate steps to preclude photography and exclude the unauthorised made it clear that what was taking place was being imparted in confidence.

The starting point for considering whether a photograph has the necessary quality of confidence is Lindsay J.'s test of whether the information contained in a photograph "has the basic attribute of inaccessibility about it". However, whilst it is a helpful starting point, it is not determinative. The information in a photograph which was taken in private, is owned by a private individual and has never been published is, strictly speaking, inaccessible. This does not necessarily mean that the information contained in it is automatically confidential. **7–020**

Take for example a photograph of a celebrity taken many years ago before he attained fame when he was a child at a friend's birthday party. Assume that the party was a private child's birthday party and it was taken **7–021**

---

[42] [2003] EWHC 786 at para.183; [2003] 3 All E.R. 996; [2003] E.M.L.R. 31.
[43] [2003] EWHC 786 at para.182 quoting Megarry J. in *Coco v AN Clark (Engineers) Ltd* [1969] R.P.C. 41 at 47; [2003] 3 All E.R. 996; [2003] E.M.L.R. 31.
[44] [2003] EWHC 786 at para.196; [2003] 3 All E.R. 996; [2003] E.M.L.R. 31.
[45] [2003] EWHC 786 at para.197; [2003] 3 All E.R. 996; [2003] E.M.L.R. 31.

by the parent of the friend. Assume also that the photograph is just a standard portrait of the celebrity as a child; the child is not doing anything particularly private, distinctive or embarrassing. Unless the parent chooses to publish the photograph, the information contained in it is "inaccessible" in the sense that one person controls access to it and it is not available to the public. It is submitted however that the photograph would not have the necessary quality of confidence about it. The only information contained in it is what the celebrity looked like as a child on a particular occasion. The mere fact it is publically inaccessible does not automatically vest the information contained in the photograph with the necessary quality of confidence. In this example, the only reason the photograph becomes of interest or acquires any kind of value is because many years after the event the child depicted has become famous. At the time the photograph was taken no one present would have considered its subject-matter to be confidential. It is submitted therefore that even if the information contained in a photograph is inaccessible, it is necessary to go on to consider whether the very substance of that information is in itself capable of being confidential. There is no reason why a mundane photograph of any person should be regarded as being confidential *per se*.

7–022    In *Campbell v MGN*[46] where photographs where published of a model outside the venue of a Narcotics Anonymous meeting, the Court of Appeal said:

"The photographs published by the defendants were of a street scene. They did not convey any information that was confidential. That information was conveyed by the captions to the photographs and the articles in which they featured."[47]

A free standing tort of a right of privacy was not pursued by the claimant in that case.[47a]

7–023    One of the problems in assessing whether a photograph contains confidential information is the difficulty in separating out the (1) necessary quality of confidence from (2) an obligation of confidence. Cases involving images reveal a tendency to bundle the two together. In both *Prince Albert v Strange*[48] and *Pollard v Photographic Co*[49] the actual content of the images did not form a part of the ratio for the court's decision. It was the underlying relationship between the owner of the images and the person disclosing them. In *Douglas v Hello*[50] the existence of elaborate security precautions was regarded as important in establishing confidentiality in the images. It is submitted that the imputation of the obligation of confidence is the essential

[46] [2002] EWCA Civ 1373; [2003] Q.B. 633.
[47] [2002] EWCA Civ 1373 at para.33, [2003] Q.B. 633; 656.
[47a] Note that the CA decision *Campbell v MGN* [2002] EWCA Civ 1373; [2003] Q.B. 633) at the time of writing is subject to an appeal to the House of Lords to be heard in February 2004.
[48] (1849) 2 De Gex. & Sm. 652; 64 E.R. 293.
[49] (1888) 40 Ch. D. 345.
[50] [2003] EWHC 786 at para.183; [2003] 3 All E.R. 996; [2003] E.M.L.R. 31.

element in protecting photographs that are mere images of physical appearance with no "added confidential value" information conveyed.

In breach of confidence cases, the court will look at the attitude of the **7–024** owner of the information in assessing whether the information can be properly regarded as confidential.[51] Whether the confider stipulates the information to be confidential[52] or whether the information is created or imparted in circumstances importing an obligation of confidence[53] are relevant factors in assessing whether information is confidential. In *Cray Valley Ltd v Deltech Europe Ltd*[54] Jacob J. referred to "the well established rule of thumb used to test whether information is to be regarded as confidential"—"given for one purpose, not to be used for another."[55] The existence of elaborate security precautions for the protection of confidential information will be persuasive in determining whether information is entitled to protection by the law of confidence.[56]

If the photograph is taken in a public place where there is no reasonable **7–025** expectation of privacy, it cannot be protected by the law of confidence. Even if the information contained therein is private, there is no prospect of that being protected by the law of confidence. If disclosure of that photograph would infringe Art.8, there is a gap in the law as the case of *Peck v UK*[57] illustrates.

### Photographic images and "necessary quality of confidence": suggested approach

It is suggested that consideration of the following questions (derived from **7–026** the cases discussed above) may assist when assessing whether a photographic image has the "necessary quality of confidence" about it:

1. What information does the image convey?

2. Is that information in itself inherently confidential in the sense that it conveys something over and above mere physical appearance? If the image does contain additional private or "added value" information that is inherently confidential, such as information about a person's medical condition or sexual life, then it will have the necessary quality of confidence about it. If it does not, then it is necessary to consider the next question.

---

[51] *Faccenda Chicken v Fowler* [1987] 1 Ch. 117; *Thomas Marshall (Exports) Ltd v Guinle* [1978] 3 All E.R. 193.
[52] *Barrymore v News Group Newspapers Ltd* [1997] F.S.R. 600, 603 *per* Jacob J. "if something is expressly said to be confidential, then it is much more likely to be held so by the courts".
[53] See below at para. 7–028.
[54] [2003] EWHC 728.
[55] [2003] EWHC 728 at para.54.
[56] [2003] EWHC 728 at para.57 quoting from F. Gurry, *Breach of Confidence* (1984).
[57] (2003) 36 E.H.R.R. 41. Discussed below at para. 7–059.

3.    Can the information in the image be said to amount to a private interest worthy of protection? Commercial value in exclusive images amounts to a protectible interest.

4.    Is the information shown accessible to the general public? If it is, then the photograph will not have the necessary quality of confidence about it. Thus, a photograph of a person in a public street cannot have the necessary quality of confidence about it. However, again this may not be absolutely determinative. For photographs in which the precise information shown is not available to the general public (in the sense that it shows a physical appearance of a person on a particular private occasion) where as the general information (the physical appearance of that person) is publically available, it is suggested that it is necessary to consider a fourth question.

**7–027**    5.    In what circumstances was the photograph taken and for what purpose? In other words did the photographer take the photograph in circumstances in which he actually knew or ought as a reasonable person to have known that the image depicted was confidential? If the photograph was taken in circumstances importing an obligation of confidence, then this in itself may be enough to imbue the information contained therein with the necessary quality of confidence. In cases (such as the Douglas wedding) where security arrangements are in place to prohibit photography and unauthorised access to a private event, photographs of that event have the necessary quality of confidence. Equally, long lens and telephoto photography may be taken in circumstances where the obligation of confidence is implied. Conversely, in the example given above, a photograph taken of a child's birthday party for the purposes of family record would not have the necessary quality of confidence about it. The fact that it was take at a private event, without more, would not render the information confidential. All the circumstances of the case need to be considered in assessing whether duty of confidence should be imposed in respect of the photographs in issue. Simply because a celebrity objects to being photographed or a person objects to publication of their image is not enough to vest the photographs with the necessary quality of confidence.

## OBLIGATION OF CONFIDENCE

**7–028**    An obligation of confidence will arise where the circumstances are such that a reasonable man standing in the shoes of the recipient of the information would have realised that the information was being given to him in confidence.[58]

---

[58] *Coco v AN Clark (Engineers) Ltd* [1969] R.P.C. 41 at 48.

Obligations of confidence may arise generally via contractual terms **7–029** obliging parties to treat certain information as confidential[59]; commercial relationships[60]; the relationship between employee and employer arising from both implied duty[61] and express terms of confidence[62]; the relationship between client and professional adviser[63]; and the relationship between spouses[64] or sexual partners.[65]

In *Pollard v Photographic Co*[66] it was held that the contract between a photographer and his customer includes an implied term that the prints taken from the negative are for the use of the customer only.[67] Interestingly *Pollard* was one of the decisions relied on by Warren and Brandeis as one of the cases in support of a law of privacy in their famous article *The Right to Privacy*.[68]

Regarding photographs, an obligation of confidence may arise via con-  **7–030** tractual conditions where images were taken for a specific purpose only[69]; where it is apparent from signs that photography is not permitted, such as a closed film set[70] or photo shoot[71]; or where what is taking place is an obviously private function from which the public are excluded, such as a wedding with a high level of obvious security.[72] Discovery of intimate photographs that have been dropped in a public place may also give rise to a duty of confidentiality.[73]

In *Douglas v Hello! Ltd (No.1)*,[74] Brooke L.J. said:  **7–031**

---

[59] *e.g. Lady Archer v Williams* [2003] EWHC 1670; [2003] E.M.L.R. 38.
[60] *Seager v Copydex Ltd (No.1)* [1967] 1 W.L.R. 923; *Saltman Engineering Co Ltd v Campbell Engineering Co Ltd* (1948) 65 R.P.C. 203; *Poly Lina Ltd v Finch* [1995] F.S.R. 751.
[61] *Robb v Green* [1895] 2 Q.B. 315; *Faccenda Chicken Ltd v Fowler* [1987] Ch. 117; *Lawrence David Ltd v Ashton* [1991] 1 All E.R. 385; *Brooks v Olyslager Oms (UK) Ltd* [1998] I.R.L.R. 590; *Intelsec Systems Ltd v Grech Cini* [2000] 1 W.L.R. 1190.
[62] *Lady Archer v Williams* [2003] EWHC Ch. 1670; [2003] E.M.L.R. 38; *Campbell v Vanessa Frisbee* [2003] E.M.L.R. 3; *Wessex Dairies v Smith* [1935] 2 K.B. 80.
[63] *e.g.* Lawyers: *Bolkiah v KPMG* [1999] 2 A.C. 222; *Ball v Druces & Attlee (A Firm)* [2002] P.N.L.R. 23; Bankers: *Tournier v National Provincial* [1924] 1 K.B. 461; *Barclays Bank Plc v Taylor* [1989] 1 W.L.R. 1066; Doctors: *Nicholson v Halton General Hospital NHS Trust* [1999] P.I.Q.R. P310; *W v Egdell* [1990] Ch. 359 (no breach of duty where disclosure in public interest).
[64] *Argyll v Argyll* [1967] Ch. 302.
[65] *Stevens v Avery* [1988] 2 W.L.R. 1280; *Barrymore v News Group Newspapers Ltd* [1997] F.S.R. 600.
[66] (1888) 40 Ch. D. 345.
[67] (1888) 40 Ch. D. 345 at 350.
[68] (1890) 4 Harvard L.R. 193 at 208.
[69] *Pollard v Photographic Company* (1888) 40 Ch. D. 345 (for facts see above at para. 7–016. And *cf.*, s.85 CDPA 1988 paras 4–044 *et seq.* above. *Lawrence v Ylla* 184 Misc. 807; 55 N.Y.S. 2d 343 (1945) (sale of photograph of pet dog for use in advertisement).
[70] *Shelley Films Ltd v Rex Features Ltd* [1994] E.M.L.R. 134 (set guarded by partrolling and static security guards, two permenant signs reading "Absolutely no photography—all film will be confiscated" and "No admittance—access to authorised persons only; on shooting days additional signs reading "closed set").
[71] *Creation Records Ltd v News Group Newspapers Ltd* [1997] E.M.L.R. 444.
[72] *Douglas v Hello! Ltd (No.6)* [2003] EWHC 786 above; [2003] 3 All E.R. 996; [2003] E.M.L.R. 31. For description of security arrangements see para. 7–017, n.40.
[73] See *obiter per* Lord Goff in *Attorney General v Guardian Newspapers Ltd (No.2)* [1990] 1 A.C. 109 at 281 giving the example of a private diary dropped in public place.
[74] [2001] Q.B. 967; [2001] 2 W.L.R. 992; [2001] 2 All E.R. 289; [2001] E.M.L.R. 9.

"if on some private occasion the prospective claimants make it clear, expressly or impliedly, that no photographic images are to be taken of them, then all those present will be bound by the obligations of confidence created by their knowledge (or imputed knowledge) of this restriction."[75]

**7–032**    It is no longer necessary to establish a pre-existing confidential relationship between the parties to establish a cause of action in breach of confidence.[76] The nature of the subject matter or the circumstances of the defendant's activities may suffice in some circumstances to give rise to liability, such as deliberate intrusion into an environment plainly intended to be private.[77] An express photography ban or presence of signs to that effect is not an essential element of establishing an obligation of confidence.[78] Intrusion into a situation where a person can reasonably expect his privacy to be respected will suffice to found a cause of action.[79]

Where a reasonable man in the shoes of the photographer would have realised that he was obtaining a view of a scene in confidence, then he is obliged by that confidentiality not to photograph the scene.[80]

If a person takes a photograph in a private place knowing that he or she is not allowed to do so, then subject to public policy justifications, an obligation not to publish the photograph will be imposed.[81] It is no answer to a claim to restrain publication of an improperly obtained photograph that the information portrayed therein is already available in the public domain.[82]

**7–033**    A duty of confidence will arise "whenever the defendant knows or ought to know" that the person with that interest can "reasonably expect his privacy to be protected".[83] A useful practical test of what is private is whether disclosure would be highly offensive to a reasonable person of ordinary sensibilities.[84]

---

[75] [2001] Q.B. 967; [2001] 2 W.L.R. 992; [2001] 2 All E.R. 289; [2001] E.M.L.R. 9 at para.71.
[76] *Douglas v Hello! Ltd (No.1) per* Keene L.J. at para. 166 [2001] Q.B. 967; [2001] 2 W.L.R. 992; [2001] 2 All E.R. 289; [2001] E.M.L.R. 9; *Secretary of State for the Home Deptartment v Wainwright* [2003] UKHL 53 at [29]; [2003] 3 W.L.R. 1137; [2003] 4 All E.R. 696.
[77] *ibid.*
[78] *Shelley Films Ltd v Rex Features Ltd* [1994] E.M.L.R. 134 at 148.
[79] *A v B plc* [2002] EWCA Civ 337 at para.11(x); [2003] Q.B. 195 at 206; [2002] E.M.L.R. 21 *per* Lord Woolf at 382; *Venables v News Group Newspapers Ltd* at para.81 [2001] 2 W.L.R. 1038; [2001] 1 All E.R. 908; [2001] E.M.L.R. 10; [2001] Fam. 430.
[80] *Creation Records Ltd v News Group Newspapers Ltd* [1997] E.M.L.R. 444.
[81] *D v L* [2003] EWCA 1169 *per* Walter L.J. at para.20; [2004] E.M.L.R. 1.
[82] *D v L* [2003] EWCA 1169 *per* Walter L.J. at para.23; [2004] E.M.L.R. 1.
[83] *A v B plc* [2002] EWCA Civ 337 at para.11(vii); and (ix) [2003] Q.B. 195 at 206; [2002] E.M.L.R. 21 *per* Lord Woolf at para.382.
[84] *A v B plc* [2002] EWCA Civ 337 at para.11(vii); [2003] Q.B. 195 at 206; [2002] E.M.L.R. 21 *per* Lord Woolf at para.382; citing Gleeson C.J.'s judgment in *Australian Broadcasting Corp v Lenah Game Meats Pty* 185 A.L.R. 1; [2001] H.C.A. 63 (High Court of Australia) at para.42; *Campbell v MGN Ltd* [2002] EWCA Civ 1373 at paras 20, 48–51, 54; [2003] Q.B. 633, 653, 659–660.

## UNAUTHORISED USE

Breach of confidence arises where the confidential information is used or **7–034** disclosed without the consent of the person to whom the duty of confidence is owed. If the information is accepted on the basis that it will be kept secret, the recipient's conscience is bound by that confidence, and it will be unconscionable for him to break that duty by publishing the information to others.[85] Negligent disclosure may give rise to liability[86] as may unconscious or inadvertent use.[87]

Normally a breach of confidence involves activity which is detrimental to the imparter of the information[88] but whether this is an essential requirement of the tort of breach of confidence is unresolved.[89]

## A MOVE AWAY FROM THE COCO V CLARK TEST

There is some suggestion that there is a move away from the *Coco v Clark* test[90] **7–035** in cases concerning personal information. In the three recent Court of Appeal cases *Douglas v Hello! Ltd (No. 1)*,[91] *A v B plc*,[92] and *Campbell v MGN Ltd*,[93] not much regard was paid to *Coco v Clark*. Although other more traditional breach of confidence cases were cited which applied that test, the Court of Appeal focussed on whether there was a private interest worthy of protection.

In, *A v B plc*[94] and *Campbell v MGN Ltd*[95] the court considered that:

> "There must be some interest of a private nature which the Claimant wishes to protect, but usually the answer to the question whether there exists a private interest worthy of protection will be obvious."[96]

In both cases the test of whether disclosure would be highly offensive to a reasonable person of ordinary sensibilities was applied.[97] In *Campbell*, the

---

[85] *Douglas v Hello (No.1)* [2001] Q.B. 967 at para.65.
[86] *Weld-Blundell v Stephens* [1920] A.C. 956.
[87] *Seager v Copydex Ltd (No.1)* [1967] 1 W.L.R. 923; *Bolkiah v KPMG* [1999] 1 All E.R. 517.
[88] *Cray Valley Ltd v Deltech Europe Ltd* [2003] EWHC 728 at para.53.
[89] e.g. *AG v Guardian Newspapers (No.2)* per Lord Keith at 256; where example given of a charity donor who wished to remain annonymous; *Campbell v MGN Ltd* [2002] EWCA Civ 1373 at para.52; [2003] Q.B. 633, 660.
[90] See above at para.7–005.
[91] [2001] Q.B. 967; [2001] 2 W.L.R. 992; [2001] 2 All E.R. 289; [2001] E.M.L.R. 9.
[92] [2002] EWCA Civ 337; [2003] Q.B. 633; [2002] 3 W.L.R. 542; [2002] E.M.L.R. 21.
[93] [2002] EWCA Civ 1373 at para.54; [2003] Q.B. 633 at 660 per Lord Phillips M.R.
[94] [2002] EWCA Civ 337, 3 W.L.R. 542; [2002] E.M.L.R. 21.
[95] [2002] EWCA Civ 1373 at para.54; [2003] Q.B. 633 at 660 per Lord Phillips M.R.
[96] *A v B plc* [2002] EWCA Civ 337 at para.11(vii); [2003] Q.B. 195 at 206; [2002] E.M.L.R. 21 per Lord Woolf at 382; approved in *Campbell v MGN Ltd* [2002] EWCA Civ 1373 at para.51; [2003] Q.B. 633 at 660 per Lord Phillips M.R.
[97] *A v B plc* [2002] EWCA Civ 337 at para.11(vii); [2003] Q.B. 195 at 206; [2002] E.M.L.R. 21 per Lord Woolf at 382; citing Gleeson C.J.'s judgment in *Australian Broadcasting Corp v Lenah Game Meats Pty* 185 A.L.R. 1; [2001] H.C.A. 63 (High Court of Australia) at para.42; *Campbell v MGN Ltd* [2002] EWCA Civ 1373 at paras 20, 48–51; 54; [2003] Q.B. 633, 653, 659–660.

Court of Appeal has doubted that the distinction between what is "highly offensive" and "offensive" is very meaningful in practice.[98]

**7–036**     The *Coco v Clark* test was applied by Lindsay J. in *Douglas v Hello*[99] but this case, it is submitted, is properly characterised as one of commercial confidence rather than private or personal information.[1] The wedding photographs were the subject of a contract worth £1m.

The "shoehorning"[2] of invasion of privacy cases into the tort of breach of confidence and the tendency of lawyers presented with a new problem "to find a pre-formed slot to pop it into, like a toddler in a play group"[3] is bound to cause problems and leave areas worthy of protection uncovered. The commercial confidence protected by the court in *Douglas v Hello (No.6)* is, it is submitted, better described as a right of publicity shoehorned into a confidence box. At the present time the way in which the law will develop is unclear.

## BEYOND CONFIDENCE: A FREE STANDING RIGHT OF PRIVACY

**7–037**     Breach of confidence and invasion of privacy are not the same.[4] Breach of confidence involves misuse or disclosure of confidential information. Invasion of privacy can occur where there is intrusion into privacy that does not involve the disclosure of private facts.[5]

**7–038**     Historically, the law of England and Wales has notoriously failed to recognise a free standing right of privacy and case law is littered with observations to this effect. Perhaps the most famous of these is in the much lamented decision of *Kaye v Robertson*[6] where a television celebrity was recovering in hospital from serious injuries. The evidence showed that he was in no fit state to give informed consent. Journalists gained access to his room and sought to publish the interview and photographs they obtained, some of which showed substantial scars to his head where severe head and brain injuries had been caused. Breach of confidence was not argued. In giving judgement Glidewell L.J. said:

"It is well known that in English law there is no right of privacy and accordingly there is no right of action for breach of a person's privacy. The facts of the present case are a graphic illustration of the desirability of

---

[98] *Campbell v MGN Ltd* [2002] EWCA Civ 1373 at para.51; [2003] Q.B. 633, 660.
[99] [2003] EWHC 786 at para.183; [2003] 3 All E.R. 996; [2003] E.M.L.R. 31.
[1] See Lindsay J. at paras 195, 196–197, 217.
[2] *Campbell v MGN* [2002] EWCA Civ 1373 at para.70; [2003] Q.B. 633, 633; [2003] 2 W.L.R. 80; [2003] 1 All E.R. 224; [2003] E.M.L.R. 2.
[3] Sedley L.J. in the Foreword to *The Law of Privacy & the Media* (Michael Tugendhat Q.C. and Iain Christie ed., 2002, Oxford University Press).
[4] *R v BSC. Ex p. BBC* [2002] Q.B. 885 at para.48; *Campbell v MGN Ltd* [2002] EWCA Civ 1373 at para.31; [2003] Q.B. 633 at 655 *per* Lord Phillips M.R.; *Peck v United Kingdom* (2003) 36 E.H.R.R. 41.
[5] *Campbell v MGN Ltd* [2002] EWCA Civ 1373, para.31; [2003] Q.B. 633, 655 *per* Lord Phillips M.R.
[6] [1991] F.S.R. 62.

Parliament considering whether and in what circumstances statutory provision can be made to protect the privacy of individuals"[7]

There had been some indications to the contrary and dicta suggesting that   **7–039** the law of the UK may in fact protect privacy separately from the law of breach of confidence. However, this was dispelled by the House of Lords in *Secretary of State for the Home Department v Wainwright*.[8] This case concerned a mother and her son who were strip searched when visiting another son of hers in prison. The claimants contended that the prison officers were liable for the tort of invasion of privacy arising from the European Convention on Human Rights. The House of Lords rejected this argument, holding that there was no tort of invasion of privacy in English law.[9] It was acknowledged that the common law of breach of confidence has reached a point at which a confidential relationship has become unnecessary.[10] Their Lordships distinguished between privacy as a value which underlies the existence of a rule of law and privacy as a principle of law in itself.[11] Privacy was thus a value underlying the common law of confidence but not a free standing tort in its own right.[12]

The law in this area is still developing. As was acknowledge in *Wainwright* the common law of confidence has expanded to include privacy type cases where there is no obligation of confidence. It is certain that in the interval between writing and publication of this work that there will be further case law and that jurisprudence will have moved on. The decision of the ECHR in *Von Hannover v Germany*[13] which was heard on November 6, 2003 but at the time of writing had not yet been published may very well impact on this question.

In the meantime the law of the UK is left in an unsatisfactory state. In *Campbell v MGN*,[14] Lord Philips MR spoke of the "shoehorning into the torn of breach of confidence of publication of information that would more happily be described as breach of privacy." Given the decision of the ECHR in *Peck v United Kingdom*[14a] recognising a breach of Art. 8 arising out of matters occurring on a public highway, it is submitted that is possible that the domestic law of the United Kingdom will yet develop to encompass a right of privacy that is independent from breach of confidence—whether this occurs via judicial development of the common law or whether ultimately statutory intervention is required remains to be seen. The ECHR were not of the view that an action for breach of confidence in the UK would have provided Mr Peck with an adequate remedy. However, it should be noted that under the present law of the UK, following the implementation of the

---

[7] [1991] F.S.R. 62 at 66.
[8] [2003] UKHL 53; [2003] 3 W.L.R. 1137; [2003] 4 All E.R. 969, HL. See below at para. 7–037.
[9] *ibid.*, at [35] *per* Lord Hoffmann.
[10] *ibid.*, at [29].
[11] *ibid.*, at [31].
[12] *Loc. cit.*
[13] App. No. 59320/00 for the facts see above at para. 7–004.
[14] [2002] EWCA Civ 1373 at para. 70; [2003] Q.B. 633, 633; [2003] 2 W.L.R. 80; [2003] 1 All E.R. 224; [2003] E.M.L.R. 2.
[14a] (2003) 36 E.H.R.R. 41. For the facts see below at para 7–059.

Data Protection Act 1998, if that case was considered today Mr Peck may very well have a remedy under that statute.[14b]

**7–040**    Professor William Prosser in his much cited article[14c] stated that the tort of privacy was not a single tort but a complex of four stating:

> "Without any attempt to exact definition, these four tort maybe described as follows:
>
> 1. Intrusion upon the plaintiff's seclusion or solitude or into his private affairs.
> 2. Public disclosure of embarrassing private facts about the plaintiff.
> 3. Publicity which places the plaintiff in a false light in the public eye.
> 4. Appropriation, for the defendant's advantage of the plaintiff's name or likeness."

This description has been cited in many cases in many jurisdictions and treated as a starting point for the tort.[14d]

**7–041**    In a recent decision of the District Court of Queensland[14e] in what was essentially a harassment action, it was held that there was an actionable right of privacy. The court expressed the view that the essential elements of such a tort would be:

(a) a willed act by the defendant;

(b) which intrudes upon the privacy or seclusion of the plaintiff;

(c) in a manner which would be considered highly offensive to a reasonable person of ordinary sensibilities

(d) and which causes the plaintiff detriment in the form of mental psychological or emotional harm or distress or which prevents or hinders the plaintiff from doing an act which she is lawfully entitled to do.[14f]

As noted above, the question of whether there is a free standing right of privacy has been answered in the negative by the House of Lords in *Secretary of State for the Home Department v Wainwright*.[14g] In the light of that decision and possible future development, it is perhaps helpful to review the existing dicta—some of which tends to support a freestanding right of privacy, some of which suggests that breach of confidence is the only actionable tort and some of which leaves it as an open question.

---

[14b] See below at para.7–061.

[14c] *Privacy* (1960) 48 California Law Review 383 at 389.

[14d] Recent examples include *Secretary of State for the Home Department v Wainwright* [2003] UKHL 53 at [16]; [2003] 3 W.L.R. 1137; [2003] 4 All E.R. 969, HL; *Australian Broadcasting Corp. v Lenah Game Meats Pty* 185 A.L.R 1; [2001] H.C.A. 63, High Court of Australia at 323; *Grosse v Purvis* June 16, 2003, Senior Judge Skoien at 430; and *Denver Pub Co v. Bueno* 54 P.3d 893, 896.

[14e] *Grosse v Purvis* June 16, 2003, Senior Judge Skoien.

[14f] *Grosse v Purvis* June 16, 2003, Senior Judge Skoien at para. 444.

[14g] *Secretary of State for the Home Department v Wainwright* [2003] UKHL 53; [2003] 3 W.L.R. 1137; [2003] 4 All E.R. 969, HL. CA decision at [2001] EWCA Civ 2081; [2002] Q.B. 1334.

## Dicta in support of a right of privacy

Sedley L.J. in *Douglas v Hello! Ltd (No. 1)*[15]     **7–042**
    What a concept of privacy does, however is accord recognition to the fact
that the law has to protect not only those people whose trust has been
abused but those who simply find themselves subjected to an unwanted
intrusion into their personal lives. The law no longer needs to construct an
artificial relationship of confidentiality between intruder and victim: it can
recognise privacy itself as a legal principle draw from the fundamental value
of personal autonomy.

> "... we have reached a point at which it can be said that with confidence
> that the law recognises and will appropriately protect a right of personal
> privacy."[16]

Lord Philips M.R. in *Campbell v MGN*[17]
    The development of the law of confidentiality since the Human Rights Act
1998 came into force has seen information described as "confidential" not
where it has been confided by one person to another, but where it relates to an
aspect of an individual's private life which he does not choose to make public.
We consider that the unjustifiable publication of such information would
better be described as breach of privacy rather than breach of confidence.

## Dicta suggesting there is no actionable right of privacy in the UK

Lord Hoffman in *Secretary of State for the Home Department v Wainwright*[17a]

> "I read these remarks [of Sedley L.J. quoted above at para. 7–042] as
> suggesting that, in relation to the publication of personal information
> obtained by intrusion, the common law of breach of confidence has
> reached the point at which a confidential relationship has become unne-
> cessary. As the underlying value protected is privacy, the action might as
> well be renamed invasion of privacy. 'To say this' said Sedley L.J., at p.
> 1001, para. 125, 'is in my belief to say little, save by way of a label, that
> our courts have not said already over the years.'
>     I do not understand Sedley L.J. to have been advocating the creation of
> a high-level principle of invasion of privacy. His observations are in my
> opinion no more (although certainly no less) than a plea for the extension
> and possibly renaming of the old action for breach of confidence. As
> Buxton L.J. pointed out in this case in the Court of Appeal at [2002] Q.B.

---

[15] At para.126 [2001] Q.B. 967, 1001; [2001] 2 W.L.R. 992; [2001] 2 All E.R. 289; [2001]
E.M.L.R. 9.
[16] At para.110.
[17] [2002] EWCA Civ 1373 at para.70; [2003] Q.B. 633; [2003] 2 W.L.R. 80; [2003] 1 All E.R. 224;
[2003] E.M.L.R. 2.
[17a] [2003] UKHL 53; [2003] 3 W.L.R. 1137; [2003] 4 All E.R. 969, HL.

1334, 1361–1362, paras 96–99, such an extension would go further than any English court has yet gone and would be contrary to some cases (such as *Kaye v Robertson* [1991] F.S.R. 62) in which it positively declined to do so. The question must wait for another day. But Sedley L.J.'s dictum does not support a principle of privacy so abstract as to include the circumstances of the present case.

There seems to me a great difference between identifying privacy as a value which underlies the existence of a rule of law (and may point the direction in which the law should develop) and privacy as a principle of law in itself. The English common law is familiar with the notion of underlying values—principles only in the broadest sense—which direct its development.

... I would reject the invitation to declare that since at the latest 1950 there has been a previously unknown tort of invasion of privacy."

**7–043**   Lord Woolf in *A v B plc*[17b]

It is most unlikely that any purpose will be served by a judge seeking to decide whether there exists a due cause of action in tort which protects privacy. In the great majority of situations, if not all situations, where the protection of privacy is justified, relating to events after the Human Rights Act came into force an action for breach of confidence now will, where this is appropriate provide appropriate protection.[18]

*Secretary of State for the Home Department v Wainwright*[19]

Court of Appeal holding that the Human Rights Act 1998 could not change the rule at common law that there was no tort of invasion of privacy, by introducing a retrospective right to privacy.

*Peck v United Kingdom*[20]

Holding that there was no remedy in the UK for disclosure of CCTV footage of an attempted suicide in a public place. Decision of the ECHR discussed below at para.7–059.

**Dicta suggesting it remains an open question**

**7–044**   Lindsay J. in *Douglas v Hello! Ltd (No.6)*[21]

Declining to hold there is an existing law of privacy for 5 reasons (1) conflicting case law; (2) claimants adequately protected in confidence (3) matter best left to Parliament (4) Lord Woolf's comment in *A v B* that no purpose would be served by a judge seeking to decide whether such a tort exists (5) it was not argued that if such a tort existed the claimants would have made any greater recovery.

---

[17b] [2002] EWCA Civ 337; [2003] Q.B. 633; [2002] 3 W.L.R. 542; [2002] E.M.L.R. 21.
[18] At para.11(vi).
[19] [2001] EWCA Civ 2081; [2002] Q.B. 1334; [2002] 3 W.L.R. 405.
[20] (2003) 36 E.H.R.R. 41 at para.63.
[21] [2003] EWHC 786 at para.229 [2003] 3 All E.R. 996; [2003] E.M.L.R 31.

Keene L.J. in *Douglas v Hello! Ltd (No. 1)* [22]

Whether the resulting liability is described as being for breach of a right to privacy may be little more than deciding what label is to be attached to that cause of action, but there would seem to be merit in recognising that the original concept of breach of confidence has in this particular category of case developed into something different from the commercial and employment relationships with which confidentiality is mainly concerned.

Brooke L.J. in *Douglas v Hello! Ltd (No. 1)* [23]

Whether [the courts give recognition to Art.8 rights] in future by an extension of the existing frontiers of the law of confidence or by recognising the existence of new relationships which give rise to enforceable legal rights ... is not for this court, on this occasion, to predict.

Lord Nicholls in *R v Khan (Sultan)* [24]

I prefer to leave open for another occasion the important question of whether the present piecemeal protection of privacy has now developed to the extent that a more comprehensive principle can be seen to exist.

*Earl Spencer v United Kingdom* [25]

A photograph of Lady Spencer had been taken with a telephoto lens while she was walking in the grounds of a private clinic where she was receiving treatment. The photograph was published under the caption "So thin: Victoria walks in the clinic grounds this week". On the basis of *Kaye v Robertson*, she did not pursue a claim in the domestic courts. The European Commission of Human Rights held that she should have pursued her remedies in the UK Courts first. They considered that it could not be concluded that:

"a breach of confidence action is ineffective or insufficient but rather a conclusion that the matter should be put to the domestic courts for consideration in order to allow those courts, through the common law system in the United Kingdom, the opportunity to develop existing rights by way of interpretation." [26]

## RELATIONSHIP BETWEEN ART.8 AND ART.10

The right to a private and family life guaranteed by Art.8 and the right to freedom of expression guaranteed by Art.10 are both fundamental human      **7–045**

---

[22] At para. 166 [2001] Q.B. 967, 1012; [2001] 2 W.L.R. 992; [2001] 2 All E.R. 289; [2001] E.M.L.R. 9.
[23] At para.88 [2001] Q.B. 967, 992; [2001] 2 W.L.R. 992; [2001] 2 All E.R. 289; [2001] E.M.L.R. 9.
[24] [1997] A.C. 558, 582–588.
[25] 25 E.H.R.R. CD105.
[26] 25 E.H.R.R. CD105 at 117–118.

rights and neither has automatic priority over the other.[27]

Article 8 and Article 10 are as follows.

## "Art. 8: Right to respect for private and family life

**7–046**    1.    Everyone has the right to respect for his private and family life, his home and his correspondence.

2.    There shall be no interference by a public authority with the exercise of this right except such as is in accordance with the law and is necessary in a democratic society in the interests of national security, public safety or the economic well-being of the country, for the prevention of disorder or crime, for the protection of health or morals, or for the protection of the rights and freedoms of others."

## "Art. 10: Freedom of expression

**7–046A**    1.    Everyone has the right to freedom of expression. This right shall include freedom to hold opinions and to receive and impart information and ideas without interference by public authority and regardless of frontiers. This Article shall not prevent States from requiring the licensing of broadcasting, television or cinema enterprises.

2.    The exercise of these freedoms, since it carries with it duties and responsibilities, may be subject to such formalities, conditions, restrictions or penalties as are prescribed by law and are necessary in a democratic society, in the interests of national security, territorial integrity or public safety, for the prevention of disorder or crime, for the protection of health or morals, for the protection of the reputation or rights of others, for preventing the disclosure of information received in confidence, or for maintaining the authority and impartiality of the judiciary."

There is much judicial comment both in Europe and in the UK domestic courts as to the importance of freedom of expression in a democratic society.[28] Articles 8 and 10 have to be balanced and Art.10 is not a trump

---

[27] *Douglas v Hello (No.1)* [2001] Q.B. 967 *per* Sedley L.J. at paras 135–137 and Keene L.J. at para.150; *Douglas v Hello (No.6)* [2003] EWHC 786 *per* Lindsay J. at para.186(v); [2003] 3 All E.R. 996; [2003] E.M.L.R. 31. *Cream Holdings v Banerjee* [2003] 2 All E.R. 318 at paras 51–4, 72–83.

[28] "Freedom of speech is the lifeblood of a democracy" *R. v Secretary of State for the Home Department. Ex p. Simms* [2000] 2 A.C. 115, 126 *per* Lord Steyn; "one of the essential foundations of [a democratic society] *Handyside v UK* (1976) 1 E.H.R.R. 737, para.49; *Ahmed v UK* (1998) 29 E.H.R.R. 1, para.52.

card.[29] The balance should be struck by applying the "methodical concept of proportionality".[30] The 15 guidelines set out by Lord Woolf in *A v B plc* are a useful starting point.[31]

Equally, the interests identified in Art.10(2) are not trump cards which **7–047** automatically override the principles of open justice and freedom of expression. The derogation only override the guaranteed rights when it is "necessary" they should do so. It is not a question of balancing the freedom of expression against one or more of the interests identified in para.2. The question is whether those who seek to bring themselves within the protection of Art.10(2) can demonstrate convincingly that they are.[32]

Article 10 applies to "everyone" whether natural or legal persons.[33] It protects political expression[34]; artistic expression[35]; advertising.[36] Detailed consideration of the application of Art.10 is outside the scope of this work.[37] As far as photography is concerned it should be noted that Art.10 extends not only the ideas and information expressed, but also to the means of expression.[38] Any restriction on the means of dissemination interferes with the right to receive and impart information.[39] Prohibition of publication of a photograph of an alleged rightwing extremist who faced trial for a letter bomb campaign in connection with a report of the criminal proceedings amounted to an interference with Art.10.[40] A restriction prohibiting publication of a photograph had the effect of limiting the choice of the press as to the form in which it could present its reports is in breach of Art.10.[41]

## CIRCUMSTANCES IN WHICH THE TAKING OF A PHOTOGRAPH MAY INFRINGE ART.8

In assessing the taking of a photograph, the ECJ and the Commission will **7–048** consider (1) whether the taking of the photograph involved an invasion of privacy; (2) whether the photograph is of a public or private act; (3) the

---

[29] *Douglas v Hello (No.6)* [2003] EWHC 786 at para.212 [2003] 3 All E.R. 996; [2003] E.M.L.R. 31.
[30] *London Regional Transport v Mayor of London* [2001] EWCA Civ 1491 at para.56; [2003] E.M.L.R. 4.
[31] [2002] EWCA Civ 337; [2003] Q.B. 195; [2002] 3 W.L.R. 542; [2002] 2 All E.R. 545; [2002] E.M.L.R. 21.
[32] *Kelly v BBC* [2001] 1 FLR 197, 210C.
[33] *Autronic AG v Switzerland* (1990) 12 E.H.R.R. 485 at para.47.
[34] *Lingens v Austria* (1986) 7 E.H.R.R. 407; *Wingrove v UK* (1997) 24 E.H.R.R. 1.
[35] *Muller v Switzerland* (1988) 13 E.H.R.R. 212.
[36] *Cascado Coca v Spain* (1994) 19 E.H.R.R. 64.
[37] See *e.g.* Lester & Pannick, *Human Rights Law and Practice* (Butterworths) and Simor & Emmerson *Human Rights Practice* (Sweet & Maxwell).
[38] *Jersild v Denmark* (1995) 19 E.H.R.R. 1, para.31. See also cases discussed above at paras 2–164 and 2–165.
[39] *Oberschlick v Austria* (1991) 19 E.H.R.R. 389, para.57.
[40] *News Verlags GmbH & Co KG v Austria* (2001) 31 E.H.R.R. 8 (ECtHR).
[41] *News Verlags GmbH & Co KG v Austria* (2001) 31 E.H.R.R. 8 (ECtHR).

purpose for which the photograph was created; and (4) the actual use of the photograph including the extent to which it was distributed to the general public.[42]

**7–049**    Where a person is photographed in a public place it is unlikely to infringe Art.8, particularly if that person is taking place in public activities.[43] Generally, in a public place anyone is free in principle to take photographs and the taking of such photographs can in most circumstances be considered a trivial act which must be tolerated by others, even if some people may consider it unpleasant that someone else should take their photograph.[44] Where a participant in a demonstration in the form of a sit-in taking place in a public passage for pedestrians was photographed by the police it was held that there was no infringement of Art.8.[45] There was no intrusion into the "inner circle" of the applicant's private life in the sense that the authorities had entered his home and taken photographs there.[46] The Commission attached weight to the respondent government's assurances that the photographs remained anonymous, were not entered into a data processing system and no steps were taken to identify the people photographed by means of data processing.[47]

**7–050**    Although the general rule is that photography in a public place does not infringe Art.8, this is not an absolute rule. Surveillance per se amounts to an interference with Art.8 although it may be justified for reasons of crime prevention or detection.[48] Even if no criminal proceedings are brought, the retention of material may be justified by considerations such as the combatting of organised terrorism,[49] or to allow future identification of suspects.[50] This does not mean that publication of the images for unrelated purposes is justified. In *Peck v United Kingdom*[51] the publication of CCTV footage of a man prior to an attempted suicide was held to infringe Art.8 even though no complaint was made about the fact of the surveillance.

The use of photographs in the course of a criminal investigation is not an interference with Art.8 where the photographs had been provided voluntarily in connection with applications for official documents or had been

---

[42] *Friedl v Austria* (1995) 21 E.H.R.R. 83; *X v United Kingdom* App. No.5877/72; 45 Coll. 90. See S.H. Naismith, *Photographs, Privacy & Freedom Of Expression* [1996] 2 E.H.R.L.R. 150 at 151.

[43] *Friedl v Austria* (1995) 21 E.H.R.R. 83. Note that this is may be affected by the decision of the ECHR in *Von Hannover v Germany* (App. No. 59320/00) which was heard on November 6, 2003 but has not yet been published. For facts see above at para. 7–004.

[44] *Friedl v Austria* (1995) 21 E.H.R.R. 83 at para. 49 (concurring opinion of Mr H Danelius). See above at n.43.

[45] *Friedl v Austria* (1995) 21 E.H.R.R. 83 at para.49.

[46] *Friedl v Austria* (1995) 21 E.H.R.R. 83; *X v United Kingdom* App. No.5877/72; 45 Coll. 90.

[47] *Friedl v Austria* (1995) 21 E.H.R.R. 83 at para.50.

[48] *e.g. Klass v Germany* (1979–80) 2 E.H.R.R. 214 and *Malone v United Kingdom* (1985) 7 E.H.R.R. 14.

[49] *Mc Veigh v United Kingdom* App. No.8022/77, 8025/77 and 8027/77; 25 D.R. 15 paras 229–231. *cf. Taylor v United Kingdom* App. No.13736/88, November 10, 1989 (seizure by police of family photo albums. Rejected for non-exhaustion of domestic remedies).

[50] *X v United Kingdom* App. No.5877/72, October 22; 1973 45 Coll. 90.

[51] (2003) 36 E.H.R.R. 41 at para.63; [2003] E.M.L.R. 15.

obtained on the occasion of a previous arrest and were not made available to the general public nor used for any purpose other than the criminal proceedings.[52]

In *Murray v United Kingdom*[53] a woman was arrested by soldiers entering her home on suspicion of being involved with the IRA and she was photographed at the army screening centre without her knowledge or consent and the photograph was kept on record along with personal details about her, her family and home. The Commission found that this constituted interference with her right to respect for private and family life and the home. However, they considered that the measures pursued the legitimate aim of the prevention of crime, which had to be viewed in the context of the fight against terrorist crime in Northern Ireland. Against this background the taking and retention of a photograph was not disproportionate to the legitimate aim of the prevention of crime. It is worth noting that in that case the Court of Appeal of Northern Ireland had observed "according to the common law there is no remedy if someone takes a photograph of another against his will."

7–051

The state has positive obligations under Art.8 such that it may be required to take steps to protect the individual even where the state itself is not responsible for the interference.[54] Resolution 428 (1970) of the Parliamentary Assembly of the Council of Europe provides:

7–052

"The right to privacy afforded by Article 8 of the Convention on Human Rights should not only protect an individual against interference by public authorities but also against interference by private persons including the mass media."[55]

The extent to which a government is required to intervene in order to prevent interference with Art.8 rights by the mass media is undecided, but the question of whether there is a domestic remedy is relevant.[56]

## CORPORATIONS, CONFIDENTIALITY AND THE RIGHT TO PRIVACY

It is not clear whether a company can claim an Art.8 right to privacy. Pannick and Lester state "there are some rights which by their nature, cannot be enjoyed by a company. For example the right to a private life, which is at its root a right to *personal* privacy."[57]

7–053

---

[52] App. No.18395/91, December 7, unpublished. Referred to in *Friedl v Austria* (1995) 21 E.H.R.R. 83 at para.48.
[53] (1995) 19 E.H.R.R. 193.
[54] *X & Y v Netherlands*, March 26, 1985, Series A No.91.
[55] Para.C7.
[56] *Winer v UK* App. No.10871/48; 48 D.R. 154 (defamation provided sufficient remedy); *Earl Spencer v United Kingdom* 25 E.H.R.R. CD105; *Whiteside v United Kingdom* App. No.20357/92 (law of harassment sufficient remedy).
[57] Lester & Pannick, *op. cit.* at p.37 n. 11 citing William L. Prosser *Privacy* (1960) 48 Calif. L.R. 383 at 408–409.

There are some suggestions that a company may enjoy limited rights such as respect for its place of business.[58] In *R. v Broadcasting Standards Commission Ex p. BBC*[59] it was held that a company could make a complaint of unwarranted infringement of its privacy. However, this decision concerned the construction of the Broadcasting Act 1996 and is of limited assistance in consideration of the wider question of whether a company has a right under Art.8.

**7–054**   In *Cream Holdings v Banerjee*,[60] Sedley L.J. said:

"If, as has been held to be the case, a corporation is capable of enjoying privacy rights under Article 8, the disclosure of its affairs—especially shameful ones—is on the face of it a breach of respect for its privacy; though the more shameful the matter disclosed, the less likely it is to survive the application of article 8(2)."

However in *Australian Broadcasting Corp v Lenah Game Meats Pty* it was said that the right to privacy is for the benefit of natural and not artificial persons and thus a corporation can have no claim to a right of privacy.[61] This is an Australian decision and should be approached with caution as obviously the court was not bound by the Convention or European jurisprudence on the matter. It was said that the tort of invasion of privacy focuses on the humiliation and intimate personal distress suffered by an individual as a result of intrusive behaviour. While a corporation may have its reputation or business damaged as a result of intrusive activity, it is not capable of emotional suffering.[62]

## WHAT IS PRIVATE?

**7–055**   There is no bright line which can be drawn between what is private and what is not and there is a large area between what is necessarily public and what is necessarily private.[63] An action is not private simply because it is not done in public.[64] The English courts have shown a reluctance to find that a photograph taken of subject matter in a public place should be restrained on the basis of confidentiality or privacy.[65] The attitude of the courts tends to

---

[58] *Colas Est v France* (No. 37971/97) April 16, 2002 (ECHR).
[59] [2001] Q.B. 885; [2000] 3 W.L.R. 1327; [2000] 3 All E.R. 989.
[60] [2003] EWCA Civ 103 at para.80; [2003] 2 All E.R. 318.
[61] *Australian Broadcasting Corp v Lenah Game Meats Pty* 185 A.L.R. 1; [2001] H.C.A. 63 (High Court of Australia).
[62] *Australian Broadcasting Corp v Lenah Game Meats Pty* 185 A.L.R. 1; [2001] H.C.A. 63 (High Court of Australia).
[63] *Australian Broadcasting Corp v Lenah Game Meats Pty* 185 A.L.R. 1; [2001] H.C.A. 63 (High Court of Australia) approved by the Court of Appeal in *A v B plc* [2002] E.M.L.R. 21 at 382.
[64] *Australian Broadcasting Corp v Lenah Game Meats Pty* 185 A.L.R. 1; [2001] H.C.A. 63 (High Court of Australia) approved by the Court of Appeal in *A v B plc* [2002] E.M.L.R. 21 at 382.
[65] e.g. *Campbell v MGN Ltd* [2002] EWCA Civ 1373; [2003] Q.B. 633; *MGN v Attard* (unrep) October 19, 2001, Connell J.

follow that of the PCC[66] as expressed in its Code, that in order for a place to be regarded as private it must be a place, whether public or private, where there is a reasonable expectation of privacy. A public street has so far not been held to give rise to a right of confidentiality or privacy by domestic courts.[67] However, it is clear from European case law discussed below that in some exceptional circumstances there may be a right of privacy in respect of an act taking place in public.

In *MGN v Attard*[68] in issue were photographs of the survivor of two **7–056** conjoined twins that were taken whilst she was being wheeled in a pushchair on a public highway. Refusing an injunction, Connell J. said:

> "... on the basis on which I approach this case no argument can be advanced that this was an infringement of the right of privacy on the basis that the photographs were taken in circumstances which might have been described properly as private. They were taken in a public street in a large city."[69]

It is submitted that it is not axiomatic that simply because a photograph is take in a public place that publication cannot be restrained on the basis of confidence or privacy. Whilst it is fair to say that this is the general rule, if the photograph's content is such that it would be offensive to the reasonable person, publication may be restrained. Such cases will be rare, as generally photography in a public place is permissible.[69a] The fact that information is known to a limited number of members of the public (such as a small group witnessing an event in public) does not prevent the information from having and retaining the character of confidentiality.[70] As was said by the High Court of New Zealand:

> "Merely because the fact is one that occurred at a public place and in view of the general public, which may have been only a few persons or merely because it can be found in a public record, does not mean that it should receive widespread publicity if it does not involve a matter of public concern. There can be such a thing as highly offensive publicity to something that happened long ago even thought it occurred in a public place."[71]

---

[66] As to which see Ch. 14, below.

[67] *cf. Peck v United Kingdom* [2003] E.M.L.R. 15; (2003) 36 E.H.R.R. 41; *Aubry v Les Éditions Vice-Versa Inc* [1998] 1 S.C.R. 591 (Supreme Court of Canada) (restraining publication of photograph of person sitting on the steps of a public library taken without her consent). Note that this is may be affected by the decision of the ECHR in *Von Hannover v Germany* (App. No. 59320/00) which was heard on November 6, 2003 but has not yet been published. For facts see above at para. 7–004.

[68] (unrep) October 19, 2001, Connell J.

[69] Transcript, p.6.

[69a] See above at paras 7–049 and 7–050.

[70] *Stephens v Avery* [1988] Ch. 449 at 454; *R. v Broadcasting Complaints Commission Ex p. Granada Televison Ltd* [1995] E.M.L.R. 163 at 168; *Creation Records Ltd v News Group Newspapers Ltd* [1997] E.M.L.R. 444 at 456; *Mills v News Group Newspapers* [2001] E.M.L.R. 957 at 968.

[71] *Bradley v Wingnut Films Ltd* 24 I.P.R. 205 (High Court of New Zealand, 1992).

**7–057**    In a case factually similar to *MGN v Attard*, the High Court of New Zealand rejected a claim that photographs taken of children of a radio broadcaster being pushed along a public footpath in a stroller were subject to a right of privacy.[72] After a very full consideration of the law on this point in the UK, the USA, Australia and New Zealand, Randerson J. concluded that the information contained in the photographs taken in a public street could not without more convey any information that was confidential. Randerson J. said:

> "There is no statutory prohibition against the taking of photographs in a public street and, in general, it must be taken to be one of the ordinary incidents of living in a free community. It is well established as a general rule, that there is nothing to prevent the taking of photographs of private property from a public place[73]: *Victoria Park Racing and Recreation Grounds Co Ltd v Taylor* (1937) 58 C.L.R. 479, 494; *Sports and General Press Agency Ltd v "Our Dogs" Publishing Co Ltd* (1916) 2 K.B. 880, affirmed (1917) 2 K.B. 125; *Bathurst City Council v Saban* (1985) 2 N.S.W.L.R. 70; and *Prosser and Keeton on Torts*, 5ᵗʰ ed., pp.855–856. The general rule must however be qualified where the taking of the photographs may infringe, for example, the laws of trespass, nuisance, or amount to a breach of confidence as suggested by Laws J in *Hellewell*. A further qualification arises where a photograph is published in a context which is defamatory: *Tolley v J S Fry and Sons Ltd* (1930) 1 K.B. 467. And if there is deliberate or persistent conduct, the offender may be subject to prohibition orders under the Harassment Act 1997.
>
> Here, no serious objection is made to the taking of the photographs. The essence of the complaint is the second defendant's intention to publish them in its magazine. I accept Mr Akel's submission that there is a difference between the fleeting glimpse of the children which passers-by may have had in the street and the publication of a semi-permanent record in the form of a photograph published in a magazine. In the latter case, there is a longer opportunity for a reader to view and identify the children. But the distinction is only one of degree and I am unable in principle to accept that the publication of photographs such as those in the present case could be actionable under any of the formulations of privacy suggested in those jurisdictions which have adopted a privacy tort or, indeed, the limited form of the tort recognised in this court.
>
> There may be exceptional cases (of which *Peck* may be a good example) where the nature of the photograph, the manner in which it was obtained, or the way in which it is later published, could amount to a breach of confidence as that action is now developing in the United Kingdom. That may be so even if the photograph is taken in a public place. Although the publication of a photograph taken in a public place will not ordinarily be

---

[72] *Hoskings v Runting* CP 527/02 (May 30, 2003), Randerson J., High Court of New Zealand, Auckland Registry; [2003] 3 N.Z.L.R. 385. NB. Court of Appeal of New Zealand gave judgment on March 25, 2004 (CA 101/03) dismissing the Claimant's appeal.

[73] For discussion of the "right" to take a photograph see above at paras 6–002 *et seq.*

actionable, there should be no automatic assumption that the media have *carte blanche*. That said, there is nothing exceptional in the present case which would warrant the intervention of the court."

The photographs in issue showed the faces of the children but they were described as "not particularly prominent". Again, the principle that a photograph taken in a public place is not actionable was upheld. The decision of Randerson J. has been appealed to the New Zealand Court of Appeal.[73a]

By contrast in *Aubry v Éditions Vice-Versa Inc*[74] a decision of the Supreme Court of Canada, damages were awarded in respect of a photograph taken in a public place. The claimant, a 17 year old, had been photographed sitting on the steps of the front of a building without consent. The photograph was published in a magazine and she sought compensatory damages. It was argued that it would amount to an infringement of freedom of expression to require a photographer to obtain the consent of all those they photograph in a public place. This was rejected by the Canadian court which held that the claimant's right to protect her image was more important than the right to publish her photograph without first obtaining her permission.    **7–058**

The extent to which an act on a public street can be protected either by a right of privacy or an expanded law of confidentiality is a question that has yet to be properly addressed by the domestic courts in the UK. However, it is clear from the decision of the ECHR in *Peck v United Kingdom* that an act that occurs on a public street can be subject to a right of privacy in certain circumstances.

In *Peck v United Kingdom*[75] the applicant was captured on CCTV walking in a town centre with a kitchen knife and attempting suicide by cutting his wrists. Stills from the CCTV footage were released by the local council accompanying an article entitled "Defused—the partnership between CCTV and the police prevents a potentially dangerous situation". Local papers published the stills which did not mask the applicant's face. A television channel then sought the CCTV footage which the council provided for use in a news programme about CCTV and it was also supplied to a BBC programme called Crime Beat which had an audience of 9.2 million viewers. Steps were taken to mask the applicant's identity but they were insufficient. The applicant instituted judicial review proceedings against the local council contending that they had no right to disclose the footage. The applicant contended that his rights under Art.8 had been violated both in isolation and together with Art.13 (effective remedy before an national authority). The publications had occurred in 1995 and 1996 prior to the Human Rights Act 1998 coming into force.    **7–059**

The ECHR held that the disclosure by the council of the CCTV footage constituted a serious interference with the applicant's right to respect for his private life.[76] The foreseeable exposure of the act was taken into account by    **7–060**

---

[73a] The New Zealand Court of Appeal gave judgment on March 25, 2004 (CA 101/03) dismissing the Claimant's appeal.

[74] [1998] 1 S.C.R. 591.

[75] (2003) 36 E.H.R.R. 41 at para.63.

[76] 36 E.H.R.R. 41.

the court. It observed that the applicant was in a public street but was not there for the purposes of participating in any public event and he was not a public figure. It was late at night and he was "deeply perturbed and in a state of some distress". The distribution of the CCTV footage via the media meant that his attempted suicide was viewed to an extent which far exceeded the degree of exposure that would be foreseeable to a person walking in that area.[77] The ECHR observed:

> "Private life is a broad term not susceptible to exhaustive definition. The court has already held that elements such as gender identification, name, sexual orientation and sexual life are important elements of the personal sphere protected by Article 8. The Article also protects a right to establish and develop relationships with other human beings and the outside world and it may include activities of professional or business nature. There is, therefore, a zone of interaction of a person with others, even in a public context which may fall within the scope of private life."[78]

**7–061**    It is submitted that an act which occurs in a public street may, in exceptional circumstances, be subject to a right of privacy (arising from implied confidentiality) depending upon the following:

(1)  the nature of the act and whether disclosure would be offensive to a reasonable person of ordinary sensibility (an attempted suicide by an obviously disturbed person is plainly well within that category);

(2)  the reasonable expectations of a person in the shoes of the claimant as to (i) the nature and number of public observers, and (ii) the probability that the information will be disseminated, and (iii) the extent to which the information is likely to be disseminated;

(3)  whether a permanent or systematic record has been made of the information.

It should be remembered that the case of *Peck v UK*[78a] primarily concerned the question of whether English law provided an adequate remedy on the specific facts of that case. In *Wainwright v Secretary of State for the Home Department*[78b] Lord Hoffman said in relation to *Peck v UK*[78c]:

> Counsel for the Wainwrights relied upon Peck's case as demonstrating the need for a general tort of invasion of privacy. But in my opinion it shows no more than the need, in English law, for a system of control of the use of film from CCTV cameras which shows greater sensitivity to the feelings of people who happen to have been caught by the lens.[78d]

---

[77] (2003) 36 E.H.R.R. 41 at para.62.
[78] (2003) 36 E.H.R.R. 41 at para.57.
[78a] [2003] E.M.L.R. 15; (2003) 36 E.H.R.R. 41.
[78b] [2003] UKHL 53 at [16]; [2003] 3 W.L.R. 1137; [2003] 4 All E.R. 969, HL.
[78c] [2003] E.M.L.R. 15; (2003) 36 E.H.R.R. 41.
[78d] [2003] UKHL 53 at [33]; [2003] 3 W.L.R. 1137; [2003] 4 All E.R. 969, HL.

However, if *Peck v United Kingdom*[78e] were on its facts to come before a UK domestic court in 2003, the claimant may have a remedy under the Data Protection Act 1998 in any event.[78f]

The substance of the Data Protection Act 1998 came into force in the UK on March 1, 2000.[78g] A data controller is under a duty to comply with the eight Data Protection principles, the first of which is that data must be processed fairly and lawfully.[78h] It is submitted that consideration of whether processing has been fair will entail consideration of whether any relevant codes have been complied with.[78i] In July 2000, the Data Protection Commissioner (as the title then was) issued a Code of Practice for Users of CCTV pursuant to her powers under s.51(3)(b).[78j] In the section concerning Access to and Disclosure of Images to Third Parties at paragraphs 6 to 8,[78k] it is stated that images should not be routinely made available to the media, if they are reasons should be documented and that images of individuals need to be disguise or blurred. Failure to do this is, it is submitted, likely to amount to unfair processing and may give rise to a claim for compensation under the Data Protection Act 1998.[78l]

### SPECIFIC CATEGORIES OF PHOTOGRAPHS

### Secret filming and telephoto lens photography

Secret filming or photography of people in a public place can amount to infringement of Art.8(1) even where there is no private element to the events filmed.[79] Secret filming is considered objectionable because it is not open to those who are the subject of the filming to take any action to prevent it.[80] However it is not objectionable, where the photography or filming may be justified for reasons of crime prevention or detection.[81] It also doubtful whether, if what is filmed, is activity in a public place with no reasonable expectation of privacy disclosure of which would not be offensive to a reasonable person whether any case of action would arise.[81a]    **7–062**

In *Hellewell v Chief Constable*—decided in 1995 well before the Human Rights Act came into force—Law J. said:

---

[78e] [2003] E.M.L.R. 15; (2003) 36 E.H.R.R. 41.
[78f] *cf.* comments of Lord Hoffman in *Wainwright v Secretary of State for the Home Department* [2003] UKHL 53 at [16]; [2003] 3 W.L.R. 1137; [2003] 4 All E.R. 969, HL.
[78g] Data Protection Act 1998 (Commencement) Order 2000 (SI 2000/183).
[78h] See below at para. 11–034.
[78i] See below at para. 11–037.
[78j] See below at para. 11–179. The Code is reproduced in full at Appendix 5, below.
[78k] See Appendix 5, below.
[78l] See below at para. 11–107.
[79] *R. v Loveridge* [2001] EWCA Crim 973, para.30; [2001] 2 Cr. App. R. 592, 599.
[80] *Broadcasting Standards Commission Ex p. BBC* [2000] 3 W.L.R. 1327.
[81] See cases cited above at para.7–050.
[81a] See above at paras 7–049 and 7–050, and 7–059 and 7–060.

"If someone with a telephoto lens were to take from some distance and with no authority a picture of another engaged in some private act, his subsequent disclosure of the photograph would in my judgment, as surely amount to a breach of confidence as if he had found or stolen a letter or diary in which the act was recounted and proceeded to publish it. In such as case, the law would protect what might reasonably be called a right of privacy, although the name accorded to the cause of action would be breach of confidence. It is elementary that, in all such cases, a defence based on the public interest would be available."[82]

**7–063**    If there is an intrusion in a situation where a person can reasonably expect his privacy to be respected, then that intrusion will be capable of giving rise to a liability in action for breach of confidence unless the intrusion can be justified.[83] Generally, the court will restrain publication of confidential information improperly or surreptitiously obtained.[84] However, the fact that the information has been obtained by unlawful activity does not mean that its publication will necessarily be restrained, but that unlawful means have been used is a compelling factor when a discretion comes to be exercised.[85]

The monitoring of the actions of an individual in a public place by the use of photographic equipment which does not record the visual data does not, as such, give rise to an interference with the individual's private life.[86]

Long lens photography of persons in private places without their consent is prohibited by the Press Complaints Commission Code[87] which the court is required to consider by virtue of s.12(4) of the Human Rights Act 1998.[88] Unless there is some type of public interest reasons for photography and/or publication, long lens photography of private acts would infringe a right to privacy.[89]

---

[82] [1995] 1 W.L.R. 804 at 807H.

[83] *A v B plc* [2002] EWCA Civ 337; [2003] Q.B. 195; [2002] E.M.L.R. 21 at 383.

[84] *D v L* [2003] EWCA 1169 at para.18 *per* Walter L.J.; [2004] E.M.L.R. 1; *Ashburton v Pape* [1913] 2 Ch. 429 at 475 *per* Swinfen Eady J. Note that there is an error in the dicta of Swinfen Eady L.J. from *Ashburton v Pape* [1913] 2 Ch. 429 at 475 as quoted in the judgment of Walter L.J. in *D v L* [2003] EWCA 1169 at para. 18. The actual quotation should read:

"The principle upon which the Court of Chancery has acted for many years has been to restrain the publication of *confidential* information improperly or surreptitiously obtained or of information imparted in confidence which ought not to be divulged." (emphasis added).

The word "confidential" is omitted in the extract in *D v L*.

[85] *A v B plc* [2002] EWCA Civ 337 at para.11(x); [2003] Q.B. 195, 206; *Douglas v Hello! Ltd (No.6)* [2003] EWHC 786 at para.186j(xii).

[86] App. Nos 32200/96; and 32201/96, *Herbecq v Belgium*; Dec. 14.1.98; D.R. 92-A, p.92.

[87] See below at Ch. 14 and Appendix 3.

[88] As to s.12(4) see below at paras 7–110 and 14–006.

[89] *Hellewell v Chief Constable of Derbyshire* [1995] 1 W.L.R. 804, 807, approved in *Douglas v Hello (No.1)* at para.166 [2001] Q.B. 967 [2001] 2 W.L.R. 992; [2001] 2 All E.R. 289; [2001] E.M.L.R. 9.

## Photographs of sexual activity

The nature of the relationship between the parties, the nature of the   **7–064**
sexual activity and all the circumstances in which it takes place affect the
attribution of the quality of confidentiality to sexual activity.[90] The impact
of the disclosure on others, for example children of the relationship, may be
relevant to the very existence of confidentiality.[91] The court is likely to view
the confidentiality of sexual relations within a marriage or a permanent
relationship differently to transient relationships or one night stands.[92]

In *Theakston v MGN Ltd*[93] an injunction was granted restraining pub-   **7–065**
lication of photographs of the claimant engaged in some forms of sexual
activity taken without his consent at a brothel. An injunction to restrain the
publication of the fact the claimant had attended the brothel was refused.
Ouseley J. said:

"The authorities cited to me showed that the courts have consistently
recognised that photographs can be particularly intrusive and have
showed a high degree of willingness to prevent the publication of photographs, taken without the consent of the person photographed but which
the photographer or someone else sought to exploit and publish. This
protection extends to photographs, taken without their consent, of people
who exploited the commercial value of their own image in similar photographs, and to photographs taken with the consent of people but who
had not consented to that particular form of commercial exploitation, as
well as to photographs taken in public or from a public place of what
could not be seen with the naked eye, then at least with the aid of powerful binoculars. I concluded that this part of the injunction involved no
particular extension of the law of confidentiality and that publication of
such photographs would be particularly intrusive into the claimant's own
individual personality. I considered that even though the fact of that the
claimant went to the brothel and the details as to what he did there were
not to be restrained from publication, the publication of photographs
taken there without his consent could still constitute an intrusion into his
private and personal life and would do so in a particularly humiliating
and damaging way."[94]

[90] *Theakston v MGN Ltd* [2002] E.M.L.R. 22 at para.58.
[91] *Theakston v MGN Ltd* [2002] E.M.L.R. 22 at para.59.
[92] *A v B plc* [2002] EWCA Civ 337 para.43; [2003] Q.B. 195, 216; [2002] E.M.L.R. 21 at 394–395,
*Theakston v MGN Ltd* [2002] E.M.L.R. 22 at para.59.
[93] [2002] E.M.L.R. 22 at para.78.
[94] [2002] E.M.L.R. 22 at para.78.

## Photographs of property

### *Exterior and interiors of homes*

**7–066**    Unauthorised photographs of a person's home and property may infringe a right to privacy.[95] It is doubtful that a mere photograph of the outside of a house would amount to an actionable breach of privacy unless (1) the photograph itself enabled the address of a person to be identified, and (2) there was a real risk that the owner or resident would suffer adverse consequences from the disclosure of the address such as death or injury or being made vulnerable to stalkers.[96] Where the evidence of a risk of such adverse consequences is slight, an injunction will be refused.[97]

In *Beckham v MGN Ltd*[98] an injunction was granted restraining publication of unauthorised photographs of the interior of the matrimonial home of David and Victoria Beckham. The claimants had been the subject of threats and were "sensitive" about the security arrangements at the property. There was a possibility that the photographs might reveal the nature of or part of the security arrangements or that items of property be revealed which they did not want to be revealed. The evidence was that they would not enter into an agreement to publish details of their domestic arrangements unless they had absolute control over which photographs would be published. An injunction was granted on the basis of an unwarranted intrusion into the claimant's privacy. An argument on the part of the defendants that the claimants should be required to give a cross-undertaking that they would not publish or permit to be published any photographs of the subject matter in the injunction was rejected as an unwarranted restriction on their freedom to contract on what terms they saw fit.

### *Other rights and property release forms*

**7–067**    Other rights that may restrict the right to take and/or publish photographs of property are copyright, trademarks, the law of defamation, and contractual terms. Passing off may possibly be relevant depending upon the use of the photograph—for example if it were represented to be an official poster of a stately home or similar—but this is not likely to be a common problem.[99]

**7–068**    Generally in the UK, photographs of the exteriors of buildings that can be viewed from public places may be taken freely and do not require property release forms for use and publication.[1] However, if the photograph is to be used commercially, particularly in advertising, a property release form

---

[95] *Beckham v MGN Ltd* (unrep) June 28, 2001, Eady J.
[96] *Mills v News Group Newspapers* [2001] E.M.L.R. 957; *Venables v News Group Newspapers Ltd* [2001] E.M.R.L. 10; *Nicholls v BBC* [1999] E.M.L.R. 791.
[97] *Mills v News Group Newspapers* [2001] E.M.L.R. 957.
[98] (unrep) June 28, 2001, Eady J.
[99] See Ch. 10, below.
[1] Although for commercial photography in certain places licences may be required from the local authority or otherwise, *e.g.* Trafalgar Square. See above at paras 6–171 to 6–179.

would be advisable.[1a] Many picture libraries will require a property release form in respect of photographs that depict identifiable property before they will accept or deal with that image. Photographs of the interiors of buildings, whether public buildings or private property, may be affected by terms and conditions imposed by the owners prohibiting photography.

Copyright does not prevent photography of buildings. The Copyright Designs & Patents Act 1988 provides that copyright in a building is not infringed by making a photograph or film of it.[2] In addition, copyright in sculptures, models for buildings and works of artistic craftsmanship that are permanently situated in a public place or in premises open to the public is not infringed by taking a photograph or making a film of the work.[3]

However, where the photograph of a property includes other copyright works that are more than incidentally included,[4] rights clearance for the copyright works would be required. Examples would be a building with an original mural painted on the side or a photograph of the stage of a theatre showing a set design.

**7–069**

The increasing trend towards registering building facades as trademarks and the potential consequences for photographers is discussed above at paras 5–038 and 5–053. Even where the building facade is registered as a trademark, in most cases the building owner could not prohibit the taking of photographs or publication of photographs of that building. As at the date of writing, those building facades that are registered as trade marks in the UK are all "logo" styled drawings of the building rather than photographs. What is protected is the logo mark and not the visual appearance of the building.

In the United Kingdom there is no recognised right of the owner in the image of his or her property. In France and other civil law jurisdictions, there are many cases where the owner of the building has been held to have the sole right to exploit his property in any form and can prohibit commercial exploitation of photographs taken without consent.[5] No such right is recognised in the United Kingdom. Absent use of a photograph of a property for advertising or in a potentially defamatory way, it is not necessary as a matter of law to obtain the consent of the owner of a building that can be viewed from a public place before publication of a photograph of that building.

If the proposed use of the image is commercial or editorial, obtaining a property release from the building owner is advisable. The best advice, even if perhaps excessively cautious, is "if in doubt, obtain a property release form". As noted above, in practice many commercial picture libraries will simply not deal in images without a property release. Depending upon the

**7–070**

---

[1a] *Cf.* Decisions of the Advertising Standards Authority concerning use of photographs of homes without permission discussed below at para. 14–084.

[2] CDPA 1988, s.62(1)(a). See above at para. 2–182.

[3] CDPA 1988, s.62(1)(b). See above at para. 2–182.

[4] As to the defence of incidental inclusion see above at para. 2–168 and below at paras 5–054 *et seq.*

[5] *e.g. Pritchett v Dubray* Court of Cassation (1999) 182 R.I.D.A. 148 and case comment by M. Cornu, (use of photograph of a café on postcards without permission of café owner prohibited).

proposed nature of the use, in extreme cases, obtaining a property release from the occupier as well (if this is a different person) may also be advisable. Owner and occupier releases would be advisable if a photograph of the building was to be used in a way that may be defamatory—for example, if it were to be used to illustrate an article about drug dealers in a manner that may suggest either the owner or the occupier of a particular property were drug dealers.[6]

## PHOTOGRAPHS OF PARTICULAR CLASSES OF PEOPLE

### Celebrities and public figures

7–071    A public figure is entitled to a private life.[7] The fact that an individual has achieved prominence in the public arena does not mean that his private life can be laid bare by the media.[8] However, such individuals need to recognise that because of their public position their actions will be more closely scrutinised by the media.[9] Those who have courted public attention have less grounds to object to intrusion into their private lives.[10] Simply because a person is the subject of media attention, for example because they are married to a public figure, does not automatically render them a role model or a public figure whose private life is a matter of legitimate interest to the public.[11] Whether the claimant has by his way of life or activities generated legitimate public interest will be relevant in assessing whether he is entitled to preserve his confidentiality.[12]

Where a public figure chooses to make untrue pronouncements about his or her private life, the press will normally be entitled to put the record straight.[13]

### Celebrities and commercial confidence

7–072    Where the overriding complaint is the misappropriation of the commercial value of an image and there is a basis to establish an obligation in

---

[6] See below at para. 7–127.

[7] *A v B plc* [2002] EWCA Civ 337 para.11(xii); [2003] Q.B. 195, 208; [2002] E.M.L.R. 21 at 384.

[8] *Campbell v MGN Ltd* [2002] EWCA Civ 1373 at para.41; [2003] Q.B. 633 at 658 *per* Lord Phillips M.R.; *D v L* [2003] EWCA 1169 at para.28 *per* Walter L.J.

[9] *A v B plc* [2002] EWCA Civ 337 para.11(xii); [2003] Q.B. 195, 208; [2002] E.M.L.R. 21 at 384; *Douglas v Hello! Ltd (No.6)* [2003] EWHC 786 at para.186(i); [2003] 3 All E.R. 996; [2003] E.M.L.R. 31.

[10] *A v B plc* [2002] EWCA Civ 337 para.11(xii); [2003] Q.B. 195, 208; [2002] E.M.L.R. 21 at 385; *Douglas v Hello! Ltd (No.6)* [2003] EWHC 786 at para.186(iv); [2003] 3 All E.R. 996; [2003] E.M.L.R. 31; *Woodward v Hutchins* [1977] 2 All E.R. 751 at 754f, 755j.

[11] *Lady Archer v Williams* [2003] EWHC 1670 at para.64; [2003] E.M.L.R. 38.

[12] *Lady Archer v Williams* [2003] EWHC 1670 at para.66; [2003] E.M.L.R. 38.

[13] *Campbell v MGN Ltd* [2002] EWCA Civ 1373 at para.43; [2003] Q.B. 633 at 658 *per* Lord Phillips M.R.; *Woodward v Hutchins* [1977] 2 All E.R. 751 at 754 *per* Lord Denning "If the image which they fostered was not a true image, it is in the public interest that it should be corrected".

confidence in respect of that image (for example by exclusion of photographers from a private event), publication of the images may be restrained on the basis of commercial confidence.[14] This is discussed further above at paras 7–012 to 7–027.

It is submitted that an action for misappropriation of the commercial value of a celebrity's image has more in common with a right of publicity than confidence. The approach of the courts in the USA to the right of publicity is interesting and warrants consideration, particularly because the focus is on the commercial value of the right which distinguishes it from the right to privacy.

## The right of publicity

The law of the United States of America and other jurisdictions such as Canada[15] (but not the UK) recognise a right of publicity. This is the inherent right of every person to control the commercial use of his or her identity. The term "right of publicity" was first coined in 1953 by Judge Jerome Franklin in the American case of *Haelen Laboratories Inc v Topps Chewing Gum*.[16] The case concerned the legal interest of a baseball player and the publication of his picture on chewing gum cards. It was said "a man has a right in the publicity value of his photograph ie. the right to grant the exclusive privilege of publishing his picture". Since then, the right of publicity has developed and is now well established in the USA in particular and several states have enacted right of publicity statutes.[17]

**7–073**

The right of publicity in the USA is a wide subject encompassing both statute and common law with a vast body of case law in its own right. This right is not presently recognised in the United Kingdom and detailed treatment of the law of other jurisdictions is outside the scope of this work. However, an overview of the principles applied by the USA courts is included here as it is submitted that the right of publicity is closer in spirit to the commercial confidence approach of Lindsay J. in *Douglas v Hello Ltd (No.6)* than either the existing UK law concerning breach of confidence or any embryonic free-standing privacy right. It is not entirely improbable that the law in the United Kingdom will, over the next decade, develop to protect commercial rights in images in a similar manner to a right of publicity. It has been said that courts in this country should be very cautious, now that the Human Rights Act 1998 is in force, in seeking to derive assistance from judgments in other jurisdictions founded on some different rights-based

**7–074**

---

[14] *Douglas v Hello! Ltd (No.6)* [2003] EWHC 786; [2003] All E.R. 996; [2003] E.M.L.R. 31.
[15] See *e.g. Krouse v Chrysler Canada Ltd* 40 D.L.R. 3d 15 (Ont. CA); *Athans v Canadian Adventure Camps* 80 D.L.R. (3d) 583 (professional water skier could recover damages for an invasion of his right to market his own personality).
[16] 202 F.2d 866 at 868 (2nd Cir. 1953).
[17] Currently 18 states have such legislation: California, Florida, Illinois, Indiana, Kentucky, Massachusetts, Nebraska, Nevada, New York, Ohio, Oklahoma, Rhode Island, Tennessee, Texas, Utah, Virginia, Washington and Wisconsin. See J. T. McCarthy, *The Rights of Publicity and Privacy* (West Group) Ch.6.

charter.[18] As indicated above, some states have right of publicity statutes and many authorities are decisions under the relevant statute. For further reading on the USA right of publicity see the excellent looseleaf work *The Rights of Publicity and Privacy* by J. Thomas McCarthy.

**7–075**     The right of publicity is a property right and a form of intellectual property.[19] Non-celebrities are entitled to object to commercial use of their identity and may maintain an action for infringement of the right where there is economic damage.[20] The right protects the plaintiff's persona or identity which includes name and likeness[21]; physical appearance (both in the form of actual photographs of the individuals[22] and the use of looka-likes[23]); voice[24]; and any distinguishing feature so closely identifiable with a persona such as to suggest endorsement including property such as a racing driver's car[25] or costume.[26]

The plaintiff must establish:

(1) ownership of an enforceable right in the identity or persona of a human being, either because the action concerns the plaintiff's own identity or because he is an assignee[27] or licensee[28] of another's right of publicity;

(2) the defendant has used some aspect of the identity or persona in such a way that the plaintiff is identifiable from that use[29];

(3) without the consent of the rights owner[30]; and

(4) the unauthorised use has or is likely to cause damage to the commercial value of the plaintiff's persona.

---

[18] *Douglas v Hello! Ltd (No.1)* para.76 [2001] Q.B. 967 at 989 *per* Brooke L.J.

[19] *Acme Circus Operating Co v Kuperstock* 711 F.2d 1538, 1541 (11th Cir. 1983).

[20] *e.g. Motschenbacher v RJ Reynolds Tobacco Co*, 498 F.2d 821, 824, n.11 (9th Cir. 1974); *Cohen v Herbal Concepts Inc* 100 A.D.2d 175, 473 N.Y.S.2d 426, 431 (1984); aff'd, 63 N.Y.2d 379, 482 N.Y.S.2d 457 (1984); *Ainsworth v Century Supply Co* 693 N.E. 2d 510, 514 (Ill. App. 1998). See further J. T. McCarthy, *The Rights of Publicity and Privacy* at para.4.16.

[21] *Brown v Ames* 201 F.3d 654, 658 (5th Cir. 2000); *Canessa v JI Kislak Inc.* 235 A.2d 62. 97 N.J. Super. 327 (1967) (use of name and picture of non-celebrity family by real estate company); *Palmer v Schonhorn Enterprises Inc* (1967) 232 A.2d 458, 96 N.J. Super. 327 (golfer Arnold Palmer).

[22] *Lerman v Chuckleberry Publishing Co* 521 F. Supp. 228, 232 (S.D. N.Y. 1981) (stills from a film); *Downing v Abercrombie & Fitch* 265 F.3d 994, 60 U.S.P.Q. 2d 1184 (9th Cir 2001).

[23] *Onassis v Christian Dior-New York Inc* 122 Misc. 2d 603, 472 N.Y.S 2d 254 (1984); affirmed 110 A.D.2d 1095; 488 N.Y.S. 2d 843 (1985); *Washington v Brown & Williamson* 223 U.S.P.Q. 1116 (E.D. Pa. 1984).

[24] *Lahr v Adell Chem Co* 300 F.2d 256, 259 (1st Cir. 1962); *Waits v Frito Lay* 978 F.2d 1093 (9th Cir. 1992); *Midler v Ford Motor Co* 849 F.2d 460 (9th Cir. 1988). And see L. A. Wohl, *The Right of Publicity and Vocal Larceny: Sounding Off on Sound-Alikes* (1988) 57 Fordham L. Rev. 445.

[25] *Motschenbacher v R J Reynolds Tobacco Co* 498 F.2d 821 (9th Cir. 1974).

[26] *Tin Pan Apple Inc v Miller Brewing Co* 737 F. Supp. 826 (S.D.N.Y. 1990).

[27] *Estate of Elvis Presley v Russen*, 513 F. Supp. 1339, 1350; 211 U.S.P.Q. 415 (D.N.J. 1981).

[28] *Re D.B. Kaplan Delicatessen* 225 U.S.P.Q. 342 (Trademark Tr. & App. Bd.).

[29] *Waits v Frito-Lay Inc* 978 F. 2d 1093; 23 U.S.P.Q.2d 1721, 1726 (9th Cir. 1992); *Negri v Schering Corp* 333 F. Supp. 101 (S.D.N.Y. 1971); *Ali v Playgirl Inc* 447 F. Supp. 723, 206 U.S.P.Q. 1021 (S.D.N.Y. 1978).

[30] *Downing v Abercrombie & Fitch*, 265 F.3d 994; 60 U.S.P.Q.2d 1184 (9th Cir. 2001).

There is no requirement that an element of falsity be made out to establish **7–076** infringement of the right of publicity and this distinguishes it from false endorsement or passing off claims.[31] Damage to commercial value is a key element of the tort. If the damage alleged is to self esteem, hurt feelings or state of mind, the proper cause of action is infringement of the right of privacy.[32] It has been observed that the right of publicity is a proprietary right with goals analogous to those of patent and copyright law and that it has little to do with protecting feelings or reputation.[33]

It is immaterial that the defendant made little profit from the use.[34] The liability arises because the defendant receives a benefit from using the celebrity's persona gratuitously. In a case concerning the use of a Jacqueline Onasiss lookalike, the court observed "The commercial hitchhiker seeking to travel on the fame of another will have to learn to pay the fare or stand on his own two feet."[35]

An interesting issue concerning the use of photographs and the right of **7–077** publicity is the extent to which the plaintiff must be identifiable in order to recover. In *Negri v Schering Corp*[36] the use of a nine inch high, full length likeness of a film actress was held to infringe under a New York statute. The photograph of the actress was a scene from a film she had appeared in. It was used in a magazine advertisement for an anti-histamine in which she was depicted with her leading man in the film. The defendants contended that the actress was not recognisable as it showed her as she was 40 years ago.

The court considered that her features were "clear and characteristic" and that it was easily recognisable as a picture of her. In addition there was evidence that a friend of her's and four others had in fact recognised her. The court took into account the fact that she was shown with her leading man plainly pointed towards recognition. It was said that the number of people who recognised the advertisement is not material to the issue of liability but may be relevant to the question of damages.[37] The question of whether the actress' appearance had changed in the 40 years from when the picture was taken was said to be "beside the point"[38] as the object of the statute was to protect unauthorised use of name or image for commercial exploitation.

In *Cheatham v Paisano Publications Inc*[39] it was accepted that a plaintiff **7–078** may have a right of publicity claim arising from a photograph that does not

---

[31] *e.g. Rogers v Grimaldi* 875 F.2d 994, 1004 (2nd Cir. 1989); *Eastwood v Superior Court* 149 Cal. App. 3d 409 (2d Dist. 1983) ("The appearance of an 'endorsement' is not the sine qua non of a claim for commercial appropriation"); *Flores v Mosler Safe Co* (1959) 196 N.Y.S. 2d 975, 980; 164 N.E. 2d 853.

[32] J. T. McCarthy, *The Rights of Publicity and Privacy* at paras 5.58 and paras 11.30.

[33] *Zacchini v Scripps-Howard Broadcasting Co* 433 U.S. 462; 53 L. Ed. 2d 965; 97 S. Ct. 2489 (1977).

[34] *Henley v Dillard Dep't Stores*, 46 F. Supp. 2d 587 (N.D. Tex. 1999).

[35] *Onassis v Christian Dior-New York Inc* 122 Misc. 2d 603; 472 N.Y.S. 2d 254 (1984); affirmed 110 A.D. 2d 1095; 488 N.Y.S. 2d 843 (1985).

[36] 333 F. Supp. 101 (S.D. N.Y. 1971).

[37] 333 F. Supp. 101 at 104 (S.D.N.Y. 1971).

[38] 333 F. Supp. 101 at 105 (S.D.N.Y. 1971).

[39] 891 F. Supp. 381 (W.D. Ky. 1995).

show her face. The plaintiff was the creator of "unique" clothing designs which she displayed at bikers' events. At a bikers' festival she wore what the court described as "one of her distinctive creations which displayed her bottom through fishnet fabric that replaced cut out portions of her jeans". A magazine published a photograph of the plaintiff's bottom as part of a photo essay about the festival. The picture did not identify the plaintiff. A year or so later, the same publishers published an advertisement for a T-shirt with a similar image on it. The plaintiff issued proceedings for commercial exploitation of a likeness and invasion of privacy. The defendant issued a motion for dismissal.

The court denied the motion stating that a cause of action could arise if the plaintiff's image was distinctive enough that her friends and customers could recognise the replica image on the T-shirt and identify this as her image. The plaintiff's claims that friends and customers did recognise her unique designs and that they had commercial value overcame the defendant's motions to dismiss at the outset.

**7–079**    In *Cohen v Herbal Concepts Inc*[40] the photograph in issue was that of a nude mother and child full length viewed from behind at an angle which did not show their faces. The photograph was taken whilst the mother and her four year old daughter were bathing in a stream located on private property without their consent. The photographer sold the photographs for use in an advertisement for an anti-cellulite product. The action was framed in invasion of privacy rather than infringement of a right of publicity but the court said "manifestly there can be no appropriation of plaintiff's identity for commercial purposes if he or she is not recognizable from the picture."[41] As far as the right of privacy was concerned it was observed that the court would need to determine "the quality and quantity of the identifiable characteristics displayed in the advertisement and this will require an assessment of the clarity of the photograph, the extent to which identifying features are visible and the distinctiveness of those features". On the facts identifying features included their hair, bone structure, body contours, stature and posture. The court dismissed the defendant's motion for summary judgment concluding that a jury could find that someone familiar with the people depicted could identify them by looking at the advertisement.

It has been held that the right of publicity protects the estates of deceased persons.[42] In addition, a number of state statutes provide for a right of publicity that survives death.[43] As the right is founded in commercial interests, a post-mortem right is reconcilable with the underlying rationale that the right is a property right.[44] This is to be distinguished from a right of privacy, which like the right to object to defamation, is a personal right which terminates on death.

---

[40] 63 N.Y. 2d 379; 472 N.E.2d 307; 482 N.Y.S.2d 457 (1984 C.A. N.Y.).
[41] 63 N.Y. 2d 379 at 384.
[42] *Estate of Elvis Presley v Russen* 513 F. Supp. 1339 (D. N.J. 1981).
[43] *e.g.* California, Florida, Illinois. See further J. T McCarthy, *The Rights of Publicity and Privacy*, Ch.6.
[44] *Estate of Elvis Presley v Russen* 513 F. Supp. 1339 at 1355 (D. N.J. 1981).

# Children

## General

No child, simply by virtue of being a child, is entitled to a right of privacy   **7–080**
or confidentiality.[45] It has been said that a child is left to whatever remedies
against the media the law would give an adult in comparable circumstances.[46]

However, in practice children enjoy greater privacy rights than adults
under the inherent jurisdiction of the Family Division of the High Court and
the extensive legislation prohibiting identification of children in relation to
court proceedings.[47]

Where the court has jurisdiction to grant an injunction, the child's rights
under Art.8 must be taken into account in order that the court complies
with its obligations under s.6 of the Human Rights Act 1998. In a case where
an injunction was sought to prevent identification of a parent accused of
murder in order to protect the privacy of her son, it was said that the court is
at least entitled to consider the grant of an injunction even if the publicity is
not directed at a child or his carers.[48]

Further, cl.6(ii) of the Press Complaints Commission (PCC) Code states
that journalists must not interview or photograph a child under the age of 16
on subjects involving the welfare of the child or any other child without the
consent of a parent or adult responsible for the children. The court is
obliged to take into account the PCC Code if relevant under s.12(4) of the
Human Rights Act.

## Children of celebrities

The starting point is that a child of a celebrity has as much right to   **7–081**
privacy as any other child. However confidentiality, as far as celebrities and
those in the public eye are concerned, is something which can be bought and
sold.[49] Where a parent has sold with consent images of their child, it is
doubtful whether the court would restrain publication of similar images.[50]

Clause 6(v) of the PCC Code states that where material about the private
life of a child is published there must be justification for publication other
than the fame, notoriety, or position of his or her parents or guardian. As
noted, the court is obliged to take into account the PCC Code if relevant
under s.12(4) of the Human Rights Act.

---

[45] *R v Central Independent Television plc* [1994] Fam. 192, 207; [1994] 2 F.L.R. 151.
[46] *Kelly v BBC* [2001] Fam. 59, 74.
[47] See above at paras 6–044 *et seq.*
[48] *Re S (A child)* [2003] EWCA Civ 963 at 75.
[49] e.g. *Douglas v Hello (No.6)* [2003] EWHC 786; [2003] 3 All E.R. 996; [2003] E.M.L.R. 31.
[50] *Attard v MGN* October 19, 2001 Connell J. And see decision of the PCC in *Attard v Manchester Evening News* PCC Report No.55 (July–Sept 2001) p.9 at p.10, referred to in Ch. 10,
below and below at paras 14–048, n. 88 and 14–056.

*Children working as models or performing*

**7–082**     A child (*i.e.* a person under 16)[51] cannot work as a model where payment is made in respect of that work either to the child or to another person unless a licence has been granted by the local authority for the area the child lives in.[52] Any photographer proposing to engage a child model where payment is being made should apply for a licence from the relevant licensing authority at least 21 days before the photo shoot.[53] This is because the local authority has power to refuse to grant a licence if the application is not received by them at least 21 days before the day on which the activity for which the licence is required takes place.[54] The form of application is set out in Sch.1 of the Children (Performances) Regulations 1968.[55]

Similar prohibitions apply to children participating in specified performances or taking part in sport for payment. The law is piecemeal and to be found in ss.22–30 of the Children & Young Persons Act 1933; ss.37–43 of the Children & Young Persons Act 1963 and Children (Performances) Regulations 1968.[56] In 1998 the Regulations were amended when the UK implemented the European Directive for the Protection of Young Persons at Work.[57]

**7–083**     In addition to work as a model for payment or participation in sport for payment, it is necessary to have a licence granted by a local authority for a child to take part in:

(a)   any performance in connection with which a charge is made (whether for admission or otherwise)[58];

(b)   any performance in licensed premises (*i.e.* within the meaning of the Licensing Act 1964)[59];

(c)   any broadcast performance[60] or performance included in a programme service within the meaning of the Broadcasting Act 1990[61];

(d)   any performance recorded by whatever means with a view to its use in a broadcast or such a service or in a film intended for public exhibition.[62]

---

[51] Children and Young Persons Act 1933, s.30(1) "a child means in relation to England and Wales a person who is not over compulsory school age construed in accordance with s.8 of the Education Act 1996". This definition is adopted in the 1963 Act by s.4(1), Children and Young Persons Act 1963. Section 8 of the Education Act 1996 defines compulsory school age as (essentially) from the ages of 5 to 16, up to and including the last day of the school year in which the child is subject to compulsory attendance.

[52] Children and Young Persons Act 1963, s.37.

[53] Children (Performances) Regulations 1968 (SI 1968/1728), reg.1.

[54] Children (Performances) Regulations 1968 (SI 1968/1728), reg.1(3).

[55] SI 1968/1728. Available on the internet at *http://www.hmso.gov.uk/si/si1998/19981678.htm*.

[56] SI 1968/1728.

[57] 94/33. Implemented by the Children (Protection at Work) Regulations 1998 (SI 1998/276).

[58] Children and Young Persons Act 1963, s.37(2)(a).

[59] Children and Young Persons Act 1963, s.37(2)(b).

[60] Children and Young Persons Act 1963, s.37(2)(c).

[61] Children and Young Persons Act 1963, s.37(2)(d).

[62] Children and Young Persons Act 1963, s.37(2)(e).

A child is treated as taking part in a performance if he takes the place of a performer in any rehearsal or in any preparation for the recording of the performance.[63] Performance is not defined in the Act and should be construed in its ordinary meaning.

In the case of performances, the person who must make the application is the person responsible for the production of the performance in which the child is to take part.[64] In the majority of cases, this is unlikely to be the photographer. However, where the licence is to cover work as a model, the applicant must be the person who proposes to engage the child as a model[65] which in some cases may very well be the photographer.

The power of the local authority to grant licences either to children taking **7–084** part in performances, working as a model, or taking part in sport for reward is not discretionary provided that certain conditions are met.[66] The local authority shall not grant a licence for a child to do anything unless they are satisfied that:

(1) the child is fit to undertake the relevant licenced activity;

(2) proper provision has been made to secure the child's health and kind treatment;

(3) the education of the child will not suffer, having regard to such provision has or will be made in that regard.[67]

However, if the local authority is satisfied these conditions have been met and they have power to grant a licence, they cannot refuse to grant the licence.[68] The local authority does have power to prescribe conditions to the licence,[69] including a condition requiring any money earned by the child to be paid into the county court or dealt with in a manner to be approved by the local authority.[70]

Licenses shall not be granted in respect of children under the age of 14 **7–085** unless:

(1) the licence is for acting and there is a declaration in the application that the part cannot be taken except by a child of that age[71]; or

(2) the licence is for a ballet (which is either just a ballet or part of an opera—in other words not simply one part of an entertainment) and there is a declaration in the application that the child's part cannot be taken except by a child of his age[72]; or

---

[63] Children and Young Persons Act 1963, s.37(2).
[64] Children (Performances) Regulations 1968 (SI 1968/1728), reg.1(2)(a).
[65] Children (Performances) Regulations 1968 (SI 1968/1728), reg.1(2)(b).
[66] Children and Young Persons Act 1963, s.37(4).
[67] Children and Young Persons Act 1963, s.37(4).
[68] Children and Young Persons Act 1963, s.37(4).
[69] Children and Young Persons Act 1963, s.37(5).
[70] Children and Young Persons Act 1963, s.37(6).
[71] Children and Young Persons Act 1963, s.38(1)(a).
[72] Children and Young Persons Act 1963, s.38(1)(b).

(3) the nature of the performance is wholly or mainly musical or the performance consists only of opera and ballet.[73]

**7–086**     There is no need for a licence where no payment is made in respect of the performance (other than defraying expenses) and the child has not taken part in any other performance[74] within the preceding six months on more than three days.[75] Similarly, the need for a licence is dispensed with where a performance (not for payment other than defraying expenses) is given under arrangements made by a school[76] or a body of persons approved by the Home Office or the local authority.[77]

Any person who causes or procures a child to do anything in contravention of the licence requirements set out in s.37 of the Children and Young Persons Act 1963 or fails to comply with any licence condition or knowingly or recklessly makes any false statement in or in connection with an application for a licence under that section, shall be liable on summary conviction to a fine not exceeding level 3[78] on the standard scale or imprisonment for a term not exceeding three months or both.[79] It is also an offence subject to the same punishment, for a parent or guardian to allow a child to do anything in contravention of s.37 of the 1963 Act.

**7–087**     Participation of children in performances of a dangerous nature such as acrobatic or contortionist performances are further regulated by the Children and Young Persons Act 1933. Detailed consideration is outside the scope of this work. In summary, no person aged 16 or under shall take part in any performance for which a licence is required under the 1968 Act in which his life or limbs are endangered.[80] There is an absolute prohibition on training a child under 12 to take part in performances of a dangerous nature.[81] For children between the ages of 12 and 16, a licence from the local authority is required for training to take part in performances of a dangerous nature.[82] There are also restrictions on persons under the age of 18 going abroad for the purposes of performing for profit which includes work as a model where a payment is made other than for defraying expenses and there are licence requirements.[83]

## Model Release Forms

**7–088**     As discussed above, the present state of the law in the United Kingdom is that generally there is no right of action in confidence in respect of matters taking place in a public place. It remains to be seen whether a free standing

---

[73] Children and Young Persons Act 1963, s.38(1)(c).
[74] To which s.37 applies—see above.
[75] Children and Young Persons Act 1963, s.37(3)(a).
[76] Within the meaning of the Education Act 1996.
[77] Children and Young Persons Act 1963, s.37(3)(b).
[78] Scale set out in *Criminal Justice Act 1982*, s.37(2). At the time of writing, level 3 is £1,000.
[79] Children and Young Persons Act 1963, s.40.
[80] Children and Young Persons Act 1933, s.23.
[81] Children and Young Persons Act 1933, s.24.
[82] Children and Young Persons Act 1933, s.24.
[83] Children and Young Persons Act 1933, s.25.

tort of privacy will yet develop although the judgment of the House of Lords in *Secretary of State for the Home Department v Wainwright*[83a] plainly rejected the idea that there was such a tort.[83b] Photographs of people in public places may be taken freely.[84] There may be exceptional circumstance where, as in *Peck v UK*,[85] the subject matter is such that publication is regarded as offensive to the reasonable person. Absent any such special circumstances, there is no requirement to obtain model release in respect of pictures taken in public places in the UK. However, caution is advised in the light of the Data Protection Act 1998 as it is unclear at the time of writing to what extent these types of photographs class as data, if at all.[85a] It is to be hoped that such images would be excluded but it is uncertain and consent may thus be required.

In any event, if the proposed use of the photograph is in advertising or other commercial use, a model release form should be obtained.[86] As with property releases, in practice many photographic libraries will not deal in images of people without a model release form. Many jurisdictions have wider rights than the UK and the lack of a model release restricts the territories in which an image can be used. Without a model release in a format approved by the photographic library, an image featuring a clearly identifiable model is often valueless in the modern commercial environment.

Where there is any risk that the use of the image may be in a defamatory **7–089** way or in a manner implying endorsement of a product, permission of the subject should be obtained. Use of a photograph, whether for commercial or editorial purposes, to illustrate a sensitive subject should always be specifically cleared with the model in respect of that specific use. Sensitive subjects would include any use that portrays the subject (or could be construed as portraying the subject) in a negative or unfavourable light or related to any of the following areas: any form of medical condition; sexual activity or sexual orientation; infidelity, divorce or relationship breakdown; drug use or other substance abuse; violence or physical abuse; any criminal activity; court processes (civil or criminal), the justice system, prison or any use that could be construed as suggesting a criminal conviction; alcohol; tobacco; political campaigns or matters. Equally any use tending to ridicule the subject should also be the subject of a model release for that specific use.

## Performer's rights

The Copyright Designs and Patents Act 1988 confers on performers the **7–090** right to require consent to the exploitation of their live performances.[87] A

---

[83a] *Secretary of State for the Home Department v Wainwright* [2003] UKHL 53; [2003] 3 W.L.R. 1137; [2003] 4 All E.R. 969, HL. CA decision at [2001] EWCA Civ 2081; [2002] QB 1334.
[83b] Discussed above at para.7–039.
[84] See above at para. 7–055.
[85] See above paras 7–059 *et seq.*
[85a] See below at paras 11–021 to 11–033.
[86] Due to the provisions of the Code of the Committee of Advertising Practice see below at para. 14–081.
[87] CDPA 1988, s.180(1).

performance means a dramatic performance (including dance or mime); a musical performance; a reading or recitation of a literary work, or a performance of a variety act or similar presentation which in all cases is a live performance given by one or more individuals.[88]

A performer's rights are infringed by a person who, without his consent, makes a recording of the whole or any substantial part of a qualifying performance directly from the live performance.[89] The right is also infringed by a live broadcast or including live in a cable programme service the whole or any substantial part of a qualifying performance[90] or by the making of a recording of the whole or any substantial part of a qualifying performance directly from a broadcast of or cable programme including the live performance.[91] A recording made by a person for his private and domestic use does not infringe a performer's rights.[92] No damages shall be awarded against a defendant who, at the time of the infringement, had reasonable grounds to believe that consent had been given.[93]

**7–091**      The rights are infringed by "recordings" or "copies of recordings" of performances. A recording is defined as meaning a film or sound recording:

(a)  made directly from the live performance,

(b)  made from a broadcast of or cable programme including the performance, or

(c)  made directly or indirectly from another recording of the performance.[94]

Section 211 provides that in Pt II of the 1988 Act (*i.e.* the section dealing with Performer's Rights) film and sound recording have the same meaning as in Pt 1 of the Act.[95]

A photograph for the purposes of the 1988 Act is defined as being a recording of light or other radiation on any medium on which an image is produced *and which is not part of a film.*[96] A photograph as defined is not part of a film. It is submitted that a performer's rights are not infringed by the taking of a photograph of a performance as this does not amount to a recording being neither a film nor a sound recording. To interpret "copy of a recording" (where recording is defined as above) as including a photograph

---

[88] CDPA 1988, s.180(2).
[89] CDPA 1988, s.182(1)(c). As to the meaning of qualifying performance see s.181—broadly either a performance given by a citizen, subject or resident of a qualifying country or a performance which takes place in a qualifying country.
[90] CDPA 1988, s.182(1)(b).
[91] CDPA 1988, s.182(1)(c).
[92] CDPA 1988, s.182(2).
[93] CDPA 1988, s.182(3).
[94] CDPA 1988, s.180(2).
[95] *i.e.* Film: s.5B "a recording on any medium from which moving image may by any means produced" and Sound Recordings: s.5A "a recording of sounds from which the sounds may be produced or a recording of the whole or any part of a literary, dramatic or musical work from which sounds reproducing the work or part may be produced regardless of the medium on which the recording is made or the method by which the sounds are reproduced or produced."
[96] CDPA 1988, s.4(2).

is to artificially stretch the meaning of "copy" in this context, but the point is not the subject of authority.[96a] This does not mean that the taking of photographs of performers is something that everyone is entitled to do. Taking photographs of actors in the theatre or singers in concert may very well be prohibited by contractual conditions on the tickets. In addition, in some circumstances such photographs may infringe other copyrights such as set design or costume design. Filming a qualifying performance without consent (other than for private and domestic use) would infringe a performer's rights however.

## Persons in custody

The use which the police may make of a photograph of a person in custody is limited by their obligations to the subject. They may make reasonable use of it for the purposes of the prevention and detection of crime, the investigation of alleged offences or the apprehension of persons unlawfully at large. The key is that they must have only these purposes in mind and must make no more than reasonable use of the picture in seeking to accomplish them.[97]

The police will not be subject to legal sanctions if they make honest and reasonable use of a suspect's photograph in the fight against crime as they will have a public interest defence.[98]

In *R. (on the application of Ellis) v The Chief Constable of Essex Police*[99] an application was made seeking to prohibit the use by the police of the photograph of a man with "numerous convictions" for offences of dishonesty and car-related crimes on a poster. The police in Brentwood had devised an "Offender Naming Scheme" developed with a view to reducing core crimes such as burglary in the area. The objectives of the scheme were to deter potential offenders and reassure the general public that the local police were arresting and convicting criminals in the area. Part of the proposed campaign was the use of a poster showing a photograph of a convicted offender below which would appear his name, the offence he had committed and the length of sentence he was serving with the words "If you come to Brentwood to do crime, expect to do the time". The claimant was proposed to be one of those included on the posters.

The Divisional Court accepted that in order to establish the legality of the scheme it has to be shown that the inclusion of the selected candidate was *necessary* for the discharge of the duty cast upon the police to formulate and

**7–092**

**7–093**

---

[96a] *Cf.* Discussion below at para. 9–049 of new exemption in respect of performers rights for photographs taken in private and domestic premises inserted in Sch. 2 to the CDPA 1988 by the Copyright and Related Rights Regulations 2003 (SI 2003/2498). This suggests a photograph may be infringing but the amendment is problematic and internally consistent as discussed below at para. 9–049.

[97] *Hellewell v Chief Constable* [1995] 1 W.L.R. 804 at 810 *per* Laws J.

[98] *Hellewell v Chief Constable* [1995] 1 W.L.R. 804 at 811 *per* Laws J. The Association of Chief Police Officers publishes guidelines as to the use of photographs of suspects and persons in custody: Media Advisory Group Guidelines (No. 8) — *Photographs* available online *http://www.acpo.police.uk/policies/index.html*.

[99] [2003] EWHC 1321; [2003] 2 FLR 566.

implement policies designed to reduce crime and disorder.[1] "Necessary" in this context requires that the action on behalf of the police should be a proportionate response. The rights of the public have to be balanced with those of the offender.

The court declined to declare whether the scheme *per se* was lawful or unlawful, saying that it will depend upon the offenders selected for inclusion and how it is operated in practice. It was doubted that it would be appropriate to use a photograph of an offender with young children as the children of an offender have Art.8 rights. The court concluded that further information needed to be obtained as to the monitoring and risk assessments used by the police before it was possible to assess whether the benefits of the Scheme are proportionate to the intrusion into an offender's Art.8 rights. The court made no order on the application, declining to declare the scheme unlawful but observed "there must be at least a doubt as to whether the benefits that are likely to be achieved justify this burden."[2]

**7–094**     A prisoner retains all his rights as a citizen other than those that are inconsistent with his status as a prisoner. The same is true of some in custody awaiting trial.[3] Covert filming of a person in custody in a magistrate's court is in contravention of the suspect's rights under Art.8(1) of the Convention.[4] Note that the United States Supreme Court has ruled that prisoners do not have any privacy interests regarding their cells.[5]

The Secretary of State has power to make regulations prescribing the time, manner of dress in which prisoners shall be measured and photographed and the number of copies of the photographs to be made and the persons to whom they shall be sent.[6] The Prison Rules 1999 provide that every prisoner may be photographed on reception and subsequently, but no copy of the photograph shall be given to any person not authorised to receive it.[6a] Every inmate in a Young Offender Institution may be photographed on reception and subsequently, but no copy of the photograph shall be given to any person not authorised to receive it.[6b]

There are also provisions in statutory instruments forbidding the taking of photographs in prisons. No outside person is permitted to view a prison unless authorised by statute or the Secretary of State.[6c] No person viewing the prison is permitted to take a photograph, make a sketch or communicate

---

[1] *ibid.*, at para.[29].
[2] *ibid.*, para.38.
[3] *R. v Loveridge* [2001] EWCA Crim 973, para.30; [2001] 2 Cr. App. R. 592, 598.
[4] *R. v Loveridge* [2001] EWCA Crim 973, paras 30 and 32; [2001] 2 Cr. App. R. 592, 599. And see cases cited at above at paras 7–062 and 7–063.
[5] *Hudson v Palmer* 468 U.S. 517 (1984).
[6] Prison Act 1952, s.16. See also Regulations for the Measuring and Photographing of Criminal Prisoners 1896 (SI 1896/762).
[6a] Prison Rules 1999 (SI 1999/72), r.42. See also *R on the Application of Saira Ali Ahmed v Secretary of State for the Home Department* [2004] EWHC 158, January 21, 2004 McCombe J. (unsuccessful application for judicial review of the decision of the Prison Service refusing the applicant permission to publish in an autobiography photographs taken in prison during and immediately after her wedding to Charles Bronson).
[6b] Young Offender Institution Rules 2000 (SI 2000/337), r.47(1).
[6c] Prison Rules 1999 (SI 1999/72), r.72(1).

with a prisoner unless authorised by statute or the Secretary of State.[6d] Similar provisions apply to Young Offender institutions,[6e] Secure Training Centres,[6f] and military detention centres.[6g]

## Corpses

In most cases, property rights will not be available to relatives of a **7–095** deceased person to assert to prevent a right to photograph the corpse. The right of privacy is regarded as personal in nature and dies with the claimant so the estate of the deceased would have no right of action in privacy. However, recourse for relatives may lie either under the Human Rights Act and the Convention or a common law right to confidentiality.

There is no property in a corpse[7] but this is subject to qualification.[8] Those people charged with the duty of burying a body have a right to its custody and possession until burial.[9] Certain statutes also make provision regarding the use of a corpse for medical purposes.[10] A corpse or body parts are capable of becoming the subject of property where work effectively transforms the corpse into an item in which there is a right of possession. Where a corpse, or part of a corpse, undergoes a process or application of human skill designed to preserve it for medical or scientific examination, it acquires a value and becomes property. Preserved specimens of human body parts have been held to be property so that a person stealing them is rightly convicted of theft.[11]

In *Doodeward v Spence*[12] an Australian case, which involved a claim for a **7–096** preserved foetus of a two-headed stillborn child, Griffith C.J. said:

> "where a person has by the lawful exercise of work or skill so dealt with a human body or part of a human body in his lawful possession that it has acquired some attributes differentiating it from a mere corpse awaiting burial, he acquires a right to retain possession of it, at least as against any person not entitled to have it delivered to him for the purpose of burial."[13]

The authors of *Clerk & Lindsell* citing *Doodeward* submit that once a **7–097** body has undergone a process or other application of human skill, such as

---

[6d] *ibid.*, r.72(2).
[6e] Young Offender Institution Rules 2000 (SI 2000/337), r.76.
[6f] Secure Training Centre Rules 1998 (SI 1998/472), r.42.
[6g] Imprisonment and Detention (Air Force) Rules 1980 (SI 1980/2005), r.110 (air force establishments); Naval Detention Quarters Rules 1973 (SI 1973/270), r.97 (naval detention).
[7] *Handyside's Case* (1749) 2 East. P.C. 652 (bodies of Siamese twins); *Williams v Williams* (1882) 20 Ch. D. 659, 662–623.
[8] *Dobson v North Tyneside Health Authority* [1997] 1 W.L.R. 596, 600D.
[9] *Edmunds v Armstrong Funeral Home Ltd* [1931] 1 DLR 676. And see *Clerk & Lindsell on Torts* (18th ed.) at 14–45.
[10] Human Tissue Act 1961; Human Organ Transplants Act 1989.
[11] *R. v Kelly (Anthony Noel)* [1999] Q.B. 621; [1999] 2 W.L.R. 384; [1998] 3 All E.R. 74 (theft of 35 human body parts from the Royal College of Surgeons).
[12] (1908) 6 C.L.R. 406.
[13] (1908) 6 C.L.R. 406 at 414.

stuffing or embalming, it can be the subject of property[14] and that conversion would lie for a skeleton or cadaver used for research or exhibition.[15] The Court of Appeal accepted that this proposition was properly arguable but expressed the view that *Doodeward* was not a decision establishing it.[16] Thus it was held that the removal and preservation of the deceased's brain in paraffin was not on a par with stuffing or embalming of a corpse and no property subsisted.[17]

There is no property in a dead body that has not undergone a process or application of human skill. Relatives of the deceased cannot therefore rely on property rights to prevent dealings with the corpse or photographs being taken.

7–098     For the purposes of the Human Rights Act 1998, any person who claims that a public authority has acted in a way which is incompatible with a Convention Right may bring proceedings under the Act only if he is (or would be) a victim of the unlawful act.[18] A person is a victim of an unlawful act only if he would be a victim for the purposes of Art.34 of the Convention if proceedings were brought in the ECtHR in respect of that Act.[19]

7–099     An application cannot be brought in the ECHR in the name of a deceased person. There are two ways in which relatives can make such an application. An heir to the estate or next of kin can bring an application in his own name as a victim.[20] Applications where relatives have been held to be direct victims tend to concern serious human rights violations concerning Art.2 (the right to life) and Art.3 (prohibition against torture).[21] The other is as an indirect victim.[22]

There is some doubt in European case law as to the extent that (1) the living may have Art.8 rights vis à vis their deceased relatives, and (2) that the rights of the living to express views as to funeral arrangements fall within Art.8.

A complaint that the applicant was unable to visit a family grave breached his right to respect for private life within the meaning of Art.8 was not upheld by the Commission on the facts of the case.[23] The observation that

---

[14] *Clerk & Lindsell on Torts* (18th ed.) at 14–45.

[15] *ibid.*, n.72.

[16] *Dobson v North Tyneside Health Authority* [1997] 1 W.L.R. 596, 600G–601E *per* Peter Gibson L.J. In accepting the proposition was arguable, the court referred to P. Matthews, *Whose Body? People As Property* [1983] C.L.P. 193; *Palmer on Bailment* 2nd ed. (1991) p.9 and R. Magnusson, "Proprietary Rights in Human Tissue" in *Interests in Goods*, Palmer and McKendrick eds (1993) p.237.

[17] *ibid.*, at 601G.

[18] Human Rights Act 1998, s.7(1).

[19] Human Rights Act 1998, s.7(7).

[20] *Cyprus v Turkey* (2002) 35 E.H.R.R. 30 at para. 989: Art.3 (torture/inhuman or degrading treatment)—whether a family member of a "disappeared person" is a victim of treatment contrary to Art.3 will depend on the existence of special factors which give the suffering of the person concerned a dimension and character distinct from the emotional distress which may be regarded as inevitably caused to relatives of a victim of serious human rights violation; *Çakici v Turkey* (2001) 31 E.H.R.R. 5; *Yasa v Turkey* (1998) 28 E.H.R.R. 408.

[21] *e.g.* cases cited above in n.20.

[22] *McCann v UK* (1995) 21 E.H.R.R. 97; *Campbell and Cosans v UK* (1981) 3 E.H.R.R. 531; *McLeod v UK* (1996) 22 E.H.R.R. CD158 (daughter could not claim to be indirect victim of violation of deceased mother's rights under Arts 6 and 8).

[23] *Habsburg Lothringen v Austria* App. No.15344/89; 64 D.R. 210.

"even assuming that an issue could arise in this respect" tends to suggest the Commission was doubtful as to whether this could amount to a violation of Art.8.

Refusal to allow a husband to see a post-mortem report on his wife cannot be an interference with his family life as the post-mortem report as such does not form part of that family life.[24] It was held that as the right to respect for family life did not confer an entitlement to receive a report containing such detailed medical information while the family unit remains in existence during the life of the spouse, Art.8 could not confer such an entitlement to receive a post-mortem report containing such information after the death of the spouse.

7–100

It has been held however that a desire of a person to have his ashes scattered in his own garden fell within Art.8.[25] It was accepted that persons may need to express their personality by the way they arrange how they are buried. However, no violation of Art.8 was found as this is not a matter solely for the persons directly concerned and that the state could regulated corpse disposal. This case does indicate that a person may have Art.8 rights in respect of his body after death.

The Press Complaints Commission Code states that "in cases involving personal grief or shock, enquiries should be carried out and approaches made with sympathy and discretion. Publication must be handled sensitively at such times but this should not be interpreted as restricting the right to report judicial proceedings." The court is obliged to take into account relevant privacy codes under s.12(4) of the Human Rights Act 1998.

7–101

Publication of photographs of a corpse is something that would almost inevitably cause distress to the immediate family. Such photographs would satisfy the test of being offensive to a reasonable person.[26] In most cases, it would not be classed as a publication "handled sensitively". Unless there was some overriding public interest, for example an argument that photographs of the bodies clearly showed that a government had carried out torture, in the vast majority of cases publication of a photograph of a dead body would not be warranted and would be restrained by the courts. In addition, it is likely that those coming into possession of photographs of the corpse, such as mortuary attendants would themselves be under a duty of confidentiality to their employer.

In a USA case *Reid v Pierce County*[27] the plaintiffs were relatives of deceased persons who brought proceedings against a county and its mortuary employees alleging that the activities of the employees in showing to

7–102

---

[24] *B v United Kingdom* App. No.11516/85 (13/05/1986).

[25] *X v Germany* App. No.8741/79; 24 D.R. 137.

[26] *A v B plc* [2002] EWCA Civ 337 at para.11(vii); [2003] Q.B. 195 at 206; [2002] E.M.L.R. 21 *per* Lord Woolf at 382; citing Gleeson C.J.'s judgment in *Australian Broadcasting Corp v Lenah Game Meats Pty* 185 A.L.R. 1; [2001] H.C.A. 63 (High Court of Australia) at para.42; *Campbell v MGN Ltd* [2002] EWCA Civ 1373 at paras 20, 48–51, 54; [2003] Q.B. 633, 653, 659–660.

[27] 136 Wn. 2d 195; 961 P.2d 333; 1998 Wash Lexis 584 (Supreme Court of Washington). See also *R v Moyer* [1994] S.C.R. 899 Supreme Court of Canada (neo-Nazi prosecuted (for an offence contrary to s.182(*b*) of the Criminal Code) for committing indignities to corpses buried in a Jewish cemetery by taking photographs depicting a simulated urination on one of the gravestones and an exhibition of a male genital organ on another gravestone).

others photographs of their relatives' corpses constituted a common law invasion of privacy. There were a number of joined cases which raised similar issues. In one case, employees of the medical examiners office appropriated autopsy photographs of corpses, showed them at cocktail parties and used them to create personal scrapbooks. The relatives became aware of this practice after the media reported that lawyers for the county had used the employee's misconduct in this regard to obtain a more favourable settlement against the County in an employment discrimination suit. In another case, photographs of a person killed as a result of an accident with a power tool were used by the accident investigator to illustrate classes he taught on road safety.

**7–103**    The defendants argued that if any right of privacy was violated it was that of the deceased and not the relatives of the deceased, contending that privacy is a personal interest and may not be brought by the relatives of the deceased person. The court rejected this argument relying on USA case law holding that relatives have a privacy interest in preventing disclosure of autopsy photographs.[28] It was held that the immediate relatives of a deceased person have a protectable privacy interest in the autopsy records of the deceased which is "grounded in maintaining the dignity of the deceased". The court said "We fail to see how autopsy photographs of the Plaintiffs do not constitute intimate details of the Plaintiff's lives or are not facts Plaintiffs do not wish exposed "before the public gaze".[29] The court did say that relatives of a deceased person must shoulder a heavy burden in establishing a cause of action in privacy but where there were unusual circumstances as in these cases, it may be that the defendant's conduct would be found to be sufficiently egregious to give rise to an independent cause of action in favour of the deceased's immediate family.

**7–104**    It is submitted that under the law of the United Kingdom relatives of a deceased person would be able to obtain an injunction to prohibit publication of photographs of the corpses of relatives. This is not rooted in any interest in rights of the deceased or maintaining the dignity of the deceased (as suggested in *Reid*) as the right to privacy is a personal right that terminates with death. Rather, the rights of the relatives to prevent publication arise out of their own rights to a private and family life which includes a right to grieve in private and their own personal dignity and interests in not seeing photographs of the bodies of their deceased relatives displayed in public.

---

[28] *Katz v National Archives & Records Admin* 862 F. Supp. 476 (D.D.C. 1994); Aff'd 68 F.3d 1438 (1995) (x-rays and autopsy photographs of President Kennedy); *Badhwar v United States Dep't of Air Force* 829 F.2d 182 (DC Cir. 1987) (families of deceased aricraft pilots have privacy interest in autopsy reports); *Douglas v Stokes* 149 S.W. 849 (1912) (parents arranged for photographs of their conjoined twin sons who died shortly after birth, photographer taking extra picture for his own use invaded their right of privacy).
[29] 136 Wn. 2d 195 at 213.

DEFENCES TO BREACH OF CONFIDENCE ACTIONS

## Elements of the Coco v Clark test are not met

Where the information is in the public domain, it is not confidential and it **7–105**
will defeat an action for breach of confidence.[30] Similarly, if there is no
obligation of confidence or if there is no misuse of the information, the cause
of action is not established.

## Public interest

The publication of confidential information will not be restrained where **7–106**
there is just cause for disclosing it but the burden lies on the defendant to
establish that there was just cause.[31] Public interest defences to breach of
confidence actions have been recognised where publication of the information was for the detection or prevention of crime or wrongdoing; the
prevention of miscarriages of justice and in the interests of maintaining
public safety.[32] A defence of public interest would also be available in cases
involving a free standing right of privacy.[33]

Cases where the public interest defence has been upheld in cases of disclosure of confidential information include: unreliability of intoximeters
approved by the government used to breathalise drivers was a matter of real
public concern[34]; disclosure by a consultant psychiatrist of a report prepared
on the instruction of a homicidal patient for a mental health review tribunal
where the information was highly relevant to the patient's dangerousness[35];
information concerning the life of pop singers "correcting" a favourable but
allegedly untrue image fostered by the singers' publicity[36]; and reasonable
use by the police of the photographs of suspects for the purposes of crime
prevention.[37]

---

[30] *Attorney-General v Guardian Newspapers Ltd (No.2)* [1990] 1 A.C. 109 at 282; [1988] 3
W.L.R. 776.
[31] *Attorney-General v Guardian Newspapers Ltd (No.2)* [1990] 1 A.C. 109 at 282; [1988] 3
W.L.R. 776.
[32] *Price Waterhouse v BCCI Holdings (Luxembourg) SA* [1992] B.C.L.C. 583.
[33] *Grosse v Purvis* (District Court of Queensland) June 16, 2003, Senior Judge Skoien at
para.447; *Australian Broadcasting Corp v Lenah Game Meats Pty* 185 A.L.R. 1; [2001] H.C.A.
63 (High Court of Australia) at para.34.
[34] *Lion Laboratories Ltd v Evans* [1985] Q.B. 526; [1984] 3 W.L.R. 539; [1984] 2 All E.R. 417.
[35] *W v Egdell* [1990] Ch. 359; [1990] 2 W.L.R. 471; [1990] 1 All E.R. 835.
[36] *Woodward v Hutchins* [1977] 2 All E.R. 751. It is submitted that this authority should be
approached with caution as the "favourable" publicity referred to seemed to be very general
rather than specifically contrary to the confidential information sought to be published. In
addition, the disclosing party was a former employee. It is doubtful whether this case would be
decided the same way today.
[37] *Hellewell v Chief Constable of Derbyshire* [1995] 1 W.L.R. 804; [1995] 4 All E.R. 473.

**7–107**    It has long been established that there is a distinction between what is in "the public interest" and what is interesting to the public.[38] However, this is somewhat difficult to reconcile with Lord Woolf's observations in *A v B*:

> "Even trivial facts relating to a public figure can be of great interest to readers and other observers of the media. In many of these situations it would be overstating the position to say that there is a public interest in the information being published. It would be more accurate to say that the public have an understandable and so a legitimate interest in being told the information. If this is situation then it can be appropriately taken into account by a court when deciding on which side of the line a case falls."[39]

In *Campbell v MGN Ltd*[40] the Court of Appeal considered that a normal person of ordinary sensibilities, upon reading that the claimant was a drug addict, would not find it offensive that it was also disclosed that she was attending meetings of Narcotics Anonymous.

Journalists may be permitted to publish the detail necessary to carry credibility which may include publication of photographs if required.[41]

### Waiver of privacy

**7–108**    It is unclear to what extent a right to privacy or confidentiality may be lost by self-publicity of one's own affairs. There is authority to the effect that if a personal relationship is put into the public domain by the parties to the relationship, any right of confidence will be lost.[42] Similarly, there is authority that where a group of pop singers promoted a particular image, they could not object to disclosures designed to correct that image.[43] Whilst these decisions have been criticised, there is modern authority in support of the idea that a person who has courted publicity has less ground to object to subsequent intrusion.[44]

### REMEDIES

**7–109**    The remedies available for breach of confidence are an injunction; damages or an account of profits; and an order for delivery up or destruction.

---

[38] *Lion Laboratories Ltd v Evans* [1985] Q.B. 526; *Francome v Mirror Group Newspapers* [1984] 2 All E.R. 408; *London Regional Transport v Mayor of London* [2003] E.M.L.R. 4, para.40; *Douglas v Hello! Ltd (No.6)* [2003] EWHC 786 at para 231.

[39] [2002] EWCA Civ 337; [2003] Q.B. 195; [2002] 3 W.L.R. 542; [2002] 2 All E.R. 545; [2002] E.M.L.R. 21.

[40] [2002] EWCA Civ 1373 at para.54; [2003] Q.B. 633 at 660 *per* Lord Phillips M.R.

[41] *Campbell v MGN Ltd* [2002] EWCA Civ 1373 at paras 63–64; [2003] Q.B. 633 at 662 *per* Lord Phillips M.R. And see cases cited above at para. 7–047.

[42] *Lennon v News Group Newspapers* [1978] F.S.R. 573.

[43] *Woodward v Hutchins* [1977] 1 W.L.R. 760.

[44] See above at para. 7–071.

## Injunctions and s.12(4) of the Human Rights Act 1998

Where there is an application for an interim injunction to restrain pub-  **7–110**
lication of information which affects the right of freedom of expression, the
starting point for the court is s.12 of the Human Rights Act 1998 which
provides as follows:

### Freedom of expression

12—(1) This section applies if a court is considering whether to grant
any relief which, if granted might affect the exercise of the Convention right to freedom of expression.

(2) If the person against whom the application for relief is made ('the
respondent') is neither present nor represented, no such relief is to
be granted unless the court is satisfied that the applicant has taken
all practicable steps to notify the respondent; or that there are
compelling reasons why the respondent should not be notified.

(3) No such relief is to be granted so as to restrain publication before
trial unless the court is satisfied that the applicant is likely to
establish that publication should not be allowed.

(4) The court must have particular regard to the importance of the
Convention right to freedom of expression and, where the proceedings relate to material which the respondent claims, or which
appears to the court, to be journalistic, literary or artistic material
(or to conduct connected with such material), to the extent to
which the material has, or is about to, become available to the
public; or it is, or would be, in the public interest for the material to
be published; any relevant privacy code.[45]

(5) In this section
'court' includes a tribunal; and 'relief' includes any remedy or
order (other than in criminal proceedings)."

Section 12(3) provides that in order to grant interim relief the court must be
satisfied that the applicant is "likely to establish that publication should not
be allowed". Precisely what this means has been given some consideration in
a number of recent cases with conflicting views and obiter comment[46] but

---

[45] As to the meaning of "relevant privacy code" see below at para. 14–006 at (2) and for the
Press Complaints Commission Code of Practice see below at paras 14–007 *et seq.* The code is
reproduced in full in Appendix 5, below.
[46] *e.g.* Holding applicant must show more than the *American Cyanamid* test threshold of a
serious issue to be tried: *Douglas v Hello! Ltd (No. 1)* [2001] E.M.L.R. 9 at para.136 and
para.150; *Mills v News Group Newspapers* [2001] E.M.L.R. 957 at para.18. *Cf. Theakston v
MGN Ltd* [2002] E.M.L.R. 22 at para.20 (more probable than not) and *Imutran Ltd v Uncaged
Campaigns Ltd* [2001] E.M.L.R. 21 where it was said "the difference between the two [*American
Cyanamid* and s.12(3)] is so small that I cannot believe that there will be many (if any) cases
which would have succeeded under the *American Cyanamid* test but will now fail because of the
terms of s.12(3)." For discussion see H. Rogers and H. Tomlinson *Privacy & Expression:
Convention Rights and Interim Injunctions in Privacy* [2003] E.H.R.L.R. Special Issue 37.

finally fell to be decided by the Court of Appeal as the central issue in *Cream Holdings Ltd v Banerjee*.[47]

**7–111**     In *Cream Holdings Ltd v Banerjee*[48] the claimants, a well-known company running nightclubs and events, obtained an injunction restraining publication by a newspaper of information passed to them by their former in-house accountant concerning a number of allegations of financial irregularities.

The Court of Appeal unanimously concluded that the test is a "real prospect of success"[49] but arrived at that conclusion for different reasons. The injunction was continued but only by a majority with Sedley L.J. dissenting.

**7–112**     Simon Brown L.J. considered that the natural and ordinary meaning of "likely" was "more likely than not"[50] but that it had to be read in a way that was compatible with Convention rights (*i.e.* a real prospect of success). Sedley L.J. considered that the ordinary meaning of "likely" was "probable in its strict sense".[51] He also considered that s.3 of the Human Rights Act[52] required the court to read down meaning of the word to a lower threshold of "real prospect of success" or "a realistic possibility of eventual success in preventing publication"[53] in order to make s.12(3) Convention compliant. He left open the question of whether the meaning had to be read down uniformly or only in cases where another competing Convention right other than freedom of expression was at stake.[54] Arden L.J. arrived at the same conclusion after consideration of existing case law.

**7–113**     This case is illustrative of the difficulty in balancing the competing interests of Art.8 and Art.10. Sedley L.J. considered that the principal matter which the newspaper wanted to publish was "incontestably a matter of serious public interest"[55] and there was no real possibility of the claimant's succeeding at trial. He dissented from the decision of the court and would have discharged the injunction. It is indicative of this difficulty that Sedley L.J. was of such a strong view that the injunction should be discharged but that the other two members of the court considered that the appeal should be dismissed and the injunction should remain.

Any relevant privacy code includes the Press Complaints Commission Code of Practice.[56] However, the court discourages advocates from seeking to rely on individual decisions of the Press Council "which at best are no more than illustrative of how the Press Council performs its different responsibilities".[57]

---

[47] [2003] EWCA Civ 103; [2003] Ch. 650; [2003] 2 All E.R. 318.
[48] [2003] EWCA Civ 103; [2003] Ch. 650; [2003] 2 All E.R. 318; [2003] E.M.L.R. 323.
[49] Sedley L.J. at para.83; Arden L.J. at para.121.
[50] Simon Brown L.J. at para.25.
[51] [2003] EWCA Civ 103 at para.71; [2003] Ch. 650; [2003] 2 All E.R. 318.
[52] Human Rights Act 1998, s.3(1) "So far as it is possible to do so, primary legislation and subordinate legislation must be read and given effect in a way which is compatible with Convention Rights."
[53] At para.83.
[54] [2003] EWCA Civ 103 at para.77.
[55] [2003] EWCA Civ 103 at para.88.
[56] As to which see below at para. 14–006 at (2) and paras 14–007 *et seq.*
[57] *A v B plc* at para.11(xv), [2003] Q.B. 195 at 210; [2002] E.M.L.R. 21 at 387.

## Damages for breach of confidence and invasion of privacy

### Court awards

The purpose of an award of damages for breach of confidence is to put **7–114** the claimant in the position he would have been in but for the breach.[58] A claimant may be required to elect whether to claim damages for breach of confidence or for infringement of copyright.[59]

General damages for injuries to feelings caused by breach of confidence should be kept to a modest level, be proportionate to the injury suffered and should be well below the level of general damages for serious physical or psychiatric injury.[60] Early indications are that awards for actions in confidence that concern personal privacy issues rather than commercial confidences will be relatively low. By contrast, there have been reported in the press settlements in actions concerning intrusive photographs at a much higher level.

In *Peck v UK*[61] the ECHR awarded €11,800 (about £7,800 at the date of **7–115** award) as non-pecuniary damage for "significant distress, embarrassment and frustration" caused by the release of CCTV footage of him carrying a large knife in the process of attempting suicide which violated his rights under Art.8.

In *Lady Archer v Williams*,[62] an award of £2,500 was made for hurt feelings following publication of an article disclosing that the claimant had undergone a facelift.

In *Douglas v Hello!*[62a] the husband and wife claimants were each awarded £3,750 for distress arising out of publication of unauthorised wedding photographs taken in breach of confidence.

In *Campbell v MGN Ltd*[63] the judge at first instance awarded £2,500 for both breach of confidence and compensation under s.13 of the Data Protection Act for publishing details and photographs of the claimant's attendance at Narcotics Anonymous meetings. A further £1,000 was awarded as aggravated damages for the highly offensive and hurtful way one of the articles "trashed her as a person". The decision on liability was reversed by the Court of Appeal.[64]

In *Cornelius v De Taranto*[65] an award of £3,000 was made for mental distress arising out of unauthorised disclosure of a medico-legal report to a GP and consultant psychiatrist. The nature and detail of the confidential material disclosed, the character of the recipients of the disclosure, and the extent of the disclosure were material factors in assessing compensation.

---

[58] *Dowson & Mason Ltd v Potter* [1986] 1 W.L.R. 1419.
[59] *Nicrotherm Electrical Co Ltd v Percy* [1957] R.P.C. 207 at 214, CA *per* Lord Evershed M.R.
[60] *Lady Archer v Williams* [2003] EWHC 1670 at para.76 *per* Jackson J; [2003] E.M.L.R. 38.
[61] [2003] E.M.L.R. 15; (2003) 36 E.H.R.R. 41.
[62] [2003] EWHC 1670 at para.78; [2003] E.M.L.R. 38.
[62a] (Damages) [2004] EWHC 63, Ch. For facts see above at para. 7–017.
[63] [2002] E.M.L.R. 30.
[64] [2002] EWCA Civ 1373; [2003] Q.B. 633.
[65] [2001] E.M.L.R. 329; upheld by the CA: [2002] E.M.L.R. 112.

*Reported settlement figures*

**7–116**    The following settlement figures are as reported in the press. They are not court awards and are not authenticated, but are included for completeness:

> £40,000 paid by a tabloid for topless photographs of an actress whilst on holiday in the grounds of a villa.[66]
>
> £50,000 settlement for nude photographs of a radio DJ with her husband taken whilst she was on honeymoon in a secluded villa on a private island in the Seychelles.[67]

In both of these cases the images involved nudity of the subject.

## DEFAMATION

### Meaning of defamatory

**7–117**    The tort of defamation protects a person's reputation. A statement is defamatory if "the words tend to lower the plaintiff in the estimation of right-thinking members of society,"[68] or if the words are "likely to affect a person adversely in the estimation of reasonable people generally."[69] Equally, any imputation which holds the claimant up to hatred, contempt or ridicule is defamatory.[70] The question of whether a particular imputation is defamatory is a question of fact for the jury, and as such will vary with the time, place and state of public opinion.[71]

Notwithstanding that what is defamatory is a question of fact that will vary from time to time, previous decisions are of value in determining whether particular words are capable of bearing a defamatory meaning.[72] Many of the examples are matters which one would expect to be defamatory, such as imputations of dishonesty and criminal behaviour or immoral conduct.

Defamatory meaning may also arise because of extraneous facts which are known to the recipients of the publication. In such circumstances, a "true" innuendo is said to arise but only where the extended meaning arises from facts that go beyond mere general knowledge.[73]

---

[66] *Holden v Express Newspapers, The Guardian*, December 12, 2001.
[67] *Sara Cox v The People, The Guardian*, June 7, 2003.
[68] *Sim v Stretch* (1936) 52 T.L.R. 669.
[69] *Gillick v BBC* [1996] E.M.L.R. 267.
[70] *Parmiter v Coupland* (1840) 6 M. & W. 105, 108.
[71] *Gatley on Libel & Slander* (10th ed.) at para. 2.18.
[72] *Gatley on Libel & Slander* (10th ed.) at para. 2.18.
[73] *Lewis v Daily Telegraph* [1964] A.C. 234. And see *Gatley on Libel & Slander* (10th ed.) at paras 3.18 *et seq.*

## Reputation in image

Photographs,[74] statues,[75] and physical representations of a person may **7–118** convey an imputation defamatory of a person. Caricatures and cartoons may tend to expose a claimant to ridicule and be defamatory.[76]

Publication of a photograph or an image of a person is not the same as publication of their name.[77] If the claimant is not named in the matter complained of, he is obliged to establish that people who saw the publication were able to identify him as the person shown.[78] In appropriate circumstances it may be proper to infer that old friends and acquaintances would have recognised the claimant.[79]

A true photograph that by its angle or other optical illusion makes the **7–119** plaintiff look ridiculous none the less may be defamatory. In an American case *Burton v Crowell Pub Co*[80] a photograph was used of the plaintiff in an advert for cigarettes with the caption "Get a lift with a Camel". He was depicted carrying a saddle from which a white girth falls loosely "in such a way that it seems to be attached to the plaintiff and not to the saddle. So regarded, the photograph becomes grotesque, monstrous, and obscene." The caption was said to reinforce the ribald interpretation which made "a preposterously ridiculous spectacle of the plaintiff". It was held the plaintiff's consent to pose for the photograph did not amount to a consent to use the offending photograph which distorted his image. Judge Learned Hand in judgment said:

> "Had such a picture been deliberately produced, surely every right-minded person would agree that he would have had a genuine grievance; and the effect is the same whether it is deliberate or not. Such a caricature affects a man's reputation, if by that is meant his position in the minds of others; the association so established may be beyond repair; he may become known indefinitely as the absurd victim of this unhappy mischance. Literally, therefore, the injury falls within the accepted rubric; it exposes the sufferer to 'ridicule' and 'contempt.' "[81]

---

[74] *Dwek v Macmillan Publishers Ltd* [2000] E.M.L.R. 284; *Garbett v Hazell, Watson & Viney Ltd* [1943] 2 All E.R. 359; *Burton v Crowell Pub Co* 82 F.2d 154 (2d Cir. 1936); *Thayer v Worcester Post Co*, 284 Mass. 160, 187 N.E. 292 (1933) (photograph with caption "principals in local divorce scandal"); *Monkton v Ralph Dunn*, *The Times*, January 20, 1907; *De Freece v News of the World*, *The Times*, February 5, 1919. For an extensive review of USA cases involving defamation and photographs see: G., Sarno, *Libel and Slander: Defamation by Photograph* (1987) 52 A.L.R. 4th 488.

[75] *Monson v Tussauds* [1894] 1 Q.B. 671; *Corelli v Wall* (1906) 22 T.L.R. 532.

[76] *Austin v Culpepper* (1684) 2. Show. 313; *Smith v Wood* (1813) 3 Camp. 323; *Vander v Zalm Times Publishers* [1979] W.W.R. 673 (cartoon depicting plaintiff pulling wings off flies—imputing cruel and sadistic nature, reversed on other grounds).

[77] *Dwek v Macmillan Publishers Ltd* [2000] E.M.L.R. 284 at 291 *per* May L.J. *Cf.* Sedley L.J. at 294: "Identification by appearance can, it seems to me, be at least as potent as direct identification by name."

[78] *Dwek v Macmillan Publishers Ltd* [2000] E.M.L.R. 284 applying *Barbaro v Amalgamated Television Services* [1985] 1 N.S.W.L.R. 30.

[79] *Dwek v Macmillan Publishers Ltd* [2000] E.M.L.R. 284.

[80] 82 F.2d 154 (2d Cir. 1936).

[81] 82 F.2d 154 (2d Cir. 1936) at 155.

In an Australian case[82] following *Burton v Crowell Pub Co* the photograph was of the the plaintiff leaving a shower. His genitals were faintly visible. It was held that as a result of that exposure the plaintiff had at least arguably been held up to ridicule and the photograph was capable of conveying a defamatory imputation.

**7–120**    A photographer will not be liable for defamation where a photograph he has taken is used in a defamatory manner and there is no evidence that the photographer knew the image would be used in that manner.[83] Thus there was no liability on the part of a photographer where a photograph showing the plaintiff looking out of her door at an adjacent property was used to illustrate an article about spying on neighbours.[84]

## Defamation and photographs: specific instances

### False endorsement

**7–121**    Publication of a person's photograph in such a way as to induce the public to believe that he endorsed or recommended the product or service advertised may be libellous.[85] In *Tolley v Fry*[86] it was held that it was open to the jury to infer from the use of a caricature of a famous golfer to advertise chocolate that it had been published with his approval. It might be inferred that he had compromised his amateur status by accepting payment for it.

However, *Tolley v Fry* is very much a decision of its time when exploiting amateur status for reward was akin to "prostituting" one's reputation.[87] It is unlikely that in the modern environment where celebrity endorsement is common that a jury would regard an allegation of false endorsement alone as defamatory. Of course, there may be circumstances where false endorsement arguably amounts to defamation, for example where the nature of the product or services advertised suggests the claimant is immoral or dishonest or where the claimant has a reputation for not endorsing commercial products and fears that such endorsement may lead others to perceive his

---

[82] *Ettingshausen v Australian Consolidated Press Ltd* (1991) 23 N.S.W.L.R. 443.
[83] *Westby v Madison Newspapers Inc* 81 Wis. 2d; 259 N.W. 2d (1977). And see s.1. Defamation Act 1996 (person not to be considered author of a statement if only involved in certain processes).
[84] *ibid.*
[85] See also *Plumb v Jeyes Sanitary Compound Co Ltd*, *The Times*, April 15, 1937 (photograph of policeman wiping his brow used with an advert for Jeyes footbath held to be defamatory as meaning he had slovenly or unclean habits such that a bath would be inadequate); *Griffiths v Bondor Hosiery Co Ltd*, *The Times*, December 11, 1935 (head and shoulders used on naked body to advertise stockings).
[86] [1931] A.C. 333 reversing [1931] K.B. 467, CA.
[87] See [1931] K.B. 467 at 479, CA reversed by [1931] A.C. 333, HL.

career was in decline.[88] Generally, in the modern commercial environment where there is false endorsement of standard[89] products or services, actions in passing off tend to be pursued rather than in libel.[90]

In *Kaye v Robertson*[91] (following an argument advanced on the basis of *Tolley v Fry*) Glidewell L.J. accepted that it was arguable that publication of an interview and photographs of an actor in hospital in "no fit condition to give informed consent" which the newspaper asserted to be a consensual exclusive, was defamatory.[92] Where an image of a person is used, the question will often be whether the claimant will be assumed to have consented to or participated in the use of her likeness.[93]

**7–122**

### Juxtaposition of photograph with captions or libellous articles

The juxtapositon of a photograph with a caption or other material may render the photograph defamatory.[94] In an American case, a photograph of a teenage girl embracing a young man in an advertisement placed directly below a diary page which read "Dear diary: I found out today that I'm pregnant what will I do now?" was held to be open to interpretation by a jury that she was a pregnant teenager.[95] As to the sufficiency of disclaimers see below at para. 7–130.

**7–123**

In *Dwek v Macmillan Publishers Ltd*[96] a photograph of the claimant seated on a sofa with a woman and another man was published in a biography of Mohammed Al Fayed. The caption stated that the woman was a prostitute and wrongly identified the claimant as Dodi Fayed. The defendant's applied to strike out the action contending that readers were unlikely to recognise

**7–124**

---

[88] This was the evidence of Dustin Hoffman in a right of publicity/unfair competition claim arising out of the superimposing of his image as the character "Tootsie" onto the bodies of models. The court observed that the plaintiff "maintains a strict policy of not endorsing commercial products for fear that he will be perceived in a negative light by his peers and motion picture industry executives, suggesting that his career is in decline and that he no longer has the business opportunities or the box office draw as before." The district court's judgment was reversed on appeal on the basis that the magazine was entitled to First Amendment protection and there was no malice. *Hoffman v Capital Cities/ABC Inc* 255 F.3d 1180 (9th Cir. 2001) Reversing 33 F. Supp. 2d 867.

[89] *i.e.* products or services with which mere association could not be defamatory as distinguished from (*e.g.*) pornographic products. See also cases cited below at para. 9–020.

[90] See Ch. 10, below and cases cited below at para. 9–020.

[91] [1991] F.S.R. 62.

[92] [1991] F.S.R. 62 at 67.

[93] *e.g. Rejent v Liberation Publications* 611 N.Y.S.2d 866, 868 (1st Dep't 1994) (plaintiff's allegation of unauthorised use of his photograph to advertise a pornographic magazine was sufficient to state a cause of action for defamation, because use of photograph carried false implication that plaintiff consented to associate with and appear in pornographic magazine).

[94] *Garbett v Hazell, Watson & Viney Ltd* [1943] 2 All E.R. 359 (photograph of plaintiff carrying on business as outdoor photographer shown with his camera and showing photographs to two women, juxtaposed with photograph of a naked woman with words stating that for extra payment the customer could have a photograph like that of the naked woman. Held: photographs and words arranged in such a manner as to be capable of a defamatory meaning).

[95] *Triangle Publications, Inc v Chumley* (1984) 253 Ga. 179; 317 S.E. 2d 534. See also *Zbyszko v New York American Inc* (1930) 228 App. Div. 277 (newspaper published a photograph of a particularly repulsive gorilla. Next to it appeared a photograph of the plaintiff above the caption: "Stanislaus Zbyszko, the Wrestler, Not Fundamentally Different from the Gorilla in Physique.").

[96] [2000] E.M.L.R. 284.

the claimant but that if they did they would conclude that the obvious intention was to refer to Dodi Fayed and the inclusion of a photograph of the claimant was a mistake. The Court of Appeal, dismissing the defendant's appeal against their failed application, held that the words taken together with the photograph were capable of meaning that the man in the photograph was a person who consorted and had sex with prostitutes. It was possible as a matter of law for it to be infered that persons might recognise the claimant from the photograph and it should be left to the jury to decide whether the inference was to be drawn in all the circumstances.

Publication of a photograph in a "rogue's gallery"[97] or other suggestion that an innocent person is a criminal is capable of being defamatory. The question of whether the photograph carries the imputation that the person portrayed is a criminal should be left to the jury.[98]

### Photographs of people wrongly identified

**7–125**    The two classic situations in which publication of photographs of a person may give rise to liability in defamation are where there is publication of:

(1) a photograph of the claimant A wrongly captioned/referenced by article text as Person B[99]; or

(2) a photograph of Person B wrongly captioned as claimant A.

Both situations are capable of giving rise to a defamatory imputation. It goes without saying that extreme care should be taken in ensuring that the photograph used is that of the person it is identified as, particularly so where the use is in connection with allegations of criminal conduct. Many cases concerning photographs of the wrong person involve the use of images of persons with identical or very similar names[1] and caution is advised.

**7–126**    In the first situation, where there is only a photograph of the claimant and he is wrongly named as another, the court may be able to infer that people might recognise the claimant from the photograph and it should be left to

---

[97] *Regan v Sullivan*, 557 F.2d 300, 308–08 (2d Cir. 1977).
[98] *Colpitts v Fine* 42 A.D.2d 551; 345 N.Y.S.2d 45 (1st Dept. 1973).
[99] e.g. *Watts v Times Newspapers* [1997] Q.B. 650; [1996] 2 W.L.R. 427; [1996] 1 All E.R. 152; [1996] E.M.L.R. 1 (photograph of a property developer instead of an author error to illustrate article alleging author had plagiarised. Newspaper published apology. Author sued alleging original article and apology were defamatory of him); *Wandt v Hearst's Chicago American* 129 Wis. 419; 109 N.W. 70 (1906) (newspaper published an article accusing a certain person of being a "suicide fiend," mistakenly accompanied by a photograph of the plaintiff. Held that even though the name of the person referred to as a "suicide fiend" was given, the juxtaposition of the plaintiff's photograph with the article was, in effect, a statement that the plaintiff was a "suicide fiend."). Statements in open Court: *O'Dowd v IPC Magazines Ltd* (14/6/2000 Lawtel:AC8001534) (photograph of claimant in error named illustrating an article about another person alleged to have suffered from schizophrenia, abused drugs and had been committed to a secure mental institution for the murder of his wife); *Thorpe v Enquirer/star Group Incorporated* (AC0002688) (photograph of the Princess of Wales and the plaintiff in the mistaken belief that he was Mr Oliver Hoare) Lawtel.
[1] e.g. *Watts v Times Newspapers* [1997] Q.B. 650; [1996] 2 W.L.R. 427; [1996] 1 All E.R. 152; [1996] E.M.L.R. 1; *O'Dowd v IPC Magazines Ltd* (14/6/2000 Lawtel:AC8001534).

the jury to decide whether the inference is to be drawn in all the circumstances.[2] However as noted above, publication of a photograph of a person is not the same as publication of their name[3] and where the claimant is not named it is necessary to establish that people who saw the publication were able to identify him as the person shown.[4]

Where a photograph of another person is wrongly captioned or identified as the claimant, whether that is libellous use will turn on whether (a) the use of the claimant's name in association with the photograph is such that what is said about the other person can reasonably be said to refer to the claimant, and (b) whether what is said about the person pictured can have defamatory meaning when applied to the claimant. It is sufficient if a sensible person in the light of any special factors could reasonably have understood the statement referred to the claimant.[5] It is for the judge to decide whether the words complained of are capable of being taken as referring to the claimant, but a question of fact for the jury as to whether they were so understood.[6]

It an American case it was held regarding publication of announcement of the claimant's engagement and wedding date together with the wrong photograph (in fact being of a woman who looked like the claimant holding a baby in her lap) that the question of whether that was capable of bearing the meaning that the claimant had been guilty of an illicit and immoral sexual affair and was the mother of an illegitimate child was a question that should be left to the jury.[7]

## Photographs of buildings

Use of photographs of buildings to illustrate articles may be defamatory of the building owners or company who operates their business from that premises. In the USA, a photograph of a car park filled with garbage with a caption identifying it as the property of a real estate company which accompanied an article that stated an "outraged" mayoral candidate had visited a tenement and seen "Five dead rats. Crumbling stairs. A lot crammed with beer cans and broken bottles." was held to be defamatory.[8]       **7–127**

A bank won a jury verdict for libel where an article on illegal banking procedures was illustrated with a photograph of the innocent claimant bank.[9]

---

[2] *Dwek v Macmillan Publishers Ltd* [2000] E.M.L.R. 284. Discussed above at para. 7–124.
[3] *Dwek v Macmillan Publishers Ltd* [2000] E.M.L.R. 284 at 291 *per* May L.J. *Cf.* Sedley L.J. at 294: "Identification by appearance can, it seems to me, be at least as potent as direct identification by name."
[4] *Dwek v Macmillan Publishers Ltd* [2000] E.M.L.R. 284 applying *Barbaro v Amalgamated Television Services* [1985] 1 N.S.W.L.R. 30.
[5] *Morgan v Oldhams Press Ltd* [1971] 1 W.L.R. 1239.
[6] *ibid. Hayward v Thompson* [1982] Q.B. 47.
[7] *Southeastern Newspapers Inc v Walker* (1947) 76 Ga. App. 57; 44 S.E. 2d 697.
[8] *Kunst v New York World Telegram Corp* (1967, 1st Dept) 28 App. Div. 2d 662; 280 N.Y.S. 2d 798.
[9] *Liccione v Collier* 117 N.Y.S. 639 (1909) (judgment reversed on other grounds and remanded for a new trial).

*Lookalikes*

**7–128**   Claims for inadvertent defamation by coincidental use of a photograph of a person who looks like the claimant are unlikely to be successful. The test to be applied in assessing whether a photograph of a person who looks like the claimant is defamatory is objective.[10] The question is "would the ordinary sensible reader of the advertisement having regard to the words complained of and the photograph in the context of the advertisement as a whole and clothed with the special knowledge of the publishes that the photograph looked like the claimant, have reasonably concluded that the woman shown was the claimant."[11]

**7–129**   In *O'Shea v MGN Ltd*[12] the defendants published on a website a porno-graphic advertisement containing a photograph of a glamour model who looked like the claimant. The claimant brought proceedings for libel con-tending that the meaning was that she was appearing or performing on a highly pornographic website. The court accepted that if the photograph had in fact been a true photograph of the claimant her claim would have been successful. However, Morland J. granted summary judgment for the defendant and said:

> "Photography and filming play a major role in modern journalism in newspapers, magazines and television in getting the message across. Pic-tures are necessary, effective, and telling adjuncts to a story.
>
> It would impose an impossible burden on a publisher if he were required to check if the true picture of someone resembled someone else who because of the context of the picture was defamed. Examples are legion: unlawful violence in street protest demonstrations, looting, hoo-liganism at football matches, people apparently leaving or entering court with criminal defendants and investigative journalism into drug dealing, corruption, child abuse and prostitution.
>
> ... The fact that in over a century no claim has been made in respect of a libel in respect of a 'look-alike' picture is an indication that there is no pressing social need for the application of the strict liability principle for the protection of the reputation of the 'look-alike'.
>
> If someone were deliberately to publish a defamatory article or broadcast a defamatory film not naming the victim but using a 'look-alike' picture of a person, perhaps a celebrity, so that those who know that person would identify that person from the 'look-alike' picture, that person would have a remedy, the tort of malicious falsehood. That in my judgment would provide sufficient protection of reputation".[13]

---

[10] *O'Shea v MGN Ltd* [2001] E.M.L.R. 40.
[11] *O'Shea v MGN Ltd* [2001] E.M.L.R. 40.
[12] [2001] E.M.L.R. 40.
[13] [2001] E.M.L.R. 40 at 995–956.

*Retouching and photo manipulation*

Where there is a clear caption or text indicating the photograph has been altered, a claim in defamation is unlikely to succeed.[14] However, words in the text of an article or in a caption will not always be efficacious to cure defamatory headlines or material and it all depends on the context.[15]   **7–130**

In *Charleston v News Group Newspaper Ltd*[16] two actors from an Australian soap opera sued a newspaper for defamation arising out of manipulated images. The newspaper had published an article comprising photographs showing the plaintiffs' faces superimposed on the near-naked bodies of models in pornographic poses. The text made it clear that the photographs had been produced by superimposing the plaintiffs' faces on the bodies of others without the knowledge or consent of the plaintiffs and castigated the makers of a pornographic computer game.

The House of Lords held that a claim for libel could not be founded on a headline or photograph in isolation from the related text.[17] The question of whether an article was defamatory had to be answered by reference to the response of the ordinary, reasonable reader to the entire publication. However, the question of whether the text of an article or a disclaimer was sufficient to neutralise an otherwise defamatory headline or photograph was a matter for the jury.[18]   **7–131**

The practical effect of this decision is that provided an article, headline, or caption makes it clear that the image is altered, a claim in defamation is unlikely to succeed. But it is only where the antidote (whether a disclaimer or otherwise) so obviously extinguishes the defamation that no issue could properly be left to the jury that the judge should rule at an interim stage that the article as a whole is not capable of being defamatory.[19]

In principle then, a digitally manipulated photograph is capable of being defamatory particularly if there is no "neutralisation" or disclaimer. In the USA, a plaintiff succeeded in actions for defamation arising out of alteration of an image where a photograph of a woman was altered to show her in prison dress implying she was a criminal.[20]

---

[14] *Cf.* approach of the court to conflicting messages in a passing off case: *Clark v Associated Newspapers Ltd* [1998] 1 W.L.R. 1558; [1998] 1 All E.R. 959; [1998] R.P.C. 261.

[15] *Charleston v News Group Newspaper Ltd* [1995] 2 A.C. 65 at 74 *per* Lord Nicholls of Birkenhead.

[16] [1995] 2 A.C. 65; [1995] 2 W.L.R. 450; [1995] 2 All E.R. 313; [1995] 3 E.M.L.R. 129.

[17] [1995] 2 A.C. 65 at 73 *per* Lord Bridge of Harwich.

[18] [1995] 2 A.C. 65 at 72 *per* Lord Bridge of Harwich.

[19] *Mark v Associated Newspapers* [2002] E.M.L.R. 839.

[20] *Morsette v "The Final Call"* (Supreme Court, Appellate Division, First Department, New York) 2003 WL 22213111. For USA cases where plaintiffs have failed regarding retouched or altered images see: *Byrd v Hustler Magazine, Inc* 433 So. 2d 593, (1983, Fla. App.) (photograph of model making a V-sign reprinted with one finger airbrushed out with caption plainly stating image had been retouched by a reader); *Bass v Straight Arrow Publishers Inc* 59 A.D. 2d 684; 398 N.Y.S. 2d 669 (N.Y.A.D. 1 Dept, 1977) (no defamation in publication of a photograph retouching the original which showed the plaintiff's dark hair blended into a dark background; to accommodate a white background in the printed version an arbitrary delineation of the plaintiff's coiffure was made, providing an inoffensive and natural appearing result); *Grant v Esquir, Inc.* (1973, S.D. N.Y.) 367 F. Supp. 876 (head of Cary Grant superimposed on a model).

## DEFENCES

**7–132**   The list of the defences to a claim for defamation which is provided below is intended merely to be a check list for practitioners. There is considerable case law in relation to each defence, particularly the question of privilege consideration which is outside the scope of this work.[21]

The following are defences to defamation actions:

(1) Justification where it is contended that the statement is true or substantially true.

(2) Fair comment where the statement is an opinion based on true facts which an honest person could hold in relation to a matter of public interest.

(3) Absolute privilege—most commonly attaching to statements made in court or parliamentary proceedings.

(4) Qualified privilege deriving from both statute and common law.[22]

(5) Innocent dissemination or secondary responsibility where the defendant had an innocent or secondary role in the publication.[23]

(6) Offer of amends.[24]

(7) Limitation.[25]

(8) Consent to publication.

## REMEDIES

**7–133**   Remedies available in defamation actions are (1) damages, (2) an injunction restraining publication, and (3) leave for the claimant to read a statement in open court with the aim of vindicating his reputation. The aim of damages is to compensate the claimant for his loss of reputation. The following factors may arise for consideration in arriving at an award of damages in a libel action:

1. The objective feature of the libel itself, such as its gravity, its prominence, the circulation of the medium in which it is published, and any repetition.

---

[21] See *Gatley on Libel & Slander* (10th ed.), Pt 2 at paras 10.1 *et seq.*
[22] *e.g.* statements made from a social or moral duty such as references by an employer or reporting of crime. And see Defamation Act 1996, s.7.
[23] Defamation Act 1996, s.1.
[24] Defamation Act 1996, s.2.
[25] Limitation period for defamation is one year: Defamation Act 1996, s.5, amending, Limitation Act 1980, s.4A.

2. The subjective effect on the plaintiff's feelings (usually characterised as aggravating features) not only from the publication itself but from the defendant's conduct thereafter both up to and including the trial itself.

3. Matters tending to mitigate damages such as the publication of an apology.

4. Matters tending to reduce damages, *e.g.* evidence of the plaintiff's bad reputation.

5. Special damages.

6. Vindication of the claimant's reputation past and present.[26]

## TRESPASS TO THE PERSON

Trespass to the person is an actionable tort and may comprise (a) battery **7–134** when there is actual infliction of unlawful physical contact, (b) assault where the claimant is caused to apprehend an immediate assault, or (c) false imprisonment.

It was submitted in *Kaye v Robertson*[27] that the taking of flashlight photography amounted to a battery. The court accepted that in principle if a bright light was shone into another person's eyes deliberately and injured his sight or damaged him in some other way, it may in law amount to a battery. However, the necessary effects were not established by the evidence as there was no evidence that the taking of the photographs caused damage.

It is submitted that it is very unlikely that simple flash photography alone is capable of amounting to a battery.

---

[26] *Campbell v News Group Newspapers Ltd* [2002] E.M.L.R. 43 at para.26; *Kiam v MGN Ltd* [2002] E.M.L.R. 25.
[27] [1991] F.S.R. 62.

# Chapter 8

# Obscenity

## INTRODUCTION

**8–001**  At common law, publication of an obscene libel was a punishable offence.[1] The first statute was the Obscene Publications Act 1857 which allowed for the destruction of immoral books but contained no provision defining obscenity. In 1868, in *R. v Hicklin*,[2] Cockburn C.J. gave a definition of obscenity that remains the basis of the modern law when he said:

> "Whether the tendency of the matter charged as obscenity is to deprave and corrupt those whose minds are open to such immoral influences and into whose hands such a publication might fall."[3]

The Select Committee of the House of Commons on Obscene Publications recommended that the test of any statutory definition should contain the words "deprave and corrupt" from *R. v Hicklin*.[4]

**8–002**  The basis of the current law are the Obscene Publications Acts 1959 and 1964, together with the Broadcasting Act 1990 which extended the law beyond films and books to include television and sound broadcasting. In addition, there are a number of other statutes which cover related matters such as the Post Office Act 1953, the Protection of Children Act 1978, and the Indecent Displays (Control) Act 1981.

## SCOPE OF THIS CHAPTER

**8–003**  This chapter contains coverage of all obscenity and indecency offences (both statutory and at common law) that are applicable to photographs or similar works. For practical purposes, the only obscenity statute which this chapter does not deal with is the Theatres Act 1968 which prohibits obscene performances of plays.

---

[1] *R. v Wilkes* (1770) 4 Burr. 2527, 2547; *R. v Hicklin* (1867–68), L.R. 3 Q.B. 360. As to obscene libel see below at para.8–030.
[2] (1868) L.R. 3 Q.B. 360.
[3] *ibid.*, at 371.
[4] HC Paper 123–1 (Session 1957–58) paras 7 and 14.

# THE OBSCENE PUBLICATIONS ACTS 1959 AND 1964

## Offences of (1) publication of obscene matter and (2) having obscene matter intended for publication for gain

Under s.2 of the Obscene Publications Act 1959 any person who, whether **8–004** or not for gain, publishes an obscene article is liable on summary conviction to a fine not exceeding the prescribed sum,[5] or to imprisonment for a term not exceeding six months.[6] On indictment a person so convicted is liable to a fine,[7] or to imprisonment not exceeding three years or both.[8] It is also an offence subject to the same penalties for a person to have an obscene article for publication for gain whether for gain to himself or gain to another.[9] Thus, there are two separate offences; publishing an obscene article and having an obscene article for publication for gain. A person is deemed to have an article for publication for gain if he has the article in his ownership, possession, or control.[10]

The test for obscenity is set out in s.1(1) of the Obscene Publications Act **8–005** 1959:

"1.(1) For the purposes of this Act an article shall be deemed to be obscene if its effect or (where the article comprises two or more distinct items) the effect of any one of its items is, if taken as a whole, such as to tend to deprave and corrupt persons who are likely, having regard to all relevant circumstances, to read, see or hear the matter contained or embodied in it."

There are two limbs to the test: (1) the article must tend to deprave and corrupt, and (2) such persons who are likely to read, see, or hear the matter contained or embodied in it. The statutory provision is compatible with Art.10 (freedom of expression) of the European Convention on Human Rights as the offence is prescribed by law for a legitimate purpose.[11]

---

[5] The prescribed sum is currently £5,000 pursuant to the Magistrates' Court Act 1980, s.32(9).
[6] Obscene Publications Act 1959, s.2(1)(a).
[7] The level of the fine is unlimited, but should be within the offender's capacity to pay: *R. v Garner* [1986] 1 All E.R. 78, [1986] 1 W.L.R. 73.
[8] Obscene Publications Act 1959, s.2(1)(b).
[9] This followed the amendment of the 1959 Act by s.1(1) of the Obscene Publications Act 1964 which was designed to deal with the lacuna caused by the decision in *Mella v Monahan* [1961] Crim. L.R. 175. See below under "publication" at para.8–009.
[10] Obscene Publications Act 1964, s.1(2). See also 1964 Act, s.1(5) "References ... in this section to publication for gain shall apply to any publication with a view to gain, whether the gain is to accrue by way of consideration for the publication or in any other way."
[11] *R. v Perrin* [2002] EWCA Crim 747. See also as to restrictions on broadcasting of offensive material not being incompatible with Art.10: *R. (On the Application of Prolife Alliance) v British Broadcasting Corporation; sub nom R. (On the Application of Quintavalle) v British Broadcasting Corporation* [2003] UKHL 23; [2003] 2 W.L.R. 1403; [2003] 2 All E.R. 977; [2003] E.M.L.R. 457 (Broadcasting Acts 1990 and 1996).

Any prosecution must be commenced within two years of the commission of the offence.[12]

**8–006**     Where the article in question is a film of 16mm width or more and the relevant publication took place or was to take place in the course of a film exhibition,[13] proceedings shall not be instituted except by or with the consent of the Director of Public Prosecutions.[14] "Relevant publication" means either (in the case of proceedings for publishing an obscene article) the publication in respect of which the defendant would have been charged,[15] or (in the case of proceedings for having an obscene article for publication for gain) the publication which, if the proceedings were brought, the defendant would be alleged to have had in contemplation.[16]

## Articles

**8–007**     The Act applies to all obscene "articles". Article is defined as meaning "any description of article containing or embodying matter to be read or looked at, or both, any sound record and any film or other record of a picture or pictures."[17] Photographs fall within this definition as do video cassettes[18] and films.[19] Digital images held on a computer disk are also included—the "article" being the computer disk.[20]

**8–008**     It had been held that photographic negatives do not come within the provisions of the 1959 Act because they are not capable of publication in the sense of being shown, played, or protected as required by s.1(3).[21] This was overcome by the Obscene Publications Act 1964, s.2 which extended the 1959 Act to include within the meaning of "articles" anything intended to be used in the reproduction or manufacture of obscene articles. This would include photographic negatives, transparencies or plates. Section 2(1) of the Obscene Publications Act 1964 reads as follows:

"2(1) The Obscene Publications Act 1959 (as amended by this Act) shall apply in relation to anything which is intended to be used, either alone or

---

[12] Obscene Publications Act 1959, s.2(3). See also *R. v Barton* [1976] Crim. L.R. 514 (rejection of argument that prosecution of an actor in obscene film commenced out of time as once the film was completed his involvement was over. Evidence he knew that the films were to be distributed for gain. Held, he was an aider and abettor of a continuing offence committed on the same dates as the principals).

[13] As to the meaning of film exhibition see below at para.8–031.

[14] Obscene Publications Act 1959, s.2(3A).

[15] *ibid.*, s.2(3A)(a).

[16] *ibid.*, s.2(3A)(b).

[17] Obscene Publications Act 1959, s.1(2).

[18] *A-G's Reference (No.5 of 1980)* [1980] 3 All E.R. 816.

[19] *Attorney-General's Reference (No.2 of 1975)* [1976] 2 All E.R. 753, 766; [1976] 1 W.L.R. 710.

[20] *R. v Fellows* [1997] 2 All E.R. 548, 557–558; [1997] 1 Cr. App. R. 244. For discussion of this case and the difficulties computer pornography poses for the 1978 Act see C. Manchester, *More About Computer Pornography* [1996] Crim. L.R. 645.

[21] *Straker v DPP* [1963] 1 All E.R. 697 at 699–700 *per* Lord Parker C.J. "The definition of the word 'article' coupled with 'publication' is quite inapt to cover a negative" at 700C. *Cf.* Protection of Children Act 1978, s.7(4) which expressly includes negatives within the definition of photographs. As to the definition of publication in the Obscene Publications Act 1959, s.1(3), see below at para.8–009.

as one of a set for the reproduction or manufacture therefrom of articles containing or embodying matter to be read, looked at or listened to, as if it were an article containing or embodying matter to be read, looked at or listened to, as if it were an article containing or embodying that matter so far as that matter is to be derived from the set."

An article is deemed to be had or kept for publication if it is had or kept for the reproduction of articles for publication.[22]

## Publication

Publication is defined by ss.1(3) and (4) which provide as follows:  **8–009**

"**1.**—(3) For the purposes of this Act a person publishes an article who—

    (a)  distributes, circulates, sells, lets on hire, gives, or lends it, or who offers it for sale or for letting on hire; or

    (b)  in the case of an article containing or embodying matter to be looked at or a record, shows, plays or projects it [, or, where the matter is data stored electronically, transmits that data.][23]

    (4) For the purposes of this Act a person also publishes an article to the extent that any matter recorded on it is included by him in a programme included in a programme service.

    (5) Where the inclusion of any matter in a programme so included would, if that matter were recorded matter, constitute the publication of an obscene article for the purposes of this Act by virtue of subsection (4) above, this Act shall have effect in relation to the inclusion of that matter in that programme as if it were recorded matter."

"Publication" falls into three distinct groups. In the first group, "sells, lets on hire, gives, or lends" publication is to an individual; in the second group ("distributes, circulates") publication is on a wider scale involving more than one person; in the third group a mere offer for sale or letting on hire constitutes publication.[24] For cases falling within the first group, the issue for the jury is whether the effect of the article was such as to tend to deprave and corrupt the individual to whom it was published. The second issue is whether any other people were likely to see the article, *i.e.* was re-publication reasonably to be expected? If so, then a third issue arises: would the article tend to deprave and corrupt the person or persons to whom republication could reasonably have been expected?[25]

The return of obscene photographs to the owners of the film by a film  **8–010** developer after development and printing constitutes publication.[26] An

---

[22] Obscene Publications Act 1964, s.2(2).
[23] Words in square brackets inserted by the Criminal Justice and Public Order Act 1994, s.168(1), Sch.9, para.3.
[24] *R. v Barker (No.1)* [1962] 1 All E.R. 748 at 749, 750; [1962] 1 W.L.R. 349 at 351 *per* Ashworth J.
[25] *ibid.*
[26] *R. v Taylor (Alan)* [1995] 1 Cr. App. R. 131; (1994) 158 J.P. 317; (1994) 91(10) L.S.G. 3.

argument that the customers remained the owners of the materials and that nothing was published to a third party failed. It was held that something new was created when the film was developed. The UK Photo Marketing Association, a trade organisation of the imaging industry, publishes guidelines for film processors as to best practice when confronted with obscene or indecent material. These guidelines are set out below at para.8–036.

**8–011**    The transmission of images on the internet to websites via an Internet Service Provider (ISP) constitutes publication.[27] The act of publication takes place when the data is transmitted to the ISP. There can be publication where images are uploaded to a website and publication where the images are downloaded elsewhere. A contention that publication occurred abroad via the internet failed.[28] The data was sent and received within the jurisdiction and therefore it was immaterial that the transmission left the jurisdiction in the interim period. Further, providing someone with a password to access an archive of obscene material on a website amounts to "showing" the material.[29]

**8–012**    Displaying a priced article in a shop does not constitute an offer for sale within the meaning of this section.[30] Accordingly, there was no offer for sale when packets of obscene photographs (wrapped in cellophane so that the top photograph was visible) were displayed in a shop with a ticket attached stating the price.[31] This gap was closed by the Obscene Publications Act 1964[32] which made it an offence to have an obscene article for publication.

"Shows, plays or projects" excludes photographic negatives as they would not be shown, played or projected to the public.[33]

Programme and programme service have the same meaning as in the Broadcasting Act 1990.[34]

---

[27] *R. v Waddon (Graham)* (Crim Div) April 6, 2000, Transcript No:99/5233/Z3; Lawtel No C7800504 (affirming decision of H.H.J. Hardy, Southwark Crown Court, June 30, 1999, [2000] Current Law 996; [1999] I.T.C.L.R. 422; [1999] Masons C.L.R. 396.)
[28] *ibid.*
[29] *R. v Fellows* [1997] 2 All E.R. 548; [1997] 1 Cr. App. R. 244.
[30] *Mella v Monahan* [1961] Crim. L.R. 175.
[31] *ibid.*
[32] S.1(1) amending the 1959 Act, s.2(1) and s.1(2).
[33] *Straker v DPP* [1963] 1 All E.R. 697. See also above negatives fall within the definition of articles following the amendment by the Obscene Publications Act 1964.
[34] Obscene Publications Act 1958, s.1(5). "Programme Service" is defined in s.201(1) Broadcasting Act 1990 as:
  (a) any television broadcasting service or other television programme service (within the meaning of Pt I of the Broadcasting Act 1990);
  (b) any sound broadcasting service or licensable sound programme service (within the meaning of Pt III of the Broadcasting Act 1990);
  (bb) any digital sound programme service (within the meaning of Pt II of the Broadcasting Act 1996);
  (c) any other service which consists in the sending, by means of a telecommunication system, of sounds or visual images or both either—
    (i) for reception at two or more places in the United Kingdom (whether they are so sent for simultaneous reception or at different times in response to requests made by different users of the service); or
    (ii) for reception at a place in the United Kingdom for the purpose of being presented there to members of the public or to any group of persons.
  "Programme" is defined by the Broadcasting Act 1990, s.202(1) as including an advertisement and, in relation to any service, includes any item included in that service.

## Tend to deprave and corrupt

The test of tending to deprave and corrupt depends upon the article itself **8–013** and the purpose or intention of the publisher is immaterial.[35] A novel should be judged as a whole, but a magazine or any other article comprising a distinct number of items is to be judged on an item by item basis.[36] If one item is obscene that is sufficient to make the whole article obscene.[37]

In proceedings for *publishing* an obscene article, the question whether an article is obscene is to be determined without regard to any publications by another person, unless that publication by the other person could reasonably have been expected to follow from publication by the person charged.[38] In proceedings for *having* an obscene article intended for publication, the question whether the article is obscene shall be determined by reference to such publication it may reasonably be inferred the defendant had in contemplation and to any further publication that could reasonably be expected to follow from it, but not to any other publication.[39]

Obscenity is not confined to matters of a sexual nature and includes **8–014** material that encourages violence[40] or that advocates drug-taking to the extent that there is a real danger that readers might be tempted to experiment with drugs.[41]

The meaning of "deprave" and "corrupt" has been the subject of considerable judicial comment. It has been said that the test suggests "thoughts of a most impure and libidinous character".[42] It has also been said:

"To 'deprave' means to make morally bad, to pervert, to debase or corrupt morally. To 'corrupt' means to render morally unsound or rotten, to destroy the moral purity or chastity, to pervert or to ruin a good quality, to debase, to defile."[43]

There is no distinction between "deprave" and "corrupt"; if someone is made or kept morally bad or worse by something, they are depraved by it.[44] An article is not necessarily obscene for the purposes of the Act because it is

---

[35] *Shaw v DPP* [1962] A.C. 220 at 227; *R. v Calder and Boyars Ltd* [1969] 1 Q.B. 151, 52 Cr. App. R. 706; *R. v Anderson* [1972] 1 Q.B. 304; [1971] 3 All E.R. 1152; *Knuller (Publishing, Printing and Promotions) Ltd v DPP* [1973] A.C. 435. See also *R. v Penguin Books Ltd* [1961] Crim. L.R. 176.
[36] *R. v Anderson* [1972] 1 Q.B. 304; [1971] 3 All E.R. 1152 at 1158.
[37] *ibid.*
[38] Obscene Publications Act 1959, s.2(6).
[39] Obscene Publications Act 1964, s.1(3)(b).
[40] *DPP v A and BC Chewing Gum* [1968] 1 Q.B. 159; [1967] 3 W.L.R. 493 (children's cards); *R. v Calder and Boyars Ltd* [1969] 1 Q.B. 151, 52 Cr. App. R. 706 (book—*Last Exist to Brooklyn*).
[41] *John Calder (Publications) v Powell* [1965] 1 Q.B. 509; [1965] 2 W.L.R. 138 (*Cain's Book* novel about heroin addiction); *R. v Grossman (Beth)* [1985] Q.B. 819; [1985] 2 W.L.R. 1001 (pamphlet about "freebasing" method of inhalation); *Kirk v Powell, Guardian,* December 11, 1964 Div. Ct.
[42] *R. v Hicklin* (1867–68) L.R. 3 Q.B. 860 at 371 *per* Cockburn J.
[43] *R. v Penguin Books Ltd* [1961] Crim. L.R. 176 at 177 *per* Byrne J. (*Lady Chatterley's Lover*).
[44] *R. v Sumner* [1977] Crim. L.R. 362.

repulsive, filthy, loathsome, or lewd.[45] Equally, articles which are of a sexually explicit nature are not necessarily obscene.[46]

**8–015**      The test of obscenity is a relative one as an article can only be obscene or be deemed to be obscene in relation to the likely viewers of it.[47] The jury must be satisfied that the effect of a book is to tend to deprave and corrupt a significant proportion of likely readers/viewers; what amounts to a significant proportion is a matter for the jury.[48] It has been said that the "significant proportion" test cannot be safely transplanted to cases of a different character, *i.e.* other than in connection with a book.[49] A "significant proportion" means a part which is not negligible[50] but may be less than half.[51] If publication is to take place abroad, the question of whether the article is obscene is to be decided according to the evidence as to whether it would tend to deprave or corrupt readers in the country of destination.[52]

**8–016**      Whether an article is obscene is a question for the jury and should normally be tried without the assistance of expert evidence.[53] Exceptionally, expert evidence may be admissible where the likely readers are a special class such that the jury cannot be expected to understand the likely impact of the material on its members without assistance.[54] For example, where the allegedly obscene matter is directed at very young children,[55] or where it is necessary for the jury to have a preliminary understanding about the effect of cocaine and the various methods by which it can be ingested.[56]

### Powers of search and seizure; orders for forfeiture

**8–017**      The powers of magistrates to issue warrants for search and seizure of obscene articles are set out in s.3 which reads as follows:

"**3.**—(1) If a justice of the peace is satisfied by information on oath that there is reasonable ground for suspecting that, in any premises in the petty sessions area for which he acts, or on any stall or vehicle in that area, being premises or a stall or vehicle specified in the information, obscene articles are, or are from time to time, kept for publication for gain, the

---

[45] *R. v Anderson* [1972] 1 Q.B. 304; [1971] 3 All E.R. 1156.

[46] *Darbo v CPS*, *The Times*, July 11, 1991, CO/929/90, (Transcript: Marten Walsh Cherer) June 28, 1991, QBD (Crown Office List) *per* Mann L.J.

[47] *DPP v Whyte* [1972] A.C. 849; [1972] 3 All E.R. 12 at 17; *Attorney-General's Reference (No.2 of 1975)* [1976] 2 All E.R. 753, 757; [1976] 1 W.L.R. 710 *per* Kenneth Jones J. upheld by CA. See also *R. v Clayton v Halsey* [1963] 1 Q.B. 163.

[48] *R. v Calder and Boyars Ltd* [1969] 1 Q.B. 151; (1968) 52 Cr. App. R. 706.

[49] *DPP v Whyte* [1972] A.C. 849 at 865; [1972] 3 All E.R. 12 at 21 *per* Lord Pearson.

[50] *ibid.*, at 886 and 22 respectively *per* Lord Pearson; 870 and 25 *per* Lord Cross.

[51] *ibid.*, at 870 and 25 respectively *per* Lord Cross.

[52] *Gold Star Publications Ltd v DPP* [1981] 1 W.L.R. 732; (1981) 73 Cr. App. R. 141.

[53] *R. v Anderson* [1972] 1 Q.B. 304; [1971] 3 All E.R. 1156; *R. v Calder and Boyars Ltd* [1969] 1 Q.B. 151; (1968) 52 Cr. App. R. 706.

[54] *DPP v Jordan* [1977] A.C. 699; [1976] 3 W.L.R. 887; [1976] 3 All E.R. 775 at 779; (1977) 64 Cr. App. R. 33 *per* Lord Wilberforce.

[55] *DPP v A and BC Chewing Gum* [1968] 1 Q.B. 159; [1967] 3 W.L.R. 493 (psychiatric evidence as to the effect children's swap cards depicting battle scenes would have on the minds of children).

[56] *R. v Skirving* [1985] Q.B. 819; (1985) 81 Cr. App. R.9.

justice may issue a warrant under his hand empowering any constable to enter (if need be by force) and search the premises, or to search the stall or vehicle ... and to seize and remove any articles found therein or thereon which the constable has reason to believe to be obscene articles and to be kept for publication for gain.

(2) A warrant under the foregoing subsection shall, if any obscene articles are seized under the warrant, also empower the seizure and removal of any documents found in the premises or, as the case may be, on the stall or vehicle which relate to a trade or business carried on at the premises or from the stall or vehicle.

(3) Subject to subsection (3A) of this section any articles seized under subsection (1) of this section shall be brought before a justice of the peace acting for the same petty sessions area as the justice who issued the warrant, and the justice before whom the articles are brought may thereupon issue a summons to the occupier of the premises or, as the case may be, the user of the stall or vehicle to appear on a day specified in the summons before a magistrates' court for that petty sessions area to show cause why the articles or any of them should not be forfeited; and if the court is satisfied, as respects any of the articles, that at the time when they were seized they were obscene articles kept for publication for gain, the court shall order those articles to be forfeited:

Provided that if the person summoned does not appear, the court shall not make an order unless service of the summons is proved.

Provided also that this subsection does not apply in relation to any article seized under subsection (1) of this section which is returned to the occupier of the premises or, as the case may be, to the user of the stall or vehicle in or on which it was found.

(3A) Without prejudice to the duty of a court to make an order for the forfeiture of an article where section 1(4) of the Obscene Publications Act 1964 applies (orders made on conviction), in a case where by virtue of subsection (3A) of section 2 of this Act proceedings under the said section 2 for having an article for publication for gain could not be instituted except by or with the consent of the Director of Public Prosecutions, no order for the forfeiture of the article shall be made under this section unless the warrant under which the article was seized was issued on an information laid by or on behalf of the Director of Public Prosecutions.

(4) In addition to the person summoned, any other person being the owner, author or maker of any of the articles brought before the court, or any other person through whose hands they had passed before being seized, shall be entitled to appear before the court on the day specified in the summons to show cause why they should not be forfeited.

(5) Where an order is made under this section for the forfeiture of any articles, any person who appeared, or was entitled to appear, to show cause against the making of the order may appeal to the Crown Court; and no such order shall take effect until the expiration of the period within which notice of appeal to the Crown Court may be given against the order, or, if before the expiration thereof notice of appeal is duly given or application is made for the statement of a case for the opinion of the

High Court, until the final determination or abandonment of the proceedings on the appeal or case.

(6) If as respects any articles brought before it the court does not order forfeiture, the court may if it thinks fit order the person on whose information the warrant for the seizure of the articles was issued to pay such costs as the court thinks reasonable to any person who has appeared before the court to show cause why those articles should not be forfeited; and costs ordered to be paid under this subsection shall be enforceable as a civil debt.

(7) For the purposes of this section the question whether an article is obscene shall be determined on the assumption that copies of it would be published in any manner likely having regard to the circumstances in which it was found, but in no other manner."

References in s.3 to publication for gain shall apply to any publication with a view to gain, whether the gain is to accrue by way of consideration for the publication or in any other way.[57]

**8–018**    A justice of the peace shall not issue a warrant under s.3(1) except on information laid by or on behalf of the Director of Public Prosecutions or by a constable.[58] The warrant is restricted to obscene articles and thus a warrant which included "any other material of a sexually explicit nature" was bad and the resulting conviction quashed.[59]

The justices must look at the articles themselves and not merely listen to the prosecutor reading out passages.[60] Any warrant issued authorises only one entry, search and seizure, and when it has been carried out it is spent.[61]

Where articles are seized pursuant to s.3 and a person is convicted of having them for publication for gain, an order for forfeiture shall be made upon his conviction.[62] Any such order shall not take effect until the expiration of the ordinary time within which an appeal may be instituted or where, an appeal is instituted, until the appeal is finally decided or abandoned.[63] An application for a case to be stated or leave to appeal is treated as the institution of a case.[64] Where a decision on appeal is subject to a further appeal, the appeal shall not be deemed to be finally decided until the expiration of the ordinary time within which a further appeal may be instituted or, where a further appeal is duly instituted, until the further appeal is finally decided or abandoned.[65]

---

[57] Obscene Publications Act 1964, s.1(5).

[58] Criminal Justice Act 1967, s.25. "Constable" means any person holding the office of constable and not a member of the police of the rank of constable: *Halsbury's Laws* (4th ed.) Vol.36, paras 201 *et seq.*

[59] *Darbo v CPS* (Crown Office List) *The Times*, July 11, 1991, CO/929/90, (Transcript: Marten Walsh Cherer) June 28, 1991 *per* Mann L.J.

[60] *Thomson v Chain Libraries* [1954] 1 W.L.R. 999; [1954] 2 All E.R. 616 (decided under Obscene Publications Act 1857 20 & 21 Vict. c.83).

[61] *R. v Adams* [1980] Q.B. 575; [1980] 3 W.L.R. 275; [1980] 1 All E.R. 473; (1980) 70 Cr. App. R. 149.

[62] Obscene Publications Act 1964, s.1(4).

[63] *ibid.*

[64] *ibid.*, s.1(4)(a).

[65] *ibid.*, s.1(4)(b).

## Defence of innocent publication or possession

A person shall not be convicted of an offence of publishing an obscene **8–019** article under s.2 of the 1959 Act if he proves that he had not examined the article in respect of which he is charged and has no reasonable cause to suspect that it was such that his publication of it would make him liable to be convicted of an offence under s.2.[66]

In the case of proceedings for having an obscene article intended for publication, a person shall not be convicted of that offence if he proves that he had not examined the article and had no reasonable cause to suspect that his having it would make him liable to be convicted of that offence.[67]

The burden of proof is on the defendant and he needs to show (1) he had **8–020** no knowledge of any obscenity in the articles he published or had for publication, (2) that there was nothing in the article or the circumstances under which it came to him which ought to have lead him to suppose that it contained obscene material, and (3) that it was not by any negligence on his part that he did not know that it was obscene.[68] A director of a publishing company who was convicted of publishing obscene libels had his conviction quashed on appeal as he had no personal knowledge of the contents of the books.[69] At the time when the order for printing was taken the appellant was absent and he apparently had not seen the books prior to publishing.

## Defence of public good

A person shall not be convicted of an offence under s.2 (nor any forfeiture **8–021** order made) if it is proved that the publication of the article in question is justified as being for the public good on the ground that it is in the interests of science, literature, art, or learning,[70] or other objects of general concern.[71] "Other objects of general concern" is a mobile phrase that may change in content as society changes,[72] but falls within the same general area of concern as science, literature, etc. It does not permit the admission of evidence that pornographic material had psycho-therapeutic value for various categories of persons such that it relieved their sexual tensions and diverted them from anti-social and possibly criminal activities directed against others.[73]

---

[66] Obscene Publications Act 1959, s.2(5).
[67] Obscene Publications Act 1964, s.1(3)(a).
[68] *Vizetelly v Mudie's Select Library* [1900] 2 Q.B. 170 at 180 *per* Romer L.J. (libel case). See also libel cases: *Weldon v Times Book Co Ltd* (1911) 28 T.L.R. 143, CA (applying *Vizetelly v Mudie's Select Library*); *Bottomley v F W Woolworth & Co Ltd* (1932) 48 T.L.R. 521, CA; *Sun Life Assurance Co of Canad v W H Smith & Co* (1933) 150 L.T. 211; [1933] All E.R. Rep 432, CA.
[69] *R. v Love (Howard Stanley)* (1955) 39 Cr. App. R. 30 citing *R. v Allison* (1888) 59 L.T. 933.
[70] See *Attorney-General's Reference (No.3 of 1977)* [1978] 1 W.L.R. 1123; [1978] 3 All E.R. 1166; (1978) 67 Cr. App. R. 393 where CA construed learning as meaning "the product of scholarship".
[71] Obscene Publications Act 1959, s.4(1).
[72] *DPP v Jordan* [1977] A.C. 699; [1976] 3 W.L.R. 887; [1976] 3 All E.R. 775 at 780; (1977) 64 Cr. App. R. 33 *per* Lord Wilberforce.
[73] *ibid.*

**8–022**     The preceding defence does not apply to films or film soundtracks which have a separate but similar defence. A person shall not be convicted of an offence against s.2 in relation to a moving picture film or a soundtrack (nor any forfeiture order made) if it is proved that the publication of the film or soundtrack is justified as being for the public good on the ground that it is in the interests of drama, opera, ballet, or any other art, or of literature or learning.[74] "Moving picture film soundtrack" means any sound record designed for playing with a moving picture film whether incorporated with the film or not.[75]

The Act provides that expert opinion as to the literary, artistic, scientific, or other merits of the article may be admitted in any proceedings to establish or negative the public good defence.[76] "Other merits" includes sociological or ethical merits.[77] Evidence may be adduced relating to other books and their literary merits to establish a "climate of literature".[78] It is not permitted to seek to prove that other works in circulation are obscene but have not been the subject of a charge.[79]

**8–023**     The test for the public good defence is set out in *R. v Calder and Boyars Ltd* in the judgment of Salmon L.J.:

> "the proper direction on a defence under s.4 ... is that the jury must consider on the one hand the number of readers they believe would tend to be depraved and corrupted by the book, the strength of the tendency to be depraved and corrupted by the book, and the nature of the depravity or corruption; on the other hand, they should assess the strength of the literary, sociological or ethical merit which they consider the book to possess. They should then weigh up all these factors and decide whether on balance the publication is proved to be justified as being for the public good."[80]

The jury must determine the issues of whether the article is obscene and whether it was published by the defendant before considering whether a defence under s.4 has been established.[81]

## Broadcasting Act 1990

**8–024**     Section 162 and Sch.15 of the Broadcasting Act 1990 amends the Obscene Publications Act 1959 and adds supplementary provisions concerning tele-

---

[74] Obscene Publications Act 1959, s.4(1A) (as inserted by the Criminal Law Act 1977, s.53).
[75] *ibid.*, s.4(3) (as inserted by the Criminal Law Act 1977, s.53).
[76] *ibid.*, s.4(2).
[77] *R. v Calder and Boyars Ltd* [1969] 1 Q.B. 151 at 171; (1968) 52 Cr. App. R. 706; *R. v Penguin Books Ltd* [1961] Crim. L.R. 176 at 177.
[78] *R. v Penguin Books Ltd* [1961] Crim. L.R. 176.
[79] *ibid.*
[80] [1968] 3 All E.R. 644 at 650.
[81] *DPP v Jordan* [1977] A.C. 699; [1976] 3 W.L.R. 887; [1976] 3 All E.R. 775; (1977) 64 Cr. App. R. 33.

vision and sound programmes. The supplementary provisions in Sch.15 are set out below.

"1 In this Schedule—
  'the 1959 Act' means the Obscene Publications Act 1959;
  'relevant programme' means a programme included in a programme
    service;
and other expressions used in this Schedule which are also used in the 1959 Act have the same meaning as in that Act.

*Liability of person providing live programme material*
  2 Where—

(a) any matter is included by any person in a relevant programme in circumstances falling within section 1(5) of the 1959 Act, and
(b) that matter has been provided, for inclusion in that programme, by some other person,

the 1959 Act shall have effect as if that matter had been included in that programme by that other person (as well as by the person referred to in sub-paragraph (a)).

*Obscene articles kept for inclusion in programmes*
  3 It is hereby declared that where a person has an obscene article in his ownership, possession or control with a view to the matter recorded on it being included in a relevant programme, the article shall be taken for the purposes of the 1959 Act to be an obscene article had or kept by that person for publication for gain.

*Requirement of consent of Director of Public Prosecutions*
  4(1) Proceedings for an offence under section 2 of the 1959 Act for publishing an obscene article shall not be instituted except by or with the consent of the Director of Public Prosecutions in any case where—

(a) the relevant publication, or
(b) the only other publication which followed from the relevant publication,

took place in the course of the inclusion of a programme in a programme service; and in this sub-paragraph 'the relevant publication' means the publication in respect of which the defendant would be charged if the proceedings were brought.

  (2) Proceedings for an offence under section 2 of the 1959 Act for having an obscene article for publication for gain shall not be instituted except by or with the consent of the Director of Public Prosecutions in any case where—

(a) the relevant publication, or
(b) the only other publication which could reasonably have been expected to follow from the relevant publication,

was to take place in the course of the inclusion of a programme in a programme service; and in this sub-paragraph 'the relevant publication' means the publication which, if the proceedings were brought, the defendant would be alleged to have had in contemplation.

(3) [Corresponds to s.3(3A) of 1959 Act above]

*Defences*

5(1) A person shall not be convicted of an offence under section 2 of the 1959 Act in respect of the inclusion of any matter in a relevant programme if he proves that he did not know and had no reason to suspect that the programme would include matter rendering him liable to be convicted of such an offence.

(2) Where the publication in issue in any proceedings under that Act consists of the inclusion of any matter in a relevant programme, section 4(1) of that Act (general defence of public good) shall not apply; but

(a) a person shall not be convicted of an offence under section 2 of that Act, and

(b) an order for forfeiture shall not be made under section 3 of that Act,

if it is proved that the inclusion of the matter in question in a relevant programme is justified as being for the public good on the ground that it is in the interests of

(i) drama, opera, ballet or any other art

(ii) science, literature or learning, or

(iii) any other objects of general concern.

(3) Section 4(2) of that Act (admissibility of opinions of experts) shall apply for the purposes of sub-paragraph (2) above as it applies for the purposes of section 4(1) and (1A) of that Act.

*Exclusion of Proceedings Under Common Law*

6. Without prejudice to section 2(4) of the 1959 Act, a person shall not be proceeded against for an offence at common law—

(a) in respect of a relevant programme or anything said or done in the course of such a programme, where it is of the essence of the common law offence that the programme or (as the case may be) what was said or done was obscene, indecent, offensive, disgusting or injurious to morality; or

(b) in respect of an agreement to cause a programme to be included in a programme service or to cause anything to be said or done in the course of a programme which is to be so included, where the common law offence consists of conspiring to corrupt public morals or to do any act contrary to public morals or decency.''

## Obscenity prosecution practice

What is regarded as obscene is notoriously hard to define—decisions are **8–025** obviously made on a case by case basis but "hard core" pornography is the main target. Generally, pornographic material that can be obtained legally in the United Kingdom is unlikely to be regarded as obscene for the purposes of a prosecution. This in turn means that the guidelines operated by the British Board of Film Classification ("BBFC") for the purposes of classifying films and videos have considerable indirect influence on practice.

Following the decision in *R. v Video Appeals Committee Ex p. British Board of Film Classification*,[82] the BBFC relaxed its guidelines and allowed videos rated R18 to show actual sexual intercourse. In that case, the BBFC had refused to classify certain pornographic video films. In order to grant a classification, the BBFC had required editing of "all shots of penetration by penis, hand or dildo, as well of all shots of a penis being masturbated or taken into a woman's mouth". The parties seeking the classification appealed to the Video Appeals Committee ("VAC") which allowed the appeal concluding that the video could be given an R18 certificate, allowing it to be sold only in licenced sex shops, as the risk that it might be viewed by, and cause harm to, children or young persons was insignificant. The BBFC applied for judicial review of the VAC's decision contending that the VAC had erred in apparently taking the view that the test set out in the Video Recordings Act 1984, s.4A as to the risk of harm to potential viewers including children did not have to be applied where there was an "unquantified risk of harm". BBFC's application was dismissed and it was held that to refuse to classify a film until a risk could be quantified would unreasonably fetter discretion.

Prior to that decision the R18 guidelines had stated "there must be no **8–026** clear sight of penetration, oral, vaginal or anal, or of masturbation." The R18 guidelines now permit films depicting "penetration by finger, penis, tongue, vibrator or dildo". Broadly, the R18 guidelines prohibit films which show non-consensual sex; violence; infliction of harm; acts which breach the criminal law; material likely to encourage an interest in abusive sexual activity such as paedophilia or incest; and activity which is degrading or dehumanising, such as bestiality or necrophilia. The full BBFC classification guidelines can be found on the BBFC website at *http://www.bbfc.co.uk/*.

## Photo Marketing Agency guidelines

The UK Photo Marketing Association ("PMA") was formed in 1988 and **8–027** forms part of PMA International.[83] PMA International began in 1924 and was then known as the Photo Finishers Association of America. It is a trade association which exists to promote the growth of the imaging industry through co-operation. In 1996, the UK PMA published guidelines for

---

[82] [2000] E.M.L.R. 850; [2000] C.O.D. 239.
[83] *http://www.pmai.org/*.

processors when confronted with potentially obscene or indecent matter. The guidelines provide useful practical guidance and are set out in full below.

## Photo marketing association (PMA) guidelines in relation to the processing of potentially indecent or obscene photographs and other dubious material[84]

### 1. Introduction

The purpose of this document is to assist photo-processors and retailers, to be aware of their legal position regarding the processing and printing of indecent and obscene photos, and other dubious material, and to offer some guidance on what to do if a photo-processor receives such material from a customer.

Photo-processors should observe the laws of the land and cannot reasonably be expected by customers to process or return material when they may commit a criminal offence in doing so. There is also a particular responsibility in relation to indecent photographs of children as the circumstances may indicate that the child is in need of care and protection.

Photo-processors should handle the very rare cases when potentially indecent or obscene photographs are received with sensitivity and discretion but if such photographs give serious cause for concern, they will need to consult the relevant authorities so that the authorities may decide whether the material warrants further investigation and or prosecution.

### 2. The legal position

The three relevant Acts are set out below:

- Obscene Publications Acts 1959 & 1963 make it an offence to publish (e.g. distribute, circulate, sell, give, lend, etc) an obscene article. An article is "deemed to be obscene if its effect .... is .... such as to tend to deprave and corrupt persons who are likely .... to see it."

- The Protection of Children Act 1978 (as amended), makes it an offence "to take or permit to be taken any indecent photograph of a child" or to possess such a photo without a legitimate reason. A child is defined as a person under 16 years of age.

- The Post Office Act 1953[85] makes it an offence to send any indecent item through the post.

### 3. What is "indecent or obscene"?

This can only be decided by the Courts as a matter of fact in the particular circumstances of the case. However, we have set out below some guidance which we have collated from the police and other sources which may help you to determine (in the first instance) whether a particular photo causes concern.

### *Photos of Children*

Each photograph should be judged individually and it should be noted that there is no statutory definition of "indecent". Indicators which may suggest that a photo of a child could potentially be indecent include

---

[84] Reproduced with permission of the Photo Marketing Association International, see above at para.8–027.
[85] Now governed by the Postal Services Act 2000 as to which see below at para.8–041.

a) Does the child appear to be under 16 years of age?

b) Is the child aware that the photo is being taken (i.e. posed)?

c) Are the genitalia exposed?

d) Does the photo have a gratuitous sexual implication?

e) Is it indecent by virtue of the context (e.g. a child included in the same photo as sexually active adults)?

*Action to Take*

If knowingly you process or print indecent material involving children, you may be committing a criminal offence if you return it to your customer. If you have received material which ~ believe to be potentially indecent, we recommend you immediately contact the police for further advice. In the case of photos involving children, you should speak to your nearest Child Protection Unit who can be contacted via your local Police Station.

*Photos of adults*

Nudity or posing in itself will not render a photo obscene. However, the following activities depicted are likely to do so:

— Sexual penetration.

— Masturbation.

— Sado-Masochism/bondage.

— Unnatural sexual practices or perversions.

*Action to Take*

Photo-processors may commit a criminal offence under the Obscene Publications Act if they process and return obscene material which is subsequently published. Publishing involves the distribution of the material to third parties whether or not for gain. Processors should not therefore return either the prints or the negatives of such material unless they are satisfied that the material is not obscene or that it will not be published. Processors should consider contacting the C.LD. at their local police station for advice.

## 4. Handling such cases

Processors should develop internal procedures for dealing with these rare cases. A system should be instituted so that an employee, who believes he has discovered a dubious photograph, immediately refers it to Manager/Director level and where possible, a committee of three people should rule on the photograph, giving reasons in writing contemporaneously for the decision reached. Processors should however, have particular regard to the following when dealing with potentially indecent or obscene material.

a. Do not return either the negatives nor the prints to the customer but instead give these to the police if requested.

b. Do not accuse your customer of taking or having indecent or obscene photos—that is a matter for the Courts to decide. You should merely state that due to the nature of the photos you have referred the matter to the police for advice.

c.   Ensure that all the people involved, e.g. your staff, suppliers, police, etc., are aware of the need for the incident to be kept entirely confidential.

d.   Do keep detailed notes of the incident for your own use should you be needed as a witness in any subsequent Court case.

e.   Ensure that any communications with customers on these issues are handled with discretion and sensitivity, for example, the matter should not be discussed with the customer concerned, where the conversation could be overhead.

## 5. Reasonableness

What the law will look for is reasonableness. That, for example, the decision for referral or non referral to the police is soundly based, that reasons are given, so that the decision is founded on proper grounds, not on the whim or the idiosyncrasies of some unbalanced individual. Reasonableness would also be a defence not only to a civil action, but to the criminal offence of publishing under the Obscene Publications Acts 1959 & 1963.

## 6. Other material

Many processors will not expect their staff to handle material which, although the handling of such material may not be illegal per se, is morally or otherwise offensive. Examples of this could include photos depicting the commission of crimes, e.g. dog-fighting, badger-baiting, the use of illegal substances, etc, etc, etc. The processor should decide whether it wishes to process and return such material but processors are reminded that they are not normally obliged to handle work which they choose not to. If you receive material which you prefer not to handle, it may not be appropriate to involve the police but you should have a private discussion with your customer to explain your policy, destroy the prints (but return the negatives), and ask the customer not to submit any similar material in future. No charge should be made.

## 7. Return of material

Processors should also consider the means of returning indecent material to customers, when they are able to do so, in view of the provisions of the Post Office Act. It may be possible to make such material available for collection or a courier service could be used.

## 8. General

This note provides general guidance but the PMA is not able to comment in relation to specific instances. Photo-processors should consult their own solicitors or the relevant authorities for further advice in such cases. There may be advantages in identifying in advance, the relevant police officer, or Child Protection Unit, at local level, who may be able to assist you.

**Sentencing**

**8–028**     A person convicted of an offence under the Obscene Publications Act 1959 is liable on summary conviction to a fine not exceeding the prescribed sum,[86] or to imprisonment for a term not exceeding six months.[87] On indictment, a person so convicted is liable to a fine[88] or to imprisonment not exceeding three years, or both.[89]

The Court of Appeal gave guidance as to sentencing in *Holloway*[90] where the appellant had been engaged in selling pornographic books, films, and video tapes on a commercial scale from a shop.

> "Experience has shown ... that fining these pornographers does not discourage them. Fines merely become an expense of the trade and are passed on to purchasers of the pornographic matter, so that prices go up and sales go on.
>
> In the judgment of this court, the only way of stamping out this filthy trade is by imposing sentences of imprisonment on first offenders and all connected with the commercial exploitation of pornography: otherwise front men will be put up and the real villains will hide behind them. It follows, in our judgment, that the salesmen, projectionists, owners and suppliers behind them should on conviction lose their liberty. For first offenders sentences need only be comparatively short, but persistent offenders should get the full rigour of the law. In addition, the courts should take the profit out of this illegal filthy trader by imposing very substantial fines".[91]

**8–029**     The following sentences have been approved by the Court of Appeal:

- 30 months' imprisonment for commercial supply of pornographic videos by mail order where the defendant had three previous convictions.[92]

- 18 months' imprisonment for a defendant employed in a shop supplying obscene videos aggravated by continuation of the offence following a police warning.[93]

- 6 months for a shopkeeper selling obscene books/videos as part of general trade together with £2,000 fine.[94]

---

[86] The prescribed sum is currently £5,000 pursuant to the Magistrates' Court Act 1980, s.32(9).
[87] Obscene Publications Act 1959, s.2(1)(a).
[88] The level of the fine is unlimited but should be within the offender's capacity to pay: *R. v Garner* [1986] 1 All E.R. 78; [1986] 1 W.L.R. 73.
[89] Obscene Publications Act 1959, s.2(1)(b).
[90] (1982) 4 Cr. App. R. (S) 128.
[91] *ibid.*, at 131 *per* Lawton L.J.
[92] *R. v Lamb* [1998] 1 Cr. App. R. (S) 77.
[93] *R. v Ibrahim* [1998] 1 Cr. App. R. (S) 157.
[94] *R. v Knight* (1990) 12 Cr. App. R. (S) 319; see also *R. v Doorgashurn* (1988) 10 Cr. App. R. (S) 195.

- 3 months' imprisonment for an employee working in a shop for the operators of the shop as a "front man" but where he was aware of the general nature of the stock.[95]

## OBSCENE LIBEL AT COMMON LAW

Publication of obscene matter is an indictable offence at common law.[96] **8–030** However, the Obscene Publications Act 1959, s.2(4) provides that a person publishing an article may not be proceeded against for an offence at common law consisting of the publication of any matter contained or embodied in the article where it is of the essence of the offence that the matter is obscene.

It has been said that "The obvious purpose of s.2(4) is to make available where the essence of the offence is tending to deprave and corrupt, the defences which are set out in the Act".[97] Section 2(4) does not prevent prosecution for the common law offence of conspiring to corrupt public morals,[98] or of outraging public decency.[99]

Similarly, the Act provides that a person shall not be proceeded against at **8–031** common law for an offence:

(a) in respect of a film exhibition (or anything said or done during the course of a film exhibition) where it is of the essence of the common law offence that the exhibition or what was said or done was obscene, indecent, offensive, disgusting, or injurious to morality[1]; or

(b) in respect of an agreement to give a film exhibition (or to cause anything to be said or done in the course of such an exhibition) where the common law offence consists of conspiring to corrupt public morals or to do any act contrary to public morals or decency.[2]

For these purposes "film exhibition" means any exhibition of moving pictures which is produced otherwise than by the simultaneous reception and exhibition of programmes included in a programme service (within the meaning of the Broadcasting Act 1990).[3]

---

[95] *R. v Pace* [1998] 1 Cr. App. R. (S) 121.
[96] *R. v Curl* (1727) 2 Str. 788. "Obscene matter" at common law has the definition set out in *R. v Hicklin* (1867–68) L.R. 3 Q.B. 360 above at para.8–001.
[97] *Knuller (Publishing, Printing and Promotions) Ltd v DPP* [1973] A.C. 435 at 456 *per* Lord Reid.
[98] *Shaw v DPP* [1962] A.C. 220; [1961] 2 W.L.R. 897; [1961] 2 All E.R. 446 (publishing advertisements for prostitutes); *Knuller (Publishing, Printing and Promotions) Ltd v DPP* [1973] A.C. 435 (advertisements for the purpose of inducing or encouraging homosexual practices).
[99] *R. v Gibson* [1990] 3 W.L.R. 595; [1991] 1 All E.R. 439 (display in a gallery of a pair of earrings made from freeze-dried human foetuses). See below at para.8–034.
[1] Obscene Publications Act 1959, s.2(4A)(a).
[2] *ibid.*, s.2(4A)(b).
[3] *ibid.*, s.2(7) applying definition of "film exhibition" in the Cinemas Act 1985, s.21. As to the meaning of "programmes" and "programme service" within the meaning of the Broadcasting Act 1990 see above at para.8–012, n.34.

COMMON LAW OFFENCE OF OUTRAGING PUBLIC DECENCY

### Outraging public decency

**8–032**    It is an indictable offence at common law to commit in public an act of such lewd, obscene, or disgusting nature as to amount to an outrage to public decency (whether or not it tends to deprave or corrupt those who see it),[4] or such act as is injurious to public morals by tending to corrupt the mind.[5] It arises where ordinary decent minded people who are not likely to become corrupted or depraved will be outraged or utterly disgusted by what they read or see.[6] The punishment is a fine, or imprisonment, or both at the discretion of the court without limit provided the sentence is not inordinate.[7]

It is not necessary to prove that the act in fact disgusted those who saw it. It is sufficient to prove that it was calculated to do so.[8]

**8–033**    For an act to be in public, more than one person must have been able to see the act complained of.[9] Not only must the offence have been seen by at least two witnesses, but it must also have been committed where there was the likelihood that it would be seen by members of the public.[10] This does not necessarily mean that it must be a public place, but it has to be a place where the public are able to see what takes place there, such as the balcony of a private house.[11]

Indecency in the context of outraging public decency is not confined to sexual indecency. It has no limit other than saying it includes anything which an ordinary decent man or woman would find shocking, disgusting, and revolting.[12] It includes for example, disinterring a corpse,[13] selling a wife,[14] or filming women as they used the lavatory in a supermarket.[15]

### Galleries and exhibitions

**8–034**    Galleries and exhibitions to which the public have access as of right, or gratis, or on payment, are included within the meaning of "in public" for the purposes of outraging public decency.[16]

---

[4] *Shaw v DPP* [1962] A.C. 220 at 281 *per* Lord Reid
[5] *Russell on Crime* (12th ed.) Vol.2, p.1423.
[6] *Knuller (Publishing, Printing & Promotions) Ltd v DPP* [1973] A.C. 435 at 457 *per* Lord Reid.
[7] *R. v Morris* [1951] 1 K.B. 394; [1950] 2 All E.R. 965; (1950) 34 Cr. App. R. 210.
[8] *R. v May (John)* (1990) 91 Cr. App. R. 157 at 159.
[9] *R. v Watson* (1847) 2 Cox C.C. 376; *R. v Webb* (1848) 3 Cox C.C. 183; *R. v Farrell* (1862) 9 Cox C.C. 446 (indecent exposure); *R. v Mayling* [1963] 2 Q.B. 717 at 724; [1963] 2 W.L.R. 709; [1963] 1 All E.R. 687; (1963) 47 Cr. App. R. 102; *R. v May (John)* (1990) 91 Cr. App. R. 157 at 159.
[10] *R. v Walker (Steven)* [1996] 1 Cr. App. R. 111 at 114; [1995] Crim. L.R. 826.
[11] *ibid.*, citing *Smith v Hughes* [1960] 1 W.L.R. 830; [1960] 2 All E.R. 859.
[12] *Knuller (Publishing, Printing & Promotions) Ltd v DPP* [1973] A.C. 435 at 458 *per* Lord Reid.
[13] *Rex v Lynn* (1788) 2 Durn. & E. 733.
[14] Cited in *Rex v Delaval* (1763) 3 Burr. 1434, 1438; 97 E.R. 915.
[15] *R. v Ching Choi* (unrep) May 7, 1999; Lawtel No.C0004944; [1999] 8 Archbold News 3, CA.
[16] *Knuller (Publishing, Printing & Promotions) Ltd v DPP* [1973] A.C. 435 at 458E *per* Lord Reid; *R. v Gibson; R. v Sylveire* [1990] 2 Q.B. 619; (1990) 91 Cr. App. R. 341. See also Indecent Displays Control Act 1981 below at para.8–063.

Outraging public decency may arise by the exhibition of articles (including photographs) such as a exhibiting a picture of a man covered in sores[17]; displaying earrings made from freeze dried human foetuses in a gallery[18]; and exhibiting deformed children.[19] Superficially hiding an exhibit if the public is expressly or impliedly invited to look behind the shield or cover does not necessarily negate a charge of outraging public decency.[20] Public touting for an outrageously indecent exhibition in private also amounts to an offence, such as inviting people to view an indecent exhibition in a booth.[21] It is not necessary to seek to draw particular attention to the obscene exhibit; a mere invitation to the public to enter the premises where it is displayed will suffice.[22]

No prosecutions of galleries for outraging public decency have been instigated in the UK for several years.[23] The last notable prosecution was in 1989 in *R. v Gibson*; *R. v Sylveire*[24] where a gallery was prosecuted for displaying earrings made out of human foetuses of about three to four months gestation. In recent years, concerns have been raised in relation to a handful of exhibitions.

In 1997, an exhibition at the Royal Academy of Arts entitled "Sensation" (which featured amongst other things a portrait of Myra Hindley[25] and *Self*, a sculpture by Marc Quinn consisting of eight pints of his blood poured into a cast of his head) caused much controversy. Calls for prosecution were resisted. However, a work[26] by Jake and Dinos Chapman which featured a "ring of mutant child mannequins with convulsive displaced genitalia" was displayed in a room with a warning notice to which only over 18s were permitted access.[26a]

In March 2001, an exhibition entitled "*I am a Camera*" was referred to the CPS in connection with photographs of children but they declined to prosecute.[27]

**8–035**

---

[17] *Reg v Grey* (1864) 4 F. & F. 73 (176 E.R. 472). Exhibition in a shop window of a life size colour picture of a man half naked to the waist covered in sores. Held to be guilty of a nuisance. "No man has a right thus to expose disgusting and offensive exhibitions in or upon a public highway."

[18] *R. v Gibson; R. v Sylveire* [1990] 2 Q.B. 619; (1990) 91 Cr. App. R. 341.

[19] *Herring v Walround* (1681) 2 Chan. Cas. 110. (22 E.R. 870). Showing embalmed Siamese twins for money held to be a misdemeanour. "Herring was delivered of two female children ... the birth was monstrous for they had two heads, four arms, four legs and but one belly where their two bodies were conjoined".

[20] *Knuller (Publishing, Printing & Promotions) Ltd v DPP* [1973] A.C. 435 at 495 *per* Lord Simon of Glaisdale.

[21] *R. v Saunders & Hitchcock* (1875) 1 Q.B.D. 15; *Knuller (Publishing, Printing & Promotions) Ltd v DPP* [1973] A.C. 435 at 495 *per* Lord Simon of Glaisdale.

[22] *R. v Gibson; R. v Sylveire* [1990] 2 Q.B. 619 at 630; (1990) 91 Cr. App. R. 341.

[23] *Cf.* In the USA an art gallery and its director faced charges of obscenity in respect of an exhibition of works of Robert Maplethorpe, an acclaimed but controversial photographer. *Maplethorpe Retrospective Sparks Pornography Debate* (1990) 87(33) L.S.G. 10.

[24] [1990] 2 Q.B. 619 at 630; (1990) 91 Cr. App. R. 341.

[25] *Myra* by Marcus Harvey based on Hindley's police photograph.

[26] *Zygotic acceleration, biogenetic de-sublimated libidinal model (enlarged x 1000)* (1995).

[26a] *Cf.* Requirements for an Adequate Warning Notice under the Indecent Displays (Control) Act 1981 below at para.8–066. But note displays only visible from within the art gallery are excluded from being a public place under that Act: see below at para.8–065.

[27] See below at para.8–051.

**8–036**   In 2002, *Body Worlds* an anatomical exhibition of real human bodies that had been preserved by a process known as plastination[28] opened in London. One of the exhibits was the bisected cadaver of an eight-months pregnant woman with her womb opened to reveal the foetus. In early 2002, the police visited the BodyWorks exhibition abroad prior to its opening in London with a view to assessing whether any offences of outraging public decency or other indecency offence would be committed.[29] They took the view that no such offences had been committed and the exhibition was never referred to the Crown Prosecution Service. No complaints in respect of the exhibition were received by the Obscene Publications Unit.[29a]

## Conspiracy to outrage public decency

**8–037**   As there is an offence at common law of conduct which outrages public decency, a conspiracy to outrage public decency is also a common law offence as an agreement to do an illegal act.[30] However, in *Shaw v DPP*[31] two judges of the House of Lords in a minority (Lords Reid and Diplock) took the view that there was no such offence. In that case the conviction in respect of conspiracy to outrage public decency was quashed as the summing up was inadequate.

## Conspiracy to corrupt public morals

**8–038**   Conspiracy to corrupt public morals is a misdemeanour which is indictable at common law.[32] "Conspiracy to corrupt public morals" means to corrupt the morals of such members of the public as may be influenced by the matter published by the accused.[33] It requires an intention to debauch and corrupt and is a separate offence from outraging public decency which raises the issue, not whether people might be corrupted, but whether the sense of decency of members of the public would be outraged.[34]

Whether matter is corrupting is a question for the jury, but they should keep in mind the current standards of ordinary decent people.[35] Corrupt is a

---

[28] Described as a unique method of preserving tissue in a lifelike state. The bodies are impregnated with a reactive polymer such as silicone rubber, epoxy, or polyester resin. The result is a specimen which is dry, odourless, durable, and retains its original surface relief. See further *http://www.plastination.com*.

[29] Author's telephone interview with Inspector Brian Ward of Obscene Publications Unit, Metropolitan Police, August 27, 2002.

[29a] See above at n.29.

[30] *Knuller (Publishing, Printing & Promotions) Ltd v DPP* [1973] A.C. 435 at 493.

[31] [1962] A.C. 220; [1961] 2 W.L.R. 897; [1961] 2 All E.R. 446, HL.

[32] *Shaw v DPP* [1962] A.C. 220, HL.

[33] *Knuller (Publishing, Printing & Promotions) Ltd v DPP* [1973] A.C. 435 at 456, HL, *per* Lord Reid.

[34] *R. v Gibson; R. v Sylveire* [1990] 2 Q.B. 619 at 623, 624, (1990) 91 Cr. App. R. 341, CA; *Knuller (Publishing, Printing & Promotions) Ltd v DPP* [1973] A.C. 435 at 468, HL.

[35] *Knuller (Publishing, Printing & Promotions) Ltd v DPP* [1973] A.C. 435 at 457, HL, *per* Lord Reid.

strong word that should not be weakened by too gentle a paraphrase or explanation.[36] "Corrupt public morals" suggests conduct which a jury might find destructive of the very fabric of society.[37]

## Overlap with Obscene Publications Act 1959/statutory indecency offences

It has been held that the bringing of a charge for conspiring to corrupt **8–039** public morals or outraging public decency is not precluded by s.2(4) of the Obscene Publications Act 1959 which prohibits prosecution at common law for offences where the essence of the offence is obscenity.[38] Section 2(4) of the Obscene Publications Act 1959 provides:

"A person publishing an article shall not be proceeded against for an offence at common law consisting of the publication of any matter contained or embodied in the article where it is of the essence of the offence that the matter is obscene."

The Court of Appeal considered that "obscene" in s.2(4) bore the limited meaning ascribed to it by s.1(1).[39] Therefore, prosecution of offences of outraging public decency and corrupting public morals offenced are not prohibited by s.2(4).

As far as corruption of public morals is concerned, this is perhaps surprising in the light of an assurance given to the House of Commons on June 3, 1964, by the Solicitor-General to the effect that "a conspiracy to corrupt public morals would not be charged so as to circumvent the statutory defence in subsection (4)."[40]

"I find nothing in the [Sexual Offences Act 1967] to indicate Parliament thought or intended to lay down that indulgence in these [homosexual] practises is not corrupting. I read the Act as saying that, even though it may be corrupting, if people choose to corrupt themselves in this way that is their affair and the law will not interfere. But no licence is given to others to encourage the practice."[41]

---

[36] *Knuller (Publishing, Printing & Promotions) Ltd v DPP* [1973] A.C. 435 at 460, HL, per Lord Morris of Borth-y-Gest.
[37] *Knuller (Publishing, Printing & Promotions) Ltd v DPP* [1973] A.C. 435 at 491 *per* Lord Simon of Glaisdale.
[38] *R. v Gibson; R. v Sylveire* [1990] 2 Q.B. 619 at 623, 624; (1990) 91 Cr. App. R. 341 at 346, CA; *Shaw v DPP* [1962] A.C. 220; *Knuller (Publishing, Printing & Promotions) Ltd v DPP* [1973] A.C. 435. As to Obscene Publications Act 1959, s.2(4) see above at para.8–030.
[39] *R. v Gibson; R. v Sylveire* [1990] 2 Q.B. 619 at 623, 625; (1990) 91 Cr. App. R. 341 at 346, CA. As to the meaning of "obscene" under s.1(1) see above at paras 8–005 and 8–013 *et seq.*
[40] *Hansard*, HC Vol.695, col.1212. Discussed in *Knuller (Publishing, Printing & Promotions) Ltd v DPP* [1973] A.C. 435 at 456, 466.
[41] *Knuller (Publishing, Printing & Promotions) Ltd v DPP* [1973] A.C. 435 at 457 *per* Lord Reid.

## BLASPHEMY

**8–040**   At common law, blasphemy is an offence. It is defined as the publication of matter which vilifies or is contemptuous of, or which denies the truth of, the Christian religion or the Bible or the Book of Common Prayer, and which is couched in indecent, scurrilous, or offensive terms likely to shock and outrage the feelings of the general body of Christian believers. It is triable on indictment only.[41a]

Blasphemy is only concerned with the Christian religion and does not extend to other religions such as Islam.[42] It has been held in Europe that the refusal of a classification certificate for a video recording on the grounds that it infringed the criminal law of blasphemy did not amount to a violation of the right to freedom of expression under Art.10 of the European Convention on Human Rights.[43]

In 1985 the Law Commission recommended that this offence be abolished.[44] In theory, it would be possible for there to be a prosecution in respect of a blasphemous photograph or image, but in the modern climate it is unlikely. Indeed, there has been only one prosecution for blasphemy since 1922.[45]

## POSTAL SERVICES ACT 2000

**8–041**   Section 85(3) of the Postal Services Act 2000 provides that it is an offence to send by post a postal packet which encloses—

(a) any indecent or obscene print, painting, photograph, lithograph, engraving, cinematograph film, or other record of a picture or pictures, book, card, or written communication, or

(b) any other indecent or obscene article (whether or not of a similar kind to those mentioned in paragraph (a)).

A person commits an offence if he sends by post a postal packet which has on the packet, or on the cover of the packet, any words, marks, or designs which are of an indecent or obscene character.[46] A postal packet means a letter, parcel, packet, or other article transmissible by post.[47]

The above offences apply in respect of packages posted on or after March 26, 2001, which was the date the section came into force.[48] Prior to that time,

---

[41a] See *Archbold* (2004) at 27-1 *et seq.*
[42] *Chief Metropolitan Stipendiary Magistrate Ex p. Choudhury* [1991] Q.B. 429.
[43] *Wingrove v UK* (1997) 24 E.H.R.R. 1.
[44] Law Com No.145.
[45] *Whitehouse v Lemon* [1979] A.C. 617; [1979] 2 W.L.R. 281; [1979] 1 All E.R. 898; (1979) 68 Cr. App. R. 381.
[46] Postal Services Act 2000, s.85(4).
[47] *ibid.*, s.125.
[48] See Postal Services Act 2000 (Commencement No.3 and Transitional and Saving Provisions) Order 2001 (SI 2001/878), arts 2, 15 and Sch.

a similar prohibition was contained in s.11 of the Post Office Act 1953 which has now been repealed,[49] but still applies to packages posted before March 26, 2001.[50]

A person convicted of any of these offences is liable on summary con- **8–042** viction, to a fine not exceeding the statutory maximum,[51] or on conviction on indictment, to a fine or to imprisonment for a term not exceeding 12 months, or to both.[52]

Under the preceding section in the Post Office Act 1953, it was held that "obscene" in this context does not have the same meaning as under the Obscene Publications Act 1959. It bears its ordinary dictionary meaning and includes things which are shocking, lewd, indecent and so on.[53] The words "indecent" and "obscene" convey one idea, namely, offending against the recognised standards of propriety, indecency being at the lower, and obscenity at the upper, end of the scale.[54] The test of indecency is objective.[55] The character of the addressee is immaterial as is the effect on the recipient.[56] The issue of obscenity or indecency is entirely one for the jury to be determined in relation to recognised standards of propriety which may vary from age to age and hence expert evidence is inadmissible.[57]

## PROTECTION OF CHILDREN ACT 1978

### Offences of taking, etc. indecent photographs of children

Taking indecent photographs of children and minors is prohibited by the **8–043** Protection of Children Act 1978. Section 1 of the Act states it is an offence for a person:

(a) to take, or permit to be taken or to make, any indecent photograph or pseudo-photograph of a child; or

(b) to distribute or show such indecent photographs or pseudo-photographs; or

(c) to have in his possession such indecent photographs or pseudo-photographs, with a view to their being distributed or shown by himself or others; or

---

[49] Postal Services Act 2000 (Commencement No.3 and Transitional Saving Provisions) Order 2001 (SI 2001/878).
[50] *ibid.*, art.4.
[51] £5,000.
[52] s.85(5).
[53] *R. v Anderson* [1972] 1 Q.B. 304 at 311, 312; (1972) 56 Cr. App. R. 155 at 122, CA.
[54] *R. v Stanley* [1965] 2 Q.B. 327; [1965] 2 W.L.R. 917; [1965] 1 All E.R. 1035; (1965) 49 Cr. App. R. 175.
[55] *R. v Straker* [1965] Crim. L.R. 239; *Kosmos Publications Ltd v DPP* [1975] Crim. L.R. 345.
[56] *ibid.*
[57] *R. v Stamford* [1972] 2 Q.B. 391.

(d) to publish or cause to be published any advertisement likely to be understood as conveying that the advertiser distributes or shows such indecent photographs or pseudo-photographs, or intends to do so.

Proceedings for an offence under the Protection of Children Act 1978 shall not be instituted except by or with the consent of the Director of Public Prosecutions.[58] Any person convicted under this Act is liable (a) upon indictment to a term of imprisonment of up to 10 years, or to a fine, or to both, and (b) upon summary conviction, to imprisonment for up to six months, or to a fine not exceeding the prescribed sum, or to both[59]

## Photographs and pseudo-photographs

### Photographs

**8–044**    Indecent films, copies of indecent photographs or films, and indecent photographs comprised in a film are to be included within the meaning of "indecent photographs".[60] "Film" includes any form of video-recording.[61] The Act provides that references to "a photograph" include the negative as well as the positive version,[62] and data stored on a computer disk or by other electronic means which is capable of conversion into a photograph.[63]

The Act was amended in 1994 to expressly include digital photographs as data stored on a computer disk.[64] Even prior to amendment, it was held that "photograph" included digital photographs held as data on a computer disk which can be converted into a screen image.[65] and that "the statutory definition"[66] was wide enough to include "later as well as contemporary forms of photograph."[67]

Downloading a photograph from the internet classes as "making" a photograph for the purposes of s.1(1)(a).[68]

### Pseudo-photographs

**8–045**    "Pseudo-photograph" is defined as "an image, whether made by computer-graphics or otherwise howsoever, which appears to be a photo-graph."[69] As with photographs, references to an "indecent pseudo-

---

[58] Protection of Children Act 1978, s1(4). See *R. v Bull* (1994) 99 Cr. App. R. 193 (consent of DPP valid if given before committal. Offence under Firearms Act 1968) distinguishing *Price v Humphries* [1958] 2 Q.B. 353; [1958] 3 W.L.R. 304. *Cf. R. v Whale* [1991] Crim. L.R. 692.
[59] Protection of Children Act 1978, s.6. See further below under "Sentencing".
[60] Protection of Children Act 1978, s.7(2).
[61] Protection of Children Act 1978, s.7(5).
[62] Protection of Children Act 1978, s.7(4)(a).
[63] Protection of Children Act 1978, s.7(4)(b) (as substituted by Criminal Justice and Public Order Act 1994, s 84(3)(b)).
[64] *ibid.*
[65] *R. v Fellows* [1997] 2 All E.R. 548, 557–558; [1997] 1 Cr. App. R. 244.
[66] At that time Protection of Children Act 1978, s.7(4) which read "References to a photograph include the negative as well as the positive version."
[67] *R. v Fellows* [1997] 2 All E.R. 548 at 557; [1997] 1 Cr. App. R. 244.
[68] *R. v Bowden* [2000] 1 Cr. App. R. 438; *Atkins v DPP* [2000] 2 Cr. App. R. 248.
[69] Protection of Children Act 1978, s.7(7).

photograph" are to be interpreted as including a copy of an indecent pseudo-photograph and data stored on a computer disk or by other electronic means which is capable of conversion into a pseudo-photograph.[70]

The statute further provides:

"If the impression conveyed by a pseudo-photograph is that the person shown is a child, the pseudo-photograph shall be treated for all purposes of this Act as showing a child and so shall a pseudo- photograph where the predominant impression conveyed is that the person shown is a child notwithstanding that some of the physical characteristics shown are those of an adult."

These provisions were inserted because technology allows the superimposition of an actual photograph of a child's face onto a pornographic photograph of an adult and by electronic manipulation the resulting image can be made to appear to be a pornographic photograph of a child.[71] It has been said *obiter* that the term "pseudo-photographs" which was introduced by the 1994 amendment is concerned with images created by computer processes rather than the storage or transmission by computers of images created originally by photography.[72]

Where an image was created by sellotaping a photograph of the lower half **8–046** of a young woman's naked body over a photograph of a child, it was held that the image did "not appear to be a photograph."[73] It was obviously two photographs sellotaped together and hence did not fall within the definition of "pseudo-photograph." However, it was said that if that exhibit were itself to be photocopied to produce a single image it could well be said to constitute a pseudo-photograph.[74] The question is whether the exhibit in question is "an image ... which appears to be a photograph."[75]

### Take or make, show or distribute, etc.

Voluntarily downloading an image from a web-page onto a computer **8–047** screen is an act of making a photograph or pseudo-photograph.[76] In reaching this conclusion, the Court of Appeal observed:

"By downloading the image, the operator is creating or causing the image to exist on the computer screen. The image may remain on the screen for a

---

[70] Protection of Children Act 1978, s.7(9).
[71] HC Official Report SC B (Criminal Justice and Public Order Bill) cols 733, 741, 742, February 15, 10004.
[72] *R. v Fellows* [1997] 2 All E.R. 548, 557–558; [1997] 1 Cr. App. R. 244.
[73] *DPP v Atkins; Goodland v DPP* [2000] 1 W.L.R. 1427; [2000] 2 All E.R. 425, 438–439; [2000] 2 Cr. App. R. 248, DC.
[74] *Loc. cit.*
[75] *Loc. cit.*
[76] *R. v Smith; R. v Jayson* [2002] EWCA Crim 683 at para.33; [2003] 1 Cr. App. R. 13; *DPP v Atkins; Goodland v DPP* [2000] 1 W.L.R. 1427; [2000] 2 All E.R. 425; [2000] 2 Cr. App. R. 248, DC; *R. v Bowden* [2001] Q.B. 88; [2000] 2 W.L.R. 1083; [2000] 2 All E.R. 418; [2000] 1 Cr. App. R. 438.

second or for a much longer period. Whether its creation amounts to an act of making cannot be determined by the length of time that the image remains on the screen."[77]

Providing another with a password which gives access to an archive of indecent material amounts to "showing" that other the material stored.[78] "Showing" means showing the photographs to another; the offence requires more than simple possession with a view to showing photographs only to oneself.[79]

A person is not guilty of an offence of "making" or being in possession of an indecent photograph contained in an email attachment, if before he opens the attachment he did not know that it contained or was likely to contain indecent photographs of a child.[80] The mens rea required is that the act of making should be a deliberate and intentional act with knowledge that the image made is or is likely to be an indecent photograph of a child.[81]

**8–048**    A computer, when being used to browse the internet, will store recently viewed material in a temporary internet cache. This helps to speed up the browsing process so that when the user re-visits the pages stored the browser can use the locally stored cache. The cache can be accessed off line until it is emptied automatically when it becomes full, but even then it is possible to retrieve the information forensically.[82] It has been suggested that whether the automatic storing of images in the cache by the computer can amount to an offence of "making" will depend on whether the defendant was aware of the cache process; making does not include unintentional copying.[83] However, a more recent case suggests that deliberate downloading is sufficient and there is no need to show an intention on the part of the defendant to store the images permanently or for future retrieval.[84]

Possession of an indecent video in the sense of physical control by an assistant in a shop selling videos was sufficient to found a charge under s.1(1)(c) as the video was in the shop clearly for the purposes of distribution.[85]

A person is to be regarded as distributing an indecent photograph or pseudo-photograph if he parts with possession of it to, or exposes or offers it for acquisition by, another person.[86]

---

[77] *R. v Smith; R. v Jayson* [2002] EWCA Crim 683 at para.33, CA; [2003] 1 Cr. App. R. 13.

[78] *R. v Fellows* [1997] 2 All E.R. 548; [1997] 1 Cr. App. R. 244.

[79] *R. v T (Child Pornography); R. v ET (Child Pornography)* (1999) 163 J.P. 349; [1999] Crim. L.R. 749.

[80] *R. v Smith; R. v Jayson* [2002] EWCA Crim 683 at paras 15, 19, CA; [2003] 1 Cr. App. R. 13.

[81] *R. v Smith; R. v Jayson* [2002] EWCA Crim 683 at para.34, CA; [2003] 1 Cr. App. R. 13.

[82] See *DPP v Atkins; Goodland v DPP* [2000] 1 W.L.R. 1427; [2000] 2 All E.R. 425, 428; [2000] 2 Cr. App. R. 248, DC.

[83] *DPP v Atkins; Goodland v DPP* [2000] 1 W.L.R. 1427; [2000] 2 All E.R. 425, 436; [2000] 2 Cr. App. R. 248, DC.

[84] *R. v Smith; R. v Jayson* [2002] EWCA Crim 683 at paras 19 and 23–37, CA; [2003] 1 Cr. App. R. 13. *Mens rea* does not require an intention to retrieve.

[85] *R. v Matrix* [1997] Crim. L.R. 901 CA (Crim Div).

[86] Protection of Children Act 1978, s.1(2).

## Test of indecency

Section 7(3) of the Protection of Children Act 1978 provides:  **8–049**

"Photographs (including those comprised in a film) shall, if they show children and are indecent, be treated for all purposes of this Act as indecent photographs of children [and so as respects pseudo-photographs]."

The question of whether a photograph is indecent is an objective test.[87] Accordingly, the circumstances in which the photograph are taken and the intention of the photographer are irrelevant when determining whether a photograph is indecent.[88] Where the defendant is charged with "taking", the question for the jury is, (1) is it proved that the defendant took the photograph produced deliberately and intentionally? (2) if so, is it indecent?[89]

Where a photograph was taken of a seven-year old boy alone after  **8–050** bathing nude with his parents who were naturists and there was no issue as to whether the taking was intentional, the photographs alone were the only material which should have gone before the jury in order for them to decide whether they were indecent.[90] Evidence as to the photographer's intention and reasons for taking the photograph were irrelevant to the question of indecency. An argument that this was incompatible with Art.10 (freedom of expression) of the European Convention on Human Rights was rejected.[91] However, the circumstances/intention of the photographer might be relevant where there is an issue as to whether the taking was intentional or accidental.[92] Exhibits indicating a defendant's interest in paedophile material and showing how a computer was used to access paedophile news groups, chatlines and websites were relevant in showing that it was more likely than not that a file containing an indecent image of a child had been created deliberately rather than accidentally.[93]

The issue of obscenity or indecency is entirely one for the jury to be determined in relation to recognised standards of propriety which may vary from age to age and hence, expert evidence is inadmissible.[94] The fact that a similar photograph could be found in a medical textbook is not the test for deciding whether a photograph is indecent or not.[95]

---

[87] *R. v Graham-Kerr* [1988] 1 W.L.R. 1098; (1989) 88 Cr. App. R. 302; *R. v Smethurst (John Russell)* [2001] EWCA Crim 772 at para.21; [2002] 1 Cr. App. R. 6, CA. See also re "indecent" under the Post Office Act 1953: *R. v Straker* [1965] Crim. L.R. 239; *Kosmos Publications Ltd v DPP* [1975] Crim. L.R. 345.
[88] *R. v Graham-Kerr* [1988] 1 W.L.R. 1098; (1989) 88 Cr. App. R. 302; *R. v Smethurst (John Russell)* [2001] EWCA Crim 772; [2002] 1 Cr. App. R. 6, CA.
[89] *R. v Graham-Kerr* [1988] 1 W.L.R. 1098 at 1105D; (1989) 88 Cr. App. R. 302, CA.
[90] *ibid.*, at 1106. *Cf R. v Owen* [1988] 1 W.L.R. 134; (1988) 86 Cr. App. R. 29, CA below at para.8–052, n.2 and accompanying text.
[91] *R. v Smethurst (John Russell)* [2001] EWCA Crim 772; [2002] 1 Cr. App. R. 6, CA.
[92] *R. v Graham-Kerr* [1988] 1 W.L.R. 1098 at 1106; (1989) 88 Cr. App. R. 302, CA.
[93] *R. v Mould* (unrep) November 6, 2000, CA (Lawtel No.C0100349).
[94] *R. v Stamford* [1972] 2 Q.B. 391; *R. v Graham-Kerr* [1988] 1 W.L.R. 1098; (1989) 88 Cr. App. R. 302; *R. v Owen* [1988] 1 W.L.R. 134; (1988) 86 Cr. App. R. 29, CA.
[95] *R. v Mould* (unrep) November 6, 2000, CA (Lawtel No.C0100349).

**8-051**     Ordinary family photographs of children unclothed do not fall within the Act. Lord Woolf in *R. v Smethurst* said "No one could possibly suggest that a family taking photographs of their own children in the ordinary way would be a situation where it would be appropriate to prosecute."[96] Indeed, when the Protection of Children Bill was being debated in the Lords, Lord Harris of Greenwich said "... I think, frankly that there is no danger that ordinary family snapshots or legitimate sex education material would be caught by the terms of the Bill."[97]

In March 2001, the Saatchi gallery was the subject of a visit from the Metropolitan Police in connection with an exhibition entitled "I am a Camera".[98] The images in respect of which the concern was raised were two images taken by the photographer Tierney Gearon. The photographs depicted the photographer's own children—aged six and four years old naked or partly naked while playing. In one, the two children are wearing identical theatrical masks and standing on a beach. In the other, the girl stands behind the boy son who is urinating in the snow; both are wearing goggles. The images were part of a series documenting family life.[99] The CPS decided not to prosecute concluding there was insufficient evidence to provide a realistic prospect of conviction under the Protection of Children Act 1978 and stating that "in reaching this decision, the CPS considered whether the photographs in question were indecent and the likely defence of the gallery, *i.e.* whether they had a legitimate reason for showing them."[1]

### Age of child portrayed

**8-052**     Section 2(3) of the Protection of Children Act 1978 provides:

"In proceedings under this Act relating to indecent photographs of children a person is to be taken as having been a child at any material time if it appears from the evidence as a whole that he was then under the age of 16."

---

[96] [2001] EWCA Crim 772 at para.22; [2002] 1 Cr. App. R. 6, CA.

[97] *Hansard*, HL Official Report 5th series, Vol.392, col.563, May 18, 1978. Citing a High Court decision in a customs case *Commissioners of Customs & Excise v Sun & Health Ltd* in 1973 where "the judge specifically said that photographs of naked boys as such would not offend against recognised standards of propriety. Some of the photographs before him were, he said, patently inoffensive and he went on to consider in relation to the remainder whether there were ingredients beside simple nakedness which would make them indecent. That is exactly how I would expect the issue under the Bill to be decided."

[98] Alan Travis, "Police Obscenity Squad Raid Saatchi Gallery", *Guardian*, March 10, 2001; "Police raid gallery over naked child pictures", *The Times*, March 10, 2001, p.3.

[99] "Family photos aren't porn insists Saatchi row artist", *Observer*, March 11, 2001; Anjana Ahuja & Carol Midgley, "Legally Indecent?", *The Times*, March 13, 2001, p.2.

[1] Alan Travis & Nick Hopkins, "No charges over Saatchi photos", *Guardian*, March 16, 2001, p.1; Stuart Tendler, "CPS Clears Saatchi Gallery", *The Times*, March 16, 2001, p.3.

The jury are entitled to have regard to the age of the child in the photograph in determining whether the photograph is indecent.[2] In reaching this conclusion, the Court of Appeal took the view that "indecent" qualifies "photograph of a child" and not the word "to take, or permit to be taken".[3]

The objective of the Act is to protect children from exploitation and degradation. There is no requirement that the prosecution establish that the defendant knew that the photographs which were found to be indecent showed a child or children.[4] Parliament did not create a statutory defence for those who did not know nor had any cause to suspect them to be photographs of a child.[5] Whether a person depicted was a child for the purposes of the 1978 Act is a question of fact for the jury based on inference without any need for formal proof. Accordingly, there is no necessity for paediatric or other expert evidence as to the age of an unknown person depicted in a photograph.[6]

## Offences by corporations

Where a company is found guilty of an offence under s.1 of the Act, in some circumstances individual directors and members of that company may be personally liable to prosecution. Section 3 of the Act provides:    **8–053**

"(1) Where a body corporate is guilty of an offence under this Act and it is proved that the offence occurred with the consent or connivance of, or was attributable to any neglect on the part of, any director, manager, secretary or other officer of the body, or any person who was purporting to act in any such capacity he, as well as the body corporate, shall be deemed to be guilty of that offence and shall be liable to be proceeded against and punished accordingly.

(2) Where the affairs of a body corporate are managed by its members, subsection (1) shall apply in relation to the acts and defaults of a member in connection with his functions of management as if he were a director of the body corporate."

## Powers of entry, search and seizure

Justices of the peace have power to issue a warrant authorising any constable to enter (if need be by force) and search premises (including stalls or vehicles) and to seize and remove any articles which he has reasonable cause to believe are, or include, indecent photographs/pseudo-photographs    **8–054**

---

[2] *R. v Owen* [1988] 1 W.L.R. 134 at 139; (1988) 86 Cr. App. R. 29, CA (photographs taken by a professional photographer of a 14 year old girl who wished to become a model some of which showed her bare breasted).
[3] Loc cit.
[4] *R. v Land (Michael)* [1999] Q.B. 65; [1998] 3 W.L.R. 322; [1998] 1 All E.R. 403 at 407; [1998] 1 Cr. App. R. 301, CA.
[5] *ibid.*
[6] *ibid.*

of children.[7] A justice of the peace may issue a warrant where he is satisfied by information on oath laid by or on behalf of the Director of Public Prosecutions or by a constable that there is reasonable ground for suspecting that, in any premises in the petty sessions area for which he acts, there is an indecent photograph or pseudo-photograph of a child.[8]

Articles seized under the authority of the warrant and not returned to the occupier of the premises, shall be brought before a justice of the peace acting for the same petty sessions area as the justice who issued the warrant.[9]

## Forfeiture

**8–055**     Where articles are brought before a justice following seizure pursuant to s.4, the justice may issue a summons to the occupier of the premises to appear before the magistrates' court for that petty sessions area to show cause why the articles should not be forfeited.[10] If photographs have been seized and a person is then convicted under the Act for offences in respect of those photographs, the court must make a forfeiture order.[11]

If the court is satisfied that the articles are in fact indecent photographs or pseudo-photographs of children, the court shall order them to be forfeited.[12] However, if the person summoned does not appear, the court cannot make an order unless service of the summons is proved.[13] Any other person who owns or made the articles, or through whose hands the articles had passed before being seized, is entitled to appear before the court on the hearing of the summons to show cause why they should not be forfeited.[14]

If a forfeiture order is made, any person who appeared or was entitled to appear to show cause against the making of the order may appeal to the Crown Court.[15]

**8–056**     Where the court does not order forfeiture of articles brought before it, the court may, if it thinks fit, order the person on whose information the warrant was issued to pay such costs as the court thinks reasonable to any person who has appeared before it to show cause why the photographs or pseudo-photographs should not be forfeited.[16] Any such costs ordered to be paid are recoverable as a civil debt.[17]

Any forfeiture order made (including an order made on appeal) shall not take effect until the expiration of the ordinary time within which an appeal may be instituted or, where such an appeal is duly instituted, until the appeal is finally decided or abandoned.[18] For this purpose:

---

[7] Protection of Children Act 1978, s.4(2).
[8] *ibid.*, s.4(1).
[9] *ibid.*, s.4(3).
[10] Protection of Children Act 1978, s.5(1).
[11] Protection of Children Act 1978, s.5(6).
[12] Protection of Children Act 1978, s.5(2).
[13] *ibid.*
[14] Protection of Children Act 1978, s.5(3).
[15] Protection of Children Act 1978, s.5(4).
[16] Protection of Children Act 1978, s.5(6).
[17] *Loc. cit.*
[18] Protection of Children Act 1978, s.5(7).

(1) an application for a case to be stated or for leave to appeal is treated as the institution of an appeal[19]; and

(2) where a decision on appeal is subject to a further appeal, the appeal is not finally decided until the expiration of the ordinary time within which a further appeal may be instituted or, where a further appeal is duly instituted, until the further appeal is finally decided or abandoned.[20]

## Defences under the Protection of Children Act 1978

Where a person is charged with an offence under s.1(1)(b) [distributing or showing] or (c) [possession with a view to distribution or showing], it shall be a defence for him to prove: **8–057**

(a) that he had a legitimate reason for distributing or showing the photographs or pseudo-photographs or (as the case may be) having them in his possession[21]; or

(b) that he had not himself seen the photographs or pseudo-photographs and did not know, nor had any cause to suspect, them to be indecent.[22]

The court will be slow to conclude that a defence of legitimate reason has been established. It has been said:

"The central question where the defence is legitimate research will be whether the defendant is essentially a person of unhealthy interests in possession of indecent photographs in the pretence of undertaking research, or by contrasts a genuine researcher with no alternative but to have this sort of unpleasant material in his possession. In other cases there will be other categories of legitimate reason advanced. They will each have to be considered on their own facts. Courts are plainly entitled to bring a measure of scepticism to bear upon such an enquiry: they should not readily conclude that the defence has been made out"[23]

As to "did not have any cause to suspect" see the cases cited under the Obscene Publications Act 1959 above at paras 8–019 and 8–020.

---

[19] Protection of Children Act, s.5(7)(a).
[20] Protection of Children Act, s.5(7)(b).
[21] Protection of Children Act 1978, s.1(3)(b).
[22] *ibid.*
[23] *DPP v Atkins; Goodland v DPP* [2000] 1 W.L.R. 1427; [2000] 2 All E.R. 425 at 432–433; [2000] 2 Cr. App. R. 248, DC.

## Sentencing

**8–058**    Offences under the Protection of Children Act 1978 are triable either on indictment or on summary conviction.[24] A person convicted on indictment is liable to imprisonment for a term of up to 10 years, or a fine, or both.[25] A person convicted summarily is liable to:

(a) to imprisonment for a term not exceeding six months; or

(b) to a fine not exceeding the prescribed sum for the purposes of s.2 of the Magistrates' Court Act 1980 (punishment on summary conviction of offences triable either way: £1,000 or other sum substituted by order under that Act), or to both.[26]

The maximum sentence of imprisonment on indictment for an offence under the Protection of Children Act 1978 was increased from 3 years to 10 years on January 11, 2001.[27] Accordingly, cases decided prior to then will be of little assistance when considering sentencing.

**8–059**    General sentencing guidance was given in *R. v Toomer*[28] which was decided prior to the increase in penalty. Factors that the court have considered to be aggravating are the degree of onward dissemination[29]; and the level of obscenity depicted in the image as it reflected the degree of corruption to which the child had been exposed.[30] Where there is commercial benefit, the court will take a strong line to discourage this kind of activity.[31] Other relevant matters include an early guilty plea, the level of co-operation with investigations, and the character of the defendant.[32]

More recent guidance was given in *R. v Oliver*[33] where it was said that the two primary factors in determining the seriousness of an offence are the nature of the material and the extent of the offender's involvement with it. The nature of the material could be graded into five levels of seriousness: (1) images depicting erotic posing with no sexual activity; (2) sexual activity between children, or solo masturbation by a child; (3) non-penetrative sexual activity between adults and children; (4) penetrative sexual activity between children and adults; and (5) sadism or bestiality. The seriousness of an offence increased with the offender's proximity to, and responsibility for, the original abuse. Locating an image on the web is less serious than

---

[24] Protection of Children Act 1978, s.6(1).

[25] Protection of Children Act 1978, s.6(2).

[26] Protection of Children Act 1978, s.6(3). The prescribed sum is currently £5,000 under s.32(9) of the Magistrates' Court Act 1980.

[27] Protection of Children Act 1978, s.6(1) as amended by the Criminal Justice and Court Services Act 2000, s 41(1) (Commencement: SI 2000/3302, art.2(a)).

[28] [2001] Crim. L.R. 149.

[29] *R. v Wild (Michael Keith) (No.2)* [2001] EWCA Crim 1433; [2002] 1 Cr. App. R. (S) 38; *R. v Toomer* [2001] Crim. L.R. 149.

[30] *ibid.*

[31] *R. v B* [2000] 1 Cr. App. R. (S.) 412; *R. v Toomer* [2001] Crim. L.R. 149.

[32] *R. v Toomer* [2001] Crim. L.R. 149.

[33] [2002] EWCA Crim 2766; [2003] 1 Cr. App. R. 28; [2003] 2 Cr. App. R. (S) 15; [2003] Crim. L.R. 127.

downloading it and a fine would normally be appropriate where the offender was in possession of material merely for his own use. The court distinguished between pseudo-photographs and photographs—offences involving pseudo-photographs will be less serious than those involving real photographs where the making had involved no exploitation, abuse or corruption of children.

In *R. v Fellows*[34] a sentence of three years, the imprisonment was upheld **8–060** by Court of Appeal for using a computer to store images in digital form, enabling it to display and print out indecent pictures of children; making data available on the internet via an archive accessible only by a password which the appellant gave only to those who were vouched for by an existing password holder, or who provided additional data of the same kind which increased the size and scope of the archive. The appellant was of previous good character and there was no financial gain. In the same case, six months, imprisonment had been imposed to the second appellant who had accessed the above data via the internet and provided additional data to the first appellant. He too was of previous good character and there had been no financial gain.

In *R. v Bayliss*[35] a sentence of nine months, imprisonment for taking indecent photographs of a child together with one count of unlawful sexual intercourse with a girl under 16 was upheld by the Court of Appeal. The appellant was 52 and had no previous convictions with "a lifetime of honourable support to the community".

## CRIMINAL JUSTICE ACT 1988: POSSESSION OF INDECENT PHOTOGRAPHS OF CHILDREN

Under s.160 of the Criminal Justice Act 1988 it is an offence to be in **8–061** possession of an indecent photograph of a child.

"160(1) It is an offence for a person to have any indecent photograph or pseudo-photograph of a child in his possession.

(2) Where a person is charged with an offence under subsection (1) above, it shall be a defence for him to prove –

(a) that he had a legitimate reason for having the photograph or pseudo-photograph in his possession; or

(b) that he had not himself seen the photograph or pseudo-photograph and did not know, nor had any cause to suspect, it to be indecent; or

(c) that the photograph or pseudo-photograph was sent to him without any prior request made by him or on his behalf and that he did not keep it for an unreasonable time.

---

[34] [1997] 2 All E.R. 548; [1997] 1 Cr. App. R. 244.
[35] [2000] 1 Cr. App. R. (S) 412.

(2A) A person shall be liable on conviction on indictment of an offence under this section to imprisonment for a term not exceeding five years or a fine, or both.

(3) A person shall be liable on summary conviction of an offence under this section to imprisonment for a term not exceeding six months or a fine not exceeding level 5 on the standard scale, or both.

(4) Sections 1(3), 2(3), 3 and 7 of the Protection of Children Act 1978 shall have effect as if any reference in them to that Act included a reference to this section."

**8–062**　The definitions of photographs and pseudo-photographs are the same as under the Protection of Children Act 1978.[36] Unlike the 1978 Act, the offence is committed by mere possession (without intent to publish for gain) of an indecent photograph of a child.[37] Proceedings shall not be instituted except by or with the consent of the DPP.[38] Directors, managers, or other officers of corporations which are convicted of an offence under this section may be deemed to be personally guilty of the offence in the same circumstances as under the Protection of Children Act 1978.[39] As to case law concerning the meaning of indecent and the statutory defences see above at paras 8–049 and 8–057 respectively.

Prior to January 11, 2001, this was a summary only offence. It was amended by the Criminal Justice and Court Services Act 2000 to insert s.2A which in addition makes the offence triable on indictment and punishable by a term of imprisonment not exceeding five years.[40]

## INDECENT DISPLAYS (CONTROL) ACT 1981

### Offence of publically displaying indecent matter

**8–063**　Under the Indecent Displays (Control) Act 1981, it is an offence for any person to make a public display of indecent matter (or to cause or permit the display to be made).[41] Anything displayed in a public place or that is visible

---

[36] Criminal Justice Act 1988, s.160(4) above applies the "Interpretation" section (s.7) of the Protection of Children Act 1978. Thus, films are included as is any form of video recording. See above at paras 8–044 to 8–046.

[37] *Cf. Case v Minister of Safety and Security* Constitutional Court (South Africa) 1 B.H.R.C. 541 holding that the Indecent or Obscene Photographic Matter Act 1967, s.2 was incompatible with the South African Constitution. The court concluded that the 1967 Act (in which "indecent and obscene photographic matter" was defined by means of an open ended list of categories) sanctioned unwarranted and unjustifiable invasions of the right to personal privacy regardless of the nature of the material possessed.

[38] Criminal Justice Act 1988, s.160(4) above applying the Protection of Children Act 1978, s.1(3).

[39] Criminal Justice Act 1988, s.160(4) above applying the Protection of Children Act 1978, s.3. See above at para.8–053.

[40] Criminal Justice and Court Services Act 2000, s.41(3)(a) and Criminal Justice and Court Services Act 2000 (Commencement No.1) Order 2000 (SI 2000/3302), art.2(a)).

[41] Indecent Displays (Control) Act 1981, s.1(1). See also common law offences of outraging public decency above at paras 8–032 *et seq.*

from a public place is deemed to be publically displayed.[42] Any person convicted under the Act is liable on summary conviction to a fine not exceeding the statutory maximum, or on indictment, to imprisonment for a term not exceeding two years, or a fine, or both.[43]

## Indecent matter

Matter includes anything capable of being displayed except for an actual **8–064** human body or any human body part.[44] In determining for the purposes of the Indecent Displays (Control) Act 1981 whether any displayed matter is indecent, any matter which is not exposed to view is to be disregarded.[45] Account may be taken of the effect of juxtaposing one thing with another.[46]

For case law concerning the meaning of indecent see above at paras 8–049 and 8–042.

## Public place

"Public place" means any place to which the public have or are permitted **8–065** to have access (whether on payment or otherwise) while that matter is displayed. There are a number of places excluded from falling within the definition of public place and/or the ambit of the Act, namely:

(1) any place to which the public have access only upon making a payment which is to see the display[47];

(2) a shop or any part of a shop to which the public can only gain access by passing beyond an adequate warning notice[48];

(3) anything included in a television broadcasting service or television programme service[49];

(4) any matter included in the display of an art gallery or museum and only visible from within the art gallery or museum[50];

(5) any matter displayed by (or with the authority of) the Crown or any local authority and visible only from within a building occupied by the Crown or any local authority[51];

---

[42] Indecent Displays (Control) Act 1981, s.1(2).
[43] Indecent Displays (Control) Act 1981, s.4(1).
[44] Indecent Displays (Control) Act 1981, s.1(5). *Cf.* common law offence at outraging public decency above at paras 8–032 to 8–036.
[45] Indecent Displays (Control) Act 1981, s.1(5)(a).
[46] Indecent Displays (Control) Act 1981, s.1(5)(a).
[47] Indecent Displays (Control) Act 1981, s.1(3)(a).
[48] Indecent Displays (Control) Act 1981, s.1(3)(b). As to adequate warning notice see below at para.8–066.
[49] Within the meaning of the Broadcasting Act 1990 as to which see above at para.8–012, n.34. Indecent Displays (Control) Act 1981, s.1(4)(a).
[50] Indecent Displays (Control) Act 1981, s.1(4)(b).
[51] Indecent Displays (Control) Act 1981, s.1(4)(c).

(6) any matter included in a performance of a play within the meaning of the Theatres Act 1968[52];

(7) any matter included in a film exhibition as defined in the Cinemas Act 1985—[53]

   (i) given in a place which as regards that exhibition is required to be licensed under s.1 of that Act or by virtue only of s.5, 7 or 8 of that Act is not required to be so licensed[54];

   (ii) which is an exhibition to which s.6 of that Act applies given by an exempted organisation as defined by subs (6) of that section.[55]

### Adequate warning notice

**8–066**    The requirements for an "adequate warning notice" are set out by the Act. An adequate warning notice must contain the following words and no others[56]:

"WARNING

Persons passing beyond this notice will find material on display which they may consider indecent. No admittance to persons under 18 years of age."

The word "WARNING" must appear as a heading.[57] No pictures or other matter shall appear on the notice.[58] The notice must be so situated that no one could reasonably gain access to the shop or part of the shop in question without being aware of the notice and it must be easily legible by any person gaining such access.[59]

---

[52] Indecent Displays (Control) Act 1981, s.1(4)(d). See Theatres Act 1968; s.18(1) " 'Play' means
   (a) any dramatic piece whether involving improvisation or not, which is given wholly or in part by one or more persons actually present and performing and in which the whole or a major proportion of what is done by the person or persons performing, whether by way of speech, singing or acting, involves the playing of a role; and
   (b) any ballet given wholly or in part by one or more persons actually present and performing, whether or not it falls within paragraph (a) of this definition."

[53] Indecent Displays (Control) Act 1981, s.1(4)(e). Cinemas Act 1985, s.21(1) defines "film exhibition" as "any exhibition of moving pictures which is produced otherwise than by the simultaneous reception and exhibition of programmes included in a programme service (within the meaning of the Broadcasting Act 1990)".

[54] Cinemas Act 1985, s.1 (in general, license required for all film exhibitions); s.5 (exhibitions in private dwelling-houses); s.7 (exhibitions in premises used occasionally); s.8 (exhibitions in movable buildings).

[55] Non-profit organisations certified by the Secretary of State under the Cinemas Act 1985.

[56] Indecent Displays (Control) Act 1981, s1(6)(a).

[57] *ibid.*, s.1(6)(b).

[58] *ibid.*, s.1(6)(c).

[59] *ibid.*, s.1(6)(d).

## Powers of arrest, seizure and entry

A constable may seize any article which he has reasonable grounds for   **8–067**
believing to be, or to contain, indecent matter and to have been used in the
commission of an offence under the Indecent Displays (Control) Act 1981.[60]

In England and Wales, if a justice of the peace is satisfied, on information
on oath, that there are reasonable grounds for suspecting that an offence
under the 1981 Act has been or is being committed on any premises, he may
issue a warrant authorising any constable to enter the premises specified in
the information or, as the case may be, evidence (if need be by force) to seize
any article which the constable has reasonable grounds for believing to be or
to contain indecent matter and to have been used in the commission of an
offence under this Act[61]

## Offences by corporations

Where a company is guilty of an offence under the Act and it is proved   **8–068**
that the offence occurred with the consent or connivance of, or was attributable to any neglect on the part of, any director, manager, secretary, or
other officer of the body, or any person who was purporting to act in any
such capacity he, as well as the body corporate, shall be deemed to be guilty
of that offence and shall be liable to be proceeded against and punished
accordingly.[62]

Where the affairs of a body corporate are managed by its members, the
same provision applies in relation to the acts and defaults of a member in
connection with his functions of management as if he were a director of the
body corporate.[63]

## CUSTOMS CONSOLIDATION ACT 1876

Importation of "Indecent or obscene prints, paintings, photographs,   **8–069**
books, cards, lithographic or other engravings, or any other indecent or
obscene articles" is prohibited by s.42 of Customs Consolidation Act 1876.
Indecent films are included within this prohibition.[64]

It is an offence contrary to the Customs and Excise Management Act 1979
to knowingly acquire possession of goods with respect to importation or
exportation which are the subject of any prohibition with intent to evade
any such prohibition or duty payable.[65] A person convicted of such an

---

[60] Indecent Displays (Control) Act 1981, s.2(2).
[61] Indecent Displays (Control) Act 1981, s.2(3).
[62] Indecent Displays (Control) Act 1981, s.3(1).
[63] Indecent Displays (Control) Act 1981, s.3(2).
[64] *Derrick v Customs and Excise Commissioners* [1972] 2 W.L.R. 359.
[65] Customs and Excise Management Act 1979, s.170(1)(iii). As to offences under the Customs
and Excise Management Act 1979 generally see *Archbold 2004* (Sweet & Maxwell) at 25–386 *et
seq.* and *Blackstone's Criminal Practice 2004* at B17.1 *et seq.*

offence is liable (a) on summary conviction, to a penalty of the prescribed sum or of three times the value of the goods, whichever is the greater, or to imprisonment for a term not exceeding six months, or to both; or (b) on conviction on indictment, to a penalty of any amount, or to imprisonment for a term not exceeding seven years, or to both.[66]

The test of obscenity is not required for the purposes of the Customs Consolidation Act 1876, s.42 as the effect of the legislation is to prohibit the manufacture and marketing in the UK of such items so that there was no lawful trade in such goods in the UK.[67] It is not contrary to the Treaty of Rome 1957, Art.30 (free movement of goods) as Art.36 allows for derogations from the right to free movement of goods on grounds of public morality.[68]

The prosecution only has to establish that the defendant knew he was importing goods subject to a prohibition and was seeking to evade the prohibition.[69] It is not necessary to show that he knew the precise nature of the goods he imported or that he knew the goods were in fact obscene/indecent pursuant to statutory provision.[70]

## CINEMATOGRAPH FILMS (ANIMALS) ACT 1937

8–070    The Cinematograph Films (Animals) Act 1937 prohibits exhibition or supply of a film if animals were harmed during the making of the film. Section 1(1) provides:

> "No person shall exhibit to the public, or supply to any person for public exhibition (whether by him or by another person), any cinematograph film (whether produced in Great Britain or elsewhere) if in connection with the production of the film any scene represented in the film was organised or directed in such a way as to involve the cruel infliction of pain or terror on any animal or the cruel goading of any animal to fury."

A cinematograph film is deemed to be exhibited to the public when, and only when, it is exhibited in a place to which for the time being members of the general public as such have access, whether on payment of money or otherwise.[71] The court may infer (without prejudice to any other form of proof) from the film, that a scene represented in the film was organised or directed in such a way as to involve the cruel infliction of pain or terror on

---

[66] Customs and Excise Management Act 1979, s.170(3).
[67] *R. v Bow Street Magistrates Court Ex p. Noncyp Ltd* [1990] 1 Q.B. 123, CA.
[68] *R. v Uxbridge Justices Ex p. Webb* (1998) 162 J.P. 198; [1994] C.O.D. 24.
[69] *R. v Forbes (Giles)* [2001] UKHL 40; [2001] 3 W.L.R. 428; [2001] 4 All E.R. 97; [2002] 1 Cr. App. R. 1 (appellant believed he was importing prohibited videos. If the videos had contained what he thought they contained, they would not in fact have been prohibited. Conviction upheld). As to "knowingly" see also *R. v Taaffe* [1984] 2 W.L.R. 326.
[70] *R. v Forbes (Giles)* [2001] UKHL 40; [2001] 3 W.L.R. 428; [2001] 4 All E.R. 97; [2002] 1 Cr. App. R. 1.
[71] Cinematograph Films (Animals) Act 1937, s.1(4)(a).

an animal or the cruel goading of an animal to fury.[72] Irrespective of whether the court draws such an inference or not, it is a defence for the defendant to prove that he believed, and had reasonable cause to believe, that no scene so represented was so organised or directed.[73]

Any person convicted of contravening the Act is liable on summary conviction to a fine not exceeding level 3 on the standard scale, or to a term of imprisonment not exceeding three months, or both.[74]

---

[72] Cinematograph Films (Animals) Act 1937, s.1(3).
[73] *ibid.*
[74] *ibid.*

# Part C

# Use of Photographs

# Chapter 9

# Internet and digital images

## INTRODUCTION AND SCOPE OF THIS CHAPTER

The development of the internet and digital photography raises specific legal **9–001** issues and problems which for the most part fall within traditional causes of action and legal topics discussed elsewhere in this work. For example, a digital photograph is easier to copy and disseminate than an analogue photograph; this is a legal problem for the rights owner governed by the law of copyright. However, technology also creates a practical problem for the rights owner as to how to police their rights.

This chapter aims (1) to highlight the particular problems concerning photographs that may arise as a result of modern technology, (2) direct the reader to other parts of the text where these issues are discussed in the context of other causes of actions, and (3) give some practical suggestions as to methods of dealing with such problems or reference points as to where further information and guidance can be obtained.

OVERVIEW OF RELEVANT TECHNOLOGY

## Digital images

**9–002**    The method in which a digital camera produces an image has already been discussed above.[1] Broadly, the image is produced by a light sensitive sensor in the camera which accumulates charge. This is then broken down into digital data that can be read by a computer in the form of binary code.

Image files are large as it takes a large amount of computer memory to store an image made up of over one million pixels. The most common forms of digital images are .jpeg[2] and .tiff[3] formats. A .jpeg image is compressed in order to keep the image size smaller and make it faster to load and easier to store. An original .tiff file is not as compressed and is therefore a preferable format where image integrity is important, for example, for use in litigation. However, .tiff files tend to be larger than .jpeg files.

## Digital manipulation

**9–003**    The ready availability and affordability of imaging programmes means that it is easy for anyone, whether professional or lay, to make alterations to photographs. Manipulation of photographs is no longer the preserve of the professional graphic designer. Access to a computer is a part of everyday life and very little expertise is required to operate imaging software at a simple level. Adobe Photoshop[4] is the best known image editing programme and dominates the market, but there are a number of other programmes available including, for example, Corel Painter and Corel DRAW[5]; Deneba Canvas[6]; Jasc Paint Shop Pro[7]; Roxio PhotoSuite[8]; and GIMP.[9]

**9–004**    Using such software permits a vast range of alterations to be made to a photograph, ranging from minor touch ups to whole scale creation of scenes that never occurred. Changes that can be made include:

- removal of minor flaws in the image, such as scratches, dust, hairs, etc.;

- brightness and contrast;

- burning and dodging (respectively making parts of the image darker or lighter, for example to de-emphasise a background);

---

[1] At paras 2–014 to 2–018.
[2] Jpeg stands for Joint Photographic Experts Group.
[3] Tiff stands for Tagged Image File Format.
[4] *http://www.adobe.com/*.
[5] *http://www.corel.com/*.
[6] *http://www.deneba.com/*.
[7] *http://www.jasc.com/*.
[8] *http://www.roxio.com/*.
[9] GNU Image Manipulation Program: *http://www.gimp.org/*.

- cropping an image;

- restoring original colours or changing colours, including colourisation of black and white images;

- reversing an image (left to right/horizontal to vertical);

- adding, moving, or deleting objects (including cloning which allows copying of existing textures and colours within the image).

## Internet

The internet is an international network of interconnected computers. **9–005**
Each computer connected to the internet has an unique identity established by its unique Internet Protocol address ("IP address"). An IP address consists of a series of numbers. A series of numbers is difficult for users to remember so the Domain Name System ("DNS") was developed which allows users to identify a computer by an alphanumeric "domain name". A domain name corresponds to a particular series of numbers that serve as routing addresses on the internet to a particular computer. Domain names are used generally as a convenient way of locating information and reaching others on the internet.

An individual computer will be connected to the internet via an ISP (Internet Service Provider) which typically occurs when the computer dials via a modem and connects to the ISP's network which may, in turn, be connected to other networks. Ultimately, a series of larger networks connect together at a higher level called Network Access Points ("NAP's). In this way it is possible for a user of an individual computer to access the interconnected computers which constitute the internet.

Protocols essentially govern the way in which one computer commu- **9–006**
nicates with another. The basic internet communication protocol is called TCP/IP (Transmission Control Protocol/Internet Protocol). The TCP/IP allows computers to receive information in a common language. The TCP breaks down the information being sent into packets and the IP ensures that each "packet" of data is sent to the receiving computer where they are reassembled into the original whole.

When a computer accesses a website via the internet it will frequently copy that information into its cache. The cache is a sub-set of the computer's memory which allows it to operate faster. Storing information in the cache allows the computer to access the copy more quickly than if it did so via its main memory. Copies of images on websites will, along with the text of pages, be, from time to time, stored into the cache of a computer used for internet access. This has caused historical debate as to whether this cache copying amounts to copyright infringement, but it is now dealt with by the Copyright Designs and Patents Act 1988.[10]

---

[10] See below at paras 9–007 to 9–014.

PARTICULAR PROBLEMS

### Visual search engines and temporary cache copies

**9–007**     A search engine is a system that searches the web and locates requested data on other websites.[11] A user who wishes to search for information on a particular subject types the desired search term into the search engine which then produces a list of web sites that contain information relating to the search term. Usually, the list of results is in text format. There are search engines that specifically search for images and return results as small pictures or photographs.[12]

**9–008**     Each miniature photograph that appears in the results returned is a copy of another photograph that exists on a third party website outside of the control of the search engine provider. Potentially, these small copies amount to copyright infringement of the images reproduced. However, it is submitted that this type of use is now covered by a new permitted Act introduced into the Copyright Designs and Patents Act 1988 by the Copyright and Related Rights Regulations 2003 which inserts s.28A:

> **"28A Making of temporary copies**
> Copyright in a literary work, other than a computer program or a database, or in a dramatic, musical or artistic work, the typographical arrangement of a published edition, a sound recording or a film, is not infringed by the making of a temporary copy which is transient or incidental, which is an integral and essential part of a technological process and the sole purpose of which is to enable–
>
> (a) a transmission of the work in a network between third parties by an intermediary; or
> (b) a lawful use of the work;
>
> and which has no independent economic significance."

**9–009**     The purpose of a thumbnail copy of an image appearing in the results returned by a search engine is to allow the user to find the image on another website. This amounts to a temporary copy which is transient or incidental. It does enable a lawful use of the work by aiming to direct the user to the lawful owner's website. As the images are, for the most part, small, low resolution thumbnails, it can be seriously contended that they have no independent economic significance. It is perhaps open to argument as to whether the reproduction of the full image can be said to be "an integral and essential part of a technological process". It would be possible to search for images and return text results with links to the images, although this would

---

[11] *e.g.* Google: *http://www.google.com/*; Alta Vista: *http://www.altavista.com/*; Yahoo: *http://www.yahoo.com/*; Ask Jeeves: *http://www.ask.com/*.
[12] *e.g.* Ditto: *http://www.ditto.com/*; Picsearch: *http://www.picsearch.com/*; Google images: *http://images.google.com/*.

defeat the object of a visual search engine.[13] Whether reproduction of an artistic work by a search engine can truly be said to be "essential" on a strict construction is open to question. However, the Directive[14] specifically mentions browsing in recital (33) which reads:

> "The exclusive right of reproduction should be subject to an exception to allow certain acts of temporary reproduction, which are transient or incidental reproductions, forming an integral and essential part of a technological process and carried out for the sole purpose of enabling either efficient transmission in a network between third parties by an intermediary, or a lawful use of a work or other subject-matter to be made. The acts of reproduction concerned should have no separate economic value on their own. *To the extent that they meet these conditions, this exception should include acts which enable browsing as well as acts of caching* to take place, including those which enable transmission systems to function efficiently, provided that the intermediary does not modify the information and does not interfere with the lawful use of technology, widely recognised and used by industry, to obtain data on the use of the information. A use should be considered lawful where it is authorised by the rightholder or not restricted by law." (emphasis added)

It is submitted, in the light of Recital (33), that reproduction of images by an image search engine falls within the s.28A exemption as an act which enables browsing. Reproduction of images in the computer memory as part of a cache does also not amount to copyright infringement as a result of s.28A, provided the conditions of the section are met.

The issue of whether reproduction of thumbnail pictures by a search **9–010** engine amounted to fair use[15] under the US Copyright Act was considered by the US Court of Appeals for the 9th Circuit in *Kelly v Arriba*[16] on two occasions. The court's first opinion of February 2002 was withdrawn by the second opinion of July 2003. The second opinion stated that the 2002 decision was not to be cited as a precedent in the Court of Appeals for the 9th Circuit or any district court. The first opinion expressed views about inline linking and framing of images which as yet has not been considered by any appellate UK court and warrants consideration for this reason.

---

[13] *Cf: Kelly v Arriba Soft Corporation* 336 F.3d 811 (9th Cir. 2003) at 821 where it was held that use of a full image thumbnail by a visual search engine was reasonable and necessary. If only part of the image was copied, it would be more difficult to identify it thereby reducing the usefulness of the visual search engine.

[14] 2001/29 on the harmonisation of certain aspects of Copyright and Related Rights in the Information Society.

[15] 17 U.S.C. 107 which states that in considering whether use is fair use the court shall take into account four factors: (1) the purpose and character of the use, including whether such use is of a commercial nature or is for nonprofit educational purposes; (2) the nature of the copyrighted work; (3) the amount and substantiality of the portion used in relation to the copyrighted work as a whole; and (4) the effect of the use upon the potential market for or value of the copyrighted work.

[16] *Kelly v Arriba Soft Corporation* 336 F.3d 811 (9th Cir, 2003) withdrawing its earlier opinion of February 2002 280 F.3d 934 (9th Cir. 2002).

Kelly, the plaintiff, was a professional photographer. The defendant, Arriba, (now known as Ditto.com) operated an internet search engine that displayed its results in the form of small pictures. Kelly discovered that his photographs were part of Arriba's search engine database and brought copyright infringement proceedings. There were three aspects to the use of the images that were in issue. First, the search engine created thumbnail images of the photographs. This was done by the computer programme crawling the web for images to index which were then downloaded in full size onto Arriba's server. The copies were then used to generate smaller, low resolution thumbnail images. Once the thumbnail images were created the program then deleted the full sized copies from the server ("Thumbnail Use").

**9–011**    The second aspect of image use in issue took place when the user clicked on the thumbnail. This resulted in production of an "image attributes" page which contained the original full-sized image imported directly from the originating web page with a link to that page. This process is known as "inline linking" whereby an image is imported from another website and is displayed as if it is part of the current website surrounded by the current website's text and advertising, etc.[17] ("Inline Linking Use").

The third aspect concerned use between July 1999 to August 2000, when clicking on the thumbnail produced two new windows. One contained the full sized image imported from the originating website and underneath was a second window displaying the originating web page ("Framed Use").

**9–012**    The first opinion of the Court of Appeals was given in February 2002. The district court had granted summary judgment to the defendant, finding there had been fair use, and Kelly appealed. The 9th Circuit held that the Thumbnail Use amounted to fair use. The thumbnails were not a substitute for the full size image and the search engine would guide users to Kelly's site rather than away from it. In considering the four factors, the court must balance in considering whether there was fair use,[18] the court found that the purpose and character of the use favoured Arriba because the search engine benefited the public by enhancing information gathering techniques on the internet and there was minimal loss of integrity to the images. The nature of the copyrighted works, namely creative photographs, only slightly weighed in favour of Kelly. The amount and substantiality of portion used was neutral as, although the whole images were copied by the engine, it was reasonable to do so to allow users to recognise the image. The final factor, the effect on the market, was in favour of Arriba as the use of thumbnails was not a substitute for the full sized images. The court concluded overall that the use was fair.

**9–013**    However, in the part of the opinion that was later withdrawn, the court considered that the display of full sized images by Inline Linked Use and Framing Use was not fair dealing. Kelly contended that this use infringed his exclusive right to display the copyrighted work publically under the USA Copyright Act. In its first opinion (later retracted) the court agreed. The

---

[17] See further re: inline linking below at para.9–015.
[18] See above at para.9–010, n.15.

court held that by allowing the public to view the full size work while visiting the Arriba website, Arriba created a public display of Kelly's work.[19] By inline linking and framing, Arriba were showing Kelly's work without his permission. It was held that this did not amount to fair use because the use of the full sized images, unlike the thumbnails, did not enhance the search engine or act as a means of access, but were rather the end product in themselves. Giving users access to the full sized images without having to visit another site did not amount to legitimate use.

The second opinion of the court given in 2003 retracted the part of the opinion concerning Inline Linking Use and Framing Use and decreed it could not be cited as a precedent in the 9th Circuit.[20] This was because the district court had given summary judgment in respect of InLine Linking and Framing Use but neither party had moved for summary judgment on those issues. A district court may not grant summary judgment when the party has not requested it. Accordingly, in its second opinion, the Court of Appeals reversed that portion of the district court's opinion and remanded it for further proceedings. The reasoning for upholding the summary judgment in respect of the Thumbnail use remained as in the first opinion.

The withdrawn conclusions of the Court of Appeals in *Kelly v Arriba* that Inline Linking Use and Framing Use of images amounted to public display raises serious questions as to whether in the UK a court would consider that such use amounted to "communication to the public" under the Copyright Designs and Patents Act 1988. This has yet to be considered by the courts, but in the light of *Kelly v Arriba* there is a real risk that UK courts would consider that this type of use amounted to copyright infringement. Until the law is settled, inline linking and imbedding of images and framing of images from external sites without copyright clearance should be avoided. At the very least such use should be approach with caution and relevant clear disclaimers stating the origin of the images is recommended.

**9–014**

## Hypertext linking

A hypertext link is the HTML (Hyper Text Mark Up Language) pro-  **9–015** gramme command which tells the web browser to go to another document or a part of the same document. It is how users can move from viewing one website page to another by clicking on the relevant link. There are various types of links:

Surface linking—   links to the homepage of another site (*i.e.* the first page/gateway of the other site).

Deep linking—   links to an interior page of another site, bypassing the homepage and attribution.

---

[19] 280 F.3d 934 (9th Cir. 2002) at 945–946.
[20] 336 F.3d 811.

Framing—    results in the display of pages of another external linked site within a frame or window of the original linking site.

Inline linking—    links to an image on an external site resulting in the display of that image imbedded on the web page of the original linking site. The image is viewed as if it appears on the linking site without transferring the user to the linked site. However, the image shown is not copied by the linking site and remains on the linked site's server. The image is called up directly from the server where it is posted and just appears as a temporary copy on the user's screen. This technique is also known as dynamic linking, or automatic linking.

**9–016**    Most simple linking does not involve the reproduction of any copyright works by the linking site—all that is reproduced is a linked web address.[21] The only copies of the website content are temporary cache copies on the computer of the user who clicks on the link and this would fall within the making of temporary copies exception in s.28A of the Copyright Designs and Patents Act 1988.[22] If the link itself actually reproduces copyright material (for example newspaper headlines or a link comprising images that are copied) there may copyright infringement.[23]

Framing and inline linking are more problematic. Both may be considered not a "lawful use of the work" within the meaning of s.28A, CDPA 1988 and outside the terms on which the original site owner allows access to his website material. It is also arguable that framing or inline linking may amount to "authorisation" of copying of the linked material by the actual user who obtains copy of the material on his computer.[24]

**9–017**    Whilst inline embedding of images or framing does not copy the image to the linking site, it is an open question as to whether this amounts to "communication to the public" which is an exclusive right of the copyright

---

[21] *e.g.* USA: *Ticketmaster Corp v Tickets.com, Inc* 2000 WL 1887522 (C.D. Cal. August 10, 2000) aff'd, 2 Fed. App. 741 (9th Cir. 2001) (deep linking); *Ford Motor Co v 2600 Enterprises,* 177 F. Supp. 2d 661 (E.D. Mich. 2001) ("fuckgeneralmotors.com" automatically linked to plaintiff's site located at "ford.com". Claim for preliminary injunction alleging trademark infringement, dilution and unfair competition by use of the Ford trade mark in the programming code establishing the link was dismised).

[22] See above at para.9–008.

[23] *Shetland Times Ltd v Wills* [1997] F.S.R. 604; [1997] E.M.L.R. 277 (Scotland, Outer House). See also *Playboy Enterprises Inc v Webbworld Inc* 991 F. Supp. 543 (N.D. Texas 1997) (downloading of images amounted to a display).

[24] Copyright Designs and Patents Act 1988, s.16(2) which provides "Copyright in a work is infringed by a person who without the license of the copyright owner does, *or authorises another to do,* any of the acts restricted by copyright" (emphasis added). As to meaning of "authorise" see: *CBS Songs Ltd v Amstrad Consumer Electronics Plc* [1988] A.C. 1013; [1988] 2 W.L.R. 1191; [1988] 2 All E.R. 484; *Pensher Security Door Co Ltd v Sunderland City Council* [2000] R.P.C. 249; *Amstrad Consumer Electronics Plc v British Phonographic Industry Ltd* [1986] F.S.R. 159; *Standen Engineering Ltd v A Spalding & Sons Ltd* [1984] F.S.R. 554. Joint tortfeasors: *MCA Records Inc v Charly Records Ltd (No.5)* [2001] EWCA Civ 1441; [2002] E.M.L.R. 1; [2002] F.S.R. 26; *PLG Research Ltd v Ardon International Ltd* [1993] F.S.R. 197.

owner.[25] It is recommended that in the light of the USA case *Kelly v Arriba* which is discussed above at para.000 that inline linking of images without copyright clearance should be avoided until the law in the UK is settled. Inline linking to images may also infringe other legal rights such as the moral rights of the photographer/image creator.[26] If the inline linked image is a trademark or a photograph of a person, the use may be trademark infringement or some form of passing off or false endorsement, depending upon the presentation of the image and the nature of its use.

## Digital manipulation

Digital photographs can be edited very easily both by adding new ele-   **9–018**
ments to, or deleting elements, in the original image, or by altering contrast or brightness. Even simple editing such as changing the brightness of an image can change the meaning, for example darkening or brightening of a photograph of an accident scene to reflect different weather conditions and visibility.

In many circumstances this is a creative advantage both commercially and for the layman, from enabling models to be re-touched to perfection and the removal of unwanted or unflattering elements (*e.g.* red eyes) from family photographs. However, the ease with which such photographs can be altered causes difficulties in two distinct areas. First, manipulation of photographs in itself may give rise to causes of action directly. Secondly, where the integrity of digital images is crucial, such as use in litigation, the availability of image manipulation programmes may call into question the authenticity of evidence.

## Digitally manipulated photographs

### *Possible causes of action*

Use of photographs that have been digitally manipulated may give rise to   **9–019**
causes of action which are discussed elsewhere in this work, in particular:

copyright infringement—   see above at paras 2–019, 2–146 and 3–017

moral rights infringement—see above at paras 4–020 and 4–028 to 4–029

---

[25] Copyright Designs and Patents Act 1988, ss.16(1)(d) and 20 as amended by The Copyright and Related Rights Regulations 2003 (SI 2003/2498), reg.6. See discussion of USA case *Kelly v Arriba* 336 F.3d 811 (9th Cir. 2003) withdrawing its earlier opinion of February 2002 280 F. 3d 934 (9th Cir. 2002) above at paras 9–010 to 9–014 in which an initial opinion of the Court of Appeals for the 9th Circuit, later withdrawn, expressed the opinion that framing and inline linking amounted to an infringement of the right to "display the work publicly" under the USA Copyright Act. See also *Playboy Enterprises Inc v Webbworld Inc* 991 F. Supp. 543 (N.D. Texas 1997) (unauthorised downloading of copyright images on to a website allowing subscribers to view the works on their computer monitors amounted to a display).
[26] Moral rights, see Ch.14, below.

| defamation— | see above at para.7–130 and see model release forms at para.7–088, and |
| passing off— | see below at paras 10–009 *et seq.*, and |
| data protection— | see below at paras 1–003 *et seq.*, and |
| in the USA infringement of right of publicity— | see above at paras 7–073 to 7–079. |

In addition, if there is a contractual term in which a model or photographic subject has the right to approve photographs, use of a manipulated image in contravention of such a term may give rise to an action in breach of contract.

Litigation concerning both the use of digitally manipulated images of people and false impressions given by suggestions of consensual posing for photographs has not been particularly successful either in the UK[27] or the USA[28] The main reason for failure seems to be that viewers would not be mislead either because it was clear that the image was digitally created or there was no suggestion of consensual endorsement.[29]

**9–020**  Digital manipulation creating a false image of a person naked or in connection with publications of sexual content may give rise to a cause of action in defamation if the suggestion is of voluntary association with the publication. In the USA, there are a number of reported decisions in this area. It has been said of Hustler magazine that "to be depicted as voluntarily associated with such a sheet ... is unquestionably degrading to a normal person."[30] The use of a photograph of a man bare chested with suggestive headlines raised a triable issue as to whether this created a false message that a person voluntarily posed nude for a magazine and in doing so implicitly endorsed the magazine and its sexual content.[31] A false suggestion of a willing interview with a tabloid via quotations and headlines could convey a message that an actor was "washed up as movie star if he

---

[27] *Charleston v News Group Newspaper Ltd* [1995] 2 A.C. 65.

[28] *e.g. Hoffman v Capital Cities/ABC Inc* 255 F.3d 1180 (9th Cir. 2001) Reversing 33 F. Supp. 2d 867. See above at para.7–121, n.88. Although cf. *Grant v Esquire Inc* 367 F. Supp. 876 (S.D.N.Y. 1973) Esquire Magazine published an image of Cary Grant's face superimposed on the body of a model. Grant had posed for the original photographs for the magazine some years earlier. Esquire's motion for summary judgment was dismissed on the basis that whether the use of the picture was for trade (to attract attention) or whether it was used in the course of legitimate comment on a public figure was a question for the jury.

[29] For further discussion of the possibility of an action in passing off arising from the publishing of a photograph suggesting endorsement of the publication *per se* in an editorial context see below at para.10–016.

[30] *Douglass v Hustler Magazine* 769 F.2d 1128 (7th Cir. 1985) (false light claim for insinuation that the plaintiff was the kind of person to pose nude for Hustler).

[31] *Solano v Playgirl Inc* 292 F.3d 1078 (9th Cir. 2002) (actor shown shirtless in swimming trunks under headline "Primetime's Sexy Young Stars Exposed" on cover of Playgirl. Actor had not posed for or given an interview to the magazine and sued alleging deliberately created false impression that he did so making it appear that he was willing to degrade himself and endorse such a magazine). *Cf. Kournikova v General Media Communications Inc* 67 U.S.P.Q. 2d 1395 (C.D. Cal. Dist. Ct, May 2, 2003) (false advertising and false endorsement claim dismissed in respect of nude photographs falsely identified by the claimant. Headline "Caught close up on nude beach" did not suggest consensual endorsement).

was courting publicity in a sensationalist tabloid."[32] By analogy, use of photographs to make the same suggestion may be actionable.

*Ethics of digital manipulation and the press*

The press regularly report instances of digital manipulation of photo-   **9–021**
graphs by others[33] and the media, in some cases notoriously, alter photographs themselves.[34] The use of digitally manipulated photographs is generally not approved by photojournalists who generally seek to uphold standards of accuracy.[35] In 1996, the National Union of Journalists, at its annual delegate meeting launched a campaign for the adoption of use of a standardised mark to indicate a photograph which had been digitally manipulated. The proposed marks were based on those developed by a study group chaired by Professor Fred Ritchin[36]

To be effective in practice, the proposed mark needs to be used within the   **9–022**
image area and not as a caption, to avoid misleading viewers if there is deep linking or in line linking directly to an image or where the image is copied electronically. The use of such a mark on the photograph in itself may be something a photographer would not appreciate, as it inevitably intrudes into the composition of the image. There does not seem to have been much use of this icon by the media to date. Captions seem to be more common where there is obvious digital manipulation.

[32] *Eastwood v National Enquirer Inc* 123 F.3d 1249 (9th Cir. 1997).
[33] "Royal Wedding's Invisible Secret", *The Times*, June 22, 1999, p.3 (Wedding of Earl and Countess of Wessex, official photograph 10 members of the family had better headshots inserted); "Schoolgirl Sees Red As Her Pink Hair Is Painted Brown", *Daily Telegraph*, February 22, 2002, p.8 (dyed pink hair of schoolgirl was digitally altered to brown in an official school photograph at the direction of the school).
[34] *e.g.* in April 2003, a Los Angeles Times photographer was dismissed for doctoring a photograph of a British soldier in Iraq: *Los Angeles Times*, April 2, 2003, A6. In July 2003, the London Evening Standard admitted that a photograph showing Iraqis celebrating the liberation of Baghdad, had been enhanced to show a larger crowd than actually existed. The image had been taken from TV footage and some extra people were added to the image in order to fill the space left by the removal of logos from the picture: *Evening Standard*, July 24, 2003, p.18; S. Bates, "Faking It", *Guardian*, May 5, 2003. See also S. Farrell and C. Midgley, "Changing Photographs Is Child's Play", *The Times*, August 12, 1997, (referring to *Time* magazine's darkening of the police mugshot of O. J. Simpson in 1994 and in December 1994 the *London Evening Standard* removing a beer bottle from a photograph of John and Pauline Prescott leaving wine glasses with a caption "champagne socialists").
[35] *e.g.* see the USA National Press Photographers Association (NPPA) 1991 Statement of Principle—Digital Manipulation Code of Ethics at *http://www.nppa.org/services/bizpract/digitalethics.html*: "As journalists we believe the guiding principle of our profession is accuracy; therefore, we believe it is wrong to alter the content of a photograph in any way that deceives the public." For further reading see F. Ritchin, *In Our Own Image: The Coming Revolution in Photography: How Computer Technology Is Changing Our View of the World (Writers and Artists on Photography)* (Aperture Press, 1999).
[36] New York School of Photography. See *http://www.londonfreelance.org/manipsym.html*.

Caution is advised where digital manipulation takes place that alters the content of the photograph creating a misrepresentation of what was actually photographed. Publishers should be alive to the possibility of infringement of legal rights, both those of the copyright owner and any persons depicted, and the use of disclaimers should be considered.[37] Digital manipulation that merely enhances the clarity of the image is unobjectionable and unlikely to result in litigation.

It should be noted that the NUJ Code of Conduct provides that journalists should not allow publication or broadcast of a digitally manipulation photograph unless that photograph is clearly marked as having been manipulated.[38] The Code reproduced in full below also makes provision that photographs should be obtained only by straightforward means, unless justified by considerations of overriding public interest.

---

[37] See copyright above at paras 2–019, 2–146 and 3–017; moral rights above at paras 4–020 and 4–028 to 4–029; defamation above at paras 7–117 *et seq.*; and use of disclaimers above at para.7–130; passing off below at paras 10–002 *et seq.* and model release forms above at para.7–088.

[38] See NUJ Code of Conduct, para.11, reproduced in full below.

# The National Union of Journalists Code of Conduct

1. A journalist has a duty to maintain the highest professional and ethical standards.

2. A journalist shall at all times defend the principle of the freedom of the press and other media in relation to the collection of information and the expression of comment and criticism. He/she shall strive to eliminate distortion, news suppression and censorship.

3. A journalist shall strive to ensure that the information he/she disseminates is fair and accurate, avoid the expression of comment and conjecture as established fact and falsification by distortion, selection or misrepresentation.

4. A journalist shall rectify promptly any harmful inaccuracies, ensure that correction and apologies receive due prominence and afford the right of reply to persons criticised when the issue is of sufficient importance.

5. A journalist shall obtain information, photographs and illustrations only by straightforward means. The use of other means can be justified only by overriding considerations of the public interest. The journalist is entitled to exercise a personal conscientious objection to the use of such means.

6. A journalist shall do nothing which entails intrusion into anybody's private life, grief or distress, subject to justification by overriding considerations of the public interest.

7. A journalist shall protect confidential sources of information.

8. A journalist shall not accept bribes nor shall he/she allow other inducements to influence the performance of his/her professional duties.

9. A journalist shall not lend himself/herself to the distortion or suppression of the truth because of advertising or other considerations.

10. A journalist shall mention a person's age, sex, race, colour, creed, illegitimacy, disability, marital status, or sexual orientation only if this information is strictly relevant. A journalist shall neither originate nor process material which encourages discrimination, ridicule, prejudice or hatred on any of the above-mentioned grounds.

11. No journalist shall knowingly cause or allow the publication or broadcast of a photograph that has been manipulated unless that photograph is clearly labelled as such. Manipulation does not include normal dodging, burning, colour balancing, spotting, contrast adjustment, cropping and obvious masking for legal or safety reasons.

12. A journalist shall not take private advantage of information gained in the course of his/her duties before the information is public knowledge.

13. A journalist shall not by way of statement, voice or appearance endorse by advertisement any commercial product or service save for the promotion of his/her own work or of the medium by which he/she is employed.

*Digital manipulation and parody*

**9–023**     Creation of photographs that parody other images is easily achieved by the use of digital manipulation. The extent to which UK copyright law adequately provides a defence for parodies is unclear. It is virtually inevitable that a digital manipulated photo-illustration which parodies another photograph will reproduce "a substantial part" of the original copyright photograph. Where there is reproduction of "a substantial part", there is no separate defence of parody.[39]

Under the Copyright Designs and Patents Act 1988, there is a defence of fair dealing with a work for the purpose of criticism or review.[40] Fair dealing for criticism or review does not infringe any copyright in the work provided that (1) it is accompanied by a sufficient acknowledgment, and (2) the work has been made lawfully available to the public. It is certainly arguable that a parody is a form of criticism.[41] But there is requirement for sufficient acknowledgment for this defence to be relied on. In fact, in other jurisdictions it has been held that the nature of parody requires the audience to have some awareness of the parodied work.[42]

Statutes in many jurisdictions specifically provide for a defence of parody.[43] If there is no defence for a genuine parody under the 1988 Act because there is no sufficient acknowledgment or otherwise, it is questionable whether the UK domestic law provides adequate protection for freedom of expression under Art.10.

---

[39] Contrary to CDPA 1988, s.16(3). If a substantial part is reproduced there is no separate defence of parody: *Williamson Music Ltd v Pearson Partnership Ltd* [1987] F.S.R. 97; *Schweppes Ltd v Wellingtons Ltd* [1984] F.S.R. 210.

[40] CDPA 1988, s.30 as amended by SI 2003/2498, reg.10.

[41] Cases in which parody has been raised include *Williamson Music Ltd v Pearson Partnership Ltd* [1987] F.S.R. 97; *Schweppes Ltd v Wellingtons Ltd* [1984] F.S.R. 210; *Joy Music Ltd v Sunday Pictorial Newspapers Ltd* [1960] 2 Q.B. 60; [1960] 2 W.L.R. 645; [1960] 1 All E.R. 703. See further Laddie, Prescott & Vitoria et al., The Modern Law of Copyright & Designs (3rd ed.) a 3.142; *Copinger and Skone James on Copyright* (14th ed.) at 9–18.

[42] *Rogers v Koons*, 960 F.2d 301, 310 (2nd Cir. 1992) where the court said "By requiring that the copied work be an object of the parody, we merely insist that the audience be aware that underlying the parody there is an original and separate expression, attributable to a different artist. This awareness may come from the fact that the copied work is publicly known or because its existence is in some manner acknowledged by the parodist in connection with the parody." See also *Leibovitz v Paramount Pictures Corp* 948 F. Supp. 1214 (S.D. N.Y., 1996) (holding that a parody of photograph by Annie Leibovitz of a pregnant Demi Moore that originally appeared on the cover of Vanity fair was fair use. The parody was a poster for the film *Naked Gun: The Final Insult 33*—which had the body of a pregnant model in a similar pose and manipulated to duplicate the skin tone of the original photograph onto which was superimposed the head of male actor Leslie Neilsen).

[43] *e.g.* French Copyright Code 1992, Art.L.122.5(4) "parody, pastiche and caricature, taking account of the laws of the genre"; Spanish Copyright Act 1987, Art.39 "The parody of a disclosed work shall not be considered such a transformation as requires the consent of the author, provided that it involves no risk of confusion with that work and does no harm to the original work or its author". See L. Gimeno, *A Parody of Songs* [1997] Ent.L.R. 18 and E. Gredley and M. Maniatis, *Parody: A Fatal Attraction? Part 1: The Nature of Parody and Its Treatment in Copyright* [1997] E.I.P.R. 339–344; (Pt 2 at [1997] E.I.P.R. 412–420).

*Integrity of digital images for use in litigation*

When involved in litigation in which digital photographs are a significant **9–024** piece of evidence, parties seeking to rely on the photographs should take care to ensure that at trial they are in a position to demonstrate the authenticity of the image. Parties involved in litigation in which the opposing party is seeking to rely on a digital photograph should be alive to the possibility that the photograph may have been altered, either deliberately or accidentally. This is not to suggest that everyone involved in litigation is busily doctoring photographs to assist their case, but merely that the possibility of alteration is something to be aware of.

There is software available that allows for data verification of visual images at the point of creation establishing a secure master reference file with imbedded data that tracks changes.[44] For such software to have any meaning, it relies on use at the time the image is created. This is all very well if the image creator is, for example, a law enforcement agency aware of the need to maintain data integrity and using data integrity software. Where the image has been created by a lay person or without use of data integrity software, it is advisable for those having custody of the image to take basic precautions in case the evidence is challenged. Images should be kept in their original file format. An original .tiff file is preferable to a .jpeg file as the latter has a greater compression.[45]

Ideally, when using digital photographs for litigation it would be sensible **9–025** to institute and maintain "a chain of evidence" type procedure where a hard copy of the original image is printed out and dated, the original file is carefully labelled and any changes or use of that file are recorded to avoid authentication problems. In cases where the photographer is a lay client who has, for example, photographed an accident scene, this will not often be possible or practical. If the "original" photographic file passes into the hands of solicitors, the solicitors should be in a position to demonstrate that the integrity of that evidence has been maintained.

In February 1998 in the United States of America, the Scientific Working Group on Digital Evidence (SWGDE) was established.[46] It was created by the Federal Crime Laboratory Directors group and original members included, amongst others, the forensic laboratories of the FBI, US Customs and the US Postal Inspection Service. SWGDE was created in order to develop standards and harmonize operations in the use of digital forensic evidence. The SWGDE publish a "Best Practices" document[47] for digital evidence laboratories which makes various recommendations including procedures for receiving and identifying evidence, maintaining the integrity of evidence, storage, examination of digital evidence, and the monitoring of equipment used to examine the evidence. In the UK, similar guidance is published by the Association of Chief Police Officers (ACPO) in conjunction

---

[44] *e.g.* Veridata (Signum Technologies) *http://www.signumtech.com/*.
[45] For differences see above at para.9–002.
[46] For further information see its website at *http://www.swgde.org/*.
[47] Available *via* the website, see above at n.46.

with the National Hi-Tech Crime Unit.[47a] The procedures suggested apply to all digital evidence, not just photographs, but would be a useful starting point for those considering establishing standard procedures for dealing with photographic evidence.

**9–026**     The SWGDE and ACPO standards are aimed at forensic work in a criminal context and are correspondingly high. At a lower level, the basic ideas set out in the standards are worth considering in a civil litigation context in cases where photographic evidence integrity may be in issue. Simple precautions such as limiting access to the image computer file would help if there were to be a suggestion that the photograph was altered in some way. It is also important to avoid degrading the quality of the image by resaving it in a different file format or further compressing an already compressed file.

*Some indicators that an image may have been manipulated*

**9–027**     The starting point is really the "look and feel" of the photograph. Albeit an imprecise and unscientific method; consider if it looks "right". More specifically, look for consistency in:

- Shadows of objects. Added or deleted objects may be indicated by an inconsistent shadow pattern.

- Object relationships and perspective. Added objects may be out of perspective or expected alignment with existing objects. Two people shown about to shake hands may have inconsistent sight lines.

- Elements concerning time and season. Consistency of level of lighting and other elements (*e.g.* a person's clothing) compared with (1) any time shown on clocks or watches, or (2) seasonal indicators.

- Reflections shown in any reflective materials pictured.

- Texture in areas in the photograph where only background appears. Any inconsistency in texture or large areas of background may indicate a removed object.

**9–028**     Digital manipulation can be done so skilfully that it would be impossible to detect. The size of image files is such, that unlike word processing programmes, a history file detailing changes cannot generally be obtained via hard drive inspection. Experts may be able to detect changes in some circumstances but not always. "Feathering" which results from transitioning one pixel to another, or within a pixel itself, may be an indicator of digital manipulation.[48] It shows as blurring of colour under magnification along the

---

[47a] The ACPO Good Practice Guide for Computer Based Electronic Evidence. Available via the National Hi-Tech Crime Unit's website at *http://www.nhtcu.org.*
[48] See V.E. Bianchini and H. Bass *A Paradigm for the Authentication of Photographic Evidence in the Digital Age* [1998] 20 Thomas Jefferson L. Rev. 303 at 311 from an interview in September 1997 with Jeff Pratt of Chrome Digital Services, a San Diego firm specialising in digital photography.

transition lines. The data file can be examined under magnification to assess whether there is any feathering. Another indication of fraudulent image creation may be where a hard copy photograph is being proffered as an original analogue image but is printed on computer photo imaging paper. Computer photo paper is usually visibly marked as such. If there is a disparity between the type of image asserted and the type of paper, a request for inspection of the original negative/transparency should be made.[49] However, the unfortunate reality is that digital alteration to images may very well be undetectable.

## *Requiring proof of authenticity of photographs in civil litigation*

The Civil Procedure Rules provide that a party is deemed to admit the authenticity of a document disclosed to him under Pt 31 (disclosure and inspection of documents) unless he serves notice that he wishes the document to be proved at trial.[50] "Document" in this context has a wide definition as meaning "anything in which information of any description is recorded",[51] and includes photographs, whether analogue or digital photograph computer files. Accordingly, if it proposed to challenge (or simply to require proof of) the authenticity of a photograph, a notice requiring proof needs to be served. Such a notice to prove a document must be served by either (a) the latest date for serving witness statements, or (b) within seven days of disclosure of the document, whichever is later.[52]

**9–029**

## RIGHTS MANAGEMENT AND DIGITAL WATERMARKS

### Digital watermarks: General

Digital watermarks are a form of "rights management" that allows an image to be marked as being the property of a particular individual or organisation. Watermarks may be either visible or invisible. In its simplest form, a digital water mark may be a visible name or logo, or copyright symbol overlaid and repeated over the image. If a visible copyright notice is layered into an image in such a way as to make it difficult for it to be cropped out, this will deter copiers. However, visible watermarks obviously interfere with and obscure the image. Invisible watermarks embed a unique digital code into an image that is invisible to the naked eye, thus permanently "tagging" the image.

**9–030**

There are several different types of software and systems for imbedding digital watermarks into an image that are invisible to the naked eye. Any digital image file will contain "noise"—random unwanted digital data present in any file. Most watermarking systems work by replacing some of

---

[49] *ibid.*
[50] CPR 1998, r.32(19)(1).
[51] CPR 1998, r.31.4.
[52] CPR 1998, r.32(19)(2).

the noise in any image with a code. As the code is imbedded throughout the image, many watermarks can, at least in theory, survive cropping, scanning, resizing, compression, and printing and re-scanning. Digital watermarks do not just simply mark an image as the copyright work of a particular person or company. Watermarks can also be used to track images and search via the web for the marks. "Web spider" programmes are used to track images via a web browser that downloads images from the internet and checks whether they contain a watermark.

**9–031**    The watermark has to be capable of extraction and can be read by the appropriate software reader. A digital watermark needs to be robust in the sense that it will survive attacks on the image, whether intentional or unintentional, that change the digital data. Stirmark is a tool which has been developed to test the robustness of watermarking systems.[53] A variety of attacks on watermarking systems have been tested using Stirmark and the authors concluded that the majority of copyright marking systems are vulnerable to attacks.[54] There is a great deal of scientific literature concerning the robustness of digital watermarks and research into the extent to which different types of watermarks survive, consideration of which is outside the scope of this work.[55]

There are various commercial watermarking software programmes available, for example, PictureMarc (which is licenced to and bundled with Adobe Photoshop), and Digimarc (Digimarc Corporation)[56]; Ewatermarc (Kowa Company)[57]; SysCopP (MediaSec Technologies)[58]; SureSign (Signum Technologies)[59]; and Datamark.[60]

**9–032**    Further developments in electronic rights management include the creation of public databases identifying image rights owners. In the UK, the Visual Creators Index (VCI) was set up in 1999 to protect the interests of photographers and creators of digital images.[61] The VCI aims to create worldwide standard formats for digital labels which identify the creator of an image. Each photographer or image creator who is registered with the VCI is given a unique Creator Code comprising of digits and letters. The idea is that this Creator Code acts as a digital watermark embedded into the image which enables anyone who needs to identify the rights owner to do so

---

[53] By A.P. Fabien, Petitcolas *et al.* See *http://www.petitcolas.net/fabien/watermarking/index.html*.

[54] A. P. Fabien, Ross Petitcolas, J. Anderson, Markus G. Kuhn, "Attacks on copyright marking systems", in David Aucsmith (ed.), *Information Hiding*, Second International Workshop, IH'98, Portland, Oregon, USA, April 15–17, 1998, Proceedings, LNCS 1525, Springer-Verlag, pp.219–239. Available online at *http://www.petitcolas.net/fabien/publications/ih98-attacks.pdf*.

[55] For Digimarc guide to its own watermark survival see: *http://www.digimarc.com/products/support/wmguide/wmguide4.asp*. There are a large number of scientific and technical papers posted in PDF format available on the internet concerning digital watermarking robustness that can easily be located via a search engine. Most are highly technical and outside the scope of this work.

[56] *http://www.digimarc.com*.

[57] *http://www.ewatermark.com/*.

[58] SysCopP = System for Copyright Protection. *http://www.mediasec.com/*.

[59] Sure Sign. *http://www.signumtech.com/*.

[60] *http://www.datamark.co.uk/*.

[61] *http://www.vci-uk.com/*.

via a publically accessible database. By April 1999, the VCI had registered over 1,200 creators of visual images whose assigned codes can be searched via the Visual Creators' Registry[62] which can be accessed through the internet.

## Removal or alteration of rights management information

As from October 31, 2003, the Copyright Designs and Patents Act 1988 was amended[63] for the purpose of implementing the European Directive[64] to harmonise copyright and related rights in the information society.   **9–033**

The changes grant rights of action in respect of circumvention of technological measures—and removal or alteration of rights management information. "Technological measures" are distinguished from electronic rights management information. Broadly, technological measures are those which protect (rather than merely identify) a copyright work, by controlling access to the work (*e.g.* encryption) or copy control mechanisms.[65] Rights management information is "any information provided by a copyright owner which identifies the work, the author, the copyright owner or the holder of any intellectual property rights or information about the terms and conditions of the use of the work and any numbers or codes that represent such information".[66]

Digital watermarks which simply identify a photograph (and do not restrict copying or access to the photograph) fall within the definition of rights management information. Rights of action are granted to the publisher of copyright works that have been watermarked against those who knowingly alter or remove such watermarks and those who import or distribute copies of the work from which the watermarks have been removed. Photographs are included as copyright works attracting this protection.[67]   **9–034**

Any person issuing copies of a work or communicating copies of a work to the public has the same rights as a copyright owner does for copyright infringement against anyone who knowingly and without authority either removes or alters rights management information, where that person knows or has reason to believe by removal or alteration he is inducing, enabling, facilitating, or concealing copyright infringement.[68] Any electronic rights management information which is either "associated with a copy of the copyright work or appears in connection with the communication to the public of the copyright work"[69] is protected.   **9–035**

---

[62] *http://www.vci-registry.org/*.

[63] By the Copyright and Related Rights Regulations 2003 (SI 2003/2498).

[64] 2001/29.

[65] "Technological measures" are defined as "any technology, device or component which is designed, in the normal course of its operation, to protect a copyright work other than a computer program" CDPA 1988, s.296ZF(1) as inserted by SI 2003/2498, reg.24.

[66] CDPA 1988, s.296ZG(7)(b), as inserted by SI 2003/2498, reg.25.

[67] CDPA 1998, s.296ZG(7)(a) (expressions defined in Pt 1 have the same meaning as in that Part) as inserted by SI 2003/2498, reg.25. For the definition of copyright work and photographs see above at paras 2–009 to 2–010.

[68] CDPA 1988, s.296ZG(1) and (3) as inserted by SI 2003/2498, reg.25.

[69] CDPA 1988, s.296ZG(1)(a) and (b) as inserted by SI 2003/2498, reg.25.

The 1988 Act also grants the same rights as a copyright owner has for copyright infringement to a person issuing or communicating copies of the work to the public against any person who distributes or imports for distribution or communicates copies to the public of a copyright work from which electronic rights management has been removed or altered.[70] Again, it is a requirement that the importer/distributer knows or has reason to believe that by doing so he is inducing, enabling, facilitating, or concealing an infringement of copyright.

**9–036**    The same rights of action (against (1) those altering/removing rights management information, and (2) those importing/distributing such altered works) are granted concurrently to the copyright owner or his exclusive licensee, where he is not the person issuing or communicating copies of the work to the public.[71]

The rights apply to photographs made before or after October 31, 2003.[72] However, no act done before the Copyright and Related Rights Regulations 2003 came into force on October 31, 2003 shall be regarded as an infringement of any new or extended right created by the Regulations.[73] Nothing in the Regulations affects any agreement made before December 22, 2002.[74] Equally, no act done after October 31, 2003, in pursuance of an agreement made before December 22, 2002, shall be regarded as an infringement of any new or extended right.[75]

### Practical security options for image use on the internet

**9–037**

| Method | Advantages | Disadvantages |
|---|---|---|
| Visible watermark | Simple, inexpensive and an obvious deterrent as plainly visible. | Interferes with image. Can be removed by cropping or cloning. |
| Digital watermark | Theoretically permanent and will survive attacks on the data. Can be tracked. Notification that images are watermarked has deterrent effect. | Questionable as to what extent watermarks do actually survive certain types of image processing. Tracking usually requires expense of subscription to tracking service. |

---

[70] CDPA 1998, s.296ZG(2) and (3) as inserted by SI 2003/2498, reg.25.
[71] CDPA 1998, ss.296ZG(4) and (5) as inserted by SI 2003/2498, reg.25.
[72] SI 2003/2498, reg.31.
[73] SI 2003/2498, reg.31(2). Commencement: reg.1.
[74] SI 2003/2498, reg.32(1).
[75] SI 2003/2498, reg.32(2).

| | | |
|---|---|---|
| Low resolution/small images/image compression | Again simple and inexpensive. Low resolution and small images are less likely to be copied. | Loss of image quality. Spoils visual appearance of website. |
| Disable users mouse right click which normally brings up the "Save As" menu. | Website designers can disable this function by using java script. Can be replaced with a text box containing (*e.g.* copyright warnings). Immediate and obvious. Stops easy downloading and saving of image. | Does not stop copying by more sophisticated users. May be irritating to users who use the right mouse button for legitimate purposes, *e.g.* to copy and paste the contact details of the business. |
| Control access to website | Requiring registration, etc. of users allows tracking of image use. Users aware of this and discouraged from copying. | Less exposure and publicity. More practical for image libraries or sites containing a large number of commercially valuable images. Less practical for other business websites that are not dealing commercially in images, as limiting access to the website defeats the object of advertising/a web presence. |
| Software that prevents downloading or encrypts a website page. | Very effective. | May restrict viewing access as may require a plug-in/ reader for images to be viewed. Expense of software. If image is licenced for publication, it will become publically available non-encrypted and is capable of being copied. |

## DIGITISATION OF ANALOGUE PHOTOGRAPHS

**9–038**   Digitization is the process of converting data into a form that can be read by a computer—*i.e.* binary codes of 0s and 1s. Analogue photographs can be digitized by scanning them into a computer. Unauthorised digitization of analogue photographs may give rise to a claim for copyright infringement by the owner of the photographic copyright.

Problems have arisen where a licence was originally granted by a copyright owner to reproduce an analogue photograph at a time when digital photographs and databases did not exist or the licence was silent about electronic use. Such cases raise the question of the extent to which subsequent digital use by the licensee of the copyright work is covered by the original licence. The most typical example is use by newspapers and periodicals copying into a new digital format (such as a CD-ROM or a searchable database) articles and photographs from back copies of their publications. In many cases, whether such use was contemplated or can be implied will depend on the contractual terms of the licence and the circumstances of the case. Today most licensing agreements will (or should) address this problem directly either by (1) expressly including "all media whether now known or hereafter to be devised" or "all media whether now existing or to be developed in the future" or similar wording, or (2) expressly excluding certain uses such as electronic use or use in media that do not yet exist.

**9–039**   If the licence agreement is silent, it is doubtful whether the court would be imply a term incorporating electronic use in the absence of some compelling evidence. The court adopts a minimalist approach to implying terms, both generally and intellectual property cases. An implication should only be made if this is necessary and then only of what is necessary and no more.[76] Unless it can be contended that the relevant electronic use was within the contemplation of the parties (*e.g.* because at the time of the licence the photographer knew that it was the periodical's practice to include the image on its website), it is unlikely that an argument that such a term should be implied would have any chance of success. It is clear from the Copyright in the Information Society Directive[77] that to communicate a work to the public by electronic transmission is a separate right of the copyright owner which covers internet use and remote access databases.[78]

**9–040**   Case law from other jurisdictions supports the view that electronic use of analogue works is a separate and new use, particularly where the electronic

---

[76] *Ray v Classic FM plc* [1998] F.S.R. 622; *Liverpool City Council v Irwin* [1977] A.C. 239. See also *R. Griggs Group Ltd v Evans* [2003] EWHC 2914 Ch and above at paras 2–089 to 2–092.
[77] 2001/29. Implemented in the UK by The Copyright and Related Rights Regulations 2003 (SI 2003/2498) amending the Copyright Designs and Patents Act 1988.
[78] Directive recital (23) "This Directive should harmonise further the author's right of communication to the public. This right should be understood in a broad sense covering all communication to the public not present at the place where the communication originates. This right should cover any such transmission of a work to the public by wire or wireless means ..." And see the CDPA 1988, s.20 as amended by reg.6 Copyright and Related Rights Regulations 2003 (SI 2003/2498).

use allows direct access to the work.[79] It is arguable that a licence to reproduce an analogue work in a periodical amounts to a licence to embed the work into a particular edition of collective work. If so, then a digital reproduction of the original analogue work in the context of that full collective work by the collective work owner is arguably within the terms of the licence.[80] This would cover electronic reproduction of the periodical, page by page, where the individual articles/photographs works can only be accessed on a copy of the full page on which they originally appeared—an electronic version of microfiche effectively. However, most electronic uses do not reproduce the individual work in this way but rather have searchable programmes where the article or photograph can be accessed directly and independently. Further, the argument (that reproduction in context where no direct access is permitted) was a permitted use analogous to microfiche archiving was rejected by a court in the USA in *Greenberg v National Geographic Society*.[81]

In *Greenberg v National Geographic Society*[82] the National Geographic Society developed a CD-ROM library that included in digital format every issue of the magazine from 1888 to 1996 in digital format. Jerry Greenberg was a photographer who had completed four photographic assignments for the Society over 30 years. The copyright in the works had been reassigned back to the photographer prior to the development of the CD-ROM. Greenberg issued copyright infringement proceedings against the National Geographic Society. The Society contended that it was entitled to reproduce the photographs because it owned the copyright in the original issues of the magazine in which they appeared. The magazines were converted to digital format by scanning each cover and page of each issue into a computer. The district court granted summary judgment to the National Geographic Society and Greenberg appealed.

The Society argued that it was the owner of the copyright in the "collective work" and that its use of the photographs on the CD-ROM amounted to "a revision" of the collective work which was permitted by the US Copyright Act, 17 U.S.C. 201(c). This argument was rejected by the Court of Appeals for the 11th Circuit who held: **9–041**

> "...common-sense copyright analysis compels the conclusion that the Society in collaboration with Mindscape has created a new product ('an original work of authorship') in a new medium, for a new market that far transcends any privilege of revision or other mere reproduction envisioned in §201(c)"[83]

---

[79] USA cases (see below): *New York Times Co Inc v Tasini* 106 F.3d 161 (2001, Sup. Ct. (US)); *Greenberg v National Geographic Society* 244 F.3d 1267 (11th Cir. 2001); *Random House Inc v Rosetta Books LLC* 150 F. Supp. 2d 613 (S.D.N.Y., 2001) affirmed 283 F.3d 490 (2nd Cir. 2002).
[80] *Cf*: regarding copyright in a typographical arrangement of a newspaper edition: *Newspaper Licensing Agency Ltd v Marks & Spencer Plc* [2001] UKHL 38; [2003] 1 A.C. 551; [2001] 3 W.L.R. 290; [2001] 3 All E.R. 977.
[81] 244 F.3d 1267 (11th Cir. 2001).
[82] 244 F.3d 1267 (11th Cir. 2001).
[83] 244 F.3d 1267 at 1273 (11th Cir. 2001).

The court took this view not withstanding that

"What the user of [the CD-ROM] sees on his computer screen ... is a reproduction of each page of the magazine that differs from the original only in size and resolution of the photographs and text. Every cover, article, advertisement and photograph appears as it did in the original paper copy of the magazine. The user can print out the image of any page of the magazine but the [CD-ROM] does not provide a means for the user to separate the photographs from the text or otherwise edit the pages in any way."

The court held that the use amounted to copyright infringement and remanded the case to the district court for assessment of damages.

**9–042**    Whilst this case concerns construction of the US Copyright Act, it is instructive for those practising in the UK as it is illustrative of an appellate court's approach to the question of whether digital reproduction amounted to a new use. The argument that it was analogous to microfiche use and was mere change in medium[84] was plainly rejected, as is clear from a footnote to the judgment where it was said:

"The Society characterizes this case as one in which there has merely been a republication of a preexisting work, without substantive change, in a new medium; specifically, digital format. As discussed in the text, however, this case is both factually and legally different than a media transformation. The Society analogizes the digitalization of the Magazine to the reproduction of the Magazine on microfilm and microfiche. While it is true that both the digital reproductions and the microfilm/microfiche reproductions require a mechanical device for viewing them, *the critical difference, from a copyright perspective, is that the computer, as opposed to the machines used for viewing microfilm and microfiche, requires the interaction of a computer program in order to accomplish the useful reproduction involved with the new medium.* These computer programs are themselves the subject matter of copyright, and may constitute original works of authorship, and thus present an additional dimension in the

---

[84] See also *Random House Inc v Rosetta Books LLC* 150 F. Supp. 2d 613 (S.D.N.Y., 2001) affirmed 283 F.3d 490 (2nd Cir. 2002) (whether an "E book" was a form of book covered by a licence to publish "in book form"). Refusing injunction "To be sure, there is some appeal to appellant's argument that an 'ebook'—a digital book that can be read on a computer screen or electronic device. ... But the law of New York, which determines the scope of Random House's contracts, has arguably adopted a restrictive view of the kinds of 'new uses' to which an exclusive license may apply when the contracting parties do not expressly provide for coverage of such future forms." See also the comments of the lower court distinguishing between analogue and electronic use: "... the 'new use'—electronic digital signals sent over the internet—is a separate medium from the original use—printed words on paper ... Ebooks take advantage of the digital medium's ability to manipulate data by allowing ebook users to electronically search the text for specific words and phrases, change the font size and style, type notes into the text and electronically organize them, highlight and bookmark, hyperlink to specific parts of the text, and, in the future, to other sites on related topics as well, and access a dictionary that pronounces words in the ebook aloud. The need for a software program to interact with the data in order to make it usable, as well as the need for a piece of hardware to enable the reader to view the text, also distinguishes analog formats from digital formats."

copyright analysis. Because this case involves not only the incorporation of a new computer program, but also the combination of the Sequence and the Replica, we need not decide in this case whether the addition of only the Program would result in the creation of a new collective work."[85] (Emphasis added).

The Supreme Court of the United States in *New York Times Co Inc v Tasini*[86] considered a similar case involving an action by a group of freelance authors who had contributed articles to two newspapers and a magazine. The publishers entered into a licence agreement with LEXIS/NEXIS to allow reproduction of articles from the newspapers and magazines in computer databases. Thus, with the permission of the periodical publishers but without the author's consent, LEXIS/NEXIS placed copies of the freelancers' articles into electronic databases. The authors issued copyright infringement proceedings against the publishers. The publishers relied on the provision of the US Copyright Act allowing owners of copyright in collective works to reproduce the collective work and revisions of the collective work.

Unlike the National Geographic case, each article was retrievable by the user in isolation, independently of the context of the original print publication. This was regarded as significant by the Supreme Court who noted that, as a result, the database did not reproduce or distribute the articles as "part of" an original edition of a collective work or as a revision. Again, a microfiche analogy was drawn by the publishers and rejected by the Supreme Court who said:    **9–043**

> "The Publishers press an analogy between the Databases, on the one hand, and microfilm and microfiche, on the other. We find the analogy wanting. Microforms typically contain continuous photographic reproductions of a periodical in the medium of miniaturized film.
>
> Accordingly, articles appear on the microforms, writ very small, in precisely the position in which the articles appeared in the newspaper. The Times, for example, printed the beginning of Blakely's 'Remembering Jane' Article on page 26 of the Magazine in the September 23, 1990, edition; the microfilm version of the Times reproduces that same Article on film in the very same position, within a film reproduction of the entire Magazine, in turn within a reproduction of the entire September 23, 1990, edition. True, the microfilm roll contains multiple editions, and the microfilm user can adjust the machine lens to focus only on the Article, to the exclusion of surrounding material. Nonetheless, the user first encounters the Article in context. In the Databases, by contrast, the Articles appear disconnected from their original context. In NEXIS and NYTO, the user sees the 'Jane' Article apart even from the remainder of page 26. In GPO, the user sees the Article within the context of page 26,

---

[85] 244 F.3d 1267 at n.12.
[86] 121 S. Ct. 2381; 106 F.3d 161 (2001, Sup. Ct. (US)). For discussion see P. Jaszi, *How Important is the Tasini Decision?* [2001] 23 (12) E.I.P.R. 595.

but clear of the context of page 25 or page 27, the rest of the Magazine, or the remainder of the day's newspaper. In short, unlike microforms, the Databases do not perceptibly reproduce articles as part of the collective work to which the author contributed or as part of any 'revision' thereo."[87]

**9–044**    It can be seen that the fact that the articles appear disconnected from their original context was an important aspect of the rejection by the Supreme Court of the publisher's arguments. However, notwithstanding that the photographs could only be accessed in context of the original publication in *Greenberg v National Geographic Society*,[88] the court in that case also held that there was copyright infringement. In the light of these cases, it is questionable whether UK courts are likely to be persuaded by an argument that a licence to use an analogue photograph in a collective work (otherwise silent about electronic use) would impliedly include a licence to use that work in an electronic full copy of the collective work, even where the individual photographs cannot be accessed individually.

## VIDEO GRABS

**9–045**    Video frame grabbing software allows the user to "grab" or capture still images from a screen (whether television broadcast, videotape, DVD, or computer game screen shot) and save them as still digital images. Generally, this will amount to a copyright infringement of the film, broadcast, or material that is copied, there being no special loophole simply because the image has been obtained by a video grab. It is governed by the law of copyright and the question would be whether the use was permitted by any defence or statutory exemption.[89]

**9–046**    Infringement by copying in relation to a film or broadcast includes making a photograph of the whole or *any substantial part of any image forming part* of the film or broadcast.[90] And as has been noted above, any act restricted by the copyright in a work includes acts in relation to the work as a whole or *any substantial part* of it.[91] A single frame of a film reproduced on a poster has been held to be part of a film.[92]

However, the Copyright Designs and Patents Act 1988 does provide that the making of a photograph for private and domestic use of a broadcast does not infringe copyright. The wording of this section was changed and expanded by the Copyright and Related Rights Regulations 2003.[93] Section 71, CDPA 1988 prior to amendment read as follows:

---

[87] 121 S. Ct. 2381 at 2392 (2001, Sup. Ct. (US)).
[88] 244 F.3d 1267 (11th Cir. 2001).
[89] See above at paras 2–157 *et seq.*
[90] CDPA 1988, s.17(4) as amended by Copyright and Related Rights Regulations 2003 (SI 2003/2498).
[91] CDPA 1988, s.16(4).
[92] *Spelling Goldberg Productions Inc v BPC Publishing Ltd* [1981] R.P.C. 280.
[93] SI 2003/2498, reg.31.

**"71 Photographs of television broadcasts or cable programme**
The making for private and domestic use of a photograph of the whole or any part of an image forming part of a television broadcast or cable programme, or a copy of such a photograph, does not infringe any copyright in the broadcast or cable programme or in any film included in it."

From October 31, 2003, the section was amended to read as follows[94]:     **9–047**

**"Photographs of Broadcasts**
**71.**—(1) The making in domestic premises for private and domestic use of a photograph of the whole or any part of an image forming part of a broadcast, or a copy of such a photograph, does not infringe any copyright in the broadcast or in any film included in it.
(2) Where a copy which would otherwise be an infringing copy is made in accordance with this section but is subsequently dealt with—

(a) it shall be treated as an infringing copy for the purposes of that dealing; and
(b) if that dealing infringes copyright, it shall be treated as an infringing copy for all subsequent purposes.

(3) In subsection (2), 'dealt with' means sold or let for hire, offered or exposed for sale or hire or communicated to the public."

The main differences are that to qualify for the exemption from copyright     **9–048**
infringement in addition to being made for private and domestic use, the photograph must now be made *in domestic premises* as well. This would exclude taking photographs of the film screen in a public cinema for example. A further change is that even if a photograph is taken in domestic premises for private and domestic use, if that photograph is sold, hired, or offered for sale or hire, or communicated to the public, it will amount to a copyright infringement. Communication to the public would include posting the photograph on a website.
The new s.71 applies to all photographs whether made before or after October 31, 2003.[95] However, no act done before the Copyright and Related Rights Regulations 2003 came into force on October 31, 2003, shall be regarded as an infringement of any new or extended right created by the Regulations.[96]
The Copyright and Related Rights Regulations 2003 also create a new     **9–049**
provision providing an exemption in respect of performance rights for photographs taken in domestic premises for private and domestic use by inserting a new paragraph 17B into Schedule 2.[96a]

---

[94] Copyright and Related Rights Regulations 2003 (SI 2003/2498), reg.20.
[95] SI 2003/2498, reg.31.
[96] SI 2003/2498, reg.31(2). Commencement: reg.1. For transitional provisions see above at para.9–036.
[96a] SI 2003/2498, reg.20(2).

**"Photographs of Broadcasts**

**17B.**—(1) The making in domestic premises for private and domestic use of a photograph of the whole or any part of an image forming part of a broadcast, or a copy of such a photograph, does not infringe any right conferred by Part 2 in relation to a performance or recording included in the broadcast.

(2) Where a recording which would otherwise be an illicit recording is made in accordance with this paragraph but is subsequently dealt with

(a) it shall be treated as an illicit recording for the purposes of that dealing; and

(b) if that dealing infringes any right conferred by Part 2, it shall be treated as an illicit recording for all subsequent purposes.

(3) In sub-paragraph (2), 'dealt with' means sold or let for hire, offered or exposed for sale or hire or communicated to the public.

(4) Expressions used in this paragraph have the same meaning as in section 71."

**9–050**   This seems to be an internally inconsistent provision. Paragraph 17B(1) refers to the making of a photograph. Paragraph 17B(2) states that where "*a recording* which would otherwise be *an illicit recording* is made in accordance with this paragraph", but in fact the paragraph makes no provision for non-illicit recordings. It only makes provision for *photographs* which are distinct from recordings. For the purposes of Pt 2 of the CDPA 1988 (which concerns performer's rights) "recording" in relation to a performance is defined as:

"a film or sound recording

(a) made directly from the live performance

(b) made from a broadcast of the performance, or

(c) made, directly or indirectly, from another recording of the performance."[97]

Paragraph 17B(4) states that expressions used in para.17B of Sch.2 have the same meaning as in s.71. This does not assist as s.71 does not use the word "recording". The practical effect of this paragraph is unclear. If the intention was to create a provision that results in a photograph of a broadcast of a performance taken in domestic premises for private and domestic use being treated as infringing performer's rights if it is dealt with commercially, it seems doubtful whether this was achieved. This would require "a recording" to mean "a photograph" both of which have distinct statutory definitions.

Presumably the intention is also to render infringing commercial dealing with a video-grab of a performance originally made for private and domestic use. It should be remembered that a still image from a film (as defined under

---

[97] CDPA 1988, s.180.

the Act) is excluded from the definition of photograph.[98] Video-grabs that are still film images electronically captured would not fall within the definition of photographs.

Paragraph 17B of Schedule 2 seems to be directed at preventing commercial dealing with domestically created photographs, video-grabs or recordings that infringe performer's rights. However, the wording of the section is somewhat problematic and the meaning is ambiguous.

---

[98] CDPA 1988, ss.4(2)(b) and 5B. See above at para.2–036.

# Chapter 10

# Passing off

## SCOPE OF THIS CHAPTER

This chapter contains an overview of the law of passing off in outline only **10–001** and deals with specific matters pertaining to photographs and images. For further information as to the law of passing off generally, see Wadlow, *The Law of Passing Off: Unfair Competition By Misrepresentation* (3rd ed., Sweet & Maxwell, 2004) and Drysdale and Silverleaf, *Passing Off* (2nd ed., Butterworths, 1995).

## ELEMENTS OF PASSING OFF

The essential requirements of the tort are a misrepresentation by a trader **10–002** that damages the goodwill of another. The classic and oft quoted formulation is that of Lord Diplock in *Warnink v Townend*[1] where he identified the five elements necessary to establish a cause of action in passing off as:

---

[1] *Erven Warnink BV v J Townend & Sons (Hull) Ltd* [1979] A.C. 731 at 742; [1979] 2 All E.R. 927; [1979] 3 W.L.R. 68; [1980] R.P.C. 31.

"(1) a misrepresentation (2) made by a trader in the course of his trade, (3) to prospective customers of his or ultimate consumers of goods or services supplied by him (4) which is calculated to injure the business or goodwill of another trader (in the sense that this is a reasonably forseeable consequence) and (5) which causes actual damage to a business or goodwill of the trader by whom the action is brought or (in a *quia timet* action) will probably do so."

This is sometimes expressed as the classic trinity of reputation, misrepresentation, and damage.[2]

## GOODWILL AND REPUTATION

**10–003**   The claimant has to establish that he has goodwill in England. Where a foreign business has no reputation or goodwill in England, an action for passing off will fail.[3]

"[Goodwill] is a thing very easy to describe, very difficult to define. It is the benefit and advantage of the good name, reputation and connection of a business. It is the attractive force which brings in custom. It is the one thing which distinguishes an old-established business from a new business at its first start. The goodwill of a business must emanate from a particular centre or source. However, widely extended or diffused its influence may be goodwill is worth noting unless it has power of attraction sufficient to bring customers home to the source from which it emanates."[4]

The purpose of a passing off action is to vindicate the claimant's exclusive right to goodwill and protect it against damage.[5] Normally the reputation in the mark will be the claimant's exclusive property but a claimant can succeed in passing off where the goodwill is shared with others.[6]

## ENTITLEMENT TO SUE

### Meaning of trader

**10–004**   Only a trader can suffer damage to the goodwill of his business. There is no limited judicial definition of "trader" and it is widely interpreted by the

---

[2] *Consorzio del Prosciutto di Parma v Marks & Spencer plc* [1991] R.P.C. 351.
[3] *Anheuser-Busch Inc v Budejovicky Budar NP* [1984] F.S.R. 413.
[4] *Inland Revenue Commissioners v Muller & Co's Margarine Ltd* [1901] A.C. 217, 223.
[5] *Irvine v Talksport Ltd* [2002] EWHC 367, Ch at para.34 *per* Laddie J.; [2002] 1 W.L.R. 2355; [2002] 2 All E.R. 414; [2002] E.M.L.R. 32; [2002] F.S.R. 60. Upheld on issue of liability by CA at [2003] EWCA Civ 423; [2003] 2 All E.R. 881; [2003] E.M.L.R. 26; [2003] F.S.R. 35.
[6] *Bollinger v Costa Brave Wine Co Ltd (No.3)* [1960] Ch. 262; *Chocosuisse Union des Fabricants Suisses de Chocolat v Cadbury Ltd* [1998] R.P.C. 117; [1998] E.T.M.R. 205 (affirmed CA: [1999] E.T.M.R.. 1020; [1999] R.P.C. 826).

courts when assessing who is a trader for the purposes of passing off. It includes those engaged in professional, artistic, and literary occupations[7]; and would certainly include a professional photographer.

Persons and organisations who have been held to be traders and capable of sustaining an action in passing off include authors and journalists[8]; artists[9]; musicians[10]; sportsmen[11]; professional ballroom dancers[12]; the BBC[13]; unincorporated associations[14]; professional associations[15]; proprietary clubs[16]; and charities.[17]

## No necessity for actual trading if sufficient reputation

Where a reputation has been established, goodwill may continue to subsist even after the claimant ceases trading.[18] Claimants have succeeded where a night-club had been closed for five years but there was an intention to re-open on alternative premises,[19] and where a hotel was being rebuilt with no trading for three years.[20] A band trading under the name "Liberty" succeeded in a passing off action notwithstanding a "low profile" for the pre ceding five years and the defendant's contention that it was defunct[21]— although it was described by the court as a borderline case.[22] It was observed that "the impact made by good musicians can last well after they have stopped performing and sometimes after their death".[23]

**10–005**

---

[7] *Kean v McGivan* [1982] F.S.R. 119.
[8] *Clark v Associated Newspapers Ltd* [1998] 1 W.L.R. 1558; [1998] 1 All E.R. 959; [1998] R.P.C. 261; *Forbes v Kemsley Newspapers* (1951) 68 R.P.C. 183; *Sykes v John Fairfax* [1978] F.S.R. 312 (Supreme Ct New South Wales).
[9] *Marengo v Daily Sketch & Sunday Graphic Ltd* [1948] 1 All E.R. 406.
[10] *Hines v Winnick* [1947] Ch. 708; [1947] 2 All E.R. 517; *Fleetwood Mac Promotions Ltd v Clifford Davis Management Ltd* [1975] F.S.R. 150 (pop group); *Sutherland v V2 Music* [2002] EWHC 14, Ch ("funk" band).
[11] *Irvine v Talksport Ltd* [2003] EWCA Civ 423; [2003] 2 All E.R. 881; [2003] E.M.L.R. 26; [2003] F.S.R. 35 (Formula 1 racing driver); *Sale v Barr* 25 C.P.R. (4th) 449 (Alberta) (figure skaters); *Paracidal v Herctum* (1983) 4 I.P.R. 201, Supreme Court of Queensland (Spanish horsemaster, trainer and rider).
[12] *Henderson v Radio Corporation Pty Ltd* [1969] R.P.C. 218; [1960] N.S.W.L.R. 279.
[13] *British Broadcasting Co v Talbot Motor Co Ltd* [1981] F.S.R. 228.
[14] *Toms and Moore v Merchant Service Guild Ltd* (1908) 25 R.P.C. 474 (the Imperial Merchant Service Guild).
[15] *Society of Accountants and Auditors v Goodway* [1907] 1 Ch. 489; *Society of Incorporated Accountants v Vincent* (1954) 71 R.P.C. 325; *BMA v Marsh* (1931) 48 R.P.C. 565; *Institute of Chartered Accountants v Hardwick* (1919) 35 T.L.R. 342.
[16] *Ad-Lib Club v Granville* [1971] 2 All E.R. 300.
[17] *British Legion v British Legion Club (Street) Ltd* (1931) 48 R.P.C. 555; *The British Diabetic Association v The Diabetic Society* [1995] 4 All E.R. 812; [1996] F.S.R. 1.
[18] *Thermawear Ltd v Vedonis Ltd* [1982] R.P.C. 44.
[19] *Ad-Lib Club v Granville* [1971] 2 All E.R. 300.
[20] *Berkeley Hotel Co Ltd v Berkeley International (Mayfair) Ltd* [1971] F.S.R. 300; [1972] R.P.C. 237.
[21] *Sutherland v V2 Music* [2002] EWHC 14, Ch; [2002] E.M.L.R. 28.
[22] *ibid.*, at para.40.
[23] *ibid.*, at para.40.

However, a claimant will only succeed in passing off where he has ceased trading if he has not abandoned the mark.[24] A proprietary right to a mark may be lost through non-use.[25]

Equally, it is also possible to have a sufficient reputation before trading commences acquired through pre-launch publicity.[26] But the claimant's reputation must exist at the time the defendant commences the activities complained of.[27]

### Foreign claimants

**10–005A**   A foreign claimant must be able to establish goodwill in England.[28]

### Importers, distributors and retailers

**10–006**   The owner of goodwill may not be the manufacturer but another party in the distribution chain.

In *MedGen Inv v Passion for Life Products Ltd*[29] the issue was who owned the goodwill in an anti-snoring product—a foreign manufacturer or the UK exclusive distributor. It was held that the goodwill belonged to the distributor as:

  (i)   the manufacturer carried on no business in the UK;

  (ii)  the packaging in which the product was sold carried no reference to the manufacturer;

  (iii) all marketing and sales were carried out by the distributor and references on the packaging and in advertisements were exclusively to the distributor; and

  (iv)  there was no evidence that either retail traders or the public knew the manufacturer was the developer of the product or responsible for its manufacture. It was also held that goodwill was local in character and whilst it was possible for a business based overseas to

---

[24] *Maxims Ltd v Dye* [1977] 1 W.L.R. 1155; [1978] 2 All E.R. 55; [1977] F.S.R. 364; *Star Industrial Co Ltd v Yap Kwee Kor* [1976] F.S.R. 256.
[25] *Norman Kark Publications v Odhams Press* [1962] 1 W.L.R. 380; [1962] 1 All E.R. 636; [1962] R.P.C. 163 (action failed due to seven years non-use of magazine title).
[26] *WH Allen v Brown Watson* [1965] R.P.C. 191; *BBC v Talbot* [1981] F.S.R. 228; *Fletcher Challenge Ltd v Fletcher Challenge Pty Ltd* [1982] F.S.R. (adoption of company name by defendant after merger announced); *My Kinda Bones v Dr Pepper's Stove* [1984] F.S.R. 289 (pre-launch advertising); *Glaxo plc v Glaxowellcome Ltd* [1996] F.S.R. 388 (adoption of company name by defendant day after merger announced); *Pontiac Marina Pte Ltd v CDL Hotels International Ltd* [1998] F.S.R. 839 (Singapore) (pre-launch advertising); but *cf. Maxwell v Hogg* (1867) L.R. 2 Ch. 307 (trading must have commenced before any cause of action).
[27] *Cadbury Schweppes Pty Ltd v Pub Squash Co Pty Ltd* [1981] R.P.C. 429; *Teleworks Ltd v Telework Group Plc* (unrep.) April 27, 2001, Christopher Floyd Q.C. sitting as a deputy High Court Judge; [2002] R.P.C. 27.
[28] *Alain Bernadin et Cie v Pavilion Properties Ltd* [1967] R.P.C. 581; *Anheuser-Busch Inc v Budejovicky Budar NP* [1984] F.S.R. 30.
[29] [2001] F.S.R. 30.

acquire goodwill in the UK by the supply of products through an agent or distributor, whether it did so depended on the facts of the case.

Wadlow observes that for a dealer or importer to succeed, the misrepresentation must be material in that the public attach importance to who has imported or distributed the goods as opposed to manufactured them.[30]

## BADGE OF RECOGNITION: MARK OR GET-UP

The claimant must have some badge of recognition, such as a logo, in which    **10–007** his reputation vests. But it is the claimant's goodwill that is protected by the tort of passing off and not the badge itself.[31] A distinguishing feature/badge of recognition has been found in personal names and nom de plumes[32]; the "get-up" in which goods are packaged[33]; and even the shape of goods packaging.[34]

It is not necessary for the claimant to demonstrate that his business is identifiable by the public by name. What is required is that the trade or the public recognise the claimant's mark as denoting the goods of a particular manufacturer so that a substantial proportion of persons buying under the mark would expect to get his goods.[35]

## PHOTOGRAPH AS A BADGE OF REPUTATION

There is no reason in principle why a photograph or image cannot be a    **10–008** badge of reputation and protected from unauthorised use in passing off. It has been said that:

"...the tort no longer anchored as in its early nineteenth century formulation to the name or trade mark of a product or business. It is wide enough to encompass other descriptive material, such as slogans or *visual images* which radio, television or newspaper advertising campaigns can lead the market to associate with a plaintiff's product, provided always that such descriptive material has become part of the good will of the

---

[30] Wadlow, *op. cit.*, at para.3–131.
[31] *Star Industrial Co Ltd v Yap Kwee Kor* [1976] F.S.R. 256 at 269 (PC); *Payton & Co v Snelling Lampard & Co* (1889) 17 R.P.C. 48, 55 (CA); affirmed [1901] A.C. 308 (HL).
[32] *Landa v Greenberg* (1908) 24 T.L.R. 441 ("Aunt Naomi"); *Hines v Winnick* [1947] Ch. 708 ("Dr Crock and his Crackpots"); *Marengo v Daily Sketch* (1948) 65 R.P.C. 242.
[33] *Sodastream v Thorn Cascade* [1982] R.P.C. 459; *Reckitt & Colman v Borden (No.3)* [1990] R.P.C. 341 (Jif Lemon).
[34] *Edge v Niccolls* [1911] A.C. 693 (laundry blue distinctive packaging with a stick).
[35] *Birmingham Vinegar Brewer Co v Powell* [1897] A.C. 710; *William Edge & Sons Ltd v William Nicols & Sons Ltd* [1911] A.C. 693, 705; *Copydex Ltd v Noso Products Ltd* (1952) 69 R.P.C. 38.

product. And the test is whether the product has derived from the goodwill of the product."[36] (emphasis added)

Unauthorised use of photographs of celebrities has been restrained in passing off.[37]

## HUMAN IMAGE AS A BADGE OF REPUTATION: FALSE ENDORSEMENT

**10–009**   It is now common for celebrities to receive income by the exploitation of their names and images by way of endorsement. The endorsee takes the benefit of the attractive force which is the reputation of the celebrity.[38] Where a defendant uses a photograph of a celebrity to misrepresent that the celebrity has endorsed his product, the celebrity can maintain an action in passing off provided that the elements of the tort are established.[39]

**10–010**   Whether use of the image of a person amounts to a representation that the person has consented to the use of his image, or amounts to use conveying endorsement, is a question of fact and depends on a variety of factors including the content and format of the material and the context in which the image appears.[40] If a person's image is used in such a way as to misrepresent that he has endorsed a product, it is immaterial whether the image is a real photograph or a digitally manipulated photograph.[41] The question is whether the image gives the impression that the person has agreed to be so depicted.[42] Where it is clear there is no endorsement, for example where it is made plain that a model is a look-a-like and not the famous person in question, there is no cause of action in passing off.[43] Accordingly, if it is in issue whether a digitally manipulated image has been so obviously doctored that it does not objectively misrepresent that the person depicted had consented to endorsement, it is advisable to obtain direct evidence to this from

---

[36] *Cadbury Schweppes Pty Ltd v Pub Squash Co Pty Ltd* [1981] R.P.C. 429.

[37] *e.g. Irvine v Talksport Ltd* [2003] EWCA Civ 423; [2003] 2 All E.R. 881; [2003] E.M.L.R. 26; [2003] F.S.R. 35 and cases cited below at paras 10–009 to 10–015.

[38] *Irvine v Talksport Ltd* [2002] EWHC 367 (Ch) at para.39. Upheld on liability by CA at [2003] EWCA Civ 423; [2003] 2 All E.R. 881; [2003] E.M.L.R. 26; [2003] F.S.R. 35.

[39] *Henderson v Radio Corporation Pty Ltd* [1969] R.P.C. 218 (High Court of New South Wales, Appellate Jurisdiction); *Irvine v Talksport Ltd* [2003] EWCA Civ 423; [2003] 2 All E.R. 881; [2003] E.M.L.R. 26; [2003] F.S.R. 35 (CA).

[40] *Honey v Australian Airlines Ltd* (1990) 18 I.P.R. 185 (Federal Court of Australia). Passing off claim by an Olympic long jumper for use of his photograph on a poster, in a magazine and a book failed on the facts. There was no representation that the plaintiff had licenced the use of the image. The images would have been perceived as promotion of sport and not an endorsement of services by the plaintiff.

[41] *Irvine v Talksport Ltd* [2003] EWCA Civ 423 at paras 81–82 *per* Jonathan Parker L.J.; [2003] 2 All E.R. 881; 898 [2003] E.M.L.R. 26; [2003] F.S.R. 35.

[42] *Irvine v Talksport Ltd* [2003] EWCA Civ 423 at para.81 *per* Jonathan Parker L.J.; [2003] 2 All E.R. 881; 898 [2003] E.M.L.R. 26; [2003] F.S.R. 35.

[43] *Newton-John v Scholl-Plough* (1986) 11 F.C.R. 233 (General Division: New South Wales District Registry, Burchett J.). Use of a model who looked similar to the actress Olivia Newton-John in Maybelline makeup advertisement with a caption "Olivia? No, Maybelline". The judge considered that "this advertisement tells even the most casual reader, at even the first glance, that in fact it is not Olivia Newton-John who is represented in the advertisement."

the relevant section of the public targeted.[44] The lack of an express statement that goods are *not* endorsed may not alone be enough to lead members of the public to believe that use of an image is authorised, particularly where the claimant is in the habit of stating that a number of its products are "official".[45] If the image is not recognisable or identifiable as being the claimant, there will be no confusion and an action in passing off will fail.[46]

Passing off merely protects the goodwill that the claimant has in his **10–011** reputation. Thus the famous person's identity indicia (name, voice, image, etc.) would only be protected in as much as they are badges of the goodwill he has in his reputation. A performer who has acquired a reputation under a particular name is entitled to protect that name; a name can become part of an individual's stock-in-trade.[47] It has been noted *obiter* by the Court of Appeal that it is arguable that the voice of an actor is part of his stock-in-trade.[48] A name or voice may be badges of goodwill and a person's image can equally be part of his stock-in-trade.

In *Irvine v Talksport Ltd*, it was said that there was no reason in principle that prevented an action in passing off succeeding in a false endorsement case.[49] In that case, the defendant radio station obtained a photograph of the claimant, a well-known racing driver, holding a mobile telephone. The photograph was digitally manipulated to replace the telephone with a radio bearing the name of the defendant. The defendants used the altered photograph on the front of a brochure sent to prospective advertisers on its radio station. It was said that in order to succeed the claimant had to establish (1) that at the time of the acts complained of he had a significant reputation or goodwill, and (2) that the actions of the defendant gave rise to

---

[44] See observations of Jonathan Parker L.J. at para.79 in *Irvine v Talksport Ltd* [2003] EWCA Civ 423; [2003] 2 All E.R. 881, 897; [2003] E.M.L.R. 26; [2003] F.S.R. 35.

[45] *Halliwell v Panini* (unrep.) June 6, 1997, Lightman J. *Ex parte* (on notice) application for an injunction to restrain distribution of an unauthorised sticker collection of images of the Spice Girls. Injunction refused on the balance of convenience doubting whether the public would consider collection to be authorised by the claimants.

[46] *Athans v Canadian Adventure Camps* (1977) 80 D.L.R. (3d) 583 (Ontario High Court) (Claim in passing off concerning use of drawings based on photographs of waterskier failed. NB: Claim for wrongful appropriation of personality succeeded. *Per* Henry J.: "... it is improbable that the relevant segments of the public who would read the advertisement and the brochure would associate the business of [the defendant] with [the plaintiff] ... There is no evidence that any but the most knowledgeable persons concerned in the sport of waterskiing would identify the drawing with [the plaintiff".); *Joseph v Daniels* (1986) 11 C.P.R. (3d) 544 (British Columbia Supreme Court) (wrongful appropriation of personality claim dismissed. Photograph only showing torso of male body builder did not take advantage of his reputation, likeness or other component which the viewer would identify with him). See also *Paracidal v Herctum Pty Ltd* (1983) 4 I.P.R. 201 (Supreme Court of Queensland) facts below at para.10–015, n.61.

[47] *Hines v Winnick* [1947] Ch. 708; [1947] 2 All E.R. 517; *Fleetwood Mac Promotions Ltd v Clifford Davis Management Ltd* [1975] F.S.R. 150 (pop group); *Sutherland v V2 Music* [2002] EWHC 14 (Ch.) ("funk" band).

[48] *Sim v HJ Heinz Co Ltd* [1959] 1 All E.R. 547 at 549 *per* Hodson L.J. (Application for an injunction regarding advertising commentary involving a "soundalike" actor). In the same case at first instance McNair J. said *obiter* at 551 "it would seem to me to be a grave defect in the law if it were possible for a party for the purposes of commercial gain, to make use of the voice of another party without his consent."

[49] [2002] EWHC 367 (Ch) at para.46 *per* Laddie J. [2002] 1 W.L.R. 2355; [2002] 2 All E.R. 414, [2002] E.M.L.R. 32, [2002] F.S.R. 60. Upheld on liability CA: [2003] EWCA Civ 423; [2003] 2 All E.R. 881; [2003] E.M.L.R. 26; [2003] F.S.R. 35.

a false message which would be understood by a not insignificant section of his market that his goods have been endorsed, recommended, or approved of by the claimant.[50]

**10–012**    At first instance, Laddie J. drew a distinction between product endorsement and character merchandising:

> "When someone endorses a product or service he tells the relevant public that he approves of the product or service or is happy to be associated with it. In effect he adds his name as an encouragement to members of the relevant public to buy or use the service or product. Merchandising is rather different. It involves exploiting images, themes or articles which have become famous. ... A example of merchandising is the sale of memorabilia relating to the late Diana, Princess of Wales. A porcelain plate bearing her image could hardly be thought of as being endorsed by her, but the enhanced sales which be achieved by virtue of the presence of her image is a form of merchandising."[51]

Upholding his decision on liability, Jonathan Parker L.J. giving the judgment of the Court of Appeal observed:

> "I find it difficult to conceive of a clearer way of conveying by way of a quasi-photographic image, the message that a celebrity has endorsed a particular radio station than by depicting the celebrity listening intently to a radio bearing the station's logo."[52]

**10–013**    *Irvine v Talksport*[53] is one of the first UK decisions in which a passing off action succeeded in a false endorsement case. Most earlier claims had failed due to a lack of a common field of activity or no real possibility of confusion,[54] but it was held in *Irvine v Talksport* that there was no requirement for a common field of activity. This extension of the law of passing off is akin to torts in other jurisdictions allowing for an action for wrongful appropriation of personality.[55]

---

[50] [2002] EWHC 367 (Ch) at para.46 see n.49, above.

[51] *Irvine v Talksport Ltd* [2002] EWHC 367 (Ch) at para.9 see above at para.10–011, n.49.

[52] *Irvine v Talksport Ltd* [2003] EWCA Civ 423 at para.82 *per* Jonathan Parker L.J.; [2003] 2 All E.R. 881, 898; [2003] E.M.L.R. 26; [2003] F.S.R. 35.

[53] [2003] EWCA Civ 423; [2003] 2 All E.R. 881; [2003] E.M.L.R. 26; [2003] F.S.R. 35. Upholding decision on liability of Laddie J. [2002] EWHC 367 (Ch); [2002] 1 W.L.R. 2355; [2002] 2 All E.R. 414; [2002] E.M.L.R. 32; [2002] F.S.R. 60.

[54] *McCullough v May* (1948) 65 R.P.C. 58; [1947] 2 All E.R. 845. "Uncle Mac" a children's broadcaster could not restrain the use of the name "Uncle Mac" as a trademark for a puffed wheat cereal as the broadcaster "Uncle Mac" was not in any way involved in producing or marketing puffed wheat; *Lyngstad v Anabas Products Ltd* [1977] F.S.R. 62: Pop group Abba failed to restrain use of their image on badges and transfers for pillowslips. The age of this decision is shown by the comment of Oliver J. at 68 where he said "indeed I do not think [that it] could be alleged on the evidence, that there is any general custom for such licences to be granted by pop singers. Indeed the available evidence is quite to the contrary." Today it is very common for such endorsement licences to be granted by pop singers, sportsmen and other personalities.

[55] Canada: *Sale v Barr* 25 C.P.R. (4th) 449 (Alberta); *Athans v Canadian Adventure Camps* (1977) 80 D.L.R. (3d) 583 (Ontario High Court); *Racine v CJRC Capitale Lee* (1977) 35 C.P.R. (2d) 28; *Krouse v Chrysler Canada Ltd* (1972) 2 O.R. 133; rev'd (1973) O.R. (2d) 225.

A wider interpretation of passing off had been applied in Australia for **10–014** many years. In *Henderson v Radio Corp Pty Ltd*,[56] professional ballroom dancers succeeded in passing off following unauthorised use of their photograph on a record sleeve of ballroom dancing music. The court concluded that the representation that the dancers recommended the record was an inducement to buy it.[57] It was held that wrongful appropriation of another's professional reputation is an injury in itself. The defendant had wrongfully deprived the plaintiffs of their right to withhold or bestow a professional recommendation which was sufficient injury upon which to grant an injunction.[58]

In *Pacific Dunlop v Hogan*,[59] the use of the eponymous character from the film *Crocodile Dundee* in a spoof advertisement was held to amount to a form of passing off. The advertisement parodied a scene from the film and featured a different actor dressed in similar clothes to the character Crocodile Dundee. The Federal Court of Australia held that the plaintiff was entitled to relief as there had been a misrepresentation of some type of association with the plaintiff, not withstanding the suggestion of association was vague. In an earlier case[60] also involving the Crocodile Dundee character, an even broader approach was taken and it was held that in Australia there was a form of passing off which protected characters even where there was no misrepresentation.

An injunction was granted restraining use of an "artist's impression" of a **10–015** photograph of a well-known horse rider to advertise a wildlife park's performing horses.[61] The photograph was of the plaintiff in a distinctive outfit upon his horse which was standing on its rear legs. The plaintiff was also said to be identifiable by his facial appearance as he had a moustache. The defendant used a poster produced by a graphic artist which consisted of a depiction of the plaintiff on his horse. It was said "even if the other matters of detail were to be disregarded entirely [the plaintiff] like most other people is recognisable by his face". It was held that the poster gave an impression that the plaintiff was the person depicted and involved passing off by the defendants of the business of the plaintiff as their own.

## USE OF A PERSON'S IMAGE TO ACCOMPANY AN INTERVIEW

Case law suggests that there is no cause of action in passing off for the non- **10–016** consensual use of a person's photograph to accompany an interview with him or other false suggestion of a consensual interview.[62] It submitted that in the modern climate of celebrity endorsement there is no reason, in principle,

---

[56] [1969] R.P.C. 218.
[57] [1969] R.P.C. 62 at 232 (40) *per* Evatt C.J. (High Court of NSW, Appellate Jurisdiction).
[58] [1969] R.P.C. 62 at 236 (15) *per* Evatt C.J.
[59] (1989) 14 I.P.R. 398; (1989) 87 A.L.R. 14.
[60] *Hogan v Koala Dundee* (1988) 12 I.P.R. 508 (use of a logo of a koala bear dressed like the character).
[61] *Paracidal v Herctum Pty Ltd* (1983) 4 I.P.R. 201 (Supreme Court of Queensland).
[62] *Kaye v Robertson* [1991] F.S.R. 62; *Harrison and Starkey v Polydor Ltd* [1977] F.S.R. 1.

why a misrepresentation that a person has voluntarily consented to an interview or posed for photographs should not sound in passing off provided that the elements of the tort are met. Both cases in support of the proposition that no action can lie in passing off are older authorities and out of step with commercial reality.

In *Kaye v Robertson*[63] a claim in passing off relating to an actor's interest in an interview with him and photographs about his recovery from an accident was rejected. Gordon Kaye, a well-known actor, was recovering from severe head injuries in hospital. A journalist and photographer from a tabloid gained unauthorised access to his room in the hospital, interviewed him and took photographs. The medical evidence was that he was in no fit condition to be interviewed or to give informed consent. The tabloid proposed to publish the story but an injunction was obtained at first instance. On appeal, it was argued that there was a cause of action in passing off. This was rejected by the court. Glidewell L.J. rejected the contention that the elements of *Warnink v Townend (No.1)*[64] were satisfied saying:

> "I think that the plaintiff is not in the position of a trader in relation to his interest in his story about his accident and his recovery, and thus fails from the start to have a right of action under this head".[65]

Bingham L.J. described the claim in passing off as hopeless.[66]

**10–017**    The pop group the Beatles also failed in passing off to prohibit the issuing of an album of taped interviews with them with photographs of the group on the record sleeve.[67] The application for an injunction was dismissed on the basis that there was no possibility of confusion. It was said:

> "the question really must be: Would anybody who is going to buy a record of pop music buy [the interview tapes] under the impression that he is getting something issued by or on behalf of the Beatles? It seems to me quite absurd to think that anything like that would happen. What is provided by the Beatles is quite clear. They are song-writers, they are composers, they are performers; but they do not on their ordinary records—and it has not been suggested that they do—provide anything else. What is here being provided is a certain amount of philosophical and other chat, intersperse with some of their music. That is quite a different production from anything which has been called to my attention as emanating from the Beatles".[68]

**10–018**    It is submitted it should be possible to maintain a successful action for passing off for a misrepresentation of a voluntary interview or voluntary posing for photographs for publication. However, the requirements of the

---

[63] [1991] F.S.R. 62.
[64] [1979] A.C. 731.
[65] [1991] F.S.R. 62, 69.
[66] *ibid.*, at 70.
[67] *Harrison and Starkey v Polydor Ltd* [1977] F.S.R. 1.
[68] *ibid.*, at 4–5 (*per* Walton J.).

*Warnick v Townend*[69] test must be met. As with an action for false endorsement, the claimant would need to establish (1) significant good will, and (2) that the actions of the defendant have given rise to a false message that the publication has been endorsed by the claimant, and (3) this has caused or is likely to cause damage.[70] In the vast majority of cases, the misrepresentation and damage elements will be difficult hurdles to surmount.

Passing off actions of this type will only have any prospect of success if there is a misrepresentation that the person has consented to publication. The media is not shy of proclaiming a non-consensual "scoop" obtained via investigative or surreptitious means.[71] An express misrepresentation that photographs have been posed for voluntarily or an interview granted consensually is, in practice, rare as it is unnecessary. Express words suggesting consent such as "exclusive interview" may amount to sufficient misrepresentation.[72] An implied representation of consent may arise from a suggestion that words were spoken directly to a journalist from the relevant publication giving the impression of a personal interview.[73]

It will be difficult to imply a misrepresentation of consensual association **10–019** with a newspaper or magazine solely from the use of a person's photograph without express words indicating consent of the subject to publication. It is submitted that mere publication of a photograph of a person in a magazine does not alone, without more, imply endorsement of the publication or that the photograph has been specifically posed for that magazine. The public must be taken to be aware that newspapers and magazines commonly use celebrities, names and photographs without making endorsement contracts and there is no prima facie inference of endorsement.[74] Accordingly, it is submitted that in the UK there is no presumption that mere publication of a person's photograph in a particular publication implies endorsement of that publication. To succeed in passing off, there needs to be some implicit representation of approval or consent.

---

[69] [1979] A.C. 731. See above at para.10–002.

[70] *Irvine v Talksport Ltd* [2003] EWCA Civ 423 at para.33 *per* Jonathan Parker L.J. approving comments of Laddie J.; [2003] 2 All E.R. 881; [2003] E.M.L.R. 26; [2003] F.S.R. 35.

[71] *e.g.* Lord Bingham of Cornhill C.J., *Opinion: Should There Be A Law to Protect Rights of Personal Privacy* [1996] E.H.R.L.R. 451 commenting on *Kaye v Robertson* that after a narrow injunction was granted prohibiting publication of an interview without a clear indication that it had been given involuntarily "The newspaper accordingly went ahead and published the interview, boasting of the fact that it had been obtained without Mr Kaye's consent."

[72] *Cf.* USA false advertising/false light cases: *Solano v Playgirl Inc* 292 F.3d 1078 (9th Cir. 2002); *Eastwood v National Enquirer Inc* 123 F.3d 1249 (9th Cir. 1997); *Kournikova v General Media Communications Inc* 67 U.S.P.Q. 2d 1395 (C.D. Cal. Dist. Ct, May 2, 2003) (Headline "Caught close up on nude beach" did not suggest consensual endorsement). See above at para.9–020.

[73] *Eastwood v National Enquirer Inc* 123 F.3d 1249 (9th Cir. 1997). A false suggestion of a willing interview with a tabloid via quotations and headlines could convey a message that an actor was "washed up as movie star if he was courting publicity in a sensationalist tabloid".

[74] See *e.g.* observations of US 9th Cir. in *Abdul-Jabbar v General Motors Corp* 75 F.3d 1391, 1397 (9th Cir. 1996) "Newspapers and magazines commonly use celebrities, names and photographs without making endorsement contracts, so the public does not infer an endorsement agreement from the use."

**10–020**     It is submitted that implied misrepresentation may occur if the use is such that readers may assume that ordinary propriety, decency, or practices would have required the publication to obtain permission of the subject.[75] The classic example of such use would be publication of posed (or apparently posed) nude, semi-nude, or pornographic pictures.[76] If passing off were established, it would be immaterial whether the image is a real photograph or a digitally manipulated photograph.[77] Where a cause of action does arise in passing off for publication of falsely created pornographic images, there will also probably be a cause of action in defamation.[78] There will be no actionable misrepresentation where it is made clear that the subject did not consent to publication of nude or pornographic photographs, such as a clear disclaimer, or where it is apparent that the images were obtained without the co-operation of the subject.[79] Whether a person is depicted in such a way as to suggest endorsement of the publication will be a question of fact in the circumstances of each case.

Proof of damage is also likely to be problematic in an action for passing off concerning endorsement of publication of a photograph and/or an interview. If the publication is in a standard magazine or newspaper, it is doubtful that there would be damage, particularly if the claimant is in the habit of giving interviews. A misrepresentation has to be material to be actionable. Where the public are not influenced by whether or not information or photographs have been published with consent, the representation is not relied on and hence not material.

**10–021**     However, misrepresentations of association with certain periodicals with lesser reputations may affect a person's relationship with advertisers and endorsement deals and amount to damage by injurious association.[80] A false suggestion of a willing interview with a tabloid via quotations and headlines could convey a message that an actor was "washed up as movie star if he was courting publicity in a sensationalist tabloid."[81] If it contended association has damaged the individual's goodwill ideally, evidence of lost sales or endorsement agreements due to the magazine publisher's conduct should be obtained. Harm may be found not only in the form of lost commercial

---

[75] See Australian case concerning unauthorised exploitation of photographs of swimmer under Trade Practices Act 1974: *Talmx Pty Ltd v Telstra Corp Ltd* (1996) 36 I.P.R. 46 (Supreme Ct Queensland CA) citing *Hogan v Pacific Dunlop Ltd* (1988) 12 I.P.R. 225.

[76] Arguably publication of a person's photograph on the cover of a magazine may also be such a use but this would probably require more than just the image. *E.g.* USA case of *Solano v Playgirl Inc* 292 F.3d 1078 (9th Cir. 2002) (actor shown shirtless in swimming trunks under headline "Primetime's Sexy Young Stars Exposed" on cover of Playgirl. Whether this created the false impression he endorsed the magazine and its sexual content was a proper question to be left to the jury).

[77] *Irvine v Talksport Ltd* [2003] EWCA Civ 423 at paras 81–82 *per* Jonathan Parker L.J.; [2003] 2 All E.R. 881; 898; [2003] E.M.L.R. 26; [2003] F.S.R. 35.

[78] See cases cited above at paras 7–128 to 7–131 and para.9–020 (digital manipulation).

[79] *Cf. Kournikova v General Media Communications Inc* 67 U.S.P.Q. 2d 1395 (C.D. Cal. Dist. Ct, May 2, 2003) (use of word "caught" in headline "Caught close up on nude beach" would not lead a reasonable reader to conclude the plaintiff had co-operated with the publication)

[80] *Annabel's (Berkeley Square) Ltd v Schock* [1972] R.P.C. 838; *Harrod's Ltd v R Harrod Ltd* (1924) 41 R.P.C. 74.

[81] *Eastwood v National Enquirer Inc* 123 F.3d 1249 (9th Cir. 1997).

profit, but also in the loss of control over one's image and the loss of control over whom or what that image is associated with.[82]

## IMAGES OF DECEASED PERSONS

Where the famous person has been dead for many years, it appears that an **10–022** action for false endorsement by use of his image will not succeed as there is no possibility of his consenting to the endorsement.[83]

It is submitted that in some circumstances it would be possible to maintain an action for passing off in respect of the image of a deceased celebrity, but such cases are likely to be extremely rare. It is plain that a reputation may survive where trading has ceased,[84] and that reputation may survive death.[85] Where the person has been dead for many years and this is well-known, it would be extremely difficult to misrepresent that there was endorsement in such a way as to mislead the public. However, it is submitted that (1) where the death is recent; (2) there is a reputation at the time of death that survives the death; (3) the misrepresentation is likely to mislead the public by suggesting the endorsement took place whilst the person was alive; and (4) it is likely to damage surviving goodwill in any continuing business of the estate, in principle an action for passing off should be maintainable.

## IMAGES OF FICTIONAL CHARACTERS

Character merchandising, where the name or image or a fictional character **10–023** is used on or in connection with consumer goods, is now a widespread commercial practice. Where there is a misrepresentation by use of a character's image that the goods on which they appear are licensed such that the public will assume the goods originate from the claimant, an action in passing off will lie.[86] The misrepresentation is that the goods are licenced and it is unclear to what extent it can be presumed that the public expect goods to be licenced from an "official" source. In some circumstances, the public may be indifferent to the source.[87]

---

[82] *Sale v Barr* 25 C.P.R. (4th) 449 (Alberta) at para.14 *per* Lee J.
[83] *Irvine v Talksport Ltd* [2002] EWHC 367 (Ch) at para.44; [2002] 1 W.L.R. 2355; [2002] 2 All E.R. 414; [2002] E.M.L.R. 32; [2002] F.S.R. 60. Upheld on liability by the CA at [2003] EWCA Civ 423; [2003] 2 All E.R. 881; [2003] E.M.L.R. 26; [2003] F.S.R. 35.
[84] See cases cited above at para.10–005.
[85] *Sutherland v V2 Music* [2002] EWHC 14 (Ch) at para.40 *per* Laddie J.; [2002] E.M.L.R. 28 "the impact made by good musicians can last well after they have stopped performing and sometimes after their death. Needless to say in the case of international stars this impact is nurtured by re-releases of their recorded music and the like."
[86] *Mirage Studios v Counter Feat Clothing Co Ltd* [1991] F.S.R. 145; *Taverner Rutledge v Trexapalm* [1977] R.P.C. 275; [1975] F.S.R. 479. See further Wadlow, *op. cit.*, at paras 7–112 *et seq.* and Drysdale & Silverleaf, *op. cit.*, at 3.53.
[87] See comments of Laddie J. in *Elvis Presley Trade Marks* [1997] R.P.C. 543 quoted above at para.5–033. Upheld on appeal at [1999] R.P.C. 567.

As indicated by the comments of Laddie J. in *Irvine v Talksport*,[88] the courts draw a distinction in passing off between endorsement by the use of a real person's image and use of images of fictional characters. A real person can exercise choice and judgment in deciding which products to endorse which may be relied on by the public; whereas a licence to merchandisers to use a fictional character does not entail any such judgment and is in reality often granted to the highest bidder. To succeed in passing off regarding character merchandising rights, it appears that it is necessary to establish that the public are aware of the claimant's practice of granting licences and that there is an exercise of quality control such that the licence guarantees quality.[89]

**10–024**   In *Tot Toys Ltd v Mitchell (t/a Stanton Manufacturing)*[90] a decision of the High Court of New Zealand it was said that in order to use passing off to protect character merchandising rights in the image of an inanimate object, it is necessary to establish that:

(1) the claimant has created in the public mind an image of that object which is of value for promotional purposes;

(2) the defendant made promotional use of the image in a way which caused deception, *e.g.* by leading the public falsely to believe that the defendant or his product had some form of association with the claimant or the claimant's product; and

(3) in consequence, the claimant suffered some form of loss beyond mere prejudice to character merchandising potential.

## MISREPRESENTATION

**10–025**   The classic misrepresentation is that the defendant's goods are those of the claimant.[91] But misrepresentation may be found in many other forms such as false endorsement[92]; that second hand goods are new[93] or a false representation that the defendant is an agent of the claimant.[94] It has been said that it is impossible to list all the ways in which a false representation may be made.[95] The defendant's mens rea is irrelevant and proof of fraud or knowledge of the claimant's mark is unnecessary.[96]

---

[88] See above at para.10–012 [2002] EWHC 367 (Ch); [2002] 1 W.L.R. 2355; [2002] 2 All E.R. 414; [2002] E.M.L.R. 32; [2002] F.S.R. 60. Upheld on liability by the CA at [2003] EWCA Civ 423; [2003] 2 All E.R. 881; [2003] E.M.L.R. 26; [2003] F.S.R. 35.
[89] *Mirage Studios v Counter Feat Clothing Co Ltd* [1991] F.S.R. 145; *Taverner Rutledge v Trexapalm* [1977] R.P.C. 275; [1975] F.S.R. 479.
[90] (1992) 25 I.P.R. 337.
[91] *Reddaway v Banham* [1896] A.C. 199 at 204.
[92] See above at paras 10–009 to 10–015.
[93] *Gillette Safety Razor Co v Franks* (1924) 41 R.P.C. 499; *Morris Motors Ltd v Lilley (trading as G &L Motors)* [1959] 1 W.L.R. 1184; [1959] 3 All E.R. 737.
[94] *Wheeler & Wilson Manufacturing Co v Shakespear* (1896) 39 L.J. Ch. 36.
[95] *Spalding (AG) & Bros v AW Gamage* (1915) 32 R.P.C. 273 *per* Lord Parker.
[96] *Spalding (AG) & Bros v AW Gamage* (1915) 32 R.P.C. 273.

Confusion alone without misrepresentation is insufficient.[97] Passing off may be established where there is misrepresentation with no confusion.[98] It is only necessary to show that a majority or substantial proportion of a group of consumers are likely to be deceived and not an entire class.[99]

The misrepresentation must be material in the sense that it is likely to **10–026** influence the consumer. But there is no requirement that the customer has to pay for the goods or services in order for passing off to arise.[1]

Many cases suggest that there is a requirement that the claimant and the defendant are engaged in a common field of activity,[2] but modern case law tends to suggest there is no such requirement.[3] It has been said that although the requirement for a common field has been relaxed, it remains relevant to the question of deception.[4]

## LIKELIHOOD OF DAMAGE

It is necessary to establish that the claimant has suffered or is really likely to **10–027** suffer damage to his property right in his business goodwill.[5] As far as future damage is concerned, there must be a serious risk or a real tangible risk of damage in the future.[6]

Damage occurs where the claimant has inferior goods passed off as his own,[7] or by association with a business of poor repute that is likely to injure the claimant's reputation.[8] Dilution or erosion of the claimant's goodwill by the defendant's use of the mark is sufficient to establish damage.[9] Damage may be found not only in the form of lost commercial profit, but also in the loss of control over one's image and the loss of control over whom or what that image is associated with.[10]

---

[97] *County Sound v Ocean Sound* [1991] F.S.R. 367; *Barnsley Brewery Co Ltd v RBNB* [1997] F.S.R. 462 at 467.

[98] *Bristol Conservatories Ltd v Conservatories Custom Built Ltd* [1989] R.P.C. 455.

[99] *Saville Perfumery Ltd v June Perfect Ltd & FW Woolworth & Co Ltd* (1941) 58 R.P.C. 147 at 176; *Neutrogena Corp v Golden Ltd* [1996] R.P.C. 473.

[1] *OT v Cumming* (1915) 32 R.P.C. 69 (Scotland); *F Hoffman La Roche & Co AG v DDSA Pharmaceuticals Ltd* [1969] F.S.R. 410.

[2] *McCulloch v Lewis A May (Produce Distributors) Ltd* [1947] 2 All E.R. 845; (1947) 5 R.P.C. 58.

[3] *Eastman Photographic Materials Co Ltd v Griffiths (John) Cycle Corp Ltd* (1898) 15 R.P.C. 105 (cameras and bicycles); *BBC v Talbot Motor Co* [1981] F.S.R. 228 (services and goods); *News Group Newspapers v Rocket Record Co* [1981] F.S.R. 89 (the Sun newspaper mark "Page 3" and pop records); *Lego Systems v Lego M Lemelstrich* [1983] F.S.R. 155 (toy bricks and garden sprinklers); *Irvine v Talksport Ltd* [2002] EWHC 367 (Ch) at para.38 discussed above at para.10–011 (sportsman and radio programme endorsement).

[4] *Nice and Safe Attitude Ltd v Piers Flook (t/a Slaam! Clothing Co)* [1997] F.S.R. 14.

[5] *Erven Warnink BV v J Townend & Sons (Hull) Ltd* [1979] A.C. 731 at 742; [1979] 2 All E.R. 927; [1979] 3 W.L.R. 68; [1980] R.P.C. 31.

[6] *British Legion v British Legion Club (Street) Ltd* (1931) 48 R.P.C. 555 at 563 *per* Farwell J.

[7] *Bollinger v Costa Brava Wine Co Ltd* [1960] Ch. 262; [1960] R.P.C. 16.

[8] *Annabel's (Berkeley Square) v Schock* [1972] R.P.C. 838 (nightclub suing escort agency using same name); *Sony v Saray* [1983] F.S.R. 302 (defendants having reputation for unpleasant manner of trading).

[9] *Tattinger SA v Allbev* [1993] F.S.R. 641 at 670, 676, 678.

[10] *Sale v Barr* 25 C.P.R. (4th) 449 (Alberta) at para.14 *per* Lee J.

In false endorsement cases, it has been said that damages for a loss of revenue arising from a lost opportunity to endorse another product is too remote.[11]

## DEFENCES

**10–028**   Defences to a claim in passing off may be found in showing:

    (a)  one or more of the essential elements of the cause of action have not been established by the claimant *e.g.*:

        (i)  mark is not distinctive of the claimant;

        (ii)  mark has not been used as a trade mark to distinguish goods[12];

        (iii)  lack of reputation;

        (iv)  no misrepresentation—for example use of mark for purposes of comparative advertising[13];

    (b)  misrepresentation by the claimant that his mark is a registered trademark[14];

    (c)  bona fide use of the defendant's own name[15];

    (d)  a concurrent/shared reputation,[16] or an earlier pre-existing reputation[17];

    (e)  delay or acquiescence;

    (f)  the claim is contrary to EEC laws concerning competition and free movement of goods[18];

    (g)  expiry of the limitation period.[18a]

---

[11] *Henderson v Radio Corporation Pty Ltd* [1969] R.P.C. 218 at 244 *per* Manning J. It was argued that because the plaintiffs' image had been used on the defendant's record, the plaintiffs were less likely to be invited to sponsor an alternative record and would lose income as a result.

[12] *Cellular Clothing Co v Maxton and Murray* [1899] A.C. 326; *Unidoor v Marks and Spencer* [1988] R.P.C. 275.

[13] *Ciba-Geigy v Parke Davis* [1994] F.S.R. 8.

[14] Success in passing off depends on reputation. A misrepresentation that a mark is registered allows a claimant to establish a reputation in the mark on the back of an unwarranted claim to a monopoly in that mark. The claimant should not be allowed to rely on a reputation acquired fraudulently. See *Intercontex v Schmidt* [1988] F.S.R. 575. It is a criminal offence to represent that a mark is registered when it is not: s.95, Trade Marks Act 1994.

[15] *Pinet (F) & Cie v Maison Louis Pinet Ltd* [1898] 1 Ch. 179; *Rodgers v Rodgers* (1924) 41 R.P.C. 277.

[16] *Macmillan v Ehrman Bros* (1904) 21 R.P.C. 647; *Everest v Camm* (1950) 67 R.P.C. 200; *Whitstable Oyster Fishery Co v Hayling Fisheries Ltd* (1900) 17 R.P.C. 461 (CA (1901) R.P.C. 434); *Southorn v Reyonolds* (1865) 12 L.T. 75; *General Electric Co v General Electric Co Ltd* [1972] 2 All E.R. 507.

[17] *Payton v Titus Ward* (1899) 17 R.P.C. 58.

[18] See *Wadlow, op. cit.*; at paras 9–21 *et seq.*

[18a] Six years: Limitation Act 1980, s.6. Note that the limitation period for malicious falsehood is one year from the date the cause of action accrued: Limitation Act 1980, s.4A.

It is possible that use of the mark as satire or parody may amount to a defence but the ambit of such a defence remains unclear.[19]

## REMEDIES

The remedies available for passing off are:

**10–029**

(1) Damages—quantified as damages that naturally flow from the unlawful act of the defendants.[20] Normally, this will be damage to goodwill and loss of sales, both of which are difficult to quantify. In cases involving passing off by false endorsement, if the celebrity charges a standard fee for the type of endorsement concerned, that is likely to be the measure of loss. In other cases, the court will approach the assessment of damages by attempting to assess the reasonable endorsement fee which would be entered into between a willing endorser and a willing endorsee.[21] Such a fee is that which on a balance of probabilities the defendant would have had to pay in order to obtain lawfully that which it in fact obtained unlawfully.[22] The court will take into account evidence of the endorsement deals the claimant has in fact entered into.[23] In *Irvine v Talksport Ltd*[24] the Court of Appeal relying on evidence of the level of the claimant's existing endorsement agreements increased the award of damages from £2,000 to £25,000 in respect of a distribution to an audience of less than 1,000 where there was no representation of endorsement made to the general public.

(2) An interim and final injunction. The fact that the claimant has granted licences to others does not preclude the grant of an interim injunction and does not necessarily indicate (via a willingness to accept royalty payments) that damages would be an adequate remedy.[25];

(3) A declaration.[26]

---

[19] *Miss World v James St. Production* [1981] F.S.R. 309 (film titled "The Alternative Miss World—no confusion); *Pacific Dunlop v Hogan* (1989) 14 IPR 398; (1989) 87 A.L.R. 14 (parody used in advertisement did amount to passing off).
[20] *Spalding (AG) & Bros v AW Gamage* (1915) 32 R.P.C. 273.
[21] *Irvine v Talksport Ltd* (CA) [2003] EWCA Civ 423 at para.106; [2003] 2 All E.R. 881; 903, [2003] E.M.L.R. 26; [2003] F.S.R. 35.
[22] *ibid.*
[23] *ibid.*, at para.111.
[24] *ibid.*
[25] *British Broadcasting Corporation v Celebrity Centre Productions Ltd* (1988) 15 I.P.R. 333 (ChD), Falconer J.
[26] *Treasure Cot Co Ltd v Hamley Bros Ltd* (1950) 67 R.P.C. 89; *Wayne V Myers & Co Ltd v LE Fields Auto Services Ltd* (1954) 71 R.P.C. 435.

(4) An account of profits. A successful claimant is entitled to elect an account of profits instead of an inquiry to damages,[27] but an account remains an equitable remedy which the court may refuse.[28]

(5) an order for delivery up or destruction.[29]

**10–030**   Interim remedies available are those usually available for infringement of a property right and include interim injunctions, search orders, and freezing injunctions.

Where actions for passing off are issued in the High Court they should be in the Chancery Division.[30]

---

[27] *Weingarten Bros v Bayer & Co* [1904–7] All E.R. 877; (1905) 22 R.P.C. 341 at 351.
[28] *McDonald's Hamburgers Ltd v Burgerking (UK) Ltd* [1987] F.S.R. 112 at 122; *Van Zeller v Mason Catley & Co* (1907) 25 R.P.C. 37.
[29] *Cf. Lissen Ltd v Mutton* (1929) 46 R.P.C. 10 (order for delivery up refused in passing off action); *Baume v Moore (No.1)* [1958] Ch. 907; [1958] 2 W.L.R. 797; [1958] 2 All E.R. 113; [1958] R.P.C. 226 (whether order for delivery up available in passing off left open).
[30] *McCain International v Country Fair Foods Ltd* [1981] R.P.C. 69.

# Chapter 11

# Data protection

## SCOPE OF THIS CHAPTER

**11–001**   This chapter contains an outline of the law of Data Protection as set out in the Data Protection Act 1998. It includes, for example, a full list of the exemptions for the sake of completeness, even where there is no relevance to photography. Specific issues concerning photography receive more detailed consideration.

As with the other chapters in this book, it is not, nor is it intended to, provide a complete commentary on the law of Data Protection. For more detailed treatment, the reader is referred to *Data Protection Law and Practice* by Rosemary Jay and Angus Hamilton (2nd ed., Sweet & Maxwell, 2003) and the *Encyclopaedia of Data Protection*, S. Charlton, S. Gaskill, *et al.* (eds) (Sweet & Maxwell).

## BACKGROUND

**11–002**   In 1972 the Younger Committee on Privacy[1] made specific recommendations for the use of computers which manipulated personal data, but its recommendations were not adopted. The Lindop Committee which was set up to consider data protection specifically, rather than the wider privacy, reported in 1978.[2] It recommended the creation of a Data Protection Authority and Codes of Practices, but again these recommendations were not adopted.

The first UK Act to deal with Data Protection was the Data Protection Act 1984. The current governing statute is the Data Protection Act 1998 which received Royal Assent on July 16, 1998. The majority of its provisions came into force on March 1, 2000.[3] The Act was the UK implementation of the European Data Protection Directive[4] which was intended to harmonise the data protection laws of the European Union. The directive stated its objective as protection of "the fundamental rights and freedoms of natural persons, and in particular their right to privacy with respect to processing of personal data".[5]

## GENERAL

**11–003**   The Act applies to personal data with special provision being made for "sensitive personal data". The first principle provides that personal data shall be processed fairly and lawfully and only provided that specified conditions are met. In the case of all data, one of the conditions in Sch.2

---

[1] (1972) Cmnd. 5012.
[2] (1978) Cmnd. 7341.
[3] Data Protection Act 1998 (Commencement) Order 2000 (SI 2000/183).
[4] 95/46.
[5] *ibid.*, Art.1.

must be met. In the case of sensitive personal data, one of the conditions in Sch.3 must also be met.

The Act should, if possible, be interpreted in a way that is consistent with the directive.[6]

## Freedom of Information Act 2000

The Freedom of Information Act 2000, when it comes fully into force, will apply to information held by public authorities. Organisations that are classed as public authorities are specified in the Act and include not just government departments but a wide range bodies, including maintained schools and certain NHS health care providers.[7] The Act will make certain amendments to the Data Protection Act 1998.    **11–004**

The Freedom of Information Act 2000 imposes obligations on public authorities to publish certain information under publication schemes. It also introduces an obligation on public authorities to provide information in response to requests. The latter is achieved both by extension of the definition of data to include "recorded information held by a public authority"[8] which results in the application of the s.7 subject access rights under the Data Protection Act 1998 to such data, and also by the introduction of a new third party access right under the Freedom of Information Act 2000[9] itself. These new access provisions are not scheduled to come into force until 2005. Some reference has been made in the text to the proposed changes where applicable but otherwise the Freedom of Information Act 2000 is not considered in this chapter.[10]

## PRELIMINARY DEFINITIONS

## Data

"Data" is defined by s.1 of the 1998 Act as information which:    **11–005**

(a)  is being processed by means of equipment operating automatically in response to instructions given for that purpose;

(b)  is recorded with the intention that it should be processed by means of such equipment;

---

[6] *Campbell v MGN Ltd* [2002] EWCA Civ 1373 at para.96; [2003] Q.B. 633 at 669 *per* Lord Phillips M.R.
[7] Freedom of Information Act 2000, Sch.1.
[8] Freedom of Information Act 2000, s.68(1), (2)(a) to come into force on November 30, 2005, unless other order made.
[9] Freedom of Information Act 2000, s.1.
[10] See further J. MacDonald *et al.*, *The Law of Freedom of Information* (Oxford University Press) and P. Birkenshaw, *Freedom of Information The Law the Practice and The Ideal* (3rd ed., Butterworths, 2001).

(c) is recorded as part of a relevant filing system or with the intention that it should form part of a relevant filing system;

(d) does not fall within paras (a) (b) or (c), but forms part of an accessible record.

This definition will be extended in 2005 by the Freedom of Information Act 2000 to include recorded information held by a public authority that does not fall within any of paras (a)–(d).[11] Information is a wide term and includes photographs and images.[12]

*Processing*

**11–006**    Processing is further defined as meaning:

"in relation to information or data, means obtaining, recording or holding the information or data or carrying out any operation or set of operations on the information or data, including—

(a) organisation, adaptation or alteration of the information or data,
(b) retrieval, consultation or use of the information or data,
(c) disclosure of the information or data by transmission, dissemination or otherwise making available, or
(d) alignment, combination, blocking, erasure or destruction of the information or data."[13]

**11–007**    As with many of the definitions under the Act, the definition of processing is very wide. The definition of processing is so wide that it embraces the relatively ephemeral operations that will normally be carried out by way of the day to day tasks, involving the use of electronic equipment such as the laptop and the modern printing press in translating information into the printed newspaper.[14] Electronic storage of images on a computer would fall within the definition of processing as it amounts to holding data. Any databases of images that are searchable are also included. Digital manipulation of images would fall within "adaption or alteration of the infor-

---

[11] By the Freedom of Information Act 2000, s.68.
[12] *Douglas v Hello (No.6)* [2003] EWHC 786; [2003] 3 All E.R. 996; [2003] E.M.L.R. 31; *Campbell v Mirror Group Newspapers Ltd* [2002] EWCA Civ 1373; [2003] Q.B. 633; [2003] 2 W.L.R. 80; [2003] 1 All E.R. 224; [2003] E.M.L.R. 2; reversing [2002] EWHC 499; [2002] E.M.L.R. 30. At first instance it was held that photographs with captions were capable of being "sensitive personal data". The fact that the photographs were "data" *per se* within the meaning of the Act was not challenged on appeal. This case is the subject of an appeal to the House of Lords to be heard in February 2004. And *cf. Handyside Films (Production) Ltd v Express Newspaper Ltd* [1986] F.S.R. 463 (Contempt of Court Act 1981; disclosure of sources), rejecting an argument that photographs were not "information".
[13] Data Protection Act 1998, s.1.
[14] *Campbell v MGN Ltd* [2002] EWCA Civ 1373 at para.122; [2003] Q.B. 633 at 674 *per* Lord Phillips M.R.

mation or data." This will probably include processing of images by pixelation or otherwise to render them anonymous.[15]

"Processing by equipment operating automatically" includes transmitting images via an ISDN line; correcting defects in images; transmitting electronic images to a printer; and in the processes used in the course of preparation for and in the course of printing.[16] Publication of images in a hard copy form that have previously been processed automatically is a processing operation and falls within the scope of the Act.[17]

## Manual and analogue data

Manual and analogue data will fall within the provisions of the Act if it has been recorded as part of a relevant filing system or with the intention that it should form part of a relevant filing system. Certain exemptions were provided in respect of manual data, but for the most part these expired on October 24, 2001. Some limited exemptions remain until October 27, 2007, but broadly they only apply to manual data that was already subject to processing that was underway immediately before October 24, 1998.[18]

**11–008**

Analogue photographs and images that are stored in a manner that amounts to a relevant filing system will be covered by the Act. The meaning of "relevant filing system" is discussed below. It would include, for example, a picture library storing transparencies in a manual filing system structured in a sufficiently sophisticated way by reference to individuals that allows specific information about the individual concerned to be obtained. Thus a filing system storing images of politicians under the name of a particular politician, sub-indexed into images of him at work, at home, etc. would be included. Any system merely storing analogue images under the names of the people depicted in a way that then requires further manual lengthy searching through many images would probably not class as a relevant filing system.

## Relevant filing system

Exactly what is meant by "a relevant filing system" is ambiguous and has been the subject of debate. In December 2003, the meaning was clarified by the Court of Appeal in *Durant v Financial Services Authority*[19] which is discussed below at para.11–011. The Act defines it as follows:

**11–009**

"relevant filing system" means any set of information relating to individuals to the extent that, although the information is not processed by means of equipment operating automatically in response to instructions

---

[15] As to anonymising data see below at para.11–168.

[16] *Douglas v Hello (No.6)* [2003] EWHC 786 at para.231 *per* Lindsay J.; [2003] 3 All E.R. 996; [2003] E.M.L.R. 31.

[17] *Douglas v Hello (No.6)* [2003] EWHC 786; [2003] 3 All E.R. 996; [2003] E.M.L.R. 31. *Campbell v Mirror Group Newspapers Ltd* [2002] EWCA Civ 1373 at paras 96–105; [2003] Q.B. 633 at 669–671; [2003] 2 W.L.R. 80; [2003] 1 All E.R. 224; [2003] E.M.L.R. 2.

[18] See below at para.11–177. Detailed consideration of the transitional provisions is outside the scope of this work and the consideration below is in outline only.

[19] [2003] EWCA Civ 1746.

given for that purpose, the set is structured, either by reference to individuals or by reference to criteria relating to individuals, in such a way that specific information relating to a particular individual is readily accessible.[20]

This covers manual filing systems that are *structured*. The directive offers little assistance as it defines a "personal data filing system" as meaning:

"any structured set of personal data which are accessible according to specific criteria, whether centralized, decentralized or dispersed on a functional or geographical basis"[21]

**11–010**     Two Recitals offer further limitations. Recital 15 provides that the process of data is covered by this directive "*only* if it is automated or if the data processed are contained or are intended to be contained in a filing system *structured according to specific criteria relating to individuals, so as to permit easy access to the personal data in question.*" (emphasis added). Recital 27 provides:

"Whereas the protection of individuals must apply as much to automatic processing of data as to *manual processing*; whereas the scope of this protection must not in effect depend on the techniques used, otherwise this would create a serious risk of circumvention; whereas, nonetheless, *as regards manual processing, this Directive covers only filing systems, not unstructured files*; whereas, in particular, the content of a filing system *must be structured according to specific criteria relating to individuals allowing easy access to the personal data*; whereas, in line with the definition in Article 2 (c), the different criteria for determining the constituents of a structured set of personal data, and the different criteria governing access to such a set, may be laid down by each Member State; *whereas files or sets of files as well as their cover pages, which are not structured according to specific criteria, shall under no circumstances fall within the scope of this Directive.*" (emphasis added).

**11–011**     The meaning of "relevant filing system" was considered by the Court of Appeal in *Durant v Financial Services Authority*.[22] The claimant, Mr Durant, had been a customer of Barclays Bank. The Financial Services Authority (the FSA) had investigated a complaint by him against Barclays Bank. The claimant thereafter sought subject access to four categories manual files held by the FSA. These consisted of:

(1)    a two volume file relating to systems and controls which Barclays Bank was required to maintain arranged in date order which con-

---

[20] Data Protection Act 1998, s.1.
[21] 95/46, Art.2(c).
[22] [2003] EWCA Civ 1746.

tained a few documents relating to part of the claimant's claim
against the bank;

(2) a complainants file relating to complaints made to the FSA by customers of Barclays Bank that was sub-divided by complaint's name
(organised alphabetically) with documents therein relating to a particular complainant filed in date order;

(3) a file relating to issues concerning Barclays Bank but not necessarily
identified by reference to an individual complainant. It did contain a
sub-file marked "Mr Durant" not indexed in any further way; and

(4) a sheaf of papers in an unmarked transparent folder held by the
FSA's Company Secretariat concerning the claimant's complaint
about the FSA's refusal to disclose details of the outcome of the
investigation of his complaint against the bank. It was not organised
by date or any other criteria. None of these files were held to be a
relevant filing system.

The Court observed that in order to constitute a relevant filing system, a
manual filing system must: (1) relate to individuals; (2) be a "set" or part of
a "set" of information; (c) be structured by reference to individuals or
criteria relating to individuals; and (d) be structured in such a way that
specific information relating to a particular individual is readily accessible.[23]
It was held that "a relevant filing system" is limited to a system:

(1) in which the files forming part of it are structured or referenced in
such a way as to clearly indicate at the outset of the search whether
specific information capable of amounting to personal data of an
individual requesting it under section 7 is held within the system and,
if so, in which files or files, it is held;[24] and

(2) which has, as part of its owns structure or referencing mechanism, a
sufficiently sophisticated and detailed means of readily indicating
whether and where in an individual file or files specific criteria or
information about the applicant can be readily located.[25]

Only manual filing systems that are sufficiently sophisticated in indexing
structure in a way that allows ready access to the information in a manner
broadly equivalent to a computerised system are included.[26] The indexing
needs to be such as to allow identification of the file in which the data is
located at the outset with reasonable certainty and speed and to enable
location of the information about the individual concerned with that file
without having to make a manual search.[27] Accordingly, a file of a collection
of images of a particular person simply with their name on the front that

---

[23] *Durant v Financial Services Authority* [2003] EWCA Civ 1746 at [46], *per* Auld L.J.
[24] *Durant v Financial Services Authority* [2003] EWCA Civ 1746 at [50], *per* Auld L.J.
[25] *ibid.*
[26] *Durant v Financial Services Authority* [2003] EWCA Civ 1746 at [47] and [50].
[27] *Durant v Financial Services Authority* [2003] EWCA Civ 1746 at [48].

requires a large number of images to be leafed through may not be included, even where they are filed in date order.[28]

Unstructured files are excluded[29] so a single card file containing a large number of photographs of one or more persons in no particular order would not fall within the definition. If the single card file is divided into sections where the images are indexed separately, by date and by depicted subject matter, this may fall within the section.[30] The more the filing system allows for "easy access" to particular pieces of data (*i.e.* the more structured and indexed it is) the more likely it would be held to be a "relevant filing system". An image library system for storing hard copy transparencies of images of people indexed by the name of the person depicted and arranged in sub-sections concerning work, home, attendance at a particular function, performance in a particular production etc would probably fall within the definition of relevant filing system.

## Accessible record

**11–012**     An accessible record[31] is:

(a) A health record[32] which consists of information relating to the physical or mental health or condition of an individual AND has been made by or on behalf of a health professional[33] in connection with the care of that individual.

(b) An education record,[34] namely any record of information (excluding information which is processed by a teacher solely for the teacher's own use[35]) which:

(i) is processed by or on behalf of the governing body of, or a teacher at any school maintained by a local education authority

---

[28] *Durant v Financial Services Authority* [2003] EWCA Civ 1746 at [48]to [49], *per* Auld L.J.
[29] See Recital 27 above at para.11–010.
[30] *Durant v Financial Services Authority* [2003] EWCA Civ 1746 at [48] to [49], *per* Auld L.J.
[31] Data Protection Act 1998, s.68.
[32] "Health record" as defined by s.68(2).
[33] "Health Professional" is defined by s.69(1) and includes (in all cases registered) medical practitioners; dentists; opticians; pharmaceutical chemists; nurses, midwives or health visitors; osteopaths; chiropractor; any person who is registered as a member of a profession to which the Professions Supplementary to Medicine Act 1960 for the time being extends; a clinical psychologist, child psychotherapist or speech therapist; a music therapist employed by a health service body and a scientist employed by such a body as a head of department. "Health Service Body" is defined in s.69(3) and includes, *inter alia*, a Health Authority established under the National Health Service Act 1977, s.8 and National Health Service Trust established under the National Health Service and Community Care Act 1990, s.5. "Registered medical practitioner" includes any person provisionally registered under the Medical Act 1983, ss.15 or 21 and engaged in such employment as mentioned in subs.(3) of that section. (*i.e.* employed in a resident medical capacity in one or more approved hospitals, approved institutions or approved medical practices).
[34] "Educational record" as defined by the Data Protection Act 1998, Sch.11.
[35] Sch.11, para.2.

or special school as defined by s.6(2) of the Education Act 1996 which is not so maintained,[36]

(ii) relates to any person who is or has been a pupil at the school[37]; and

(iii) originated from or was supplied by either an employee of the LEA which maintains the school; or a pupil to whom the record relates; or a parent[38] of that pupil; or in the case of a voluntary aided foundation or foundation special school or a non-LEA-maintained special school, a teacher or other employee at the school including an educational psychologist engaged by the governing body under a contract of services.[39]

(c) An accessible public record which in England and Wales means the following specified records held by the stated authorities[40]:

Housing Act local authority—information held for the purpose of any of the authorities tenancies.
Local social services authority—information held for any purpose of the authorities social services functions.

## Data controller

The Act places obligations on the "data controller". This is defined as "a person who (either alone or jointly or in common with other persons) determines the purposes for which and the manner in which any personal data are, or are to be, processed."[41]   **11–013**

Where personal data are processed only for purposes for which they are required by or under any enactment to be processed, the person on whom the obligation to process the data is imposed by or under that enactment is for the purposes of this Act the data controller.[42]

## Data subject

The Act grants certain rights to the data subject. The data subject is defined as "an individual who is the subject of personal data".[43] This requires consideration of what amounts to personal data which is dealt with in the next paragraph. A person who appears in a photograph from which they can be identified will be a data subject.   **11–014**

---

[36] Sch.11, paras 2(a) and 3.
[37] Sch.11, para.2(b).
[38] As defined by the Education Act 1996, s.576(1).
[39] Data Protection Act 1998, Sch.11, para.4.
[40] Sch.12, paras 1–3.
[41] Data Protection Act 1998, s.1.
[42] Data Protection Act 1998, s.1(4).
[43] Data Protection Act 1998, s.1.

## Personal data

**11–015**   Personal data is defined in s.1(1) of the Data Protection Act 1998 as meaning "data which relate to a living individual who can be identified:

(a) from those data; or

(b) from those data and other information which is in the possession of, or is likely to come into the possession of the data controller

and includes any expression of opinion about the individual and any indication of the intentions of the data controller or any other person in respect of the individual."[44] As s.1(1) makes clear, the Act only applies to living individuals, and once a person has died the Act is of no application.[45]

The above definition derives from Art.2(a) of the directive which provides:

" 'Personal data' shall mean any information relating to an identified or identifiable natural person ('data subject'); an identifiable person is one who can be identified, directly or indirectly, in particular by reference to an identification number or to one or more factors specific to his physical, physiological, mental, economic, cultural or social identity."

**11–016**   The directive differentiates between (1) an identified person, and (2) an identifiable person. Recital 26 of the Directive also assists in interpretation of this distinction as it provides:

"Whereas the principles of protection must apply to any information concerning an identified or identifiable person; whereas, to determine whether a person is identifiable, account should be taken of all the means likely reasonably to be used either by the controller or by any other person to identify the said person; whereas the principles of protection shall not apply to data rendered anonymous in such a way that the data subject is no longer identifiable . . ."

Mere mention of a data subject's name in a document held by a data controller does not necessarily amount to his personal data.[46] Whether it does so in any particular instance depends upon where it falls in a continuum of relevance or proximity to the data subject.[47] The information should have the data subject as its focus rather than some other transaction or event in which he may have figured.[48] The information also needs to be

---

[44] Data Protection Act 1998, s.1(1).
[45] *cf* Freedom of Information (Scotland) Act 2002, s.38 which extends an exemption to the medical records of a deceased person.
[46] *Durant v Financial Services Authority* [2003] EWCA Civ 1746 at [28], *per* Auld L.J.
[47] *ibid.*
[48] *Durant v Financial Services Authority* [2003] EWCA Civ 1746 at [28], *per* Auld L.J. Such as an investigation into a third party's conduct which the data subject has merely instigated.

biographical in a significant sense, that is going beyond the recording of the data subjects involvement in an event that has no personal connotations, a life event in respect of which his privacy could not be said to be compromised.[49] It covers information that affects his privacy, whether in his personal or family life, business or professional capacity.[50]

The definition of personal data potentially has a very broad scope and includes photographs of an identified or identifiable person.[51] Precisely what is meant by "identifiable" and the degree of information which is necessary for a person to be identifiable within the meaning of the Act is unclear.

## Photographs as personal data

Photographs and images of people are capable of being personal data.[52] Images of people are information which relate to an individual and from which an individual can be identified.[53] Some types of images of people are plainly classed as personal data. If the photograph or image is stored in any way identifying the person shown by name or otherwise directly linked to the name of the person shown will be personal data. Accordingly, digital images, whether still or moving (or analogue photographs in a relevant filing system), stored under the name of the person are classed as personal data. As long as the image and the name of the person depicted are linked or are capable of being linked, then the person shown can be identified and the image is classed as personal data.

**11–017**

Photographs of celebrities held by an image library or a newspaper are personal data because the data (the image) is of an identified person. Equally, photographs of students held by a college or school are personal data again because the images are of identified persons. Model portfolios held by model agencies containing photographs of models they represent would amount to personal data. The question of whether personal data includes "anonymous" images that show enough of a person's face for that person to be identified but where the specific name or identity of the person is unknown to the data controller is more problematic and discussed below.

If the image of the person can be cross-matched with other information enabling identification which is in the possession of, or is likely to come into the possession of the data controller, the image is personal data. It is

**11–018**

[49] *Durant v Financial Services Authority* [2003] EWCA Civ 1746 at [28], *per* Auld L.J.
[50] *ibid.*
[51] *Douglas v Hello (No.6)* [2003] EWHC 786; [2003] 3 All E.R. 996; [2003] E.M.L.R. 31; *Campbell v Mirror Group Newspapers Ltd* [2002] EWCA Civ 1373; [2003] Q.B. 633; [2003] 2 W.L.R. 80; [2003] 1 All E.R. 224; [2003] E.M.L.R. 2; reversing [2002] EWHC 499; [2002] E.M.L.R. 30 *per* Morland J. At first instance it was held that photographs with captions were capable of being "sensitive personal data".
[52] *Douglas v Hello (No.6)* [2003] EWHC 786; [2003] 3 All E.R. 996; [2003] E.M.L.R. 31; *Campbell v Mirror Group Newspapers Ltd* [2002] EWCA Civ 1373; [2003] Q.B. 633; [2003] 2 W.L.R. 80; [2003] 1 All E.R. 224; [2003] E.M.L.R. 2; reversing [2002] EWHC 499; [2002] E.M.L.R. 30.
[53] *Douglas v Hello (No.6)* [2003] EWHC 786; [2003] 3 All E.R. 996; [2003] E.M.L.R. 31; *Campbell v Mirror Group Newspapers Ltd* [2002] EWCA Civ 1373; [2003] Q.B. 633; [2003] 2 W.L.R. 80; [2003] 1 All E.R. 224; [2003] E.M.L.R. 2; reversing [2002] EWHC 499; [2002] E.M.L.R. 30.

possible for photographs or images of people that do not *per se* reveal sufficient information to enable them to be identified (*e.g.* images taken from a distance not showing facial detail) to nevertheless fall within the definition of personal data if the individual shown can be identified from other information in the possession of, or likely to come into the possession of, the data controller. CCTV footage may be capable of being cross-matched with identifying information about individuals. CCTV cameras in shops and banks that film persons entering the premises may be able to cross-reference the time of credit card or banking transactions. Film footage of crowds in a sports stadia may be able to be cross-referenced with records about who had purchased tickets for particular seats.

**11–019**     Photographs or images of a person from behind or otherwise not showing their face may amount to personal data. Such images may reveal information enabling the subject to be identified because of distinguishing physical features such as a distinctive tattoo or the combination of physical appearance in conjunction with location, or other information revealed in the image. This would be a question of fact. If indistinct images or images not showing someone's face are captioned or stored in a manner where they are labelled as being images of particular individuals, then taken together it amounts to data from which an individual can be identified.

The definition of "data" also includes the situation where an individual can be identified from data together with information likely to come into the possession of the data controller. The Information Commissioner's Guidance in relation to this category gives the following example:

> Another way in which information may come into the possession of a data controller is in relation to an image captured on CCTV. This might produce an image which is not of a distinguishable individual, but the actual identity of that individual may become apparent from other information likely to come into the possession of the data controller.

Personal data also includes all data that *relate* to a living individual who can be identified from the data. It is not therefore limited to photographs of people. Potentially, it would include photographs of, for example, a person's home in conjunction with information identifying who lives in the property.

**11–020**     Examples of images that may fall within the definition of personal data include:

- a digital photograph of John Smith stored under an identifying file name—smith.jpg, johnsmith.jpg, jsmith.jpg, john.jpg, js.jpg;

- a digital photograph of John Smith stored under a random numerical file name which when opened shows his image and a caption "John Smith";

- a digital photograph of John Smith, the director of Company X, stored under a random numerical file name which when opened shows his image and a caption "the director of Company X.";

- a digital photograph of John Smith taken by a health club stored on computer as part of John Smith's records;

- an analogue transparency of a person stored in a card mount with name of the person written on to the card mount;

- a digital photograph of a schoolgirl Jane Brown taken as part of a series of individual portrait photographs of a school class photographed in alphabetical order which whilst not stored under her name or with a caption can be cross matched with the class register to reveal her identity. By cross matching the second person photographed with the second name on the class register of those photographed, she can be identified;

- a CCTV image of a person taking money out of a cashpoint that can be cross matched by date and time with the account name and number that the withdrawal was made from;

- an x-ray labelled with the name of the person x-rayed.

### Photographs and the meaning of "can be identified"

The phrase "can be identified from those data" causes difficulty in the **11–021** case of images of people. The problem is whether "can be identified from those data" means "can be actually identified as a named or otherwise specified person" or whether it means "theoretically capable of identification." A photograph or image of a person that clearly shows sufficient parts of their face to enable them to be recognised and hence identified (hereafter an "ID Image") is information from which that person *can* be identified. Facial information alone can be sufficient to enable a person to be identified. It is a classic means of identification of criminal suspects via the publicising of photo-fit images or CCTV footage. On a literal reading of the statute, ID Images are information from which a person can be identified. However, on its own an image of an anonymous person without the name is just that. The fact that the person depicted can theoretically be identified by persons known to him may not be enough to make it information from which a person "can be identified" within the personal data definition. If "can be identified" is taken to mean "theoretically can be identified" then all ID Images class as personal data. In this section, the term "Abstract Identification" is used to refer to hypothetically possible identification from a human image that is essentially anonymous to the data controller but would permit identification by recognition by those who knew the person depicted.

Conversely "can be identified" may require identification as a specified **11–022** person. If so, only images that were able to be matched with a name (or other information to link the image to a specified person) by the data controller would be included (hereafter referred to as Specific Identification). This would include ID Images that were stored under names—for example databases of student photographs held by schools or university, or images of celebrities held by media organisations. It would also include ID

Images that could be cross-matched with other data such as CCTV footage from a cashpoint which by time could be matched up with the account accessed by the person. However, it would exclude totally anonymous photographs of people in public places and images where no information to link the image to a specified person was or was likely to come into possession of the data controller.

There are some matters in the directive, the Act, and the Information Commissioner's Legal Guidance that support the Specific Identification interpretation, and some matters that support the Abstract Identification interpretation.

**11–023**   The Office of the Information Commissioner has published legal guidance to assist in interpretation of the Act in a document entitled *Data Protection Act 1998—Legal Guidance*.[54] In support of a definition of personal data including Abstract Identification, the Guidance states that an individual may be "identified" even where his or her name or address is not necessarily known.[55] However, the Guidance goes on to give the following example:

**11–030**       "The capture of an image of an individual by a CCTV camera may be done in such a way that distinguishable features of that individual are processed and identified from the captured images. However, in order to be able to identify that individual it will be necessary to match the image to a photograh, a physical description, or a physical person. If this can be done the CCTV footage will be personal data."[56]

The Commissioner's view is that "it is sufficient if the data are capable of being processed to enable the controller to distinguish the data subject from any other individual".[57] The guidance goes on to states "One element to be taken into account would be whether a data controller can form a connection between the data and the individual."[58] These latter observations generally tend to support an interpretation of personal data requiring Specific Identification or the possibility of Specific Identification.

**11–024**   Whether the definition of personal data only includes Specific Identification or whether it also includes Abstract Identification, is an important question, particularly for photographers taking photographs of strangers in public places. Do photographs of anonymous people class as personal data? If a photographer takes a photograph of a stranger in the street whose identity he does not know, does not take steps to ascertain, and is not likely to come into possession of information enabling identification, does that class as personal data? In other words, does a photograph of a person alone without more information, amount to data from which a person can be

---

[54] Available on the Information Commissioner's website at *http://www.dataprotection.gov.uk*.
[55] *Office of the Information Commissioner Data Protection Act 1998 Legal Guidance* at para.2.2.3.
[56] *Office of the Information Commissioner Data Protection Act 1998 Legal Guidance* at para.2.2.3, p.12.
[57] *Office of the Information Commissioner Data Protection Act 1998 Legal Guidance* at para.2.2.3, p.11.
[58] *Office of the Information Commissioner Data Protection Act 1998 Legal Guidance* at para.2.2.1, p.11.

identified within the meaning of the Act? It is submitted that such an image should not class as data under the Act and that the Specific Identification interpretation is to be preferred.[59]

It is certainly arguable that, taking the natural and ordinary meaning of the words of the section, the definition of personal data in the Act should be interpreted as meaning Abstract Identification.[60] *Any* photograph that records a person's face sufficient for him to be recognized amounts to data from which a person can be identified. If the image is clear enough to show a person's face to a degree allowing identification, then that person is capable of identification from the image alone, even if the data controller does not know or is likely to come into possession of the subject's name. A person's face is the paradigm example of a single piece of information which enables a particular individual to be identified. Other standard data such as a name or an address taken alone do not necessarily allow for such precise identification. For example, there may be many people who share the same name.

On such a construction, all photographs or images containing enough **11–025** information to enable the subject to be recognised would amount to personal data. It is immaterial whether the photograph is of one person alone, or a group of people, provided that those individuals pictured are identifiable. Support for this construction may be found in the directive. The directive definition of an identifiable person as "one who *can* be identified, *directly or indirectly*, in particular by reference to an identification number or *to one or more factors specific to his physical*, physiological, mental, economic, cultural or social identity"(emphasis added) would include a bare photograph or image from which a person is recognisable irrespective of whether in fact that image is matched to a physical description.

The Commissioner's Guidance gives a further example which tends to **11–026** support the Abstract Identification interpretation:

"If the information about a particular web user is built up over a period of time, perhaps through the use of tracking technology, with the intention that it may later be linked to a name and address, that information is personal data. Information may be compiled about a particular web user, but there might not be any intention of linking it to a name and address or e-mail address. There might merely be an intention to target that particular user with advertising, or to offer discounts when they re-visit a particular web site, on the basis of the profile built up, without any ability to locate that user in the physical world. The Commissioner takes the view that such information is, nevertheless, personal data. In the context of the on-line world the information that identifies an individual is that which uniquely locates him in that world, by distinguishing him from others."[61]

---

[59] See below at paras 11–031 to 11–033.
[60] As defined above at para.11–021.
[61] *Office of the Information Commissioner Data Protection Act 1998 Legal Guidance* at para.2.2.3, p.12.

If mere anonymous association with a computer is enough to amount to information enabling a person to be identified for the purposes of the Act, then an ID Image should also be sufficient. As the authors of *Data Protection Law and Practice* observe: "The issue is a simple one; while several people can share a computer they cannot share a face".[62] It is of course the case that there are people who look alike and mistaken identification from images is possible. But, in reality, it remains the case that Abstract Identification is possible from an ID Image of a person alone.

11–027   The CCTV Code of Practice suggests the Information Commissioner takes the view that any image from which an image can be identifiable is "personal" data as the glossary states:

> "The definition of personal data is not therefore limited to circumstances where a data controller can attribute a name to a particular image. If images of distinguishable individuals' features are processed and an individual can be identified from these images they will amount to personal data."[63]

If it is the case that any photograph showing enough of a person's face to make them identifiable is personal data, then this has far reaching consequences, perhaps beyond that which the Act was intended. Photographs of groups of people in public places would amount to personal data in respect of each person whose face was visible and identifiable.

11–028   A similar issue was considered by the Hong Kong Court of Appeal in *Eastweek Publisher Ltd v Privacy Commissioner for Personal Data.*[64] The complainant was a woman who had been photographed without her knowledge or consent by a photographer working for a magazine using a long range lens. After taking the picture, the photographer attempted to reach her to seek her consent for use, but because of crowded conditions, he failed to reach her. The photograph was published as part of an article on fashion sense of Hong Kong women but contained unflattering comments about the complainant's fashion sense. The Privacy Commissioner held that the requirement to collect personal data by means which "are fair in the circumstances of the case" had been contravened. He considered that whilst it was not *per se* unfair to have failed to seek prior consent because of a desire to capture the complainant in a natural pose, it was unfair to have taken her picture without her knowledge using a long lens. The magazine sought judicial review of the Commissioner's decision.

11–029   The application for judicial review was dismissed but the judge expressed doubts as to whether the photograph amounted to data about the complainant. The magazine then appealed to the Court of Appeal of Hong Kong. The definitions of "data" and "personal data" under the Hong Kong Personal Data (Privacy) Ordinance of 1996 are not that dissimilar to those

---

[62] R. Jay and A. Hamilton, *Data Protection Law and Practice* (2nd ed., Sweet & Maxwell, 2003) at p.82.
[63] *CCTV Code of Practice*, Pt II, 1. Definitions, p.20. See Appendix 5, below.
[64] [2000] 2 H.K.L.R.D. 83; [2000] 1 H.K.C. 692.

in the Data Protection Act 1998.[65] The Ordinance was also based on the provisions of the directive as is the UK Act. The Court of Appeal held by a majority of 2–1 that whilst a photograph was capable of being personal data, the Ordinance was directed at data users who were compiling information about a person already identified or whom the data user intended to identify. Taking a photograph of an anonymous subject did not fall with the Ordinance. Ribeiro J.A. said:

> "It is, in my view, of the essence of the required act of personal data collection that the data user must thereby be compiling information about an identified person or about a person whom the data user intends or seeks to identify. The data collected must be an item of personal information attaching to the identified subject, as the above-mentioned definitions of 'personal data' and 'data subject' suggest. This is missing in the present case. What is crucial here is the complainant's anonymity and the irrelevance of her identity so far as the photographer, the reporter and Eastweek were concerned. Indeed, they remained completely indifferent to and ignorant of her identity right up to and after publication of the offending issue of the magazine. She would have remained anonymous to Eastweek if she had not lodged a complaint and made her identity known. In my view, to take her photograph in such circumstances did not constitute an act of personal data collection relating to the complainant."[66]

In support of this interpretation the court referred to other aspects of the statute which could only operate on the basis that the data collected related to a subject whose identity was known to the data user, including an individual's right to request information held about him by a data user; requirements to inform the data subject of proposed use; requirements to obtain consent of the data user. It was held that the fact that a photograph, when published, was capable of conveying the identity of the subject to a reader who happened to be acquainted with that person did not make the act of taking the photograph an act of data collection if the photographer and his principals acted without knowing or being at all interested in ascertaining the identity of the person being photographed. A distinction was made between "informational privacy" which was protected, and a general right to personal privacy which was not. One of the curious consequences of this conclusion is that under the law of Hong Kong, a photographer is potentially in a better position if he does not approach or seek to obtain the name or identity of the anonymous subject.

**11–030**

---

[65] Personal Data (Privacy) Ordinance (Cap.486): "Data" means "any representation of information ... in any document". "Personal data" means "any data.
  (a) relating directly or indirectly to a living individual;
  (b) from which it is practicable for the identity of the individual to be directly or indirectly ascertained; and
  (c) in a form in which access to or processing of the data is practicable."
A copy of the full text of the Ordinance can be obtained via the website of the Office of the Privacy Commissioner for Personal Data, Hong Kong at *http://www.pco.org.hk/*.
[66] [2000] 2 H.K.L.R.D. 83 at 90–91 *per* Ribeiro J.

The approach of the Hong Kong Court of Appeal is equally applicable to the Data Protection Act 1998. If it is considered that personal data only includes Specific Identification, an anonymous photograph of a person taken in *Eastweek* circumstances where there is no prospect that the subject be identified does not fall within the meaning of "personal data". It is submitted that the second limb of the definition of personal data in the Data Protection Act 1998 tends against inclusion of Abstract Identification. The second limb provides that personal data is:

> "data which relate to a living individual who can be identified ... from those data and other information which is in the possession of, *or is likely to come into the possession of* the data controller"[67] (emphasis added).

This reference to identification data *together with* other information likely to come into possession of the data controller suggests that the directive is aimed at Specific Identification. It suggests identification of the nature that allows the data controller to connect the data with a specific person. A photographer taking a picture of a stranger in the street and thereafter processing the image, cannot as data controller identify the person. Equally, he is not likely to have information coming into his possession that would enable him to identify that person.

**11–031**     It is submitted that the directive and the Act are directed at informational privacy and not intended to create an absolute right of privacy that attaches to any image of an unnamed person who happens to be captured on camera or film in public.[68] This is supported by the Commissioner's view expressed in the Legal Guidance that it is sufficient if the data are capable of being processed by the data controller to enable the data controller to distinguish the data subject from any other individual. This would be the case if a data subject could be treated differently from other individuals.[69] Further, the UK Court of Appeal in *Durant v Financial Services Authority*[70] held that, in order to amount to "personal data" within the meaning of the 1998 Act, the information revealed needed to be significant in a biographical sense that went beyond mere recording of a life event that did not compromise the subject's privacy. Accordingly, it is submitted that "personal data" should be construed as requiring Specific Identification (including possible Specific Identification by information likely to come into the data controller's possession) and not as Abstract Identification.

**11–032**     As with the Hong Kong Ordinance, the 1998 Act has many provisions that are predicated on the basis that the data controller is able to identify a specific person and is able to make a connection between the data and an

---

[67] Data Protection Act 1998, s.1(1).
[68] This is also supported by dicta in *Durant v Financial Services Authority* [2003] EWCA Civ 1746 at [28] where it was said that personal data was "information that affects [the subject's] privacy, whether in his personal or family life, business or professional capacity."
[69] Office of the Information Commissioner Data Protection Act 1998 Legal Guidance at para.2.2.3, p.13.
[70] [2003] EWCA Civ 1746.

individual. The rights of the data subject include a right to be informed whether personal data of which he is the subject is being processed by the data controller.[71] If the data controller has an image of a person whose identity he does not know, he will not be able to connect the two. Obviously, the person seeking information could supply the data controller with his photograph, but it is only that very act that allows the data controller in these circumstances to actually identify the data subject as a specific person. There are other examples of provisions that indicates that the Act is directed at protecting specific individuals and is concerned with Specific Identification.[72] Further, all ID Images that are personal data are inevitably sensitive data because they disclose information as to ethnic or racial origin. If "personal data" is construed as meaning Abstract Identification, this has a potentially severe impact on the freedom to take and otherwise process photographs of people in public places.[73]

Further, the directive does not apply to anonymised data.[74] The exclusion of anonymised data again suggests that the directive does not create an absolute privacy right, but is aimed at the informational privacy of an identified person. Although a photograph of a person whose identity is not known nor is likely to be known to the data controller is not equivalent to anonymised data, by analogy because it does not permit or anticipate Specific Identification, such a photograph should fall outside the Act.

It is submitted therefore that a photograph of a person taken in the street in *Eastweek* type circumstances where the identity of the person is unknown and not likely to become known should, as the Hong Kong Court of Appeal held, be excluded from data protection. This interpretation would not exclude CCTV images as the purpose of CCTV footage is security and its aim is to be able to record and identify those committing criminal activity. It is therefore data where it is reasonably likely that information may come into the possession of the data controller allowing Specific Identification as that is the ultimate aim of the filming. Equally, such an interpretation would not give carte blanche to publish all reportage photographs of people taken in public or quasi-public places if publication would in some way infringe their right to a private and family life under Art.8.[75]

This question is not the subject of direct authority in the United Kingdom

**11–033**

---

[71] Data Protection Act 1998, s.7(1).

[72] *e.g.* Right to prevent automated decision taking (s.12); right to be informed of logic of automated decision taking for the purpose of evaluating matters relating to an individual (s.7(1)(d); research exception only applies if "data is not processed to support measures or decisions with respect to particular individuals" (s.33(1)(a)).

[73] See comments below at para.11–051.

[74] Directive 95/46, Recital 26 "... whereas the principles of protection shall not apply to data rendered anonymous in such a way that the data subject is no longer identifiable". *R. v Department of Health Ex p. Source Informatics Ltd (No.1)* [2001] Q.B. 424; [2000] 2 W.L.R. 940; [2000] 1 All E.R. 786; [2001] F.S.R. 8.

[75] As to breach of confidence, privacy and Art.8, see Ch.7, above.

at the present time.[76] It is of course possible that if it fell to be considered that the UK courts may take a different view from the Hong Kong Court of Appeals and hold that "personal data" does include Abstract Identification material. Until such time as there is a definitive decision, the safest course to be adopted by those processing images of people would be to proceed on the basis that Abstract Identification is included with the 1998 Act and seek consent for use from those persons depicted in the image.[77] In any case involving this type of problem, the s.32 exception (journalism, artistic, and literary purposes) may be of application and should be considered.[78]

## THE DATA PROTECTION PRINCIPLES

**11–034**   Every data controller is under a duty to comply with the eight Data Protection principles which are set out in Sch.1 to the 1998 Act.[79] The eight principles are:

---

1. Personal data shall be processed fairly and lawfully and in particular shall not be processed unless:

   (a) at least one of the conditions in Sch.2 is met; and
   (b) in the case of sensitive personal data, at least one of the conditions in Sch.3 is also met.

2. Personal data shall be obtained only for one or more specified and lawful purposes, and shall not be further processed in any manner incompatible with that purpose or those purposes.

3. Personal data shall be adequate, relevant and not excessive in relation to the purpose or purposes for which they are processed.

4. Personal data shall be accurate and, where necessary, kept up to date.

5. Personal data processed for any purpose or purposes shall not be kept for longer than is necessary for that purpose or those purposes.

---

[76] In December 2003, the UK Court of Appeal in *Durant v Financial Services Authority* [2003] EWCA Civ 1746 held that, in order to amount to "personal data" within the meaning of the 1998 Act, the information revealed needed to be significant in a biographical sense that went beyond mere recording of a life event that did not compromise the subject's privacy, but this case did not concern the issue of what is meant by "can be identified" in relation to photographic images. There also remains the question as to what extent photographs taken of a person in a public place without their consent can amount to infringement of privacy: as to which see above at paras 7–055 to 7–061.

[77] See Practical Guidance below at paras 11–182 *et seq.*

[78] See below at paras 11–141 *et seq.*

[79] s.4(4).

6. Personal data shall be processed in accordance with the rights of data subjects under the Data Protection Act 1998.

7. Appropriate technical and organisational measures shall be taken against unauthorised or unlawful processing of personal data and against accidental loss or destruction of, or damage to, personal data.

8. Personal data shall not be transferred to a country or territory outside the European Economic Area unless that country or territory ensures an adequate level of protection for the rights and freedoms of data subjects in relation to the processing of personal data.

### First Principle: Fair and lawful processing

Personal data shall be processed fairly and lawfully and in particular shall not be processed unless: **11–035**

(a) at least one of the conditions in Sch.2 is met; and

(b) in the case of sensitive personal data, at least one of the conditions in Sch.3 is also met.

#### *Lawfully*

Both lawfulness and fairness are objective standards.[80] "Lawfully" certainly requires compliance with statutory provisions, both those of the Data Protection Act and other statutes and the common law. In a case decided under the 1984 Act, the Registrar's views that *unlawful* included *ultra vires* acts or those in breach of confidence were upheld by the Data Protection Tribunal.[81] **11–036**

#### *Fairly*

Provisions for the interpretation of "processed fairly" are set out in Pt II of Sch.1 to the Data Protection Act 1998. Unfair processing occurs when a person from whom data is obtained is not informed of the purpose for which that data is being obtained.[82] In determining whether personal data is processed fairly, regard is to be had to the method by which the data is obtained, including whether the person from whom the data is obtained is **11–037**

---

[80] Under the previous statute, the Data Protection Registrar stated "Standards of fairness and lawfulness must be objectively assessed and applied." *The Guidelines*, 3rd series, November 1994 at p.59.
[81] *British Gas Trading Ltd v Data Protection Registrar*, March 1998; [1997–98] Info. T.L.R. 393, Data Protection Tr.
[82] *Innovations (Mail Order) Ltd v Data Protection Registrar* (DA9231/49/1) September 1993 (1984 Act)—failure by mail order company to inform customers of the possibility of their details used as part of a traded mailing list was unfair.

deceived or misled as to the purpose or purposes for which they are to be processed.[83] It is submitted that consideration of whether processing is "fair" will also entail consideration of any relevant professional guidelines or relevant codes.[84]

Surreptitiously obtained images, whether taken via long lense photography, covert surveillance or in breach of an implied obligation of confidence, will almost certainly be treated as unfair processing.[85] A covert photograph is not fairly obtained because the subject has not been given an opportunity to refuse to be photographed.[86]

**11–038**  Data is treated as being obtained fairly if it is obtained from a person who is authorised by an enactment to supply it or is required to supply it by an enactment.[87]

Personal data is not to be treated as having been processed fairly unless, when information is obtained from the data subject, the data controller ensures so far as is reasonably practicable that the data subject has been provided with the following information[88]:

(a) the identity of the data controller;

(b) the identity of any representative of the data controller;

(c) the purpose or purposes for which the data is intended to be processed; and

(d) any further information which is necessary having regard to the specific circumstances in which the data are to be processed.

The right to receive this information is given a special status in that (subject to the exemption provisions in the Data Protection Act 1998), the provisions are to have effect notwithstanding any enactment or rule of law that prohibits or restricts the disclosure or authorises the withholding of information.[89]

**11–039**  Where the information is not obtained from the data subject, in order for the processing to be fair, the data controller must ensure, so far as is practicable, that before the first processing of the data or first disclosure to a

---

[83] Data Protection Act 1998, Sch.1, Pt II, para.1(1).

[84] Not just the s.32 designated codes, but any other Guidance which the data controller should have taken into consideration. Some examples are the CCTV Code of Practice, the NUJ Code of Practice, and the Statement by International Committee of Medical Journal Editors (see below at para.11–185) but there will be others.

[85] *Douglas v Hello (No.6)* [2003] EWHC 786 at para.236; [2003] 3 All E.R. 996; [2003] E.M.L.R. 31; *Campell v MGN Ltd* [2002] EWCA Civ 1373; [2003] Q.B. 633; [2003] 2 W.L.R. 80; [2003] 1 All E.R. 224; [2003] E.M.L.R. 2, CA. And see Morland J.'s observations below [2002] EWHC 499 at paras 108–111; [2002] E.M.L.R. 30 at 645.

[86] *Campell v MGN Ltd* [2002] EWCA Civ 1373 at paras 87–88; [2003] Q.B. 633, 667; [2003] 2 W.L.R. 80; [2003] 1 All E.R. 224; [2003] E.M.L.R. 2.

[87] Sch.1, Pt II, para.1(2)—including any Convention or other instrument imposing an international obligation on the UK.

[88] Sch.1, Pt II, paras 2(1) and 2(3).

[89] Data Protection Act 1998, s.27(5).

third party that the data subject has or has made readily available to him the information listed above.[90] This does not apply where (1) the provision of that information would involve a disproportionate effect, nor where (2) the recording of the data is necessary for compliance by the data controller with legal obligations (other than contractual obligations)[91] provided that certain additional conditions are met.[92] To rely on the exemption, the data controller must not have received notice in writing from the data subject requesting the information.[93] Further, if it is contended that the provision of the information would involve disproportionate effect, the data controller must record his reasons for this conclusion.[94]

Finally, the interpretation provisions in Sch.1 also state that personal data containing "a general identifier" (such as a number or code used for identification purposes) falling with descriptions to be prescribed by the Secretary of State are not to be treated as processed fairly and lawfully unless they are processed in compliance with any conditions so prescribed.[95] There are not as yet any regulations made relating to "general identifiers".

The Human Rights Act 1998 provides that Acts of Parliament must be read and given effect in a way which is compatible with the Convention rights so far as it is possible to do so.[96] The meaning of "fairly" should therefore be interpreted in a way that is compatible with Art.8 (right to a private and family life). The right of freedom of expression in Art.10 may justify an "unfair" processing that is in breach of Art.8. But in considering whether the processing is "fair", the court will need to have regard to Art.8 at the outset. In this regard it should be remembered that the objective of the directive as set out in Art.1 reads: **11–040**

"In accordance with this Directive, Member States shall protect the fundamental rights and freedoms of natural persons, and *in particular their right to privacy* with respect to the processing of personal data." (emphasis added)

### First Principle Conditions: Legitimate processing

It is a mandatory requirement of the first principle that data shall not be processed, that at least one condition in Sch.2 must be satisfied. **11–041**

---

[90] Sch.1, Pt II, para.2(1)(b). Also para.2(2) defining "relevant time" by which data subject must have have the information either provided or made readily available.

[91] Sch.1, Pt II, para.(3).

[92] Data Protection (Conditions under Paragraph 3 of Part II of Schedule 1) Order 2000 (SI 2000/185).

[93] Data Protection (Conditions under Paragraph 3 of Part II of Schedule 1) Order 2000 (SI 2000/185), arts 3 and 4.

[94] Data Protection (Conditions under Paragraph 3 of Part II of Schedule 1) Order 2000 (SI 2000/185), arts 3 and 5.

[95] Data Protection Act 1998, Sch.1, Pt II, para.2(4).

[96] Human Rights Act 1998, s.3(1).

---

**Schedule 2 Conditions: Mandatory that at least one is met**

1. The data subject has given his consent to the processing.

2. The processing is necessary:

   (a) for the performance of a contract to which the data subject is a party; or

   (b) for the taking of steps at the request of the data subject with a view to entering into a contract.

3. The processing is necessary for compliance with any legal obligations to which the data controller is subject, other than an obligation imposed by contract.

4. The processing is necessary in order to protect the vital interests of the data subject.

5. The processing is necessary:

   (a) for the administration of justice;

   (b) for the exercise of any functions conferred on any person by or under any enactment;

   (c) for the exercise of any functions of the Crown, a Minister of the Crown or a government department; or

   (d) for the exercise of any other functions of a public nature exercised in the public interest by any person.

6. The processing is necessary for the purpose of legitimate interests pursued by the data controller or by the third party or parties to whom the data are disclosed, except where the processing is unwarranted in any particular case by reason of prejudice to the rights and freedoms or legitimate interests of the data subject.

---

**Condition 1: Consent of subject**

**11–042**      *The data subject has given his consent to the processing.*

"Consent" in the first condition of Sch.2 is to be distinguished from the "explicit consent" of the data subject which is required for processing of sensitive personal data.[97] The requirement for "consent" presumably includes implied consent, being in contrast with explicit consent. In the context of photography, a person who poses for photographs by arrangement may be taken to have given implied consent even where no model release form or explicit consent is given.

However, the directive by contrast states that personal data may only be processed if the data subject has unambiguously given his consent.[98] This

---

[97] Data Protection Act 1998, Sch.3, para.1.
[98] 95/46, Art.7(1).

would include a subject knowingly and obviously posing for photographs (*e.g.* turning up to a photo shoot in studio), but would exclude photographs taken of a person in a public place without prior arrangement. Even if the person was aware they were being photographed and acted in such a way as to suggest consent (for example looking towards the camera and smiling), this is unlikely to amount to be "unambiguous" consent. This is supported by the directive's definition of consent as meaning "any freely given specific and informed indication of his wishes by which the data subject signifies his agreement to personal data relating to him being processed."[99]

The consent must be given for the actual processing. A data controller **11–043** who obtains consent for one purpose will fall outside this condition if he processes it for another purpose. Thus where consent, express or implied, is given by a person to use their photograph for a particular purpose, use for another purpose would be contrary to the first condition. Also excluded from any implied consent would be use which the subject could not be taken to expect. For example, the release of CCTV footage of a man in a public street in a state of some distress late at night to the broadcast media (which resulted in the moment being viewed to an extent which far exceeded any exposure to a passer by or security observation) was not use which could have been foreseen by that man.[1]

### Condition 2: Performance of contracts/taking of steps at the request of the subject with a view to entering contracts

*The processing is necessary:* **11–044**

*(a) for the performance of a contract to which the data subject is a party; or*

*(b) for the taking of steps at the request of the data subject with a view to entering into a contract.*

The processing has to be "necessary" to comply with either part of this condition. Necessary is not further defined by the Act. The Information Commissioner's Guidance suggests that the question of whether something is "necessary" should take into account an objective assessment of whether (1) the purposes for which the data are being processed are valid; (2) such purposes can only be achieved by the processing of personal data; and (3) the processing is proportionate to the aim pursued.[2]

### Condition 3: Compliance with legal obligations (not contractual)

*The processing is necessary for compliance with any legal obligations to* **11–045** *which the data controller is subject, other than an obligation imposed by contract.*

---

[99] 95/46, Art.2(h).
[1] *Peck v United Kingdom* (2003) 36 E.H.R.R. 41 at 738–739, para.62.
[2] *Office of the Information Commissioner Data Protection Act 1998 Legal Guidance* at para.3.1.6, p.30.

As with the preceding condition, in order to fall within the third condition, the processing must be *necessary* for compliance with any legal obligations to which the data controller is subject, other than an obligation imposed by contract. This would include statutory obligations.

### Condition 4: Vital interests of the subject

**11–046**    *The processing is necessary in order to protect the vital interests of the data subject.*

This condition is satisfied where the processing is *necessary* in order to protect the vital interests of the data subject. The Information Commissioner's Guidance states that reliance on this condition may only be claimed where the processing is necessary for matters of life and death, for example, the disclosure of a data subject's medical history to a hospital casualty department treating the data subject after a serious road accident.[3] This is only the interpretation of the Information Commissioner and it is possible that a court might construe "vital interests" more widely.

### Condition 5: Necessary for interests of justice/public functions

**11–047**    *The processing is necessary:*

   *(a) for the administration of justice;*

   *(b) for the exercise of any functions conferred on any person by or under any enactment;*

   *(c) for the exercise of any functions of the Crown, a Minister of the Crown or a government department; or*

   *(d) for the exercise of any other functions of a public nature exercised in the public interest by any person.*

Again the word "necessary" is used.[4] This condition is aimed at public authorities and bodies or persons carrying out functions of a public nature. Although condition 5(d) is widely framed, it does not extend to the media. The commercial publication of newspapers does not amount to the exercise of a function of a public nature within condition 5(d).[5]

### Condition 6: Data controller's legitimate interests

**11–048**    *The processing is necessary for the purpose of legitimate interests pursued by the data controller or by the third party or parties to whom the data are disclosed, except where the processing is unwarranted in any particular case by*

---

[3] *Office of the Information Commissioner Data Protection Act 1998 Legal Guidance* at para.3.1.1, p.20.
[4] As to the meaning of necessary see above at para.11–044.
[5] *Campbell v MGN Ltd* [2002] EWHC 499 at para.115 *per* Morland J. [2002] E.M.L.R. 30 at 646. The Court of Appeal agreed with this view, see [2002] EWCA Civ 1373 at paras 87–88; [2003] Q.B. 633, 667–668; [2003] 2 W.L.R. 80; [2003] 1 All E.R. 224; [2003] E.M.L.R. 2.

*reason of prejudice to the rights and freedoms or legitimate interests of the data subject.*

Condition 6 allows processing where it is necessary for the purpose of legitimate interests pursued by the data controller or by the third party or parties to whom the data are disclosed, except where the processing is unwarranted in any particular case by reason of prejudice to the rights and freedoms or legitimate interests of the data subject.

The Information Commissioner takes a wide view of the legitimate interests condition and recommends that two tests be applied to establish whether this condition may be appropriate in any particular case.[6] First the legitimacy of the interests pursued by the data controller or the third party to whom the data are to be disclosed must be established. Secondly, it must be considered whether the processing is unwarranted in any particular case by reason of prejudice to the rights and freedoms or legitimate interests of the data subject whose interests override those of the data controller. The Commissioner considers that the fact that the processing of the personal data may prejudice a particular data subject does not necessarily render the whole processing operation prejudicial to all the data subjects.

## Sensitive personal data

The first principle provides that sensitive personal data shall not be processed unless at least one of the conditions in Sch.3 is also met. This is in addition to the requirements that (1) the processing be fair and lawful, and (2) that at least one of the Sch.2 conditions is met.   **11–049**

### Meaning of sensitive personal data

Sensitive personal data is defined as personal data consisting of information as to[7]:   **11–050**

    (a)  the racial or ethnic origin of the data subject,

    (b)  his political opinions,

    (c)  his religious beliefs or other beliefs of a similar nature,

    (d)  whether he is a member of a trade union (within the meaning of the Trade Union and Labour Relations (Consolidation) Act 1992),

    (e)  his physical or mental health or condition,

    (f)  his sex life,

    (g)  the commission or alleged commission by him of any offence, or

---

[6] *Office of the Information Commissioner Data Protection Act 1998 Legal Guidance* at para.3.1.1, p.25.
[7] Data Protection Act 1998, s.2.

(h) any proceedings for any offence committed or alleged to have been committed by him, the disposal of such proceedings or the sentence of any court in such proceedings.

**11–051**    Photographs and images which consist of information as to any of the above categories will amount to sensitive personal data. Thus, photographs of a well-known model leaving a Narcotics Anonymous meeting, in conjunction with captions to that effect, were held to be sensitive personal data as the information concerned her physical or mental health or condition; namely her drug addiction.[8] Even if the data does not specify directly and precisely information within the categories, it may nevertheless be sensitive personal data if it can be understood to convey such information by implication.[9]

Potentially, any image of an identified person inherently classes as sensitive personal data because it inevitably reveals information concerning their racial or ethnic origin—in particular skin colour. Even in cases where the information that can be gleaned from the image is imprecise, it still remains information about the subject's ethnic origin. A black and white image of a person may not enable an observer to categorically identify whether the person depicted was (for example) Caucasian, Asian, native American, or mixed race. However, it might indicate that the person was not (for example) Afrocaribbean or Chinese—which remains information about the subject's racial or ethnic origin.

**11–052**    In *Durant v Financial Services Authority*[10] it was held that, in order to amount to "personal data" within the meaning of the 1998 Act, the information revealed needed to be significant in a biographical sense that went beyond mere recording of a life event that did not compromise the subject's privacy.[11] It is arguable that the part of a person's image that just shows visually self-evident information about racial origin does not, without more, amount to personal data at all. The information is visible to all and hence, arguably not biographically significant in a way that compromises privacy. In some circumstances, that self evident racial origin information may become biographically significant if cross-matched with other data.

However, photographs were not specifically considered in *Durant v Financial Services Authority*.[12] There remains the possibility that the mere

---

[8] *Campbell v Mirror Group Newspapers Ltd* [2002] EWHC 499 at paras 89–92; [2002] E.M.L.R. 30, 640. Reversed on other grounds [2002] EWCA Civ 1373; [2003] Q.B. 633; [2003] 2 W.L.R. 80; [2003] 1 All E.R. 224; [2003] E.M.L.R. 2. The CA agreed with the finding that the photographs were sensitive personal data: at paras 87–88. Note this case is the subject of an appeal to the House of Lords to be heard in February 2004.
[9] *Lord Ashcroft v Attorney-General* [2002] EWHC 1122, QB, Gray J. (unrep) at para.30. Application to amend Particulars of Claim to allege that a memorandum constituted "sensitive personal data" because it bore the meaning that the subject had allegedly committed a criminal offence. The court rejected the defendant's objection that the memorandum did not fall within s.2(g) because it did not specify a particular offence. It was held to be arguable that a reference to laundry arrangements would be understood to be a reference to the criminal offence of money-laundering.
[10] [2003] EWCA Civ 1746.
[11] *ibid.* at [28] *per* Auld L.J.
[12] [2003] EWCA Civ 1746.

fact that an image shows a person's skin colour will result in its classification as information as to ethnic or racial origin. If the image qualifies as "personal data" then it is arguable that it is automatically "sensitive personal data". Although this may appear to be somewhat surprising, the words "data consisting of information as to the racial or ethnic origin of the data subject" cannot logically be read in any way that would exclude the information about skin colour and ethnic identity shown in an image. To do otherwise would be to strain the construction of the meaning of the word "information" by importing words that are not there, such as "excluding information visible to all". It is a simple fact that a person's image does contain information about that individual's racial origin. Until this is clarified by the courts, the position is unclear. Given the possibility that the meaning of "personal data" may include all ID Images of people,[13] potentially all ID Images are sensitive data.

As discussed above, at paras 11–022 *et seq.*, it is submitted that anonymous images of individual public places should not be treated as falling within the meaning of personal data, but this is not yet the subject of authority. However, if it is the case that (1) the Data Protection Act covers any image of a person even where that person cannot be specifically identified by name or otherwise,[14] (2) a mere image of a person showing their skin colour is sensitive data, this potentially causes serious difficulty for photographers who photograph people in public. In order to process sensitive data, one of the Sch.3 conditions *must* be complied with. In cases of photographs of people in public places, there are only two that are likely to be of relevance—Condition 1 (explicit consent) and Condition 5 (information made public by the data subject). Explicit consent is all very well if the photographer is able to obtain a model release from the subject. In many cases this will be impractical—for example the person is too far away, the conditions are crowded, the person is on/ in moving transport or for other reasons, the photographer is unable to obtain consent.

The difficulty with Condition 5 is that it requires the information to be made public as the result of "steps taken deliberately" by the data subject. This would include celebrities who regularly consent to photo-shoots but may not include non-public figures in public places. As discussed below "deliberate" connotes conscious choice. It is arguable that merely going out in public anonymously cannot amount to deliberate steps to make ones racial or ethnic origin public, as there is no real choice. **11–053**

If neither Condition 1 or Condition 5 of the Sch.3 conditions apply, then a photographer, in order to process the information contained in his images, would need to rely on the s.32 special purposes (journalistic, artistic, literary purposes) exemption. This in itself requires compliance with four separate conditions, one of which is that compliance with the provision of the Data Protection Act 1998 in respect of which the exemption is sought is incom-

---

[13] *i.e.* an image that is sufficient (in terms of facial depiction and clarity) to enable the person shown to be identified. For author's definition of ID Image in this context and discussion of the problem of whether the statutory definition of personal data includes Abstract Identification or requires Specific Identification see above at para.11–022.

[14] *i.e.* abstract identification. Discussed above at para. 11–022.

patible with the special purposes. Unless s.32 is given a wide interpretation by the courts, it will be difficult for anyone, whether photographers, picture libraries, or the media to take and process images of non-public figures taken in public places.

**11–054**   In *Campbell v MGN Ltd* at first instance Morland J. considered the fact that photographs showing the model Naomi Campbell leaving Narcotics Anonymous also showed that she was black was irrelevant to the case:

> "In my judgment the contention, that the published photographs of the claimant are sensitive personal data because they consist of information as to her racial or ethnic origin, has no materiality or relevance to the circumstances of this case. The claimant is proud to be a leading black fashion model and it is part of her life style and profession to be photographed as a black woman. She has suffered no damage or distress because the photographs disclose that she is black.
>
> However, it should not be understood that I am ruling that images whether photographic or otherwise that disclose whether from physical characteristic or dress, racial or ethnic origins cannot amount to sensitive personal data".[15]

On the facts of that case, whether the "ethnic origin" information rendered the photographs sensitive data was irrelevant because, as stated above, the judge concluded that they were sensitive data in any event for other reasons.

**11–055**   The fact that the claimant was "proud to be a leading black fashion model" and was photographed as part of her job is irrelevant to the question of whether a photograph showing she is black amounted to sensitive personal data. It would certainly go to the issue of consent but that is a separate question from whether in the first place the photograph is sensitive personal data. In addition, on the facts, by virtue of her job as a black model Condition 5 (information made public by the data subject) would apply. The statutory test for what is "sensitive personal data" is not subjective. A photograph of an identifiable person reveals information about the racial or ethnic origin of a person and therefore logically will fall within the definition of "sensitive personal data" despite the potentially unsatisfactory consequences.

### Schedule 3 Conditions: For sensitive personal data

**11–056**   In addition to compliance with one of the Sch.2 conditions, where the data is "sensitive personal data", one of the Sch.3 conditions must also be satisfied. Additional circumstances in which sensitive personal data may be processed are set out in statutory instruments made under Sch.3.[16]

---

[15] *Campbell v Mirror Group Newspapers Ltd* [2002] EWHC 499 at paras 90–91; [2002] E.M.L.R. 30, 640. Reversed on other grounds [2002] EWCA Civ 1373; [2003] Q.B. 633.
[16] The Data Protection (Processing of Sensitive Personal Data) Order 2000 (SI 2000/ 417); Data Protection (Processing of Sensitive Data)(Elective Representatives) Order 2002 (SI 2002/2905).

---

**Sensitive Data: Overview of Conditions Permitting Processing**
**Schedule 3 Conditions**

1.  Explicit consent.

2.  Employment law obligations.

3.  Necessary to protect vital interests of data subject or another person.

4.  Non-profit organisations existing for political, philosophical, religious or trade-union purposes

5.  Information made public by the data subject.

6.  Legal proceedings or for defending legal rights.

7.  Public functions (administration of justice, Crown etc)

8.  Medical purposes.

9.  Monitoring of racial equality.

*Additional Conditions in Statutory Instruments*

10. Detection or prevention of unlawful act in the public interest

11. Protection of public against dishonesty, malpractice or improper conduct.

12. Disclosure of unlawful act, dishonesty, malpractice or improper conduct for publication in the public interest.

13. Confidential counselling.

14. Insurance business.

15. Insurance business—data already subject to processing immediately before 1 March 2000.

16. Monitoring of equal opportunities: religious beliefs and physical or mental disabilities.

17. Political opinions processed by political parties.

18. Research purposes.

19. Processing by police constables.

20. Processing by elective representatives.

---

## Explicit consent

*The data subject has given his explicit consent to the processing of the*   **11–057**
*personal data.*

The Act does not require that "explicit consent" be given in writing. Oral consent will suffice provided it is explicit. However, as a matter of evidence, written consent will always be preferable from the perspective of the data controller. The Directive states that personal data may only be processed if the data subject has unambiguously given his consent.[17] The definition in the Directive of consent as "any freely given *specific and informed indication* of his wishes by which the data subject signifies his agreement to personal data relating to him being processed".[18] Explicit consent under Sch.3 therefore requires the consent to be (1) unambiguous, (2) informed, and (3) specific. The requirement to "signify" agreement indicates that silence or inaction will not suffice.

**11–058**    The requirement in this condition that the data subject must give explicit consent *to the processing of the personal data* indicates that the subject must be informed of the proposed processing. The Information Commissioner in the Legal Guidance states "the Commissioner's view is that consent is not particularly easy to achieve and that data controllers should consider other conditions in Schedule 2 (and Schedule 3 if processing personal data) before looking at consent".[19]

As discussed above, it is possible that any image of a person that shows their skin colour amounts to sensitive personal data as consisting of information about their ethnic or racial origin.[20] In the case of professional models and celebrities who have previously been the subject of published photographs, Condition 5 (information made public as the result of steps taken deliberately) will apply in respect of such information about ethnic or racial origin as can be gleaned visually. In all cases, but particularly those involving images of non-public figures, it would be prudent to obtain specific written consent in the form of a model release that includes consent to specified processing under the Data Protection Act 1998. The proposed uses (*i.e.* proposed types of processing) should be identified as far as possible and as precisely as possible. As discussed above, at para.7–088, in practice many picture libraries will not deal in images without model release forms in any event.

*Employment law obligations*

**11–059**    Schedule 3, para.2 provides:

"(1) The processing is necessary for the purposes of exercising or performing any right or obligation which is conferred or imposed by law on the data controller in connection with employment.

(2) The Secretary of State may by order—

(a) exclude the application of sub-paragraph (1) in such cases as may be specified, or

---

[17] 95/46, Art.7(1).
[18] 95/46, Art.2(h).
[19] *Office of the Information Commissioner Data Protection Act 1998 Legal Guidance* at para.3.1.5, p.29.
[20] See above at paras 11–051 to 11–055.

(b) provide that, in such cases as may be specified, the condition in sub-paragraph (1) is not to be regarded as satisfied unless such further conditions as may be specified in the order are also satisfied."

To date no order has been made under this paragraph. Again, there is the requirement that the processing be "necessary".[21] The condition extends to obligations imposed by law on the data controller "in connection with employment" and is accordingly not restricted merely to employers.

## *Vital interests of data subject or another person*

Schedule 3, para.3 provides:                                          **11–060**

"The processing is necessary—

(a) in order to protect the vital interests of the data subject or another person, in a case where—
    (i) consent cannot be given by or on behalf of the data subject, or
    (ii) the data controller cannot reasonably be expected to obtain the consent of the data subject, or
(b) in order to protect the vital interests of another person, in a case where consent by or on behalf of the data subject has been unreasonably withheld."

As to the meaning of "necessary" and "vital interests" see above.[22]

## *Non-profit organisations*

The legitimate activities of non-profit organisations which exist for spe-   **11–061**
cified purposes is covered by Sch.3, Condition 4 which reads:

"The processing

(a) is carried out in the course of its legitimate activities by any body or association which—
    (i) is not established or conducted for profit, and
    (ii) exists for political, philosophical, religious or trade-union purposes,
(b) is carried out with appropriate safeguards for the rights and freedoms of data subjects,
(c) relates only to individuals who either are members of the body or association or have regular contact with it in connection with its purposes, and
(d) does not involve disclosure of the personal data to a third party without the consent of the data subject."

---

[21] As to meaning of "necessary" see above at para.11–044.
[22] "Necessary", see above at para.11–044, "Vital Interests", see above at para.11–046.

There are a number of separate conditions contained in the provision, all of which must be satisfied in order for the processing to fall within this condition. The processing must be (1) in the course of legitimate activities, by (2) a body not established or conducted for profit, and (3) exists for political, philosophical, religious, or trade-union purposes (4) carried out with appropriate safeguards, (5) relate only to members of the body or those who have regular contact with it in connection with its purposes, and (6) does not involve disclosure to third parties without the consent of the data subject.

### Information made public by the data subject

11–062    The Sch.3, para.5 condition provides:

> "The information contained in the personal data has been made public as a result of steps deliberately taken by the data subject."

This condition raises two interpretive problems: (1) what is meant by "made public", and (2) what amounts to "deliberate steps"? This is of particular relevance to photographs and images of people. Certain information concerning a person is made public merely by virtue of the person being in public and being visible. Skin colour, facial features, and in some cases dress, reveal information about the person's ethnic origin and race. Information as to religious beliefs may be conveyed by dress and physical appearance, such as the wearing of a yarmulke skullcap (Judiasm), payos hair curls (Hassidic Judiasm), or a turban (Sikhism). Information about a person's physical condition may also be inherently obvious where, for example, that person is in a wheelchair or otherwise suffering from a visually indicated disability.

11–063    The question is whether this type of visually self-evident information is "made public as the result of steps deliberately taken by the data subject" simply by the fact of them leaving their home and going into the public street.

The words "deliberate steps" suggest an element of conscious choice and intention. In other contexts, a statutory requirement of "deliberate" has been interpreted as requiring knowledge and intention on the part of the person acting. "Deliberate commission of a breach of duty" has been held to exclude circumstances where the actor was unaware he was committing a breach of duty.[23] The House of Lords considered that an act that was intentional but not done in the knowledge that there was a breach of duty did not amount to a deliberate commission of a breach of duty.[24] A "deliberate exposure to exceptional danger" in an insurance policy was held to mean conscious exposure to such a danger.[25] It was held that the question of whether an act was "deliberate" imported a subjective test.[26] "Deliberate"

[23] *Cave v Robinson Jarvis & Rolf* [2002] UKHL 18; [2003] 1 A.C. 384; [2002] 2 W.L.R. 1107; [2002] 2 All E.R. 641 (s.32(2) Limitation Act 1980).
[24] *ibid.*
[25] *Beller v Hayden* [1978] Q.B. 694; [1978] 2 W.L.R. 845; [1978] 3 All E.R. 111.

failure to pay rent under the Housing Act 1985 did not include a failure to pay rent as a result of real financial difficulties and a genuine inability to make ends meet.[27]

It would be a curious construction, if visually self evident information **11–064** that is effectively available for all the world to see was not regarded as having been made public as a result of deliberate steps in this context. However, if it is the case that "deliberate steps" requires a conscious and knowing decision, it is arguable that merely going out in public does not amount to *deliberate* steps to make one's ethnic origin or other visually self-evident information public, as there is no real choice. To keep visually self-evident information out of the sight of the public would require either never leaving private premises or going out dressed in such away that the entire body was fully concealed. In addition, the fact that an anonymous person in public is visible to strangers passing them in the street does not mean that their racial or ethnic origin has been made public in a way connected with their name and identity. For example, the ethnic origin of a reclusive writer who never gives interviews and writes under a pseudonym may be unknown to the public at large. Can it really be said that merely by emerging into the street he has taken deliberate steps to make his ethnic origin public? There is no clear answer to this question and cases will need to be determined on their own facts.

Certainly there will be cases where it will be clear that visually self-evident information has been made public by deliberate steps on the part of the data subject. A black model who as part of her job makes a deliberate and conscious choice to be photographed has plainly taken deliberate steps to make visually self-evident information public.[28] Statements about sensitive personal data made via press releases or to the media can certainly be regarded as "made public".

More borderline cases will raise difficulties. It is submitted that there are **11–065** three elements that need to be considered when ascertaining whether something has been made public: (1) the number of people to whom the disclosure has been made, (2) the manner in which the communication took place (in particular whether any purported obligation of confidence was imposed), and (3) the circumstances in which the communication took place (including the relationship between the data subject and disclosees, and whether it was in private, in public, or in a quasi-public place). Thus, an announcement to five journalists at a poorly attended press conference may be regarded as having been made public, whereas an announcement to five friends having dinner together in a restaurant may not be.

Unless it is obvious that the information has been made public (as in the case of a public figure giving an interview to the press), data controllers seeking to process sensitive personal data would be advised to look for another of the Sch.3 conditions to rely on. As with all the Sch.3 conditions, even if it can be established that the information has been made public as the

---

[27] *R. v Wandsworth LBC Ex p.* Hawthorne [1994] 1 W.L.R. 1442; [1995] 2 All E.R. 331.
[28] As in *Campbell v Mirror Group Newspapers Ltd* [2002] EWHC 499 see comments of Morland J. at paras 90–91 quoted in full above at para.11–054.

result of deliberate steps by the data subject, it is still necessary to establish that a Sch.2 condition is satisfied.

### *Legal proceedings or for defending legal rights*

**11–066**     Schedule 3, Condition 6 provides as follows:

"The processing—

    (a)  is necessary for the purpose of, or in connection with, any legal proceedings (including prospective legal proceedings),

    (b)  is necessary for the purpose of obtaining legal advice, or

    (c)  is otherwise necessary for the purposes of establishing, exercising or defending legal rights."

Again the word "necessary" appears in all the provisions—as to meaning of which see above at para.11–044. Condition 6(c) is extremely wide. The Information Commissioner's Guidance states that the Commissioner's view is that 6(c) is of limited scope and that data controllers should adopt a narrow interpretation and rely on another Sch.3 condition if there is any doubt as to whether it applies.[29] The Guidance also states that Condition 6(c) should not be used to construct a legal right where none exists.[30]

It should also be noted that personal data (as opposed to sensitive personal data) is exempt from the non-disclosure provisions where the disclosure is necessary for the purpose of legal proceedings.[31]

### *Public functions (administration of Justice, Crown, etc.)*

**11–067**     Schedule 3, Condition 7 concerns processing necessary for public functions and states:

"(1) The processing is necessary—

    (a)  for the administration of justice,

    (b)  for the exercise of any functions conferred on any person by or under an enactment, or

    (c)  for the exercise of any functions of the Crown, a Minister of the Crown or a government department.

(2) The Secretary of State may by order—

    (a)  exclude the application of sub-paragraph (1) in such cases as may be specified, or

    (b)  provide that, in such cases as may be specified, the condition in sub-paragraph (1) is not to be regarded as satisfied unless such

---

[29] *Office of the Information Commissioner Data Protection Act 1998 Legal Guidance* at para.3.1.3, pp.22–23.

[30] *ibid.*, at p.23.

[31] Data Protection Act 1998, s.35. See below at para.11–070.

further conditions as may be specified in the order are also satisfied."

The wording is very similar to the Sch.2 condition, as to which see above at para.11–047. As at October 31, 2003, no orders had been made under Condition 7(2).

### Medical purposes

Schedule 3, Condition 8 is satisfied when processing is *necessary* as follows:

**11–068**

"(1) The processing is necessary for medical purposes and is undertaken by—

  (a) a health professional, or

  (b) a person who in the circumstances owes a duty of confidentiality which is equivalent to that which would arise if that person were a health professional.

(2) In this paragraph 'medical purposes' includes the purposes of preventative medicine, medical diagnosis, medical research, the provision of care and treatment and the management of healthcare services."

Condition 8 only applies to processing undertaken by either (1) health professionals, or (2) people who owe a duty of confidentiality which is equivalent to that which would arise if that person were a health professional. Health professional is defined by s.69 of the 1998 Act which lists a number of categories of registered health professionals including doctors and dentists.[32]

"Medical research" is included in the definition of "medical purposes" and would include processing of images of patients in this context, but only where this was "necessary" to the research.[33]

### Monitoring of racial equality

The final condition in Sch.3 permits processing in connection with monitoring of racial equality and provides:

**11–069**

"(1) The processing—

  (a) is of sensitive personal data consisting of information as to racial or ethnic origin,

  (b) is necessary for the purpose of identifying or keeping under review the existence or absence of equality of opportunity or treatment between persons of different racial or ethnic origins, with a view to enabling such equality to be promoted or maintained, and

---

[32] Data Protection Act 1998, s.69(1). The full list is set out above at para.11–012, n.33.

[33] For professional guidelines about medical images see below at para.11–185, n.48 and accompanying text.

(c) is carried out with appropriate safeguards for the rights and free-doms of data subjects.

(2) The Secretary of State may by order specify circumstances in which processing falling within sub-paragraph (1)(a) and (b) is, or is not, to be taken for the purposes of sub-paragraph (1)(c) to be carried out with appropriate safeguards for the rights and freedoms of data subjects."

It should be noted that this provision is limited *only* to racial or ethnic origin information.

### *Further SI conditions permitting processing of sensitive personal data*

**11–070**    The Data Protection (Processing of Sensitive Personal Data) Order[34] sets out 10 further circumstances in which sensitive personal data may be pro-cessed. It remains a requirement that in addition to establishing one of the Statutory Instrument conditions, the data controller still needs to show that a Sch.2 ground applies. The Data Protection (Processing of Sensitive Data)(Elective Representatives) Order 2002[35] also provides for processing by, and disclosure to, elective representatives such as MPs and MEPs.

The Data Protection (Processing of Sensitive Personal Data) Order per-mits processing of sensitive personal data in the following instances:

### *Detection or prevention of unlawful act in the public interest*

**11–071**    To fall within the first condition provided by the statutory instrument, the processing must:

(a) be in the substantial public interest;

(b) be necessary for the purposes of the prevention or detection of any unlawful act (including a failure to act); and

(c) necessarily be carried out without the explicit consent of the data subject being sought so as not to prejudice those purposes.[36]

This will include processing by the police in connection with criminal acts, but would also include processing in connection with unlawful acts amounting to breaches of civil obligations. It is essential that if the explicit consent of the data subject were obtained, it would prejudice the purposes.

### *Protection of public against dishonesty, malpractice or improper conduct*

**11–072**    Sensitive personal data may be processed where the processing:

---

[34] SI 2000/417.
[35] SI 2002/2905.
[36] Data Protection (Processing of Sensitive Personal Data) Order 2000 (SI 2000/417), Sch.1, para.1.

(a) is in the substantial public interest;

(b) is necessary for the discharge of any function which is designed for protecting members of the public against:

    (i) dishonesty, malpractice, or other seriously improper conduct by, or the unfitness or incompetence of, any person, or

    (ii) mismanagement in the administration of, or failures in services provided by, any body or association; and

(c) must necessarily be carried out without the explicit consent of the data subject being sought so as not to prejudice the discharge of that function.[37]

The wording "dishonesty, malpractice or seriously improper conduct" is the same as appears in the s.31(2)(a) exemption for public watch dogs and regulatory activity. As with the preceding condition, it is necessary that obtaining the explicit consent of the data subject would prejudice the function of protection of members of the public.

### *Disclosure of unlawful act, dishonesty, malpractice or improper conduct: publication in the public interest*

This provision permits *disclosure* (rather than processing) of personal data where the disclosure is for one of the special purposes namely journalistic, artistic, or literary purposes.[38] The practical effect is to permit disclosure of sensitive personal data to or by the media where publication is in the public interest. The other "special purposes" literary or artistic purposes are unlikely to be relevant in this context.     **11–073**

The specified circumstances permit the disclosure of personal data where the disclosure:     **11–074**

(a) is in the substantial public interest;

(b) is in connection with—

    (i) the commission by any person of any unlawful act (whether alleged or established),

    (ii) dishonesty, malpractice, or other seriously improper conduct by, or the unfitness or incompetence of, any person (whether alleged or established), or

    (iii) mismanagement in the administration of, or failures in services provided by, any body or association (whether alleged or established);

(c) is for the special purposes as defined in s.3 of the 1998 Act (journalistic, artistic and literary purposes); and

---

[37] Data Protection (Processing of Sensitive Personal Data) Order 2000 (SI 2000/417), Sch.1, para.2.
[38] As to meaning of "special purposes" see below at para.11–141.

(d) is made with a view to the publication of those data by any person and the data controller reasonably believes that such publication would be in the public interest.[39]

"Act" is defined as including a failure to act.[40] This ground is of limited application as it only permits disclosure of information and would not cover retaining and other processing of such sensitive personal data.

The disclosure need only be "in connection" with wrongdoing and does not have to be evidence *per se* of wrong doing, but it must be made "with a view" to publication.

## Confidential counselling

**11–075**    This ground permits processing of sensitive personal data which is in the substantial public interest and:

(a) is necessary for the discharge of any function which is designed for the provision of confidential counselling, advice, support or any other service; and

(b) is carried out without the explicit consent of the data subject because the processing:

    (i) is necessary in a case where consent cannot be given by the data subject; or

    (ii) is necessary in a case where the data controller cannot reasonably be expected to obtain the explicit consent of the data subject, or

    (iii) must necessarily be carried out without the explicit consent of the data subject being sought so as not to prejudice the provision of that counselling, advice, support or other service.[41]

## Insurance and pensions business

**11–076**    Two grounds permit processing of sensitive personal data that is necessary for the purpose of carrying on insurance business or making determinations in connection with determining eligibility for an occupational pension scheme as defined under s.1 of the Pension Schemes Act 1993.

The first ground permits processing of sensitive personal data about the physical or mental health or condition of a parent, grandparent, great grandparent or sibling of the insured person/pension scheme member. The ground only covers processing that is necessary where the data controller

---

[39] Data Protection (Processing of Sensitive Personal Data) Order 2000 (SI 2000/417), Sch.1, para.3.
[40] Data Protection (Processing of Sensitive Personal Data) Order 2000 (SI 2000/417), Sch.1, para.3(2).
[41] Data Protection (Processing of Sensitive Personal Data) Order 2000 (SI 2000/417), Sch.1, para.4.

cannot reasonably expect to obtain the explicit consent of that data subject and the data controller is not aware of the data subject withholding his consent.[42]

The second ground permits similar processing of sensitive personal data that is necessary for the purposes of insurance or pension business that was already underway prior to March 1, 2000.[43]

### Monitoring of equal opportunities: religious beliefs and physical or mental disabilities

This ground does not apply where the data subject gives written notice requiring that the data controller cease processing. That aside, this ground permits processing of sensitive personal data consisting of information falling within s.2(c) [religious beliefs or beliefs of a similar nature] or 2(e) [physical or mental health or condition] of the 1998 Act where the processing:

**11–077**

(1) is necessary for the purpose of identifying or keeping under review the existence or absence of equality of opportunity or treatment between persons:

    (i) holding different religious beliefs or beliefs of a similar nature;

    (ii) of different states of physical or mental health or different physical or mental conditions

with a view to enabling such equality to be promoted or maintained;

(2) does not support measures or decisions with respect to any particular data subject otherwise than with the explicit consent of that data subject; and

(3) does not cause, nor is likely to cause, substantial damage or substantial distress to the data subject or any other person.[44]

The Statutory Instrument also provides that where a data subject gives written notice to any data controller who is processing personal data about that data subject under this ground requiring that data controller to cease processing the personal data at the end of such period as is reasonable in the circumstances, that data controller must have ceased processing those personal data at the end of that period.[45]

---

[42] Data Protection (Processing of Sensitive Personal Data) Order 2000 (SI 2000/417), Sch.1, para.5.
[43] Data Protection (Processing of Sensitive Personal Data) Order 2000 (SI 2000/417), Sch.1, para.6.
[44] Data Protection (Processing of Sensitive Personal Data) Order 2000 (SI 2000/417), Sch.1, para.7.
[45] Data Protection (Processing of Sensitive Personal Data) Order 2000 (SI 2000/417), Sch.1, para.7(2).

*Political opinions processed by political parties*

**11–078**   This ground permits processing of information about the data subject's political beliefs that is carried out by any person or organisation included in the register maintained pursuant to s.1 Registration of Political Parties Act 1998 in the course of his/its legitimate political activities.[46] There is also provision for the data subject to give written notice requiring the data controller to cease processing data under this ground within a period that is reasonable in the circumstances.[47]

*Research purposes*

**11–079**   Processing of sensitive personal data is permitted where the processing:

(a)  is in the substantial public interest;

(b)  is necessary for research purposes;

(c)  does not support measures or decisions with respect to any particular data subject otherwise than with the explicit consent of that data subject; and

(d)  does not cause, nor is likely to cause, substantial damage or substantial distress to the data subject or any other person.[48]

Research purposes has the same meaning as in s.33 of the Data Protection Act 1998 namely including "statistical or historical purposes".

*Processing by police constables*

**11–080**   The final ground in the SI that permits the processing of sensitive personal data simply states:

"The processing is necessary for the exercise of any functions conferred on a constable by any rule of law".[49]

*Processing by elective representatives*

**11–081**   The Data Protection (Processing of Sensitive Data)(Elective Representatives) Order 2002[50] which came into force on December 17, 2002,[51] set out further circumstances in which personal sensitive data can be processed or disclosed.

---

[46] Data Protection (Processing of Sensitive Personal Data) Order 2000 (SI 2000/417), Sch.1, para.8.
[47] Data Protection (Processing of Sensitive Personal Data) Order 2000 (SI 2000/417.), Sch.1, para.8(2).
[48] Data Protection (Processing of Sensitive Personal Data) Order 2000 (SI 2000/417), Sch.1, para.9.
[49] Data Protection (Processing of Sensitive Personal Data) Order 2000 (SI 2000/417), Sch.1, para.10.
[50] SI 2002/2905.
[51] SI 2002/2905, para.1.

It permits processing by and disclosure to elected representatives[52] (including persons acting with their authority) in certain circumstances. Processing by elected representatives is permitted in connection with the discharge of their function as an elected representative:

(1) pursuant to request made by the data subject to the elected repre-   **11–110**
    sentative to take action on his behalf or on behalf of another where
    the processing is necessary for action by the representative pursuant
    to the request.[53]

(2) pursuant to a request made by a third party to the elected repre-
    sentative to take action on behalf of the data subject or other indi-
    vidual and where the processing is necessary for any action taken in
    response to the request. In such circumstances the processing can only
    be without the explicit consent of the data subject if (a) the data
    subject cannot give consent, (b) the elected representative cannot
    reasonably be expected to obtain the explicit consent of the data
    subject, (c) must necessarily be carried out without the explicit con-
    sent of the data subject being sought so as not to prejudice the action
    taken by the elected representative, (d) is necessary in the interests of
    another individual in a case where the explicit consent of the data
    subject has been unreasonably withheld.[54]

Disclosure to an elected representative is permitted where the disclosure:   **11–082**

(1) is made

    (a) in response to a communication to the data controller from the
        elected representative acting pursuant to a request made by the
        data subject;
    (b) is of sensitive personal data which are relevant to the subject
        matter of that communication; and
    (c) is necessary for the purpose of responding to that communica-
        tion.[55]

(2) is made

---

[52] Defined by Sch.1, para.1 as meaning an elected member of: (1) the House of Commons, the National Assembly for Wales, the Scottish Parliament or the Northern Ireland Assembly; (2) of the European Parliament elected in the UK; (3) a local authority a county council, a district council, a London borough council or a parish council (England) or a county council, a county borough council or a community council (Wales); and (3) an elected mayor of a local authority within the meaning the Local Government Act 2000 (Pt II); (4) the Mayor of London or an elected member of the London Assembly; (5) an elected member of the Common Council of the City of London, or the Council of the Isles of Scilly; (6) an elected member of a council constituted under the Local Government, etc. (Scotland) Act 1994, s.2; or (7) an elected member of a district council within the meaning of the Local Government Act (Northern Ireland) 1972.
[53] SI 2002/2905, para.3.
[54] Data Protection (Processing of Sensitive Data)(Elective Representatives) Order 2002 (SI 2002/2905), Sch.3, para.4.
[55] Data Protection (Processing of Sensitive Data)(Elective Representatives) Order 2002 (SI 2002/2905), Sch.3, para.5.

(a)  in response to a communication to the data controller from the elected representative acting pursuant to a request made by *an individual other than the data subject*;

(b)  is of sensitive personal data which are relevant to the subject matter of that communication;

(c)  is necessary for the purpose of responding to that communication; and

(d)  is carried out without the explicit consent of the data subject because the disclosure:

    (i)  is necessary in a case where explicit consent cannot be given by the data subject,

    (ii)  is necessary in a case where the data controller cannot reasonably be expected to obtain the explicit consent of the data subject,

    (iii)  must necessarily be carried out without the explicit consent of the data subject being sought so as not to prejudice the action taken by the elected representative, and

    (iv)  is necessary in the interests of another individual in a case where the explicit consent of the data subject has been unreasonably withheld.[56]

### Second Principle: Processed only for specified purposes

**11–083**    *Personal data shall be obtained only for one or more specified and lawful purposes, and shall not be further processed in any manner incompatible with that purpose or those purposes.*

The purpose for which personal data is obtained may be specified in a notice given to the data subject[57] or by notification to the Commissioner.[58] However, this principle cannot be satisfied by mere notification of the purpose for which the data is processed and decisions about purpose cannot be made retrospectively by data controllers after the data has been obtained.[59] In considering whether disclosure of data is compatible with the purposes for which it was obtained, regard will be had to the purposes for which the data is intended to be processed by the third party to whom it is to be disclosed.[60]

---

[56] Data Protection (Processing of Sensitive Data)(Elective Representatives) Order 2002 (SI 2002/2905), para.6.
[57] Data Protection Act 1998, Sch.1, Pt II, para.(5)(a).
[58] Under Pt III of the Act. Data Protection Act 1998, Sch.1, Pt II, para.(5)(b).
[59] Office of the Information Commissioner Data Protection Act 1998 Legal Guidance at para.3.2, p.35.
[60] Data Protection Act 1998, Sch.1, Pt II, para.(6).

## Third Principle: Data to be adequate, relevant and not excessive

*Personal data shall be adequate, relevant and not excessive in relation to the* **11–084**
*purpose or purposes for which they are processed.*

There are no interpretation provisions in Sch.1 of the Act in respect of this principle. The third principle basically requires that data controllers should seek to identify and only obtain the minimum amount of information that is required in order to fulfill their purpose.[61] If additional information is required, data controllers should seek to identify the specific cases in which additional information is required and ensure the further information is obtained only in those cases.

The Information Commissioner's Guidance states that it is not acceptable for information to be held on the basis that it might possibly be useful in the future without a view of how it will be used. This is distinguished from information held in case of a foreseeable contingency. The example given is holding details of blood groups of employees engaged in hazardous occupations.[62]

The CCTV Code of Practice issued by the Information Commissioner under s.51(3)(b) of the Data Protection Act 1998 states that consideration should be given to ensure CCTV cameras do not record more information than is necessary.[63] Thus, if there is a risk of crime only at night, recording should only take place between particular hours. Care should be taken to ensure cameras do not record private residences or overlook back gardens, etc. Data may be inadequate if images recorded are blurred or indistinct because of media quality, poor light, or if the equipment is damaged or poorly maintained.

## Fourth Principle: Accurate and up to date

*Personal data shall be accurate and, where necessary kept up to date.* **11–085**

"Inaccurate" is defined by the Act as being data that is "incorrect or misleading as to any matter of fact."[64] The requirement for accuracy is absolute, but the requirement that information be kept up to date is qualified as being "where necessary".

The interpretation provisions for the Fourth Principle in Sch.1 provide that:

---

[61] *Community Charge Registration Office of Runnymede BC v Data Protection Registrar* Case DA/90 24/49/3 in *Encyclopaedia of Data Protection* (Sweet & Maxwell) at 6-001 (decided under 1984 Act) but endorsed in relation to the 1998 Act in *Office of the Information Commissioner Data Protection Act 1998 Legal Guidance* at para.3.3, p.36.
[62] *Office of the Information Commissioner Data Protection Act 1998 Legal Guidance* at para.3.3, p.37.
[63] The CCTV Code of Practice is reproduced in full in Appendix 5, below.
[64] Data Protection Act 1998, s.70(2).

"The fourth principle is not to be regarded as being contravened by reason of any inaccuracy in personal data which accurately record information obtained by the data controller from the data subject or a third party in a case where—

(a) having regard to the purpose or purposes for which the data were obtained and further processed, the data controller has taken reasonable steps to ensure the accuracy of the data, and

(b) if the data subject has notified the data controller of the data subject's view that the data are inaccurate, the data indicate that fact."

Accuracy in relation to photographs and images of people stored for identification purposes requires that the images are clear and recorded on to a medium of sufficient quality. If the medium on to which the images are recorded deteriorates, the images should be discarded. Images may be degraded by changes of file format or compression resulting in a loss of resolution and clarity, and hence accuracy.[65]

**11–086**     The requirement for accuracy impacts upon digital photographs that have been digitally manipulated. If the digital manipulation does not give an incorrect or misleading impression of fact about the person shown, the principle will not be breached. Simple retouching that improves the clarity of a photograph or minor removal of flaws would not be incorrect or misleading as to matters of fact.

However, if a digital photograph of a person is manipulated in such a way as to be incorrect or misleading as to matters of fact, then it would fall foul of this requirement. Any digital manipulation that causes an image to misrepresent facts about the person shown would infringe this principle. So, for example, creating images of people meeting each other who have never met, or images that suggest the people shown are in a sexual relationship who are not, or images that suggest the person shown undertaking an activity that they do not, would fall foul of this requirement. If digital manipulation of this type has taken place, then for the purposes of the Data Protection Act, in order for there to be any argument that the data not to be inaccurate, it would be necessary for the images to be stored in such a way as to clearly mark the fact that they had been altered and how they had been altered. However, it is doubtful whether the data controller could claim the benefit of the Sch.1 interpretation exemption that he has taken reasonable steps to ensure accuracy where he is responsible for the inaccuracy (*i.e.* the manipulation).[66] Digital manipulation for artistic purposes or journalistic purposes may be covered by the s.32 special purposes exemption.[67]

**11–087**     The CCTV Code of Practice[68] issued by the Information Commissioner under s.51(3)(b) of the Data Protection Act 1998 contains further guidance

---

[65] As to file formats and compression see above at para.9–002.
[66] See R. Jay and A. Hamilton, *Data Protection Law and Practice* (2nd ed., Sweet & Maxwell, 2003) at p.167.
[67] See below at paras 11–141 *et seq.*
[68] The CCTV Code of Practice is reproduced in full in Appendix 5, below.

to ensure use of CCTV cameras complies with the Fourth Principle, in particular that:

- the tapes or recording media should be of good quality;

- if the system records time and dates, this should be accurate and there should be a documented procedure for ensuring such accuracy;

- images should be clear enough to enable identification;

- cameras should be property maintained to ensure clear recording.

## Fifth Principle: Not kept for longer than necessary

*Personal data processed for any purpose or purposes shall not be kept for longer than is necessary for that purpose or those purposes.*   **11–088**

The Information Commissioner's Guidance suggest that the fifth principle requires that data controllers review the data they hold regularly and institute systems to delete information which is no longer required.[69] Schedule 1 of the Act does not give any further interpretation of this principle.

It is submitted that anonymisation of data and images would enable compliance with this provision as well as deletion.[70]

The CCTV Code of Practice[71] recommends that data controllers should have a policy on the time periods for retention of images which takes into account the nature of the images and the purpose for which it is being collected.[72] It is suggested that where images are recorded for the purpose of crime prevention, that the only images that may need to be retained are those relating to specific incidents of criminal activity and the rest could be erased after a short period. Other examples given are that publicans may not need to keep images for longer than seven days because they would soon be aware of any incident such as a fight occurring on their premises; town centre image recordings may not need to be retained for longer than 31 days unless they are required for evidential purposes in legal proceedings.[73]

## Sixth Principle: Processed in accordance with data subject's rights

*Personal data shall be processed in accordance with the rights of data subjects under the Data Protection Act 1998.*   **11–089**

Further interpretation of the sixth principle is set out in Sch.1 as follows:

---

[69] *Office of the Information Commissioner Data Protection Act 1998 Legal Guidance* at para.3.5, p.39.
[70] As to anonymisation see below at para.11–168.
[71] The CCTV Code of Practice is reproduced in full in Appendix 5, below.
[72] *CCTV Code of Practice*, Pt 3, Fifth Data Protection Principle, p.28. See Appendix 5, below.
[73] *CCTV Code of Practice*, Pt 1, Processing the Images, Standard 1, p.11. See Appendix 5, below.

"A person is to be regarded as contravening the sixth principle if, but only if—

    (a) he contravenes section 7 by failing to supply information in accordance with that section,

    (b) he contravenes section 10 by failing to comply with a notice given under subsection (1) of that section to the extent that the notice is justified or by failing to give a notice under subsection (3) of that section,

    (c) he contravenes section 11 by failing to comply with a notice given under subsection (1) of that section, or

    (d) he contravenes section 12 by failing to comply with a notice given under subsection (1) or (2)(b) of that section or by failing to give a notification under subsection (2)(a) of that section or a notice under subsection (3) of that section"

This means that the sixth principle is breached where the data controller fails to comply with a subject access request (s.7); continues processing likely to cause damage and distress after a request to cease doing so (s.10); fails to comply with a notice to cease direct marketing (s.11); or fails to comply with the provisions related to automated decision taking (s.12).

### Seventh Principle: Security

**11–090**    *Appropriate technical and organisational measures shall be taken against unauthorised or unlawful processing of personal data and against accidental loss or destruction of, or damage to, personal data.*

The Act gives further guidance as to the interpretation of the seventh principle. It provides that the measures must ensure a level of security appropriate to—

    (a) the harm that might result from such unauthorised or unlawful processing or accidental loss, destruction or damage as are mentioned in the seventh principle, and

    (b) the nature of the data to be protected.[74]

However, what is an appropriate measure may have regard to the state of technological development and the cost of implementing any measures.[75]

The data controller must take reasonable steps to ensure the reliability of any employees of his who have access to the personal data.[76]

**11–091**    If the processing of personal data is carried out by a third party on behalf of the data controller, in order to comply with the seventh principle, the data controller must:

---

[74] Data Protection Act 1998, Sch.1, Pt II, para.9.
[75] *ibid.*
[76] Data Protection Act 1998, Sch.1, Pt II, para.10.

(a) choose a data processor providing sufficient guarantees in respect of the technical and organisational security measures governing the processing to be carried out, and

(b) take reasonable steps to ensure compliance with those measures.[77]

In addition, if the processing is carried out by a third party on behalf of a data controller, in order for the data controller to comply with the seventh principle, the processing must be carried out under a contract made or evidenced in writing.[78] The contract must also provide that the data processor is to act only on instructions from the data controller.[79] Finally, the contract must require the third party data processor to comply with obligations equivalent to those imposed on a data controller by the seventh principle.[80]

The Information Commissioner Guidance in relation to the seventh principle suggests the carrying out of standard risk assessment and risk management techniques which identify potential threats to the system, the vulnerability of the system, and counter measures to put in place to reduce and manage the risk.[81] The Guidance sets out a list of suggested security controls for consideration, including the implementation of security management policies; controlling access to the information by physical controlled access to rooms or buildings, and password systems; ensuring business continuity by having back-up copies; training of staff; and systems for detecting, tracking, and dealing with security breaches.[82]

### Eighth Principle: Not transferred to countries without protection

*Personal data shall not be transferred to a country or territory outside the European Economic Area unless that country or territory ensures an adequate level of protection for the rights and freedoms of data subjects in relation to the processing of personal data.*   **11–092**

Matters that must be taken into account in deciding whether a non-EEA country has an adequate level of protection are set out in Sch.1 which provides[83]:

"An adequate level of protection is one which is adequate in all the circumstances of the case, having regard in particular to   **11–093**

(a) the nature of the personal data,

---

[77] Data Protection Act 1998, Sch.1, Pt II, para.11.
[78] Data Protection Act 1998, Sch.1, Pt II, para.12(a)(i).
[79] Data Protection Act 1998, Sch.1, Pt II, para.12(a)(ii).
[80] Data Protection Act 1998, Sch.1, Pt II, para.12(b).
[81] *Office of the Information Commissioner Data Protection Act 1998 Legal Guidance* at para.3.7, p.41.
[82] *Office of the Information Commissioner Data Protection Act 1998 Legal Guidance* at para.3.7, pp.41–42.
[83] Data Protection Act 1998, Sch.1, Pt II, para.13.

(b) the country or territory of origin of the information contained in the data,

(c) the country or territory of final destination of that information,

(d) the purposes for which and period during which the data are intended to be processed,

(e) the law in force in the country or territory in question,

(f) the international obligations of that country or territory,

(g) any relevant codes of conduct or other rules which are enforceable in that country or territory (whether generally or by arrangement in particular cases), and

(h) any security measures taken in respect of the data in that country or territory."

There are a number of exemptions to the eighth principle which are set out in Sch.4 of the Data Protection Act 1998, including where the data subject has given his consent to the transfer.[84]

**11–094**   A finding of the European Commission under s.31(2) of the Data Protection Directive that a particular territory does or does not ensure an adequate level of protection is binding.[85] Switzerland and Hungary have been held to have adequate protection for personal data.[86] Canada has been held to provide adequate protection for certain types of transfers only.[87] The position *vis-à-vis* the USA is problematic due to a lack of a comprehensive federal data protection law. "Safe Harbor" agreements have been reached allowing US companies to declare themselves compliant with European Union data protection law. The law governing overseas transfer of personal data is complex and outside the consideration of this work. The reader is referred to other specialist texts.[88]

## RIGHTS OF THE DATA SUBJECT

**11–095**   The data subject (defined as "an individual who is the subject of personal data"[89]) is granted a number of rights by the Data Protection Act 1998. All individuals have rights to make subject access requests, including minors. In England and Wales, the guidance is that a child by the age of 12 may be

---

[84] Reference should be made to Sch.4 for the full exemptions. In outline, in addition to (1) consensual transfers the eighth principle does not apply to transfers (2) necessary for performance of contract between data subject or data controller (3) other contracts entered into at request of or in interests of data subject (4) in the public interest (5) for legal proceedings (6) for the protection of vital interests of data subject (7) of data on public register (8) of kind approved by Commissioner or (9) authorised by the Commissioner.

[85] Data Protection Act 1998, Sch.1, Pt II, para.15.

[86] Commission Decision of July 26, 2000 [2000] O.J L214/1–3; Commission Decision July 26, 2000 [2000] O.J. L215/4–6.

[87] Commission Decision December 20, 2001 [2001] O.J. L2/12–16.

[88] See R. Jay and A. Hamilton, *Data Protection Law and Practice* (2nd ed.) (Sweet & Maxwell, 2003) Ch.8; S. Charlton, S. Gaskill, *et al.* (eds) *Encyclopaedia of Data Protection* (Sweet & Maxwell) at 1-386 *et seq.*

[89] Data Protection Act 1998, s.1(1).

expected to have sufficient maturity to understand the nature of the request.[90] Accordingly, if a data controller receives a subject access request from a minor aged 12 or over who understands the nature of the request, the data controller will need to comply with the request. In Scotland, a child is not deemed to have legal capacity until the age of 16. In order to bring the law in Scotland into line with England and Wales, the 1998 Act provides that if the question falls for decision in Scotland, a person of 12 years or more is presumed to have sufficient maturity and understanding to exercise rights under the Act.[91]

---

**Individual's Rights Under the Data Protection Act 1998**

1. Right to access to Personal Data (s.7)

2. Right to prevent Processing Likely to Cause Damage or Distress (s.10)

3. Right to prevent Processing for Direct Marketing (s.11)

4. Right to prevent Automated Decision Making (s.12)

5. Right to seek Compensation (s.13)

6. Right to Rectification, Blocking, Erasure and Destruction of Inaccurate Data (s.14)

7. Right to Request An Information Commissioner's Assessment

---

## Notices

Rights are exercised by a notice or request made in writing to the data controller. The Act does not specify any format for such a request. Any request in writing may be made by electronic means as long as it is in legible form and capable of being used for subsequent reference.[92]    **11–096**

## Right of access to personal data: s.7

An individual has the right to be informed by any data controller whether personal data of which that individual is the data subject are being processed by or on behalf of that data controller.[93] If the data controller is processing such data about that individual, then the individual also has the right to be given by the data controller a description of[94]:    **11–097**

(i)  the personal data of which that individual is the data subject,

---

[90] *Office of the Information Commissioner Data Protection Act 1998 Legal Guidance* at para.4.1.6, p.52.
[91] Data Protection Act 1998, s.66.
[92] Data Protection Act 1998, s.64.
[93] Data Protection Act 1998, s.7(1)(a).
[94] Data Protection Act 1998, s.7(1)(b).

(ii)   the purposes for which they are being or are to be processed, and

(iii)   the recipients or classes of recipients to whom they are or may be disclosed.

The individual has the right to have communicated to him in an intelligible form the information constituting his personal data and any information available to the data controller as to the source of the information.[95] In addition, where there is automatic processing of personal data for the purpose of evaluating matters relating to an individual (such as work performance credit worthiness, reliability, or conduct) which has constituted or is likely to constitute the sole basis for any decision significantly affecting him, the individual has the right to be informed by the data controller of the logic involved in that decision-taking.[96] The s.7 rights are given a special status in that (subject to the exemption provisions in the Data Protection Act 1998), they are to have effect notwithstanding any enactment or rule of law that prohibits or restricts the disclosure or authorises the withholding of information.[97]

**11–098**   If the data controller fails to comply with a request under s.7, on the application of the person who made the request, the court may make an order requiring the data controller to comply with the request.[98] Both the High Court and county court have jurisdiction to make such an order.[99]

The information supplied must be a copy of the information in a permanent form unless (1) the supply of such a copy is not possible, (2) it would involve a disproportionate effect, or (3) the data subject agrees otherwise.[1] Disproportionate effect is not defined by the Act. The Information Commissioner's Guidance states that matters to be taken into account include the cost of provision, the length of time it may take to provide the information, how difficult or otherwise it may be for the data controller to provide, and the size of the organisation of which the request has been made.[2] These matters will be balanced against the effect on the data subject.

The data controller is not under an obligation to supply any of the above information unless he has received a request in writing[3] and the prescribed fee,[4] which is generally a flat rate of £10.[5] The data controller should be supplied with information from the person making the request such that the data controller reasonably requires to satisfy himself as to the identity of the

---

[95] Data Protection Act 1998, s.7(1)(c).
[96] Data Protection Act 1998, s.7(1)(d).
[97] Data Protection Act 1998, s.27(5).
[98] Data Protection Act 1998, s.7(9).
[99] Data Protection Act 1998, s.15(1).
[1] Data Protection Act 1998, s.8(2).
[2] Office of the Information Commissioner Data Protection Act 1998 Legal Guidance at para.4.1, p.46.
[3] Data Protection Act 1998, s.7(2)(a).
[4] Data Protection Act 1998, s.7(2)(b).
[5] Data Protection (Subject Access) (Fees and Miscellaneous Provisions) Regulations 2000 (SI 2000/191). There are exceptions: credit reference agencies (maximum fee £2); educational records (no fee chargeable but may recover some of copying charges on a sliding scale); certain health records that are part of a manual system (maximum fee £50).

person making the request and in order to locate the information sought.[6] If the data subject does not supply such information after the data controller has informed the data subject of the requirement for further information, the data controller is not obliged to comply with the access request.[7] However, the data controller needs to act promptly in requesting any further information necessary to fulfill the request and a deliberate delay is not acceptable.[8]

The data controller must comply with any subject access request made **11–099** under s.7 of the 1998 Act promptly.[9] In any event, generally the request must be complied with within 40 days of either the receipt of the request by the data controller or the date on which the data controller has both the request and the required fee, which ever is the later.[10] There are different time limits for credit files[11] and school pupil records.[12]

Data controllers do not need to comply with requests under s.7 where they have already complied with an earlier identical or similar request by the same individual unless a reasonable interval has elapsed between compliance with the previous request and the making of the current request.[13] A "reasonable interval" is to be determined by regard to the nature of the data, the purpose for which the data are processed, and the frequency with which the data are altered.[14]

Special provisions apply where the data controller cannot comply with a **11–100** request without disclosing information relating to another individual who can be identified from that information. If that is the case, then generally the data controller is not obliged to comply with the request unless the other individual has consented to the disclosure to the person making the subject access request or it is reasonable in all the circumstances to comply with the request without the consent of the other individual.[15] However, the data

---

[6] Data Protection Act 1998, s.7(3). As amended by *Freedom of Information Act 2000*, s.73, Sch.6, para.1 on May 14, 2001 (See SI 2001/1637, art.2(d)).
[7] *ibid.*
[8] *Office of the Information Commissioner Data Protection Act 1998 Legal Guidance* at para.4.1, p.47.
[9] Data Protection Act 1998, s.7(8).
[10] Data Protection Act 1998, s.7(8) and (10).
[11] Seven working days: Data Protection (Subject Access) (Fees and Miscellaneous Provisions) Regulations 2000 (SI 2000/191), reg.4.
[12] 15 school days: Data Protection (Subject Access) (Fees and Miscellaneous Provisions) Regulations 2000 (SI 2000/191), reg.5.
[13] Data Protection Act 1998, s.8(3).
[14] Data Protection Act 1998, s.8(4).
[15] Data Protection Act 1998, s.7(4). For discussion of the two stage process contemplated by s.7(4) see *Durant v Financial Services Authority* [2003] EWCA Civ 1746 at [64]–[67]. Note that in cases concerning data about physical or mental health there is a further circumstance obliging the data controller to comply with the request which will identify a third party, namely where "the information is contained in a health record and the other individual is a health professional who has compiled or contributed to the health record or has been involved in the care of the data subject in his capacity as a health professional": Data Protection (Subject Access Modification) (Health) Order 2000 (SI 2000/413), art.8. However, the Order also amends (for the purposes of access to health data only) s.7(9) which, as amended, provides that any person at risk of serious harm to his physical or mental health arising from s.7 disclosure can make an application to the court for an order that the data controller does not comply with the s.7 provisions (SI 2000/413, art.8). This allows for the protection of health professionals who are potentially at risk in respect of disclosure of information about the health care they have provided to (for example) dangerous patients suffering from mental health conditions.

controller is not relieved from his obligation to comply with the request if it is possible to communicate information without disclosing the identity of the other person by omitting names or other identifying particulars.[16] In determining whether it is reasonable in all the circumstances to comply with the request without the consent of the other individual concerned, regard shall be had to any duty of confidentiality owed to the other individual; any steps taken by the data controller with a view to seeking the consent of the other individual; whether the other individual is capable of giving consent; and any express refusal of consent by the other individual.[17]

**11–101**    Special provisions also apply where the information requested consists of information as to the physical or mental health of the data subject as set out in the Data Protection (Subject Access Modification) (Health) Order 2000[18] If the data controller is not a health professional as defined in the Order, the information should not be provided unless the appropriate health professional has been consulted.[19] Personal data concerning physical or mental health may also be exempt from disclosure where it would be likely to cause serious harm to the physical or mental health, or condition of the data subject or any other person.[20] Disclosure of educational records[21] and social work records[22] may in some circumstances also be exempt from the s.7 rights where disclosure would cause serious harm to the physical or mental health of the data subject or any other person.

The Freedom of Information Act 2000 will make further amendments to the provisions concerning subject access requests in respect of access to "unstructured personal data" held by public authorities which are presently not yet in force.[23] "Unstructured personal data" means data other than information which is recorded as part of, or with the intention that it should form part of any set of information relating to individuals to the extent that the set is structured by reference to individuals or by reference to criteria relating to individuals.[24] When they come into force, the provisions will insert a new s.9A which provides that a public authority is not obliged to comply with a s.7 request in respect of "unstructured personal data" unless (1) the request under that section contains a description of the data,[25] and (2) the authority estimates that the cost of complying with the request so far as relating to those data would exceed the appropriate limit (as prescribed).[26]

---

[16] Data Protection Act 1998, s.7(5).
[17] Data Protection Act 1998, s.7(6).
[18] SI 2000/413.
[19] SI 2000/413, art.6.
[20] Data Protection (Subject Access Modification) (Health) Order 2000 (SI 2000/413), art.5.
[21] See further Data Protection (Subject Access Modification) (Education) Order 2000, (SI 2000/414).
[22] See further Data Protection (Subject Access Modification) (Social Work) Order 2000, (SI 2000/415).
[23] Inserting a new s.9A into the Data Protection Act 1998: Freedom of Information Act 2000, s.69(2). Will come into force on November 30, 2005, unless the Secretary of State appoints an earlier date: Freedom of Information Act 2000, s.87(1)(m).
[24] Data Protection Act 1998, s.9A(1), to be inserted, see n.99 above.
[25] Data Protection Act 1998, s.9A(2) to be inserted, see n.99 above.
[26] Data Protection Act 1998, s.9(A)(3) to be inserted, see n.99 above.

## Right to prevent processing likely to cause damage or distress: s.10

Section 10 of the Data Protection Act 1998 gives individuals a right to **11–102** prevent processing likely to cause damage or distress. An individual is entitled at any time by notice *in writing* to a data controller to require the data controller at the end of such period as is reasonable in the circumstances, to cease, or not to begin, processing, or processing for a specified purpose or in a specified manner, any personal data in respect of which he is the data subject, on the ground that, for specified reasons:

(1)  the processing of the data, or for that purpose, or in that manner, is causing or is likely to cause substantial damage or substantial distress to him or to another, and

(2)  that damage or distress is or would be unwarranted.

Damage and distress is not further defined other than the qualification that it must be "substantial." The Information Commissioner's Legal Guidance states that the Commissioner takes the view that a data subject notice under this section is only likely to be appropriate where the particular processing has caused, or is likely to cause, someone to suffer loss or harm, or upset or anguish of a real nature over and above annoyance level without justification.[27]

This right does not apply where any of the conditions in paras 1 to 4 of **11–103** Sch.2 are met, namely where[28]:

1.  The data subject has given his consent to the processing;

2.  The processing is necessary:

    (a)  for the performance of a contract to which the data subject is a party; or

    (b)  for the taking of steps at the request of the data subject with a view to entering into a contract.

3.  The processing is necessary for compliance with any legal obligations to which the data controller is subject, other than an obligation imposed by contract.

4.  The processing is necessary in order to protect the vital interests of the data subject.

There is also provision for the Secretary of State to make orders prescribing other exemptions, but as at November 1, 2003, no orders had been made under that provision.[29]

---

[27] *Office of the Information Commissioner Data Protection Act 1998 Legal Guidance* at para.4.2.1, p.54.

[28] Data Protection Act 1998, s.10(2)(a).

[29] Data Protection Act 1998, s.10(2)(b).

**11–104**     Relying on consent under para.1 of Sch.2 may prove problematic for a data controller, depending on the terms in which the consent was framed. Consent can be withdrawn. It may be arguable that consent is irrevocable in the circumstances of the case in relation to the specific processing contemplated. If not, a notice under s.10 would impliedly be a withdrawal of consent.

Within 21 days of receiving a notice under s.10, the data controller must either (1) serve the data subject who served the s.10 notice with a written notice stating he has complied with the data subject notice, or (2) stating his reasons for regarding the data subject notice as to any extent unjustified and the extent (if any) to which he has complied or intends to comply with it.[30]

On the application of any person who has given a notice under s.10 which appears to the court to be justified (or to be justified to any extent), if the court considers that the data controller in question has failed to comply with the notice, the court may order him to take such steps for complying with the notice (or for complying with it to that extent) as the court thinks fit.[31] Both the High Court and county court have jurisdiction to make such an order.[32]

### Right to preventing processing for purposes direct marketing: s.11

**11–105**     This is of little relevance to data protection in connection with images and is not considered in any detail here. The right entitles a person to serve a notice in writing on a data controller requiring the data controller, within a reasonable period, to cease processing for the purposes of direct marketing personal data in respect of which he is the data subject.[33]

### Right to prevent automated decision making: s.12

**11–106**     This right relates only to automated processing of data carried out in order to make assessments or take decisions about individuals. The decision must be solely automated and therefore any human input will take the processing outside this provision. An example of automated decision making would be a financial institution using a computer programme that selects individuals to be offered loans or credit cards. The right to prevent automated decision making is unlikely to impact on use of photographs and images and is not considered here.

In summary, s.12 grants an individual the right to serve a notice in writing requiring the data controller to ensure that no decision taken by or on behalf of the data controller which significantly affects that individual is based solely on the processing by automatic means of personal data in respect of which that individual is the data subject for the purpose of

---

[30] Data Protection Act 1998, s.10(3).
[31] Data Protection Act 1998, s.10(4).
[32] Data Protection Act 1998, s.15(1).
[33] Data Protection Act 1998, s.11.

evaluating matters relating to him such as, for example, his performance at work, his creditworthiness, his reliability, or his conduct.[34]

## Remedies

### *Compensation: s.13*

This is a particularly important provision as it grants individuals a right to seek compensation from data controllers in respect of failures to comply with the requirements of the Data Protection Act 1998. Compensation may be awarded by either the High Court or the county court.[35] Section 13 in full provides as follows: **11–107**

> **"Compensation for failure to comply with certain requirements**
> **13.**—(1) An individual who suffers damage by reason of any contravention by a data controller of any of the requirements of this Act is entitled to compensation from the data controller for that damage.
>
> (2) An individual who suffers distress by reason of any contravention by a data controller of any of the requirements of this Act is entitled to compensation from the data controller for that distress if
>
> (a) the individual also suffers damage by reason of the contravention, or
> (b) the contravention relates to the processing of personal data for the special purposes.
>
> (3) In proceedings brought against a person by virtue of this section it is a defence to prove that he had taken such care as in all the circumstances was reasonably required to comply with the requirement concerned."

An individual who suffers damage by reason of any contravention by a data controller of any requirements of the Data Protection Act 1998 is *entitled* to compensation.[36] It is not limited to the data subject and includes any individuals suffering damage. "Any contravention" is a wide provision and would include any failure to comply with the requirements for fair and lawful processing and any breach of the Data Protection Principles. The requirement that the damage be suffered "by reason" of the contravention suggests that the court must consider whether actual compliance with the data protection principles would have made a difference to the damage suffered.[37] **11–108**

Compensation is also available for distress where there is damage by reason of the contravention.[38] Compensation for distress where the individual does not suffer damage is available only if the contravention relates to

---

[34] Data Protection Act 1998, s.12(1).
[35] Data Protection Act 1998, s.15(1).
[36] Data Protection Act 1998, s.13(1).
[37] *Douglas v Hello! Ltd (No.6)* [2003] EWHC 786 at para.239 *per* Lindsay J.; [2003] 3 All E.R. 996; [2003] E.M.L.R. 31.
[38] Data Protection Act 1998, s.13(2)(a).

the processing of data for the purposes of journalism or artistic or literary purposes.[39]

It is a defence to any claim for compensation for contravention of a requirement for the data controller to prove that he had taken such care as in all the circumstances was reasonably required to comply with the requirement concerned.[40]

## Level of compensation

**11–109**     Early indications are that levels of damages awarded as compensation under the Data Protection Act 1998 in respect of image processing will be fairly modest. The fact that compensation is for damage or distress caused "by reason" of any contravention of the Act means that if the damage or distress was primarily caused by breaches of other civil law obligations that give rise to a sufficient remedy, any compensation awarded under s.13 will only be nominal.[41]

However, there is no reason in principle why exemplary damages could not be awarded provided that the case falls within one of the relevant categories identified by Lord Devlin in *Rookes v Barnard (No.1)*[42] namely: (1) cases where there has been "oppressive arbitrary or unconstitutional action by servants of the government",[43] or (2) cases where "the defendant's conduct has been calculated by him to make a profit for himself which may exceed the compensation payable to the plaintiff."[44]

**11–110**   *Campbell v MGN*[45]

At first instance (decision on liability reversed by the CA), damages were assessed at £2,500 with aggravated damages in the sum of £1,000 for publication of photographs of the claimant leaving a Narcotics anonymous meeting. Note this case is the subject of an appeal to the House of Lords to be heard in February 2004.

*Adeniji v London Borough of Newham*[46]

A settlement of £5,000 was approved by the court in respect of an action by a child (through her litigation friend) for alleged misuse of photographs taken of her at a nursery in breach of confidence, contrary to the Human

---

[39] *i.e.* the "special purposes" as defined by s.3; Data Protection Act 1998, s.13(2)(b).
[40] Data Protection Act 1998, s.13(3).
[41] *Douglas v Hello! Ltd (No.6)* [2003] EWHC 786 at para.239 *per* Lindsay J.; [2003] 3 All E.R. 996; [2003] E.M.L.R. 31.
[42] [1964] A.C. 1129; *Broome v Cassell & Co Ltd (No.1)* [1972] A.C. 1027; *Kuddus v Chief Constable of Leicestershire* [2001] UKHL 29; [2002] 2 A.C. 122; [2001] 2 W.L.R. 1789; [2001] 3 All E.R. 193.
[43] [1964] A.C. 1129 at 1226.
[44] *ibid.* A third category of cases was included that is not relevant here—namely where exemplary damages are expressly authorised by statute.
[45] *Campbell v Mirror Group Newspapers Ltd* [2002] EWHC 499; [2002] E.M.L.R. 30 *per* Morland J. Reversed [2002] EWCA Civ 1373; [2003] Q.B. 633; [2003] 2 W.L.R. 80; [2003] 1 All E.R. 224; [2003] E.M.L.R. 2.
[46] (unrep) Garland J., October 16, 2001.

Rights Act 1998 and in breach of the Data Protection Act 1998. The child suffered from spinal muscular atrophy and sickle cell anaemia. Photographs were taken of her whilst she was attending a nursery run by the social services department of the defendant. The photographs were then published by the defendant in various brochures which gave the public information about services on offer by its social services department, in particular in a brochure titled *A strategy for children and young people who are affected or infected by HIV/AIDS*.

## Douglas v Hello![47]

A nominal award of £50 each was made to Michael Douglas and Catherine Zeta Jones as damages under the Data Protection Act 1998 arising out of unauthorised publication of photographs of their wedding where the damage was primarily caused as a result of breaches of other civil law obligations that provided as sufficient remedy.

## Rectification, blocking, erasure and destruction: s.14

If a court is satisfied on the application of a data subject that personal **11–111** data of which the applicant is the subject are inaccurate, the court may order the data controller to rectify, block, erase, or destroy those data.[48] The court may also make such an order in respect of any other personal data in respect of which the defendant is the data controller and which contain an expression of opinion which appears to the court to be based on the inaccurate data.[49] "Inaccurate data" is defined as data which is "incorrect or misleading as to any matter of fact."[50] As with any of the rights contained in ss.10–14, both the High Court and county court have jurisdiction to make such an order.[51]

The power of the court to make such an order applies whether or not the data accurately records information received or obtained by the data controller from the data subject or a third party.[52] Where the data accurately records such information, then if the data controller has complied with the requirements of Sch.1, Pt II, para.7 (no contravention of fourth principle if data controller has taken reasonable steps to verify accuracy, or data indicates data subject's view as notified to the data controller that it is accurate) the court may make an order requiring the data to be supplemented by such statement of the true facts relating to the matters dealt with by the data as the court may approve.[53] If all or any of those requirements have not been complied with, the court may make such order as it thinks fit for securing compliance with those requirements, with or without a further order requiring the data to be supplemented by such a statement of true facts.[54]

---

[47] [2003] EWHC 2629 Ch.
[48] Data Protection Act 1998, s.14(1).
[49] Data Protection Act 1998, s.14(1).
[50] Data Protection Act 1998, s.70(2).
[51] Data Protection Act 1998, s.15(1).
[52] Data Protection Act 1998, s.14(2).
[53] Data Protection Act 1998, s.14(2)(a).
[54] Data Protection Act 1998, s.14(2)(b).

**11–112**    The court has a range of options under s.14 and has power to make an order requiring the data controller to:

(1)  rectify the data,

(2)  block the data,

(3)  erase the data, or

(4)  destroy the data.

The meaning of rectify, erase, and destroy are fairly plain. The right to apply for an order rectifying or erasing accurate data existed under the 1984 Act.[55] The right to apply for an order "blocking" data is a new provision.

An order "blocking the data" presumably will permit a data controller to retain the information but render it inaccessible to certain persons.[56] Authors Jay and Hamilton observe that it is unclear whether blocking only limits disclosure of the data, or whether the use of the data can be blocked.[57] It has also been pointed out that whilst the ability to block data may have technical advantages, continued processing would be in breach of the fourth principle to ensure data is accurate.[58]

**11–113**    Where the court does make an order under s.14(1), or if it is satisfied that personal data which has been rectified, blocked, erased, or destroyed was inaccurate, then the court may, where it considers it reasonably practicable, order the data controller to notify third parties to whom the data have been disclosed of the rectification, blocking, erasure, or destruction.[59]

It is not only the case that rectification/destruction orders may be made where the data is inaccurate. Section 14(4) provides that an order for rectification, blocking, erasure, or destruction of data may also be made where the court is satisfied that the data controller has contravened any of the requirements of the Act in circumstances entitling the data subject to compensation under s.13, and there is a substantial risk of further contravention in respect of those data in such circumstances.[60] If such an order is made under s.14(4), the court may, if reasonably practicable,[61] order the data controller to notify third parties to whom the data has been disclosed of the rectification, blocking, erasure, or destruction.[62]

---

[55] Data Protection Act 1984, s.24.
[56] See discussion of blocking orders in R. Jay and A. Hamilton, *Data Protection Law and Practice* (2nd ed., Sweet & Maxwell, 2003) at p.347.
[57] R. Jay and A. Hamilton, *Data Protection Law and Practice* (2nd ed., Sweet & Maxwell, 2003) at p.83.
[58] See S. Charlton, S. Gaskill *et al.* (eds) *Encyclopaedia of Data Protection* (Sweet & Maxwell) at 1–242.
[59] Data Protection Act 1984, s.14(3).
[60] Data Protection Act 1984, s.14(4).
[61] Data Protection Act 1984, s.14(6) provides "In determining whether it is reasonably practicable to require such notification ... the court shall have regard, in particular, to the number of persons who would have to be notified."
[62] Data Protection Act 1998, s.14(5).

*Remedies obtainable via the Information Commissioner*

The Information Commissioner has power to make an assessment as to **11–114** whether the information is being processed in contravention of the Act.[63] The Commissioner also has powers to issue information notices, special information notices, and enforcement notices.[64] Anyone served with any of the notices has a right of appeal to the Information Tribunal.[65]

An individual can make a request that the Information Commissioner make an assessment or make a formal complaint requesting that an enforcement notice be served. However, once that is done, all further matters are dealt with by the Commissioner and an individual has a very limited right to receive information from the Commissioner about his assessment or enforcement activities. Further, the Commissioner has no power to award compensation and his enforcement powers are weaker than the courts. Accordingly, in many cases where there is a serious violation of the Data Protection Act 1998 that gives rise to a claim for compensation, legal proceedings will be preferable. The powers of the Information Commissioner are therefore dealt with here in outline only.[66]

## Request for assessment: s.42

A person may ask the Information Commissioner for an assessment of **11–115** any processing by which he believes himself to be directly affected as to whether it is likely or unlikely that the processing has been, or is being carried out, in compliance with the provisions of the 1998 Act.[67] "Any person" may make a request, presumably including legal persons, as the right to request an assessment is not expressed to be limited to living individuals.[68]

The Commissioner has an absolute duty to make an assessment when requested.[69] The effect of this is diluted by the fact that he may make an assessment "in such a manner as appears to him to be appropriate". In determining in what manner it is appropriate to make an assessment, the Commissioner may have regard to the extent to which the request appears to him to raise a matter of substance; any undue delay in making the request, and whether or not the person making the request is entitled to make an application under s.7 in respect of the personal data in question.[70]

---

[63] Data Protection Act 1998, s.42.
[64] See Data Protection Act 1998, ss.40–50.
[65] Data Protection Act 1998, s.48. See below at para.11–120.
[66] For further information see R. Jay and A. Hamilton, *Data Protection Law and Practice* (2nd ed., Sweet & Maxwell, 2003) Ch.20 and pp.356–359; S. Charlton, S. Gaskill *et al.* (eds) *Encyclopaedia of Data Protection* (Sweet & Maxwell) at 1–060/10 *et seq*, 1–229 *et seq*. and 1–146/2.
[67] Data Protection Act 1998, s.42.
[68] Unlike the definition of "personal data" in s.1 as "data which relate to living individuals."
[69] Data Protection Act 1998, s.42(2), "the Commissioner *shall* make an assessment..."
[70] Data Protection Act 1998, s.42(3).

The Information Commissioner has published a *Policy on Handling Assessments* which can be downloaded via the internet.[71]

The Commissioner is under no obligation to disclose the format or details of the assessment to the requesting party. He only has to notify the requesting party of (1) whether he has in fact made an assessment as a result of the request, and (2) the extent that he considers appropriate (in particular with regard to any s.7 exemptions) of any view formed, or action taken, as a result of the request.[72]

## Information notice

**11–116**    Where the Commissioner has received a s.42 assessment request, or otherwise reasonably requires information in order to determine whether the data controller has complied with the data protection principles, he may serve the data controller with an information notice.[73] The information notice requires the data controller to supply the Commissioner the information specified within the stated time.[74]

Failure to comply with an information notice is a criminal offence.[75] It is a defence to prove the exercise of all due diligence in an attempt to comply.[76]

There is a right of appeal against an information notice to the Information Tribunal.[77] Appeals to the Information Tribunal are governed by Sch.6 of the Act and the Data Protection Tribunal (Enforcement Appeals) Rules 2000.[78] Generally, a notice of appeal must be served on the Tribunal within 28 days of the date on which the notice relating to the disputed decision was served on, or given to the appellant.[79] However, the Tribunal may accept a notice of appeal served after the 28 day period if it is of the opinion that, by reason of special circumstances, it is just and right to do so.[80]

## Special information notices

**11–117**    "Special information notices" allow the Commissioner to obtain information with a view to establishing whether personal data is being processed only for the special purposes (*i.e.* journalistic, literary, or artistic purposes),[81] or whether data is being processed with a view to publication by any person

---

[71] At *http://www.dataprotection.gov.uk/dpr/dpdoc.nsf.* Access via Home Page under the "Guidance & Other Publications" button.
[72] Data Protection Act 1998, s.42(4).
[73] Data Protection Act 1998, s.43.
[74] Data Protection Act 1998, s.43. s.43 requires certain other information to be contained in the notice.
[75] Data Protection Act 1998, s.47.
[76] Data Protection Act 1998, s.47(3).
[77] Data Protection Act 1998, s.48.
[78] SI 2000/189 as amended by the Information Tribunal (Enforcement Appeals) (Amendment) Rules 2002, (SI 2002/2722).
[79] Data Protection Tribunal (Enforcement Appeals) Rules 2000 (SI 2000/189), r.4(1).
[80] Data Protection Tribunal (Enforcement Appeals) Rules 2000 (SI 2000/189), r.4(1).
[81] As defined in the Data Protection Act 1998, s.3.

of any journalistic, literary, or artistic material which has not previously been published by the data controller.[82]

A special information notice may only be served where the Commissioner **11–118** has received an assessment request under s.42, or where proceedings have been stayed under s.32.[83] Even where proceedings have been stayed under s.32, the Commissioner may only serve a special information notice if he:

(1) has reasonable grounds for suspecting that the personal data to which the proceedings relate—

(a) are not being processed only for the special purposes, or
(b) are not being processed with a view to the publication by any person of any journalistic, literary, or artistic material which has not previously been published by the data controller.

Failure to comply with a special information notice is a criminal offence.[84] It is a defence to prove the exercise of all due diligence in an attempt to comply.[85]

There is a right of appeal against a special information notice to the **11–119** Information Tribunal.[86] Appeals to the Information Tribunal are governed by Sch.6 of the Act and the Data Protection Tribunal (Enforcement Appeals) Rules 2000.[87] Generally, a notice of appeal must be served on the Tribunal within 28 days of the date on which the notice relating to the disputed decision was served on or given to the appellant.[88] However, the Tribunal may accept a notice of appeal served after the 28 day period if it is of the opinion that, by reason of special circumstances, it is just and right to do so.[89]

## Enforcement notices

The Information Commissioner has power to serve an enforcement notice **11–120** on any data controller whom the Commissioner is satisfied has contravened or is contravening any of the data protection principles.[90] The enforcement notice may require the data controller, in order to comply with the principle(s) in question, to do either or both of the following:

(1) to take or refrain from taking specified steps within a stated time[91];

---

[82] Data Protection Act 1998, s.44(2).
[83] Data Protection Act 1998, s.44.
[84] Data Protection Act 1998, s.47.
[85] Data Protection Act 1998, s.47(3).
[86] Data Protection Act 1998, s.48.
[87] SI 2000/189 as amended by the Information Tribunal (Enforcement Appeals) (Amendment) Rules 2002 (SI 2002/2722).
[88] Data Protection Tribunal (Enforcement Appeals) Rules 2000 (SI 2000/189), r.4(1).
[89] Data Protection Tribunal (Enforcement Appeals) Rules 2000 (SI (2000/189), r.4(1).
[90] Data Protection Act 1998, s.40(1).
[91] Data Protection Act 1998, s.40(1)(a).

(2) refrain from processing any (or any specified) personal data, or to refrain from processing them for a purpose so specified or in a manner so specified after such time as may be so specified.[92]

Failure to comply with an enforcement notice is a criminal offence.[93] It is a defence to prove the exercise of all due diligence in order to comply with the notice.[94]

Any person served with an enforcement notice has a right of appeal to the Information Tribunal.[95] Appeals to the Information Tribunal are governed by Sch.6 of the Act and the Data Protection Tribunal (Enforcement Appeals) Rules 2000.[96] Generally, a notice of appeal must be served on the Tribunal within 28 days of the date on which the notice relating to the disputed decision was served on or given to the appellant.[97] However, the Tribunal may accept a notice of appeal served after the 28 day period if it is of the opinion that, by reason of special circumstances, it is just and right to do so.[98]

## EXEMPTIONS

**11–121**   Certain types of data processing are exempt from certain provisions in the Data Protection Act 1998. There are a large number of categories of processing which are exempt, but the provisions they are exempt from varies from category to category. In addition, there are some transitional exemptions. Many of these exemptions, whilst they in theory will apply to photographs and images in so far as they are personal data, in reality are unlikely to be of much relevance in practice to those advising in respect of images. All the exemptions are referred to here in outline. There is only detailed consideration of exemptions likely to be relevant to the question of photographs and images in practice.

---

**Overview of Exemptions**

**11–122**

*Exemptions: A List*
*Under the 1998 Act*

| | |
|---|---|
| National Security | s.28 |
| Crime and Taxation | s.29 |
| Serious Harm to Physical or Mental Health | s.30 + SI 2000/413 |

---

[92] Data Protection Act 1998, s.40(1)(b).
[93] Data Protection Act 1998, s.47.
[94] Data Protection Act 1998, s.47(3).
[95] Data Protection Act 1998, s.48.
[96] SI 2000/189 as amended by the Information Tribunal (Enforcement Appeals) (Amendment) Rules 2002 (SI 2002/2722).
[97] Data Protection Tribunal (Enforcement Appeals) Rules 2000 (SI 2000/189), r.4(1).
[98] Data Protection Tribunal (Enforcement Appeals) Rules 2000 (SI 2000/189), r.4(1).

| | |
|---|---|
| Education | s.30 + SI 2000/414 |
| Social Work | s.30 + SI 2000/415 |
| Regulatory Activity | s.31 |
| Journalism, Literature and Art | s.32 |
| Research History and Statistics | s.33 |
| Information Made Available to the Public By Enactment | s.34 |
| Disclosure Required By Law or For Legal Proceedings | s.35 |
| Domestic Purposes | s.35 |
| Confidential references | Sch 7 |
| Armed forces | Sch 7 |
| Judicial appointments and honours | Sch 7 |
| Crown employment and Crown or Ministerial appointments | Sch 7 |
| Management forecasts etc | Sch 7 |
| Corporate finance | Sch 7 |
| Negotiations | Sch 7 |
| Examination Marks | Sch 7 |
| Examination Scripts | Sch 7 |
| Legal Professional Privilege | Sch 7 |
| Self—Incrimination | Sch 7 |

*Data Protection (Miscellaneous Subject Access Exemptions) Order 2000 SI 2000/419*
Human Fertilisation and Embrylogy
Adoption Records
Special Educational Needs
Parental Records and Reports
Public Registers

The part of the Act dealing with exemptions begins by defining two categories of provisions—the subject information provisions, and the non-disclosure provisions. This categorisation enables a short hand and convenient way for the various exemptions to exclude either or both of these sets of provisions. It is therefore necessary to understand what is included within these definitions when considering the exemptions.

*Subject Information Provisions*

The "Subject Information Provisions" are defined as:                    **11–123**

(a) the first data protection principle to the extent to which it requires compliance with para.2 of Pt II of Sch.1, and

(b) s.7.[99]

---

[99] Data Protection Act 1998, s.27(2).

This essentially means the rights of the data subject to receive information and the right of access to personal data in particular:

(1) The right of the data subject to be provided with the information about the identity of the data controller and any representative of the data controller; the purposes for which the data is intended to be processed, and any further information which is necessary having regard to the specific circumstances in which the data are to be processed.[1]

(2) The right of access to personal data as set out in s.7; namely the right to be informed of whether personal data is processed; the right to a description of the personal data, the purpose of processing and the recipients to whom it is being disclosed; and the right to have communicated in intelligible form the information constituting the personal data.

*Non-disclosure provisions*

**11–124**   "Non-disclosure provisions" mean, to the extent that they are inconsistent with the disclosure in question[2]:

(1) the First Data Protection Principle (fair and lawful processing) except to the extent to which it requires compliance with the conditions in Schs 2 and 3;

(2) the Second (specified and lawful purpose), Third (adequate, relevant and not excessive) Fourth (accurate and up to date) and Fifth (not kept for longer than necessary) Data Protection Principles, and

(3) the right to prevent processing likely to cause damage or distress (s.10)

(4) the right to rectification, blocking, erasure, and destructions (s.14(1) to (3)).

## National security: s.28

**11–125**   Personal data are exempt from the following provisions if the exemption is required for the purpose of safeguarding national security[3]:

(a) all of the data protection principles;

(b) the rights of data subjects (Pt II of the Act in its entirety);

(c) the notification provisions (Pt III of the Act in its entirety);

(d) enforcement provisions (Pt V of the Act in its entirety);

---

[1] Sch.1, Pt II, paras 2(1) and 2(3).
[2] Data Protection Act 1998, s.27(3) and (4).
[3] Data Protection Act 1998, s.28.

(e) the offence of unlawfully obtaining or disclosing personal data set out in s.55.

A minister who is a member of the Cabinet (or the Attorney General or Lord Advocate) can issue a certificate certifying that an exemption is required for the purpose of safeguarding national security.[4] Such a certificate may identify the personal data covered by "a general description" and can be issued in respect of processing that is yet to take place.[5] Any certificate so issued is to be regarded as conclusive evidence that the exemption is required for the purpose of safeguarding national security.[6]

Any person directly affected by the issuing of such a certificate may appeal against the certificate to the Information Tribunal.[7] Appeals to the Information Tribunal under s.28 are governed by Sch.6 of the Act and the Data Protection Tribunal (National Security Appeals) Rules 2000.[8]

## Crime and taxation: s.29

This exemption applies to any personal data processed for any of the following purposes:   **11–126**

(1) the prevention or detection of crime,

(2) the apprehension or prosecution of offenders,

(3) the assessment or collection of any tax,

(4) the assessment or collection of any duty,

(5) the assessment or collection of any imposition of a similar nature to a tax or a duty.[9]

### *Crime and taxation: first exemption*

In any case where the application would be likely to prejudice those purposes, personal data processed for any of those purposes are exempt from:   **11–127**

---

[4] Data Protection Act 1998, s.28(2) and (10).
[5] Data Protection Act 1998, s.28(3).
[6] Data Protection Act 1998, s.28(2).
[7] Data Protection Act 1998, s.28(4).
[8] SI 2000/206. For appeals to the National Security Appeals Panel of the Information Tribunal see (1) *Norman Baker MP v Sec. of State Home Department*, October 1, 2001 (no reasonable grounds for issuing a certificate of "unnecessarily wide effect") *Encyclopaedia of Data Protection* (Sweet & Maxwell) at 6–681. Full report *via* Department of Constitutional Affairs (formerly the Lord Chancellor's Department) website *http://www.lcd.gov.uk/foi/ bakerfin.pdf*; (2) *Al-Fayed v Sec. of State for Home Dept*, February 28, 2002 *http://www.lcd.gov.uk/foi/ alfayedfin.pdf*; (3) *Gosling v Sec. of State for Home Dept*, August 1, 2003 *http://www.lcd.gov.uk/ foi/goslingfin.pdf*; (4) *Hitchens v Sec. of State for Home Dept*, August 4, 2003 *http:// www.lcd.gov.uk/foi/hitchensfin.pdf*.
[9] Data Protection Act 1998, s.29.

- the First Data Protection Principle, but not the requirement to comply with Sch.2 and/or Sch.3 conditions[10];

- the subject access provisions in s.7.[11]

Accordingly, the processing needs to be carried out on legitimate grounds. Sensitive personal data cannot be processed unless one of the Sch.3 conditions is met.

It has been held by the Administrative Court that "likely" is this context means more than "a real risk".[12] It connotes "a degree of probability where there is a very significant and weighty chance of prejudice to the identified public interests. The degree of risk must be such that there 'may very well' be prejudice to those interests even if the risk falls short of being more probable than not."[13]

## Crime and taxation: second exemption

**11–128**    Personal data processed for the purpose of discharging *statutory functions* and which was obtained from a person who had it in his possession for any of the purposes stated above at (1) to (5) are exempt from

"the subject information provisions to the extent to which the application of the provisions would be likely to prejudice any of the crime and taxation purposes."[14]

## Crime and taxation: third exemption

**11–129**    Personal data are exempt from the non-disclosure provisions in any case in where disclosure is for any of the crime or taxation purposes and where the application of those provisions in relation to the disclosure would be likely to prejudice[15] any of the crime or taxation purposes.[16]

"In any case" means "in any particular case". If the data controller wishes to rely on the s.29 exemption, he needs to show that one of the statutory objectives is likely to be prejudiced in the particular case in which the question arises.[17]

---

[10] Data Protection Act 1998, s.29(1).

[11] *ibid.*

[12] *R. (on the application of Alan Lord) v Secretary of State for the Home Department* [2003] EWHC 2073 (Admin) *per* Munby J. at paras 99–100.

[13] *ibid.*, at para.100.

[14] Data Protection Act 1998, s.29(2). As to the meaning of "likely" in s.29(1) see above at para.11–127, n.12 and accompanying text.

[15] As to the meaning of "likely to prejudice" see above at para.11–127, n.12 and accompanying text.

[16] Data Protection Act 1998, s.29(3).

[17] *R. (on the application of Alan Lord) v Secretary of State for the Home Department* [2003] EWHC 2073 (Admin) *per* Munby J. at para.94; *Equifax Europe Ltd v The Data Protection Registrar* (Case DA/90 25/49/7); *Encyclopaedia of Data Protection* Vol.IV, paras 6–099 *et seq.*

## Crime and taxation: fourth exemption

The fourth exemption applies to government departments, local authorities (or any authority administering council tax or housing benefits) processing personal data for any of the crime and taxation purposes.[18] The exemption only applies where the personal data consists of a classification applied to the data subject as part of a risk assessment system which is operated by that authority for either (a) the assessment or collection of any tax, duty, or similar imposition, or (b) the prevention or detection of crime, or apprehension or prosecution of offenders, where the offence concerned involves any unlawful claim for any payment out of, or any unlawful application of, public funds. If these requirements are met, there is an exemption from the subject access provisions to the extent to which such exemption is required in the interests of the operation of the risk assessment system.[19]

**11–130**

# Health

The Data Protection (Subject Access Modification)(Health) Order 2000[20] was made under s.30(1) of the Data Protection Act 1998 which gives the Secretary of State power to exempt or modify the subject information provisions with respect to data consisting of information about the physical or mental health or condition of the data subject.

**11–131**

## Serious harm to physical or mental health

Personal data consisting of information as to the physical or mental health or condition of the data subject are exempt from the s.7 rights of access in any case to the extent to which the application of s.7 would be likely to cause serious harm to the physical or mental health, or condition of the data subject, or any other person.[21]

**11–132**

A data controller who is not a health professional as defined[22] cannot withhold information under this exemption without first consulting the appropriate health professional.[23] The data controller must consult the person who appears to the data controller to be the appropriate health professional on the question whether or not the exemption applies with respect to the information (*i.e.* whether or not disclosure is likely to cause harm to physical or mental health). There is no need to consult the appropriate health professional where that health professional has given an opinion in writing that all information that is the subject of the request is covered by the exemption,[24] but controllers cannot rely on a written state-

---

[18] Data Protection Act 1998, s.29(4) and (5).
[19] *ibid.*
[20] SI 2000/413. In force March 1, 2000.
[21] Data Protection (Subject Access Modification) (Health) Order 2000 (SI 2000/413), art.5.
[22] Defined in Data Protection (Subject Access Modification) (Health) Order 2000 (SI 2000/413), art.2.
[23] Data Protection (Subject Access Modification) (Health) Order 2000 (SI 2000/413), art.5(2).
[24] Data Protection (Subject Access Modification) (Health) Order 2000 (SI 2000/413), art.7.

ment that is more than six months old, or if it is reasonable to re-consult the health professional.[25]

Equally, a data controller who is not a health professional must not communicate any personal data as to physical or mental condition in response to a request without first consulting the appropriate health professional.[26] This does not apply to information which the data controller is satisfied has previously been seen by the data subject or is already within the knowledge of the data subject.[27]

### *Court proceedings involving children*

**11–133**    Personal data consisting of information as to the physical or mental health of the subject is exempt from the subject information provisions where it is processed by a court in specified proceedings involving children,[28] and is in the form of information supplied to the court in a report or other evidence given to the court by a local authority, Health and Social Services Board, Health and Social Services Trust, probation officer, or other person.[29] The exemption only applies where, in accordance with any of the provisions of the relevant court rules, the information may be withheld from the data subject in whole or in part.[30]

### *Access by third parties acting on behalf of the data subject*

**11–134**    Where an application for s.7 access is made by either (1) a person with parental responsibility on behalf of a child data subject, or (2) a person appointed by the court in respect of a data subject who is incapable of managing his affairs, mental or physical health data are exempt from s.7 in any case to the extent to which the application of that section would disclose information:

(a) provided by the data subject in the expectation that it would not be disclosed to the person making the request (unless the data subject has expressly indicated that he no longer has that expectation)[31];

(b) obtained as a result of any examination or investigation to which the data subject consented in the expectation that the information would not be so disclosed (unless the data subject has expressly indicated that he no longer has that expectation)[32]; or

---

[25] Data Protection (Subject Access Modification) (Health) Order 2000 (SI 2000/413), art.7(2).
[26] Data Protection (Subject Access Modification) (Health) Order 2000 (SI 2000/413), art.6(1).
[27] Data Protection (Subject Access Modification) (Health) Order 2000 SI (2000/413), art.6(2).
[28] Any proceedings to which any of the following apply: the Family Proceedings Courts (Children Act 1989) Rules 1991; the Magistrates' Courts (Children and Young Persons) Rules 1992; the Magistrates' Courts (Criminal Justice (Children)) Rules (Northern Ireland) 1999; the Act of Sederunt (Child Care and Maintenance Rules) 1997 or the Children's Hearings (Scotland) Rules 1996 apply where, in accordance with a provision of any of those Rules, the information may be withheld by the court in whole or in part from the data subject.
[29] Data Protection (Subject Access Modification) (Health) Order 2000 (SI 2000/413), art.4.
[30] Data Protection (Subject Access Modification) (Health) Order 2000 (SI 2000/413), art.4(2).
[31] Data Protection (Subject Access Modification) (Health) Order 2000 (SI 2000/413), art.5(a).
[32] Data Protection (Subject Access Modification) (Health) Order 2000 (SI 2000/413), art.5(b).

(c) which the data subject has expressly indicated should not be so disclosed.[33]

## Education

The Data Protection (Subject Access Modification) (Education) Order 2000[34] was made under s.30(2) of the Data Protection Act 1998 which gives the Secretary of State power to exempt or modify the subject information provisions with respect to data controllers who are schools or teachers and regarding information relating to current and former pupils.

**11-135**

The exemptions in the Education Order apply to personal data consisting of information constituting an educational record as defined in para.1 of Sch.11 to the Act.[35] Broadly, this is any record of information relating to any person who is or has been a pupil at the school that is processed by or on behalf of the governing body of, or a teacher at any school in England and Wales, and originated from any one or more of a number of specified people including the pupil, his parents, and employees of the local authority maintaining the school.[36] It excludes information which is processed by a teacher solely for the teacher's own use. Reference should be made to Sch.11 for the full definition.

The Education Order does not apply to data consisting of information as to the physical or mental health or condition of the data subject to which the Data Protection (Subject Access Modification) (Health) Order 2000.[37]

### Educational records

An educational record is exempt from s.7 subject access in any case to the extent to which the application of that section would be likely to cause serious harm to the physical or mental health or condition of the data subject or any other person.[38]

**11-136**

Where an application for s.7 access is made by either (1) a person with parental responsibility on behalf of a child data subject, or (2) a person appointed by the court in respect of a data subject who is incapable of managing his affairs, an educational record is exempt from s.7 in any case to the extent to which the application of that section would not be in the best interests of that data subject and where the personal data consisting of information as to whether or not the data subject is, has been, or is, at risk of being the subject of child abuse.[39]

---

[33] Data Protection (Subject Access Modification) (Health) Order 2000 (SI 2000/413), art.5(c).
[34] SI 2000/414. In force March 1, 2000.
[35] Data Protection (Subject Access Modification) (Education) Order 2000 (SI 2000/414), art.3(1).
[36] Data Protection Act 1998, Sch.11, paras 1 *et seq.*
[37] SI 2000/413. As to the provisions of this order see above at paras 11–131 to 11–134.
[38] Data Protection (Subject Access Modification) (Education) Order 2000 (SI 2000/414), art.5.
[39] Data Protection (Subject Access Modification) (Education) Order 2000 (SI 2000/414), art.5(2).

*Court proceedings*

**11–137**    Personal data consisting of an educational record is exempt from the subject information provisions where it is processed by a court in proceedings covered by specified rules[40] and consists of information supplied in a report or other evidence given to the court in the course of those proceedings and in accordance with a provision of any of the specified rules, the information may be withheld by the court in whole or in part from the data subject.[41]

## Social work

**11–138**    The Data Protection (Subject Access Modification) (Social Work) Order 2000[42] was made under s.30(3) of the Data Protection Act 1998 which gives the Secretary of State power to exempt or modify the subject information provisions with respect to data controllers who are government departments, local authorities, or other designated bodies, and regarding information processed for the purposes of social work. The power to confer exemptions or make modifications is limited by s.30(3) to cases where the application of the subject access provisions is likely to prejudice the carrying out of social work.

The Social Work Order does not apply any data consisting of information as to the physical or mental health or condition of the data subject to which the Data Protection (Subject Access Modification) (Health) Order 2000 or the Data Protection (Subject Access Modification) (Education) Order 2000 applies.

**11–139**    The data to which the Data Protection (Subject Access Modification) (Social Work) Order 2000[43] (and hence the exemptions) applies are identified in Sch.1 of the order to which reference should be made. It includes, for example, data processed by a local authority in connection with its social services functions and by a probation committee.

Personal data to which the Order are exempt from the obligations in s.7(1)(b) to (d) of the Act in any case to the extent to which the application of those provisions would be likely to prejudice the carrying out of social work by reason of the fact that serious harm to the physical or mental health or condition of the data subject or any other person would be likely to be caused.[44]

"Social work" personal data processed by a court and consisting of information supplied in a report or other evidence given to the court by a local authority, Health and Social Services Board, Health and Social Ser-

---

[40] Any proceedings to which the following apply: Magistrates' Courts (Children and Young Persons) Rules 1992; the Magistrates' Courts (Criminal Justice (Children)) Rules (Northern Ireland) 1999; the Act of Sederunt (Child Care and Maintenance Rules) 1997 or the Children's Hearings (Scotland) Rules 1996.
[41] Data Protection (Subject Access Modification) (Education) Order 2000 (SI 2000/414), art.4.
[42] SI 2000/415. In force March 1, 2000.
[43] SI 2000/415. In force March 1, 2000.
[44] Data Protection (Subject Access Modification) (Social Work) Order 2000 (SI 2000/415), art.5(1).

vices Trust, probation officer, or other person in the course of any specified proceedings are exempt from the subject access provisions.[45]

## Regulatory activity: s.31

Personal data processed for the purposes of discharging certain regulatory **11–140** functions specified in s.31 are exempt from the subject information provisions in any case to the extent to which the application of those provisions to the data would be likely to prejudice the proper discharge of those functions.

A large number of relevant functions are set out in s.31 to which reference should be made. Generally, the application is to public watch dogs who are concerned with protecting the public, charities, or fair competition in business.

## Journalism, literature, and art: s.32

"Special purposes" means any one or more of the following[46]:   **11–141**

- the purposes of journalism,
- artistic purposes,
- literary purposes.

Processing for special purposes (if four conditions are satisfied under s.32) qualifies for potential exemption from the vast majority of provisions of the Data Protection Act 1998. The "Special Purposes" exemption is the most significant of the exemptions for the purposes of considering photographs.

### Overview of special purposes exemptions

The four conditions that must be satisfied to claim any exemption under **11–142** s.32 are:

1. The personal data is being processed *only* for the special purposes.

2. The processing is undertaken with a view to the publication by any person of any journalistic, literary, or artistic material.

3. The data controller reasonably believes that, taking account in particular of the special importance of the public interest in freedom of expression, publication would be in the public interest.

4. The data controller reasonably believes that, in all the circumstances, compliance with the provision in respect of which the exemption is claimed is incompatible with the special purposes.

---

[45] Data Protection (Subject Access Modification)(Social Work) Order 2000 (SI 2000/415), art.4 and Sch.1, para.2.
[46] Data Protection Act 1998, s.3.

**11–143**    If all of these conditions are met, then the s.32 exemption is available in respect of the following:

- all of the Data Protection Principles with the sole exception of the Seventh Data Protection Principle (measures to be taken to prevent unauthorised processing, etc.);

- subject access under s.7;

- right to prevent processing likely to cause damage or distress: s.10;

- rights in relation to automated decision taking: s.12;

- rectification, blocking, erasure, or destruction of certain inaccurate manual data during the transitional periods: s.12A;

- rectification, blocking, erasure, and destruction of inaccurate data: s.14(1)–(3).

The s.32 exemption, if applicable, applies both before and after publication.[47] The requirements of the Act in the absence of s.32 would impose restrictions on the media which would radically restrict the freedom of the press.[48]

*Section 32*

**11–144**    Section 32 is set out below in full.

---

**Journalism, Literature and Art**

**32.**—(1) Personal data which are processed only for the special purposes are exempt from any provision to which this subsection relates if
  (a)  the processing is undertaken with a view to the publication by any person of any journalistic, literary or artistic material,
  (b)  the data controller reasonably believes that, having regard in particular to the special importance of the public interest in freedom of expression, publication would be in the public interest, and
  (c)  the data controller reasonably believes that, in all the circumstances, compliance with that provision is incompatible with the special purposes.

(2) Subsection (1) relates to the provisions of—
  (a)  the data protection principles except the seventh data protection principle,
  (b)  section 7,
  (c)  section 10,
  (d)  section 12,

---

[47] *Campbell v MGN Ltd* [2002] EWCA Civ 1373 at para.120; [2003] Q.B. 633 at 674 *per* Lord Phillips M.R. Note this case is the subject of an appeal to the House of Lords to be heard in February 2004.
[48] *Campbell v MGN Ltd* [2002] EWCA Civ 1373 at para.123; [2003] Q.B. 633 at 674 *per* Lord Phillips M.R. Note this case is the subject of an appeal to the House of Lords to be heard in February 2004.

[*(dd)* *section 12A,*] and
   (e) section 14(1) to (3).

(3) In considering for the purposes of subsection (1)(b) whether the belief of a data controller that publication would be in the public interest was or is a reasonable one, regard may be had to his compliance with any code of practice which
   (a) is relevant to the publication in question, and
   (b) is designated by the Secretary of State by order for the purposes of this subsection.

(4) Where at any time ("the relevant time") in any proceedings against a data controller under section 7(9), 10(4), 12(8)[, *12A(3)*] or 14 or by virtue of section 13 the data controller claims, or it appears to the court, that any personal data to which the proceedings relate are being processed
   (a) only for the special purposes, and
   (b) with a view to the publication by any person of any journalistic, literary or artistic material which, at the time twenty-four hours immediately before the relevant time, had not previously been published by the data controller,
the court shall stay the proceedings until either of the conditions in subsection (5) is met.

(5) Those conditions are
   (a) that a determination of the Commissioner under section 45 with respect to the data in question takes effect, or
   (b) in a case where the proceedings were stayed on the making of a claim, that the claim is withdrawn.

(6) For the purposes of this Act "publish", in relation to journalistic, literary or artistic material, means make available to the public or any section of the public.

[The words in italics and within square brackets are part of the transitional provisions inserted temporarily until October 23, 2007.[49]]

## Meaning of purposes of journalism, artistic and literary purposes

The special purposes,[50] being the purposes of journalism, artistic purposes, and literary purposes, are not further defined. It should be remembered that the Human Rights Act 1998 provides that in so far as it is possible to do so, primary legislation must be read and given effect in a way which is compatible with the Convention Rights.[51]    **11–145**

It is probable therefore that in order to ensure compliance with Art.10 **11–146** that the meaning of each of the three special purposes will be given a wider, rather than a narrower construction. This is particularly the case with the phrase "purposes of journalism". There is considerable judicial comment to the effect that freedom of expression is a vital part of a democracy.[52] A vital aspect of protection of freedom of expression is the protection of the freedom of the press. It is submitted that "purposes of journalism" would

---

[49] By the Data Protection Act 1998, s.72, Sch.13, para.2(a) and (b) respectively.
[50] Identified in Data Protection Act 1998, s.3.
[51] Human Rights Act 1998, s.3(1).
[52] See above at para.7–046, n.28.

include any processing in connection with journalistic reporting in any media and encompass both the recording of facts and the expression of opinion.

**11–147**     "Literary purposes" is capable of covering an extremely wide range of processing. Under the Copyright Designs and Patents Act 1988, copyright subsists in "an original work of literature"[53] which is widely defined as "any work other than a dramatic or musical work which is written, spoken or sung" and includes tables, computer programs, and databases. This provision is not interpreted as requiring any literary merit but it has been said that a literary work is one intended to afford information, instruction, or pleasure.[54] If one takes as a starting point that literary purposes are any purposes in connection with preparation of "a work of literature" meaning anything written, then literary purposes would include not just novels or non-fiction books, but tables, instruction leaflets, and possibly even computer programs. It is arguable that "literary purposes" would include processing of photographic images in connection with a work of literature, for example photographs of individuals in a biography.

Again when considering "artistic purposes", some assistance may be derived from the Copyright Designs and Patents Act 1988 ("CDPA 1988") which defines "an artistic work" as including a graphic work, photographs, sculptures, collages, and architecture.[55] Unlike the statutory definition of literary work which does not specifically state there is no requirement for literary merit, the CDPA 1988 specifically states graphic works are included "irrespective of artistic quality".[56] Artistic purposes will include processing in connection with creation of graphic artistic works. In its widest definition of "artistic" it encompasses "the arts" in general, including music, drama, opera, etc.

**11–148**     Photographs that are created and processed for artistic purposes would be included within the special purposes. In some cases, it will be clear that a photograph is processed for artistic purposes—such as photographs processed with a view to inclusion in a photographic exhibition, or digitally manipulated images that become more in the nature of photo-illustrations. Equally, at the other end of the scale, will be photographs that are plainly not processed for artistic purposes such as police "mug-shots", post-mortem photographs, or other photographs taken and processed as evidential records. In between these two extremes falls a wide variety of images and the extent to which the processing of such images can be said to be for "artistic purposes" depends upon the interpretation that the court will give to that phrase. It is submitted that any kind of processing of images for illustrative use is capable of amounting to artistic purposes, which would include images of buildings used in prospectuses or other quasi-documentary images published as illustrations.

---

[53] Copyright Designs and Patents Act 1988, s.1.
[54] *Exxon Corp v Exxon Insurance Consultants International Ltd* [1982] Ch. 119; [1981] 3 All E.R. 241; [1982] R.P.C. 69.
[55] Copyright Designs and Patents Act 1988, s.3.
[56] Copyright Designs and Patents Act 1988, s.4(1)(a).

*Condition 1: Processed only for special purposes*

Although s.32 contains three conditions in subss.(1)–(3), in reality there    **11–149**
are four conditions. The first part of s.32 states that exemption applies to
"Personal data which are processed *only* for the special purposes ... "

The "only" qualification relates to the processing and not to the creation
of the data. Accordingly, the exemption can be claimed in respect of a
photograph or image created for other purposes that is then *processed* for
one of the special purposes. Take for example, a CCTV camera that records
images for the purpose of security. If, however, it happened to record a
politician engaged in some criminal activity, if the media were to process
that image in the form of preparation for publication in a newspaper,
potentially the s.32 "journalistic purposes" exemption could be claimed as
the *processing* was for one of the special purposes.

*Condition 2: With a view to publication*

Section 32(1)(a) provides that the exemption can only be claimed if "The    **11–150**
processing is undertaken with a view to the publication by any person of any
journalistic, literary or artistic material." It is unclear what is meant by
"with a view to publication". Would it for example cover photographic
images kept on file "just in case"? It is submitted that given that the aim of
s.32 is essentially to protect freedom of expression, to interpret the provision
as covering theoretical publication in the future where there is no immediate
intention to publish is to construe the section too widely. It is submitted that
this provision should be interpreted as meaning "with a genuine view to
publication within a reasonably foreseeable period" as opposed to "a possible view to publication at some indeterminate point in the future."

"Publish" is defined in s.32(6) as meaning "material available to the
public or any section of the public". When the Bill was debated in the Lords,
it was made clear that this definition of publish was intended to cover all
media and "includes any means of making available, including broadcasting, Internet and so forth."[57]

*Condition 3: Publication in the public interest*

Section 32(1)(b) provides the third condition that must be satisfied in    **11–151**
order to claim the exemption, namely "the data controller reasonably
believes that, having regard in particular to the special importance of the
public interest in freedom of expression, publication would be in the public
interest."

---

[57] *Hansard* Lords Grand Committee Vol.586, No.110, col.90, February 25, 1998, Lord Williams
of Mostyn who went on to say "We believe that the value of using the general term 'publishing'
is that it is apt to accommodate in the future any further developments."

**Designated codes**

**11–152**   In considering for the purposes of subs.(1)(b) whether the belief of a data controller that publication would be in the public interest was, or is, a reasonable one, regard may be had to his compliance with any designated code of practice which is relevant to the publication in question.

The designated codes are specified by Order[58] and are:

1.   the Press Complaints Commission Code of Practice[59];

2.   the Producers' Guidelines published by the British Broadcasting Corporation;

3.   the Broadcasting Standards Commission Code on Fairness and Privacy[60];

4.   the Independent Television Commission Programme Code[61];

5.   Radio Authority Code.[62]

It should be noted that the Codes numbered 3 to 5 above are likely to change in the near future. The Office of Communications Act 2002 (together with the Communications Act 2003) creates a new unified regulator for media, radio, and telecommunications called Ofcom, together with a new regulatory regime. Ofcom will replace the Radio Authority, the Broadcasting Standards Commission, and the Independent Television Commission. It is anticipated that Ofcom will become vested with its full powers on December 29, 2003.[63]

**11–153**   The CCTV Code of Practice made by the Information Commissioner under s.51(3)(b) of the Data Protection Act 1998 is not a designated code of practice for the purposes of the s.32 special purposes exemption. It remains relevant in so far as its provisions should be taken into account in determining whether processing has been fair under the First Data Protection Principle.

**11–154**   Each of the Codes numbered 1 to 4 contain guidelines relevant to the obtaining and use of images of people. The Press Complaints Commission Code is likely to be of particular relevance to photographic images, as it covers the use of photograph by the print media. A number of provisions are directly applicable, in particular the clauses concerning:

Accuracy        duty not to publish inaccurate, misleading, or distorted material, including pictures: cl.1(i).

---

[58] Data Protection (Designated Codes of Practice) (No.2) Order 2000 (SI 2000/1864).
[59] See Ch.14, below. The PCC Code is reproduced in full at Appendix 3, below.
[60] Under the Broadcasting Act 1996, s.107. NB: this section will be amended by the Communications Act 2003, s.360(3), Sch.15, Pt 2, paras 132(1) and (2) from a date to be appointed.
[61] Under the Broadcasting Act 1990, s.7. NB: this is to be repealed by the Communications Act 2003, ss.360(3), 406(7), Sch.15, Pt 1, para.4, Sch.19(1) from a date to be appointed.
[62] Under the Broadcasting Act 1990, s.91.
[63] For latest information see what is described as the Ofcom transitional website at *http://www.ofcom.org.uk/*.

Privacy     Respect for his or her private and family life, home, health, and correspondence; use of long lens photography to photograph people in private places without their consent unacceptable: cl.3.

Harassment     No photographing of individuals in private places without their consent; must not persist in pursuing or photographing individuals after having been asked to desist; must not remain on their property after having been asked to leave and must not follow them: cl.4(ii).

The PCC Code is considered in more detail in Chapter 14, below, and the Code itself is set out in full in Appendix 3, below.

The BBC Producer's Guidelines contain a number of provisions con- **11–155** cerning obtaining and use of images. The Guidelines state that generally, surreptitious recording is only normally permitted for one of four purposes: (1) as an investigative tool regarding issues of serious anti-social or criminal behaviour, (2) to gather material which could not be obtained openly in countries where the local law is contrary to democratic freedoms and principles, (3) for social research where no other method could reasonably capture the relevant behaviour, or (4) for purely entertainment purposes where the secret recording and any deception are an intrinsic part of the entertainment.[64] There are also guidelines concerning use of computer graphics and digitally manipulated images which hold that viewers must not be mislead and that where composite images are created it should be clear that the graphic is not a simple photographic image.[65] The Guidelines also cover use of CCTV footage[66] and contain general guidance on privacy.[67]

The Independent Television Commission Programme Code,[68] Section 2 **11–156** contains guidance as to Privacy Fairness and Gathering of Information. Guidance includes that editors and producers filming in public places must satisfy themselves that words spoken or actions taken by individuals are sufficiently in the public domain to justify their being communicated to the television audience.[69] The Code recommends that when filming in semi-public places, if the appearance of a person in the film is not incidental, random or anonymous, or where though unnamed the person is shown in a particularly sensitive situation (such as intensive care patients), that individual written consents be obtained.[70] Secret filming is acceptable "only where it is clear that the material so acquired is essential to establish the credibility and authority of a story where this cannot or is unlikely to be

---

[64] BBC Producer's Guidelines, Part 5 Surreptitious Recording, General Principles, p.66. Available on line at *http://www.bbc.co.uk/info/policies/producer_guides/*.

[65] BBC Producer's Guidelines, Part 2 Impartiality and Accuracy, (8) Computer Graphics p.48.

[66] BBC Producer's Guidelines, Part 4 Privacy, (6) CCTV footage p.63. See under CCTV footage below at para.11–179.

[67] BBC Producer's Guidelines, Part 4 Privacy.

[68] Available online at *http://www.itc.org.uk/*.

[69] Independent Television Commission Programme Code 2.2(i).

[70] Independent Television Commission Programme Code 2.2(ii).

achieved using 'open' filming or recording techniques or where the story itself is equally clearly of public interest."[71]

### "Public Interest"

**11–157**     The meaning of "public interest" has received detailed consideration by the courts in connection with other areas of law, in particular breach of confidence[72] and copyright infringement. Generally, the courts have upheld publication in the public interest where there has been iniquity or fraud, or other misdeeds of similar gravity.[73] There is a distinction between what is in "the public interest" and what it is interesting to the public.[74] Although recent judicial comment has suggested that, in connection with public figures, the understandable and legitimate interest of the public interest in being told even trivial information can be taken into account.[75] Publication to correct untrue pronouncements made by a public figure is in the public interest as the press is entitled to put the record straight.[76]

The inclusion of the phrase "having regard in particular to the special importance of the public interest in freedom of expression" suggests that "public interest" in the context of s.32 is intended to include freedom of expression *per se*. In other words, for publication to be in the public interest in this context, it does not need to be of material in connection with "traditional" serious and grave public interest matters, such as public security or fraud. If it can be established that to prevent publication is an unwarranted infringement of the right to freedom of expression in itself, then publication would be in the public interest simply by virtue of the public interest in having the right to freedom of expression upheld. If a more narrow definition of "public interest" is applied here, then it would tend to render the inclusion of artistic and literary purposes nugatory.

*Condition 4: compliance with relevant provision is incompatible with special purposes*

**11–158**     The fourth condition is set out in s.32(1)(c) and requires that "the data controller reasonably believes that, in all the circumstances, compliance with that provision is incompatible with the special purposes." This means that in respect of *each* of the provisions which the data controller seeks to claim an exemption from, he has to show that compliance *with that provision* is incompatible with the special purposes.

---

[71] Independent Television Commission Programme Code 2.4.
[72] See above at paras 7–106 and 7–107.
[73] *Beloff v Presdram* [1973] 1 All E.R. 241, 260.
[74] *Lion Laboratories Ltd v Evans* [1985] Q.B. 526; *Francome v Mirror Group Newspapers* [1984] 2 All E.R. 408; *London Regional Transport v Mayor of London* [2003] E.M.L.R. 4, para.40; *Douglas v Hello! Ltd (No.6)* [2003] EWHC 786 at para.231; [2003] 3 All E.R. 996; [2003] E.M.L.R. 31.
[75] *A v B* [2002] EWCA Civ 337; [2003] Q.B. 195; [2002] 3 W.L.R. 542; [2002] 2 All E.R. 545; [2002] E.M.L.R. 21. See comments of Lord Woolf quoted above at para.7–107.
[76] *Campbell v MGN Ltd* [2002] EWCA Civ 1373; [2003] Q.B. 633.

In cases concerning photographs of people taken without consent processed for artistic purposes where it is sought to rely on s.32, this condition is likely to cause difficulty. The starting point is that the principles of the Act need to be complied with *unless* compliance is incompatible with the special purposes. The First Data Protection Principle requires fair and lawful processing, including compliance with at least one of the Sch.2 conditions. In most cases, the only relevant condition is likely to be the consent of the data subject. Further, as discussed above,[77] it is arguable that all photographs showing an identifiable person are sensitive personal data as they reveal information about a person's ethnic or racial origin in which case compliance with a Sch.3 condition is also required. If the photograph is of a crowd scene, there is a good argument that requiring consent from every person would be incompatible with artistic purposes. Where photographs and images are of individuals or small groups of people, it will be difficult in many cases to genuinely claim that obtaining the explicit consent of the data subject was incompatible with artistic purposes.

Take for example a "naturalistic" photograph taken of a person in the street. As discussed above,[78] it is unclear whether any photograph, even of an anonymous person whose named identity is unknown, amounts to personal data. It is submitted above, that it does not. Assume for present purposes that such a photograph does amount to personal data. Certainly, there is a valid argument that obtaining consent in advance is incompatible with the artistic purpose of obtaining a naturalistic pose. However, there is no reason why obtaining consent to further processing from the data subject after the photograph has been taken would be incompatible with artistic purposes. The photographer could approach the subject and request consent. If for some valid reason the photographer is not able to request consent, such as crowded conditions meaning he fails to reach the subject,[79] then compliance with the Sch.2 condition may very well be incompatible with the artistic purposes. If however, he reaches the subject and consent is refused, it is very doubtful whether it could be contended thereafter (if the photograph is processed and published) that compliance with the First Data Protection Principle was on the facts genuinely incompatible with the special purposes. The very fact that consent was requested suggests that compliance with the First Data Protection Principle was possible and hence not incompatible with the artistic purpose. The fact that the subject refused cannot be discounted. The rights of the subject have to be weighed against freedom of expression. This is made clear by Recital 37 of the Directive which provides

**11–159**

"Whereas the processing of personal data for purposes of journalism or for purposes of literary of artistic expression, in particular in the audiovisual field, should qualify for exemption from the requirements of certain provisions of this Directive in so far as this is necessary to reconcile the

---

[77] See above at para.11–050 to 11–055.
[78] See above at paras 11–21 to 11–033.
[79] As in *Eastweek Publisher Ltd v Privacy Commissioner for Personal Data* [2000] 2 H.K.L.R.D. 83; [2000] 1 H.K.C. 692 discussed above at paras 11–028 *et seq.*

fundamental rights of individuals with freedom of information and notably the right to receive and impart information, as guaranteed in particular in Article 10 of the European Convention for the Protection of Human Rights and Fundamental Freedoms; whereas Member States should therefore lay down exemptions and derogations necessary for the purpose of balance between fundamental rights as regards general measures on the legitimacy of data processing, measures on the transfer of data to third countries and the power of the supervisory authority..."[80]

**11–160**   If the photographs are processed for journalistic purposes, there are better prospects of being able to establish that compliance with the First Data Protection Principle, in particular the requirements to establish a Sch.2 condition (and for sensitive personal data, a Sch.3 condition) are incompatible. As far as publication of photographic material for journalistic purposes is concerned, the only Sch.2 condition that is likely to be relevant is the first condition that the consent of the data subject has been given. If consent is requested and refused, then it is not possible to publish in compliance with the First Data Protection Principle (unless another Sch.2 condition is met). Where the purposes are journalistic purposes, the court may be more willing to conclude that if publication is in itself justifiable in the public interest, publication without the consent of the data subject is warranted.[81] In order to make the publication, it may not be reasonably practical to comply with the data protection principles.[82]

### Stay of proceedings

**11–161**   In certain circumstances involving special purposes, the court shall stay proceedings against a data controller under any of the following provisions:

- s.7(9) (failure to comply with s.7 access request),

- s.10(4) (failure to comply with s.10 notice to prevent processing likely to cause damage or distress),

- s.12(8) (failure to comply with notice re: automated decision taking),

- s.12A(3) (failure to comply with s.12A notice in relation to exempted manual data),

- s.14 (application for order for rectification, blocking, erasure, or destruction),

- s.13 (claim for compensation for damage or distress).

**11–162**   Until either of two specified conditions are met, proceedings will be stayed where at any time ("the relevant time") the data controller claims, or it

---

[80] 95/46/EC, Recital 37.
[81] See *Campbell v MGN Ltd* [2002] EWCA Civ 1373 at para.132; [2003] Q.B. 633 at 677 *per* Lord Phillips M.R. Note this case is the subject of an appeal to the House of Lords to be heard in February 2004.
[82] *ibid.*

appears to the court, that any personal data to which the proceedings relate are being processed[83]:

(a) only for the special purposes, and

(b) with a view to the publication by any person of any journalistic, literary, or artistic material which, at the time, 24, hours immediately before the relevant time, had not previously been published by the data controller.

Those conditions that must be met before the stay is lifted are either[84]:

(a) that a determination of the Commissioner under s.45 with respect to the data in question takes effect, or

(b) in a case where the proceedings were stayed on the making of a claim, that the claim is withdrawn.

### *Special purposes and powers of the Commissioner*

The Commissioner has particular powers to deal with personal data processed for special purposes which are considered above.[85]    **11–163**

In addition, if proposed proceedings involve processing for one of the special purposes, any party has the right to apply to the Commissioner for assistance in relation to those proceedings[86] which may include bearing the cost of legal advice, representation, and related matters.[87]

## Research history and statistics: s.33

"Research purposes" is stated to include "statistical and historical pur-    **11–164** poses"[88] but is not further defined. All the exemptions provided for the use of personal data for research purposes require compliance with two safe-guard conditions—that the data is not used to take decisions with respect to individuals, and the use is not likely to cause damage or distress to the data subject. Compliance with these conditions gives exemption from the s.7 subject access and the Second (obtaining/processing for specified purposes) and Fifth (not kept longer than necessary) Data Protection Principles.

Personal data which are processed only for research purposes are exempt from the s.7 subject access provisions provided that:

(1) the data are not processed to support measures or decisions with respect to particular individuals[89]; and

---

[83] Data Protection Act 1998, s.32(4).
[84] Data Protection Act 1998, s.32(4).
[85] See above at para.11–117.
[86] Data Protection Act 1998, s.53(1).
[87] Data Protection Act 1998, Sch.10.
[88] Data Protection Act 1998, s.33.
[89] Data Protection Act 1998, s.33(1)(a) and (4).

(2) the data are not processed in such a way that substantial damage or substantial distress is, or is likely to be, caused to any data subject[90]; and

(3) the results of the research or any resulting statistics are not made available in a form which identifies data subjects or any of them.[91]

**11–165**    The Second Data Protection Principle provides that personal data shall be obtained only for one or more specified and lawful purposes, and shall not be further processed in any manner incompatible with that purpose or those purposes.[92] Further processing of personal data *only* for research purposes will not breach the Second Data Protection Principle and is not to be regarded as being incompatible with the original purposes that the data was obtained provided that:

(1) the data are not processed to support measures or decisions with respect to particular individuals[93]; and

(2) the data are not processed in such a way that substantial damage or substantial distress is, or is likely to be, caused to any data subject.[94]

Equally, if those conditions are met, the Fifth Principle, which requires that data not be kept longer than necessary for the purposes for which it was processed, does not apply. Personal data processed for research purposes in compliance with those conditions may be kept indefinitely.[95]

**11–166**    The right to rely on the exemption on the basis that the processing is for research purposes only will not be lost merely because the data is disclosed:

(1) to any other person for research purposes only[96];

(2) to the data subject or someone acting on his behalf[97];

(3) at the request, or with the consent, of the data subject or a person acting on his behalf[98]; or

(4) in circumstances in which the person making the disclosure has reasonable grounds for believing that the disclosure falls within either of the above categories (1) to (3).[99]

**11–167**    In addition to the above exemption, there are a number of grounds set out within the main provisions of the Act that may permit processing for

---

[90] Data Protection Act 1998, s.33(1)(b) and (4).
[91] Data Protection Act 1998, s.33(4))(b).
[92] Data Protection Act 1998, Sch.1, Pt 1 and 2.
[93] Data Protection Act 1998, s.33(1)(a) and (2).
[94] Data Protection Act 1998, s.33(1)(b) and (2).
[95] Data Protection Act 1998, s.33(3).
[96] Data Protection Act 1998, s.33(5)(a).
[97] Data Protection Act 1998, s.33(5)(b).
[98] Data Protection Act 1998, s.33(5)(c).
[99] Data Protection Act 1998, s.33(5)(d).

research. In order for personal data to be processed, one of the requirements of Sch.2 must be met.[1] The Sch.2 conditions include Condition 1 (data subject has given consent),[2] and Condition 6 (process necessary for legitimate interests of data controller or third parties) which may be relevant.[3] In order for sensitive personal data to be processed one of the requirements of Sch.3 must be met.[4] The Sch.3 conditions include Condition 1 (data subject has given explicit consent),[5] Condition 8 (process necessary for medical purposes including medical research),[6] and Condition 9 (monitoring of racial or ethnic date for equality purposes) which may be relevant.[7]

Processing of medical information is subject to additional regulation and professional guidance, consideration of which is outside the scope of this work.[8]

## Anonymised data

Anonymised data is not included within the ambit of the Data Protection **11–168** Act 1998. Hence, truly anonymised data may be used for research. Recital 26 of the Directive provides "... whereas the principles of protection shall not apply to data rendered anonymous in such a way that the data subject is no longer identifiable ..."[9] A person processing anonymised data for research falls outside the Act. However, in order to be rendered anonymous, the data itself must undergo processing. It is an open question as to whether this processing, if it is of personal data as defined, will need to comply with the Act. The Commissioner takes the view that the process of anonymising amounts to processing and therefore a data controller who undertakes the process of anonymising will need to comply with the Data Protection Act 1998.[10]

In *R. v Dept of Health Ex p. Source Informatics*[11] it was acknowledged that anonymised data fell outside the Directive.[12] It was submitted in argument that the Directive equally did not apply to *the process* of anonymising. The court stated obiter that "common sense and justice alike" would appear to favour this contention.[13] The Commissioner's Legal Guidance on anonymisation states:

---

[1] First Data Protection Principle, Sch.1, Pt 1, 1(a).
[2] As to Sch.2, Condition 1 see above at para.11–042.
[3] As to Sch.2, Condition 1 see above at para.11–048.
[4] First Data Protection Principle, Sch.1, Pt 1, 1(b).
[5] As to Sch.3, Condition 1 see above at para.11–057.
[6] As to Sch.3, Condition 8 see above at para.11–068.
[7] As to Sch.2, Condition 9 see above at para.11–069.
[8] *e.g.* Health Service (Control of Patient Information) Regulations 2002 (SI 2002/1438); the General Medical Council Guidance on confidentiality. For other guidance concerning images see below at para.11–185.
[9] 95/46.
[10] *Office of the Information Commissioner Data Protection Act 1998 Legal Guidance* at para.2.2.5, p.13.
[11] [2001] Q.B. 424; [2000] 2 W.L.R. 940; [2000] 1 All E.R. 786.
[12] [2001] Q.B. 424; [2000] 2 W.L.R. 940; [2000] 1 All E.R. 786 at 798–799 *per* Simon Brown L.J.
[13] [2001] Q.B. 424; [2000] 2 W.L.R. 940; [2000] 1 All E.R. 786 at 799 *per* Simon Brown L.J.

"The Commissioner considers anonymisation of personal data difficult to achieve because the data controller may retain the original data set from which the personal identifiers have been stripped to create the 'anonymised' data. The fact that the data controller is in possession of this data set which, if linked to the data which have been stripped of all personal identifiers, will enable a living individual to be identified, means that all the data, including the data stripped of personal identifiers, remain personal data in the hands of the data controller and cannot be said to have been anonymised. The fact that the data controller may have no intention of linking these two data sets is immaterial."[14]

## Information made available to the public by enactment: s.34

**11–169**    Where the data consists of information which the data controller is obliged by or under any enactment (excluding enactments contained in the Freedom of Information Act 2000) to make available *to the public*, whether by publishing it, by making it available for inspection, or otherwise, and whether gratuitously or on payment of a fee, the personal data are exempt from[15]:

- the subject information provisions,[16]
- the Fourth Data Protection Principle (accuracy),[17]
- the non-disclosure provisions.[18]

It only applies to information that the data controller is required to publish by the relevant enactment.

## Disclosure required by law or for legal proceedings: s.35

**11–170**    Personal data are exempt from the non-disclosure provisions where the disclosure is required by or under any enactment, by any rule of law or by the order of a court.[19]

Personal data are exempt from the non-disclosure provisions where the disclosure is necessary:

(1) for the purpose of, or in connection with, any legal proceedings (including prospective legal proceedings), or

(2) for the purpose of obtaining legal advice, or

---

[14] *Office of the Information Commissioner Data Protection Act 1998 Legal Guidance* at para.2.2.5.
[15] Data Protection Act 1998, s.33.
[16] For definition of "subject information provisions" see above at para.11–123.
[17] As to which see above at para.11–085.
[18] For definition of "non disclosure provisions" see above at para.11–124.
[19] Data Protection Act 1998, s.35(1). For definition of "non disclosure provisions" see above at para.11–124.

(3) for the purposes of establishing, exercising, or defending legal rights.[20]

## Domestic purposes

Personal data processed by an individual only for the purposes of that **11–171** individual's personal, family, or household affairs (including recreational purposes) are exempt from all of the data protection principles, the provisions of Pt II (Rights of Data Subjects and Others) and Pt III (Notification by Data Controllers).[21]

## Miscellaneous exemptions

*Schedule 7: miscellaneous exemptions* **11–172**

Schedule 7 sets out a number of further miscellaneous exemptions which are:

*Confidential references*—exempt from s.7 subject access,[22]

*Armed forces*—exempt from subject information provisions to the extent to which the application would be likely to prejudice the combat effectiveness of the Crown's armed forces.[23]

*Judicial appointments and honours*—processing to assess suitability for judicial office or for the conferring of an honour by the Crown exempt from subject information provisions.[24]

*Crown employment and Crown or Ministerial appointments*—processing for the purposes of assessing any person's suitability for Crown employment or Ministerial appointment exempt from the subject information provisions.[25]

*Management forecasts, etc.*—processing for the purposes of management **11–173** forecasting or planning to assist the data controller in the conduct of any business or other activity are exempt from the subject information provisions to the extent to which the application of those provisions would be likely to prejudice the conduct of that business or other activity.[26]

---

[20] Data Protection Act 1998, s.35(2). For definition of "non disclosure provisions" see above at para.11–124.
[21] Data Protection Act 1998, s.36.
[22] Data Protection Act 1998, Sch.7, para.1.
[23] Data Protection Act 1998, Sch.7, para.2. For definition of "subject information provisions" see above at para.11–123.
[24] Data Protection Act 1998, Sch.7, para.3. For definition of "subject information provisions" see above at para.11–123.
[25] Data Protection Act 1998, Sch.7, para.4. For definition of "subject information provisions" see above at para.11–123.
[26] Data Protection Act 1998, Sch.7, para.5.

*Corporate finance*—exempt from subject information provisions where application could (or is reasonably believed) to affect the price of any instrument.[27]

*Negotiations*—processing of records of the intentions of the data controller in relation to any negotiations with the data subject are exempt from the subject information provisions in any case to the extent to which the application of those provisions would be likely to prejudice those negotiations.[28]

**11–174**    *Examination Marks*—time for compliance with a s.7 subject access request extended until earlier of five months from day request received or 40 days from announcement of results.[29]

*Examination Scripts*—personal data consisting of information recorded by candidates during an academic, professional, or other examination are exempt from s.7 subject access.[30]

*Legal Professional Privilege*—exempt from the subject information provisions if the data consist of information in respect of which a claim to legal professional privilege could be maintained in legal proceedings.[31]

**11–175**    *Self-Incrimination*—A person need not comply with any request or order under s.7 to the extent that compliance would, by revealing evidence of the commission of any offence other than an offence under this Act, expose him to proceedings for that offence.[32]

*Other miscellaneous exemptions*

**11–176**    Section 38(1) gives the Secretary of State power to make further exemptions by order. The Data Protection (Miscellaneous Subject Access Exemptions) Order 2000[33] was made pursuant to this power. It specifies a number of instruments and enactments which restrict disclosure of certain information in respect of which a s.7 subject access exemption is granted. The Order covers information relating to human fertilisation and embryology, adoption records, children's special educational needs, and parental order records.

---

[27] Data Protection Act 1998, Sch.7, para.6.
[28] Data Protection Act 1998, Sch.7, para.7.
[29] Data Protection Act 1998, Sch.7, para.8.
[30] Data Protection Act 1998, Sch.7, para.9, .
[31] Data Protection Act 1998, Sch.7, para.10.
[32] Data Protection Act 1998, Sch.7, para.11.
[33] SI 2000/419 as amended by Data Protection (Miscellaneous Subject Access Exemptions) (Amendment) Order 2000 (SI 2000/186).

## Transitional provisions

The transitional provisions are set out in Sch.8. The first transitional **11–177** period ended on October 23, 2001, and the exemptions available under Pt II of Sch.8 have now expired.

A second transitional period is provided for which runs from October 23, 2001, until October 24, 2007. This provides an exemption that applies to:

(1) eligible manual data[34] which were held immediately before October 24, 1998, and

(2) other personal data [not falling with (1) above] which forms part of an accessible record and does not fall within the other categories (a) to (c) of the s.1 definition of data [*i.e.* is not processed by automatic equipment operating in response to instruction; is not recorded with the intention that it should be processed by such equipment; and is not part of (or intended to be part of) a relevant filing system].

It does not include eligible manual data processed only for historical research within the meaning of para.16, Sch 8.

Data to which the exemption applies are exempt until October 24, 2007, **11–178** from:

- the first data protection principle except to the extent to which it requires compliance with para.2 of Pt II of Sch.1 (data not to be regarded as processed fairly unless information as to identity of data controller, etc. made available to data subject);

- the Second (obtained for specified purposes), Third (adequate relevant and not excessive), Fourth (accurate and up to date), and Fifth (not kept longer than necessary) data protection principles;

- s.14(1) to (3).

For further information and detail as to the transitional provisions, the reader is referred to other works.[35]

## CLOSE CIRCUIT TELEVISION

Closed Circuit Television (CCTV) is very common and can be found on **11–179** public streets, quasi-public places such as banks, restaurants, or museums, and in some cases in private homes. Virtually any use of CCTV footage will amount to processing including filming, storing transferring, copying,

---

[34] As defined by Sch.8, para.1(2) non-automated data which is subject to processing that was already under way immediately before October 24, 1998.

[35] See R. Jay and A. Hamilton, *Data Protection Law and Practice* (2nd ed., Sweet & Maxwell, 2003) Ch.22; *Encyclopaedia of Data Protection* (Sweet & Maxwell) Vol 1, 1–199/3.

viewing, editing, or printing images in hard copy. CCTV images of people that can be identified, whether by cross-referencing data or because their faces are clearly visible, will amount to personal data. If the images recorded do not enable a person to be identified, either visually or by cross referencing, they will effectively amount to anonymised data. In most cases, the reason for installing CCTV is usually for security reasons and if the images are truly anonymous it would defeat the object. Accordingly, virtually all CCTV footage will be caught by the Act.

However, recital 16 of the Directive provides:

"Whereas the processing of sound and image data, such as in cases of video surveillance, does not come within the scope of this Directive if it is carried out for the purposes of public security, defence, national security or in the course of State activities relating to the area of criminal law or of other activities which do not come within the scope of Community law."

**11–180**    "Public security" presumably only encompasses surveillance carried out by public authorities for the purposes of public security. It would not include private CCTV which, although it may be relevant to the public (for example CCTV outside a public house filming in the street), is not for the purposes of public security but rather for the private security interests of the CCTV owner.

In July 2000, the Data Protection Commissioner (as the title then was) issued a Code of Practice for users of CCTV pursuant to her powers under s.51(3)(b). The Code is not intended to apply to surveillance covered by the Regulation of Investigatory Powers Act; surveillance of employees to monitor compliance with their employment contracts; private security equipment installed in homes for home security; or the use of cameras by the broadcast media for the purposes of journalism; or for artistic or literary purposes.

The Code is reproduced in full at Appendix 5, below, to which reference should be made. It is not a designated Code for the purposes of the s.32 exemption and as noted it is not intended to apply to the broadcast media. It however would certainly be taken into account by the court in assessing whether any CCTV image processing has been fair in accordance with the First Data Protection Principle.

**11–181**    The use of CCTV footage by the media must be used with caution as the case of *Peck v UK*[36] illustrates. If it is possible to anonymise the images, this will generally be the safest course. A major difficulty for the media is that the detailed provenance of the images and how they came into existence will often be unknown. The BBC Producer's Guidelines state:

"When dealing with Close Circuit Television (CCTV) video or recordings provided by the emergency services or other bodies or individuals, special care must be taken over issues such as privacy anonymity and defamation. Our ignorance of the circumstances surrounding the recording

---

[36] (2003) 36 E.H.R.R. 41. Discussed above at para.7–059.

increase the risk in using it and we must apply the same ethical, editorial considerations as we would to material we record ourselves. The principles in this chapter [Privacy] and Chapter 5: Surreptitious Recording apply. If illegal or anti-social activity is shown there may be real risks of defamation or contempt. If in doubt seek legal advice."[37]

## PRACTICAL GUIDANCE

The Data Protection Act 1998, which came into force on March 1, 2000,[38] has only been considered by the courts in a relatively small number of cases. A large number of the provisions are worded in such a way as to have potentially very wide application. In the case of images of people, depending on statutory construction, it is possible that any image of an identifiable person amounts to "data from which a person can be identified"[39] even if the name of that person is not known to the data controller nor likely to be known.[40] How widely (or narrowly) the courts will construe the s.32 exemption which applies to the special purposes (artistic, literary, and journalism) remains relatively untested. Accordingly, it would be prudent for anyone processing images—including those dealing with images commercially and any organisations holding images of people (whether schools, hospitals, health clubs, or employers)—to err on the side of caution in so far as compliance with the provisions of the Data Protection Act is concerned. The following are suggested by way of practical guidance:

**11–182**

1. abide by any relevant professional guidance or relevant codes;

2. obtain consent for use if possible;

3. consider use of opt-out provisions;

4. consider anonymisation of the images if practical;

5  in the absence of consent, use another image if possible.

### Abide by any relevant professional guidance or relevant codes

Many public authorities and organisations provide statements of good practice and publish guidelines about the use of images within their particular fields. Processing "fairly" will inevitably take into account relevant ethical and professional standards. A failure to comply with the applicable ethical guidelines will be a prima facie indication that processing is not fair.

**11–183**

---

[37] BBC Producer's Guidelines, Part 4 Privacy, (6) CCTV footage p.63. Available online at *http://www.bbc.co.uk/info/policies/producer_guides/*.
[38] Data Protection Act 1998 (Commencement) Order 2000, (SI 2000/183).
[39] The definition of "personal data" in s.1(1) of the Act. See above at paras 11–015 and 11–016.
[40] See discussion of abstract identification and specific identification above at paras 11–021 to 11–033.

There are a large number of organisations that produce such guidelines. The following are only a few examples, not an exhaustive list:

**11–184    Guidelines For Use By the Media.**    Relevant guidelines may include the Press Complaints Commission Code[41]; the Broadcasting Standards Commission Code of Guidance on Privacy; the Independent Television Commission Programme Code[42]; the BBC Producers Guidelines[43]; and the NUJ Code of Conduct.[44]

**11–185    Guidelines For Use By the Medical Profession.**    The General Medical Council (GMC) publishes guidelines entitled *Making and Using Visual and Audio Recordings of Patients*.[45] Other relevant guidance published by the GMC includes *Research: The Role and Responsibilities of Doctors*[46] which has provisions concerning confidentiality and consent, and *Media Inquiries about Patients*.[47] Most medical publishers take the view that the old traditional method of anonymisation by printing a black band across the eyes of a patient depicted is inadequate.[48]

**11–186    Guidelines for CCTV Users.**    Code of Practice for users of CCTV issued by the Data Protection Commissioner (as the title then was) issued pursuant to her powers under s.51(3)(b).[49]

### Obtain consent for use if possible

**11–187**    If possible, the consent of the person in the image should be obtained for the particular use contemplated. Use of a photograph for different purposes other than which it was obtained is likely to infringe the First Principle (fair and lawful processing) and the Second Principle (obtained only for one or more specified and lawful purposes and not be further processed in a

---

[41] Reproduced at Appendix 3 and Ch.14, below.
[42] Available online at *http://www.itc.org.uk/*.
[43] Available online at *http://www.bbc.co.uk/info/policies/producer_guides/*.
[44] Reproduced above after para.9–022.
[45] Available on line at *http://www.gmc-uk.org/standards/AUD_VID.HTM*. or via the home page *http://www.gmc-uk.org/* under "Ethical Guidance".
[46] Available on line at *http://www.gmc-uk.org/standards/default.htm* or via the home page *http://www.gmc-uk.org/* under "Ethical Guidance".
[47] *ibid.*
[48] See *e.g. Protection of Patients' Rights to Privacy*, Statement by International Committee of Medical Journal Editors 1995 B.M.J. 311:1272 (November 11) which included the following:
"Identifying details should be omitted if they are not essential, but patient data should never be altered or falsified in an attempt to attain anonymity. Complete anonymity is difficult to achieve, and informed consent should be obtained if there is any doubt. For example, masking of the eye region in photographs of patients is inadequate protection of anonymity."
The B.M.J. (formerly British Medical Journal) editorial policy on patient confidentiality and consent available on line at: *http://bmj.bmjjournals.com/advice/editorial_policies.shtml* states "Black bands across the eyes are wholly ineffective in disguising the patient, and changing details of patients to try to disguise them is bad scientific practice." See also C.A. Hood, C.A. Hope, T. Hope and P. Dove, *Videos, photographs, and patient consent* B.M.J. 1998; 316:1009–1011 (March 28).
[49] Reproduced at Appendix 5, below.

manner incompatible with those purposes). Thus, for example, a passport photograph image supplied to a university as part of an application process should not be publically displayed without the consent of the person featured.

### Photographing of individuals

If photographing individuals or small groups, their consent should be **11–188** obtained *before* the photograph is taken. Implied consent will suffice for data that is not sensitive personal data. However, a photograph of an identifiable person will reveal information about a person's ethnic origin and therefore may class as sensitive personal data. Even where the data is sensitive personal data, there is no requirement that explicit consent be in writing and oral consent will suffice. However, express written consent to the processing intended is always preferable from an evidential point of view, such as a model release form that details the proposed use. Details of the proposed use should include the intended use of the image, who or which organisations will have access to them, and if relevant and/or possible where, when, and which publication it is intended they be published in.

If photographing individuals in naturalistic poses, where it is important that they are unaware that they are being photographed, it is prudent to seek consent afterwards. It should be noted that if the UK courts followed the approach of the Hong Kong courts in *Eastweek Publisher Ltd v Privacy Commissioner for Personal Data*[50] that a photographer who does not know the identity of the person he photographed may, by virtue of that fact, fall outside the provisions of the Data Protection Act 1998. However, the position in the United Kingdom is not yet the subject of judicial authority and in such circumstances, caution and hence express consent is sensible.

### Photographs of larger groups and crowds in public places

Obtaining the permission of everyone in a crowd scene is impractical and **11–189** in many cases would be impossible (unless done by an opt-out provision on a ticket or as part of entry conditions to a venue). For this reason, obtaining consent of everyone in a crowd would be regarded as incompatible with artistic or journalistic purposes and would not defeat an attempt to rely on the s.32 exemption.[51] Many people in crowd scenes are not likely to be identifiable in any event.

If the photograph is likely to show clearly the faces of people in the foreground, it would be sensible for a photographer to announce that he intends to take a photograph for publication or for whatever use is intended, thus giving people the opportunity to move away. Equally, making it obvious that a photograph is about to be taken should give individuals time and opportunity to move out of shot.

---

[50] [2000] 2 H.K.L.R.D. 83; [2000] 1 H.K.C. 692. See above at para.11–028.
[51] As to the s.32 special purposes exemption see above at para.11–141.

### Consider use of opt-out provisions

**11–190**   Give individuals the opportunity to opt-out of being photographed or having images they have supplied being used by the organisation they have been supplied to.

Thus, if passport photographs are being supplied to (for example) a college as part of an application process, the application form could state that if the application is successful the photograph will be used on a bulletin board to enable staff and students to identify each other and giving the applicant the opportunity to opt out of that procedure and refuse consent.

### Consider anonymisation of the images if practical

**11–191**   If consent cannot be obtained and it is a practical option, which would not destroy the point of use of the image, the image can be anonymised. Anonymisation of images needs to strip the image of the person's identity which may include obliteration not just of facial features but also of identifying marks such as tattoos.

### In the absence of consent, use another image if possible

**11–192**   If there is no consent or consent is refused, another image of another person who has consented should be used if this is possible. In some cases, this will not be a realistic option. In many other cases, where the general image content is all that is required and it is not vital which person appears in the image, it should be possible to obtain an alternative image. For example, if what is required is a general photograph of some students for a prospectus, it is unimportant precisely which students are depicted. If there is one image with no consent attached, the simplest way to ensure Data Protection compliance is to either re-shoot the image with consent or obtain a library image which has consent attached. If use of another image which has subject consent is possible, this course should be adopted until the courts have further clarified the ambit of the Data Protection Act 1998.

# Chapter 12

# Picture libraries

## SCOPE OF THIS CHAPTER

This chapter contains an introduction to picture libraries for practitioners **12–001** unfamiliar with this area and focuses on issues arising from the loss and destruction of analogue images. The majority of picture libraries today deal in digital images, either solely or primarily. Even analogue images can be scanned into a digital format. Issues arising from loss and destruction of hard copy original analogue images will become increasingly rare. However, there are still libraries who continue to deal in analogue images. Thus, causes of action arising from damage or destruction of analogue images still remains of commercial relevance and are considered here.

**12–002**    There is also an outline of matters that are taken into consideration in arriving at the level of reproduction fee with respect to different media which is of application to both analogue and digital images. The majority of legal issues considered elsewhere in this work are of direct relevance to the picture library industry, irrespective of whether the images are analogue or digital. The moral rights of the photographer; copyright infringement of library stock; questions of whether image content infringes third party rights[1] or is otherwise against the law[2]; data protection; and control of the use of the image by the licencee to prevent infringement of third party rights (together with appropriate indemnities) all impact on the business of image licencing. Reference should be made to the relevant chapters.

## INTRODUCTION

**12–003**    The term "picture libraries" encompasses a wide variety of organisations ranging from international corporations, like Corbis and Getty, to smaller specialist collections run out of private houses, to the sole photographer only dealing with his own work. In addition, some art galleries, museums, and other organisations, such as the Kennel Club, have their own picture libraries. All deal in the commercial supply and licensing of images. Libraries enable picture users and researchers to locate suitable images quickly and easily.

**12–004**    The larger corporations license all types of images across an extremely broad spectrum of themes including stock editorial images used to illustrate books and magazines, topical breaking news photographs, photographs of celebrities, and creative photo-illustrations. Some of the smaller libraries limit their stock to narrower topics. The range of specialist subjects covered is fascinatingly comprehensive. By way of example, there are specialist libraries only or primarily dealing with images of: fire and firefighters; health and medicine; maps; plants and gardens; horses; golf; Russia and the Soviet Union; polar exploration; and even UFOs and strange phenomena.

The British Association of Picture Libraries and Agencies (BAPLA)[3] is the trade association for the picture library industry in the United Kingdom. It was founded in 1975 and initially had seven or eight members and worked to

---

[1] Including the rights of people depicted and whether the image itself shows other copyright works or trademarks.

[2] For example, in contempt of court or contrary to the laws of obscenity.

[3] *http://www.bapla.org.uk*. See also CEPIC (Co-ordination of European Picture Agencies and Libraries (a European Economic Interest Group representing the interests of picture associations, agencies and libraries in Europe) *http://www.cepic.org/*.

establish the basic principles and practices now commonplace in the picture library business. BAPLA now has over 400 members. BAPLA's work includes the promotion of the picture library industry and good trade practice. All members must adhere to BAPLA's Code of Professional Ethics.[4]

## HOW PICTURE LIBRARIES OPERATE

Picture libraries dealing with analogue (as opposed to digital) images will supply original colour transparencies to third parties requesting particular types of images. Libraries dealing exclusively or mainly with digital images will supply them electronically, often via the internet, so many of the problems concerning loss and damage of original transparencies that affect analogue libraries do not apply. The picture library industry has increasingly abandoned use of analogue images as consumers have demanded digital images. Analogue images, in order to be commercially viable, need to be scanned into digital format. However, there are picture libraries who continue to deal in analogue images where loss and damage to the stock remains a real issue. This section primarily concerns the issues arising in connection with such loss and damage. Other issues which affect digital libraries such as copyright infringement, image content, and image use are dealt with elsewhere in this work

**12–005**

Picture libraries dealing with analogue images will supply original colour transparencies. A transparency is essentially the same as a "slide". The colour transparency is the first generation image—*i.e.* what is recorded by the camera on to the film. Most amateur/tourist photographers use colour negative film which needs to be developed and printed to show the true colours of the image. A transparency is a first generation record of the image as seen.

A photographic print developed from a colour negative film is thus a second generation image. The highest quality image is the first generation transparency. A second-stage image, whether a duplicate of the transparency or the developed print, will inevitably suffer some deterioration in image quality simply by virtue of the fact that it is second generation. Accordingly, most analogue picture libraries supply original transparencies. Black and white photographs are created from a negative in a similar way to colour negative film. Occasionally, duplicates may be supplied where the original is particularly valuable or has become damaged. Generally the supply is of originals.

**12–006**

Photographers supply the libraries with transparencies from which the libraries select which images they wish to retain. The relationship between the photographer and the library again will vary from library to library. Many of the larger libraries have standard contracts/terms and conditions. Other libraries deal with photographers on a more informal basis, sometimes surprisingly without any kind of written contract at all.

---

[4] Available on line at *http://www.bapla.org.uk/static/bapla/CodeConduct.php* or *via* the home page *http://www.bapla.org.uk/* under menu item "BAPLA".

**12–007**   Typically, if a picture researcher is requesting images of a specific subject, the library will send a number of transparencies for consideration. The transparencies should be accompanied by a delivery note. The British Photographer's Liaison Committee produces a standard form "Terms & Conditions of Submission and Reproduction of Images"[4a] which is prevalent, but some libraries use variations or their own form. Issues arising from the delivery note will invariably be a matter of contract law to be determined on the specific terms in issue.

**12–008**   Standard delivery notes usually provide that the images are sent on loan to the client and remain the property of the picture library. Images are typically loaned for about 30 days or 60 days for book publishers. If the client selects an image or images from those sent which it wishes to reproduce, it will then enter into a licence agreement with the library. The delivery note and sending of the images does not constitute a right to use the images. The reproduction rights and fees for reproduction are agreed separately. The delivery note should state on the front page the fees for loss or damage. Potential fees incurred by the use of an analogue library are as follows:

**Search & service fee.**   Fees for searching time of library to provide images, packaging, post, etc. This is payable in any event.

**Reproduction fee.**   Where the client decides it wishes to reproduce image(s), a reproduction fee is paid. The relevant fee will depend on the nature of the use.[5]

**Loss fee.**   If the supplied transparency or print is lost or damaged by the client, then a loss fee becomes payable. The level of the loss fee will depend on the terms set by the library and the nature of the image.[6]

**Holding fee.**   This becomes payable when the images have not been returned by the specified return date. The holding fee is the equivalent of an "overdue" payment to a book library. Rates vary but are roughly in the region of £3.00 to £4.00 per week per image.

**Failure to credit fee.**   The British Photographer's Liaison Committee[7] Terms and Conditions[8] provide for an addition at 50 per cent of the licence

---

[4a] See below at para. 12–008, nn. 7 and 8.
[5] See below at paras 12–040 to 12–048.
[6] See below at paras 12–029 to 12–039.
[7] The British Photographer's Liaison Committee is an organisation that aims to promote and protect the rights and interest of photographers. Its members include: the Association of Photographers; the British Association of Picture Libraries and Agencies; the Design and Artists Copyright Society; Institute of Medical Illustrators; and the National Union of Journalists.
[8] © Copyright 2001 British Photographer's Liaison Committee/Finers Stephens Innocent as agreed by BAPLA, AOP, NUJ, MPA and the BFP. Available from, *inter alia*, The Association of Photographers, 81 Leonard Street, London EC2A 4QS. Telephone 020 7739 6669 *http://www.the-aop.org* and from BAPLA, 18 Vine Hill London EC1R 5DZ Telephone: 020 7713 1780 *http://www.bapla.org.uk/*.

fee to become payable if there is a failure to credit the library and the photographer when the image is reproduced.[9]

The level of payment to the photographer will vary according to the terms of the picture library concerned. A common percentage appears to be in the region 50:50 with the photographer receiving half of the fee. **12–009**

Legal problems arising most frequently for analogue picture libraries are copyright infringement and the loss or damage of transparencies. Copyright infringement is dealt with in Chapters 2 and 3. This chapter focuses on the loss of images and quantification of damages for such loss. Guidelines for valuing the use of an image in relation to copyright infringement are set out below at para. 12–040 and above at para. 2–191.

## LOSS OR DAMAGE OF TRANSPARENCIES: WHERE THERE IS NO CONTRACT

In the majority of cases, where transparencies are lost or damaged the relationship between the respective parties (the photographer and the library, or the library and the third party client) will be governed by contract. Where there is a delivery note with terms and conditions, the specific provisions will govern. However, there may be circumstances where there is no contract (such as a photographer sending transparencies to a library speculatively) or where it is desired to frame a claim in tort. What is the position if in such circumstances the transparencies are lost or damaged? **12–010**

## Wrongful interference with goods

Photographs and transparencies are chattels and as such a defendant who wrongfully interferes with the claimant's chattels may be liable for either (1) trespass to goods, (2) conversion, or (3) damage to the reversion. **12–011**

## Trespass to goods

Trespass to goods arises where there is direct and immediate wrongful interference with goods in the claimant's possession.[10] It is unlikely to arise in the context of picture libraries as in most cases, the images will not be in the possession of either the owner (usually the photographer) or the library.[11] The images will usually be lawfully in the possession of either the library or the client of the library and as such trespass to goods is of minor relevance. Causes of action arising are more likely to lie in an action for conversion. **12–012**

---

[9] British Photographer's Liaison Committee Terms and Conditions of Submission and Reproduction of Images, Cl.14. *Cf.* Damages for loss of publicity for failure to identify author, above at para. 4–061.

[10] For further information on Trespass to Goods see *Clerk & Lindsell on Torts* (18th ed., Sweet & Maxwell) 14–134 and N. Palmer, *Bailment* (2nd ed., Sweet & Maxwell, 1991).

[11] There are exceptions to the rule that the claimant must be in possession; none of which are relevant here (i) trustees, (ii) executors or admintrators of an estate before probate/letters of administration are granted, (iii) owner of a franchise, (iv) bailment determinable at will: see *Clerk & Lindsell on Torts* (18th ed., Sweet & Maxwell) 14–136.

## Damage to the reversion

**12–013**    Where an owner out of possession has no immediate right to possession (*e.g.* hire purchase or lent to a third party), he cannot recover in either trespass or conversion if his goods are taken or destroyed. However, he can maintain an action where he can prove actual loss for damage to the reversion.[12] Once the period of loan of images has expired, the picture library will be entitled to possession and if the images are not returned following a specific demand, or are returned damaged, the library will be able to maintain an action in conversion. Damage to the reversion is only of importance where the claimant is a non-possessor, in the sense that he has no right to possession, of the goods. Therefore, for most cases involving picture libraries damage to the reversion will be of little relevance as there will be a cause of action in conversion or contract.

## Conversion

**12–014**    Bailment is broadly defined as the delivery of actual or constructive possession of a chattel by the bailor to the bailee on trust for some purpose on condition that the chattel will be redelivered to the bailor as soon as the purpose for bailment has been accomplished or the time for which they were bailed has elapsed.[13]

Conversion is an act of deliberately dealing with a chattel in a manner inconsistent with the rights of the owner (or person entitled to possession) which deprives the owner of the use and possession of it. It is an act of conversion when property is wrongfully taken or received by someone not entitled to do so or when it is wrongfully retained. By statute, conversion also includes inadvertent action, where a bailee's breach of duty results in the loss or destruction of the bailed item.[14]

**12–015**    Conversion of goods does not include interference with intellectual property rights. Conversion is subject to the Torts (Interference with Goods) Act 1977 which defines goods as all personal chattels other than things in action and money.[15] This does not include intellectual property rights. Accordingly, when considering actions for conversion of images, it is important to remember that the copyright is not actionable in conversion.[16] The damages that can be claimed are purely those flowing from the loss of the physical image itself.

---

[12] See *Clerk & Lindsell on Torts*, (18th ed., Sweet & Maxwell) 14–04 and 14–142.
[13] *Re S Davis & Co Ltd* [1945] Ch. 402.
[14] Torts (Interference With Goods) Act 1977, s.2(2).
[15] Torts (Interference With Goods) Act 1977, s.14(1). Following the recommendation of the Law Reform Committee (Cmnd. 4774) that wrongful interference should not extend to any form of intellectual property.
[16] Copyright Act 1956, s.18(1) did permit actions for conversion. However, following the recommendations of the Whitford Committee (Cmnd. 6732) at para.943, conversion for copyright was not included in the Copyright, Designs & Patents Act 1988. The 1956 Act, s.18(1) applies now only to actions commenced before August 1, 1989: s.127 and Sch.1, para.1. Accordingly, it is of limited practical relevance today. To all intents and purposes, no conversion actions lie for infringement of copyright.

Where a picture library receives transparencies or prints, they become bailees of the images and owe the photographer (or owner of the images) a duty of care. Similarly, when a client of the library receives images from the library, they become bailees of the library and strictly sub-bailees of the photographer or owner of the images.

The most likely instances of conversion that will be encountered in the context of analogue images and picture libraries will be:   **12–016**

(1) by clients of the picture library who have received images—wrongfully (*i.e.* without the permission of the library bailor), destroying deliberately,[17] destroying or losing negligently,[18] parting with,[19] refusing to surrender goods on demand after the expiry of authorised period,[20] or otherwise dealing with images in a manner which constitutes denial of title of the picture library;

(2) by the picture library—the same acts as above in relation to either (a) images it retains with the authority of the photographer as part of its collection, or (b) images it has received unsolicited from photographers as involuntary bailee.[21]

## DUTY OWED BY THE BAILEE

The duties discussed below are those in bailment, but a bailee's duty to take care of the chattel can lie in contract and in tort as well as bailment.[22]   **12–017**

The extent of the duty in bailment owed by the bailee will depend on the nature of the bailment. Broadly, for present purposes, there are three types of bailment[23]:

---

[17] *Heald v Carey* (1852) 11 C.B. 977; *Richardson v Atkinson* (1723) 1 Stra. 576.

[18] Torts (Interference With Goods) Act 1977, s.2(2).

[19] *Martindale v Smith* (1841) 1 Q.B. 389; *M'Combie v Davies* (1805) 6 East 658; *R.H. Willis & Son v British Car Auctions Ltd* [1978] 1 W.L.R. 438; *Motis Exports Ltd v Dampskibsselskabet AF1912, Aktieselskab (No. 1)* [1999] 1 Lloyd's Rep. 837 (aff'm CA [2000] 1 All E.R. (Comm) 91; [2000] 1 Lloyd's Rep. 211)—misdelivery; *City Television v Conference & Training Office Ltd* [2001] E.W.C.A. Civ. 1770, CA (Sedley L.J., Arden L.J.) November 16, 2001 (negligent return of goods to third party in breach of duty to seek bailor's permission to do so).

[20] Unpermitted possession alone is not sufficient: *Barclays Mercantile Finance Ltd v Sibec Developments Ltd* [1992] 1 W.L.R. 1253, 1257. Conversion arises where the detention is contrary to the rights of the owner, *e.g.* refusal to surrender goods on specific demand: *Rushworth v Taylor* (1842) 2 Q.B. 699; *Secretary of State for Defence v Guardian Newspapers Ltd*, *The Times*, December 16, 1983 and [1985] A.C. 339. Note that a demand must be brought to the knowledge of the defendant before issue and a letter posted but not received by the defendant will not suffice: *King v Walsh* [1932] I.R. 178.

[21] See below at para. 12–021.

[22] *Jackson v Mayfair Window Cleaning Co Ltd* [1952] 1 All E.R. 215.

[23] Pawn or pledge is another class but unlikely to be of relevance here. Gratuitous bailment and bailment for reward can be subdivided into further categories (a) deposit of goods for custody (*e.g.* warehousing, cloakrooms), (b) deposit for work to be done (*e.g.* clothes repairs), (c) deposit for use of the goods by the bailee (*e.g.* photographic images, loan of a carpet cleaner, etc). See also *Coggs v Bernard* (1703) 2 Ld. Raym. 909 where bailment was divided into 5 classes by Holt C.J.: (1) gratuitous deposit of a chattel with a bailee for custody, (2) gratuitous delivery to a bailee who is to do something to or with the chattel, (3) gratuitous loan for the bailee to use the chattel, (4) pawn or pledge, (5) hire of a chattel or services to the bailee for reward.

(1) bailment for reward—the loan of a chattel for payment (as in the photographic library supplying original transparencies to third party clients) or storage for payment;

(2) gratuitous bailment—where a bailee receives goods to hold or work on or use without reward;

(3) involuntary bailment—where a bailee receives goods without request or unsolicited.

**12-018**    The courts have moved away from classifying categories of bailment and have adopted a more flexible approach depending upon the facts of the particular case in issue.[24] It is right that there is little distinction in modern authorities between the duty owed by a gratuitous bailee or a bailee for reward. However, it remains the case that the authorities draw a distinction between the standard of care required of an involuntary bailee on the one hand, and gratuitous bailees and bailees for reward on the other.

### Gratuitous bailment or bailment for reward

**12-019**    The common law duty of the bailee is to take reasonable care of the bailor's goods and not to convert them.[25] The standard of care required will depend upon the particular circumstances of the case.[26] The bailee must take reasonable care to ensure that the chattel is kept in a place that is fit and proper for the purpose.[27] The bailee must return the chattel to the bailor on demand, or deliver it in accordance with his instructions.[28]

**12-020**    The burden of proof is on the bailee, whether gratuitous or for reward, to show that the loss of or damage to any goods bailed to him was not caused by any fault on his part or that of his servants or agents.[29]

Sub-bailment arises where a bailee who has a present right to possession transfers possession of the goods to a third party (the sub-bailee). Thus the photographer is the bailor (provided he has not transferred ownership of the images to the library, in which case the library is the owner and principal bailor), the library is the bailee and the third party client receiving images is the sub-bailee. Where there is a sub-bailment for reward, the sub-bailee will

---

[24] *AVX Ltd v E.G.M. Solders Ltd, The Times*, July 7, 1982. Staughton J. stated that the court "should not classify the type of bailment, or even ... ascertain whether it is truly a bailment at all, in order to determine what duty of care, if any is owed" (transcript p.7 quoted in *N.* Palmer, *Bailment* (2nd ed., Sweet & Maxwell, 1991) p.686); *Houghland v RR Low (Luxury Coaches) Ltd* [1962] 1 Q.B. 694, 698; [1962] 2 All E.R. 159, 161; *Morris v CW Martin & Sons Ltd* [1966] 1 Q.B. 716, 731.

[25] *Morris v CW Martin & Sons Ltd* [1966] 1 Q.B. 716 at 726, 732, 738; [1965] 2 All E.R. 725 at 731, 735, 738.

[26] *Houghland v RR Low (Luxury Coaches) Ltd* [1962] 1 Q.B. 694, 698; [1962] 2 All E.R. 159, 161.

[27] *Searle v Laverick* (1873–74) LR 9 Q.B. 122; *British Road Services Ltd v Arthur V. Crutchley & Co Ltd (No. 1)* [1968] 1 All E.R. 811; [1968] 1 Lloyd's Rep. 271.

[28] *Hooper v London & North Western Rly Co* (1880) 50 L.J.Q.B. 103, 105; *Alexander v Railway Executive* [1951] 2 K.B. 882, 884–885.

[29] *Port Swettenham Authority v T.W.Wu & Co* [1979] A.C. 580, 590 *per* Lord Salmon.

owe to the bailor all the duties of a bailee for reward.[30] The original bailee's duties are not extinguished by the sub-bailment and the sub-bailee's duties are owed concurrently with the original bailee.[31]

## Involuntary bailment

An involuntary bailee has been defined as a person whose possession of a chattel, although known to him and the result of circumstances of which he is aware, occurs through events over which he has no proper control and to which he has given no effective prior consent.[32]    **12–021**

This will arise where a library receives unsolicited images from photographers. However, if the library holds itself out as willing to consider unsolicited images and receives specific images knowingly with a promise to consider them, it will not be an involuntary bailee. Any action amounting to effective prior consent will negate involuntary bailment.

Where a manuscript was left with a publisher and the author was told on leaving it that it would be submitted to a reader, it was held that the publisher was not a gratuitous bailee since the opportunity given to him of reading the manuscript was in good consideration.[33] In the absence of an agreement to the contrary, where a manuscript submitted to a publisher is lost or destroyed through his negligence (or that of his employees), the author may recover its value.[34] A slight assumption of control by the defendant may lead to a duty.[35]    **12–022**

Conversely, where a manuscript of a play was sent voluntarily to a defendant theatre manager who had never asked for it, it was held that the defendant owed no duty in respect of the manuscript.[36] Similarly, where a miniature painting was sent to the defendant's house without the defen-

---

[30] *Morris v CW Martin & Sons Ltd* [1966] 1 Q.B. 716, 729 *per* Lord Denning M.R.

[31] *Morris v CW Martin & Sons Ltd* [1966] 1 Q.B. 716, 728; *Gilchrist Watt and Sanderson Pty Ltd v York Products Pty Ltd* [1970] 3 All E.R. 825, 829; *Metaalhandel JA Magnus BV v Ardfields Transport Ltd and Eastfell Ltd* [1988] 1 Lloyd's Rep. 197.

[32] N. Palmer, *Bailment*, (2nd ed., Sweet & Maxwell, 1991) at p.677. Citing, *inter alia*, *Property Life Insurance Ltd v Edgar* (unreported, NZ Supreme Court, March 15, 1980), Mahon J. a person "who has come into possession of good without any volition on his part, as for example . . . the recipient by delivery of unsolicited goods".

[33] *Stone v Long* [1901–04] Mac C.C. 66.

[34] *ibid.*

[35] *Newman v Bourne and Holingsworth* (1915) 31 T.L.R. 209.

[36] *Howard v Harris* (1884) Cababé & Ellis 253. The plaintiff wrote to the defendant who was a manager of a theatre stating he had written a play and asking the defendant to assist him in producing it. The defendant replied that if the plaintiff would send him the scene, plot and sketch of the play he would look through it. The plaintiff sent them to the defendant but also sent the manuscript of the play itself which was lost. The claim was for the return of the manuscript *not* the scene, plot and sketch. This decision has been criticised on the basis that it in fact involved an ordinary gratuitous deposit and as the defendant had acquiesced in the receipt, he could not be regarded as in any better position than a finder of the play. See Palmer, *op. cit.* (1991) at p.681.

dant's knowledge or request and was damaged whilst in the defendant's possession, there was no liability.[37]

The position therefore appears to be that there is only involuntary bailment where there is a true and unrequested submission. However, where images are received knowingly with a promise to consider them, or where there is other activity which amounts to effective prior consent, a duty does arise, probably as a gratuitous bailee.[38].

**12–023**    The duty of an involuntary bailee is a narrow one and has been described as a "low-level" and a "very limited" duty.[39] Where the conduct of an involuntary bailee does not amount to conversion, he will only rarely be liable for any loss or damage to the goods. It has been said that an involuntary bailee is not liable for mere negligence, but must abstain from wilful damage.[40] As far as conversion is concerned, an involuntary bailee who in good faith carries out an action which would amount to conversion of goods, is only liable if he did so without reasonable care.[41] It has been said that "in the absence of clear notice by [the involuntary bailees] to the bailor that with effect from a specified date [the bailees] would regard themselves as discharged from any liability for the moulds if they were not collected, [the bailees] ... remained subject to a duty not to convert or inflict wilful damage on the moulds and perhaps a duty not to be grossly negligent in relation to them."[42]

It should be noted that the Torts (Interference with Goods) Act 1977 provides that contributory negligence is no defence to conversion actions.[43] Palmer however suggest that if an involuntary bailee is indeed liable only for those conversions occasioned by his lack of reasonable care, the action should, for these purposes, be characterised as one in negligence and the defence should, in appropriate circumstances, be allowed.[44]

## RIGHT OF ACTION

**12–024**    The claimant must have had at the time of the conversion either actual possession or the immediate right to possession.[45] It is not necessary to prove ownership and thus, an agent with an interest less than ownership

---

[37] *Lethbridge v Philips* (1894) 2 Stark. 544. See also *Neuwith v Over Darwen Co-operative Society* (1894) 63 L.J.Q.B. 290 (doublebass damaged after being left in hall following rehearsal; no bailment as instrument not enstrusted to the defendants and they had given no undertaking to be responsible for its safety).

[38] See *Stone v Long* [1901–04] Mac C.C. 66 above at para. 12–022, n.33, criticism of *Howard v Harris*.

[39] *JJD SA (a company) v Avon Tyres Ltd* (unrep) CA February 23, 2000, CA, *per* Lord Bingham C.J.

[40] Palmer, *op. cit.* (1991) at p.683.

[41] *Elvin and Powell Ltd v Plummer Roddis Ltd* (1933) 50 T.L.R. 158; *AVX Ltd v E.G.M. Solders Ltd, The Times,* July 7, 1982; *Batistoni v Dance, The Times,* January 18, 1908.

[42] *JJD SA (a company) v Avon Tyres Ltd* (unrep) February 23, 2000, CA, *per* Lord Bingham C.J.

[43] s.11(1).

[44] Palmer, *op. cit.* (1991) at p.696.

[45] *Wilbraham v Snow* (1669) 2 Wms. Saund. 47a.

may sue in conversion.[46] Where images are lost by a client of the library, the library having the immediate right to possession of the images will be entitled to sue. In such circumstances, whether the photographer also has a right to sue in conversion will depend upon the terms of his arrangement with the library—*i.e.* has he transferred ownership of his transparencies to the library or is it a bailment arrangement? Where an owner has consented to a sub-bailment, he will be bound by the terms of any contract governing the sub-bailment but he has concurrent rights with the bailee against the sub-bailor.[47]

DEFENCES

The following is a list of some common defences to an action for conversion. It is not definitive and is intended as a starting point. Reference should be made to other works for further detail[48]:     **12–025**

(1)  element of the tort are not met, *e.g.*:

    (a)  claimant has no title to sue because he did not have actual possession or the immediate right to possession, or because the defendant is a co-owner[49];

    (b)  subject matter of action not personal chattels but is a chose in action or money[50];

    (c)  an involuntary bailee acted with reasonable care[51];

(2)  third party has a better right to the goods than the claimant[52];

(3)  defendant acted pursuant to statutory authority[53] or is otherwise protected by statute[54];

(4)  defendant acted with the permission or licence of the claimant[55];

---

[46] *Morrison v Gray* (1824) 2 Bing. 260.
[47] *Singer Co (UK) Ltd v Tees and Hartlepool Port Authority* [1988] 1 Lloyd's Rep. 164.
[48] N. Palmer, *Bailment*, (2nd ed. Sweet & Maxwell, 1991); *Clerk & Lindsell on Torts*, (18th ed., Sweet & Maxwell) 14–73 *et seq.*; *Atkins Court Forms* Vol.39 (2000 Issue) pp.200 *et seq.*
[49] *Torts (Interference With Goods) Act 1977*, s.10(1)(a), (b). Co-owner is only liable to another if he destroys the goods or in cases of wrongful sale and disposals which give good title. No cause of action lies against a joint owner for acts consistent with his ownership: *Nyberg v Handelaar* [1892] 2 Q.B. 202; *Fennings v Lord Grenville* (1808) 1 Taunt. 241; 127 E.R. 825.
[50] *Torts (Interference With Goods) Act 1977*, s.14(1).
[51] See above at para.12–023.
[52] Torts (Interference With Goods) Act 1977, s.8(1).
[53] *e.g.* Police and Criminal Evidence Act 1984.
[54] *e.g.* Insolvency Act 1986, s.307(4) (dealing with bankrupt's property in ignorance of the bankruptcy); Insolvency Act 1986, s.234(3) (liquidator, administrative receiver and receivers not liable for any loss or damage resulting from the seizure or disposal of goods which he reasonably believes to be the company's property except in so far as that loss or damage is caused by the office-holder's own negligence).
[55] *Aikins v Brunton* (1866) 14 W.R. 636; *Ancaster v Milling* (1832) 2 Dow. & Ry. K.B. 714.

(5) defendant (bailee) acted on bailor's order without any notice of defect in the bailor's title[56];

(6) defendant has already paid damages to a the claimant's sub-bailee or payment to claimant would otherwise amount to double liability[57];

(7) other general defences to tortious claim such as limitation.[58]

## REMEDIES FOR CONVERSION

**12–026**   By s.3 of the *Torts* (Interference With Goods Act) 1977, the remedies available for conversion are one only of the following:

(1) an order for delivery up of the goods and consequential damages— s.3(2)(a); or

(2) an order for delivery up of the goods, but giving the defendant the alternative of paying damages by reference to the value of the goods, together in either case with consequential damages—s.3(2)(b); or

(3) damages—s.3(2)(c).

Relief under category (1)—s.3(2)(a)—is at the discretion of the court.[59] It does not give the defendant the option of paying damages to the value of the goods instead of delivering up. In many cases, where goods have been lost or destroyed there will be no value in seeking an order under s.3(2)(a) as the goods are not capable of delivery up.

**12–027**   Damages are at large and aggravated damages are available for conversion.[60] The damages for deprivation which is normally the market value of the goods together with any special loss which flows naturally and directly from the wrong.[61] If the property has been lost, the starting point for the calculation of the damages is the value of the property converted.[62] The market value of the goods is the amount the goods can be sold for not, the value of replacement.[63] However, if the replacement cost is more than the market value, the replacement cost may be recoverable if it is reasonable to

---

[56] *Hollins v Fowler* (1874–75) L.R. 7 H.L. 757; *RH Willis and Son v British Car Auctions* [1978] 1 W.L.R. 438 (auctioneer).
[57] *Torts (Interference With Goods) Act 1977*, ss.7 and 8.
[58] Limitation Act 1980, s.2.
[59] s.3(3).
[60] *Owen and Smith v Reo Motors (Britain) Ltd* [1934] All E.R. 734.
[61] *Chabbra Corp Pte Ltd v Owners of the Jag Shakti (The Jag Shakti)* [1986] A.C. 337; [1986] 2 W.L.R. 87. And see generally *McGregor on Damages* (16th ed. (Sweet & Maxwell, 1997) at paras 1362 *et seq.*
[62] *Martin v Norbury* (unrep) July 21, 1999, CA (Judge L.J., May L.J., Sedley L.J.) applying *The Jag Shakti* above.
[63] *Smith Kline & French Laboratories Ltd v Long* [1988] 3 All E.R. 887; [1989] 1 W.L.R. 1 (cause of action deceit, applying conversion principles to damages); *Chubb Cash v John Crilley & Son* [1983] 1 W.L.R. 599.

replace.[64] Where the articles converted have a low intrinsic worth but have a high potential or exchange value, courts allow claimants in actions for conversion to recover, in effect, the value of the rights or benefits which the document or other token represents and which has been impaired.[65] Thus it should be possible to recover more per item than the mere replacement value where the original has been lost.

Historically, the time of conversion has normally been regarded as the relevant time for assessment of the value of the goods.[66] More recently, it has been said that damages for conversion ought not to be arbitrarily assessed as at either the date of the conversion or the date of the judgment, and there is no absolute rule regarding the date as to which the goods are to be valued.[67] The method of valuation and date of valuation will depend on the circumstances.[68] Damages ought to be such as fairly compensated the owner for the loss of the goods, taking into account such matters as whether he would have kept the goods if they had not been converted; if not, when he would have sold or replaced them; if they were kept, whether they had increased in value, and whether the owner had suffered damage for loss or use.[69] **12–028**

Consequential losses are recoverable where they are reasonably foreseeable and the direct result of the conversion. This includes the loss of profits to be made from the goods.[70] Loss of profit for transparencies/images not available to be licenced by the library are thus recoverable.

An action for conversion concerns only the physical photographs/transparencies and not the copyright in the images themselves.[71] The cause of action is for the loss of the specific physical images only. This is the case even where the items lost were the only copies and the only embodiment of the copyright work. It is important to appreciate that the loss of opportunity to exploit the copyright is a loss flowing from the conversion of the physical photograph. It is not damages for a separate cause of action for conversion of the copyright.

---

[64] *Dominion Mosaics and Tile Co v Trafalgar Trucking* [1990] 2 All E.R. 246; *J & E Hall v Barclay* [1937] 3 All E.R. 620, 623.

[65] N. Palmer, *Bailment* (2nd ed., Sweet & Maxwell, 1991) at p.228.

[66] *Mercer v Jones* (1813) 3 Camp. 477. Later authorities have taken the value at the date of judgment but subject to qualifications, *e.g. Sachs v Miklos* [1948] 2 K.B. 23, CA and *Munro v Willmott* [1949] 1 K.B. 295. *McGregor* submits that the "soundest approach is to start off with the value at the time of conversion as the prima facie measure; this is in accord with the general principle that damages are to be assessed at the date of the wrong. The effect upon this measure of damages of increases or decreases in the value between wrong and judgment must then be considered." *McGregor on Damages* (16th ed., Sweet & Maxwell) at para.1386. See generally *McGregor on Damages* (16th ed.) paras 1384 *et seq.*

[67] *IBL Ltd v Coussens* [1991] 2 All E.R. 133, 143j *per* Nicholls L.J.

[68] *IBL Ltd v Coussens* [1991] 2 All E.R. 133, 139j *per* Neill L.J.

[69] *IBL Ltd v Coussens* [1991] 2 All E.R. 133, 139–140.

[70] *Bodley v Reynolds* (1846) 8 Q.B. 779 (tools of trade); *Liesbosch Dredger v S.S. Edison* [1933] A.C. 449, 463–464 and 468–470 (dredger sunk by defendant—true value of ship included loss of carrying out pending contracts during period of delay between sinking and replacement).

[71] Torts (Interferences With Goods) Act 1977, s.14(1)—things in action (*i.e.* intellectual property rights) are excluded from actions in conversion. See above at para. 12–015.

ASSESSMENT OF DAMAGES: LOSS OR DAMAGE OF TRANSPARENCIES
AND HOLDING FEES

**12–029**   The level of damages and method of assessment will depend on whether the claim is one based in contract for stated loss fees on a delivery note or in tort (including conversion).

### Contract: delivery note loss fees

**12–030**   As referred to above, standard delivery notes will usually state on the form what the loss/damage fee for the prints or transparencies is.

At the time of writing, a standard loss fee in the United Kingdom is about £500. A survey conducted in 1998[72] found that on average, picture libraries stated around £500 as a loss fee on delivery notes. The main range of loss fees for basic stock photographs was between £400–£750, although there were some higher and lower figures quoted. Loss fees do vary and some types of images will have a higher loss fee stated, such as aerial photography or for "special images". It is important to distinguish between standard "stock" images and special images which are of higher value and may be difficult or impossible to recreate—for example, documentary photographs, celebrity portraits. The same survey found that for special images, a loss fee was more likely to be in the region of £1,000 and higher depending on the specific nature of the image.

Photographic library loss fees have been held to be a genuine pre-estimation of damage and not a penalty and are thus enforceable.[73] In proceedings where a point is taken about the validity of the loss fee, it is advisable even if relying on a delivery note, to plead in the alternative the actual replacement value and to have evidence of the actual value to adduce in order to justify the level of the loss fees in the event. For issues arising out of the specific terms of a particular contract, reference should be made to *Chitty on Contract* and other standard texts on contract.

### Contract: delivery note holding fees

**12–031**   In *Interfoto v Stilletto*[74] the plaintiff picture library sent 47 transparencies to the defendant as requested with a delivery note which stated that the transparencies were to be returned in 14 days. The note stated that a holding fee of £5 per day (plus VAT) for each transparency would be charged if they

---

[72] By Sal Shuel, Collections picture library, formerly Administrator of BAPLA.

[73] *Studio Press Holland t/a Stockcolour International Ltd v Galaxy Publications Ltd* (unrep) November 24, 1988, High Court, Queen's Bench Div. Gareth Williams Q.C. sitting as a Deputy. The loss fee claimed were in respect of 20 lost transparencies at the rate of 750 Dutch guilders as per contract. The judge went on to say that if he was wrong in his view that it was not a penalty, he had been satisfied that 750 guilders was a reasonable valuation in respect of each photograph.

[74] *Interfoto Picture Library Ltd v Stiletto Visual Programmes Ltd* [1989] Q.B. 433; [1988] 1 All E.R. 348. Applying *Thornton v Shoe Lane Parking* [1971] 2 Q.B. 163.

were not returned by the due date. The defendants did not use the transparencies but did not return them. The plaintiff sent an invoice for £3,783 in
holding fees. The defendants refused to pay, and at first instance plaintiff
obtained judgment.

The Court of Appeal held that where clauses incorporated into a contract
contained a particularly onerous or unusual condition, the party seeking to
enforce that condition had to show that it had been brought fairly and
reasonably to the attention of the other party. The plaintiff had done
nothing to draw the defendants' attention to condition 2 which was an
onerous clause,[75] the condition never became a part of the contract. The
defendants were relieved from liability under the clause and the plaintiffs
could only recover a holding fee assessed on the basis of quantum meruit.

At first instance, it was held that on a quantum merit, a reasonable charge
would have been £3.50 per transparency per week and not £5 per day.
Evidence was adduced of loss fees charged by about 10 other photographic
libraries, most of which charged less than £3.50 per week and only one of
which charged more than £4 per transparency per week.[76] The Court of
Appeal reduced the amount of the judgment to a quantum meruit holding
fee which was assessed as £3.50 per transparency per week for the retention
of the transparencies beyond a reasonable period which was held to be 14
days from the date of their receipt by the defendants.

**12–032**

Today, the standard form delivery note provides for loss fees to be clearly
stated on the front of the form. Where the British Photographer's Liaison
Committee Standard Terms[77] are being used, the issues arising in *Interfoto*
are unlikely to apply, as there is provision to state the loss fees clearly on the
front.

## Valuation of lost or damaged images: non-contractual

Valuation of loss or damaged transparencies where, for whatever reason,
there is no contractual claim for a stated loss fee is more problematic. The
starting point is that damages for a tort should put the claimant in the
position he would have been in had the tort not occurred.[78]

**12–033**

The normal measure of damages for goods lost or destroyed is the market
value of the goods destroyed at the time and place of destruction, although
this is subject to recent qualification.[79] If the replacement cost is more than
the market value, that cost is still recoverable if it is reasonable to replace.
The claimant will not be entitled to the cost of a replacement where it is
unreasonable to demand an exact replacement.[80]

As far as compensation of the image owner is concerned, there are three
possible methods of valuing the loss of the image:

---

[75] *per* Dillon L.J; [1989] Q.B. 433, 438.
[76] [1989] Q.B. 433, 436.
[77] See above at para. 12–008, nn.7 and 8.
[78] *Livingstone v Raywards Coal Co* (1880) 5 App. Cas at para. 12–026. 25, 39.
[79] See above "Remedies for Conversion".
[80] *Uctkos v Mazzetta* [1956] 1 Lloyd's Rep. 209; *Dominion Mosaics and Tile Co v Trafalgar Trucking* [1990] 2 All E.R. 246, 255B.

(1) where the image was not an original (a duplicate or a print) the cost of reprinting the image or creating a new duplicate;

(2) if the image was original, either:

(i) the cost of re-shooting the images if practicable and not unreasonable; or

(ii) the value of the physical image itself (the cost of the film or development of a print) which for one image may be negligible but for many images may be substantial together with the likely income the transparency would have generated.

### Re-shooting

**12–034**    In many cases, re-shooting will be impossible, for example contemporary news photographs; sports matches; photographs of deceased persons; or structures like the Berlin wall which no longer exist. Where re-shooting is a realistic possibility, a claim on this basis will need to be valued according to the costs of a re-shoot specific to the recreation of those images by that photographer. Possible heads of claim would include the time of the photographer; cost of film and expenses; accommodation and travel (if images of a particular place); and model fees if applicable.

However, damages for a re-shoot will not automatically be recoverable if the cost of re-shooting is unreasonable.[81]

### Loss of profit from lost or damaged images

**12–035**    The enormous amount of variable factors mean that valuation of the likely future worth of images will be difficult and in almost all cases expert evidence will be necessary. Some of the factors which affect the likely future income of an image are outlined below.

The hypothetical future demand of a particular image is the basis for assessment but is inevitably difficult to assess. An experienced picture librarian will be able to express an opinion, but demand varies according to fashion.[82] Unforseen events may affect image demand. Following the attack on the World Trade Center on September 11, 2001, images of the original twin towers were in demand.[83] Images which do not easily date (such as unchanging landscapes, flora and fauna) are likely to continue to generate

---

[81] See for example *Uctkos v Mazzetta* [1956] 1 Lloyd's Rep. 209. Held that the owner of a totally destroyed motorboat was only entitled to the reasonable cost of another craft which reasonably met his needs and not to damages on the basis that he was entitled to the replacement of his boat. The boat was of an unusual type which would require a very large expenditure to construct a similar one.

[82] In considering subjects having a "dormant patch", Sal Shuel of Collections Picture Library gives the example of a high demand for images of the 1960s during the 1980s but at that time there was little interest in images of the 1970s. By contrast, during the 1990s, the demand was for images of the 1970s.

[83] See for example E. Vulliamy and E. Helmore, "Ghouls cash in on grieving families", *Observer Sunday* October 7, 2001 (t-shirts and gifts sold with pictures of the World Trade Center); H. Cotter, "Amid the Ashes, Creativity", *New York Times*, February 1, 2002 (account of various galleries exhibiting works related to September 11, including older skyline images).

income for many years. Even images which are dated may generate future income by virtue of the fact they have become history—for example pictures of the Berlin Wall coming down.[84]

Photographs of celebrities and other public figures can have an extremely **12–036** high value depending on the fame of the subject, which should be taken into account. Certain types of photographs which are difficult to obtain are also likely to attract a higher rate of income and a higher replacement value. Sports photography is one example. To gain access to most, if not all, professional venues and stadia, the photographer needs to be accredited. In many cases the photographer will be allocated a specific location within the venue and not permitted to take photographs from other places. Successful sports images retain a long term value as images are in demand for newspapers and magazine interviews, biographies, and historical accounts.

Most analogue libraries do not keep duplicate copies of all stock images as the expense and time of replicating images is not cost effective and the storage space required would be double. An argument that a library is contributorily negligent for failing to keep duplicates of stock material is likely to fail in the face of expert evidence that it is not industry practice.[85] However, duplicates are sometimes made of some particularly valuable or rare images. It may be an issue as to whether the specific image in question was such that the reasonably competent image library would have made duplicate. This is likely only to apply to a very small number of highly valuable images. It should be remembered that in conversion actions, contributory negligence is no defence.[86]

*Karadia v Thames Water Utilities*[87] is a useful illustration of how a court **12–037** approaches quantification of damages in lost transparency cases. In that case, a number of transparencies were damaged as a result of a burst water main belonging to the defendant. The defendant admitted liability under s.6 of the Water Act 1981 and the issue was quantification of damages. The defendant also contended that the plaintiff was contributorily negligence for failing to take duplicates.[88] This was rejected by the court. There were three different groups of images lost: (1) 120 unique paranoramic shots and other $6 \times 6$ shots of the Berlin Wall at the time it came down, (2) 33 fashion photographs and 6 rolls of unedited film (around 240 images); the evidence was that many of these images would have been discarded, and (3) current affairs photographs taken in the Middle East including some taken in the royal palace of Saudi Arabia which required special permission.

---

[84] See below at para. 12–037—*Karadia v Thames Water Utilities* (unrep) March 5, 1999, High Court, Queen's Bench Division, HHJ MacDuff Q.C.
[85] See below at para. 12–037—*Karadia v Thames Water Utilities* (unrep) March 5, 1999, High Court, Queen's Bench Division, HHJ MacDuff Q.C.
[86] Torts (Interference With Goods) Act 1977, s.11(1).
[87] (unrep) March 5, 1999, High Court, Queen's Bench Division, HHJ MacDuff Q.C.
[88] This was a claim in negligence. Note that contributory negligence is not a defence to conversion actions, Torts (Interference With Goods) Act 1977, s.11(1).

In assessing damages, the judge applied[89] the approach set out in *Allied Maples v Simonds and Simonds*.[90] It was stated in *Allied Maples* that where the quantification of the claimant's loss depends on future uncertain events (such as in this case whether photographs would continue to earn at the same rate in the future), the issue is decided not on the balance of probability but rather on the court's assessment, often expressed in percentage terms, of the events occurring or not occurring which depends in part on the hypothetical acts of a third party (in the case of images, the hypothetical third party licensee).

**12–038**     In applying the *Allied Maples* approach, the judge took into account the risk that the photographs may not have sold or would have taken longer to sell. The judge also took into account the following factors:

(i)   The fact that 13 of the Berlin Wall images were retained by the plaintiff in good condition and were likely to generate income.

(ii)  The law of diminishing returns—namely the fact that images of the same subject matter would not generate income in direct proportion to the number of images involved. Thus 200 images of one type would not generate double the income of 100 images of the same type, although the income would be somewhat higher. As he said "I think it is wrong to look just at individual photographs and their earning capacity. There is not an inelastic demand."[91]

(iii) The background of the plaintiff's earnings for the previous 10 years.

(iv)  Discounted for accelerate receipt due to the fact that the majority of the income for the Berlin Wall images would lie in the future (10th anniversary of wall coming down, 25th anniversary, etc.).

(v)   The fact that the photographs could have sold more than once.

**12–039**     On the facts of the case and in the light of the expert evidence, damages were awarded for the images as follows:

(1)   Berlin Wall images £40,000 including a discount of 0.4.

(2)   Fashion photographs £10,000. The expert evidence had valued them at £23,200, but the judge discounted to allow for images not selling.

(3)   Current affairs photographs £5,000.

There was also an agreed figure of £500 for the loss of the value of the film.

---

[89] Transcript, p.19F.
[90] [1995] 1 W.L.R. 1602 at 1609H–1610C *per* Stuart-Smith L.J. (solicitor's negligence action for failure to obtain warranty for plaintiff purchasers of a company against liability for former tenant's obligations under assigned leases. Causation and quantification of damages turned on what the plaintiff and the third party (from whom they were buying the company) hypothetically would have done if they had been given the correct advice).
[91] Transcript 21H–22A.

The application of the law of diminishing returns means that in cases where the loss is of many images of the same or similar subject matter, the value of each image individually will not be accepted by the court as a realistic valuation. Some account needs to be taken of the fact that there is not an unending demand for one type of image.

## DAMAGES FOR INFRINGEMENT AND MARKET ROYALTY RATES: VALUING THE IMAGE

BAPLA[92] historically published, for distribution to its members only, information on the range of fees charged by its members for various types of image during the previous calendar year, called the *Fee Negotiation Guide*. In 2001, this was revised to ensure compliance with the Competition Act 1998 and changed format to a historical analysis of fees charged and negotiating structures used by those picture library members surveyed. It was published under the title *Pricing Trends Survey 2001*.[93]    **12–040**

The survey states that it "is not intended to offer recommendation or guidance on pricing." It is, however, an extremely useful starting point for lawyers attempting to place a value on use of an image as it indicates the matters that are taken into account when licencing images for particular uses (*e.g.* territories, size of image, etc.). Although it is historical, it gives a rough idea of the value of different types of image use. The BAPLA *Pricing Trends Survey 2001* is a good starting point for those wishing to understand how image libraries negotiate fees and attempting to place a value on use of a stock image in a particular media.

For lawyers attempting to assess a likely reproduction fee for a standard stock image used in an infringing manner, an alternative method of valuing would be to contact a number of picture libraries dealing in similar images and request information as to the likely rates. It will be essential to know the specific nature of the use for which a quote is sought. It is not a simple question of asking for example "How much would it cost to reproduce an image of a parachute jump?". The fee paid to the picture library will vary according to the specific nature of the use. The medium used, the size of the image, the duration and territory of the licence, and the number in the print run will all affect the fee.    **12–041**

This is a method of attempting to put a value on use of a standard stock image. If the image is a special (*i.e.* a non-standard image) and has high value, for example pictures of celebrities or images of newsworthy moments that will not reoccur, the relevant value and licence fee will probably need to be established by expert evidence.[94]

The following list is an indication of the factors that affect the repro-    **12–042** duction fees in different categories. It should provide a starting point for

---

[92] British Association of Picture Libraries and Agencies.
[93] Available from BAPLA, 18 Vine Hill, London EC1R 5DZ Telephone: 020 7713 1780 *http://www.bapla.org.uk/*.
[94] See above at paras 12–035 to 12–036.

seeking information as to current market rates. These factors are not likely to be of great assistance in valuing future income of lost transparencies as, for the reasons set out above, this will turn on the hypothetical future demand for which expert evidence will be invariably necessary.

The following are guidelines as to the type of factors that affect the market royalty rate for particular uses of standard images. For further information as to the assessment of damages in copyright infringement cases, see above at para. 2–191.

## Advertising

**12–043**   Cost will vary according to:

(1)  Nature of the media.

   (a)  National newspapers and major magazines will tend to cost more than reproduction in provincial or trade periodicals. Fees will depend upon which newspaper or magazine the images are reproduced in. Unsurprisingly, the charge tends to be higher for higher circulation magazines.

   (b)  Television advertising—fees will vary according to whether the use is on UK regional television, network, satellite, or world-wide.

   (c)  Cinema advertising

(2)  Use of the image and length of use

   (a)  Periodicals—variables affecting fee—(i) Size of the advert—not the size of the image, (ii) number of uses or length of time (*e.g.* reproduction fees for one month, six months, etc.)

   (b)  Television—variables affecting fee—(i) first use or a test, (ii) weekend broadcast, (iii) licence period duration.

   (c)  Cinema—variables affecting fee—(i) duration of use in advert; a common dividing point is four seconds with differing rates for use for less than four seconds and for more than four seconds, (ii) length of licence period, (one month, six months, etc.).

## Promotional material

**12–044**   Cost will vary according to:

(1)  Nature of the medium

   Use of an image on any of the following will have different market rates according to the medium the image is produced on: showcards; posters; brochures; calendars; carrier bags; ceramics; cheques; gift wrap; greetings cards; jigsaw puzzles; match boxes; mouse mats; general packaging; commemorative packaging; phone cards; playing cards; records and CDs; stamps; stickers; trays; t-shirts.

(2) Size of the print run.

(3) Size of the item or the image (*e.g.* a full page in a leaflet will cost more than a 1/4 page).

(4) Area of distribution—UK, Europe or worldwide.

## Audio visual works

Fees will vary according to:                                    **12–045**

(1) Nature of the medium—rates will vary for video, slide showings, CDI or CD-ROMs for corporate use, CD ROMs for entertainment use. Use in an entertainment CD will tend to be marginally less than use in a corporate CD ROM.

(2) Size of the print run where applicable, or if showing to an audience (*e.g.* slide showing) the number of showings.

(3) Area of distribution where applicable—UK, Europe or worldwide.

(4) Internet use—variables affecting fee—(i) whether use is editorial, advertising, or commercial/business; (ii) whether use is for internet or closed network company intranet; (iii) size of webpage area the reproduced image occupies; (iv) position on site home page, or use on a menu page may attract a higher fee; (v) duration of licence (one month, six months, etc.); (vi) use as an icon is commonly calculated by reference to the equivalent rate for 1/4 of a page with a percentage reduction. Each use of the image icon within the site will attract a per cent uplift.

## Museum exhibitions and other displays

Factors affecting fees include:                                **12–046**

(1) Place of display—museums and educational use; promotional and trade fair display; shop window decoration; and restaurant or office use all attract different rates.

(2) Duration of use—(one day, one week, one month, permanent, etc.).

(3) Size of the image.

## Editorial usage

(1) Books—variables affecting fee include—(i) territory book is to be   **12–047** published in; (ii) size of image; (iii) use on the cover; (iv) use on the back cover; (v) use on a jacket wrap; (v) use as chapter opener/end paper; (vi) number of editions of the book the licence is for; (vii) size of the print run.

(2) Magazines and newspapers—(i) level of circulation: international and foreign magazines, free magazines, in-house publications, national newspapers and provincial newspapers will all attract different rates; (ii) size of image reproduced; (iii) newsworthy pictures will be subject to negotiation relating to the current "news" value of the image and fees may vary significantly depending upon the specific image.

(3) Television—(i) territory: the BBC Tel Pic contract—a standard contract for use by the BBC in obtaining photographic supplies is a good illustration of standard territories. The BBC Tel Pic contract (which does not apply to news or current affairs) divides the word into rights areas and the relevant fee depends on the area of usage. The areas are UK; Commonwealth; Australia; USA1 (main commercial networks); USA2 (other); Europe; Rest of the World (excluding previous categories); and the World; (ii) further exploitation after initial terrestrial broadcast—*e.g.* selling programme on video, etc.; (iii) cable and satellite usage will have different rates to terrestrial broadcasting; (iv) nature of audience where applicable, *e.g.* non-paying educational; trapped audience (*e.g.* aircraft or prison).

### Artist's reference fees

**12–048**   Where the image is being used by an artist as a basis for a drawing or painting of the image or part of the image, an artist's reference fee is payable. The BAPLA *Pricing Trends Survey 2001*[95] records that there are three main approaches to dealing with artist reference fees: (1) charging a fixed fee for use irrespective of the nature of the final artwork or amount of the image used; (2) charging a range of fees dependent on the end use of the artwork; and (3) charging a range of fees dependent on the degree to which the image is recognisable.[96]

In practice, if the artist's work is an exact (or near enough) replication of the entire image, the full standard licence fee is payable. If only part of the image is used by the artist, then a discount may be given.

---

[95] Available from BAPLA, 18 Vine Hill, London EC1R 5DZ Telephone: 020 7713 1780 *http://www.bapla.org.uk/* See above at para. 12–040.
[96] BAPLA *Pricing Trends Survey 2001* at p.14.

# Chapter 13

# Collecting societies

## Scope of the chapter

This chapter contains a brief history of collecting societies and an outline of the work of the UK collecting society for visual artists, the Design and Artists' Copyright Society (DACS). **13–001**

This chapter deals with two related matters, namely (1) the resale right due to be introduced into the UK in 2006 for living artists (which in many countries is collectively administered), and (2) some general practical guidance concerning copyright clearance and locating the rights owner.

For more detailed information about collecting societies, including the other UK collecting societies mentioned, the reader is referred to other works.[1]

---

[1] Laddie, Prescott and Vitora *et al., The Modern Law of Copyright and Designs* (3rd ed., Butterworths) at 25.1 *et seq.* and *Copinger and Skone James on Copyright* (14th ed., Sweet & Maxwell) at 28–37.

# INTRODUCTION

**13–002**    Collecting societies is a term used to describe organisations, generally non-profit, that administer the copyrights owned by their members and in particular collect and distribute royalties accrued in respect of the use of those copyrights. The underlying rationale is that it is easier, more efficient, and more financially viable to enforce certain authors' rights collectively, particularly secondary rights,[2] rather than to leave enforcement to the individual.

Collecting societies do not take assignments of the copyright in the works. They are authorised by their members to act as agents on behalf of those members in respect of the licensing of their works. Collecting societies thus enter into licensing agreements on their member's behalf. Collecting societies also monitor use of the relevant works and collect and distribute royalties to its members. The majority of collecting societies have entered into reciprocal arrangements with foreign collecting societies operating with respect to the same rights. In this way, collecting societies are able to ensure the collection and distribution of royalties to foreign copyrights owners and the receipt and distribution of royalties earned overseas to the home membership.

## THE ORIGINS OF COLLECTING SOCIETIES

**13–003**    The origin of collecting societies dates back to 1850 when the *Agence Centrale pour la Perception Droits Auteurs et Compositeurs de Musique* was founded by the songwriter Ernest Bourget, the composers Victor Parizot and Paul Henrion together with the publisher Jules Colombier.[3] Together they had brought a lawsuit against a Parisian concert café called the Ambassadeurs, objecting to the fact that they had to pay for their seats and meals, whereas no one had to pay for their works being performed by the orchestra.[4] They were successful in their litigation and the Agence was founded to enforce their new rights. This was replaced in 1851 by SACEM (Société des Auteurs, Compositeurs et Éditeurs de Musique) which was established in France to administer performance rights in musical works and is still in operation today.[5]

**13–004**    The end of the 19th century and the opening decades of the 20th century saw the formation of similar collecting societies across Europe and inter-

---

[2] The term "primary rights" is used to refer to uses of the work that can be directly controlled by the author such as the original commissioning or first sale, subsequent licensing on a poster, etc. Primary rights are often dealt with by the individual artist personally. "Secondary rights" is generally taken to mean rights subsequent to the primary use which are difficult to control as an individual—or rights that the artist is unable to exercise other than collectively. This would include (for example) photocopying, public lending, or re-transmission of broadcasts.
[3] *Introduction to Collective Management of Copyright and Related Rights* (World Intellectual Property Organization, Geneva) at para.26.
[4] *ibid.*
[5] *http://www.sacem.fr/*.

nationally, many of which still exist today. GEMA[6], the German society for performing and mechanical reproduction rights in respect of musical works, was founded in 1903. The Mechanical Copyright Licences Company Ltd (Mecolico), established in 1910, was the first UK collecting society. Mecolico was established to collect and distribute mechanical rights royalties from the producers of sound recordings. In the same year the Copyright Protection Society Ltd was also founded in the UK. In 1924, these two licensing societies merged to form the Mechanical Copyright Protections Society (MCPS) which still continues to administer mechancial music copyrights. The American Society of Composers, Authors & Publishers (ASCAP) was established in 1914 as was the Performing Rights Society (PRS) in the UK. The Australasian Performing Right Association Ltd (APRA) was founded 1926.

By 1926 there were enough societies to form an international organisation. In June 1926, 18 author's rights societies from around the world set up the International Confederation of Societies of Authors and Composers (CISAC). By 2003, CISAC had 209 member societies from over 108 different countries.[7]

The development of technology, and in particular multi-media formats, is problematic from a collective licensing perspective as a large number of licences will be needed for one product which may encompass music, still and moving images, text, and other literary or dramatic works. An organisation proposing to produce a multi-media work may need to negotiate with a large number of other bodies including picture libraries, film studios, television companies, book publishers, record companies, software designers, and publishers. In response to this problem, a number of umbrella collecting societies or one-stop-shops have been set up on behalf of all creators whose works are used in multi-media works. The one-stop-shop consists of a number of collecting societies co-operating to allow a multi-media producer to obtain all relevant licences from a single organisation. Such organisations include SESAM[8] in France, CMMV[9] in Germany and MCCI in Ireland.[10]    **13–005**

There are other projects on similar lines in the European Community seeking to take multimedia rights clearance to a European level. The European VERDI (Very Extensive Rights Data Information) project aims to facilitate multimedia rights trading by creating a European-wide rights information and licensing network between national collectively managed

---

[6] GEMA stands for Gesellschaft für musikalische Aufführungs und mechanische Vervielfältigungsrechte. GEMA's website is at *http://www.gema.de*.
[7] See the CISAC website at *http://www.cisac.org/*.
[8] Société de gestion des droits d'auteur dans le multimédia. *http://www.sesam.org*.
[9] Clearingstelle Multimedia für Verwertungsgesellschaften von Urheber- und Leistungsschutzrechten GmbH. *http://www.cmmv.de/*.
[10] Others countries with similar organisations include: Finland (KOPIOSTO); Italy (SIAE); Netherlands (CEDAR); Norway (CLARA); Spain (OM); Sweden (Copyswede) and Switzerland (SMCC).

clearance services.[11] Other projects such as Compas, which focusses on multimedia rights clearance for educational establishments, have narrower remits.[12]

Ultimately, the success of these initiatives will depend upon the willingness of both individual collecting societies and individual rights owners to participate.

## Collecting societies in the UK

**13–006**    A collecting society is inevitably in a dominant position in the market and may have a monopoly. In order to provide some form of public control and guard against abuse, independent supervision is provided for in the UK by the Copyright Tribunal and also the Competition Commission.[13]

The Copyright Tribunal has jurisdiction over licensing schemes of licensing bodies, including collecting societies.[14] A licensing body is defined as "a society or other organisation which has as its main object, or one of its main objects, the negotiation or granting, either as owner or prospective owner of copyright or as agent for him, of copyright licences, and whose objects include the granting of licences covering works of more than one author."[15] The Design and Artists Copyright Society is a licensing body within this definition.[16]

**13–007**    The function of the Copyright Tribunal is to hear and determine proceedings arising in connection with licensing schemes of licensing bodies under various specified statutory provisions.[17] These include references concerning the license scheme as a whole[18]; references by applicants who have been refused licences by an existing licensing body or where the terms of the proposed licence excluding him are unreasonable[19]; and general references concerning the terms of a proposed licence.[20]

The majority of references to the Copyright Tribunal concern the level of tariffs to be paid by the licensees under the schemes.[21] Frequently, these

---

[11] *http://www.verdi-project.com/*.

[12] Compas at *http://www.odl.net/compas/*. Other projects included Bonafide, Indecs and Prisam. See further *http://www.cordis.lu/econtent/mmrcs/home.html*.

[13] The Competition Commission replaced the Monopolies and Mergers Commission on April 1, 1999: *http://www.competition-commission.org.uk/*.

[14] The procedure before the Copyright Tribunal is governed by Copyright Tribunal Rules 1989 SI 1989/1129 (as amended by the Copyright Tribunal (Amendment) Rules SI 1991/201 and SI 1992/467; and the Copyright and Related Rights Regulations, SI 2003/ 2498). For further information about the Copyright Tribunal see Laddie, Prescott and Vitora *et al., The Modern Law of Copyright and Designs* (3rd ed., Butterworths) Ch.26 and *Copinger and Skone James on Copyright* (14th ed., Sweet & Maxwell) at 29–76 *et seq.*

[15] Copyright Designs and Patents Act 1988, s.116(2).

[16] *Universities UK Ltd v Copyright Licensing Agency Ltd* [2002] E.M.L.R. 35, 756; [2002] R.P.C. 36 at para.4.

[17] Copyright Designs and Patents Act 1988, s.149.

[18] Copyright Designs and Patents Act 1988, ss.118–120.

[19] Copyright Designs and Patents Act 1988, ss.121–122.

[20] Copyright Designs and patents Act 1988, s.125.

[21] See Laddie, Prescott and Vitora *et al. The Modern Law of Copyright and Designs* (3rd ed.) (Butterworths) at 26.17.

references concern musical works and recording rights. For example, as at October 2003, the Copyright Tribunal website stated that it had four pending cases.[22] Of these four cases, two concerned the PPL[23]; one concerned MCPS[24]; the last was against the Performing Rights Society, but concerned classical music licences.[25]

References concerning licensing schemes for the use of artistic works are relatively uncommon. In 2002, the Copyright Tribunal considered the terms of a licensing scheme operated by the Copyright Licensing Agency Ltd[26] (CLA) with respect to photocopying by higher education institutions which excluded "course packs" and "separate illustrations, diagrams and photographs". The Design and Artists Copyright Society Ltd intervened in the proceedings, as it had appointed CLA as its agent for the purpose of granting higher education institutions the right to make photocopies of its artistic works. The Tribunal took the view that in context the proper construction of "separate" photographs meant works on a separate page that were not necessary for the understanding of the text.[27] However, all parties agreed that the exclusion should be removed and that the blanket licence should included separate artistic works which was reflected in a 5p uplift in the royalty. **13–008**

## UK COLLECTING SOCIETIES: A LIST

The following is a list of the main UK collecting societies. In addition to these organisations there are other trade associations and organisations who administer certain types of rights on behalf of their members.[28] **13–009**

### Artistic works, literature and printed matter

| | | |
|---|---|---|
| ALCA: Authors Licensing and Collecting Society[29] | administers copying, broadcasting, and recording of literary and dramatic works on behalf of writers; | **13–010** |
| CLA: Copyright Licensing Agency[30] | administers copying of printed matter in particular books, journals, magazines, and periodicals. Licences may also include artistic works by virtue of its | |

---

[22] *http://www.patent.gov.uk/copy/tribunal/tribappsrefs.htm.*
[23] *Malcolm Finlayson v Phonographic Performance Ltd* (CT 78/02); *MBS Datacom Ltd v Phonographic Performance Ltd* (CT 64/98).
[24] *British Phonographic Industry Ltd v Mechanical-Copyright Protection Society Ltd* (CT 79/03).
[25] *The Association of British Concert Promoters v Performing Rights Society* (CT 77/02).
[26] *Universities UK Ltd v Copyright Licensing Agency Ltd* [2002] E.M.L.R. 35; [2002] R.P.C. 36.
[27] *Universities UK Ltd v Copyright Licensing Agency Ltd*, [2002] E.M.L.R. 35, 779; [2002] R.P.C. 36 at para.104.
[28] *e.g.* Christian Copyright Licensing International (CCLI) (copying of religious music); Compact Collections Ltd (royalties for film and television producers).
[29] *http://www.alcs.co.uk/.*
[30] *http://www.cla.co.uk/.*

DACS: Design and Artists Copyright Society[31]

agency agreement with the Design and Artists Copyright Society; administers rights in artistic works;

NLA: Newspaper Licensing Agency[32]

administers reprographic copying of newspapers and newspaper articles;

PLS: Publishers Licensing Society[33]

represents publishers and mandates the Copyright Licensing Agency to licence reprographic non-digital copying on its behalf.

### Music and sound recordings; film and television; and performers' rights

**13–011**

ALPA Authors' and Performers' Lending Agency Ltd

joint venture between BECS and ALCS for collective licensing of lending rights granted to authors and performers under the Copyright Directive.

AURA Association of United Recording Artists[34]

collecting society for performers who have released or producers of commercially released records.

BECS British Equity Collecting Society Ltd[35]

administers performer's remuneration arising from rental of sound recordings or video tapes, etc. of films and television.

DRPS Directors and Producers Rights Society[36]

administer rights on behalf of film and television directors for certain uses of their work both in the UK and abroad.

ERA Educational Recording Agency Ltd[37]

licences recording and use by educational establishments of broadcasts and cable programmes.

PRS Performing Right Society[38]

administers public performance, broadcasting, and use in a cable programme of musical works. Has an operational alliance with MCPS known as the MCPS-PRS Alliance.

MCPS Mechanical-Copyright Protection Society[39]

administers mechanical copyright in musical works, including the making, selling, and importing of sound recordings in all formats. Has an operational alliance with PRS.

---

[31] *http://www.dacs.org.uk/*. See below at para. 13–012.
[32] *http://www.nla.co.uk*.
[33] *http://www.pls.org.uk/*.
[34] *http://www.aurauk.com/*.
[35] *http://www.equitycollecting.org.uk/*.
[36] *http://www.dprs.org/intro.htm*.
[37] *http://www.era.org.uk/*.
[38] *http://www.prs.co.uk/*. See also PRS MCPS Alliance at *http://www.mcps-prs-alliance.co.uk/*.
[39] *http://www.mcps.co.uk/* See also PRS MCPS Alliance at *http://www.mcps-prs-alliance.co.uk/*.

| PPL Phonographic Performance Limited[40] | administers performing rights and dubbing of sound recordings on behalf of record companies. |
| VPL Video Performance Limited | Enforces public performance and broadcasting of music videos. |

## Design and artists copyright society (DACS)

DACS[41] is a non-profit collecting society for visual artists in the UK. It was founded in December 1983 by a group of artists.[42] Membership is open to any visual artist of any discipline (including photographers, photo-journalists, and illustrators) who are resident in the UK or the Republic of Ireland. DACS represents 16,000 British commercial artists and 36,000 international fine artists by virtue of reciprocal agreements with foreign collecting societies.[43] In 2002, DACS collected over £3,080,000 in rights revenue[44] which had risen from £1,850,000 (2001) and £1,567,000 (2000) in the preceding years.[45]

**13–012**

In November 2003, DACS had two categories of membership; ordinary membership (living artists), and successor membership (for surviving relatives or beneficiaries) but a revision of the membership categories is anticipated in 2004.[46] Under the existing ordinary membership agreement, DACS is granted an exclusive licence by the artist for both primary and secondary rights.[47] This means that for those living photographers whose work is dealt with by agents or who have their work licenced to picture libraries, membership of DACS under the present system is not an option because they cannot grant an exclusive reproduction licence to DACS. As at November 2003, it was not possible to be a living ordinary member of DACS and be represented by DACS for secondary rights only. However, the proposal to revise the membership categories may address this difficulty.

In addition to licensing of particular individuals' works, DACS also distributes collective copyright licensing income from blanket licensing schemes. DACS has operated an annual distribution scheme (called Payback) since 2000 in which visual artists are invited to register to claim a share of money collected under various blanket licence schemes such as the CLA photocopying licence. Any artist—whether or not a member of DACS—can make a claim under the Payback scheme. Under the 2002

**13–013**

[40] *http://www.ppluk.com/*.
[41] *http://www.dacs.co.uk/* Design and Artists Copyright Society Ltd, Parchment House,13 Northburgh Street, London, EC1V 0JP.
[42] John Alexander Sinclair, Philip Dahan-Bouchard, Susan Hiller, Elaine Kowalsky, Eduardo Paolozzi, Michael Rizzello and David Shepherd, DACS Annual Report 2002.
[43] DACS Annual Report 2002, p.8.
[44] DACS Annual Report 2003, p.4.
[45] DACS Annual Report 2002, p.4.
[46] The author is grateful to Janet Tod, Membership and Development Officer of DACS for this information.
[47] Ordinary Membership Agreement, Cl.1.

Payback scheme, over £500,000 was available for artists to claim.[48] Photographers comprised 49 per cent of successful claimants for use in publications and 58 per cent of successful claimants for use in television.[49] In that year, 22 of the 50 claimants receiving the highest payment were photographers.[50]

If a photographer is represented by DACS and an individual wishes to reproduce his work, an application can be made to DACS for a licence. DACS operates various different schemes which have varying terms and conditions dependent upon the particular form of reproduction proposed. The slide collection licensing scheme, for example, covers the reproduction of all artistic works, including photographs, on to slides for educational purposes. The appropriate Request for Permission form needs to be completed and returned to DACS. DACS will then process the application. In 2003, DACS suggested that applicants allow up to four weeks for processing of the request as further information (as to layouts, etc.) may prolong the administration time.[51] If the request is granted, a License Agreement will be issued. Fees are calculated by reference to the published tariffs in force at the time.

## INTERNATIONAL VISUAL ARTISTS COLLECTING SOCIETIES

**13–014**    The International Confederation of Societies of Authors and Composers[52] (CISAC) is an international organisation concerned with the protection of creator's rights, including improving the quality of collective administration. Many of its members are collecting societies; further information about collecting societies; collective administration is available on the CISRAC website.

**13–015**    The following is a list of collecting societies within the respective country that deals with the collective administration of the work of visual artists including photographs. Many of these societies have reciprocal or unilateral agreements with each other. Those underlined are some of the societies that have agreements with DACS.

| | | |
|---|---|---|
| Australia | **VISCOPY**[53] | (visual arts); and The Copyright Agency Ltd[54] (writers, visual artists, print publishers) |
| Austria | VBK | (Verbund für Bildung und Kultur) |
| Belgium | **SABAM**[55] | (Société Belge des Auteurs, Compositeurs et Éditeurs) and |

---

[48] DACS Annual Report 2002.
[49] DACS Payback 2002 Report at p.3
[50] DACS Payback 2002 Report at p.16.
[51] DACS Factsheet *Licensing Reproduction Rights A Step-By-Step Procedure*.
[52] *http://www.cisac.com.*
[53] *http://www.viscopy.com.au/.*
[54] *http://www.copyright.com.au/.*
[55] *http://www.sabam.be/.*

|          | **SOFAM**              | (Société Multimedia des Auteurs des Arts Visuels) |
| Brazil   | SBAT[56]               | (Sociedade Brasileira De Autores) |
| Canada   | SODRAC[57]             | (Société du Droit de Reproduction des Auteurs, Compositeurs et Éditeurs au Canada)—musical works and artistic works; |
|          | **SODART**[58]         | (Société de Droits d'Auteur en Arts Visuels)—visual arts—and |
|          | CARCC[59]              | (Canadian Artists Representation Copyright Collective Inc)—visual and media artists. |
| Chile    | CREAIMAGEN[60]         | |
| Czech Republic | OOA-S[61]        | |
| Denmark  | **COPY-DAN**[62]       | |
| Estonia  | **EAU**[63]            | (Eesti Autorite Ühing) |
| Finland  | **Kuvasto**[64]        | |
| France:  | **ADAGP**[65]          | (Société des Auteurs Dans les Arts Graphiques et Plastiques) |
|          | SAIF[66]               | (Société des Auteurs des Arts Visuels et de l'Image Fixe) |
| Germany  | **Bild-Kunst**[67]     | |
| Greece   | OSDEETE                | |
| Hungary  | **HUNGART**[68]        | |
| Iceland  | MYNDSTEF[69]           | |
| Italy    | **SIAE**[70]           | (Società Italiana degli Autori ed Editori) |
| Japan    | JVACS;                 | |
|          | **APG-JAPAN:**[71]     | |
|          | **JAA**[72]            | (Japanese Artists Association) |
| Korea    | **SACK**[73]           | (Society of Artist's Copyright of Korea) |
| Latvia   | **AKKA/LAA**           | |

---

[56] *http://www.sbat.com.br/.*
[57] *http://www.sodrac.com/.*
[58] *http://www.sodart.org/.*
[59] *http://www.carcc.ca/.*
[60] *http://www.creaimagen.cl/.*
[61] *http://www.ooas.cz.*
[62] *http://www.copydan.dk/.*
[63] *http://www.eau.org/.*
[64] *http://www.kuvastory.fi/.*
[65] *http://www.adagp.fr/.*
[66] *http://saif.free.fr/.*
[67] *http://www.bildkunst.de/.*
[68] *http://www.kibernet.hu/hungart/.*
[69] *http://www.myndstef.is/.*
[70] *http://www.siae.it/.*
[71] *http://www.apg.gr.jp/.*
[72] *http://www.jaa-iaa.or.jp.*
[73] *http://www.sack.or.kr/.*

| Lithuania | **LATGA-A**[74] | (Lietuvos Autori_ Teisi_ Gynimo Asociacijos Agent_ra) |
| Mexico | **SOMAAP**[75] | |
| Netherlands (visual artists) | **Beeldrecht**[76] | |
| | **Burafo**[77] | (collective administration of photographer's rights) |
| Norway | **BONO**[78] | (Billedkunst Opphavsrett i Norge/ Norwegian Visual Artists Copyright Society) |
| Portugal | **SPA**[79] | (Sociedade Portuguesa de Autores/ Portugese Authors Society representing literary and visual artists) |
| Romania | VISARTA | |
| Russia Fed. | **RAO**[80] | |
| South Africa | **DALRO**[81] | (Dramatic, Artistic and Literary Rights Organisation) |
| Spain | **VEGAP**[82] | |
| Sweden | **BUS**[83] | Bildkonst Upphovsrätt i Sverige |
| Switzerland | **ProLitteris,**[84] | |
| USA | **ARS** | (Artists Rights Society) |
| | VAGA | (Visual Artists and Galleries Association) |
| Venezula | AUTORARTE | |

## DROIT DE SUITE (RESALE RIGHT)

**13–016**    The European Directive on the resale right for the benefit of the author of an original work of art (hereafter "Resale Right Directive") was adopted on September 27, 2001.[85] The Directive provides for an artists' resale right in respect of copyright works. This is the right of an author of an original work of art and his heirs to share in the proceeds of sale of a work when it is resold. The subject matter of the right is the physical work, the medium in which the copyright work is embodied.[86] It does not apply to the first original sale by the creator but only to subsequent sales, including sales at auction. The resale right is also known by its French name, droit de suite,

---

[74] *http://www.latga.lt/.*
[75] *http://www.m3w3.com.mx/somaap/index.htm.*
[76] *http://www.beeldrecht.nl; http://www.cedar.nl/beeldrecht/.*
[77] *http://www.burafo.nl/.*
[78] *http://www.bono.no.*
[79] *http://www.spautores.pt.*
[80] *http://www.rao.ru.*
[81] *http://www.pgw.org/sacfo/dalro.htm.*
[82] *http://www.vegap.es/.*
[83] *http://www.bus.se/.*
[84] *http://www.prolitteris.ch.*
[85] 2001/84.
[86] Recital (2).

which literally means the right of following. Prior to the Directive, the resale right was recognised in the legislation of 11 of the 15 Member States of the European Union but not the United Kingdom. In many countries, droit de suite is collectively administered and the Resale Right Directive provides for either compulsory or optional collective management of the royalty.[87] If the right is to be collectively administered in the UK, of the existing collecting societies, DACS is the most likely candidate.[88] In other jurisdictions there has been litigation as to which collecting society has the right to collect droit de suite.[89]

The Resale Right Directive must be implemented in the United Kingdom, **13–017** as indeed in all Member States, by January 1, 2006.[90] However, Member States (such as the UK) who do not apply the resale right as at September 27, 2001, are not required to apply the resale right in respect of dead artists for the benefit of those entitled as heirs or otherwise until January 1, 2010.[91] A further period of two more years to implement the provisions in respect of the work of deceased artists "if necessary to enable the economic operations in that Member State to adapt gradually to the resale right system while maintaining their economic viability".[92] This reflects the lobbying by the United Kingdom Government, who joined with the UK art market in opposing the introduction of a resale right as it was feared that it would lead to vendors who pay the royalties moving sales out of England to territories where there is no such law.[93] The resale right for living artists must be implemented in the UK by January 1, 2006. As at November 1, 2003, the Directive was not implemented in the UK and no draft Statutory Instrument was available.

The Resale Right Directive requires Member States to implement laws **13–018** providing for a resale right which is defined as "an inalienable right, which cannot be waived, even in advance, to receive a royalty based on the sale price obtained for any resale of the work, subsequent to the first transfer of the work by the author."[94]

---

[87] Resale Right Directive 2001/84, Art.6(1).
[88] As at November 2003, the DACS Ordinary Membership Agreement at Cl.1(m) includes resale right (droit de suite) as one of the rights in respect of which members appoint DACS as exclusive licensee.
[89] *Bildkonst Upphovsratt i Sverige v DUR* [2003] E.C.D.R. 4 Hogsta Domstolen (Sweden) (dispute between two Swedish collecting societies as to which was the appropriate body to collect droit de suite royalties).
[90] Art.12(1).
[91] Art.8(2).
[92] Art.8(3). At least 12 months before the end of the period, the Member State is required to give the Commission its reasons.
[93] The UK has by far the largest international art market in Europe, accounting for between 60–70 per cent of the total EU market with an annual turnover of £2.2 billion. See further: C-E., Renault, *Resale rights: Toward a European Harmonisation* [2003] 14(2) Ent. L.R. 2003 44; S. Stokes, *Implementing the Artists' Resale Right (Droit de Suite) Directive into English Law* [2002] 13(7) Ent. L.R. 153; D.L. Booton, *A Critical Analysis of the European Commission's proposal for a directive harmonising the droit de suite* [1998] 2 I.P.Q. 165; S. Hughes, *Droit de Suite: A Critical Analysis of the Approved Directive* [1997] 19(12) E.I.P.R. 694.
[94] Art.1(1).

The resale right applies to all original works of graphic art[95] including photographs "provided that they are made by the artist himself or are copies considered to be original works of art".[96] This is likely to cause some difficulty in the case of photographs as many "original" photographs can be reprinted from the same transparency or digital file. Limited editions are included by Art.2(2) which provides:

"Copies of works of art covered by this Directive, which have been made in limited numbers by the artist himself or under his authority, shall be considered to be original works of art for the purposes of this Directive. Such copies will normally have been numbered, signed or otherwise duly authorised by the artist."

**13–019**     Accordingly, any resale of one copy photograph from a limited set of prints of an original photograph signed by the artist will be included. Practically, this right is of limited relevance to the majority of living photographers. An artist or sculptor can sell both the original work which has a rarity value as original and also limited edition prints. By contrast, the original work of the photographer is the negative, transparency, or digital file, which itself may be used to produce limited edition prints. In the modern environment, the original work is a digital file that can be easily copied and thus the photographer's resale market at auction is realistically limited to limited edition prints. It is relatively rare for prints of photographic works of *living* photographers, even the most famous, to sell at auction at the high levels that are often attained for original paintings or sculptures by artists of comparable status.[97]

**13–020**     Member States may set a minimum sale price before droit de suite applies, but this must not be more than €3,000.[98] If the UK adopts this figure, then in order for a photographer to claim any resale royalty sale of the limited edition print or original transparency, it will need to be in excess of €3,000[99] which is a relatively high figure for such a work unless it is either by a very

---

[95] Art.2(1) which provides in full "For the purposes of this Directive, 'original work of art' means works of graphic or plastic art such as pictures, collages, paintings, drawings, engravings, prints, lithographs, sculptures, tapestries, ceramics, glassware and photographs, provided they are made by the artist himself or are copies considered to be original works of art."

[96] Resale Right Directive. 2001/84 Art.2(1).

[97] The following examples are not intended to provide information about current or historical market value of works by any named photographer. These random examples are included as general illustration of the point that even the works of famous photographers tend not to sell for millions or even hundreds of thousands of pounds and photographic works tend at auction to make less than original paintings or sculptures by painters or artists of similar status. *E.g.* David Bailey print 35×27 cm of a portrait of Man Ray sold for £564 (Sotheby's, London, May 10, 1990); David Bailey Gelatin silver print 46×46 cm Picasso one eye sold for £470 (Bloomsbury, London, May 23, 2003); Annie Liebovitz cibachrome print 36×30 cm of a pregnant Demi Moore sold for equivalent of £2,406 (Christie's, Melbourne, April 27, 1999); Antony Armstrong Jones, 1st Earl of Snowdon (Lord Snowdon) vintage gelatin silver print 30×25 cm of Charlie Chaplin sold for DM 1,600 (equivalent £492) (Villa Grisebach, Berlin, June 28, 2001). Source: Artprice. *http://www.artprice.com.*

[98] Resale Right Directive 2001/84, Art.3. On November 1, 2003, €3,000 was equivalent to about £2,051.

[99] Resale Right Directive 2001/84, Art.3. On November 1, 2003, €3,000 was equivalent to about £2,051.

famous photographer or is of historical value. The royalty to be paid is proportional to the sale price in Euros as follows:

(a)  4 % of the sale price up to sales of €50,000;

(b)  3 % of the sale price from sales between €50,000.01 to €200,000;

(c)  1 % of the sale price for sales between €200,000.01 to €350,000;

(d)  0.5 % for the portion of the sale price from €350,000.01 to €500,000;

(e)  0.25 % for the portion of the sale price exceeding €500,000.[1]

The total amount of the royalty may not exceed €12,500.[2]

The Directive states that the royalty is to be paid by the seller.[3] Member States are free to provide that any intermediary art market professional such as salesrooms, art galleries, or art dealers is alone liable to pay the royalty or is liable to share liability to pay the royalty with the seller.[4]

The person entitled to receive the royalty is either the author of the work or those entitled after his death.[5] The resale right lasts for life of the author plus 70 years.[6]

## RIGHTS CLEARANCE FOR PHOTOGRAPHS: SOME PRACTICAL GUIDANCE

Unless the proposed use of a photograph that is protected by copyright falls within one of the permitted acts, any copying of an image or issuing of copies of the image to the public requires the licence of the copyright owner. If the image is being obtained via a picture library, the rights clearance will normally be dealt with by that library and the terms of the licence specified. If it is desired to reproduce a photograph taken by a particular photographer and it is not licenced by a picture library, it can sometimes be problematic tracking down the rights owner. The wealth of information available on the internet has contributed to making this process considerably easier. The following are some suggested starting points.   **13–021**

### Original publisher

If the image has already been published in a newspaper, periodical, book, or other work, the image will very often have a copyright notice printed either next to it or in a list of acknowledgments. The information in the copyright notice is usually the best and most obvious starting point. Even if   **13–022**

---

[1] Art.4(1).
[2] *ibid.* On November 1, 2003, €12,500 was equivalent to about £8,548.
[3] Art.1(4).
[4] Art.1(2) and (4).
[5] Art.6(1).
[6] Art.8(1).

there is no copyright notice, the publisher may have information about the photograph's copyright owner. The publisher may in fact be the copyright owner.

## WATCH database

**13–023**    WATCH (Writers, Artists, and their Copyright Holders) database, available freely online, enables location of the copyright owner of the works of artists and writers.[7] It contains primarily the names and addresses of copyright holders or contacts for authors and artists whose archives are housed, in whole or in part, in libraries and archives in North America and the United Kingdom. It is a joint project of the University of Reading in England and the Harry Ransom Humanities Research Center at The University of Texas, Austin, Texas, USA.

## Galleries and museums

**13–024**    Galleries currently dealing with, or which have historically dealt with a photographer's work may be able to assist as to who the copyright owner is and provide contact details. Many museums and galleries, particularly the larger ones, will have a copyright officer or rights department who may be prepared to forward requests to the copyright owner or holder.

Internet search engines are useful in locating the whereabouts of work. There are also online databases such as *Art In Context*[8] which is an online reference library containing information about artists, including photographers, and where to find their work.

---

[7] *http://tyler.hrc.utexas.edu/*.
[8] *http://www.artincontext.com/*.

# Chapter 14

# Public regulation and codes of conduct

## SCOPE OF THE CHAPTER

**14–001** This chapter contains an overview of the structure of media self-regulation and focuses on the two bodies of most practical relevance to the use of photographs by the print media—the Press Complaints Commission and the Advertising Standards Authority. There is also an outline of the relevant provisions of the BBC Producers' Guidelines. Although the Guidelines are directed at broadcast television rather than still images, they contain useful guidance that may be applicable to the use of photographs. The Codes of Broadcasting Standards Commission and the Independent Television Commission are not covered in this chapter. Both bodies are due to be replaced by the unified regulator OFCOM at the end of 2003 as will their Codes.[1] The Radio Authority which regulates independent radio is also not considered.

## INTRODUCTION

**14–002** There are a number of media bodies that operate self-regulatory codes of practice. These provide a mechanism for members of the public to complain about failures of the media to adhere to the standards set in the Codes. The main advantage over legal proceedings is that the process of making a complaint is free and resolution is usually fairly speedy. However, although these public bodies can impose varying sanctions, in general their powers are extremely limited. A major disadvantage is that at the present time there is no power to award compensation.

The main regulatory bodies (relevant to image and photograph usage) and their respective codes are as follows:

| Regulatory Body | Media Covered | Codes |
|---|---|---|
| Press Complaints Commission | Newspaper and magazine publishing | Press Complaints Commission Code of Practice |
| Committee of Advertising Practice (and the Advertising Standards Authority) | Non-broadcast advertising | British Code of Advertising, Sales Promotion and Direct Marketing (11th ed.) |
| Broadcasting Standards Commission (to be replaced by OFCOM) | All UK broadcasting— television and radio, both terrestrial and satellite | BSC Code on Fairness and Privacy BSC Code on Standards |

---

[1] See below at para.14–004.

| Regulatory Body | Media Covered | Codes | |
|---|---|---|---|
| Independent Television Commission (to be replaced by OFCOM) | Commercial television services in the UK except S4C (Wales) | Various ITC Programme Code; ITC Advertising Standards Code; Code for Text Services | **14–003** |
| OFCOM (expected to begin full operation on December 29, 2003)[2] | Broadcasting, telecommunications and radio—taking over the functions of the Broadcasting Standards Commission, the Independent Television Commission, Oftel, the Radio Authority and the Radio-communications Agency[3] | As at November 1, 2003, not yet published.[4] | |

OFCOM, a unified communications regulator, will replace the five **14–004** existing regulators named above and is expected to be fully operational from December 29, 2003.[5] The existing codes of the other regulators are likely to be replaced.

In addition to the above regulatory bodies, the British Broadcasting **14–005** Corporation has published the BBC Producers' Guidelines in respect of which complaints can be made to the BBC Programme Complaints Unit.

### RELEVANCE OF THE CODES

Any particular Code may be relevant in a number of ways: **14–006**

(1) In itself it provides a free method of complaint to the relevant body.

(2) As a "relevant privacy code"; s.12(4) of the Human Rights Act 1998 which governs applications for relief that affects the right of freedom

---

[2] See *http://www.ofcom.org.uk/*.
[3] Communications Act 2003, s.2 and Sch.1.
[4] OFCOM is required by statute to draw up and review various codes: *e.g.* Codes relating to: avoidance of unjust or unfair treatment or interference with privacy in broadcasts (s.107, Broadcasting Act 1996 as amended by the Communications Act 2003, s.360(3), Sch.15); standards for the content of television and radio programmes (Communications Act 2003, s.319); provision for the deaf and visually impaired (Communications Act 2003, s.303); and electronic programme guides (Communications Act 2003, s.310).
[5] Communications Act 2003, s.2 and Sch.1.

of expression provides that one of the matters the court must take into account is "any relevant privacy code".[6] This has been held to include the Press Complaints Commission Code.[7] In the course of Parliamentary debate, it was also said that a relevant code could also be the Broadcasting Standards Commission Code, the Independent Television Commission Code or a broadcaster's internal code, such as the BBC Producers' Guidelines.[8] It also includes relevant internal codes of newspapers or other organisations.[9]

(3) In determining whether personal data has been processed fairly. Under the First Principle of the Data Protection Act 1998, personal data which is required to be processed "fairly".[10] Fairness, it is submitted, should take into account whether the processor has abided by any applicable code.

(4) Certain specified codes are to be taken into account under the Data Protection Act 1998 in assessing whether, under the s.32 exemption for journalist, artistic or literary purposes, the data controller had a reasonable belief that publication would be in the public interest.[11] The designated codes are specified by Order[12] and are: the Press Complaints Commission Code of Practice[13]; the Producers' Guidelines published by the British Broadcasting Corporation; the Broadcasting Standards Commission Code on Fairness and Privacy[14]; the Independent Television Commission Programme Code[15]; and the Radio Authority Code.[16] The BSC Code, the ITC Code and the Radio Authority Code are likely to change following the replacement

---

[6] Human Rights Act 1998, s.12 is set out in full above at para. 7–110.
[7] As to the Press Complaints Commission Code of Practice see below at para. 14–007 and Appendix 3, below.
[8] *Hansard*, HC (6th Series) Vol.315, col.538, July 2, 1998. The bound Volume Debates of Hansard from 1988 can be searched and viewed on line via the UK Parliament website at *http://www.parliament.uk/index.cfm*.
[9] *Hansard*, HC (6th Series) Vol.315, col.539, July 2, 1998. In debate it was asserted that all newspapers and broadcasters ought to have their own internal standards. The Secretary of State was then asked, if it was shown that such internal standards had been breached, whether the standards would class as a "relevant privacy code" under the legislation. The Secretary of State replied in response:
> "First, the hon. Gentleman asserts that all those organisations ought to have their own privacy code. I understand his point, but I do not think that it is up to us to assert that an individual private newspaper ought to have its own privacy code. However, it is very much in newspapers' interests to have such a code, because otherwise they would not get the benefit of the relevant limb, which is subsection (4)(b) of the new clause."
[10] See above at para. 11–037 and Ch.11 generally.
[11] Data Protection Act 1998, s.32(3). See above at para. 11–141.
[12] *Data Protection (Designated Codes of Practice) (No.2) Order 2000* (SI 2000/1864).
[13] See below at paras 14–007 *et seq.* and Appendix 3, below.
[14] Under of the Broadcasting Act 1996, s.107. NB: this section will be amended by the Communications Act 2003, s.360(3), Sch.15, Pt 2, para.132(1) and (2) from a date to be appointed.
[15] Under the Broadcasting Act 1990, s.7. NB: this is to be repealed by the Communications Act 2003, ss.360(3), 406(7), Sch.15, Pt 1, para.4, Sch.19(1) from a date to be appointed.
[16] Under of the Broadcasting Act 1990, s.91.

of the respective bodies with the unified regulator Ofcom which is expected to become fully operational on December 29, 2003.[17]

## THE PRESS COMPLAINTS COMMISSION

The Press Complaints Commission[18] is an independent body which deals with complaints from members of the public about the editorial content of newspapers and magazines. It was created in 1991, following publication of the Report of the Calcutt Committee[19] in June 1990. The Calcutt Committee concluded that the existing Press Council was ineffective as an adjudicating body. It had recommended a new self-regulatory body be created in its placed which would have 18 months to demonstrate that non-statutory self-regulation could be made to work effectively.

**14–007**

The Press Complaints Commission Code of Practice is written by a committee of editors and ratified by the Commission. It was first published in 1991 and has undergone a number of changes since then. Key changes of relevance are:

**14–008**

| | |
|---|---|
| October 1993 | A footnote defining private property was introduced into cl.4 (Privacy) and cl.8 (Harassment) was amended to refer to this definition with regard to the taking of long lens photographs. |
| May 1995 | This definition of private property was altered to clarify that privately-owned land which could easily be seen by passers-by would not be considered a private place. |
| January 1998 | Clause 1 (Accuracy) was extended to deal with photo manipulation and the privacy clause, which became cl.3, was substantially reworded.[20] |

## Judicial review

The Press Complaints Commission ("PCC") has been the subject of judicial review applications that were unsuccessful on the merits, but the question of whether the PCC was capable of judicial review was not finally determined.[21] In *R. v Press Complaints Commission. Ex p. Stewart-Brady*[22] the PCC reserved its position as to whether it was a body subject to judicial

**14–009**

---

[17] For latest information see what is described as the Ofcom transitional website at *http:// www.ofcom.org.uk/*.

[18] *http://www.pcc.org.uk/*.

[19] Report of the Committee on Privacy and Related Matters (Cm. 1102, 1990) chaired by David Calcutt Q.C.

[20] For both the current and earlier wording of the privacy clause see below at paras 14–021 to 14–022.

[21] *R. (on the application of Ford) v Press Complaints Commission* [2001] E.W.H.C. Admin 683; [2002] E.M.L.R. 5 (application for permission); *R. v Press Complaints Commission. Ex p. Stewart-Brady* [1997] E.M.L.R. 185; (1997) 9 Admin L.R. 274; [1997] C.O.D. 203 (renewed application for leave).

[22] [1997] E.M.L.R. 185; (1997) 9 Admin. L.R. 274; [1997] C.O.D. 203.

review. The court proceeded on an assumption there was jurisdiction and considered it was at least arguable that the PCC was subject to judicial review.[23] In *R. (on the application of Ford) v Press Complaints Commission*,[24] the PCC accepted that it was arguable whether it is a public authority for the purposes of s.6 of the Human Rights Act 1998 and amenable to judicial review.[25]

Section 6(1) of the Human Rights Act 1998 provides that it is unlawful for a public authority to act in a way which is incompatible with a Convention right. If the PCC is a public authority, then it must act in a way that is compatible with the rights provided for in the European Convention. A public authority is defined in s.6(3)(b) as including any person certain of whose functions are functions of a public nature.[26] But this definition is qualified by the statement that in relation to a particular act, a person is not a public authority by virtue only of subs. (3)(b) if the nature of the act is private.[27]

**14–010**     The Parliamentary debates on the Human Rights Bill reveal that there was initial uncertainty on the part of the government as to whether the PCC was a public authority. However, later it was accepted by the government that the PCC was a public authority and it was primarily as a result of this that s.12 of the Human Rights Act was introduced to, safeguard freedom of expression.[28] During debate in the House of Lords, Lord Wakeham, then Chairman of the Press Complaints Commission, said:

> "As the noble and learned Lord the Lord Chancellor knows, there was until recently legal opinion from a most distinguished quarter that the PCC was not within the terms of the Bill. However, an article in The Times last week by David Pannick QC[29] asserted, in stark contrast, that the PCC is caught by the definition. In addition, during the Second Reading debate the noble Lord, Lord Williams of Mostyn, suggested that this was a matter for the courts to determine.
>
> It would have been unusual to proceed with such uncertainty because it left open an ambiguity which might have the effect of bringing disputes between newspapers and individuals within the scope of the Bill only by virtue of the fact that the PCC was declared a public authority. However, I can now answer my own question–and I am most grateful to the noble and learned Lord the Lord Chancellor for assisting me in this. He wrote to me this morning to confirm that, in his view, the PCC is a public authority within the terms of the Bill."[30]

---

[23] [1997] E.M.L.R. 185 at 189 *per* Lord Woolf M.R.
[24] [2001] E.W.H.C. Admin 683; [2002] E.M.L.R. 5.
[25] [2001] E.W.H.C. Admin 683 at para.11; [2002] E.M.L.R. 5 at 100 *per* Silber J.
[26] Human Rights Act 1998, s.6(3)(b).
[27] Human Rights Act 1998, s.6(5).
[28] See Lord Lester and D. Pannick, *Human Rights Law and Practice* (Butterworths, 1999) at pp.45–46.
[29] *The Times*, November 18, 1997.
[30] *Hansard*, HL Official Report (5th series), Vol.583, cols 771–774, November 24, 1997.

During debate in the House of Commons, the Home Secretary Jack Straw also said "It will ultimately be a matter for the courts, but our considered view is that the Press Complaints Commission undertakes public functions but the press does not, which is crucial."[31]

It has been said that whether a body is amenable to judicial review is of assistance in considering whether it is a public authority, but it is not determinative.[32] In considering whether a parochial church council serving notice to repair a chancel was a public authority under the Human Rights Act 1998, the House of Lords held that a public authority under s.6 could either be a core public authority (exercising functions that were broadly governmental), or a hybrid public authority (exercising both public and non-public functions).[33] A non-governmental organisation ought not to be regarded as a core public authority.[34] In the case of hybrid public authorities, there is no assumption that everything done by that body is a public function. Section 6(3) requires a distinction to be drawn between functions that are public and those which are private.[35] It is the function that the person is performing that is determinative of the question whether it is for the purposes of a given case, a hybrid public authority.[36] The House of Lords held that the church council was not a public authority as it was acting in the sectional and not in the public interest; it was essentially a domestic religious body.[37]

**14–011**

It has been held that in taking a decision that affected a person's right of access to a public market, the Hampshire Farmers Markets Ltd (a private limited company that stepped into the shoes of an organisation originally set up by a County Council under a later repealed local government statute) was acting as a public authority.[38] The source of the power is not critical, but what is required is the existence of a public law element; the fact that the decision of the body concerned access to a public market was critical.[39]

**14–012**

On the basis of this case law the Press Complaints Commission (not being a governmental organisation) is not a core public authority and can only be a hybrid authority. The House of Lords has held the question of whether a body is acting as a hybrid public authority is determined by reference to the function that the person is performing.[40] It is submitted that when giving adjudications, the PCC is acting in its capacity as the self-regulatory body of

---

[31] *Hansard*, HC Official Report (6th Series) Vol.314, col.414, June 17, 1998.
[32] *Aston Cantlow and Wilmcote with Billesley Parochial Church Council v Wallbank* [2003] UKHL 37, HL, at para.52; [2003] 3 W.L.R. 283 *per* Lord Hope; *R. (on the application of Heather) v Leonard Cheshire Foundation* [2002] E.W.C.A. Civ. 366; [2002] 2 All E.R. 936.
[33] *Aston Cantlow and Wilmcote with Billesley Parochial Church Council v Wallbank* [2003] UKHL 37, HL, at paras 8–10 *per* Lord Nicholls and para.41 *per* Lord Hope; [2003] 3 W.L.R. 283 at 287–288 and 296.
[34] *ibid.*, at para.47; [2003] 3 W.L.R. 283 at 298 *per* Lord Hope.
[35] *ibid.*, at para.41; [2003] 3 W.L.R. 283 at 296 *per* Lord Hope.
[36] [2003] 3 W.L.R. 283.
[37] *ibid.*, at para.86; [2003] 3 W.L.R. 283 at 310 *per* Lord Hobhouse.
[38] *R. (on the Application of Beer) v Hampshire Farmers' Markets Ltd* [2003] E.W.C.A. Civ. 1056, CA.
[39] *R. (on the Application of Beer) v Hampshire Farmers' Markets Ltd* [2003] E.W.C.A. Civ. 1056, CA at para.34.
[40] [2003] 3 W.L.R. 283.

the press and is therefore acting in public capacity. Thus it is submitted the PCC's adjudications are capable of being subject to judicial review and in that capacity it is acting as a hybrid public authority.[41] It is clear that the Advertising Standards Authority is amenable to judicial review and is carrying out a public function in respect of its adjudications.[42] The PCC is in an analogous position.

If, as is submitted, the PCC is subject to judicial review, the court exercises a regulatory function in judicial review proceedings and would only interfere with decisions of the PCC where it is *clearly* desirable.[43]

## Press Complaints Commission Code as "a relevant privacy code"

**14–013**     Section 12(4) of the Human Rights Act 1998 which governs applications for relief that affects the right of freedom of expression provides that one of the matters the court must take into account is "any relevant privacy code".[44] The PCC Code is capable of being "a relevant privacy code" for the purposes of this section.[45]

The PCC Code may not merely be relevant to claims against those sections of the press who are subject to the PCC jurisdiction. It has been held that it is arguable that the PCC Code is "a relevant code" for the purposes of a claim against an individual press informant.[46] The Court of Appeal considered that it is arguable that where the code indicates that publication of a story is legitimate, the Code is of relevance in considering the legitimacy of the act of the informant in providing the story to the media.[47]

### Complaints procedure

**14–014**     The PCC suggest that in the first instance a complainant writes to the editor of the newspaper as that "is usually the quickest way of getting a correction or apology for an inaccuracy or intrusion."[48] Normally, the Commission will only consider complaints from those directly affected by the publication complained. Exceptionally the Commission may in its discretion consider a complaint from a third party but only if it raises a matter

---

[41] For further discussion as to whether media regulators are "public authorities" see : *The Law of Privacy and the Media* (Michael Tugendhat Q.C. and Iain Christie ed. (Oxford University Press, 2002) at paras 13.135 *et seq.* and 1st supplement.

[42] See below at para. 14–065.

[43] [1997] E.M.L.R. 185, 190; (1997) 9 Admin. L.R. 274, 279B *per* Lord Woolf M.R.

[44] Human Rights Act 1998, s.12 is set out in full above at para. 7–110.

[45] *Av B plc* at para.11(xiv); [2003] Q.B. 195 at 210; [2002] E.M.L.R. 21 at 386; *Theakston v MGN Ltd* [2002] E.W.H.C. 137; [2002] E.M.L.R. 22. As to the meaning of "relevant privacy code" see above at para. 14–006(2).

[46] *Campbell v Frisbee* [2002] E.W.C.A. Civ. 1374 at paras 24–25; [2003] E.M.L.R. 3 at 84 (*per* Lord Philips M.R.). The Court of Appeal reversed Lightman J. ([2002] E.W.H.C. 328; [2002] E.M.L.R. 31) who held that the Code was not relevant as it was of no application to an individual defendant as it had no jurisdiction in respect of her conduct.

[47] *Campbell v Frisbee* [2002] E.W.C.A. Civ. 1374 at paras 24–25; [2003] E.M.L.R. 3 at 84 (*per* Lord Philips M.R.).

[48] PCC Guidance Making A Complaint. Available online at *http://www.pcc.org.uk/complaint/how_complaint.htm*.

of significant public interest. Complaints to the PCC should be made in writing and within one month of the publication of the article or within a period of one month after the close of correspondence with the relevant editor with regard to the matter. Complaints will not be dealt with outside this time unless there are special circumstances. A copy of the complete article identifying the name of the publication and the date on which it was published should be sent with the written complaint. The PCC aims to deal with complaints within 40 working days.[49] Like the Advertising Standards Authority, it does not hold oral hearings and will not deal with complaints which are the subject of legal proceedings. The PCC will also not deal with complaints about print advertisements. Complaints about print advertisements should be made to the Advertising Standards Authority.[50] In 2002, the PCC received 2,630 complaints of which 2,390 were from ordinary people, not public figures.[51]

Complaints may be resolved to the satisfaction of the complainant **14–015** without the necessity of an adjudication by the PCC where the newspaper or publication takes appropriate remedial action. This may include publishing an apology, a correction or clarification, or a letter from the complainant. In cases of images, remedial action may include deleting of images from an archive or database and an undertaking not to republish them.

If the PCC finds that the Code has been breached, then its adjudication is required to be published by the relevant publication that was the subject of the complaint. This is an extremely limited form of sanction and can be contrasted with the wider sanctions open to the Advertising Standards Authority.[52]

## Adjudications of the PCC concerning photographs

The Commission attempts to maintain consistency in its decisions. It **14–016** therefore refers to its previous decisions and has a case law approach to its adjudications.[53] Substantial changes were made to the Code of Practice at the end of 1997 which came into force on January 1, 1998.[54] Care should be taken if seeking to rely on pre-1998 decisions when advising or considering whether to make a complaint, as the wording of some of the clauses changed significantly, particularly the privacy clause. Where an adjudication referred to in this section was made under a pre–1998 Code it is indicated in the footnote.

Questions of taste and matters for editorial judgment are generally outside the remit of the Code. However, a complaint was upheld in respect of "explicit and horrifying pictures" illustrating a story about cannibalism as "an extreme breach of the spirit of the Code of Practice and the standards

---

[49] PCC Complainants Charter, para.2.
[50] As to which see below at paras 14–063 *et seq.*
[51] Press Complaints Commission, Annual Review 2002, p.6.
[52] See below at para. 14–070.
[53] *Bright v Daily Mail* PCC Report No.44 (Oct–Dec 1998) p.12 at p.13.
[54] For a copy of the pre-1998 Code see PCC Report No.40 (Oct–Dec 1997) at p.38.

which the newspaper industry sets itself."[55] No *prima facie* breach of the Code has been found in respect of publications in the national newspaper of Gulf War pictures of captured airmen[56]; or publication in a family magazine of nude sunbathers from a "completely unnecessary" angle[57]; use of a photograph of a house to illustrate an article about a slump in the property market where previous publications had not been objected to[58]; and for the use of an out-of-date photograph of a club where two of the members shown had since died but the caption showed it was a "flash-back" picture.[59]

**14–017**    The Commission has also stated that copyright issues are a legal matter outside the remit of the Code.[60] The Commission has declined to find breaches of the Code where in issue is the question of whether photographs were taken in breach of contract and contrary to terms of admission prohibiting photographs.[61]

The clauses of the Code in respect of which there is commentary on previous adjudications below are only those under which issues concerning photographs most frequently arise. The adjudications referred to are predominantly cases involving photographs. However, there are some references to non-photographic cases in which guideline principles have been established.

It should be noted that the Court of Appeal has stated that it discourages advocates from seeking to rely on individual decisions of the Press Council "which at best are no more than illustrative of how the Press Council performs its different responsibilities".[62] Given however that the PCC itself applies the Code by reference to its previous decisions and has a precedential approach to its adjudications,[63] to view the Code in isolation without actual reference to the manner in which it is actually applied is artificial.

---

[55] *Walsh v Sunday Sport* PCC Report No.2 (July–Sept 1991) p.23 ("no more than the exploitation of an appetite for horror and necrophily". Pre–1998 Code adjudication).

[56] PCC Report No.1 (Jan–June 1991) p.24. Case no.5.

[57] PCC Report No.1 (Jan–June 1991) p.26. Case no.21

[58] PCC Report No.13 (Sept 1992) p.12. Case no.8.

[59] PCC Report No.13 (Sept 1992) p.14. Case no.21.

[60] PCC Report No.17 (March–April 1993) p.31 Case no.31; *Shipman v The Mirror* PCC Report No.56/57 (Oct 2001–March 2002) p.11 (publication of private correspondence).

[61] *Andrews v The Mirror* PCC Report No 56/57 (Oct 2001–March 2002) p.12 (photographs in prison). See below at para. 14–034.

[62] *A v B plc* at para.11(xv); [2003] Q.B. 195 at 210; [2002] E.M.L.R. 21 at 387. See also *Theakston v MGN Ltd* [2002] E.W.H.C. 137 at para.13; [2002] E.M.L.R. 22, 404 where Ouseley J. said "The editor of [the newspaper] ... produced some examples of the Press Complaints Commission adjudications which he thought were helpful. I did not regard his assessment of how that body would react to any complaint by the claimant to the proposed article as persuasive. As the editor in question, and a member of the Commission his views were not wholly disinterested."

[63] *Bright v Daily Mail* PCC Report No.44 (Oct–Dec 1998) p.12 at p.13.

## *Public interest exception*

A number of the clauses of the PCC Code are identified as principles to which publication in the public interest may warrant and justify breach.[64] Public interest is defined by the Code as including: **14–018**

   (i)  detecting or exposing crime or a serious misdemeanour;

  (ii)  protecting public health and safety;

 (iii)  preventing the public from being misled by some statement or action from an individual or organisation.

If it is sought to rely on the public interest exception, the PCC will require a full explanation from the relevant editor demonstrating how the public interest was served.[65] Exceptional public interest will need to be demonstrated in cases involving children.[66] The public interest is unlikely to be served by publication of a person's photograph for purely illustrative purposes.[67]

## Accuracy: Clause 1

*Clause 1(i)—inaccurate, misleading or distorted material, including pictures*

This clause covers any kind of inaccurate use of images, including digital manipulation that is inaccurate or misleading and incorrect attributions of images. It is not the Commission's job to find out whether allegations of disputed fact are true or not.[68] Its task is to consider whether editors have taken care not to publish inaccurate, misleading, or distorted material that are in breach of the Code. **14–019**

It is important to complain the first time an image is used in an inaccurate way, as failure to complain about first use may result in complaints being rejected for subsequent use. Where a photograph has been used in a particular way and no complaint is made, the Commission has taken the view that it is in the public domain and declined to uphold a complaint for inaccurate use of the photograph where it was used again in the same way.[69] **14–020**

Complaints have been upheld in respect of:

- a photograph of a child who suffered from Moebius syndrome and was thus unable to smile openly was digitally manipulated without

---

[64] These are Privacy (cl.3); Harrassement (cl.4); Children (cl.6); Children in Sex Cases (cl.7); Listening Devices (cl.8); Hospitals (cl.9); Reporting of Crime (cl.10); Misrepresentation (cl.11); Payment for Articles (cl.16).

[65] PCC Code, The Public Interest, para.2.

[66] PCC Code, The Public Interest, para.2.

[67] *Eves v Brecon & Radnor Express* PCC Report No.56/57 (Oct 2001–March 2002) p.21 (photograph of 14 year old boy at school).

[68] *Harkishin v Sunday Sport* PCC Report No.58/59 (April–Sept 2002) p.10.

[69] *A woman v News Shopper* PCC Report No.61 (October 2, 2002).

the consent of the parents to alter her mouth to produce a smile. The altered photograph was produced on the same page as the original.[70]

- photographs of an interior of a house subsequently sold to a well-known actress which showed possessions of the previous owner (the complainant). The complaint was that the feature was misleading because it failed to make clear the photographs were taken before the house was sold and gave the impression the complainants had sold their possessions including a treasured wedding gift. The complaint was upheld as there was nothing in the feature to suggest the photographs had been taken before the house was sold. The Code's requirement not to publish misleading material had been breached.[71]

- a photograph of a woman taken while she was smoking a cigarette in a public place used in an article about women smokers and lung cancer. It inaccurately implied that she was a heavy smoker when she was not.[72]

- a photograph of a man who had not died of AIDS included in a gallery of 21 photographs of famous people claiming they were all victims of AIDS.[73]

**Privacy: Clause 3**

14–021    Clause 3 states:

> *"(i)  Everyone is entitled to respect for his or her private and family life, home, health and correspondence. A publication will be expected to justify intrusions into any individual's private life without consent*
> *(ii)  The use of long lens photography to take pictures of people in private places without their consent is unacceptable. Note—Private places are public or private property where there is a reasonable expectation of privacy."*

Privacy is one of the clauses to which there may be an exception on the basis of public interest. The Commission will consider the nature of the material published and whether there is anything inherently personal or private about it.[74] The extent to which material is publically available is relevant and

---

[70] *Scott and Daily Mirror* PCC Report No.35 (July–Sept 1996) p.35 (the wording of cl.1(i) in both the pre-1998 Code and current Code remained the same).
[71] *Hello!* PCC Report No.55 (July–Sept 2001) p.5
[72] *Cunningham and Scotland on Sunday* PCC Report No.17 (March–April 1993) p.10
[73] *Biddle & Co (on behalf of the estate of Malcolm Forbes) v Daily Sport* PCC Report No.15 (Nov–Dec 1992) p.6. (cl.1(Accuracy) pre-1998 Code).
[74] *Theodore Goddard (on behalf of Steve Bing) v The Mirror* PCC Report No.58/59 (April–Sept 2002) p.7 (rejecting a complaint in respect of publication of the main switchboard number of the complaint's work with an encouragement to readers to call to express their views on his conduct. The complainant had been involved in a high profile relationship and the PCC considered "scrutiny by the press in these circumstances was inevitable"). As to public interest see above at para. 14–018.

thus a complaint was rejected in respect of publication of a telephone number that was in the telephone directory.[75]

The wording of the privacy clause changed in 1998. Before January 1, 1998, privacy was dealt with in Clause 4 of the Code and had a substantially different wording as follows:

**"Press Complaints Commission Code of Practice prior to 1998 amendment**   **14–022**
**Clause 4. Privacy [Replaced by Clause 3 above on 1st January 1998]**

(*i*)  *intrusions and enquiries into an individual's private life without his or her consent, including the use of long-lens photography to take pictures of people on private property without their consent, are only acceptable when it can be shown that these are, or reasonably believed to be in the public interest*

(*ii*) *Publication of material obtained under (i) above is only justified when the facts show that the public interest is served.*

*Note—Private property is defined as (i) any private residence, together with its garden and outbuildings, but excluding any adjacent fields or parkland and the surrounding parts of the property within the unaided view of passers-by (ii) hotel bedrooms (but not other areas in a hotel) and (iii) those parts of a hospital or nursing home where patients are treated or accommodated."*

Some of the adjudications referred to in this section were decided under the pre-1998 Code and on the basis of the old privacy clause. Caution is advised when seeking to rely on these older adjudications because of the substantial change of wording. The old clause is set out in full above for assistance. However, it is interesting that the adjudications of the PCC concerning privacy post-amendment still tend to focus on whether the material was "within the unaided view of passers-by" even though this wording is not repeated in the current clause.

The test applied by the Commission for breach of the current Clause 3   **14–023**
(Privacy) in relation to photographs is:

(i)   Was the picture taken in a public place?

(ii)  Does it relate to a matter of public interest?

(iii) Has the individual done anything to put issues relating to him in the public domain—and therefore provided de facto consent for the story?

(iv)  Has the individual taken steps to protect their privacy?[76]

---

[75] *ibid.*
[76] *E.Rex Makin (on behalf of Ian Stewart-Brady) v Liverpool Echo* PCC Report No.49 (Jan–March 2000) p.14.

**14-024**    Privacy is the right of an infant as much as a child or an adult.[77] Prisoners are entitled to a right of privacy under this clause,[78] as indeed are all persons convicted "no matter how horrendous their crimes".[79] The Commission considers that the deceased have no right of privacy.[80] Thus, it declined to consider a complaint in respect of a photograph of a person (taken in circumstances that were in breach of privacy) that was published after that person's death.[81]

A private place is defined by the Code as a public or private property where there is "a reasonable expectation of privacy".[82] Historically, the PCC adjudications reveal a consistent interpretation of this phrase as excluding quasi-public places, such as hotels or shops, that are accessible or visible to the public. However, more recent adjudications have tended towards accepting that there may be places to which the public have access in which individuals will still have a reasonable expectation of privacy.[83]

**14-025**    In *R. (on the application of Ford) v Press Complaints Commission*[84] it was argued for the complainant that "a reasonable expectation of privacy" did not merely mean a reasonable expectation of not being observed, but also meant a reasonable expectation of not having one's photograph appearing all over the media. This was rejected by the court on the basis that Clause 3(ii) concerned the taking of the photograph rather than publication.[85] In that case Anna Ford, the newsreader, and her partner had been photographed using a long lens camera whilst they were dressed in swimwear on a beach. The PCC rejected the complaint as it considered that as the beach was accessible to the general public there was no expectation of privacy[86] and the court declined to interfere. However, it is clear from subsequent decisions of the European Court of Human Rights, that the Art.8 right to privacy under the European Convention can be breached by publication by the media of acts that occurred in public to an extent which far exceeded the degree of exposure that would be foreseeable to a person in that public place.[87]

**14-026**    The PCC adjudication in *Ford* can be contrasted with another adjudication also concerning photographs taken on a beach. In 2001, the PCC upheld a complaint by the author J.K. Rowling in respect of photographs

---

[77] *Zachs v The Herald* PCC Report No.38 (April–June 1997) p.9 at p.15; *Evans v Bristol Evening Post* PCC Report No.44 (Oct–Dec 1998) p.10 (approving *Zachs v The Herald*).

[78] *Andrews v The Mirror* PCC Report No.56/57 (Oct 2001–March 2002) p.12 (complaint not upheld).

[79] *Rampton Hospital Authority v The Sun* PCC Report No.50 (April–June 2000) p30; *E.Rex Makin (on behalf of Ian Stewart-Brady) v Liverpool Echo* PCC Report No.49 (Jan–March 2000) p.14.

[80] *Messrs Manches on behalf of the Tolkien Family v Sunday Mercury* PCC Report No.62 (January 26, 2003).

[81] *Messrs Manches on behalf of the Tolkien Family v Sunday Mercury* PCC Report No.62 (January 26, 2003).

[82] Code of Practice, definition in Note to cl.3.

[83] *Tunbridge v Dorking Advertiser* PCC Report No.58/59 (April–Sept 2002) (complaint date: February 22, 2002) p.5 (complaint under cl.4 Harassment).

[84] [2001] E.W.H.C. Admin 683; [2002] E.M.L.R. 5.

[85] [2001] E.W.H.C. Admin 683 at para.36; [2002] E.M.L.R. 5 at p.107 *per* Silber J.

[86] *Bindmans (on behalf of Anna Ford and David Scott)* PCC Report No.52 (Oct–Dec 2000) p.11.

[87] *Peck v United Kingdom* [2003] E.M.L.R. 15; (2003) 36 E.H.R.R.R. 41 at para.62.

published of her eight year old daughter taken on a beach only accessible to residents of a particular hotel.[88] Possibly with the *Ford* decision in mind the adjudication began "while the commission may have regard to its previous decisions, circumstances will necessarily vary from case to case and it therefore considers each complaint on its merits." It was, however, noted that the complainant had previously gone to considerable lengths to protect her daughter's privacy. The beach was not overlooked by other holiday apartments and the family had gone there in low season to avoid unwanted attention. In addition, the complaint concerned a child (and was also made under Clause 6 (Children) and a higher level of privacy protection is given to children.

The Commission has adjudicated that there is no reasonable expectation **14–027** of privacy on public roads or pavements or through a glass shop front in full view of passers-by[89]; on a public bridge (suicide jump)[90]; in a front garden open to a public highway[91]; a publicly accessible beach[92] when moving between a public hospital entrance and an ambulance[93] in a police van travelling through a public area where the person inside is visible to anyone outside through the window[94]; millennium New Year's Eve at the Millennium Dome[95]; the lounge and bar of a hotel and outside a hotel[96]; and a private car park of a block of flats visible from a public street.[97]

---

[88] *Rowling v OK! Magazine* PCC Report No.56/57 (Oct 2001–March 2002) p.5.

[89] *Kingston & Haertel and Hello!* PCC Report No.55 (July–Sept 2001) p.10.

[90] *Curnos and Edinburgh Evening News* PCC Report No.40 (Oct–Dec 1997) p.6 (public interest in a tragic story which had happened in a public place. "The Commission has never sought to adjudicate on matters of taste and offensiveness which rightly do not fall under the Code." Decided under Privacy, cl.4 pre-1998 Code.). *Cf. Peck v United Kingdom* 36 E.H.R.R. 41 (ECtHR holding that Art.8 right to private life was infringed by media publication of part of CCTV footage of a man in a public street who was in distress and attempted suicide. The ECtHR considered that his CCTV footage was viewed to an extent which far exceeded the degree of exposure that would be foreseeable to a person walking in that area.).

[91] *Tindall and Sunday People* PCC Report No.52 (Oct–Dec 2000) p.6. *Cf de Valero Wills and News of the World* PCC Report No.26 (Aug–Sept 1994) p.14 (Complaint upheld in respect of photograph of couple on private property by their front door with their child. Note this was an adjudication under cl.4 (Privacy) of the pre-1998 Code which referred to private property defined as any private residence together with its garden and outbuildings and not "reasonable expectation of privacy".)

[92] *Bindmans (on behalf of Anna Ford and David Scott)* PCC Report No.52 (Oct–Dec 2000) p.11—long lens photographs of Anna Ford and her companion on a beach while wearing swimwear. Once the Commission had concluded that the complainants were not in a place where they could reasonably expect privacy, the only issue was whether the fact that they were shown in swimwear showed a lack of respect for their private lives. It was concluded it did not as the photographs were "innocuous" and did not "intrude into any intimacy nor left the complainants open to ridicule". The complainant made an unsuccessful application for permission to judicially review this decision.

[93] *Rampton Hospital Authority v The Sun* PCC Report No.50 (April–June 2000) p.30.

[94] *E.Rex Makin (on behalf of Ian Stewart-Brady) v Liverpool Echo* PCC Report No.49 (Jan–March 2000) p.14.

[95] *Carberry v Daily Mail* PPC Report No.49 (Jan–March 2000) p.17.

[96] *Nancy Seltzer Ass (on behalf of Sean Connery) v Sunday Mail* PCC Report No.47 (July–Sept 1999) p.17.

[97] *Unwin v News of the World* PCC Report No.28 (Jan–Feb 1995) p.7 (Note this was an adjudication under cl.4 (Privacy) of the pre-1998 Code which referred to private property defined as any private residence together with its garden and outbuildings).

**14–028**      Complaints have been upheld in respect of photographs of: a guest relaxing at the home of a celebrity[98]; a television presenter who was topless whilst at her own property where she could not be observed by members of the public[99]; undercover video footage of a private party[1]; a woman at work inside her private office taken from the garden of the office[2]; a couple on the deck of a private yacht moored near a private island on which the general public were not permitted[3]; individuals inside a cathedral[4]; a woman walking in the private grounds of an addiction clinic[5]; individuals in a private garden[6]; a royal couple kissing on private land at Balmoral[7]; Prince William travelling during his year off between school and university[8]; the home of an MP in an article about a local planning issue where the use did not add to the story[9]; and where photographs were provided on the understanding that the subject would not be identified (shown in dark silhouette only) where, in breach of agreement, the individual was identified.[10]

**14–029**      The approach of the PCC in this area has been criticised as inconsistent.[11] For example, the adjudication concerning Prince William effectively held that there was a reasonable expectation of privacy in a public place in Chile.[12] However, Prince William may be regarded as an atypical complai

---

[98] *Eversheds (on behalf of Sir Elton John) v Daily Sport* PPC Report No.54 (April–June 2001) p.16; *Eversheds (on behalf of Sir Elton John) v Esquire Magazine* PPC Report No.49 (Jan–March 2000) p.6 (Nos 2 and 3).

[99] *Granada plc v Sunday Sport* PCC Report No.55 (July–Sept 2001) p.11 ("There is no justification for publishing photographs which are taken when people are so clearly in a place where they have a reasonable expectation of privacy.")

[1] *Ryle v News of the World* PCC Report No.53 (Jan–March 2001) p.10.

[2] *MacQuarrie v Scotland on Sunday* PCC Report No.47 (July–Sept 1999) p.14 ("the inside of an office is a place where there is a reasonable expectation of privacy").

[3] *Allen & Overy (on behalf of the Begum Aga Khan)* PCC Report No.46 (April–June 1999) p.10.

[4] *McCartney and Hello!* PCC Report No.43 (July–Sept 1998) p.12 (the family of Sir Paul McCartney lighting a candle in Notre Dame Cathedral in memory of his recently deceased wife. The Commission "deplored" publication and stated it expected journalists to respect the sanctity of individuals acts of worship. It was stated a cathedral is "a clear example of a place where there is a reasonable expectation of privacy").

[5] *Spencer and News of the World* PCC Report No.29 (March–April 1995) p.6 (cl.4 (Privacy) of the pre-1998 Code).

[6] *Lancashire and The Sun* PCC Report No.26 (Aug–Sept 1994) p.14 (Note this was an adjudication under cl.4 (Privacy) of the pre-1998 Code which referred to private property defined as any private residence together with its garden and outbuildings and not "reasonable expectation of privacy"); *Miss Julie Goodyear MBE and The People* PCC Report No.62 October 6, 2002 (long lens photography).

[7] *Anson (on behalf of HRH Prince Edward) and Today* PCC Report No.25 (May–July 1994) p.5–9 (cl.4 (Privacy) of the pre-1998 Code).

[8] *Lamport (on behalf of HRH Prince William) v OK! Magazine* PCC Report No.52 (Oct–Dec 2000) p.8.

[9] *Winterton and Evening Sentinel* PCC Report No.19 (May 1993) p.7 (pre-1998 Code).

[10] *Evening Chronicle (Newcastle)* PCC Report No.31 (Aug–Oct 1995) p.14 (An argument that it was justified in the public interest as it showed for the first time the apparently serious nature of the relationship was rejected; cl.4 (Privacy) of the pre-1998 Code).

[11] See G. Robertson and A. Nicol, *Media Law* (4th ed., Sweet & Maxwell, 2000) at p.690 where the authors observe "What constitutes 'a reasonable expectation of privacy' has been the subject of a number of conflicting decisions, some plainly influenced by the status of the complaint."

[12] *Lamport (on behalf of HRH Prince William) v OK! Magazine* PCC Report No.52 (Oct–Dec 2000) p.8.

nant and had already been the subject of special PCC guidelines.[13] Whilst it is true that there are some decisions which conflict[14], it is submitted that consideration of the PCC adjudications shows that some common threads are discernable.

Any public road or public street is not regarded by the PCC as a place where there is a reasonable expectation of privacy.[15] The PCC will need to reconsider this approach in the light of the decision of the European Court of Human Rights in *Peck v United Kingdom*.[16] In adjudicating under the current code, the PCC tend to consider that there is also no reasonable expectation of privacy in respect of private property that is clearly visible from the public street such that passers-by can see what is occurring there unaided.[17] This can be contrasted with the approach under the old pre-1998 privacy clause which specifically provided that a private residence and its garden was private property. Many of the apparently conflicting decisions concerning gardens visible from the street are explicable due to the change in this part of the Code.

In considering privacy in respect of quasi-public places or private places **14–030** visible from the street, there is a marked emphasis by the PCC as to whether the person is visible and recognisable from the street unaided (*i.e.* no long lens equipment required).[18] There is a reasonable expectation of privacy if the property is private and the person is not visible from the street.[19] If a long lens is necessary to photograph the complainant with any clarity, this tends to support a reasonable expectation of privacy.[20] Quasi-public places, even if accessible to the public, at which the activity being carried out is essentially private also attract a reasonable expectation of privacy—such as a cathedral where one might carry out mourning or other acts of worship that are reasonably expected to be private.[21]

Generally, places open to the general public (such as public areas of hotels[22] or the millennium dome[23]) have not been considered to be places where there is a reasonable expectation of privacy by the PCC. However, an adjudication in 2002 took a slightly different approach to this question.

---

[13] *Prince William and Privacy* (Speech by the Rt Hon Lord Wakeham, then Chairman of the Press Complaints Commission, at St Bride's Institute, Fleet Street, June 28, 2000); *Prince William and Privacy—Statement by Les Hinton, Chairman of the editors' Code of Practice Committee*, June 28, 2000.
[14] *Cf. Bindmans (on behalf of Anna Ford and David Scott)* PCC Report No.52 (Oct–Dec 2000) p.11 and *Rowling v OK! Magazine* PCC Report No.56/57 (Oct 2001—March 2002) p.5.
[15] See adjudications cited in above at para. 14–027, nn.89 to 97 and accompanying text.
[16] (2003) 36 E.H.R.R. 41.
[17] See adjudications cited at para. 14–027, nn. 89 to 97 above and accompanying text.
[18] *Miss Julie Goodyear MBE and The People* PCC Report No.62 October 6, 2002 (long lens photography); *Tunbridge v Dorking Advertiser* PCC Report No.58/59 (April–Sept 2002) (Complaint date: February 22, 2002) p.5 (complaint under cl.4 Harrassment).
[19] See adjudications referred above at para. 14–028, nn. 98, 99 and 1 and accompanying text.
[20] *Goodyear v The People* PCC Report No.60/61 (Oct 2002—March 2003), p.19.
[21] *McCartney and Hello!* PCC Report No.43 (July–Sept 1998) p.12. For facts see n.4 above.
[22] *Nancy Seltzer Ass (on behalf of Sean Connery) v Sunday Mail* PCC Report No.47 (July–Sept 1999) p.17.
[23] *Carberry v Daily Mail* PPC Report No.49 (Jan–March 2000) p.17.

**14–031**      In *Tunbridge v Dorking Advertiser*,[24] the article complained of was a review of a local restaurant including a photograph in which the complainant and his dining companion were clearly visible. The complainant contended the photographs were taken secretly and made a complaint under Clause 4 (Harassment). The Commission said that customers of a quite café could expect to be able to sit inside without having to worry whether surreptitious photographs would be taken. The restaurant was judged to be a place where the complainant had a reasonable expectation of privacy. The fact they were not "easily visible from the street" was specifically referred to. This suggests that if the complainant had been sitting in the window and visible from the street, the Commission's view may have been different.

The Commission relied on its earlier decision in *Ryle v News of the World*[25] in support of the contention that "the Commission has made clear before ... that there may be places such as hotels which are accessible to the public where an individual will still have a reasonable expectation of privacy".[26] The reliance on *Ryle* was misplaced as that complaint concerned private rooms in a hotel that had been booked and were not open to the public. *Ryle* did not concern unrestricted public areas of the hotel as seems to be suggested. In fact, the PCC had previously found that a genuinely public area of a hotel did not give rise to a reasonable expectation of privacy.[27] However, *Tunbridge* is a significant change in approach of the PCC as indicating a willingness to find a reasonable expectation of privacy in a quasi-public place to which the public have access.

**14–032**      It is possible for a person to become disentitled to privacy protection under the Code where they themselves have put matters into the public domain.[28] However, the fact that a person has sought publicity in the past or has put matters concerning their private life into the public domain does not mean that the press are entitled to publish articles on any subject involving the complainant or their families.[29] Where articles complained of concern the same areas of personal life as those put into the public domain by the

---

[24] *Tunbridge v Dorking Advertiser* PCC Report No.58/59 (April–Sept 2002) (Complaint date: February 22, 2002) p.5 (complaint under cl.4 Harassment).

[25] *Ryle v News of the World* PCC Report No.53 (Jan–March 2001) p.10.

[26] *Tunbridge v Dorking Advertiser* PCC Report No.58/59 (April–Sept 2002) (complaint date: February 22, 2002) p.5 (complaint under cl.4 Harassment).

[27] *Nancy Seltzer Ass (on behalf of Sean Connery) v Sunday Mail* PCC Report No.47 (July–Sept 1999) p.17 (hotel lounge and bar. Photograph taken when complainant was heading for the street. The Commission noted "the property was not owned by an individual, but by a hotel where by definition members of the public unknown to the complainant would congregate").

[28] *E.Rex Makin (on behalf of Ian Stewart-Brady) v Liverpool Echo* PCC Report No.49 (Jan–March 2000) p.14; *Attard v Manchester Evening News* PCC Report No.55 (July–Sept 2001) p.9 at p.10; *Guppy v The Sun* PCC Report No.32 (Nov–Dec 1995) p.5 (Newspaper failed to demonstrate that the complainant had placed her private life into the public domain in such a way or to such an extent that the protection of the Code did not apply; cl.4 (Privacy) of the pre-1998 Code); *Carling v The Sun* PCC Report No.32 (Nov–Dec 1995) p.9 (complainant had placed details of her past and current relationships into the public domain; cl.4 (Privacy) of the pre-1998 Code).

[29] *Carling v The Sun* PCC Report No.32 (Nov–Dec 1995) p.9 at p.10 (cl.4 (Privacy) of the pre-1998 Code); *Spencer v News of the World* PCC Report No.29 (March–April 1995) p.6 (health of wife; cl.4 (Privacy) of the pre-1998 Code).

complainant, it is likely that publication will not breach the Code.[30] A complaint will not be upheld where the complained of material was proportional to that already in the public domain.[31] The Commission will take into account whether the complainant has ever discussed similar matters or profited from revealing details.[32]

Normally, publication of a photograph of the home of a celebrity that does not enable identification of the location will not constitute a breach of the owner's privacy.[33] In a case involving an ordinary person, it was said that generally the Commission would not hold the publication of a photograph of someone's house, taken from a public place, constituted an invasion into their privacy.[34] However, the Commission has made clear that when publishing details of the home of a celebrity without consent, newspapers must take care to ensure that they do not publish the precise address or material that might enable people to find the location of the home.[35] It was judged that there was no intrusion into privacy where a newspaper had identified a street in which the complainant had recently bought a house where the street contained 31 residential buildings[36]; nor where the address of the complainant is already in the public domain.[37] Equally, if images of the interior of a home have been put into the public domain by the police, there will be no invasion of privacy from publication of those photographs.[38] Publication of the precise address or details that enable the home to be found will amount to a breach and the Commission is mindful of security problems celebrities may encounter.[39]

**14–033**

The Commission will not deal with contractual disputes or matters subject to legal proceedings. This may cause difficulty where photography is

**14–034**

---

[30] *Carling v The Sun* PCC Report No.32 (Nov–Dec 1995) p.9 at p.10 (cl.4 (Privacy) of the pre-1998 Code).

[31] *ibid.*

[32] *Granada Media plc (on behalf of Miss N Russell) v Sunday Sport* PCC Report No 56/57 (Oct 2001–March 2002) p.14.

[33] *The Mail on Sunday* PCC Report No.51 (July–Sept 2000) p.8 (2 photographs of celebrity's home–one aerial. Complaint not upheld. Commission did not consider the article revealed sufficient information to identify the whereabouts of the home.) *Cf. Gardiner v Daily Star* PCC Report No.34 (April–June 1996) p.22 (A lottery winner bought houses for 3 of his friends in the same cul-de-sac in which he lived. Complaint upheld in respect of publication of an aerial photograph specifically identifying the complainants property as well as those of other residents even where address not published. Note this was decided under cl.4 (Privacy) of the pre-1998 Code). *Cf.* approach of the Advertising Standards Authority to publication of images of homes in advertisements below at para. 14–084.

[34] *A Man v The Herfordshire Mercury* PCC Report No.44 February 19, 1999 (publication of a photograph of house together with name of village).

[35] *ibid. Coltrane v Daily Mirror* PCC Report No.33 (Jan–March 1996) p.21 (photograph together with article identifying whereabouts. Newspaper apologised. Cl.4 (Privacy) of the pre-1998 Code). And see Editorial, PCC Report 12 (1992).

[36] *Wyman v The Times* PCC Report No.34 (April–June 1996) p.21 (cl.4 (Privacy) of the pre-1998 Code).

[37] *Dunne and Sunday Mercury* PCC Report No.33 (Jan–March 1996) p.24 (Gatley Park—photograph and simplified map published; cl.4 (Privacy) of the pre-1998 Code); *A Man and The Herfordshire Mercury* PCC Report No.44 February 19, 1999 (addresses reported in public domain as a result of court case).

[38] *Ms Karen Tomlinson v Peterborough, Evening Telegraph*, May 20, 2002.

[39] *Ms Dynamite* PCC Report No.63, (March 26, 2003) (Complaint upheld in respect of a report that the singer Ms Dynamite had purchased a new property in North London naming the street with photo of the specific property).

prohibited by contract. A complainant who had been convicted of murder two weeks previously was photographed in prison in the audience of a concert within the prison.[40] It was alleged that the photograph had been taken by subterfuge as the photographer had only been allowed access to the prison for the event having signed a contract requiring him not to take photographs of prisoners without their written consent. Somewhat surprisingly the PCC did not find a breach of the Code and in its adjudication said:

> "The Commission sympathised with the view that any prisoner has an expectation that they will not be exposed to unwanted press photographs while they are in prison, although it understood that circumstances will vary and that there may be occasions where such photographs are permissible in the public interest. However, responsibility for ensuring that the prison was somewhere where prisoners had a reasonable expectation of privacy rested with the prison authorities which exercised absolute control over the prison environment. As they had apparently not secured the complainant's privacy and not taken action against the newspaper despite the existence of the contract, it was not for the Commission to criticise the newspaper".[41]

14–035    The newspaper had not accepted that it had breached the contract and the Prison Service had indicated that it would not sue the newspaper. However, the Commission went on to say that there was nothing to suggest that the Commission was a more appropriate forum for considering what in essence was a complaint about breach of contract. A complaint had also been made under Clause 11 (Misrepresentation/Subterfuge) and the Commission stated that it could not take a view without effectively concluding whether or not the contract had been breached. This it considered would have intruded into legal issues that would more appropriately be dealt with in court between the parties to the contract. It remained for the prison authorities to pursue the matter if they thought that their contract with the journalist had been breached.

14–036    It is submitted that this case is a good illustration of the limitations of the PCC. A photograph had been taken in a place which was private and one to which the public had no access. Although the Commission accepted that the claimant had a right to privacy in principle, it declined to uphold the complaint simply because there was a contract which may have been breached. This fails to take into account the fact that the contract itself effectively reinforced the privacy right by specifically prohibiting photography without the subject's consent. It is submitted that the question of whether the photograph *per se* was an infringement of privacy was a discrete matter that the PCC could have adjudicated upon. If this approach is followed in other cases, it may cause difficulty as there are many quasi-private places where entry is governed by terms and conditions prohibiting pho-

---

[40] *Andrews v The Mirror* PCC Report No.56/57 (Oct 2001–March 2002) (June 2, 2001) p.12.
[41] *Andrews v The Mirror* PCC Report No.56/57 (Oct 2001–March 2002) (June 2, 2001) p.13.

tography. Certain private functions may also have similar arrangements.[42] It appears in the light of this adjudication that if there is an issue as to whether a contract prohibiting photography has been breached, the Commission will decline to make a finding at all.

A very wide view of what is encompassed by "legal matters" (which results in the PCC declining to make a finding) may mean a significant reduction of cases involving photographs which the Commission is prepared to deal with in the light of the Data Protection Act 1998. The Data Protection Act 1998 may give rise to concurrent rights of action in many cases involving photographs of identifiable individuals which are classed as personal data.[43] In practice, an adjudication that there was a breach may be in some cases tantamount to a finding that the processing was unfair.[44] If the PCC adopts a too restrictive approach in declining to make findings simply because it may have some consequences as a matter of law, however tangential, then it will find that, particularly in cases involving photographs, it has a very restricted ambit. It would in theory be possible for the PCC to decline jurisdiction by hiding behind the Data Protection Act 1998.     **14–037**

Complaints as to invasion of privacy have not be upheld in respect of material that is in the public domain, where the individual is not identifiable, nor where publication is a question of taste or decency. Complaints were rejected in respect of photographs of: a four week old infant being carried by its father in a public place where the child's face was only partially visible[45]; a severed head and dismembered body parts of soldiers[46]; a boy's grave[47]; a covered body of a murdered child being carried from a crime scene[48]; one of the largest houses to be built in Britain in recent years taken from a helicopter which had not flown below the legal limit of 500 ft[49]; and where the photograph was in the public domain and had been used in promotional material.[50]     **14–038**

---

[42] *e.g.* celebrity weddings where the staff are under confidentiality agreements.

[43] See Ch.11, above.

[44] In contravention of the First Data Protection Principle. This is not necessarily the same as a finding that the complainant has a good cause of action as there may be other issues. *E.g.* in order to claim compensation under s.13 of the Data Protection Act 1998 damage or distress is required; there may be an issue as to whether the s.32 exemption (journalistic or artistic purposes) applies, etc. But an adjudication that the Code had been breached would almost certainly be equivalent in practice to a finding that processing was contrary to the First Principle (fair and lawful processing) which may be considered a matter of law.

[45] *Kingston & Haertel v Hello!* PCC Report No.55 (July–Sept 2001) p.10.

[46] *Raviv v Al Hayat* PCC Report No.40 (Oct–Dec 1997) p.12 (Privacy cl.4 of pre-1998 Code) complaint by Ambassador of Israel in respect of photographs of deceased Israeli soldiers— "matters of taste and decency must be left to editorial judgment. The Commission is not there to act as a censor."

[47] *Smith v Daily Record* PCC Report No.37 (Jan–March 1997) p.13 (cl.4 (Privacy) of pre-1998 Code).

[48] *Garvey v Yorkshire Evening Post* PCC Report No.20 (Aug–Sept 1993) p.9 (Use was acceptable to illustrate a tragic event; cl.4 (Privacy) of pre-1998 Code).

[49] *Sullivan v The Daily Mail* PCC Report No.8 (April 1992) p.6 (building of house was of public interest; cl.4 (Privacy) of pre-1998 Code).

[50] *News of the World* PCC Report No.24 (March–April 1994) p.13 (cl.4 (Privacy) of pre-1998 Code).

**Harassment: Clause 4**

**14–039**   Clause 4 states:

> "*(i)   Journalists and photographers must neither obtain nor seek to obtain information or pictures through intimidation, harassment or persistent pursuit*
>
> *(ii)   They must not photograph individuals in private places (as defined by the note to clause 3) without their consent; must not persist in telephoning, questioning, pursuing or photographing individuals after having been asked to desist; must not remain on their property after having been asked to leave and must not follow them.*
>
> *(iii)   Editors must ensure that those working for them comply with these requirements and must not publish material from other sources which does not meet these requirements.*"

The harassment clause is identified as being subject to the public interest exception.

**14–040**   This clause overlaps to a degree with the privacy Clause 3 as it prohibits photographing individuals in private places as defined in the Clause 3 note. The meaning of "private places" and the approach of the Commission to determining what is a private place is discussed above. The Commission will not deal with matters that are the subject of legal proceedings nor make findings of law. Nor will it make judgments as to whether journalists accused of harassment have trespassed or caused criminal damage, as these are matters of law.[51]

In *Tunbridge v Dorking Advertiser*,[52] which concerned a photograph taken inside a public restaurant, the complaint was made under the harassment clause rather than the privacy clause. The complaint was upheld on the basis that the restaurant was held in the circumstances to be a place where there was a reasonable expectation of privacy.[53] Previous decisions of the PCC had tended to hold that public places like restaurants did not give rise to an expectation of privacy.[54] Complaints have been upheld where the place that the images were acquired was private, such as undercover video footage taken at a party taking place within private rooms in a hotel which were not open to the public.[55]

**14–041**   A complaint was upheld in respect of photographs of Prince William travelling in Chile obtained as a result of persistent pursuit.[56] The Commission concluded it was clear that the photographs could only have been taken by people who had pursued Prince William in South America as he was in a place where photographers would not normally have been. The

---

[51] *Crompton v Evening Standard* PCC Report No.58/59 (April–Sept 2002) p.11.
[52] PCC Report No.58/59 (April–Sept 2002) (Complaint date: February 22, 2002) p.5.
[53] For further consideration of this decision see above at para. 14–031.
[54] See above at paras 14–027 *et seq.*
[55] *Ryle v News of the World* PCC Report No.53 (Jan–March 2001) p.10.
[56] *Lamport (on behalf of HRH Prince William) v OK! Magazine* PCC Report No.52 (Oct–Dec 2000) p.8. See also "Prince William and Privacy" speech given by Rt Hon Lord Wakeham, Chairman of PCC of June 28, 2000, reproduced in PCC Report No.51, p.21.

Commission stated that it wished to remind "all publications of the need carefully to check the origins of photographs such as this before considering whether or not to publish them."[57]

A complaint was rejected where the complainant had apparently posed for pictures before allegedly becoming angry and there was no evidence of harassment.[58] A reporter and a photographer sitting in a car at a school for a few hours outside an event, to which other members of the press had been invited and which members of the Royal Family were attending, did not amount to harassing behaviour.[59]

## Intrusion into grief or shock: Clause 5

Clause 5 concerning intrusion into grief or shock states:                    **14–042**

*"In cases involving personal grief or shock, enquiries must be carried out and approaches made with sympathy and discretion. Publication must be handled sensitively at such times but this should not be interpreted as restricting the right to report judicial proceedings."*

The three criteria used to assess whether there is a breach of Clause 5 are:

(1) whether a publication can be shown to have broken the news of an injury or death to a victim's family;

(2) whether a publication has trivialised an incident or reported it a gratuitously humourous way; and

(3) whether there is any evidence that the victims have been distressed by the presence of the press and the taking of photographs at the scene of the accident.[60]

Complaints have been upheld in respect of photographs of people    **14–043** attending a funeral taken outside a crematorium when the photographer had been asked to leave[61]; a family lighting a candle inside a Cathedral in memory of a recently deceased wife and mother[62]; and a journalist pushing his way into the house of grieving relatives.[63]

Complaints were rejected regarding:

---

[57] *Lamport (on behalf of HRH Prince William) v OK! Magazine* PCC Report No.52 (Oct–Dec 2000) p.8 at p.9.
[58] *Nancy Seltzer Ass (on behalf of Sean Connery) v Daily Record* PCC Report No.47 (July–Sept 1999) p.16.
[59] *Crompton v Evening Standard* PCC Report No.58/59 (April–Sept 2002) p.11.
[60] *Salisbury v Lancashire Evening Post* PPC Report No.51 (July–Sept 2000) p.9; *Clarkson Hirst (on behalf of Rodney Telford) v Lancaster Guardian* PPC Report No.50 (April–June 2000) p.19.
[61] *Dibb Lupton Alsop (on behalf of Carol Smillie) v Sunday Mail* PCC Report No.50 (April–June 2000) p.14.
[62] *McCartney v Hello!* PCC Report No.43 (July–Sept 1998) p.12.
[63] *Clement v South Yorkshire Times* PCC Report No.43 (July–Sept 1998) p.20.

- photographs of a traffic accident in which a woman and her two daughters were seriously injured. The faces of the woman and her eldest daughter were visible. The Commission did not find any evidence that the victims had been troubled by the presence of the press at the accident scene.[64]

- photograph a victim of a traffic accident being cut free from the wreckage of his car where (1) the photograph had been taken by an official who was at the scene recording the incident not a member of the press, (2) the news was not broken to the family by the article being published two days later, by which time it would have been reasonable to assume the immediate family would have been informed, (3) the text of the article did not make light of a serious situation and appeared to be a straightforward news report of an event that occurred in public.[65]

### Children: Clause 6

**14–044**    Clause 6 provides:

"*(i)   Young people should be free to complete their time at school without unnecessary intrusion.*
*(ii)   Journalists must not interview or photograph a child under the age of 16 on subjects involving the welfare of the child or any other child in the absence of or without the consent of a parent or other adult who is responsible for the children.*
*(iii)   Pupils must not be approached or photographed while at school without the permission of the school authorities.*
*(iv)   There must be no payment to minors for material involving the welfare of children nor payments to parents or guardians for material about their children or wards unless it is demonstrably in the child's interest.*
*(v)   Where material about the private life of a child is published, there must be justification for publication other than the fame, notoriety or position of his or her parents or guardian.*"

This is a clause that may be overridden by public interest, but an exceptionally high level of public interest is required in cases involving children as the interests of the child are normally paramount.[66] The Commission tends to apply this very strictly. The public interest will not be served by publication of a photograph of a child that is purely illustrative.[67]

---

[64] *Salisbury v Lancashire Evening Post* PCC Report No.51 (July–Sept 2000) p.9.
[65] *Clarkson Hirst (on behalf of Rodney Telford) v Lancaster Guardian* PCC Report No.50 (April–June 2000) p.19.
[66] PCC Code, Public Interest para.4. See further above at para. 14–018.
[67] *Eves v Brecon & Radnor Express(1)* PCC Report No.56/57 (Oct 2001–March 2002) p.21 (photograph of 14 year old boy at school).

A complaint was upheld for the naming of a child as a victim of suspected **14–045** tuberculosis.[68] The argument that this was in the public interest on the basis that readers needed to be informed of the identity of a child with a notifiable disease was rejected. The Commission took the view that the public interest was not so exceptional as to override the interests of the child and it could have been served without naming the child. Conversely, where the report concerned a boy's disruptive conduct that had lead to a high profile debate about exclusions from schools, there was a public interest in reporting the matter particularly where the circumstances were in the public domain.[69]

Newspapers should take particular care to seek full and proper consent when publishing pictures of children that might embarrass them, interrupt their schooling, or damage their welfare in some other way.[70] It is irrelevant whether the child herself consents as the Code plainly requires parental consent.[71] The purpose of cl.6 is to protect the welfare of the child. Publication of photographs which do not show a child's face and in such a way that he is not identifiable are unlikely to have an adverse impact on the child's welfare.[72]

Privacy is the right of an infant as much as a child or an adult.[73] Even when **14–046** individuals do put matters concerning the private lives of their families into the public domain, the press cannot reasonably justify thereafter publishing any articles on any subject concerning them.[74] Where the complained of material was proportional to that already in the public domain, a complaint would not be upheld.[75] The Commission has stated that privacy is best maintained when not compromised in any way.[76] Thus, where a child begins to acquire a public profile in their own right, for example by making public appearances, it becomes more difficult for that child to be protected by the Code.[77]

Clause 6(v) specifically provides that the fame of a child's parents alone is not sufficient to justify publication about a child's private life. The Commission has said that the test to be applied in considering publication of material concerning the children of public figures is whether a newspaper

---

[68] *A Couple v Evening Express; A Couple v Press and Journal* PCC Report No.56/57 (Oct 2001– March 2002) pp.8–11.

[69] *Aldred v Daily Mail* PCC Report No.60/61 (Oct 2002–March 2003), p.9.

[70] *Blair v Daily Sport* PCC Report No.49 (Jan–March 2000) p.5. See below at n.81 and accompanying text; *Rowling v OK! Magazine* PCC Report No.56/57 (Oct 2001–March 2002) p.6.

[71] *Granton v Daily Post* PCC Report No.58/59 (April–Sept 2002) p.17 at p.18.

[72] *A Woman v The Daily Telegraph* PCC Report No.58/59 (April–Sept 2002) p.15 (article about a care home including photographs of the complainant's son which did not show his face. Complaint not upheld).

[73] *Zachs v The Herald* PCC Report No.38 (April–June 1997) p.9 at p.15; *Evans v Bristol Evening Post* PCC Report No.44 (Oct–Dec 1998) p.10 (approving *Zachs v The Herald*).

[74] *Carling v Daily Mail* PCC Report No.50 (April–June 2000) p 23 at p.24 (interview with complainant's ex-husband about his attempt to gain access to his children who lived with the complainant. Complaint not upheld as published material proportionate to matters relating to the children already put into the public domain by the complainant.)

[75] *ibid.*

[76] *Blair v The Daily Telegraph, Daily Mail* PCC Report No.56/57 (Oct 2001–March 2002) (December 8, 2001) p.19 at p.21.

[77] *ibid.*

would write such a story if it was about an ordinary person.[78] Academic achievement or successful entrance to a university might well fall into such a category but private choices about the nature of such an application or private details about an individual's time at university would not.[79]

**14–047**    Breaches of the Code in respect of children have been found in respect of the following:

where a press agency obtained a photograph from a child of a relative for publication[80]; photographs of the son of a politician at a ball dancing with and kissing a girl[81]; photographs of an eight year old daughter of a well-known writer on a hotel beach in her swimwear[82]; photographs of children between the ages of 12–16 at youth centre discos accompanied by text about adolescence notwithstanding the children were not named[83]; a photograph which was two years old (but still identified the child) of a nine year old girl accompanying an article about the breakdown of her grandparents' marriage[84]; where the photographer had adequate notice that the parent he requested permission from to photograph the children may not have been the appropriate parent to give consent[85]; and where two boys were photographed (after being asked by the photographer, without parental consent) to skate in an area in respect of which a new by-law had been introduced to fine skaters[86].

**14–048**    Complaints which were rejected in respect of alleged breaches of the provisions concerning children include:

Photograph of a four week old infant, a child of an actress, being carried by its father in a public place where the child's face was only partially visible. Public roads or pavements were not places where people could have a reasonable expectation of privacy. A glass shop front in full view of passers by was in the same category. "Mere publication of child's

---

[78] *Blair v The Daily Telegraph, Daily Mail* PCC Report No.56/57 (Oct 2001–March 2002) (December 8, 2001) p.19 at p.20.

[79] *ibid.*

[80] *Raymonds Press Agency*, PCC Report No.1 (Jan–June 1991) p.15. Photographer attended address of woman who had agreed to become a surrogate mother. 11 year old boy answered door and photographer asked him if he had a photograph of the woman which he could borrow. Photograph provided by child. Adjudication stated it was wrong for a journalist to have dealings with a child with a view to publication without the consent of an adult in a position of authority. Described as "a particularly bad example of picture snatching."

[81] *Blair v Daily Sport* PCC Report No.49 (Jan–March 2000) p.5 (complaint upheld as photograph clearly might embarrass, interrupt schooling, or damage welfare and no parental consent had been obtained. None of the other children in the photograph were identified other than the politician's son in breach of cl.6(v)).

[82] *Rowling v OK! Magazine* PCC Report No.56/57 (Oct 2001–March 2002) p.6 and see above under Privacy (Clause 1).

[83] *Price v The Observer* PCC Report No.49 (Jan–March 2000) p.12 (children were clearly identifiable to those who knew them and pictures were of an embarrassing nature).

[84] *Caldin v Chat* PCC Report No.45 (Jan–March 1999) p.16.

[85] *Ackroyd v Woman* PCC Report No.39 (July–Sept 1997) p.10 (Interviewing Children cl.12 of pre-1998 Code).

[86] *Jones v The Daily Telegraph* PCC Report No.39 (July–Sept 1997) p.17 (Interviewing Children Clause 12 of pre-1998 Code).

image cannot breach the Code when it is taken in a public place and is unaccompanied by any private details or material that might embarrass or inconvenience the child."[87]

A simple photograph of a child's image was not a matter that could reasonably be considered to concern the child's welfare and no consent was required.[88] Mere publication of a child's image unaccompanied by details of its private life when he or she is in a public place is not in breach of the Code.[89]

Publication of Christian name of child of a celebrity, mentioning the fact **14–049** of his birth with photographs of the mother's home where the location was unidentifiable did not contain any material that could reasonably be considered to be about the child's welfare or private life.[90]

No breach of cl.6 for publication of an unauthorised photograph of a child where similar photographs of a child were to published with the consent of the parents in other media.[91] The commission observed that privacy is a commodity which can be sold. Where a complainant releases or sells information or photographs then they may become disentitled to the protection of the Code in certain circumstances.

### Children in sex cases: Clause 7

A complaint was upheld where children who were the alleged victims of **14–050** indecent assault were identifiable through jigsaw identification.[92] "Jigsaw identification" is identification by the public by the combining of different pieces of information published in separate news sources.[93] Where a photograph was published of a small children's home where an alleged gang rape had taken place, the complaint was upheld as there was a risk it could have lead to identification of the children. The Council had asked the newspaper not to publish the name of the home or its picture as all the children were wards of court.[94]

### Hospitals: Clause 9

Clause 9 provides: **14–051**

> "*(i)  Journalists or photographers making enquiries at hospitals or similar institutions must identify themselves to a responsible executive and obtain permission before entering non-public areas.*

---

[87] *Kingston & Haertel v Hello!* PCC Report No.55 (July–Sept 2001) p.10.
[88] *Attard v Manchester Evening News* PCC Report No. 55 (July–Sept 2001) p.9 at p.10. *Donald v Hello! Magazine* PCC Report No. 52 (Oct–Dec 2000) p.5.
[89] *Donald v Hello! Magazine* PCC Report No. 52 (Oct–Dec 2000) p.5.
[90] *The Mail on Sunday* PCC Report No.51 (July–Sept 2000) p.8.
[91] *Attard v Manchester Evening News* PCC Report No.55 (July–Sept 2001) p.9 at p.10.
[92] *Hazzledine v The Times* PCC Report No.30 (May–July 1995) p.6 (cl.13 (Children in Sex Cases) of the pre-1998 Code).
[93] See further above at paras 6–080 to 6–082.
[94] *Leadbetter v Manchester Evening News* PCC Report No.2 (July–Sept 1991) p.14 (pre-1998 Code).

    *(ii) The restrictions on intruding into privacy are particularly relevant to enquiries about individuals in hospitals or similar institutions"*

"A hospital or similar institution" has been held by the PCC to include a residential home for the elderly where a large number of residents were in need of supervision for medical conditions.[95]

This is one of the clauses to which there may be a public interest defence. However, the Commission has stated that public interest exemptions concerning individuals in hospitals will be rare.[96] A very strong public interest defence is required to breach this clause.[97]

A complaint was upheld in respect of a photograph taken without permission of a patient who had suffered injuries in the Canary Wharf bomb blast.[98] It was said that even where it was important to describe the devastation caused, such reporting took second place to the welfare of the victim which was paramount. A complaint was also upheld in respect of an interview carried out in hospital with a man who had recently regained consciousness from a coma and "barely knew his own name".[99]

**14–052**    Complaints were rejected in respect of:

- A photograph of a woman whilst a hospital patient who had been kicked in the head by her boyfriend. The article sought to contrast the level of punishment of the offender with the level of injury to the woman. The photograph had been taken at the invitation of the woman's parents but the photographer had failed to obtain permission from a responsible executive of the hospital. The Commission concluded that the taking and publishing of the photograph was in the public interest. The Commission has stated that public interest exemptions to cl.9 are likely to remain rare since the Code is particularly strict on protecting those who are most vulnerable in hospital.[1]

- Photographs of elderly patients who had been placed on trollies to await treatment, taken by photographer (who had failed to identify himself to a responsible executive) which accompanied a report making serious allegations about the conditions which members of the public were facing in the hospital was an investigation in the public interest.[2]

---

[95] *A Man v Daily Mail* PCC Report No.58/59 (April–Sept 2002) p.8.
[96] *Northwick Park Hospital v Evening Standard* PCC Report No.56/57 (Oct 2001–March 2002) p.22 at p.24; *Taunton & Somerset NHS Trust v The Mirror* PCC Report No.54 (April–June 2001) p.15. As to the public Interest exemption see above at para. 14–018.
[97] *ibid.*
[98] *Hutchinson v News of the World* PCC Report No.37 (Jan–March 1997) p.15.
[99] *Jennings v Eastbourne Gazette* PCC Report No.60/61 (Oct 2002–March 2003), p.6.
[1] *Taunton & Somerset NHS Trust v The Mirror* PCC Report No.54 (April–June 2001) p.15.
[2] *Harrison v Daily Mail* PCC Report No.46 (April–June 1999) p.15.

- A photograph of a hospital patient taken with a long lense as she moved between a hospital entrance and the ambulance where it was a non-public area of the hospital.[3]

- A photograph of "a notorious child murderer" standing at a window in Ashworth hospital taken with a telephoto lens.[4]

- An article concerning serious allegations made by a family about the manner in which their relative had been treated by a hospital in the hours before his death where the newspaper was investigating in the public interest and at the instigation of the family. The Commission held that the public interest justified breach of cl.9.[5]

14–053

## Reporting of crime: Clause 10

Clause 10 concerns reporting identifying innocent relatives of those accused or convicted of crime and provides:

14–054

"(i) *The press must avoid identifying relatives or friends of persons convicted or accused of crime without their consent.*

(ii) *Particular regard should be paid to the potentially vulnerable position of children who are witnesses to, or victims of, crime. This should not be interpreted as restricting the right to report judicial proceedings.*"

A complaint was upheld where a newspaper published a topless photograph of a former girlfriend of a convicted rapist accompanied by a caption which named her, gave her city of residence and stated she had been a girlfriend of the convicted man.[6] A complaint was also upheld under this clause for publication of a photograph of children in connection with an article about their mother (the complainant's ex-wife) who had reportedly been cautioned by the police for fraud after exaggerating the number of Christmas presents that had been taken from her house by burglars.[7] The Commission considered that the children were clearly identified as being related to someone accused of crime and viewed it as an unjustified intrusion.

## Misrepresentation: Clause 11

Clause 11 of the PCC Code states:

14–055

"(i) *Journalists must not generally obtain or seek to obtain information or pictures through misrepresentation or subterfuge.*

---

[3] *Brown v The Sun* PCC Report No.50 (April–June 2000) p.30.
[4] *Kaye v The Sun* PCC Report No.31 (Aug–Oct Dec 1995) p.9 (photographs of Ian Brady—justified scrutiny of him in public interest; clause.6 (Hospitals) of the pre-1998 Code).
[5] *Northwick Park Hospital v Evening Standard* PCC Report No.56/57 (Oct 2001–March 2002) p.22 at p.24 (Complaints in respect of article headlined "Dying Man is dragged from A & E by nurses" rejected).
[6] *A woman v Daily Star* PCC Report No. 47 (July–Sept 1999) p.19. (there was no public interest justification for naming her and she was entitled to believe that such an intimate photograph would have remained private).
[7] *A man v Bolton Evening News* PCC Report No.41 (Jan–March 1998) p.22.

*(ii)   Documents or photographs should be removed only with the consent of the owner.*

*(iii)   Subterfuge can be justified only in the public interest and only when material cannot be obtained by any other means."*

Clause 8 also prohibits use of clandestine listening devices by journalists or the interception of telephone call.[7a] Subterfuge is only justified where the use is in the public interest and only then if the material cannot be obtained by any other means. The Commission will not deal with complaints concerning contractual matters. Complaints in respect of photographs taken by subterfuge that are arguably in breach of a contract preventing photography will be rejected.[8]

A complaint was upheld where a photograph of the complainant was obtained by a reporter posing to be a public relations agent for a third party at a meeting with the complainant to purchase some of his goods. There was evidence that the complainant was not involved in any wrongdoing and the use of subterfuge seeking to obtain a story to show he was, was unjustified.[9]

**14–056**    Complaints were rejected where:

- A photograph was taken with a long lens of parents of conjoined twins (one of whom died after an operation to separate them) together with the surviving child by a photographer invited to photograph the surgical team. The photographs were taken after people thought the photographer had left the site. It did not contravene cl.11. "To say otherwise would imply that any photograph taken by undetected or surreptitious photographer would breach the code."[10]

- A reporter using an alias gained entry to and took photographs of the premises of a man involved in a hard-core video copying business which had been raided by the police. It was held that exposure of the crime was in the public interest, and while the initial action had been taken by the police this was no bar to further investigations. The use of subterfuge was justified by public interest.[11]

### Victims of sexual assault: Clause 12

**14–057**    Clause 12 states:

*"The press must not identify victims of sexual assault or publish material likely to contribute to such identification unless there is adequate justification and, by law, they are free to do so."*

---

[7a] See Appendix 3, below.
[8] *Andrews v The Mirror* PCC Report No.56/57 (Oct 2001–March 2002) (June 2, 2001) p.12.
[9] *Hagan v Sunday Post* PCC Report No.17 (March–April 1993) p.19. (serviceman selling Gulf War propaganda leaflets where Ministry of Defence had no criticism of him; cl.6 (Misrepresentation) pre–1998 Code).
[10] *Attard v Manchester Evening News* PCC Report No.55 (July–Sept 2001) p.9. There was also an invasion of privacy complaint which was not dealt with by the PCC as the matter had been decided by a court.
[11] *Wingrove v News of the World* PCC Report No.16 (Jan–Feb 1993) p.7. (cl.7(i) (Misrepresentation) pre-1998 Code).

There is no public interest defence to breaches of this clause.

The Commission guidelines regarding photographs and identity of victims point out that photographs may lead to identification of victims even if there are no names in the captions and the faces are obscured. The Commission has stated:

> "Editors should consider carefully whether or not their pictures offer clues, albeit unwittingly, that will allow some readers to put a name to the individual concerned. Such clues may well be found in unusual hairstyles or in distinctive clothing. They may also be found in pictures which illustrate a particular relationship between victims and family members, friends or locations. The choice of colour photography instead of black and white could also lead to easier identification in some cases. ... While black and white photographs may not be a complete answer, silhouettes may greatly reduce the probability of identification."[12]

Other suggestions were consultation before publication with the person involved; careful consideration of clothes, hairstyle and setting; or use of models depending on the individual circumstances. **14–058**

Any details beyond the most basic—no matter how small—can identify a victim to someone who does not know of the crime to which that person has been subjected.[13] The Commission has said that it is crucial in the light of the extreme vulnerability of such victims, that editors follow this clause of the Code to the letter.[14]

## Discrimination: Clause 13

A complaint was rejected in respect of the publication of photographs of 16 convicted drug dealers all of whom were black, headlined "Faces of Evil". It was adjudged that the presentation was not prejudicial or pejorative other than to the drug dealing community. The identity of convicted criminals, unless prohibited by law, was a matter of public record.[15] **14–059**

## Payment for articles including pictures: Clause 16

The general principles applied by the Commission are: **14–060**

(1) the Commission will bear in mind the legal framework provided for by Parliament within which people are not allowed to profit from their crimes when adjudicating on ethical matters of public policy;

---

[12] *Editorial* PCC Report No.21 (Oct–Nov 1993) p.5.
[13] *Thames Valley Police v The London Metro* PCC Report No.58/59 (April–Sept 2002), p.16 (complaint upheld re an article concerning the rape of a young woman that named the town where the assault took place and other details including her age, recent health problems and a describe of the family home).
[14] *ibid.*
[15] *Primarolo v Bristol Evening Post* PCC Report No.34 (April–June 1996) p.24 (cl.15 (Discrimination) of the pre-1998 Code).

(2) the provisions of the Code are not intended to stop all those who have ever been convicted of a crime from being paid for their story—only to stop those stories which do not contain a public interest element;

(3) if there is a public interest element, then a payment—including exclusivity—is permissible, even though such payments may be distasteful and offensive. It is recognised that payment is increasingly demanded by people for a variety of circumstances.[16]

The Commission also has taken into account:

(1) the extent to which the newspaper has thought through the issue of payment against the background of the Code before deciding to offer payment, including whether it has identified issues of public interest, considered whether payment was necessary, and whether payment would make new material available to the public[17];

(2) the time payment was made in relation to any criminal proceedings[18];

(3) whether payment was in fact necessary.[19]

**14–061**     The Commission has said that it will apply five key tests that are applied in considering payments to witnesses in criminal cases:

(1) Did the journalists take every possible step to ensure that any financial dealings had no influence on the evidence that the witnesses gave?

(2) Were the payments disclosed to the prosecution and defence?

(3) Was the material in the public interest?

(4) Was there an overriding need for offers of payment to be made?

(5) Was any money offered dependent on conviction?[20]

**14–062**     A complaint was not upheld in respect of payment made to the mother of an English nanny convicted of the manslaughter of an infant in America. It was concluded there was a clear public interest in questioning the convictions, the interviews contained new information and were integral to the campaign and there was evident need for payment.[21]

---

[16] *Re: Mary Bell and Parry & MacLauchlan* PCC Report No.43 (July–Sept 1998) p.5; *Bright v Daily Mail* PCC Report No.44 (Oct–Dec 1998) p.12.
[17] *Bright v Daily Mail* PCC Report No.44 (Oct–Dec 1998) p.12 at p.14.
[18] *Bright v Daily Mail* PCC Report No.44 (Oct–Dec 1998) p.12 at p.14. (Louise Woodward case—payment to mother of nanny convicted of manslaughter. Payment made not during trial but during a window between the first and second verdicts where their was genuine controversy about the trial).
[19] *Bright v Daily Mail* PCC Report No.44 (Oct–Dec 1998) p.12 at p.15.
[20] *A reader v News of the World, the Mail on Sunday, Daily Mail, Sunday People and Sunday Mirror* PCC Report No.56/57 (Oct 2001–March 2002) (January 25, 2002), p.25.
[21] *Bright v Daily Mail* PCC Report No.44 (Oct–Dec 1998) p.12 at p.17.

Complaints have been upheld for an account of the impact of a crime by the perpetrator's daughter which did not reveal any material of genuine public interest and gave no new information about, or perspective on the crime.[22] It is not acceptable to offer money on conditional on a defendant being convicted.[23]

## THE ADVERTISING STANDARDS AUTHORITY

All non-broadcast advertising in the UK must comply with the British Code of Advertising, Sales Promotion and Direct Marketing. The Committee of Advertising Practice (CAP) was founded in 1961 and produced the first edition of the British Code of Advertising Practice. In 1962, CAP established the Advertising Standards Authority (ASA), an independent body that would adjudicate in respect of the British Code of Advertising Practice.    **14–063**

Today, the applicable code is the British Code of Advertising, Sales Promotion and Direct Marketing (11th ed.) which came into force on March 4, 2003. It supercedes the 10th edition which came into force on October 1, 1999. In addition to the general rules set out in the Code there are also specific rules that deal with:

(1)   Sales Promotion;

(2)   Direct Marketing;

(3)   Alcoholic Drinks[24];

(4)   Children[25];

(5)   Motoring[26];

(6)   Environmental Claims[27];

(7)   Health & Beauty Products and Therapies[28];

(8)   Weight Control[29];

(9)   Employment and Business Opportunities[30];

(10)   Financial Products[31];

---

[22] *Barlow v The Daily Telegraph* PCC Report No.47 (July–Sept 1999) (article by daughter of Jonathan Aitken) p.10.
[23] *Taylor v News of the World* PCC Report No.48 (Oct–Nov 1999) p.5; *A reader v News of the World, the Mail on Sunday, Daily Mail, Sunday People and Sunday Mirror* PCC Report No.56/57 (Oct 2001–March 2002), p.25.
[24] British Code of Advertising, Sales Promotion and Direct Marketing (11th ed.) cl. 46.
[25] British Code of Advertising, Sales Promotion and Direct Marketing (11th ed.).
[26] *Ibid.*, cl.48.
[27] *Ibid.*, cl.49.
[28] *Ibid.*, cl.50.
[29] Clause 51, *Ibid.*
[30] *Ibid.*, cl.52.
[31] *Ibid.*, cl.53.

(11)   Betting and Gaming[32];

(12)   Tobacco, Rolling Papers and Filters.[33]

**14–064**    In addition, advertising in relation to certain subject matter may be governed by further rules[34] either statutory (*e.g.* medicines[35]; aerial advertising[36]) or by other non-legislative regulation such as the codes of conduct of professional bodies (*e.g.* barristers[37] solicitors[38]; and accountants[39]).

CAP itself provides a free Copy Advice Service which is a confidential service for marketers, agencies and media owners who want to check an advertisement against the requirements of the Code before publication.[40]

### Judicial review

**14–065**    The decisions of the ASA are amenable to judicial review as it is exercising a public law function and is thus a public authority.[41] The court exercises a supervisory role and will only interfere with a decision of the ASA on grounds of irrationality, illegality, or procedural impropriety.[42] If there is a band of reasonable interpretation in relation to any particular advertisement, the court will not interfere simply because another reasonable view can be taken unless it is shown that the court's decision is plainly wrong.[43]

Whether material is part of an advertisement cannot be the subject of a clear cut test and it is a matter for the ASA to decide.[44] The court will not

---

[32] *Ibid.*, cl.54.

[33] *Ibid.*, cl.55.

[34] For further information about specific categories of regulation see: G., Crown, *Advertising Law and Regulation* (Butterworths, 1998), Pt 2.

[35] Medicines Act 1968, s.92 to 97 and regulations made under s.95, Medicines (Advertising) Regulations 1994 (SI 1994/1932) as amended by inter alia (SI 1996/1552) Medicines (Monitoring of Advertising) Amendment Regulations 1999 (SI 1999/267) and (SI 1999/784).

[36] Civil Aviation Act 1982, s.82 ("Save in such circumstances as may be prescribed, no aircraft while in the air over any part of the United Kingdom shall be used, whether wholly or partly for emitting or displaying any advertisement or other communication in such a way that the advertisement or communication is audible or visible from the ground.") Civil Aviation (Aerial Advertising) Regulations 1995 (SI 1995/2943).

[37] Bar Council Code of Conduct, para.710 incorporating by reference the British Codes of Advertising and Sales Promotion but with certain qualifications, *e.g.* advertising must not include statements about the barrister's success rate. Available online at *http://www.barcouncil.org.uk/*.

[38] Law Society of England and Wales Publicity Code.

[39] Institute of Chartered Accountants in England and Wales Guide to Professional Ethics, para.1.211. Available on line at *http://www.icaew.co.uk/*.

[40] The Copy Advice Team can be contacted on 020 7580 1400 or by email at copyadvice@cap.org.uk. See further *http://www.cap.org.uk/*.

[41] *R. v Advertising Standards Authority Ltd. Ex p. Insurance Services Plc* [1990] C.O.D. 42; (1990) 2 Admin. L.R. 77; *R. v Advertising Standards Authority Ltd Ex p. Vernons Organisation Ltd* [1992] 1 W.L.R. 1289, 1292; [1993] 2 All E.R. 202.

[42] *R. v Advertising Standards Authority. Ex p. DSG Retail Ltd (t/a Dixons)* [1997] C.O.D. 232 *per* Popplewell J.

[43] *R. v Advertising Standards Authority Ex p. DSG Retail Ltd (t/a Dixons)* [1997] C.O.D. 232.

[44] *R. v Advertising Standards Authority Ltd Ex p. Charles Robertson (Developments) Ltd* [2000] E.M.L.R. 463 at 475 *per* Moses J.

interfere unless the decision of the ASA is contrary to the only reasonable conclusion.[45]

The Administrative Court has held that the Code, although a restriction on advertising, is consistent with the Art.10 right to freedom of expression.[46] The Code is not a blanket ban and the advertiser is free to advertise his product within the Code which is designed for the protection of the public.[47] The Code has been held to be "prescribed by law" for the purposes of Art.10(2) and albeit short of direct statutory effect it meets the purposive intentions of Art.10(2).[48] The ASA adjudication procedures are not incompatible with Art.6 (right to a fair trial).[49]     **14–066**

Unless there are exceptional circumstances, an interim injunction will not be granted to restrain publication of an ASA adjudication pending an application for judicial review.[50] This is in accordance with the normal principles that expressions of opinion and conveyance of information will not be restrained by the courts except on pressing grounds, where for example, damage caused might be irreparable.[51]

An injunction was granted in one case where the subject of the ASA adjudication had wrongly been informed that the investigation had been suspended and had not been given adequate opportunity to give further comment on the adjudication.[52] Where a body acting in a judicial or quasi-judicial capacity published its decisions, it was under a duty to give all parties ample opportunity to make whatever representations would normally be appropriate in the circumstances.[53]     **14–067**

## ASA procedure

Any person, organisation, or company may make a complaint to the ASA. The identities of members of the public who complain are neither published by the ASA or revealed by the ASA to marketers without express     **14–068**

---

[45] *ibid.*
[46] *SmithKline Beecham Plc v Advertising Standards Authority* [2001] E.W.H.C. Admin 6; [2001] E.M.L.R. 23, para.14 *per* Hunt J.; *R. v Advertising Standards Authority. Ex p. Rath* [2001] E.M.L.R. 22; [2001] H.R.L.R. 22.
[47] *SmithKline Beecham Plc v Advertising Standards Authority* [2001] E.W.H.C. Admin 6; [2001] E.M.L.R. 23, para.14 *per* Hunt J.
[48] *R v Advertising Standards Authority Ex p. Rath* [2001] E.M.L.R. 22; [2001] H.R.L.R. 22 at para.26 *per* Turner J.
[49] *Stephen Buxton (t/a the Jewelry Vault) v Advertising Standards Authority* [2002] E.W.H.C. 2433, QBD (Admin), (unrep.) (Sullivan J., October 31, 2002.
[50] *R. v Advertising Standards Authority Ltd Ex p. Vernons Organisation Ltd* [1992] 1 W.L.R. 1289, 1292; [1993] 2 All E.R. 202.
[51] *ibid.*, at 1293–1294 *per* Laws J.
[52] *R. v Advertising Standards Authority Ltd Ex p. Direct Line Financial Services Ltd* [1998] C.O.D. 20 (Popplewell J., August 8, 1997) distinguishing *R v Advertising Standards Authority Ltd. Ex p. Vernons Organisation Ltd* [1992] 1 W.L.R. 1289. *Cf. R. v Advertising Standards Authority. Ex p. Rath* [2001] E.M.L.R. 22; [2001] H.R.L.R. 22 *per* Turner J. preferring *Ex p. Vernons Organisation Ltd.*
[53] *ibid.*

permission.[54] In order to deter retaliatory complaints, complainants who are competitors may be required to justify their complaint.[55]

Complaints must be made within three months of the marketing communication's publication.[56] Complaints about older marketing communications will only be considered in exceptional circumstances.[57] The ASA requires that complaints be made in writing[58] and also makes provision for complaints to be made online.[59] The complaint should be accompanied by a copy of the advertisement or a note of when and where it appeared.[60] If there are extant legal proceedings or threatened legal proceedings in respect of the matters complained of, the ASA will not normally pursue the complaint.[61]

All complaints are dealt with in writing and on the basis of submitted documentary evidence. No provision is made for oral hearings.[62] Once a complaint has been received, if it falls within the ambit of the Code, the ASA will conduct an investigation.[63] The ASA will ask the advertiser to comment on the complaint and supply any evidence necessary. The advertisement is then considered and a draft recommendation will be made by the investigating executive to the ASA Council. The ASA will then make a final adjudication which the complainant and the advertiser are informed of. A copy of the adjudication is published by the ASA.

**14–069**   There is provision for reconsideration of an adjudication by an Independent Reviewer on two grounds:

(1)   where additional evidence becomes available; an explanation as to why the evidence was not submitted previously will be required;

(2)   where there is a substantial flaw in the ASA's adjudication or in the process by which the adjudication was made.[64]

Requests for a review must be in writing, contain a full statement of the grounds and should be sent within 21 days of the date on the ASA's letter of notification of adjudication.[65]

---

[54] British Code of Advertising, Sales Promotion and Direct Marketing (11th ed.) cl.60.29.
[55] British Code of Advertising, Sales Promotion and Direct Marketing (11th ed.) cl.60.30.
[56] British Code of Advertising, Sales Promotion and Direct Marketing (11th ed.) cl.60.28.
[57] *ibid.*
[58] *ibid.*
[59] There is an online complaints form on the ASA website (*http://www.asa.org.uk/*) accessible under "How to Complain".
[60] British Code of Advertising, Sales Promotion and Direct Marketing (11th ed.) cl.60.28.
[61] British Code of Advertising, Sales Promotion and Direct Marketing (11th ed.) cl.60.32. Or an Independent Review: cl.60.38.
[62] British Code of Advertising, Sales Promotion and Direct Marketing (11th ed.) cl.60.37. This is not incompatible with Art. 6 (right to a fair trial) see above at para. 14–066.
[63] British Code of Advertising, Sales Promotion and Direct Marketing (11th ed.) cl.60.34.
[64] British Code of Advertising, Sales Promotion and Direct Marketing (11th ed.) cl.60.38.
[65] *ibid.*

## Sanctions

If a complaint is upheld, the marketers responsible for the advertisement **14–070** are told by the ASA to amend or withdraw the complaint. Most do so voluntarily but if they do not, sanctions are applied.[66] Sanctions focus on ensuring that non-compliant advertisements are amended, withdrawn, or stopped as quickly as possible.

The publicising of the ASA adjudications is damaging to most marketeers and the adverse publicity also serves to warn the public. In addition, CAP may issued Ad Alerts to its members, including the media, advising them to withhold their services from non-compliant marketers or deny them advertising sapace.[67] Trading sanctions may be imposed by the relevant trade association or professional body by withdrawal, revocation, or temporary suspension of recognition and trading privileges.[68] Persistent offenders may be required to have some or all of their advertisements undergo pre-publication vetting by the CAP Copy Advice Team.[69]

## Application of the Code

Broadly, the British Code of Advertising, Sales Promotion and Direct **14–071** Marketing applies to all forms of advertising in any form of non-broadcast media. The regulation of the broadcast media is currently the province of the Radio Authority, the Broadcasting Standards Commission and the Independent Television Commission—all of which are due to be replaced by a single unified regulator Ofcom at the end of December 2003.[70]

The British Code of Advertising, Sales Promotion and Direct Marketing is stated to apply to[71]:

(a) advertisements in newspapers, magazines, brochures, leaflets, circulars, mailings, e mails, text transmissions, fax transmissions, catalogues, follow-up literature, and other electronic and printed material;

(b) posters and other promotional media in public places, including moving images;

(c) cinema and video commercials;

(d) advertisements in non-broadcast electronic media, including online advertisements in paid-for space (*e.g.* banner and pop-up advertisements);

---

[66] British Code of Advertising, Sales Promotion and Direct Marketing (11th ed.) cl.61.6.
[67] British Code of Advertising, Sales Promotion and Direct Marketing (11th ed.) cl.61.6.
[68] British Code of Advertising, Sales Promotion and Direct Marketing (11th ed.) cl.61.7.
[69] British Code of Advertising, Sales Promotion and Direct Marketing (11th ed.) cl.61.8.
[70] Pursuant to the Office of Communications Act 2002 and the Communications Act 2003. It is anticipated that OfCOM will become vested with its full powers on December 29, 2003. For latest information the OfCOM website at *http://www.ofcom.org.uk/*
[71] Cl.1.1 British Code of Advertising, Sales Promotion and Direct Marketing (11th ed.).

(e)  viewdata services;

(f)  marketing databases containing consumers' personal information;

(g)  sales promotions; and

(h)  advertisement promotions.

**14–072**    The following are excluded from the application of the Code[72]:

(a)  broadcast commercials;

(b)  the contents of premium rate telephone services;

(c)  marketing communications in foreign media[73];

(d)  health-related claims in marketing communications addressed only to the medical, dental, veterinary, and allied professions;

(e)  classified private advertisements, including online private advertisements;

(f)  statutory, public, police, and other official notices/non-marketing communications, produced by public authorities;

(g)  works of art exhibited in public or private;

(h)  private correspondence including correspondence between companies and their customers about existing relationships or past purchases;

(i)  oral communications, including telephone calls;

(j)  press releases and other public relations material that does not fall within any of the categories of matters to which the Code does apply[74];

(k)  editorial content, for example of the media and of books;

(l)  regular competitions such as crosswords;

(m) flyposting;

(n)  packages, wrappers, labels, tickets, timetables, and price lists unless they advertise another product, a sales promotion, or are visible in a marketing communication;

(o)  point of sale displays, except those covered by the sales promotion rules;

---

[72] C.1.2.

[73] The Code states at cl.1.2(c) as follows: "Direct marketing that originates outside the UK but is targeted at UK consumers will be subject to the jurisdiction of the relevant authority in the country where it originates so long as that authority operates a suitable cross-border complaint system. If it does not, the ASA will take what action it can. All members of the European Union, and many non-European countries, have self-regulatory organisations that are members of the European Advertising Standards Alliance (EASA). EASA co-ordinates the cross-border complaints system for its members (which include the ASA)."

[74] Listed above at para.14–071 (a) to (j).

(p) election advertisements[75];

(q) website content, except sales promotions and advertisements in paid-for space;

(r) sponsorship; marketing communications that refer to sponsorship are covered by the Code; and

(s) customer charters and codes of practice.

### Use of photographs in advertisements

The general rules of the Code which apply to all advertisements apply **14–073** equally to the use of any photographs contained within them. These general rules provide that all marketing communications should:

- be legal, decent, honest, and truthful[76];

- be prepared with a sense of responsibility to consumers and society[77];

- respect the principles of fair competition generally accepted in business.[78]

No marketing communication should bring advertising into disrepute.[79] There are also general prohibitions against advertising that is likely to cause serious or widespread offence[80]; fear or distress[81]; or that condones or encourages unsafe practices,[82] violence or anti-social behaviour.[83]

In addition to the general provisions, there are some clauses that are of particular relevance to the use of photographs. The following paragraphs set out these clauses and consider adjudications made by the ASA in relation to images under the respective clauses.

---

[75] As defined in cl.12. Essentially party political advertising whose principal function is to influence voters in local, regional, national or international elections or referendums.
[76] British Code of Advertising, Sales Promotion and Direct Marketing (11th ed.), cl.2.1.
[77] British Code of Advertising, Sales Promotion and Direct Marketing (11th ed.), cl.2.2.
[78] British Code of Advertising, Sales Promotion and Direct Marketing (11th ed.), cl.2.3.
[79] British Code of Advertising, Sales Promotion and Direct Marketing (11th ed.), cl.2.3.
[80] *ibid.*, 5.
[81] *ibid.*, cl.9.
[82] *ibid.*, cl.10. Including images of people working in an unsafe way, *e.g. Postbox Mail Order Ltd, Ankalad* (December 4, 2002) (complaint upheld in respect of a photograph of a man, standing on a ladder, leaning to one side to cut the top of a hedge with a powered trimming machine); *Harvey Nichols & Co Ltd* (June 11, 2003) Poster (driver putting on lipstick while driving).
[83] British Code of Advertising, Sales Promotion and Direct Marketing (11th ed.), cl.11. See *e.g.*: *Shark AG* (July 3, 2002) Poster (images showing men and women with scratch marks, bruising and bites in context could be seen to condone sexual violence).

## Decency: Clause 5

**14–075**   *"Marketing communications should contain nothing that is likely to cause serious or widespread offence. Particular care should be taken to avoid causing offence on the grounds of race, religion, sex, sexual orientation, or disability. Compliance with the Code will be judged on the context, medium, audience, product, and prevailing standards of decency.*

*Marketing communications may be distasteful without necessarily conflicting with above. Marketers are urged to consider public sensitivities before using potentially offensive material.*

*The fact that a particular product is offensive to some people is not sufficient grounds for objecting to a marketing communication for it."*

Complaints have been upheld in respect of advertisements that use images that: ridiculed and exploited mentally disabled people and encouraged prejudice against them[84]; were degrading to women (particularly images showing bound, handcuffed, or otherwise subjugated women)[85]; were degrading to particular racial groups[86]; were offensive to members of a religion[87]; and depicted male on male violence.[88] Complaints have also been upheld with regard to the use of sexually suggestive images of women that were gratuitous and irrelevant to the product.[89]

---

[84] *365 Corporation plc t/a eckoh* (January 16, 2002) Magazine (image of two dribbling men in torn and dirty clothing and a small picture of a clean-cut, smiling man labelled "Our weird brother. ... He just ain't like the rest of the family no more. Our Brother is A Freak."); *Neat Ideas Ltd* (May 21, 2003) Catalogue (photographs of a distressed-looking man in a straight-jacket).

[85] *Ann Summers Ltd* (April 9, 2003) Poster (complaint upheld re: photograph of the back of a woman's torso wearing only a bra and a thong with her hands handcuffed behind her back); *Mascot Models* (October 23, 2002) Magazine (images of models of women suggested that the women depicted were being subjugated and that violence towards women was acceptable). Images of women in revealing clothing are not necessarily degrading. See *Anne Summers* above and *Cantor Index Ltd* (April 17, 2002) Insert, Magazine, National press, Poster (complaint not upheld, image of a woman wearing a suit with a short skirt and an buttoned jacket with no blouse beneath); *Fusion 107.3* (February 6, 2002) Poster (naked torso of woman with radio dials shown on her breasts).

[86] *Journey 2000* (February 20, 2002) Leaflet (image of ladyboy for competition to win a trip to Thailand denigrated the people of Thailand). *Cf. Lever Faberge Ltd* (August 14, 2002) (Complaint not upheld for use of image of a Thai woman).

[87] *Bayer plc* (May 8, 2002) Regional Press (photograph of a man and a woman both sitting in the lotus position making the "namaste" greeting over stamped "RUBBISH!" in an advert for pain relief tablets judged to be offensive to Hindus). *Cf Time Out Magazine Ltd t/a Time Out* (May 28, 2003) Poster (complaint not upheld re: poster of a naked man holding a photograph of Pope John Paul II over his genital area. Whilst may have caused offence to some Roman Catholics, unlikely to cause serious or widespread offence).

[88] *Easynet Ltd* (December 4, 2002) Regional Press (photograph of a man being punched in the face by another man with caption to the effect "when your boss finds out you are spending too much on your internet connection". ASA considered the advertisements would not generally be seen as humorous).

[89] *Daisy Communications Ltd* (October 22, 2003) Magazine (*e.g.*, woman was facing away from the camera and wearing a thong); *Fusion 107.3* (February 6, 2002) Poster (naked torso of woman with radio dials shown on her breasts. ASA considered the image was sexist and irrelevant to the product being advertised); *Francois Legrand Editions* (August 28, 2002) Direct Mail (overtly sexual images of a woman and men embracing with some nudity was considered gratuitous notwithstanding the product was a potency pill).

As clause 5.1 makes clear, whether an advertisement complies with the   **14–076**
decency requirements will be judged on the context, medium, and audience.
The ASA will take into account whether the images have been displayed in a
responsible way in context[90] or directed to a limited and appropriate target
audience.[91] Use of images for campaigns requiring a hard-hitting approach,
such as anti-drugs, may not be judged offensive in the light of the target
audience.[92]

Advertising featuring sexual symbolism in a magazine with a readership
consisting of 95 per cent men, two-thirds of whom were single and mostly in
their twenties was judged unlikely to offend readers of the magazine in
which it appeared.[93] Complaints have been upheld in respect of advertising
in magazines with an adult target audience (*e.g.* film review or mens
magazines) where the imagery is sexually suggestive such that it is likely to
cause widespread offence.[94]

The likelihood that images will be seen by children is important when   **14–077**
considering complaints about offensive material. The use of sexually explicit
images in posters used publically are likely to be seen by children and as a
result be in breach of the Code.[95] If children are likely to look at the
advertising medium which advertises adult material, it should contain a
warning of adult content.[96] Complaints have not been upheld in respect of
adult material that is unlikely to be seen by children.[97]

---

[90] *Jigsaw-Junior* (October 23, 2002) Leaflet (complaint not upheld about a leaflet for childrens'
clothing featuring photographs of girls including one in a bikini. Complaint that the images
showed young girls in a suggestive sexual way and the leaflet was likely to appeal to paedophiles
was rejected); *Portfolio Gallery* (March 20, 2002) Insert (insert in a magazine for photographer
showing a distressing image. Complaint not upheld as unlikely to cause serious or widespread
offence to members of a photography association who would understand the creative nature of
the image).

[91] *News Group Newspapers Ltd t/a News of the World* (November 6, 2002) Direct Mail (complaint not upheld re. direct mailing featuring enlarged photographs of celebrities' legs, breasts
and bottoms targeted to readers of Sunday tabloid newspapers).

[92] *Brent Council* (November 5, 2003) Poster (drugs awareness centre). See also cl.9.2 of the Code
below at para. 14–080.

[93] *Club 18–30* (April 24, 2002) Magazine; *Gucci Ltd* (February 26, 2003) Magazine (sexual
nature of image was unlikely to offend the fashion conscious readership of Vogue).

[94] *EMAP Elan Ltd t/a FHM* (November 5, 2003) Magazine (photograph of a woman crouching
seeming to be performing oral sex on a man. In the foreground was the bottom half of two
women in an embrace; one woman was holding up the other woman's leg).

[95] *Calvin Klein Cosmetics* (August 21, 2002) (Complaint upheld: perfume poster of man and
woman naked from the waist up kissing open mouthed, man's hand inside waist band of
woman's trousers); *Patrick Cox* (June 4, 2003) Magazine (image unsuitable for readership of
15–17 year olds). *Cf. MacHo Ltd t/a The Erotic Print Society* (June 12, 2002) National press
(advert for catalogue of erotic pictures showing a photograph of a woman's bottom captioned
"A Spanking good offer". Advertisers argued that a national newspaper should not refuse to
publish content merely because it may be seen by minors. The complaint was not upheld as the
ASA considered that the advertisement was unlikely to cause serious or widespread offence and
was suitable for the medium.); *Wisepart Productions* (November 6, 2002) Brochure, Poster
(advertisement for play showing naked couple in shadow reflected theme of emotional intimacy
and would not harm children. Complaint not upheld).

[96] *BCA t/a Video Direct* (February 6, 2002) Leaflet (Leaflet for video supplier which had pictures of children's films on the front, children likely to pick it up).

[97] *BCA Book and Music Clubs t/a World Books* (January 9, 2002) Brochure (brochure included
books for children but considered that it was targeted at adults and was unlikely to be seen by
children; image of naked man and woman unlikely to offend target audience).

If the images are used in a genuinely humourous way and are in bad taste rather than offensive, complaints may not be upheld. Complaints were not upheld where the use of double-entendres and "tongue-in-cheek" style advertising was humorous and not offensive.[98] The fact that advertising is in bad taste does not necessarily mean a complaint will be upheld, particularly if it is clear that an image is not genuine.[99]

*Truthfulness*

**14–078**    *No marketing communication should mislead, or be likely to mislead, by inaccuracy, ambiguity, exaggeration, omission or otherwise.*

The court has held that an advertisement is misleading if it makes a false claim making it likely that people reading it will buy the product.[1]

The ASA, when making adjudications, will consider what most readers would understand from the advertising and if that majority would not infer that it was misleading, complaints will not be upheld.[2] Exaggerated images

---

[98] *Bargain Booze* (June 4, 2003) Leaflet, Regional press (photographs of "scantily dressed women" to advertise alcohol with sexual innuendo captions); *Central Trains Ltd* (May 21, 2003) Poster (humorous depiction of a stereotypical compromising situation).

[99] *Body Shock Ltd* (December 4, 2002) Magazine (complaint not upheld re. advertisement for body jewellery with photograph of a cat with a nasal piercing captioned "Pierced pussy" with a disclaimer: "No living creatures have been harmed by Body Shock during this campaign. It is strongly recommended that you do not try this at home"). See also *Gucci Ltd* (February 26, 2003) Magazine (image likely to be considered tasteless by some readers but unlikely to cause serious or widespread offence); *Ryanair Ltd* (June 11, 2003) National Press (adverts with images of Sadam Hussein and humorous captions although distasteful were not likely to cause serious or widespread offence).

[1] *SmithKline Beecham Plc v Advertising Standards Authority* [2001] E.W.H.C. Admin 6; [2001] E.M.L.R. 23; *Director General of Fair Trading v Tobyward Ltd* [1989] 2 All E.R. 266; [1989] 1 W.L.R. 517 (Control of Misleading Advertising Regulations 1988).

[2] *Central Office of Information t/a DVLA* (February 20, 2002) Poster (Objections to advertisements featuring Chitty Chitty Bang Bang and James Bond's Aston Martin clamped stating no exemptions to car tax. Complainant who understood that the cars shown were over 25 years old and therefore exempt from road tax, objected that the posters misleadingly implied that such cars needed to be taxed. Complaint rejected because the cars and their owners were obviously fictional and readers were unlikely to take the advertisements literally); *Womankind Worldwide* (April 3, 2002) Poster cll.2.2, 7.1 (Ed 10) (poster for domestic violence charity showing a collage of a woman's face that was made from photographs of several women's faces. Complaint that it trivialised domestic violence against men and was misleading not upheld as considered that most readers would understand that the poster was creating awareness about domestic violence against women); *Scottish Executive* (March 27, 2002) Regional press, cll.3.1, 7.1 (Ed 10) (Complaint not upheld in part as most readers would understand that the advertisement was raising awareness about the domestic abuse of women and would not infer that men did not experience abuse).

may be misleading,[3] as are images that do not represent the product or the services with enough accuracy.[4]

In determining whether images are genuine (particularly "before and after **14–079** photographs"), the ASA may require signed affidavits from the photographer and the model proving that the photographs were genuine and related to the advertised product.[5] Advertisements that use photographs that are stated to be take "6 months ago" or "12 months ago" in respect of treatments should either make clear when the photographs were taken or the fact that the reference is to the time taken for the treatment to show its effects.[6]

In cases involving digital manipulation or photo-illustrations, if the image is stated not to be a photograph or otherwise identified as a created image, there will be no inaccuracy and it will not be regarded as misleading.[7] Conversely, advertisers using simulated images that are not identified as such are at risk of complaints against them being upheld.[8]

---

[3] *Samuel Phillips & Co* (August 28, 2002) Regional Press (Advert legal service headlined "Did the Doctor Or Nurse Make You Worse?" with a photograph of a man wearing a hospital patient's gown and balancing on crutches, with a bandage around his head and wrist and with one leg in plaster and the other leg bandaged at the knee and toe. The ASA upheld the complaint as the image exaggerated the possible consequences of medical negligence and could mislead. The Authority told the advertisers to ensure that images used in future advertisements were representative of true medical negligence.)

[4] *Phoenix Dance Theatre* (June 25, 2003) Leaflet, cl.7.1 (Ed 10) (complaint upheld re. a leaflet for a performance using an image of two naked dancers leaping through the air. Complainant, who had seen the performance, objected that the leaflet was misleading as the images did not resemble the actual performance. The ASA noted that one image of naked dancers appeared next to a list of performance times and dates; another photograph appeared next to reviewers' comments. The ASA thus considered that readers were likely to expect that the performances contained naked dancers. It asked the advertisers to ensure that if they used similar naked images in leaflets again they made clear in the copy that performances were fully clothed); *Loudoun Castle Theme Park* (June 26, 2002) National press (photographs of theme park rides that were not available); *B&Q plc* (February 26, 2003) National press (illustration included a toilet seat and bath end panel which were not included in the price).

[5] *Kingstown Associates Ltd t/a Healthy Living Direct* (June 11, 2003) Catalogue (before and after photographs of tooth stain removal, complaint upheld as advertisers unable to provide evidence from photographer and model); *Growth Hair Clinic* (August 20, 2003) Regional press (before and after photographs of genetic hair graft treatment. Complaint not upheld as sent original copies of the photographs that were signed and dated by the model provided which the ASA were satisfied that the photographs were genuine.)

[6] *Pentoc Ltd t/a Advanced Hair Studio* (February 13, 2002) National Press (hair loss treatment).

[7] *United Utilities Green Energy* (November 5, 2003) Regional Press (complaint rejected in case of a photograph with a caption stating "A visualisation of how the proposed ... wind farm will look ...". ASA considered that the advertorial made clear that the picture shown was an impression, not an exact replica.

[8] *Sharp Corporation* (July 16, 2003) National press (mobile telephone image with a simulated picture of a woman on the phone screen. Complaint was that the advertisement exaggerated the quality of the picture that the phone could achieve. Complaint upheld as the advertisers had not demonstrated that their phone could achieve the picture quality featured in the advertisement). Cf. *Panasonic UK Ltd* (February 19, 2003) National press (complaint not upheld in respect of use of picture library photograph on the screen of a picture messaging mobile phone because the phone's image quality was comparable to that featured in the advertisement because (following demonstration by the advertisers) the Authority concluded that the advertisement accurately represented the picture quality the phone could achieve.)

*Fear and distress*

**14–080**   Clause 9 provides:

> "9.1 No marketing communication should cause fear or distress without good reason. Marketers should not use shocking claims or images merely to attract attention.
>    9.2 Marketers may use an appeal to fear to encourage prudent behaviour or to discourage dangerous or ill-advised actions; the fear likely to be aroused should not be disproportionate to the risk."

In many cases complaints made under cl.9 (fear and distress) will overlap with complaints under cl.5 (decency). Many of the reported adjudications concern both and adjudications discussed under cl.5 above should be referred to. As with complaints about decency, in respect of fear and distress complaints the ASA will look at the audience receiving the material in order to assess whether that audience would be distressed.[9]

Complaints are likely to be upheld with regard to images of a graphic nature that imply violence, particularly in an untargeted media that could be seen by children.[10] Complaints have been upheld for use of an image of a slaughtered pig[11] and images of people shown bleeding.[12]

Use of shocking images may be justified under cl.9.2 or where the subject matter is such that use is justified in order to raise public awareness.[13]

*Protection of privacy*

**14–081**   Clause 13 concerns privacy and reads as follows:

> "13.1 Marketers should not unfairly portray or refer to people in an adverse or offensive way. Marketers are urged to obtain written permission before:
>    (a) referring to or portraying members of the public or their identifiable possessions; the use of crowd scenes or general public locations may be acceptable without permission;
>    (b) referring to people with a public profile; references that accurately reflect the contents of books, articles or films may be acceptable without permission

---

[9] *Portfolio Gallery* (March 20, 2002) Insert (insert in a photography association magazine showing a distressing image. Complaint not upheld as unlikely to cause serious or widespread offence to photographers who would understand the creative nature of the image); *Konami of Europe GmbH* (August 20, 2003) Cinema (commercial for a computer game unlikely to cause distress to a cinema audience aged 15 years and over.)

[10] *Midway Games Ltd* (April 23, 2003) Poster (advert for console game with image of a hooded youth wiping his bloodied hand on the shoulder of a white, middle-aged businessman); *Mercury Records Ltd* (January 16, 2002) Poster (for music album showing a man with a bleeding nose and red and black blood running over his mouth, chin and neck).

[11] *Viva!* (January 29, 2003) Leaflet (pressure group).

[12] See adjudications under n.10, above.

[13] *British Heart Foundation* (June 19, 2002) Magazine, National Press (complaint under cl.9.1 not upheld re. a photograph of an elderly woman in her nightwear; the woman had a clear plastic bag over her head. ASA acknowledged that the image was shocking and distressing but approach was justified in the context of raising awareness about heart failure.)

(c) implying any personal approval of the advertised product; marketers should recognise that those who do not wish to be associated with the product may have a legal claim.

13.2 Prior permission may not be needed when the marketing communication contains nothing that is inconsistent with the position or views of the person featured.

13.3 References to anyone who is deceased should be handled with particular care to avoid causing offence or distress

13.4 Members of the Royal Family should not normally be shown or mentioned in marketing communications without their prior permission. Incidental references unconnected with the advertised product, or references to material such as books, articles or films about members of the Royal Family, may be acceptable.

13.5 The Royal Arms and Emblems should be used only with the prior permission of the Lord Chamberlain's office. References to Royal Warrants should be checked with the Royal Warrant Holders' Association."

Complaints will invariably be upheld for uses of human images of individual members of the public without permission[14] as will use of celebrity images implying endorsement.[15] But whilst the Code *urges* advertisers to obtain written permission before referring to or portraying individuals in advertisements, it does not *require* written permission to be obtained.[16] In addition, cl.13.1(a) states that use of crowd scenes may be acceptable.    **14–082**

Clause 13 needs to be read in conjunction with cl.14 (testimonials and endorsements). Any use of human image in such a way as to suggest endorsement must comply with requirements of cl.14.[17] In particular, advertisers are required to hold signed and dated proof including a contact address for any endorsement or testimonial. If the advertiser supplies written proof of endorsements, complaints will not be upheld.[18] Use of human images in a way that misrepresents endorsements may in any event give rise to a cause of action in passing off.[19]

It is to be noted by virtue of cl.13(c) advertisers should obtain permission even where there is only implied personal approval of the advertised product. Mere use of an employee's name may be sufficient to imply approval.[20]    **14–083**

---

[14] *The Financial Training Company* (November 3, 1999) Magazine cll. 7.1, 13.1, 20.1 (Ed 9) (permission from 10 of 14 people referred to, unable to contact the others and had therefore included their names but not their photographs); *British Sky Broadcasting Ltd* (April 5, 2000) Leaflet, National press, cl.13.1 (Ed 9) (first complaint upheld).

[15] *Key 103 & Magic 1152* (June 9, 1999) Poster, cl.13.2 (Ed 9) (poster for a radio station showing the heads of a footballer superimposed on very muscular bodies could be seen to imply that the footballer endorsed the radio station; could diminish his reputation or affect his future income from genuine endorsements.)

[16] Noted by the ASA in *Easyjet Airline Co Ltd* (October 8, 2003) National press, cl.5.1, 9.1, 13.1, 13.2 (Ed 11). For facts of this adjudication see below at para. 14–083, n.21.

[17] For text of cl.14 see Appendix 4, below.

[18] *147 Racing Ltd* (April 9, 2003) Direct Mail (photograph of snooker players Peter Ebdon and John Parrot); *The Hair Extension Centre* (June 9, 1999) Magazine (photographs of a supermodel and TV personality endorsing hair extensions).

[19] See Ch.10, above.

[20] *Balmoral Publishing Ltd* (June 19, 2002) Facsimile.

However, if the reference to a person merely states information that is in the public domain and the use is humourous or not unfair, the complaint may not be upheld.[21] Complaints have not been upheld in respect of humourous reference and use of images of those who had sought publicity and had not personally objected.[22] Targeting a Prime Minister in his capacity as head of the government and parodying his style may not amount to portrayal in an adverse way.[23] Use of an image of a public figure in his official capacity may still amount to unfair portrayal under cl.13.1 if presented with misleading information.[24]

Use of an image or a name that does not imply endorsement may not breach cl.13, particularly if general permission to use an image has been granted. A complaint was not upheld for use of a person's image where the subject of a photograph had signed a general release form, and complained in respect of particular use in an advertisement where his image was used in conjunction with a general statement as to advantages of a service and not as an endorsement of a particular product.[25] A complaint was not upheld in respect of the use of a photograph of a pop singer in advertising for a promotion to win "a dream" with words "... Your dream may be to have VIP tickets to see [Pop Singer] in concert." The ASA held that a suggestion that entrants might want the tickets as a prize did not imply an endorsement of the advertisers' products by the pop singer.[26]

---

[21] Complaints under cl.13 not upheld: *Toshiba Air Conditioning* (August 11, 1999) Magazine (advert featuring a well known transsexual with reference to "starting life with a very different anatomy"); *Serversys Ltd* (May 16, 2001) National Press (reference to a politician's loss of memory that had been widely publicised); *Easyjet Airline Co Ltd* (October 8, 2003) National press, cll. 5.1, 9.1, 13.1, 13.2 (Ed 11) (a photograph of Major and Mrs Ingram (who had been convicted of procuring a £1m prize in a TV Game show by deception) under the headline "Need a cheap getaway?" Beneath the photograph it stated "(No Major fraud required!). Lowest fares to the sun ...". Major and Mrs Ingram complained the use constituted an invasion of their privacy because their image was used without their permission and it was distressing to them. The ASA did not uphold the complaints. The ASA noted that the image was already in the public domain and, although it understood that the complainants maintained their innocence, it concluded that the advertisement portrayed the complainants in a way that was consistent with the verdicts in their court case and not in an unfairly adverse way. The ASA considered that the advertisers had not breached the Code by not seeking the complainants' permission before portraying them in the advertisement.)

[22] *Channel 5 Broadcasting Ltd* (October 17, 2001) National Press.

[23] *Multiple Sclerosis Society* (June 14, 2000) National Press (complaint not upheld for use of a caricature of Tony Blair standing alone, arms wide open, with a background that resembled a church).

[24] *Licensed Taxi Drivers Association* (September 24, 2003) Poster cl.13.1 (Ed 11) (use of official photograph of Sir John Stevens, Commissioner of the Metropolitan Police released by the Metropolitan Police Service press office was unfair portrayal as it was used without permission in an advertisement alongside misleading statistics).

[25] *British Sky Broadcasting Ltd* (April 5, 2000) Leaflet, National press, cl.13.1 (Ed 9).

[26] *Mars Confectionery* (March 8, 2000) National press, cll. 13.1, 13.2, 13.3 (Ed 9).

Complaints have been upheld in respect of the use of a photograph of a person's home without their permission or identification of an address,[27] as has use of a home misleadingly suggesting that estate agents had sold the home.[28]

    **14–084**

If the house is shown as part of a public street, then the use without the occupant's permission may be acceptable. The ASA rejected a complaint regarding the use of a picture on a brochure for a new housing development that featured a large house (identified by a caption) in the foreground with a Maypole just visible in the background. The complainant, who lived in the house featured objected that the brochure showed her house without her permission and was an intrusion into her privacy. The house was of historical interest, was closely linked with the village where the development was and carried a blue heritage plaque. The ASA concluded that, because the house was of historical significance and the picture featured the main street, the brochure was acceptable.[29]

## THE BBC PRODUCERS' GUIDELINES

The BBC is constitutionally established by a 1996 Royal Charter and an Agreement[30] which places various obligations on the Governors in connection with broadcasting standards. The Governors are required to satisfy themselves that all the activities of the Corporation are carried out in accordance with "the highest standards of probity, propriety and value for money in the use of the Licence Revenue."[31] The Governors are also required to monitor and supervise the BBC's fulfilment of its legal and contractual obligations, in particular ensuring that the BBC, its employees, and programme makers comply with the provisions of any code which the Corporation is required to draw up for the treatment of controversial subjects with due accuracy and impartiality and complies with any other code or guidelines applicable to programme content and standards.[32]

    **14–085**

    Under the 1996 Agreement, the BBC is obliged to draw up (and from time to time review) a code giving guidance and rules to ensure that controversial subjects are treated with due accuracy and impartiality.[33] The BBC is also

---

[27] *Basildon District Council; Eaga Services* (June 9, 1999) Regional press, cl.13.1a (Ed 10); *George David & Co* (April 11, 2001) Circular, cl.13.1a (Ed 10) (complaint upheld in respect of a circular for estate agency services which identified by address the complainant's house); *Select Homes (Tayside) Ltd* (January 13, 1999) Regional press, cl.13.1 (Ed 9) (a photograph advertising a proposed new building site included the image of a single house in the background implied the advertisers had built the house and had wrongly featured the complainant's house without permission); *Sunshine Conservatories* (June 14, 2000) Leaflet (complaint upheld for use of a photograph of a conservatory without permission stating products had been installed at identified address and owners of property now enjoying benefit).

[28] *Abbotts Countrywide* (April 18, 2001) Leaflet, cll. 3.1, 7.1, 13.1 (Ed 10).

[29] *Barratt Developments plc* (July 24, 2002) Brochure, cl.13.1a (Ed 10).

[30] Made between Her Majesty's Secretary of State for National Heritage and the British Broadcasting Corporation on January 25, 1996.

[31] Royal Charter, May 1, 1996, Cmnd. 3248, para.7(1)(b).

[32] Royal Charter, May 1, 1996, Cmnd. 3248, para.7(1)(f).

[33] Agreement (n.30), para.5.3.

obliged to comply with any lawful directions given to it by the Broadcasting Complaints Commission or the Broadcasting Standards Council.[34] In addition, any BBC code is required by statute "to reflect the general effect" in so far as is relevant, the Code of the BSC (and when replaced, any Ofcom Code).[35]

**14–086**    The BBC has a Programme Complaints Unit (PCU) which deals with serious editorial complaints about all publicly funded BBC services. Public complaints within the UK must refer to a breach of the BBC Producers' Guidelines. The BBC Producers' Guidelines are a publically available code of ethics for BBC programme makers.[36] All the guidelines are applicable to the use of images in a broadcast sense but some are of particular relevance to human image and photography. Detailed consideration of the codes of conduct applicable to television and broadcasting is outside the scope of this work. However, the BBC Producers' Guidelines provide some helpful practical guidance that is transferable to print media—for example the observations on anonymity. This section is intended merely to identify relevant sections for the sake of completeness and facilitate cross-reference to the Producers' Guidelines which are available online. The following sections of the Guidelines may be relevant to photographs and still images:

## Impartiality and accuracy: Part 2

**14–087**    In particular the following sections:

**7. Staging and Restaging Events.**    Guidelines for when reconstruction is permissible.

**8. Use of Computer Graphics.**    This provision provides that viewers must not be misled into believing something is a "real" document or event when it is in fact the creation of a graphic artist. Where composite photographs are created it should be clear that the graphic is not a simple photographic image. It may be appropriate to signal verbally or visually that what is being depicted is an illustration.

## Fairness and straight dealing: Part 3

**14–088**    **8. Anonymity.**    This section sets out guidelines as to when anonymity is appropriate (*e.g.* legal reasons, avoiding undue embarrassment, or reasons of safety). The Guidelines state:

"Where anonymity is necessary producers must make it effective. Both picture and voice may need to be disguised . . .

---

[34] Royal Charter, May 1, 1996, Cmnd. 3248, para.7(1)(f).
[35] Broadcasting Act 1996, ss.107(2) and (5) and 108(2) as amended by the Communications Act 2003, s.360(3), Sch.15.
[36] The Guidelines are available online at *http://www.bbc.co.uk/info/policies/producer_guides/* or via the home page under "About the BBC".

Great care needs to be taken over pictures. Blurring rather than "pixilation" (which can be reversed) is the best way of ensuring anonymity in pictures. If absolute anonymity is essential, programme makers must ensure there is no evidence of the contributor's identity even on the original recording or in any documentation..."

## Privacy: Part 4

The whole of Pt 4 of the BBC Producers' Guidelines concerns the privacy of individuals and reference should be made to that part in its entirety.[37] It is underpinned with the general principle that the BBC should respect the privacy of individuals, recognising that any intrusions have to be justified by serving a greater good.[38] The right to privacy is stated, for the purposes of the Guidelines, to be qualified by the public interest, criminal and seriously anti-social behaviour and by location (public/private). The following parts are particularly relevant

**14–089**

**2. Private Lives and Public Issues.**   Guidelines as to the reporting of personal affairs of public figures. In general, private legal behaviour of public figures should not be reported unless broader public issues are raised.

**14–090**

**5. Media Scrums.**   Concerning procedure when, as a result of a news story, large numbers of the media gather outside a private home in an attempt to secure pictures or interviews. The Guidelines state "In such cases it is important that the combined effect of legitimate news gathering does not become intimidating or unreasonably intrusive. We must not harass people unfairly ... with repeated knocks at the door or by obstructing them as they come and go ..."

**6. CCTV Footage.**   Guidelines as to use of CCTV Footage. This section is quoted in full above at para. 11–181.

**14–091**

**7. Missing People.**Guidelines as to broadcast of details of missing persons, in particular observing that care should be taken in deciding what details to broadcast and to consider that not all missing people wish to be traced.

## Surreptitious recording: Part 5

Part 5 contains guidelines as to the use of hidden cameras and microphones. The entire part concerns surreptitious recording and reference should be made to it in its entirety.[39] In addition to the general principles,

**14–092**

---

[37] The Guidelines are available online at *http://www.bbc.co.uk/info/policies/producer_guides/* or via the home page under "About the BBC".
[38] Part 4, General Principles, para.1.
[39] As to the circumstances when surreptitious recording is permitted under the Guidelines see above at para. 11–155.

guidelines in Pt 5 that are particularly relevant to photographs and still images include:

**4. Grief and Distress.**   The Guidelines suggest that use of surreptitious recording of identifiable people in grief and distress will usually only be justified if permission has been granted by the individuals concerned or someone acting on their behalf.

**5.1 Disguising Identities.**   This section sets out guidelines for considering whether, when there has been surreptitious recording of persons engaged in criminal or anti-social behaviour, their identities should be disguised. It recommends that in all cases where innocent but clearly recognisable bystanders are caught on camera in this context, whether in a public or private place, they should be disguised.

Further reference should be made to the full text of the BBC Producers' Guidelines.

# Appendix 1

## A table showing a comparison of statutory provisions in various national copyright laws for photographic works concerning originality, existence of related rights and duration of protection

**NB: This table concerns basic terms of protection only. It does not deal with transitional provisions or other exceptions such as anonymous or pseudonymous works. It should not be taken as providing a definitive guide for the duration of or copyright protection of any given photograph from a particular jurisdiction. For specific issues concerning copyright subsistence under foreign statutes, advice should be sought from specialists in the copyright law of the jurisdiction in question. See further the Introduction to Appendix 2, below.**

The Table is an analysis of the legislative provisions set out in Appendix 2 and reference should be made to Appendix 2 for further details.

**Statutory Language:** The column headed "Original" indicates the use of the word "original" in the relevant statute as per English translations identified in Appendix 2. The column headed Creating or Creation/Intellectual Production/Works of the Mind is basically intended to assist the reader in distinguishing between the pure English common law type requirement of "originality" and other statutory provisions. This column includes statutes which use phrases such as "creation of any intellectual work"; "intellectual creation"; "creative effort"; "creations of the mind"; "result of creative activity" and "intellectual production". Statutes which refer to (for example) an "original creative work" are marked in both columns. Some statutes (*e.g.* Liechtenstein) merely state *e.g.* "literary and artistic works" are protected and make no reference originality or creativity—this is indicated where there are no entries at all under the Statutory language columns.

The symbol "–" denotes that the status is not known to the author.

"pma" means *post mortem auctoris*—after the death of the author.

**Related Rights:** Identifies countries which draw some type of statutory distinction between an original photographic work which attracts copyright and a "simple" non-original photograph but nonetheless extend a type of protection to the latter.

**Duration:** Many national statutes have various duration provisions that have different periods of protection in specific cases (for example) anonymous and pseudonymous works; published and unpublished works; sound recordings, etc. The duration provisions referred to here compare the term of protection for photographs with the basic terms of protection for "core" copyright works (*i.e.* original literary, artistic, dramatic and musical works). "Years from publication", etc. usually means from the end of the calendar year in which publication took place. Reference should be made to the extracts of statutes in Appendix 2 for the respective country.

| Country | Date of Principal Law (as amended) | Statutory language Regarding Originality | | | | Related Rights | Duration | | Other Observations |
|---|---|---|---|---|---|---|---|---|---|
| | | Original | Creating or Creation Intellectual production Works of the mind | Enable author to be distinguished/ work which gives author a particular identity | Innovative/ Innovated/ Novel elements[1] | Distinction between Creative & Non Creative Photographs | Same basic term as other works | Shorter period/ or different period from other works | |
| Albania | 1992 | ■ | ■ | | | | | 50 yrs from work first made available to public or after the making of work | |
| Algeria | 1973[2] | | ■ | | | | | 10 yrs from publication (NB: this information pre-dates 1997 Act) | |
| Angola | 1990 | ■ | ■ | | | | | 25 yrs pma | |

[1] NB: Observations regarding translation, see above at para.3-078, n.72a.
[2] This information has been superseded by a further statute passed in 1997. The author has been unable to obtain a copy.

| Country (Year) | Term for works | Term from publication / photographs | Provisions / Notes |
|---|---|---|---|
| Argentina 1933 (1989) | | 20 yrs from first publication | |
| Australia 1968 (2000) | | 50 years from end of year of first publication | |
| Austria 1936 (1998) | 70 pma for works | 50 yrs from first publication for simple photographs | |
| Bahrain 1993 | | 50 yrs from publication | Provision that the Rights to photographic works do not prohibit others from taking photographs of the photographed matter even if the new photographs were taken from the same place and in the same circumstances. |
| Bangladesh 1962 (1978) | | 50 yrs from publication | |
| Barbados 1998 | 50 yrs pma | | |
| Belgium 1994 (1995) | 70 yrs pma | | |
| Belize 2000 | 50 yrs pma | | |
| Benin 1984 | | 25 yrs after work made | Only photographs of "an artistic or documentary nature" are protected |

| Country | Date of Principal Law (as amended) | Statutory language Regarding Originality | | | | Related Rights | Duration | | Other Observations |
|---|---|---|---|---|---|---|---|---|---|
| | | Original | Creating or Creation Intellectual production Works of the mind | Enable author to be distinguished/ work which gives author a particular identity | Innovative/ Innovated/ Novel elements[2a] | Distinction between Creative & Non Creative Photographs | Same basic term as other works | Shorter period/ or different period from other works | |
| Brazil | 1998 | | ■ | | | | | 70 yrs from January 1 of the year following disclosure | |
| Bulgaria | 1993 (2000) | | ■ | | | | 70 yrs pma | | |
| Burkina Faso | 1983 | ■ | | | | | 50 yrs pma | | |
| Burundi | 1978 | ■ | ■ | | | | 50 yrs pma | | |
| Cameroon | 2000 | ■ | ■ | ■ | | | 50 yrs pma | | 1982 statute gave a shorter term of protection namely 50 yrs from publication |
| Canada | 1924 (1997) | ■ | | | | | 50 yrs pma | 50 yrs from making of photograph if author is a corporation | |
| Chile | 1990 | | ■ | | | | 30 yrs pma | | |

[2a] NB: Observations regarding translation, see above at para.3–078, n.72a.

| Country | Year | | | Term (pma) | Term (from publication/making) | Notes |
|---|---|---|---|---|---|---|
| China | 1990 (2001) | | | | 50 yrs from first publication | Protection only to "artistic photographs" |
| Colombia | 1982 | | ■ | 80 yrs pma | | |
| Costa Rica | 1982 (2000) | ■ | ■ | 70 yrs pma | | |
| Côte d'Ivoire | 1996 | ■ | ■ | | 99 yrs from end of year of publication | |
| Croatia | 1999 | | ■ | 70 yrs from January 1 pma | | |
| Cuba | 1977 | ■ | | | 10 yrs from "utilization of the work" | |
| Cyprus | 1976 (1993) | ■ | | | 50 yrs from first publication | |
| Czech Republic | 2000 | | ■ | 70 yrs pma | | |
| Democratic Republic of the Congo | 1982 | ■ | | | 25 yrs from making of the work | Only photographs of "an artistic or documentary nature" are protected |
| Denmark | 2003 | | ■ | 70 yrs pma works | 50 yrs from end of year taken non-works | Distinction is between "photographic works" and "photographic pictures" |

| Country | Date of Principal Law (as amended) | Statutory language Regarding Originality | | | | Related Rights | Duration | | Other Observations |
|---|---|---|---|---|---|---|---|---|---|
| | | Original | Creating or Creation Intellectual production Works of the mind | Enable author to be distinguished/work which gives author a particular identity | Innovative/Innovated/Novel elements[3] | Distinction between Creative & Non Creative Photographs | Same basic term as other works | Shorter period/or different period from other works | |
| Djibouti | 1996 | | ■ | | | | | 25 yrs from making of photograph | |
| Dominican Republic | 1986[4] | | ■ | | | | | 10 yrs from publication | Protection only when photographs possess "sufficient artistic merit" |
| Ecuador | 1998 | | ■ | | | ■ | 70 yrs pma for photographic works | 25 yrs from making, disclosure or publication | Distinction between a photograph work and "an ordinary photograph .... that does not have the character of a photographic work" |

[3] NB: Observations regarding translation, see above at para.3–078, n.72a.
[4] This law has been superseded by the Law of 2000. See Appendix 2, below.

| | | | | | Term | | Notes |
|---|---|---|---|---|---|---|---|
| Egypt | 2002 | ■ | | | 50 yrs pma | | Under the previous statute No. 354 of June 24, 1954 Egypt distinguished between creative photographs (protected for 50 years) and photographic and cinematographic works having no original character and limited to a simple mechanical reproduction of scenes (protected for 15 years from first publication. This is not included in the 2002 statute. |
| El Salvador | 1993 | ■ | ■ | | 50 yrs pma | | |
| Estonia | 1992 (2002) | ■ | ■ | | 70 yrs pma | | Previously photographs were protected for a shorter term, being 50 yrs after making available to the public. This distinction has now been removed. |
| Finland | 1961 (1997) | | ■ | ■ | 70 yrs pma for photographic works | 50 yrs from creation of work | |
| France | 1992 (1997) | | ■ | | 70 yrs pma | | |
| Gabon | 1987 | ■ | ■ | | | 50 yrs from making available to public | |

| Country | Date of Principal Law (as amended) | Statutory language Regarding Originality | | | | Related Rights | Duration | | Other Observations |
|---|---|---|---|---|---|---|---|---|---|
| | | Original | Creating or Creation Intellectual production Works of the mind | Enable author to be distinguished/ work which gives author a particular identity | Innovative/ Innovated/ Novel elements[5] | Distinction between Creative & Non Creative Photographs | Same basic term as other works | Shorter period/ or different period from other works | |
| Gambia | 1915[6] | ■ | | | | | | | |
| Germany | 1965 (1998) | | ■ | | | ■ | 70 yrs pma for creative photographs | 50 yrs from publication for non-creative photographs | Distinction between "photographic works" and "photographs and products manufactured in a similar way to photographs" |
| Ghana | 1985 | ■ | | | | | | 50 yrs from making of work | Original if "the product of the independent efforts of the author" |
| Greece | 1993 (1996) | ■ | ■ | | | | 70 yrs pma | | |
| Guinea | 1980 | ■ | | | | | | 40 yrs pma | |
| Hong Kong | 1997 (1998) | ■ | | | | | 50 yrs pma | | |

[5] NB: Observations regarding translation, see above at para.3-078, n.72a.
[6] This is the most recent information on the UNESCO website. It is uncertain whether it has been superseded.

| Country | Year | | | Term (pma) | Term (publication/creation) | Notes |
|---|---|---|---|---|---|---|
| Hungary | 1999 (2001) | ■ | ■ | 70 yrs pma | | The previous Act of 1969 as amended provided for a related right which distinguished between "scientific or artistic creations" and "photographs which do not enjoy copyright protection". No such distinction is contained in the 1999 Act which only protects artistic photographs. |
| Iceland | 1972 (1998) | | ■ | 70 yrs pma for artistic photographs | 25 yrs from creation for non-copyright photographs | |
| India | 1957 (1999) | ■ | | | 60 yrs from publication | |
| Indonesia | 2002 | | ■ | | 50 yrs from first publication | Unusually full description of author as a person "upon whose inspiration a **Work** is produced, based on the intellectual ability, imagination, dexterity, skill or expertise manifested in a distinctive form and is of a personal nature." |
| Iran | 1970 | ■ | | | 30 yrs from publication | |

| Country | Date of Principal Law (as amended) | Statutory language Regarding Originality | | | | Related Rights | Duration | | Other Observations |
|---|---|---|---|---|---|---|---|---|---|
| | | Original | Creating or Creation Intellectual production Works of the mind | Enable author to be distinguished/work which gives author a particular identity | Innovative/Innovated/Novel elements[7] | Distinction between Creative & Non Creative Photographs | Same basic term as other works | Shorter period/or different period from other works | |
| Iraq | 1971 | | | | ■ | ■ | 25 yrs pma or 50 yrs from publication whichever is longer for copyright photographs | 5 yrs from date of publication for "mechanical transmission of scenery" non-copyright photographs | 1. Provision that the rights to photographic works do not prohibit others from taking photographs of the photographed matter even if the new photographs were taken from the same place or in the same conditions.<br><br>2. Neighbouring rights apply to photographs which are limited to the mechanical transmission of scenery. |
| Ireland | 2000 | ■ | | | | | 70 yrs pma | | |
| Israel | 1911 (1968) | ■ | | | | | | 50 yrs from production | |

[7] NB: Observations regarding translation, see above at para.3–078, n.72a.

| Country | | | | | | 70 yrs pma copyright photographs | 20 yrs from making of negative simple photographs | Neighbouring rights distinction between "simple photographs" and "works of photographic art" |
|---|---|---|---|---|---|---|---|---|
| Italy | 1941 (1997) | ■ | | | ■ | 70 yrs pma copyright photographs | 20 yrs from making of negative simple photographs | |
| Japan | 1970 (2003) | ■ | | | | 50 yrs pma | | |
| Jordan | 1992 (2001) | | | ■ | | | 25 yrs from date taken | Provision that copyright in photographic work does not prohibit others from taking photographs of the photographed matter even if the new photographs were taken from the same place or in the same circumstances. Prior to the 2001 amendment Jordan had neighbouring rights protection for photographic works that are not of creative character in that they are mere mechanical reproductions of panoramic scenes 30 years from publication). Creative photographs were protected for 30 yrs pma. |
| Kazakhstan | 1996 | ■ | | | | 50 yrs pma | | |

| Country | Date of Principal Law (as amended) | Statutory language Regarding Originality | | | | Related Rights | Duration | | Other Observations |
|---|---|---|---|---|---|---|---|---|---|
| | | Original | Creating or Creation Intellectual production Works of the mind | Enable author to be distinguished/ work which gives author a particular identity | Innovative/ Innovated/ Novel elements[8] | Distinction between Creative & Non Creative Photographs | Same basic term as other works | Shorter period/ or different period from other works | |
| Kenya | 2001 | ■ | | | | | | 50 yrs from the end of the year of either making, first being made available to the public or first publication whichever is the latest | |
| Latvia | 2000 | | ■ | | | | 70 yrs pma | | |
| Lebanon | 1924 (1946) | | | | | | | 50 yrs from publication | Protected works are "all works manifesting human intelligence" |
| Lesotho | 1989 | ■ | | | | | | 25 yrs from making | |
| Liberia | 1972 | – | – | – | – | – | – | – | – |

[8] NB: Observations regarding translation, see above at para.3–078, n.72a.

| Country | Year | | | | Duration (copyright photographs) | Duration (other photographs) | Notes |
|---|---|---|---|---|---|---|---|
| Libya | 1968 | ■ | | | 25 yrs pma or 50 yrs from first publication which ever is longer for copyright photographs | 5 years from publication for other photographs | 1 Provision that the rights to photographic works do not prohibit others from taking photographs of the photographed matter even if the new photographs were taken from the same place or in the same circumstances.<br><br>2. Neighbouring rights apply to photographs which merely involve photographing by technical means. |
| Liechtenstein | 1999 | | ■ | | 70 yrs pma | | The predecessor 1928 statute provided that copyright in a photograph does not exclude the right of any other person to take a new photograph of the same object even if the new photograph is taken from the same position and in a general manner under the same conditions as the first. |
| Luxembourg | 1972 (1997) | ■ | ■ | | 70 yrs pma for original works | 50 yrs from making for non-original photographs | The neighbouring right distinction is between photographic works that are "original in the sense that they are an intellectual creation specific to their author" and those that are not. |

| Country | Date of Principal Law (as amended) | Statutory language Regarding Originality | | | | Related Rights | Duration | | Other Observations |
|---|---|---|---|---|---|---|---|---|---|
| | | Original | Creating or Creation Intellectual production Works of the mind | Enable author to be distinguished/work which gives author a particular identity | Innovative/Innovated/Novel elements[9] | Distinction between Creative & Non Creative Photographs | Same basic term as other works | Shorter period/ or different period from other works | |
| Macau, SAR of China | 1999 | ■ | ■ | | | | | 25 yrs from date taken (completion) | Only photographs which by the choice of its subject or the manner of its execution, may be considered a personal artistic creation of the author are protected by copyright. Photographs that have mere documentary value, such as photographs of writings and documents, business papers, technical drawings and similar material, are not be protected |
| Madagascar | 1995 | | ■ | | | – | – | – | – |
| Malawi | 1989 | ■ | | | | | | 25 yrs from publication or making | |

[9] NB: Observations regarding translation, see above at para.3–078, n.72a.

| Country | Year | | | | | | | | Notes |
|---|---|---|---|---|---|---|---|---|---|
| Malaysia | 1987 (2000) | ■ | | | | | 50 yrs pma | | Prior to April 1, 1999, photographs had a different term of protection namely 50 yrs from start of year following publication. |
| Mali | 1977[10] | ■ | ■ | | | | | 50 yrs from publication | Work is defined as any original creation particularly as regards for which is a manifestation of the author's personality. |
| Malta | 2000 | ■ | | | | | 70 yrs pma | | Previous Act of 1976 gave photographs a shorter term than other works being 25 yrs from publication and "sufficient effort" was the criteria for originality. |
| Mauritius | 1997 | ■ | | | | | | 25 yrs from making | Original work is defined as "the product of a person's skill or labour". |
| Mexico | 1997 | ■ | | | | | 75 yrs pma | | |
| Moldova (Republic of) | 1994 (2000) | | ■ | | | | 50 yrs pma | | The previous statute of 1970 gave photographs a shorter term of 50 yrs from publication or creation if not published. |
| Monaco | 1948 | | | | | | 50 yrs pma | | |

[10] This statute has been repealed. See Appendix 2, below.

| Country | Date of Principal Law (as amended) | Statutory language Regarding Originality | | | | Related Rights | Duration | | Other Observations |
|---|---|---|---|---|---|---|---|---|---|
| | | Original | Creating or Creation Intellectual production Works of the mind | Enable author to be distinguished/ work which gives author a particular identity | Innovative/ Innovated/ Novel elements[11] | Distinction between Creative & Non Creative Photographs | Same basic term as other works | Shorter period or different period from other works | |
| Mongolia | 1993 (1999) | | ■ | | | | | 25 yrs from making | Prior to amendment, the 1993 Act had given photographs the same term as other works, 50 yrs pma. |
| Morocco | 2000 | ■ | | | ■ | | | 50 yrs from publication | |
| Nepal | 1966[12] | | ■ | | | | 50 yrs pma | | |
| Netherlands | 1912 (1999) | | | | | | 70 yrs pma | | |
| New Zealand | 1994 (2003) | ■ | | | | | 50 yrs pma | | |
| Nicaragua | 1999 | | | | | | 70 yrs pma | | |
| Nigeria | 1988 (1999) | ■ | | | | | | 50 yrs from publication | "Sufficient effort" criteria for originality |

[11] NB: Observations regarding translation, see above at para.3–078, n.72a.
[12] This statute has now been repealed. See Appendix 2, below.

| | | | | | | | 70 yrs pma for creative works | 15 yrs pma for non-works | Neighbouring rights distinction is between "photographic works" and "photographic pictures". |
|---|---|---|---|---|---|---|---|---|---|
| Norway | 1961 (2001) | | ■ | | | ■ | | | Neighbouring rights distinction is between "photographic works" and "photographic pictures". |
| Oman | 2000 | ■ | | | ■ | | | 50 yrs from publication | |
| Pakistan | 1962 (2000) | | | | | | | 50 yrs from publication | |
| Panama | 1994 | ■ | ■ | | | | 50 yrs pma | | |
| Paraguay | 1998 | | ■ | | | ■ | 70 yrs pma for creative works | 25 yrs from taking of photograph for non-works | |
| Peru | 1996 | | ■ | | | ■ | 70 yrs pma for copyright works | 70 yrs from 1 January following taking of the photograph for non-copyright works | Neighbouring rights distinction is between "a photographic work" (ie. a work of the mind) and a photograph that does not qualify as a work. |
| Philippines | 1998 | ■ | ■ | | | | | 50 yrs from publication or making | |
| Poland | 1994 | | ■ | | | | 50 yrs pma | | |

| Country | Date of Principal Law (as amended) | Statutory language Regarding Originality | | | | Related Rights | Duration | | Other Observations |
|---|---|---|---|---|---|---|---|---|---|
| | | Original | Creating or Creation Intellectual production Works of the mind | Enable author to be distinguished/ work which gives author a particular identity | Innovative/ Innovated/ Novel elements[13] | Distinction between Creative & Non Creative Photographs | Same basic term as other works | Shorter period/ or different period from other works | |
| Portugal | 1985 (1991)[14] | | ■ | | | | | 25 yrs after work carried out | Before a photograph qualifies for protection "the choice of a photograph's subject and conditions of creation must be deemed to be a personal artistic creation of the author." |
| Qatar | 2002 | ■ | | | | | 50 yrs pma | | The predecessor 1995 statute granted a shorter term to photographic works of 25 yrs from completion. |
| Republic of Korea | 1986 | ■ | | | | | 50 yrs from January 1 pma | | |
| Romania | 1996 | ■ | ■ | | | | 70 yrs pma | | Photographs of letters, deeds, documents, etc. do not attract copyright. |

[13] NB: Observations regarding translation, see above at para.3–078, n.72a.

[14] This statute was last amended in 2001. See Appendix 2, below.

| Country | Year | Term | Provision that it is lawful to take new photographs of a previously photographed object even if the new photographs are taken from the same place and in the same circumstances as the first. |
|---|---|---|---|
| Russian Federation | 1993 (1995) | 50 yrs pma | |
| Rwanda | 1983 | 50 yrs pma | |
| Saint Vincent and the Grenadines | 1989 | 50 years from making available to public | |
| San Marino | 1991 | 30 yrs from date taken | |
| Saudi Arabia | 1989 | 25 yrs from publication | ■ |
| Senegal | 1973 (1986) | 25 yrs pma | |
| Sierra Leone | 1965 | 50 yrs from publication | |
| Singapore | 1987 | 50 yrs from publication | |
| Slovakia | 1997 (2000) | 70 yrs pma | |
| Slovenia | 1995 | 70 yrs pma | |

| Country | Date of Principal Law (as amended) | Statutory language Regarding Originality | | | | Related Rights | Duration | | Other Observations |
|---|---|---|---|---|---|---|---|---|---|
| | | Original | Creating or Creation Intellectual production Works of the mind | Enable author to be distinguished/ work which gives author a particular identity | Innovative/ Innovated/ Novel elements[15] | Distinction between Creative & Non Creative Photographs | Same basic term as other works | Shorter period/ or different period from other works | |
| South Africa | 1978 (2002) | ■ | | | | | | 50 yrs from publication with consent of author. If no publication within 50 years from making, then duration is 50 years from end of year in which work made | |
| Spain | 1996 (1998) | ■ | ■ | | | ■ | 70 yrs pma for copyright photographs | 25 yrs from making for non-copyright photographs | |
| Sudan | 1996 | ■ | | | | | | 25 yrs from publication | |

[15] NB: Observations regarding translation, see above at para.3-078, n.72a.

| | | | | | | 70 yrs pma for copyright photographs | 50 yrs from publication for non-copyright photographs | |
|---|---|---|---|---|---|---|---|---|
| Sweden | 1960 (1995) | ■ | | | | | ■ | |
| Switzerland | 1992 (1994) | | ■ | | | 70 yrs pma | | |
| Thailand | 1994 | | | ■ | | | 50 yrs from authorship or if published within that period, 50 yrs from publication | |
| Togo | 1991 | ■ | | | ■ | | 25 yrs pma | |
| Tonga | 1985 | ■ | | | | | 25 yrs from making | |
| Trinidad & Tobago | 1997 | ■ | | ■ | | 50 yrs pma | | |
| Tunisia | 1994 | ■ | | | | | 25 Gregorian yrs from making | |
| Turkey | 1951 (1995)[16] | | ■ | | | | 70 yrs from publication | Specific unfair competition rule regarding transmissions of images applies to non-works. |

[16] This statute was further amended in 2001. See Appendix 2, below.

| Country | Date of Principal Law (as amended) | Statutory language Regarding Originality | | | | Related Rights | Duration | | Other Observations |
|---|---|---|---|---|---|---|---|---|---|
| | | Original | Creating or Creation Intellectual production Works of the mind | Enable author to be distinguished/ work which gives author a particular identity | Innovative/ Innovated/ Novel elements[17] | Distinction between Creative & Non Creative Photographs | Same basic term as other works | Shorter period/ or different period from other works | |
| Ukraine | 1993 | | ■ | | | | 50 yrs pma | | |
| Uganda | 1964 | ■ | | | | | 50 yrs from pma or publication whichever is later | | Requires "sufficient effort" to be expended on a work to give it an original character. |
| United Arab Emirates | 2002 | | ■ | | | | 50 yrs pma | | The previous 1992 statute gave photographs a shorter term of protection than other works being 10 yrs from publication |
| United Kingdom | 1988 (2003) | ■ | | | | | 70 yrs pma | | |
| United Republic of Tanzania | 1966 | ■ | | | | | | 20 yrs from end of year in which work made lawfully accessible to public | Requires "sufficient effort" to be expended on a work to give it an original character. |

[17] NB: Observations regarding translation, see above at para.3-078, n.72a.

| Country | Year | | | Term | Provision |
|---|---|---|---|---|---|
| United States of America | 1976 (2002) | ■ | | 70 yrs pma; works for hire | Provision that a third person may make new photographs of the object depicted even in the same place and circumstances as those in which the first photograph was made |
| Uruguay | 1937 (1990)[18] | | ■ | 40 yrs pma | |
| Uzbekistan | 1996 | | ■ | 50 yrs pma | |
| Venezuela | 1993 | | ■ | 60 yrs from disclosure or 60 yrs from creation if not disclosed within that period | |
| Yemen | 1994 | ■ | | 30 yrs from January 1 pma | |
| Zambia | 1994 | ■ | ■ | 50 yrs pma | |

[18] This Act was further amended in 2003, but no official English translation was available.

# Appendix 2

# Extracts from various national copyright laws for photographic works concerning originality, existence of neighbouring rights and duration of protection with selected commentary

This Appendix sets out relevant extracts (as translated into English by the respective sources) of various national statutes considered or otherwise outlines the general position as to the protection of photographs in that country. It accompanies the Table in Appendix 1. In respect of some selected countries, there is additional commentary as to the manner in which these provisions are interpreted. The primary purpose is to give a global overview of the varying approaches to originality in photographs with the intention of discerning common themes.

As noted in the introductory comments to the Table in Appendix 1, many national statutes have various duration provisions that provide for different periods of protection in specific cases—for example, anonymous and pseudonymous works; published and unpublished works; sound recordings; ownership by legal entities, etc. These further duration provisions are not considered here at all. The provisions included here refer to specific terms of protection for photographs and/or the basic terms of protection for "core" copyright works (*i.e.* original literary, artistic, dramatic and musical works) by an identifiable human author. Equally, transitional provisions of statutes are not referred to either.

**Accordingly, PLEASE NOTE this section should not be taken as providing a definitive guide for the duration of or copyright protection of any given photograph from a particular jurisdiction. A number of the statutes are originally written in a different language and are reproduced here as translated into English which may result in meaning change (*e.g.* "droit d'auteur" (author's rights) translated as copyright). For specific issues concerning copyright subsistence under foreign statutes, advice should be sought from specialists in the copyright law of the jurisdiction in question.**

A large number, but not all, of the statutory texts are taken from copies or translations on the UNESCO World Copyright Law database[1] at *http://www.*

---

[1] © UNESCO. At the time this Appendix was written, the UNESCO World Copyright Law website held English translations of all national copyright laws included in the database. Since that time, the website has been revised. In some cases, the official translation of the copyright and related rights legislation which has been provided to UNESCO is not in English, but in another of the official languages of UNESCO. Where the UNESCO Collection is cited as a source, if the law is now no longer available in English on that website the English translation was taken from the version historically available. As a consequence of this change, some of the URL links cited in the footnotes are now no longer active. They have been left to indicate source. As at February 2003, the Unesco Collection of Copyright Laws is available at *http://portal.unesco.org/culture/en/ev.php@URL_ID=14076&URL_DO=DO_TOPIC&URL_SECTION=201.html*. In the event that this link is broken or has changed by the date of publication, the Collection of Laws database can be accessed via the UNESCO homepage at *www.unesco.org* by selecting "Culture" from the menu and then "Collection of National Copyright Laws".

*unesco.org/culture/copy/index.shtml* or the WIPO collection of electronic laws[2] at *http://clea.wipo.int/* or Abu-Ghazaleh Intellectual Property (AGIP) at *http://www.agip.com/*.

Such statutes included herein are as up to date as the material held by those databases respectively.

## Albania

Law No. 7564 of May 19, 1992 (by virtue of Art. 16 of the Law No. 7491 of April 29, 1991, "On the Main Constitutional Provisions", upon proposal by the Council of Ministers

s.1    This Law provides protection for literary, artistic and journalistic works (hereinafter referred to as "works"), including every original, intellectual creation in this domain, irrespective of the form of expression, such as ... i) photographic works ... Protection is independent of the mode or form of expression, of the quality and of the purpose of the work. No protection shall extend to any idea, procedure, process, system, method of operation, concept, principle or discovery expressed, described, explained or embodied in a work.

s.17    Unless provided otherwise in this chapter, the moral and economic rights in a work shall be protected during life of the author and for 50 years after his death.

s.20    The moral and economic rights in a collective work, a photographic work or an audiovisual work shall be protected until the expiration of 50 years after such a work has been lawfully made available to the public or, failing such an event within 50 years from the making of such a work, 50 years after the making.

s.22    Calculation of terms
         Every term under this chapter shall run to the end of the calendar year.

## Algeria

Excerpt from The Constitution of the People's Democratic Republic of Algeria[3]

Art. (54)    The freedom of intellectual, artistic and scientific innovation for the citizen shall be guaranteed under the law, and copyrights shall be legally protected.

Order No. 14–73 dated Safar 29,1393 AH.corresponding to April 3, 1973 in relation to copyright

Art. 1    The creation of any intellectual work, whatever may be its type, the mode or form of its expression, its merit or its purpose, confers on its author a right called "copyright" which is defined and protected in accordance with the provisions of this Ordinance.

---

[2] Reproduced with permission of WIPO. Material sourced from WIPO Collection of Laws for Electronic Access (CLEA). The Secretariat of WIPO assumes no liability or responsibility with regard to the transformation of this data.

[3] *http://www.agip.com/laws/algeria/c.htm.*

| Art. 2 | The works to which copyright protection extends are ... photographic works to which are assimilated works expressed by a process analogous to photography ...[4] |
|---|---|
| Art. 64 | For photographic works and works of the applied arts, the term of protection shall be 10 years from the beginning of the calendar year which follows publication of the work. |

The basic term of protection of economic right for other works was life of the author plus 25 years.[5] Algerian law gives photographs a much shorter protection period. From 1997, the basic term of protection became life of the author plus 70 years.

## Angola

## Law on Authors" Rights (No. 4/90 of March 10, 1990)

| Art. 1 | The purpose of this Law is to protect authors" rights and stimulate the production of intellectual creations in the literary, artistic and scientific fields by promoting their use by society with a view to edifying a culture corresponding to the new social order that is being established in the People's Republic of Angola.[6] |
|---|---|
| Art. 3(1) | Copyright means the exclusive right of the authors of literary, artistic or scientific works to enjoy the benefit of those works and to use them or to authorize the use thereof, in whole or in part, within the limits and terms of this Law. |
| Art. 6 | For the purposes of this Law, the following, in particular, are considered original works: ... (j) photographic works or works produced by processes analogous to photography; |
| Art. 20(1) | The author's economic rights shall last for his lifetime and, for the benefit of his heirs under the applicable legislation, 50 years after his death or 25 years, in the case of photographic works or works of applied art, as from January 1 of the year following that of his death. |

## Argentina

## Law No. 11.723 on Copyright (as amended up to October 18, 1989)[7]

| Art. 1 | For the purposes of this Law, scientific, literary and artistic works shall include: writings of all kinds and of any length ... drawings, paintings, works of sculpture and architecture; ... photographs, engravings and phonograms; in short, every scientific, literary, artistic or educational production, whatever its process of reproduction. |
|---|---|
| Art. 2 | Copyright in a scientific, literary or artistic work shall entitle the author to dispose of, publish, publicly perform and exhibit, alienate, translate or adapt it, or authorize its translation, as well as to reproduce it in any form. |
| Art. 31 | The photographic portrait of a person shall not be used for commercial purposes without the express consent of the person concerned or, following his death, that of the spouse and children, or of the direct descendants of the children, or, if none exists, that of the father or |

---

[4] *http://www.unesco.org/culture/copy/copyright/algeria/fr_sommaire.html*. See n. 1, above.
[5] Art. 60.
[6] http://www.unesco.org/culture/copy/copyright/angola/fr_sommaire.html. See n. 1, above.
[7] *http://www.unesco.org/culture/copy/copyright/argentina/fr_sommaire.html*. See n. 1, above.

mother of the person concerned. If there be no spouse, children, father or mother, or direct descendants of the children, publication is free. The person who has given his consent may subsequently revoke it, subject to an indemnity for any damages occasioned. The publication of a portrait shall be free if made in connection with scientific, educational and, in general, cultural purposes, or with matters or events of public interest or which may have taken place in public.

Art. 34   For photographic works the term of copyright shall be twenty years from first publication.

**Commentary:**   The copyright statute[8] in force in Argentina is a law which attributes concept of property to the rights of the author, with some reservations and limits flowing from author's rights. It is analagous to Spanish and Portugese law.[9] Article 1 of the Argentinian statute provides that the general purpose is for the protection of scientific, literary and artistic works and then lists specific categories, but the list is open.[10] The list includes "three-dimensional works, engravings and photographs".[11] Only creative photographs are protected under Argentinian law. Protection lasts for 20 years from the end of publication of the photograph.[12] Isidoro Stananowsky comments that photographs "true to life, without originality, without personality, are simply not protected".[13] Nimmer & Geller cite two quotations from Argentinian courts

> "Photographs which demonstrate the ability, art or technique of the photographer are protected by the law, because of the sharpness of the details, light-and-shadow effects, and the clarity of the impression."[14]

However:

> "Photographs which possess journalist value may be artistic works ... for their intrinsic value alone".[15]

This suggests that there is some prospect for protection of a non-creative photograph if it has journalistic value. This is to apply a level of pragmatism in protecting a non-creative photograph which is valuable.

Article 34 provides that for photographic works the term of copyright shall be 20 years from first publication, which is shorter than the general term of life of the author plus 50 years.

---

[8] Law No. 11,723 of September 26, 1933. See Nimmer & Geller ARG 7 §1.
[9] Comments of main proponent of statute, Senator Matias Sanchez Sorondo, quoted in Nimmer & Geller ARG-11 §[2].
[10] Nimmer & Geller ARG 12 §[2][2].
[11] Nimmer & Geller ARG-16 §[2][2][h].
[12] Nimmer & Geller ARG-30 §3[2][b].
[13] Isidoro Satanowsky *Derecho Intelectual* (Intellectual Property) Vol. 1, p.227 (Tea 1994) quoted in Nimmer & Geller ARG-17 §2[2][h][i].
[14] C. Civ la Capital December 30, 1998, L.L.13–504 quoted in Nimmer & Geller ARG-17 §2[2][h][i].
[15] C.N. Crim & Correc., Sala III August 24, 1976, -D-333 quoted in Nimmer & Geller ARG-17 §2[2][h][i].

## Australia

### Copyright Act 1968 as amended.[16]

10.—(1)  In this Act, unless the contrary intention appears: ...
    "artistic work" means ... (a) a painting, sculpture, drawing, engraving or photograph, whether the work is of artistic quality or not; ...
    ... "author", in relation to a photograph, means the person who took the photograph ...
    ... "photograph" means a product of photography or of a process similar to photography, other than an article or thing in which visual images forming part of a cinematograph film have been embodied, and includes a product of xerography, and "photographic" has a corresponding meaning; ...

32(1)  Subject to this Act, copyright subsists in an original literary, dramatic, musical or artistic work that is unpublished ...

33(6)  Copyright subsisting in a photograph by virtue of this Part continues to subsist until the expiration of 50 years after the expiration of the calendar year in which the photograph is first published.

65(2)  The copyright in a work to which this section applies [sculptures and to works of artistic craftsmanship] that is situated, otherwise than temporarily, in a public place, or in premises open to the public, is not infringed by the making of a painting, drawing, engraving or photograph of the work or by the inclusion of the work in a cinematograph film or in a television broadcast.

The copyright term is shorter than for other works which are protected for life of the author plus 50 years.

## Austria

### Copyright Act, Federal Law Gazette No. 111/1936[17]

§§1(1)  Works within the meaning of this Act shall be original intellectual productions in the fields of literature, music, art and cinematography.

§§3(1)  Works of art within the meaning of this Act shall include works of photography, architecture and industrial art.(applied art (handicraft))

    (2)  Works of photography are works produced by a photographic process or a process similar to photography.

§§73(1)  Photographs in the sense of this Act shall be images produced by a photographic process. A process similar to photography shall also be considered a photographic process.

    (2)  The moving images (cinematographic productions) so produced are subject to the provisions applicable to photographs, without prejudice to the provisions relating to copyright in cinematographic works.

§§74(1)  The person who takes a photograph (the producer) shall have the exclusive right, within the limitations set forth in this Act, to multiply, distribute, publicly exhibit by means of optical contrivances, or broadcast by radio, the said photograph. In the case of photographs commercially produced, the owner of the enterprise shall be considered the producer.

    (2)  The rights of exploitation granted under paragraph (1) to the producer shall be subject to inheritance and alienation.

---

[16] *http://www.unesco.org/culture/copy/copyright/australia/fr_sommaire.html.* See n. 1, above.
[17] *http://www.unesco.org/culture/copy/copyright/austria/fr_page1.html.* See n. 1, above.

(3) Where the producer has designated his name (or pseudonym or trade name) on a photograph, copies thereof made by other persons and destined for distribution must likewise bear reference to the producer. Where a copy with such designation reproduces the photograph with substantial alterations, the designation of the producer shall bear an appropriate additional reference.

(4) In the case of multiplied copies bearing the designation of the producer, the designation of the subject matter may deviate from that given by the producer only insofar as is compatible with the customs of honest dealing.

(5) After the death of the producer the protection granted by paragraphs (3) and (4) shall accrue to the persons upon whom devolve the rights of exploitation. Where the rights of exploitation are transferred to another person, the transferee may acquire the right to be designated as the producer of the photograph. In such case the transferee shall thereafter be deemed the producer and, provided he is named as such on the photographs, he shall enjoy protection under the provisions of paragraphs (3) and (4).

(6) The protection of photographs shall terminate fifty years after they have been taken, or, where the photograph is made public before the expiration of that term, thirty years from the date when it is first made public. The terms shall be computed in accordance with §§64.

(7) §§§§5, 7 to 9, 11 to 13, 14, paragraph 2, §§15, paragraph 1, §§§§16, 16a, 16b, 17, 17a, 17b, 18, paragraph 3, §§23, paragraphs 2 and 4, §§§§24, 25, paragraphs 2 to 6, §§§§26, 27, paragraphs 1, 3, 4 and 5, §§31, paragraph 1, §§32, paragraph 1, §§33, paragraph 2, §§§§36, 37, 41, 42a, 42b, 42c, 54, paragraph 1, Berne Copyright Union and Montevideo Copyright Convention and paragraph 2, §§§§56, 56a, 56b. 59a and 59b shall apply to pictures, §§§§56c and 56d to cinematographic products *mutatis mutandis*; however, §§42a, second sentence of this law shall not apply to reproductions of commercially manufactured pictures on the basis of a model obtained by means of a photographic process.

**Commentary:** Austrian law distinguishes between photographic works (s.3(1)) and simple photographs which are not creative works (ss.73–75). The former are protected as works for 70 yrs pma and the latter for 50 years from the taking of the photograph or date of first publication. In order for simple photographs to be protected, a minimum photographic activity is required to distinguish mere copying from photography.[18]

The *sui generis* protection for simple photographs was originally for 20 years from the making of the photograph or first publication (if within the first 20 year period). In 1972, this was amended to extend the term from 20 years to 30 years and again extended to 50 years in 1996. However, the 1996 extension to 50 years applies only if the photograph was still protected on July 1, 1995, in Austria or any Member State of the European Union or the European Economic Area.[19]

---

[18] Water, Michel, Austria in *Copyright and Photographs: An International Survey*, Gendreau, Y, Nordemann and Oesch, R (eds) Kluwer Law Int. at p.50.
[19] *ibid.*, at 59.

## Bahrain[20]

## Law Decree No. (10) for 1993 in respect of the Protection of Copyrights

Art. (1)    An author is the person who prepares or creates a work in the field of literature, science or art, or any written or innovative work related to any branch of knowledge, and the work is attributed to him by having his name expressly mentioned on it, by using a pseudonym or by any other means whatsoever, unless there is evidence to the contrary.

Art. (2)1   This law shall protect the authors of innovative literary, scientific, artistic and cultural works in general, whatever the value, type, method of expression used in them or the purpose of their creation is.

2   The said protection shall include the authors of the following works: ... e) Paintings, sculpture, decoration, engraving and photography

Art. (3)1 ...   However, the rights to photographic works shall not result in prohibiting others from taking photographs of the photographed matter, even if the new photos were taken from the same place, and in general, in the same circumstances in which the first photographs were taken.

Art. (31)1   The work's protection period expires after fifty years according to the Gregorian Calendar have elapsed. 2. The work's protection period shall expire fifty years, according to the Gregorian Calendar have elapsed, as from the date of publication with respect to the following works: ... a) Cinematographic films, works of applied arts and photographs.

## Bangladesh

## The Copyright Ordinance 1962[21]

2.1—   In this Ordinance, unless there is anything repugnant in the subject or context...
(c) "artistic work" means:
(i) a painting, a sculpture, a drawing (including a diagram, map, chart or plan), an engraving or a photograph whether or not any such work possesses artistic quality

...   (zd) "photograph" includes photo-lithograph and any work produced by any process analogous to photography but does not include any part of a cinematographic work;

10(1)   Subject to the provisions of this section and to the other provisions of this Ordinance, copyright shall subsist throughout Bangladesh in the following classes of works, that is to say: ... (a) original literary, dramatic, musical and artistic works

Under s.20, copyright in photographs subsists until 50 years from the beginning of the calendar year next following the year in which the photograph is published unlike the normal term of life of the author plus 50 years.

---

[20] *http://www.agip.com/laws/bahrain/c.htm.*
[21] *http://www.unesco.org/culture/copy/copyright/bangladesh/fr_sommaire.html.* See n. 1, above.

## Barbados

### Copyright Act 1998[22]

2—(1)  For the purposes of this Act
...    "artistic work" means
(a) a graphic work, photograph, sculpture or collage, whether the work is of artistic quality or not,
...    "photograph" means a recording of light or other radiation on any medium on which an image is produced or from which an image may by any means be produced, and which is not part of a film;
...    "work" means (a) a literary, dramatic, musical or artistic work...

6(1)   Copyright is a property right which, subject to the provisions of this section, may subsist in the following categories of work:
(a)  original literary, dramatic, musical or artistic works;
(b)  sound recordings, films, broadcasts or cable programmes;
(c)  typographical arrangements of published editions and copyright may subsist in a work irrespective of its quality or the purpose for which it was created.

10(1)  Subject to the provisions of this section, copyright in any literary, dramatic, musical or artistic work exists for the life of the author and for the fifty calendar years following his death.

(2)   When copyright in a work referred to in subsection (1) is vested jointly in more than one author, the copyright exists for the life of the last surviving author and for fifty calendar years immediately following the year of his death.

(3)   Where the author of a work referred to in subsection (1) is unknown, copyright in that work exists for the fifty calendar years immediately following the year in which the work was first published; but if during that period the identity of the author is revealed, or his identity is no longer in doubt, copyright exists, for such period specified in subsection (1) or (2), as the circumstances require

(4)   Subsections (1) and (2) do not apply to a computer-generated work, the copyright in which expires at the end of the period of fifty calendar years following the calendar year in which the work was made.

(5)   This section does not apply to copyright that subsists by virtue of section 144.[23]

17     Subject to section 41, a person who for private and domestic purposes commissions the taking of a photograph or the making of a film has, where the resulting work is a protected work, the right not to have
(a)  copies of the work issued to the public;
(b)  the work exhibited or shown in public; or
(c)  the work broadcast or included in a cable programme service.

41     The right conferred by section 17 in relation to a commissioned photograph or film is infringed by a person who does or authorises the doing of any act mentioned in that section in relation to that work; but the right is not infringed by any act which, pursuant to Part V, would not be an infringement of the copyright in the work.

The 1998 Copyright Act of Barbados is very similar to the UK 1988 Act. Photographs have the same term of protection as any other work. This is a change from the previous Copyright Act 1981 of Barbados which provided that the basic term of copyright was life of the author plus 50 years.[24] Photographs were previously pro-

---

[22] *http://clea.wipo.int*
[23] Copyright owned by international organisations.
[24] Copyright Act of Barbados 1981, s.17.

tected for 50 years immediately following the year in which the work was first made available to the public.[25]

## Belgium

## Law on Copyright and Neighbouring Rights of June 30, 1994, as amended by the Law of April 3, 1995[26]

Art. 1—(1)    The author of a literary or artistic work alone shall have the right to reproduce his work or to have it reproduced in any manner or form whatsoever.

Art. 2—(1)    Copyright shall subsist for 70 years after the death of the author to the benefit of the person he has designated to such effect...

(5)    The term of protection for photographs that are original in that they constitute the author's own intellectual creation, shall be determined in accordance with the foregoing paragraphs.

Belgian copyright law is contained in two statutes; the Copyright Act 1994 and the Software Act 1995.[27] Belgium law exhibits the open and broad approach typical of civil law jurisdictions. Protection is given to "the author of a literary or artistic work"[28] and in applying the law courts require originality and creation.[29] A photograph is protected as an artistic work if original. Article 2(5) of the Belgium Copyright Act provides that photographs are:

"original in that they constitute the author's own intellectual creation"

which implements Art. 6 of the Term Directive.

Following a decision of the Supreme Court,[30] there is no longer a requirement that a photograph possess an artistic or aesthetic character to be protected as an artistic work.[31] Pictures of plants[32] and photographs illustrating a quiz in a multimedia game[33] have been protected.

Corbet & Strowel comment that the requirements of originality and creation continue to be based on open-ended notions and:

"As a result, future decisions are likely to follow sliding-scale analyses just like past case law in determining what copyright protects as well as the scope of that protection."[34]

---

[25] *ibid.*, s.21(1).
[26] *http://www.unesco.org/culture/copy/copyright/belgium/fr_sommaire.html*. See n. 1, above.
[27] Nimmer & Geller BEL §1[1].
[28] Art. 1, Belgium Copyright Act 1994, Nimmer & Geller BEL §2[1][b].
[29] *loc cit.*
[30] Cass, April 27, 1989, Pas., 1989 I 908, cited in Nimmer & Geller BEL 17 §2[2].
[31] *e.g.* Trib. Brussels September 21, 1990, Revue générale de droit civil, 1991/3, 292 and see other cases cited in Nimmer & Geller BEL 17 §2[2], n 25.
[32] Trib Brussels, November 12, 1993, J.L.M.B 1995 918 cited in Nimmer & Geller BEL 17 §2[2].
[33] Brussels May 2, 1996, A & M 1996 416 cited in Nimmer & Geller BEL 17 §2[2].
[34] In Nimmer & Geller BEL 16 §[2][1][b].

## Belize

### Copyright Act 2000 (Ch. 252) 22/06/2000, No. 12[35]

3(1)    For the purposes of this Act, unless the context otherwise requires "artistic work" means –
(a) a graphic work, photograph, sculpture or collage, irrespective of artistic quality;
...  "photograph" means a recording of light or other radiation on any medium on which an image is produced or from which an image may by any means be produced, and which is not part of a film;
...  "work" means—(a) a literary, dramatic, musical or artistic work...

7(1)    Subject to this section, the categories of works in which copyright under this Act may subsist are:
(a) original literary, dramatic, musical or artistic works...

10(1)   Subject to the provisions of this section, copyright in any literary, dramatic, musical or artistic work expires at the end of the period of fifty years from the end of the calendar year in which the author dies.

18      A person who for private and domestic purposes commissions the taking of a photograph or the making of a film shall have where the resulting work is a protected work, the right not to have
(a) copies of the work issued to the public;
(b) the work exhibited or shown in public; or
(c) the work broadcast or included in a cable programme service.

45      The right conferred by section 18 in relation to a commissioned photograph or film is infringed by a person who does or authorises the doing of any act mentioned in that section in relation to that work; but the right is not infringed by any of the following acts to the extent that pursuant to Part VI, such act would not infringe copyright in the work—
(a) the incidental inclusion of the work in an artistic work, film broadcast or cable programme (section 59);
(b) acts done for the purposes of parliamentary or judicial proceedings, or statutory enquiries (section 71).

## Benin

### Law on the Protection of Copyright which came into force March 15, 1984[36]

Art. 1.      The author of any original work of the mind, whether it be literary, artistic or scientific, shall enjoy in that work, by the mere fact of its creation, an exclusive, incorporeal property right which shall be enforceable against all persons

Art. 5        "Original work" shall mean a work whose characteristic elements and whose form, or whose form alone, enable its author to be distinguished

Art. 8        The following shall be deemed works of the mind within the meaning of this Law, whereby this list shall not be exhaustive ... (11) photographic works of an artistic or documentary nature, to which shall be assimilated for the purposes of this Law, those expressed by a process analogous to photography;

Art. 43(1)   Copyright shall last for the whole lifetime of the author and for fifty (50) calendar years after the end of the year of his death, with the exception of ... -photographic works and works of applied art for which the duration of protection shall expire twenty-five (25) years after the work has been made.

## Brazil

### The current statute is the Copyright Act Law No. 9610 of 1998[37]

Art. 7      The intellectual works that are protected are creations of the mind, whatever their mode of expression or the medium, tangible or intangible, known or susceptible of invention in the future, in which they are fixed, such as:
     ... (VII)   photographic works and other works produced by a process analogous to photography[38];

Art. 44      The economic rights in audiovisual and photographic works shall be protected for a period of 70 years from the first of January of the year following that of their disclosure.

Art. 48      Works permanently located in public places may be freely represented by painting, drawing, photography and audiovisual processes.
...

     Chapter IV Use of a Photographic Work

Art. 79      The author of a photographic work has the right to reproduce it and to offer it for sale, with due regard to the restrictions applicable to the display, reproduction and sale of portraits, and without prejudice to the author's rights in the work photographed in the case of a protected work of three-dimensional art.

     (1)      Any photograph shall legibly mention the name of" its author when used by third parties.

     (2)      Any reproduction of a photographic work that is not perfectly true to the original is prohibited unless previously authorized by the author.

The previous Copyright Act 1973 protected "creations of the mind".[39] An open list of protected works provided in Art. 6(vii) for

"photographic works and works produced by any process analagous to photography, provided that by reason of the selection of subject matter and of the conditions of execution, they may be considered artistic creations".[40]

Creative features were thus required for protection.

## Bulgaria

### Copyright and Neighbouring Rights Act No. 56/29.06. 1993[41]

Art. 3(1)      Any literary, artistic and scientific work resulting from a creative endeavour and expressed by any mode and in any objective form shall be the object of copyright such as
     ... 7.    photographic works to which are assimilated works expressed by a process analogous to photography;

---

[37] Nimmer & Geller SA1.
[38] http://www.unesco.org/culture/copy/copyright/brazil/fr_sommaire.html. See n. 1, above.
[39] Nimmer & Geller BRA-8 §2[1][a].
[40] Nimmer & Geller BRA-10 §2[2].
[41] *http://clea.wipo.int.*

Art. 13      Copyright over works of fine art or photography constituting a portrait of a person different from the author shall belong to the author. The author may negotiate with the person who appears on the portrait the terms of the use of such works.

Art. 27(1)   Copyright shall be protected for the life of the author and seventy years after his death. (Amended SG. No. 28/2000)

Photographs are, following the 2000 amendment, protected for 70 yrs pma. This is a change from the previous law. Prior to the 1993 Act, the 1951 Law Decree No. 207 provided that copyright in works of applied art and artistic photography extended for 25 years for each publication, phonogram or program, from January 1 of the year following the year of first publication. This contrasted to 50 yrs pma for other works. The 1951 Decree also provided that the copyright in works of artistic photography or works expressed by a process analogous to photography were protected only if the name of the author is indicated on each copy as well as the place and year of publication. The words "artistic photography" imply that non-creative works were not protected unde the 1951 Decree.

## Burkina Faso

## Ordinance Affording Protection to Copyright

Art. 1       The authors of original intellectual works, literary, artistic and scientific, shall enjoy protection of their works in accordance with the provisions of this Ordinance ... Works shall be protected irrespective of their value and purpose.

Art. 6       Intellectual works, literary, artistic and scientific, within the meaning of his Ordinance, shall include, in particular: ... (h) photographic works of artistic or documentary character, including works expressed by a process analogous to photography;

Art. 16      Works of art, including works of architecture permanently located in a public place, may be reproduced and made accessible to the public by means of cinematography, photography or television.

The term of protection is life of the author plus 50 years.[42] There is no separate term for photographs

## Burundi

## Copyright Statute Decree-Law No. 1/9 Regulating the Rights of Authors and Intellectual Property in Burundi (Law No. 119) of May 4, 1978[43]

Art. 2       The provisions of this Decree-Law protect the rights of authors of all intellectual works, regardless of their kind, form of expression, merit or purpose. The following in particular shall be considered intellectual works within the meaning of this Decree-Law ... photographic works of an artistic or documentary character, and works of the same character produced by a process analogous to photography

---

[42] Art. 39.
[43] *http://www.unesco.org/culture/copy/copyright/burundi/fr_sommaire.html.* See n. 1, above.

The basic term of protection is life of the author plus 50 years. There are no separate provisions for photographs.

## Cameroon

## Law No. 2000/011 of December 19, 2000 on Copyright and Neighbouring Rights[44]

2     For the implementation of this law and subsequent statutory instruments arising therefrom
    1. "original work" shall mean one which, by virtue of its characteristics or expression, can be differentiated from previous works;

3(1)     This law shall protect all literary or artistic works, irrespective of the mode, worth, genre or purpose of the expression, notably
    ... (j) photographic works including works expressed by a process similar to photography.

(2)     Copyright shall relate to the expression through which ideas are described, explained and illustrated. It shall cover the distinctive features of works, such as the plan of a literary work insofar as it is materially linked to the expression.

(3)     This law shall protect only expressions or original distinctive features resulting from a creation.

7(1)     The author shall be the individual who created a literary or artistic work. The author shall equally be the individual who designed the work and initiated its realization by an automatic process.

(2)     The author of a work protected by virtue of this law shall be the holder of the copyright in the said work.

(3)     The work shall be deemed to be created independently of any disclosure, solely from the personal though incomplete realization of the design, even where such design is incomplete. A photographic work or any other work resulting from a realization through an automatic process shall be considered as a created work.

37(1)     The patrimonial rights of an author shall last for his lifetime. They shall subsist after his death throughout the current calendar year and for the next fifty years. They shall also subsist for all his successors or rightful claimants during the year of the death of the last surviving co-author plus fifty years for joint works.

The following extract from the earlier statute is included for historical interest.

## Law No. 82–18 to Regulate Copyright of November 26, 1982[45]

s.2     Literary and artistic works shall comprise all original works in the literary, artistic and scientific fields regardless of the means and form of their expression. They shall include in particular: ... (xi) artistic or documentary photographic works, including works with like modes of expressions

s.4     Under the present law, the undermentioned terms and definitions shall apply
    (i) "original work": work whose characteristics and form give its author a particular identity

s.33     Subject to abiding by the legal provisions in force, works of art including works of architecture permanently erected in public places may be repro-

---

[44] *http://clea.wipo.int/*.
[45] *http://www.unesco.org/culture/copy/copyright/cameroon/fr_sommaire.html*. See n. 1, above.

duced and made available to the public by means of photography, cinematography or television

Under s.40(3) the term of protection for photographs was for 50 years with effect
from the calendar year in which the work was lawfully made available to the public.
This is a shorter period than most other works which are protected under s.40(2) for
life of the author plus 50 years. This distinction was removed in the 2000 Act.

## Canada

### Copyright Act 1924 as amended[46]

2. In this Act,
   "artistic work" includes ... photographs...
   "every original literary, dramatic, musical and artistic work" includes every
   original production in the literary, scientific or artistic domain,
   whatever may be the mode or form of its expression, such as compilations, books, pamphlets and other
   "photograph" includes photo-lithograph and any work expressed by any
   process analogous to photography;

5(1)   Subject to this Act, copyright shall subsist in Canada, for the term hereinafter mentioned, in every original literary, dramatic, musical and artistic
   work...

6   The term for which copyright shall subsist shall, except as otherwise
   expressly provided by this Act, be the life of the author, the remainder of the
   calendar year in which the author dies, and a period of fifty years following
   the end of that calendar year.

10(1)   Where the owner referred to in subsection (2) is a corporation, the term for
   which copyright subsists in a photograph shall be the remainder of the year
   of the making of the initial negative or plate from which the photograph was
   derived or, if there is no negative or plate, of the initial photograph, plus a
   period of fifty years.

(1.1)   Where the owner is a corporation, the majority of the voting shares of which
   are owned by a natural person who would have qualified as the author of the
   photograph except for subsection (2), the term of copyright is the term set
   out in section 6.

(2)   The person who
   (a) was the owner of the initial negative or other plate at the time when that
       negative or other plate was made, or
   (b) was the owner of the initial photograph at the time when that photo-
       graph was made, where there was no negative or other plate,
   is deemed to be the author of the photograph and, where that owner is a
   body corporate, the body corporate is deemed for the purposes of this Act to
   be ordinarily resident in a treaty country if it has established a place of
   business therein.

**Commentary:**[47]   The UK Copyright Act 1911 provided the model for the 1924
Copyright Act of Canada which was heavily amended and underpins the present
statute which was consolidating. British case law is regularly cited in Canadian
courts, but French jurisprudence also has an influence in Quebec courts and in the
Federal court.[48] Copyright subsists in "every original, literary, dramatic, musical and

---

[46] *http://www.unesco.org/culture/copy/copyright/canada/fr_sommaire.html.* See n. 1, above.
[47] See also Gendreau, Y, *Canada in Copyright and Photographs: An International Survey*,
Gendreau, Y, Nordemann and Oesch, R (eds) Kluwer Law Int. at p.99.
[48] Nimmer & Geller CAN-9 §1[1][b].

artistic work".[49] Only "original" works are protected.[50] "Artistic work" is defined to include photographs.[51] Vaver states that photographs should be protected whether or not any aesthetic intention was present so long as the work falls within the ordinary meaning of the category term.[52]

From 1994 the definition of photograph includes photolithograph and any work "expressed" by any process analogous to photography.[53] The 1994 amendment replaced the previous definition "produced" by any analagous process with "expressed".

A work must be the product of more than negligible skill, judgment taste and labour in its creation. For example, the arrangement of information in a yellow-pages telephone directory was denied protection as originality implied ingenuity or creativity—mere work was not enough.[54]

Previously, photographs had a different term of protection from other works and were only protected for 50 years from the making of the initial photograph or the negative or other plate from which the photograph was derived. That has now been altered as above so that the normal term is 50 yrs pma save where the owner is a corporation in which case the term is 50 years from the making of the photograph or negative. However, where the majority of the voting shares in a corporation are owned by a person who is the author of the photograph, the term of protection is 50 yrs pma.

## Chile

## The relevant statute is the Copyright Act Law No. 17.336 on Copyright as amended up to February 22, 1990

| | |
|---|---|
| Art. 1 | The present law protects the rights that authors of intellectual works in the literary, artistic and scientific domains acquire by the sole fact of creation of the work, whatever its form of expression, and such neighbouring rights as the law may specify. |
| Art. 3 | The following are specially protected by virtue of the present law: ... (7) Photographs, engravings and lithographs; |
| Art. 34 | The photographer has the exclusive right to reproduce, display, publish and sell his photographs, with the exception of those made by virtue of a contract, in which case the said right belongs to the person who ordered the work, without prejudice to the provisions of Article 24(1) (c). Assignment of the negative or like means of reproduction of the photograph implies assignment of the exclusive right recognise by this Article. |
| Art. 35 | In order to enjoy the protection referred to above, copies of photographs must bear the following indications: (1) The name of the photographer or of the person who ordered the work; (2) The year of reproduction of the photograph; (3) The name of the author of the work of art photographed, if there be one; and (4) The words "Prohibida la reproduccion". When the copy of the photograph does not bear the above particulars, it may be freely reproduced. |

---

[49] Copyright Act R.S.C. 1985, ch. C-42.
[50] Copyright Act R.S.C. 1985, ch. C-42, s.5(1) Nimmer & Geller CAN-13 §2[1][b].
[51] Copyright Act R.S.C. 1985, ch. C-42, s.2 Nimmer & Geller CAN-21 §2[2][d].
[52] David Vaver in Nimmer & Geller CAN-21 §2[2][d].
[53] Copyright Act R.S.C. 1985, ch. C-42, s.2 as modified by NAFTA implementation act S.C. 1993, ch.44, s.23(2) Nimmer & Geller CAN-22 §2[2][d].
[54] *Tele-Direct (Publications) Inc v American Business Information Inc* (1997) 76 CPR (3d) 296, 303–304 (Fed. CA).

Art. 43    The reproduction of works of architecture by means of photographs, cinematography, television and any other analogous process, as well as the publication of corresponding photographs in newspapers, magazines and school textbooks, is free and is not subject to remuneration in respect of copyright.

Art. 44    All monuments and, in general, artistic works that adorn public squares, avenues and places may be freely reproduced by means of photography, drawing, or any other process. Publication and sale of such reproductions is lawful.

Art. 45    The rules established by Articles 30 and 35 do not apply to films and photographs designed for purposes of publicity or propaganda.

Protection term is life of the author plus 30 years. No special term for photographs.

## China

## Copyright Act 1990[55]

Art. 1    This Law is enacted, in accordance with the Constitution, for the purposes of protecting the copyright of authors in their literary, artistic and scientific works and the rights related to copyright, of encouraging the creation and dissemination of works which would contribute to the construction of socialist spiritual and material civilization, and of promoting the development and flourishing of socialist culture and sciences

Art. 3    For the purposes of this Law, the term "works" includes works of literature, art, natural science, social science, engineering technology and the like which are expressed in the following forms: ... (4) works of fine art and photographic works

Under Art. 21 the basic term of protection for an author is the lifetime of the author and 50 years after his death, expiring on December 31 of the 50th year after his death. Photographic works are protected for 50 years, expiring on December 31 of the 50th year after the first publication of such work, provided that any such work that has not been published within 50 years after the completion of its creation shall no longer be protected under this Law.

The first Chinese copyright statute was the Copyright Act of September 7, 1990, which came into effect on June 1, 1991.[56] The Chinese Copyright Act 1990 protects works created by the author. The term works refers to "creations" in literary, artistic and scientific domains.[57] Works are required to be original in the sense of the author's own intellectual activities, but there is no requirement that a work must have any merit.[58] Article 3 defines works as protecting "works of literature, art, natural science, social science, engineering, technology and the like which are expressed in the following form ..." Nine categories are identified in Art. 3 which are further defined in regulations.[59] "Works of fine art and photographic works" are included. Photographic works are those created by recording images on light sensitive material with the aid of devices.[60]

---

[55] http://www.unesco.org/culture/copy/copyright/china/fr_sommaire.html. See n. 1, above.
[56] Nimmer & Geller CHI-5 §1[1].
[57] Nimmer & Geller CHI-17 §2[1][b].
[58] *loc cit.*
[59] Nimmer & Geller CHI-18 §2[2].
[60] Nimmer & Geller CHI-19 §2[2].

## Colombia[61]

| | |
|---|---|
| Art. 2 | Copyright shall subsist in scientific, literary and artistic works, which shall be understood as being all creations of the mind in the scientific, literary and artistic domain, whatever may be their mode or form of expression and purpose, such as ... photographic works to which are assimilated works expressed by a process analogous to photography ... and finally, any production in the scientific, literary or artistic field that can be reproduced or executed by any form of printing or reproduction, or by phonographic, radiophonic or any other known or future means. |
| Art. 8 | For the purposes of this Law:<br>(a) "artistic, scientific and literary works" means, among other things books, musical works, pictures in oils, water colour or pastel, drawings, woodcuts, calligraphic and chrysographic works, works produced by cutting, engraving, damascening, etc., in metal, stone, wood or other materials, statues, reliefs, sculptures, artistic photographs, mimed or other choreographic works; (emphasis added) |
| Art. 39 | It shall be permissible to reproduce, by painting, drawing, photography or cinematography, works that are permanently located on public highways, streets or squares, and to distribute such reproductions or works and communicate them to the public. With regard to works of architecture, this provision shall be applicable solely to outward views. |
| Art. 89 | The author of a photographic work that has sufficient artistic merit to be protected by this Law shall have the right to reproduce, distribute and display it and place it on sale, subject to the limitations of the foregoing Articles and without prejudice to the copyright in the case of photographs of other works of figurative art. Any print or reproduction of the photograph shall bear, visibly printed on it, the name of the author and the year in which it was made. |
| Art. 90 | The publication of photographs or cinematograph films of surgical operations, or other fixations of scientific character, shall be authorized by the patient or his heirs or by the surgeon or head of the medical team concerned. |

Photographs are protected as artistic works for the life of the author plus 80 years and are not subject to a separate term.

## Costa Rica

## Law No. 6683 on Copyright and Related Rights as last amended by Law No. 7979 of January 31, 2000[62]

| | |
|---|---|
| Art. 1 | Original intellectual products confer on their authors the rights to which this Law relates. The authors of literary and artistic works shall be the ov [sic] economic and moral rights therein."Literary and artistic works" shall be taken all productions in the literary and artistic domain whatever the form of expression thereof, such as ... photographic works and works expressed by a process analogous to photography |

---

[61] Translation from *http://www.unesco.org/culture/copy/copyright/colombia/fr_sommaire.html*. See n. 1, above.
[62] *http://www.unesco.org/culture/copy/copyright/costarica/fr_sommaire.html*. See n. 1, above.

Art. 71      It shall be lawful to make reproductions by photographic or other pictorial processes of statues, monuments and other works of art acquired by the authorities that are displayed in streets, parks and museums.

Period of protection is life of the author plus 70 years.[63] There is no special term for photographs.

## Côte d'Ivoire

## Law No. 96–564 of July 25, 1996 on the Protection of Intellectual Works and the Rights of Authors, Performers and Phonogram and Videogram Producers[64]

Art. 1       The term "intellectual work" means any creation or production in the literary, artistic or scientific field, regardless of its mode of expression, as specified in Article 6.

Art. 6       The protection of the rights of authors applies to all original works, regardless of the genre, merit, purpose or manner or form of expression thereof,including: ... 11.photographic works of artistic or documentary character, to which, for the purposes of this Law, works expressed by a process analogous to photography are assimilated;

Under Art. 45(3)(a) the term of protection for photographs is 99 years following the end of the calendar year in the course of which the work was lawfully made available to the public. Photographs are treated differently from other works—the standard term is life of the author plus 99 years under Art. 45(1).

## Croatia

## Copyright Law of 30 June 1999[65]

Art. 3       Unless otherwise provided in this Law, a creation in the literary, scientific or artistic field or in any other field of creation, whatever may be the kind, method or form of expression thereof, shall be considered an author's work.
             The following, in particular, shall be considered authors" works:...
             – photographic works and works produced by a process analogous to photography;

Art. 81      Authors" economic rights shall last during the author's life and seventy years after his death, and if such rights belong jointly to the collaborators in the creation of the author's work, this term shall be counted from the death of the last deceased collaborator.
             years respectively as from the creation a computer program.

...          The terms referred to in this Article shall begin with January 1 of the year following immediately the year in which the author died, or as the case may be, the year in which the work was published or created respectively.

---

[63] Art. 58.
[64] *http://www.unesco.org/culture/copy/copyright/coteivoire/fr_sommaire.html.* See n. 1, above.
[65] Republic of Croatia, State Intellectual Property Office: *http://public.srce.hr/patent/eng/nn/ autor.html.*

There are no special provisions for photographs and the normal term of copyright being 70 yrs pma applies.

## Cuba

## Relevant statute is the Copyright Act (No. 14): December 28, 1977[66]

Art. 1    This Law has for its object to provide due protection for copyright in the Republic of Cuba in harmony with the interests, objectives and principles of our Socialist Republic.

Art. 2    Copyright regulated by this Law refers to scientific, artistic, literary and educational works of an original character, which have been or may be brought to public knowledge by any lawful means, whatever their form of expression, their contents, their value or purpose.

Art. 7    The scientific, artistic, literary and educational works to which reference is made in Article 2 are those which involve creative activity on the part of their authors, basically: ... (h) photographic works and works of similar character;

Art. 22   Copyright in respect of a photographic work or in respect of a work created by a process analogous to photography is only recognized if every copy is duly identified in accordance with established regulations.

Art. 47   The period in which copyright in respect of a photographic work or a work created by a process analogous to photography, or in respect of a work of applied art, continues for ten years from the utilization of the work.

## Cyprus

## The Copyright Laws 1976 to 1993 (Law No. 59, of December 3, 1976, as last amended by Law No. 18(1), 1993)[66a]

2—(1)   In this Law, unless the context otherwise requires ... "artistic work" means, irrespective of artistic quality, any of the following, or works similar thereto ...
(d) photographs not comprised in a cinematograph film; "photograph" means the product of photography or of any other process akin to photography other than a part of a cinematographic film;

3(1)    Subject to the provisions of this section, copyright shall subsist in the following works ... (f) photographs;

(2)    No copyright shall subsist in a literary, musical or artistic work unless it is of an original character, and has been reduced to writing, audio recorded, recorded in any way by electronic or other means or has otherwise been reduced to some material form.

By s.4(2) the term of copyright for photographs is 50 years from first publication. The basic term for core works is life of the author plus 50 years.

Previously, the UK Copyright Act 1911 was in force in Cyprus. In some ways this Act is similar to earlier UK legislation in that it provides that the author of a

---

[66] *http://www.unesco.org/culture/copy/copyright/cuba/fr_sommaire.html.* See n. 1, above.
[66a] See the WIPO CLEA database at *http://clea.wipo.int/.* This statute was further amended by Law No. 12(1) of February 2001, but an official English translation was not available on that site at the time of writing.

photograph is the person who, at the time when the photograph is taken, is the owner of the material on which it is taken.[67]

## Czech Republic

## Law No. 121/2000 Coll. of April 7, 2000 on Copyright, Rights Related to Copyright and on the Amendment of Certain Laws (Copyright Act)

| | |
|---|---|
| Art. 2(1) | The subject of copyright shall be a literary work or other work of art or a scientific work which are the unique outcome of the creative activity of the author and are expressed in any objectively perceivable manner including electronic form, permanent or temporary irrespective of their scope, purpose or significance(henceforth referred to as "work"). A work shall be namely a literary work expressed by speech or in writing ... a photographic work and a work produced by a process similar to photography ... |
| (2) | A computer program shall also be considered a work if it is original in the sense of being the author's own intellectual creation; a database shall be considered a work if due to the manner of its selection or arrangement of its content it is the author's own intellectual creation; a photograph which is original in the sense of the first clause shall be protected as a photographic work. |
| Art. 37(2) | Copyright shall not be infringed by whoever |
| | ... (2)   makes a reproduction of a photographic work which is his own portrait and has been commissioned for a charge. |

Photographic works are now protected for the same basic term as other works, namely life of the author and 70 years after his death.[67a] Under the previous Law of 1965, the term of protection was life of the author plus 50 years. Unlike the previous law, the Law of 2000 specifically requires a photograph to be original in the sense of being the author's own intellectual creation. The comparable parts of the Law of 1965 are quoted below for historical interest:

## Law No. 35 of March 25, 1965, on Literary, Scientific and Artistic Works (Copyright Law)(as last amended by Law No. 86 of March 14, 1996)[68]

| | |
|---|---|
| Art. 2(1) | Copyright shall subsist in literary, scientific and artistic works that are the result of the creative activity of authors, particularly literary, theatrical and musical works and works of fine art, including works of architecture and applied art, and cinematographic, photographic and cartographic work. |
| Art. 15(1) | The use of an idea contained in another person's work for the creation of a new original work shall not infringe copyright. |
| (2) | The author's consent to use of his work shall not be required and the obligation to pay remuneration shall not apply to a person who... |
| | (f)   adapts a work of art located in a public place to other branches of art; photographs of a work of art thus located may also be reproduced and distributed without the consent of the author; ... |

---

[67] s.2(1).
[67a] Art. 27(1).
[68] *http://www.unesco.org/culture/copy/copyright/czech/fr_sommaire.html*. See n. 1, above.

(iii)   reproduces or has reproduced for his own personal use or for free distribution, a photographic work which portrays him and which was commissioned for payment;

. . .

(6)   The right to protection of authorship shall not be limited in time.

Art. 2(1) of the 1965 Copyright Law defined protected works as "literary, scientific, and artistic works which are the result of their authors" creative activity."[69] Photographic works are protected only if they display individuality as the photographer's expression, even in the case of reportage and documentary photographs.[70]

Under Art. 33 of the Law of 1965 photographs were subject to the same basic term of protection as other works—namely life of the author plus 50 years.

## Democratic Republic of the Congo

## Law on Copyright and Neighbouring Rights Law No. 24/82 of July 7, 1982[71]

Art. 6   Authors of original literary, artistic and scientific works shall be entitled to protection of their works in accordance with the intellectual and moral rights and with the economic rights laid down by this Law.

Art. 7   Literary, artistic and scientific works shall comprise: . . . -photographic works of an artistic or documentary nature, to which are assimilated, for the purposes of this Law, works expressed by a process analogous to photography;

Art. 8   Works shall be protected irrespective of their quality, their purpose, their mode or their form of expression, without being subject to any formality.

Under Art. 65 photographs are protected for 25 years as from the making of the work, this is considerably shorter than the general term of life of the author plus 50 years.[72]

## Denmark

## Consolidated Act No. 164 of March 12, 2003[73]

s.1—(1)   The person creating a literary or artistic work shall have copyright therein, be it expressed in writing or in speech as a fictional or a descriptive representation, or whether it be a musical or dramatic work, cinematographic or photographic work, or a work of fine art, architecture, applied art, or expressed in some other manner.

s.63—(1)   The copyright in a work shall last for 70 years after the year of the author's death . . .

s.70—(1)   The person who produces a photographic picture (the photographer) shall enjoy the exclusive right to make copies of it and make it available to the public.

---

[69] Nimmer & Geller CZE-7 §2[2].
[70] Nimmer & Geller CZE-8 §2[3].
[71] *http://www.unesco.org/culture/copy/copyright/congo/fr_sommaire.html.* See n. 1, above.
[72] Art. 61.
[73] *http://www.unesco.org/culture/copy/copyright/denmark/fr_sommaire.html.* See n. 1, above.

(2)      The rights in a photographic picture shall last until 50 years have elapsed from the end of the year in which the picture was taken.

(3)      The provisions of Section 2(2)[74] and (3), Sections 3, 7, 9 and 11, Section 12(1) and (2)(iv) Sections 13 to 16, Section 17(3), Section 18(1) and (2), Section 19(1) and (2), Sections 20, 21 and 23, Section 24(1) and (2), Sections 25, 27, 28, 30, 31 and Sections 33 to 35, Section 36(2), and Sections 39 to 47 and 49 to 58, and Sections 60 to 62 shall apply correspondingly to photographic pictures. If a photographic picture is subject to copyright according to Section 1, such rights may also be enforced.

There is a distinction between photographic pictures (*i.e.* non-copyright works) and photographic works.[75] Section 70 grants to "simple" photographs the same rights as for photographic works but by s.70(2) the term of protection is 50 years from the taking of the picture rather than 70 yrs pma.

## Djibouti

## Law No. 114/96/3rd L on the Protection of Copyright[76]

Art. 1      The author of an intellectual work enjoys in that work, by virtue of the mere fact of its creation, an exclusive incorporeal property right that is enforceable against all persons

Art. 3      The following in particular shall be considered intellectual works within the meaning of this Law: ... (9) photographic works, to which works expressed by a process analogous to photography are assimilated for the purposes of this Law...

Under Art. 63 photographs are protected for 25 years following the making of the work which is shorter than the standard protection of life plus 25 years.

---

[74] The listed sections are respectively: 2(2) (recording of the work on devices capable of reproducing considered copies); 2(3) (making work available to public); 3 (conditions for reproduction); 7 (signature presumption of authorship); 8 (definition of making work public); 9 (public document); 11 (limitations on authors rights); 12(1) (entitlement to make single copy for private use of public works); 12(2)(iv) (single copy entitlement prohibits copying digitized works); 13–16 (exception reproduction in education, hospitals, archives etc); 17(3) (government and other reproductions for handicapped); 18(1)(2) (use in anthologies after five years from publication excluding educational use); 19 (distribution of copies); 20, 21, 23 (exhibitions, public perf, etc.); 24(1), (2)(inclusion in art sale catalogues & reproduction of permanently public works); 25 (reporting current events); 27 (demand of works lodged with administrative authority; 28 (judicial proceedings); 29 (altering articles for everyday use); 30, 33–35 (radio and television use provisions & broadcasting); 36(2) (backup copies etc of works in digitised form); 39–47 (remuneration for private use); 49(1) (limitation period for remuneration claims); 50(1) (extended collective licence provisions); 60–62 (author cannot exercise rights in commissioned portraits without consent of commissioner; inheritance and creditor proceedings).

[75] For further discussion of the law in Denmark see Oesch, R, *Nordic Countries* in *Copyright and Photographs: An International Survey*, Gendreau, Y, Nordemann and Oesch, R (ed.s) Kluwer Law Int. at p.231.

[76] *http://www.unesco.org/culture/copy/copyright/djibouti/fr_page1.html.* See n. 1, above.

## Dominican Republic

The current law is Law No. 65–00 on Copyright, August 2000.[76a]

The previous act was the Copyright Statute (No.32–86) of July 4, 1986.[77]

| | |
|---|---|
| Art. 2 | Copyright and neighbouring rights shall subsist in literary and artistic works, as well as in the literary and artistic forms of scientific works, including all creations of the mind in the domains mentioned, whatever may be their mode or form of fixation or communication and their purpose, including but not confined to ... photographic works to which are assimilated works expressed by a process analogous to photography ... and, finally, any production in the literary or artistic field or any literary or artistic expression in the scientific field that can be reproduced or fixed by any form of printing or reproduction, or by phonographic, radiophonic, photocopying, microfilming or any other known or future means. |
| Art. 26 | In the case of photographs, copyright shall last for 10 years from the date of their first publication or public exhibition |
| Art. 32 | Any article, photograph, illustration and commentary concerning a current event, published by the press or broadcast by radio or television, may be reproduced insofar as this has not been expressly prohibited. |
| Art. 38 | Works that are permanently located on public highways, streets or squares may be reproduced by painting, drawing, photography or cinematography and such reproductions or works may be distributed and communicated to the public. In the case of works or architecture this provision shall apply solely to their external aspect. |
| Art. 53 | The author of a photographic work or a work obtained by a process analogous to photography, when such works possess sufficient artistic merit to enjoy protection under this Law, shall have the exclusive right to reproduce, distribute, display and put on sale the work in question, subject to the limitations laid down in this Law and without prejudice to the copyright in the case of photographs of other works of figurative art. |
| Art. 54 | In order to enjoy the protection provided for in the preceding Article, any print or reproduction of the photograph or the work obtained by any process analogous to photography shall bear, visibly printed on it, the name of the author and the place and date of its execution |
| Art. 55 | Publication of photographs or cinematographic films of surgical operations, or other fixations of a scientific character, shall be authorized by the patient or his heirs or by the surgeon or head of the medical team concerned. |

## Ecuador

Intellectual Property Law 08/05/1998 No. 83[78]

| | |
|---|---|
| 8 | Copyright protection shall cover all works of the mind in the literary or artistic field, regardless of their type, form of expression, merit or purpose. The right |

---

[76a] No English translation was available online at the time of writing.
[77] *http://www.unesco.org/culture/copy/copyright/dominicanrepublic/fr_sommaire.html.* See n. 1, above.
[78] *http://clea.wipo.int/.*

recognized by this Title shall be independent of the ownership of the material object in which the work is embodied, and their enjoyment and exercise shall not be subject to the requirement of registration or compliance with any other formality

Protected works shall include the following among other things:

... (i) photographic works and works expressed by processes analogous to photography;

41    The author of a photographic work or the taker of an ordinary photograph of a person must have the authorization of the person photographed, or after his death that of his successors in title, for the exercise of his copyright or related rights, as the case may be. The authorization shall be in writing and shall refer specifically to the type of use of the likeness that has been authorized. Nevertheless, use of the image shall be lawful where it has been taken in the normal course of public events and serves cultural or information purposes, or takes place in connection with news or events in the public interest.

The exceptions provided for in the foregoing paragraph shall not affect the copyright in the work of which the image forms part.

80    Economic rights shall last for the lifetime of the author and for 70 years following his death, regardless of the country of origin of the work ...

103    Any person who takes an ordinary photograph or by means of a comparable process makes another fixation that does not have the character of a photographic work shall enjoy the exclusive right to effect, authorize or prohibit the reproduction, distribution and communication to the public thereof on the same conditions as the creators of photographic works. This right shall last for 25 years counted from the first day of the year following the date of the making, disclosure or publication, as the case may be.

    The general period of protection is life of the author plus 70 years.[79] An "ordinary" photograph being not a protected work, has a shorter term of protection for 25 years from January 1, following the date of making, disclosure or publication.

## Egypt

## Law No. 82 of 2002 Pertaining to the Protection of Intellectual Property Rights[79a]

Part III

Copyrights and Neighboring Rights

Art. 138    The following terms shall in the application of the provisions of the Law herein, be deemed to have the following meaning: –

        1—Work:    Any innovated[80] work, in the literary, artistic or scientific domain whatever the type, manner of expression, significance or purpose of classification thereof is.

        2—Creativity:    The element of innovation that bestows authenticity upon the work.

Art. 140    The rights of the authors to their literary and artistic works shall be protected by the law herein, and particularly the following works ...

10- Photographic works and analogous works. Protection shall include the title of the work, provided that such title is innovated.

---

[79] Art. 88.

[79a] For observations regarding the translation of the word "innovated" see above at para. 3–078, n. 72a.

[80] *http://www.agip.com/laws/egypt/c.htm*

| Art. 160 | The protection term for financial rights of the Author granted by the law herein shall be the life of the author and fifty years calculated from the author's death. |
|---|---|
| Art. 178 | Any person taking a photograph of another, may not publish, exhibit or distribute the original or copies thereof, without permission therefrom or from all persons appearing in the photograph, unless otherwise agreed upon. Nevertheless, the photograph may be published: i) In an incident that has publicly taken place; ii) If the photograph is related to official, public characters, or national or international celebrities; or iii) If the competent Public Authorities have permitted such publication for the public welfare;Provided that the exhibition or circulation of the photograph, in such cases, shall not be prejudicial to the honor, reputation or recognition of such person. The person appearing in such photograph may authorize the publication thereof in press and other publication means, even if the photographer did not permit such publication; unless otherwise agreed upon.Such provisions shall apply to photographs, whatever the manner of taking such photographs, including drawing, engraving or any other manner. |

Egypt used to have a type of neighbouring right for non-original photographic works under its previous law No. 354 of June 24, 1954 (amended by Law (No. 34): June 17, 1975). (There were further amendments in 1993 (Law No:38) to include protection of computer programs and in 1994 to amend computer software duration period.)[81]

| Art. (1) | Any intellectual production, whatever its type, form and method of expression are, and whatever its value and intention are, shall entitle its originator to a right called copyright which shall be determined and protected according to the provisions of this order. |
|---|---|
| Art. (2) | The works which shall be protected by copyright shall be the following: ... 9- Works of photography, and works obtained in a manner similar to photography. |
| Art. (3) | ... However, the rights of the author of a photographic work do not exclude the right of any other person to take further photographs of the same object, even when such further photographs are taken from the same standpoint or under the same general conditions as the first photograph was taken |
| Art.(20) | Without prejudice to the provisions of Article 8, the rights of pecuniary exploitation specified in Articles 5, 6 and 7 shall terminate fifty years after the death of the author. However, insofar as [concerns photographic and cinematographic works having no original character, and limited to a simple mechanical reproduction of scenes, the said rights shall terminate upon the expiration of fifteen years from first publication of the work.] |

## El Salvador

## Law on the Promotion and Protection of Intellectual Property (Decree No. 604 of July 15, 1993)[82]

| Art. 4 | The author of a literary, artistic or scientific work shall have an exclusive property right in it called copyright |
|---|---|

---

[81] http://www.agip.com/laws/egypt/d.htm.
[82] *http://www.unesco.org/culture/copy/copyright/elsalvador/fr_sommaire.html*. See n. 1, above.

| | |
|---|---|
| Art. 12 | This Law shall protect works of the mind expressed in tangible form, whatever the means or form of expression, merit or purpose thereof, provided that the said works have the character of intellectual or personal creations, that is, originality. |
| Art. 13 | The creations referred to in the foregoing Article shall include all literary, scientific and artistic works, such as books, pamphlets and writings of whatever nature and length, including ... photographs, lithographs and engravings ... all other works that by analogy may be considered included within the same generic categories as the works specified.[83] |

The term of protection is life of the author plus 50 years[84]. There is no special term for photographs.

## Estonia

## Copyright Law (of November 11, 1992) as amended up to November 18, 2002[85]

| | |
|---|---|
| s.1(1) | The purpose of the Copyright Act is to ensure the consistent development of culture and protection of cultural achievements, the development of copyright-based industries and international trade, and to create favourable conditions for authors, performers, producers of phonograms, broadcasting organisations, producers of first fixations of films, makers of databases and other persons specified in this Act for the creation and use of works and other cultural achievements. |
| (2) | The Copyright Act provides for: (1) the protection of a specific right (copyright) of authors of literary, artistic and scientific works for the results of their creative activity ... |
| s.4(1) | Copyright subsists in literary, artistic and scientific works. |
| (2) | For the purposes of this Act, "works" means any original results in the literary, artistic or scientific domain which are expressed in an objective form and can be perceived and reproduced in this form either directly or by means of technical devices. A work is original if it is the author's own intellectual creation. |
| (3) | Works in which copyright subsists are: ... 17. photographic works and works expressed by a process analogous to photography, slides and slide films... |
| (4) | The author shall also enjoy copyright in the results of intermediate stages of the creation of his work (sketches, drafts, plans, drawings, chapters, etc.), if these are in compliance with the provisions of subsection (2) of this Section. |
| s.5 | This Act does not apply to: ... 6. news of the day; 7. mere facts and data |
| s.20 | It is permitted, without the authorisation of the author and without payment of remuneration, to reproduce works of architecture, works of visual art, works of applied art or photographic works which are permanently located in places open to the public by any means except for mechanical contact copying, and to communicate such reproductions of works to the public except if the work is the main subject of the reproduction and it is intended to be used for direct commercial pur- |

---

[83] Also includes "models or creations that have artistic value in the field of clothing, furniture, decoration, ornamentation, hairdressing and jewellery or precious objets".

[84] Art. 86.

[85] *http://www.unesco.org/culture/copy/copyright/estonia/fr_sommaire.html.* See n. 1, above.

poses. If the work specified in this section carries the name of its author, it shall be indicated in communicating the reproduction to the public.

The basic copyright term is life of the author plus 70 years under s.38. Prior to the 1999 amendment, the copyright term was life of the author plus 50 years. Photographs previously had a shorter term of protection of 50 years after the work has been lawfully made available to the public but this distinction has now been removed.[86]

## Finland

## Copyright Act (Law No. 404 of July 8, 1961, as last amended by Law No. 365 of April 25, 1997)

| | |
|---|---|
| Art. 1 | A person who has created a literary or artistic work shall have copyright therein, whether it be a fictional or descriptive representation in writing or speech, and whether it be a musical, dramatic, or cinematographic work, a work of fine art, architecture, artistic handicraft, industrial art, or expressed in some other manner. |
| Art. 25 | When a copy of a work of art has been sold or otherwise permanently transferred with the consent of the author, or when a work of art has been published, the work of art may be incorporated in a photograph, a film or a television program, provided its use is of secondary importance to the photograph, film or program. |
| Art. 40c | The party commissioning a portrait to be made by photographic means has the right, even if the photographer has reserved the right to the work for himself, to authorize the inclusion of the portrait in a newspaper, periodical or a biographical work, except where the photographer has separately reserved the right to prohibit such inclusion. |
| Art 43 | Copyright shall subsist until the end of the seventieth year after the year in which the author dies... |
| Art. 49a | A photographer shall have the exclusive right to exploit his photographic picture, unaltered or altered:<br>(1) by making copies thereof;<br>(2) by exhibiting it publicly.<br>The rights in a photographic picture shall apply until 50 years have elapsed from the end of the year in which the photographic picture was made. The provisions of the second paragraph of Article 2, the first and second paragraphs of Article 3,[87] Articles 7 to 9 and 11, the first and second paragraphs of Article 12, Article 13, the first and third paragraphs of Article 14, Articles 15, 16, 18, 20, 22 and 25, the first and second paragraphs of Article 25a, Articles 25b, 25d, 25f to 25i, 26, 26a to 26h, 27 to 29, 39, 40 and 40c, and also Articles 41 and 42, shall apply as appropriate to the photographic picture referred to in this Article. If a photographic picture is subject to copyright, the corresponding rights may be claimed. |

---

[86] s.41.

[87] Broadly these sections are as follows: 3 (moral rights); 7–9 (signature deemed author, definition of published, no copyright in decrees of public bodies); 11 (general limitations); 12 (reproduction for private use); 13 (photocopying); 14 (educational reproduction); 15,16,18 (reproduction in institutions and archives, etc); 20 (display of works after copy sold); 22 (quotation); 25 (various permissible reproductions of disseminated works—see above) 40c (see above); 41, 42 (transfer on death, legal seizure).

A distinction is drawn between photographic works (which receive full copyright protection for 70 yrs pma) and photographic pictures which are protected for 50 years from the creation of the work. Only the reproduction right and the right of public exhibition are granted to simple photographs.[88]

## France

### The French Intellectual Property Code of 1992[89] provides the basis of current French copyright law

Art. L.111–1   The author of a work of the mind shall by the mere fact of its creation enjoy an exclusive incorporeal property right in that work as against all persons.

Art. L.112–1   The provisions of this Code shall protect the rights of authors in all works of the mind whatever their kind, form of expression, merit or purpose.

Art. L.112–2   The following, in particular, shall be considered works of the mind within the meaning of this Code:
...9.   photographic works and works produced by techniques analagous to photography;

Art. L.123–1   The author shall enjoy, during his life time, the exclusive right to exploit his work in any form whatsoever and to derive monetary profit therefrom.
On the death of the author, that right shall subsist for his successors in title during the current calendar year and the 70 years thereafter.

A work of the mind is not defined, but only "original" works of the mind are protected.[90] The traditional French view is that originality consists of the imprint of the author's personality.[91] Originality has also been described as "intellectual contribution."[92] A non-exhaustive list of protected works in Art. L112–2 includes at para. 9:

"photographic works and other works produced by techniques analagous to photography"

The wording of the legislation covering photography has undergone notable revision. The Copyright Act of 1957 protected only "photographic works of an artistic or documentary character". This wording still applies to photographs taken before January 1, 1986.[93]

It has been observed that in France originality is traditionally thought to arise when an author puts a personal imprint on a work by exercising creative choice, irrespective of the mechanics of the art.[94] The necessary degree of choice has been found in selecting shots to optimize the impact of resulting photographs where the photographer has made choices of the most opportune moments and methods of

---

[88] For further discussion of copyright law in its application to photographs in Finland see Oesch, R, Nordic *Countries in Copyright and Photographs: An International Survey*, Gendreau, Y, Nordemann and Oesch, R (eds) Kluwer Law Int. at p.231.

[89] Law No. 92–597 of July 1, 1992, http://clea.wipo.int/.

[90] Referred to in the Code in Art.L112–4 (titles) and Art.L112–3 (derivative works).

[91] Nimmer & Geller FRA-18 §2[1][b][ii][A].

[92] *Pachot* case, Cass. Ass. plen. March 7, 1986 RIDA no 129, 136.

[93] Nimmer & Geller FRA-25 §2[2][b].

[94] Nimmer & Geller FRA-25 §2[2][b].

getting shots.[95] By contrast, there was held to be no copyright in shots of technician furnishing references point during the shooting of a film.[96] Adjusting camera and lighting to produce the desired effects has also been held to be sufficient.[97]

Similarly, even where a third party was selecting and grouping objects, a photographer was held to be the author of a work of the mind because he set the lighting, adjusted contrasts and focus, timed the pose and chose the optimum moment to take the photograph where these choices reflected his personality and aesthetic sense.[98] However, the activities undertaken in creating the work to be photographed may be enough to confer copyright protection. A stylist who chooses objects, arranges and decorates a set to be photographed is not necessarily performing a mere technical function and may be worthy of copyright protection.[99]

It has been proposed that in the case of mechanically taken photographs a neighbouring or related right be legislated.[1]

## Gabon

## Copyright Statute Date of Law (No. 1/87): July 29, 1987[2]

Art. 2       The author of any original work of the mind, whether it be literary, artistic or scientific, shall enjoy in that work, by the mere fact of its creation, an incorporeal, exclusive property right, known as copyright, enforceable against all persons

Art. 4       The following, in particular, shall be considered works of the mind within the meaning of this Law: ... photographic works of an artistic or documentary character, to which shall be assimilated works expressed by a process analogous to photography ...

Art. 37      Works of art, including architectural works, permanently located in a public place, may be reproduced and made available to the public by means of cinematography, photography or television.

Under Art. 60 the term of protection for photographs is 50 years as from the end of the calendar year in which the work was made lawfully available to the public. This is shorter than the basic term for other works which is life of the author plus 50 years.

## Gambia

## Copyright Act—Date of Law (No. 9): July 15, 1915[3]

The Copyright Act, 1911, of the United Kingdom (I and 2 Geo. V. c. 46) was applied to Bathurst and Kombo Saint Mary by a proclamation dated July 1, 1912, and to the Provinces by an Order in Council of His Majesty dated June 24, 1912. But its ss. 11 and 12 applied only to the United Kingdom. This Act enacts the provisions of those

[95] Cass civ. I 12 Jan 1994 RIDA 1994 no 162, 427.
[96] Cass civ. I 1 March 1988 RIDA 1988 no. 137, 103.
[97] Versailles 12e ch. 28 April 1988 RIDA 1988 no.138, 319; Paris 8 e ch., June 17, 1988, D.S. 1989 somm. 44 obs. Colombet.
[98] Gaz. Pal. 27 June 1999 10 note Frémond see Nimmer & Geller FRA-25 §2[2][b] n 83.
[99] Paris 8e ch. 17 June 1988 D.S. 1989, somm 44 obs Colombet cited in Nimmer & Geller FRA-25 §2[2][b].
[1] H. Desbois, *Le droit de auteur en France* no. 85 (3rd ed. Paris 1978).
[2] http://www.unesco.org/culture/copy/copyright/gabon/fr_sommaire.html. See n.1 (1st ser.), above.
[3] *http://www.unesco.org/culture/copy/copyright/gambia/fr_gambia.html*. See n.1 (1st ser.), above.

sections in the Gambia, and also provisions consequential to s.14 of the Act of the United Kingdom.

## Germany

## Law on Copyright and Neighbouring Rights (Copyright Law) (of September 9, 1965, as last amended by the Law of July 19, 1996[4]

| | |
|---|---|
| Art. 1 | Authors of literary, scientific and artistic works shall enjoy protection for their works in accordance with this Law |
| Art. 2—(1) | Protected literary, scientific and artistic works shall include, in particular: ... 5. photographic works, including works produced by processes similar to photography; |
| (2) | Personal intellectual creations alone shall constitute works within the meaning of this Law. |
| Art. 59–(1) | It shall be permissible to reproduce, by painting, drawing, photography or cinematography, works which are permanently located on public ways, streets or places and to distribute and publicly communicate such copies. For works of architecture, this provision shall be applicable only to the external appearance |
| Art. 72–(1) | Photographs and products manufactured in a similar way to photographs shall be protected, mutatis mutandis, by the provisions of Part I applicable to photographic works. |
| (2) | The right afforded by paragraph (1) shall belong to the photographer. |
| (3) | The right under paragraph (1) shall expire 50 years after publication of the photograph or after its first lawful communication to the pubic where such communication took place at an earlier date, but in any event 50 years after its manufacture if the photograph has not been published or has not been lawfully communicated to the public within that period. (Amended by the Law of June 24, 1985, and by the Law of June 23, 1995.) |

The relevant statute is the Act dealing with Copyright and Related Rights of September 9, 1965, which came into force on January 1, 1966, and has subsequently been amended. Section 1 of the 1965 Act provides "authors of literary, scientific and artistic works shall enjoy protection for their works in the manner prescribed by this Act". Section 2(2) states that works include only "personal intellectual creations". German law also has the small change doctrine (kleine Münze) which affords some degree of copyright protection to works with a lesser degree of creativity such as directories, printed forms and catalogues. Section 2(1) provides an open list of works protected by copyright and includes photographic works including works produced by processes analogous to photography.

From July 1, 1995, a non-creative photograph (*i.e.* one without sufficient creativity to attract copyright) is protected under s.72 for a term of 50 years from the year that the photograph is first made available to the public or, if not published, the year it is taken.[5] For creative photographs the normal copyright terms apply.

Prior to July 1, 1995, a distinction was drawn between non-creative photographs (previously protected for 25 years) and photographs possessing a historical documentary character which were protected for 50 years. From July 1, 1995, no further distinction was drawn and all simple non-creative photographs are protected for a 50 year term subject to transitional provisions.[6]

---

[4] *http://www.unesco.org/culture/copy/copyright/germany/fr_sommaire.html.* See n.1 (1st ser.), above.
[5] Nimmer & Geller GER-36 §3[2][a][i].
[6] Nimmer & Geller GER-36 §3[2][a][i].

The bilateral Agreement for the Mutual Protection of Copyright between the United States and Germany of January 15, 1892.[7] It has been suggested that this agreement may continue to apply to non-original photographs.[8]

## Ghana

### Copyright Law 1985[9]

2. (1) Subject to the provisions of this section the following works are eligible for copyright: ... (b) artistic works,
   (2) A work is not eligible for copyright unless:
   (a) it is original in character, ...
   (3) The eligibility of a work for copyright is not affected by its artistic quality, the purpose of the author in creating it or by the manner or form of its expression.
   (4) For the purposes of this section a work is original if it is the product of the independent efforts of the author
15. In the case of a photographic work the rights of the author referred to in subsection (1) of section 6 of this Law are protected until the expiration of fifty (50) years from the date of the making of the work
53. In this Law unless the context otherwise requires:
   "partistic work" means irrespective of artistic quality any of the following works: ...
   (b) photography not comprised in a cinematograph film;

Photographs are protected as artistic works albeit with a shorter term of protection as indicated in s.15.

## Greece

### Copyright, Related Rights and Cultural Matters (Law No. 2121/1993 as last amended by Law No. 2435 of August 2, 1996[10]

Art. 1–(1) Authors shall have, with the creation of the work, the right of copyright in that work, which includes, as exclusive and absolute rights, the right to exploit the work (economic right) and the right to protect their personal connection with the work (moral right).

Art. 2–(1) The term "work" shall designate any original intellectual literary, artistic or scientific creation, expressed in any form, notably ... works of architecture and photographs

Art. 26 The occasional reproduction and communication by the mass media of images of architectural works, fine art works, photographs or works of applied art, which are sited permanently in a public place, shall be permissible, without the consent of the author and without payment.

---

[7] The agreement was formally renewed by Germany by the law of May 18, 1922. After World War II its continuing applicability was confirmed by diplomatic correspondence between the German Federal Government and the U.S High Commissioner for Germany in 1950. See Nimmer & Geller GER-79 §6[3].

[8] Nimmer & Geller §6[3].

[9] *http://www.unesco.org/culture/copy/copyright/ghana/fr_sommaire.html*. See n.1 (1st ser.), above.

[10] *http://www.unesco.org/culture/copy/copyright/greece/fr_sommaire.html*. See n.1 (1st ser.), above.

**Photographers" Rights**

Art. 38–(1)   In the absence of an agreement to the contrary, a transfer of the economic right or exploitation contract or license dealing with the publication of a photograph in a newspaper, periodical or other mass media shall refer only to the publication of the photograph in the particular newspaper, periodical or mass media specified in the transfer or exploitation contract or license and to the archiving of the photograph. Every subsequent act of publication shall be subject to payment of a fee equal to half the current fee. The publication of a transferred photograph from the archive of a newspaper, periodical or other mass media shall be permitted only when accompanied by a reference to the title of the newspaper or of the periodical or to the name of the mass media, into whose archive the photograph was initially and lawfully placed.

(2)   Where the publication of a photograph is facilitated by the surrender of the photographic negative, use shall be made of the negative, in the absence of an agreement to the contrary, only for the first publication of the photograph, after which the negative shall be returned to the photographer.

(3)   The photographer shall retain the right to access and request the return to him of his photographs, which have been the object of an exploitation contract or license arrangement with a particular newspaper, periodical or other mass media and which have remained unpublished three months after the date of the exploitation contract or license.

(4)   Each act of publication of a photograph shall be accompanied by a mentioning of the photographer's name. This shall apply likewise when the archive of a newspaper or of a periodical or of another mass media is transferred.

(5)   The owner of a newspaper or of a periodical shall not be entitled to publish a photograph created by a photographer, employed by him, in a book or album publication without the employee's consent. This shall apply likewise to the lending of a photograph.

The general term is life of the author plus 70 years.[11] There is no separate term for photographs.

The relevant statute is the Copyright Act of 1993.[12] Copyright is understood in the European sense of "author's right". Every original mental creation of literature, art or science expressed in any form is eligible for protection.[13] Under Art. 2(1) a work is defined as "any original creation", but originality is not defined. Koumantos in Nimmer & Geller observes:

"A work that expresses the personality of the author would be original; a work that is only the product of mere routine would not be even if skill or labor have been necessary to produce it".[14]

The Act contains a non-exhaustive list of works eligible for protect which include:

"works of the visual arts, including ... photographs".[15]

---

[11] Art. 29(1).
[12] Act No. 2121/1993. See Nimmer & Geller GRE- 5 § [1].
[13] Nimmer & Geller GRE-8 §2[3].
[14] Nimmer & Geller GRE-7 § [2][2][b].
[15] Nimmer & Geller GRE-8 §2[3].

Kounmantos also observes that modern Greek commentary "suggests that criterion of "statistical uniqueness"—a work would be original if according to the law of probability it is different from anything that could be created by any other person even if this person was pursuing the same aims under the same circumstances".[16] But continues that "the dominant opinion is that to be protected by copyright a work must at least display some modicum of creativity which may be considered as an element of the very notion of the work."

## Guinea

### Law Adopting Provisions on Copyright and Neighbouring Rights in the Revolutionary People's Republic of Guinea Law No. 043/APN/CP): August 9, 1980[17]

Art. 1    The author of any original intellectual work (literary, scientific or artistic) shall, by the mere fact of its creation, enjoy an exclusive incorporeal property right in the work, effective against all persons. The following in particular shall be considered intellectual works within the meaning of this Law ... (xi) photographic works of artistic or documentary character, to which are assimilated, for the purposes of this Law, works expressed by a process analogous to photography ...

Under Art. 43 photographs are protected for 40 calendar years from the end of the year of the author's death. The basic term for most works is life of the author plus 80 years.

## Hong Kong

### Copyright Ordinance (Cap. 528 Consolidation) 27/06/1997 (1999)No. 92 (No. 95)[18]

s.2 (1)  Copyright is a property right which subsists in accordance with this Part in the following descriptions of work
(a) original literary, dramatic, musical or artistic works; ...
s.5      In this Part ... an "artistic work" means:
(a) a graphic work, photograph, sculpture or collage, irrespective of artistic quality;
... "photograph" means a recording of light or other radiation on any medium on which an image is produced or from which an image may by any means be produced, and which is not part of a film
s.17(1)  The following provisions have effect with respect to the duration of copyright in a literary, dramatic, musical or artistic work,
(2)   Copyright expires at the end of the period of 50 years from the end of the calendar year in which the author dies, subject as follows ...

The relevant statute is the Copyright Ordinance 1997 (amended in 1999) which superseded the 1956 UK Copyright Act.[19] The protection criteria unsurprisingly are

---

[16] Nimmer & Geller GRE-7 §2[2].
[17] *http://www.unesco.org/culture/copy/copyright/guinea/fr_sommaire.html*. See n.1 (1st ser.), above.
[18] *http://clea.wipo.int/*.
[19] Nimmer & Geller HK-7 §1[2].

virtually identical to the UK. A copyright work must be original in the sense of originating from its creator with a sufficient degree of labour and skill. Artistic works are protected which include "photographs ... irrespective of artistic quality". The term of protection is only 50 yrs pma.

## Hungary

### Act No. LXXVI of 1999 (as amended by Act No. XLVIII of 2001 on Designs and the Act No. LXXVII of 2001)[19a]

| | |
|---|---|
| Art. 1(1) | This Act shall provide protection for literary, scientific and art creations. |
| (2) | All creations of literature, science and art—whether or not specified by this Act—shall fall under the protection of this Act, in particular:<br>... i)  artistic photographs |
| (3) | The copyright protection shall derive from the individual and original nature of the creation conceived by the intellectual activity of the author and it shall not be subject to any quantitative, qualitative and aesthetic characteristics or to value judgments relating to the standard of creation. |

By virtue of Art. 31, the basic term of protection is life of the author plus 70 years. The predecessor Act of 1969 as amended provided for a related right for non-copyright photographs. This distinction was removed by the Act of 1999. The relevant part of the Act of 1969 is set out below:

### Act No. III of 1969 on Copyright (as last amended by Act No. LXXII of 1994)[20]

| | |
|---|---|
| Art. 1—(1) | This Act shall provide protection for literary, scientific and artistic creations |
| Art. 44(1) | Copyright in works of architecture and other engineering structures shall belong to the owner of the design. |
| ... (3) | The user of a work shall tolerate its presentation to the public and the taking of photographs of it, if this does not prejudice his legitimate interests. |
| Chapter XI—<br>Art. 51—(1) | Protection of Photographs, Illustrations and Other Visual Aids<br>Photographs, figures, technical drawings, maps, graphic illustrations or aids and films which do not enjoy copyright protection as scientific or artistic works shall nevertheless enjoy protection if they bear the name of the maker and the year of publication or disclosure. |
| (2) | The duration of protection shall be 15 years from the end of the year of publication or disclosure. |
| (3) | Use of photographs, pictures, technical drawings, maps, graphic illustrations or aids and films enjoying protection shall be subject to the authorization of the maker and the mention of his name. It |

---

[19a] Available via the UNESCO Collection of National Copyright Laws at *http://portal.unesco.org/culture/en/ev.php@URL_ID=14076&URL_DO=DO_TOPI-C&URL_SECTION=201.html*. In the event this link has changed by the date of publication the Collection of National Copyright Laws may be accessed via the home page at *http://www.unesco.org* and clicking on the tab marked "Copyright" on the bar across the top of the screen. This information is correct as at February 2004.
[20] *http://www.unesco.org/culture/copy/copyright/hungary/fr_sommaire.html*. See n.1 (1st ser.), above.

shall not be necessary to obtain authorization and to mention the name of the maker in those cases in which such is not required for the use of works enjoying copyright protection.

The 1969 Act applied the normal term of life of the author plus 70 years to artistic photographs.[21] Non-copyright photographs were protected for 15 years from publication under Art. 51 above provided they bore the name of the maker and the year of publication or disclosure. There is no longer a related right for non-copyright photographs under the 1999 law.

Originality was always a requirement for protection. Fiesor in Nimmer & Geller states "A work has to be a creation, that is, the author has to create something that has not existed before".[22] The 1969 Act itself did not contain a list of protected works. Such a list is contained in the 1969 implementing decree which, in Art. 1 lists "artistic photographs" only. However, apparently the decree did stress that although some literary, scientific or artistic works are not mentioned it does not mean that they were not eligible for protection.[23]

## Iceland

## Copyright Act Law (No. 73) of May 29, 1972as amended up to May 30, 1984[24]

Art. 1    The author of a literary or artistic work shall have copyright therein within the limitations specified in this Act. Literary and artistic works shall comprise any composed text, be it expressed in writing or in speech, dramatic work, musical work, fine art, work of architecture, cinematographic work, photography, applied art and other similar art forms, by whatever technique and in whatever form the work is disseminated.

Art. 16    It is permitted to take and reproduce pictures of buildings, and of works of art, which have been situated permanently out of doors in a public place. if a building, which enjoys protection under the rules applying to architectural art, or a work of art such as that mentioned in the preceding paragraph, constitutes the chief motif of a picture which is used for commercial purposes, then the author shall be entitled to remuneration, unless the pictures are intended for reproduction in newspapers or on television.

Art. 49    The reproduction of photographs, which do not enjoy the protection of this Act as artistic works (cf. the provisions of paragraph 2 of Article 1), shall be prohibited without the consent of the photographer or the person who has acquired his rights. If such a photograph is made available to the public for commercial or employment purposes, then the photographer, or the subsequent holder of his rights, shall be entitled to remuneration. The protection of a photograph in accordance with the provisions of this Article shall be valid until twenty-five years have elapsed from the end of the year in which it was made. The provisions of Chapter II of this Act shall likewise apply to the photographs mentioned under paragraph 1 of this Article, as seen to be fit.

---

[21] Art. 15(1).
[22] Nimmer & Geller HUN-12 §2[1][b].
[23] Nimmer & Geller HUN-14 §2[2].
[24] Law (No. 73): May 29, 1972.

The normal copyright term is life of the author plus 70 years and copyright photographic works attract this term.[25] Non-copyright photographs enjoy the limited protection under Art. 49 of 25 years from the making of the photograph.

## India

### Copyright Act 1957[26]

2      In this Act, unless the context otherwise requires (c) "artistic work" means (i) a painting, a sculpture, a drawing (including a diagram, map, chart or plan), an engraving or a photograph, whether or not any such work possesses artistic quality

...     (s) "photograph" includes photo-lithograph and any work produced by any process analogous to photography but does not include any part of a cinematograph film...

13–(1)   Subject to the provisions of this section and the other provisions of this Act, copyright shall subsist throughout India in the following classes of works, that is to say
(a) original literary, dramatic, musical and artistic works...

25     In the case of a photograph, copyright shall subsist until sixty years from the beginning of the calendar year next following the year in which the photograph is published.

The relevant statute is the Copyright Act 1957 as amended.[27] Under s.13 original artistic works are protected. It seems that the UK approach to originality is applied with the "work, labour and skill" test being applied.[28] Section 2(c) defines artistic works as including "a photograph, whether or not any such work possesses artistic quality". Photographs have a shorter term of protection than other works (which are protected for life of the author plus 60 years[29]) and are protected for 60 years from the beginning of the calendar year following that in which the photograph is first published.[30]

## Indonesia

### Law No. 19 of 2002 Regarding Copyright[30a]

Art. 1(1)   Copyright shall mean an exclusive right for an Author or the recipient of the right to publish or reproduce his Work or to grant permission for said purposes, without decreasing the limits according to the prevailing laws and regulations.

(2)     Author shall mean a person or several persons jointly upon whose inspiration a Work is produced, based on the intellectual ability, imagination, dexterity, skill or expertise manifested in a distinctive form and is of a personal nature.

---

[25] Art. 43.
[26] *http://www.unesco.org/culture/copy/copyright/india/fr_sommaire.html.* As to the UNESCO site, see n.1 (1st ser.), above. *http://clea.wipo.int/.*
[27] Act 14 of 1957, Nimmer & Geller IND-9 §1[1].
[28] See Nimmer & Geller IND-13 §2[1][b].
[29] s.22 and see Nimmer & Geller IND-20 §2[4][d].
[30] Art. 25, and seeeNimmer & Geller IND-22 §3[2][a].
[30a] Available via the Unesco portal. See n.1 (1st ser.), above, See also the website of the Indonesian Directorate General of Intellectual Property Rights at *http://www.dgip.go.id/.*

(3)       Work shall mean any results of an Author which shows originality in the field of science, arts and literature.

Art. 12(1)       In this Law, a work that is protected shall be the work in the field of science, arts and literature which includes:
... j.   photography ...

Under Art. 30(1) copyright in photographic works subsists for 50 years from first publication. The basic term for other works is life of the author and 50 years after his death: Art. 29(1). The predecessor statute had a similar but slightly different test for copyright work:

## Copyright Act (No. 6): April 12, 1982 as amended up to 1987[31]

Art. 1       Meant in this Act by:
(a) author, is somebody or are several persons jointly whose inspiration has called into being a creation based on intellectual capability, imagination, dexterity, proficiency or skillfulness, laid down in an exclusive and personal form;

...       (c) work, is any result of an author's work in an exclusive form, whatever it may be, in the field of science, arts and literature;

Art. 11       (1) Works protected under this Act are works in the fields of science, arts and literature, covering the following works ... (j) photographic works; ...

Under the 1982 Act, Art. 27(2) copyright in a photograph expired 25 years after it is first publicized. The basic protection for books, etc. was life of the author plus 50 years.

## Iran

## Law of January 12, 1970[32]

Art. 1       All writers, composers, and artists will hereafter be called "author", and the product of their knowledge, originality or art, irrespective of the method used. therein, will hereafter be called "work"

Art. 2       Works protected by copyright law are as follows: ... 8. Photographic works produced by any original methods.

Art. 16       In the following cases, the author's financial rights will be valid for a period of 30 years from the date of publication or public presentation: 1. Photographic or cinematographic works [the normal period is life of author plus 30 years]

---

[31] *http://www.unesco.org/culture/copy/copyright/indonesia/fr_sommaire.html*. See n.1 (1st ser.), above.
[32] *http://www.unesco.org/culture/copy/copyright/iran/fr_iran.html*. See n.1 (1st ser.), above.

## Iraq

### Copyright Law No. (3) for the Year 1971 for the Protection of Copyright[33]

Art. (1)1    This law protects the authors of innovated[33a] literary, artistic and scientific works, whatever their type, method of expression, importance and purpose.

Art. (2)    The protection shall include the works whose method of expression is in writing, sound, drawing, painting or movement, and in particular the following:- ... 7-Photographic and cinematic works.

Art. (4) ...    However, the copyright of a photographic work shall not entail preventing others from taking new photographs of the photographed object, even if the new photograph has been taken from the same place or in the same conditions of the first photograph.

Art. (20)    Without prejudice to the provisions of Article (9) of this law, the financial utilization rights provided for in Articles 7, 8 and 10 shall expire with the elapse of twenty five years after the death of the author, provided that the total period of protection shall not be less than fifty years as from the date of publication of the work. However, with respect to photographic and cinematic works which are limited to the mechanical transmission of scenery, such rights shall expire with the elapse of five years as from the date of first publication of the work. While the period of protection for joint works shall be calculated as from the date of death of the last author who survived. If the author is a body corporate, public or private, the financial utilization rights shall expire after the elapse of thirty years as from the date of first publication of the work.

There is thus a type of neighbouring right for photographs which are "the mechanical transmission of scenery."

## Ireland

### Copyright and Related Rights Act 2000[34]

s.2(1)...    "artistic work" includes a work of any of the following descriptions, irrespective of their artistic quality
    (a)    photographs, paintings, drawings, diagrams, maps, charts, plans, engravings, etchings, lithographs, woodcuts, prints or similar works, collages or sculptures (including any cast or model made for the purposes of a sculpture)...
    "photograph" means a recording of light, or any other radiation on any medium on which an image is produced, or from which an image may by any means be produced and which is not part of a film[35];

s.17(2)    Copyright subsists in accordance with this Act,
    (a)    original literary, dramatic, or musical works...

s.24(1)    The copyright in a literary, dramatic, musical or artistic work, or an original database shall expire 70 years after the death of the author, irre-

---

[33] *http://www.agip.com/laws/iraq/c.htm/.*
[33a] For observations regarding the translation of the word "innovated" see above at para. 3–078, n. 72a.
[34] *http://clea.wipo.int/.*
[35] Compare previous definition in 1963 Act which was "any product of photography or of any process akin to photography, other than a part of a cinematograph film".

spective of the date on which the work is first lawfully made available to the public.

s.35  Where a term of copyright is provided for in this Act, the term shall be calculated from the first day of January of the year following the event that gives rise to that term

s.114(1)  Subject to the exceptions specified in subsection (3), a person who, for private and domestic purposes, commissions the taking of a photograph or the making of a film has, where copyright subsists in the resulting work, the right not to have the work or copies of the work made available to the public.

(2)  Subject to subsection (3), the act of making available to the public, or authorising the making available to the public, of a work or copies of a work referred to in subsection (1) without the authority of the person who commissions the work infringes the right conferred by subsection (1).

(3)  The right conferred by subsection (1) shall not be infringed by an act which under section 52, 71, 72, 76 or 88[36] would not infringe the copyright in the work.

Photographs now receive the same period of protection as other works, being 70 yrs pma. Under the previous Copyright Act 1963, photographs had a shorter term of protection than other works being a period of 50 years from the end of the year in which the photograph is first published.[37] The 1963 Act provided that the basic term of protection was life of the author plus 50 years.[38]

## Israel

The relevant statute is the Copyright Act of 1911 as amended.[39] Israel is another jurisdiction in which English copyright law has an historical influence and the originals of its laws lie in the UK Copyright Act which was extended to Palestine in 1924 and maintained in force in Israel.[40] Under s.1 originality is a requirement for copyright protection.[41]

Creativity is the test preferred by the courts rather than labour and skill or the Feist notion of "sweat of the brow".[42] Artistic works are protected and are defined to include photographs.

Israeli courts draw a distinction between a documentary photograph (which may be protected) and its content which need not be. In *Tele-Event Ltd v Arutzey Zahav O.M*[43] it was held that copyright did not prohibit photographs of a Wimbledon tennis tournament which was not protected by copyright or performer's rights. Further, a documentary photograph of an event not staged by the photographer was protected by copyright. In *Keren v Shavit*[44] the court considered that the time, energy and talent which went into the making of the photograph as shown in the timing of the picture, the choice of angle and the light were sufficient to warrant copyright protection.

---

[36] Various permitted acts—respectively incidental inclusion; parliamentary and judicial proceedings; statutory inquiries; statutory authority; and anonymous and pseudonymous works.
[37] s.9(7).
[38] s.8(4).
[39] Nimmer & Geller ISR-5 §1.
[40] *http://www.unesco.org/culture/copy/copyright/israel/fr_israel.html*. See n.1 (1st ser.), above.
[41] Nimmer & Geller ISR-7 §2[1][b].
[42] Nimmer & Geller ISR-7 citing *Lev v Hamashbir Hamerkazi* CA 448/60 16 P.D. (4) 2688, 2696.
[43] (Tel Aviv) 931/92 P.M. 5754 (2) 328.
[44] (Magistrate, Tel Aviv) 24478/87 P.M. 5751(1)139 cited in Nimmer & Geller ISR-8 §2[1][b].

Photographs are accorded a shorter term, namely 50 years from the making of the negative from which the photograph was derived, than other copyright works which attract life plus 70 years.[45]

## Italy

## Law for the Protection of Copyright and Neighbouring Rights (Law No. 633 of April 22, 1941) as last amended by Decree Law No. 154 of May 26, 1997[46]

Art. 1    Works of the mind having a creative character and belonging to literature, music, figurative arts, architecture, theater or cinematography, whatever their mode or form of expression, shall be protected in accordance with this Law

Art. 2    In particular, protection shall extend to: ... (7) works of photographic art and works expressed with processes analogous to photograph provided they are not simple photographs protected in accordance with the provisions of Chapter V of Part II;

Art. 6    Copyright shall be acquired on the creation of a work that constitutes the particular expression of an intellectual effort.

Art. 32bis    The exploitation rights in photographic works shall lapse at the end of the 70th year following the author's death

### Chapter V Rights in Photographs

Art. 87    The images of persons or of aspects, elements or events of natural or social life, obtained by photographic or analogous processes, including reproductions of works of figurative art and stills of cinematographic film, shall be considered photographs for the purposes of this Chapter. This provision shall not apply to photographs of writings, documents, business papers, material objects, technical drawings and similar products.

Art. 88    The exclusive right of reproduction, dissemination and marketing of a photograph shall belong to the photographer, subject to the provisions of Section II of Chapter VI of this Part insofar as portraits are concerned, and without prejudice to any copyright in works of figurative art reproduced in photographs. However, if the work has been produced in the execution of a contract of employment or of service, the exclusive right shall belong to the employer within the limits of the object and purpose of the contract. In the absence of agreement to the contrary, the same shall apply in favour of the person who commissions photographs of objects in his possession, subject to the payment of equitable remuneration to the photographer by any person who commercially utilizes the reproduction. The President of the Council of Ministers may, in accordance with the provisions of the regulations, set suitable rates for the remuneration to be paid by any user of such photograph.

Art. 89    In the absence of agreement to the contrary, transfer of the negative or similar means of reproduction of a photograph shall imply transfer of the rights referred to in the foregoing Article, provided that such rights are the property of the transferor.

Art. 90    The copies of the photograph must bear the following particulars:

---

[45] Nimmer & Geller ISR-15 §3[2].

[46] *http://www.unesco.org/culture/copy/copyright/italy/fr_sommaire.html.* See n.1 (1st ser.), above.

(1)   the name of the photographer or, in the cases referred to in the first paragraph of Article 88, the name of the firm to which he belongs or of the person who commissioned the photograph;

(2)   the year of production of the photograph;

(3)   the name of the author of the work of art which has been photographed. If the copies do not bear these particulars, their reproduction shall not be deemed abusive and the remuneration laid down in Articles 91 and 98 shall not become due unless the photographer proves bad faith on the part of the reproducer.

Art. 91   The reproduction of photographs in anthologies intended for school use and, in general, in scientific or didactic works, shall be lawful, subject to the payment of equitable remuneration which shall be determined in the manner provided in the regulations. The name of the photographer and the year of production of the photograph shall be given on the reproduction if they are given on the original photograph. The reproduction of photographs published in newspapers or other periodicals, and which concern persons or current events or matters of any public interest, shall be lawful, subject to the payment of equitable remuneration. The provisions of the final paragraph of Article 88 shall be applicable.

Art. 92   The exclusive right in respect of photographs shall subsist for 20 years as from the making of the photograph.

The underlying statute is the Copyright Act of 1941[47] which is amended and supplemented by other laws. Italian copyright law is in spirit an author's right system (*diritto di autore*) which grants an independent and absolute right arising from the author's creative act. The only condition for protection is that the work should result from creative activity.[48] Article 1 provides for the protection of works having a "creative character". Article 6 grants copyright protection for "creation of the work as the result of an intellectual effort". Article 2(7) provides for the protection of:

"Works of photographic art and those expressed by processes analogous to photography, provided that they are not simple photographs protected by neighbouring rights, according to the provisions of chapter V of Part II of this law."[49]

Under Italian law, photographs with creative character following the Decree No. 19 of January 8, 1979, which inserted the phrase "works of photographic art and those expressed by processes analogous to photography" into Art. 2.[50] Works of photographic art are distinguished in Italian law from simple photographs with no creative character; examples given are banal snapshots or mechanically produced photographs.[51] Such photographs are protected by neighbouring rights.

Simple photographs have a shorter term of protection than artistic photographs. Under Art. 92, simple photographs are protected for 20 years from the making of the negative from which the photograph was directly or indirectly derived.[52] Film or video that, for lack of creativity, may be considered to be a series of photographs such as documentaries or news footage is also protected for 20 years.

---

[47] Law No. 633 of April 22, 1941, Nimmer & Geller ITA-5 §1[1].

[48] Nimmer & Geller ITA-8 §2[1][b].

[49] Quoted in Nimmer & Geller ITA-9 §2[2].

[50] Nimmer & Geller ITA-13 §2[3][g].

[51] Nimmer & Geller ITA-73 §9[1][a][v].

[52] Nimmer & Geller ITA-24 §3[2][a][ii].

The Italian Act does not define either works of photographic art protected by copyright or simple photographs protected by neighbouring rights.[53] Dr Mario Fabiani in Nimmer & Geller comments:

"...and the last clause of Art 87 introduces a gap between them in excluding photographs of such products as writings, documents and technical plans. Accordingly one court refused all protection to photographs of banknotes and accompanying documents which originally illustrated a book on the history of money but were reproduced without authorization in a catalog of bank notes of the past century.

The distinction between works of photographic art and simple photographs can be critical for practical purposes. Most notably, while, with an exception for portraits, general rules on point apply to works of photographic art made on the job or commission, special rules apply to photographs made in such agency relations. Art 88(2) of the Act provides that, absent agreement to the contrary, rights in a simple photograph belong to the principal of a photographer acting as agent, that is, an employee or on commission, within the limits of the object and purpose of any agency relation. Article 88(3) applies the same provision in favour of any person who commissions a simple photograph of objects in his possession, subject to the payment of equitable remuneration to the photographer by any person who commercially utilizes the reproduction."[54]

In addition, although copyright is conferred automatically without formalities on works of photographic art, simple photographs have prescribed formalities in order to attract protection. Under Art. 90 where simple photographs do not bear a notice indicating the name of the photographer and the year of reproduction, copying of such photographs is not deemed wrongful under the neighbouring right.[55] Reproduction of newsworthy photographs published in newspapers or other periodicals is lawful subject to the payment of equitable remuneration.

## Japan

The relevant statute is the Copyright Act of 1970 as amended.[56] Article 2(1)(ii) provides that a work of authorship is "a production in which thoughts or emotions are expressed in a creative way and which fall in the literary, scientific, artistic or musical domain."[57]

A certain amount of creative effort is necessary before a work will receive copyright protection, for example a classified telephone directory has been held to be a work of authorship whereas a simple list of personal names was not.[58] Commentators suggest that the law of Japan would not protect a photograph which has no creativity such as a photograph of a painting or picture on a television screen.[59] Article 10(1) sets out a non-exhaustive list of protectable works which includes at (viii) photographic works.[60] By Art. 2(4), photographic works include "works expressed by a

---

[53] Nimmer & Geller ITA-73 §9[1][a][v].

[54] Nimmer & Geller ITA-73 §9[1][a][v]. The case referred to is Court of Cassation, January 13, 1988, Decision no. 183, Giustizia civile, 1988, I, 955.

[55] Nimmer & Geller ITA-74 §9[1][a][vi].

[56] Law No. 48, last amended by Law No. 85 of June 18, 2003. For text see *http://www.u-nesco.org/culture/copy/copyright/japan/fr_sommaire.html* and *http://www.cric.or.jp/*.

[57] Nimmer & Geller JAP-9 §2[1][b].

[58] Nimmer & Geller JAP-9 §2[1][b].

[59] Moriyuki Kato cited by Doi, Teruo in *Japan* in *Copyright and Photographs: An International Survey, Gendreau, Y*, Nordemann and Oesch, R (eds) Kluwer Law Int. at p.183.

[60] Nimmer & Geller JAP-11 §2[2].

process analagous to photography". There is no statutory distinction between creative and non-creative photographs or neighbouring rights provision.

From March 25, 1997, photographs in Japan became subject to the normal term of protection, *i.e.* life of the author plus 50 years under Art. 51. Prior to that there had been a shorter term of 50 years from publication or 50 years from creation for photographic works. That distinction was removed by the 1996 amendment which repealed Art. 55.[61]

## Jordan

### Amended Copyright Law of 2001[62]

| | |
|---|---|
| Art. 3A | Innovated literary, artistic and scientific woks regardless of their kind, importance or the purpose of their production shall enjoy protection by virtue of this law. |
| | (1)　The protection shall encompass works which are expressed in writing, sound, drawing, photography or movement and in particular: |
| | 6. Works of painting, photography, sculpture, engraving, architecture and applied and ornamentation arts. |
| Art. 16 | The copyright of a photographic work shall not lead to prohibiting others from taking one or more photographs of the same item subject of the work, even if the photograph or photographs were taken from the same spot and in the same conditions in which the first photograph of the work was taken. |
| Art. 30 | The protection of the financial copyrights stipulated in this law shall remain in effect during the lifetime of the author in addition to fifty years after his death, or the death of the last survivor of those participating in the work if there were more than are author. For the purposes of calculating the protection period, the date of death shall be considered as taking place on the first of January of the calendar year following the actual date of death of the author. |
| Art. 32 | The protection period for the following works shall be in effect for twenty five years starting from the assumed date of achieving the work which is the first of January of the calendar year in which the work was actually achieved. |
| | (1)　Photographic works. |

The predecessor Jordanian statue had a type of neighbouring right for non-creative photographic works which was removed by the 2001 amendment. The Law on the Protection of Copyright 1992 (No. 22 of 1992) provided as follows:[63]

| | |
|---|---|
| Art. 3—(a) | Works created in the fields of literature, art and science, whatever their nature, their importance or the purpose for which they were made, shall enjoy protection in accordance with this Law |
| (b) | The said protection shall extend to works expressed in writing, sound, drawing, painting or movement, and in particular ... |
| | drawings, paintings, sculptures, etchings, and works of architecture and of applied and decorative art [NB: photographs not specifically listed here] |
| Art. 16 | The copyright in a photographic work shall not prevent a third party from taking one or more photographs of the subject that constitutes the work, even if the new photograph or photographs are taken from |

---

[61] Nimmer & Geller JAP-22 §3[2][b].
[62] *http://www.agip.com/laws/jordan/c.htm/*.
[63] *http://www.unesco.org/culture/copy/copyright/jordan/fr_jordan.html.* See n.1 (1st ser.), above.

the same place and in the same circumstances as the first photographic work.

Art. 30    The rights conferred on the author by this Law shall be protected for his lifetime and for 30 years after his death, or after the death of the last surviving coauthor in the case of a work of joint authorship

Art. 31    The following works shall be protected for 30 years from the date of publication thereof: ...

(a)    cinematographic, televised and photographic works that are not of creative character inasmuch as they are mere mechanical reproductions of panoramic scenes;

## Kazakhstan

## Law on Copyright and Neighbouring Rights[64]

Art. 2     For the purposes of this Law, the terms given below shall have the following meanings: "author" means the natural person whose creative effort has brought about the creation of the work;

Art. 6—(1)    Copyright shall extend to scientific, literary and artistic works that are the outcome of creative effort whatever their purpose, content, merit or manner or form of expression. (2) Copyright shall protect both disclosed works and undisclosed works that exist in an objective form, namely: .... figurative form (drawing, sketch, painting, plan, industrial design, still from a cinematographic or television or video film, photograph, etc.); ...

Art. 7—(1)    The following shall be protected by copyright ... photographic works and works obtained by processes analogous to photography;

Under Art. 28 the term of protection is life of the author plus 50 years. There is no separate term for photographs.

## Kenya

## The Copyright Act 2001, No. 12 of 2001[65]

2—(1)     In this Act, unless the context otherwise requires-"**artistic work**" means, irrespective of artistic quality, any of the following, or works similar thereto- ... (d) photographs not comprised in audio-visual works;

22—(1)    Subject to this section, the following works shall be eligible for copyright- ... (c) artistic works;.

(3)    A literary, musical or artistic work shall not be eligible for copyright unless
(a)    sufficient effort has been expended on making the work to give it an original character; and
(b)    the work has been written down, recorded or otherwise reduced to material form

Under s.23(2) the term of protection for photographs is 50 years from the end of the year in which the work was either made, first made available to the public or first published, whichever is latest. The standard term for other works is life plus 50 years. There are no neighbouring rights provisions.

---

[64] *http://www.unesco.org/culture/copy/copyright/kazakstan/fr_sommaire.html.* See n.1 (1st ser.), above.

[65] *http://www.unesco.org/culture/copy/copyright/kenya/fr_page1.html.* See n.1 (1sr ser.), above.

# Latvia

## Copyright Act of 6 April 2000[66]

s.1 The following terms are used in this Law
...2. "work"—the original creation of an author in any material form, as well as an improvisation performed in public at the time of its performance...

s.4 The subject matter of copyright, regardless of the manner or form of expression, shall comprise the following works of authors:
...(9) photographic works and works which are expressed by a process analogous to photography;

s.36 (1) Copyright shall subsist for the entire lifetime of the author and for 70 years after the death of an author...

The general term of copyright is life of the author plus 70 years. There is no special term of protection for photographs.

# Lebanon

## Decree Providing Regulation of Commercial and Industrial Property Rights in Syria and Lebanon as amended up to January 31, 1946[67]

Art. 138 This Decree protects all works manifesting human intelligence, whether written, plastic, graphic. or oral. Without the following enumeration being regarded as in any way limitative, such works include, for example ... photographs ... works of art of all kinds, whether or not they have an industrial character and whatever their merit, importance, designation, the material composing them, the nationality of their author and the place of their creation.

Under Art. 153 photographic works or works produced by a process analogous to photography have a different term of protection, being 50 years, calculated from the date of their publication. By Art. 143 the standard term is life of the author plus 50 years.

# Lesotho

## Copyright Order 1989[68]

"literary artistic and scientific" includes...
(h) photographic works, including works expressed by processes analogous to photography

3. (1) Authors of original literary, artistic and scientific works shall be entitled to copyright protection for their work under this Order, by the sole fact of the creation of such works

---

[66] *http://clea.wipo.int/*.
[67] *http://www.unesco.org/culture/copy/copyright/lebanon/fr_lebanon.html*. See n.1 (1sr ser.), above.
[68] *http://www.unesco.org/culture/copy/copyright/lesotho/fr_sommaire.html*. See n.1 (1sr ser.), above.

By s.13(5) rights in photographs are protected for a shorter period namely, until the expiration of 25 years from the making of the work. The standard protection term is life of the author plus 50 years.

## Liberia

## Act Adopting a New Patent, Copyright and Trademark Law of May 24, 1972[69]

§§2.1   Definitions*(c)* the term "literary, scientific or artistic work," irrespective of the value and the manner or form of expression shall include the following: ... 6. cinematographic and photographic works;

## Libya

## Law on the protection of copyright law (No. 9): 16 March 1968[70]

Art. 1      Authors of original literary, artistic and scientific works shall enjoy the protection provided under this Law, regardless of the kind of work, the form of its expression, its importance, or the purpose for which it was created.

Art. 2      Protection shall extend, in particular, to authors of: ... photographic or cinematographic works

Art. 3      ... However, the rights of authors of photographic works shall not be prejudicial to the rights of third parties who also photograph the same view, even if the new pictures are taken from the same place and, in particular, in the same circumstances as the first picture

Art. 20     Subject to the provisions of Article 8, the economic exploitation of the rights provided under this Law shall terminate twenty-five years after the death of the author; however, the total period of protection shall not be less than fifty years from the date of the first publication of the work. In the case of photographic or cinematographic works which merely involve photographing or filming by technical means, the period of protection shall be five years from the date on which they are first made available to the public.

Libya under Art. 20 has a type of neighbouring right for works which merely involve photographing or filming by technical means and the period of protection is only five years from publication.

## Liechtenstein

## Law of May 19, 1999 regarding the Copyright and Neighbouring Rights (Copyright Law)[70a]

Art. 2(1)   Works shall mean literary and artistic creations of the mind, irrespective of their value or purpose, that possess an individual nature.

(2)   They include, in particular:

---

[69] *http://www.unesco.org/culture/copy/copyright/liberia/fr_page1.html.* See n.1 (1st ser.), above.
[70] *http://www.unesco.org/culture/copy/copyright/lybia/fr_lybia.html.* See n.1 (1st ser.), above. Also at *http://www.agip.com/laws/laws.htm.*
[70a] Available via the UNESCO portal, see n.1 (1st ser.), above.

... (g)   photographic, cinematographic and other visual or audiovisual works.

The basic term for protection of all works including photographs is life of the author plus 70 years as provided by Art. 32. The predecessor statute had a specific provision that a copyright in a photograph did not exclude the right of another person to take a similar photograph:

## Law concerning Copyright in Literary and Artistic Works of October 26, 1928 as amended by Law: August 8, 1959[71]

Art. 2   This Law protects photographic works, including works obtained by any process analogous to photography.

5.   New photographs of objects already photographed
Art. 16   Copyright in a photographic work shall not exclude the right of any other person to take a new photograph of the same object, even if such new photograph is taken from the same position and, in a general manner, under the same conditions as the first.

The basic term of protection of a work published during the author's lifetime was life of the author plus 50 years which has now been increased to 70 years.[72] There ws no special term for photographs.

## Luxembourg

## Law of March 29, 1972, on Copyright as last amended on September 8, 1997[73]

Art. 1   The author of a literary or artistic work shall enjoy therein an exclusive incorporeal property right which shall be exclusive and enforceable against all persons.

...   The expression literary and artistic works" shall include all productions in the literary, scientific and artistic domain, regardless of the mode or form of expression thereof, such as ... photographic works to which are assimilated works expressed by a process analogous to photography ...

Art. 2   Except as otherwise provided in this Law, copyright shall subsist for 70 years after the death of the author in favour of his heirs or successors in title.

Art. 4   The copyright in photographic works and works of applied art shall subsist for 50 years from the date on which such works were made. However, photographic works shall enjoy a term equal to that provided for in Article 2 if they are original in the sense that they are an intellectual creation specific to their author.

---

[71] *http://www.unesco.org/culture/copy/copyright/liechtenstein/fr_sommaire.html.* See n.1 (1st ser.), above.
[72] Art. 36.
[73] *http://www.unesco.org/culture/copy/copyright/luxembourg/fr_page1.html.* See n.1 (1st ser.), above.

## Macau, Special Administrative Region of the People's Republic of China

The Copyright Decree of Macau has some particularly interesting provisions relating to originality in photography. It specifies that only photographs where the choice of its subject or the manner of its execution result in a personal artistic creation of the author are protected by copyright.

## Copyright, Decree-Law (Consolidation), 30/07/1999 (2000), No. 43/99/M[74]

Art. 1(1)   Intellectual creations in the literary, scientific and artistic fields, whatever may be their type, form of expression, merit, form of communication or purpose, shall be protected by copyright.

(2)   Ideas, processes, systems, operational methods, concepts, principles or discoveries, alone and as such, shall not be protected by copyright.

(4)   A work is original where it is the result of the author's own creative effort and not merely the appropriation of another person's creation.

Art. 2   The following in particular are protected works in so far as they are original:
...(h)   photographic works and works produced by processes analogous to photography;...

### SECTION VII PHOTOGRAPHIC WORKS

Art. 149   Demarcation of Protection
(1)   The only photograph that is protected by copyright is that which, by the choice of its subject or the manner of its execution, may be considered a personal artistic creation of the author.
(2)   Photographs that have mere documentary value, such as photographs of writings and documents, business papers, technical drawings and similar material, shall not be protected
(3)   Stills from cinematographic films shall be considered photographs.

Art. 150   Rights of Others
The copyright in a photographic work shall be understood as being without prejudice to the provisions regarding the exhibition, reproduction and marketing of portraits or to the copyright in the work photographed.

Art. 151   Commissioned Photographs
(1)   Unless otherwise agreed, a commissioned photograph may be reproduced or its reproduction authorized by the person portrayed or by his successors independently of authorization by the photographer.
(2)   Remuneration shall be payable to the author where a reproduction of the portrait, made by the person photographed or his successors under the foregoing paragraph, has commercial character.

Art. 152   Photographs Published in Periodicals
It shall be lawful, independently of authorization by the author but without prejudice to the right to remuneration, to reproduce photographs published in newspapers, magazines or other periodicals where they relate to persons or current events or are of general interest in any way and the reproduction is intended for inclusion in another similar periodical.

---

[74] *http://clea.wipo.int/.*

Art. 153  Disposal of Negatives
Unless otherwise agreed, disposal of the negatives of a photographic work shall imply transfer of the economic rights in the work.

Art. 154  Compulsory Information
(1) Where the author has affixed his identity or the date on which it was made on the photograph, that information shall also appear on any reproductions that may be made of it.
(2) Photographs of works of three-dimensional art shall give the name of the author of the work photographed.

Art. 155  Lapse
The copyright in photographic works shall lapse 25 years after their completion, even if they have never been disclosed or published.

Art. 156  Extension
The provisions in this Section shall be applicable to works produced by any means analogous to photography.


## Madagascar

The current law is Law No. 94–036 of September 1995. The author was unable to locate an English translation.

## Ordinance Amending Certain Provisions of Law No. 57–298 of March 11, 1957 on Literary and Artistic Property[75]

By a letter dated March 24, 1967, The Minister of Foreign Affairs of the Malagasy Republic informed the Director-General of Unesco that the French Law of March 11, 1957 on Literary and Artistic Property remains in force in the Malagasy Republic.

Art. 3  The following in particular shall be considered intellectual works within the meaning of this Law: ... photographic works of an artistic or documentary character, and other works of the same character produced by processes analogous to photography

## Malawi

### Copyright Act 1989[76]

2.  In this Act, unless the context otherwise requires ... "artistic work", irrespective of artistic quality, means any of the following works:
(a) paintings, drawings, etchings, lithographs, woodcuts, engravings, product of photogravure and prints;
(b) photography not comprised in a cinematograph film ...
"photograph" includes photolithograph and other work produced by any process analogous to photography but does not include any part of an audiovisual work;

5.(1) Literary, dramatic, musical or artistic work shall not be eligible for copyright under this Part unless:
(a) it is original in character; or

---

[75] *http://www.unesco.org/culture/copy/copyright/madagascar/fr_madagascar.html.* See n.1 (1st ser.), above.
[76] *http://www.unesco.org/culture/copy/copyright/malawi/fr_sommaire.html.* See n.1 (1st ser.), above.

(b)   it is derivative work, and it is in writing or recorded or otherwise reduced to material form

Under s.13(1)(g) photographs are only protected until the expiration of 25 years from the date on which the work was first published or made, a shorter period than the life plus 50 years for most works.

## Malaysia

### Copyright Act 1987 as amended up to June 27, 2000[77]

3          In this Act, unless the context otherwise requires:...
           "artistic work" includes: ... (e) photographs not comprised in a film;...
           "author,": ... (d) in relation to photographs, means the person by whom the arrangements for the taking of the photograph were undertaken; ... "photograph" means a recording of light or other radiation on any medium on which an image is produced or from which an image may by any means be produced and which is not part of a film ...
7. (1)     Subject to this section, the following works shall be eligible for copyright: ... (c) artistic works;...
   (2)     Works shall be protected irrespective of their quality and the purpose for which they were created.
   (3)     A literary, musical or artistic work shall not be eligible for copyright unless
           (a)  sufficient effort has been expended to make the work original in character; and
           (b)  the work has been written down, recorded or otherwise reduced to material form.

Photographs are protected for the same basic term as other works namely, life of the author and 50 years: s.17(1). The Copyright (Amendment) Act 1997 which came into force on April 1, 1999 deleted s.21 of the Copyright Act 1987. Section 21 had provided for a different term of copyright protection for photographs. Under s.21 copyright subsisted in photographs until "fifty years from the beginning or the calendar year next following the year in which the photograph was first published." The standard term for other works at that time was also life of the author plus 50 years.

## Mali

The current statute is the Copyright Law (No. 84/AN–RM): October 1994 which replaced the 1977 Law below. No English translation was available.

### Copyright statute (No. 77–46 CMLN): July 12, 1977[78]

Art. 1     The author of an intellectual work shall, by the mere fact of its creation enjoy an exclusive incorporeal property right in the work, effective against all persons
Art. 7     "Work" means any original creation, particularly as regards form, which is a manifestation of the author's personality. The work shall comprise both the work in its original form and any form derived from

---

[77] *http://www.unesco.org/culture/copy/copyright/malaysia/fr_sommaire.html.* See n.1 (1st ser.), above.
[78] *http://www.unesco.org/culture/copy/copyright/mali/fr_sommaire.html.* See n.1 (1st ser.), above.

the original.The following in particular shall be considered works: ... photographic works, to which are assimilated, for the purposes of this Ordinance, works expressed by a process similar to photography;

Under Art. 85 photographs are protected for 50 years from the date on which the work is lawfully made accessible to the public. The normal term for other works is life of the author plus 50 years.

## Malta

### Copyright Act 25/04/2000, No. XIII[79]

2.(1)  In this Act, unless the context otherwise requires "artistic work" shall include, irrespective of artistic quality, any of the following, or works similar thereto:
        ... (d) photographs not comprised in an audiovisual work;

3(1)  Subject to the provisions of this section the following works shall be eligible for copyright:
       (a)  artistic works; ...

  (2)  A literary, musical, or artistic work shall not be eligible for copyright unless the work has an *original character* and it has been written down, recorded, fixed or otherwise reduced to material form.

By s.4(4) the term of copyright for all artistic works is 70 years after the end of the year in which the author dies, irrespective of the date when the work is lawfully made available to the public. The previous statute, the Copyright Act of 1967[80] had a different definition of originality as follows:

3(2)  A literary, musical or artistic work shall not be eligible for copyright unless:
       (a)  sufficient effort has been expended on making the work to give it an original character; and
       (b)  the work has been written down, recorded or otherwise reduced to material form.

The 1976 Act gave photographs a shorter term of protection, 25 years after the end of the year which the work was first made accessible to the public by the owner of the copyright.[81] The basic term for other works was life of the author plus 25 years.

## Mauritius

### The Copyright Act 1997 (Act No. 12 of 1997)[82]

2.(1)  In this Act ...
        "artistic, literary or scientific work":
        (a)  means a production in the artistic, literary or scientific domain;
        (b)  includes: ... (x) a photographic work; ...
  ...   "author":

---

[79] *http://clea.wipo.int/*.
[80] *http://www.unesco.org/culture/copy/copyright/malta/fr_malta.html.* See n.1 (1st ser.), above.
[81] s.4(2)(ii).
[82] *http://www.unesco.org/culture/copy/copyright/mauritius/fr_sommaire.html.* See n.1 (1st ser.), above.

    (a)  means the person who has intellectually created a work

    (b)  includes: ... (iii) in the case of a photograph, the person responsible for its composition; ...

...    "original work":

    (a)  means a work which is the product of a person's skill or labour;

    (b)  does not include a work which is essentially a copy of another work

...    "photographic work" includes a work expressed by a process analogous to photography;

3.—(1)  Subject to this Act, the author of an artistic, literary or scientific work or of a derivative work shall, irrespective of the quality of the work and the purpose for which the work may have been created, be entitled to protection for his work where it is

    (a)  an original work; and

    (b)  written down, recorded, fixed or otherwise reduced to any material form.

Under s.12(6) economic rights relating to a photographic work are protected until the expiry of 25 years from the making of the work. This is shorter than the basic term for other works of life of the author plus 50 years

## Mexico

### Federal Law on Copyright of 24 December, 1996[83] amended May 19, 1997

| | |
|---|---|
| Art. 3 | The works protected by this Law are originally created works susceptible of disclosure or reproduction in any form or medium. |
| Art. 4 | The works qualifying for protection may be: ...<br>(C) in terms of their origin:<br>original works: those that are themselves original creations and not based on other, preexisting works, or which, being based on another work, possess characteristics that testify to the originality thereof;<br>derived works: those that are the result of the adaptation, translation or other transformation of an original work; |
| Art. 13 | The copyright referred to in this Law is recognized in respect of works in the following categories: ... photographic works ... |
| Art. 86 | Professional photographers may only display photographs produced on commission, as specimens of their work, after authorization has been obtained. |
| Art. 148 | Literary and artistic works that have already been disclosed may only be used in the following cases without the consent of the owner of the economic rights and without remuneration, provided that the normal exploitation of the work is not adversely affected thereby and provided also that the source is invariably mentioned and that no alteration is made to the work ...<br>reproduction, communication and distribution in drawings, paintings, photographs and audiovisual processes of works that are visible from public places. |

The basic term of protection is life of the author plus 75 years.[84] There is no separate term for the protection of photographs.

---

[83] *http://www.unesco.org/culture/copy/copyright/mexico/fr_sommaire.html.* See n.1 (1st ser.), above.

[84] Art 29.

## Moldova (Republic of)

### Law on Copyright and Neighbouring Rights(No. 293-XIII, of November 23, 1994) as last amended by No. 1207–XIV July 2000[85]

Art. 4—(1)   This Law shall protect as copyright works of the mind created in the literary, artistic and scientific fields, expressed in any material form that permits their reproduction, whether they have been disclosed or not, and whatever their form, purpose, value or means of reproduction

Art. 6—(2)   Copyright protection shall extend to: ... (i) photographic works and works obtained by processes analogous to photography...

Art. 17(4)   Copyright in audiovisual works [or photographs] shall be protected for 50 years and copyright in works of applied art for 25 years computed from the day of lawful publication of such works or from the day of their creation if they have not been published, or computed as from January 1 of the year following that of publication or of creation of the work

The basic term of protection under Art. 17(3) is the life of the author plus 50 years which now applies to photographs. Historically, photographs as copyright works received a shorter term of protection under Art. 17(4), but the words "or photographs" in square brackets above have been removed. There are no neighbouring rights for photographs.

## Monaco

### Law on the Protection of Literary and Artistic Works (Law No. 491) of November 24, 1948 as amended[86]

Art. 1   The rights of authors in their literary or artistic works are guaranteed by Law.

Art. 2(1)   The term "literary and artistic works" shall include every production in the literary, scientific and artistic domain, whatever may be the mode or form of its expression, such as ... photographic works and works produced by a process analogous to photography...

The basic period of protection is life of the author plus 50 years under Art. 12. There are no separate provisions for photographs.

## Mongolia

### Copyright, Act (Consolidation), 22/06/1993 (21/05/1999)[87]

Art. 3(1)   The subject matter of copyright shall include the following works irrespective of their content, purpose, form, merit, mode of creation or availability to the public:
...(8) photographic works and all works expressed by a process analogous to photography;

---

[85] *http://www.unesco.org/culture/copy/copyright/moldova/fr_sommaire.html.* See n.1 (1st ser.), above.
[86] *http://www.unesco.org/culture/copy/copyright/monaco/fr_monaco.html.* See n.1 (1st ser.), above.
[87] *http://clea.wipo.int/.*

...(13) any other works expressing the intellectual creative activity of the author

Art. 17(1)    The term of copyright in a particular work shall be deemed to begin from the day of its making.

(2)    The term of exclusive rights in copyrighted works shall be the life of the author and fifty years after his or her death. The term of exclusive rights in copyrighted works after the death of the author shall be deemed to begin on 1 January of the year following the death. In the case of joint authorship this term shall be deemed to begin on 1 January of the year following the death of the last surviving author.

(4)    The term of any copyrighted work where the author is a legal person shall last for a period of 75 years from 1 January of the year following the year of the making of the work.

(6)    The term of copyright of photographic works and works of applied art shall be 25 years from the making of such work.

Art. 17(6) was inserted by amendment on May 21, 1999 and provides for a shorter term of protection for photographic works, namely 25 years from the making of the work. Prior to amendment, photographs enjoyed the same term of protection as other works, namely life of the author plus 50 years. This is unusual, as the general trend in national statute amendment has been a movement towards repealing such distinctions and giving photographs the same protection as other works, rather than introducing new distinctions.

## Morocco

## Law No. 2–00 of Copyrights and Neighboring rights February 2000[88]

Art. 1    The expressions used in this law and their different substitutes shall have the following meanings:

...9.    It is considered "a photographic work" any recording of light or any other radiation on a support which produces a picture or which a picture can be produced thereof, no matter what the technical nature of the technique by which this recording was executed (chemical, electronic, ... et).

Every picture extracted from an audio-visual work shall not be considered a photographic work. It will be considered a part of an audio-visual work.

Art. 3    This law shall be applied to literary and artistic works, which shall hereinafter be referred to as "works" which are original innovations in the literary and artistic fields such as: ... J- Photographic works. The protection is not associated with the type of expression, the type of work or its purpose.

Art. 25    Regardless of the contradictory requirements to what is contained in this part, the financial rights of the author of a certain work is protected during his life as well as for fifty years after his death. The moral rights are not limited by time and can not prescribed or cancelled and are transferred after his death to his right holders.

The previous statute was Dahir (Act) Relating to the Protection of Literary and Artistic Works, 1970[89] which provided

---

[88] *http://www.agip.com/laws/morocco/c.htm.*
[89] *http://www.unesco.org/culture/copy/copyright/morocco/fr_sommaire.html.* See n.1 (1st ser.), above.

Art. 3     A work is original when its characteristic features and its form, or its form alone, make possible the identification of its author.

Art. 6     The following shall in particular be considered intellectual works: ... (8) photographic works, to which are assimilated works expressed by a process analogous to photography, on condition that the name of the author is expressly indicated

Under Art. 51 of the 1970 statute the term of protection for photographs is 50 years from the end of the year during which the work is disclosed as opposed to life plus 50 years for other works. The 2000 statute gives photographs the same term as other works.

## Nepal

The current statute is the Copyright Act of 2002. No English language translation was obtainable by the authors.

## Copyright Act of 1966, 2022[90]

2.   In this Act, unless the subject or context otherwise requires: (a) "Work" shall mean: ... (3) Any drawing, map or photograph made, engraved or photographed, or any other direct drawing or creative work, or any part thereof... or (5) Any other kind of creative work relating to literature, music or art, or any part thereof

There was no specific reference to creativity or originality in the 1966 statute other than above.

Under s.8 the basic term of copyright under the 1966 Act was life of the author plus 50 years. There was no separate provision for photographs.

## Netherlands

The relevant statute is the Copyright Act of 1912 as last amended by Act No. 303, 1999.[91] Under Art. 10(2) protection is afforded to "every production in the literary, scientific or artistic fields whatever may be the mode or form of its expression."[92] The Act does not expressly require originality. According to the Dutch Supreme Court, to be protected a work must have "a distinctive, original character, that is one bearing the designer's personal imprint."[93] or an individual original character bearing the personal mark of the maker.[94] Herman Cohen Jehoram in Nimmer & Geller observes:

> "This criterion does not imply any requirement of literary or artistic value: for example ... a snapshot ... can meet the originality test."[95]

---

[90] *http://www.unesco.org/culture/copy/copyright/nepal/fr_nepal.html*. See n.1 (1st ser.), above.

[91] Available via the UNESCO portal. See n.1 (1st ser.), above.

[92] Nimmer & Geller NETH-13 §2[1][b]; and see Hugenholtz, P. Bernt *Dutch Copyright Law 1995–2000* (Jan 2001) 187 RIDA 111, 115.

[93] *loc cit.*

[94] See Van Oerle, Richard, *Netherlands in Copyright and Photographs: An International Survey* (Gendreau, Y., Nordemann, A, and Oesch, R eds) Kluwer Law Int. (1999) at p.140.

[95] Nimmer & Geller NETH-14 §2[1][b]; Hugenholtz above n. 88 at p.115.

The Dutch law as to originality has more in common with the French and German civil law systems than the UK "skill and labour" and the US pre-Feist approaches. The Dutch Supreme Court held that factual data per se does not qualify for copyright protection and that in order to be protected a compilation needs to be "the result of a selection process expressing its maker's personal views."[96]

Article 10(1) sets out a non-exhaustive list of types of protected works and includes at sub-para. (ix) photographic works. There are no separate provision for simple photographs. The term of protection for photographs is as for other works, namely life of the author plus 70 years.

## New Zealand

## Copyright Act 1994[96a] as amended by 2003 No. 111

2(1)   In this Act, unless the context otherwise requires; "Artistic work" (a) Means: ... A graphic work, photograph, sculpture, collage, or model, irrespective of artistic quality; ...
"Photograph" means a recording of light or other radiation on any medium on which an image is produced or from which an image may by any means be produced; but does not include a film or part of a film.

14(1)   Copyright is a property right that exists, in accordance with this Act, in original works of the following descriptions: (a) Literary, dramatic, musical, or artistic works...

14(2)   A work is not original if:
(a)  It is, or to the extent that it is, a copy of another work;
(b)  It infringes the copyright in, or to the extent that it infringes the copyright in, another work.

73(1)   This section applies to the following works:
(a)  Buildings; (b) Works (being sculptures, models for buildings, or works of artistic craftsmanship) that are permanently situated in a public place or in premises open to the public.

(2)   Copyright in a work to which this section applies is not infringed by: ... (b) Copying the work by making a photograph or film of it...

Under s.22 photographs as artistic works receive the same basic term of protection as other works, *i.e.* life of the author plus 50 years from the end of the calendar year in which the author dies.

## Nicaragua

The applicable statute is Law No. 312 on Copyright and Neighbouring Rights, August 1999. The author was unable to obtain an official English translation. The official text in Spanish is available online.[96b] The term of protection is now life of the author plus 70 years under s.27 of the 1999 Act. Previously, the Copyright Provisions were contained in the 1904 Civil Code[97]

---

[96] *Grote van Dale* decision Supreme Court, January 4, 1991 NJ, 608 note Verkade, IER 1991/4,99 cited in Nimmer & Geller, *ibid.*
[96a] Available online at http://www.legislation.govt.nz/.
[96b] Via both the UNESCO portal, see n.1, (1st ser.), above, and the WIPO Collection of Laws for Electronic Access at *http://clea.wipo.int/*.
[97] *http://www.unesco.org/culture/copy/copyright/nicaragua/fr_sommaire.html*. See n.1 (1st ser.), above.

Art. 725 The ownership of products of work and industry shall be regulated by the laws of property in general, except in those cases in respect of which this Code establishes special rules

Art. 726 Every author or inventor shall enjoy the ownership of his work or of his discovery for such time as this Code may determine.

Art. 789 The following shall have the exclusive right of reproduction of their original works: ... (3) Painters, engravers, lithographers, photographers and photoengravers.

There was no list of works in the Civil Code. Photographs were not subject to a special term.

## Nigeria

## Copyright Act as last amended by the Copyright (Amendment) Decree No. 42 of 1999[98]

1(2) A literary, musical or artistic work shall not be eligible for copyright unless (a) sufficient effort has been expended on making the work to give it an original character ...

39—(1) In this Decree, unless the context otherwise requires ... "artistic work" includes, irrespective of artistic quality, any of the following works or works similar thereto ... (d) photographs not comprised in cinematograph film;

Under the First Schedule to the Act the term of protection for all photographs is 50 years after the end of the year in which the work was first published. The normal term for most works is life of the author plus 70 years.

## Norway

## Act No. 2 of May 12, 1961, Relating to Copyright in Literary, Scientific and Artistic Works, etc., With Subsequent Amendments Up to June 30, 1995 (as last amended by Law No. 52 of June 2001)[99]

s.1 Any person who creates a literary, scientific or artistic work shall have the copyright therein. By such a work is meant in this Act a literary, scientific or artistic work of any kind, irrespective of the manner or form of expression, such as: ... (6) photographic works...
In the case of photographic pictures which are not a literary, scientific or artistic work, Section 43a shall apply.

s.24 Works of art and photographic works which form part of a collection or which are exhibited or offered for sale may be depicted in catalogues of the collection and in announcements of the exhibition or sale. Works of art and photographic works may also be depicted when they are permanently located in or near a public place or thoroughfare. However, this shall not apply when the work is clearly the main motif and the reproduction is exploited commercially. Buildings may be freely depicted.

---

[98] *http://www.unesco.org/culture/copy/copyright/nigeria/fr_sommaire.html.* See n.1 (1st ser.), above.
[99] *http://www.unesco.org/culture/copy/copyright/norway/fr_sommaire.html.* See n.1 (1st ser.), above.

s.43a    A person who produces a photographic picture shall have the exclusive right to make copies thereof by photography, printing, drawing or any other process, and to make it available to the public. The exclusive right to a photographic picture shall subsist during the lifetime of the photographer and for 15 years after the expiry of the year in which he died, but for not less than 50 years from the expiry of the year in which the picture was produced. If the exclusive right is shared by two or more persons, the term of protection shall run from the expiry of the year in which the last surviving person died. The provisions of Sections 2, second and third paragraphs, 3, 6 to 9, 11 to 21, 23 to 28, 30, 31, 33 to 39f and 39j to 39l shall apply correspondingly to photographic pictures to the same extent that they apply to photographic works. If a photograph is subject to copyright, such right may also be enforced.

s.45c    Photographs of a person shall not be reproduced or publicly exhibited without the consent of the subject of the picture, except when
(a) the picture is of current or of general interest,
(b) the picture of the person is less important than the main contents of the picture.
(c) the subject of the picture is a group assembled for a meeting, an outdoor procession or situations or events of general interest,
(d) a copy of the picture is exhibited in the usual manner as an advertisement of the photographer's work and the subject of the picture does not prohibit this, or
(e) the picture is used as specified in Section 23,[1] first paragraph, third sentence, or Section 27,[2] second paragraph.
The term of protection shall apply during the lifetime of the subject of the picture and for 15 years after the expiry of the year in which the subject died.

s.58 ...   The provision in Section 43a shall apply to photographic pictures first published in the realm or which have been produced by a person who is a national of or resident in or who has his registered office in a country within the European Economic Area. The same shall apply to photographs placed in buildings or permanent structures situated in a country within the said area.

The law of Norway draws a distinction between the copyright photograph and a "ordinary" photographic picture.[3] The rights granted in respect of a photographic picture are only the reproduction right and the distribution right.[4] The term granted to simple photographs is 15 years pma or 50 years from the taking of the picture, whichever is longer.

## Oman

## Decree No. 37/2000: The Law for the Protection of Copyright and Neighboring Rights[5]

Photographs are not specifically named as a protected category of work.

---

[1] An issued portrait may be reproduced in a publication containing biographical material.
[2] Use in connection with a search, an investigation or as evidence.
[3] For further discussion of the law in Norway see Oesch, R, *Nordic Countries in Copyright and Photographs: An International Survey*, Gendreau, Y, Nordemann and Oesch, R (eds) Kluwer Law Int. at p.231.
[4] s.43a.
[5] *http://www.agip.com/laws/oman/c.htm/*.

Art. 1    In applying the rules of this law, the following words and phrases will have the meanings opposite them unless the context of text necessitates otherwise.
Author: The natural person who created the work.
Work: Any innovative[5a] literary, scientific or artistic work.

Art. 2    The authors of original works of art in literature, science, arts, and culture in general shall enjoy the protection of this law irrespective of the value of those works of art, the type thereof, the manner of expression or the purpose for which they were created. The said protection shall comprise, in particular, the authors of the following works of art:
Books, computer programs and other writings
Works of art delivered orally such as lectures, addresses and sermons.
Dramatic works of art and musical plays.
Musical works of art whether numbered or not and whether accompanied with words or not.
Works of art relating to dance designing and pantomime.
Cinematographic, television, radio, audio and audio-visual works of art.
Works of art of drawings, painting, architecture, sculpture, ornamentation and engraving.
The applied works of art whether handicraft or industrial.
Illustrations, geographical maps, plans and sketches and formative works of art relating to geography, topography, architecture and science.
Folklore.
The title of the work if it is distinctive and innovative and is not a current term used to denote the topic of the work of art.

Art. 7    Financial rights are granted to the author during his lifetime and fifty calendar years starting from the beginning of the first calendar year following his death.

Art. 8    Protection of financial right are granted to the author for fifty calendar years from the date of first publication for the following works:
Movies, applied art works and photographs.

## Law on the Protection of Copyright as approved by Royal Decree of No. 47 of 1996[6]

Art. 2    The protection afforded by this Law shall be enjoyed, in general, by the authors of original literary. scientific, artistic and cultural works, whatever their value, nature, mode of expression or purpose. Such protection shall he enjoyed in particular by the authors of the following works: ... (g) works of drawing, painting and graphics, of architecture, of sculpture, of' decorative art and of engraving; (h) works of applied art, whether works of handicraft or works produced by industrial processes;

[NB: As with the amended statute, photographs not specifically named]

Under Art. 8 of the 1996 Statute photographs were protected for 25 years from the publication date of the work. The standard term was life of the author plus 50 years.

---

[5a] For observations about the translation of the word "innovative" see above at para. 3–078, n. 72a.
[6] *http://www.unesco.org/culture/copy/copyright/oman/fr_page1.html*. See n.1 (1st ser.), above.

**Pakistan**

Copyright Ordinance, 1962 as amended up to 2000[7]

2.    In this Ordinance, unless there is anything repugnant in the subject or context ... (c)
      "artistic work" means ... a painting, a sculpture, a drawing (including a diagram, map, chart or plan), an engraving or a photograph, whether or not any such work possesses artistic quality; ...
      (w) "photograph" includes photo-lithograph and any work produced by any process analogous to photography but does not include any part of a cinematographic work;

57(1)    The following acts shall not constitute an infringement of copyright, namely: ...
      (r) the making or publishing of a painting, drawing, engraving or photograph of an architectural work of art;
      (s) the making or publishing of a painting, drawing, engraving or photograph of a sculpture or other artistic work if such work is permanently situated in a public place or any premises to which the public has access; ...

Under s.20 copyright subsists in photographs until 50 years from the beginning of the calendar year next following the year in which the photograph is published. The basic term for other works is life of the author plus 50 years.

**Panama**

Law on Copyright and Neighbouring Rights and Enacting Other Provisions (Law No. 15 of August 8, 1994)[8]

Art. 2(14)    "work" means an original intellectual creation of artistic, scientific or literary character that is susceptible of disclosure or reproduction in any form;

Art. 7    The subject matter of copyright is the work, as the result of intellectual creation. The following in particular shall be considered included among works protected by law ... photographic works and works expressed by a process analogous to photography

Art. 48    With regard to works that have already been lawfully disclosed, the following shall be allowed without authorization from the author or remuneration: 6. the reproduction of a work of art on permanent display in a street, square or other public place by means of an artistic technique different from that used for the making of the original; with regard to buildings, this exception shall be confined to the outer façade;

The general term is life of the author plus 50 years.[9] There is no special term for photographs.

---

[7] *http://www.unesco.org/culture/copy/copyright/pakistan/fr_sommaire.html.* See n.1 (1st ser.), above.
[8] *http://www.unesco.org/culture/copy/copyright/panama/fr_sommaire.html.* See n.1 (1st ser.), above.
[9] Art. 42.

# Paraguay

## Law No. 1328/98 on Copyright and Related Rights[9a]

| | |
|---|---|
| Art. 2 | For the purposes of this Law, the following expressions and their various derived forms shall have the meanings specified<br>(16) "work" any original intellectual creation in the literary or artistic field that is capable of being disclosed or reproduced in any known or as yet unknown form |
| Art. 3 | Copyright protection shall cover all intellectual works of creative character in the literary or artistic field, regardless of their type, form of expression, merit or purpose, the nationality or residence of the author or owner of the rights concerned and the place of publication of the work. |
| Art. 4 | The works to which the foregoing Article refers include the following in particular:...<br>(10) photographic works and works expressed by a process analogous to photography; |
| Art. 47 | Economic rights shall subsist throughout the life of the author and for 70 years thereafter, and shall be transferred on his death in accordance with the provisions of the Civil Code |
| Art. 135 | Any person who takes a photograph or makes another fixation by a comparable process that does not qualify as a work according to the definition contained in subparagraph 16 of Article 2 and the provisions of Title II of this Law shall have the exclusive right to authorize its reproduction, distribution and communication to the public on the same terms as are accorded to the authors of photographic works.<br>The term of this right shall be 50 years counted from the first of January of the year following that of the taking of the photograph. |

The previous copyright law was contained in the Civil Code Law (No. 1183): December 18, 1985, which came into force on January 1, 1987.[10] That provided as follows:

| | |
|---|---|
| Art. 2165 | Scientific, literary and artistic creations shall enjoy the protection afforded by this Code. |
| Art. 2175 | Anyone who has produced an original photographic image of a panorama, a landscape or a view, shall likewise enjoy in his capacity as owner of such image all rights afforded by this Code to artistic production. |

The general term of protection is life of the author plus 70 years. There is a special term for photographs which do not amount to creative works. Such simple photographs have the benefit of distribution, publication and reproduction rights for 50 years following the taking of the photograph.

---

[9a] Available in Spanish via the UNESCO Collection of National Laws. See n.1 (1st ser.), above.
[10] *http://www.unesco.org/culture/copy/copyright/paraguay/fr_paraguay.html*. See n.1 (1st ser.), above.

## Peru

### Copyright Law (Legislative Decree No. 822 of April 24, 1996)[11]

| | |
|---|---|
| Art. 3 | Copyright protection shall be accorded to all works of the mind in the literary or artistic field, whatever their kind, manner of expression, merit or purpose. |
| Art. 2 | For the purposes of this Law, the expressions that follow, and the various derived forms thereof, shall have the meanings specified... <br> (17)  work: any personal and original intellectual creation capable of being disclosed or reproduced in any form that is or may yet become known; |
| Art. 5 | Protected works shall include the following:... <br> (h)  photographic works and works expressed by a process analogous to photography |
| Art. 144 | Any person who takes a photograph or makes another form of fixation by means of a comparable process that does not qualify as a work according to the definition in this Law shall enjoy the exclusive right to authorize the reproduction, distribution and communication to the public thereof on the same conditions as are accorded to the authors of photographs. The term of this right shall be 70 years counted from the first of January of the year following that of the taking of the photograph. |

The term for a photographic copyright work is life of the author plus 70 years.[12]

## Philippines

### Intellectual Property Code of the Philippines (Republic Act No. 8293)[13]

| | |
|---|---|
| 172.1 | Literary and artistic works, hereinafter referred to as "works", are original intellectual creations in the literary and artistic domain protected from the moment of their creation and shall include in particular: ... (k) Photographic works including works produced by a process analogous to photography; lantern slides; |
| 213.5 | In case of photographic works, the protection shall be for fifty (50) years from publication of the work and, if unpublished, fifty (50) years from the making. |
| 213.6 | In case of audio-visual works including those produced by process analogous to photography or any process for making audio-visual recordings, the term shall be fifty (50) years from date of publication and, if unpublished, from the date of making. |

Other works generally receive protection for life of the author plus 50 years. Photographs thus receive a shorter term.

---

[11] *http://www.unesco.org/culture/copy/copyright/peru/fr_sommaire.html*. See n.1 (1st ser.), above.
[12] Art. 52.
[13] *http://www.unesco.org/culture/copy/copyright/philippines/fr_sommaire.html*. See n.1 (1st ser.), above.

# Poland

## Law of February 4, 1994, on Copyright and Neighbouring Rights[14]

Art. 1–1    The subject matter of copyright is any expression of creative activity having individual character and manifested in any material form, regardless of the value, intended purpose and manner of expression thereof (work).

2    The subject matter of copyright includes the following in particular: ... (3) photographic works

The relevant statute is the Copyright and Neighbouring Rights Act of 1994.[15] According to Nimmer & Geller, Art. 1.1 provides that "the scope of copyright encompasses any manifestation of creative activity of [an] individual nature, no matter in what form it comes into being and regardless of its value, purpose or manner of its expression."[16-17] Article 1.2 provides a non-exhaustive list of protected works which includes at para. (3) "photographic works". There is no distinction between creative and non-creative photographic works or neighbouring rights in respect of photographs. There is no special term provision for photographs either.

# Portugal

## Code of Copyright and Related Rights No. 45/85 of September 17, 1985, as last amended by Law No. 114/91 of September 3, 1991[18]

This Code was last amended by Decree No. 83/2001, August 2001 on organisations for the collective exercise and management of copyright and related rights societies. The extracts reproduced here are from the official translation which only included amendments up to 1991.

Art. 1(1)    Works shall mean intellectual creations in the literary, scientific and artistic fields, in whatever form, and as such they shall be protected under the present Code, as shall the rights of their authors.

Art. 2(1)    Intellectual works in the literary, scientific and artistic fields, whatever their type, form of expression, merits, mode of communication or objective, include, in particular: ... (h) photographic works and works produced by processes analogous to photography

Art. 34.(1)    Copyright in photographic works or in works obtained by a process analogous to photography, as well as works of applied art, shall lapse 25 years after the work has been carried out.(2) Where the work has not been made available to the public with the author's consent, the copyright referred to in the preceding paragraph shall also lapse 25 years after the work has been carried out.

---

[14] *http://www.unesco.org/culture/copy/copyright/poland/fr_sommaire.html.* See n.1 (1st ser.), above.
[15] Nimmer & Geller POL–7 §1.
[16-17] Nimmer & Geller POL–8 §2[1][a].
[18] *http://www.unesco.org/culture/copy/copyright/portugal/fr_sommaire.html.* See n.1 (1st ser.), above.

### SECTION VIII Photographic Works

Conditions for protection

Art. 164(1)   The choice of a photograph's subject and the conditions of its creation must be deemed to be a personal artistic creation by the author before a photograph may qualify for protection.

(2)   The provisions contained in this section shall not apply to photographs of writings, documents, business papers, technical drawings and similar objects.

(3)   Photograms of cinematographic films shall be deemed to be photographs.

Rights of authors of photographic works

Art. 165(1)   The author of a photographic work shall have the exclusive right to reproduce, disseminate and sell the work, subject to the restrictions concerning exhibition, reproduction and sale of portraits and without prejudice to copyright in the reproduced work in the case of photographs of works of plastic art.

(2)   Where a photograph has been made under an employment contract or on commission, the right referred to in this Article shall be deemed to belong to the employer or the commissioner.

(3)   Any person who uses a photographic reproduction for commercial purposes shall pay the author equitable remuneration.

Transfer of negatives

Art. 166   Unless otherwise agreed, transfer of the negative of a photographic work shall imply transfer of the rights referred to in the preceding Articles.

Compulsory information

Art. 167(1)   Copies of a photographic work shall bear the following information:
(a)   the name of the photographer;
(b)   in the case of photographs of works of plastic art, the name of the author of the work photographed.

(2)   Only the unlawful reproduction of photographs bearing the above-mentioned information may be punished. In the absence of such information, the author may not claim the compensation provided for in the present Code, unless the photographer can show evidence of bad faith on the part of the person making the reproduction.

Reproduction of commissioned photographs

Art. 168(1)   Unless otherwise agreed, when the photograph of a person has been made on commission, it may be published, reproduced or given for reproduction by the person photographed or by his heirs or transferees, without the photographer's consent.

(2)   Where the name of the photographer appeared on the original photograph, it shall also appear on the copies.

The standard term of protection under Art. 31 is life of the author plus 50 years. Photographs therefore under Art. 34(1) above receive a lesser protection. Only "creative" photographs within the meaning of Art. 164(1) are protected.

## Qatar

### Law No. 7 of 2002, Law on the Protection of Copyright and Neighboring Rights[19]

| | |
|---|---|
| Art. 2 | Protection under this Law is conferred to authors of original literary and artistic works, irrespective of the value, quality, purpose or mode of expression of these works. |
| | Protection shall cover particularly the following works: ... |
| | (7)  photographic and similar works |
| Art. 14 | A person who takes photographs or of a person shall be prohibited from publishing, displaying or distributing the original picture or copy thereof without the permission of the said person; this provision shall not apply if the publication of the photograph or portrait was done on the occasion of a public event, or if relating to public figures or world known celebrities, or if authorized by public authorities for the public interest. |
| | The person represented in the photograph may authorize its publication in newspapers and magazines and other similar publications without the authorization of the photographer, unless otherwise agreed. |
| | These provisions shall apply irrespective of the method used to produce the photograph. |
| Art. 15 | The economic rights shall be protected during the life of the Author andfor fifty calendar years after his death. |

The previous law was Law No. 25 of 1995 Concerning the Protection of Works of the Intellect and Authors" Rights.[20] The provisions relating to photographs provided as follows:

| | |
|---|---|
| Art. 2 | The protection provided by this Law shall be enjoyed by authors of original works of literature, art and science, whatever their value or nature, the purpose for which they were made and the manner of their expression. |
| Art. 3 | Protection shall generally cover works that are expressed in writing, by sound, by drawing, by painting or by movement, and in particular: ... photographic works, including works expressed by processes analogous to photography, such as still photographs, transmitted by television that are not incorporated in a physical medium; |
| Art. 17 | The following uses of protected works shall be considered legal even if they have not been consented to by the authors: ... the taking of new photographs of anything that has been previously photographed, and the earlier photograph having been published, even if the new photograph is taken in the same place and under the same circumstances as those in which the earlier photograph was taken. |

Under Art. 25 of the 1995 Statute photographs were protected for 25 calendar years from the completion date of the work. The standard period of protection was life of the author plus 50 years. The 2000 Statute gives photographs the same period of protection as other works.

---

[19] *http://www.agip.com/laws/qatar/c.htm/.*
[20] *http://www.unesco.org/culture/copy/copyright/qatar/fr_page1.html.* See n.1 (1st ser.), above.

## Republic of Korea

### Copyright Act 1986[21]

Art. 2      The definitions of the terms used in this Act shall be as follows:1. "work" shall mean original literary, scientific or artistic work

Art. 4(1)      The following shall be the examples of works referred to in this Act: ... 6. photographic works including those prepared by same means of photographs and other similar production methods;

Art. 10(1)      Authors shall have the rights prescribed in Articles 11 through 13 (hereinafter referred to as "moral rights") and the rights prescribed in Articles 10 to 21 (hereinafter referred to as "economic rights")

Art. 36(1)      Except as provided otherwise in this Sub-Chapter, the economic rights shall not be extinguished for the lifetime of the author and 50 years thereafter: Provided that the economic rights in a work released after 40 years and before 50 years after the author's death shall not be extinguished for 10 years from the date of its release.

Photographs are not the subject of separate duration or neighbouring rights provisions.

## Romania

### Law on Copyright and Neighbouring Rights No. 8 of March 14, 1996 which came into force on June 25, 1996[22]

Art. 1—(1)      The copyright in a literary, artistic or scientific work and in any similar work of intellectual creation shall be recognized and guaranteed as provided in this Law.

Art. 7      The subject matter of copyright shall be original works of intellectual creation in the literary, artistic, or scientific field, regardless of their manner of creation, specific form or mode of expression and independently of their merit and purpose, such as: ... (f) photographic works and any other works expressed by a process analogous to photography ...

Art. 85—(1)      Still photographs from cinematographic films shall be considered photographic works.

(2)      Photographs of letters, deeds, documents of any kind, technical drawings and other similar material do not qualify for legal protection by copyright.

Art. 86—(1)      The right of the author of a photographic work to exploit his own work shall not prejudice the rights of the author of the artistic work reproduced in the photographic work.

(2)      The economic rights in a photographic work created under an individual employment contract or commission contract shall be presumed to belong to the employer or commissioning party for a period of three years, unless otherwise provided in the contract.

(3)      Disposal of the negative of a photographic work shall have the effect of transfer of the economic rights of the owner of the copyright in the said work, unless otherwise provided in the contract.

---

[21] *http://www.unesco.org/culture/copy/copyright/republicofkorea/fr_sommaire.html.* See n.1 (1st ser.), above.

[22] *http://www.unesco.org/culture/copy/copyright/romania/fr_sommaire.html.* See n.1 (1st ser.), above.

Art. 87—(1) A photograph of a person, when made to order, may be published or reproduced by the person photographed or his successors without the author's consent, unless otherwise agreed.

(2) If the name of the author appears on the original photograph, it must also be shown on the reproductions

The basic term of protection which applies to photographs is life of the author plus 70 years. Article 85(2) provides that some photographs of specified items (letters, deeds, documents of any kind, technical drawings and other similar material) do attract copyright.

## Russian Federation

## Law on Copyright and Neighbouring Rights (No. 5 3 5 14): July 9, 1993[23]

Art. 4       For the purposes of this Law, the terms given below shall have the meanings specified:"author" means the natural person whose creative effort has brought about the creation of a work;..

Art. 6(1)    Copyright extends to scientific, literary and artistic works that are the product of creative work, regardless of the purpose, the merit and the manner of expression thereof

   2         Copyright protects disclosed works and also undisclosed works that exist in an objective form, namely: ... -figurative form (drawing, sketch, painting, plan, industrial design, still picture from a cinematographic or television or video film, photograph, etc.);

Art. 7(1)    The following are protected by copyright: ... photographic works and works obtained by processes analogous to photography...

Under Art. 27 photographs receive the basic term of protect that other works receive, namely lifetime of the author and 50 years after his death.

## Rwanda

## Copyright Law No. 27/1983 of November 15, 1983[24]

Art. 1       Authors of original literary, artistic and scientific works shall be entitled to the protection of their works as provided by this Law."-Original work" shall mean a work whose characteristic elements and whose form, or whose form alone, enable its author to be distinguished.

Art. 2       Protected literary, artistic and scientific works shall include, in particular:...
             (h) photographic works, including works expressed by processes similar to photography

By Art. 26 the term of protection is life of the author plus 50 years. There are no special provisions for photographs.

---

[23] *http://www.unesco.org/culture/copy/copyright/russianfederation/fr_sommaire.html.* See n.1 (1st ser.), above.
[24] *http://www.unesco.org/culture/copy/copyright/rwanda/fr_sommaire.html.* See n.1 (1st ser.), above.

## Saint Vincent and the Grenadines

## Copyright Act, 1989 (No. 53 of December 27, 1989)[25]

s.2    In this Act, except where the context otherwise requires-
"photograph" includes photolithograph and any work produced by a process analogous to photography but does not include any part of an audio-visual work; and "photographic work" has a corresponding meaning;

s.4    Literary, artistic and scientific works include-...
(h)   photographic works, including works expressed by processes analogous to photography;

5(1)  Authors of original literary, artistic and scientific works shall be entitled to protection of their works under this Part.

(2)   Works shall be protected irrespective of their quality and the purpose for which they were created.

Under s.23 photographs are protected for 50 years immediately following the year in which the work was first made available to the public. The standard term is life of the author plus 50 years.

## San Marino

## Law on the Protection of Copyright (No. 8 of January 25, 1991)[26]

Art. 5    The following original works are protected ... (a) works of literary, dramatic, musical or artistic character

Art. 9    Graphic works, photographs, sculptures and all combinations thereof ... are deemed to be works of artistic character ... Photographs are understood to be all forms of printing of visible light or other rays by means of which an image is formed or may be reproduced by any method or with the aid of any device, and which do not form part of an audiovisual work.

### Chapter IV: Photographs

Art. 84   The term of protection of photographs shall be 30 years from the date on which they were taken.

Art. 85   Where the photograph has been taken during the currency of or pursuant to a contract for the rendering of services or the making of a work or on commission, the employer or the person who commissioned the work shall, unless otherwise agreed, be deemed to be the assignee of the right of economic exploitation of the work.

Art. 86   Notwithstanding the provisions of Article 48, the transfer of the original negative or of an equivalent means of reproducing the photograph, even if not evidenced in writing, shall, unless otherwise agreed, constitute assignment of the right of economic exploitation of the work.

Art. 87   Copies of the photograph shall carry a notice stating the date on which it was taken and the name of the author; in the case referred to in Article 85, they shall also give the name of the employer or of the person who commissioned the work.

---

[25] *http://www.unesco.org/culture/copy/copyright/stvincent/fr_sommaire.html.* See n.1 (1st ser.), above.

[26] *http://www.unesco.org/culture/copy/copyright/sanmarino/fr_sommaire.html.* See n.1 (1st ser.), above.

The general term of protection is life plus 50 years under Art. 36. Photographs have a much shorter term of protection.

## Saudi Arabia

## Law Protecting Copyright of December 17, 1989 (corresponding to 19/5/1410 of Hegira) which came into force: January 12, 1990[27]

Art. 1     For the purposes of this Law: "work" shall mean any literary, scientific or artistic work not previously published; "creation" shall mean any composition comprising novel elements or characterized by special features previously unknown

Art. 2     The protection afforded by this Law shall be enjoyed by works created in the fields of science, letters and art, whatever their nature, means of expression or importance or whatever the aim pursued in their creation.

Art. 3     Protection shall extend generally to authors of works of which the means of expression is writing, sound, drawing, photography or movement, and more particularly the following works: ... (g) photographic works, including works expressed by a process analogous to photography, such as still photographs transmitted by television, but not fixed on a physical medium

Art. 8     Notwithstanding Article 7, it shall be lawful, without the consent of the author, to use a protected work, whether in the original language or in translation, in the following way: ... (j) take new photographs of an object of which a photograph has already been published, even if the new photographs are taken from the same place as the initial photograph and in the same circumstances.

Under Art. 24 photographs are protected for 25 years as from the date of publication of the work. Other works are generally protected for life of the author plus 50 years.

## Senegal

## The Copyright Act 1973 as amended up to January 24, 1986[28]

Art. 1     The author of an original intellectual (literary, scientific or artistic) work shall, by the mere fact of its creation, enjoy an exclusive incorporeal property right in the work which shall be effective against all persons.The following in particular shall be considered intellectual works within the meaning of this Law: ... photographic works of artistic or documentary character, to which are assimilated, for the purposes of this Law, works expressed by a process analogous to photography.

Under Art. 41 the term of protection for photographs is 25 years from the end of the year of the author's death. The standard term for other works is life of the author plus 50 years.

---

[27] *http://www.unesco.org/culture/copy/copyright/saudiarabia/fr_sommaire.html.* See n.1 (1st ser.), above.

[28] *http://www.unesco.org/culture/copy/copyright/senegal/fr_sommaire.html.* See n.1 (1st ser.), above.

## Sierra Leon

## Copyright Act 1965[29]

2(1)    In this Act, except in so far as the context otherwise requires, the following expressions have the meanings hereby assigned to them respectively, that is to say- ... "photograph" means any product of photography or of any process akin to photography, other than a part of a cinematograph film, and "author", in relation to a photograph, means the person who, at the time when the photograph is taken, is the owner of the material on which it is taken;

4(1)    Copyright shall subsist, subject to the provisions of this Act, in every original literary, dramatic or musical work which is unpublished...

5(1)    In this Act "artistic work" means a work of any of the following descriptions, that is to say ... (a) the following irrespective of artistic quality, namely paintings, sculptures, drawings, engravings and photographs

11(3)   The copyright in a work to which this subsection applies which is permanently situated in a public place, or in premises open to the public, is not infringed by the making of a painting, drawing, engraving or photograph of the work, or the inclusion of the work in a cinematograph film or in a television broadcast.

By s.5(4)(b) copyright subsists in a photograph until the end of the period of 50 years from the end of the calendar year in which the photograph is first published. The normal term is life of the author plus 50 years.

## Singapore

## Copyright Act Law (No. 2): 1987[30]

7(1)    In this Act, unless the context otherwise requires...
        "artistic work" means ... (a) a painting, sculpture, drawing, engraving or photograph, whether the work is of artistic quality or not; ...
        "author," in relation to a photograph, means the person who took the photograph;
        "photograph" means a product of photography or of a process similar to photography, other than an article or thing in which visual images forming part of a cinematograph film have been embodied, and includes a product of xerography, and photography shall have a corresponding meaning; "work" means a literary, dramatic, musical or artistic work;

27(1)   Subject to the provisions of this Act, copyright shall subsist in an original literary, dramatic, musical or artistic work that is unpublished...

63(2)   The copyright in a work to which this section applies that is situated, otherwise than temporarily, in a public place, or in premises open to the public, is not infringed by the making of a painting, drawing, engraving or photograph of the work or by the inclusion of the work in a cinematograph film or in a television broadcast.

---

[29] *http://www.unesco.org/culture/copy/copyright/sierraleone/fr_sommaire.html*. See n.1 (1st ser.), above.
[30] *http://www.unesco.org/culture/copy/copyright/sierraleone/fr_sommaire.html*. See n.1 (1st ser.), above.

Under s.28(6) copyright subsists in a photograph until the expiration of 50 years after the expiration of the calendar year in which the photograph is first published. The basic term for other works is life of the author plus 50 years.

## Slovakia

### Copyright Act 1997(No. 383/1997) as amended by Act No. 234/2000 of June 2000[31]

§5(4)  Photographic work is a recording of light or other radiation at any medium on which an image is produced irrespective of the method by which this recording was made: a still picture from the audiovisual work shall not be considered as a photographic work but as a part of the audiovisual work.

§6(1)  The subject of copyright is literary work, scientific work and artistic work which is the result of the author's own creative intellectual activity, in particular—... g) photographic work...

§18(1)  The copyright shall last throughout the life of author and 70 years after his/her death.

§19  The calculation of duration of copyright shall start from the first day of the year following the year in which the event decisive for the calculation occurred.

There is no separate duration provision for photographs nor any neighbouring rights provisions for non-original photographs.

## Slovenia

### Copyright and Related Rights Act of March 30, 1995[32]

Art. 5—(1)  Copyright works are individual intellectual creations in the domain of literature, science and art, which are expressed in any medium, unless otherwise provided in this Act.

(2)  The following in particular are considered copyright works: ... 6. photographic works and works produced by a process comparable to photography

Under Art. 59, the copyright term is life of the author plus 70 years. There are no special duration provisions for photographs and no neighbouring rights.

## South Africa

### Copyright Act 1978 as last amended by Copyright Amendment Act 9 of 2002[33]

1(1)  In this Act, unless the context otherwise indicates— ... "artistic work" means, irrespective of the artistic quality thereof (a) paintings, sculptures, drawings, engravings and photographs...

---

[31] *http://clea.wipo.int/*.
[32] *http://www.unesco.org/culture/copy/copyright/slovenia/fr_sommaire.html*. See n.1 (1st ser.), above.
[33] Available through the UNESCO website. See n.1 (1st ser.), above.

"photograph" means any product of photography or of any process analogous to photography, but does not include any part of a cinematograph
film;

2—(1) Subject to the provisions of this Act, the following works, if they are original, shall be eligible for copyright ... (c) artistic works ...

Originality is a matter of degree depending on the amount of skill, judgment or
labour involved in making the work.[34] A work can still be original notwithstanding
that it has been copied from a previous work provided sufficient skill and effort have
been embodied in creating the subsequent work.[35] The standard of originality
required by the Act is a low one.[36]

The basic term is life of the author plus 50 years. A shorter term for photographs
is provided in s.3(2)(b) which provides for a term of 50 years from the end of the year
in which the work is made available to the public with the consent of the owner of the
copyright or first published whichever is the longer. If neither event occurs within 50
years from the making of the work, then the term is 50 years from the end of the year
in which the work is made.

## Spain

## Consolidated Text of the Law on Intellectual Property 12 April 12 1996, as amended by Law 5/1998 of March 6, 1998[37]

Art. 10—(1)  The subject matter of intellectual property shall be all original, literary,
artistic or scientific creations expressed in any manner or medium,
whether tangible or intangible, that is known at present or may be
invented in the future, including the following: ...
(h) photographic works and works expressed by a process analogous
to photography

Art. 26  The exploitation rights in the work shall last for the lifetime of the
author and 70 years following his natural or declared death.

Art. 35  Works permanently located in parks, streets, squares or other public
places may be freely reproduced, distributed and communicated by
means of paintings, drawings, photographs and audiovisual processes

Art. 128  Any person who makes a photograph or other reproduction produced
by means of a process analogous to photography shall, when neither
has the character of protected work in terms of Book I, enjoy the
exclusive right to authorize its reproduction, distribution and communication to the public on the same terms as are accorded by this
Law to the authors of photographic works.

That right shall have a term of 25 years counted from January 1 of
the year following the date of the making of the photograph or
reproduction.

Under Art. 10 there is a requirement of originality for protection of all literary,
artistic and scientific creations. Bercovitz and Bercovitz in Nimmer & Geller observe:

---

[34] *Accesso CC v Allforms (pty) Ltd* (Case No II) Case No 2798/96 unrep cited in Dean quoting
from *Ladbroke Ltd v William Hill Ltd* [1964].
[35] Dean at 3.3.1 citing inter alia *Adonis Knitwear Holding Ltd v OK Bazaars (1929) Ltd* 335 JOC
W.
[36] *Accesso CC v Allforms (pty) Ltd* above.
[37] *http:clea.wipo.int/*.

"The Spanish Supreme Court does not impose high standards of protectability often finding originality in the combination of different elements, none of which alone displays a high level of originality."[38]

Article 10 of the Spanish Act contains a non-exhaustive list of protected works which includes at subpara. (1)(h) "photographic works and works expressed by a process analogous to photography".[39]

Spanish copyright law does draw a distinction between photographic works of an artistic nature and so called "mere photographs" which are protected by a related right for a shorter term under Art. 128.[40] As in Italian law, this distinction is extended to encompass part of audio visual works. The concept covers "all works" and "any other reproduction produced by techniques analogous to photography. Any "mere" image that is part of an audiovisual work but not protected by copyright, may be protected as a mere photograph.[41]

Artistic "copyright" photographs are protected for 70 years following either year of death of the author or lawful disclosure. However, a photograph or analagous product (*i.e.* a "mere" photograph) is protected for a term of 25 years from the start of the year in which it was made.[42]

Related rights in mere photographs are protected pursuant to Spain's Treaty Commitments or conditionally on reciprocity.[43]

## The Copyright and Neighbouring Rights Protection Act 1996[43a]

s.5(1)  Subject to the provisions of Part IV of this Act, the protection prescribed by this Act shall without fulfilment of any formality apply to any original intellectual work in the field of literature, science and arts whatever the manner of expression, value or object of such work is and such works shall in particular include:
... (e)  photographic works.
... (j)  other works known or to be developed.

s.6  The protection prescribed by this Act shall not extend to:
(a)  works which have fallen into the public domain;
(b)  official documents;
(c)  daily news or other occurrences of like nature published in news-papers, magazines or other periodicals or broadcast by radio or television.
(d)  ideas, methods, state emblems and symbols.

s.13(1)  The protection of moral rights mentioned in s.8(1) shall be during the life of the author.

(2)  The protection of economic rights in a work shall last during the author's life and 50 years after his death.

(3)  The term of protection shall last 25 years from the date of publication of the following works:
(a)  photographic pictures and cinematographic films and other audio-visual works; ...

Photographs receive a shorter term of protection than other artistic works, namely 25 years from the date of publication under s.13(3)(a). The 1996 Act requires a work

---

[38] Nimmer & Geller SPA-17 §2 [1][b].
[39] Nimmer & Geller SPA-18 §2[2].
[40] Nimmer & Geller SPA-19 §2[2].
[41] Nimmer & Geller SPA-19 §2[2].
[42] Nimmer & Geller SPA-26 §3[2][a][i].
[43] Nimmer & Geller SPA-48 §6[1][b].
[43a] The author is grateful to Professor Akolda M. Tier of the University of Khartoum for a copy of this statute as translated into English.

to be an "original intellectual work" to be capable of protection. The predecessor statute the Copyright Protection Act 1974 as translated into English had a test of "innovation" and "novel." However, it has been suggested that these words were misleading and a better translation would have been "original."[43b]

Sudan has a system for copyright registration, provided for in s.23 of the 1996 Act, which is now optional.[43c] Under the predecessor statute, the Copyright Protection Act 1974, registration and deposit of a copy of the work were obligatory.[43d] However, the registration of contracts that transfer the author's economic rights to a user remains obligatory under the 1996 Act.[43e]

## Sweden

## Act on Copyright in Literary and Artistic Works (Law No. 729, of December 30, 1960, as last amended by Law No. 1274, of December 7, 1995[44])

The text was further amended by Law No. 92 of 2000.

Art. 1    Anyone who has created a literary or artistic work shall have copyright in that work, regardless of whether it is . . .
5. a photographic work or another work of fine art . . . 7. a work expressed in some other manner

Art. 49a    Anyone who has produced a photographic picture has an exclusive right to reproduce the picture and to make it available to the public. This right applies regardless of whether the picture is used in its original form or in an altered form and regardless of which technique has been used. A picture which has been produced by a process analogous to photography is also considered a photographic picture. The right under the first paragraph subsists until 50 years have elapsed from the year in which the picture was produced.The provisions of Articles 2, second and third paragraphs, 3, 7 to 9, 11, 12, first paragraph, 13, 15, 16, 18 to 20, 23, 24, first paragraph, 25 to 26b, 26d to 26f, 26i to 28, 31 to 38, 41, 42 and 50 to 52 shall apply to pictures referred to in this Article. If such a picture is subject to copyright, copyright protection may also be claimed.

The relevant statute is the Copyright Act of 1960 with related regulations.[45] In Swedish jurisprudence decisions of other courts are not formally binding, however, in practice decisions of the Supreme Court are followed until superseded by statute.[46]

Original artistic works are protected by copyright. A work is original if it is its authors "own intellectual creation" and has "a modicum of creativity".[47] Section 1(1) gives a non-exhaustive list of protected works which includes "a photographic

---

[43b] See above at para. 3–078, n.72a.
[43c] For further information as to the copyright law of Sudan see Tier, Akolda, M., "Protection of Copyright Under Sudanese Law" (1991) 6 Arab Law Quarterly 161; Tier, Akolda, M., "The Sudan's Copyright and Neighbouring Rights Protection Act 1996: An Evaluation" UNESCO Copyright Bulletin XXXII (1998) No. 3, p.43–53.
[43d] Copyright Protection Act 1974 of Sudan, s.14.
[43e] The Copyright and Neighbouring Rights Protection Act 1996 of Sudan, s.23.
[44] *http://www.unesco.org/culture/copy/copyright/sweden/fr_sommaire.html*. See n.1 (1st ser.), above.
[45] 1960:729 Nimmer & Geller SWE-5 §1[2][a].
[46] Nimmer & Geller SWE-10 §1[5].
[47] Nimmer & Geller SWE-11 §2[1][b].

work". An artistic work is a non-literary work created with an eye to generating an artistic effect and this criterion applies to photographs.[48]

Under s.49(a) photographs which are insufficiently creative to attract copyright are protected by neighbouring rights as "photographic pictures."[49] There are no formalities necessary to attract the neighbouring right in non-creative photographs.[50]

Copyright in a copyright photograph is protected for the same term as other copyright works—generally 70 years from the death of the author.[51] Non-creative photographic pictures are protected for a shorter term of 50 years from the end of the year in which the picture is produced.[52] Prior to 1994, the Photography Act of 1960 drew a distinction between photographs of an artistic or scientific value (protected for 50 years from the death of the photographer) and other photographic pictures which were protected for 25 years from the year of production.[53]

Sweden remains bound by one bilateral agreement—that of April 5, 1986, made with the Soviet Union to the effect that national treatment would be given to the citizens of the other state independent of the date of creation or publication of a work or photographic picture for which at the date of signature the legal period of protection had not expired. The agreement is in force between Sweden and at least the Russian Federation and Belorussia.[54]

## Switzerland

### Federal Law on Copyright and Neighbouring Rights (Federal Copyright Law) of October 9, 1992, as amended by the Law of December 16, 1994[55]

Art. 2(1)  Works shall mean literary and artistic creations of the mind, irrespective of their value or purpose, that possess an individual nature.

(2)  They include, in particular: ... g. photographic, cinematographic and other visual or audiovisual works;

The relevant statute is the Copyright Act of 1992.[56] Switzerland does not apply stare decisis and Swiss decisions from one cantonal jurisdiction are persuasive but not binding on others. However, most courts will follow decisions of the Federal Tribunal.[57]

Article 2(1) protects "any literary or artistic creation of the mind whatever its value which evidences an individual character". The requirement for "individual character" basically requires (1) the creator has personal input, and (2) "an objective ascertainable modicum of creativity".[58] It is necessary for a work to be distinct from other works. This test was developed from the theory of Professor Max Kummer who suggested a test of "statistical uniqueness" (statistische Einmaligkeit). Under this test a work is protected if, statistically it was probable that no other work could be identical to it.[59] However, the Federal Tribunal decided that uniqueness was not

---

[48] Nimmer & Geller SWE-12 §2[2].
[49] Nimmer & Geller SWE-12 §2[1][b].
[50] Nimmer & Geller SWE-11 §2[1][a].
[51] Nimmer & Geller SWE-18–19 §3[1] and §3[1][2][a][ii].
[52] Nimmer & Geller SWE-19 §3[1][2][a][ii].
[53] *loc cit.*
[54] Nimmer & Geller SWE-36 §6[4].
[55] *http://www.unesco.org/culture/copy/copyright/switzerland/fr_sommaire.html.* See n.1 (1st ser.), above.
[56] The Federal Act on Copyright and Neighbouring Rights of October 9, 1992.
[57] Nimmer & Geller SWI-14 §1[1].
[58] Nimmer & Geller SWI-16 §2[1][b].
[59] Nimmer & Geller SWI-17 §2[1][b].

an absolute requirement in that a building may be protected even where a "twin" building by another architect is found to exist elsewhere.[60]

Copyright protection has been denied in Switzerland due to a lack of an individual creative concept to technical photographs of models; x-ray images taken by a doctor; and a standard photograph of a man leaning forward resting on a table holding a file as it lacked "statistical uniqueness".[61]

Article 2(2) provides a non-exhaustive list of protected works and includes "photographic, cinematographic and other visual or audiovisual works."[62] François Dessemontet in Nimmer & Geller comments:

> "In including "photographic works" with "cinematographic and other visual or audiovisual works", the legislature endeavoured to clarify that all sort of visual works are protectable, be they video clips, holograms, video samplings, multi-media works etc. Nonetheless some courts had previously taken a rigorous approach to the requirement of creativity as applied to photographs and the Third Expert Committee explicitly rejected a proposal to overturn the current case law. Except for the Unfair Competition Act, there is no other law available to protect photographs. Thus the 1992 Act might leave many press photographs lacking individuality without protection."[63]

There is no legislative distinction between creative and non-creative photographs. Photographs are subject to the same term of copyright as other works—generally life of the author plus 70 years.

## Thailand

### Copyright Act, B.E. 2537 (1994)[64]

s.4   In this Act:...
"Author" means a person who makes or creates any work which is a copyright work by virtue of this Act. "Artistic work" means a work of one or more of the following descriptions:...
(5) photographic work, which means a creation of pictures with the use of image-recording apparatus which allows the light to pass through a lens to a film or glass and developed with liquid chemical of specific formula or by any process that creates a picture or an image recorded by any other apparatus or method;...

s.6   Copyright work under this Act means a work of authorship in the form of a literary, dramatic, artistic, musical, audiovisual, cinematographic, sound recording, sound and video broadcasting work or any other work in the literary, scientific or artistic field whatever the mode or form of its expression

s.21  Copyright in a photographic work ... shall subsist for 50 years as from authorship; if the work is published during such period, copyright shall subsist for 50 years as from first publication

s.37  A drawing, painting, construction, engraving, moulding, carving, lithography, photograph, film, video broadcast or any similar use of an artistic work, except

---

[60] ATF 117 II 466, cited in Nimmer & Geller at SWI-17 §2[1][b].
[61] Cited by Hug, G, *Switzerland* in *Copyright and Photographs: An International Survey*, Gendreau, Y, Nordemann and Oesch, R (eds) Kluwer Law Int. at p.260. Respectively (1972) Blätter für Zürcherische Rechtsprechung (ZR), No. 94, p.288 (models); (1986) ZR No. 57 p.144 (x-rays); (1985) SMI p.221 (man with file).
[62] Nimmer & Geller SWI-18 §2[2][a].
[63] Nimmer & Geller SWI-20 §2[1][b].
[64] *http://www.unesco.org/culture/copy/copyright/thailand/fr_page1.html*. See n.1 (1st ser.), above.

for an architectural work, which is openly located in a public place shall not be deemed an infringement of copyright in the artistic work.

s.39 A photograph, film or video broadcast of a work of which an artistic work is a component shall not be deemed an infringement of copyright in the artistic work.

The standard term is life of the author plus 50 years. Photographs receive a shorter protection period under s.21.

## Togo

## Law on the Protection of Copyright, Folklore and Neighbouring Rights Date of Law (No. 91–12): June 10, 1991[65]

Art. 2     The author of any original intellectual work (literary, artistic or scientific) shall enjoy in relation to that work, by virtue of the mere fact of the creation thereof, an exclusive incorporeal property right binding on all persons called "copyright."

Art. 6     The following in particular shall be considered intellectual works within the meaning of this Law: ... photographic works of artistic or documentary character to which shall be assimilated, for the purposes of this Law, works expressed by processes analogous to photography ...

Art. 8     For the purposes of this Law: "original work" means a work which, by its characteristic features and its form or by its form only, allows its author to be identified;

Under Art. 37 photographs are protected for a shorter term of 25 years following the end of the year of the death of the author rather than life plus 50 years.

## Tonga

## Copyright Act 1985, Act No. 20 of 1985[66]

5(1)   Authors of original literary, artistic and scientific works shall be entitled to copyright protection for their works under this Act, by the sole fact of the creation of such works.

(2)    Literary, artistic and scientific works shall include in particular: ... (h) photographic works, including works expressed by processes analogous to photography; ...

Under s.13(5) photographs are protected for 25 years from the making of the work which is a shorter period than other works which receive life of the author plus 50 years.

---

[65] *http://www.unesco.org/culture/copy/copyright/togo/fr_sommaire.html*. See n.1 (1st ser.), above.
[66] *http://www.unesco.org/culture/copy/copyright/tonga/fr_tonga.html*. See n.1 (1st ser.), above.

## Trinidad & Tobago

## The Copyright Act, 1997 (No. 8 of 1997)[67]

s.3     For the purposes of this Act, the following terms have the following meaning...

"photographic work" is the recording of light or other radiation on any medium on which an image is produced or from which an image may be produced, irrespective of the technique (chemical, electronic or other) by which such recording is made; a still picture extracted from an audiovisual work shall not be considered a "photographic work" but a part of the audiovisual work concerned;

5(1)     Copyright is a property right which subsists in literary and artistic works that are original intellectual creations in the literary and artistic domain, including in particular:...

(i) photographic works;

The general term of protection is life of the author plus 50 years.[68] There is no special term for photographs.

## Tunisia

## Law No. 94–36 of February 24, 1994, on Literary and Artistic Property[69]

Art. 1     Copyright shall subsist in all original literary, scientific or artistic works whatever their value, purpose, mode or form of expression, as also in the title of works. It shall apply equally to a work in its original form and in any form derived from the original. The works in which copyright subsists shall include: ... photographic works, to which shall be assimilated for the purposes of this Law works expressed by a process analogous to photography...

Under Art. 19 photographs are protected for 25 Gregorian years as from the year during which the work was made. Under Art. 18 the standard term is lifetime of the author and 50 Gregorian years.

## Turkey

## Law on Artistic and Intellectual Works No. 5846 of December 5, 1951, as last amended in 1995[70]

This Act was futher amended by Law No. 4630, March 2001 but the extracts reproduced here are from a translation including amendments up to 1995 only.

---

[67] *http://www.unesco.org/culture/copy/copyright/trinidadandtobago/fr_sommaire.html.* See n.1 (1st ser.), above.

[68] s.19(1).

[69] http://www.unesco.org/culture/copy/copyright/tunisia/fr_page1.html. See n.1 (1st ser.), above.

[70] *http://www.unesco.org/culture/copy/copyright/turkey/fr_sommaire.html.* See n.1 (1st ser.), above.

| Art. 1 | For the purposes of this Law, work means any intellectual or artistic creation bearing the mark of its author and which, in accordance with the provisions below, is deemed a scientific, literary, musical, artistic or cinematographic work. |
|---|---|
| Art. 2 | The following shall be deemed scientific or literary works: ... 3. all types of photographic works of a technical or scientific nature, all types of maps, plans, projects, sketches, drawings, three-dimensional works relating to geography and topography, all types of architectural and urban designs and projects, architectural models, industrial, environmental and theatrical designs and projects, not being of an aesthetic nature. |
| Art. 4 | The following works, being of an aesthetic nature, shall be deemed artistic works: ...<br>5. photographic works |
| Art. 29 | The term of protection for handicraft, minor works of art, photographic and cinematographic works shall be 70 years as from the date on which the work has been made public. |
| Art. 30 | The rights afforded authors shall not prevent a work from being used as evidence in court or before other authorities or from being the subject matter of penal or criminal proceedings. Photographs may be reproduced and published in any form by the authorities or on their instructions for reasons of public policy or for judicial reasons without the author's consent. |
| Art. 40 | Works of art permanently situated on public streets, avenues or squares may be reproduced, publicly projected on a screen or broadcast by radio or similar means in the form of drawings, graphics, photographs and the like. In the case of works of architecture, permission shall extend to their exterior form only. |
| Art. 84 | Any person who fixes signs, sounds or images on a device permitting the transmission of such elements or who lawfully reproduces or distributes the same for commercial purposes, may prohibit others from reproducing or distributing the same signs, sounds or images by use of the same means. The provisions on unfair competition shall apply to persons who infringe the provisions of the first paragraph of this Article even if they are not acting by way of business. The provisions of this Article shall also apply to those photographs that do not qualify as works, to images fixed by similar means and to cinematographic productions. |

The standard term of protection is life of the author plus 70 years. Photographs receive a shorter protection period.

## Ukraine

## Law of Ukraine on Copyright and Related Rights (of December 23, 1993)[71]

| Art. 4 | In this Law, the terms used shall have the following meaning: "author"— a natural person through whose creative effort a work is created |
|---|---|
| Art. 5–1 | This Law protects works in the field of science, literature and art, namely: ...<br>8. photographs |

[71] *http://www.unesco.org/culture/copy/copyright/ukraine/fr_ukraine.html.* See n.1 (1st ser.), above.

The basic term of protection under Art. 24 is life of the author plus 50 years. There are no separate provisions for photographs under this Act.

## Uganda

### Copyright Act 1964[72]

§§1(2)  A literary, musical or artistic work shall not be eligible for copyright unless (a) sufficient effort has been expended on making the work to give it an original character

§§15(1)  In this Act unless the context otherwise requires "artistic work" means, irrespective of artistic quality, any of the following or works similar thereto, that is to say ... (b) photographs not comprised in a cinematograph film

The duration provisions are set out in the Third Schedule to the Act and provide that copyright expires 50 years after the end of the year in which the author dies or 50 years after the end of the year in which the work was first published, which ever is the later.

## United Arab Emirates

### Federal Law No. (7) of the year 2002 concerning Copyrights and Neighboring Rights[73]

Art. (1)  In applying the provisions of this law the following words denote the definitions explained before each one of them, unless the context denotes otherwise:
"Creation": The creativeness that gives genuineness and distinctiveness to the work

Art. 2  Authors of the works and the holders of the neighboring rights, shall enjoy the protection of this law in case that an infringement against their rights occurs in the State, namely in the following works: ... 9- Photographic works and works analogous to photography

Art. 3  Protection does not extend to mere ideas, procedures, methods of work, mathematical concepts, principles, and abstract facts, but extend to creative expression in any of them.

Art. 20(1)  The financial rights of the author stipulated in this law shall be protected through his lifetime and an additional fifty years beginning from the first day of the calendar year following his death.

Art. 43  Anyone who photographs any one else by anyway, has no right to exhibit, publish or distribute the original or its copies without a written permission from the photographed party unless otherwise agreed, or the publication of the photo of accidents occurred in public or was of famous, public or official figures or that the publication was permitted by public authority in favor of public interest provided that the exhibition of the photo or circulating it will not affect the status of the photographed person.

---

[72] *http://www.unesco.org/culture/copy/copyright/uganda/fr_page1.html*. See n.1 (1st ser.), above.
[73] *http://www.agip.com/laws/uae/c.htm/*.

> The person in the photo may permit publishing it in newspapers or other publication media, even if the photographer did not permit, unless agreed otherwise.

## Federal Law No. 40 of 1992 on the Protection of Intellectual Works and Copyright (of September 28, 1992)[74]

s.2—(1)  Authors of intellectual works created in the fields of literature, arts and science shall be entitled to the protection provided by this Law, whatever the value, nature, purpose or mode of expression, of the work.

(2)  Protection shall extend to the following intellectual works ... (f) photographic works

Under s.20 of the 1992 Law, the author's right in photographs expired after 10 years from the date of publication. The normal term was life of the author plus 25 years. The Law of 2002 gives photographs the same protection as other works namely life of the author plus 50 years.

## United Kingdom

## Copyright Designs and Patents Act 1988 as last amended in 2003

s.1(1)  Copyright is a property right which subsist in accordance with this part in the following descriptions of work—
(a)  original literary, dramatic, musical or artistic works...

s.4(1)  In this Part "artistic work" means—
(a)  a graphic work, photograph, sculpture or collage irrespective of artistic quality; ..

(2)  (b)  "photograph" means a recording of light or other radiation on any medium on which an image is produced of from which an image may by any means be produced and which is not part of a film;

. . .

Photographs of Broadcasts

s.71(1)  The making in domestic premises for private and domestic use of a photograph of the whole or any part of an image forming part of a broadcast, or a copy of such a photograph, does not infringe any copyright in the broadcast or in any film included in it.

(2)  Where a copy which would otherwise be an infringing copy is made in accordance with this section but is subsequently dealt with—
(a)  it shall be treated as an infringing copy for the purposes of that dealing; and
(b)  if that dealing infringes copyright, it shall be treated as an infringing copy for all subsequent purposes.

(3)  In subsection (2), "dealt with" means sold or let for hire, offered or exposed for sale or hire or communicated to the public.

Right to privacy of certain photographs and films

s.85(1)  A person who for private and domestic purposes commissions the taking of a photograph or the making of a film has, where copyright subsists in the resulting work, the right not to have
(a)  copies of the work issued to the public,
(b)  the work exhibited or shown in public, or
(c)  the work communicated to the public;

---

[74] *http://www.unesco.org/culture/copy/copyright/unitedarabemirates/fr_page1.html.* See n.1 (1st ser.), above.

and, except as mentioned in subsection (2), a person who does or authorises the doing of any of those acts infringes that right.

(2) The right is not infringed by an act which by virtue of any of the following provisions would not infringe copyright in the work
  (a) section 31 (incidental inclusion of work in an artistic work, film or broadcast);
  (b) section 45 (parliamentary and judicial proceedings);
  (c) section 46 (Royal Commissions and statutory inquiries
  (d) section 50 (acts done under statutory authority);
  (e) section 57 or 66A (acts permitted on assumptions as to expiry of copyright, &c).

The standard term of life of the author plus 70 years applies to photographs as artistic works under s.12(1). There is no related right for non-original photographs.

## United Republic of Tanzania

The current statute is the Copyright and Neighbouring Rights Act No. 7 of December 1999. No official translation was available on the WIPO or UNESCO site at the time of writing.

### Copyright Act 1966[75]

2(I)  In this Act, unless the context otherwise requires "artistic work" means a work, irrespective of its artistic quality, of any of the following descriptions: ... (d) photographs not comprised in a cinematograph film...

3(1)  Subject to the provisions of this section the following works shall be eligible for copyright ... (c) artistic works...

(2)   A literary, musical or artistic work shall not be eligible for copyright unless
  (a) sufficient effort has been expended on making the work to give it an original character

Under s.4, photographs have a separate protection period being 20 years after the end of the year in which the work was first made lawfully accessible to the public. The normal term is life of the author plus 25 years.

## United States of America

### Title 17. Copyrights Copyright Law of 1976 (Public Law 94–553 of October 19, 1976), as last amended by Public Law 107–321 of December 4, 2002

§§101.  Definitions
Except as otherwise provided in this title, as used in this title, the following terms and their variant forms mean the following: ...

A "work of visual art" is: ...
  (2) a still photographic image produced for exhibition purposes only, existing in a single copy that is signed by the author, or in a limited edition of 200 copies or fewer that are signed and consecutively numbered by the author.

---

[75] *http://www.unesco.org/culture/copy/copyright/unitedrepublicoftanzania/fr_unitedrepublicoftanzania.html.* See n.1 (1st ser.), above.

"Pictorial, graphic, and sculptural works" include two-dimensional and three-dimensional works of fine, graphic, and applied art, photographs, prints and art reproductions, maps, globes, charts, diagrams, models, and technical drawings, including architectural plans

§102. Subject matter of copyright: In general

(a) Copyright protection subsists, in accordance with this title, in original works of authorship fixed in any tangible medium of expression, now known or later developed, from which they can be perceived, reproduced, or otherwise communicated, either directly or with the aid of a machine or device. Works of authorship include the following categories: ... (5) pictorial, graphic, and sculptural works;

Photograph is not defined. Under §302, copyright subsists in a work for the life of the author and 70 years after the author's death. Photographs are not subject to a special term of protection and are protected along with other works. For discussion of the approach of the courts of the USA to originality in photographs see above at paras 3–013 *et seq.*

"The requisite degree of originality subsists in virtually any photograph given the photographer's personal choices as to subject, lighting, angle, etc. Originality is lacking only when a photograph exactly reproduces an earlier photograph as by photocopying [*Gracen v Bradford Exch* 698 F.2d 300 (7th Circ. 1983)] or a recreation of the identical subject, lighting, angle, etc. used in a prior photograph [grosss]."[76]

# Uruguay

## Law No. 9739 concerning Literary and Artistic Copyright. The underlying statute is of: December 15 and 17, 1937 as amended[77]

This Act was further amended in 2003, but no official English translation was available on either the WIPO or UNESCO site at the time of writing.[77a]

Art. 1     This Law protects the moral right of the author of every literary, scientific or artistic creation and recognizes his property right in the products of his intellect, science, or art, subject to the general rules of law and the following articles.

Art. 5     For the purposes of this Law, intellectual, scientific or artistic productions shall include ... photographs;

Art. 45     The following shall not be deemed to be unlawful reproductions: ... (8) The photographic reproduction of pictures, monuments or allegorical figures displayed in museums, parks or public promenades, provided that the works in question can be deemed to have passed into the public domain

---

[76] Nimmer & Geller USA-24 §2[2][e][iv].

[77] *http://www.unesco.org/culture/copy/copyright/uruguay/fr_sommaire.html.* See n.1 (1st ser.), above.

[77a] The 1937 Law as amended by the Law of Copyright and Related Rights of January 10, 2003 is available in Spanish via the UNESCO Collection of National Copyright Laws, see n.1 (1st ser.), above.

The general economic rights term is life of the author plus 40 years.[78] There is no special term for the photographs.

## Uzbekistan

## Law on Copyright and Neighbouring Rights which came into force September 17, 1996[79]

Art. 5       Copyright extends to those scientific, literary and artistic works that are the result of creative effort, whatever their purpose and merit and regardless of their form of expression

Art. 6       The following are protected by copyright: ... photographic works and works obtained by processes analogous to photography; ...

Under Art. 38, photographs are protected for life of the author plus 50 years with other works.

## Venezuela

## Law of Copyright of August 14, 1993 which came into force on October 15, 1993[80]

Art. 1       The provisions of this Law shall protect the rights of authors in all creative intellectual works, whether literary, scientific or artistic in character and whatever their nature, form of expression, merit or purpose.

Art. 2       The following in particular shall be considered included among the intellectual works referred to in the foregoing Article ...: books, pamphlets, and other literary, artistic and scientific writings, including, engraving or lithography ... and, finally, any literary, scientific or artistic product susceptible of disclosure or publication by any means or process.

NB: Photographs not specifically listed, but Art. 38 provides:

Art. 38      Photographs and also reproductions and prints obtained by a comparable process shall be protected in the same way as the intellectual works mentioned in Article I of this Law. The rights of the photographer and his successors in title shall expire after 60 years following the disclosure of the work. Nevertheless, they shall expire 60 years after having been made if they have not been disclosed during that period. Such periods shall be counted from January 1 of the year following that of disclosure or making, as the case may be. The right to exploit a photograph taken by a professional photographer may be assigned on the same conditions as a photograph taken in the course of employment relations, as provided in Article 59 of this Law. Images recorded on audiovisual tape shall be deemed equivalent to photographs insofar as they do not themselves constitute audiovisual works.

---

[78] Art. 14.
[79] http://www.unesco.org/culture/copy/copyright/uzbekistan/fr_page1.html. See n.1 (1st ser.), above.
[80] *http://www.unesco.org/culture/copy/copyright/venezuela/fr_sommaire.html.* See n.1 (1st ser.), above.

The basic copyright term for other works is life of the author plus 60 years.[81]

## Yemen

### Law No. 19 of 1994 on Intellectual Property[82]

Art. 2      Copyright shall have for a subject matter any original work created in the field of literature, arts or science, whatever may be the form, purpose, value or manner of production of the work and whether the work can be classified in any of the known branches of creation or not.

Art. 3(1)      Copyright shall have for a subject matter any work expressed by writing, sound, drawing, shaping or other means, including ... photographic and cinematographic works...

(5)      Copyright shall extend to photographic products; however, a third person may make new photographs of the object depicted in the initial photograph even in the same place and circumstances as those in which the latter was made.

Under Art. 24 the basic period of protection is the life of the author plus a period of 30 years calculated from January 1 of the year of the death of the author. There is no separate term for photographs.

## Zambia

### Copyright and Performance Rights Act, 1994[83]

2.      In this Act, unless the context otherwise requires ... "artistic works" includes ... (e) photographs ...

"photograph" means a recording of light or other radiation on any medium on which an image is produced or from which an image may by any means be produced, but does not include a part of an audiovisual work; "work" means a product of creativity in a category referred to in section 8.

8—(1)      The products of creativity in which copyright may subsist under this Act are the following categories of works:

(a) original ... artistic works...

Under s.12 copyright expires at the end of the period of 50 years from the end of the calendar year in which the author dies. There is no separate term for photographs.

---

[81] Art. 25.

[82] http://www.unesco.org/culture/copy/copyright/yemen/fr_page1.html. See n.1 (1st ser.), above.

[83] *http://www.unesco.org/culture/copy/copyright/zambia/fr_sommaire.html.* See n.1 (1st ser.), above.

# Appendix 3

# Press Complaints Commission: Code of Practice[1]

## Code of Practice

The Press Complaints Commission is charged with enforcing the following Code of Practice which was framed by the newspaper and periodical industry and ratified by the Press Complaints Commission, March 19, 2003.

All members of the press have a duty to maintain the highest professional and ethical standards. This code sets the benchmark for those standards. It both protects the rights of the individual and upholds the public's right to know. The Code is the cornerstone of the system of self-regulation to which the industry has made a binding commitment. Editors and publishers must ensure that the Code is observed rigorously not only by their staff but also by anyone who contributes to their publications.

It is essential to the workings of an agreed code that it be honoured not only to the letter but in the full spirit. The Code should not be interpreted so narrowly as to compromise its commitment to respect the rights of the individual, nor so broadly that it prevents publication in the public interest.

It is the responsibility of editors to co-operate with the PCC as swiftly as possible in the resolution of complaints.

Any publication which is criticised by the PCC under on of the following clauses must print the adjudication which follows in full and with due prominence.

## 1   Accuracy

i)    Newspapers and periodicals should take care not to publish inaccurate, misleading or distorted material including pictures.

ii)   Whenever it is recognised that a significant inaccuracy, misleading statement or distorted report has been published, it should be corrected promptly and with due prominence.

iii)  An apology must be published whenever appropriate.

iv)   Newspapers, whilst free to be partisan, must distinguish clearly between comment, conjecture and fact

v)    A newspaper or periodical must report fairly and accurately the outcome of an action for defamation to which it has been a party.

## 2   Opportunity to reply

A fair opportunity for reply to inaccuracies must be given to individuals or organisations when reasonably called for.

---

[1] Reproduced with permission of the Press Complaints Commission.

## 3 *Privacy

(i) Everyone is entitled to respect for his or her private and family life, home, health and correspondence. A publication will be expected to justify intrusions into any individual's private life without consent

ii) The use of long lens photography to take pictures of people in private places without their consent is unacceptable.

Note — Private places are public or private property where there is a reasonable expectation of privacy.

## 4 *Harassment

i) Journalists and photographers must neither obtain nor seek to obtain information or pictures through intimidation, harassment or persistent pursuit

ii) They must not photograph individuals in private places (as defined by the note to clause 3) without their consent; must not persist in telephoning, questioning, pursuing or photographing individuals after having been asked to desist; must not remain on their property after having been asked to leave and must not follow them.

iii) Editors must ensure that those working for them comply with these requirements and must not publish material from other sources which does not meet these requirements.

## 5 Intrusion into grief or shock

In cases involving personal grief or shock, enquiries should be carried out and approaches made with sympathy and discretion. Publication must be handled sensitively at such times but this should not be interpreted as restricting the right to report judicial proceedings.

## 6 *Children

i) Young people should be free to complete their time at school without unnecessary intrusion.

ii) Journalists must not interview or photograph a child under the age of 16 on subjects involving the welfare of the child or any other child in the absence of or without the consent of a parent or other adult who is responsible for the children.

iii) Pupils must not be approached or photographed while at school without the permission of the school authorities.

iv) There must be no payment to minors for material involving the welfare of children nor payments to parents or guardians for material about their children or wards unless it is demonstrably in the child's interest.

v) Where material about the private life of a child is published, there must be justification for publication other than the fame, notoriety or position of his or her parents or guardian.

## 7   *Children in sex cases

1. The press must not, even where the law does not prohibit it, identify children under the age of 16 who are involved in cases concerning sexual offences, whether as victims or as witnesses.

2. In any press report of a case involving a sexual offence against a child —

    i)   The child must not be identified.
    ii)  The adult may be identified.
    iii) The word "incest" must not be used where a child victim might be identified.
    iv)  Care must be taken that nothing in the report implies the relationship between the accused and the child.

## 8   *Listening Devices

Journalists must not obtain or publish material obtained by using clandestine listening devices or by intercepting private telephone conversations.

## 9   *Hospitals

i)  Journalists or photographers making enquiries at hospitals or similar institutions should identify themselves to a responsible executive and obtain permission before entering non-public areas.

ii) The restrictions on intruding into privacy are particularly relevant to enquiries about individuals in hospitals or similar institutions.

## 10   *Reporting of crime.

(i)  The press must avoid identifying relatives or friends of persons convicted or accused of crime without their consent.

(ii) Particular regard should be paid to the potentially vulnerable position of children who are witnesses to, or victims of, crime. This should not be interpreted as restricting the right to report judicial proceedings.

## 11   *Misrepresentation

i)   Journalists must not generally obtain or seek to obtain information or pictures through misrepresentation or subterfuge.

ii)  Documents or photographs should be removed only with the consent of the owner.

iii) Subterfuge can be justified only in the public interest and only when material cannot be obtained by any other means.

## 12   Victims of sexual assault

The press must not identify victims of sexual assault or publish material likely to contribute to such identification unless there is adequate justification and, by law, they are free to do so.

## 13   Discrimination

i) The press must avoid prejudicial or pejorative reference to a person's race, colour, religion, sex or sexual orientation or to any physical or mental illness or disability.

ii) It must avoid publishing details of a person's race, colour, religion, sexual orientation, physical or mental illness or disability unless these are directly relevant to the story.

## 14   Financial journalism

i) Even where the law does not prohibit it, journalists must not use for their own profit financial information they receive in advance of its general publication, nor should they pass such information to others.

ii) They must not write about shares or securities in whose performance they know that they or their close families have a significant financial interest without disclosing the interest to the editor or financial editor.

iii) They must not buy or sell, either directly or through nominees or agents, shares or securities about which they have written recently or about which they intend to write in the near future.

## 15   Confidential sources

Journalists have a moral obligation to protect confidential sources of information.

## 16   Witness payments in criminal trials

i) No payment or offer of payment to a witness—or any person who may reasonably be expected to be called as a witness—should be made in any case once proceedings are active as defined by the Contempt of Court Act 1981.

This prohibition lasts until the suspect has been freed unconditionally by police without charge or bail or the proceedings are otherwise discontinued; or has entered a guilty plea to the court; or, in the event of a not guilty plea, the court has announced its verdict.

*ii) Where proceedings are not yet active but are likely and foreseeable, editors must not make or offer payment to any person who may reasonably be expected to be called as a witness, unless the information concerned ought demonstrably to be published in the public interest and there is an over-riding need to make or promise payment for this to be done; and all reasonable steps have been taken to ensure no financial dealings influence the evidence those witnesses give. In no circumstances should such payment be conditional on the outcome of a trial.

*iii) Any payment or offer of payment made to a person later cited to give evidence in proceedings must be disclosed to the prosecution and defence. The witness must be advised of this requirement.

## *17   Payment to criminals

Payment or offers of payment for stories, pictures or information, must not be made directly or through agents to convicted or confessed criminals or to their associates— who may include family, friends and colleagues—except where the material concerned ought to be published in the public interest and payment is necessary for this to be done.

# The public interest

There may be exceptions to the clauses marked * where they can be demonstrated to be in the public interest.

1. The public interest includes:

i) Detecting or exposing crime or a serious misdemeanour.

ii) Protecting public health and safety.

iii) Preventing the public from being misled by some statement or action of an individual or organisation.

2. In any case where the public interest is invoked, the Press Complaints Commission will require a full explanation by the editor demonstrating how the public interest was served.

3. There is a public interest in freedom of expression itself. The Commission will therefore have regard to the extent to which material has, or is about to, become available to the public.

4. In cases involving children editors must demonstrate an exceptional public interest to over-ride the normally paramount interest of the child

# Appendix 4

# The British Code of Advertising, Sales Promotion and Direct Marketing[1]

## (Clauses 1.1 to 24.1)

## Introduction

This eleventh edition of the Code comes into force on 4 March 2003. It replaces all previous editions.

## 1.1 The Code applies to:

a    advertisements in newspapers, magazines, brochures, leaflets, circulars, mailings, e-mails, text transmissions, fax transmissions, catalogues, follow-up literature and other electronic and printed material

b    posters and other promotional media in public places, including moving images

c    cinema and video commercials

d    advertisements in non-broadcast electronic media, including online advertisements in paid-for space (eg banner and pop-up advertisements)

e    viewdata services

f    marketing databases containing consumers personal information

g    sales promotions

h    advertisement promotions

## 1.2 The Code does not apply to:

a    broadcast commercials, which are the responsibility of the Independent Television Commission or the Radio Authority (soon to be incorporated into OFCOM)

b    the contents of premium rate services, which are the responsibility of the Independent Committee for the Supervision of Standards of Telephone Information Services; marketing communications that refer to these services are covered by the Code

c    marketing communications in foreign media. Direct marketing that originates outside the UK but is targeted at UK consumers will be subject to the jurisdiction of the relevant authority in the country where it originates so

---

[1] Reproduced with permission of The Committee of Advertising Practice (CAP). CAP run a Copy Advice Service, which is a free, fast and confidential service for marketers, agencies and media owners who want to check an advertisement against the rules before publication. The Copy Advice team can be contacted on 020 7580 4100 or by email at copyadvice@cap.org.uk

long as that authority operates a suitable cross-border complaint system. If it does not, the ASA will take what action it can. All members of the European Union, and many non-European countries, have self-regulatory organisations that are members of the European Advertising Standards Alliance (EASA). EASA co-ordinates the cross-border complaints system for its members (which include the ASA).

d    Health-related claims in marketing communications addressed only to the medical, dental, veterinary and allied professions

e    classified private advertisements, including those appearing online

f    statutory, public, police and other official notices/information, as opposed to marketing communications, produced by public authorities and the like

g    works of art exhibited in public or private

h    private correspondence, including correspondence between companies and their customers about existing relationships or past purchases

i    oral communications, including telephone calls

j    press releases and other public relations material, so long as they do not fall under 1.1 above

k    editorial content, for example of the media and of books

l    regular competitions such as crosswords

m    flyposting (most of which is illegal)

n    packages, wrappers, labels, tickets, timetables and price lists unless they advertise another product, a sales promotion or are visible in a marketing communication

o    point of sale displays, except those covered by the sales promotion rules

p    election advertisements as defined in clause 12.1

q    website content, except sales promotions and advertisements in paid-for space

r    sponsorship; marketing communications that refer to sponsorship are covered by the Code

s    customer charters and codes of practice.

## 1.3    These definitions apply to the Code:

a    a *product* encompasses goods, services, ideas, causes, opportunities, prizes or gifts

b    a *consumer* is anyone who is likely to see a given marketing communication, whether in the course of business or not

c    the *United Kingdom* rules cover the Isle of Man and the Channel Islands

d    a *claim* can be implied or direct, written, spoken or visual

e    the Code is divided into numbered *clauses*

f    a *marketing communication* includes all forms of communication listed in 1.1

g    a *marketer* includes an advertiser, promoter or direct marketer h    a *supplier* is anyone who supplies products that are sold by distance selling marketing communications (and may also be the marketer)

i    a *child* is anyone under 16.

## 1.4   These criteria apply to the Code:

a    the ASA Council's interpretation of the Code is final

b    conformity with the Code is assessed according to the marketing communication's probable impact when taken as a whole and in context. This will depend on the medium in which the marketing communication appeared, the audience and its likely response, the nature of the product and any additional material distributed to consumers

c    the Code is indivisible; marketers must conform with all appropriate rules

d    the Code does not have the force of law and its interpretation will reflect its flexibility. The Code operates alongside the law; the Courts may also make rulings on matters covered by the Code

e    an indication of the statutory rules governing marketing is given on www.cap.org.uk; professional advice should be taken if there is any doubt about their application

f    no spoken or written communications with the ASA or CAP should be understood as containing legal advice

g    the Code is primarily concerned with the content of advertisements, promotions and direct marketing communications and not with terms of business or products themselves. Some rules, however, go beyond the content, for example those that cover the administration of sales promotions, the suitability of promotional items, the delivery of products ordered through an advertisement and the use of personal information in direct marketing. Editorial content is specifically excluded from the remit of the Code (see 1.2k), although it might be a factor in determining the context in which marketing communications are judged (see 1.4b)

h    the rules make due allowance for public sensitivities but will not be used by the ASA to diminish freedom of speech unjustifiably

i    the ASA does not arbitrate between conflicting ideologies.

## General rules

## Principles

2.1    All marketing communications should be legal, decent, honest and truthful.

2.2    All marketing communications should be prepared with a sense of responsibility to consumers and to society.

2.3    All marketing communications should respect the principles of fair competition generally accepted in business.

2.4    No marketing communication should bring advertising into disrepute.

2.5    Marketing communications must conform with the Code. Primary responsibility for observing the Code falls on marketers. Others involved in preparing and publishing marketing communications such as agencies, publishers and other service suppliers also accept an obligation to abide by the Code.

2.6 Any unreasonable delay in responding to the ASA's enquiries may be considered a breach of the Code.

2.7 The ASA and CAP will on request treat in confidence any genuinely private or secret material supplied unless the Courts or officials acting within their statutory powers compel its disclosure.

2.8 The Code is applied in the spirit as well as in the letter.

## Substantiation

3.1 Before distributing or submitting a marketing communication for publication, marketers must hold documentary evidence to prove all claims, whether direct or implied, that are capable of objective substantiation.

Relevant evidence should be sent without delay if requested by the ASA or CAP. The adequacy of evidence will be judged on whether it supports both the detailed claims and the overall impression created by the marketing communication. The full name and geographical business address of marketers should be provided without delay if requested by the ASA or CAP.

3.2 If there is a significant division of informed opinion about any claims made in a marketing communication they should not be portrayed as generally agreed.

3.3 Claims for the content of non-fiction books, tapes, videos and the like that have not been independently substantiated should not exaggerate the value, accuracy, scientific validity or practical usefulness of the product.

3.4 Obvious untruths or exaggerations that are unlikely to mislead and incidental minor errors and unorthodox spellings are all allowed provided they do not affect the accuracy or perception of the marketing communication in any material way.

## Legality

4.1 Marketers have primary responsibility for ensuring that their marketing communications are legal. Marketing communications should comply with the law and should not incite anyone to break it.

## Decency (i.e. avoiding serious or widespread offence)

5.1 Marketing communications should contain nothing that is likely to cause serious or widespread offence. Particular care should be taken to avoid causing offence on the grounds of race, religion, sex, sexual orientation or disability. Compliance with the Code will be judged on the context, medium, audience, product and prevailing standards of decency.

5.2 Marketing communications may be distasteful without necessarily conflicting with 5.1 above. Marketers are urged to consider public sensitivities before using potentially offensive material.

5.3 The fact that a particular product is offensive to some people is not sufficient grounds for objecting to a marketing communication for it.

## Honesty

6.1 Marketers should not exploit the credulity, lack of knowledge or inexperience of consumers.

## Truthfulness

7.1 No marketing communication should mislead, or be likely to mislead, by inaccuracy, ambiguity, exaggeration, omission or otherwise.

## Matters of opinion

8.1 Marketers may give a view about any matter, including the qualities or desirability of their products, provided it is clear that they are expressing their own opinion rather than stating a fact. Assertions that go beyond subjective opinions are subject to 3.1 above (also see 12.1 below).

## Fear and distress

9.1 No marketing communication should cause fear or distress without good reason. Marketers should not use shocking claims or images merely to attract attention.

9.2 Marketers may use an appeal to fear to encourage prudent behaviour or to discourage dangerous or ill-advised actions; the fear likely to be aroused should not be disproportionate to the risk.

## Safety

10.1 Marketing communications should not condone or encourage unsafe practices. Particular care should be taken with marketing communications addressed to or depicting children (see section 47).

10.2 Consumers should not be encouraged to drink and drive. Marketing communications should, where appropriate, include a prominent warning on the dangers of drinking and driving and should not suggest that the effects of drinking alcohol can be masked.

## Violence and anti-social behaviour

11.1 Marketing communications should contain nothing that condones or is likely to provoke violence or anti-social behaviour.

## Political advertising

12.1 Any advertisement or direct marketing communication, whenever published or distributed, whose principal function is to influence voters in local, regional, national or international elections or referendums is exempt from the Code.

12.2 There is a formal distinction between Government policy and that of political parties. Marketing communications (see clauses 1.1 and 1.2) by central or local government, as distinct from those concerning party policy, are subject to the Code.

## Protection of privacy

13.1 Marketers should not unfairly portray or refer to people in an adverse or offensive way. Marketers are urged to obtain written permission before:

a    referring to or portraying members of the public or their identifiable possessions; the use of crowd scenes or general public locations may be acceptable without permission

b    referring to people with a public profile; references that accurately reflect the contents of books, articles or films may be acceptable without permission

c    implying any personal approval of the advertised product; marketers should recognise that those who do not wish to be associated with the product may have a legal claim.

13.2 Prior permission may not be needed when the marketing communication contains nothing that is inconsistent with the position or views of the person featured.

13.3 References to anyone who is deceased should be handled with particular care to avoid causing offence or distress.

13.4 Members of the Royal Family should not normally be shown or mentioned in marketing communications without their prior permission. Incidental references unconnected with the advertised product, or references to material such as books, articles or films about members of the Royal Family, may be acceptable.

13.5 The Royal Arms and Emblems should be used only with the prior permission of the Lord Chamberlain's office. References to Royal Warrants should be checked with the Royal Warrant Holders' Association.

## Testimonials and endorsements

14.1 Marketers should hold signed and dated proof, including a contact address, for any testimonial they use. Unless they are genuine opinions taken from a published source, testimonials should be used only with the written permission of those giving them.

14.2 Testimonials should relate to the product being advertised.

14.3 Testimonials alone do not constitute substantiation and the opinions expressed in them must be supported, where necessary, with independent evidence of their accuracy. Any claims based on a testimonial must conform with the Code.

14.4 Fictitious testimonials should not be presented as though they are genuine.

14.5 Unless they are genuine statements taken from a published source, references to tests, trials, professional endorsements, research facilities and professional journals should be used only with the permission of those concerned.

14.6 Marketers should not refer in marketing communications to advice received from CAP or imply any endorsement by the ASA or CAP.

## Prices

**(see CAP Help Notes on Lowest Price Claims and Price Promises and on Retailers' Price Comparisons)**

15.1  Any stated price should be clear and should relate to the product advertised. Marketers should ensure that prices match the products illustrated (see 48.7).

15.2  Prices quoted in marketing communications addressed to the public should include VAT and other non-optional taxes and duties imposed on all buyers. In some circumstances, for example where marketing communications are likely to be read mainly by businesses able to recover VAT, prices may be quoted exclusive of VAT or other taxes and duties, provided prominence is given to the amount or rate of any additional costs.

15.3  If the price of one product is dependent on the purchase of another, the extent of any commitment by consumers must be made clear.

15.4  Price claims such as "up to" and "from" should not exaggerate the availability of benefits likely to be obtained by consumers.

15.5  A recommended retail price (RRP), or similar, used as a basis of comparison should be genuine; it should not differ significantly from the price at which the product is generally sold.

## Availability of products

16.1  Marketers must make it clear if stocks are limited. Products must not be advertised unless marketers can demonstrate that they have reasonable grounds for believing that they can satisfy demand. If a product becomes unavailable, marketers will be required to show evidence of stock monitoring, communications with outlets and swift withdrawal of marketing communications whenever possible.

16.2  Products which cannot be supplied should not normally be advertised as a way of assessing potential demand unless it is clear that this is the purpose of the marketing communication.

16.3  Marketers must not use the technique of switch selling, where their sales staff criticise the advertised product or suggest that it is not available and recommend the purchase of a more expensive alternative. They should not place obstacles in the way of purchasing the product or delivering it promptly.

## Guarantees

**(see CAP Help Note on Lowest Price Claims and Price Promises)**

17.1  Guarantees may be legally binding on those offering them. The word "guarantee" should not be used in a way that could cause confusion about consumers' legal rights. Substantial limitations on the guarantee should be spelled out in the marketing communication. Before commitment, consumers should be able to obtain the full terms of the guarantee from marketers.

17.2  Marketers should inform consumers about the nature and extent of any additional rights provided by the guarantee, over and above those given to them by law, and should make clear how to obtain redress.

17.3 Marketers should provide a cash refund, postal order or personal cheque promptly to those claiming redress under a money-back guarantee.

## Comparisons with identified competitors and/or their products

18.1 Comparative claims are permitted in the interests of vigorous competition and public information. They should neither mislead nor be likely to mislead.

18.2 They should compare products meeting the same needs or intended for the same purpose.

18.3 They should objectively compare one or more material, relevant, verifiable and representative features of those products, which may include price.

18.4 They should not create confusion between marketers and competitors or between marketers' products, trade marks, trade names or other distinguishing marks and those of competitors.

18.5 Certain EU agricultural products and foods are, because of their unique geographical area and method of production, given special protection by being registered as having a "designation of origin". Products with a designation of origin should be compared only with other products with the same designation.

## Other comparisons

19.1 Other comparisons, for example those with marketers' own products, those with products of others who are not competitors or those that do not identify competitors or their products explicitly or by implication, should be clear and fair. They should neither mislead nor be likely to mislead. The elements of comparisons should not be selected in a way that gives the marketers an artificial advantage.

## Denigration and unfair advantage

20.1 Although comparative claims are permitted, marketing communications that include comparisons with identifiable competitors and/or their products should not discredit or denigrate the products, trade marks, trade names, other distinguishing marks, activities or circumstances of competitors. Other marketing communications should not unfairly attack or discredit businesses or their products.

20.2 Marketers should not take unfair advantage of the reputation of trade marks, trade names or other distinguishing marks of organisations or of the designation of origin of competing products.

## Imitation

21.1 No marketing communication should so closely resemble any other that it misleads, is likely to mislead or causes confusion.

21.2 Marketers making comparisons with identifiable competitors and/or their products should not present products as imitations or replicas of products bearing a protected trade mark or trade name.

## Recognising marketing communications and identifying marketers

22.1 Marketers, publishers and owners of other media should ensure that marketing communications are designed and presented in such a way that it is clear that they are marketing communications. Unsolicited e-mail marketing communications should be clearly identifiable as marketing communications without the need to open them (see also clause 43.4c).

22.2 Distance selling marketing communications that require payment before products are received and have written response mechanisms should contain the full name and geographical address of the marketers (and the suppliers if different) (see also clause 42.2a).

Sales promotions and marketing communications for one day sales, homework schemes, business opportunities and the like should contain the full name and geographical address of the marketers.

Other unsolicited e-mail marketing communications, marketing communications for employment agencies and distance selling marketing communications that require payment before products are received and have telephone response mechanisms only should contain the full name and contact details of the marketers.

Distance selling marketing communications that do not require payment before products are received should state the full name of the marketers (and suppliers if different).

The law requires marketers to identify themselves in some other marketing communications. Marketers should take legal advice.

## Advertisement features

**(see CAP Help Note on Advertisement Features)**

23.1 Advertisement features, announcements or promotions, sometimes referred to as "advertorials", that are disseminated in exchange for a payment or other reciprocal arrangement should comply with the Code if their content is controlled by the marketers rather than the publishers.

23.2 Marketers and publishers should make clear that advertisement features are advertisements, for example by heading them "advertisement feature".

## Free offers

24.1 See clauses 32.1 to 32.3.

# Appendix 5

# The CCTV Code of Practice[1]

## Foreword

Closed circuit television (CCTV) surveillance is an increasing feature of our daily lives. There is an ongoing debate over how effective CCTV is in reducing and preventing crime, but one thing is certain, its deployment is commonplace in a variety of areas to which members of the public have free access. We might be caught on camera while walking down the high street, visiting a shop or bank or travelling through a railway station or airport. The House of Lords Select Committee on Science and Technology expressed their view that if public confidence in CCTV systems was to be maintained there needed to be some tighter control over their deployment and use (5th Report—Digital Images as Evidence).

There was no statutory basis for systematic legal control of CCTV surveillance over public areas until 1 March 2000 when the Data Protection Act came into force. The definitions in this new Act are broader than those of the Data Protection Act 1984 and so more readily cover the processing of images of individuals caught by CCTV cameras than did the previous data protection legislation. The same legally enforceable information handling standards as have previously applied to those processing personal data on computer now cover CCTV. An important new feature of the recent legislation is a power for me to issue a Commissioner's Code of Practice (section 51(3)(b) DPA ''98) setting out guidance for the following of good practice. In my 14th Annual Report to Parliament I signalled my intention to use this power to provide guidance on the operation of CCTV as soon as those new powers became available to me. This Code of Practice is the first Commissioner's Code to be issued under the Data Protection Act 1998.

This code deals with surveillance in areas to which the public have largely free and unrestricted access because, as the House of Lords Committee highlighted, there is particular concern about a lack of regulation and central guidance in this area. Although the Data Protection Act 1998 covers other uses of CCTV this Code addresses the area of widest concern. Many of its provisions will be relevant to other uses of CCTV and will be referred to as appropriate when we develop other guidance. There are some existing standards that have been developed by representatives of CCTV system operators and, more particularly, the British Standards Institute. While such standards are helpful, they are not legally enforceable. The changes in data protection legislation mean that for the first time legally enforceable standards will apply to the collection and processing of images relating to individuals.

This Code of Practice has the dual purpose of assisting operators of CCTV systems to understand their legal obligations while also reassuring the public about the safeguards that should be in place. It sets out the measures which must be adopted to comply with the Data Protection Act 1998, and goes on to set out guidance for the following of good data protection practice. The Code makes clear the standards which must be followed to ensure compliance with the Data Protection Act 1998 and

---

[1] Reproduced with permission of the Information Commissioner's Office.

then indicates those which are not a strict legal requirement but do represent the following of good practice.

Before issuing this Code I consulted representatives of relevant data controllers and data subjects, and published a draft copy of the Code on my website. I am grateful to all those consultees who responded and have taken account of their comments in producing this version.

Our experience of the Codes of Practice which were put forward under the 1984 Act was that they needed to remain relevant to the day to day activities of data controllers. They need to be "living" documents, which are updated as practices, and understanding of the law develops.

This code will therefore be kept under review to ensure that it remains relevant in the context of changing technology, use and jurisprudence. In this context it is likely that the Human Rights Act 1998, which comes into force on 2 October 2000, and provides important legal safeguards for individuals, will lead to developments in legal interpretation which will require review of the Code.

It is my intention that this Code of Practice should help those operating CCTV schemes monitoring members of the public to do so in full compliance of the Data Protection Act 1998 and in adherence to high standards of good practice. There does seem to be public support for the widespread deployment of this surveillance technology, but public confidence has to be earned and maintained. Compliance with this Code will not only help CCTV scheme operators' process personal data in compliance with the law but also help to maintain that public confidence without which they cannot operate.

**Elizabeth France**
**Data Protection Commissioner**
July 2000

## Introduction

This is a code of practice issued by the Data Protection Commissioner in accordance with her powers under Section 51 (3)(b) of the Data Protection Act 1998 (the "1998 Act"). It is intended to provide guidance as to good practice for users of CCTV (closed circuit television) and similar surveillance equipment.

It is not intended that the contents of this Code should apply to:—

- Targeted and intrusive surveillance activities, which are covered by the provisions of the forthcoming Regulation of Investigatory Powers Act.

- Use of surveillance techniques by employers to monitor their employees' compliance with their contracts of employment.[1]

- Security equipment (including cameras) installed in homes by individuals for home security purposes.[2]

- Use of cameras and similar equipment by the broadcast media for the purposes of journalism, or for artistic or literary purposes.

This Code of Practice is drafted in two parts:

# Part I

This sets out:

- the standards which must be met if the requirements of the 1998 Act are to be complied with. These are based on the Data Protection Principles which say that data must be

  - fairly and lawfully processed;
  - processed for limited purposes and not in any manner incompatible with those purposes;
  - adequate, relevant and not excessive;
  - accurate;
  - not kept for longer than is necessary
  - processed in accordance with individuals' rights;
  - secure;
  - not transferred to countries without adequate protection.

- guidance on good practice,

- examples of how to implement the standards and good practice.

The Data Protection Commissioner has the power to issue Enforcement Notices where she considers that there has been a breach of one or more of the Data Protection Principles. An Enforcement Notice[3] would set out the remedial action that the Commissioner requires to ensure future compliance with the requirements of the Act. The Data Protection Commissioner will take into account the extent to which users of CCTV and similar surveillance equipment have complied with this Code of Practice when determining whether they have met their legal obligations when exercising her powers of enforcement.

# Part II—Glossary

This sets out the interpretation of the 1998 Act on which Part I is based. Part I is cross-referenced to Part II to try to clarify the reasoning behind the standard or guidance.

It is intended that this Code of Practice will be revised on a regular basis in order to take account of developments in the interpretation of the provisions of the data protection legislation, developments in the technology involved in the recording of images, and developments in the use of such technologies, the use of sound recording, facial recognition techniques and the increased use of digital technology.

# Please Note

Shaded text indicates good practice.

# Initial Assessment Procedures

Before installing and using CCTV and similar surveillance equipment, users will need to establish the purpose or purposes for which they intend to use the equipment.[4] This equipment may be used for a number of different purposes—for example, prevention, investigation and detection of crime, apprehension and prosecution of offenders (including use of images as evidence in criminal proceedings), public and employee safety, monitoring security of premises etc.

# Standards

---

1. establish who is the person(s) or organisation(s) legally responsible for the proposed scheme.[5]

2. assess the appropriateness of, and reasons for, using CCTV or similar surveillance equipment (First Data Protection Principle).

3. *document this assessment process and the reasons for the installation of the scheme.*

4. establish the purpose of the Scheme (First and Second Data Protection Principle).[6]

5. *document the purpose of the scheme.*

6. ensure that the notification lodged with the Office of the Data Protection Commissioner covers the purposes for which this equipment is used[7]

7. *establish and document the person(s) or organisation(s) who are responsible for ensuring the day-to-day compliance with the requirements of this Code of Practice (if different from above)*

8. *establish and document security and disclosure policies.*

## Siting the Cameras

It is essential that the location of the equipment is carefully considered, because the way in which images are captured will need to comply with the First Data Protection Principle. Detailed guidance on the interpretation of the First Data Protection Principle is provided in Part II, but the standards to be met under this Code of Practice are set out below.

## Standards

1. The equipment should be sited in such a way that it only monitors those spaces which are intended to be covered by the equipment (First and Third Data Protection Principles).

2. If domestic areas such as gardens or areas not intended to be covered by the scheme border those spaces which are intended to be covered by the equipment, then the user should consult with the owners of such spaces if images from those spaces might be recorded. In the case of back gardens, this would be the resident of the property overlooked (First and Third Data Protection Principles).

3. Operators must be aware of the purpose(s) for which the scheme has been established (Second and Seventh Data Protection Principles).

4. Operators must be aware that they are only able to use the equipment in order to achieve the purpose(s) for which it has been installed (First and Second Data Protection Principles).

5. If cameras are adjustable by the operators, this should be restricted so that operators cannot adjust or manipulate them to overlook spaces which are

not intended to be covered by the scheme (First and Third Data Protection Principles).

6. If it is not possible physically to restrict the equipment to avoid recording images from those spaces not intended to be covered by the scheme, then operators should be trained in recognising the privacy implications of such spaces being covered (First and Third Data Protection Principles).

**For example**—individuals sunbathing in their back gardens may have a greater expectation of privacy than individuals mowing the lawn of their front garden.

**For example**—it may be appropriate for the equipment to be used to protect the safety of individuals when using ATMs, but images of PIN numbers, balance enquiries etc should not be captured.

7. Signs should be placed so that the public are aware that they are entering a zone which is covered by surveillance equipment (First Data Protection Principle).

8. The signs should be clearly visible and legible to members of the public (First Data Protection Principle)

9. The size of signs will vary according to circumstances:

**For example**—*a sign on the entrance door to a building society office may* only need to be A4 size because it is at eye level of those entering the premises.

**For example**—*signs at the entrances of car parks alerting drivers to the fact* that the car park is covered by such equipment will usually need to be large, for example, probably A3 size as they are likely to be viewed from further away, for example by a driver sitting in a car.

10. The signs should contain the following information:

    a) Identity of the person or organisation responsible for the scheme.
    b) The purposes of the scheme.
    c) Details of whom to contact regarding the scheme.
       (First Data Protection Principle)

    **For example**—Where an image of a camera is not used on a sign—the following wording is recommended:
    "Images are being monitored for the purposes of crime prevention and public safety. This scheme is controlled by the Greentown Safety Partnership.
    For further information contact 01234–567–890"

    **For example**—Where an image of a camera is used on a sign—the following wording is recommended:
    "This scheme is controlled by the Greentown Safety Partnership.
    For further information contact 01234–567–890"

11. In exceptional and limited cases, if it is assessed that the use of signs would not be appropriate, the user of the scheme must ensure that they have:

    a) Identified specific criminal activity.
    b) Identified the need to use surveillance to obtain evidence of that criminal activity.
    c) Assessed whether the use of signs would prejudice success in obtaining such evidence.

d)   Assessed how long the covert monitoring should take place to ensure that it is not carried out for longer than is necessary.

e)   *Documented (a) to (d) above.*[8]

12.   Information so obtained must only be obtained for prevention or detection of criminal activity, or the apprehension and prosecution of offenders.[9] It should not be retained and used for any other purpose. If the equipment used has a sound recording facility, this should not be used to record conversations between members of the public (First and Third Data Protection Principles).

## Quality of the Images

It is important that the images produced by the equipment are as clear as possible in order that they are effective for the purpose(s) for which they are intended. This is why it is essential that the purpose of the scheme is clearly identified. For example if a system has been installed to prevent and detect crime, then it is essential that the images are adequate for that purpose. The Third, Fourth and Fifth Data Protection Principles are concerned with the quality of personal data, and they are outlined in more detail in Part II. The standards to be met under this Code of Practice are set out below.

## Standards

1.   Upon installation an initial check should be undertaken to ensure that the equipment performs properly.

2.   If tapes are used, it should be ensured that they are good quality tapes (Third and Fourth Data Protection Principles).

3.   The medium on which the images are captured should be cleaned so that images are not recorded on top of images recorded previously (Third and Fourth Data Protection Principles).

4.   The medium on which the images have been recorded should not be used when it has become apparent that the quality of images has deteriorated. (Third Data Protection Principle).

5.   If the system records features such as the location of the camera and/or date and time reference, these should be accurate (Third and Fourth Data Protection Principles).

6.   *If their system includes such features, users should ensure that they have a documented procedure for ensuring their accuracy.*

7.   Cameras should be situated so that they will capture images relevant to the purpose for which the scheme has been established (Third Data Protection Principle)

**For example**, if the purpose of the scheme is the prevention and detection of crime and/or apprehension and prosecution of offenders, the cameras should be sited so that images enabling identification of perpetrators are captured.

**For example**, if the scheme has been established with a view to monitoring traffic flow, the cameras should be situated so that they do not capture the details of the vehicles or drivers.

8. If an automatic facial recognition system is used to match images captured against a database of images, then both sets of images should be clear enough to ensure an accurate match (Third and Fourth Data Protection Principles).

9. If an automatic facial recognition system is used, procedures should be set up to ensure that the match is also verified by a human operator, who will assess the match and determine what action, if any, should be taken (First and Seventh Data Protection Principles).[10]

10. *The result of the assessment by the human operator should be recorded whether or not they determine there is a match.*

11. When installing cameras, consideration must be given to the physical conditions in which the cameras are located (Third and Fourth Data Protection Principles).

   **For example**—infrared equipment may need to be installed in poorly lit areas.

12. Users should assess whether it is necessary to carry out constant real time recording, or whether the activity or activities about which they are concerned occur at specific times (First and Third Data Protection Principles)

   **For example**—it may be that criminal activity only occurs at night, in which case constant recording of images might only be carried out for a limited period e.g. 10.00 pm to 7.00 am

13. Cameras should be properly maintained and serviced to ensure that clear images are recorded (Third and Fourth Data Protection Principles)

14. Cameras should be protected from vandalism in order to ensure that they remain in working order (Seventh Data Protection Principle)

15. *A maintenance log should be kept.*

16. If a camera is damaged, there should be clear procedures for:

   a) *Defining the person responsible for making arrangements for ensuring that the camera is fixed.*
   b) Ensuring that the camera is fixed within a specific time period (Third and Fourth Data Protection Principle).
   c) *Monitoring the quality of the maintenance work.*

## Processing the images

Images, which are not required for the purpose(s) for which the equipment is being used, should not be retained for longer than is necessary. While images are retained, it is essential that their integrity be maintained, whether it is to ensure their evidential value or to protect the rights of people whose images may have been recorded. It is therefore important that access to and security of the images is controlled in accordance with the requirements of the 1998 Act. The Seventh Data Protection Principle sets out the security requirements of the 1998 Data Protection Act. This is discussed in more depth at Part II. However, the standards required by this Code of Practice are set out below.

**Standards**

---

1. Images should not be retained for longer than is necessary (Fifth Data Protection Principle)

   **For example**—publicans may need to keep recorded images for no longer than seven days because they will soon be aware of any incident such as a fight occurring on their premises.

   **For example**—images recorded by equipment covering town centres and streets may not need to be retained for longer than 31 days unless they are required for evidential purposes in legal proceedings.

   **For example**—images recorded from equipment protecting individuals' safety at ATMs might need to be retained for a period of three months in order to resolve customer disputes about cash withdrawals. The retention period of three months is based on the interval at which individuals receive their account statements.

2. Once the retention period has expired, the images should be removed or erased (Fifth Data Protection Principle).

3. If the images are retained for evidential purposes, they should be retained in a secure place to which access is controlled (Fifth and Seventh Data Protection Principles).

4. On removing the medium on which the images have been recorded for the use in legal proceedings, the operator should ensure that they have documented:

   a) The date on which the images were removed from the general system for use in legal proceedings.
   b) The reason why they were removed from the system.
   c) Any crime incident number to which the images may be relevant.
   d) The location of the images.
      **For example**—if the images were handed to a police officer for retention, the name and station of that police officer.
   e) The signature of the collecting police officer, where appropriate (see below) (Third and Seventh Data Protection Principles).

5. Monitors displaying images from areas in which individuals would have an expectation of privacy should not be viewed by anyone other than authorised employees of the user of the equipment (Seventh Data Protection Principle).

6. Access to the recorded images should be restricted to a manager or designated member of staff who will decide whether to allow requests for access by third parties in accordance with the user's documented disclosure policies (Seventh Data Protection Principle).[11]

7. Viewing of the recorded images should take place in a restricted area, for example, in a manager's or designated member of staff's office. Other employees should not be allowed to have access to that area when a viewing is taking place (Seventh Data Protection Principle).

8. Removal of the medium on which images are recorded, for viewing purposes, should be documented as follows:

   a) *The date and time of removal*
   b) *The name of the person removing the images*

c)   *The name(s) of the person(s) viewing the images. If this should include* third parties, this include the organisation of that third party
d)   *The reason for the viewing*
e)   *The outcome, if any, of the viewing*
f)   *The date and time the images were returned to the system or secure place,* if they have been retained for evidential purposes

9.   All operators and employees with access to images should be aware of the procedure which need to be followed when accessing the recorded images (Seventh Data Protection Principle).

10.  All operators should be trained in their responsibilities under this Code of Practice i.e. they should be aware of:

   a)   The user's security policy e.g. procedures to have access to recorded images.
   b)   The user's disclosure policy.[12]
   c)   Rights of individuals in relation to their recorded images.[13]

   (Seventh Data Protection Principle)

## Access to and disclosure of images to third parties

It is important that access to, and disclosure of, the images recorded by CCTV and similar surveillance equipment is restricted and carefully controlled, not only to ensure that the rights of individuals are preserved, but also to ensure that the chain of evidence remains intact should the images be required for evidential purposes. Users of CCTV will also need to ensure that the reason(s) for which they may disclose copies of the images are compatible with the reason(s) or purpose(s) for which they originally obtained those images. These aspects of this Code are to be found in the Second and Seventh Data Protection Principles, which are discussed in more depth at Part II. However, the standards required by this Code are set out below.

## Standards

All employees should be aware of the restrictions set out in this code of practice in relation to access to, and disclosure of, recorded images.

1.   Access to recorded images should be restricted to those staff who need to have access in order to achieve the purpose(s) of using the equipment (Seventh Data Protection Principle).[14]

2.   All access to the medium on which the images are recorded should be documented (Seventh Data Protection Principle).[15]

3.   Disclosure of the recorded images to third parties should only made in limited and prescribed circumstances (Second and Seventh Data Protection Principles).

   **For example**—if the purpose of the system is the prevention and detection of crime, then disclosure to third parties should be limited to the following:

   • Law enforcement agencies where the images recorded would assist in a specific criminal enquiry
   • Prosecution agencies
   • Relevant legal representatives

- The media, where it is decided that the public's assistance is needed in order to assist in the identification of victim, witness or perpetrator in relation to a criminal incident. As part of that decision, the wishes of the victim of an incident should be taken into account
- People whose images have been recorded and retained (unless disclosure to the individual would prejudice criminal enquiries or criminal proceedings)

4. All requests for access or for disclosure should be recorded. If access or disclosure is denied, the reason should be documented (Seventh Data Protection Principle)

5. If access to or disclosure of the images is allowed, then the following should be documented:

    a) *The date and time at which access was allowed or the date on which* disclosure was made
    b) *The identification of any third party who was allowed access or to whom* disclosure was made
    c) *The reason for allowing access or disclosure*
    d) *The extent of the information to which access was allowed or which was* disclosed[16]

6. Recorded images should not be made more widely available—for example they should not be routinely made available to the media or placed on the Internet
    (Second, Seventh and Eighth Data Protection Principles).

7. If it is intended that images will be made more widely available, that decision should be made by the manager or designated member of staff. The reason for that decision should be documented (Seventh Data Protection Principle).

8. If it is decided that images will be disclosed to the media (other than in the circumstances outlined above), the images of individuals will need to be disguised or blurred so that they are not readily identifiable (First, Second and Seventh Data Protection Principles).

9. *If the system does not have the facilities to carry out that type of editing, an* editing company may need to be hired to carry it out.

10. If an editing company is hired, then the manager or designated member of staff needs to ensure that:

    a) There is a contractual relationship between the data controller and the editing company.
    b) That the editing company has given appropriate guarantees regarding the security measures they take in relation to the images.
    c) The manager has checked to ensure that those guarantees are met
    d) The written contract makes it explicit that the editing company can only use the images in accordance with the instructions of the manager or designated member of staff.
    e) The written contract makes the security guarantees provided by the editing company explicit.

    (Seventh Data Protection Principle)

11. If the media organisation receiving the images undertakes to carry out the editing, then (a) to (e) will still apply (Seventh Data Protection Principle)

## Access by data subjects

This is a right, which is provided by section 7 of the 1998 Act. A detailed explanation of the interpretation of this right is given in Part II. The standards of this Code of Practice are set out below.

## Standards

---

1. All staff involved in operating the equipment must be able to recognise a request for access to recorded images by data subjects (Sixth and Seventh Data Protection Principles).

2. *Data subjects should be provided with a standard subject access request form which:*

   a) *Indicates the information required in order to locate the images requested.*

   For example—*an individual may have to provide dates and times of when they visited the premises of the user of the equipment.*

   b) *Indicates the information required in order to identify the person making* the request.

      **For example**—*if the individual making the request is unknown to the user* of the equipment, a photograph of the individual may be requested in order to locate the correct image.

   c) *Indicates the fee that will be charged for carrying out the search for the* images requested. A maximum of £10.00 may be charged for the search.

   d) *Asks whether the individual would be satisfied with merely viewing the* images recorded.

   e) *Indicates that the response will be provided promptly and in any event* within 40 days of receiving the required fee and information.

   f) *Explains the rights provided by the 1998 Act.*

3. Individuals should also be provided with a leaflet which describes the types images which are recorded and retained, the purposes for which those images are recorded and retained, and information about the disclosure policy in relation to those images (Sixth Data Protection Principle).[17]

4. This should be provided at the time that the standard subject access request form is provided to an individual (Sixth Data Protection Principle).[18]

5. *All subject access requests should be dealt with by a manager or designated* member of staff.

6. *The manager or designated member of staff should locate the images requested*

7. The manager or designated member of staff should determine whether disclosure to the individual would entail disclosing images of third parties (Sixth Data Protection Principle).[19]

8. The manager or designated member of staff will need to determine whether the images of third parties are held under a duty of confidence (First and Sixth Data Protection Principle).[20]

   **For example**—it may be that members of the public whose images have been recorded when they were in town centres or streets have less expectation that their images are held under a duty of confidence than individuals whose images have been recorded in more private space such as the waiting room of a doctor's surgery.

9.   If third party images are not to be disclosed, the manager or designated member of staff shall arrange for the third party images to be disguised or blurred (Sixth Data Protection Principle).[21]

10.   *If the system does not have the facilities to carry out that type of editing, a third party or company may be hired to carry it out*

11.   If a third party or company is hired, then the manager or designated member of staff needs to ensure that:

a)   There is a contractual relationship between the data controller and the third party or company.

b)   That the third party or company has given appropriate guarantees regarding the security measures they take in relation to the images.

c)   The manager has checked to ensure that those guarantees are met.

d)   The written contract makes it explicit that the third party or company can only use the images in accordance with the instructions of the manager or designated member of staff.

e)   The written contract makes the security guarantees provided by the third party or company explicit

(Seventh Data Protection Principle)

12.   If the manager or designated member of staff decides that a subject access request from an individual is not to be complied with, the following should be documented:

a)   The identity of the individual making the request

b)   The date of the request

c)   The reason for refusing to supply the images requested

d)   The name and signature of the manager or designated member of staff making the decision.[22]

13.   All staff should be aware of individuals' rights under this section of the Code of Practice (Seventh Data Protection Principle)

## Other rights

A detailed explanation of the other rights under Sections 10, 12 and 13 of the Act are provided in Part II of this Code. The standards of this Code are set out below.

## Standards

1.   All staff involved in operating the equipment must be able to recognise a request from an individual to:

a)   Prevent processing likely to cause substantial and unwarranted damage to that individual.[23]

b)   Prevent automated decision taking in relation to that individual.[24]

2.   *All staff must be aware of the manager or designated member of staff who is responsible for responding to such requests.*

3. In relation to a request to prevent processing likely to cause substantial and unwarranted damage, the manager or designated officer's response should indicate whether he or she will comply with the request or not.[25]

4. The manager or designated member of staff must provide a written response to the individual within 21 days of receiving the request setting out their decision on the request.[26]

5. If the manager or designated member of staff decide that the request will not be complied with, they must set out their reasons in the response to the individual.[27]

6. *A copy of the request and response should be retained.*

7. If an automated decision is made about an individual, the manager or designated member of staff must notify the individual of that decision.[28]

8. If, within 21 days of that notification, the individual requires, in writing, the decision to be reconsidered, the manager or designated staff member shall reconsider the automated decision.[29]

9. On receipt of a request to reconsider the automated decision, the manager or designated member of staff shall respond within 21 days setting out the steps that they intend to take to comply with the individual's request.[30]

10. *The manager or designated member of staff shall document:*

   a) *The original decision.*
   b) *The request from the individual.*
   c) *Their response to the request from the individual.*

## Monitoring compliance with this code of practice

### Standards

1. The contact point indicated on the sign should be available to members of the public during office hours. Employees staffing that contact point should be aware of the policies and procedures governing the use of this equipment.

2. *Enquiries should be provided on request with one or more of the following:*

   a) *The leaflet which individuals receive when they make a subject access* request as general information
   b) *A copy of this code of practice*
   c) *A subject access request form if required or requested*
   d) *The complaints procedure to be followed if they have concerns about the* use of the system
   e) *The complaints procedure to be followed if they have concerns about non-* compliance with the provisions of this Code of Practice

3. *A complaints procedure should be clearly documented.*

4. *A record of the number and nature of complaints or enquiries received should* be maintained together with an outline of the action taken.

5. *A report on those numbers should be collected by the manager or designated*

member of staff in order to assess public reaction to and opinion of the use of the system.

6. A manager or designated member of staff should undertake regular reviews of the documented procedures to ensure that the provisions of this Code are being complied with (Seventh Data Protection Principle).

7. *A report on those reviews should be provided to the data controller(s) in order that compliance with legal obligations and provisions with this Code of Practice can be monitored.*

8. *An internal annual assessment should be undertaken which evaluates the effectiveness of the system.*

9. *The results of the report should be assessed against the stated purpose of the scheme. If the scheme is not achieving its purpose, it should be discontinued or modified.*

10. *The result of those reports should be made publicly available.*

# PART II

## Glossary

## The Data Protection Act 1998.

## 1. Definitions

There are several definitions in Sections 1 and 2 of the 1998 Act which users of CCTV systems or similar surveillance equipment must consider in order to determine whether they need to comply with the requirements of the 1998 Act, and if so, to what extent the 1998 Act applies to them:

### a) Data Controller

"A person who (either alone or jointly or in common with other persons) determines the purposes for which and the manner in which any personal data are, or are to be, processed".

**For example**: if a police force and local authority enter into a partnership to install CCTV in a town centre with a view to:

- Preventing and detecting crime.
- Apprehending and prosecuting offenders.
- Protecting public safety.

They will both be data controllers for the purpose of the scheme.

**For example**—if a police force, local authority and local retailers decide to install a CCTV scheme in a town centre or shopping centre, for the purposes of:

- Prevention or detection crime.

- Apprehending or prosecuting offenders.

- Protecting public safety.

All will be data controllers for the purposes of the scheme. It is the data controllers who should set out the purposes of the scheme (as outlined above) and who should set out the policies on the use of the images (as outlined in the Standards section of this Code of Practice).

The data controller(s) may devolve day-to-day running of the scheme to a manager, but that manager is not the data controller—he or she can only manage the scheme according to the instructions of the data controller(s), and according to the policies set out by the data controller(s).

If the manager of the scheme is an employee of one or more of the data controllers, then the manager will not have any personal data protection responsibilities as a data controller. However, the manager should be aware that if he or she acts outside the instructions of the data controller(s) in relation to obtaining or disclosing the images, they may commit a criminal offence contrary to Section 55 of the 1998 Act, as well as breach their contract of employment.

If the manager is a third party such as a security company employed by the data controller to run the scheme, then the manager may be deemed a data processor. This is "any person (other than an employee of the data controller) who processes the personal data on behalf of the data controller. If the data controller(s) are considering using a data processor, they will need to consider their compliance with the Seventh Data Protection Principle in terms of this relationship.

### b) Personal Data

"Data which relate to a living individual who can be identified:

    a)   from those data, or
    b)   from those data and other information which is in the possession of, or is likely to come into the possession of, the data controller".

The provisions of the 1998 Act are based on the requirements of a European Directive,[31] which at, Article 2, defines, personal data as follows:
"Personal data" shall mean any information relating to an identified or identifiable natural person; an identifiable person is one who can be identified, directly or indirectly, in particular by reference to an identification number or to one or more factors specific to his physical, physiological, mental, economic, cultural or social identity.

The definition of personal data is not therefore limited to circumstances where a data controller can attribute a name to a particular image. If images of distinguishable individuals' features are processed and an individual can be identified from these images, they will amount to personal data.

### c) Sensitive Personal Data

Section 2 of the 1998 Act separates out distinct categories of personal data, which are deemed sensitive. The most significant of these categories for the purposes of this code of practice are information about:[32]

- the commission or alleged commission of any offences

- any proceedings for any offence committed, or alleged to have been committed, the disposal of such proceedings or the sentence of any court in such proceedings.

This latter bullet point will be particularly significant for those CCTV schemes which are established by retailers in conjunction with the local police force, which use other information to identify known and convicted shoplifters from images, with a view to reducing the amount of organised shoplifting in a retail centre.

It is essential that data controllers determine whether they are processing sensitive personal data because it has particular implications for their compliance with the First Data Protection Principle.

**d) Processing**

Section 1 of the 1998 Act sets out the type of operations that can constitute processing:

> "In relation to information or data, means obtaining, processing, recording or holding the information or data or carrying out any operation or set of operations on the information or data, including:
>
> a)   organisation, adaptation or alteration of the information or data,
> b)   retrieval, consultation or use of the information or data,
> c)   disclosure of the information or data by transmission, dissemination or otherwise making available, or
> d)   alignment, combination, blocking, erasure or destruction of the information or data."

The definition is wide enough to cover the simple recording and holding of images for a limited period of time, even if no further reference is made to those images. It is also wide enough to cover real-time transmission of the images. Thus if the images of individuals passing in front of a camera are shown in real time on a monitor, this constitutes "transmission, dissemination or otherwise making available. Thus even the least sophisticated capturing and use of images falls within the definition of processing in the 1998 Act.

## 2. Purposes for which personal data/images are processed

Before considering compliance with the Data Protection Principles, a user of CCTV or similar surveillance equipment, will need to determine two issues:

- What type of personal data are being processed i.e. are there any personal data which fall within the definition of sensitive personal data as defined by Section 2 of the 1998 Act.

- For what purpose(s) are both personal data and sensitive personal data being processed?

Users of surveillance equipment should be clear about the purposes for which they intend to use the information/images captured by their equipment. The equipment may be used for a number of purposes:

- Prevention, investigation and/or detection of crime.

- Apprehension and/or prosecution of offenders (including images being entered as evidence in criminal proceedings).

- Public and employee safety.

- Staff discipline.

- Traffic flow monitoring.

Using information captured by a surveillance system will not always require the processing of personal data or the processing of sensitive personal data. For example, use of the system to monitor traffic flow in order to provide the public with up to date information about traffic jams, will not necessarily require the processing of personal data.

## 3. Data protection principles

*THE FIRST DATA PROTECTION PRINCIPLE*

This requires that

"Personal data shall be processed fairly and lawfully, and, in particular, shall not be processed unless:

a)   at least one of the conditions in Schedule 2 is met, and
b)   in the case of sensitive personal data, at least one of the conditions in Schedule 3 is also met".

To assess compliance with this Principle, it is recommended that the data controller address the following questions:

**a)  Are personal data and/or sensitive personal data processed?**
The definition of sensitive personal data[33] has been discussed above and it is essential that the data controller has determined whether they are processing information/images, which fall into that category in order to assess which criteria to consider when deciding whether there is a legitimate basis for the processing of that information/images.

**b)  Has a condition for processing been met?**
The First Data Protection Principle requires that the *data controller* have a legitimate basis for processing. It is for the data controller to be clear about which grounds to rely on in this respect. These are set out in Schedules 2 and 3 to the Act.

Users of schemes which monitor spaces to which the public have access, such as town centres, may be able to rely on Paragraph 5 (d) of Schedule 2 because the processing is for the exercise of any other function of a public nature exercised in the public interest by any person. This could include purposes such as prevention and detection of crime, apprehension and prosecution of offenders or public/employee safety.

Users of schemes which monitor spaces in shops or retail centres to which the public have access may be able to rely on Paragraph 6(1) of Schedule 2 because the processing is necessary for the purposes of legitimate interests pursued by the data controller or the third party or third parties to whom the data are disclosed, except where the processing is unwarranted in any particular case by reason of prejudice to the rights and freedoms or legitimate interests of the data subject.

It should be noted that while this criterion may provide a general ground for processing, in an individual case, the interests of the data controller i.e. the user of the surveillance equipment might not outweigh the rights of an individual.

If the data controller has determined that he or she is processing sensitive personal data, then the data controller will also need to determine whether he or she has a legitimate basis for doing so under Schedule 3. It should be noted that Schedule 3 does not contain the grounds cited above in relation to Schedule 2.

Users of surveillance equipment in town centres, particularly where the local authority or police force (or a partnership of the two) are the data controllers may be able to rely on Paragraph 7(1)(b) of Schedule 3 because the processing is necessary for the exercise of any functions conferred on any person by or under an enactment. It may be that the use of such information/images by a public authority in order to meet the objectives of the Crime and Disorder Act 1998 would satisfy this criterion.

Users of information/images recorded in a shop or retail centre may be able to rely on one of the grounds contained in the Order made under Schedule 3(10) of the 1998 Act.[34]

**For example—**
"(1) The processing:

a)    is in the substantial public interest;
b)    is necessary for the purposes of the prevention and detection of any unlawful act; and
c)    must necessarily be carried out without the explicit consent of the data subject so as not to prejudice those purposes"

It is for the data controller to be sure that he or she has legitimate grounds for their processing and therefore it is essential that the data controller has identified:

- what categories of data are processed, and

- why.

### c)  Are the information/images processed lawfully?

The fact that the data controller has a legitimate basis for processing does not mean that this element of the First Data Protection Principle is automatically satisfied. The data controller will also need to consider whether the information/images processed are subject to any other legal duties or responsibilities such as the common law duty of confidentiality. Public sector bodies will need to consider their legal powers under administrative law in order to determine whether there are restrictions or prohibitions on their ability to process such data. They will also need to consider the implications of the Human Rights Act 1998.

### d)  Are the information/images processed fairly?

The fact that a data controller has a legitimate basis for processing the information/images will not automatically mean that this element of the First Data Protection Principle is satisfied.

The interpretative provisions[35] of the Act set out what is required in order to process fairly. In order to process fairly, the following information, at least, must be provided to the individuals at the point of obtaining their images:

- the identity of the data controller

- the identity of a representative the data controller has nominated for the purposes of the Act

- the purpose or purposes for which the data are intended to be processed, and

- any information which is necessary, having regard to the specific circumstances in which the data are or are to be processed, to enable processing in respect of the individual to be fair.

### e)  Circumstances in which the requirement for signs may be set aside

The Act does not make specific reference to the use of covert processing of (sensitive) personal data but it does provide a limited exemption from the requirement of fair processing. Because fair processing (as indicated above) requires that individuals are made aware that they are entering an area where their images may be captured, by the use of signs, it follows that the use of covert processing i.e. removal or failure to provide signs, is prima facie a breach of the fairness requirement of the First Data Protection Principle. However, a breach of this requirement will not arise if an exemption can be relied on. Such an exemption may be found at Section 29(l) of the Act, which states that:

"Personal data processed for any of the following purposes:

a) prevention or detection of crime
b) apprehension or prosecution of offenders

are exempt from the first data protection principle (except to the extent to which it requires compliance with the conditions in Schedules 2 and 3) . . . in any case to the extent to which the application of those provisions to the data would be likely to prejudice any of the matters mentioned . . ."

This means that if the data controller processes images for either or both of the purposes listed in the exemption, he or she may be able to obtain and process images without signs without breaching the fairness requirements of the First Data Protection Principle.

## THE SECOND DATA PROTECTION PRINCIPLE

This requires that

"Personal data shall be obtained only for one or more specified and lawful purposes, and shall not be further processed in any manner incompatible with that purpose or those purposes".

In order to ascertain whether the data controller can comply with this Data Protection Principle, it is essential that he or she is clear about the purpose(s) for which the images are processed.

Specified purposes may be those, which have been notified to the Commissioner or to the individuals.

There are a number of issues to be considered when determining lawfulness:

- Whether the data controller has a legitimate basis (see First Data Protection Principle) for the processing.

- Whether the images are processed in accordance with any other legal duties to which the data controller may be subject e.g. the common law duty of confidence, administrative law in relation to public sector powers etc.

It is quite clear from the interpretative provisions to the Principle that the requirement of compatibility is particularly significant when considering making a disclosure to a third party or developing a policy on disclosures to third parties. If the data controller intends to make a disclosure to a third party, regard must be had to the purpose(s) for which the third party may process the data.

This means, for example, that if the purpose(s) for which images are processed is:

- Prevention or detection of crime
- Apprehension or prosecution of offenders

The data controller may only disclose to third parties who intend processing the data for compatible purposes. Thus, for example, where there is an investigation into criminal activity, disclosure of footage relating to that criminal activity to the media in order to seek assistance from the public in identifying either the perpetrator, the victim or witnesses, may be appropriate. However, it would be an incompatible use if images from equipment installed to prevent or detect crime were disclosed to the media merely for entertainment purposes. For example, it might be appropriate to disclose to the media images of drunken individuals stumbling around a town centre on a Saturday night to show proper use of policing resources to combat anti-social behaviour. However, it would not be appropriate for the same images to be provided to a media company merely for inclusion in a "humorous" video.

If it is determined that a particular disclosure is compatible with the purposes for which the data controller processes images, then the extent of disclosure will need to be considered. If the footage, which is to be disclosed contains images of unrelated third parties, the data controller will need to ensure that those images are disguised in such a way that they cannot be identified.

If the data controller does not have the facilities to carry out such editing, he or she may agree with the media organisation that it will ensure that those images are disguised. This will mean that the media organisation is carrying out processing, albeit of a limited nature on behalf of the data controller which is likely to render it a data processor. In which case the data controller will need to ensure that the relationship with the media organisation complies with the Seventh Data Protection Principle.

## THE THIRD DATA PROTECTION PRINCIPLE

This requires that

> "Personal data shall be adequate, relevant and not excessive in relation to the purpose or purposes for which they are processed".

This means that consideration must be given to the situation of the cameras so that they do not record more information than is necessary for the purpose for which they were installed. For example cameras installed for the purpose of recording acts of vandalism in a car park should not overlook private residences. Furthermore, if the recorded images on the tapes are blurred or indistinct, it may well be that this will constitute inadequate data. For example, if the purpose of the system is to collect evidence of criminal activity, blurred or indistinct images from degraded tapes or poorly maintained equipment will not provide legally sound evidence, and may therefore be inadequate for its purpose.

## THE FOURTH DATA PROTECTION PRINCIPLE

This requires that

> "Personal data shall be accurate and, where necessary, kept up to date".

This principle requires that the personal information that is recorded and stored must be accurate. This is particularly important if the personal information taken from the system is to be used as evidence in cases of criminal conduct or in disciplinary disputes with employees. The Commissioner recommends that efforts are made to ensure the clarity of the images, such as using only good quality tapes in recording the information, cleaning the tapes prior to re-use and not simply recording over existing images, and replacing tapes on a regular basis to avoid degradation from over-use.

If the data controller's system uses features such as time references and even location references, then these should be accurate. This means having a documented procedure to ensure the accuracy of such features are checked and if necessary, amended or altered.

Care should be exercised when using digital-enhancement and compression technologies to produce stills for evidence from tapes because these technologies often contain pre-programmed presumptions as to the likely nature of sections of the image. Thus the user cannot be certain that the images taken from the tape are an accurate representation of the actual scene. This may create evidential difficulties if they are to be relied on either in court or an internal employee disciplinary hearing.

## THE FIFTH DATA PROTECTION PRINCIPLE

This requires that

> "Personal data processed for any purpose or purposes shall not be kept for longer than is necessary for that purpose or those purposes".

This principle requires that the information shall not be held for longer than is necessary for the purpose for which it is to be used. The tapes that have recorded the relevant activities should be retained until such time as the proceedings are completed and the possibility of any appeal has been exhausted. After that time, the tapes should be erased. Apart from those circumstances, stored or recorded images should not be kept for any undue length of time. A policy on periods for retention of the images should be developed which takes into account the nature of the information and the purpose for which it is being collected. For example where images are being recorded for the purposes of crime prevention in a shopping area, it may be that the only images that need to be retained are those relating to specific incidents of criminal activity; the rest could be erased after a very short period. The Commissioner understands that generally town centre schemes do not retain recorded images for more than 28 days unless the images are required for evidential purposes.

## THE SIXTH DATA PROTECTION PRINCIPLE

This requires that

> "Personal data shall be processed in accordance with the rights of data subjects under this Act".

The Act provides individuals with a number of rights in relation to the processing of their personal data. Contravening the following rights will amount to a contravention of the Sixth Data Protection Principle:

- The right to be provided, in appropriate cases, with a copy of the information constituting the personal data held about them—Section 7.[36]

- The right to prevent processing which is likely to cause damage or distress—Section 10.[37]

- Rights in relation to automated decision-taking—Section 12.[38]

## THE SEVENTH DATA PROTECTION PRINCIPLE[39]

This requires that

> "Appropriate technical and organisational measures shall be taken against unauthorised or unlawful processing of personal data and against accidental loss or destruction of, or damage to, personal data".

In order to assess the level of security the data controller needs to take to ensure compliance with this Principle, he or she needs to assess: —

- the harm that might result from unauthorised or unlawful processing or accidental loss, destruction or damage of the personal data.[40] While it is clear that breach of this Principle may have a detrimental effect on the purpose(s) of the scheme e.g. the evidence or images might not stand up in court, or the public may lose confidence in your use of surveillance equipment due to inappropriate disclosure, the harm test required by the Act also requires primarily the effect on the people recorded to be taken into account;

• the nature of the data to be protected must be considered. Sensitive personal data was defined at the beginning of this part of the Code, but there may be other aspects, which need to be considered. For example, a town centre scheme may coincidentally record the image of a couple kissing in a parked car, or a retailer's scheme may record images of people in changing rooms (in order to prevent items of clothing being stolen). Whilst these images may not fall within the sensitive categories as set in Section 2 (described above), it is clear that the people whose images have been captured will consider that information or personal data should be processed with greater care.

### THE EIGHTH DATA PROTECTION PRINCIPLE

This requires that

"Personal data shall not be transferred to a country or territory outside the European Economic Area unless that country or territory ensures an adequate level of protection for the rights and freedoms of data subjects in relation to the processing of personal data".

This Principle places limitations on the ability to transfer personal data to countries and territories outside of the EEA.[41] It is unlikely that the data controller would want, in general, to make such transfers of personal data overseas, but the data controller should refrain from putting the images on the Internet or on their website. In order to ensure that this Principle is not breached, the data controller should consider the provisions of Schedule 4 of the 1998 Act.

## 4. Right of subject access

Upon making a request in writing (which includes transmission by electronic means) and upon paying the fee to the data controller an individual is entitled:

• To be told by the data controller whether they or someone else on their behalf is processing that individual's personal data.

• If so, to be given a description of:

    a) the personal data,
    b) the purposes for which they are being processed, and
    c) those to whom they are or may be disclosed.

• To be told, in an intelligible manner, of:

    a) all the information, which forms any such personal data. This information must be supplied in permanent form by way of a copy, except where the supply of such a copy is not possible or would involve disproportionate effort or the individual agrees otherwise. If any of the information in the copy is not intelligible without explanation, the individual should be given an explanation of that information, e.g. where the data controller holds the information in coded form which cannot be understood without the key to the code, and

b)   any information as to the source of those data. However, in some instances the data controller is not obliged to disclose such information where the source of the data is, or can be identified as, an individual.

A data controller may charge a fee (subject to a maximum) for dealing with subject access. A data controller must comply with a subject access request promptly, and in any event within forty days of receipt of the request or, if later, within forty days of receipt of:

- the information required (i.e. to satisfy himself as to the identity of the person making the request and to locate the information which that person seeks); and

- the fee.

However, unless the data controller has received a request in writing, the prescribed fee and, if necessary, the said information the data controller need not comply with the request. If the data controller receives a request without the required fee and/or information, they should request whichever is outstanding as soon as possible in order that they can comply with the request promptly and in any event within 40 days. A data controller does not need to comply with a request where they have already complied with an identical or similar request by the same individual unless a reasonable interval has elapsed between compliance with the previous request and the making of the current request. In deciding what amounts to a reasonable interval, the following factors should be considered: the nature of the data, the purpose for which the data are processed and the frequency with which the data are altered.

The information given in response to a subject access request should be all that which is contained in the personal data at the time the request was received. However, routine amendments and deletions of the data may continue between the date of the request and the date of the reply. To this extent, the information revealed to the individual may differ from the personal data which were held at the time the request was received, even to the extent that data are no longer held. But, having received a request, the data controller must not make any special amendment or deletion which would not otherwise have been made. The information must not be tampered with in order to make it acceptable to the individual.

A particular problem arises for data controllers who may find that in complying with a subject access request they will disclose information relating to an individual other than the individual who has made the request, who can be identified from that information, including the situation where the information enables that other individual to be identified as the source of the information. The Act recognises this problem and sets out only two circumstances in which the data controller is obliged to comply with the subject access request in such circumstances, namely:

- where the other individual has consented to the disclosure of the information, or

- where it is reasonable in all the circumstances to comply with the request without the consent of the other individual.

The Act assists in interpreting whether it is reasonable in all the circumstances to comply with the request without the consent of the other individual concerned. In deciding this question regard shall be had, in particular, to:

- any duty of confidentiality owed to the other individual,

- any steps taken by the data controller with a view to seeking the consent of the other individual,

- whether the other individual is capable of giving consent, and

- any express refusal of consent by the other individual.

If a data controller is satisfied that the individual will not be able to identify the other individual from the information, taking into account any other information which, in the reasonable belief of the data controller, is likely to be in (or to come into) the possession of the individual, then the data controller must provide the information.

If an individual believes that a data controller has failed to comply with a subject access request in contravention of the Act they may apply to Court for an order that the data controller complies with the request. An order may be made if the Court is satisfied that the data controller has failed to comply with the request in contravention of the Act.

## 5. Exemptions to subject access rights

There are a limited number of exemptions to an individuals right of access. One of potential relevance to CCTV images is found at Section 29 of the Act. This provides an exemption from the subject access rights, which is similar to that discussed in relation to the exemption to the fairness requirements of the First Data Protection Principle. This means that where personal data are held for the purposes of: —

- prevention or detection of crime,

- apprehension or prosecution of offenders,

the data controller will be entitled to withhold personal data from an individual making a subject access request, where it has been adjudged that to disclose the personal data would be likely to prejudice one or both of the above purposes. Like the exemption to the fairness requirements of the First Data Protection Principle, this judgement must be made on a case-by-case basis, and in relation to each element of the personal data held about the individual. It is likely that this exemption may only be appropriately relied upon where the data controller has recorded personal data about an individual in accordance with guidance set out in relation to the fairness requirements of the First Data Protection Principle.[42]

## 6. Other rights

*Right to Prevent Processing Likely to Cause Damage or Distress*

Under Section 10 of the Act, an individual is entitled to serve a notice on a data controller requiring the data controller not to begin, or to cease, processing personal data relating to that individual. Such a notice could only be served on the grounds that the processing in question is likely to cause substantial, unwarranted damage or distress to that individual or another person. There are certain limited situations where this right to serve a notice does not apply. These are where the individual has consented; the processing is in connection with performance of a contract with the data subject, or in compliance with a legal obligation on the data controller, or in order to protect the vital interests of the individual. If a data controller receives such a notice they must respond within 21 days indicating either compliance with the notice or why the notice is not justified.

*Rights in Relation to Automated Decision-Taking*

Under section 12 of the Act individuals also have certain rights to prevent automated decision taking where a decision, which significantly affects them is based solely on automated processing. The Act draws particular attention to decisions taken aimed at evaluating matters such as the individual's performance at work and their reliability or conduct. The Act does provide exemption for certain decisions reached by automated means and these cover decisions which have been taken in the course of contractual arrangements with the individual, where a decision is authorised or required by statute, where the decision is to grant a request of the individual or where steps have been taken to safeguard the legitimate interests of individuals. This latter point may include matters such as allowing them to make representations about a decision before it is implemented.

Where no notice has been served by an individual and a decision which significantly affects the individual based solely on automated processing will be made, then there is still an obligation on the data controller to notify the individual that the decision was taken on the basis of automated processing as soon as reasonably practicable. The individual may, within 21 days of receiving such a notification, request the data controller to reconsider the decision or take another decision on a new basis. Having received such a notice the data controller has 21 days in which to respond, specifying the steps that they intend to take to comply with the notice.

In the context of CCTV surveillance it may be the case that certain automated decision-making techniques are deployed, such as with automatic facial recognition. It is important therefore that any system takes account of an individual's rights in relation to automated decision taking. It should be noted that these rights are founded on decisions, which are taken solely on the basis of automated processing. If a decision whether to take particular action in relation to a particular identified individual is taken further to human intervention, then such a decision would not be based solely on automated processing.

The individual's rights to prevent processing in certain circumstances and in connection with automated decision taking are underpinned by an individual's right to seek a Court Order should any notice served by the individual not be complied with.

*Compensation for Failure to Comply with Certain Requirements*

Under Section 13 of the Act, individuals who suffer unwarranted damage or damage and distress as a result of any contravention of the requirements of the Act are entitled to go to court to seek compensation in certain circumstances. This right to claim compensation for a breach of the Act is in addition to an individual's right to request the Data Protection Commissioner to make an assessment as to whether processing is likely or unlikely to comply with the Act.

---

**Endnotes**

[1] It is intended that employers' use of personal data to monitor employee compliance with contracts of employment will be covered by the Data Protection Commissioner's forthcoming code of practice on use of employee personal data.

[2] It is likely that the use of cameras by individuals to protect their own property is excluded from the provisions of the Act under the exemption at Section 36 of the Act.

[3] The Commissioner's powers to issue an Enforcement Notice may be found in section 40 of the Act.

[4] The First Data Protection Principle requires data controllers to have a legitimate basis for processing personal data, in this case images of individuals. The Act sets out criteria for processing, one of which must be met in order to demonstrate that there is a legitimate basis for processing the images.

[5] Section 4(4) of the Act places all data controllers under a duty to comply with the data protection principles in relation to all personal data with respect to which he is the data controller as defined by section 1(1) of the Act. See the section on definitions.

[6] See the First Data Protection Principle requires data controllers to have a legitimate basis for processing, one of which must be met in order to demonstrate that there is a legitimate basis for processing the images.

[7] Section 17 of the Act prohibits the processing of personal data unless the data controller has notified the Data Protection Commissioner. The notification scheme requires that the purpose(s) of the processing be identified.

[8] Section 29 of the Act sets out the circumstances in which the fair processing requirements of the First Data Protection Principle are set aside.

[9] It may be that the particular problem identified is theft from cars in a car park. Following the appropriate assessment, surveillance equipment is installed but signs are not. If the equipment co-incidentally records images relating to other criminality for example a sexual assault, it will not be inappropriate for those images to be used in the detection of that crime or in order to apprehend and prosecute the offender. However, it might be inappropriate for images so obtained to be used in civil proceedings or disciplinary proceedings eg the car park attendant is recorded committing a minor disciplinary misdemeanour.

[10] Users of such systems should be aware of the affect of Section 12 of the 1998 Act regarding individuals' rights in relation to automated decision taking.

[11] See the section on access to and disclosure of images to third parties.

[12] See the section on access to and disclosure of images to third parties.

[13] See the section on individual's rights.

[14] See the section on the seventh data protection principle.

[15] See the section on access to and disclosure of images to third parties.

[16] See the section on access to and disclosure of images to third parties.

[17] See the section on the right of subject access.

[18] See the section on the right of subject access.

[19] See the section on the right of subject access.

[20] See the section on the right of subject access.

[21] See the section on the right of subject access.

[22] See the section on the right of subject access.

[23] Section 10 of the Act provides individuals with the right to prevent processing likely to cause damage or distress. See the section on other rights.

[24] Users of such a system should be aware of the effects of section 12 of the Act regarding individuals' rights in relation to automated decision taking.

[25] Section 10 of the Act provides individuals with the right to prevent processing likely to cause substantial damage or distress. See the section on other rights.

[26] Section 10 of the Act provides individuals with the right to prevent processing likely to cause substantial damage or distress. See the section on other rights.

[27] Section 10 of the Act provides individuals with the right to prevent processing likely to cause substantial damage or distress. See the section on other rights.

[28] Users of such systems should be aware of the effect of section 12 of the 1998 Act regarding individuals' rights in relation to automated decision taking.

[29] Users of such systems should be aware of the effect of section 12 of the 1998 Act regarding individuals' rights in relation to automated decision taking.

[30] Users of such systems should be aware of the effect of section 12 of the 1998 Act regarding individuals' rights in relation to automated decision taking.

[31] European Directive 95/46/EC on the protection of individuals with regard to the processing of personal data and on the free movement of such data.

[32] Section 2 of Act sets out the full list of categories of sensitive personal data. This part of the Code only refers to some of the categories, which may have particular relevance for users of CCTV. For a full list, please see the relevant section of the Act.

[33] Section 2 of Act sets out the full list of categories of sensitive personal data. This part of the Code only refers to some of the categories, which may have particular relevance for users of CCTV. For a full list, please see the relevant section of the Act.

[34] The Data Protection (Processing of Sensitive Personal Data) Order 2000 (S.I No 417).

[35] Schedule 1 Part II Sections 1–4 of the Act.

[36] See the section on the right of subject access.

[37] Section 2 of the Act sets out the full list of categories of sensitive personal data. This part of the Code only refers to some of the categories, which may have particular relevance for users of CCTV. For a full list, please see the relevant section of the Act.

[38] Users of such systems should be aware of the effect of section 12 of the 1998 Act regarding individuals' rights in relation to automated decision taking.

[39] British Standard Institute—BS 7958:1991 "Closed Circuit Television (CCTV)—Management and Operation Code of Practice" provides guidance on issues of security, tape management etc.
[40] Schedule 1, Part II, Paragraph 9 of the Act.
[41] Schedule 1, Part II, Paragraphs 13–15 of the Act.
[42] See the subsection on circumstances in which the requirements for signs may be set aside.

# Appendix 6

## Countries Enjoying Protection in Respect of all Works Except Broadcasts and Cable Programmes

### Schedule 1 to the Copyright (Applications to Other Countries) Order 1999 (SI 1999/1751)

(The countries specified in this Schedule either are parties to the Berne Copyright Convention and/or the Universal Copyright Convention and/or the Agreement establishing the World Trade Organisation (including the Agreement on Trade-Related Aspects of Intellectual Property Rights) and/or are member States of the European Community or otherwise give adequate protection under their law.)

Albania
Algeria
Andorra (27th September 1957)
Angola
Antigua and Barbuda
Argentina
Australia (including Norfolk Island)
Austria
Azerbaijan
Bahamas
Bahrain
Bangladesh
Barbados
Belarus
Belgium
Belize
Benin
Bolivia
Bosnia-Herzegovina
Botswana
Brazil
Brunei Darussalam
Bulgaria
Burkina Faso
Burundi
Cameroon
Canada
Cape Verde
Central African Republic
Chad
Chile
China (including Hong Kong)

Colombia
Congo
Costa Rica
Cote d'Ivoire
Croatia
Cuba
Cyprus, Republic of
Czech Republic
Democratic Republic of the Congo
Denmark (including Greenland and the Faeroe Islands)
Djibouti
Dominica
Dominican Republic
Ecuador
Egypt
El Salvador
Equatorial Guinea
Estonia
Fiji
Finland
France (including all Overseas Departments and Territories)
Gabon
Gambia
Georgia
Germany
Ghana
Greece
Grenada
Guatemala
Guinea
Guinea-Bissau

Guyana
Haiti
Holy See
Honduras
Hungary
Iceland
India
Indonesia
Ireland, Republic of
Israel
Italy
Jamaica
Japan
Kampuchea (27th September 1957)
Kazakhstan
Kenya
Korea, Republic of
Kuwait
Kyrgyz Republic
Laos (27th September 1957)
Latvia
Lebanon
Lesotho
Liberia
Libya
Liechtenstein
Lithuania
Luxembourg
Macau
Macedonia
Madagascar
Malawi
Malaysia
Maldives

Moldova
Mali
Malta
Mauritania
Mauritius
Mexico
Monaco
Mongolia
Morocco
Mozambique
Myanmar
Namibia
Netherlands (including
    Aruba and the
    Netherlands Antilles)
New Zealand
Nicaragua
Niger
Nigeria
Norway
Pakistan
Panama
Papua New Guinea
Paraguay
Peru
Philippines

Poland
Portugal
Qatar
Romania
Russian Federation
Rwanda
Saint Kitts and Nevis
Saint Lucia
Saint Vincent and the
    Grenadines
Saudi Arabia (13th July
    1994)
Senegal
Sierra Leone
Singapore
Slovak Republic
Slovenia
Solomon Islands
South Africa
Soviet Union (27th May
    1973)
Spain
Sri Lanka
Suriname
Swaziland
Sweden

Switzerland
Taiwan (10th July 1985)
Tajikistan (25th
    December 1991)
Tanzania
Thailand
Togo
Trinidad and Tobago
Tunisia
Turkey
Uganda
Ukraine
United Arab Emirates
United States of
    America (including
    Puerto Rico and all
    territories and
    possessions)
Uruguay
Venezuela
Yugoslavia
Zaire
Zambia
Zimbabwe

# Selected Bibliography

## Books & Texts

Abu-Ghazaleh Intellectual Property (TMP Agents), *Intellectual Property Laws of the Arab Countries* (Kluwer Law International, 2000)

Arnold, R., *Performers' Rights* (2nd ed., Sweet & Maxwell, 1997)

Association of Photographers (ed. J.Kelley) *Beyond the Lens* (Association of Photographers,1996)

Beloff, M.J. *et al, Sport Law* (Hart Publishing, 1999)

Bidner, J., *Digital Photography A Basic Guide to New Technology* Kodak Workshop Series (Silver Pixel Press, 2000)

Bracewell, J *et al, The Family Court Practice 2001* (Jordan Publishing, 2001)

Cassell, D., *The Photographer & the Law* (3rd ed., BFB Books, 1997)

Charlton, S., Gaskill, S., *et al* (eds), *Encylopaedia of Data Protection* (Looseleaf, Sweet & Maxwell)

Chernoff, G., *Photography and the Law* (5th ed., Amphoto,1978)

Cooper, J. (ed.), *Privacy* EHRLR Special Issue (Sweet & Maxwell, 2003)

Copinger, W.A., *The Law of Copyright* (2nd ed., Stevens & Haynes, 1881)

Crown, G., *Advertising Law and Regulation* (Butterworths, 1998)

Dean, O. H. , *Handbook of South African Copyright Law*, (Jutta & Co Ltd South Africa, 1987)

Drysdale, J. & Silverleaf, M., *Passing Off—Law and Practice* (2nd ed., Butterworths, 1995)

Dugdale, A.M. *et al, Clerk & Lindsell on Torts* (18th ed., Sweet & Maxwell, 2000)

Eady, D. & Smith, A.T.H., *Arlidge, Eady & Smith on Contempt* (2nd ed., Sweet & Maxwell, 1999)

Freeman, M. *The Complete Guide to Digital Photography* (Thames & Hudson, 2001).

Garnett,K., Rayner-James J. & Davies, G, *Copinger and Skone James on Copyright* (14th ed., Sweet & Maxwell, 1999)

Garrison, D.L. (ed) *Intellectual Property: Eastern Europe & Commonwealth of Independent States* (Looseleaf, Oceana Publications)

Gendreau, Y., Nordemann, A, and Oesch, R (eds) *Copyright and Photographs: An International Survey* ( Kluwer Law International, 1999)

Gringras, C, *The Laws of the Internet* (2nd ed., Butterworths, 2003)

Hughes, R.T., *Hughes on Copyright and Industrial Design* (Looseleaf, Butterworths Canada)

Jay, R. and Hamilton, A., *Data Protection Law and Practice* (2nd ed., Sweet & Maxwell, 2003)

Kabel, J.J.C. & Mom, G.(eds), *Intellectual Property and Information Law* (Kluwer Law International, 1998)

Kitchin, D., Llewelyn, D. *et al, Kerly's Law of Trade Marks and Trade Names* (13th ed., Sweet & Maxwell, 2001)

Laddie, H., Prescott, P. *et al, The Modern Law of Copyright and Designs* (3rd ed., Butterworths, 2000)

Laddie, H., Prescott,P. and Vitoria, M. ,*The Modern Law of Copyright and Designs* (2nd ed., Butterworths, 1995)

Lahore, J, *Copyright and Designs* (Looseleaf, Butterworths Australia)

Langford, M., *Story of Photography* (2nd ed., Focal Press, 1997)

Lord Lester & Pannick, D., *Human Rights Law and Practice* (Butterworths,1999)

Lewis, A. & Taylor, J., *Sport: Law and Practice* (Butterworths, 2003)

Lowe, N. & Sufrin, B., *Borrie & Lowe The Law of Contempt* (3rd ed., Butterworths, 1996)

McCarthy, J.T., *The Rights of Publicity and Privacy* (Looseleaf, West Group)

McClean, J. D. (ed) *et al, Shawcross and Beaumont:Air Law* (4th ed., Butterworths, 2001)

McGregor, H., *McGregor on Damages* (16th ed., Sweet & Maxwell, 1997)

McGregor, H., *McGregor on Damages* (17th ed., Sweet & Maxwell, 2003)

Morcom, C., Roughton, A. and Graham, J., *The Modern Law of Trade Marks* (Butterworths, 1999)

Milller, C. J., *Contempt of Court* (3rd ed., Oxford University Press, 2000)

Nelson,V., *The Law of Entertainment and Broadcasting* (2nd ed., Sweet & Maxwell, 1999)

Newhall, B., *The History of Photography* (5th ed., Bulfinch Press, New York, 1982)

Nimmer, M.B. & Geller, P.E., *International Copyright Law and Practice* (Looseleaf, Matthew Bender)

Nimmer, M.B. & Nimmer D. *Nimmer on Copyright* (Looseleaf, Matthew Bender)

Palmer, N., *Bailment* (2nd ed., Sweet & Maxwell, 1991)

Richardson, P.J (ed) *et al*, *Archbold 2003* (Sweet & Maxwell, 2003)

Ricketson, S., *The Berne Convention for the Protection of Literary and Artistic Works 1886-1986* (Centre for Commercial Law Studies, Queen Mary College, Kluwer, 1987)

Ritchin, F., *In Our Own Image: The Coming Revolution in Photography: How Computer Technology Is Changing Our View of the World (Writers and Artists on Photography)* (Aperture, 1999)

Robertson, G. & Nicol, A., *Media Law* (4th ed., Sweet & Maxwell, 2000)

Skone-James, E.P., *Copinger and Skone-James on Copyright* (11th ed., Sweet & Maxwell, 1971)

Skone-James, F.E & Skone-James, E.P., *Copinger and Skone-James on Copyright* (9th ed., Sweet & Maxwell, 1958)

Smith, S., *Image, Persona and the Law Special Report* (Sweet & Maxwell, 2001)

Sterling, J.A.L., *World Copyright Law* (Sweet & Maxwell, 1998)

Tugendhat, M & Christie, I. (eds), *The Law of Privacy & the Media* (Oxford University Press, 2002)

Wadlow, C., *The Law of Passing Off* (2nd ed., Sweet & Maxwell 1995)

Wadlow, C., *The Law of Passing Off: Unfair Competition by Misrepresentation* (3rd ed., Sweet & Maxwell 2004)

## Articles

Baade, P.L., "Photographer's Rights: Case for Sufficient Originality Test in Copyright" Fall, 1996, 30 J. Marshall L.Rev. 149

Bianchini, V.E. and Bass H., "A Paradigm for the Authentication of Photographic Evidence in the Digital Age" [1998] 20 Thomas Jefferson L.Rev. 303

Lord Bingham of Cornhill C.J., "Opinion: Should There Be A Law to Protect Rights of Personal Privacy" [1996] E.H.R.L.R. 451

Burgunder, L.B., "Commercial Photographs of Famous Buildings: The Sixth Circuit Fails to Make the Hall of Fame" (1999) 89 Trademark Reporter 791

Busuttil, G., "Power for Use When Necessary" [2002] Nov/Dec Issue 42 Media Lawyer 40

Camp, W., "Practical Uses of Digital Photography in Litigation" 2. Ann. 2000, Association of Trial Lawyers of America, C.L.E. 1463

Christ, K., "Eddifice Complex: Protecting Landmark Buildings As Intellectual Property—A Critique of Available Protections and A Proposal" (2002) 92 Trademark Reporter 1041

Connolly Butler, K., "Keeping the World Safe from Naked-Chicks-in-Art Refrigerator Magnets: The Plot to Control Art Images in the Public Domain through Copyrights in Photographic and Digital Reproductions" (Fall, 1998) 21 Hastings Comm. & Ent. L.J. 55

Corbet, J., " Five Years Later: A First Assessment of the New Belgian Law on Author's Rights" (Jan 200) 183 R.I.D.A 200

Corbet, S., "The Digital Photograph: Intellectual property of whom? "[2001] 6(2) Comm. Law 46

Davis, J., "European Trade Mark Law and the Enclosure of the Commons" [2002] I.P.Q. 342

De La Loi, S., "Snap happy (Question & Answer)" [2001] (6) D.P. & P.P 42–43

Dietz, A., "Copyright Law Developments in Germany From 1993 to Mid-1997" 175 R.I.D.A. 96

Deazley, R., "Photographing Paintings in the Public Domain: A Response to Garnett" [2001] E.I.P.R. 179

Deazley, R., "Collecting Photographs, Copyrights and Cash" [2001] E.I.P.R. 551.

Dixon, J., "Children and the Statutory Restraints on Publicity" [2001] 31(Oct) Fam. Law 757

Doi, T., "WIPO Copyright Treaty and Japanese Copyright Law" 186 R.I.D.A. 155.

Dreier, T. & Karnell,G., "Originality of the Copyrighted Work: A European Perspective" [1992] 39(4) Journal of the Copyright Society of the USA 289

Franço, A., "Authors' Rights Beyond Frontiers: A Comparison of Civil Law and Common Law Conceptions" (1991) R.I.D.A. 2

Garnett, K., "Copyright in Photographs" [2000] E.I.P.R. 229

Garnett, K. & Abbott, A., "Who is the 'Author' of a Photograph?" [1998] E.I.P.R. 204

Gendreau, Y., "Copyright Ownership of Photographs in Anglo-American Law" [1993] E.I.P.R. 207

Gimeno, L., "Photographs, Commercial Exploitation of the Image and Copyright in Spain" [1998] Ent. L.R. 131

Gimeno, L. "A Parody of Songs" [1997] Ent. L.R. 18

Gimeno, L, "Copyright Subject Matter in Spain" [1996] E.I.P.R. 352

Gredley, E, and Maniatis, M., "Parody: A Fatal Attraction? Part 1: The Nature of Parody and Its Treatment in Copyright" [1997] E.I.P.R. 339; Part 2 at [1997] E.I.P.R 412

Hood, C.A., Hope, T. and Dove, P., "Videos, Photographs, and Patient Consent" 1998 B.M.J. 316:1009-1011 (March 28)

Hugenholtz, P., "Bernt Dutch Copyright Law 1995-2000" (Jan 2001) 187 R.I.D.A. 111

International Committee of Medical Journal Editors, "Protection of Patients' Rights to Privacy" 1995 B.M.J. 311:1272 (November 11)

Isaac, B., "Merchandising or Fundraising? Trade Marks and the Diana, Princess of Wales Memorial Fund" [1998] E.I.P.R. 441

Jaszi, P., "How Important is the Tasini Decision?" [2001] E.I.P.R. 595

Jay, R., "Eastweek and Photo-Journalism" [2000] 3 (Sum) D.P. & P.P. 14-18

Jones, P.,"Manipulating the Law Against Misleading Imagery: Photo-Montage and Appropriation of Well-Known Personality" [1999] E.I.P.R. 28

Karnell, G.W.G., "European Originality: A Copyright Chimera" in Kabel, J.J.C. & Mom, G (eds), *Intellectual Property and Information Law* (Kluwer Law International, 1998) at p. 201

Kun, S., "Race Horses and Intellectual Property Rights: Racing Towards Recognition" (1997) 17 Q.L.R. 207

Lai, S., "Digital Copyright and Watermarking" [1999] E.I.P.R. 171

Lesieutre Honan, A., "The Skyscraping Reach of the Lanham Act: How Far Should the Protection of Famous Building Design Trademarks Be Extended?" (2000) 94 Northwestern University Law Review 1509

Lupton, K., "Photographs and the Concept of Originality in Copyright Law" [1988] E.I.P.R. 257

Mitchener, J., "Intellectual Property in Image - A Mere Inconvenience" [2003] I.P.Q. 163

Munro, C., "Photographs and Legality" [1997] Ent. L.R. 197

Naismith, S.H., "Photographs, Privacy & Freedom Of Expression" [1996] 2 E.H.R.L.R. 150.

Nimmer, M.B and Price, M.E., "Moral Rights & Beyond: Considerations for the College Art Association" in *Occasional Papers In Intellectual Property* from Benjamin N. Cardozo School of Law, Yeshiva University, Number 3, *Resuscitating A Collaboration With Melville Nimmer: Moral Rights and Beyond.* Available on line at http://www.cardozo.yu.edu/ip_program/papers/3.pdf

Oberman,M.S. & Lloyd,T, "Copyright Protection for Photographs in the Age of New Technologies" 2 B.U. J. Sci. & Tech. L. 10

Olsson, J.T, "Rights in Fine Art Photography: Through a Lens Darkly" May, 1992, 70 Tex. L. Rev. 1489

Oppenoorth, Fritis, "Facets of Dutch Portrait Law" Copyright World, 28 (March 1993) 38

Pendleton, M.D., "Character Merchandising, Personality and Sponsorship Rights Strike A Snag in Hong Kong: The Andy Lau Case" [1999] E.I.P.R. 521

Porter, H., "Character Merchandising: Does English Law Recognise a Property Right in Name and Likeness" [1999] Ent. L.R. 180

Ricketson, S., "The Concept of Originality in Anglo-Australian Copyright Law" (1991) 9(2) Journal of Copyright Society of Australia 1

Rozenberg, J., "The Pinochet Case and Cameras In Court" [1999] (Sum) P.L. 178

Sarno, G., "Libel and Slander: Defamation by Photograph" (1987) 52 A.L.R. 4th 488

Schønning, P., Eskola, J, *et al,* "News from the Nordic Countries" 174 R.I.D.A 125.

Soler Masota, "Photography and Copyright" (April 2000) 184 R.I.D.A. 60

Stokes, S., "Letter, Photographing Paintings in the Public Domain: A Response to Garnett" [2001] E.I.P.R. 354

Stokes, S., "Graves' Case Revisited in the USA" [2000] Ent.L.R. 104

Warren, S and Brandeis, L., "The Right to Privacy" (1890) 4 Harvard L.R. 193

Wohl, L. A., "The Right of Publicity and Vocal Larceny: Sounding Off on Sound-Alikes" (1988) 57 Fordham L.Rev. 445

## Other

Report of the Copyright Committee of 1952, Cmd. 8662

Report of the Committee to Consider the Law on Copyright and Designs (1977), Cmnd. 6732

Trade Marks Registry Works Manual

Newspapers: *The Times, The Daily Telegraph; The Guardian; London Evening Standard.*

# Index

*All references are to paragraph numbers*

**Advertising Standards Authority**—*cont.*
privacy, 14–081–14–084
procedure for complaints, 14–068–14–069
public authority, as, 14–065
public figures, 14–082–14–083
race, causing offence on grounds of, 14–075
reconsideration of adjudication, 14–069
religion, causing offence on grounds of, 14–075
representations, making, 14–067
sanctions, 14–070
shocking images, 14–080
sex, causing offence on grounds of, 14–075
time limits, 14–068
truthfulness, 14–078–14–079
violence, use of images of, 14–075, 14–080
**Aerial photographs**
airspace, invasion of, 6–094–6–095
Canada, 3–026
height, flights at a reasonable, 6–094–6–095
helicopters, hovering, 6–094, 6–132
low flying aircraft, 6–094, 6–132
nuisance, 6–132
originality copyright, 3–025–3–026, 3–034
orthophotos, 3–025–3–026
privacy, 14–033, 14–038
surveillance by, 6–132
trespass to land, 6–094–6–095
**Aesthetic merit**, 3–004
**Agence Centrale pour la Perception Droits Auteurs et Compositeurs de Musique,** 13–003
**Agents, copyright and,** 2–053
**Aggravated damages**, 6–103, 7–115, 11–109, 12–027
**Airspace, invasion of**, 6–094–6–095
**Alarm or distress, harassment causing**, 6–140
**Albania, copyright protection,** Appendix 2
**Algeria, copyright protection,** Appendix 2
**Altered or treated by someone else, works which have been,** 4–020
**Amends, offers of,** 7–132
**Analogue photographs**
collective works, 9–040–9–044
colour transparencies, 12–005–12–006
copyright,
author, 2–052
definition of, 2–010
first ownership, 2–073
generally, 2–012–2–013
qualifying conditions, 2–038
term of protection, 2–093
term of protection flow chart, 2–100
data protection, 11–008
destruction and loss of,12–001, 12–005, 12–016
damages for loss of, 12–029–12–039
digital photography, 2–015
digitisation of,copyright work, as, 2–145
implied licence, 9–039
originality, 3–020
process, 9–038–9–044
film frames, 2–036
fees, 12–002, 12–008–12–009
history, 1–001

**Analogue photographs**—*cont.*
licences, 9–038–9–039, 9–044
picture libraries, 12–001, 12–005–12–006, 12–014–12–024
scanning, 9–038
United States, 9–040–9–044
**Angola, copyright protection**, Appendix 2
**Animals,** 8–070. *See also* **Wildlife photography**
**Anonymity**
anonymous or pseudonymous works, 2–181, 4–035
BBC Producers' Guidelines, 14–088
breach of agreement to ensure, 14–028
Copyright, Designs and Patents Act 1988, 2–181
data protection,
anonymised data, 11–168
data, 11–166, 11–180, 11–186
images, 11–017, 11–021–11–022, 11–024, 11–032, 11–088
fair dealing, 2–181
guidelines, to maintain
BBC Producers Guidelines, 14–088
General Medical Council, 11–185
Press Complaints Commission, 14–057
jigsaw identification. *See* **Jigsaw Identification**
identification, 11–021, 11–023–11–024, 11–026, 11–030–11–033
Information Commissioner, 11–166
infringement, 2–181
integrity, right of, 4–035
Press Complaints Commission guidance re victims of sexual assault, 14–057
Pixilation, 14–088
privacy, 4–052
sexual offences, 6–069–6–077, 6–080
term of protection, 2–181, 4–035, 4–052
**Anonymous or pseudonymous works,** 2–181, 4–035
**Antiques, originality in photographs of.** *See* **Three Dimensional Objects.**
**Apologies, 4–060, 14–014, 14–015**
**Appeals**
Attorney-General on a point of law, 6–078–6–079
contempt and, 6–036
Court of Appeal, 6–036, 6–041
data protection, 11–115, 11–118–11–119
enforcement notices, 11–119
forfeiture orders, 8–056
indecent photographs of children, 8–056
information notices, 11–115
obscenity, search and seizure and, 8–018
special information notices, 11–118
street trading in the City of London, 6–174
Video Appeals Committee, 8–025
**Apprenticeship, ownership of copyright and,** 2–074
**Approval of photographs,** 9–019
**APRA (Australasian Performing Right Association Ltd),** 13–004
**Archer, Frederick Scott,** 1–004
**Architects' drawings,** 2–183